A Quick Guide to Working with Primary Sources

This quick guide provides some basic steps for analyzing the documents and visual sources in this book. For more detailed help in working with primary sources, see pp. xlv–xlix.

Reading and Analyzing a Written Document

The following questions will help you understand and analyze a written document:

- Who wrote the document?

- When and where was it written?

- What type of document is it (for example, a letter to a friend, a political decree, an exposition of a religious teaching)?

- Why was the document written? Under what circumstances was it composed?

- What point of view does it reflect?

- Who was its intended audience?

- What about the document is believable and what is not?

- What can the document tell us about the individual that produced it and the society from which he or she came?

Viewing and Analyzing a Visual Source

These questions will help you to understand and analyze a visual source:

- When and where was the image or artifact made?

- Who made the image or artifact? How was it made?

- Who paid for or commissioned it?

- Where might the image or artifact have originally been displayed or used?

- For what audience(s) was it intended?

- What message(s) is it trying to convey?

- How could it be interpreted differently depending on who viewed or used it?

- What can this image tell us about the individual that produced it and the society from which he or she came?

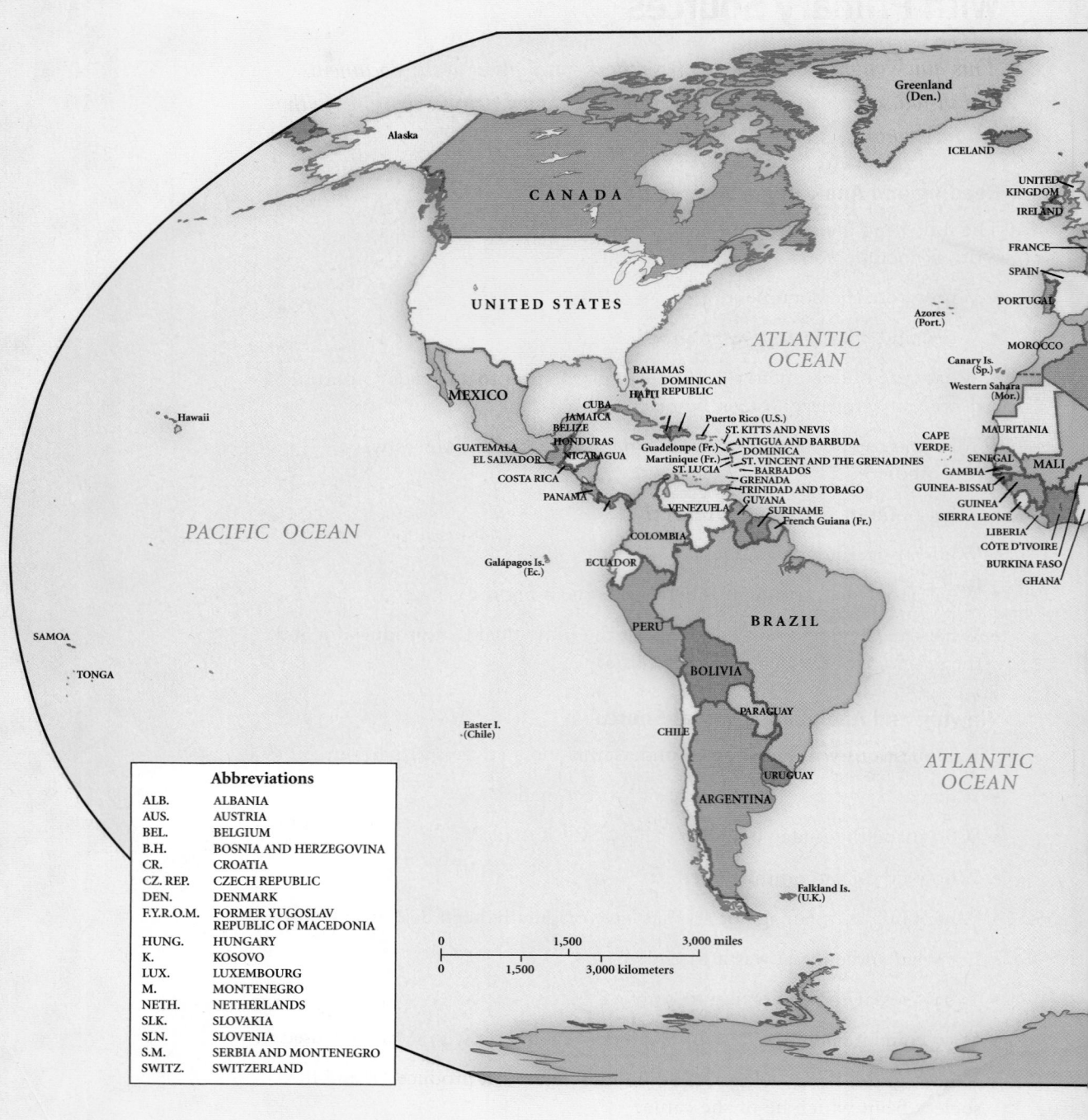

Greenland
(Den.)

ICELAND

Alaska

CANADA

UNITED
KINGDOM

IRELAND

FRANCE

SPAIN

PORTUGAL

UNITED STATES

ATLANTIC
OCEAN

Azores
(Port.)

MOROCCO

Hawaii

MEXICO

BAHAMAS
DOMINICAN
REPUBLIC
HAITI

Canary Is.
(Sp.)

Western Sahara
(Mor.)

CUBA
JAMAICA
BELIZE
HONDURAS

Puerto Rico (U.S.)
ST. KITTS AND NEVIS
ANTIGUA AND BARBUDA
DOMINICA

MAURITANIA

GUATEMALA
EL SALVADOR
NICARAGUA

Guadeloupe (Fr.)
Martinique (Fr.)
ST. LUCIA

ST. VINCENT AND THE GRENADINES
BARBADOS

CAPE
VERDE

SENEGAL

MALI

COSTA RICA

GRENADA
TRINIDAD AND TOBAGO
GUYANA

GAMBIA
GUINEA-BISSAU

PANAMA

VENEZUELA

SURINAME
French Guiana (Fr.)

GUINEA
SIERRA LEONE

PACIFIC OCEAN

COLOMBIA

LIBERIA
CÔTE D'IVOIRE

Galápagos Is.
(Ec.)

ECUADOR

BURKINA FASO
GHANA

PERU

BRAZIL

SAMOA

BOLIVIA

TONGA

PARAGUAY

Easter I.
(Chile)

CHILE

ARGENTINA

URUGUAY

ATLANTIC
OCEAN

Falkland Is.
(U.K.)

Abbreviations

ALB.	ALBANIA
AUS.	AUSTRIA
BEL.	BELGIUM
B.H.	BOSNIA AND HERZEGOVINA
CR.	CROATIA
CZ. REP.	CZECH REPUBLIC
DEN.	DENMARK
F.Y.R.O.M.	FORMER YUGOSLAV REPUBLIC OF MACEDONIA
HUNG.	HUNGARY
K.	KOSOVO
LUX.	LUXEMBOURG
M.	MONTENEGRO
NETH.	NETHERLANDS
SLK.	SLOVAKIA
SLN.	SLOVENIA
S.M.	SERBIA AND MONTENEGRO
SWITZ.	SWITZERLAND

0   1,500   3,000 miles

0   1,500   3,000 kilometers

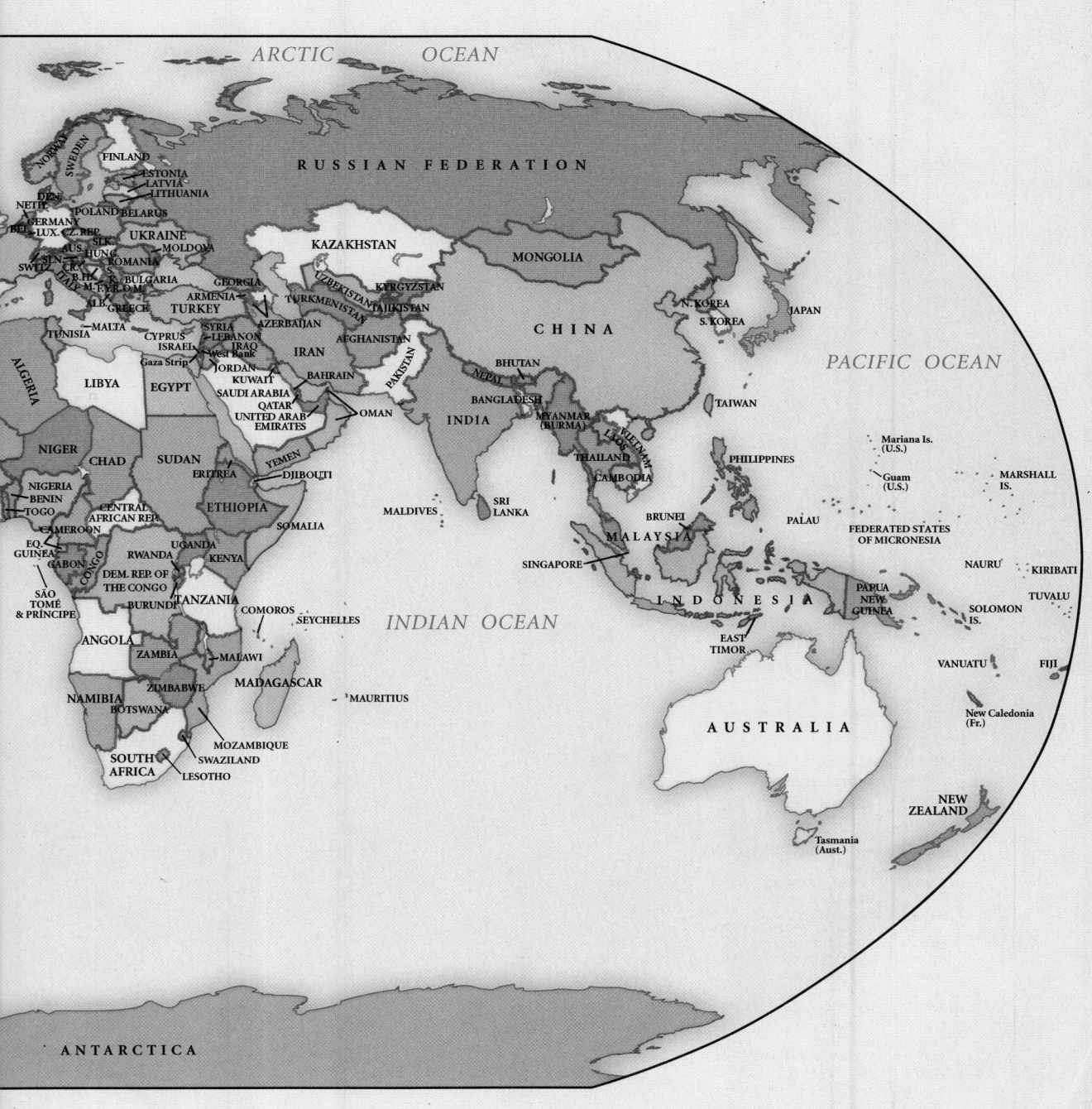

Ways of the World

A Brief Global History

with Sources

Ways of the World

A Brief Global History with Sources

ROBERT W. STRAYER

California State University, Monterey Bay

Bedford/St. Martin's

Boston • New York

For Gina, Nicole, Alisa, and their generation

For Bedford/St. Martin's
Executive Editor for History: Mary Dougherty
Director of Development for History:
    Jane Knetzger
Executive Editor for History:
    Tracy Mueller Crowell
Developmental Editor: Kathryn Abbott
Senior Production Editor: Bridget Leahy
Senior Production Supervisor: Joe Ford
Executive Marketing Manager:
    Jenna Bookin Barry
Editorial Assistant: Robin Soule
Production Assistant: Lidia MacDonald-Carr
Copyeditor: Janet Renard
Editorial Consultant: Eric W. Nelson,
    Missouri State University
Text and Cover Design: Joyce Weston
Photo Research: Carole Frohlich, The Visual
    Connection Image Research, Inc.

Indexer: Leoni Z. McVey
Cover Art: Codex Duran: Fol. 208v. Meeting
    between Hernán Cortés and Moctezuma.
    Bridgeman Art Library.
Frontispiece: Miguel Cabrera (1695–1768),
    Mestizo family. Scala/Art Resource, NY
Cartography: Mapping Specialists Limited
Composition: NK Graphics
Printing and Binding: RR Donnelley
    and Sons

President: Joan E. Feinberg
Editorial Director: Denise B. Wydra
Director of Marketing: Karen R. Soeltz
Director of Editing, Design, and Production:
    Susan W. Brown
*Assistant Director of Editing, Design, and
    Production:* Elise S. Kaiser
Managing Editor: Elizabeth M. Schaaf

Library of Congress Control Number: 2010920404

Manufactured in the United States of America.

1   2   3   4   5   6   14   13   12   11   10

For information, write: Bedford/St. Martin's, 75 Arlington Street, Boston, MA 02116
(617-399-4000)

ISBN-10: 0-312-48916-1   ISBN-13: 978-0-312-48916-8   (combined edition)
ISBN-10: 0-312-48917-X   ISBN-13: 978-0-312-48917-5   (Vol. 1)
ISBN-10: 0-312-48918-8   ISBN-13: 978-0-312-48918-2   (Vol. 2)
ISBN-10: 0-312-64466-3   ISBN-13: 978-0-312-64466-6   (high school edition)

Preface

WAYS OF THE WORLD FIRST APPEARED in September 2008 and was warmly welcomed by students and teachers, who seemed to like its brevity, clarity, and accessibility. Among the responses that the book provoked, however, was the call for a set of primary sources keyed to its narrative. This version of *Ways of the World* addresses that need in what Bedford/St. Martin's calls a "docutext" format. Each chapter narrative is now followed by a group of related documents and, separately, a collection of visual sources, both of which are organized around particular themes or questions from the chapter. Thus this docutext version of *Ways of the World* presents an integrated package of text and sources that offers instructors a wide range of pedagogical possibilities. For students, it provides a "laboratory" experience, enabling them to engage the evidence directly and to draw conclusions from sources—in short to "do history" rather than simply read history.

The history that students encounter in *Ways of the World* is now widely known as world or global history, a rather new and remarkably ambitious field of study that has come of age during my own career in the academy and particularly during the past quarter of a century. Those of us who practice world history, as teachers or textbook authors, are seldom specialists in the particulars of what we study and teach. Rather we are "specialists of the whole," seeking to find the richest, most suggestive, and most meaningful contexts in which to embed those particulars. We look for the big-picture processes and changes that have marked the human journey; we are alert to the possibilities for comparison across cultural boundaries; and we pay special attention to the multiple interactions among human communities. Our task, fundamentally, is to teach contextual thinking. The documents and visual sources presented here frequently add a personal dimension to these big-picture themes by evoking the words and images of particular historical actors who lived, worked, played, suffered, triumphed, and interacted over the many centuries of the human journey.

What's in a Title?

The title of a book should evoke something of its character and outlook. The main title of *Ways of the World* is intended to suggest at least three dimensions of this text.

The first is **diversity** or **variation**, for the "ways of the world," or the ways of being human in the world, have been many and constantly changing. World history was conceived in part to counteract a Eurocentric perspective on the human past, deriving from several centuries of Western dominance on the world stage. This book seeks to embrace the experience of humankind in its vast diversity, while noticing the changing location of particular centers of innovation and wider influence.

Second, the title *Ways of the World* invokes major **panoramas**, **patterns**, or **pathways** in world history, as opposed to highly detailed narratives. Many world history instructors have found that students often feel overwhelmed by the sheer quantity of data that a course in global history can require of them. In the narrative sections of this book, the larger patterns or the "big pictures" of world history appear in the foreground on center stage, while the still plentiful details, data, and facts occupy the background, serving in supporting roles.

A third implication of the book's title lies in a certain **reflective** or **musing quality** of *Ways of the World*, which appears especially in the Big Picture essays that introduce each part of the book and in a Reflections section at the end of each chapter. This dimension of the text is a product of my own growing appreciation that history of any kind, and world history in particular, offers endless raw material for contemplating large questions. Here are some of the issues that are addressed in this fashion:

- How can we tell when one period of history ends and another begins? What marks off the classical era, for example, or the early modern period of world history? Does the twentieth century deserve to be considered a separate period of time?

- In what ways and why do historians and religious believers sometimes rub each other the wrong way?

- How can we, or should we, make moral judgments in the face of the vast ambiguity of most historical phenomena?

- Are there clear "lessons" to be learned from the past? And does history really repeat itself, as so many students seem to believe?

- How can we avoid Eurocentrism when dealing with recent centuries, in which Europeans were in fact increasingly central to the human story?

- How can we retain a sense of surprise, unexpectedness, contingency, or luck in our telling of the human story, particularly when we know the outcomes of those stories?

None of these questions have clear or easy answers, but the opportunity to contemplate them is among the great gifts that the study of history offers to us all.

Integrating Narrative and Sources: The Docutext Approach

The subtitle of this book, *A Brief Global History with Sources*, refers to its docutext format. Following the narrative portion of each chapter are a set of written primary sources and then another set of visual primary sources. Each collection is organized around a particular theme, issue, or question that derives from the chapter narrative. As the title of these features suggests, they enable students to "consider the evidence" and thus begin to understand the craft of historians as well as their conclusions. All of them are thoroughly cross-referenced with the text, are furnished with brief head-notes providing context for the sources, and are accompanied by a series of probing Using the Evidence questions appropriate for in-class discussion and writing assignments.

Many of these Considering the Evidence features are broadly comparative or cross-cultural. For example, the Documents feature for Chapter 5 invites students to consider the nature of the good life and good society in the thinking of Confucius, the *Bhagavad Gita*, Socrates, and Jesus. Likewise the Visual Sources feature for Chapter 15 raises questions about the display of status derived from items acquired in the transregional commerce of the early modern era, with examples from Europe, the Ottoman Empire, colonial Mexico, and the West African kingdom of Dahomey. Other features are regionally focused, providing a more in-depth look at certain elements of specific societies. In Chapter 7, for example, the Documents feature allows students to explore the history of Axum through a series of texts from the early centuries of the Common Era, while the Visual Sources feature of Chapter 22 examines the communist vision of the future in Mao's China via its poster art.

Achieving Coherence

The great virtue of world history lies in its inclusiveness, for it allows us to see the world and to see it whole. But that virtue is also the source of world history's greatest difficulty—telling a coherent story. How can we meaningfully present the planet's many and distinct peoples and their intersections with one another in the confines of a single book or a single term? What prevents that telling from bogging down in the endless detail of various civilizations or cultures, from losing the forest for the trees, from implying that history is just "one damned thing after another"?

Less Can Be More

Ways of the World seeks to cope with that fundamental conundrum of world history—the tension between inclusion and coherence—in several ways. The first is the relative brevity of the narrative and a corresponding selectivity. This means, of course, leaving some things out or treating them more succinctly than some instructors might expect. But the docutext format allows for exploration of particular topics in greater depth via the Documents and Visual Sources features. The positive side of narrative brevity is that the textbook need not overwhelm students or dominate the pedagogy of the course. It allows for more professorial creativity in constructing individual world history courses and in mixing and matching text and sources.

Narrative brevity also encourages a "themes and cases" rather than a "civilization-by-civilization" approach to the global past. Thus most chapters in this book focus on a broad theme, explored on a global or transregional scale: agricultural revolutions in Chapter 2; classical-era empires in Chapter 4; axial-age religions in Chapter 5; long-distance commerce in Chapters 8 and 15; the colonial experience of the long nineteenth century in Chapter 20; the Communist experiment in Chapter 22; twentieth-century globalization in Chapter 24. Docutext features add substantially to the "themes and cases" dimension of the book.

The Three Cs of World History: Change, Comparison, Connection

As a further aid to achieving coherence on a global scale, *Ways of the World* refers repeatedly to what I call the "**three Cs**" of world history. They represent some of the distinctive perspectives of world history as an academic discipline and are introduced more extensively in the prologue.

The first "C" emphasizes large-scale **changes**, both within and especially across major regions of the world. Change, of course, is a central theme in all historical study and serves to challenge "essentialist" descriptions of particular cultures or peoples. Among the macrochanges highlighted in *Ways of the World* are the peopling of the planet in Chapter 1; the emergence of "civilization" in Chapter 3; the rise of universal religions in Chapter 5; the changing shape of the Islamic world in Chapter 11; the breakthrough of industrialization in Chapter 18; the development of European global dominance in Chapters 19 and 20; the rise and fall of world communism in Chapter 22; the acceleration of globalization in Chapter 24.

The second "C" involves frequent **comparison**. It is a technique of integration through juxtaposition, of bringing several regions or cultures into our field of vision at the same time. It encourages reflection both on the common elements of the human experience and on its many variations. Such comparisons are pervasive throughout the book, informing both the chapter narratives and many of the docutext features. We examine the difference, for example, between the Agricultural Revolution in the Eastern and Western Hemispheres in Chapter 2; between the beginnings of Buddhism and the early period of Christianity in Chapter 5; between patriarchy in Athens and in Sparta in Chapter 6; between European and Asian empires of the early modern era in Chapter 14; between the Chinese and the Japanese response to European intrusion in Chapter 19; between postures toward Islam in twentieth-century Turkey and in Iran in Chapter 23; and many more.

The final "C" emphasizes **connections**, networks of communication and exchange that increasingly shaped the character of those societies that participated in them. For world historians, cross-cultural interaction becomes one of the major motors of historical change. Such connections are addressed in nearly every chapter narrative and many docutext features. For example, Chapter 3 explores the clash of the Greeks and the Persians during the classical era; Chapter 8 highlights the long-distance commercial networks that linked the Afro-Eurasian world, while its Visual Sources feature illustrates Central Asia as a cultural crossroads; Chapter 11 focuses attention on the numerous cross-cultural encounters spawned by the spread of Islam; Chapters 14 and 15 explore various facets of the transhemispheric Columbian exchange of the early modern era; Chapter 17 probes the linkages among the Atlantic revolutions of the late eighteenth and early nineteenth centuries, and its Documents feature displays the interplay of the idea of "rights" across the region; Chapter 24 concludes the book with an examination of globalization, highlighting its economic, feminist, religious, and environmental dimensions.

Organizing World History: Chronology, Theme, and Region

Organizing a world history textbook or a world history course is, to put it mildly, a daunting task. How should we divide up the seamless stream of human experience into manageable and accessible pieces, while recognizing always that such divisions are both artificial and to some extent arbitrary? Historians, of course, debate the issue endlessly. In structuring *Ways of the World*, I have drawn on my own sense of "what works" in the classroom, on a personal penchant for organizational clarity, and on established practice in the field. The outcome has been an effort to balance three principles of organization—chronology, theme, and region—in a flexible format that can accommodate a variety of teaching approaches and organizational strategies.

The chronological principle is expressed most clearly in the overall structure of the book, which divides world history into six major periods. Each of these six "parts" begins with a brief **Big Picture essay** that introduces the general patterns of a particular period and raises questions about the problems historians face in dividing up the human past into meaningful chunks of time.

Part One (to 500 B.C.E.) deals in three separate chapters with beginnings—of human migration and social construction in the Paleolithic era, of agriculture, and of civilization. Each of them pursues an important theme on a global scale and illustrates that theme with regional examples treated comparatively.

Part Two, on the classical era (500 B.C.E. to 500 C.E.), likewise employs the thematic principle in exploring the major civilizations of Eurasia (Chinese, Indian, Persian, and Mediterranean), with separate chapters focusing on their empires (Chapter 4), cultural traditions (Chapter 5), and social organization (Chapter 6). This structure represents a departure from conventional practice, which usually treats the classical era on a civilization-by-civilization basis, but it allows for more effective and pointed comparison. These Eurasian chapters are followed by a single chapter (Chapter 7) that examines regionally the classical era in sub-Saharan Africa and the Americas, while asking whether their histories largely follow Eurasian patterns or depart from them.

Part Three embraces the thousand years between 500 and 1500 C.E., often known simply, and not very helpfully, as the "postclassical" era. The Big Picture essay for Part Three spotlights and seeks to explain a certain vagueness in our descriptions of this period of time, pointing out the various distinctive civilizational patterns of that millennium as well as the accelerating interactions among them. The six chapters of Part Three reflect a mix of thematic and regional principles. Chapter 8 focuses topically on commercial networks, while Chapters 9, 10, and 11 deal regionally with the Chinese, Christian, and Islamic worlds respectively. Chapter 12 treats pastoral societies as a broad theme and the Mongols as the most dramatic illustration of their impact on the larger stage of world history. Chapter 13, which bridges the two volumes of the book, presents an around-the-world tour in the fifteenth century, which serves both to conclude Volume 1 and to open Volume 2.

In considering the early modern era (1450–1750), **Part Four** treats each of its three constituent chapters thematically. Chapter 14 compares European and Asian empires; Chapter 15 lays out the major patterns of global commerce and their consequences (trade in spices, silver, furs, and slaves); and Chapter 16 focuses on cultural patterns, including the globalization of Christianity and the rise of modern science.

Part Five takes up the era of maximum European influence in the world, from 1750 to 1914. Here the Big Picture essay probes how we might avoid Eurocentrism, while describing a period of time in which Europeans were in fact increasingly central to the global story. Part Five, which charts the emergence of a distinctively modern society in Europe, devotes separate chapters to the Atlantic revolutions (Chapter 17) and the Industrial Revolution (Chapter 18). Then it turns to the growing impact of those societies on the rest of humankind—on China, the Ottoman Empire, and Japan, which are treated comparatively in Chapter 19; and on the world of formal colonies in Chapter 20.

The most recent century (1914–2010), which is treated in **Part Six**, is perhaps the most problematic for world historians, given the abundance of data and the absence of time to sort out what is fundamental and what is peripheral. The Big Picture essay that opens Part Six explores this difficulty, asking whether that century deserves the status of a separate period in the human story. Chapters 21, 22, and 23 examine respectively three major regions of the world in that century—the Western or industrial world, the communist world, and the third or developing world—while Chapter 24 explores the multiple processes of globalization, which have both linked and divided the human community in new ways.

Promoting Active Learning

As all instructors know, students can often "do the assignment" or read the required chapter and yet have nearly no understanding of it when they come to class. The problem, frequently, is passive studying—a quick once-over, perhaps some highlighting of the text—but little sustained involvement with the material. A central pedagogical problem in all teaching at every level is how to encourage more active, engaged styles of learning. How can we push students to articulate in their own words the major ideas of a particular chapter or section of the text? How can we encourage them to recognize arguments, even in a textbook, and to identify and evaluate the evidence on which those arguments are based? Active learning seeks to enable students to manipulate the information of the book, using its ideas and data to answer questions, to make comparisons, to draw conclusions, to criticize assumptions, and to infer implications that are not explicitly disclosed in the book itself. This ability to use and rearrange the material of a text, not simply to recall it, lies at the heart of active college-level learning.

This docutext version of *Ways of the World* incorporates a wealth of opportunities to promote active learning, to assist students in reading the book, and to generate livelier classroom exchanges.

- Chief among those opportunities are the docutext **Considering the Evidence features**. Both written and visual sources call for interpretation and imagination, an understanding of context, and consideration of point of view. Working with those sources virtually requires active engagement. A series of prompts for each document or image and the integrative Using the Evidence questions at the end of every feature serve to guide that engagement.

- The part-opening **Big Picture essays** preview for students what follows in the subsequent chapters. In doing so, they provide a larger context for those chapters; they enable students to make comparisons with greater ease; they facilitate making connections across several chapters; and they raise questions about periodization.

- Each Big Picture essay is followed by a **Landmarks timeline**, providing a chronological overview of what follows in that particular part of the book. Each of these Landmarks is organized in a series of parallel regional timelines, allowing students to see at a glance significant developments in various regions of the world during the same time.

- A **contemporary vignette** opens each chapter with a story that links the past and the present. Chapter 1, for example, presents Gudo Mahiya, a twenty-first-century member of a gathering and hunting society in Tanzania, who rejects an opportunity to become a settled farmer or herder. Chapter 15, which describes the Atlantic slave trade, opens with a brief account of an African American woman who in 2002 visits what had been a slave port in Ghana. These vignettes seek to show the continuing resonance of the past in the lives of contemporary people.

- To encourage active learning explicitly, a series of **questions in the margins** provides students with "something to look for" as they read particular sections. Those notations also indicate what kind of question is being asked—about change, comparison, or connection, for example.

- The **Reflections** section at the end of each chapter raises provocative, sometimes quasi-philosophical questions about the craft of the historian and the unfolding of the human story. It provides grist for the mill of vigorous class discussions and personal pondering.

- To further foster active learning, the **Second Thoughts** section at the end of each chapter provides a list of particulars (people, places, events, processes, concepts) under the heading "**What's the Significance?**" inviting students to check their grasp of that chapter's material. The next part of the Second

Thoughts section is a set of **Big Picture Questions**. Unlike the marginal questions, which are keyed specifically to the adjacent material, these Big Picture Questions are not directly addressed in the text. Instead, they provide opportunities for integration, comparison, analysis, and sometimes speculation. Such questions might well become the basis for engaging writing assignments, class discussions, or exam items. Finally, a limited **list of suggested readings**—books, articles, and Web sites–invites further exploration of the material in the chapter.

- **Snapshots** appear in every chapter and present succinct glimpses of particular themes, regions, or time periods, adding some trees to the forest of world history.

- As is always true of books published by Bedford/St. Martin's, a **rich program of maps and images** accompanies the narrative. Because history and geography are so closely related, more than 100 maps have been included in the two volumes of the book. About 150 images, most of them contemporary to the times and places they illustrate, punctuate the narrative text, while dozens of others in the various Visual Sources features provide multiple occasions for students to assess visual sources as historical evidence.

Supplements

A comprehensive collection of print and electronic resources for students and instructors accompanies this book. Developed with my collaboration, they are designed to provide a host of practical learning and teaching aids. You can learn more about the accompanying materials by visiting bedfordstmartins.com/strayersources/catalog.

For Students

***Ways of the World: A Brief Global History with Sources* e-Book.** This easy-to-use, searchable e-book integrates the narrative, maps, and images from *Ways of the World* with resources from the Online Study Guide, making it a dynamic learning and study tool. Instructors can share annotations as well as add documents, images, and other materials to customize the text. The e-book can be packaged free with the print text or purchased stand-alone at a discount.

FREE Student Center at bedfordstmartins.com/strayer. The Student Center is a free resource to help students master themes and information presented in the textbook and improve their historical skills. **The Online Study Guide** provides students with self-review quizzes and activities for each chapter, including a multiple-choice self-test that focuses on important conceptual ideas; an identification quiz that helps students remember key people, places, and events; a flashcard activity that tests students' knowledge of key terms; and two interactive map activities intended to strengthen students' geography skills. Instructors can monitor students' progress through an online Quiz Gradebook or receive e-mail updates. The Student Center also features **History Research and Writing Help**, which includes *History Research and Reference Sources*, with links to history-related databases, indexes, and journals, plus contact information for state, provincial, local, and professional history organizations; *More Sources and How to Format a History Paper*, with clear advice on how to integrate primary and secondary sources into research papers, how to cite sources correctly, and how to format in MLA, APA, *Chicago*, or CBE style; *Build a Bibliography*, a simple but powerful Web-based tool that addresses the process of collecting sources and generates bibliographies in four commonly used documentation styles; and *Tips on Avoiding Plagiarism*, an online tutorial that reviews the consequences of plagiarism and explains what sources to acknowledge, how to keep good notes, how to organize research, and how to integrate sources appropriately and includes exercises to help students practice integrating sources and recognize acceptable summaries.

For Instructors

HistoryClass for *Ways of the World: A Brief Global History with Sources.* Bedford/St. Martin's online learning space for history gives you the right tools and the rich content to create your course, your way. An interactive e-book enables you to easily assign relevant textbook sections. Additional primary sources supplement the textbook and provide more options for class discussion and assignments. Other resources include guidelines for analyzing primary materials, avoiding plagiarism, and citing sources. Access to the acclaimed content library Make History provides unlimited access to thousands of maps, images, documents, and Web links. Online Study Guide content offers a range of activities to help students assess their progress, study more effectively, and improve their critical thinking skills. Customize the provided content and mix in your own with ease—everything in HistoryClass is integrated to work together in the same space.

Instructor's Resource Manual at bedfordstmartins.com/strayersources/ catalog. This extensive manual by Eric W. Nelson (Missouri State University) and Phyllis G. Jestice (University of Southern Mississippi) offers both experienced and first-time instructors tools for presenting the book's material in exciting and engaging ways. Introductory essays cover teaching with the docutext and analyzing primary written and visual sources. Also included are chapter learning objectives; annotated chapter outlines; lecture strategies; tips for helping students with common misconceptions and difficult topics; a list of key terms and definitions; answer guidelines for in-text chapter questions; and suggestions for in-class activities (including using film, video, and literature), ways to start discussions, topics for debate, and analyzing primary sources. For the Documents and Visual Sources features in each textbook chapter, the instructor's manual includes answers to headnote questions and to the Considering the Evidence comparative questions. The manual also provides suggestions for in-class and out-of-class activities for the Documents and Visual Sources features. Each chapter concludes with a guide to all the chapter-specific supplements available with *Ways of the World*. A guide for first-time teaching assistants, two sample syllabi, a list of useful books for the first-time world history professor, and a list of books that form the basis of a world history reference library are also included.

Instructor's Resource CD-ROM. This disc provides instructors with ready-made and customizable PowerPoint multimedia presentations built around chapter outlines, maps, figures, and all images from the docutext, plus jpeg versions of these maps, figures, and images. Also included are chapter questions formatted in PowerPoint and MS Word for use with i<clicker, a classroom response system, and blank outline maps in PDF format. Many of these resources are also available for download at bedfordstmartins.com/strayersources/catalog.

Computerized Test Bank. Written by Eric W. Nelson (Missouri State University) and Phyllis G. Jestice (University of Southern Mississippi), the test bank provides more than thirty exercises per chapter, including multiple-choice, fill-in-the-blank, short-answer, and full-length essay questions. The answer key includes textbook page numbers, correct answers, and essay outlines. Instructors can customize quizzes, add or edit both questions and answers, and export questions and answers to a variety of formats, including WebCT and Blackboard.

FREE Student Center with Instructor Resources at bedfordstmartins.com/strayer. The Student Center for *Ways of the World* gathers not only all the electronic resources for students but also those for instructors in one easy-to-use site. Instructors can keep track of their students' progress in the Online Study Guide by using the Quiz Gradebook and can also gain access to lecture, assignment, and research materials; PowerPoint chapter outlines and images; and the digital libraries at Make History.

Make History at bedfordstmartins.com/makehistory. Free and open to instructors and students, Make History combines the best Web resources with hundreds of maps and images, to make finding source material simple. Users can browse the collection of thousands of resources by course or by topic, date, and type. Each item has been carefully chosen and helpfully annotated. Instructors can also create collections to share with students or for use in lectures and presentations.

Content for Course Management Systems. A variety of student and instructor resources developed for this textbook is ready for use in course management systems such as Blackboard, WebCT, and other platforms. This e-content includes the book's Online Study Guide, online instructor's resources, and the book's test bank.

Videos and Multimedia. A wide assortment of videos and multimedia CD-ROMs on various topics in world history is available to qualified adopters. Contact your Bedford/St. Martin's representative for more information.

Packaging Opportunities

In addition to using book-specific supplements, instructors have numerous options for packaging other Bedford/St. Martin's titles with *Ways of the World* for free or at a discount. Visit bedfordstmartins.com/strayer/catalog for more information.

Rand McNally Historical Atlas of the World. This collection of almost seventy full-color maps illustrates the eras and civilizations in world history from the emergence of human societies to the present. *Available for $3.00 when packaged with the text.*

The Bedford Glossary for World History. This handy supplement for the survey course gives students historically contextualized definitions for hundreds of terms—from *abolitionism* to *Zoroastrianism*—that students will encounter in lectures, reading, and exams. *Free when packaged with the text.*

World History Matters: A Student Guide to World History Online. Based on the popular World History Matters Web site produced by the Center for History and New Media, this unique resource, edited by Kristin Lehner (The Johns Hopkins University), Kelly Schrum (George Mason University), and T. Mills Kelly (George Mason University), combines reviews of 150 of the most useful and reliable world history Web sites with an introduction that guides students in locating, evaluating, and correctly citing online sources. *Free when packaged with the text.*

The Bedford Series in History and Culture. More than 100 titles in this highly praised series combine first-rate scholarship, historical narrative, and important primary documents for undergraduate courses. Each book is brief, inexpensive, and focused on a specific topic or period. *Package discounts are available.*

Trade Books. Titles published by sister companies Farrar, Straus and Giroux; Henry Holt and Company; Hill and Wang; Picador; St. Martin's Press; and Palgrave Macmillan are *available at a 50 percent discount* when packaged with Bedford/St. Martin's textbooks. For more information, visit bedfordstmartins.com/tradeup.

"It Takes a Village"

In any enterprise of significance, "it takes a village," as they say. Bringing *Ways of the World* to life, it seems, has occupied the energies of several villages.

The largest of these villages consists of those many people who read the manuscript at various stages, and commented on it, sometimes at great length. I continue to be surprised at the power of this kind of collaboration. Frequently, passages I had regarded as polished to a gleaming perfection benefited greatly from the collective wisdom and experience of these thoughtful reviewers. Reviewers in the early phases of this project provided detailed and invaluable advice on the Documents and Visual

Sources features for this docutext. Reviewers commissioned by Bedford/St. Martin's are listed here in alphabetical order, with my great thanks:

Sanjam Ahluwalia, *Northern Arizona University*
Abel Alves, *Ball State University*
Cynthia Bisson, *Belmont University*
Deborah Buffton, *University of Wisconsin–La Crosse*
Brian D. Bunk, *University of Massachusetts–Amherst*
Allen Dieterich-Ward, *Shippensburg University*
Jonathan Dresner, *Pittsburg State University*
Deborah Gerish, *Emporia State University*
Nicholas Germana, *Keene State College*
Terrell Goddard, *Northwest Vista College*
L. Dana Goodrich, *Northwest Vista College*
Andrew Goss, *University of New Orleans*
Candace Gregory-Abbott, *California State University–Sacramento*
Jeanne Harrie, *California State University–Bakersfield*
Stephen Hernon, *Notre Dame Academy (NY)*
Marianne Holdzkom, *Southern Polytechnic State University*
Bryan Jack, *Winston–Salem State University*
Theresa Jordan, *Washington State University*
Jared Brent Krebsbach, *University of Memphis*
John LaValle, *Western New Mexico University*
Otto W. Mandahl Jr., *Skagit Valley College*
Kathryn Mapstone, *Bunker Hill Community College*
John Maunu, *Grosse Ile High School*
Mario D. Mazzarella, *Christopher Newport University*
Mark W. McLeod, *University of Delaware*
Eben Miller, *Southern Maine Community College*
Theodore A. Nitz, *Gonzaga University*
Kenneth Osgood, *Florida Atlantic University*
John Pinheiro, *Aquinas College*
Anthony R. Santoro, *Christopher Newport University*
Alyssa Goldstein Sepinwall, *California State University–San Marcos*
David Simonelli, *Youngstown State University*
Helene Sinnreich, *Youngstown State University*
Steven Stofferahn, *Indiana State University*
Lisa Tran, *California State University–Fullerton*
Wendy Turner, *Augusta State University*
Elaine C. P. Turney, *University of Texas–San Antonio*
Michael Vann, *California State University–Sacramento*
Kurt J. Wertmuller, *Azusa Pacific University*
Nathaniel P. Weston, *Seattle Central Community College*
James Wood, *North Carolina A&T State University*.

Others in the village of reviewers have been friends, family, and colleagues who graciously agreed to read portions of the manuscript and offer helpful counsel: Kabir Helminski, James Horn, Elisabeth Jay, David Northrup, Lynn Parsons, Katherine Poethig, Kevin Reilly, and Julie Shackford–Bradley.

The "Bedford village" has been a second community supporting this enterprise and the one most directly responsible for the book's appearance in print. It would be difficult for any author to imagine a more encouraging and professional publishing team. Developmental editor Kathryn Abbott, herself an experienced professor of history, has been my primary point of contact with the Bedford village as this docutext version of *Ways of the World* unfolded. She has helped to conceptualize the entire project, masterfully summarized and analyzed the numerous reviews of the manuscript, added her own thoughtful suggestions to the mix, and generally kept the project on track—all with grace and courtesy. In a similar role, Jim Strandberg guided the development of the original text with the sensitivity of a fine historian as well as the skill of an outstanding editor. Eric Nelson of Missouri State University has served as a general consultant for the docutext, as well as the co-author of the fine instructor's manual that accompanies the book. A number of the ideas for Considering the Evidence features came from him, and his careful reading of all the features in draft form was extremely helpful. To all of these close collaborators, I acknowledge a debt of gratitude that I am unable to adequately repay.

Publisher Mary Dougherty first broached the idea of my writing a world history text for Bedford and later surprised me with the suggestion for a docutext version of the book. With a manner as lovely as it is professional, she has provided overall editorial leadership and a calming balm to authorial anxieties. More recently these tasks have passed to executive editor Traci Mueller, who has undertaken them with a similar combination of kindness and competence. Jane Knetzger, director of development, has overseen the project from its beginning, bore my many questions with forbearance, and, even better, provided timely answers. Company president Joan Feinberg has, to my surprise and delight, periodically kept her own experienced hand in this pot, while executive editor Beth Welch, though fully engaged in her own projects, has served as counselor from the sidelines. Photo researcher Carole Frohlich identified and acquired the many images that grace *Ways of the World: A Brief Global History with Sources* and did so with amazing efficiency and courtesy. Working with her has been an aesthetic education for me and a personal delight.

Operating more behind the scenes in the Bedford village, a series of highly competent and always supportive people have shepherded this book along its way. Lynn Sternberger and Robin Soule provided invaluable assistance in handling the manuscript, contacting reviewers, and keeping on top of the endless details that such an enterprise demands. Bridget Leahy served as project editor during the book's production and, often under considerable pressure, did so with both grace and efficiency. Copy editor Janet Renard polished the prose and sorted out my inconsistent usages with a seasoned and perceptive eye.

Jenna Bookin Barry and Sally Constable have overseen the marketing process, while history specialist John Hunger and a cadre of humanities specialists and sales representatives have introduced the book to the academic world. Jack Cashman supervised the development of ancillary materials to support the book, and Donna Dennison ably coordinated research for the lovely covers that mark *Ways of the World*.

Yet another "village" that contributed much to *Ways of the World* consists in that group of distinguished scholars and teachers who worked with me on an earlier world history text, *The Making of the Modern World*, published by St. Martin's Press (1988, 1995). They include Sandria Freitag, Edwin Hirschmann, Donald Holsinger, James Horn, Robert Marks, Joe Moore, Lynn Parsons, and Robert Smith. That collective effort resembled participation in an extended seminar, from which I benefited immensely. Their ideas and insights have shaped my own understanding of world history in many ways and greatly enriched *Ways of the World*.

A final and much smaller community sustained this project and its author. It is that most intimate of villages that we know as a marriage. Here I pay wholly inadequate tribute to its other member, my wife, Suzanne Sturn. She knows how I feel, and no one else needs to.

To all my fellow villagers, I offer deep thanks for perhaps the richest intellectual experience of my professional life. I am grateful beyond measure.

Robert Strayer
La Selva Beach, California

Brief Contents

Preface v

Working with Primary Sources xlv

Prologue: From Cosmic History to Human History li

PART ONE First Things First: Beginnings in History, to 500 B.C.E. 2

THE BIG PICTURE Turning Points in Early World History 3

1. First Peoples: Populating the Planet, to 10,000 B.C.E. 11
2. First Farmers: The Revolutions of Agriculture, 10,000 B.C.E.–3000 B.C.E. 49
3. First Civilizations: Cities, States, and Unequal Societies, 3500 B.C.E.–500 B.C.E. 85

PART TWO The Classical Era in World History, 500 B.C.E.–500 C.E. 132

THE BIG PICTURE After the First Civilizations: What Changed and What Didn't? 133

4. Eurasian Empires, 500 B.C.E.–500 C.E. 143
5. Eurasian Cultural Traditions, 500 B.C.E.–500 C.E. 189
6. Eurasian Social Hierarchies, 500 B.C.E.–500 C.E. 237
7. Classical Era Variations: Africa and the Americas, 500 B.C.E.–1200 C.E. 281

PART THREE An Age of Accelerating Connections, 500–1500 324

THE BIG PICTURE Defining a Millennium 325

8. Commerce and Culture, 500–1500 333
9. China and the World: East Asian Connections, 500–1300 379
10. The Worlds of European Christendom: Connected and Divided, 500–1300 425
11. The Worlds of Islam: Afro-Eurasian Connections, 600–1500 473
12. Pastoral Peoples on the Global Stage: The Mongol Moment, 1200–1500 521
13. The Worlds of the Fifteenth Century 569

PART FOUR   The Early Modern World, 1450–1750   618

THE BIG PICTURE   Debating the Character of an Era   619

14. Empires and Encounters, 1450–1750   625
15. Global Commerce, 1450–1750   673
16. Religion and Science, 1450–1750   721

PART FIVE   The European Moment in World History, 1750–1914   770

THE BIG PICTURE   European Centrality and the Problem of Eurocentrism   771

17. Atlantic Revolutions and Their Echoes, 1750–1914   **779**
18. Revolutions of Industrialization, 1750–1914   825
19. Internal Troubles, External Threats: China, the Ottoman Empire, and Japan, 1800–1914   877
20. Colonial Encounters, 1750–1914   923

PART SIX   The Most Recent Century, 1914–2010   968

THE BIG PICTURE   The Twentieth Century: A New Period in World History?   969

21. The Collapse and Recovery of Europe, 1914–1970s   977
22. The Rise and Fall of World Communism, 1917–Present   1029
23. Independence and Development in the Global South, 1914–Present   1081
24. Accelerating Global Interaction, Since 1945   1133

Notes   1189
Index   1209

Contents

Preface   *v*
Maps   *xxxix*
Special Features   *xliii*
Working with Primary Sources   *xlv*

Prologue: From Cosmic History to Human History   *li*

The History of the Universe • The History of a
Planet • The History of the Human Species in
a Single Paragraph: A Preview • Why World
History? • Comparison, Connection, and Change:
The Three Cs of World History

Snapshot: **A History of the Universe as a Cosmic
Calendar**   *lii*

PART ONE
First Things First: Beginnings in History, to 500 B.C.E.   *2*

THE BIG PICTURE Turning Points in Early
World History   *3*

The Emergence of Humankind • The
Globalization of Humankind • The Revolution
of Farming and Herding • The Turning Point of
Civilization • A Note on Dates

Landmarks of Early World History,
to 500 B.C.E.   *8*

1. First Peoples: Populating the Planet, to 10,000 B.C.E.   *11*

Out of Africa to the Ends of the Earth: First
Migrations   *12*
   *Into Eurasia • Into Australia • Into the Americas
   • Into the Pacific*
The Ways We Were   *20*
   *The First Human Societies • Economy and the
   Environment • The Realm of the Spirit • Settling
   Down: The Great Transition*
Comparing Paleolithic Societies   *24*
   *The San of Southern Africa • The Chumash of
   Southern California*
Reflections: The Uses of the Paleolithic   *31*
Second Thoughts   *32*
   *What's the Significance? • Big Picture Questions
   • Next Steps: For Further Study*
Snapshot: **The Long Road to the Global Presence
of Humankind**   *13*
Snapshot: **The Paleolithic Era in Perspective**   *23*

CONSIDERING THE EVIDENCE
Documents Glimpses of Paleolithic Life   *34*
   *1.1—A Paleolithic Woman in the Twentieth
   Century: Nisa, The Life and Words of an !Kung
   Woman, 1969–1976 • 1.2—Australian Aboriginal
   Mythology: Stories from the Dreamtime, twentieth
   century*
Using the Evidence   *41*

Visual Sources The Aboriginal Rock Painting of
   Australia   *42*
   *Namondjok, Namarrgon (Lightning Man), and
   Barrginj • Nabulwinjbulwinj • A Hunting Scene*
Using the Evidence   *47*

2. First Farmers: The Revolutions of Agriculture, 10,000 B.C.E.–3000 B.C.E.   *49*

The Agricultural Revolution in World History   *50*
Comparing Agricultural Beginnings   *51*
   Common Patterns • Variations
The Globalization of Agriculture   *56*
   *Triumph and Resistance • The Culture of
   Agriculture*
Social Variation in the Age of Agriculture   *62*
   *Pastoral Societies • Agricultural Village Societies
   • Chiefdoms*
Reflections: The Legacies of Agriculture   *66*
Second Thoughts   *67*
   *What's the Significance? • Big Picture Questions
   • Next Steps: For Further Study*
Snapshot: **Agricultural Breakthroughs**   *52*
Snapshot: **The History of Maize/Corn**   *57*

CONSIDERING THE EVIDENCE
Documents Agricultural Village Societies   *68*
   *2.1—Germanic Peoples of Central Europe: Tacitus,
   Germania, first century* C.E. *• 2.2—Social
   Organization among the Gikuyu: Jomo Kenyatta,
   Facing Mount Kenya, 1938 • 2.3—Religion in a
   Caribbean Chiefdom: Bartolomé de Las Casas,
   Apologetic History of the Indies, 1566*
Using the Evidence   *75*

Visual Sources Art and Life in the Early
   Agrarian Era   *76*
   *Çatalhüyük: An Early Map and Landscape Painting
   • Women, Men, and Religion in Çatalhüyük • An
   African Pastoral Community • The Mystery of
   Stonehenge • A Sculpture from the Nok Culture*
Using the Evidence   *83*

3. First Civilizations: Cities, States, and Unequal Societies, 3500 B.C.E.–500 B.C.E.   *85*

Something New: The Emergence of
   Civilizations   *86*
   *Introducing the First Civilizations • The Question
   of Origins • An Urban Revolution*
The Erosion of Equality   *94*
   *Hierarchies of Class • Hierarchies of Gender •
   Patriarchy in Practice*
The Rise of the State   *99*
   *Coercion and Consent • Writing and Accounting
   • The Grandeur of Kings*
Comparing Mesopotamia and Egypt   *103*
   *Environment and Culture • Cities and States
   • Interaction and Exchange*
Reflections: "Civilization": What's in a Word?   *112*
Second Thoughts   *113*
   *What's the Significance? • Big Picture Questions
   • Next Steps: For Further Study*
Snapshot: **Writing in Ancient Civilizations**   *101*
Snapshot: **Key Moments in Mesopotamian
   History**   *104*
Snapshot: **Key Moments in Nile Valley
   Civilizations**   *107*

CONSIDERING THE EVIDENCE

Documents Life and Afterlife in Mesopotamia
  and Egypt   *115*

  *3.1—In Search of Eternal Life: The Epic of
  Gilgamesh, ca. 2700 B.C.E.–2500 B.C.E. • 3.2—Law
  and Justice in Ancient Mesopotamia: The Law Code
  of Hammurabi, ca. 1800 B.C.E. • 3.3—The Afterlife
  of a Pharaoh: A Pyramid Text, 2333 B.C.E. •
  3.4—A New Basis for Egyptian Immortality:
  Book of the Dead, ca. 1550–1064 B.C.E. •
  3.5—The Occupations of Old Egypt: Be a Scribe,
  ca. 2066–1650 B.C.E.*

Using the Evidence   *125*

Visual Sources Indus Valley Civilization   *126*

  *Ancient Harappa • A Seal from the Indus Valley
  • Man from Mohenjo Daro • Dancing Girl*

Using the Evidence   *131*

PART TWO
The Classical Era in
World History,
500 B.C.E.–500 C.E.   *132*

THE BIG PICTURE After the First Civilizations:
  What Changed and What Didn't   *133*

Continuities in Civilization • Changes in
Civilization • Classical Civilizations

Landmarks of the Classical Era, 500 B.C.E. to
  500 C.E.   *140*

Snapshot: **World Population during the Age of
  Agricultural Civilization**   *135*

4. Eurasian Empires, 500 B.C.E.–
500 C.E.   *143*

Empires and Civilizations in Collision: The Persians
  and the Greeks   *145*

  *The Persian Empire • The Greeks • Collision: The
  Greco-Persian Wars • Collision: Alexander and the
  Hellenistic Era*

Comparing Empires: Roman and Chinese   *154*

  *Rome: From City-State to Empire • China: From
  Warring States to Empire • Consolidating the Roman
  and Chinese Empires • The Collapse of Empires*

Intermittent Empire: The Case of India   *165*

Reflections: Classical Empires and the Twentieth
  Century   *167*

Second Thoughts   *168*

  *What's the Significance? • Big Picture Questions
  • Next Steps: For Further Study*

Snapshot: **Key Moments in Classical Greek
  History**   *150*

Snapshot: **Key Moments in the History of the
  Roman Empire**   *157*

Snapshot: **Key Moments in Classical Chinese
  History**   *162*

CONSIDERING THE EVIDENCE

Documents Political Authority in Classical
  Civilizations   *170*

  *4.1—In Praise of Athenian Democracy: Pericles,
  Funeral Oration, 431–430 B.C.E. • 4.2—In Praise
  of the Roman Empire: Aelius Aristides, The Roman
  Oration, 155 C.E. • 4.3—Governing a Chinese
  Empire: The Writings of Master Han Fei, third
  century B.C.E. • 4.4—Governing an Indian Empire:
  Ashoka, The Rock Edicts, ca. 268–232 B.C.E.*

Using the Evidence   *178*

Visual Sources Qin Shihuangdi and China's
Eternal Empire *180*

*An Eighteenth-Century Representation of Qin
Shihuangdi • The Terra-Cotta Army of Shihuangdi •
Terra-Cotta Infantry • Terra-Cotta Archer • A Bronze
Horse-Drawn Chariot*

Using the Evidence *187*

5. Eurasian Cultural Traditions,
500 B.C.E.–500 C.E.   *189*

China and the Search for Order *192*
  *The Legalist Answer • The Confucian Answer
  • The Daoist Answer*
Cultural Traditions of Classical India *197*
  *South Asian Religion: From Ritual Sacrifice to
  Philosophical Speculation • The Buddhist Challenge
  • Hinduism as a Religion of Duty and Devotion*
Moving toward Monotheism: The Search for God
  in the Middle East *202*
  Zoroastrianism • Judaism
The Cultural Tradition of Classical Greece: The
  Search for a Rational Order *205*
  The Greek Way of Knowing • The Greek Legacy
Comparing Jesus and the Buddha *209*
  *The Lives of the Founders • Establishing New
  Religions • Creating Institutions*
Reflections: Religion and Historians *214*
Second Thoughts *215*
  *What's the Significance? • Big Picture Questions
  • Next Steps: For Further Study*
Snapshot: Thinkers and Philosophies of the
  Classical Era *191*
Snapshot: Reflections on Human Love from
  Mediterranean Civilization *209*

CONSIDERING THE EVIDENCE
Documents The Good Life in Classical Eurasia *217*
  *5.1—Reflections from Confucius: Confucius, The
  Analects, ca. 479–221 B.C.E. • 5.2—Reflections
  from the Hindu Scriptures: Bhagavad Gita, ca. fifth
  to second century B.C.E. • 5.3—Reflections
  from Socrates: Plato, Apology, ca. 399 B.C.E. •
  5.4—Reflections from Jesus: The Gospel of Matthew,
  ca. 70–100 C.E.*
Using the Evidence *226*
Visual Sources Representations of the
  Buddha *227*
  *Footprints of the Buddha • A Classic Indian Buddha
  • A Bodhisattva of Compassion: Kannon of 1,000
  Arms • The Chinese Maitreya Buddha • The
  Amitabha Buddha*
Using the Evidence *235*

6. Eurasian Social Hierarchies,
500 B.C.E.–500 C.E.   *237*

Society and the State in Classical China *238*
  *An Elite of Officials • The Landlord Class
  • Peasants • Merchants*
Class and Caste in India *242*
  Caste as Varna *• Caste as* Jati *• The Functions of Caste*
Slavery in the Classical Era: The Case of the
  Roman Empire *247*
  *Slavery and Civilization • The Making of a Slave
  Society: The Case of Rome • Resistance and Rebellion*
Comparing Patriarchies of the Classical Era *252*
  *A Changing Patriarchy: The Case of China •
  Contrasting Patriarchies in Athens and Sparta*
Reflections: Arguing with Solomon and the
  Buddha *259*

Second Thoughts   *260*

*What's the Significance? • Big Picture Questions
• Next Steps: For Further Study*

Snapshot: **Social Life and Duty in Classical India**   *244*

Snapshot: **Comparing Greco-Roman and American Slavery**   *248*

CONSIDERING THE EVIDENCE

Documents   Patriarchy and Women's Voices in the Classical Era   *262*

6.1—A Male View of Chinese Women's Lives: Fu Xuan, How Sad It Is to Be a Woman, third century C.E. *• 6.2—A Chinese Woman's Instructions to Her Daughters: Ban Zhao, Lessons for Women, late first century* C.E. *• 6.3—An Alternative to Patriarchy in India: Psalms of the Sisters, first century* B.C.E. *• 6.4—Roman Women in Protest: Livy, History of Rome, late first century* B.C.E. *to early first century* C.E.

Using the Evidence   *271*

Visual Sources   Pompeii as a Window on the Roman World   *272*

Terentius Neo and His Wife • A Pompeii Banquet • Scenes in a Pompeii Tavern • A Domestic Shrine • Mystery Religions: The Cult of Dionysus

Using the Evidence   *279*

7. Classical Era Variations: Africa and the Americas, 500 B.C.E.–1200 C.E.   *281*

The African Northeast   *283*

Meroë: Continuing a Nile Valley Civilization • Axum: The Making of a Christian Kingdom

Along the Niger River: Cities without States   *288*

South of the Equator: The World of Bantu Africa   *290*

Cultural Encounters • Society and Religion

Civilizations of Mesoamerica   *292*

The Maya: Writing and Warfare • Teotihuacán: The Americas' Greatest City

Civilizations of the Andes   *297*

Chavín: A Pan-Andean Religious Movement • Moche: A Regional Andean Civilization

North America in the Classical Era: From Chaco to Cahokia   *301*

Pit Houses and Great Houses: The Ancestral Pueblo • The Mound Builders of the Eastern Woodlands

Reflections: Deciding What's Important: Balance in World History   *305*

Second Thoughts   *306*

What's the Significance? • Big Picture Questions • Next Steps: For Further Study

Snapshot: **Continental Population in the Classical Era**   *283*

CONSIDERING THE EVIDENCE

Documents   Axum and the World   *307*

7.1—A Guidebook to the World of Indian Ocean Commerce: The Periplus of the Erythraean Sea, first century C.E. *• 7.2—The Making of an Axumite Empire: Inscription on a Stone Throne, second or third century* C.E. *• 7.3—The Coming of Christianity to Axum: Rufinus, On the Evangelization of Abyssinia, late fourth century* C.E. *• 7.4—A Byzantine View of an Axumite Monarch: Julian, Report to the Byzantine Emperor on Axum, 530–531 • 7.5—Axum and the Gold Trade: Cosmas, The Christian Topography, sixth century* C.E.

Using the Evidence   *315*

Visual Sources   Art and the Maya Elite   *316*

Shield Jaguar and Lady Xok: A Royal Couple of Yaxchilan • The Presentation of Captives • A Bloodletting Ritual • The Ball Game • An Embracing Couple

Using the Evidence   *323*

PART THREE
An Age of Accelerating Connections, 500–1500   *324*

THE BIG PICTURE Defining a Millennium   325

Third-Wave Civilizations: Something New, Something Old, Something Blended • The Ties That Bind: Transregional Interaction in the Postclassical Era

Landmarks in the Era of Accelerating Connections, 500 to 1500   *330*

8. Commerce and Culture, 500–1500   *333*

Silk Roads: Exchange across Eurasia   *335*
  The Growth of the Silk Roads • Goods in Transit • Cultures in Transit • Disease in Transit

Sea Roads: Exchange across the Indian Ocean   *341*
  Weaving the Web of an Indian Ocean World • Sea Roads as a Catalyst for Change: Southeast Asia and Srivijaya • Sea Roads as a Catalyst for Change: East Africa and Swahili Civilization

Sand Roads: Exchange across the Sahara   *348*
  Commercial Beginnings in West Africa • Gold, Salt, and Slaves: Trade and Empire in West Africa

An American Network: Commerce and Connection in the Western Hemisphere   *351*

Reflections: Economic Globalization—Ancient and Modern   *354*

Second Thoughts   *355*
  What's the Significance? • Big Picture Questions • Next Steps: For Further Study

Snapshot: **Economic Exchange along the Silk Roads**   *337*

Snapshot: **Economic Exchange in the Indian Ocean Basin**   *343*

CONSIDERING THE EVIDENCE

Documents Travelers' Tales and Observations   *356*
  8.1—A Chinese Buddhist in India: Huili, A Biography of the Tripitaka Master and Xuanzang, Record of the Western Region, Seventh Century C.E. *• 8.2—A European Christian in China: Marco Polo, The Travels of Marco Polo, 1299 • 8.3—An Arab Muslim in West Africa: Ibn Battuta, Travels in Asia and Africa, 1354*

Using the Evidence   *366*

Visual Sources Art, Religion, and Cultural Exchange in Central Asia   *367*
  Greek Culture, Buddhism, and the Kushans • Buddhist Monks on the Silk Road • Manichaean Scribes • The Mongols in China • Islam, Shamanism, and the Turks

Using the Evidence   *377*

9. China and the World: East Asian Connections, 500–1300   *379*

The Reemergence of a Unified China   *380*
  A "Golden Age" of Chinese Achievement • Women in the Song Dynasty

China and the Northern Nomads: A Chinese World Order in the Making   *385*
  The Tribute System in Theory • The Tribute System in Practice • Cultural Influence across an Ecological Frontier

Coping with China: Comparing Korea, Vietnam, and Japan   *390*

Korea and China • Vietnam and China • Japan and China

China and the Eurasian World Economy *397*
Spillovers: China's Impact on Eurasia • On the Receiving End: China as Economic Beneficiary

China and Buddhism *399*
Making Buddhism Chinese • Losing State Support: The Crisis of Chinese Buddhism

Reflections: Why Do Things Change? *403*

Second Thoughts *405*
What's the Significance? • Big Picture Questions • Next Steps: For Further Study

Snapshot: **Key Moments in the History of Postclassical China** *386*

CONSIDERING THE EVIDENCE

Documents The Making of Japanese Civilization *406*
9.1—Japanese Political Ideals: Shotoku, The Seventeen Article Constitution, 604 • 9.2—Buddhism in Japan: The Zen Tradition: Dogen, Writings on Zen Buddhism, thirteenth century • 9.3—The Uniqueness of Japan: Kitabatake Chikafusa, The Chronicle of the Direct Descent of Gods and Sovereigns, 1339 • 9.4—Social Life at Court: Sei Shonagon, Pillow Book, ca. 1000 • 9.5—The Way of the Warrior: Shiba Yosimasa, Advice to Young Samurai, ca. 1400, and Imagawa Ryoshun, The Imagawa Letter, 1412

Using the Evidence *416*

Visual Sources The Leisure Life of China's Elites *417*
A Banquet with the Emperor • At Table with the Empress • A Literary Gathering • Solitary Reflection • An Elite Night Party

Using the Evidence *422*

10. The Worlds of European Christendom: Connected and Divided, 500–1300 *425*

Eastern Christendom: Building on the Roman Past *427*
The Byzantine State • The Byzantine Church and Christian Divergence • Byzantium and the World • The Conversion of Russia

Western Christendom: Rebuilding in the Wake of Roman Collapse *434*
Political Life in Western Europe, 500–1000 • Society and the Church, 500–1000 • Accelerating Change in the West, 1000–1300 • Europe Outward Bound: The Crusading Tradition

The West in Comparative Perspective *445*
Catching Up • Pluralism in Politics • Reason and Faith

Reflections: Remembering and Forgetting: Continuity and Surprise in the Worlds of Christendom *452*

Second Thoughts *453*
What's the Significance? • Big Picture Questions • Next Steps: For Further Study

Snapshot: **Key Moments in Byzantine History** *427*

Snapshot: **Key Moments in the Evolution of Western Civilization** *434*

CONSIDERING THE EVIDENCE

Documents The Making of Christian Europe… and a Chinese Counterpoint *455*
10.1—The Conversion of Clovis: Gregory of Tours, History of the Franks, late sixth century • 10.2—Advice on Dealing with "Pagans": Pope Gregory, Advice to the English Church, 601 •

10.3—*Charlemagne and the Saxons: Charlemagne, Capitulary on Saxony, 785* • 10.4 *and* 10.5—*The Persistence of Tradition: Willibald, Life of Boniface, ca 760* C.E., *and The Leechbook, tenth century* • 10.6—*The Jesus Sutras in China: The Jesus Sutras, 635–1005*

Using the Evidence   *464*

Visual Sources Reading Byzantine Icons   *466*
Christ Pantokrator • *The Nativity* • *Ladder of Divine Ascent*

Using the Evidence   *471*

11. The Worlds of Islam: Afro-Eurasian Connections, 600–1500   *473*

The Birth of a New Religion   *474*
The Homeland of Islam • *The Messenger and the Message* • *The Transformation of Arabia*

The Making of an Arab Empire   *480*
War and Conquest • *Conversion to Islam* • *Divisions and Controversies* • *Women and Men in Early Islam*

Islam and Cultural Encounter: A Four-Way Comparison   *488*
The Case of India • *The Case of Anatolia* • *The Case of West Africa* • *The Case of Spain*

The World of Islam as a New Civilization   *495*
Networks of Faith • *Networks of Exchange*

Reflections: Past and Present: Choosing Our History   *500*

Second Thoughts   *501*
What's the Significance? • *Big Picture Questions* • *Next Steps: For Further Study*

Snapshot: Key Moments in the Early History of Islam   *476*

Snapshot: Key Achievements in Islamic Science and Scholarship   *499*

CONSIDERING THE EVIDENCE
Documents Voices of Islam   *502*
11.1—The Voice of Allah: The Quran, seventh century • *11.2—The Voice of the Prophet Muhammad: The Hadith, eighth and ninth centuries* • *11.3—The Voice of the Law: The Sharia, ninth century* • *11.4—The Voice of the Sufis: Inscription in Rumi's Tomb, thirteenth century; Rumi, Poem, thirteenth century; and Rumi, "Drowned in God," Mathnawi, thirteenth century*

Using the Evidence   *511*

Visual Sources Islamic Civilization in Persian Miniature Paintings   *512*
An Arab Camp Scene • *City Life in Islamic Persia* • *The Night Journey of Muhammad*

Using the Evidence   *519*

12. Pastoral Peoples on the Global Stage: The Mongol Moment, 1200–1500   *521*

Looking Back and Looking Around: The Long History of Pastoral Nomads   *522*
The World of Pastoral Societies • *The Xiongnu: An Early Nomadic Empire* • *The Arabs and the Turks* • *The Masai of East Africa*

Breakout: The Mongol Empire   *529*
From Temujin to Chinggis Khan: The Rise of the Mongol Empire • *Explaining the Mongol Moment*

Encountering the Mongols: Comparing Three Cases   *536*
China and the Mongols • *Persia and the Mongols* • *Russia and the Mongols*

The Mongol Empire as a Eurasian Network   *541*
  *Toward a World Economy • Diplomacy on a
  Eurasian Scale • Cultural Exchange in the Mongol
  Realm • The Plague: A Eurasian Pandemic*
Reflections: Changing Images of Nomadic
  Peoples   *547*
Second Thoughts   *548*
  *What's the Significance? • Big Picture Questions
  • Next Steps: For Further Study*

Snapshot: **Varieties of Pastoral Societies**   *523*

Snapshot: **Key Moments in Mongol History**   *531*

CONSIDERING THE EVIDENCE

Documents Perspectives on the Mongols   *550*
  *12.1—Mongol History from a Mongol Source:
  The Secret History of the Mongols, ca. 1240 •
  12.2—A Letter from Chinggis Khan: Chinggis
  Khan, Letter to Changchun, 1219 • 12.3—A Russian
  View of the Mongols: The Chronicle of Novgorod,
  1238 • 12.4—Chinese Perceptions of the Mongols:
  Epitaph for the Honorable Menggu, 1274
  • 12.5—Mongol Women through European Eyes:
  William of Rubruck, Journey to the Land of the
  Mongols, ca. 1255*
Using the Evidence   *559*

Visual Sources The Black Death and Religion in
  Western Europe   *560*
  *The Flagellants • Burying the Dead • A Culture of
  Death • In the Face of Catastrophe—Questioning
  or Affirming the Faith*
Using the Evidence   *567*

**13. The Worlds of the Fifteenth
Century   569**

The Shapes of Human Communities   *571*
  *Paleolithic Persistence • Agricultural Village Societies
  • Herding Peoples*
Civilizations of the Fifteenth Century: Comparing
  China and Europe   *575*
  *Ming Dynasty China • European Comparisons:
  State Building and Cultural Renewal • European
  Comparisons: Maritime Voyaging*
Civilizations of the Fifteenth Century: The Islamic
  World   *584*
  *In the Islamic Heartland: The Ottoman and Safavid
  Empires • On the Frontiers of Islam: The Songhay
  and Mughal Empires*
Civilizations of the Fifteenth Century: The
  Americas   *588*
  The Aztec Empire • The Inca Empire
Webs of Connection   *594*
A Preview of Coming Attractions: Looking Ahead
  to the Modern Era, 1500–2010   *596*
Reflections: What If? Chance and Contingency
  in World History   *599*
Second Thoughts   *599*
  *What's the Significance? • Big Picture Questions •
  Next Steps: For Further Study*

Snapshot: **Major Developments around the World
  in the Fifteenth Century**   *570*

Snapshot: **Key Moments in European Maritime
  Voyaging**   *581*

Snapshot: **World Population Growth, 1000–2000**
  597

CONSIDERING THE EVIDENCE

Documents The Aztecs and the Incas through
Spanish Eyes   601

*13.1—Diego Duran on the Aztecs: King
Moctezuma I, Laws, Ordinances and Regulations,
ca. 1450, and Diego Duran, Book of the Gods and
Rites, 1574–76 • 13.2—Pedro de Cieza de Léon
on the Incas: Pedro de Cieza de Léon, Chronicles of
the Incas, ca. 1550*

Using the Evidence   607

Visual Sources Sacred Places in the World of the
Fifteenth Century   608

*The Hall of Prayer for Good Harvest at the Temple
of Heaven, Beijing, China • Kinkakuji: A Buddhist
Temple in Japan • The Dome of the Rock, Jerusalem
• The Church of St. George, Lalibela, Ethiopia*

Using the Evidence   616

PART FOUR
The Early Modern World,
1450–1750   *618*

THE BIG PICTURE Debating the Character of
an Era   *619*

An Early Modern Era? • A Late Agrarian Era?
Landmarks in the Early Modern Era,
1450–1750   *622*

14. Empires and Encounters,
1450–1750   *625*

European Empires in the Americas   *626*
*The European Advantage • The Great Dying • The
Columbian Exchange*

Comparing Colonial Societies in the Americas   *631*
*In the Lands of the Aztecs and the Incas • Colonies
of Sugar • Settler Colonies in North America*

The Steppes and Siberia: The Making of a Russian
Empire   *639*
*Experiencing the Russian Empire • Russians and
Empire*

Asian Empires   *643*
*Making China an Empire • Muslims and Hindus
in the Mughal Empire • Muslims, Christians, and
the Ottoman Empire*

Reflections: Countering Eurocentrism … or
Reflecting It?   *650*

Second Thoughts   *651*
*What's the Significance? • Big Picture Questions
• Next Steps: For Further Study*

Snapshot: **Ethnic Composition of Colonial
Societies in Latin America (1825)**   *636*

CONSIDERING THE EVIDENCE

Documents State Building in the Early
Modern Era   *652*
*14.1—The "Self-Portrait" of a Chinese Emperor:
The Emperor Kangxi, Reflections, 1671–1722 •
14.2—The Memoirs of Emperor Jahangir: Jahangir,
Memoirs, 1605–1627 • 14.3—An Outsider's View of
Suleiman I: Ogier Ghiselin de Busbecq, The Turkish
Letters, 1555–1562 • 14.4 and 14.5—French State-
Building and Louis XIV: Louis XIV, Memoirs, 1670,
and Jean-Baptiste Colbert, Instructions for
Intendants, 1680*

Using the Evidence   *663*

Visual Sources The Conquest of Mexico Through
Aztec Eyes   *664*
*Disaster Foretold • Moctezuma and Cortés • The
Massacre of the Nobles • The Spanish Retreat from
Tenochtitlán • Smallpox: Disease and Defeat*

Using the Evidence   *671*

15. Global Commerce,
1450–1750   *673*

Europeans and Asian Commerce   *674*
  *A Portuguese Empire of Commerce • Spain and the
  Philippines • The East India Companies • Asian
  Commerce*
Silver and Global Commerce   *682*
The "World Hunt": Fur in Global Commerce   *685*
Commerce in People: The Atlantic Slave Trade   *689*
  *The Slave Trade in Context • The Slave Trade in
  Practice • Comparing Consequences: The Impact of
  the Slave Trade in Africa*
Reflections: Economic Globalization—Then and
  Now   *697*
Second Thoughts   *698*
  *What's the Significance? • Big Picture Questions •
  Next Steps: For Further Study*
Snapshot: **Key Moments in the European
  Encounter with Asia**   *678*
Snapshot: **The Slave Trade in Numbers
  (1501–1866)**   *694*

CONSIDERING THE EVIDENCE
Documents Voices from the Slave Trade   *700*
  *15.1—The Journey to Slavery: Olaudah Equiano,
  The Interesting Narrative of the Life of Olaudah
  Equiano, 1789 • 15.2—The Business of the Slave
  Trade: Thomas Phillips, A Journal of a Voyage Made
  in the Hannibal of London, 1694 • 15.3—The Slave
  Trade and the Kingdom of Kongo: King Affonso I,
  Letters to King Jao of Portugal, 1526 • 15.4—The
  Slave Trade and the Kingdom of Asante: Osei
  Bonsu, Conversation with Joseph Dupuis, 1820*
Using the Evidence   *710*

Visual Sources Exchange and Status in the Early
  Modern World   *711*
  *Tea and Porcelain in Europe • A Chocolate Party in
  Spain • An Ottoman Coffeehouse • Clothing and
  Status in Colonial Mexico • Procession and Display
  in the Kingdom of Dahomey*
Using the Evidence   *719*

16. Religion and Science,
1450–1750   *721*

The Globalization of Christianity   *722*
  *Western Christendom Fragmented: The Protestant
  Reformation • Christianity Outward Bound •
  Conversion and Adaptation in Spanish America
  • An Asian Comparison: China and the Jesuits*
Persistence and Change in Afro-Asian Cultural
  Traditions   *732*
  *Expansion and Renewal in the Islamic World •
  China: New Directions in an Old Tradition • India:
  Bridging the Hindu/Muslim Divide*
A New Way of Thinking: The Birth of Modern
  Science   *737*
  *The Question of Origins: Why Europe? • Science as
  Cultural Revolution • Science and Enlightenment •
  Looking Ahead: Science in the Nineteenth Century
  • European Science beyond the West*
Reflections: Cultural Borrowing and Its
  Hazards   *746*
Second Thoughts   *747*
  *What's the Significance? • Big Picture Questions •
  Next Steps: For Further Study*
Snapshot: **Catholic/Protestant Differences in the
  Sixteenth Century**   *724*

Snapshot: **Major Thinkers and Achievements of the Scientific Revolution** *740*

CONSIDERING THE EVIDENCE
Documents Cultural Change in the Early Modern World *749*

16.1—Luther's Protest: Martin Luther, Table Talk, early sixteenth century • 16.2—Progress and Enlightenment: Marquis de Condorcet, Sketch of the Progress of the Human Mind, 1793–1794 • 16.3—Debating Confucianism: Wang Yangming, Conversations, early sixteenth century • 16.4—The Wahhabi Perspective on Islam: Abdullah Wahhab, History and Doctrines of the Wahhabis, 1803 • 16.5—The Poetry of Kabîr: Kabîr, Poetry, ca. late fifteenth century

Using the Evidence   *759*

Visual Sources Global Christianity in the Early Modern Era   *761*

Pieter Seanredam, Interior of a Dutch Reformed Church • Catholic Baroque: Interior of Pilgrimage Church, Mariazell, Austria • Cultural Blending in Andean Christianity • Making Christianity Chinese • Christian Art at the Mughal Court

Using the Evidence   *769*

PART FIVE
The European Moment In World History, 1750–1914   *770*

THE BIG PICTURE European Centrality and the Problem of Eurocentrism   *771*

Eurocentric Geography and History • Countering Eurocentrism

Landmarks of the European Moment in World History, 1750–1914   *776*

17. Atlantic Revolutions and Their Echoes, 1750–1914   *779*

Comparing Atlantic Revolutions   *780*

The North American Revolution, 1775–1787 • The French Revolution, 1789–1815 • The Haitian Revolution, 1791–1804 • Spanish American Revolutions, 1810–1825

Echoes of Revolution   *793*

The Abolition of Slavery • Nations and Nationalism • Feminist Beginnings

Reflections: Revolutions Pro and Con   *803*

Second Thoughts   *804*

What's the Significance? • Big Picture Questions • Next Steps: For Further Study

Snapshot: **Key Moments in the History of Atlantic Revolutions**   *781*

Snapshot: **Key Moments in the Growth of Nationalism**   *797*

CONSIDERING THE EVIDENCE
Documents Claiming Rights   *806*

17.1—The French Revolution and the "Rights of Man": The Declaration of the Rights of Man and Citizen, 1789 • 17.2—The Rights of Women: Mary Wollstonecraft, A Vindication of the Rights of Woman, 1792 • 17.3—Rights and National Independence: Simón Bolívar, The Jamaica Letter, 1815 • 17.4—Rights and Slavery: Frederick Douglass, What to the Slave Is the Fourth of July?, 1852 • 17.5—Rights in the Colonial World: Raden Adjeng Kartini, Letter to a Friend, 1899

Using the Evidence   *816*

Visual Sources Representing the French
Revolution *817*

*The Early Years of the French Revolution: "The
Joyous Accord" • A Reversal of Roles: The Three
Estates of the Old Regime • Revolution and
Religion: "Patience, Monsignor, your turn will come."
• An English Response to Revolution: "Hell Broke
Loose or, the Murder of Louis" • Revolution, War,
and Resistance: A German View of Napoleon*

Using the Evidence   *823*

18. Revolutions of Industrialization, 1750–1914   *825*

Explaining the Industrial Revolution   *826*
    Why Europe? • Why Britain?
The First Industrial Society   *832*
    *The British Aristocracy • The Middle Classes •
    The Laboring Classes • Social Protest*
Variations on a Theme: Comparing Industrialization
    in the United States and Russia   *840*
    *The United States: Industrialization without
    Socialism • Russia: Industrialization and Revolution*
The Industrial Revolution and Latin America in
    the Nineteenth Century   *846*
    *After Independence in Latin America • Facing the
    World Economy • Becoming like Europe?*
Reflections: History and Horse Races   *853*
Second Thoughts   *854*
    *What's the Significance? • Big Picture Questions
    • Next Steps: For Further Study*
Snapshot: **Measuring the Industrial
    Revolution**   *833*
Snapshot: **The Industrial Revolution and the
    Global Divide**   *847*

CONSIDERING THE EVIDENCE
Documents Varieties of European Marxism   *855*

*18.1—Socialism According to Marx: Karl Marx
and Friedrich Engels, The Communist Manifesto,
1848 • 18.2—Socialism without Revolution:
Eduard Bernstein, Evolutionary Socialism, 1899
• 18.3—Socialism and Women: Clara Zetkin,
The German Socialist Women's Movement, 1909 •
18.4—Socialism in Song: Eugene Pottier, The
Internationale, 1871 • 18.5—Lenin and Russian
Socialism: V. I. Lenin, What Is To Be Done?, 1902*

Using the Evidence   *866*
Visual Sources Art and the Industrial
Revolution   *867*

*The Machinery Department of the Crystal Palace
• The Railroad as a Symbol of the Industrial Era •
Outside the Factory: Eyre Crowe, The Dinner
Hour, Wigan • Inside the Factory: Lewis Hine,
Child Labor, 1912 • Philip James de Loutherbourg,
Coalbrookdale by Night • John Leech, Capital and
Labour*

Using the Evidence   *875*

19. Internal Troubles, External Threats: China, the Ottoman Empire, and Japan, 1800–1914   *877*

The External Challenge: European Industry and
    Empire   879
    *New Motives, New Means • New Perceptions of the
    "Other"*
Reversal of Fortune: China's Century of Crisis   *882*
    *The Crisis Within • Western Pressures • The Failure
    of Conservative Modernization*
The Ottoman Empire and the West in the
    Nineteenth Century   *889*

*"The Sick Man of Europe" • Reform and Its
Opponents • Outcomes: Comparing China and the
Ottoman Empire*

The Japanese Difference: The Rise of a New East
Asian Power   *894*

    *The Tokugawa Background • American Intrusion
and the Meiji Restoration • Modernization Japanese
Style • Japan and the World*

Reflections: Success and Failure in History   *903*

Second Thoughts   *903*

    *What's the Significance? • Big Picture Questions
• Next Steps: For Further Study*

Snapshot: **Chinese/British Trade at Canton,
1835–1836**   *885*

Snapshot: **Key Moments in the Rise of Japan in
the Nineteenth Century and Beyond**   *899*

CONSIDERING THE EVIDENCE

Documents Voices from the Opium War   *905*

    *19.1—A Chinese Response to Lord Macartney:
Emperor Qianlong, Message to King George III, 1793
• 19.2 and 19.3—Debating the Opium Problem:
Xu Naiji, An Argument for Legalization, 1836, and
Yuan Yulin, An Argument for Suppression, 1836 •
19.4—A Moral Appeal to Queen Victoria:
Commissioner Lin Zexu, Letter to Queen Victoria,
1839 • 19.5—War and Defeat: The Treaty of
Nanjing, 1842*

Using the Evidence   *913*

Visual Sources Japanese Perceptions of
the West   *915*

    *The Black Ships • Depicting the Americans •
Women and Westernization • Kobayashi Kiyochika's
Critique of Wholesale Westernization • Japan, China,
and Europe: A Reversal of Roles*

Using the Evidence   *921*

20. Colonial Encounters,
1750–1914   *923*

A Second Wave of European Conquests   *924*

Under European Rule   *928*

    *Cooperation and Rebellion • Colonial Empires with
a Difference*

Ways of Working: Comparing Colonial
Economies   *932*

    *Economies of Coercion: Forced Labor and the Power
of the State • Economies of Cash-Crop Agriculture:
The Pull of the Market • Economies of Wage Labor:
Working for Europeans • Women and the Colonial
Economy: An African Case Study • Assessing
Colonial Development*

Believing and Belonging: Identity and Cultural
Change in the Colonial Era   *941*

    Education • Religion • "Race" and "Tribe"

Reflections: Who Makes History?   *947*

Second Thoughts   *948*

    *What's the Significance? • Big Picture Questions
• Next Steps: For Further Study*

Snapshot: **Long-Distance Migration in an Age of
Empire, 1846–1940**   *940*

CONSIDERING THE EVIDENCE

Documents Indian Responses to Empire   *950*

    *20.1—The Wonders of British Calcutta: Nawab
Muhabbat Khan, On Calcutta, late eighteenth century
• 20.2—Seeking Western Education: Ram Mohan
Roy, Letter to Lord Amherst, 1823 • 20.3—The
Indian Rebellion: Bahadur Shah, The Azamgarh
Proclamation, 1857 • 20.4—The Credits and Debits
of British Rule in India: Dadabhai Naoroji, Speech
to a London Audience, 1871 • 20.5—Gandhi on
Modern Civilization: Mahatma Gandhi, Indian
Home Rule, 1908*

Using the Evidence   959
Visual Sources The Scramble for Africa   960
Prelude to the Scramble • Conquest and Competition • From the Cape to Cairo • A French Critique of the Boer War • The Ethiopian Exception
Using the Evidence   967

PART SIX
The Most Recent Century,
1914–2010   *968*

THE BIG PICTURE The Twentieth Century: A New Period in World History?   *969*

Old and New in the Twentieth Century • Three Regions—One World
Landmarks of the Most Recent Century, 1914–2010   *974*

21. The Collapse and Recovery of Europe, 1914–1970s   *977*

The First World War: European Civilization in Crisis, 1914–1918   *978*
An Accident Waiting to Happen • Legacies of the Great War
Capitalism Unraveling: The Great Depression   *985*
Democracy Denied: Comparing Italy, Germany, and Japan   *988*
The Fascist Alternative in Europe • Hitler and the Nazis • Japanese Authoritarianism
A Second World War   *996*
The Road to War in Asia • The Road to War in Europe • The Outcomes of Global Conflict
The Recovery of Europe   *1005*
Reflections: War and Remembrance: Learning from History   *1008*
Second Thoughts   *1009*
What's the Significance? • Big Picture Questions • Next Steps: For Further Study

Snapshot: **Comparing the Impact of the Depression**   *987*
Snapshot: **Key Moments in the History of World War II**   *1001*

CONSIDERING THE EVIDENCE
Documents Ideologies of the Axis Powers   *1010*
21.1—Mussolini on Fascism: Benito Mussolini, The Political and Social Doctrine of Fascism, 1933 • 21.2—Hitler on Nazism: Adolph Hitler, Mein Kampf (My Struggle), 1925–1926 • Document 21.3—The Japanese Way: Cardinal Principles of the National Entity of Japan, 1937
Using the Evidence   *1017*
Visual Sources Propaganda and Critique in World War I   *1019*
Women and the War • Defining the Enemy • War and the Colonies • The Battlefield • The Aftermath of War
Using the Evidence   *1027*

22. The Rise and Fall of World Communism, 1917–Present   *1029*

Global Communism   *1030*
Comparing Revolutions as a Path to Communism   *1032*
Russia: Revolution in a Single Year • China: A Prolonged Revolutionary Struggle

Building Socialism in Two Countries   *1038*

 *Communist Feminism • Socialism in the
Countryside • Communism and Industrial
Development • The Search for Enemies*

East versus West: A Global Divide and a
 Cold War   *1045*

 *Military Conflict and the Cold War • Nuclear
Standoff and Third World Rivalry • The United
States: Superpower of the West, 1945–1975 • The
Communist World, 1950s–1970s*

Comparing Paths to the End of Communism   *1051*

 *China: Abandoning Communism and Maintaining
the Party • The Soviet Union: The Collapse of
Communism and Country*

Reflections: To Judge or Not to Judge   *1057*

Second Thoughts   *1058*

 *What's the Significance? • Big Picture Questions
• Next Steps: For Further Study*

Snapshot: **China under Mao, 1949–1976**   *1042*

CONSIDERING THE EVIDENCE

Documents Experiencing Stalinism   *1060*

 *22.1—Stalin on Stalinism: Joseph Stalin, The Results
of the First Five-Year Plan, 1933 • 22.2—Living
through Collectivization: Maurice Hindus, Red Bread,
1931 • 22.3—Living through Industrialization:
Personal Accounts of Soviet Industrialization, 1930s
• 22.4—Living through the Terror: Personal Accounts
of the Terror, 1930s*

Using the Evidence   *1070*

Visual Sources Poster Art in Mao's China   *1071*

 *Smashing the Old Society • Building the New
Society: The People's Commune • Women, Nature,
and Industrialization • The Cult of Mao •
Propaganda Posters after Mao*

Using the Evidence   *1079*

23. Independence and Development in the Global South, 1914–Present   *1081*

Toward Freedom: Struggles for Independence   *1082*

 *The End of Empire in World History • Explaining
African and Asian Independence*

Comparing Freedom Struggles   *1086*

 *The Case of India: Ending British Rule • The Case
of South Africa: Ending Apartheid*

Experiments with Freedom   *1094*

 *Experiments in Political Order: Comparing African
Nations and India • Experiments in Economic
Development: Changing Priorities, Varying Outcomes
• Experiments with Culture: The Role of Islam in
Turkey and Iran*

Reflections: History in the Middle of the
 Stream   *1108*

Second Thoughts   *1109*

 *What's the Significance? • Big Picture Questions
• Next Steps: For Further Study*

Snapshot: **Key Moments in South African
History**   *1090*

Snapshot: **Economic Development in the Global
South by the Early Twenty-first Century**   *1100*

CONSIDERING THE EVIDENCE

Documents Debating Development in Africa
1110

 *23.1—The Colonial Legacy for Modern
Development: A. Adu Boahen, African Perspectives
on Colonialism, 1987 • 23.2—Development and
African Unity: Kwame Nkrumah, Africa Must
Unite, 1963 • 23.3—Development, Socialism,
and Self-Reliance: Julius Nyerere, The Arusha
Declaration, 1967 • 23.4—Development and*

*Women: Mildred Malineo Tau, Women: Critical to
African Development, 1981 • 23.5—Development,
Elites, and the State: George B. N. Ayittey, Africa
Betrayed, 1992, and Africa in Chaos, 1998*
Using the Evidence   *1121*
Visual Sources Representing Independence   *1122*
*Non-Co-operation Tree and Mahatma Gandhi •
African National Congress • Vietnamese Independence
and Victory over the United States • Winning a
Jewish National State • A Palestinian Nation in
the Making*
Using the Evidence   *1131*

24. Accelerating Global Interaction, Since 1945   *1133*

The Transformation of the World Economy   *1134*
*Reglobalization • Growth, Instability, and Inequality
• Globalization and an American Empire*
The Globalization of Liberation: Comparing
Feminist Movements   *1145*
*Feminism in the West • Feminism in the Global
South • International Feminism*
Religion and Global Modernity   *1150*
*Fundamentalism on a Global Scale • Creating
Islamic Societies: Resistance and Renewal in the
World of Islam • Religious Alternatives to
Fundamentalism*
The World's Environment and the Globalization
of Environmentalism   *1158*
*The Global Environment Transformed • Green and
Global*
Final Reflections: Pondering the Uses of
History   *1163*

Second Thoughts   1166
*What's the Significance? • Big Picture Questions •
Next Steps: For Further Study*
Snapshot: Indicators of Reglobalization   *1138*
Snapshot: World Population Growth,
1950–2005   *1159*

CONSIDERING THE EVIDENCE
Documents Contending for Islam   *1167*
*24.1—A Secular State for an Islamic Society in
Turkey: Mustafa Kemal Atatürk, Speech to the
General Congress of the Republican Party, 1927 •
24.2—Egypt's Muslim Brotherhood: Hassan al-
Banna, Toward the Light, 1936 • 24.3—The Ideas
of the Ayatollah Khomeini: Ayatollah Khomeini,
Sayings of the Ayatollah Khomeini, 1980 •
24.4—A Liberal Viewpoint from an Islamic Woman:
Benazir Bhutto, Politics and the Muslim Woman,
1985 • 24.5—Islam and 9/11: Kabir Helminski:
"Islam and Human Values," 2009*
Using the Evidence   *1178*
Visual Sources Experiencing Globalization   *1180*
*Globalization and Work • Globalization and
Consumerism • Globalization and Migration •
Globalization and Protest • Globalization: One
World or Many?*
Using the Evidence   *1187*

Notes   *1189*
Acknowledgments   *1207*
Index   *1209*
About the Author   *Inside back cover*

Maps

MAP 1.1   The Global Dispersion of Humankind   14
MAP 1.2   Migration of Austronesian-Speaking People   19
SPOT MAP   The San of Southern Africa   25
SPOT MAP   The Chumash of Southern California   29

MAP 2.1   The Fertile Crescent   54
MAP 2.2   The Global Spread of Agriculture   58
SPOT MAP   Bantu Migrations   60

MAP 3.1   First Civilizations   88
MAP 3.2   Mesopotamia   105
MAP 3.3   An Egyptian Empire   110

MAP 4.1   The Persian Empire   146
MAP 4.2   Classical Greece   148
MAP 4.3   Alexander's Empire and Successor States   152
MAP 4.4   The Roman Empire   156
MAP 4.5   Classical China   159
MAP 4.6   Empire in South Asia   166

SPOT MAP   Ancient Israel   204
MAP 5.1   The Spread of Early Christianity and Buddhism   213

SPOT MAP   Yellow Turban Rebellion   241
SPOT MAP   The Rebellion of Spartacus   251

MAP 7.1   Africa in the Classical Era   285
SPOT MAP   Classical Civilizations of Mesoamerica   293
SPOT MAP   Classical Civilizations of the Andes   297
SPOT MAP   North America in the Classical Era   301

MAP 8.1   The Silk Roads   335
MAP 8.2   The Sea Roads   342
SPOT MAP   Southeast Asia, ca. 1200 C.E.   345
SPOT MAP   The Swahili Coast of East Africa   347
MAP 8.3   The Sand Roads   350
MAP 8.4   The American Web   352

MAP 9.1   Tang and Song Dynasty China   381
SPOT MAP   Korean Kingdoms about 500 C.E.   391
SPOT MAP   Vietnam   392
SPOT MAP   Japan   394
MAP 9.2   The World of Asian Buddhism   400

MAP 10.1   The Byzantine Empire   428
MAP 10.2   Western Europe in the Ninth Century   436
MAP 10.3   Europe in the High Middle Ages   439
MAP 10.4   The Crusades   443

SPOT MAP   Arabia at the Time of Muhammad   475
MAP 11.1   The Arab Empire and the Initial Expansion of Islam, 622–900 C.E.   481
MAP 11.2   The Growing World of Islam (900–1500)   489
SPOT MAP   The Sultanate of Delhi   490
MAP 11.3   The Ottoman Empire by the Mid-Fifteenth Century   492
MAP 11.4   West Africa and the World of Islam   493

SPOT MAP   The Xiongnu Confederacy   526
SPOT MAP   The Masai of East Africa   528
MAP 12.1   The Mongol Empire   530
MAP 12.2   Trade and Disease in the Fourteenth Century   543

MAP 13.1   Asia in the Fifteenth Century   576
MAP 13.2   Europe in 1500   579
MAP 13.3   Africa in the Fifteenth Century   582
MAP 13.4   Empires of the Islamic World   585
MAP 13.5   The Americas in the Fifteenth Century   589
MAP 13.6   Religion and Commerce in the Afro-Eurasian World   596

MAP 14.1   European Colonial Empires in the Americas   627
MAP 14.2   The Russian Empire   640
SPOT MAP   China's Qing Dynasty Empire   644
SPOT MAP   The Mughal Empire   645
MAP 14.3   The Ottoman Empire   647

MAP 15.1   Europeans in Asia in the Early Modern Era   676
MAP 15.2   The Global Silver Trade   682
MAP 15.3   The North American Fur Trade   686
MAP 15.4   The Atlantic Slave Trade   689

MAP 16.1   Reformation Europe in the Sixteenth Century   726
SPOT MAP   The Expansion of Wahhabi Islam   734

MAP 17.1   The Expansion of the United States   782
MAP 17.2   Napoleon's European Empire   788
MAP 17.3   Latin American Independence   791
MAP 17.4   The Nations and Empires of Europe, ca. 1880   798

MAP 18.1   The Early Phase of Europe's Industrial Revolution   829
MAP 18.2   The Industrial United States in 1900   841
SPOT MAP   The 1905 Revolution in Russia   845
MAP 18.3   Latin America and the World, 1825–1935   850

MAP 19.1   China and the World in the Nineteenth Century   887
MAP 19.2   The Contraction of the Ottoman Empire   890
MAP 19.3   The Rise of Japan   902

MAP 20.1   Colonial Asia in the Early Twentieth Century   925
MAP 20.2   Conquest and Resistance in Colonial Africa   927

MAP 21.1   The World in 1914   978
MAP 21.2   Europe on the Eve of World War I   980
MAP 21.3   Europe and the Middle East after World War I   983
MAP 21.4   World War II in Asia   998
MAP 21.5   World War II in Europe   1000
MAP 21.6   The Growth of European Integration   1007

MAP 22.1   Russia in 1917   1033
MAP 22.2   The Rise of Communism in China   1037
MAP 22.3   The Global Cold War   1046
MAP 22.4   The Collapse of the Soviet Empire   1056

MAP 23.1   The End of European Empires   1084
SPOT MAP   The Independence of British South Asia   1089
MAP 23.2   South Africa after Apartheid   1093
MAP 23.3   The "Worlds" of the Twentieth Century   1095
SPOT MAP   Iran, Turkey, and the Middle East   1103

MAP 24.1   Globalization in Action: Foreign Direct Investment in the Late Twentieth Century   1136
MAP 24.2   Global Inequality: Population and Economic Development   1140
MAP 24.3   Two Faces of an "American Empire"   1143
MAP 24.4   The Islamic World in the Early Twenty-first Century   1154
MAP 24.5   Carbon Dioxide Emissions in the Twentieth Century   1160

Special Features

Landmarks

PART 1   Landmarks of Early World History, to 500 B.C.E.   8
PART 2   Landmarks of the Classical Era, 500 B.C.E.–500 C.E.   140
PART 3   Landmarks in the Era of Accelerating Connections, 500–1500   330
PART 4   Landmarks in the Early Modern Era, 1450–1750   622
PART 5   Landmarks of the European Moment in World History, 1750–1914   776
PART 6   Landmarks of the Most Recent Century, 1914–2010   974

Snapshots

A History of the Universe as a Cosmic Calendar   lii
The Long Road to the Global Presence of Humankind   13
The Paleolithic Era in Perspective   23
Agricultural Breakthroughs   52
The History of Maize/Corn   57
Writing in Ancient Civilizations   101
Key Moments in Mesopotamian History   104
Key Moments in Nile Valley Civilizations   107
World Population during the Age of Agricultural Civilization   135
Key Moments in Classical Greek History   150
Key Moments in the History of the Roman Empire   157
Key Moments in Classical Chinese History   162
Thinkers and Philosophies of the Classical Era   191
Reflections on Human Love from Mediterranean Civilization   209
Social Life and Duty in Classical India   244
Comparing Greco-Roman and American Slavery   248
Continental Population in the Classical Era   283
Economic Exchange along the Silk Roads   337
Economic Exchange in the Indian Ocean Basin   343
Key Moments in the History of Postclassical China   386
Key Moments in Byzantine History   427
Key Moments in the Evolution of Western Civilization   434
Key Moments in the Early History of Islam   476
Key Achievements in Islamic Science and Scholarship   499
Varieties of Pastoral Societies   523
Key Moments in Mongol History   531
Major Developments around the World in the Fifteenth Century   570

Key Moments in European Maritime Voyaging   581
World Population Growth, 1000–2000   597
Ethnic Composition of Colonial Societies in Latin America (1825)   636
Key Moments in the European Encounter with Asia   678
The Slave Trade in Numbers (1501–1866)   694
Catholic/Protestant Differences in the Sixteenth Century   724
Major Thinkers and Achievements of the Scientific Revolution   740
Key Moments in the History of Atlantic Revolutions   781
Key Moments in the Growth of Nationalism   797
Measuring the Industrial Revolution   833
The Industrial Revolution and the Global Divide   847
Chinese/British Trade at Canton, 1835–1836   885
Key Moments in the Rise of Japan in the Nineteenth Century and Beyond   899
Long-Distance Migration in an Age of Empire, 1846–1940   940
Comparing the Impact of the Depression   987
Key Moments in the History of World War II   1001
China under Mao, 1949–1976   1042
Key Moments in South African History   1090
Economic Development in the Global South by the Early Twenty-first Century   1100
Indicators of Reglobalization   1138
World Population Growth, 1950–2005   1159

Working with Primary Sources

Introduction

Historians interpret the past by examining what they refer to as "primary" or "original" sources—documents, images, or objects produced by the very people we are studying and at the time of or soon after the events that they describe or depict. These sources—the "raw material" of the historian's craft—can take many forms: recorded versions of oral traditions, handed down over many centuries; an endless variety of written materials; images and artifacts such as paintings and pottery. Such sources are precious windows into the past. Their survival in large part determines what history can be recovered and what is forever lost. For instance, only the chance survival of the well-preserved agricultural settlement at Çatalhüyük that is among the subjects of Chapter 2's Visual Sources feature allows us to examine what may be the first surviving map in human history.

Using primary sources effectively is no easy task. Unlike textbooks, which are written explicitly for twenty-first-century students, the sources that historians work with were not aimed at you. They were produced in circumstances and with cultural assumptions that are often quite unfamiliar to contemporary readers. And so they require effort: critical reading and observation, systematic analysis, and historical imagination. Working with them is like listening in on conversations from the past, eavesdropping, as it were, on our ancestors. Each source potentially provides a valuable glimpse into the past, but all sources must be analyzed carefully because, like ourselves, our ancestors' understandings of their own lives and time were subject to distortions, fabrications, misunderstandings, and ambiguity.

Working with Written Documents

Written documents are the most common type of primary source that historians use. Typical written sources include personal records, such as diaries, memoirs, business account books, and private correspondence; and public records, including sacred texts, autobiographies, travelers' accounts, newspaper articles, legislation and law codes, court rulings, and wills. Indeed, nearly every written record is potentially a useful primary source depending on the questions that historians are trying to answer. Usually historians are able to draw stronger conclusions when they can locate and examine sources on the same topic from a number of different perspectives. For example, in the Documents feature of Chapter 15, the Atlantic slave trade is explored from the perspective of a slave, a European slave trader, and several African rulers, building up a more complex picture of the trade than any one of these documents could convey on its own. However, even a single source, when analyzed effectively, can provide a window into the past.

Reading a Document

Reading a document requires careful analysis and an understanding of the context in which the document was produced. The following questions provide the basis for understanding and analyzing any primary document:

- Who wrote the document?
- When and where was it written?
- What type of document is it (for example, a letter to a friend, a political decree, an exposition of a religious teaching)?
- Why was the document written? Under what circumstances was it composed? What point of view does it reflect? What other views or opinions is the document arguing against?
- Who was its intended audience?
- What about the document is believable, and what is not?
- What might historians learn from this document?
- What can the document tell us about the individual who produced it and the society from which he or she came from?

Many documents do not answer the first three questions directly. In *Ways of the World: A Brief Global History with Sources*, questions that cannot be answered directly are addressed in the introductory headnote to the document. These headnotes may help you to establish a context for understanding the document and to identify its point of view or potential biases and the larger discourse of which it is a part.

Once these three basic questions are answered, a historian is then likely to consider the next two questions, which often shape what is written and how ideas are presented—why the document was written and who the intended audience was. The document itself and sometimes its headnote will provide information essential for answering these questions. Inspiration and intention are crucial factors that shape the form and content of a source. For instance, one might examine a document differently depending on whether it was intended for a private or a public readership or whether it was intended to be read by a small elite or a wider audience.

Finally, through both establishing the context in which the document was written and carefully reading the document, historians seek to come to some conclusions about the document by asking whether the document is believable, in what ways it sheds light on the past, and what the document tells us about the person who produced it and the time period in which it was generated. In answering these more complex questions, historical imagination is essential. Your imagination, informed by knowledge of the context, enables you to read the document through the eyes of its author and its audience. How might this document have been understood at the time it was written? But in using your imagination, you must take care not to read into the documents your own assumptions and understandings. It is a delicate balance, a kind of dance that historians constantly undertake. Even documents that contain material that historians find unbelievable can be useful, for we seek not only to know the "truth" about what happened in the past but also to grasp the world as our ancestors understood it. Historians sometimes even speak about reading documents "against the grain," seeking understandings that authors certainly did not intend to convey. For example, the Law Code of Hammurabi in Chapter 3's Documents feature depicts an impressive system of justice in ancient Mesopotamia, but it can also be read as an account of the numerous problems or conflicts that that society had to confront.

Reading Documents Together

While each document must be read and understood individually, historians typically draw their strongest conclusions when they analyze a number of documents together. The essays in the Documents features in *Ways of the World* are designed to explore sets of primary sources that address a central theme of the chapter and frequently include several related documents. When considered together, these sources from different perspectives allow the historian to understand the issue or event more fully. A good example of this approach can be found in the Documents feature for Chapter 11, which explores the emergence of Islam through both holy texts such as the Quran and later interpretations of these texts by Sharia legal scholars and Sufi mystics.

The broad theme and approach introduced at the opening of each essay is further defined by the Using the Evidence questions at its conclusion. For instance, Chapter 13's Documents feature, "The Aztecs and Incas through Spanish Eyes," explores the advantages and disadvantages of using sources written by conquerors to reconstruct conquered societies that left few written records of their own.

Working with Visual Sources

Artifacts that derive from the material culture of the past, religious icons or paintings that add to our understanding of belief systems, a family portrait that provides insight into presentations of self in a particular time and place, a building whose layout reveals how power and authority were displayed in a specific empire—all of these visual sources represent another category of primary sources that historians can use to re-create and understand the past. However, visual evidence can be more difficult to interpret than written documents because most people are not trained in visual analysis. Furthermore, it may be more difficult to discern what meanings animated the creators of particular images or artifacts and what understandings they conveyed to those who viewed or used them.

To use visual sources, we must be able to see these pieces of evidence through the eyes of the societies that produced them and to decode the symbols and other features that imbue these visual sources with meaning. The values of past cultures are often far removed from our own; thus the symbols in these images and artifacts are often unfamiliar to our eyes. Nevertheless, interpreting visual sources effectively can provide insights not offered by written documents. Indeed, for some preliterate societies, archeological and artistic evidence is all that remains of their history.

Analyzing an Image or Artifact

Just as with written documents, context is crucial for analyzing visual evidence. Context provides critical information needed to see the visual source through the eyes of its creator and of those for whom it was created. Sometimes the image or artifact will provide this information, but more often in *Ways of the World: A Brief Global History with Sources*, the Visual Sources essay will provide essential context for your interpretation, as in Chapter 16's Visual Sources feature, where the specific contexts in which Christian images were created are critical to their interpretation and analysis.

Once again, a set of fundamental questions, similar to those you would ask a written document, will help you understand and analyze a visual source:

- When and where was the image or artifact made?
- Who made the image or artifact? How was it made?
- Who paid for or commissioned it?
- Where might the image or artifact have originally been displayed or used?
- Where is it now, and how did it get there?
- For what audience(s) was it intended?
- What message(s) is it trying to convey?
- How could it be interpreted differently depending on who viewed or used it?
- What are the meanings of the symbols or other abstract features in the visual source?

While these questions do not always have a single, clear answer, being aware of the possibilities will shape your examination of the source.

Once you have established the context in which the piece of visual evidence was produced, you should then focus on a careful examination of the source itself, asking the following questions:

- If the source is an image, who or what is depicted?
- What information can be gleaned from the positioning of figures, their clothing, hairstyles, and other visual cues?
- What activities are depicted?
- If it is a specifically religious image, what is depicted, and what likely purpose did the image serve?
- If it is an artifact, what function did it serve?
- What can the image tell us about the society that produced it and the time period in which it was created?

Addressing this question can take a historian down many different lines of inquiry. Depending on the visual sources under examination, additional questions arise, such as the following:

- What types of technology or techniques were used to produce the visual source?

- What was the relationship between those who made the visual source and those who used or viewed it?

Considering Visual Evidence Collectively

As with written documents, each piece of visual evidence must be examined and understood in its own right, although historians draw their strongest conclusions when they analyze a number of visual sources together rather than relying on a single source. The Visual Sources essays in *Ways of the World* explore sets of visual sources that address a central theme in the chapter and frequently include several related images that, when considered together, allow the historian to become aware of how multiple perspectives on a single topic can enhance understanding. Moreover, these essays often explore the strengths and weaknesses of a type of visual source for answering questions posed by historians.

The broad theme and approach are introduced at the opening of each essay and are further defined by the Using the Evidence questions at its conclusion. For instance, the Visual Sources feature for Chapter 13, "Sacred Places in the World of the Fifteenth Century," explores the intersections between sacred sites and political authority in fifteenth-century Africa and Eurasia. While each source considered individually speaks to a specific region and has distinctive characteristics, collectively the sources show that these sorts of sites across Africa and Eurasia were frequently set apart from the profane or ordinary world and were linked to a wider sacred geography.

Finally, as you begin to explore the Documents and Visual Sources features in *Ways of the World*, you might think of the experience as a kind of "history laboratory." In working with these materials, you are "doing history," much like lab experiments in chemistry courses represent "doing science." Furthermore, you will probably recognize connections between particular documents and visual sources. When that happens, the work of "doing history" has truly begun, as most historians use visual sources in conjunction with written documents to create an even more complete picture of the past. Enjoy!

Prologue

From Cosmic History to Human History

IN THE BEGINNING, ACCORDING TO THE NAVAHO, the world was created by Holy People, who had long lived underground and were forced to the surface by a great flood, from which they escaped through a hollow reed. First Man and First Woman were later formed from ears of white and yellow corn. To some of the ancient Greeks, an original Cosmic Egg, floating on a formless mixture of air, water, and matter, gave birth to the deities of Earth and Sky, who then created the earth and all its living creatures, as well as the sun, moon, and stars. For the Hebrews of biblical times, God brought order out of a primordial chaos, creating light and darkness, the earth, and all its living creatures. Pronouncing the creation good, God then made the first humans, placing them in the Garden of Eden, where they soon encountered temptation and choice in the form of a serpent.

These are among the multitude of stories, or myths of origin, that seek to answer that fundamentally human question: what happened in the beginning? Such stories seek to anchor particular societies in a larger context, providing their people with a sense of place, purpose, and belonging. Modern scholars, like earlier tellers of creation stories, also seek to puzzle out the beginnings of the cosmos, of the earth, of life, and of humankind. Unlike myths of origin, though, modern creation stories rely largely on those fields of study that emerged from the Scientific Revolution of the sixteenth century and later—astronomy, physics, geology, biology. Such accounts claim to be truer and more certain, at least in a literal sense, for they can be checked and verified rather than simply accepted and believed. They are, however, stronger on *how* things began than on *why*. Although they provide a more factually detailed account of beginnings, they may have less to offer about the meaning of it all. Therefore, many people in the modern world have tried hard to reconcile scientifically derived understandings of "in the beginning" with the meaning-based accounts contained in long-standing religious traditions.

The History of the Universe

World historians, although largely focused on the unfolding of all things human, have recently begun to situate that remarkable story in the larger contexts of both cosmic history and planetary history. The most inclusive of these modern frameworks

Snapshot   **The History of the Universe as a Cosmic Calendar**[1]

Big bang	January 1	13.7 billion years ago
Stars and galaxies begin to form	End of January/ mid-February	12 billion years ago
Milky Way galaxy forms	March/early April	10 billion years ago
Origin of the solar system	September 9	4.7 billion years ago
Formation of the earth	September 15	4.5 billion years ago
Earliest life on earth	Late September/ early October	4 billion years ago
Oxygen forms on earth	December 1	1.3 billion years ago
First worms	December 16	658 million years ago
First fish, first vertebrates	December 19	534 million years ago
First reptiles, first trees	December 23	370 million years ago
Age of dinosaurs	December 24–28	329–164 million years ago
First humanlike creatures	December 31 (late evening)	2.7 million years ago
First agriculture	December 31: 11:59:35	12,000 years ago
Birth of the Buddha/ Greek civilization	December 31: 11:59:55	2,500 years ago
Birth of Jesus	December 31: 11:59:56	2,000 years ago
Aztec and Inca empires	December 31: 11:59:59	500 years ago

■ Change

What have been the major turning points in the prehuman phases of "big history"?

is sometimes called "big history." It is really the "history of everything" from the big bang to the present, and it extends over the enormous, almost unimaginable time-scale of some 13.7 billion years, the current rough estimate of the age of the universe.[2]

To make this vast expanse of time even remotely comprehensible, some scholars have depicted the history of the cosmos as if it were a single calendar year (see the Snapshot). On that cosmic calendar, most of the action took place in the first few milliseconds of January 1. As astronomers, physicists, and chemists tell it, the universe that we know began in an eruption of inconceivable power and heat. Out of that explosion of creation emerged matter, energy, gravity, electromagnetism, and the "strong" and "weak" forces that govern the behavior of atomic nuclei. As gravity pulled the rapidly expanding cosmic gases into increasingly dense masses, stars formed, with the first ones lighting up around 1 to 2 billion years after the big bang, or the end of January to mid-February on the cosmic calendar.

Hundreds of billions of stars followed, each with its own history, though following common patterns. They emerge, flourish for a time, and then collapse and die, and in doing so they sometimes generate supernova, black holes, and pulsars—phenomena at least as fantastic as the most exotic of earlier creation stories. Within the stars, enormous nuclear reactions gave rise to the elements that are reflected in the periodic table known to all students of chemistry. Over eons, these stars came together in galaxies, such as our own Milky Way, which probably emerged in March or early April, and in even larger structures called groups, clusters, and superclusters. Adding to the strangeness of our picture of the cosmos is the recent and controversial notion that perhaps 90 percent or more of the total mass of the universe is invisible to us, consisting of a mysterious and mathematically predicted substance known to scholars only as "dark matter."

The contemplation of cosmic history has prompted profound religious or philosophical questions about the meaning of human life. For some, it has engendered a sense of great insignificance in the face of cosmic vastness. In disputing the earth- and human-centered view of the Catholic Church, Voltaire, an eighteenth-century French thinker, wrote: "This little globe, nothing more than a point, rolls in space like so many other globes; we are lost in this immensity."[3] Nonetheless, human awareness of the mystery of this immeasurable universe renders us unique and generates for many people feelings of awe and humility that are almost religious. As tiny but knowing observers of this majestic cosmos, we have found ourselves living in a grander home than ever we knew before.

The History of a Planet

For most of us, one star, our own sun, is far more important than all the others, despite its quite ordinary standing among the billions of stars in the universe and its somewhat remote location on the outer edge of the Milky Way galaxy. Circling that star are a series of planets, formed of leftover materials from the sun's birth. One of those planets, the third from the sun and the fifth largest, is home to all of us. Human history—our history—takes place not only on the earth but also as part of the planet's history.

That history began with the emergence of the entire solar system about two-thirds of the way through cosmic history, some 4.7 billion years ago, or early September on the cosmic calendar. Geologists have learned a great deal about the history of the earth—the formation of its rocks and atmosphere, the movement of its continents, the collision of the tectonic plates that make up its crust, and the constantly changing landscape as mountains formed, volcanoes erupted, and erosion transformed the surface of the planet. All of this has been happening for more than 4 billion years and continues still.

The most remarkable feature of the earth's history—and so far as we know unrepeated elsewhere—was the emergence of life from the chemical soup of the early planet. It happened rather quickly, only about 600 million years after the earth itself took shape, or late September on the cosmic calendar. Then for some 3 billion years, life remained at the level of microscopic single-celled organisms. According to biologists, the many species of larger multicelled creatures—all of the flowers, shrubs, and trees as well as all of the animals of land, sea, and air—have evolved in an explosive proliferation of life-forms, punctuated by massive die-offs as well, over the past 600 million years, or since mid-December on the cosmic calendar.

Each of these species has also had a history as its members struggled to find resources, cope with changing environments, and deal with competitors. The history of dinosaurs, for example, from their rise to their extinction, occupied about 165 million years, or about five days in late December on the cosmic calendar. Egocentric creatures that we are, however, human beings have usually focused their history books and history courses entirely on a single species—our own, *Homo sapiens*, humankind. On the cosmic calendar, *Homo sapiens* is an upstart primate whose entire history occurred in the last few minutes of December 31. Almost all of what we normally study in history courses—agriculture, writing, civilizations, empires, industrialization—took place in the very last minute of that cosmic year. The entire history of the United States occurred in the last second.

Yet during that brief time, humankind has had a career more remarkable and arguably more consequential for the planet than any other species. At the heart of human uniqueness lies our amazing capacity for accumulating knowledge and skills. Other animals learn, of course, but they learn the same things over and over again. Twenty-first-century chimpanzees in the wild master the same skills as their ancestors did a million years ago, but the exceptional communication abilities provided by human language allow us to learn from one another, to express that learning in abstract symbols, and then to pass it on, cumulatively, to future generations. Thus we have moved from stone-tipped spears to nuclear weapons, from "talking drums" to the Internet, from grass huts to the Taj Mahal and Notre Dame cathedral.

This extraordinary ability has translated into a human impact on the earth that is unprecedented among all living species.[4] Human populations have multiplied far more extensively and have come to occupy a far greater range of environments than has any other large animal. Through our ingenious technologies, we have appropriated for ourselves, according to recent calculations, some 25 to 40 percent of the solar energy that enters the food chain. We have recently gained access to the stored solar energy of coal, gas, and oil, all of which have been many millions of years in the making, and we have the capacity to deplete these resources in a few hundred or a few thousand years. Other forms of life have felt the impact of human activity, as numerous extinct or threatened species testify. Human beings have even affected the atmosphere itself, and global warming is altering the climate of the planet. Thus human history has been, and remains, of great significance not for ourselves alone but also for the earth itself and for the many other living creatures with which we share it.

The History of the Human Species in a Single Paragraph: A Preview

The history of our species has occupied roughly the last 250,000 years, conventionally divided into three major phases, based on the kind of technology that was most widely practiced. The enormously long Paleolithic age, with its gathering and hunting way of life, accounts for 95 percent or more of the time that humans have occupied the planet. People utilizing a Paleolithic technology initially settled every major landmass on the planet and constructed the first human societies (see Chapter 1). Then beginning about 12,000 years ago with the first Agricultural Revolution, the domestication of plants and animals increasingly became the primary means of sustaining human life and societies. In giving rise to farming village societies, to pastoral communities depending on their herds of animals, and to state- and city-based civilizations, this agrarian way of life changed virtually everything and fundamentally shaped the human experience ever since. Finally around 1750, a quite sudden spurt in the rate of technological change, which we know as the Industrial Revolution, took hold. That vast increase in productivity, wealth, and human control over nature once again transformed almost every aspect of human life and gave rise to new kinds of societies that we call "modern."

Here then, in a single paragraph, is the history of humankind—the Paleolithic era, the agricultural era, and, most recently and briefly, the modern industrial era. Clearly this is a world history perspective, based on the notion that the human species as a whole has a history that transcends any of its particular and distinctive cultures. That perspective—known variously as planetary, global, or world history—has become increasingly prominent among those who study the past. Why should this be so?

Why World History?

Not long ago—in the mid-twentieth century, for example—virtually all college-level history courses were organized in terms of particular civilizations or nations. In the United States, courses such as Western Civilization or some version of American History served to introduce students to the study of the past. Since then, however, a set of profound changes has pushed much of the historical profession in a different direction.

The world wars of the twentieth century, revealing as they did the horrendous consequences of unchecked nationalism, persuaded some historians that a broader view of the past might contribute to a sense of global citizenship. Economic and cultural globalization has highlighted both the interdependence of the world's peoples and their very unequal positions within that world. Moreover, we are aware as never before that our problems—whether they involve economic well-being, environmental deterioration, disease, or terrorism—respect no national boundaries. To many thoughtful people, a global present seemed to call for a global past. Furthermore, as

■ Change

Why has world history achieved an increasingly prominent place in American education in recent decades?

colonial empires shrank and newly defined third-world peoples asserted themselves on the world stage, these peoples also insisted that their histories be accorded equivalent treatment with those of Europe. An explosion of new knowledge about the histories of Asia, Africa, and pre-Columbian America erupted from the research of scholars around the world. All of this has generated a "world history movement," reflected in college and high school curricula, in numerous conferences and specialized studies, and in a proliferation of textbooks, of which this is one.

This world history movement has attempted to create a global understanding of the human past that highlights broad patterns cutting across particular civilizations and countries, while acknowledging in an inclusive fashion the distinctive histories of its many peoples. This is, to put it mildly, a tall order. How is it possible to encompass within a single book or course the separate stories of the world's various peoples? Surely it must be something more than just recounting the history of one civilization or culture after another. How can we distill a common history of humankind as a whole from the distinct trajectories of particular peoples? Because no world history book or course can cover everything, what criteria should we use for deciding what to include and what to leave out? Such questions have ensured no end of controversy among students, teachers, and scholars of world history, making it one of the most exciting fields of historical inquiry.

Comparison, Connection, and Change: The Three Cs of World History

Despite much debate and argument, one thing is reasonably clear: in world history, nothing stands alone. Every event, every historical figure, every culture, society, or civilization gains significance from its inclusion in some larger context. Most world historians would probably agree on three such contexts that define their field of study. Each of them confronts a particular problem in our understanding of the past.

The first is constant **comparison**. Whatever else it may be, world history is a comparative discipline, seeking to identify similarities and differences in the experience of the world's peoples. What is the difference between the development of agriculture in the Middle East and in Mesoamerica? Was the experience of women largely the same in all patriarchal societies? What did the Roman Empire and Han dynasty China have in common? Why did the Industrial Revolution and a modern way of life evolve first in Western Europe rather than somewhere else? What distinguished the Russian and Chinese revolutions? What different postures toward modernity emerged within the Islamic world? Describing and, if possible, explaining such similarities and differences are among the major tasks of world history. Comparison, then, is a recurring theme in this book, with expressions in every chapter.

Comparison has proven an effective tool in the struggle against Eurocentrism, the notion that Europeans or people of European descent have long been the primary movers and shakers of the historical process. That notion arose in recent centuries when Europeans were in fact the major source of innovation in the world and did for a time exercise something close to world domination. This temporary pre-eminence decisively shaped the way Europeans thought and wrote about their own histories and those of other people. In their own eyes, Europeans alone were progressive people, thanks to some cultural or racial superiority. Everyone else was to some degree stagnant, backward, savage, or barbarian. The unusual power of Europeans allowed them for a time to act on those beliefs and to impose such ways of thinking on much of the world. But comparative world history sets European achievements in a global and historical context, helping us to sort out what was distinctive about its development and what similarities it bore to other major regions of the world. Puncturing the pretensions of Eurocentrism has been high on the agenda of world history.

The art of comparison is a learned skill, entailing several steps. It requires, first of all, asking explicitly comparative questions and determining what particular cases will be involved. If you want to compare revolutions, for example, you would need to decide which ones you are considering—American, French, Russian, Chinese, Cuban. Defining categories of comparison is a further step. Precisely which characteristics of these revolutions will you compare—their origins, their ideologies, the social classes involved, their outcomes? Finally, how will you present your comparison? You might choose a case-by-case analysis in which you would describe, say, the American Revolution first, followed by an account of the Cuban Revolution, which makes explicit comparisons with the former. Or you might choose a thematic approach in which you would consider first the origins of both revolutions, followed by a comparison of their ideologies, and so on. You will find examples of both approaches in this book.

A second context that informs world history involves the interaction, encounters, and **connections** among different and often distant peoples. What happened when people of distinct civilizations or cultures met? Focusing on cross-cultural connections represents an effort to counteract a habit of thinking about particular peoples, states, or cultures as self-contained and isolated communities. Despite the historical emergence of separate and distinct societies, none of them developed alone. Each was embedded in a network of relationships with both near and more distant peoples. Moreover, these cross-cultural connections did not begin with the voyages of Columbus. The Chinese, for example, interacted continuously with the nomadic peoples on their northern border; generated technologies that diffused across all of Eurasia; transmitted elements of their culture to Japan, Korea, and Vietnam; and assimilated a foreign religious tradition, Buddhism, which had originated in India. Though clearly distinctive, China was not a self-contained or isolated civilization. The encounter with strangers, or at least with strange ideas and practices, was everywhere one of the most powerful motors of change in human societies. Thus world history pays attention not only to the internal developments of particular civilizations or peoples but also to the networks, webs, and cross-cultural encounters in which they were enmeshed.

A third context in which the particulars of world history can be situated is found in that perennial question that historians everywhere seek to explore: what changes, what persists, and why. In world history, it is the "big picture" **changes**—those that impact large segments of humankind—that are of greatest interest. How did the transition from a gathering and hunting economy to one based on agriculture take place? How did cities, empires, and civilizations take shape in various parts of the world? What generated the amazing transformations of the "revolution of modernity" in recent centuries? World historians also pay attention to the changes that occur within and between particular civilizations. How can we explain the dramatic collapse of Maya civilization or the fall of the Roman Empire? How did Buddhism change when it entered China? How was Islam transformed when it encountered West African societies? What lay behind the emergence of a new balance of global power after 1500, one that featured the growing prominence of Europe on the world stage?

Both change and comparison provide an antidote to a persistent tendency of human thinking that historians call "essentialism." A more common term is "stereotyping." It refers to our inclination to define particular groups of people with an unchanging or essential set of characteristics. Women are nurturing; peasants are conservative; Americans are aggressive; Hindus are religious. Serious students of history soon become aware that every significant category of people contains endless divisions and conflicts and that human communities are constantly in flux. Peasants may often accept the status quo, except of course when they rebel, as they frequently have. Americans have experienced periods of isolationism and withdrawal from the world as well as times of aggressive engagement with it. Things change.

But some things persist, even if they also change. We should not allow an emphasis on change to blind us to the continuities of human experience. A recognizably Chinese state has operated for more than 2,000 years. Slavery and patriarchy persisted as human institutions for thousands of years until they were challenged in recent centuries, and in various forms they exist still. The teachings of Buddhism, Christianity, and Islam have endured for centuries, though with endless variations and transformations.

Comparisons, connections, and changes—all of them operating on a global scale—represent three contexts or frameworks that can help us bring some coherence to the multiple and complex stories of world history. They will recur repeatedly in the pages that follow.

Second Thoughts

What's the Significance?

myths of origin   big history   the three Cs
cosmic calendar   comparative history

To assess your mastery of the material in this prologue, see the **Online Study Guide** at bedfordstmartins.com/strayer.

For Web sites and documents related to this prologue, see **Make History** at bedfordstmartins.com/strayer.

Big Picture Questions

1. What is the difference between religiously based myths of origin and creation stories derived from scientific accounts?
2. How do you respond personally to modern notions of the immense size and age of the universe?
3. What examples of comparison, connection, and change in world history would you like to explore further as your course unfolds?

Next Steps: For Further Study

David Christian, *Maps of Time* (2004). A brilliant survey of "big history" by a leading world historian.

Ross Dunn, ed., *The New World History* (2000). A collection of articles dealing with the teaching of world history.

Patrick Manning, *Navigating World History* (2003). An up-to-date overview of the growth of world history, the field's achievements, and the debates within it.

J. R. McNeill and William H. McNeill, *The Human Web* (2003). An approach to world history that emphasizes the changing webs of connection among human communities.

David Northrup, "Globalization and the Great Convergence: Rethinking World History in the Long Term," *Journal of World History* (September 2005). A thoughtful essay identifying broad patterns of human history.

"The Cosmic Time-Line," http://visav.phys.uvic.ca/~babul/AstroCourses/P303/BB-slide.htm. A more detailed cosmic calendar.

"World History for Us All," http://worldhistoryforusall.sdsu.edu/dev/default.htm. A model world history curriculum for high school courses.

Ways of the World

A Brief Global History

with Sources

PART ONE

First Things First

Beginnings in History

TO 500 B.C.E.

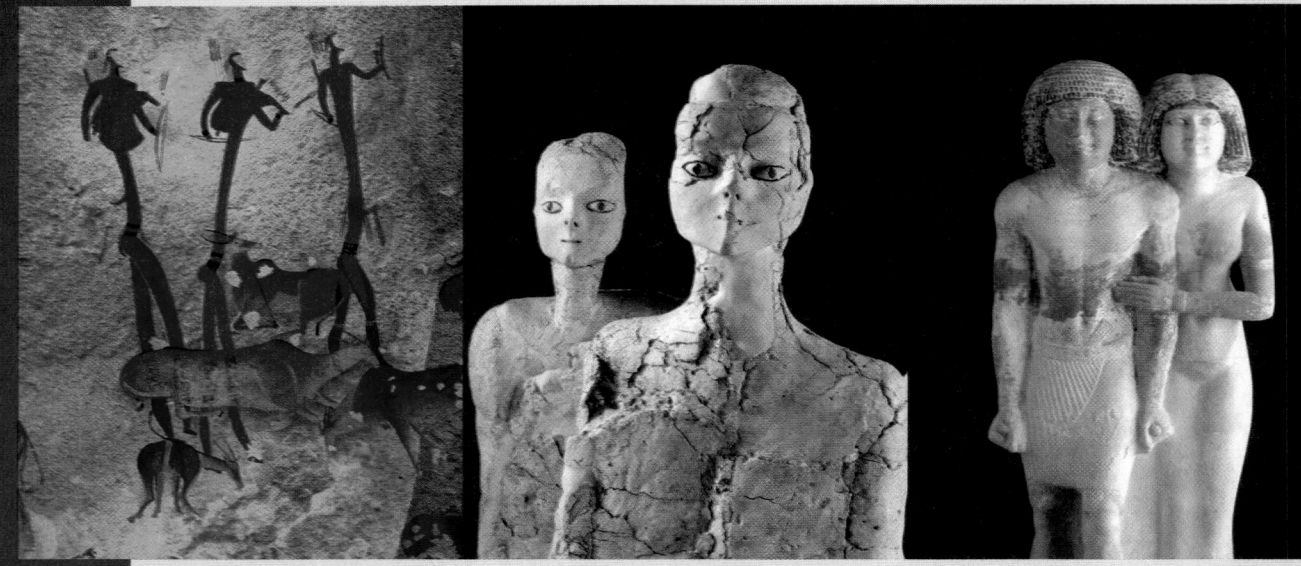

Contents

Chapter 1. First Peoples: Populating the Planet, to 10,000 B.C.E.

Chapter 2. First Farmers: The Revolutions of Agriculture, 10,000 B.C.E.–3000 B.C.E.

Chapter 3. First Civilizations: Cities, States, and Unequal Societies, 3500 B.C.E.–500 B.C.E.

Turning Points in Early World History

Both the ancient sages who developed their societies' creation myths and the grand-parents who still relate the histories of their families have had to decide at what point to begin their stories and what major turning points in those stories to highlight. So too must historians, whether they narrate the tale of a village, a city, a nation, a civilization, or the entire human community. For world historians, concerned with humankind as a whole, four major "beginnings," each of them an extended histor-ical process, have charted the initial stages of the human journey.

The Emergence of Humankind

Ever since Charles Darwin, most scholars have come to view human beginnings in the context of biological change on the planet. In considering this enormous process, we operate on a timescale quite different from the billions of years that mark the history of the universe and of the earth. According to archeologists and anthropologists, the evolutionary line of descent leading to *Homo sapiens* diverged from that leading to chimpanzees, our closest primate relatives, some 5 million to 6 million years ago, and it happened in eastern and southern Africa. There, perhaps twenty or thirty different species emerged, all of them members of the Homininae (or hominid) family of humanlike creatures. What they all shared was bipedalism, the ability to walk upright on two legs. In 1976, the archeologist Mary Leakey uncovered in what is now Tanzania a series of footprints of three such hominid individuals, preserved in cooling volcanic ash about 3.5 million years ago. Two of them walked side by side, perhaps holding hands.

Over time, these hominid species changed. Their brains grew larger, as evidenced by the size of their skulls. About 2.3 million years ago, a hominid creature known as *Homo habilis* began to make and use simple stone tools. Others started to eat meat, at least occasionally. By 1 million years ago, some hominid species, especially *Homo erectus*, began to migrate out of Africa, and their remains have been found in various parts of Eurasia. This species is also associated with the first controlled use of fire.

Eventually all of these earlier hominid species died out, except one: *Homo sapi-ens*, ourselves. We too emerged first in Africa and quite recently, probably no more than 250,000 years ago, although there is constant debate among specialists about these matters. For a long time, all of the small number of *Homo sapiens* lived in Africa, but sometime after 100,000 years ago, they too began to migrate out of Africa onto the Eurasian landmass, then to Australia, and ultimately into the Western Hemisphere and the Pacific islands. The great experiment of human history had begun.

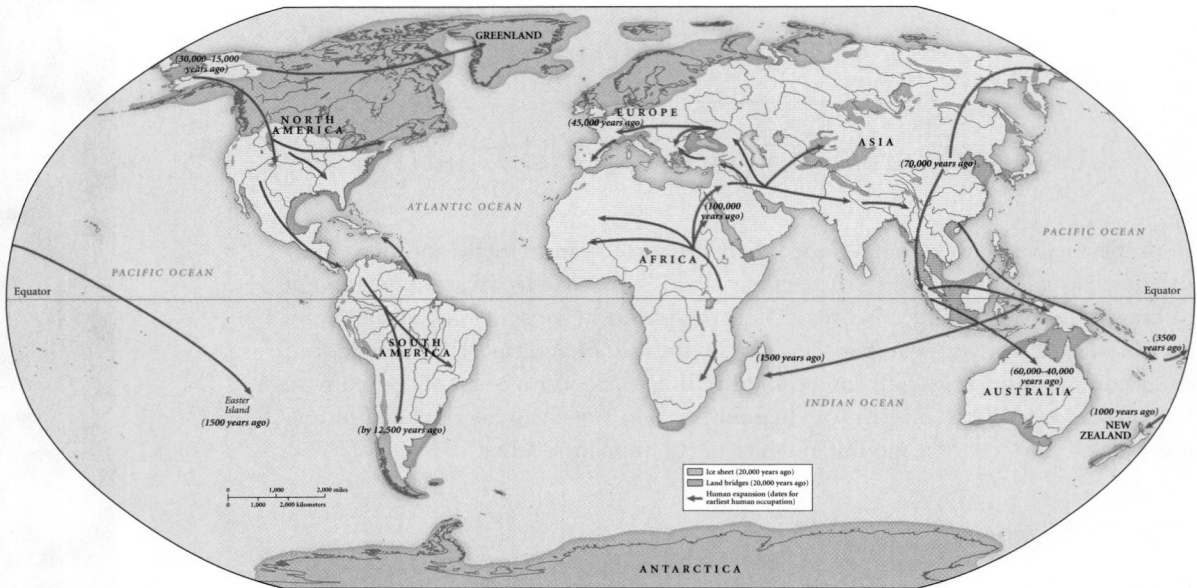

The Global Dispersion of
Humankind (p. 14)

The Globalization of Humankind

Today, every significant landmass on earth is occupied by human beings, but it was not always so. A mere half million years ago our species did not exist, and only 100,000 years ago that species was limited to Africa and numbered, some scholars believe, fewer than 10,000 individuals. These ancient ancestors of ours, rather small in stature and not fast on foot, were armed with a very limited technology of stone tools with which to confront the multiple dangers of the natural world. But then, in perhaps the most amazing tale in all of human history, they moved from this very modest and geographically limited role in the scheme of things to a worldwide and increasingly dominant presence. What kinds of societies, technologies, and understandings of the world accompanied, and perhaps facilitated, this globalization of humankind?

The phase of human history during which these initial migrations took place is known to scholars as the Paleolithic era. The word "Paleolithic" literally means the "old stone age," but it refers more generally to a food-collecting or gathering and hunting way of life, before agriculture allowed people to grow food or raise animals deliberately. Lasting until roughly 11,000 years ago, the Paleolithic era represents over 95 percent of the time that human beings have inhabited the earth, although it accounts for only about 12 percent of the total number of people who have lived on the planet.

It was during this time that *Homo sapiens* colonized the world, making themselves at home in every environmental niche, from the frigid Arctic to the rain forests of Central Africa and Brazil, in mountains, deserts, and plains. It was an amazing achievement, accomplished by no other large species. Accompanying this global

migration were slow changes in the technological tool kits of early humankind
as well as early attempts to impose meaning on the world through art, ritual, and
religion. Although often neglected by
historians and history textbooks, this
long period of the human experience
merits greater attention and is the focus
of Chapter 1.

The Revolution of Farming and Herding

In late 2009, almost all of the world's
6.8 billion people lived from the food

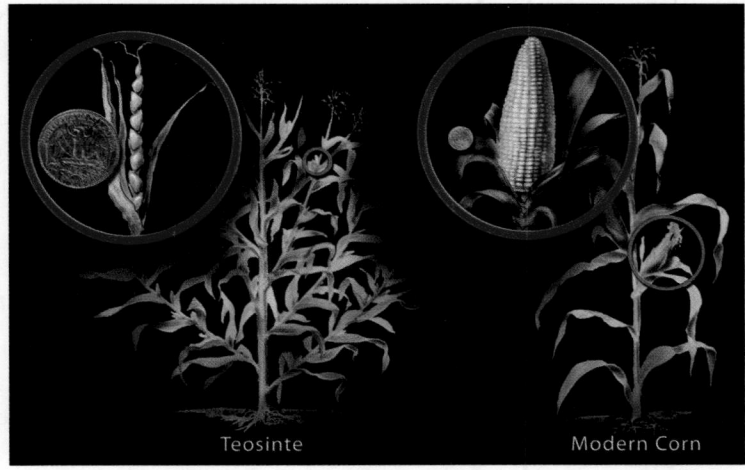

Teosinte   Modern Corn

Teosinte and Maize/Corn
(p. 56)

grown on farms and gardens and from domesticated animals raised for their meat,
milk, or eggs, but this was not always so. In fact, before 11,000 years ago, no one
survived in this fashion. Then, repeatedly and fairly rapidly, at least in world history
terms, human communities in parts of the Middle East, Asia, Africa, and the
Americas began the laborious process of domesticating animals and selecting seeds
to be planted. This momentous accomplishment represents another "first" in the
human story. After countless millennia of relying on the gathering of wild foods and
the hunting of wild animals, why and how did human societies begin to practice
agriculture and herding? What changes to human life did this new technology bring
with it?

   This food-producing revolution, considered in Chapter 2, surely marks the single
most significant and enduring transformation of the human condition, providing
the foundation for virtually everything that followed. The entire period from the
beginning of agriculture to the Industrial Revolution around 1750 might be considered a single phase of the human story—the age of agriculture—calculated now
on a timescale of millennia or centuries rather than the more extended periods of
earlier eras. Although the age of agriculture was far shorter than the immense Paleolithic era that preceded it, farming and herding allowed for a substantial increase in
human numbers.

   In the various beginnings of food production lay the foundations for some of
the most enduring divisions within the larger human community. Much depended
on the luck of the draw—on the climate and soils, on the various wild plants and
animals that were available for domestication. Many agricultural peoples lived in
small settled villages, independent of larger political structures, while drawing their
food supply from their own gardens and farms. Some depended on root crops,
such as potatoes in the Andes; others relied on tree crops, such as the banana; the
most favored areas were those where highly nutritious wild grains such as rice,
wheat, or corn could be domesticated. In more arid regions where farming was
difficult, some peoples, known as pastoralists, came to depend heavily on their

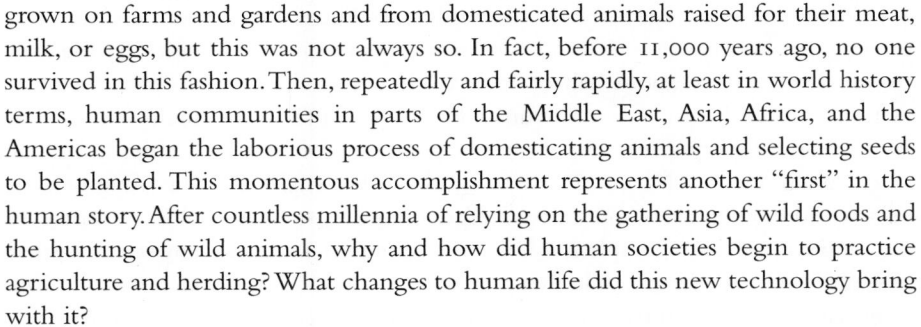

herds of domesticated animals. Because they moved frequently and in regular patterns, in search of pasturelands, they are often referred to as nomads. With regard to animal husbandry, the Americas were at a distinct disadvantage, for there were few large animals that could be tamed—no goats, sheep, pigs, horses, camels, or cattle. In the Afro-Eurasian world, conflicts between settled agricultural peoples and more mobile pastoral peoples represented an enduring pattern of interaction across the region.

The Turning Point of Civilization

The most prominent and powerful human communities to emerge from the Agricultural Revolution were those we often designate as "civilizations," societies that were based in bustling cities and governed by powerful states. Virtually all of the world's people now live in a state with a formal political authority that controls a particular territory, whether it is a single city such as Singapore, a tiny country such as The Gambia, or a huge territory such as Russia. The political, economic, and cultural life of state-based societies everywhere gives prominence to cities. By the early twenty-first century, about half of the world's population lived in urban centers. States and cities have become so common as to seem almost natural.

In world history terms, however, the appearance of states and cities is a rather recent phenomenon. Not until several thousand years *after* the beginning of agriculture did the first cities and states emerge, around 3500 B.C.E. Well after 1000 C.E., substantial numbers of people still lived in communities without any state or urban structures. Nonetheless, people living in state- and city-based societies or civilizations have long constituted the most powerful and innovative human communities on the planet. They gave rise to empires of increasing size, to enduring cultural and religious traditions, to new technologies, to sharp class inequalities, to male domination (patriarchy), and to large-scale warfare.

For all of these reasons, civilizations have featured prominently in accounts of world history, sometimes crowding out the stories of other kinds of human communities. The earliest civilizations, which emerged between 3500 and 500 B.C.E., have long fascinated professional historians and lovers of history everywhere. In at least six separate places—Mesopotamia (present-day Iraq), Egypt, Pakistan and northern India, China, Peru, and Mexico—such state- and city-based societies emerged. What was their relationship to the Agricultural Revolution? What new ways of life did they bring to the experience of humankind? These are the questions that are examined in Chapter 3.

A Note on Dates

Recently it has become standard in the Western world to refer to dates prior to the birth of Christ as B.C.E. (before the Common Era), replacing the earlier B.C. (before Christ) usage. This convention is an effort to become less Christian-centered and

Eurocentric in our use of language, although the chronology remains linked to the birth of Jesus. Similarly, the time following the birth of Christ is referred to as C.E. (the Common Era) rather than A.D. (*Anno Domini*, Latin for "year of the Lord"). Dates in the more distant past are designated in this book simply as so many "years ago." Of course, these conventions are only some of the many ways that human societies have reckoned time. The Chinese frequently dated important events in terms of the reign of particular emperors, while Muslims created a new calendar beginning with Year 1, marking Muhammad's emigration to Medina in 622 C.E. As with so much else, the ways that we measure time reflect the cultures in which we have been born and the historical experience of our societies.

Landmarks of Early World History, to 500 B.C.E.

27,000	26,000	25,000	24,000	23,000	22,000	21,000	20,000	19,000	18,000	17,000	16,000	15,000	14,000

Africa

250,000 years ago
Emergence of *Homo sapiens*

100,000 years ago
Human migration out of Africa into Eurasia

16,000–9000 B.C.E.
Development of distinctive regional cultures

Eurasia

60,000 years ago
Human entry into Australia

45,000 years ago
Human entry into Europe

15,000 B.C.E.
Lascaux cave paintings in southern France

The Americas

30,000–15,000 years ago
Human entry into the Americas

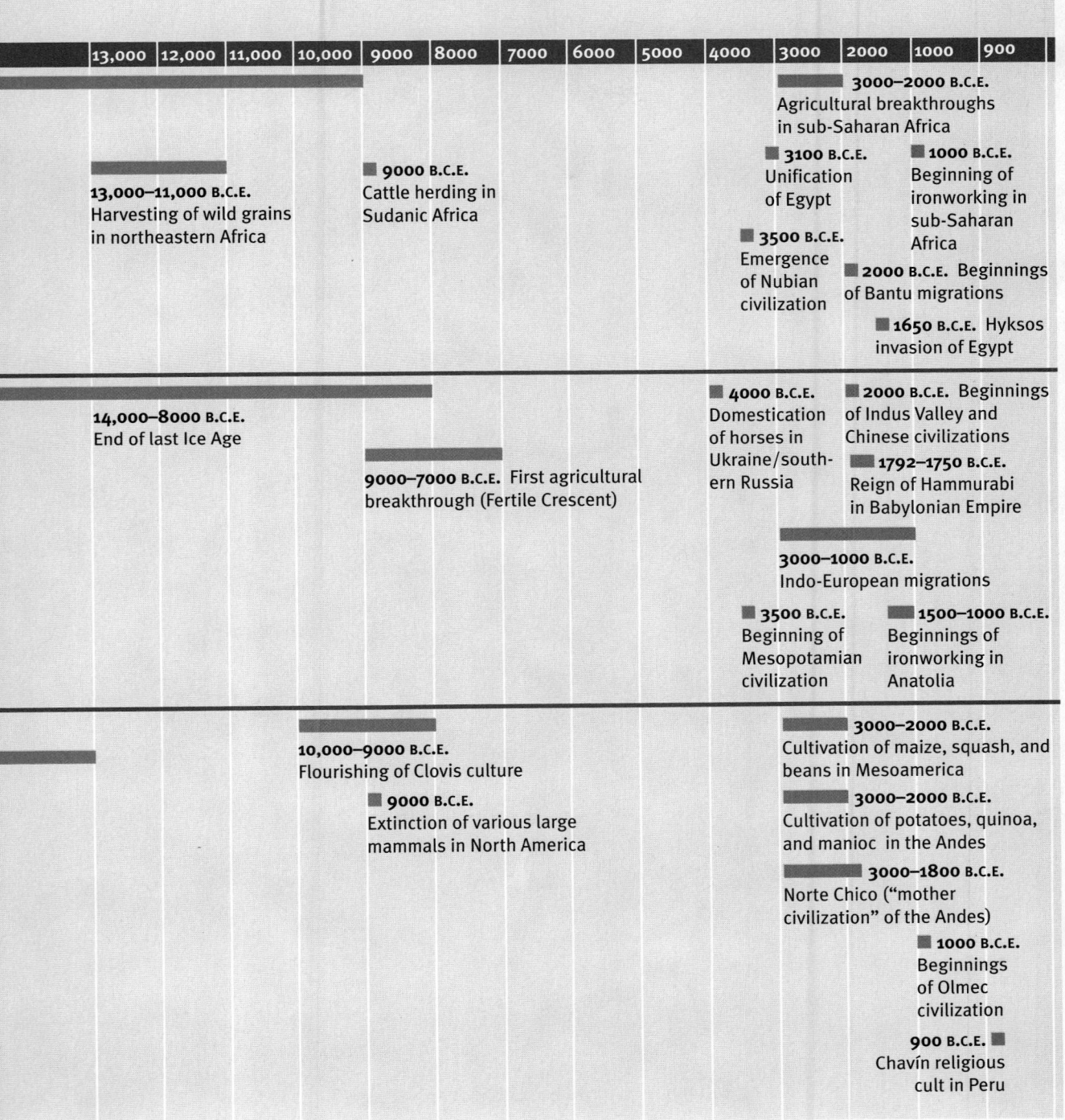

13,000 | 12,000 | 11,000 | 10,000 | 9000 | 8000 | 7000 | 6000 | 5000 | 4000 | 3000 | 2000 | 1000 | 900

3000–2000 B.C.E.
Agricultural breakthroughs
in sub-Saharan Africa

3100 B.C.E.
Unification
of Egypt

1000 B.C.E.
Beginning of
ironworking in
sub-Saharan
Africa

13,000–11,000 B.C.E.
Harvesting of wild grains
in northeastern Africa

9000 B.C.E.
Cattle herding in
Sudanic Africa

3500 B.C.E.
Emergence
of Nubian
civilization

2000 B.C.E. Beginnings
of Bantu migrations

1650 B.C.E. Hyksos
invasion of Egypt

14,000–8000 B.C.E.
End of last Ice Age

4000 B.C.E.
Domestication
of horses in
Ukraine/south-
ern Russia

2000 B.C.E. Beginnings
of Indus Valley and
Chinese civilizations

1792–1750 B.C.E.
Reign of Hammurabi
in Babylonian Empire

9000–7000 B.C.E. First agricultural
breakthrough (Fertile Crescent)

3000–1000 B.C.E.
Indo-European migrations

3500 B.C.E.
Beginning of
Mesopotamian
civilization

1500–1000 B.C.E.
Beginnings of
ironworking in
Anatolia

10,000–9000 B.C.E.
Flourishing of Clovis culture

3000–2000 B.C.E.
Cultivation of maize, squash, and
beans in Mesoamerica

9000 B.C.E.
Extinction of various large
mammals in North America

3000–2000 B.C.E.
Cultivation of potatoes, quinoa,
and manioc in the Andes

3000–1800 B.C.E.
Norte Chico ("mother
civilization" of the Andes)

1000 B.C.E.
Beginnings
of Olmec
civilization

900 B.C.E.
Chavín religious
cult in Peru

First Peoples

Populating the Planet

TO 10,000 B.C.E.

Out of Africa to the Ends of the
  Earth: First Migrations
  Into Eurasia
  Into Australia
  Into the Americas
  Into the Pacific
The Ways We Were
  The First Human Societies
  Economy and the Environment
  The Realm of the Spirit
  Settling Down: The Great
    Transition
Comparing Paleolithic Societies
  The San of Southern Africa
  The Chumash of Southern
    California
Reflections: The Uses of the
  Paleolithic
Considering the Evidence
  Documents: Glimpses of
    Paleolithic Life
  Visual Sources: The Aboriginal
    Rock Painting of Australia

"We do not want cattle, just wild animals to hunt and water that we can drink."[1] That was the view of Gudo Mahiya, a prominent member of the Hadza people of northern Tanzania, when he was questioned in 1997 about his interest in a settled life of farming and cattle raising. With only about 1,000 total members, the Hadza represent one of the very last peoples on earth to continue a way of life that was universal among humankind until 10,000 to 12,000 years ago. At the beginning of the twenty-first century, several hundred Hadza still made a living by hunting game, collecting honey, digging up roots, and gathering berries and fruit. They lived in quickly assembled grass huts located in small mobile camps averaging eighteen people and moved frequently around their remote region. Almost certainly their way of life is doomed, as farmers, governments, missionaries, and now tourists descend on them. The likely disappearance of their culture parallels the experience of many other such societies, which have been on the defensive against more numerous and powerful neighbors for 10,000 years.

NONETHELESS, THAT WAY OF LIFE SUSTAINED HUMANKIND for more than 95 percent of the time that our species has inhabited the earth. During countless centuries, human beings successfully adapted to a wide variety of environments without benefit of deliberate farming or animal husbandry. Instead, our early ancestors wrested a livelihood by gathering wild foods such as berries, nuts, roots, and grain; by scavenging dead animals; by hunting live animals; and

Paleolithic Art: The rock art of gathering and hunting peoples has been found in Africa, Europe, Australia, and elsewhere. This image from the San people of southern Africa represents aspects of their outer life in the form of wild animals and hunters with bows as well as the inner life of their shamans during a trance, reflected in the elongated figures with both human and animal features. (Image courtesy of S.A. Tourism)

by fishing. Known to scholars as "gathering and hunting" peoples, they were foragers or food collectors rather than food producers. Instead of requiring the earth to produce what they wanted, they took—or perhaps borrowed—what nature had to offer. Because they used stone rather than metal tools, they also have been labeled "Paleolithic," or "old stone age," peoples.

History courses and history books often neglect this long phase of the human journey and instead choose to begin the story with the coming of agriculture about 12,000 years ago or with the advent of civilizations about 5,000 years ago. Some historians identify "real history" with writing and so dismiss the Paleolithic era as largely unknowable because its people did not write. Others, impressed with the rapid pace of change in human affairs since the coming of agriculture, assume that nothing much of real significance happened in the Paleolithic era—and no change meant no history.

But does it make sense to ignore the first 200,000 years or more of human experience? Although written records are absent, scholars have learned a great deal about Paleolithic peoples through their material remains: stones and bones, fossilized seeds, rock paintings and engravings, and much more. Archeologists, biologists, botanists, demographers, linguists, and anthropologists have contributed much to our growing understanding of gathering and hunting peoples. Furthermore, the achievements of Paleolithic peoples—the initial settlement of the planet, the creation of the earliest human societies, the beginning of reflection on the great questions of life and death—deserve our attention. The changes they wrought, though far slower than those of more recent times, were extraordinarily rapid in comparison to the transformation experienced by any other species. Those changes were almost entirely cultural or learned, rather than the product of biological evolution, and they provided the foundation on which all subsequent human history was constructed. Our grasp of the human past is incomplete—massively so—if we choose to disregard the Paleolithic era.

Out of Africa to the Ends of the Earth: First Migrations

The first 150,000 years or more of human experience was an exclusively African story. Around 250,000 years ago, in the grasslands of eastern and southern Africa, *Homo sapiens* first emerged, following in the footsteps of many other hominid species before it. Time and climate have erased much of the record of these early people, and Africa has witnessed much less archeological research than have other parts of the world, especially Europe. Nonetheless, scholars have turned up evidence of distinctly human behavior in Africa long before its appearance elsewhere. Africa, almost certainly, was the place where the "human revolution" occurred, where "culture," defined as learned or invented ways of living, became more important than biology in shaping behavior.

What kinds of uniquely human activity show up in the early African record?[2] In the first place, human beings began to inhabit new environments within Africa—forests and deserts—where no hominids had lived before. Accompanying these movements of people were technological innovations of various kinds: stone blades

Snapshot   **The Long Road to the Global Presence of Humankind**

(all dates approximate)	Years Ago
Earliest bipedal hominids (walking upright on two legs)	7 million to 6 million
Homo habilis (earliest use of stone tools)	2.5 million
Homo erectus (first controlled use of fire and first hominid migrations out of Africa)	1.9 million to 200,000
Earliest *Homo sapiens* in Africa	250,000
Beginnings of human migration out of Africa	100,000–60,000
Human entry into eastern Asia	70,000
Human entry into Australia (first use of boats)	60,000–40,000
Human entry into Europe	45,000
Extinction of large mammals in Australia	30,000
Human entry into the Americas	30,000–15,000
Cave art in Europe	25,000
Extinction of Neanderthals	25,000
End of last Ice Age (global warming)	16,000–10,000
Earliest agricultural revolutions	12,000–10,000
Extinction of large mammals in North America	11,000
Austronesian migration to Pacific islands and Madagascar	3,500–1,000
Human entry into New Zealand (last major region to receive human settlers)	1,000

and points fastened to shafts replaced the earlier hand axes; tools made from bones appeared, and so did grindstones. Evidence of hunting and fishing, not just the scavenging of dead animals, marks a new phase in human food collection. Settlements were planned around the seasonal movement of game and fish. Patterns of exchange over a distance of almost 200 miles indicate larger networks of human communication. The use of body ornaments, beads, and pigments such as ocher as well as possible planned burials suggest the kind of social and symbolic behavior that has characterized human activity ever since. All of this occurred before 100,000 years ago and, based on current evidence, long before such activity surfaced elsewhere in the world.

Then, sometime between 100,000 and 60,000 years ago, human beings began their long trek out of Africa and into Eurasia, Australia, the Americas, and, much later,

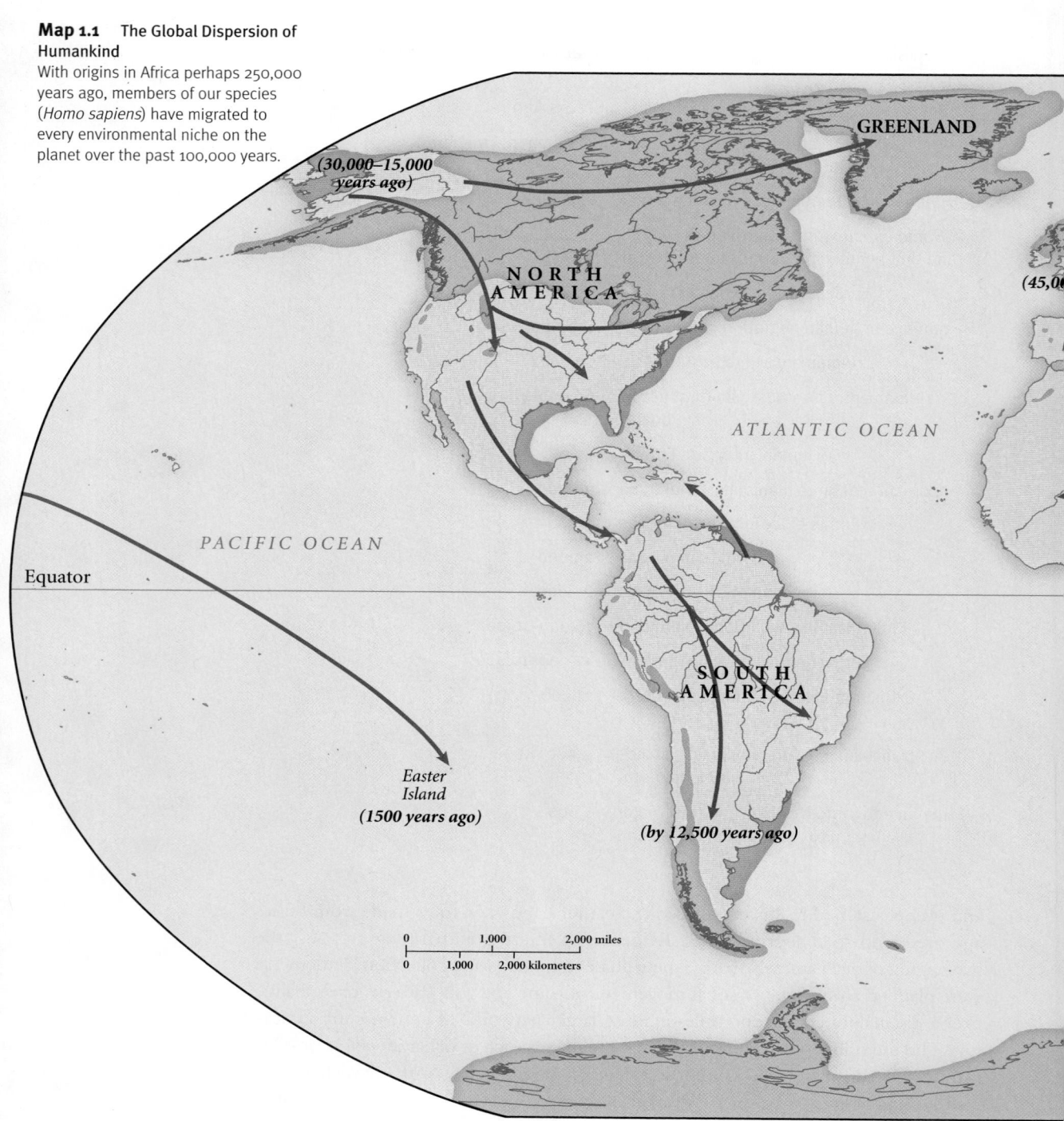

Map 1.1 The Global Dispersion of Humankind

With origins in Africa perhaps 250,000 years ago, members of our species (*Homo sapiens*) have migrated to every environmental niche on the planet over the past 100,000 years.

GREENLAND

(30,000–15,000 years ago)

NORTH AMERICA

(45,0

ATLANTIC OCEAN

PACIFIC OCEAN

Equator

SOUTH AMERICA

Easter Island

(1500 years ago)

(by 12,500 years ago)

0   1,000   2,000 miles

0   1,000   2,000 kilometers

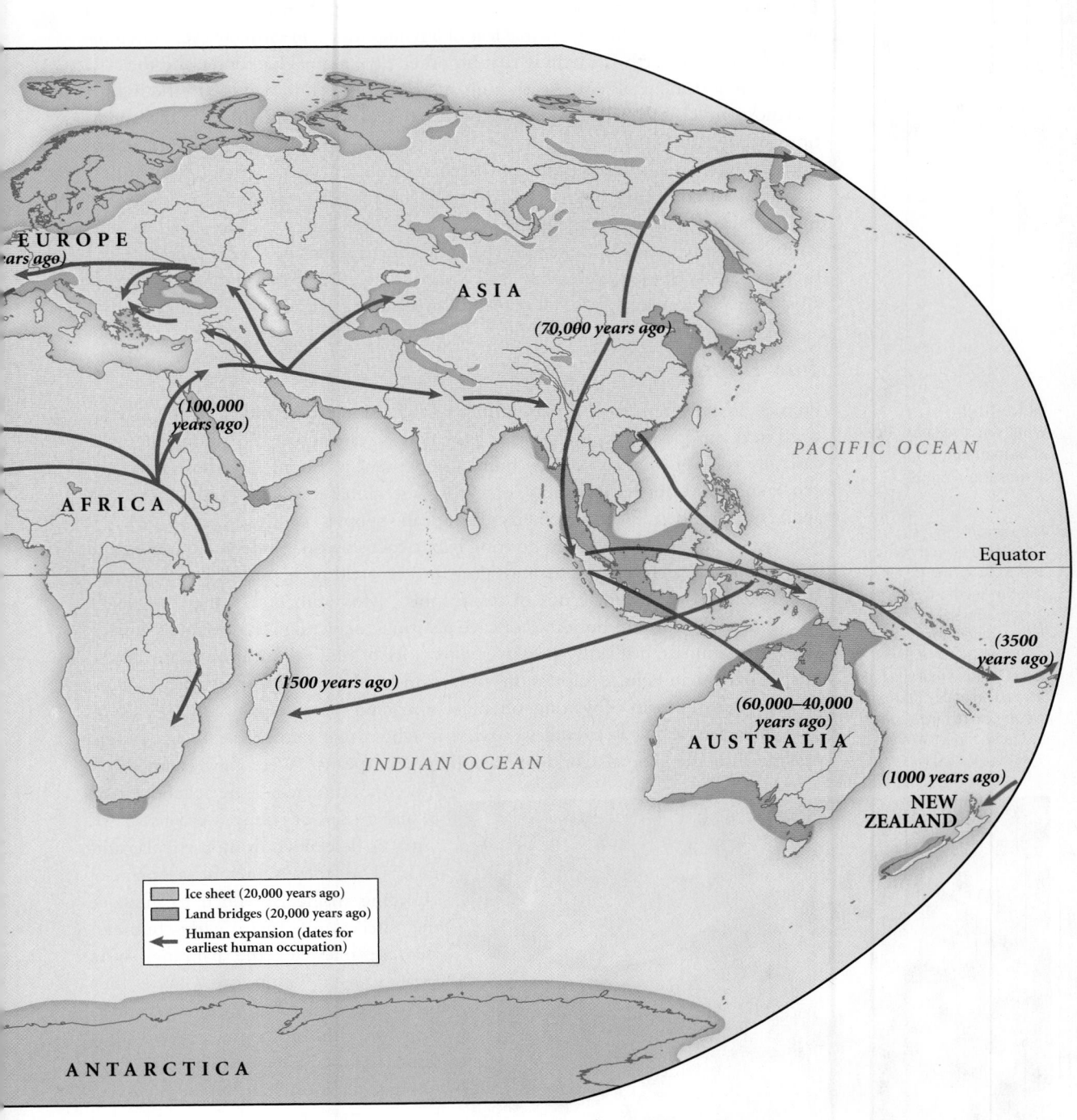

EUROPE
(ars ago)

ASIA

(70,000 years ago)

(100,000
years ago)

PACIFIC OCEAN

AFRICA

Equator

(3500
years ago)

(1500 years ago)

(60,000–40,000
years ago)

INDIAN OCEAN

AUSTRALIA

(1000 years ago)
NEW
ZEALAND

Ice sheet (20,000 years ago)
Land bridges (20,000 years ago)
Human expansion (dates for
earliest human occupation)

ANTARCTICA

15

the islands of the Pacific (see Map 1.1). In occupying the planet, members of our species accomplished the remarkable feat of learning to live in virtually every environmental niche on earth, something that no other large animal had done; and they did it with only stone tools and a gathering and hunting technology to aid them. Furthermore, much of this long journey occurred during the difficult climatic conditions of the last Ice Age (at its peak around 20,000 years ago), when thick ice sheets covered much of northern Eurasia and North America. The Ice Age did give these outward-bound human beings one advantage, however: the amount of water frozen in northern glaciers lowered sea levels around the planet, creating land bridges among various regions that were separated after the glaciers melted. Britain was then joined to Europe; eastern Siberia was connected to Alaska; and New Guinea, Australia, and Tasmania were all part of a huge supercontinent known as Sahul.

Into Eurasia

■ **Change**
What was the sequence of human migration across the planet?

The Lascaux Caves
Discovered by four teenage boys in 1940, the Lascaux caves in southern France contain some 2,000 images, dating to perhaps 17,000 years ago. Many of them depict in quite realistic form the wild animals of the region—oxen, bulls, horses, ibex, and birds. (JM Labat/ Photo Researchers, Inc.)

Human migration out of Africa led first to the Middle East and from there westward into Europe about 45,000 years ago and eastward into Asia. Among the most carefully researched areas of early human settlement in Eurasia are those in southern France and northern Spain. Colder Ice Age climates around 20,000 years ago apparently pushed more northerly European peoples southward into warmer regions. There they altered their hunting habits, focusing on reindeer and horses, and developed new technologies such as spear throwers and perhaps the bow and arrow as well as many different kinds of stone tools.[3] Most remarkably, they also left a record of their world in hundreds of cave paintings, depicting reindeer, bulls, horses, and other animals, brilliantly portrayed in colors of red, yellow, brown, and black. Images of human beings, impressions of human hands, and various abstract designs, perhaps an early form of writing, often accompanied the cave paintings.

Scholars have debated endlessly what insights these remarkable images might provide into the mental world of Paleolithic Europeans.[4] Were they examples of "totemic" thinking—the belief that particular groups of people were associated with, or descended from, particular animals? Did they represent a form of "hunting magic" intended to enhance the success of these early hunters? Because many of the paintings were located deep within caves, were they perhaps part of religious or ritual practices or rites of passage? Were they designed to pass on information to future generations? Or did they symbolize, as some recent scholars contend, a coded representation of a Paleolithic worldview divided into male and female

realms, both opposed to and balancing each other? We simply do not know. Nonetheless, these images excite our imagination still, 20,000 years or more after they were created. In them we sense a kinship with the humanity of our distant ancestors.

Farther east, archeologists have uncovered still other remarkable Paleolithic adaptations to Ice Age conditions. Across the vast plains of Central Europe, Ukraine, and Russia, new technologies emerged, including bone needles, multilayered clothing, weaving, nets, storage pits, baskets, and pottery. Partially underground dwellings constructed from the bones and tusks of mammoths compensated for the absence of caves and rock shelters. All of this suggests that some of these people had lived in more permanent settlements, at least temporarily abandoning their nomadic journeys. Associated with these Eastern European peoples were numerous female figurines, the earliest of which was uncovered in 2008 in Germany and dated to at least 35,000 years ago. Carved from stone, antlers, mammoth tusks, or, occasionally, baked clay, these so-called Venus figurines depict the female form, often with exaggerated breasts, buttocks, hips, and stomachs (see image, p. 22). They were not limited to a single region but have been found all across Europe, from Spain to Russia, suggesting a network of human communication and cultural diffusion over a wide area.

Into Australia

Early human migration to Australia, currently dated to around 60,000 years ago, came from Indonesia and involved another first in human affairs—the use of boats. Over time, people settled in most regions of this huge continent, though quite sparsely. Scholars estimate the population of Australia at about 300,000 people in 1788, when the first Europeans arrived. Over tens of thousands of years, these people had developed perhaps 250 languages; collected a wide variety of bulbs, tubers, roots, seeds, and cereal grasses; and hunted large and small animals, as well as birds, fish, and other marine life. A relatively simple technology, appropriate to a gathering and hunting economy, sustained Australia's Aboriginal people into modern times. When outsiders arrived in the late eighteenth century, all of the continent's people still practiced that ancient way of life, despite the presence of agriculture in nearby New Guinea.

Accompanying their technological simplicity and traditionalism was the development of an elaborate and complex outlook on the world, known as the Dreamtime. Expressed in endless stories, in extended ceremonies, and in the evocative rock art of the continent's peoples, the Dreamtime recounted the beginning of things: how ancestral beings crisscrossed the land, creating its rivers, hills, rocks, and waterholes; how various peoples came to inhabit the land; and how they related to animals and to one another. In this view of the world, everything in the natural order was a vibration, an echo, a footprint of these ancient happenings, which link the current inhabitants intimately to particular places and to timeless events in the past. (See Document 1.2, pp. 39–41, and Visual Sources: The Aboriginal Rock Painting of Australia, pp. 42–47.)

The journeys of the Dreamtime's ancestral beings reflect in a general way the networks of migration, communication, and exchange that linked the continent's many Paleolithic peoples. Far from isolated groups, they had long exchanged particular stones, pigments, materials for ropes and baskets, wood for spears, feathers and shells for ornaments, and an addictive psychoactive drug known as *pituri* over distances of hundreds of miles.[5] Songs, dances, stories, and rituals likewise circulated. Precisely how far back in time these networks extend is difficult to pinpoint, but it seems clear that Paleolithic Australia, like ancient Europe, was both many separate worlds and, at the same time, one loosely connected world.

Into the Americas

The earliest settlement of the Western Hemisphere occurred much later than that of Australia, for it took some time for human beings to penetrate the frigid lands of eastern Siberia, which was the jumping-off point for the move into the Americas. Experts continue to argue about precisely when the first migrations occurred (somewhere between 30,000 and 15,000 years ago), about the route of migration (by land across the Bering Strait or by sea down the west coast of North America), about how many separate migrations took place, and about how long it took for people to penetrate to the tip of South America.[6] There is, however, good evidence of human activity in southern Chile by 12,500 years ago.

The first clearly defined and widespread cultural tradition in the Americas is associated with people who made a distinctive projectile point, known to archeologists as a Clovis point. Scattered all over North America, Clovis culture flourished around 12,000 to 11,000 years ago. Scattered bands of Clovis people ranged over huge areas, camping along rivers, springs, and waterholes, where large animals congregated. Although they certainly hunted smaller animals and gathered many wild plants, Clovis people show up in the archeological record most dramatically as hunters of very large mammals, such as mammoths and bison. Killing a single mammoth could provide food for many weeks or, in cold weather, for much of the winter. The wide distribution of Clovis point technology suggests yet again a regional pattern of cultural diffusion and at least indirect communication over a large area.

Then, about 10,900 years ago, all trace of the Clovis people disappears from the archeological record at the same time that many species of large animals, including the mammoth and several species of horses and camels, also became extinct. Did the Clovis people hunt these animals to extinction and then vanish themselves as their source of food disappeared? Or did the drier climate that came with the end of the Ice Age cause this megafaunal extinction? Experts disagree, but what happened next was the creation of a much greater diversity of cultures as people adapted to this new situation in various ways. Hunters on the Great Plains continued to pursue bison, which largely avoided the fate of the mammoths. Others learned to live in the desert, taking advantage of seasonal plants and smaller animals, while those who lived near the sea, lakes, or streams drew on local fish and birds. Many peoples retained their gathering and hunting way of life into modern times, while others became farmers and, in a few favored regions, later developed cities and large-scale states.[7]

Into the Pacific

The last phase of the great human migration to the ends of the earth took place in the Pacific Ocean and was distinctive in many ways. In the first place, it occurred quite recently, jumping off only about 3,500 years ago from the Bismarck and Solomon islands near New Guinea as well as from the islands of the Philippines. It was everywhere a waterborne migration, making use of oceangoing canoes and remarkable navigational skills, and it happened very quickly and over a huge area of the planet. Speaking Austronesian languages that trace back to southern China, these oceanic voyagers had settled every habitable piece of land in the Pacific basin within about 2,500 years. Other Austronesians had sailed west from Indonesia across the Indian Ocean to settle the island of Madagascar off the coast of eastern Africa. This extraordinary process of expansion—both rapid and extensive—made the Austronesian family of languages the most widespread in the world. With the occupation of Aotearoa (New Zealand) about 1300 C.E., the initial human settlement of the planet was finally complete (see Map 1.2).

In contrast with all of the other migrations, these Pacific voyages were undertaken by people with an agricultural technology, who carried both domesticated plants and animals in their canoes. Both men and women made these journeys, suggesting a deliberate intention to colonize new lands. Virtually everywhere they went, two developments followed. One was the creation of highly stratified societies or chiefdoms, of which ancient Hawaiian society is a prime example. In Hawaii, an elite class of chiefs with political and military power ruled over a mass of commoners. The other development was the dramatic impact that these migrations had on the environment of previously uninhabited islands. Many species of

■ **Comparison**

How did Austronesian migrations differ from other early patterns of human movement?

Map 1.2 Migration of Austronesian-Speaking People

People speaking Austronesian languages completed the human settlement of the earth quite recently as they settled the islands of the vast Pacific and penetrated the Indian Ocean to Madagascar, off the coast of southeast Africa.

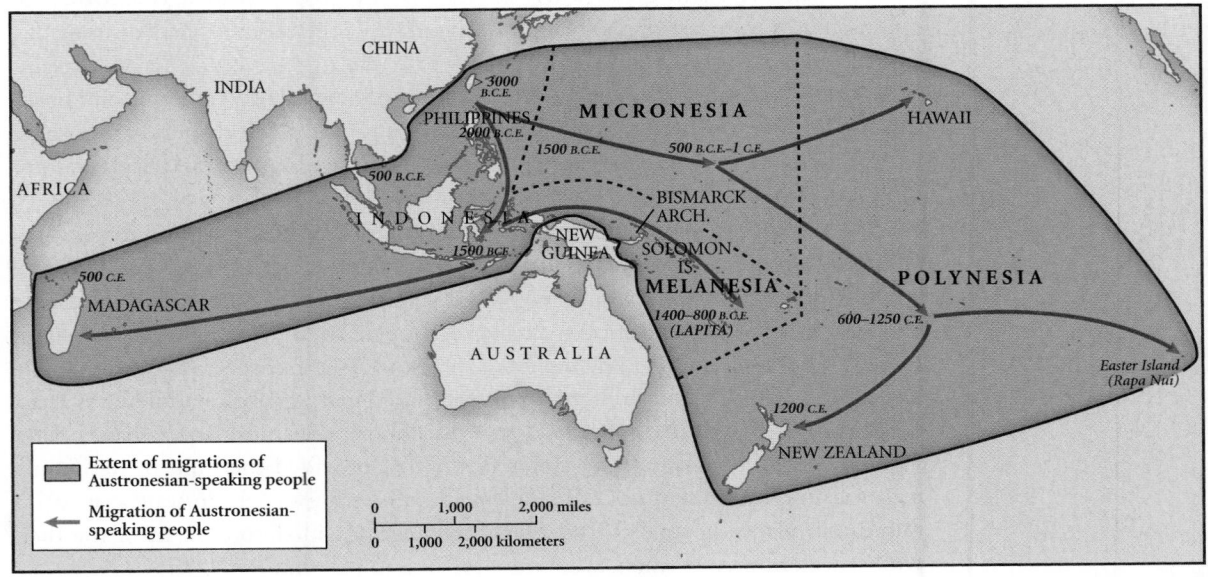

animals quickly became extinct, especially large flightless birds. The destruction of the forests of Rapa Nui (Easter Island) between the fifteenth and seventeenth centuries C.E. brought famine, violent conflict, and a sharp population decline to this small island society, while the absence of large trees ensured that no one could leave the island, for they could no longer build the canoes that had brought them there.[8]

The Ways We Were

During their long journeys across the earth, Paleolithic people created a multitude of separate and distinct societies, each with its own history, culture, language, identity, stories, and rituals, but the limitations of a gathering and hunting technology using stone tools imposed some commonalities on these ancient people. Based on the archeological record and on the example of gathering and hunting societies that still existed in modern times, scholars have sketched out some of the common features of these early societies.

The First Human Societies

■ Change
In what ways did a gathering and hunting economy shape other aspects of Paleolithic societies?

Above all else, these Paleolithic societies were small, consisting of bands of twenty-five to fifty people, in which all relationships were intensely personal and normally understood in terms of kinship. No anonymity or hiding in the crowd was possible in a society of relatives. The available technology permitted only a very low population density and ensured an extremely slow rate of population growth. Scholars estimate that world population may have been as low as 10,000 people around 100,000 years ago and grew slowly to 500,000 by 30,000 years ago and then to 6 million by 10,000 years ago.[9] Paleolithic bands were seasonally mobile or nomadic, moving frequently and in regular patterns to exploit the resources of wild plants and animals on which they depended. The low productivity of a gathering and hunting economy normally did not allow the production of much surplus, and because people were on the move so often, transporting an accumulation of goods was out of the question.

All of this resulted in highly egalitarian societies, lacking the many inequalities of wealth and power that came with later agricultural and urban life. With no formal chiefs, kings, bureaucrats, soldiers, nobles, or priests, Paleolithic people were perhaps freer of tyranny and oppression than any subsequent kind of human society, even if they were more constrained by the forces of nature. Without specialists, most people possessed the same set of skills, although male and female tasks often differed sharply. Relationships between women and men usually were far more equal than in later societies. As the primary food gatherers, women provided the bulk of the family income. One study of a modern gathering and hunting society in southern Africa found that plants, normally gathered by women, provided 70 percent of the diet, while meat, hunted by men, accounted for just 30 percent.[10]

When the British navigator and explorer Captain James Cook first encountered the gathering and hunting peoples of Australia in 1770, he described them, perhaps a little enviously, in this way:

> They live in a Tranquillity which is not disturb'd by the Inequality of Conditions: The Earth and sea of their own accord furnishes them with all things necessary for life, they covet not Magnificient houses, Household-stuff.... In short they seem'd to set no value upon any thing we gave them.... They think themselves provided with all the necessarys of Life.[11]

Native Australians
A number of Aboriginal Australians maintained their gathering and hunting way of life well into the twentieth century. Here an older woman shows two young boys how to dig for honey ants, a popular food. (Bill Bachman/Alamy)

The Europeans who settled permanently among such people some twenty years later, however, found a society in which physical competition among men was expressed in frequent one-on-one combat and in formalized but bloody battles. It also meant recurrent, public, and quite brutal beatings of wives by their husbands.[12] Although sometimes romanticized by Europeans, the relative social equality of Paleolithic peoples did not always ensure a utopia of social harmony.

Like all other human cultures, Paleolithic societies had rules and structures. A gender-based division of labor usually cast men as hunters and women as gatherers. Values emphasizing reciprocal sharing of goods resulted in clearly defined rules about distributing the meat from an animal kill. Rules about incest and adultery governed sexual behavior, while understandings about who could hunt or gather in particular territories regulated economic activity. Leaders arose as needed to organize a task such as a hunt, but without conferring permanent power on individuals.

Economy and the Environment

For a long time, gathering and hunting peoples were viewed as primitive, impoverished, barely eking out a living from the land. In more recent decades, anthropologists studying contemporary Paleolithic societies—those that survived into the twentieth century—began to paint a different picture. They noted that gathering and hunting people frequently worked fewer hours to meet their material needs than did people in agricultural or industrial societies and so had more leisure time. One scholar referred to them as "the original affluent society," not because they had so much, but because they wanted or needed so little.[13] Nonetheless, life expectancy was low, probably little more than thirty-five years on average. Life in the wild was surely dangerous, and dependency on the vagaries of nature rendered it insecure as well.

But Paleolithic people also acted to alter the natural environment substantially. The use of deliberately set fires to encourage the growth of particular plants certainly changed the landscape and in Australia led to the proliferation of fire-resistant eucalyptus trees at the expense of other plant species. In many parts of the world—Australia, North America, Siberia, Madagascar, Pacific islands—the extinction of various large animals followed fairly quickly after the arrival of human beings, leading scholars to suggest that Paleolithic humankind played a major role, coupled perhaps with changing climates, in the disappearance of these animals. Other hominid, or humanlike, species, such as the Neanderthals in Europe or the recently discovered Flores man in Indonesia, also perished after living side by side with *Homo sapiens* for millennia. Whether their disappearance occurred through massacre, interbreeding, or peaceful competition, they were among the casualties of the rise of humankind. Thus the biological environment inhabited by gathering and hunting peoples was not wholly natural but was shaped in part by their own hands.

The Realm of the Spirit

The religious or spiritual dimension of Paleolithic culture has been hard to pin down because bones and stones tell us little about what people thought, art is subject to many interpretations, and the experience of contemporary gathering and hunting peoples may not reflect the distant past. There is, however, clear evidence for a rich ceremonial life. The presence of rock art deep inside caves and far from living spaces suggests a "ceremonial space" separate from ordinary life. (See Visual Sources: The Aboriginal Rock Painting of Australia, pp. 42–47.) The extended rituals of contemporary Australian Aboriginal people, which sometimes last for weeks, confirm this impression, as do numerous and elaborate burial sites found throughout the world. No full-time religious specialists or priests led these ceremonies, but part-time shamans (people believed to be especially skilled at dealing with the spirit world) emerged as the need arose. Such people often entered an altered state of consciousness or a trance while performing the ceremonies, often with the aid of psychoactive drugs.

Precisely how Paleolithic people understood the nonmaterial world is hard to reconstruct, and speculation abounds. Linguistic evidence from ancient Africa suggests a variety of understandings: some Paleolithic societies were apparently monotheistic; others saw several levels of supernatural beings, including a Creator Deity, various territorial spirits, and the spirits of dead ancestors; still others believed in an impersonal force suffused throughout the natural order that could be accessed by shamans during a trance dance.[14] The prevalence of Venus figurines and other symbols all across Europe has convinced some scholars, but not all, that Paleolithic religious thought had a strongly feminine dimension, embodied in a Great Goddess and concerned with the regeneration and renewal of life.[15] Many gathering and hunting peoples likely developed a cyclical view of time that drew on the changing phases of the moon and on the cycles of female fertility—birth, menstruation,

The Willendorf Venus
Less than four and a half inches in height and dating to about 25,000 years ago, this female figure, which was found near the town of Willendorf in Austria, has become the most famous of the many Venus figurines. Certain features—the absence of both face and feet, the coils of hair around her head, the prominence of her breasts and sexual organs—have prompted much speculation among scholars about the significance of these intriguing carvings. (Naturhistorisches Museum, Vienna, Austria/The Bridgeman Art Library)

Snapshot   **The Paleolithic Era in Perspective**[16]

	Paleolithic Era (from 250,000 to 10,000 years ago)	Agricultural Era (from 10,000 to 200 years ago)	Modern Industrial Era (since 1800)
Duration of each era, as a percentage of 250,000 years	96%	4%	0.08%
Percent of people who lived, out of 80 billion total	12%	68%	20%
Percent of years lived in each era (reflects changing life expectancies)	9%	62%	29%

pregnancy, new birth, and death. Such understandings of the cosmos, which saw endlessly repeated patterns of regeneration and disintegration, differed from later Western views, which saw time moving in a straight line toward some predetermined goal.[17]

Settling Down: The Great Transition

Though glacially slow by contemporary standards, changes in Paleolithic cultures occurred over time as people moved into new environments, as populations grew, as climates altered, and as different human groups interacted with one another. For example, all over the Afro-Eurasian world after 25,000 years ago, a tendency toward the miniaturization of stone tools is evident. Known as micro-blades, these smaller and more refined spear points, arrowheads, knives, and scrapers were carefully struck from larger cores and often mounted in antler, bone, or wooden handles.[18] This ancient and global technological change was similar perhaps to the miniaturization of electronic components in the twentieth century. Another important change in the strategies of Paleolithic people was the collection of wild grains, which represented a major addition to the food supply beyond the use of roots, berries, and nuts. This innovation originated in northeastern Africa around 16,000 years ago.

But the most striking and significant change in the lives of Paleolithic peoples occurred as the last Ice Age came to an end between 16,000 and 10,000 years ago. What followed was a general global warming, though one with periodic fluctuations and cold snaps. Unlike the contemporary global warming, generated by human activity and especially the burning of fossil fuels, this ancient warming phase was a wholly natural phenomenon, part of a long cycle of repeated heating and

■ Change

Why did some Paleolithic peoples abandon earlier, more nomadic ways and begin to live a more settled life?

cooling characteristic of the earth's climatic history. Plants and animals unable to survive in the Ice Age climate now flourished and increased their range, providing a much richer and more diverse environment for many human societies. Under these improved conditions, human populations grew, and some previously nomadic gathering and hunting communities, but not all of them, found it possible to settle down and live in more permanent settlements or villages. These societies were becoming both larger and more complex, and it was less possible to simply move away if trouble struck. Settlement also meant that households could store and accumulate goods to a greater degree than previously. Because some people were more energetic, more talented, or luckier than others, the thin edge of inequality gradually began to wear away the egalitarianism of Paleolithic communities.

Changes along these lines emerged in many places. Paleolithic societies in Japan, known as Jomon, settled down in villages by the sea, where they greatly expanded the number of animals, both land and marine, that they consumed. They also created some of the world's first pottery, along with dugout canoes, paddles, bows, bowls, and tool handles, all made from wood. A similar pattern of permanent settlement, a broader range of food sources, and specialized technologies is evident in parts of Scandinavia, Southeast Asia, North America, and the Middle East between 12,000 and 4,000 years ago. Bows and arrows seem to have been invented separately in Europe, Africa, and the Middle East during this period and spread later to the Americas. In Labrador, longhouses accommodating 100 people appear in the archeological record. Far more elaborate burial sites in many places testify to the growing complexity of human communities and the kinship systems that bound them together. Separate cemeteries for dogs suggest that humankind's best friend was also our first domesticated animal friend.

This process of settling down among gathering and hunting peoples—and the changes that followed from it—marked a major turn in human history, away from countless millennia of nomadic journeys by very small communities. It also provided the setting within which the next great transition would occur. Growing numbers of people, living in settled communities, placed a much greater demand on the environment than did small bands of wandering people. Therefore, it is perhaps not surprising that among the innovations that emerged in these more complex gathering and hunting societies was yet another way for increasing the food supply—agriculture. That epic transition is the subject of the next chapter.

Comparing Paleolithic Societies

Over the 200,000 years or more of the Paleolithic era, human societies naturally differed from one another—in their tool kits, their adaptation to the environment, their beliefs, their social organization, and much more. Here we examine more carefully two such societies, the San of southern Africa and the Chumash of southern California. What they shared was a gathering and hunting way of life and a continuing existence into modern times. Unlike the gathering and hunting peoples who

Jomon Figurines
Female figurines, dating to perhaps 4,000 years ago, have been found among Japan's Paleolithic people, known as the Jomon. Many scholars believe these carvings had a ritual function, associated with fertility. (Tokyo National Museum, Collection of Mrs. Kane Yamazaka)

succumbed to the relentless expansion of agricultural or industrial societies, the San and the Chumash maintained their ancient way of life into the eighteenth, nineteenth, and twentieth centuries. Even though modern gathering and hunting societies studied by anthropologists surely differed in many ways from their ancient counterparts, they do allow us to see the human face of a way of life long vanished from most parts of the earth.

The San of Southern Africa

On the northern fringe of the Kalahari Desert, in an area including Angola, Namibia, and Botswana, lies the country of the San people, who numbered 50,000 to 80,000 at the start of the twenty-first century. Linguistically, they are related to the great Khoisan language family, whose speakers have lived throughout eastern and southern Africa for many millennia. The immediate ancestors of the San have inhabited southern Africa for at least 5,000 years. Economically, Khoisan-speaking peoples practiced a gathering and hunting way of life with a technology of stone tools that was recognizable to their twentieth-century San descendants. Another cultural practice of long standing was the remarkable rock art of southern Africa, depicting people and animals, especially the antelope, in thousands of naturalistic scenes of hunts, battles, and dances. Dating to as far back as 26,000 years ago, this tradition persisted into the nineteenth century, making it the "oldest artistic tradition of humankind."[19] Modern scholars suggest that this art reflected the religious experience of trance healers, who were likely the artists who painted these images. (See chapter opening photo on p. 10.) When a late-nineteenth-century anthropologist showed some of these rock paintings to an elderly San couple, the woman began to sing and dance, while the man became sad, remembering the old songs.[20] In these and other ways, contemporary San people are linked to an ancient cultural tradition that is deeply rooted in the African past.

Most Khoisan gathering and hunting peoples had long ago been absorbed or displaced by the arrival of Bantu-speaking peoples bearing agriculture, domesticated animals, and iron tools, but the San, living in a relatively remote location, endured. Even the colonization of southern Africa by Europeans left the San largely intact until the 1960s and later, but not completely, for they traded with their agricultural neighbors and sometimes worked for them. The San also began to use iron arrowheads, fashioned from metals introduced by the newcomers. Drums, borrowed from their Bantu-speaking neighbors, now supplemented their own stringed instruments and became part of San musical tradition. Despite these borrowings, when anthropologists descended on the San in the 1950s and 1960s and studied every aspect of their culture, they found a people still practicing an ancient way of life. (See Document 1.1, pp. 34–39, for a description of San life from a twentieth-century woman's perspective.) The following account of San culture is drawn largely from the work of Richard Lee, an anthropologist who lived with and was adopted by one of

■ **Description**
What are the most prominent features of San life?

The San of Southern Africa

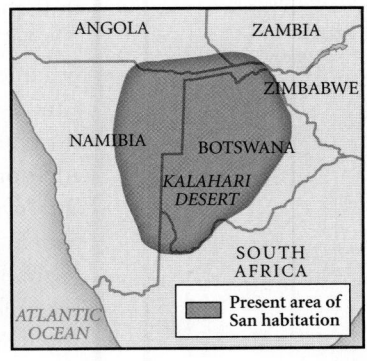

ANGOLA   ZAMBIA

ZIMBABWE

NAMIBIA   BOTSWANA

KALAHARI DESERT

SOUTH AFRICA

ATLANTIC OCEAN

▨ Present area of San habitation

the San groups who called themselves the Ju/'hoansi.[21] The term literally means "real people"; the slash and the apostrophe in the name denote "clicks," which are a distinctive sound in the San language.

In the semidesert conditions of the northern Kalahari, the Ju/'hoansi have drawn a livelihood from a harsh land using some twenty-eight tools for gathering, hunting, and preparing food. The most important implements include an all-purpose wooden digging stick, a large leather garment used for carrying things and also as a blanket, woven ropes, nets, a knife, a spear, a bow, and arrows tipped with a potent poison. The Ju/'hoansi have identified and named some 260 species of wild animals, of which the kudu, wildebeest, and gemsbok are the most commonly hunted, entirely by men. More than 100 species of wild plants, including various nuts, berries, roots, fruits, melons, and greens, were collected, largely by women.

What kind of life did they create for themselves with this modest technology? According to Richard Lee, it was a "happy combination of an adequate diet and a short workweek." He calculated that the Ju/'hoansi consumed 2,355 calories on average every day, about 30 percent from meat and 70 percent from vegetables, well balanced with sufficient protein, vitamins, and minerals—and, he concluded, they "[did] not have to work very hard" to achieve this standard of living. An average workweek involved about seventeen hours of labor in getting food and another twenty-five hours in housework and making and fixing tools, with the total work divided quite equally between men and women. This left plenty of leisure time for resting, visiting, talking, and conducting rituals and ceremonies. Still, it was an uncertain and perpetually anxious life, with fluctuating rainfall, periodic droughts, seasonal depletion of plants, and the unpredictable movement of animals.

What made the Ju/'hoansi way of life possible was a particular kind of society, one characterized by mobility, sharing, and equality. The basic unit of social organization was a band or camp of roughly ten to thirty people, who were connected by ties of exchange and kinship with similar camps across a wide area. The membership of a camp fluctuated over time as many people claimed membership in more than one band. Furthermore, the camps themselves, consisting of quickly built grass huts, were moved frequently, with the Ju/'hoansi seldom staying more than a few months in any one place. The flexibility of this arrangement allowed them to adjust rapidly to the changing seasonal patterns of their desert environment.

At one level, Ju/'hoansi society was extremely simple. No formal leaders, chiefs, headmen, priests, or craft specialists existed, and decisions were made by individual families and camps after much discussion. On another level, social relationships were extremely complex, and it took Richard Lee several years to penetrate them. In addition to common kinship relations of marriage and descent, there were "joking" and "avoidance" relationships that determined the degree of familiarity with which people engaged one another. A further element of complexity lay in a unique "naming" system, which created a deep bond among people with the same name, even though they were not biologically related. For example, a man could not marry any woman who bore the same name as his mother or sister.

At the heart of such a small-scale society of intense personal relationships were values of modesty, cooperation, and equality, which the Ju/'hoansi went to great lengths to inculcate and maintain. One technique, known as "insulting the meat," involved highly negative comments about the size or quality of an animal killed by a hunter and the expectation that a successful hunter would disparage his own kill. As one man put it:

> When a young man kills much meat, he comes to think of himself as a chief or a big man, and he thinks of the rest of us as his servants or inferiors. We can't accept this. We refuse one who boasts, for someday his pride will make him kill someone. So we always speak of his meat as worthless. In this way we cool his heart and make him gentle.

Another practice tending toward equality was the principle that the owner of the arrow that killed an animal, not the successful hunter himself, had the right to distribute the meat from that animal. Because arrows were widely shared, and sometimes owned by women, this custom spread the prestige of meat distribution widely within the society and countered any possibility that the hunter might regard the meat as his private property.

Beyond the sharing of food within a camp was a system of unequal gift exchange among members of different camps. For example, I give you something today, and many months later, you may give me a gift that need not be equivalent in value. When Richard Lee appeared puzzled by the inequality of the exchange, he was told: "We don't trade with things; we trade with people." This system of exchange had more to do with establishing social relations than with accumulating goods. One famous and highly respected hunter named Toma "gave away everything that came into his hands.... [I]n exchange for his self-imposed poverty, he won the respect and following of all the people."[22] It was an economic system that aimed at leveling wealth, not accumulating it, and that defined security in terms of possessing friends or people with obligations to oneself, rather than possessing goods.

Social equality extended also to relations between women and men. Richard Lee noted "relative equality between the sexes with no-one having the upper hand." Teenagers engaged quite freely in sex play, and the concept of female virginity was apparently unknown, as were rape, wife beating, and the sexual double standard. Although polygamy was permitted, most marriages were in fact monogamous because women strongly resisted sharing a husband with another wife. Frequent divorce among very young couples allowed women to leave unsatisfactory marriages easily. Lee found that longer-term marriages seemed to be generally fulfilling and stable. Both men and women expected a satisfying sexual relationship, and both occasionally took lovers, although discreetly.

But not all was sweetness and light among the Ju/'hoansi. Frequent arguments about the distribution of meat or the laziness or stinginess of particular people generated conflict, as did rivalries among men over women. Lee identified twenty-two murders that had occurred between 1920 and 1955 and several cases in which the community came together to conduct an execution of particularly disruptive individuals. Lesser tensions were handled through talk; more serious disputes might result in separation, with some people leaving to join another camp or to start their own.

In confronting the world beyond material and social life, the Ju/'hoansi reflected beliefs and practices that were arguably tens of thousands of years old. Unlike later peoples with their many gods, goddesses, spirits, and powers, the San populated the spiritual universe in a quite limited way. A Creator God, Gao Na, gave rise to the earth, men, women, animals, waterholes, and all other things; but like the Greek gods, Gao Na was a capricious deity who often visited misfortune on humankind, simply because he chose to do so. A lesser god, Gauwa, was even more destructive, spreading disease, conflict, and death, but also on occasion providing assistance to beleaguered humans. The most serious threat to human welfare came from the ghosts of dead ancestors, the *gauwasi,* who were viewed as primarily malevolent. Asked why the ancestral spirits were so destructive, one woman healer replied:

> Longing for the living is what drives the dead to make people sick. . . . They are very very sad. . . . They miss their people on earth. And so they come back to us. They hover near the villages and put sickness into people, saying "Come, come here to me."

The Ju/'hoansi had one powerful resource for counteracting these evil influences from the world of the gods and ancestors. It was *n/um,* a spiritual potency that lies in the stomach and becomes activated during "curing dances," powerful nightlong rituals held frequently, especially during the dry season when several camps converged on the remaining waterholes. Around a fire, an inner circle of women clapped and sang, while men danced in a circle behind them. Then someone went into a trance and, in that altered state of consciousness, sought to share his or her activated *n/um* with everyone in the camp, pulling the evil out of them. Doing so had the power to heal the sick, to bring harmony to the community, to affect the rainfall and the supply of animals, and to protect everyone from the evil designs of the ancestors.[23]

Recent analysis suggests that the rock art of southern Africa represents the visions achieved by ancient trance dancers as they did battle with the supernatural world. (See chapter opening photo on p. 10.) If so, the Ju/'hoansi of the twentieth century were participating in the longest and most continuous religious tradition in world history.

The trance dance was in many ways a distinctive tradition. It did not seek communion with the supernatural; no gifts or sacrifices were offered to the gods or the ancestors, and few prayers were made for their assistance. Viewing the gods as the source of disease, conflict, and death, the Ju/'hoansi hurled at them words of reproach, abuse, and rejection, seeking to ward them off, to expel them from society. It was, as one scholar put it, a "war with God."[24] The leaders of this war, the trance dancers, were not possessed by any supernatural being but used the trance state to activate their own internal *n/um*. Nor were they a priestly elite. Men and women alike could become healers, although a fearful and extended process of spiritual preparation awaited them. Almost half of the men and one-third of the women whom Lee encountered had entered the trance state. It was a much-sought-after role, but it conveyed no permanent power or authority. Finally, Ju/'hoansi religious thinking located the source of evil and misfortune outside of the community in the activity of the gods and ancestors rather than within society in the form of sorcerers or witches. The curing dances brought the community together, united against the external and supernatural enemy.

The Chumash of Southern California

If the San Ju/'hoansi people provide a window into the life of at least one nomadic and long-established gathering and hunting society, the Chumash are more representative of those later post–Ice Age Paleolithic peoples who settled in permanent villages and constructed more complex societies. Together the San and the Chumash illustrate the immense variation that was possible within the limits of a gathering and hunting way of life.

Located in southern California in the vicinity of present-day Santa Barbara, the Chumash occupied a richer and more varied environment than did the San. Speaking a series of related dialects, they lived along the coast, in the immediate interior, and on a series of offshore islands. Thus they were able to draw on the resources of the sea as well as those of the land to support a much more densely settled population of perhaps 20,000 people when they first encountered the Spanish in the sixteenth century.

Although the area had been sparsely occupied for about 10,000 years, the history of its people comes into sharper focus only in the centuries of the Common Era. The first millennium C.E. witnessed a growing population, the overhunting and depletion of deer herds in the interior, likely food shortages, and consequently increasing levels of violence and warfare among rival groups. Evidence for this violence is found in the large number of skeletons with bashed-in skulls or arrow and spear wounds. Then, in the several centuries after 1150 C.E., the Chumash, according to a noted scholar, "created an entirely new society."[25] Whereas the history of the San is marked by long-term continuities with a distant past, the Chumash experienced an extraordinary transformation.

A major element of that transformation lay in a remarkable technological innovation—the creation of a planked canoe, or *tomol*—an ocean-going vessel some twenty to thirty feet long and with a cargo capacity of two tons. Called "the most technically sophisticated watercraft developed in the New World," the tomol came into general use around 1000 C.E.[26] Building or owning one of these vessels brought immense prestige, wealth, and power, injecting a new element of inequality into Chumash society. The

■ **Comparison**

In what ways, and why, did Chumash culture differ from that of the San?

The Chumash of Southern California

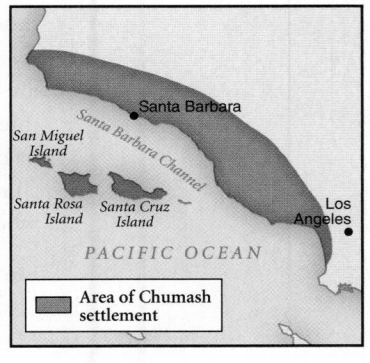

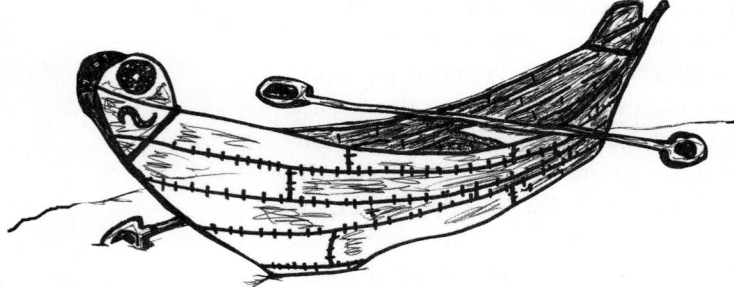

A Chumash Tomol
A technologically sophisticated seagoing canoe, the tomol, shown here in a contemporary drawing, was constructed from redwood or pine planks sewn together and caulked with hard tar and pine pitch. In recent decades, Chumash descendants have built several tomols and paddled them from the California mainland to the Channel Islands, re-creating a voyage that their distant ancestors had made many times. These reenactments were part of an effort to preserve for future generations the culture and traditions of the ancient Chumash. (Gaviota Coast Conservancy/Redrawn by © Elizabeth Leahy)

boatbuilders organized themselves into an elite craft guild, the Brotherhood of the Tomol, which monopolized canoe production and held the tools, knowledge, and sacred medicine associated with these boats. The tomol stimulated a blossoming of trade along the coast and between the coast and the islands as plant food, animal products, tools, and beads now moved regularly among Chumash communities. The boats also made possible deep-sea fishing, with swordfish, central to Chumash religious practice, being the most highly prized and prestigious catch.

In other ways as well, the material life of the Chumash was far more elaborate than that of the San. They lived in round, permanent, substantial houses, covered by grass or reeds, some of them fifty feet in diameter and able to hold up to seventy people. Every village had its own sweathouse, built partially underground and entered through an opening in the roof. Soapstone bowls, wooden plates, beautifully decorated reed baskets, and a variety of items made from bone or shell reflected a pattern of technological innovation far beyond that of the San.

A resource-rich environment, a growing and settled population, flourishing commerce, and technological innovation combined to produce something that scholars not long ago would have considered impossible—a market economy among a gathering and hunting people. Whereas the economic life of the San was regulated almost entirely by custom and tradition, that of the Chumash involved important elements of a market-based system: individuals acting out of a profit motive; the use of money, in the form of stringed beads; regulation of the supply of money to prevent inflation; specialized production of goods such as beads, stone tools, canoes, and baskets; prices attached to various items; payment for services provided by dancers, healers, and buriers; and private ownership of canoes, stores of food, and some tools. This is how an early Spanish observer described the Chumash in 1792:

> All these Indians are fond of traffic and commerce. They trade frequently with those of the mountains, bringing them fish and beadwork which they exchange for seeds and shawls of foxskin and a kind of blanket.... When they trade for profit, beads circulate among them as if they were money, being strung on long threads, according to the greater or smaller wealth of each one.... These strings of beads ... are used by the men to adorn their heads and for collars.... They all make a show of their wealth which they always wear in sight on their heads, whence it is taken for gambling and trafficking.[27]

How different is all this from the life of the Ju/'hoansi! Permanently settled villages, ranging in size from several hundred to a thousand people, would have struck the San as unsustainably large compared to their own mobile camps of twenty-five to fifty people. The specialized skills of the Chumash probably would have surprised the Ju/'hoansi, because all San people possessed pretty much the same set of skills. The San no doubt would have been appalled by the public display of wealth, the impulse toward private accumulation, and the inequalities of Chumash society. A bearskin cape, worn only by the elite of canoe owners and village chiefs, marked the beginnings of class distinctions, as did burials, which were far more elaborate for the wealthy and their children than for commoners. Members of the Brotherhood of the Tomol often were buried with parts of their canoes.

Perhaps most offensive to the egalitarian and independent Ju/'hoansi would have been the emergence of a permanent and hereditary political elite among the Chumash. High-ranking Chumash chiefs, who inherited their positions through the male line, exercised control over a number of communities, but each village also had its own chief, some of whom were women. These political leaders, all of whom were also canoe owners, led their people in war, presided over religious rituals, and regulated the flourishing trade that followed the invention of the tomol. They also named the dates for periodic feasts, during which donations and collections from the wealthy were used to feed the poor and to set aside something for a rainy day. This effort at redistributing wealth might have earned the approval of the Ju/'hoansi, who continually sought to level any social and economic distinctions among themselves.

Whatever the Ju/'hoansi might have thought, these transformations—technological, economic, social, and political—created a more unified and more peaceful life among the Chumash in the several centuries after 1150. Earlier patterns of violence apparently subsided as specialized crafts and enhanced trade evened out the distribution of food, making various Chumash communities dependent on one another. More formal political leadership enabled the peaceful resolution of disputes, which formerly had been resolved in battle. Frequent celebrations served to bring various Chumash villages together, while a society-wide organization of ritual experts provided yet another integrating mechanism. These transformations represent a remarkable achievement, especially because they introduced in a gathering and hunting society many social elements normally associated only with agricultural peoples. However, the coming of the Europeans, with their guns, diseases, and missionaries, largely destroyed Chumash society in the centuries following that epic encounter. The mobile San, in their remote location, were able to preserve their ways of life far longer than the more settled, and therefore vulnerable, Chumash, who were unable to avoid the powerful newcomers.

⊢⊣ Reflections: The Uses of the Paleolithic

Even when it is about a past as distant as the Paleolithic era, the study of history is also about those who tell it in the present. We search the past, always, for our own purposes. For a long time, modern people were inclined to view their Paleolithic ancestors as primitive or superstitious, unable to exercise control over nature, and ignorant of its workings. Such a view was, of course, a kind of self-congratulation, designed to highlight the "progress" of modern humankind. It was a way of saying, "Look how far we have come."

In more recent decades, growing numbers of people, disillusioned with modernity, have looked to the Paleolithic era for material with which to criticize, rather than celebrate, contemporary life. Feminists have found in gathering and hunting peoples a much more gender-equal society and religious thinking that featured the divine feminine, qualities that encouragingly suggested that patriarchy was neither inevitable nor eternal. Environmentalists have sometimes identified peoples in the distant past who were uniquely in tune with the natural environment rather than seeking to dominate it. Some nutritionists have advocated a "Paleolithic diet" of wild plants and animals as well suited to our physiology. Critics of modern materialism and competitive capitalism have been delighted to discover societies in which values of sharing and equality predominated over those of accumulation and hierarchy. Still others have asked, in light of the long Paleolithic era, whether the explosive population and economic growth of recent centuries should be considered normal or natural. Perhaps they should be regarded as extraordinary, possibly even pathological. Finally, research about the Paleolithic era has been extremely important in efforts by contemporary gathering and hunting peoples, or their descendants, to maintain or recover their older identities amid the conflicting currents of modern life. All of these uses of the Paleolithic have been a way of asking, "What have we lost in the mad rush to modernity, and how can we recover it?"

Both those who look with disdain on Paleolithic "backwardness" and those who praise, often quite romantically, its simplicity and equality seek to use these ancient people for their own purposes. In our efforts to puzzle out the past, all of us—historians and students of history very much included—stand somewhere. None of us can be entirely detached when we view the past, but this is not necessarily a matter for regret. What we may lose in objectivity, we gain in passionate involvement with the historical record and the many people who inhabit it. Despite its remoteness from us in time and manner of living, the Paleolithic era resonates still in the twenty-first century, reminding us of our kinship with these distant people and the significance of that kinship to finding our own way in a very different world.

Second Thoughts

What's the Significance?

Paleolithic rock art	Austronesian migrations	Paleolithic settling down
Venus figurines	"the original affluent	San culture
Dreamtime	society"	"insulting the meat"
Clovis culture	shamans	Chumash culture
megafaunal extinction	trance dance	Brotherhood of the Tomol

Big Picture Questions

1. What is the significance of the Paleolithic era in world history?
2. In what ways did various Paleolithic societies differ from one another, and how did they change over time?
3. Which statements in this chapter seem to be reliable and solidly based on facts, and which ones are more speculative and uncertain?
4. How might our attitudes toward the modern world influence our assessment of Paleolithic societies?

Next Steps: For Further Study

David Christian, *This Fleeting World: A Short History of Humanity* (2008). A lovely essay by a leading world historian, the first part of which provides a succinct survey of the Paleolithic era.

Brian M. Fagan, *People of the Earth: An Introduction to World Prehistory* (2006). A global account of early human history, written by a leading archeologist.

Clive Gamble, *Timewalkers: The Prehistory of Global Colonization* (2003). A beautifully written account of the initial human settlement of the earth.

Sally McBreatry and Alison S. Brooks, "The Revolution That Wasn't: A New Interpretation of the Origin of Modern Human Behavior," *Journal of Human Evolution* 39 (2000). A long scholarly article laying out the archeological evidence for the emergence of humankind in Africa.

Marjorie Shostak, *Nisa: The Life and Words of an !Kung Woman* (2000). A vivid first-person account of a San woman's life in a twentieth-century gathering and hunting society.

"Prehistoric Art," http://witcombe.sbc.edu/ARTHprehistoric.html#general. An art history Web site with a wealth of links to Paleolithic art around the world.

For Web sites and additional documents related to this chapter, see **Make History** at bedfordstmartins.com/strayer.

Documents

Considering the Evidence:
Glimpses of Paleolithic Life

For historians accustomed to working with documents written during the time period they are studying, the Paleolithic era has often been an exercise in frustration. No such documents exist for the long era of gathering and hunting societies, for writing did not develop until quite late in the history of humankind—around 3500 B.C.E., with the emergence of the first civilizations. Thus historians have been dependent on the slender archeological remains of Paleolithic people—their bones, tools, fossilized seeds, paintings, and sculptures—for understanding the lives of these most distant of our ancestors.

In the twentieth century, anthropologists and other scholars descended on the few remaining gathering and hunting peoples, studying their cultures and collecting their stories, myths, and oral traditions. Historians are often skeptical about the usefulness of such material for understanding the distant past of Paleolithic societies. After all, gatherers and hunters in the modern era have often mixed and mingled with agricultural societies, have come under European colonial rule, or have been in contact with elements of modern civilization. Thus their cultures may well have changed substantially from earlier patterns of Paleolithic life.

While recognizing that twentieth-century accounts may not precisely describe earlier gathering and hunting societies, we are nonetheless fortunate to have these more recent materials. Despite their limitations, they provide us at least a glimpse into ways of living and thinking that have almost completely vanished from the earth. The two documents that follow represent this kind of material.

Document 1.1

A Paleolithic Woman in the Twentieth Century

In 1971 the American anthropologist Marjorie Shostak was conducting research among the San people of the Kalahari Desert on the border of Botswana and South Africa (see map, p. 25). There she became acquainted with a fifty-year-old woman called Nisa. Although Nisa had interacted with neighboring cattle-keeping people and with Europeans, she had lived most of her life "in the

bush," fully participating in the gathering and hunting culture of her ancestors. Nisa proved willing to share with Shostak the intimate details of her life,
including her memories of childhood, her five marriages, the birth of her
children, her relationships with various lovers, and the deaths of loved ones.
Those interviews became the basis for the remarkable book from which the
following excerpts derive.

- What conflicts in San life does Nisa's account reveal?

- What does her story indicate about San attitudes toward sex and
  marriage? How might you compare those attitudes with those of
  contemporary society?

- How does Nisa understand God, or the divine?

- How does she understand the purpose of the curing rituals in which
  she took part?

- How would you describe Nisa's overall assessment of San life? Do you
  find it romanticized, realistic, or critical? What evidence from the passages
  supports your conclusions?

- How does this insider's account of San life support, contradict, or supplement the description of San culture found on pages 25–29?

NISA

The Life and Words of an !Kung Woman
1969–1976

We are people who live in the bush, and who belong in the bush. We are not village people. I have no goats. I have no cattle. I am a person who owns nothing. That's what people say I am: a poor person.... No donkey, either. I still carry things myself, in my kaross when I travel, and that's why I live in the bush....

Family Life

We lived and lived, and as I kept growing, I started to carry my little brother around on my shoulders.

Source: Marjorie Shostak, *Nisa: The Life and Words of an !Kung Woman* (Cambridge, Mass.: Harvard University Press, 1981), 41, 69, 87–89, 153–55, 166, 210–11, 226–27, 271, 299, 301–2, 316–17.

My heart was happy then; I had grown to love him and carried him everywhere. I'd play with him for a while and whenever he would start to cry, I'd take him to Mother so he could nurse. Then I'd take him back with me and we'd play together again.

That was when Kumsa was little. But once he was older and started to talk and then to run around, that's when we were mean to each other and hit and fought all the time. Because that's how children play. One child does mean things and the other children do mean things back. If your father goes out hunting one day, you think, "Won't Daddy bring home meat? Then I can eat it, but I can also *stinge* it!" When your father does come home with meat, you say, "My daddy brought back meat and I won't let you have *any* of it!" The other children say, "How come we play together yet you always treat us so badly?"

When Kumsa was bigger, we were like that all the time. Sometimes we'd hit each other. Other times, I'd grab him and bite him and said, "Oooo…what is this thing that has such a horrible face and no brains and is so mean? How come it is so mean to me when I'm not doing anything to it?" Then he'd say, "I'm going to *hit* you! What's protecting you that I shouldn't?" And I'd say, "You're just a baby! I, *I* am the one who's going to hit *you!* Why are you so miserable to me?" I'd insult him and he'd insult me and I'd insult him back. We'd just stay together and play like that.…

Life in the Bush

We lived in the bush and my father set traps and killed steenbok and duiker and gemsbok and we lived, eating the animals and foods of the bush. We collected food, ground it in a mortar, and ate it. We also ate sweet nin berries and tsin beans. When I was growing up, there were no cows or goats.… I had never seen other peoples and didn't know anything other than life in the bush. That's where we lived and where we grew up.

Whenever my father killed an animal and I saw him coming home with meat draped over a stick, balanced on one shoulder—that's what made me happy. I'd cry out, "Mommy! Daddy's coming and he's bringing *meat!*" My heart would be happy when I greeted him, "Ho, ho, Daddy! We're going to eat meat!"

Or honey. Sometimes he'd go out and come home with honey. I'd be sitting around with my mother and then see something coming from way out in the bush. I'd look hard. Then, "Oooh, Daddy found a beehive! Oh, I'm going to eat honey! Daddy's come back with honey for us to eat!" And I'd thank him and call him wonderful names.

Sometimes my mother would be the one to see the honey. The two of us would be walking around gathering food and she'd find a beehive deep inside a termite mound or in a tree. I remember one time when she found it. I jumped and ran all around and was so excited I couldn't stop moving. We went to the village to get some containers, then went back to the termite mound. I watched as she took the honey out. Then, we went home.…

When we were living in the bush, some people gave and others stinged. But there were always enough people around who shared, people who liked one another, who were happy living together, and who didn't fight. And even if one person did stinge, the other person would just get up and yell about it, whether it was meat or anything else, "What's doing this to you, making you not give us meat?"

When I was growing up, receiving food made my heart happy. There really wasn't anything, other than stingy people, that made me unhappy. I didn't like people who wouldn't give a little of what they had.…

It's the same today. Here I am, long since an adult, yet even now, if a person doesn't give something to me, I won't give anything to that person.…

Marriage

…The day of the wedding, everyone was there. All of Tashay's friends were sitting around, laughing and laughing. His younger brother said, "Tashay, you're too old. Get out of the way so I can marry her. Give her to me." And his nephew said, "Uncle, you're already old. Now, let *me* marry her." They were all sitting around, talking like that. They all wanted me.

I went to my mother's hut and sat there. I was wearing lots of beads and my hair was completely covered and full with ornaments.

That night there was another dance. We danced, and some people fell asleep and others kept dancing.…

The next day they started [to build the marriage hut]. There were lots of people there—Tashay's mother, my mother, and my aunt worked on the hut; everyone else sat around, talking. Late in the day, the young men went and brought Tashay to the finished hut. They set him down beside it and stayed there with him, sitting around the fire.…

They came and brought me back. Then they laid me down inside the hut. I cried and cried. People told me, "A man is not something that kills you; he is someone who marries you, who becomes like your father or your older brother. He kills animals and gives you things to eat. Even tomorrow, while you are crying, Tashay may kill an animal. But when he returns, he won't give you any meat; only he will eat. Beads, too. He will get beads but he won't give them to you. Why are you so afraid of your husband and what are you crying about?"

I listened and was quiet. Later, we went to sleep. Tashay lay down beside the opening of the hut, near the fire, and I lay down inside; he thought I might try and run away again. He covered himself with a blanket and slept....

We began to live together, but I ran away, again and again. A part of my heart kept thinking, "How come I'm a child and have taken another husband?"...

We lived and lived, the two of us, together, and after a while I started to really like him and then, to love him. I had finally grown up and had learned how to love. I thought, "A man has sex with you. Yes, that's what a man does. I had thought that perhaps he didn't."

We lived on and I loved him and he loved me. I loved him the way a young adult knows how to love; I just *loved* him. Whenever he went away and I stayed behind, I'd miss him. I'd think, "Oh, when is my husband ever coming home? How come he's been gone so long?" I'd miss him and want him. When he'd come back my heart would be happy, "Eh, hey! My husband left and once again has come back."

We lived and when he wanted me, I didn't refuse; he just lay with me....

I...gave myself to him, gave and gave. We lay with each other and my breasts were very large. I was becoming a woman.

Loss

It was while we were visiting in the Tswana village and just after Kxau was born that Tashay died....

I lay there and thought, "Why did this happen? The two of us gave so much to each other and lived together so happily. Now I am alone, without a husband. I am already a widow. Why did God

trick me and take my husband? God is stingy! He just takes them from you. God's heart is truly far from people."...

Then I was without my husband and my heart was miserable. Every night I missed him and every night I cried, "I am without the man I married." I thought, "Where will I see the food that will help my children grow? Who is going to help me raise this newborn? My older brother and my younger brother are far away. Who is going to help me now?" Because Kxau had only just been born; he was so small he almost didn't exist. Then I said, "Everyday food will do it. I will start today to gather the food that will bring them up," and I went out and brought back what I could....

In your heart, your child, your mother, and your father are all equal. When any one of them dies, your heart feels pain. When your child dies, you think, "How come this little thing I held beside me and watched all that she did, today has died and left me? She was the only child I had with me; there wasn't another I spent my days with. We two stayed together and talked together. This God...his ways are foul! Why did he give me a little one and then take her away?"...

The death of your parents, husband, or children—they are equal in the amount of pain you feel when you lose them. But when they all die and you have no family left, then you really feel pain. There is no one to take care of you; you are completely alone....

That's the way it is. God is the one who destroys. It isn't people who do it. It is God himself.

Lovers

...Besa [Nisa's fourth husband] and I did argue a lot, usually about sex. He was just like a young man, almost a child, who lies with his wife day after day after day....

Every night Besa wanted me and every night he would make love to me. That Besa, something was wrong with his brain!...

We argued like that all the time....That man, he wanted sex more than anything else! After a while, I realized I didn't like his ways. That's when I thought, "Perhaps I will leave him. Perhaps I'll find another man and see what he is like."

I didn't leave him, not for many years. But I did have lovers and so did he. Because, as I am Nisa, my lovers have been many. At that time, there was Tsaa and Nanau. One day Tsaa would make love to me, another day Nanau. They were jealous of each other, and once Tsaa even went to Besa and told him that Nanau and I were lovers. Besa said, "What can I do about it?"...

Because affairs—one married person making love to another not her husband—is something that even people from long ago knew. Even my father's father's father's father knew. There have also always been fights where poison arrows are shot and people are killed because of that. Having affairs is one of the things God gave us.

I have told you about my lovers, but I haven't finished telling you about all of them, because they are as many as my fingers and toes. Some have died and others are still alive.... When you are a woman, you don't just sit still and do nothing—you have lovers. You don't just sit with the man of your hut, with just one man. One man can give you very little. One man gives you only one kind of food to eat. But when you have lovers, one brings you something and another brings you something else. One comes at night with meat, another with money, another with beads. Your husband also does things and gives them to you.

But sitting with just one man? We don't do that. Does one man have enough thoughts for you?...

A Healing Ritual

...N/um—the power to heal—is a very good thing. This is a medicine very much like your medicine because it is strong. As your medicine helps people, our n/um helps people. But to heal with n/um means knowing how to trance. Because, it is in trance that the healing power sitting inside the healer's body—the n/um—starts to work. Both men and women learn how to cure with it, but not everyone wants to. Trance-medicine really hurts! As you begin to trance, the n/um slowly heats inside

you and pulls at you. It rises until it grabs your insides and takes your thoughts away. Your mind and your senses leave and you don't think clearly. Things become strange and start to change. You can't listen to people or understand what they say. You look at them and they suddenly become very tiny. You think, "What's happening? Is God doing this?" All that is inside you is the n/um; that is all you can feel.

You touch people, laying on hands, curing those you touch. When you finish, other people hold you and blow around your head and your face. Suddenly your senses go "Phah!" and come back to you. You think, "Eh hey, there are people here," and you see again as you usually do....

N/um is powerful, but it is also very tricky. Sometimes it helps and sometimes it doesn't, because God doesn't always want a sick person to get better....

I was a young woman when my mother and her younger sister started to teach me about drum-medicine. There is a root that helps you learn to trance, which they dug for me. My mother put it in my little leather pouch and said, "Now you will start learning this, because you are a young woman already." She had me keep it in my pouch for a few days. Then one day, she took it and pounded it along with some bulbs and some beans and cooked them together. It had a horrible taste and made my mouth feel foul. I threw some of it up. If she hadn't pounded it with the other foods, my stomach would have been much more upset and I would have thrown it all up; then it wouldn't have done anything for me. I drank it a number of times and threw up again and again. Finally I started to tremble. People rubbed my body as I sat there, feeling the effect getting stronger and stronger. My body shook harder and I started to cry. I cried while people touched me and helped me with what was happening to me.

Eventually, I learned how to break out of my self and trance. When the drum-medicine songs sounded, that's when I would start. Others would string beads and copper rings into my hair. As I began to trance, the women would say, "She's started to trance, now, so watch her carefully.

Don't let her fall." They would take care of me, touching me and helping. If another woman was also in a trance, she laid on hands and helped me.

They rubbed oil on my face and I stood there—a lovely young woman, trembling—until I was finished.

Document 1.2

Australian Aboriginal Mythology

The Aboriginal, or native, peoples of Australia have lived on their island/continent for probably 60,000 years. Until the arrival of Europeans in the late eighteenth century, they practiced a gathering and hunting way of life. That culture persisted into the twentieth century, and a small number of Aboriginal people practice it still. Over many centuries, an elaborate body of myths, legends, and stories evolved, reflecting Aboriginal understandings of the world. Known collectively as the Dreamtime, such stories served to anchor the landscape and its human and animal inhabitants to distant events and mythical ancestors. A contemporary Aboriginal artist, Semon Deeb, explains:

> Around the beginning the Ancestral Beings rose from the folds of the earth and stretching up to the scorching sun they called, "I am!" As each Ancestor sang out their name, "I am Snake," "I am Honey Ant," they created the most sacred of their songs. Slowly they began to move across the barren land naming all things and thus bringing them into being. Their words forming verses as the Ancestors walked about, they sang mountains, rivers and deserts into existence. Wherever they went, their songs remained, creating a web of Songlines over the Country. As they travelled the Ancestors hunted, ate, made love, sang and danced leaving a trail of Dreaming along the songlines. Finally at the end of their journey the Ancestral Beings sang "back into" the earth where they can be seen as land formations, sleeping.[28]

Transmitted orally and changing over time, numerous Dreamtime stories have been collected and set down in writing over the past two centuries. The tale presented here deals with the relationship of men and women, surely among the great themes of human reflection everywhere.

- What does this story suggest about the relationships between women and men? Does it support or undermine notions of gender equality among Paleolithic peoples? Is it consistent with the story associated with Visual Source 1.2 (see p. 45)?

- How are the familiar features of the known world—rivers, mountains, humans, animals, and male dominance—linked to ancient happenings in the Dreamtime?

- What aspects of a gathering and hunting way of life are reflected in this tale?

Stories from the Dreamtime
Twentieth Century

In the Dreamtime, in the land of the Murinbata people, a great river flowed from the hills through a wide plain to the sea. As it is today, the land then was rich with much fish and game. From the river rose at one place a series of high hills, where lived an old woman named Mutjinga, a woman of power. She it was who called the invisible spirits to her side with secret incantations that none other knew. She was a *kirman*, leader of the ceremonies in which the people sang and danced the exploits of the totemic beings so their spirits would be pleased and would bring food in its season and many children for the people. In those days, all the things in the world had both a physical form that could be touched, seen, and felt, and a spirit form, which was invisible. When living things died, their spirits went to a secret cave where they remained until it was time for them to be born again. Mutjinga was caretaker of this cave. Only she knew where it was. In the cave, she kept the sacred totems to which the spirits returned.

Mutjinga could speak with the spirits. Because she had this power, she could do many things which the men could not. She could send the spirits to frighten away game, to waylay people at night, or to cause a child to be born without life. The men feared the power of Mutjinga and did not consort with her. They called upon her to lead their dances and teach them songs, but none came to sit by her fire.

Mutjinga became lonely and sent for her young granddaughter to keep her company.

Mutjinga and the girl gathered bulbs and nuts and caught small game, but Mutjinga found no satisfaction in this food, for she craved the flesh of men....

[The story then recounts how Mutjinga dug a hole and covered it with branches in order to trap unsuspecting hunters. Magically turning herself into a goanna (a lizard), she

Source: Louis A. Allen, *Time Before Morning* (New York: Thomas Y. Crowell, 1975), 145–48.

appeared to hunters, led them to their deaths in the hole, and then ate them. This fate befell even the younger brother of her granddaughter, despite the girl's unsuccessful efforts to save him. He too was killed and partially eaten, while Mutjinga kept the rest of his body in a nearby stream.]

The next morning, the little girl was at her early chores when she saw two men coming up the hillside. As she watched, recognition lit her face and she turned toward Mutjinga.

"It is my father and brother who come. Please do not harm them," she implored.

"I crave their flesh. If you trick me again I shall eat you, as well as your father and brother," Mutjinga warned. "This time I shall wait beside you until the men appear so you cannot deceive me."

The men approached the fire, paid their respects to the old woman, and greeted the child warmly. "Daughter, have you seen your brother who came hunting this way yesterday?" the father asked.

Mutjinga hastened to reply for the child. "No, we have not seen him," she said. "It is too bad, for nearby are many goanna holes. There is a large goanna right there," and she pointed to the hole where she kept the club.

"I thirst. First give me water," said the father.

"There is cold water in the stream," the little girl told him as she pointed down the hill.

The two men walked through the bush to the stream. As the father bent to drink, he saw the leg of his elder son, which Mutjinga had weighted down in the water with a large rock. At once he understood.

"The old woman will kill us unless we kill her first," he said to his younger son, and the two men returned to the fire.

"The goanna went into the tall grass," Mutjinga told them when they appeared. "Leave your spears and light a fire to burn the grass. This will drive the goanna out, and when it runs toward its hole, you can kill it with your spears."

The men went to fire the grass. As soon as they were out of sight, the father said, "Son, climb this tree and watch the old woman closely. She works powerful magic."

This the son did, and he saw Mutjinga speak the magic words. She repeated them twice. He watched as the woman and the girl changed into goannas. From the limb of the tree, he observed the larger goanna chase the smaller one into the bush. Soon great billows of smoke were rising from the burning grass. The small goanna scuttled from the bush, its companion nipping at its heels. They ran past the hunters and disappeared down the hole.

"Get the spears," the father commanded and ran toward the hole. Just as the son returned, spears in hand, the ground beneath the father gave way and he plunged through. Waiting at the bottom was Mutjinga, club raised for the kill. But the son hurled his spear and Mutjinga fell bleeding to the ground.

The father seized her roughly. "Say the magic words that will release my daughter or we shall kill you," he threatened.

Painfully Mutjinga did as she was bidden. The daughter changed into her human form and the two men and the girl climbed from the hole.

"Daughter, show us the secret cave where the spirits are hidden," said the father, "and teach us the magic words you have learned from the old woman. We shall take the spirits to another place, and we shall have the power."

And so it was. The father took the totems from that place and hid them in another cave. He became the *kirman*, the song leader, and he taught the people the sacred dances and ceremonies. To him they brought their problems and he judged between them when they quarreled. And to this day, the men have kept the power.

Using the Evidence:
Glimpses of Paleolithic Life

1. **Considering human commonality and diversity:** The study of world history highlights both the common humanity of people from all times and places as well as the vast differences that have separated particular cultures from one another. How might these texts, as well as the paintings in the Visual Sources section (pp. 42–47), serve to illustrate both of these perspectives?

2. **Linking documents and text narrative:** How do these documents and images support or amplify particular statements made about Paleolithic life in this chapter? How might they challenge or contradict that narrative?

3. **Considering the relationship of technology and culture:** How might the gathering and hunting technology of the South African and Australian peoples discussed in this chapter have shaped their cultural understandings as expressed in these documents and images? In what ways might cultural expression, as a product of human imagination, have developed independently of their technology? Does it make sense to evaluate technology as more or less "advanced"? Should culture be assessed in the same way?

Visual Sources

Considering the Evidence:
The Aboriginal Rock Painting of Australia

The rock paintings of the Aboriginal peoples of Australia represent what may be the longest continuously practiced artistic tradition in world history. Scholars have found evidence of these paintings dating to some 40,000 years ago, and the tradition has continued into the twentieth century and beyond as contemporary artists retouched and repainted ancient images and created new ones. A contemporary Aboriginal artist explained what those paintings meant to him:

> When I look at my [dreaming] paintings it makes me feel good—happy in heart, spirit. Everything is there: all there in the caves, not lost. This is my secret side. This is my home—inside me....Our dreaming, secret side—we must hold on to this, like our fathers, looking after it....We give to our sons when we die. The sons keep this from their fathers, grandfathers. The sons will remember, they can carry on, not be lost. And it is still there—fathers' country with rock hole, painted cave....The people keep their ceremony things and pictures—they make them new. They bring young boys for learning to the caves, telling the stories, giving the laws from grandfathers' fathers, learning to do the paintings—[the dreaming] way.[29]

For native peoples of Australia, whose way of life has been so thoroughly disrupted by more than two centuries of European invasion and domination, this continuing artistic tradition provides a link to the past.

Created in caves and protected rock shelters all over this giant island/continent, these paintings were the products of the many distinct peoples of Paleolithic Australia. While they shared a common gathering and hunting way of life, each had its own language, stories, and ceremonies, which found expression in their paintings. Many of them depicted spirit figures or ancestors from the Dreamtime. Such images were often regarded, not as works of art by human artists, but as the actual ancestral beings themselves, able to convey their spiritual energy to their descendants. In this respect, they served something of the same purpose as the much later icons or religious paintings in the Christian world, said to convey the very presence of the divine. (See Visual Sources: Reading Byzantine Icons, pp. 466–71.)

Beyond religious or ceremonial purposes, Aboriginal rock painting also depicted various animals, some of them now extinct; stenciled images of human hands; and abstract designs, believed by scholars to represent coded symbols understood only by those who underwent proper ceremonial initiation. Other paintings portrayed scenes from daily life and were particularly focused on hunting. Still others recorded historical events such as the visits of fishermen from what is now Indonesia to the northern coasts of Australia. Images of European sailing ships, rifles, tools, and animals also found a place in the more recent expressions of Aboriginal rock painting.

The three images shown in this section are from the Kakudu National Park in Australia's Northern Territory, an area inhabited by humans for some 20,000 years. Some of the fading images in the park were repainted in the 1960s by Nayambolmi, one of the last of the traditional rock-art painters. As you examine these images, keep in mind that even the experts do not really know what they meant to the people who created them thousands of years ago. Our task is to appreciate, to imagine, and to speculate about these remarkable paintings rather than to decipher them with any precision.

In Visual Source 1.1, the largest and main figure at the top is Namondjok, a Creation Ancestor, who according to some accounts can be seen in the sky at night as a dark spot in the Milky Way galaxy. Other stories recount that Namondjok violated incest laws by sleeping with a woman from his clan who would have been considered his sister. To the right is Namarrgon, or Lightning Man, who generates the tremendous lightning storms that occur during the rainy season. The arc around his body represents the lightning, while the axes on his head, elbow, and feet are used to split the dark clouds, creating thunder and lightning. The female figure beneath Namondjok is Barrginj, the wife of Lightning Man, while the people below her, elaborately dressed, are perhaps on their way to a ceremony.

■ What could an Aboriginal viewer learn about nature from this painting?

■ What might he or she understand about the cosmic hierarchy?

■ Why do you think the artist positioned people at the bottom of the picture? Might the positioning of Barrginj have meaning as well?

■ How might you interpret the relative size of the various images in the painting?

Visual Source 1.1 Namondjok, Namarrgon (Lightning Man), and Barrginj (J. Marshall/Visual Connection Archive)

Visual Source 1.2 depicts Nabulwinjbulwinj, said to be a wicked and dangerous male spirit who kills females by hitting them with a yam and then eating them.

■ What message might such a story seek to convey?

■ Does this story seem consistent with Document 1.2, which seeks to explain why men have power over women?

Visual Sources 1.1 and 1.2 both reflect a distinctive style of Aboriginal painting known as the X-ray tradition, in which the internal bones and organs of human or animal figures are depicted while also showing their outward appearance.

■ What internal structures can you distinguish in these images?

■ What purposes or intentions might lay behind such a style?

Visual Source 1.2 Nabulwinjbulwinj (J. Marshall/Visual Connection Archive)

Visual Source 1.3 A Hunting Scene (Oz Outback Internet Services, Queensland, Australia)

Visual Source 1.3 depicts a hunting scene, featuring either people or the thin Mimi spirits, said to inhabit the nooks and crannies of the area's rock formations. Notice the spears that the hunters carry. Various kinds of spears and spear-throwing devices had earlier replaced or supplemented the boomerang, while bows and arrows were unknown to the hunters of Australia before contact with Europeans.

- If the painting depicts real people or actual hunters, what purposes might it serve?

- What different understandings might emerge if the painting is seen as portraying Mimi spirits?

- How might a contemporary Aboriginal artist, such as the one quoted on page 42, understand this painting?

Using the Evidence:
The Aboriginal Rock Painting of Australia

1. **Comparing rock art traditions:** How do these Paleolithic-era paintings compare with those from South Africa and southern France shown on pages 00 and 00?

2. **Considering art and religion:** How do these images reflect the religious understandings of the Dreamtime (see Document 1.2, pp. 39–41)?

3. **Seeking further evidence:** What additional information might help you to understand these images more fully?

4. **Connecting past and present:** In what ways do these paintings retain their ability to speak to people living in industrial societies of the twenty-first century? Or do they have meaning only for those who made them?

CHAPTER TWO

First Farmers

The Revolutions of Agriculture

10,000 B.C.E.—3000 B.C.E.

The Agricultural Revolution in
  World History
Comparing Agricultural Beginnings
  Common Patterns
  Variations
The Globalization of Agriculture
  Triumph and Resistance
  The Culture of Agriculture
Social Variation in the Age
  of Agriculture
  Pastoral Societies
  Agricultural Village Societies
  Chiefdoms
Reflections: The Legacies
  of Agriculture
Considering the Evidence
  Documents: Agricultural Village
    Societies
  Visual Sources: Art and Life in the
    Early Agrarian Era

"After me, I suppose there will be nothing here," remarked seventy-two-year-old Elsie Eiler in 2005. At the time, she was the sole remaining resident of the farm town of Monowi, Nebraska. "There is just no employment for people. Farming is hard and all the small farms have had to merge into bigger ones, and the young people just want to go away to college and a city. Few of them come back." Founded in 1902 by Czech immigrants, Monowi in the early twentieth century boasted a post office, two banks, a high school, a church, and rows of well-built homes. By the early twenty-first century, the church was boarded up, many houses had collapsed, deer and wild elk roamed the town's empty spaces, and flocks of birds nested in thick weeds along what had once been Main Street. With the death of her husband in 2004, Mrs. Eiler became the only living soul in Monowi, where she served as the town's mayor and ran its only business, a tavern whose customers came from passing traffic and nearby settlements.[1]

MRS. EILER'S STORY AND THAT OF HER TOWN were part of a much larger global process taking place over the past several centuries of the industrial age—a dramatic decline in the number of people directly earning their living as farmers. The United States represents an extreme case of this worldwide phenomenon: at the beginning of the twenty-first century, only about 5 percent of Americans lived on farms, and many of them were over the age of sixty-five. Despite the

---

The Statues of Ain Ghazal: Among the largest of the early agricultural settlements investigated by archeologists is that of Ain Ghazal, located in the modern state of Jordan. Inhabited from about 7200 to 5000 B.C.E., in its prime it was home to some 3,000 people, who lived in multiroomed stone houses; cultivated barley, wheat, peas, and lentils; and herded domesticated goats. These remarkable statues, around three feet tall and made of limestone plaster applied to a core of bundled reeds, were among the most startling finds at that site. Did they represent heroes, gods, goddesses, or ordinary people? No one really knows. (Courtesy, Department of Antiquities of Jordan [DoA]. Photo: Freer Gallery of Art and Arthur M. Sackler Gallery, Washington, DC)

small number of American farmers, modern agriculture was so productive that those few people were able to feed the entire country and to export a large amount of food as well. This modern retreat from the farm marked a dramatic reversal of a much more ancient pattern in which growing numbers of people began to farm and agriculture became for the first time the primary occupation for the vast majority of humankind. The beginnings of that epic process represent the central theme of this chapter.

The Agricultural Revolution in World History

The chief feature of the long Paleolithic era—and the first human process to operate on a global scale—was the initial settlement of the earth. Then, beginning around 12,000 years ago, a second global pattern began to unfold—agriculture. The term "Neolithic" (New Stone Age) or "Agricultural Revolution" refers to the deliberate cultivation of particular plants as well as the taming and breeding of particular animals. Thus a whole new way of life gradually replaced the earlier practices of gathering and hunting in most parts of the world. Although it took place over centuries and millennia, the coming of agriculture represented a genuinely revolutionary transformation of human life all across the planet and provided the foundation for almost everything that followed: growing populations, settled villages, animal-borne diseases, horse-drawn chariot warfare, cities, states, empires, civilizations, writing, literature, and much more.

Among the most revolutionary aspects of the age of agriculture was a new relationship between humankind and other living things, for now men and women were not simply using what they found in nature but were actively changing nature as well. They were consciously "directing" the process of evolution. The actions of farmers in the Americas, for example, transformed corn from a plant with a cob of an inch or so to one measuring about six inches by 1500. Later efforts more than doubled that length. Farmers everywhere stamped the landscape with a human imprint in the form of fields with boundaries, terraced hillsides, irrigation ditches, and canals. Animals too were transformed as selective breeding produced sheep that grew more wool, cows that gave more milk, and chickens that laid more eggs than their wild counterparts.

This was "domestication"—the taming, and the changing, of nature for the benefit of humankind—but it created a new kind of mutual dependence. Many domesticated plants and animals could no longer survive in the wild and relied on human action or protection in order to reproduce successfully. Similarly, human beings in the agricultural era lost the skills of their gathering and hunting ancestors, and in any event there were now too many people to live in that older fashion. As a consequence, farmers and herders became dependent on their domesticated plants and animals. From an outside point of view, it might well seem that corn and cows had tamed human beings, using people to ensure their own survival and growth as a species, as much as the other way around.

A further revolutionary aspect of the agricultural age is summed up in the term "intensification." It means getting more for less, in this case more food and resources—far more—from a much smaller area of land than was possible with a gathering and hunting technology. More food meant more people. Growing populations in turn required an even greater need for the intensive exploitation of the environment. And so was launched the continuing human effort to "subdue the earth" and to "have dominion over it," as the biblical story in Genesis recorded God's command to Adam and Eve.

Comparing Agricultural Beginnings

Perhaps the most extraordinary feature of the Neolithic or Agricultural Revolution was that it occurred, separately and independently, in many widely scattered parts of the world: the Fertile Crescent of Southwest Asia, several places in sub-Saharan Africa, China, New Guinea, Mesoamerica, the Andes, and eastern North America (see the Snapshot on p. 52). Even more remarkably, all of this took place at roughly the same time (at least as measured by the 250,000-year span of human history on the planet)—between 12,000 and 4,000 years ago. These facts have generated many questions with which historians and other scholars have long struggled. Why was the Agricultural Revolution so late in the history of humankind? What was unique about the period after 10,000 B.C.E. that may have triggered or facilitated this vast upheaval? In what different ways did the Agricultural Revolution take shape in its various locations? How did it spread from its several points of origin to the rest of the earth? And what impact did it have on the making of human societies?

Common Patterns

It is no accident that the Agricultural Revolution coincided with the end of the last Ice Age, a process of global warming that began some 16,000 years ago. By about 11,000 years ago, the Ice Age was over, and climatic conditions similar to those of our own time generally prevailed. This was but the latest of some twenty-five periods of glaciation and warming that have occurred over the past several million years of the earth's history and which are caused by minor periodic changes in the earth's orbit around the sun. The end of the last Ice Age, however, coincided with the migration of *Homo sapiens* across the planet and created new conditions that made agriculture possible. Combined with active hunting by human societies, climate change in some areas helped to push into extinction various species of large mammals on which Paleolithic people had depended, thus adding to the pressure to find new food sources. The warmer, wetter, and more stable conditions, particularly in the tropical and temperate regions of the earth, also permitted the flourishing of more wild plants, especially cereal grasses, which were the ancestors of many domesticated crops. What climate change took away with one hand, it apparently gave back with the other.

■ **Change**
What accounts for the emergence of agriculture after countless millennia of human life without it?

Snapshot   **Agricultural Breakthroughs**[2]

Location	Dates (B.C.E.)	Plants	Animals
Southwest Asia (Fertile Crescent)	9000–7000	barley, wheat, lentils, figs	goats, sheep, cattle, pigs
China	6500–5000	rice, millet, soybeans	pigs, chickens, water buffalo
Saharan and sub-Saharan Africa	3000–2000	sorghum, millet, yams, teff	cattle (perhaps 8000 B.C.E.)
Highland New Guinea	7000–4000	taro, bananas, yams, sugarcane	—
Andes region	3000–2000	potatoes, quinoa, manioc	llamas, alpaca, guinea pig
Mesoamerica	3000–2000	maize, squash (perhaps 7000 B.C.E.), beans	turkey
Eastern woodlands of North America	2000–1000	sunflower, goosefoot, sumpweed	—

Over their long history, gathering and hunting peoples had already developed a deep knowledge of the natural world and in some cases an ability to manage it actively. They had learned to make use of a large number of plants and to hunt and eat both small and large animals, creating what archeologists call a "broad spectrum diet." In the Middle East, people had developed sickles for cutting newly available wild grain, baskets to carry it, mortars and pestles to remove the husk, and storage pits to preserve it. Peoples of the Amazon and elsewhere had learned to cut back some plants to encourage the growth of their favorites. Native Australians had built elaborate traps in which they could capture, store, and harvest large numbers of eels.

In hindsight, much of this looks like a kind of preparation for agriculture. Because women in particular had long been intimately associated with collecting wild plants, most scholars believe that they were the likely innovators who led the way to deliberate farming, with men perhaps taking the lead in domesticating animals. Clearly the knowledge and technology necessary for agriculture were part of a longer process involving more intense human exploitation of the earth. Nowhere was agriculture an overnight invention.

Using such technologies, and benefiting from the global warming at the end of the last Ice Age, gathering and hunting peoples in various places were able to settle down and establish more permanent villages, abandoning their nomadic ways and more intensively exploiting the local area. This was particularly the case in resource-rich areas close to seas, lakes, marshes, and rivers. In settling down, however, they soon lost some of the skills of their ancestors and found themselves now required to support growing populations. Evidence for increasing human numbers around the world during this period of global warming has persuaded some scholars that agriculture was a response to an impending "food crisis."[3] If the number of people outstripped the local resources, or if sudden fluctuations in climate—prolonged drought or a cold snap, for example—diminished those resources, these newly settled communities were in trouble. It was no longer so easy to simply move away. These vagaries surely motivated people to experiment and to innovate in an effort to increase the food supply. Clearly, many of the breakthroughs to agriculture occurred only *after* gathering and hunting peoples had already grown substantially in numbers and had established a sedentary way of life.

These were some of the common patterns that facilitated the Agricultural Revolution. New opportunities appeared with the improved conditions that came at the end of the Ice Age. New knowledge and technology emerged as human communities explored and exploited that changed environment. The disappearance of many large mammals, growing populations, newly settled ways of life, and fluctuations in the process of global warming—all of these represented pressures or incentives to increase food production and thus to minimize the risks of life in a new era.[4] From some combination of these opportunities and incentives emerged the profoundly transforming process of the Agricultural Revolution.

This new way of life initially operated everywhere with a simple technology—the digging stick or hoe (the plow was developed only later). But the several transitions to this hoe-based agriculture, commonly known as horticulture, varied considerably, depending on what plants and animals were available locally. For example, potatoes were found in the Andes region, but not in Africa or Asia; wheat and wild pigs existed in the Fertile Crescent, but not in the Americas. Furthermore, of the world's 200,000 plant species, only several hundred have been domesticated, and just five of these—wheat, corn, rice, barley, and sorghum—supply more than half of the calories that sustain human life. Only fourteen species of large mammals have been successfully domesticated, of which sheep, pigs, goats, cattle, and horses have been the most important. Because they are stubborn, nervous, solitary, or finicky, many animals simply cannot be readily domesticated.[5] In short, the kind of Agricultural Revolution that unfolded in particular places depended very much on what happened to be available locally, and that in turn depended on sheer luck.

Variations

Among the most favored areas—and the first to experience a full Agricultural Revolution—was the Fertile Crescent, an area sometimes known as Southwest Asia, consisting of present-day Iraq, Syria, Israel/Palestine, and southern Turkey (see Map 2.1). In this region, an extraordinary variety of wild plants and animals capable of domestication provided a rich array of species on which the now largely settled gathering and hunting people could draw. What triggered the transition to agriculture, it seems, was a cold and dry spell between 11,000 and 9500 B.C.E., a temporary

■ **Comparison**
In what different ways did the Agricultural Revolution take shape in various parts of the world?

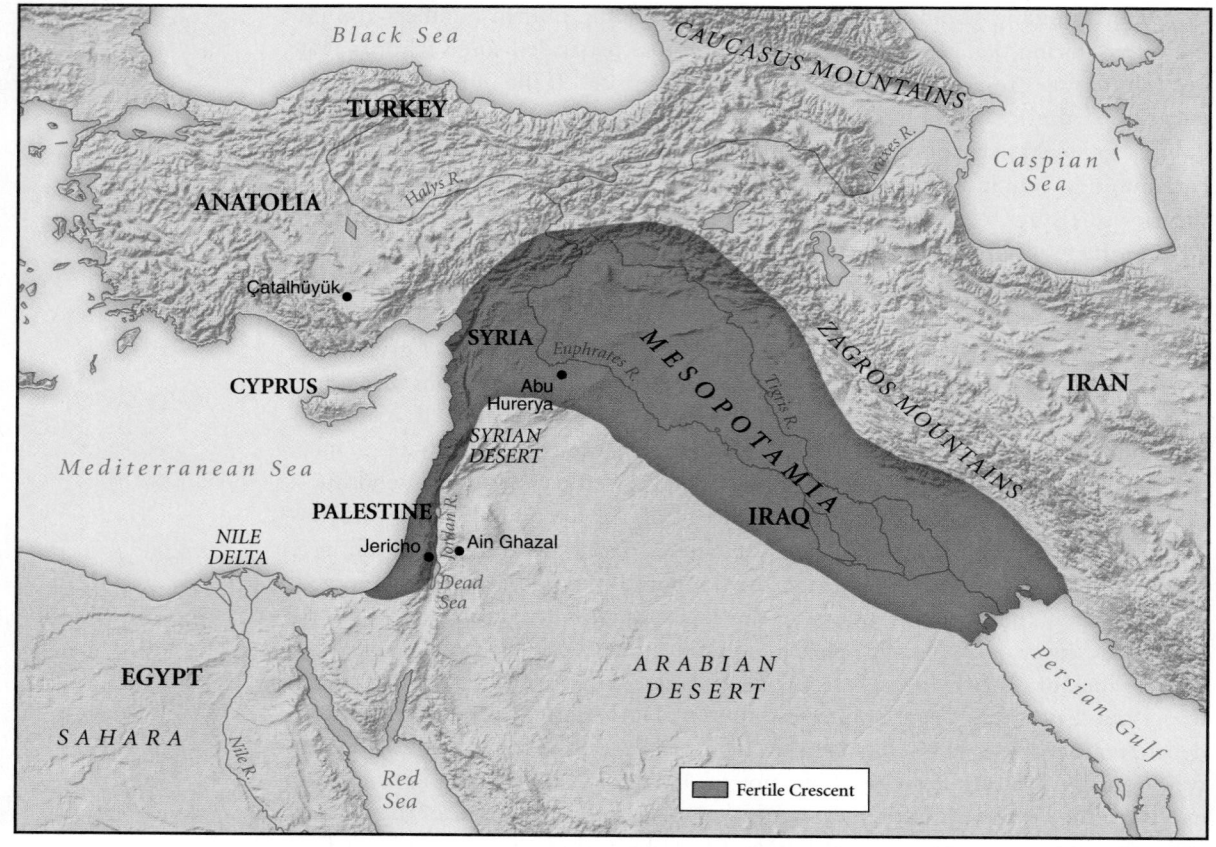

Map 2.1   The Fertile Crescent
Located in what is now called the Middle East, the Fertile Crescent was the site of many significant processes in early world history, including the first breakthrough to agriculture and later the development of some of the First Civilizations.

interruption in the general process of global warming. Larger settled populations were now threatened with the loss of the wild plants and animals on which they had come to depend. Their solution was domestication. In the millennium or so after 9000 B.C.E., figs, wheat, barley, rye, peas, lentils, sheep, goats, pigs, and cattle all came under human control, providing the foundation for the world's first, and most productive, agricultural societies.

Archeological evidence suggests that the transition to a fully agricultural way of life in this region sometimes took place quite quickly, within as few as 500 years. Signs of that transformation included large increases in the size of settlements, which now housed as many as several thousand people. In these agricultural settings, archeologists have found major innovations: the use of sun-dried mud bricks; the appearance of monuments or shrinelike buildings; displays of cattle skulls; more elaborate human burials, including the removal of the skull; and more sophisticated tools, such as sickles, polished axes, and awls.[6] Environmental deterioration in ecologically fragile regions was yet another indication of this new way of life. Numerous settlements in the Jordan River valley and Palestine were abandoned as growing populations of people and goats stripped the area of trees and ground cover, leading to soil erosion and food shortages, which required their human inhabitants to scatter.[7] (See the chapter opening photograph, p. 48, for sculptures from the early agricultural settlement of Ain Ghazal in the Middle East.)

At roughly the same time, perhaps a bit later, another process of domestication was unfolding on the African continent in a most unlikely place—the eastern part of what is now the Sahara in present-day Sudan. Between 10,000 and 5,000 years ago, however, "the Saharan desert . . . effectively did not exist," according to scholars, as the region received more rainfall than currently, had extensive grassland vegetation, and was "relatively hospitable to human life."[8] It seems likely that cattle were domesticated in this region about 1,000 years before they were separately brought under human control in the Middle East and India. At about the same time, the donkey also was domesticated in northeastern Africa near the Red Sea and spread from there into Southwest Asia, even as the practice of raising sheep and goats moved in the other direction. In Africa, animal domestication thus preceded the domestication of plants, while elsewhere in the world it was the other way around.

In terms of farming, the African pattern again was somewhat different. Unlike the Fertile Crescent, where a number of plants were domesticated in a small area, sub-Saharan Africa witnessed the emergence of several widely scattered farming practices. Sorghum, which grows well in arid conditions, was the first grain to be "tamed" in the eastern Sahara region. In the highlands of Ethiopia, teff, a tiny, highly nutritious grain, as well as enset, a relative of the banana, came under cultivation. In the forested region of West Africa, yams, oil palm trees, okra, and the kola nut (still used as a flavoring for Coca-Cola and Pepsi) emerged as important crops. The scattered location of these domestications generated a less productive agriculture than in the more favored and compact Fertile Crescent, but a number of the African domesticates—sorghum, castor beans, gourds, millet, the donkey—subsequently spread to enrich the agricultural practices of Eurasian peoples.

Yet another pattern of agricultural development took shape in the Americas. Like the Agricultural Revolution in Africa, the domestication of plants in the Americas occurred separately in a number of locations—in the coastal Andean regions of western South America, in Mesoamerica, in the Mississippi valley, and perhaps in the Amazon basin—but surely its most distinctive feature lay in the absence of animals that could be domesticated. Of the fourteen major species of large mammals that have been brought under human control, only one, the llama/alpaca, existed in the Western Hemisphere. Without goats, sheep, pigs, cattle, or horses, the peoples of the Americas lacked the sources of protein, manure (for fertilizer), and power (to draw plows or pull carts, for example) that were widely available to societies in the Afro-Eurasian world. Because they could not depend on domesticated animals for meat, agricultural peoples in the Americas relied more on hunting and fishing than did peoples in the Eastern Hemisphere.

Furthermore, the Americas lacked the rich cereal grains that were widely available in Afro-Eurasia. Instead they had maize or corn, first domesticated in southern Mexico by 4000 to 3000 B.C.E. Unlike the cereal grains of the Fertile Crescent, which closely resemble their wild predecessors, the ancestor of corn, a mountain grass

Teosinte   Modern Corn

Teosinte and Maize/Corn
The sharp difference in size between the tiny cobs of teosinte, a wild grass, and usable forms of domesticated maize meant that the Agricultural Revolution took place more slowly in Mesoamerica than it had in Mesopotamia. (Nicolle Rager Fuller, National Science Foundation)

called *teosinte*, looks nothing like what we now know as corn or maize. Thousands of years of selective adaptation were required to develop a sufficiently large cob and number of kernels to sustain a productive agriculture, an achievement that one geneticist has called "arguably man's first, and perhaps his greatest, feat of genetic engineering."[9] Even then, corn was nutritionally poorer than the protein-rich cereals of the Fertile Crescent. To provide sufficient dietary protein, corn had to be supplemented with squash and beans, which were also domesticated in the Americas.

Thus while Middle Eastern societies quite rapidly replaced their gathering and hunting economy with agriculture, that process took 3,500 years in Mesoamerica.

Another difference in the progress of the Agricultural Revolution lay in the north/south orientation of the Americas, which required agricultural practices to move through, and adapt to, quite distinct climatic and vegetation zones if they were to spread. The east/west axis of Eurasia meant that agricultural innovations could spread more rapidly because they were entering roughly similar environments. Thus corn, beans, and squash, which were first domesticated in Mesoamerica, took several thousand years to travel the few hundred miles from their Mexican homeland to the southwestern United States and another thousand years or more to arrive in eastern North America. The llama, guinea pig, and potato, which were domesticated in the Andean highlands, never reached Mesoamerica.[10]

The Globalization of Agriculture

■ **Connection**
In what ways did agriculture spread? Where and why was it sometimes resisted?

From the various places where it originated, agriculture spread to much of the rest of the earth, although for a long time it coexisted with gathering and hunting ways of life (see Map 2.2). Broadly speaking, this extension of farming occurred in two ways. The first is called diffusion, which refers to the gradual spread of agricultural techniques, and perhaps of the plants and animals themselves, but without the extensive movement of agricultural people. Neighboring groups exchanged ideas and products in a down-the-line pattern of communication. A second process involved the slow colonization or migration of agricultural peoples as growing populations pushed them outward. Often this meant the conquest, absorption, or displacement of the earlier gatherers and hunters, along with the spread of the languages and cultures of the migrating farmers. In many places, both processes took place.[11] The spread of corn-based agriculture in the Americas, highlighted in the Snapshot on page 57, illustrates the process.

Snapshot   The History of Maize/Corn[12]

The earliest domestication of teosinte—a grass from which modern maize/corn subsequently developed in a process of adaptation and "genetic engineering" over thousands of years—occurs in southern Mexico. It may have been used for the sugary syrup found in its stalk as well as the nutritional value of its kernels.	9000–8000 B.C.E.
Maize cultivation spreads to South America (Ecuador, Peru).	2300–1000 B.C.E.
Maize cob reaches length of about six centimeters. There is evidence that corn was ground with stone mortars and baked in flat bread.	by 2000 B.C.E.
Maize becomes the staple of Mesoamerican agriculture. Its cultural importance was reflected in its prominence in various myths of origin. Such stories among the Maya, for example, held that humankind was made first of mud, then of wood, and finally, and most successfully, from maize dough.	1500 B.C.E.
Maize spreads to the southwestern United States as farming people migrate.	1000 B.C.E.
In Peru, the average size of a maize cob doubles. Maize is used for making maize beer.	500 B.C.E.–1 C.E.
Maize cultivation reaches the eastern woodlands of the Mississippi River valley, largely through diffusion, although people of this region had already domesticated several minor crops, such as sunflowers.	500 C.E.
Maize farming is introduced in New England and is widespread by 1300, about 300 years before the arrival of the Pilgrims.	1000 C.E.
Maize spreads to Europe, Africa, and Asia, following European conquest of the Americas.	16th–18th centuries C.E.

Triumph and Resistance

Some combination of diffusion and migration took the original agricultural package of Southwest Asia and spread it widely into Europe, Central Asia, Egypt, and North Africa between 6500 and 4000 B.C.E. Languages originating in the core region accompanied this movement of people and farming practices. Thus Indo-European languages, which originated probably in Turkey and are widely spoken even today from India to Europe, reflect this movement of culture associated with the spread of agriculture. In a similar process, the Chinese farming system moved into Southeast Asia and elsewhere, and with it a number of related language families developed. India received agricultural influences from the Middle East, Africa, and China alike.

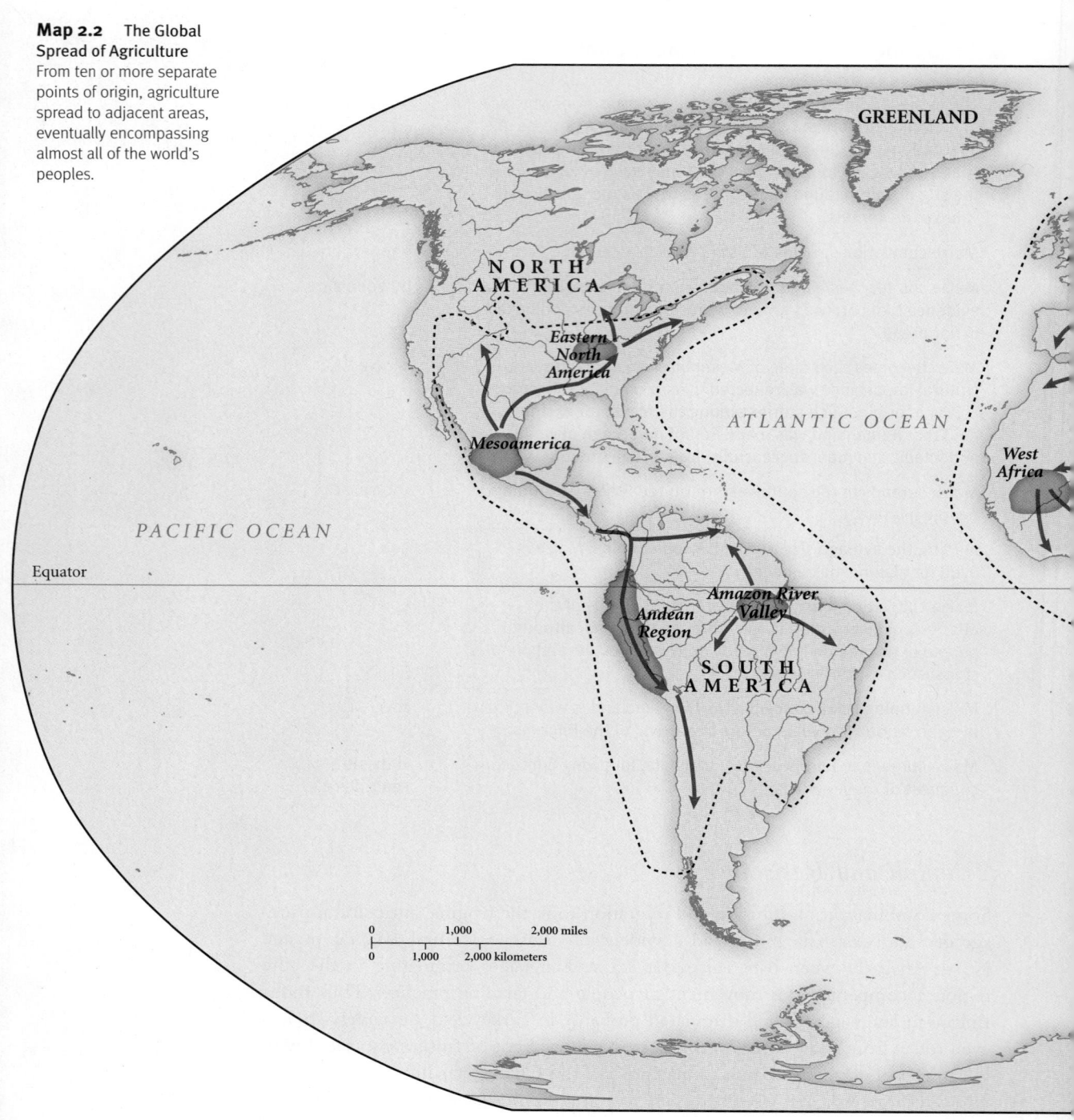

Map 2.2 The Global Spread of Agriculture From ten or more separate points of origin, agriculture spread to adjacent areas, eventually encompassing almost all of the world's peoples.

GREENLAND

NORTH AMERICA

Eastern North America

ATLANTIC OCEAN

West Africa

Mesoamerica

PACIFIC OCEAN

Equator

Amazon River Valley

Andean Region

SOUTH AMERICA

0   1,000   2,000 miles
0 1,000 2,000 kilometers

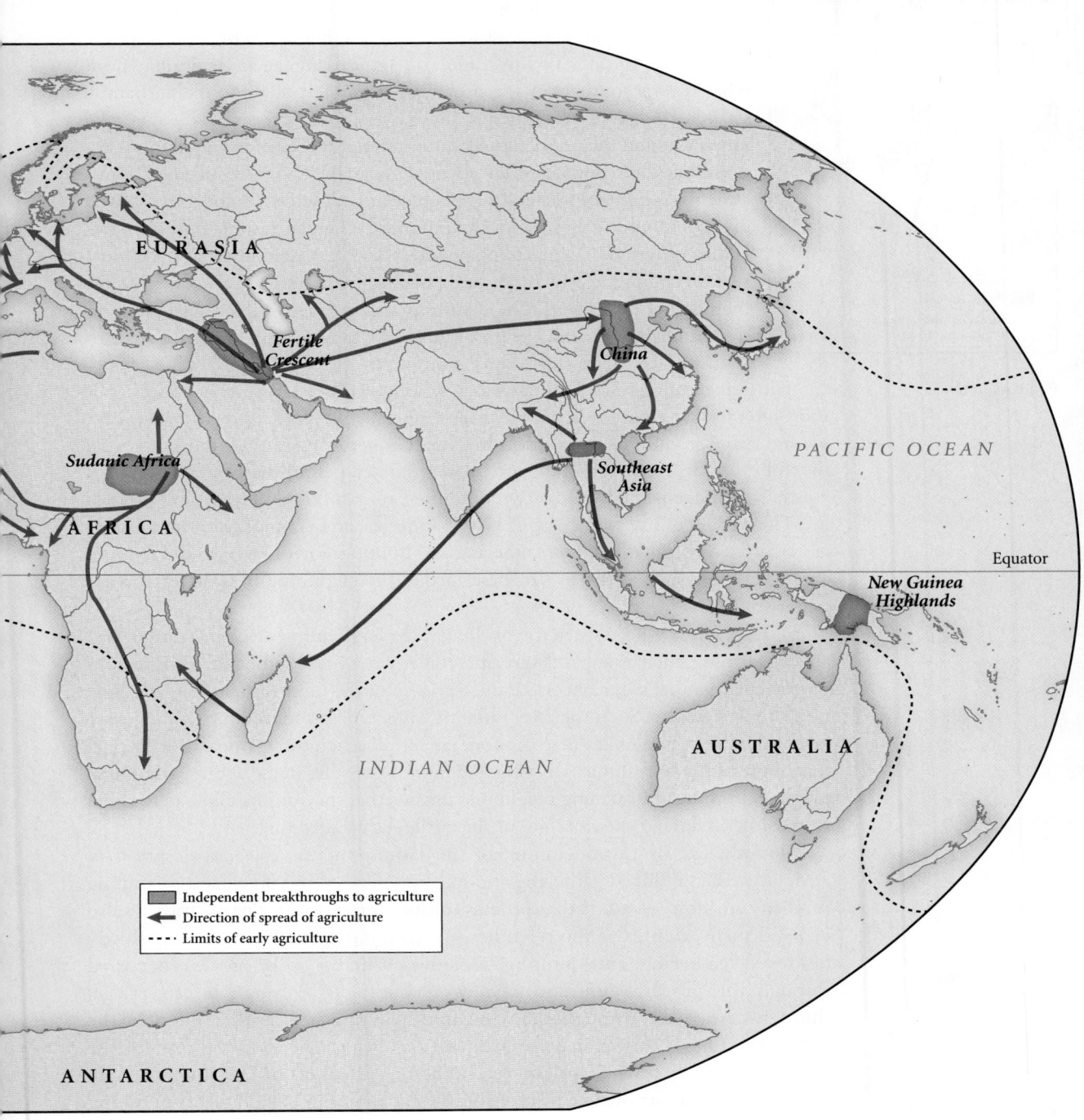

EURASIA

Fertile
Crescent

China

PACIFIC OCEAN

Sudanic Africa

Southeast
Asia

AFRICA

Equator

New Guinea
Highlands

AUSTRALIA

INDIAN OCEAN

Independent breakthroughs to agriculture
Direction of spread of agriculture
Limits of early agriculture

ANTARCTICA

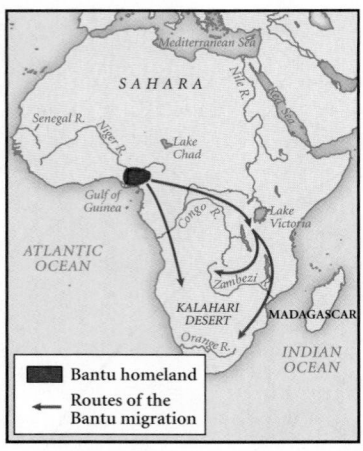

Bantu Migrations

Within Africa, the development of agricultural societies in the southern half of the continent is associated with the migration of peoples speaking one or another of the some 400 Bantu languages. Beginning from what is now southern Nigeria or Cameroon around 3000 B.C.E., Bantu-speaking people moved east and south over the next several millennia, taking with them their agricultural, cattle-raising, and, later, ironworking skills, as well as their languages. The Bantus generally absorbed, killed, or drove away the indigenous Paleolithic peoples or exposed them to animal-borne diseases to which they had no immunities. A similar process brought agricultural Austronesian-speaking people, who originated in southern China, to the Philippine and Indonesian islands, with similar consequences for their earlier inhabitants. Later, Austronesian speakers carried agriculture to the uninhabited islands of the Pacific and to Madagascar off the coast of southeastern Africa (see Map 1.2 on p. 19).

The globalization of agriculture was a prolonged process, lasting 10,000 years or more after its first emergence in the Fertile Crescent, but it did not take hold everywhere. The Agricultural Revolution in New Guinea, for example, did not spread much beyond its core region. In particular, it did not pass to the nearby peoples of Australia, who remained steadfastly committed to gathering and hunting ways of life. The people of the west coast of North America, arctic regions, and southwestern Africa also maintained their gathering and hunting way of life into the modern era. A very few, such as the Hadza, described at the beginning of Chapter 1, practice it still.

Some of those who resisted the swelling tide of agriculture lived in areas unsuitable to farming, such as harsh desert or arctic environments; others lived in regions of particular natural abundance, like the territory of the Chumash, so they felt little need for agriculture. Such societies found it easier to resist agriculture if they were not in the direct line of advance of more powerful agricultural people. But the fact that many of the remaining gathering and hunting peoples knew about agricultural practices from nearby farming neighbors suggests that they quite deliberately chose to resist it, preferring the freer life of their Paleolithic ancestors.

Nonetheless, by the beginning of the Common Era, the global spread of agriculture had reduced gathering and hunting peoples to a small and dwindling minority of humankind. If that process meant "progress" in certain ways, it also claimed many victims as the relentlessly expanding agricultural frontier slowly destroyed gathering and hunting societies. Whether this process occurred through the peaceful diffusion of new technologies, through intermarriage, through disease, or through the violent displacement of earlier peoples, the steady erosion of this ancient way of life has been a persistent thread of the human story over the past 10,000 years. The final chapters of that long story are being written in our own century. After the Agricultural Revolution, the future, almost everywhere, lay with the farmers and herders and with the distinctive societies that they created.

The Culture of Agriculture

What did that future look like? In what ways did societies based on the domestication of plants and animals differ from those rooted in a gathering and hunting economy? In the first place, the Agricultural Revolution led to an increase in human population, as the greater productivity of agriculture was able to support much larger numbers. An early agricultural settlement uncovered near Jericho in present-day Israel probably had 2,000 people, a vast increase in the size of human communities compared to much smaller Paleolithic bands. On a global level, scholars estimate that the world's population was about 6 million around 10,000 years ago, before the Agricultural Revolution got under way, and shot up to some 50 million by 5,000 years ago and 250 million by the beginning of the Common Era. Here was the real beginning of the human dominance over other forms of life on the planet.

But larger communities and more people did not necessarily mean an improved life for ordinary people. Farming involved hard work and more of it than in many earlier gathering and hunting societies. The remains of early agricultural people show some deterioration in health—more tooth decay and anemia, a shorter physical stature, and diminished life expectancy. Living close to animals subjected humans to new diseases—smallpox, flu, measles, chicken pox, malaria, tuberculosis, rabies—while living in larger communities generated epidemics for the first time in human history.[13] Furthermore, relying on a small number of plants or animals rendered early agricultural societies vulnerable to famine, in case of crop failure, drought, or other catastrophes. The advent of agriculture bore costs as well as benefits.

Agriculture also imposed constraints on human communities. Some Paleolithic people had settled in permanent villages, but all agricultural people did so, as farming required a settled life. A good example of an early agricultural settlement comes from northern China, one of the original independent sources of agriculture, where rice, millet, pig, and chicken farming gave rise to settled communities by about 7,000 years ago. In 1953, workers digging the foundation for a factory uncovered the remains of an ancient village, now called Banpo, near the present-day city of Xian. Millet, pigs, and dogs had been domesticated, but diets were supplemented with wild plants, animals, and fish. Some forty-five houses covered with thatch laid over wooden beams provided homes to perhaps 500 people. More than 200 storage pits permitted the accumulation of grain, and six kilns and pottery wheels enabled the production of various pots, vases, and dishes, many decorated with geometric designs and human and animal images. A large central space suggests an area for public religious or political activity, and a trench surrounding the village indicates some common effort to defend the community.

Early agricultural villages such as Banpo reveal another feature of the age of agriculture—an explosion of technological innovation. Mobile Paleolithic peoples had little use for pots, but such vessels were essential for settled societies, and their creation and elaboration accompanied agriculture everywhere. So too did the weaving of textiles, made possible by collecting the fibers of domesticated plants (cotton

■ **Change**
What was revolutionary about the Agricultural Revolution?

Women and Weaving
During the Paleolithic era and beyond, the weaving of cloth was widely regarded as women's work. It still is in many places, as this picture from an early twenty-first-century carpet-weaving workshop in Isfahn (Iran) illustrates. (Phil Weymout/Lonely Planet Images/Getty Images)

and flax, for example) and animals such as sheep. Evidence for the invention of looms of several kinds dates back to 7,000 years ago, and textiles, some elaborately decorated, show up in Peru, Switzerland, China, and Egypt. Like agriculture itself, weaving clearly seems to be a technology in which women were the primary innovators. It was a task that was compatible with child-rearing responsibilities, which virtually all human societies assigned primarily to women.[14] Another technology associated with the Agricultural Revolution was metallurgy. The working of gold and copper, then bronze, and, later, iron became part of the jewelry-, tool-, and weapon-making skill set of humankind. The long "stone age" of human technological history was coming to an end, and the age of metals was beginning.

A further set of technological changes, beginning around 4000 B.C.E., has been labeled the "secondary products revolution."[15] These technological innovations involved new uses for domesticated animals, beyond their meat and hides. Agricultural people in parts of Europe, Asia, and Africa learned to milk their animals, to harvest their wool, and to enrich the soil with their manure. Even more important, they learned to ride horses and camels and to hitch various animals to plows and carts. Because these types of animals did not exist in the Americas, this revolutionary new source of power and transportation was available only in the Eastern Hemisphere.

A final feature of early agricultural societies lay in their growing impact on the environment, as farming and herding peoples deliberately altered the natural ecosystem by removing the natural ground cover for their fields, by making use of irrigation, and by grazing their now-domesticated animals. In parts of the Middle East within a thousand years after the beginning of settled agricultural life, some villages were abandoned when soil erosion and deforestation led to declining crop yields, which could not support mounting populations.[16] The advent of more intensive agriculture associated with city-based civilizations only heightened this human impact on the landscape (see Chapter 3).

Social Variation in the Age of Agriculture

■ **Comparison**
What different kinds of societies emerged out of the Agricultural Revolution?

The resources generated by the Agricultural Revolution opened up vast new possibilities for the construction of human societies, but they led to no single or common outcome. Differences in the natural environment, the encounter with strangers, and sometimes deliberate choices gave rise to several distinct kinds of societies early on in the age of agriculture, all of which have endured into modern times.

Pastoral Societies

One variation of great significance grew out of the difference between the domestication of plants and the domestication of animals. Many societies made use of both, but in regions where farming was difficult or impossible—arctic tundra, some grasslands, and deserts—some people came to depend far more extensively on their animals, such as sheep, goats, cattle, horses, camels, or reindeer. Animal husbandry was a "distinct form of food-producing economy," relying on the milk, meat, and blood of animals.[17] Known as herders, pastoralists, or nomads, such people emerged in Central Asia, the Arabian Peninsula, the Sahara, and in parts of eastern and southern Africa. What they had in common was mobility, for they moved seasonally as they followed the changing patterns of vegetation necessary as pasture for their animals.

The particular animals central to pastoral economies differed from region to region. The domestication of horses by 4000 B.C.E. and the later mastery of horseback-riding skills enabled the growth of pastoral peoples all across the steppes of Central Asia by the first millennium B.C.E. Although organized primarily in kinship-based clans or tribes, these nomads periodically created powerful military confederations, which played a major role in the history of Eurasia for thousands of years. In the Inner Asian, Arabian, and Saharan deserts, domesticated camels made possible the human occupation of forbidding environments. The grasslands south of the Sahara and in parts of eastern Africa supported cattle-raising pastoralists. The absence of large animals capable of domestication meant that no pastoral societies emerged in the Americas.

The relationship between nomadic herders and their farming neighbors has been one of the enduring themes of Afro-Eurasian history. Frequently, it was a relationship of conflict as pastoral peoples, unable to produce their own agricultural products, were attracted to the wealth and sophistication of agrarian societies and sought access to their richer grazing lands as well as their food crops and manufactured products. The biblical story of the deadly rivalry between two brothers—Cain, a "tiller of the ground," and Abel, a "keeper of sheep"—reflects this ancient conflict, which persisted well into modern times. But not all was conflict between pastoral and agricultural peoples. The more peaceful exchange of technologies, ideas, products, and people across the ecological frontier of pastoral and agricultural societies also served to enrich and to change both sides. In the chapters that follow, and especially in Chapter 12, we will encounter pastoral

The Domestication of Animals
Although farming often gets top billing in discussions of the Neolithic Revolution, the raising of animals was equally important, for they provided meat, pulling power, transportation (in the case of horses and camels), and manure. Animal husbandry also made possible pastoral societies, which were largely dependent on their domesticated animals. In this Egyptian carving, dating to about 2380 B.C.E., two workers lead a prime bull to the fields. (G. Dagli Orti/The Art Archive)

societies repeatedly, particularly as they interact with neighboring agricultural and "civilized" peoples. (See Visual Source 2.3, p. 80, for a rock-art painting of an early pastoral community in the Sahara.)

Agricultural Village Societies

The most characteristic early agricultural societies were those of settled village-based farmers, such as those living in Banpo or Jericho. Such societies retained much of the equality and freedom of gathering and hunting communities, as they continued to do without kings, chiefs, bureaucrats, or aristocracies.

An example of this type of social order can be found at Çatalhüyük, a very early agricultural village in southern Turkey. A careful excavation of the site revealed a population of several thousand people who buried their dead under their houses and then filled the houses with dirt and built new ones on top, layer upon layer. No streets divided the houses, which were constructed adjacent to one another. People moved about the village on adjoining rooftops, from which they entered their homes. Despite the presence of many specialized crafts, few signs of inherited social inequality have surfaced. Nor is there any indication of male or female dominance, although men were more closely associated with hunting wild animals and women with plants and agriculture. "Both men and women," concludes one scholar, "could carry out a series of roles and enjoy a range of positions, from making tools to grinding grain and baking to heading a household."[18] (See Visual Sources: Art and Life in the Early Agrarian Era, pp. 76–83, for additional images from Çatalhüyük and for other architectural and artistic expressions of early agricultural settlements.)

Many such village-based agricultural societies flourished well into the modern era, usually organizing themselves in terms of kinship groups or lineages, which incorporated large numbers of people well beyond the immediate or extended family. Such people traced their descent through either the male or the female line to some common ancestor, real or mythical. In many African societies, for example, a lineage system provided the framework within which large numbers of people could make and enforce rules, maintain order, and settle disputes without going to war. In short, the lineage system performed the functions of government, but without the formal apparatus of government, and thus did not require kings or queens, chiefs, or permanent officials associated with a state organization. (See Document 2.2, pp. 71–73 for a description of an East African agricultural village society, the Gikuyu.) The Tiv of central Nigeria organized close to a million people in this fashion at the end of the nineteenth century. Theirs was a system in which power was dispersed

Çatalhüyük
Since the 1960s, archeologists have uncovered the connected homes of Çatalhüyük, shown here in a photo of the excavation, as well as many artifacts, murals, and sculptures from this early agricultural settlement in southern Turkey. (Courtesy, James Mellaart/Çatalhöyük Research Project)

throughout the society rather than being concentrated in particular people or institutions. In fact, the Tiv had no word for "politics" as a separate aspect of life, for there was no state that specialized in political matters.

Despite their democratic qualities and the absence of centralized authority, village-based lineage societies sometimes developed modest social and economic inequalities. Elders could exploit the labor of junior members of the community and sought particularly to control women's reproductive powers, which were essential for the growth of the lineage. Among the Igbo of southern Nigeria, "title societies" enabled men and women of wealth and character to earn a series of increasingly prestigious "titles" that set them apart from other members of their community, although these honors could not be inherited. Lineages also sought to expand their numbers, and hence their prestige and power, by incorporating war captives or migrants in subordinate positions, sometimes as slaves.

Many agricultural societies, in Africa and elsewhere, conducted their affairs without formal centralized states or full-time rulers, even when they were aware of these institutions and practices from nearby peoples. Given the frequent oppressiveness of organized political power in human history, such experiments with "stateless societies" represent an intriguing alternative to states, kingdoms, and empires, so frequently highlighted in the historical record. These agricultural village societies pioneered the human settlement of vast areas; adapted to a variety of environments; created numerous cultural, artistic, and religious traditions; incorporated new crops, institutions, and people into their cultures; and interacted continuously with their neighbors.

Chiefdoms

In other places, agricultural village societies came to be organized politically as chiefdoms, in which inherited positions of power and privilege introduced a more distinct element of inequality, but unlike later "kings," chiefs could seldom use force to compel the obedience of their subjects. Instead they relied on their generosity or gift giving, their ritual status, or their personal charisma to persuade their followers. The earliest such chiefdoms seem to have emerged in the Tigris-Euphrates river valley called Mesopotamia (present-day Iraq), sometime after 6000 B.C.E., when temple priests organized irrigation systems and controlled trade with nearby societies.

Many chiefdoms followed in all parts of the world, and the more recent ones have been much studied by anthropologists. (See Documents 2.1, pp. 68–71, and 2.3, pp. 73–75, for examples of chiefdoms in Europe and the Caribbean.) For example, chiefdoms emerged everywhere in the Pacific islands, which had been colonized by agricultural Polynesian peoples. Chiefs usually derived from a senior lineage, tracing their descent to the first son of an imagined ancestor. With both religious and secular functions, chiefs led important rituals and ceremonies, organized the community for warfare, directed its economic life, and sought to resolve internal conflicts. They collected tribute from commoners in the form of food, manufactured goods, and raw materials. These items in turn were redistributed to warriors, craftsmen, religious specialists, and other subordinates, while the chief kept enough to maintain

■ **Comparison**
How did chiefdoms differ from stateless agricultural village societies?

Cahokia
Pictured here in an artist's reconstruction, Cahokia (near St. Louis, Missouri) was the center of an important agricultural chiefdom around 1100 C.E. See Chapter 7 for details. (Cahokia Mounds State Historic Site, Illinois. Painting by Lloyd K. Townsend)

his prestigious position and his imposing lifestyle.[19] In North America as well, a remarkable series of chiefdoms emerged in the eastern woodlands, where an extensive array of large earthen mounds testify to the organizational capacity of these early societies. The largest of them, known as Cahokia, flourished around 1100 C.E. In such agricultural chiefdoms—both ancient and more recent—the distinction between elite and commoner, based on birth rather than age or achievement, began to take root. It was a fateful turn in the organization of human societies—one that was replicated, elaborated, and assumed to be natural in all later states and civilizations.

Reflections: The Legacies of Agriculture

Because it is practiced around the world and has achieved virtually universal acceptance, agriculture, or domestication, may seem to be a natural or inevitable feature of the human story. In terms of world history, however, it is a recent development, an adaptation to the unique conditions of the latest interglacial period. Who can say how long those conditions will last or whether agriculture would remain a viable way of life in a renewed Ice Age?

No matter how it turns out in the very long run, during the last 10,000 years or so, the Agricultural Revolution has radically transformed both the trajectory of the human journey and the evolution of life on the planet. This epic transformation granted to one species, *Homo sapiens*, a growing power over many other species of plants and animals. Agriculture made possible an increase in human numbers far beyond what a gathering and hunting economy could support, and it enabled human beings to control and manipulate both plants and animals for their own purposes far more than ever before.

But if agriculture provided humankind with the power to dominate nature, it also, increasingly, enabled some people to dominate others. This was not immediately apparent, and for several thousand years, and much longer in some places, agricultural villages retained much of the social equality that had characterized

Paleolithic life. Slowly, though, many of the resources released by the Agricultural Revolution accumulated in the hands of a few. Rich and poor, chiefs and common- ers, landowners and dependent peasants, rulers and subjects, dominant men and subordinate women, slaves and free people—these distinctions, so common in the record of world history, took shape most extensively in highly productive agricul- tural settings, which generated a substantial economic surplus. There the endless elaboration of such distinctions, for better or worse, became a major feature of those distinctive agricultural societies known to us as "civilizations."

Second Thoughts

What's the Significance?

end of the last Ice Age	Bantu migration	pastoral societies
"broad spectrum diet"	peoples of Australia	Çatalhüyük
Fertile Crescent	Banpo	"stateless societies"
teosinte	"secondary products	chiefdoms
diffusion	revolution"	

To assess your mastery of the material in this chapter, visit the **Student Center** at bedfordstmartins.com/strayer.

Big Picture Questions

1. The Agricultural Revolution marked a decisive turning point in human history. What evidence might you offer to support this claim, and how might you argue against it?
2. How did early agricultural societies differ from those of the Paleolithic era? How does the example of settled gathering and hunting peoples such as the Chumash complicate this comparison?
3. Was the Agricultural Revolution inevitable? Why did it occur so late in the story of humankind?
4. "The Agricultural Revolution provides evidence for 'progress' in human affairs." How would you evaluate this statement?

Next Steps: For Further Study

Elizabeth Wayland Barber, *Women's Work: The First 20,000 Years* (1994). Explores the role of women in early technological development, particularly textile making.

Peter Bellwood, *First Farmers* (2005). A recent and up-to-date account of the Agricultural Revolution, considered on a global basis.

Mark Nathan Cohen, *The Food Crisis in Prehistory* (1977). An older work arguing that mounting human population triggered the breakthrough to agriculture.

Jared Diamond, *Guns, Germs, and Steel* (1997). A provocative and much-publicized explanation for regional economic differences, based on variations among early agricultural revolutions.

Steven Mithen, *After the Ice: A Global Human History, 20,000–5000 B.C.* (2004). An imaginative tour of world archeological sites during the Agricultural Revolution.

Neil Roberts, *The Holocene: An Environmental History* (1998). Explores the role of climate change and human activity in shaping the global environment during the age of agriculture.

"The Agricultural Revolution," http://www.wsu.edu/gened/learn-modules/top_agrev/agrev-index .html. A Web-based tutorial from Washington State University.

For Web sites and additional documents related to this chapter, see **Make History** at bedfordstmartins.com/strayer.

Documents

Considering the Evidence:
Agricultural Village Societies

The Agricultural Revolution was arguably the most significant turning point in the larger story of humankind, at least before the Industrial Revolution. And the most celebrated outcome of the agricultural breakthrough was "civilization"—the early city- and state-based societies of Egypt, Mesopotamia, India, China, Peru, and elsewhere (see Chapter 3). Yet the domestication of plants and animals did not everywhere and always lead to civilizations, and certainly not immediately. In the Middle East and Northeastern Africa, for example, thousands of years passed before the transition to agriculture generated a recognizable civilization. Elsewhere, fully agricultural societies without the characteristic features of civilization—cities, empires, written languages, and pronounced social inequalities—persisted well into modern times.

The earliest agricultural village societies, which emerged well before writing had been developed anywhere, have passed into history leaving no documentary record. Therefore, we focus here on three much later examples of such societies—the Germanic neighbors of the Roman Empire during the first century C.E., the Gikuyu people of East Africa in the early twentieth century, and the Taino of the Caribbean islands during the sixteenth century. Since these peoples lacked writing, our documentary evidence about them derives from the descriptions of literate outsiders or from more recent accounts by educated insiders. While varying greatly in their historical and cultural settings, the documents that follow and the peoples they describe nonetheless provide us with some exposure to those agricultural village societies and chiefdoms that were among the major outcomes of the Agricultural Revolution.

Document 2.1

Germanic Peoples of Central Europe

Ancient Germanic-speaking peoples, occupying much of Central Europe north of the Roman Empire, were never a single "nation" but rather a collection of tribes, clans, and chiefdoms, regarded by the Romans as barbarians though admired and feared for their military skills (see Map 4.4, p. 156). They were famously described by Tacitus (56–117 C.E.), a Roman official and well-known historian. Tacitus himself had never visited the lands of the people he describes; rather, he relied on earlier written documents and interviews with merchants and soldiers who had traveled and lived in the region.

■ What can we learn from Tacitus's account about the economy, politics, society, and culture of the Germanic peoples of the first century C.E.?

■ Which statements of Tacitus might you regard as reliable and which are more suspect? Why?

■ Why did Tacitus regard Germanic peoples as distinctly inferior to Romans? How might he have responded to the idea that these people would play a major role in the collapse of the Roman Empire several centuries later?

■ Modern scholars have argued that Tacitus used the Germanic peoples to criticize aspects of his own Roman culture. What evidence might support this point of view?

TACITUS

Germania
First Century C.E.

The Germans themselves I should regard as aboriginal, and not mixed at all with other races through immigration or intercourse.... [W]ho would leave Asia, or Africa, or Italy for Germany, with its wild country, its inclement skies, its sullen manners and aspect, unless indeed it were his home? In their ancient songs, their only way of remembering or recording the past, they celebrate an earth-born god, Tuisco, and his son Mannus, as the origin of their race, as their founders....

The tribes of Germany are free from all taint of intermarriages with foreign nations, and they appear as a distinct, unmixed race, like none but themselves. Hence, too, the same physical peculiarities throughout so vast a population. All have fierce blue eyes, red hair, huge frames, fit only for a sudden exertion. They are less able to bear laborious work. Heat and thirst they cannot in the least endure; to

cold and hunger their climate and their soil inure them....

They choose their kings by birth, their generals by merit. These kings have not unlimited or arbitrary power, and the generals do more by example than by authority.... But to reprimand, to imprison, even to flog, is permitted to the priests alone, and that not as a punishment, or at the general's bidding, but, as it were, by the mandate of the god whom they believe to inspire the warrior.... And what most stimulates their courage is that their squadrons or battalions, instead of being formed by chance or by a fortuitous gathering, are composed of families and clans. Close by them, too, are those dearest to them, so that they hear the shrieks of women, the cries of infants....

Tradition says that armies already wavering and giving way have been rallied by women who, with earnest entreaties and bosoms laid bare, have vividly represented the horrors of captivity, which the Germans fear with such extreme dread on behalf of their women.... They even believe that the sex

Source: Alfred John Church and William Jackson Brodribb, *The Agricola and Germania of Tacitus* (London: Macmillan, 1877), pp. 87ff.

has a certain sanctity and prescience, and they do not despise their counsels, or make light of their answers....

Mercury is the deity whom they chiefly worship, and on certain days they deem it right to sacrifice to him even with human victims....

Augury and divination by lot no people practice more diligently. The use of lots is simple. A little bough is lopped off a fruit-bearing tree, and cut into small pieces; these are distinguished by certain marks, and thrown carelessly and at random over a white garment. In public questions the priest of the particular state, in private the father of the family invokes the gods, and, with his eyes toward heaven, takes up each piece three times, and finds in them a meaning according to the mark previously impression on them....

When they go into battle, it is a disgrace for the chief to be surpassed in valor, a disgrace for his followers not to equal the valor of the chief. And it is an infamy and a reproach for life to have survived the chief, and return from the field. To defend, to protect him, to ascribe one's own brave deeds to his renown, is the height of loyalty. The chief fights for victory; his vassals fight for their chief.... Feasts and entertainments, which though inelegant, are plentifully furnished, are their only pay. The means of this bounty come from war or rapine.° Nor are they as easily persuaded to plough the earth and to wait for the year's produce as to challenge an enemy and earn the honor of wounds. Nay, they actually think it tame and stupid to acquire by the sweat of toil what they might win by their blood.

Whenever they are not fighting, they pass much of their time in the chase, and still more in idleness giving themselves up to sleep and to feasting, the bravest and the most warlike doing nothing, and surrendering the management of the household of the home, and of the land, to the women, the old men, and all the weakest members of the family.... It is the custom of the states to bestow by voluntary and individual contribution on the chief a present of cattle or of grain, which, while accepted as a compliment, supplies their wants. They are particularly delighted by gifts from neighboring tribes... such as choice

steeds, heavy armor, trappings, and neckchains. We have now taught them to accept money also.

It is well known that the nations of Germany have no cities, and that they do not even tolerate closely contiguous dwellings. They live scattered and apart, just as a spring, a meadow, or a wood has attracted them. Their villages they do not arrange in our fashion,... but every person surrounds his dwelling with an open space, either as a precaution against the disasters of fire, or because they do not know how to build. No use is made by them of stone or tile; they employ timber for all purposes, rude masses without ornament or attractiveness....

They all wrap themselves in a cloak which is fastened with a clasp, or, if this is not forthcoming, with a thorn, leaving the rest of their persons bare.... They also wear the skins of wild beasts....

Their marriage code, however, is strict, and indeed no part of their manners is more praiseworthy. Almost alone among barbarians they are content with one wife, except a very few among them.... Lest the woman should think herself to stand apart from aspirations after noble deeds and from the perils of war, she is reminded by the ceremony which inaugurates marriage that she is her husband's partner in toil and danger, destined to suffer and to dare with him alike both in peace and in war....

Very rare for so numerous a population is adultery, the punishment of which is prompt, and in the husband's power. Having cut off the hair of the adulteress and stripped her naked, he expels her from the house in the presence of her kinfolk, and then flogs her through the whole village. The loss of chastity meets with no indulgence; neither beauty, youth, nor wealth will procure the culprit a husband. No one in Germany laughs at vice, nor do they call it the fashion to corrupt and to be corrupted.... To limit the number of their children or to destroy any of their subsequent offspring is accounted infamous, and good habits are here more effectual than good laws elsewhere....

It is the duty among them to adopt the feuds as well as the friendships of a father or a kinsman. These feuds are not implacable; even homicide is expiated by the payment of a certain number of cattle and of sheep, and the satisfaction is accepted by the entire family, greatly to the advantage of the state, since

---

°**rapine:** a seizure or robbery.

feuds are dangerous in proportion to a people's freedom....

[S]laves are not employed after our manner with distinct domestic duties assigned to them, but each one has the management of a house and home of his own. The master requires from the slave a certain quantity of grain, of cattle, and of clothing, as he would from a tenant, and this is the limit of subjection. All other household functions are discharged by the wife and children....

Of lending money on interest and increasing it by compound interest they know nothing—a more effectual safeguard than if it were prohibited.

Land proportioned to the number of inhabitants is occupied by the whole community in turn, and afterward divided among them according to rank. A wide expanse of plains makes the partition easy. They till fresh fields every year, and they have still more land than enough;... corn [wheat] is the only produce required from the earth.

Document 2.2

Social Organization among the Gikuyu

Occupying the fertile highlands of central Kenya in East Africa, the Gikuyu were an agricultural, iron-working, and Bantu-speaking people who were incorporated into the British Empire during the late nineteenth century (see the map on p. 60). They were among the many "stateless societies" of world history, for they did not organize themselves in a large-scale centralized political authority. Over many centuries, however, they had developed or adapted from their neighbors a mechanism known as age-sets to facilitate social integration and political decision-making. Age-sets were groups of men who were initiated at the same time and then rose collectively through a series of age-grades, or ranks, over the course of their lives. Here, the Gikuyu age-set system, as well as its gendered division of labor, is described by Jomo Kenyatta, a well-known nationalist leader in colonial Kenya and the country's first African president. In his book *Facing Mount Kenya*, published in 1938, Kenyatta described Gikuyu life in a positive (perhaps idealized) fashion, intended to counteract negative British images of African life as primitive, backward, or savage.

■ How does Kenyatta describe the division of labor and marriage practices in Gikuyu families? Does his description suggest gender equality or patriarchy?

■ What were the major stages through which Gikuyu men passed during their lives? What duties were associated with each of the age-grades?

■ How did the age-set system perform some of the functions of states, while avoiding their often oppressive features? How might you define the advantages and disadvantages of a stateless society in comparison to human communities organized around a formal government or state?

■ In light of the colonial setting in which Kenyatta was living, what message was he trying to convey?

JOMO KENYATTA
Facing Mount Kenya
1938

The chief occupations among the Gikuyu are agriculture and the rearing of livestock, such as cattle, sheep, and goats. Each family, i.e., a man, his wife or wives, and their children, constitute an economic unit. This is controlled and strengthened by the system of division of labor according to sex....

In house-building, the heavy work of cutting timbers and putting up the framework falls on men. Carrying and cutting of the grass for thatching and plastering the wall with clay or cow-dung is the work of women.... The entire housework naturally falls within the sphere of women's activities. They cook, bring water from the rivers, wash utensils, and fetch firewood from the forests and bush. They also perform the task of carrying the loads on their backs....

In cultivating the fields, men clear the brush and cut big trees, and also break the virgin soil with digging sticks and hoes. Women come behind them and prepare the ground for sowing seeds. Planting is shared by both sexes.... Weeding is done collectively.... Harvesting is done chiefly by women.... Tending of cattle, sheep, and goats and also slaughtering and distributing the meat and preparing the skins is entirely men's duty. Dressmaking, pottery, and weaving of baskets is exclusively women's profession.... The brewing of beer is done jointly by both men and women.... Trading is done by both sexes....

The Gikuyu customary law of marriage provides that a man may have as many wives as he can support, and that the larger one's family, the better it is for him and the tribe.... The custom also provides that all women must be under the protection of men... and that all women must be married in their teens, i.e., fifteen to twenty. Thus there is no term in the Gikuyu language for "unmarried" or "old maids."...

The teaching of social obligations is... emphasized by the classification of age-groups.... This binds together those of the same status in ties of closest loyalty and devotion. Men circumcised at the same time stand in the very closest relationship to each other....

The fellowship and unity of these age-groups is rather a remarkable thing. It binds men from all parts of the country, and though they may have been circumcised in places hundreds of miles apart, it is of no consequence. They are like old boys of the same school, though I question whether the Europeans have any association with the same high standards of mutual obligation.... Age-groups further emphasize the social grades of junior and senior, inferior and superior.... The older group takes precedence over the younger and has rights to service and courtesy which the younger must acknowledge.

...The circumcision ceremony was the only qualification which gave a man the recognition of manhood and the full rights of citizenship.... As soon as his circumcision wounds heal, he joins the national council of junior warriors. At this stage his father provides him with necessary weapons, namely spear, shield, and sword; then a sheep or a male goat is given to the senior warriors of the district.... The animal is killed for a ceremony of introducing the young warrior into the general activities and etiquette of the warrior class.

The second stage in warriorhood was celebrated about eighty-two moons or twelve rain seasons following the circumcision ceremony. At this juncture the junior warrior was promoted to the council of the senior warriors.... The initiation fee to this rank was two sheep or goats....

The third stage in manhood is marriage. When a man is married and has established his own homestead, he is required to join the council of elders

Source: Jomo Kenyatta, *Facing Mount Kenya* (London: Martin Secker and Warburg, 1938), 53–55, 174, 115–16, 198–205.

(*kiama*); he pays one male goat or sheep and then he is initiated into a first grade of eldership.... [They] act as messengers to the *kiama*, and help to skin animals, to light fires, to bring firewood, to roast meat for the senior elders, and to carry ceremonial articles to and from the *kiama* assemblies. They must not eat kidneys, spleen, or loin, for these are reserved for the senior elders.

Next... comes the council of peace. This stage is reached when a man has a son or daughter older enough to be circumcised.... After this [an elaborate ceremony of induction into this new age-grade], the candidate is invested with his staff of office and a bunch of sacred leaves. This signifies that he is now a peaceful man, that he is no longer a carrier of spear and shield, or a pursuer of the vanity of war and plunder. That he has now attained a stage where he has to take the responsibility of carrying the symbols of peace and to assume the duties of peace-maker in the community....

The last and most honored status in the man's life history is the religious and sacrificial council. This stage is reached when a man has had practically all his children circumcised, and his wife (or wives) has passed the child-bearing age.... The elders of this grade assume a role of "holy men." They are the high priests. All religious and ethical ceremonies are in their hands.

Document 2.3

Religion in a Caribbean Chiefdom

When Christopher Columbus arrived in the Caribbean region in the late fifteenth century, he found a densely settled agricultural people known as the Taino inhabiting the islands now called Hispaniola (modern Haiti and Dominican Republic), Cuba, Jamaica, and Puerto Rico. Organized into substantial village communities governed by a hierarchy of chiefs (*cacique*), Taino society featured modest class distinctions. An elite group of chiefs, warriors, artists, and religious specialists enjoyed a higher status than commoners, who worked the fields, fished, and hunted. Within a half century of Columbus's arrival, almost all of the Taino had perished, victims of Spanish brutality and Old World diseases. Among the witnesses to this catastrophe was the Spanish missionary and Dominican priest Bartolomé de Las Casas (1474–1566). His extensive writings contained a vehement denunciation of Spanish actions in the Americas as well as an informed description of Taino life and culture. Here, Las Casas describes his understanding of Taino religion.

■ Based on this account, how might you describe Taino religious practice?

■ To what extent does Las Casas's Christian perspective color his account of Taino religion?

■ What was the function of the *zemis* in Taino culture?

■ What was the relationship between Taino political authorities and the "priests," or *behiques*?

■ Which features of Taino religious life did Las Casas appreciate and which did he find offensive or erroneous?

BARTOLOMÉ DE LAS CASAS
Apologetic History of the Indies
1566

The people of this island Hispaniola had a certain faith in and knowledge of a one and true God, who was immortal and invisible, for none can see him, who had no beginning, whose dwelling place and residence is heaven, and they called him Yócahu Vagua Maórocoti. . . .

Into this true and catholic knowledge of the true God these errors intruded, to wit: that God had a mother, whose name was Atabex, and a brother Guaca, and other relatives in like fashion. They must have been like people without a guide on the road of the truth; rather there was one who would lead them astray, clouding the light of their natural reason that could have guided them. . . .

[T]hey had some idols or good-luck statues, and these were generally called *zemis*. . . . They believed these zemis gave them water and wind and sun when they had need of them, and likewise children and other things they wanted to have. Some of these were made of wood and others of stone. . . .

[P]riests, who are called *behiques* in the language of these islands and who were their theologians, prophets, and soothsayers, practiced some deceptions upon these people, primarily when they acted as physicians, in accordance with what the devil, from the domain allowed to him, dictated to them what they were to say or do. They led the people to believe they spoke with those statues and that the statues revealed their secrets to them, and they find out from those secrets everything they want to know. And it must have been so, because the devil surely spoke in those statues. . . .

They had other idols or images of stone which those priests and physicians made the people believe they took out of the bodies of those who were sick, and these stones were of three kinds. I never saw their form, but they held each one to have its own power: one had the power to favor their sown lands; the second, so that women would have good fortune in childbirth; the power of the third was that they would have water and good rains when they had need of them. Thus they must have been like the gods of the ancients, each one of whom had the responsibility of presiding in his domain, although these peoples sensed this more crudely and simply than the ancients. The kings and lords boasted, and in this the other people must have followed them, about their zemis or gods and considered them more glorious, saying that they had better zemis than the other peoples and lords, and they endeavored to steal them from each other; and although they took great care in guarding these statues or idols or whatever they may have been from other Indians from other kingdoms and dominions, they took incomparably greater care in guarding and concealing them from the Spaniards, and when they suspected their approach, they would take them and hide them in the mountains. . . .

We found that in the season when they gathered the harvest of the fields they had sown and cultivated, which consisted of the bread made from roots, yams, sweet potatoes, and corn, they donated a certain portion as first fruits, almost as if they were giving thanks for benefits received. Since they had no designated temples or houses of religion, as has been said above, they put this portion of first fruits of the crops in the great house of the lords and caciques, which they called *caney*, and they offered and dedicated it to the zemi. They said the zemi sent the water and brought the sun and nurtured all those fruits and gave them children and the other benefits which were there in abundance. All the things offered in this way were left there either until they rotted or the children took them or played with them or until they were spoiled, and thus they were consumed. . . .

Source: Bartolomé de Las Casas, "Apologetic History of the Indies, 1566," in *Taino: Pre-Columbian Art and Culture from the Caribbean*, edited by Fatima Bercht et al., translated by Susan C. Griswold (New York: Monacelli Press, 1997), 175–79.

When I would ask the Indians at times:"Who is this zemi you name?" they answered me:"He who makes it rain and makes the sun shine and gives us children and the other benefits we desire.".…

I saw them celebrate their cohoba° a few times, and it was something to see how they took it and what they said. The first to begin was the lord, and while he took it everyone kept silent; when he had taken his cohoba (which is to inhale those powders through the nostrils…), and they took it seated on some low but very well carved benches which they called *duhos*…, he would stay a while with his head turned to one side and his arms placed on his knees, and afterward he would lift his face toward heaven and speak his certain words, which must have been his prayer to the true God, or to the one whom he held to be a god; then everyone would respond almost like when we respond amen, and they would do this with a great clamor of voices

or sounds, and then they would give thanks to him, and they must have flattered him with praises, winning his benevolence and begging him to tell what he had seen. He would give them an account of his vision, saying that the zemi had spoken and assured him of good or adverse times, or that there were to be children, or that there was to be a death among them, or that they were to have some contention or war with their neighbors, and other foolishness that came to their imagination, stirred up by that intoxication, or that the devil, perhaps and haplessly, had insinuated to them so as to deceive them and inculcate in them a devotion to him.…

[One particular] zemi brought diseases to men, according to their belief, for which they sought the help of the priests or behiques, who were their prophets and theologians as has been said; these priests would respond that the disease had befallen them because they had been negligent or forgetful in bringing cassava bread and yams and other things to eat to the ministers who swept and cleaned the house or hermitage of Vaybrama, good zemi, and that he had told him so.

_____

°**cohoba:** a hallucinogenic drug used in religious ceremonies.

Using the Evidence:
Agricultural Village Societies

1. **Comparing agricultural societies:** How would you compare the social organization of the three societies described in Documents 2.1, 2.2, and 2.3?

2. **Comparing agricultural and Paleolithic societies:** What features of gathering and hunting societies persisted among agricultural peoples? In what ways did they differ from their Paleolithic ancestors?

3. **Evaluating documents:** Documents 2.1 and 2.3 derive from outsiders to the societies they portray. In what ways did their outsider status influence the authors' understanding of these societies? And how did Kenyatta's position as a modern and Western-educated Gikuyu living in a colonial setting shape his description of his own people in Document 2.2? What assumptions and purposes did each of these writers bring to his task?

4. **Assessing the credibility of sources:** Consider these documents as sources of historical information about the societies they describe. What statements might historians reliably use as evidence and what might they discard or view with skepticism?

Visual Sources

Considering the Evidence:
Art and Life in the Early Agrarian Era

The long period of world history between the beginnings of settled agriculture and the rise of civilizations is known as the early agrarian era or sometimes the Neolithic age. It was a time when the revolutionary implications of the breakthrough to agriculture began to be felt. Since these transformations took place before the advent of writing, historians depend heavily on material remains—art, artifacts, and architecture—for understanding the life of these people. In the absence of written records, scholars are sometimes hard-pressed to know precisely what motivated the creation of these works or what they signified to those who made them. Inference, imagination, and sometimes speculation play an important role in the analysis of this evidence.

Given human creativity and the global scope of the early agrarian era, generalizations about Neolithic art as a whole are difficult to make. But in comparison with the Paleolithic era, the new economy generated by agriculture gave rise to many artistic innovations. Weaving and pottery making became major industries, offering new opportunities for creative expression. Larger-scale stone structures, known as megaliths, appeared in various places, and settled farming communities required more elaborate dwellings, including some substantial stone fortifications. Agrarian societies also produced much larger sculptures than did gathering and hunting societies. Finally, while animals continued to be a focus of Neolithic art, human figures became more prominent and were more realistically depicted than in the cave paintings and Venus figurines of the Paleolithic era.

The art of the early agrarian era sometimes included representations of the distinctive social and economic patterns of this new phase of human history. One example is a remarkable wall painting from Çatalhüyük, an early farming community located in south-central Turkey (see pp. 64–65 and Map 2.1, p. 54). Dated to about 6200 B.C.E., the painting is apparently a stylized portrayal of the village itself, showing some eighty buildings arranged on rising terraces. Behind the town rises an erupting twin-peaked volcano, resembling the nearby actual volcano of Hasan Dag, which was active during the time that Çatalhüyük flourished. In this painting, we have a record of one of the most distinctive outcomes of the Agricultural Revolution—the establishment of settled agricultural villages. It is also perhaps the earliest map and landscape painting

Visual Source 2.1 Çatalhüyük: An Early Map and Landscape Painting (James Mellaart/Çatalhöyuk Research Project)

uncovered to date. Visual Source 2.1 is a reconstruction of that image, which was about ten feet long in its original form.

- What particular features of the mountain/volcano can you identify? What do you think the dots on the mountain represent? Notice that the volcano is venting from both the top and the base of the mountain, as volcanoes often do.

- Compare the map with the photograph on page 64 of the uncovered remains of Çatalhüyük. What similar features do you see?

- Notice that this image contains neither human nor animal figures. What might be the significance of this absence?

- What do you think the purpose of such an image might have been? Keep in mind that obsidian (black volcanic glass) found at the base of the mountain was a very valuable, and perhaps sacred, item in Çatalhüyük and an important product in regional trading patterns.

Archeological investigation at Çatalhüyük has generated a major debate about the role of women in the religious and social life of this early agricultural village. The first major dig at the site, undertaken by James Mellaart in the 1960s, uncovered a number of small female figurines, the most famous of which is shown here as Visual Source 2.2. It dates to about 5000 B.C.E. and is some eight inches in height. The baked-clay figure depicts a seated female whose arms are resting on two lionesses or leopards. For Mellaart, this was evidence for an ancient and powerful cult of the "mother Goddess," an idea that proved compelling to a number of feminist scholars and goddess worshippers. This understanding also gained support from the absence of similar male figurines. Some goddess devotees have come to view Çatalhüyük as a pilgrimage site.

Visual Source 2.2 Women, Men, and Religion in Çatalhüyük (Museum of Anatolian Civilization, Ankara/Gianni Dagli Orti/The Art Archive)

- What features of this statue might support such a view?

- How might the fact that this figurine was discovered in an abandoned grain bin affect your thinking about its significance?

- Why might feminist scholars have been attracted to Mellaart's interpretation of this figure?

- What alternative understandings of this figure can you imagine?

Later archeological research, ongoing since 1993 under the leadership of Ian Hodder, has called some aspects of this "mother Goddess" interpretation into question. Hodder, for example, doubts the existence of an organized cult with an attached priesthood, as Mellaart theorized. Rather, Hodder noted that the image suggests "a close connection between ritual and daily functions." He added:

> I do not think that there was a separate religious elite. I think the religion was an integral part of daily life. It may be wrong to think of the Çatal art as religious or symbolic at all. It may be more that people thought that they had to paint, or make relief sculptures, in order to achieve certain practical ends (such as make the crops grow, or prevent children from dying).[20]

Furthermore, Hodder suggested that while women were certainly prominent in the symbolism of the village, there is little evidence for a "matriarchal society" in which women dominated. Rather, he wrote that "men and women had the same social status. There was a balance of power."[21]

■ Why do you think the life of this small Neolithic village some 7,000 or more years ago continues to provoke such passionate debate? (You might want to do a little research about the controversies surrounding Çatalhüyük.)

The Neolithic or Agricultural Revolution gave rise not only to settled farming communities but also to pastoral nomadic societies, dependent on their herds of domesticated animals (see p. 63). Nowhere has this transformation been more thoroughly documented than in the rock art of the central Sahara region of Africa. There the domestication of cattle actually preceded the development of farming and from perhaps 4500 B.C.E. or earlier, pastoral societies flourished in the area. Later, horses and camels were introduced into the region as well. Visual Source 2.3, a rock-art painting from Tassili-n-Ajjer, in southeastern Algeria, illustrates the early development of such pastoral societies. The multiple colors of the cattle indicate that they were a long-domesticated species.

■ On the left, women and children are attending a line of calves roped together. What might this suggest to historians seeking to understand this society?

■ How would you describe the activities of the other human figures, presumably men? Does this suggest anything about the division of labor in such societies?

■ Notice that the herd of cattle is portrayed in front of some huts, indicated by stylized circles. What might this indicate about the nature of this community?

■ How might you compare the society depicted in this image with that of Çatalhüyük in Visual Source 2.1?

Among the most famous sites of the early agrarian era is Stonehenge, a series of earthworks accompanied by circles of standing stones located in

Visual Source 2.3 An African Pastoral Community (Henri Lhote)

southern England, where the Agricultural Revolution emerged around 4000 B.C.E. Construction of the Stonehenge site began around 3100 B.C.E. and continued intermittently for another 1,500 years.

■ Have a close look at the aerial photograph of Stonehenge in Visual Source 2.4. How would you describe its major features to someone who had never seen it? What questions about the site come to mind?

Almost everything about Stonehenge has been a matter of controversy and speculation among those scholars who have studied it. Prominent among those debates have been the questions of motivation and function. Why was it constructed? What purposes did it serve for those early farming peoples who used it? The discovery of the cremated remains of some 240 individuals, dating to the first five centuries of its existence, has convinced some scholars that it was a burial site, perhaps for members of a single high-ranking family. It was the "domain of the dead" or an abode of the ancestors, remarked one archeologist, linked ritually perhaps to a nearby village of Durrington Walls, a "land of the living" consisting of 300 to 1,000 homes.[22] Others have cast Stonehenge as an astronomical observatory, aligned with the solstices and able to predict eclipses and the movement of heavenly bodies, or perhaps a center of sun worship. Most recently, it has been depicted as "a place of pilgrimage for the sick and injured of the Neolithic world," based on the number of burials in the area that show signs of serious illness, trauma, or deformity as well as the presence of many bluestone rock chips thought to have magical healing properties.[23]

Whatever its purposes, still other controversies surround the manner of its construction. How were those huge slabs of rock, some as heavy as fifty tons and others coming from a location 240 miles away, transported to Stonehenge and put into place? Were they dragged overland or transported partway by boat along the Avon River? Or did the movement of earlier glaciers deposit them in the region?

Visual Source 2.4 The Mystery of Stonehenge (© Skyscan/Corbis)

■ What does a structure of the magnitude of Stonehenge suggest about the Neolithic societies that created it?

■ What kinds of additional evidence would be most useful to scholars seeking to puzzle out the mysteries of Stonehenge?

The first millennium B.C.E. witnessed the flourishing of an impressive artistic tradition, arising out of the Nok culture, among the agricultural peoples of what is now northern Nigeria. Unlike the earlier Neolithic peoples highlighted in this section, they had learned to make and use iron. Amid the stone axes, iron implements, and pottery found in the region, the material remains of this ancient African culture also yielded a treasure of terra-cotta (fired clay) figures, often life-size, depicting animals and especially people. The highly stylized human figures shared several features: elongated heads often disproportionately large in comparison to their bodies; triangular eyes; pierced noses,

Visual Source 2.5 A Sculpture from the Nok Culture
(Musée du Quai Branly/Scala/Art Resource, NY)

pupils, ears, and lips (perhaps to vent the air during the firing process); and elaborate attention to hairstyles, ornamentation, and dress. The artistic sophistication of these pieces has suggested to some scholars that their creators drew on an even earlier, as yet undiscovered, tradition. Some similarities with much later sculptures from Ife and Benin in southern Nigeria suggest the possibility of a long-lasting and widespread artistic tradition in West Africa. Visual Source 2.5 presents one of these Nok sculptures, dating to somewhere between 600 B.C.E. and 600 C.E.

■ What features of Nok sculpture, described above, can you identify in this figure?

■ How might you describe the mood that this figure evokes? Some scholars have dubbed this and many similar Nok sculptures "thinkers." Does it seem more likely that this notion reflects a present-day sensibility or that it might be an insight into the mentality of the ancient artist who created the image? Why?

■ What might you infer about the status of the person represented in this sculpture?

■ No one actually knows the purpose of these works. What possibilities come to mind as you consider Visual Source 2.5?

Using the Evidence:
Art and Life in the Early Agrarian Era

1. **Assessing personal reactions:** How do you respond personally to Visual Sources 2.1–2.5? What do you find surprising or impressive about them? Which of them are most accessible to a person of the early twenty-first century? Which are least accessible? Do you find these images easier to understand than the Paleolithic rock art featured in Chapter 1? Why or why not?

2. **Considering art as evidence:** What insights about early agrarian life might we derive from these images? In what ways do they reflect the technological or economic changes of the Agricultural Revolution?

3. **Reflecting on speculation:** You will notice that our understanding of all of these works is highly uncertain, inviting a considerable amount of speculation, guesswork, or imagination. Why are historians willing to articulate uncertain interpretations of ancient art? Is this an appropriate undertaking for historians, or should scholars remain silent when the evidence does not allow them to speak with certainty and authority?

CHAPTER THREE

First Civilizations

Cities, States, and Unequal Societies

3500 B.C.E.—500 B.C.E.

Something New: The Emergence of
Civilizations
  Introducing the First Civilizations
  The Question of Origins
  An Urban Revolution
The Erosion of Equality
  Hierarchies of Class
  Hierarchies of Gender
  Patriarchy in Practice
The Rise of the State
  Coercion and Consent
  Writing and Accounting
  The Grandeur of Kings
Comparing Mesopotamia
  and Egypt
  Environment and Culture
  Cities and States
  Interaction and Exchange
Reflections: "Civilization": What's
  in a Word?
Considering the Evidence
  Documents: Life and Afterlife in
    Mesopotamia and Egypt
  Visual Sources: Indus Valley
    Civilization

"Over 100 miles of wilderness, deep exploration into pristine lands, the solitude of backcountry camping, 4×4 trails, and ancient American Indian rock art and ruins. You can't find a better way to escape civilization!"[1] So goes an advertisement for a vacation in Utah's Canyonlands National Park, one of thousands of similar attempts to lure apparently constrained, beleaguered, and "civilized" city-dwellers into the spacious freedom of the wild and the imagined simplicity of earlier times. This urge to "escape from civilization" has long been a central feature in modern life. It is a major theme in Mark Twain's famous novel *The Adventures of Huckleberry Finn*, in which the restless and rebellious Huck resists all efforts to "sivilize" him by fleeing to the freedom of life on the river. It is a large part of the "cowboy" image in American culture, and it permeates environmentalist efforts to protect the remaining wilderness areas of the country. Nor has this impulse been limited to modern societies and the Western world. The ancient Chinese teachers of Daoism likewise urged their followers to abandon the structured and demanding world of urban and civilized life and to immerse themselves in the eternal patterns of the natural order. It is a strange paradox that we count the creation of civilization among the major achievements of humankind and yet people within these civilizations have often sought to escape the constraints, artificiality, hierarchies, and other discontents of city living.

WHAT EXACTLY ARE THESE CIVILIZATIONS that have generated such ambivalent responses among their inhabitants? When, where,

Raherka and Mersankh: Writing was among the defining features of civilizations almost everywhere. In ancient Egyptian civilization, the scribes who possessed this skill enjoyed both social prestige and political influence. This famous statue shows Raherka, the chief of the scribes during Egypt's Fifth Dynasty (about 2350 B.C.E.), in an affectionate pose with his wife, Mersankh. (Réunion des Musées Nationaux/Art Resource, NY)

and how did they first arise in human history? What changes did they bring to the people who lived within them? Why might some people criticize or seek to escape from them? These are the issues addressed in this chapter.

As historians commonly use the term, civilization represents a new and particular type of human society, made possible by the immense productivity of the Agricultural Revolution. Such societies encompassed far larger populations than any earlier form of human community and for the first time concentrated some of those people in sizable cities, numbering in the many tens of thousands. In these cities, people were organized and controlled by powerful states whose leaders could use force to compel obedience. Profound differences in economic function, skill, wealth, and status sharply divided the people of civilizations, making them far less equal, and subject to much greater oppression, than had been the case in earlier agricultural villages, pastoral societies, and chiefdoms. Pyramids, temples, palaces, elaborate sculptures, written literature, complex calendars, as well as class, slavery, patriarchy, and large-scale warfare—all of these have been among the cultural products of civilization.

Something New: The Emergence of Civilizations

■ **Change**

When and where did the First Civilizations emerge?

Like agriculture, civilization was a global phenomenon, showing up independently in six major locations scattered around the world during the several millennia after 3500 B.C.E. and in a number of other smaller expressions as well (see Map 3.1). At the time, these breakthroughs to a new way of life were small islands of innovation in a sea of people living in much older ways. In the long run of human history, however, civilizations gradually absorbed, overran, or displaced people practicing other ways of living. Over the next 5,000 years, civilization, as a unique kind of human community, gradually encompassed ever-larger numbers of people and extended over ever-larger territories, even as particular civilizations rose, fell, revived, and changed.

Introducing the First Civilizations

The earliest of these civilizations emerged around 3500 B.C.E. to 3000 B.C.E. in three places. One was the "cradle" of Middle Eastern civilization, expressed in the many and competing city-states of Sumer in southern Mesopotamia (located in present-day Iraq). Much studied by archeologists and historians, Sumerian civilization gave rise to the world's earliest written language, which was used initially by officials to record the goods received by various temples. Almost simultaneously, the Nile River valley in northeastern Africa witnessed the emergence of Egyptian civilization, famous for its pharaohs and pyramids, as well as a separate civilization known as Nubia, farther south along the Nile. Unlike the city-states of Sumer, Egyptian civilization took shape as a unified territorial state in which cities were rather less prominent. Later in this chapter, we will explore these two First Civilizations in greater detail.

Less well known and only recently investigated by scholars was a third early civilization that was developing along the central coast of Peru from roughly 3000 B.C.E. to 1800 B.C.E., at about the same time as the civilizations of Egypt and Sumer. This desert region received very little rainfall, but it was punctuated by dozens of rivers that brought the snowmelt of the adjacent Andes Mountains to the Pacific Ocean. Along a thirty-mile stretch of that coast and in the nearby interior, a series of some twenty-five urban centers emerged in an area known as Norte Chico, the largest of which was Caral, in the Supe River valley. In Norte Chico, archeologists have found monumental architecture in the form of earthen platform mounds, one of them measuring 60 feet tall and 500 feet long, as well as large public ceremonial structures, stone buildings with residential apartments, and other signs of urban life.

Norte Chico was a distinctive civilization in many ways. Its cities were smaller than those of Mesopotamia and show less evidence of economic specialization. The economy was based to an unusual degree on an extremely rich fishing industry in anchovies and sardines along the coast. These items apparently were exchanged for cotton, essential for fishing nets, as well as food crops such as squash, beans, and guava, all of which were grown by inland people in the river valleys using irrigation agriculture. Unlike Egypt and Mesopotamia, Peruvian civilization did not rest upon grain-based farming; the people of Norte Chico did not develop pottery or writing; and few sculptures, carvings, or drawings have been uncovered so far. Archeologists have, however, found a 5,000-year-old *quipu* (a series of knotted cords, later used extensively by the Inca for accounting purposes), which some scholars have suggested may have been an alternative form of writing. Furthermore, the cities of Norte Chico lacked defensive walls, and archeologists have discovered little evidence of warfare, such as burned buildings and mutilated corpses. It was also an unusually self-contained civilization. Whereas Egypt and Mesopotamia had long interacted with each other, the only import from the outside world evident in Norte Chico, or in Andean civilization generally, was maize (corn), which was derived ultimately from Mesoamerica, though without direct contact between the two regions. Norte Chico apparently "lighted a cultural fire" in the Andes and established a pattern for the many Andean civilizations that followed—Chavín, Moche, Nazca, and, much later, the Inca.[2]

Somewhat later, three additional First Civilizations made their appearance. In the Indus and Saraswati river valleys of what is now Pakistan, a remarkable civilization arose during the third millennium B.C.E. By 2000 B.C.E., it embraced a far larger area than Mesopotamia, Egypt, or coastal Peru and was expressed primarily in its elaborately planned cities. All across this huge area, about twice the size of Texas, common patterns prevailed: standardized weights, measures, architectural styles, even the size of bricks. As elsewhere, irrigated agriculture provided the economic foundation for the civilization, and a written language, thus far undeciphered, provides evidence of a literate culture.

Unlike its Middle Eastern counterparts, the Indus Valley civilization apparently generated no palaces, temples, elaborate graves, kings, or warrior classes. In short,

Map 3.1 First Civilizations

Six First Civilizations emerged independently in locations scattered across the planet, all within a few thousand years, from 3500 to 1000 B.C.E.

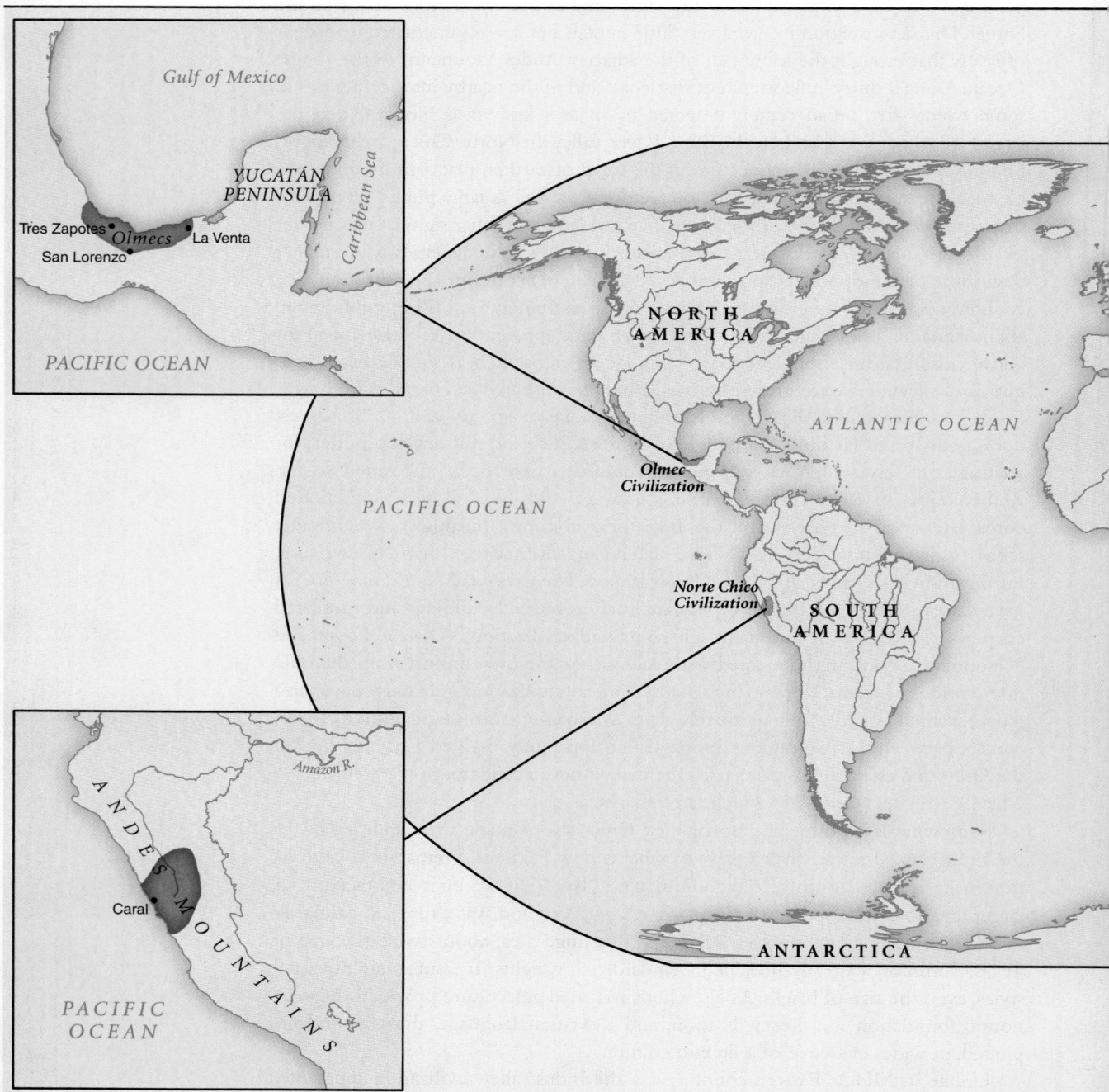

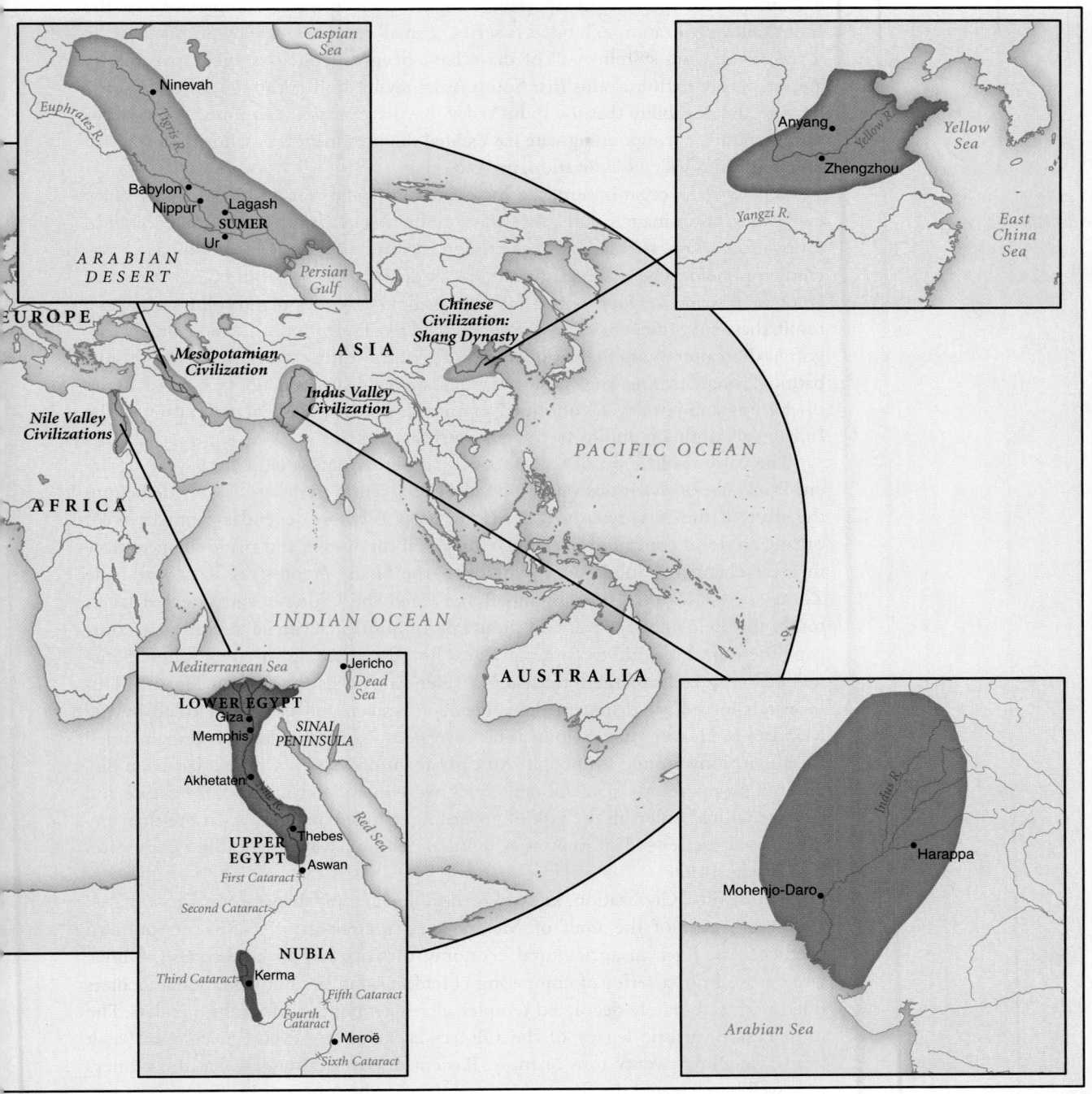

Caspian
Sea

Euphrates R.

Ninevah

Tigris R.

Babylon
Nippur   Lagash
                SUMER
                Ur

ARABIAN
DESERT   Persian
                        Gulf

EUROPE

ASIA

Mesopotamian
Civilization

Chinese
Civilization:
Shang Dynasty

Indus Valley
Civilization

Anyang
          Zhengzhou

Yellow
River

Yellow
Sea

East
China
Sea

Yangzi R.

Nile Valley
Civilizations

AFRICA

PACIFIC OCEAN

INDIAN OCEAN

AUSTRALIA

Mediterranean Sea   Jericho
                       Dead
                       Sea

LOWER EGYPT
     Giza
     Memphis   SINAI
                      PENINSULA
     Akhetaten

                      Red Sea

          Thebes
UPPER
EGYPT   Aswan
First Cataract

Second Cataract

          NUBIA
Third Cataract Kerma
                    Fifth Cataract
          Fourth
          Cataract

              Meroë
                Sixth Cataract

Indus R.

Harappa

Mohenjo-Daro

Arabian Sea

the archeological evidence provides little indication of a political hierarchy or centralized state. This absence of evidence has sent scholars scrambling to provide an explanation for the obvious specialization, coordination, and complexity that the Indus Valley civilization exhibited. A series of small republics, rule by priests, an early form of the caste system—all of these have been suggested as alternative mechanisms of integration in this first South Asian civilization. Although no one knows for sure, the possibility that the Indus Valley may have housed a sophisticated civilization without a corresponding state has excited the imagination of scholars. (See Visual Sources: Indus Valley Civilization, pp. 126–31.)

Whatever its organization, the local environmental impact of the Indus Valley civilization, as in many others, was heavy and eventually undermined its ecological foundations. Repeated irrigation increased the amount of salt in the soil and lowered crop yields. The making of mud bricks, dried in ovens, required an enormous amount of wood for fuel, generating large-scale deforestation and soil erosion. As a result, these magnificent cities were abandoned by about 1700 B.C.E. and largely forgotten thereafter. Nonetheless, many features of this early civilization—ceremonial bathing, ritual burning, yoga positions, bulls and elephants as religious symbols, styles of clothing and jewelry—continued to nourish the later classical civilization of the Indian subcontinent and in fact persist into the present.[3]

The early civilization of China, dating to perhaps 2200 B.C.E., was very different from that of the Indus Valley. The ideal of a centralized state was evident from the days of the Xia dynasty (2200–1766 B.C.E.), whose legendary monarch Wu organized flood control projects that "mastered the waters and made them to flow in great channels." Subsequent dynasties—the Shang (1766–1122 B.C.E.) and the Zhou (1122–256 B.C.E.)—substantially enlarged the Chinese state, erected lavish tombs for their rulers, and buried thousands of human sacrificial victims to accompany them in the world to come. By the Zhou dynasty, a distinctive Chinese political ideology had emerged, featuring a ruler, known as the Son of Heaven. This monarch served as an intermediary between heaven and earth and ruled by the Mandate of Heaven only so long as he governed with benevolence and maintained social harmony among his people. An early form of written Chinese has been discovered on numerous oracle bones, which were intended to predict the future and to assist China's rulers in the task of governing. Chinese civilization, more than any other, has experienced an impressive cultural continuity from its earliest expression into modern times.

A final First Civilization, known as the Olmec, took shape around 1200 B.C.E. along the coast of the Gulf of Mexico near present-day Veracruz in southern Mexico. Based on an agricultural economy of maize, beans, and squash, Olmec cities arose from a series of competing chiefdoms and became ceremonial centers filled with elaborately decorated temples, altars, pyramids, and tombs of rulers. The most famous artistic legacy of the Olmecs lay in some seventeen colossal basalt heads, weighing twenty tons or more. Recent discoveries suggest that the Olmecs may well have created the first written language in the Americas by about 900 B.C.E.

Sometimes regarded as the "mother civilization" of Mesoamerica, Olmec cultural patterns—mound building, artistic styles, urban planning, a game played with a rubber ball, ritual sacrifice, and bloodletting by rulers—spread widely throughout the region and influenced subsequent civilizations, such as the Maya and Teotihuacán.

Beyond these six First Civilizations, other, smaller civilizations also flourished. Lying south of Egypt in the Nile Valley, Nubian civilization was clearly distinctive and independent of its northern neighbor, although Nubia was involved in a long and often contentious relationship with Egypt. Likewise in China, a large city known as Sanxingdui, rich in bronze sculptures

Shang Dynasty Bronze
This bronze tiger, created around 1100 B.C.E., illustrates Chinese skill in working with bronze and the mythological or religious significance of the tiger as a messenger between heaven and the human world. (Jiangxi Provincial Museum, Nanchang/Visual Connection Archive)

and much else, arose separately but at the same time as the more well-known Shang dynasty. As a new way of living and a new form of human society, civilization was beginning its long march toward encompassing almost all of humankind by the twentieth century.

The Question of Origins

The first question that historians ask about almost everything is "How did it get started?" Scholars of all kinds—archeologists, anthropologists, sociologists, and historians—have been arguing about the origins of civilization for a very long time, with no end in sight.[4] Amid all the controversy, one thing seems reasonably clear: civilizations had their roots in the Agricultural Revolution. That is the reason they appeared so late in the human story, for only an agricultural technology permitted human communities to produce sufficient surplus to support large populations and the specialized or elite minorities who did not themselves produce food. Furthermore, all of the First Civilizations emerged from earlier and competing chiefdoms, in which some social ranking and economic specialization had already developed. It was a gradual and evolutionary process. However, not all agricultural societies or chiefdoms developed into civilizations, so something else must have been involved. It is the search for this "something else" that has provoked such great debate among scholars.

Some scholars have emphasized the need to organize large-scale irrigation projects as a stimulus for the earliest civilizations, but archeologists have found that the more complex water control systems appeared long after states and civilizations

■ Change
What accounts for the initial breakthroughs to civilization?

had already been established. Others have suggested that powerful states were useful in protecting the privileges of favored groups. Warfare and trade have figured in still other explanations for the rise of civilizations. Anthropologist Robert Carneiro combined several of these factors in a thoughtful approach to the question.[5] He argued that a growing density of population, producing more congested and competitive societies, was a fundamental motor of change, and especially in areas where rich agricultural land was limited, either by geography (oceans, deserts, mountains) or by powerful competing societies. Such settings provided incentives for innovations, such as irrigation or plows that could produce more food, because opportunities for territorial expansion were not readily available. But circumscribed environments with dense populations also generated intense competition among rival groups, which led to repeated warfare. A strong and highly organized state was a decided advantage in such competition. Because losers could not easily flee to new lands, they were absorbed into the winner's society as a lower class. Successful leaders of the winning side emerged as an elite with an enlarged base of land, a class of subordinated workers, and a powerful state at their disposal—in short, a civilization.

Although such a process was relatively rapid by world history standards, it took many generations, centuries, or perhaps millennia to evolve. It was, of course, an unconscious undertaking in which the participants had little sense of the long-term outcome as they coped with the practical problems of survival on a day-to-day basis. What is surprising, though, is the rough similarity of the result in many widely separated places from about 3500 B.C.E. to the beginning of the Common Era.

However they got started (and much about this is still guesswork), the First Civilizations, once established, represented a very different kind of human society than anything that came before. All of them were based on highly productive agricultural economies. Various forms of irrigation, drainage, terracing, and flood control enabled these early civilizations to tap the food-producing potential of their regions. In dry lands with good soil, such as northern China and southern Iraq, water made all the difference and vastly increased the agricultural output. In all these civilizations, pottery likewise enhanced the productivity of farming, as did animal-drawn plows and metalworking in Afro-Eurasia. Ritual sacrifice, often including people, usually accompanied the growth of civilization, and the new rulers normally served as high priests or were seen as divine beings, their right to rule legitimated by association with the sacred.

An Urban Revolution

■ **Change**
What was the role of cities in the early civilizations?

It was the resources from agriculture that made possible one of the most distinctive features of the First Civilizations—cities. What would an agricultural villager have made of Uruk, ancient Mesopotamia's largest city? Uruk had walls more than twenty feet tall and a population around 50,000 in the third millennium B.C.E. The city's center, visible for miles around, was a stepped pyramid, or ziggurat, topped with a temple (see the photo on p. 100). Inside the city, our village visitor would have found other temples as well, serving as centers of worship and as places for the redistribution of stored food. Numerous craftspeople labored as masons, copper workers, weavers, and in many other specialties, while bureaucrats helped administer the city. It was, surely, a "vibrant, noisy, smelly, sometimes bewildering and dangerous, but also exciting place."[6] Here is how the *Epic of Gilgamesh*, Mesopotamia's ancient epic poem, describes the city:

> Come then, Enkidu, to ramparted Uruk,
> Where fellows are resplendent in holiday clothing,
> Where every day is set for celebration,
> Where harps and drums are played.
> And the harlots too, they are fairest of form,
> Rich in beauty, full of delights,
> Even the great gods are kept from sleeping at night.[7]

Equally impressive to a village visitor would have been the city of Mohenjo Daro, which flourished along the banks of the Indus River around 2000 B.C.E. With a population of perhaps 40,000, Mohenjo Daro and its sister city of Harappa featured large, richly built houses of two or three stories, complete with indoor plumbing, luxurious bathrooms, and private wells. Streets were laid out in a gridlike pattern, and beneath the streets ran a complex sewage system. Workers lived in row upon row of standardized two-room houses. Grand public buildings, including what seems to be a huge public bath, graced the city, while an enormous citadel was surrounded by a brick wall some forty-five feet high (see Visual Source 3.1, p. 127).

Even larger, though considerably later, was the Mesoamerican city of Teotihuacán, located in the central valley of Mexico. It housed perhaps 200,000 people in the middle of the first millennium C.E. Broad avenues, dozens of temples, two huge pyramids, endless stone carvings and many bright frescoes, small apartments for the ordinary, palatial homes for the wealthy—all of this must have seemed another world for a new visitor from a distant village. In shopping for obsidian blades, how was she to decide among the 350 workshops in the city? In seeking relatives, how could she find her way among many different compounds, each surrounded by a wall and housing a different lineage? And what would she make of a neighborhood composed entirely of Mayan merchants from the distant coastal lowlands?

Cities, then, lay at the heart of all of the First Civilizations. They were

Mohenjo Daro
Flourishing around 2000 B.C.E., Mohenjo Daro was by far the largest city of the Indus Valley civilization, covering more than 600 acres. This photograph shows a small part of that city as it has been uncovered by archeologists during the past century. The large watertight tank or pool, shown in the foreground, probably offered bathers an opportunity for ritual purification. In the ruins of Mohenjo Daro, writes archeologist Gregory Possehl, "one can walk down streets well defined by the high walls of homes and other buildings, climb the stairways used in antiquity, peer down ancient wells, and stand in bathing rooms used over 4,000 years ago." (Harappa Images)

political/administrative capitals; they were centers for the production of culture, including art, architecture, literature, ritual, and ceremony; they served as marketplaces for both local and long-distance exchange; and they housed most manufacturing activity. Everywhere they generated a unique kind of society, compared to earlier agricultural villages. Urban society was impersonal, for it was no longer possible to know everyone. Relationships of class and occupation were at least as important as those of kinship and village loyalty. Most notably, the degree of specialization and inequality far surpassed that of all preceding human communities.

The Erosion of Equality

Among the most novel features of early urban life, at least to our imaginary village visitor, was the amazing specialization of work. In Document 3.5 (pp. 123–25), an Egyptian teacher tries to persuade a reluctant student, preparing to be a scribe (a literate public official), to take his lessons seriously by pointing out the disadvantages of the many other occupations that await him. In ancient Mesopotamia, even scribes were subdivided into many categories: junior and senior scribes, temple scribes and royal scribes, scribes for particular administrative or official functions.[8] None of these people, of course, grew their own food; they were supported by the highly productive agriculture of farmers.

Hierarchies of Class

■ Change
In what ways was social inequality expressed in early civilizations?

Alongside the occupational specialization of the First Civilizations lay their vast inequalities—in wealth, status, and power. Here we confront a remarkable and persistent feature of the human journey. As ingenuity and technology created more-productive economies, the greater wealth now available to societies was everywhere piled up rather than spread out. Early signs of this erosion of equality were evident in the more settled and complex gathering and hunting societies such as the Chumash and in agricultural chiefdoms such as Cahokia, but the advent of urban-based civilizations multiplied and magnified these inequalities many times over, as the egalitarian values of earlier cultures were everywhere displaced. This transition represents one of the major turning points in the social history of humankind.

As the First Civilizations took shape, inequality and hierarchy soon came to be regarded as normal and natural. Upper classes everywhere enjoyed great wealth in land or salaries, were able to avoid physical labor, had the finest of everything, and occupied the top positions in political, military, and religious life. Frequently, they were distinguished by the clothing they wore, the houses they lived in, and the manner of their burial. Early Chinese monarchs bestowed special clothing, banners, chariots, weapons, and ornaments on their regional officials, and all of these items were graded according to the officials' precise location in the hierarchy. In Mesopotamia, the punishments prescribed in the famous Code of Hammurabi depended on social status (see Document 3.2, pp. 118–21). A free-born commoner who struck a person of equal rank had to pay a small fine, but if he struck "a man who is his superior, he shall receive 60 strokes with an oxtail whip in public." Clearly, class had consequences.

In all civilizations, free commoners represented the vast majority of the population and included artisans of all kinds, lower-level officials, soldiers and police, servants, and, most numerous of all, farmers. It was their surplus production—appropriated through a variety of taxes, rents, required labor, and tribute payments—that supported the upper classes. At least some of these people were aware of, and resented, these forced extractions and their position in the social hierarchy. Most Chinese peasants, for example, owned little land of their own and worked on plots granted to them by royal or aristocratic landowners. An ancient poem compared the exploiting landlords to rats and expressed the farmers' vision of a better life:

> Large rats! Large rats!
> Do not eat our spring grain!
> Three years have we had to do with you.
> And you have not been willing to think of our toil.
> We will leave you,
> And go to those happy borders.
> Happy borders, happy borders!
> Who will there make us always to groan?[9]

At the bottom of social hierarchies everywhere were slaves. Slavery and civilization, in fact, seem to have emerged together. (For early references to slavery, see Document 3.2, pp. 118–21). Female slaves, captured in the many wars among rival Mesopotamian cities, were put to work in large-scale semi-industrial weaving enterprises, while males helped to maintain irrigation canals and construct ziggurats. Others worked as domestic servants in the households of their owners. In all of the First Civilizations, slaves—derived from prisoners of war, criminals, and debtors— were available for sale; for work in the fields, mines, homes, and shops of their owner; or on occasion for sacrifice. From the days of the earliest civilizations until the nineteenth century, the practice of "people owning people" was an enduring feature of state-based societies everywhere.

The practice of slavery in ancient times varied considerably from place to place. Egypt and the Indus Valley civilizations initially had far fewer slaves than did Mesopotamia, which was highly militarized. Later, the Greeks of Athens and the Romans employed slaves far more extensively than did the Chinese or Indians (see Chapter 6). Furthermore, most ancient slavery differed from the type of slavery practiced in the Americas during recent centuries; in the early civilizations, slaves were not a primary agricultural labor force, many children of slaves could become free people, and slavery was not associated primarily with "blackness" or with Africa.

Hierarchies of Gender

■ Change

In what ways have historians tried to explain the origins of patriarchy?

Accompanying the hierarchies of class were those of gender, as civilizations everywhere undermined the earlier and more equal relationships between men and women. Most scholars agree that early horticultural societies, those using a hoe or digging stick, continued the relative gender equality that had characterized Paleolithic peoples. In such societies, women were much involved in agricultural labor, which generated most of the food for the village. Women were also engaged in spinning, weaving, and pottery making—activities that were compatible with their role as mothers. Their central economic function, together with their amazing capacity to produce new life, gave women considerable respect and, arguably, a status generally equal to that of men. Some scholars have seen this respect and status reflected, at least in Europe and the Middle East, in a proliferation of figurines, masks, signs, symbols, and myths, all featuring women and feminine themes dealing with birth, growth, death, and regeneration.[10]

But as the First Civilizations took shape, the institutions and values of male dominance, often referred to as patriarchy, gradually emerged. The big question, of course, lies in trying to explain this momentous change. What was it about civilization that seemed to generate patriarchy?

One approach to answering this question highlights the role of a new and more intensive form of agriculture, involving the use of animal-drawn plows and the keeping and milking of large herds of animals. Unlike earlier farming practices that relied on a hoe or digging stick, plow-based agriculture meant heavier work, which men were better able to perform. Taking place at a distance from the village, this new form of agriculture was perhaps less compatible with women's primary responsibility for child rearing. Furthermore, the growing population of civilizations meant that women were more often pregnant and even more deeply involved in child care than before. Thus, in plow-based communities, men took over most of the farming work, and the status of women declined correspondingly, even though their other productive activities—weaving and food preparation, for example—continued. "As women were increasingly relegated to secondary tasks . . . ," writes archeologist Margaret Ehrenberg, "they had fewer personal resources with which to assert their status."[11]

Because patriarchy also developed in civilizations untouched by plow agriculture, such as those of Mesoamerica and the Andes, perhaps something else was at work as well. Historian David Christian suggests that the declining position of women was connected more generally to the growth of social complexity in civilizations as economic, religious, and political "specialists" became more prominent. Because men were less important in the household, they may have been more available to assume the powerful and prestigious specialist roles. From these positions of authority, men were able to shape the values and practices of their societies in ways that benefited themselves at the expense of women. Here, perhaps, lies the origin of an ancient distinction between the realm of the home, defined as the domain of women, and the world of public life, associated with men.[12]

Women have long been identified not only with the home but also with nature, for they are intimately involved in the fundamental natural process of reproduction. But civilization seemed to highlight culture, or the human mastery of nature, through agriculture, monumental art and architecture, and the creation of large-scale cities and states. Did this mean, as some scholars have suggested, that women were now associated with an inferior dimension of human life (nature), while men assumed responsibility for the higher order of culture?[13]

A further aspect of civilization that may well have contributed to patriarchy was warfare. Large-scale military conflict with professionally led armies was a feature of almost all of the First Civilizations, and female prisoners of war often were the first slaves. With military service largely restricted to men, its growing prominence in the affairs of civilizations served to enhance the power and prestige of a male warrior class. So too, perhaps, did private property and commerce, central elements of the First Civilizations. Without sharp restrictions on women's sexual activity, how could a father be certain that family property would be inherited by his offspring? In addition, the buying and selling associated with commerce were soon applied to male rights over women, as female slaves, concubines, and wives were exchanged among men.

Patriarchy in Practice

Whatever the precise origins of patriarchy, male dominance permeated the First Civilizations, marking a gradual change from the more equal relationships of men and women within agricultural villages or Paleolithic bands. Historian Gerda Lerner documented this transition in ancient Mesopotamian civilization. By the second millennium B.C.E., various written laws codified and sought to enforce a patriarchal family life that offered women a measure of paternalistic protection while insisting on their submission to the unquestioned authority of men. Central to these laws was the regulation of female sexuality. A wife caught sleeping with another man might be drowned at her husband's discretion, whereas he was permitted to enjoy sexual relations with his female servants, though not with another man's wife. Divorce was far easier for the husband than for the wife. Rape was a serious offense, but the injured party was primarily the father or the husband of the victim, rather than the violated woman herself. Even elite women, who were often allowed to act on behalf of their powerful husbands, saw themselves as dependent. "Let all be well with [my husband]," prayed one such wife, "that I may prosper under his protection."[14]

■ **Comparison**
How did Mesopotamian and Egyptian patriarchy differ from each other?

Furthermore, women in Mesopotamian civilization were sometimes divided into two sharply distinguished categories. Respectable women, those under the protection and sexual control of one man, were required to be veiled when outside the home, whereas nonrespectable women, such as slaves and prostitutes, were forbidden to wear veils and were subject to severe punishment if they presumed to cover their heads.

Finally, the powerful goddesses of earlier times were gradually relegated to the home and hearth. They were replaced in the public arena by dominant male deities, who now were credited with the power of creation and fertility and viewed as the patrons of wisdom and learning. The culmination of this "demotion of the goddess," argues Gerda Lerner, lies in the Hebrew Scriptures, in which a single male deity, Yahweh, alone undertakes the act of creation without any participation of a female goddess.

Patriarchy was not everywhere the same, however. Egypt, while clearly patriarchal, afforded its women greater opportunities than did most other First Civilizations. In Egypt, women were recognized as legal equals to men, able to own property and slaves, to administer and sell land, to make their own wills, to sign their own marriage contracts, and to initiate divorce. Royal women occasionally exercised significant political power, acting as regents for their young sons or, more rarely, as queens in their own right. Clearly, though, this was seen as abnormal, for Egypt's most famous queen, Hatshepsut (reigned 1472–1457 B.C.E.), was sometimes portrayed in statues as a man, dressed in male clothing and sporting the traditional false beard of the pharaoh. Moreover, married women in Egypt were not veiled as in Mesopotamia. Statues and paintings often showed men and women in affectionate poses and as equal partners, as can be seen in the photo (p. 84) at the beginning of this chapter. Although marriages were clearly arranged by parents, the love poetry of New Kingdom Egypt (1550–1064 B.C.E.) suggests an element of romance and longing. One lovesick boy lamented the absence of his beloved, referred to as a "sister":

> Seven days since I saw my sister,
> and sickness invaded me; . . .
> The sight of her makes me well . . .
> Her speaking makes me strong;
> Embracing her expels my malady. . . .

And a young woman exults at the sight of her love:

> I passed before his house,
> I found his door ajar;
> My brother stood by his mother; . . .
> He looked at me as I passed by, . . .
> How my heart exulted in gladness,
> My brother, at your sight.[15]

The Rise of the State

What, we might reasonably ask, held ancient civilizations together despite the many tensions and complexities of urban living and the vast inequalities of civilized societies? Why did they not fly apart amid the resentments born of class and gender hierarchies? The answer, in large part, lay in yet another distinctive feature of the First Civilizations—states. Organized around particular cities or larger territories, early states were headed almost everywhere by kings, who employed a variety of ranked officials, exercised a measure of control over society, and defended the state against external enemies. To modern people, the state is such a familiar reality that we find it difficult to imagine life without it. Nonetheless, it is a quite recent invention in human history, with the state replacing, or at least supplementing, kinship as the basic organizing principle of society and exercising far greater authority than earlier chiefdoms.

Coercion and Consent

Early states in Mesopotamia, Egypt, China, Mesoamerica, and elsewhere drew their power from various sources, all of which assisted in providing cohesion for the First Civilizations. One basis of power was the recognition that the complexity of life in cities or densely populated territories required some authority to coordinate and regulate the community. Someone had to organize the irrigation systems of river valley civilizations. Someone had to adjudicate conflicts among the many different peoples, unrelated to one another, who rubbed elbows in the early cities. Someone had to direct efforts to defend the city or territory against aggressive outsiders. The state, in short, solved certain widely shared problems and therefore had a measure of voluntary support among the population. For many people, it was surely useful.

■ **Change**
What were the sources of state authority in the First Civilizations?

The state, however, was more useful for some people than for others, for it also served to protect the privileges of the upper classes, to require farmers to give up a portion of their product to support city-dwellers, and to demand work on large public projects such as pyramids and fortifications. If necessary, state authorities had the ability, and the willingness, to use force to compel obedience. The Egyptian teacher mentioned earlier described to his reluctant student what happens to a peasant unable to pay his tax in grain:

> Now the scribe lands on the shore. He surveys the harvest. Attendants are behind him with staffs, Nubians with clubs. One says [to the peasant], "Give grain." There is none. He is beaten savagely. He is bound, thrown into a well, submerged head down. His wife is bound in his presence. His children are in fetters. His neighbors abandon them and flee.[16]

Such was the power of the state, as rulers accumulated the resources to pay for officials, soldiers, police, and attendants. This capacity for violence and coercion marked

A Mesopotamian Ziggurat
This massive ziggurat/temple to the Mesopotamian moon god Nanna was built around 2100 B.C.E. in the city of Ur. The solitary figure standing atop the staircase illustrates the size of this huge structure. (Richard Ashworth/Robert Harding World Imagery/Corbis)

off the states of the First Civilizations from earlier chiefdoms, whose leaders had only persuasion, prestige, and gifts to back up their authority.

Force, however, was not always necessary, for the First Civilizations soon generated ideas suggesting that state authority and class and gender inequalities were normal, natural, and ordained by the gods. Kingship everywhere was associated with the sacred. Ancient Chinese kings were known as the Son of Heaven, and they alone could perform the rituals and sacrifices necessary to keep the cosmos in balance. Mesopotamian rulers were thought to be the stewards of their city's patron gods. Their symbols of kingship—crown, throne, scepter, mace—were said to be of divine origin, sent to earth when the gods established monarchy. Egyptians, most of all, invested their pharaohs with divine qualities. Rulers claimed to embody all the major gods of Egypt, and their supernatural power ensured the regular flooding of the Nile and the defeat of the country's enemies.

But if religion served most often to justify unequal power and privilege, it might also on occasion be used to restrain, or even undermine, the established order. Hammurabi claimed that his law code was inspired by Marduk, the chief god of Babylon, and was intended to "bring about the rule of righteousness in the land, to destroy the wicked and the evil-doers; so that the strong should not harm the weak."[17] Another Mesopotamian monarch, Urukagina from the city of Lagash, claimed authority from the city's patron god for reforms aimed at ending the corruption and tyranny of a previous ruler. In China during the Zhou dynasty (1122–256 B.C.E.), emperors ruled by the Mandate of Heaven, but their bad behavior could result in the removal of that mandate and their overthrow.

Writing and Accounting

A further support for state authority lay in the remarkable invention of writing. It was a powerful and transforming innovation, regarded almost everywhere as a gift from the gods, while people without writing often saw it as something magical or supernatural. Distinctive forms of writing emerged in all of the First Civilizations

Snapshot Writing in Ancient Civilizations

Most of the early writing systems were "logophonetic," using symbols to designate both whole words and particular sounds or syllables. Chinese characters, which indicated only words, were an exception. None of the early writing systems employed alphabets.

Location	Type	Initial Use	Example	Comment
Sumer	Cuneiform: wedge-shaped symbols on clay tablets representing objects, abstract ideas, sounds, and syllables	Records of economic transactions, such as temple payments and taxes	bird	Regarded as the world's first written language; other languages such as Babylonian and Assryian were written with Sumerian script
Egypt	Hieroglyphs ("sacred carvings"): a series of signs that denote words and consonants (but not vowels or syllables)	Business and administrative purposes; later used for religious inscriptions, stories, poetry, hymns, and mathematics	rain, dew, storm	For everyday use, less formal systems of cursive writing (known as "hieratic" and "demotic") were developed
Andes	Quipu: a complex system of knotted cords in which the color, length, type, and location of knots conveyed mostly numerical meaning	Various accounting functions; perhaps also used to express words	numerical data (possibly in codes), words, and ideas	Widely used in the Inca Empire; recent discoveries place quipus in Caral some 5,000 years ago
Indus River Valley	Some 400 pictographic symbols representing sounds and words, probably expressing a Dravidian language currently spoken in southern India	Found on thousands of clay seals and pottery; probably used to mark merchandise	6 fish	As yet undeciphered
China	Oracle bone script: pictographs (stylized drawings) with no phonetic meaning	Inscribed on turtle shells or animal bones; used for divination (predicting the future) in the royal court of Shang dynasty rulers	horse	Direct ancestor of contemporary Chinese characters
Olmec	Signs that represent sounds (syllables) and words; numbering system using bars and dots	Used to record the names and deeds of rulers and shamans, as well as battles and astronomical data	jaguar	Structurally similar to later Mayan script; Olmec calendars were highly accurate and the basis for later Mesoamerican calendars

except the Andes, although some scholars now regard their knotted strings, or quipus, as a kind of writing.[18]

Writing sustained the First Civilizations and their successors in many ways. Literacy defined elite status and conveyed enormous prestige to those who possessed it. (See Document 3.5, pp. 123–25, for a celebration of writing.) Because it can be learned, writing also provided a means for some commoners to join the charmed circle of the literate. Writing as propaganda, celebrating the great deeds of the kings, was prominent, especially among the Egyptians and later among the Maya. A hymn to the pharaoh, dating to about 1850 B.C.E., extravagantly praised the ruler:

> He has come unto us . . . and has given peace to the two Riverbanks
> . . . and has made Egypt to live; he hath banished its suffering;
> . . . he has caused the throat of the subjects to breathe
> . . . and has trodden down foreign countries
> . . . he has delivered them that were robbed
> . . . he has come unto us, that we may [nurture up?] our children and bury our aged ones.[19]

In Mesopotamia and elsewhere, writing served an accounting function, recording who had paid their taxes, who owed what to the temple, and how much workers had earned. Thus it immensely strengthened bureaucracy. Complex calendars indicated precisely when certain rituals should be performed. Writing also gave weight and specificity to orders, regulations, and laws. Hammurabi's famous law code (see Document 3.2, pp. 118–21), while correcting certain abuses, made crystal clear that fundamental distinctions divided men and women and separated slaves, commoners, and people of higher rank.

Once it had been developed, writing, like religion, proved hard to control and operated as a wild card in human affairs. It gave rise to literature and philosophy, to astronomy and mathematics, and, in some places, to history. On occasion, the written word proved threatening, rather than supportive, to rulers. China's so-called First Emperor, Qin Shihuangdi (reigned 221–210 B.C.E.), allegedly buried alive some 460 scholars and burned their books when they challenged his brutal efforts to unify China's many warring states, or so his later critics claimed (see Chapter 4). Thus writing became a major arena for social and political conflict, and rulers always have sought to control it.

The Grandeur of Kings

Yet another source of state authority derived from the lavish lifestyle of elites, the impressive rituals they arranged, and the imposing structures they created. Everywhere, kings, high officials, and their families lived in luxurious palaces, dressed in splendid clothing, bedecked themselves with the loveliest jewelry, and were attended by endless servants. Their deaths triggered elaborate burials, of which the pyramids of the Egyptian pharaohs were perhaps the most ostentatious. Almost all of the First

Civilizations accompanied high-status funerals with the human sacrifice of numerous retainers, who would nourish the souls or serve the needs of their rulers in the afterlife. Monumental palaces, temples, ziggurats, pyramids, and statues conveyed the immense power of the state and its elite rulers. The Olmec civilization of Mesoamerica (1200–400 B.C.E.) erected enormous human heads, more than ten feet tall and weighing at least twenty tons, carved from blocks of basalt and probably representing particular rulers. Somewhat later the Maya Temple of the Giant Jaguar, towering 154 feet tall, was the most impressive among many temples, pyramids, and palaces that graced the city of Tikal. All of this must have seemed overwhelming to common people in the cities and villages of the First Civilizations.

Olmec Head
This colossal statue, some six feet high and five feet wide, is one of seventeen such carvings, dating to the first millennium B.C.E., that were discovered in the territory of the ancient Olmec civilization. Thought to represent individual rulers, each of the statues has a distinct and realistically portrayed face. (Danny Lehman/Corbis)

Comparing Mesopotamia and Egypt

A productive agricultural technology, city living, immense class inequalities, patriarchy, the emerging power of states—all of these were common features of First Civilizations across the world and also of those that followed. Still, these civilizations were not everywhere the same, for differences in political organization, religious beliefs and practices, the role of women, and much more gave rise to distinctive traditions. Nor were they static. Like all human communities, they changed over the centuries. Finally, these civilizations did not exist in isolation, for they participated in networks of interactions with near and sometimes more distant neighbors. In looking more closely at two of these First Civilizations—Mesopotamia and Egypt—we can catch a glimpse of the differences, changes, and connections that characterized early civilizations.

■ **Comparison**
In what ways did Mesopotamian and Egyptian civilizations differ from each other?

Environment and Culture

The civilizations of both Mesopotamia and Egypt grew up in river valleys and depended on their rivers to sustain a productive agriculture in otherwise arid lands. Those rivers, however, were radically different. At the heart of Egyptian life was the Nile, "that green gash of teeming life," which rose predictably every year to bring the soil and water that nurtured a rich Egyptian agriculture. The Tigris and Euphrates rivers, which gave life to Mesopotamian civilization, also rose annually, but "unpredictably and fitfully, breaking man's dikes and submerging his crops."[20]

Snapshot   Key Moments in Mesopotamian History

Beginning of irrigated agriculture	6000 B.C.E.
Period of independent Sumerian city-states	3200–2350 B.C.E.
Earliest cuneiform texts	3000 B.C.E.
First Sumerian law codes	2500 B.C.E.
First Mesopotamian empire: conquest of Sumer by Sargon of Akkad	2350 B.C.E.
Epic of Gilgamesh compiled	after 2000 B.C.E.
Babylonian empire	1900–1500 B.C.E.
Reign of Hammurabi	1792–1750 B.C.E.
Assyrian rule in Mesopotamia	900–612 B.C.E.
Assyrian conquest of Israel	722 B.C.E.
Babylonian conquest of Judah by King Nebuchadnezzar	586 B.C.E.
Mesopotamia incorporated into Persian empire	by 500 B.C.E.

(See Map 3.2.) Furthermore, an open environment without serious obstacles to travel made Mesopotamia far more vulnerable to invasion than the much more protected space of Egypt, which was surrounded by deserts, mountains, seas, and cataracts. For long periods of its history, Egypt enjoyed a kind of "free security" from external attack that Mesopotamians could only have envied.

Does the physical environment shape the human cultures that develop within it? Most historians are reluctant to endorse any kind of determinism, especially one suggesting that "geography is destiny," but in the case of Mesopotamia and Egypt, many scholars have seen some relationship between the physical setting and culture.

In at least some of its literature, the Mesopotamian outlook on life, which developed within a precarious, unpredictable, and often violent environment, viewed humankind as caught in an inherently disorderly world, subject to the whims of capricious and quarreling gods, and facing death without much hope of a pleasant life beyond. A Mesopotamian poet complained: "I have prayed to the gods and sacrificed, but who can understand the gods in heaven? Who knows what they plan for us? Who has ever been able to understand a god's conduct?"[21] The famous Mesopotamian *Epic of Gilgamesh*, excerpted in Document 3.1, pages 115–18, likewise depicted a rather pessimistic view of the gods and of the possibility for eternal life.

By contrast, elite literate culture in Egypt, developing in a more stable, predictable, and beneficent environment, produced a rather more cheerful and hopeful outlook on the world. The rebirth of the sun every day and of the river every year seemed to assure Egyptians that life would prevail over death. The amazing

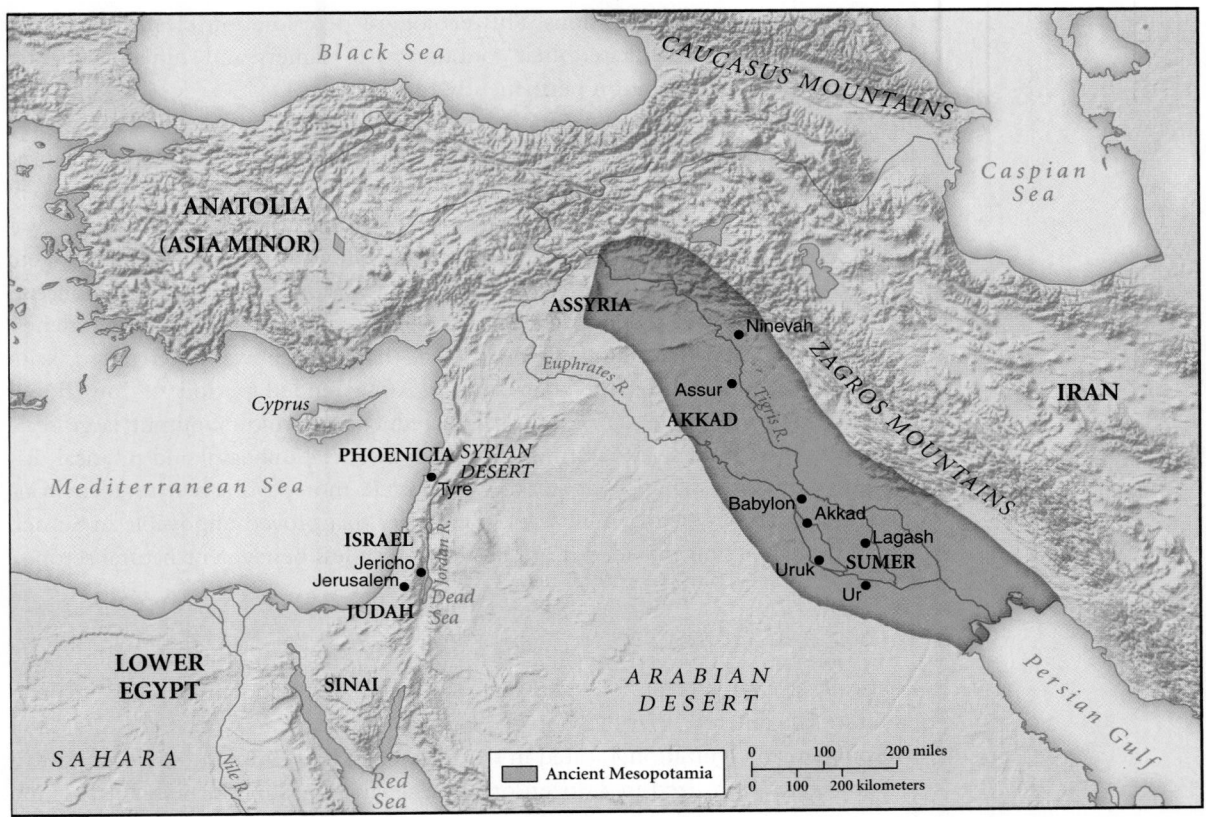

Map 3.2 Mesopotamia After about 1,000 years of independent and competitive existence, the city-states of Sumer were incorporated into a number of larger imperial states based in Akkad, Babylon, and then Assyria.

pyramids, constructed during Egypt's Old Kingdom (2663–2195 B.C.E.), reflected the firm belief that at least the pharaohs and other high-ranking people could successfully make the journey to eternal life in the Land of the West. Incantations for the dead, such as those illustrated in Document 3.3, describe an afterlife that Gilgamesh could only have envied. Over time, larger groups of people, beyond the pharaoh and his entourage, came to believe that they could gain access to the afterlife if they followed proper procedures and lived a morally upright life (see Documents 3.3 and 3.4, pp. 121–23). Thus Egyptian civilization not only affirmed the possibility of eternal life but also expanded access to it.

If the different environments of Mesopotamia and Egypt shaped their societies and cultures, those civilizations, with their mounting populations and growing demand for resources, likewise had an impact on the environment.[22] In Sumer (southern Mesopotamia), deforestation and soil erosion decreased crop yields by some 65 percent between 2400 and 1700 B.C.E. Also contributing to this disaster was the increasing salinization of the soil, a long-term outcome of intensive irrigation. By 2000 B.C.E., there were reports that "the earth turned white" as salt accumulated in the soil. As a result, wheat was largely replaced by barley, which is far more tolerant of salty conditions. This ecological deterioration clearly weakened Sumerian city-states, facilitated their conquest by foreigners, and shifted the center of Mesopotamian civilization permanently to the north.

Egypt, by contrast, created a more sustainable agricultural system, which lasted for thousands of years and contributed to the remarkable continuity of its civilization. Whereas Sumerian irrigation involved a complex and artificial network of canals and dikes that led to the salinization of the soil, its Egyptian counterpart was much less intrusive, simply regulating the natural flow of the Nile. Such a system avoided the problem of salty soils, allowing Egyptian agriculture to emphasize wheat production, but it depended on the general regularity and relative gentleness of the Nile's annual flooding. On occasion, that pattern was interrupted, with serious consequences for Egyptian society. An extended period of low floods between 2250 and 1950 B.C.E. led to sharply reduced agricultural output, large-scale starvation, the loss of livestock, and, consequently, social upheaval and political disruption. Nonetheless, Egypt's ability to work *with* its more favorable natural environment enabled a degree of stability and continuity that proved impossible in Sumer, where human action intruded more heavily into a less benevolent natural setting.

Cities and States

Politically as well as culturally and environmentally, Mesopotamian and Egyptian civilizations differed sharply. For its first thousand years (3200–2350 B.C.E.), Mesopotamian civilization, located in the southern Tigris-Euphrates region known as Sumer, was organized in a dozen or more separate and independent city-states. Each city-state was ruled by a king, who claimed to represent the city's patron deity and who controlled the affairs of the walled city and surrounding rural area. Quite remarkably, some 80 percent of the population of Sumer lived in one or another of these city-states, making Mesopotamia the most thoroughly urbanized society of ancient times. The chief reason for this massive urbanization, however, lay in the great flaw of this system, for frequent warfare among these Sumerian city-states caused people living in rural areas to flee to the walled cities for protection. With no overarching authority, rivalry over land and water often led to violent conflict. After one such conflict destroyed the city of Ur and desecrated its temple, a poet lamented the city's sad fate:

> After your city had been destroyed, how now can you exist!
> After your house had been destroyed, how has your heart led you on!
> Your city has become a strange city . . .
> Your house has become a house of tears.[23]

These conflicts, together with environmental devastation, eventually left Sumerian cities vulnerable to outside forces, and after about 2350 B.C.E., stronger peoples from northern Mesopotamia conquered Sumer's warring cities, bringing an end to the Sumerian phase of Mesopotamian civilization. First the Akkadians (2350–2000 B.C.E.) and later the Babylonians (1900–1500 B.C.E.) and the Assyrians (900–612

B.C.E.) created larger territorial states or bureaucratic empires that encompassed all or most of Mesopotamia. Periods of political unity now descended upon this First Civilization, but it was unity imposed from outside. Much later, a similar process befell the Greek city-states, whose endemic warfare invited Macedonian invasion and their subsequent incorporation into the empires of Alexander the Great and then of the Romans (see Chapter 4).

Egyptian civilization, by contrast, began its history around 3100 B.C.E., with the merger of several earlier states or chiefdoms into a unified territory that stretched some 1,000 miles along the Nile. For an amazing 3,000 years, Egypt maintained that unity and independence, though with occasional interruptions. A combination of wind patterns that made it easy to sail south along the Nile and a current flowing north facilitated communication, exchange, unity, and stability within the Nile Valley. Here was a record of political longevity and continuity that the Mesopotamians and many other ancient peoples might well have envied.

Cities in Egypt were less important than in Mesopotamia, although political capitals, market centers, and major burial sites gave Egypt an urban presence as well. Most people lived in agricultural villages along the river rather than in urban centers, perhaps because Egypt's greater security made it less necessary for people to

$Snapshot$ **Key Moments in Nile Valley Civilizations**

Small-scale states in Sudanic Africa	5000 B.C.E.
Nubian kingdom of Ta-Seti	3400–3200 B.C.E.
Unification of Egypt as a single state	3100 B.C.E.
Frequent warfare between Egypt and Nubian states	3100–2600 B.C.E.
Old Kingdom Egypt (high point of pharaohs' power and pyramid building)	2663–2195 B.C.E.
Nubian kingdom of Kush established	2500 B.C.E.
Egyptian commercial expeditions to Nubia	2300 B.C.E.
Hyksos invasion and rule of Egypt	1650–1550 B.C.E.
New Kingdom Egypt	1550–1064 B.C.E.
Emergence of Egyptian empire	1500 B.C.E.
Queen Hatshepsut launches expeditions to Land of Punt, probably along the East African coast	1473–1458 B.C.E.
Kush conquest of Egypt	760–660 B.C.E.
Assyrian conquest of Egypt	671–651 B.C.E.
Persian rule in Egypt	525–404 B.C.E.
Roman conquest of Egypt	30 B.C.E.

gather in fortified towns. The focus of the Egyptian state resided in the pharaoh, believed to be a god in human form. He alone ensured the daily rising of the sun and the annual flooding of the Nile. All of the country's many officials served at his pleasure; the law of the land was simply the pharaoh's edict; and access to the after-life lay in proximity to him and burial in or near his towering pyramids.

This image of the pharaoh and his role as an enduring symbol of Egyptian civilization persisted over the course of three millennia, but the realities of Egyptian political life changed over time. By 2400 B.C.E., the power of the pharaoh had diminished, as local officials and nobles, who had been awarded their own land and were able to pass their positions on to their sons, assumed greater authority. When changes in the weather resulted in the Nile's repeated failure to flood properly around 2200 B.C.E., the authority of the pharaoh was severely discredited, and Egypt dissolved for several centuries into a series of local principalities.

Even when centralized rule was restored around 2000 B.C.E., the pharaohs never regained their old power and prestige. Kings were now warned that they too would have to account for their actions at the Day of Judgment. Nobles no longer sought to be buried near the pharaoh's pyramid but instead created their own more modest tombs in their own areas. Osiris, the god of the dead, became increasingly prominent, and "all men who were worthy . . . not merely those who had known the pharaoh in life" could aspire to immortality in his realm.[24]

Interaction and Exchange

■ Connection

In what ways were Mesopotamian and Egyptian civilizations shaped by their interactions with near and distant neighbors?

Although Mesopotamia and Egypt represented separate and distinct civilizations, they interacted frequently with each other and with both near and more distant neighbors. Even in these ancient times, the First Civilizations were embedded in larger networks of commerce, culture, and power. None of them stood alone.

The early beginnings of Egyptian civilization illustrate the point. Its agriculture drew upon wheat and barley, which reached Egypt from Mesopotamia, as well as gourds, watermelon, domesticated donkeys, and cattle, which derived from Sudan. Some scholars argue that Egypt's step pyramids and its system of writing were stimulated by Mesopotamian models. The practice of "divine kingship" seems to have derived from the central or eastern Sudan, where small-scale agricultural communities had long viewed their rulers as sacred and buried them with various servants and officials. From this complex of influences, the Egyptians created something distinct and unique, but that civilization had roots in both Africa and Southwest Asia.[25]

Furthermore, once they were established, both Mesopotamia and Egypt carried on extensive long-distance trade. Sumerian merchants had established seaborne contact with the Indus Valley civilization as early as 2300 B.C.E. Other trade routes connected it to Anatolia (present-day Turkey), Egypt, Iran, and Afghanistan. During Akkadian rule over Mesopotamia, a Sumerian poet described its capital of Agade:

In those days the dwellings of Agade were filled with gold,
   its bright-shining houses were filled with silver,
   into its granaries were brought copper, tin, slabs of
   lapis lazuli [a blue gemstone], its silos bulged at the sides . . .
   its quay where the boats docked were all bustle. . . .[26]

All of this and more came from far away.

Egyptian trade likewise extended far afield. Beyond its involvement with the Mediterranean and the Middle East, Egyptian trading journeys extended deep into Africa, including Nubia, south of Egypt in the Nile Valley, and Punt, along the East African coast of Ethiopia and Somalia. One Egyptian official described his return from an expedition to Nubia: "I came down with three hundred donkeys laden with incense, ebony, . . . panther skins, elephant tusks, throw sticks, and all sorts of good products."[27] What most intrigued the very young pharaoh who sent him, however, was a dancing dwarf that accompanied the expedition back to Egypt.

Along with trade goods went cultural influence from the civilizations of Mesopotamia and Egypt. Among the smaller societies of the region to feel this influence were the Hebrews, who had migrated from Mesopotamia to Palestine and Egypt early in their history. Their sacred writings, recorded in the Old Testament, showed the influence of Mesopotamia in the "eye for an eye" principle of their legal system and in the story of a flood that destroyed the world. Unique to the Hebrews, however, was their emerging awareness of a merciful and single deity, Yahweh, who demanded an ethical life from his people. This conception subsequently achieved global significance when it was taken over by Christianity and Islam.

The Phoenicians, who were commercially active in the Mediterranean basin from their homeland in present-day Lebanon, also were influenced by Mesopotamian civilization. They adopted the Mesopotamian fertility goddess Ishtar, renaming her Astarte. They also adapted the Sumerian cuneiform method of writing to a much easier alphabetic system, which later became the basis for Greek and Latin writing. Various Indo-European peoples, dispersing probably from north-central Anatolia, also

Egypt and Nubia
By the fourteenth century B.C.E., Nubia was a part of an Egyptian empire. This wall painting shows Nubian princes bringing gifts or tribute, including rings and bags of gold, to Huy, the Egyptian viceroy of Nubia. The mural comes from Huy's tomb. (Courtesy of the Trustees of the British Museum)

Map 3.3 An Egyptian Empire

During the New Kingdom period after 1550 B.C.E., Egypt became for several centuries an empire, extending its political control southward into Nubia and northward into Palestine.

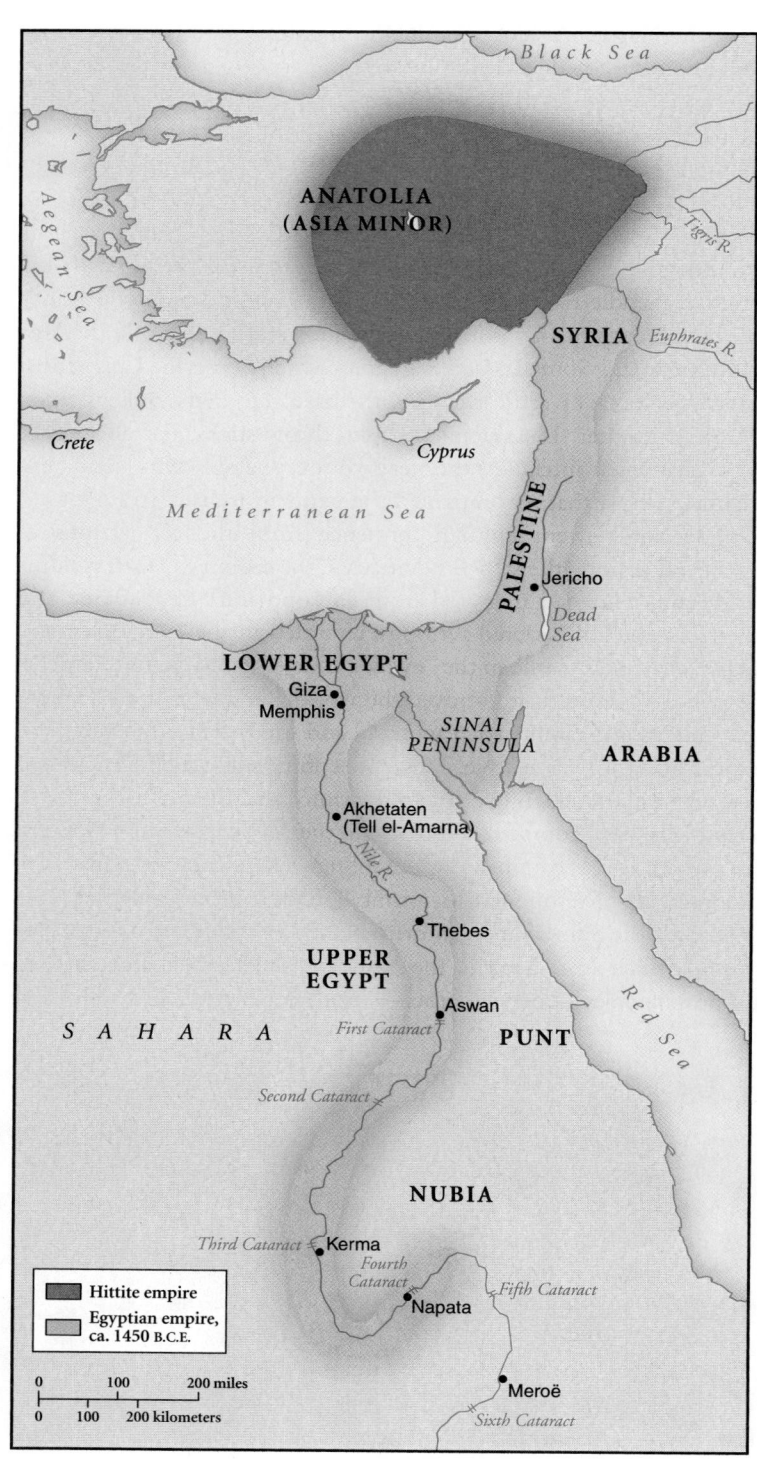

incorporated Sumerian deities into their own religions as well as bronze metallurgy and the wheel into their economies. When their widespread migrations carried them across much of Eurasia, they took these Sumerian cultural artifacts with them.

Egyptian cultural influence likewise spread in several directions. Nubia, located to the south of Egypt in the Nile Valley, not only traded with its more powerful neighbor but also was subject to periodic military intervention and political control from Egypt. Skilled Nubian archers were actively recruited for service as mercenaries in Egyptian armies. They often married Egyptian women and were buried in Egyptian style. All of this led to the diffusion of Egyptian culture in Nubia, expressed in building Egyptian-style pyramids, worshipping Egyptian gods and goddesses, and making use of Egyptian hieroglyphic writing. Despite this cultural borrowing, Nubia remained a distinct civilization, developing its own alphabetic script, retaining many of its own gods, developing a major ironworking industry by 500 B.C.E., and asserting its political independence whenever possible. The Nubian kingdom of Kush, in fact, invaded Egypt in 760 B.C.E. and ruled it for about 100 years.

In the Mediterranean basin, clear Egyptian influence is visible in the art of the Minoan civilization, which emerged on the island of Crete about 2500 B.C.E. More controversial has been the claim by historian Martin Bernal in a much-publicized book, *Black Athena* (1987), that ancient Greek culture—its art, religion, philosophy, and language—drew heavily upon Egyptian as well as Mesopotamian precedents. His book lit up a passionate debate among scholars. To some of his critics, Bernal seemed to undermine the originality of Greek civilization by suggesting that it had Afro-Asian origins. His supporters accused the critics of Eurocentrism. Whatever its outcome, the controversy surrounding Bernal's book served to focus attention on Egypt's relationship to black Africa and to the world of the Mediterranean basin.

Influence was not a one-way street, however, as Egypt and Mesopotamia likewise felt the impact of neighboring peoples. Pastoral peoples, speaking Indo-European languages and living in what is now southern Russia, had domesticated the horse by perhaps 4000 B.C.E. and later learned to tie that powerful animal to wheeled carts and chariots. This new technology provided a fearsome military potential that enabled various chariot-driving peoples to temporarily overwhelm ancient civilizations. Based in Anatolia, the Hittites overran the powerful Babylonian empire of Mesopotamia in 1595 B.C.E. About the same time, another pastoral group with chariots, the Hyksos, invaded Egypt and ruled it for more than a century (1650–1535 B.C.E.). But chariot technology was portable, and soon both the Egyptians and the Mesopotamians incorporated it into their own military forces. In fact, this powerful military innovation, together with the knowledge of bronze metallurgy, spread quickly and widely, reaching China by 1200 B.C.E. There it enabled the creation of a strong Chinese state ruled by the Shang dynasty. All of these developments provide evidence of at least indirect connections across the entire Eurasian landmass in ancient times. Even then, no civilization was wholly isolated from larger patterns of interaction.

In Egypt, the intrusion of the chariot-driving Hyksos shattered the sense of security that this Nile Valley civilization had long enjoyed. It also stimulated the normally complacent Egyptians to adopt a number of technologies pioneered earlier in Asia, including the horse-drawn chariot; new kinds of armor, bows, daggers, and swords; improved methods of spinning and weaving; new musical instruments; and olive and pomegranate trees. Absorbing these foreign innovations, Egyptians expelled the Hyksos and went on to create their own empire, both in Nubia and in the eastern Mediterranean regions of Syria and Palestine. By 1500 B.C.E., the previously self-contained Egypt became for several centuries an imperial state bridging Africa and Asia, ruling over substantial numbers of non-Egyptian peoples (see Map 3.3). It also became part of an international political system that included the Babylonian and later Assyrian empires of Mesopotamia as well as many other peoples of the region. Egyptian and Babylonian rulers engaged in regular diplomatic correspondence, referred to one another as "brother," exchanged gifts, and married their daughters into one another's families. One Babylonian king complained to an Egyptian pharaoh that the delegation that had come to take his daughter to Egypt contained only five carriages. What would his courtiers say about the daughter of a great ruler traveling with such a paltry escort?[28]

⊢⊣ Reflections: "Civilization": What's in a Word?

In examining the cultures of ancient Mesopotamia and Egypt, we are worlds away from life in agricultural villages or Paleolithic camps. Much the same holds for those of the Indus Valley, China, Mesoamerica, and the Andes. Strangely enough, historians have been somewhat uncertain as to how to refer to these new forms of human community. Following common practice, I have called them "civilizations," but scholars have reservations about the term for two reasons. The first is its implication of superiority. In popular usage, "civilization" suggests refined behavior, a "higher" form of society, something unreservedly positive. The opposite of "civilized"—"barbarian," "savage," or "uncivilized"—is normally understood as an insult implying inferiority. That, of course, is precisely how the inhabitants of many civilizations have viewed those outside their own societies, particularly those neighboring peoples living without the alleged benefit of cities and states.

Modern assessments of the First Civilizations reveal a profound ambiguity about these new, larger, and more complex societies. On the one hand, these civilizations have given us inspiring art, profound reflections on the meaning of life, more productive technologies, increased control over nature, and the art of writing—all of which have been cause for celebration. On the other hand, as anthropologist Marvin Harris noted, "[H]uman beings learned for the first time how to bow, grovel, kneel, and kowtow."[29] Massive inequalities, state oppression, slavery, large-scale warfare, the subordination of women, and epidemic disease also accompanied the rise of civilization, generating discontent, rebellion, and sometimes the urge to escape. This ambiguity about the character of civilizations has led some historians to avoid the word, referring to early Egypt, Mesopotamia, and other regions instead as complex societies, urban-based societies, state-organized societies, or some more neutral term.

A second reservation about using the term "civilization" derives from its implication of solidity—the idea that civilizations represent distinct and widely shared identities with clear boundaries that mark them off from other such units. It is unlikely, however, that many people living in Mesopotamia, Norte Chico, or ancient China felt themselves part of a shared culture. Local identities defined by occupation, clan affiliation, village, city, or region were surely more important for most people than those of some larger civilization. At best, members of an educated upper class who shared a common literary tradition may have felt themselves part of some more inclusive civilization, but that left out most of the population. Moreover, unlike modern nations, none of the earlier civilizations had definite borders. Any identification with that civilization surely faded as distance from its core region increased. Finally, the line between civilizations and other kinds of societies is not always clear. Just when does a village or town become a city? At what point does a chiefdom become a state? Scholars continue to argue about these distinctions.

Given these reservations, should historians discard the notion of civilization? Maybe so, but this book continues to use it both because it is so deeply embedded in our way of thinking about the world and because no alternative concept has achieved widespread usage for making distinctions among different kinds of human communities. When the term appears in the text, try to keep in mind two points. First, as used by historians, "civilization" is a purely descriptive term, designating a particular type of human society—one with cities and states—and does not imply any judgment or assessment, any sense of superiority or inferiority. Second, it is used to define broad cultural patterns in particular geographic regions—Mesopotamia, the Peruvian coast, or China, for example—even though many people living in those regions may have been more aware of differences and conflicts than of those commonalities.

Second Thoughts

What's the Significance?

Norte Chico/Caral	Mohenjo Daro/Harappa	*Epic of Gilgamesh*
Indus Valley civilization	Code of Hammurabi	Egypt: "the gift of the Nile"
Olmec civilization	patriarchy	Nubia
Uruk	rise of the state	Hyksos

To assess your mastery of the material in this chapter, visit the **Student Center** at bedfordstmartins.com/strayer.

Big Picture Questions

1. What distinguished civilizations from other forms of human community?
2. How does the use of the term "civilization" by historians differ from that of popular usage? How do you use the term?
3. "Civilizations were held together largely by force." Do you agree with this assessment, or were there other mechanisms of integration as well?
4. In the development of the First Civilizations, what was gained for humankind, and what was lost?

Next Steps: For Further Study

For Web sites and additional documents related to this chapter, see **Make History** at bedfordstmartins.com/strayer.

Cyril Aldred, *The Egyptians* (1998). A brief and up-to-date account from a widely recognized expert.

Samuel Noah Kramer, *History Begins at Sumer* (1981). A classic account of Sumerian civilization, filled with wonderful stories and anecdotes.

David B. O'Connor, *Ancient Nubia: Egypt's Rival in Africa* (1994). An overview of this ancient African civilization, with lovely illustrations based on a museum exhibit.

Christopher A. Pool, *Olmec Archeology and Early Mesoamerica* (2007). A scholarly and up-to-date account of the earliest civilization in Mesoamerica.

Lauren Ristvet, *In the Beginning* (2007). A sweeping examination of the early phases of world history, from human evolution to the First Civilizations.

"The Ancient Indus Civilization," http://www.harappa.com/har/haro.html. Hundreds of vivid pictures and several brief essays on the Indus Valley civilization.

The British Museum, "Ancient Egypt," http://www.ancientegypt.co.uk/menu.html. An interactive exploration of Egyptian civilization.

Documents

Considering the Evidence:
Life and Afterlife in Mesopotamia and Egypt

The advent of writing was not only a central feature of the First Civilizations but also a great boon to later historians. Access to early written records from these civilizations allows us some insight, in their own words, as to how these ancient peoples thought about their societies and their place in the larger scheme of things. Such documents, of course, tell only a small part of the story, for they most often reflect the thinking of the literate few—usually male, upper-class, powerful, and well-to-do—rather than the outlook of the vast majority who lacked such privileged positions. Nonetheless, historians have been grateful for even this limited window on the life of at least some of our ancient ancestors.

Among the First Civilizations, accessible written records are most widely available for Mesopotamia and Egypt. Those excerpted here disclose something about those peoples' beliefs regarding life in this world—class and gender, crime and justice, occupation and kingship—as well as about what awaits in the life beyond. Such reflections about life and afterlife allow us to catch a glimpse of the social organization and cultural outlook of these First Civilizations.

Document 3.1

In Search of Eternal Life

The most well-known of the writings from the world of the First Civilizations is surely the *Epic of Gilgamesh*. Inscribed on clay tablets in various versions, the Gilgamesh epic has been pieced together by scholars over the past century or so. Its origins no doubt go back to stories and legends circulating during the life of the historical Gilgamesh, the powerful ruler of the Sumerian city of Uruk around 2700 B.C.E., although the earliest written version of the epic dates to around 2000 B.C.E. (see Map 3.2, p. 105).

The epic poem itself recounts the adventures of Gilgamesh, said to be part human and part divine. As the story opens, he is the energetic and yet oppressive ruler of Uruk. The pleas of his people persuade the gods to send Enkidu, an uncivilized man from the wilderness, to counteract this oppression. But before he can confront the erring monarch, Enkidu must become civilized, a process that occurs at the hands of a seductive harlot. When the two men finally meet, they engage in a titanic wrestling match from which Gilgamesh emerges victorious. Thereafter they bond in a deep friendship and undertake a series of adventures together. In the course of these adventures, they offend the gods, who then determine that Enkidu must die. Devastated by the loss of his friend and the realization of his own mortality, Gilgamesh undertakes an extended search for eternal life. During this search, he meets a tavern owner, a wise woman named Siduri, as well as Utnapishtim, the only human being ever granted immortality by the gods. In the end, however, Gilgamesh learns that eternal life is not available to mere mortals and thus his quest proves futile.

The excerpts that follow illustrate something of Mesopotamian views of kingship, of the gods, and of the possibilities of life and afterlife.

- How would you define the Mesopotamian ideal of kingship? What is the basis of the monarch's legitimacy?

- What understanding of the afterlife does the epic suggest?

- What philosophy of life comes across in the Gilgamesh story?

- How does the *Epic of Gilgamesh* portray the gods and their relationship to humankind?

The Epic of Gilgamesh
ca. 2700 B.C.E.–2500 B.C.E.

On Kingship

[These first selections deal with the nature of kingship. They tell of the great deeds of Gilgamesh and his oppression of the people as well as recounting the instructions about kingship from Enlil, the chief Sumerian god, who is responsible for determining the destinies of humankind.]

I will proclaim to the world the deeds of Gilgamesh. This was the man to whom all things were known; this was the king who knew the countries of the world. He was wise, he saw mysteries and knew secret things, he brought us a tale of the days before the flood. He went on a long journey, was weary, worn-out with labor, returning he rested, he engraved on a stone the whole story.

When the gods created Gilgamesh they gave him a perfect body. Shamash the glorious sun endowed him with beauty, Adad the god of the storm endowed him with courage, the great gods made his beauty perfect, surpassing all others, terrifying like a great wild bull. Two-thirds they made him god and one-third man.

In Uruk he built walls, a great rampart, and the temple of blessed Eanna for the god of the firmament Anu, and for Ishtar the goddess of love. Look at it still today: the outer wall where the cornice runs, it shines with the brilliance of copper; and the inner wall, it has no equal. Touch the threshold, it is ancient. Approach Eanna the dwelling of Ishtar, our lady of love and war, the like of which no latter-day king, no man alive can equal. Climb upon the wall of Uruk; walk along it, I say; regard the foundation terrace and examine the masonry: is it not burnt brick and good? The seven sages laid the foundations.

Gilgamesh went abroad in the world, but he met with none who could withstand his arms till he

Source: *The Epic of Gilgamesh*, translated by N. K. Sanders (London: Penguin, 1972), 61–62; 70; 92–93; 101–2; 106–11.

came to Uruk. But the men of Uruk muttered in their houses, "Gilgamesh sounds the tocsin for his amusement, his arrogance has no bounds by day or night. No son is left with his father, for Gilgamesh takes them all, even the children; yet the king should be a shepherd to his people. His lust leaves no virgin to her lover, neither the warrior's daughter nor the wife of the noble; yet this is the shepherd of the city, wise, comely, and resolute."

Enlil of the mountain, the father of the gods, had decreed the destiny of Gilgamesh. So Gilgamesh dreamed and Enkidu said, "The meaning of the dream is this. The father of the gods has given you kingship, such is your destiny; everlasting life is not your destiny. Because of this do not be sad at heart, do not be grieved or oppressed. He has given you power to bind and to loose, to be the darkness and the light of mankind. He has given you unexampled supremacy over the people, victory in battle from which no fugitive returns, in forays and assaults from which there is no going back. But do not abuse this power, deal justly with your servants in the palace, deal justly before Shamash.

On the Search for Immortality

[As Enkidu lies dying, he tells Gilgamesh of a dream he had about the afterlife.]

"[T]his is the dream I dreamed last night. The heavens roared, and earth rumbled back an answer; between them stood I before an awful being, the somber-faced man-bird; he had directed on me his purpose. His was a vampire face, his foot was a lion's foot, his hand was an eagle's talon. He fell on me and his claws were in my hair, he held me fast and I smothered; then he transformed me so that my arms became wings covered with feathers. He turned his stare toward me, and he led me away to the palace of Irkalla, the Queen of Darkness, to the house from which none who enters ever returns, down the road from which there is no coming back.

"There is the house whose people sit in darkness; dust is their food and clay their meat. They are clothed like birds with wings for covering, they see no light, they sit in darkness. I entered the house of dust and I saw the kings of the earth, their crowns put away for ever; rulers and princes, all those who once wore kingly crowns and ruled the world in the days of old. They who had stood in the place of the gods like Anu and Enlil, stood now like servants to fetch baked meats in the house of dust, to carry cooked meat and cold water from the water-skin. In the house of dust which I entered were high priests and acolytes, priests of the incantation and of ecstasy....Then I awoke like a man drained of blood who wanders alone in a waste of rushes."

[When Gilgamesh in his quest for immortality meets Siduri, the tavern keeper, he confesses to her his fear and anguish, and receives some wise counsel in return.]

"[M]y friend who was very dear to me and who endured dangers beside me, Enkidu my brother, whom I loved, the end of mortality has overtaken him. I wept for him seven days and nights till the worm fastened to him. Because of my brother I am afraid of death, because of my brother I stray through the wilderness and cannot rest. But now, young woman, maker of wine, since I have seen your face do not let me see the face of death which I dread so much."

She answered, "Gilgamesh, where are you hurrying to? You will never find that life for which you are looking. When the gods created man they allotted to him death, but life they retained in their own keeping. As for you, Gilgamesh, fill your belly with good things; day and night, night and day, dance and be merry, feast and rejoice. Let your clothes be fresh, bathe yourself in water, cherish the little child that holds your hand, and make your wife happy in your embrace; for this too is the lot of man."

[Later, when Gilgamesh reaches Utnapishtim, the only man to survive the great flood and receive eternal life from the gods, he hears a similar message.]

Utnapishtim said, "There is no permanence. Do we build a house to stand forever, do we seal a contract to hold for all time? Do brothers divide an inheritance to keep forever, does the flood-time of rivers endure?... From the days of old there is no permanence. The sleeping and the dead, how alike they are, they are like a painted death. What is there between the master and the servant when both have fulfilled their doom? When the Anunnaki, the judges, come together, and Mammetun the mother of destinies, together they decree the fates of men. Life and death they allot but the day of death they do not disclose."

On the Gods

[In his conversation with Utnapishtim, Gilgamesh learns something about the nature of Mesopotamian gods and the origins of the great flood, which ages ago had destroyed humankind.]

"You know the city Shurrupak, it stands on the banks of the Euphrates? That city grew old and the gods that were in it were old. There was Anu, lord of the firmament, their father, and warrior Enlil their counselor, Ninurta the helper, and Ennugi watcher over canals; and with them also was Ea. In those days the world teemed, the people multiplied, the world bellowed like a wild bull, and the great god was aroused by the clamor. Enlil heard the clamor and he said to the gods in council, 'The uproar of mankind is intolerable and sleep is no longer possible by reason of the babel.' So the gods agreed to exterminate mankind....

"With the first light of dawn a black cloud came from the horizon; it thundered within where Adad, lord of the storm, was riding. In front over hill and plain Shullat and Hanish, heralds of the storm, led on. Then the gods of the abyss rose up; Nergal pulled out the dams of the nether waters, Ninurta the war-lord threw down the dykes, and the seven judges of hell, the Annunaki, raised their torches, lighting the land with their livid flame. A stupor of despair went up to heaven when the god of the storm turned daylight to darkness, when he smashed the land like a cup. One whole day the tempest raged, gathering fury as it went, it poured over the people like the tides of battle; a man could not see his brother nor the people be seen from heaven. Even the gods were terrified at the flood, they fled to the highest heaven, the firmament of Anu; they crouched against the walls, cowering like curs. Then Ishtar the sweet-voiced Queen of Heaven cried out like a woman in travail: 'Alas the days of old are turned to dust because I commanded evil; why did I command this evil in the council of all the gods? I commanded wars to destroy the people, but are they not my people, for I brought them forth? Now like the spawn of fish they float in the ocean.' The great gods of heaven and of hell wept, they covered their mouths."

Document 3.2

Law and Justice in Ancient Mesopotamia

If the *Epic of Gilgamesh* affords us some insight into Mesopotamian cultural and religious thinking, the so-called Code of Hammurabi provides a glimpse of this First Civilization's social and economic life. Hammurabi (reigned ca. 1795–1750 B.C.E.) was the ruler of the Babylonian Empire, which for a time gave a measure of political unity to the rival cities and kingdoms of Mesopotamia. Sometime during his reign he ordered inscribed on a large stone pillar a number of laws, judgments, or decrees. They were intended, in Hammurabi's words, "to bring about the rule of righteousness in the land, to destroy the wicked and the evil-doers; so that the strong should not harm the weak..., to further the well-being of mankind."

■ If you knew nothing else about ancient Mesopotamia, what could you conclude from the Code of Hammurabi about the economy and society of this civilization in the eighteenth century B.C.E.? How might you describe the economy of the region? What distinct social groups are mentioned in the code? What rights did women enjoy and to what restrictions were they subject?

■ What can you infer from the code about the kind of social problems that afflicted ancient Mesopotamia?

■ How would you define the principles of justice that underlay Hammurabi's code? In what different ways might twenty-first-century observers and those living at the time of Hammurabi assess that system of justice?

■ How did the code seek to realize the aims of Hammurabi as described above?

The Law Code of Hammurabi
ca. 1800 B.C.E.

On Crime, Punishment, and Justice

2. If any one bring an accusation against a man, and the accused go to the river and leap into the river, if he sink in the river his accuser shall take possession of his house. But if the river prove that the accused is not guilty, and he escape unhurt, then he who had brought the accusation shall be put to death, while he who leaped into the river shall take possession of the house that had belonged to his accuser....

3. If any one bring an accusation of any crime before the elders, and does not prove what he has charged, he shall, if it be a capital offense charged, be put to death....

5. If a judge try a case, reach a decision, and present his judgment in writing; if later error shall appear in his decision, and it be through his own fault, then he shall pay twelve times the fine set by him in the case, and he shall be publicly removed from the judge's bench, and never again shall he sit there to render judgment....

22. If any one is committing a robbery and is caught, then he shall be put to death....

196. If a man put out the eye of another man, his eye shall be put out.

197. If he break another man's bone, his bone shall be broken....

On the Economy

26. If a chieftain or a man [common soldier], who has been ordered to go upon the king's highway for war does not go, but hires a mercenary, if he withholds the compensation, then shall this officer or man be put to death, and he who represented him shall take possession of his house....

30. If a chieftain or a man leave his house, garden, and field and hires it out, and some one else takes possession of his house, garden, and field and uses it for three years: if the first owner return and claims his house, garden, and field, it shall not be given to him, but he who has taken possession of it and used it shall continue to use it....

Source: *The Code of Hammurabi*, translated by L. W. King, 1915.

53. If any one be too lazy to keep his dam in proper condition, and does not so keep it; if then the dam break and all the fields be flooded, then shall he in whose dam the break occurred be sold for money, and the money shall replace the corn which he has caused to be ruined....

104. If a merchant give an agent corn, wool, oil, or any other goods to transport, the agent shall give a receipt for the amount, and compensate the merchant therefore. Then he shall obtain a receipt from the merchant for the money that he gives the merchant....

122. If any one give another silver, gold, or anything else to keep, he shall show everything to some witness, draw up a contract, and then hand it over for safe keeping....

229. If a builder build a house for some one, and does not construct it properly, and the house which he built fall in and kill its owner, then that builder shall be put to death....

253. If any one agree with another to tend his field, give him seed, entrust a yoke of oxen to him, and bind him to cultivate the field, if he steal the corn or plants, and take them for himself, his hands shall be hewn off....

271. If any one hire oxen, cart, and driver, he shall pay one hundred and eighty ka of corn per day....

On Class and Slavery

8. If any one steal cattle or sheep, or an ass, or a pig or a goat, if it belong to a god or to the court, the thief shall pay thirtyfold therefore; if they belonged to a freed man of the king he shall pay tenfold; if the thief has nothing with which to pay, he shall be put to death....

15. If any one take a male or female slave of the court, or a male or female slave of a freed man, outside the city gates, he shall be put to death....

17. If any one find runaway male or female slaves in the open country and bring them to their masters, the master of the slaves shall pay him two shekels of silver....

117. If any one fail to meet a claim for debt, and sell himself, his wife, his son, and daughter for money or give them away to forced labor: they shall work for three years in the house of the man who bought them, or the proprietor, and in the fourth year they shall be set free....

198. If he put out the eye of a freed man, or break the bone of a freed man, he shall pay one gold mina.

199. If he put out the eye of a man's slave, or break the bone of a man's slave, he shall pay one-half of its value....

202. If any one strike the body of a man higher in rank than he, he shall receive sixty blows with an ox-whip in public....

215. If a physician make a large incision with an operating knife and cure it, or if he open a tumor [over the eye] with an operating knife, and saves the eye, he shall receive ten shekels in money.

216. If the patient be a freed man, he receives five shekels.

217. If he be the slave of some one, his owner shall give the physician two shekels....

On Men and Women

110. If a "sister of a god" [a woman formally dedicated to the temple of a god] open a tavern, or enter a tavern to drink, then shall this woman be burned to death....

128. If a man take a woman to wife, but have no intercourse with her, this woman is no wife to him.

129. If a man's wife be surprised with another man, both shall be tied and thrown into the water, but the husband may pardon his wife and the king his slaves.

130. If a man violate the wife [betrothed wife or child-wife] of another man, who has never known a man, and still lives in her father's house, and sleep with her and be surprised, this man shall be put to death, but the wife is blameless.

131. If a man bring a charge against one's wife, but she is not surprised with another man, she must take an oath and then may return to her house.

132. If the "finger is pointed" at a man's wife about another man, but she is not caught sleeping with the other man, she shall jump into the river for her husband....

136. If any one leave his house, run away, and then his wife go to another house, if then he return, and wishes to take his wife back: because he fled from his home and ran away, the wife of this runaway shall not return to her husband.

137. If a man wish to separate from a woman who has borne him children, or from his wife who has borne him children: then he shall give that wife her dowry, and a part of the usufruct [the right to use] of field, garden, and property, so that she can rear her children. When she has brought up her children... she may then marry the man of her heart....

142. If a woman quarrel with her husband, and say: "You are not congenial to me," the reasons for her prejudice must be presented. If she is guiltless, and there is no fault on her part, but he leaves and neglects her, then no guilt attaches to this woman, she shall take her dowry and go back to her father's house.

143. If she is not innocent, but leaves her husband, and ruins her house, neglecting her husband, this woman shall be cast into the water....

148. If a man take a wife, and she be seized by disease, if he then desire to take a second wife, he shall not put away his wife who has been attacked by disease, but he shall keep her in the house which he has built and support her so long as she lives.

Document 3.3

The Afterlife of a Pharaoh

Egyptian thinking about life, death, and afterlife bears comparison with that of Mesopotamia. In the selections that follow, we catch a glimpse of several Egyptian ways of understanding these fundamental human concerns. The first excerpt comes from a group of so-called pyramid texts, inscribed on the walls of a royal tomb as spells, incantations, or prayers to assist the pharaoh in entering the realm of eternal life among the gods in the Land of the West. This one was discovered in the tomb of the Egyptian king Teti, who ruled between roughly 2345 and 2333 B.C.E. Such texts represent the oldest religious writings in world history.

■ How is the afterlife of the pharaoh represented in this text?

■ How does it compare with depictions of the afterlife in the *Epic of Gilgamesh*?

A Pyramid Text
2333 B.C.E.

Oho! Oho! Rise up, O Teti!
Take your head, collect your bones,

Gather your limbs, shake the earth from your
    flesh!
Take your bread that rots not, your beer that sours
    not,
Stand at the gates that bar the common people!
The gatekeeper comes out to you, he grasps your
    hand,

Source: Miriam Lichtheim, *Ancient Egyptian Literature* (Berkeley: University of California Press, 1975), 1:41–42.

Takes you into heaven, to you father Geb.
He rejoices at your coming, gives you his hands,
Kisses you, caresses you,
Sets you before the spirits, the imperishable
   stars....
The hidden ones worship you,
The great ones surround you,
The watchers wait on you,

Barley is threshed for you,
Emmer° is reaped for you,
Your monthly feasts are made with it,
Your half-month feasts are made with it,
As ordered done for you by Geb, your father,
Rise up, O Teti, you shall not die!

_____

°**Emmer:** a variety of wheat

Document 3.4

A New Basis for Egyptian Immortality

Much later, during the New Kingdom period of ancient Egyptian history (1550–1064 B.C.E.), the *Book of the Dead* was compiled, gathering together a number of magical spells designed to ensure a smooth passage to eternal life. Written on papyrus, the spells could be purchased by anyone who could afford them. The owner then inscribed his own name and title and had the document placed in his tomb. The most famous of these texts is the so-called Negative Confession, which portrays the deceased person appearing before the gods in a place of judgment to demonstrate his moral life and his fitness for a place in the Land of the West. Such practices extended to people other than just the pharaoh the possibility of magical assistance in gaining eternal life with the gods.

- What changes in Egyptian religious thinking does the Negative Confession mark?

- On what basis are the users of the Negative Confession making their claim for eternal life?

- What does the Negative Confession suggest about the sources of conflict and discord in New Kingdom Egypt? How do these compare with the social problems revealed in the Code of Hammurabi?

Book of the Dead
ca. 1550–1064 B.C.E.

When the deceased enters the hall of the goddesses of Truth, he says:

Homage to thee, O great god, thou Lord of Truth. I have come to thee, my Lord, and I have brought myself hither that I may see thy beauties. I know thee, I know thy name. I know the names of the Two-and-Forty gods who live with thee in this Hall of Maati. In truth I have come to thee. I have brought Truth to thee. I have destroyed wickedness for thee.

I have not sinned against men.
I have not oppressed (or wronged) [my] kinsfolk.

_____

Source: E. A. Wallis Budge, *Osiris, the Egyptian Religion of Resurrection* (London: P. L. Warner; New York: G. P. Putnam's Sons, 1911), 1:337–39.

I have not committed evil in the place of truth.°

I have not known worthless men.

I have not committed acts of abomination.

I have not caused my name to appear for honors.

I have not domineered over slaves.

I have not thought scorn of the god.

I have not defrauded the poor man of his goods.

I have not caused harm to be done to the slave by his master.

I have caused no man to suffer.

I have allowed no man to go hungry.

I have made no man weep. I have slain no man.

I have not given the order for any man to be slain.

I have not caused pain to the multitude.

I have not filched the offerings in the temples.

I have not purloined the cakes of the gods.

I have not stolen the offerings of the spirits.

_____

°**place of truth:** a temple or burial place.

I have not defiled myself in the pure places of the god of my city.

I have not cheated in measuring of grain.

I have not filched land or added thereto.

I have not encroached upon the fields of others.

I have not added to the weight of the balance.

I have not cheated with the pointer of the scales.

I have not taken away the milk from the mouths of the babes.

I have not driven away the beasts from their pastures.

I have not netted the geese of the preserves of the gods.

I have not obstructed water when it should run.

I have not cut a cutting in a canal of rating water.

I have not extinguished a flame when it ought to burn.

I have not abrogated the days of offering the chosen offerings.

I have not turned off cattle from the property of the gods.

I am pure. I am pure. I am pure. I am pure.

Document 3.5

The Occupations of Old Egypt

Compared to small Paleolithic communities and later agricultural village societies, civilizations developed a far more complex division of labor and a much greater sense of social hierarchy. Such features of the First Civilizations are on display in the Egyptian text commonly known as "Be a Scribe." Dating from the Middle Kingdom period (2066–1650 B.C.E.), it was a school text that students training for administrative positions would copy in an effort to improve their writing. It also conveyed to them the exalted position of a scribe in contrast to many other occupations. One such text suggested that writing granted a kind of immortality to the scribe: "Man decays; his corpse is dust; all his kin have perished. But a book makes him remembered through the mouth of its reciter."[30]

■ What might historians learn from this text about the occupational and social structure of Middle Kingdom Egypt?

■ What does learning to write offer to a young Egyptian? What advantages of a scribal position are suggested in the document?

■ What timeless frustrations of a teacher are evident in this text?

Be a Scribe

ca. 2066–1650 B.C.E.

Apply yourself to [this] noble profession....You will find it useful.... You will be advanced by your superiors. You will be sent on a mission....Love writing, shun dancing; then you become a worthy official.... By day write with your fingers; recite by night. Befriend the scroll, the palette. It pleases more than wine. Writing for him who knows it is better than all other professions. It pleases more than bread and beer, more than clothing and ointment. It is worth more than an inheritance in Egypt, than a tomb in the west.

Young fellow, how conceited you are!... But though I beat you with every kind of stick, you do not listen....You are a person fit for writing, though you have not yet known a woman. Your heart discerns, your fingers are skilled, your mouth is apt for reciting....

But though I spend the day telling you "Write," it seems like a plague to you....

See for yourself with your own eye. The occupations lie before you.

The washerman's day is going up, going down. All his limbs are weak, [from] whitening his neighbor's clothes every day, from washing their linen.

The maker of pots is smeared with soil.... [H]e is like one who lives in the bog.

The cobbler mingles with vats. His odor is penetrating. His hands are red..., like one who is smeared with blood....

The watchman prepares garlands and polishes vase-stands. He spends a night of toil just as one on whom the sun shines.

The merchants travel downstream and upstream. They are as busy as can be, carrying goods from one town to another. They supply him who has wants. But the tax collectors carry off the gold, that most precious of metals.

The ships' crews from every house [of commerce], they receive their loads. They depart from Egypt for Syria, and each man's god is with him. [But] not one of them says: "We shall see Egypt again!"

[The] outworker who is in the fields, his is the toughest of all the jobs. He spends the day loaded with his tools, tied to his toolbox. When he returns home at night, he is loaded with the toolbox and the timbers, his drinking mug, and his whetstones....

Let me also expound to you the situation of the peasant, that other tough occupation. [Comes] the inundation and soaks him..., he attends to his equipment. By day he cuts his farming tools; by night he twists rope. Even his midday hour he spends on farm labor. He equips himself to go to the field as if he were a warrior....When he reaches his field he finds [it?] broken up. He spends time cultivating, and the snake is after him. It finishes off the seed as it is cast to the ground. He does not see a green blade. He does three plowings with borrowed grain. His wife has gone down to the merchants and found nothing for barter....

If you have any sense, be a scribe. If you have learned about the peasant, you will not be able to be one.... Look, I instruct you to...make you become one whom the king trusts; to make you gain entrance to treasury and granary. To make you receive the shipload at the gate of the granary. To make you issue the offerings on feast days. You are dressed in fine clothes; you own horses. Your boat is on the river; you are supplied with attendants. You stride about inspecting. A mansion is built in your town. You have a powerful office, given you by the king. Male and female slaves are about you. Those who are in the fields grasp your hand, on plots that you have made....Put the writings in your heart, and you will be protected from all kinds of toil. You will become a worthy official.

Do you not recall the [fate of] the unskilled man? His name is not known. He is ever burdened

---

Source: Miriam Lichtheim, *Ancient Egyptian Literature* (Berkeley: University of California Press, 1975), 2:168–72.

[like an ass carrying things] in front of the scribe who knows what he is about.

Come, [let me tell] you the woes of the soldier, and how many are his superiors: the general, the troop-commander, the officer who leads, the standard-bearer, the lieutenant, the scribe, the commander of fifty, and the garrison-captain. They go in and out in the halls of the palace, saying: "Get laborers!" He is awakened at any hour. One is after him as [after] a donkey. He toils until the Aten sets in his darkness of night. He is hungry, his belly hurts; he is dead while yet alive. When he receives the grain-ration, having been released from duty, it is not good for grinding.

He is called up for Syria. He may not rest. There are no clothes, no sandals....His march is uphill through mountains. He drinks water every third day; it is smelly and tastes of salt. His body is ravaged by illness. The enemy comes, surrounds him with missiles, and life recedes from him. He is told: "Quick, forward, valiant soldier! Win for yourself a good name!" He does not know what he is about. His body is weak, his legs fail him. When victory is won, the captives are handed over to his majesty, to be taken to Egypt....His wife and children are in their village; he dies and does not reach it. If he comes out alive, he is worn out from marching....

Be a scribe, and be spared from soldiering! You call and one says: "Here I am." You are safe from torments. Every man seeks to raise himself up. Take note of it!

Using the Evidence:
Life and Afterlife in Mesopotamia and Egypt

1. **Defining civilization:** What features of civilization, described in Chapter 3, do these documents illustrate?

2. **Making comparisons:** What similarities and differences between ancient Mesopotamian and Egyptian civilizations can you infer from these documents? How might you account for the differences?

3. **Considering past and present:** What elements of thought and practice from these early pieces of written literature resonate still in the twenty-first century? What elements remain strange or unfamiliar to modern sensibilities?

4. **Seeking further evidence:** What dimensions of these civilizations' social life and religious thinking are not addressed in these documents? What other perspectives might you want to seek out?

5. **Reading between the lines:** Historians often use documents to obtain insights or information that the authors did not intend to convey. How might these documents be used in this fashion? What are the advantages and dangers in this use of ancient texts?

Visual Sources

Considering the Evidence:
Indus Valley Civilization

In most accounts of the First Civilizations, Egypt and Mesopotamia hold center stage. And yet the civilization of the Indus River valley was much larger, and its archeological treasures have been equally impressive, though clearly distinctive (see pp. 86–91). This civilization arose around 2600 B.C.E., about a thousand years later than its better-known counterparts in the Middle East and North Africa. By 1500 B.C.E. Indus Valley civilization was in decline, as the center of Indian or South Asian civilization shifted gradually eastward to the plains of the Ganges River. In the process, all distinct memory of the earlier Indus Valley civilization vanished, to be rediscovered only in the early twentieth century as archeologists uncovered its remarkable remains. Here is yet another contrast with Egypt and Mesopotamia, where a memory of earlier achievements persisted long after those civilizations had passed into history. The images that follow are drawn from archeological investigations of the Indus Valley civilization and offer us a glimpse of its many achievements and unique features. Since its written language was limited in extent and has not yet been deciphered, scholars have been highly dependent on its physical remains for understanding this First Civilization.

Among the most distinctive elements of Indus Valley civilization were its cities, of which Mohenjo Daro and Harappa were the largest and are the most thoroughly investigated. Laid out systematically on a grid pattern and clearly planned, they were surrounded by substantial walls made from mud bricks of a standardized size and interrupted by imposing gateways. Inside the walls, public buildings, market areas, large and small houses, and craft workshops stood in each of the cities' various neighborhoods. Many houses had indoor latrines, while wide main streets and narrow side lanes had drains to carry away polluted water and sewage. Visual Source 3.1 is a modern drawing of ancient Harappa by one of the leading archeologists of the city, Jonathan M. Kenoyer. Also see the photo on page 93, which shows a section of the excavated city of Mohenjo Daro.

- Based on these images, how would you describe an Indus Valley city to someone who had never seen it?

- Compare these images of Indus Valley cities with those of the early agrarian village of Çatalhüyük (see the photo on p. 64 and Visual

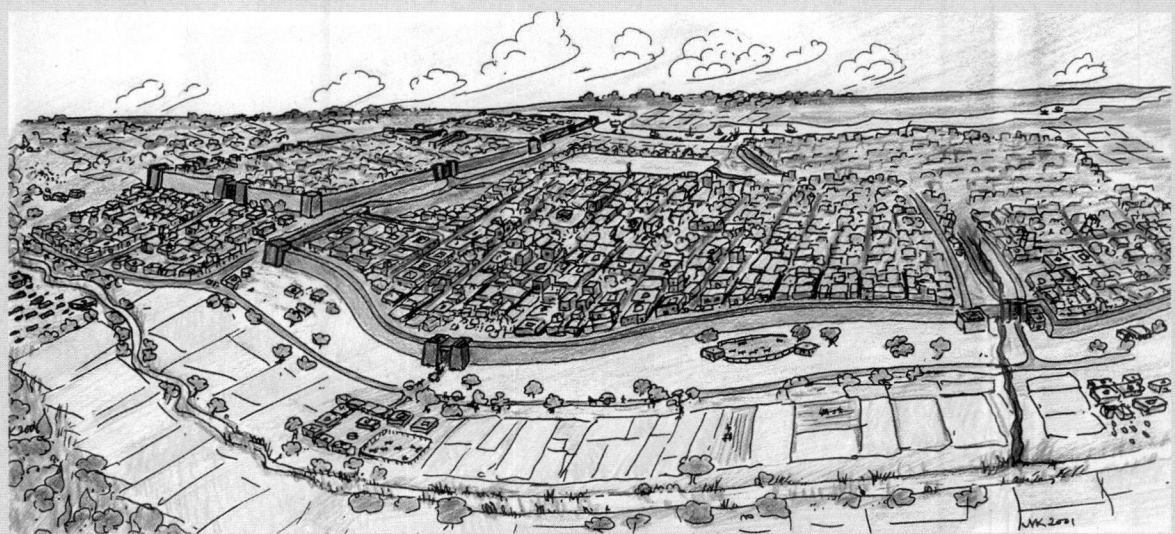

Visual Source 3.1 Ancient Harappa (J. Mark Kenoyer/Harappa Images)

Source 2.1 on p. 77). What differences can you identify between these two types of settlements? What had changed in the intervening centuries?

In many ancient and more recent societies, seals have been used for imprinting an image on a document or a product. Such seals have been among the most numerous artifacts found in the Indus Valley cities. They generally carried the image of an animal—a bull, an elephant, a crocodile, a buffalo, or even a mythic creature such as a unicorn—as well as a title or inscription in the still undeciphered script of this civilization. Thus the seals were accessible to an illiterate worker loading goods on a boat as well as to literate merchants or officials. Particular seals may well have represented a specific clan, a high official, or a prominent individual. Unicorn seals have been the most numerous finds and were often used to make impressions on clay tags attached to bundled goods, suggesting that their owners were involved in trade or commerce. Because bull seals, such as that shown in Visual Source 3.2, were rarer, their owners may have been high-ranking officials or members of a particularly powerful clan. The bull, speculates archeologist Jonathan Kenoyer, "may symbolize the leader of the herd, whose strength and virility protects the herd and ensures the procreation of the species, or it may stand for a sacrificial animal."[31] Indus Valley seals, as well as pottery, have been found in Mesopotamia, indicating a well-developed trade between these two First Civilizations.

■ How might a prominent landowner, a leading official, a clan head, or a merchant make use of such a seal?

■ What meaning might you attach to the use of animals as totems or symbols of a particular group or individual?

Visual Source 3.2 A Seal from the Indus Valley (J. Mark Kenoyer/Harappa Images)

■ Notice the five characters of the Indus Valley script at the top of the seal. Do a little research on the script with an eye to understanding why it has proved so difficult to decipher.

The most intriguing features of Indus Valley civilization involve what is missing, at least in comparison with ancient Egypt and Mesopotamia. No grand temples or palaces; no elite burial places filled with great wealth; no images of warfare, conquest, or the seizing of captives; no monuments to celebrate powerful rulers. These absences have left scholars guessing about the social and political organization of this civilization. Kenoyer has suggested that the great cities were likely controlled not by a single ruler, but by "a small group of elites, comprised of merchants, landowners, and ritual specialists."[32] Visual Source 3.3, a statue seven inches tall and found in Mohenjo Daro, likely depicts one of these elite men.

■ What specific features of the statue can you point out?

■ What possible indication of elite status can you identify?

■ What overall impression does the statue convey?

Visual Source 3.3 Man from Mohenjo Daro (Department of Archaeology and Museums, Karachi, Pakistan)

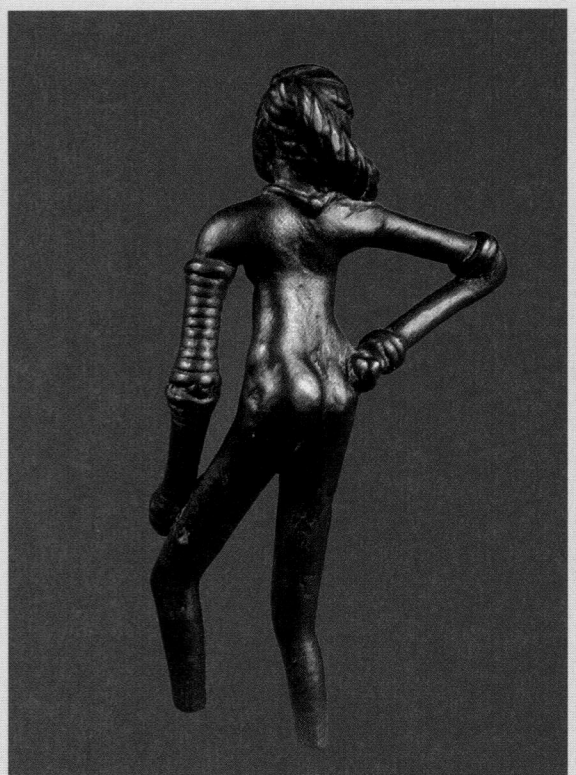 

Visual Source 3.4 Dancing Girl (Courtesy, National Museum, New Delhi. Photo: Professor Gregory Possehl, Curator, Asian Department, University of Pennsylvania Museum)

Limited archeological evidence suggests that at least some urban women played important social and religious roles in the Indus Valley civilization. Figurines of women or goddesses are more common than those of men. Women, apparently, were buried near their mothers and grandmothers, while men were not interred with their male relatives. The great variety of clothing, hairstyles, and decorations displayed on female figurines indicates considerable class, ethnic, and perhaps individual variation.

Among the most delightful discoveries in the Indus Valley cities is the evocative statue shown in Visual Source 3.4. It is about four inches tall and dated to around 2500 B.C.E. This young female nude is known generally as the "dancing girl." Cast in bronze using a sophisticated "lost wax" method, this statue provides evidence for a well-developed copper/bronze industry. The figure herself was portrayed in a dancer's pose, her hair gathered in a bun and her left arm covered with bangles and holding a small bowl. Both her arms and legs seem disproportionately long. She has been described variously as a queen, a high-status woman, a sacred temple dancer, and a tribal girl.

Although no one really knows her precise identity, she has evoked wide admiration and appreciation. Mortimer Wheeler, a famous British archeologist, described her as "a girl perfectly, for the moment, perfectly confident of herself and the world." American archeologist Gregory Possehl, also active in the archeology of the Indus Valley civilization, commented: "We may not be certain that she was a dancer, but she was good at what she did and she knew it."[33]

■ What features of this statue may have provoked such observations?

■ How do you react to this statue? What qualities does she evoke?

■ What does Visual Source 3.4 suggest about views of women, images of female beauty, and attitudes about sexuality and the body?

Using the Evidence: Indus Valley Civilization

1. **Using art as evidence:** What can we learn about Indus Valley civilization from these visual sources? How does our level of understanding of this civilization differ from that of Egypt and Mesopotamia where plentiful written records are available?

2. **Considering art without writing:** Based on these visual sources and those in Chapters 1 and 2, consider the problem of interpreting history through art, artifacts, or archeological sites in the absence of writing. What can we know with some certainty? What can we only guess at?

3. **Comparing art across time:** How would you compare the rock art of Australian Paleolithic peoples (Chapter 1), the art of early agricultural and pastoral peoples (Chapter 2), and the art from the Indus Valley? Consider issues of style, content, and accessibility to people of the twenty-first century. Is it possible to speak of artistic "progress" or "development," or should we be content with simply noticing differences?

4. **Comparing representations of people:** Notice the various ways that human figures were portrayed in the visual sources shown in Chapters 1–3. How might you define those differences? What variations in the depiction of men and women can you identify?

5. **Seeking further evidence:** What additional kinds of archeological discoveries would be helpful in furthering our understanding of Indus Valley civilization?

PART TWO

The Classical Era in World History

500 B.C.E.–500 C.E.

Contents

Chapter 4. Eurasian Empires, 500 B.C.E.–500 C.E.
Chapter 5. Eurasian Cultural Traditions, 500 B.C.E.–500 C.E.
Chapter 6. Eurasian Social Hierarchies, 500 B.C.E.–500 C.E.
Chapter 7. Classical Era Variations: Africa and the Americas, 500 B.C.E.–1200 C.E.

After the First Civilizations: What Changed and What Didn't?

Studying world history has much in common with using the zoom lens of a camera. Sometimes, we pull the lens back in order to get a picture of the broadest possible panorama. At other times, we zoom in a bit for a middle-range shot, or even farther for a close-up of some particular feature of the historical landscape. Students of world history soon become comfortable with moving back and forth among these several perspectives.

As we bid farewell to the First Civilizations, we will take the opportunity to pull back the lens and look broadly, and briefly, at the entire age of agricultural civilizations, a period from about 3500 B.C.E., when the earliest of the First Civilizations arose, to about 1750 C.E., when the first Industrial Revolution launched a new and distinctively modern phase of world history. During these more than 5,000 years, the most prominent large-scale trend was the globalization of civilization as this new form of human community increasingly spread across the planet, encompassing more people and larger territories.

The first wave of that process, addressed in Chapter 3, was already global in scope, with expressions in Asia, Africa, and the Americas. Those First Civilizations generated the most impressive and powerful human societies created thus far, but they proved fragile and vulnerable as well. The always-quarreling city-states of ancient Mesopotamia had long ago been absorbed into the larger empires of Babylon and Assyria. During the first millennium B.C.E., Egypt too fell victim to a series of foreign invaders, including the forces of Nubia, Assyria, Alexander the Great, and the Roman Empire. The Indus Valley civilization likewise declined sharply, as deforestation, topsoil erosion, and decreased rainfall led to desertification and political collapse by 1500 B.C.E. Norte Chico civilization seems to have faded away by 1800 B.C.E. The end of Olmec civilization around 400 B.C.E. has long puzzled historians, for it seems that the Olmecs themselves razed and then abandoned their major cities even as their civilizational style spread to neighboring peoples. About the same time, China's unified political system fragmented into a series of warring states.

Even if particular First Civilizations broke down, there was no going back. Civilization as a form of human community proved durable and resilient as well as periodically fragile. Thus, in the thousand years between 500 B.C.E. and 500 C.E., new or enlarged urban-centered and state-based societies emerged to replace the First Civilizations in the Mediterranean basin, the Middle East, India, China, Mesoamerica, and the Andes. Furthermore, smaller expressions of civilization began to take shape elsewhere—in Ethiopia and West Africa, in Japan and Indonesia, in Vietnam and Cambodia. In short, the development of civilization was becoming a global process.

Many of these "second wave" civilizations likewise perished, as the collapses of the Roman Empire, Han dynasty China, and the Mayan cities remind us. They were followed by yet a "third wave" of civilizations (roughly 500 to 1500 C.E.; see Part Three). Some of them represented the persistence or renewal of older patterns, as in the case of China, for example, while elsewhere—such as in Western Europe, Russia, Japan, and West Africa—new civilizations emerged, all of which borrowed heavily from their more-established neighbors. The largest of these, Islamic civilization, incorporated a number of older centers of civilization, Egypt and Mesopotamia for example, under the umbrella of a new religion. The globalization of civilization continued apace.

The size and prominence of these civilizations sometimes lead historians and history textbooks to ignore those cultures that did not embrace the city- and state-centered characteristic of civilizations. World history, as a field of study, has often been slanted in the direction of civilizations at the expense of other forms of human community. To counteract that tendency, the following chapters will, on occasion, point out the continuing historical development of gathering and hunting peoples, agricultural societies organized around kinship principles and village life, emerging chiefdoms, and pastoral peoples.

Continuities in Civilization

The renewal and expansion of civilization, however, remains the leading story. As this account of the human journey moves into the second and third waves of civilization, the question arises as to how they differed from the first ones. From a panoramic perspective, the answer is "not much." States and empires rose, expanded, and collapsed with a tiresome regularity, requiring history students to remember who was up and who was down at various times. It is arguable, however, that little fundamental change occurred amid these constant fluctuations. Monarchs continued to rule most of the new civilizations; men continued to dominate women; a sharp divide between the elite and everyone else persisted almost everywhere, as did the practice of slavery.[1]

Furthermore, no technological or economic breakthrough occurred to create new kinds of human societies as the Agricultural Revolution had done earlier or as the Industrial Revolution would do in later centuries. Landowning elites had little incentive to innovate, for they benefited enormously from simply expropriating the surplus that peasant farmers produced. Nor would peasants have any reason to invest much effort in creating new forms of production when they knew full well that any gains they might generate would be seized by their social superiors. Merchants, who often were risk takers, might have spawned innovations, but they usually were dominated by powerful states and were viewed with suspicion and condescension by more prestigious social groups.

Many fluctuations, repetitive cycles, and minor changes characterize this long era of agricultural civilization, but no fundamental or revolutionary transformation of social or economic life took place. The major turning points in human history had occurred earlier with the emergence of agriculture and the birth of the First Civilizations and would occur later with the breakthrough of industrialization.

Changes in Civilization

While this panoramic perspective allows us to see the broadest outlines of the human journey, it also obscures much of great importance that took place during the second and third waves of the age of agrarian civilization. If we zoom in a bit more closely, significant changes emerge, even if they did not result in a thorough transformation of human life. Population, for example, grew more rapidly than ever before during this period, as the Snapshot illustrates. Even though the overall trend was up, important fluctuations interrupted the pattern, especially during the first millennium C.E., when no overall growth took place. Moreover, the rate of growth, though rapid in comparison with Paleolithic times, was quite slow if we measure it against the explosive expansion of recent centuries, when human numbers quadrupled in the twentieth century alone. This modest and interrupted pattern of population growth during the age of agrarian civilization reflected the absence of any fundamental economic breakthrough, which could have supported much larger numbers.

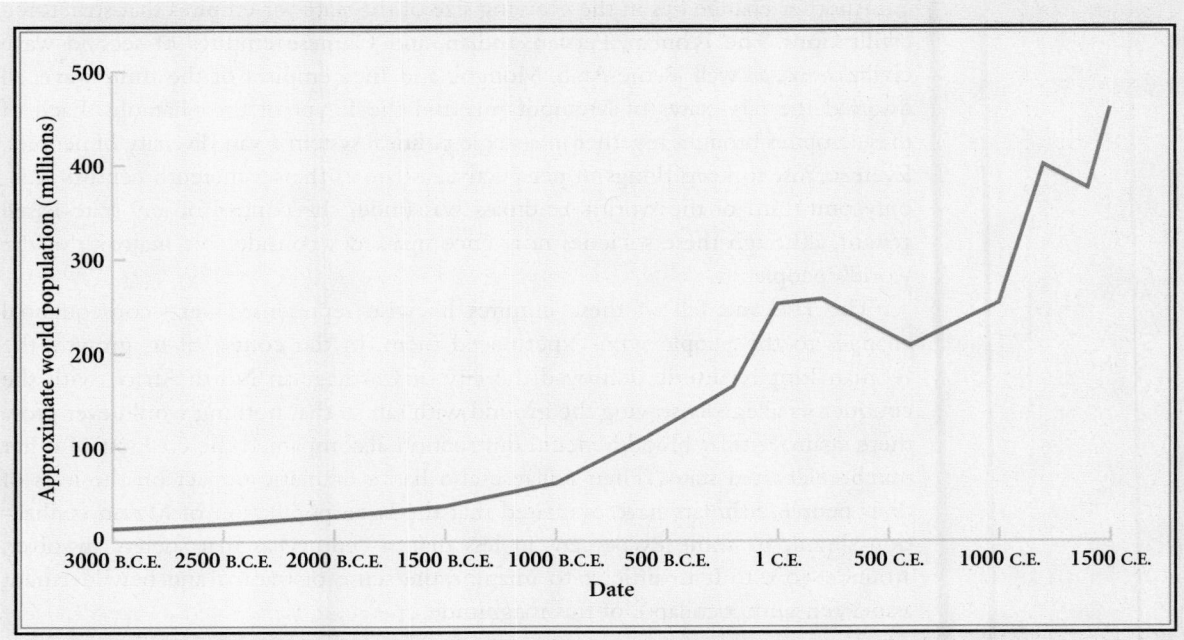

Snapshot   **World Population during the Age of Agricultural Civilization**[2]

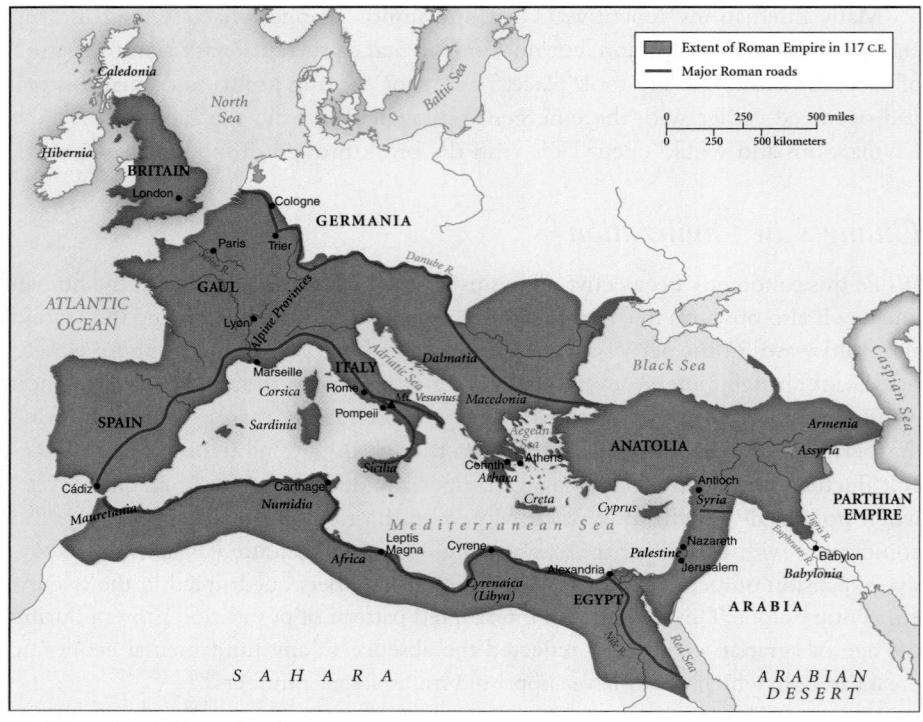

The Roman Empire (p. 156)

Another change lies in the growing size of the states or empires that structured civilizations. The Roman, Persian, Indian, and Chinese empires of second-wave civilizations, as well as the Arab, Mongol, and Inca empires of the third wave, all dwarfed the city-states of Mesopotamia and the Egypt of the pharaohs. Each of these empires brought together in a single political system a vast diversity of peoples. Even so, just to keep things in perspective, as late as the seventeenth century C.E., only one-third of the world's landmass was under the control of any state-based system, although these societies now encompassed a considerable majority of the world's people.

The rise and fall of these empires likewise represented very consequential changes to the people who experienced them. In the course of its growth, the Roman Empire utterly destroyed the city of Carthage in North Africa, with the conquerors allegedly sowing the ground with salt so that nothing would ever grow there again. Similar bloodshed and destruction accompanied the creation of other much-celebrated states. Their collapse also had a dramatic impact on the lives of their people. Scholars have estimated that the large population of Mayan civilization shrank by some 85 percent in less than a century as that society dissolved around 840 C.E. It is difficult to imagine the sense of trauma and bewilderment associated with a collapse of this magnitude.

Second- and third-wave civilizations also generated important innovations in many spheres. Those in the cultural realm have been perhaps the most widespread and enduring. Distinctive "wisdom traditions"—the great philosophical/religious systems of Confucianism and Daoism in China; Hinduism and Buddhism in India; Greek rationalism in the Mediterranean; and Judaism, Zoroastrianism, Christianity, and Islam in the Middle East—have provided the moral and spiritual framework within which most of the world's peoples have sought to order their lives and define their relationship to the mysteries of life and death. All of these philosophical and religious systems are the product of second- and third-wave civilizations.

Although no technological breakthrough equivalent to the Agricultural or Industrial Revolution took place during the second and third waves of agrarian civilizations, more modest innovations considerably enhanced human potential for manipulating the environment. China was a primary source of such technological change, though by no means the only one. "Chinese inventions and discoveries," wrote one prominent historian, "passed in a continuous flood from East to West for twenty centuries before the scientific revolution."[3] They included piston bellows, the draw-loom, silk-handling machinery, the wheelbarrow, a better harness for draft animals, the crossbow, iron casting, the iron-chain suspension bridge, gunpowder, firearms, the magnetic compass, paper, printing, and porcelain. India pioneered the crystallization of sugar and techniques for the manufacture of cotton textiles. Roman technological achievements were particularly apparent in construction and civil engineering—the building of roads, bridges, aqueducts, and fortifications—and in the art of glassblowing.

A further process of change following the end of the First Civilizations lay in the emergence of far more elaborate, widespread, and dense networks of communication and exchange that connected many of the world's peoples to one another. Many of the technologies mentioned here diffused widely across large areas. Sugar production provides a telling example. The syrup from sugarcane, which was initially domesticated in New Guinea early in the age of agriculture, was first processed into crystallized sugar in India by 500 C.E. During the early centuries of the Islamic era, Arab traders brought this technology from India to the Middle East and the Mediterranean, where Europeans learned about it during the Crusades. Europeans then transferred the practice of making sugar to the Atlantic islands and finally to the Americas, where it played a major role in stimulating a plantation economy and the Atlantic slave trade.[4]

Long-distance trade routes represented another form of transregional interaction. Caravan trade across northern Eurasia, seaborne commerce within the Indian Ocean basin, the exchange of goods across the Sahara, river-based commerce in the eastern woodlands of North America, various trading networks radiating from Mesoamerica—all of these carried goods, and sometimes culture as well. Buddhism, Hinduism, Christianity, and especially Islam spread widely beyond their places of origin, often carried on the camels and ships of merchants, creating ties of culture and religion among distant peoples within the Afro-Eurasian zone. Disease also increasingly linked distant human communities. According to the famous Greek historian Thucydides, a mysterious plague "from parts of Ethiopia above Egypt" descended on Athens in 430 B.C.E. and decimated the city, "inflicting a blow on Athenian society from which it never entirely recovered."[5]

Thus the second and third waves of civilization gave rise to much larger empires, new and distinctive cultural/religious traditions, any number of technological innovations, and novel patterns of interaction among far-flung societies. In these ways, the world became quite different from what it had been in the age of the First Civilizations, even though fundamental economic and social patterns had not substantially changed.

Classical Civilizations

At this point, and in the four chapters that follow, our historical lens zooms in to a middle-range focus on the major second-wave civilizations during the thousand years between 500 B.C.E. and 500 C.E. Historians frequently refer to this period of time as the "classical era" of world history, a term that highlights enduring traditions that have lasted into modern times and persist still in the twenty-first century. Confucianism, Hinduism, Buddhism, Judaism, and Christianity all took shape during this era of second-wave civilizations, and all of them remain very much alive at the dawn of the third millennium C.E. Despite the many and profound transformations of modernity, billions of people in the contemporary world still guide their lives, or at least claim to, according to teachings that first appeared 2,000 or more years ago.

Beyond the practices of individuals, the current identities of entire countries, regions, and civilizations are still linked to the achievements of the classical era. In 1971, a largely Muslim Iran mounted a lavish and much-criticized celebration of the 2,500th anniversary of the ancient Persian Empire. In 2004, a still communist China permitted public celebrations to mark the 2,555th birthday of its ancient sage Confucius. Students in Western schools and universities continue to read the works of Plato and Aristotle, produce the plays of Aeschylus and Sophocles, and admire the accomplishments of Athens. Many Indians still embrace the ancient religious texts called the Vedas and the Upanishads and continue to deal with the realities of caste. These are the continuities and enduring legacies that are reflected in the notion of "classical civilizations."

Designating the millennium between 500 B.C.E. and 500 C.E. as a "classical era" in world history is derived largely from the experience of Eurasian peoples, for it was on the outer rim of that huge continent that the largest and most influential civilizations took shape—in China, India, Persia, and the Mediterranean basin. Furthermore, that continent housed the vast majority of the world's people, some 80 percent or more.[6] Thus the first three chapters of Part Two focus exclusively on these Eurasian civilizations. Chapter 4 introduces them by examining and comparing their political frameworks and especially the empires (great or terrible, depending on your point of view) in which most of them were expressed. Chapter 5 looks at the cultural or religious traditions that each of them generated, while Chapter 6 probes their social organization—class, caste, slavery, and gender. Chapter 7 turns the spotlight on Africa and the Americas, asking whether their histories during the classical era paralleled Eurasian patterns or explored alternative possibilities.

In recalling the classical era, we will have occasion to compare the experiences of its various peoples, to note their remarkable achievements, to lament the tragedies that befell them and the suffering to which they gave rise, and to ponder their continuing power to fascinate us still.

Landmarks of the Classical Era, 500 B.C.E.–500 C.E.

	700 B.C.E.	600 B.C.E.	500 B.C.E.	400 B.C.E.	300 B.C.E.	200 B.C.E.	100 B.C.E.	0

China

551–479 B.C.E. Confucius

221–206 B.C.E. Qin dynasty

6th century B.C.E.(?) Laozi

500–221 B.C.E. Political fragmentation (age of "warring states")

206 B.C.E. –220 C.E. Han dynasty

S. Asia/India

◀ **by 750 B.C.E.** Urban centers in Ganges valley

563–483 B.C.E. Life of the Buddha

321–185 B.C.E. Mauryan dynasty

327 B.C.E. Invasion of India by Alexander

◀ **800–400 B.C.E.** Compilation of Upanishads

268–232 B.C.E. Reign of Ashoka

Middle East/Persia

539 B.C.E. Cyrus allows Jews to return from exile

383–323 B.C.E. Seleucid dynasty (Greek)

334 B.C.E. Invasion of Alexander the Great

553–330 B.C.E. Achaemenid dynasty

247 B.C.E.–224 C.E. Parthian dynasty

7th–6th century B.C.E. (?) Life of Zarathustra

Mediterranean Basin

336–323 B.C.E. Reign of Alexander the Great

4 B.C.E.–EARLY 30S C.E. Life of Jesus

◀ **800–336 B.C.E.** Era of Greek city-states

◀ **800–500 B.C.E.** Hebrew prophets

470–322 B.C.E. Socates, Plato, Aristotle

500–479 B.C.E. Greco-Persian Wars

509 B.C.E. Founding of Roman Republic

200 B.C.E.–200 C.E. High point of Roman Empire

Africa

◀ **760 B.C.E.** Kush conquest of Egypt

300 B.C.E.–100 C.E. Nubian kingdom of Meroë

The Americas

◀ **9th century B.C.E.** Chavín religious cult in Andes

400 B.C.E. Decline of Olmec civilization

200 B.C.E.–500 C.E. Nazca culture

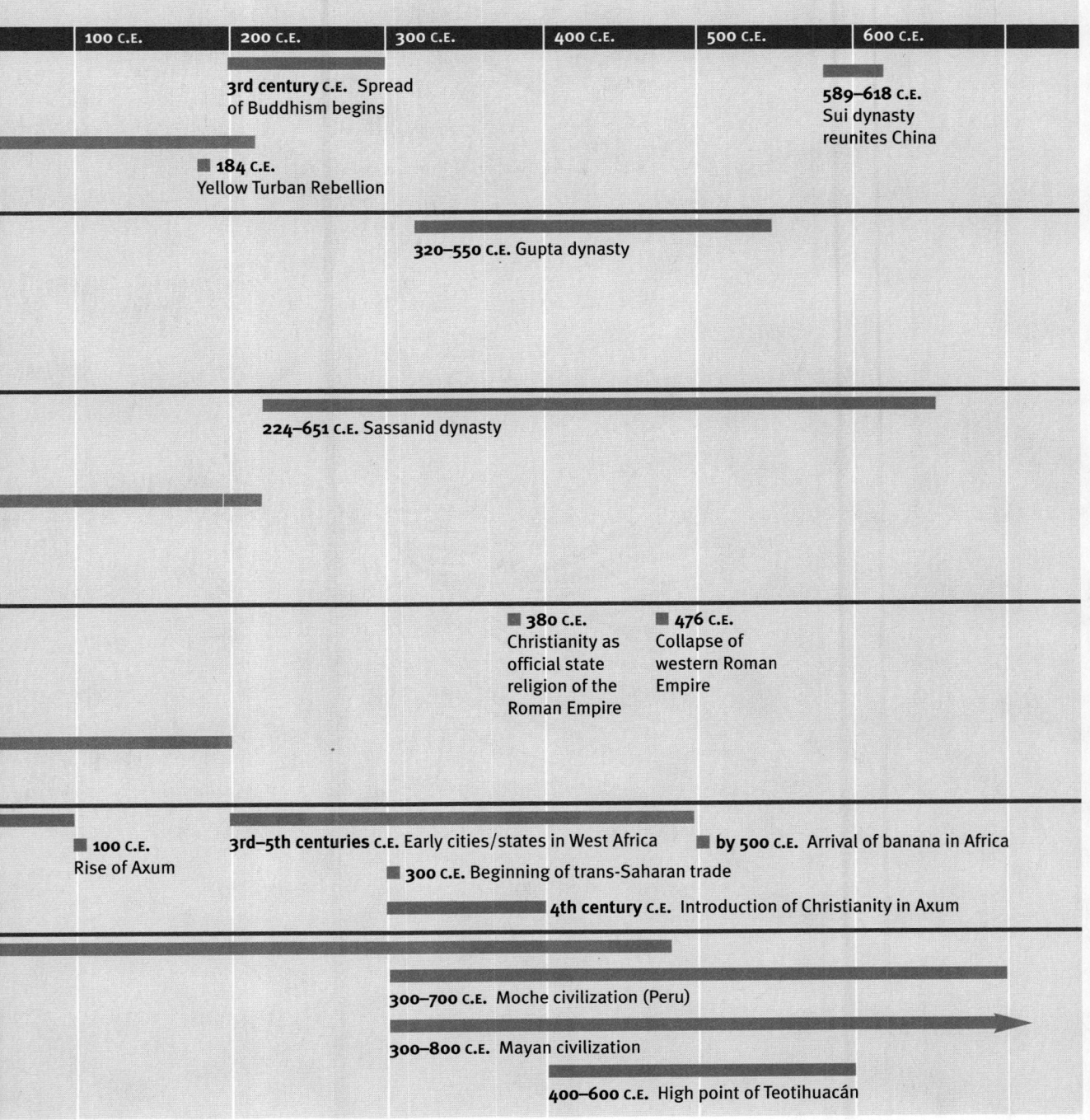

100 C.E.　200 C.E.　300 C.E.　400 C.E.　500 C.E.　600 C.E.

3rd century C.E.　Spread of Buddhism begins

589–618 C.E. Sui dynasty reunites China

■ **184** C.E. Yellow Turban Rebellion

320–550 C.E. Gupta dynasty

224–651 C.E. Sassanid dynasty

■ **380** C.E. Christianity as official state religion of the Roman Empire

■ **476** C.E. Collapse of western Roman Empire

■ **100** C.E. Rise of Axum

3rd–5th centuries C.E. Early cities/states in West Africa

■ **by 500** C.E.　Arrival of banana in Africa

■ **300** C.E. Beginning of trans-Saharan trade

4th century C.E.　Introduction of Christianity in Axum

300–700 C.E.　Moche civilization (Peru)

300–800 C.E.　Mayan civilization

400–600 C.E.　High point of Teotihuacán

CHAPTER FOUR

Eurasian Empires

500 B.C.E.—500 C.E.

Empires and Civilizations in
   Collision: The Persians and the
   Greeks
   The Persian Empire
   The Greeks
   Collision: The Greco-Persian Wars
   Collision: Alexander and the
    Hellenistic Era
Comparing Empires: Roman and
   Chinese
   Rome: From City-State to Empire
   China: From Warring States to
    Empire
   Consolidating the Roman and
    Chinese Empires
   The Collapse of Empires
Intermittent Empire: The Case of
   India
Reflections: Classical Empires and
   the Twentieth Century
Considering the Evidence
   Documents: Political Authority in
    Classical Civilizations
   Visual Sources: Qin Shihuangdi
    and China's Eternal Empire

Are We Rome? It was the title of a thoughtful book, published in 2007, asking what had become a familiar question in the early twenty-first century: "Is the United States the new Roman Empire?"[1] With the collapse of the Soviet Union by 1991 and the subsequent U.S. invasions of Afghanistan and Iraq, some commentators began to make the comparison. The United States' enormous multicultural society, its technological achievements, its economically draining and overstretched armed forces, its sense of itself as unique and endowed with a global mission, its concern about foreigners penetrating its borders, its apparent determination to maintain military superiority—all of this invited comparison with the Roman Empire. Supporters of a dominant role for the United States argue that Americans must face up to their responsibilities as "the undisputed master of the world" as the Romans did in their time. Critics warn that the Roman Empire became overextended abroad and corrupt and dictatorial at home and then collapsed, suggesting that a similar fate may await the American empire. Either way, the point of reference was an empire that had passed into history some 1,500 years earlier, a continuing reminder of the relevance of the distant past to our contemporary world. In fact, for at least several centuries, that empire has been a source of metaphors and "lessons" about personal morality, corruption, political life, military expansion, and much more.

    Even in a world largely critical of empires, they still excite the imagination of historians and readers of history. The earliest ones

Statue of Augustus: Likely dating from about 20 B.C.E., this statue has become symbolic of the emerging Roman Empire. Commemorating a major Roman military victory, it shows Augustus as imperator, or military commander, with his right arm extended as if he were addressing his troops. According to some scholars, his barefoot posture suggests divinity. So does the small figure of Cupid riding a dolphin at the base, for Cupid was the son of the Roman goddess Venus and serves to link Augustus to this much beloved deity. (Scala/Art Resource, NY)

show up in the era of the First Civilizations when Akkadian, Babylonian, and Assyrian empires encompassed the city-states of Mesopotamia and established an enduring imperial tradition in the Middle East. Egypt became an imperial state when it temporarily ruled Nubia and the lands of the eastern Mediterranean. Following in their wake were many more empires, whose rise and fall have been central features of world history for the past 4,000 years.

BUT WHAT EXACTLY IS AN EMPIRE? At one level, empires are simply states, political systems that exercise coercive power. The term, however, is normally reserved for larger and more aggressive states, those that conquer, rule, and extract resources from other states and peoples. Thus empires have generally encompassed a considerable variety of peoples and cultures within a single political system, and they have often been associated with political and cultural oppression. No clear line divides empires and small multiethnic states, and the distinction between them is arbitrary and subjective. Frequently, empires have given political expression to a civilization or culture, as in the Chinese and Persian empires. Civilizations have also flourished without a single all-encompassing state or empire, as in the competing city-states of Mesopotamia, Greece, and the Maya or the many rival states of post-Roman Europe. In such cases, civilizations were expressed in elements of a common culture rather than in a unified political system.

The Eurasian empires of the classical era—those of Persia, Greece under Alexander the Great, Rome, China during the Qin and Han dynasties, India during the Mauryan and Gupta dynasties—shared a set of common problems. Would they seek to impose the culture of the imperial heartland on their varied subjects? Would they rule conquered people directly or through established local authorities? How could they extract the wealth of empire in the form of taxes, tribute, and labor while maintaining order in conquered territories? And, no matter how impressive they were at their peak, they all sooner or later collapsed, providing a useful reminder to their descendants of the fleeting nature of all human creation.

Why have these and other empires been of such lasting fascination to both ancient and modern people? Perhaps in part because they were so big, creating a looming presence in their respective regions. Their armies and their tax collectors were hard to avoid. Maybe also because they were so bloody. Conquest and the violence that accompanies it easily grab our attention, and certainly, all of these empires were founded and sustained at a great cost in human life. The collapse of these once-powerful states is likewise intriguing, for the fall of the mighty seems somehow satisfying, perhaps even a delayed form of justice. The study of empires also sets off by contrast those times and places in which civilizations have prospered without an enduring imperial state.

But empires have also commanded attention simply because they were important. Very large numbers of people—probably the majority of humankind before the twentieth century—have lived out their lives in empires, where they were often governed by rulers culturally different from themselves. These imperial states brought together people of quite different traditions and religions and so stimulated the exchange of ideas, cultures, and values. The Roman Empire, for example, provided the arena within which Christianity was transformed from a small Jewish sect into a world religion. Despite their violence, exploitation, and oppression, empires also imposed substantial periods of peace and security, which fostered economic and artistic development, commercial exchange, and cultural mixing.

Empires and Civilizations in Collision: The Persians and the Greeks

The classical era in Eurasia witnessed the flowering of second-wave civilizations in the Mediterranean world, the Middle East, India, and China. For the most part, these distant civilizations did not directly encounter one another, as each established its own political system, cultural values, and ways of organizing society. A great exception to that rule lay in the Mediterranean world and in the Middle East, where the emerging Persian Empire and Greek civilization, physically adjacent to each other, experienced a centuries-long interaction and clash. It was one of the most consequential cultural encounters of the classical world.

The Persian Empire

In 500 B.C.E., the largest and most impressive of the world's empires was that of the Persians, an Indo-European people whose homeland lay on the Iranian plateau just north of the Persian Gulf. Living on the margins of the earlier Mesopotamian civilization, the Persians constructed an imperial system that drew upon previous examples, such as the Babylonian and Assyrian empires, but far surpassed them all in size and splendor. Under the leadership of the famous monarchs Cyrus (reigned 557–530 B.C.E.) and Darius (reigned 522–486 B.C.E.), Persian conquests quickly reached from Egypt to India, encompassing in a single state some 35 million people, an immensely diverse realm containing dozens of peoples, states, languages, and cultural traditions (see Map 4.1).

■ **Comparison**
How did Persian and Greek civilizations differ in their political organization and values?

The Persian Empire centered on an elaborate cult of kingship in which the monarch, secluded in royal magnificence, could be approached only through an elaborate ritual. When the king died, sacred fires all across the land were extinguished, Persians were expected to shave their hair in mourning, and the manes of horses were cut short. Ruling by the will of the great Persian god Ahura Mazda, kings were absolute monarchs, more than willing to crush rebellious regions or officials. Interrupted on one occasion while he was with his wife, Darius ordered the offender, a high-ranking nobleman, killed, along with his entire clan. In the eyes of many, Persian monarchs fully deserved their effusive title—"Great king, King of kings, King of countries containing all kinds of men, King in this great earth far and wide." Darius himself best expressed the authority of the Persian ruler when he observed: "what was said to them by me, night and day, it was done."[2]

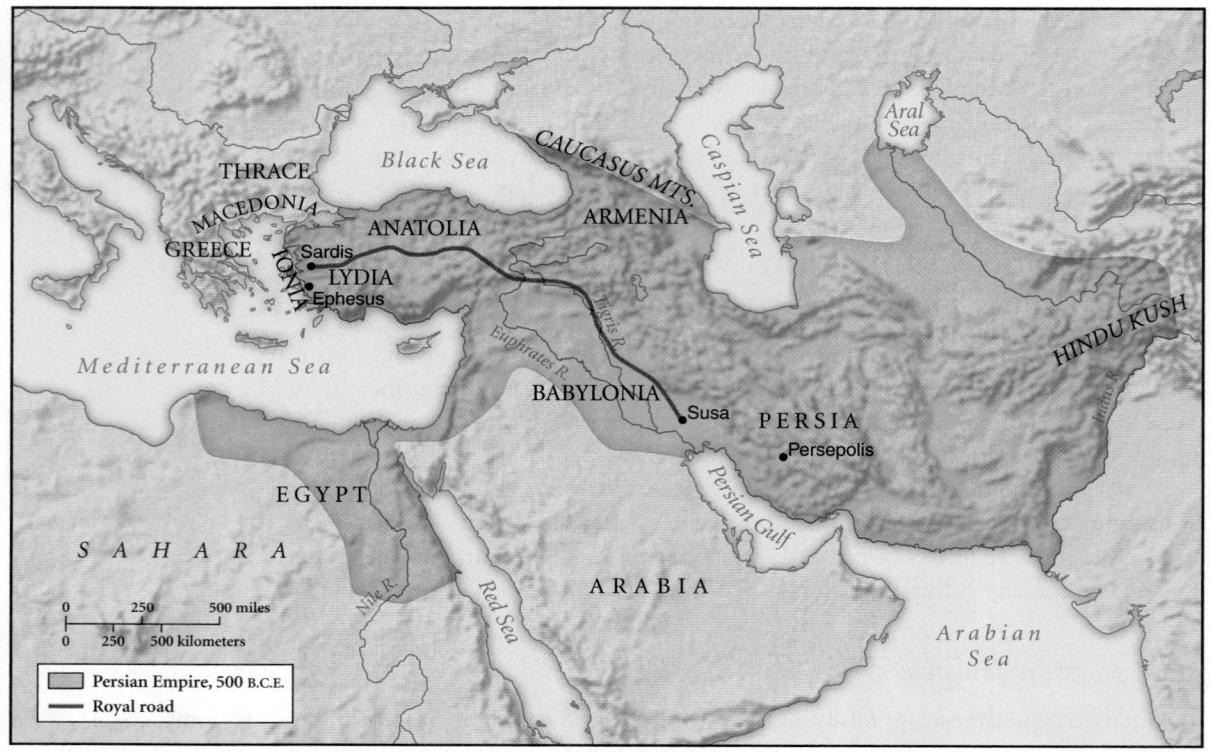

Map 4.1   The Persian Empire
At its height, the Persian Empire was the largest in the world. It dominated the lands of the First Civilizations in the Middle East and was commercially connected to neighboring regions.

But more than conquest and royal decree held the empire together. An effective administrative system placed Persian governors, called *satraps*, in each of the empire's twenty-three provinces, while lower-level officials were drawn from local authorities. A system of imperial spies, known as the "eyes and ears of the King," represented a further imperial presence in the far reaches of the empire. A general policy of respect for the empire's many non-Persian cultural traditions also cemented the state's authority. Cyrus won the gratitude of the Jews when in 539 B.C.E. he allowed those exiled in Babylon to return to their homeland and rebuild their temple in Jerusalem. In Egypt and Babylon, Persian kings took care to uphold local religious cults in an effort to gain the support of their followers and officials. The Greek historian Herodotus commented that "there is no nation which so readily adopts foreign customs. They have taken the dress of the Medes and in war they wear the Egyptian breastplate. As soon as they hear of any luxury, they instantly make it their own."[3] For the next 1,000 years or more, Persian imperial bureaucracy and court life, replete with administrators, tax collectors, record keepers, and translators, provided a model for all subsequent regimes in the region, including, later, those of the Islamic world.

The infrastructure of empire included a system of standardized coinage, predictable taxes levied on each province, and a newly dug canal linking the Nile with the Red Sea, which greatly expanded commerce and enriched Egypt. A "royal road," some 1,700 miles in length, facilitated communication and commerce across this vast empire. Caravans of merchants could traverse this highway in three months, but agents of the imperial courier service, using a fresh supply of horses every twenty-five to thirty miles, could carry a message from one end of the road to another in a week or two. Herodotus was impressed. "Neither snow, nor rain, nor heat, nor darkness of night," he wrote, "prevents them from accomplishing the task proposed to them with utmost speed." That description of the imperial Persian postal system was much later adopted as the unofficial motto for its counterpart in the United States Postal Service.

Persepolis
The largest palace in Persepolis, the Persian Empire's ancient capital, was the Audience Hall. The emperor officially greeted visiting dignitaries at this palace, which was constructed around 500 B.C.E. This relief, which shows a lion attacking a bull and Persian guards at attention, adorns a staircase leading to the Audience Hall. (Gianni Dagli Orti/Corbis)

The immense wealth and power of the Persian Empire were reflected in the construction of elaborate imperial centers, particularly Susa and Persepolis. Palaces, audience halls, quarters for the harem, monuments, and carvings made these cities into powerful symbols of imperial authority. Materials and workers alike were drawn from all corners of the empire and beyond. Inscribed in the foundation of Persepolis was Darius's commentary on what he had set in motion: "And Ahura Mazda was of such a mind, together with all the other gods, that this fortress [should] be built. And [so] I built it. And I built it secure and beautiful and adequate, just as I was intending to."[4]

The Greeks

It would be hard to imagine a sharper contrast than that between the huge and centralized Persian Empire, governed by an absolute and almost unapproachable monarch, and the small competing city-states of classical Greece, which allowed varying degrees of popular participation in political life. Like the Persians, the Greeks were an Indo-European people whose early history drew on the legacy of the First Civilizations. The classical Greece of historical fame emerged around 750 B.C.E. as a new civilization and flourished for about 400 years before it was incorporated into a succession of foreign empires. During that relatively short period, the civilization of Athens and Sparta, of Plato and Aristotle, of Zeus and Apollo took shape and collided with its giant neighbor to the east.

Calling themselves Hellenes, the Greeks created a civilization that was distinctive in many ways, particularly in comparison with the Persians. The total population of

■ **Change**
Why did semidemocratic governments emerge in some of the Greek city-states?

Greece and the Aegean basin was just 2 million to 3 million, a fraction of that of the Persian Empire. Furthermore, Greek civilization took shape on a small peninsula, deeply divided by steep mountains and valleys. Its geography certainly contributed to the political shape of that civilization, which found expression not in a Persian-style empire, but in hundreds of city-states or small settlements (see Map 4.2). Most were quite modest in size, with between 500 and 5,000 male citizens. Each of these city-states was fiercely independent and in frequent conflict with its neighbors, yet they had much in common, speaking the same language and worshipping the same gods. Every four years they temporarily suspended their persisting rivalries to participate together in the Olympic Games, which had begun in 776 B.C.E. Despite this emerging sense of Greek cultural identity, it did

Map 4.2   Classical Greece
The classical civilization of Greece was centered on a small peninsula of southeastern Europe, but Greek settlers spread that civilization along the coasts of the Mediterranean and Black seas.

little to overcome the endemic political rivalries of the larger city-states—Athens, Sparta, Thebes, Corinth, and many others.

Like the Persians, the Greeks were an expansive people, but their expansion took the form of settlement in distant places rather than conquest and empire. Pushed by a growing population, Greek traders in search of iron and impoverished Greek farmers in search of land stimulated a remarkable emigration. Between 750 and 500 B.C.E., Greek settlements were established all around the Mediterranean basin and the rim of the Black Sea. Settlers brought Greek culture, language, and building styles to these new lands, even as they fought, traded, and intermarried with their non-Greek neighbors.

The most distinctive feature of Greek civilization, and the greatest contrast with Persia, lay in the extent of popular participation in political life that occurred within at least some of the city-states. It was the idea of "citizenship," of free people running the affairs of state, of equality for all citizens before the law, that was so unique. A foreign king, observing the operation of the public assembly in Athens, was amazed that male citizens as a whole actually voted on matters of policy: "I find it astonishing," he noted, "that here wise men speak on public affairs, while fools decide them."[5] Compared to the rigid hierarchies, inequalities, and absolute monarchies of Persia and other ancient civilizations, the Athenian experiment was remarkable. This is how one modern scholar defined it:

> Among the Greeks the question of who should reign arose in a new way. Previously the most that had been asked was whether one man or another should govern and whether one alone or several together. But now the question was whether all the citizens, including the poor, might govern and whether it would be possible for them to govern as citizens, without specializing in politics. In other words, should the governed themselves actively participate in politics on a regular basis?[6]

The extent of participation and the role of "citizens" varied considerably, both over time and from city to city. Early in Greek history, only the wealthy and well-born had the rights of full citizenship, such as speaking and voting in the assembly, holding public office, and fighting in the army. Gradually, middle- and lower-class men, mostly small-scale farmers, also obtained these rights. At least in part, this broadening of political rights was associated with the growing number of men able to afford the armor and weapons that would allow them to serve as *hoplites*, or infantrymen, in the armies of the city-states. In many places, strong but benevolent rulers known as *tyrants* emerged for a time, usually with the support of the poorer classes, to challenge the prerogatives of the wealthy. Sparta—famous for its extreme forms of military discipline and its large population of *helots*, conquered people who lived in slavelike conditions—vested most political authority in its Council of Elders. The council was composed of twenty-eight men over the age of sixty, derived from the wealthier and more influential segment of society, who served for life and provided political leadership for Sparta.

Snapshot   Key Moments in Classical Greek History

Traditional date for first Olympic Games	776 B.C.E.
Emergence of Greek city-states and overseas colonization	750–700 B.C.E.
Evolution of hoplite military tactics	700–650 B.C.E.
Tyrants rule in many city-states	670–500 B.C.E.
Sparta dominant in Peloponnesus	550 B.C.E.
Cleisthenes' political reforms in Athens	507 B.C.E.
Greco-Persian Wars	490–479 B.C.E.
Golden Age of Athens (building of Parthenon; Athenian democracy, rule of Pericles)	479–429 B.C.E.
Helot rebellion in Sparta	463 B.C.E.
Peloponnesian War	431–404 B.C.E.
Macedonian conquest of Greece	338 B.C.E.
Conquests of Alexander the Great	333–323 B.C.E.
Hellenistic era	323–30 B.C.E.
Greece comes under Roman control	2nd century B.C.E.

It was in Athens that the Greek experiment in political participation achieved its most distinctive expression. Early steps in this direction were the product of intense class conflict, leading almost to civil war. A reforming leader named Solon emerged in 594 B.C.E. to push Athenian politics in a more democratic direction, breaking the hold of a small group of aristocratic families. Debt slavery was abolished, access to public office was opened to a wider group of men, and all citizens were allowed to take part in the Assembly. Later reformers such as Cleisthenes and Pericles extended the rights of citizens even further. By 450 B.C.E., all holders of public office were chosen by lot and were paid, so that even the poorest could serve. The Assembly, where all citizens could participate, became the center of political life.

Athenian democracy, however, was different from modern democracy. It was direct, rather than representative, democracy, and it was distinctly limited. Women, slaves, and foreigners, together far more than half of the population, were wholly excluded from political participation. Nonetheless, political life in Athens was a world away from that of the Persian Empire and even from that of many other Greek cities.

■ Connection

What were the consequences for both sides of the encounter between the Persians and the Greeks?

Collision: The Greco-Persian Wars

If ever there was an unequal conflict between civilizations, surely it was the collision of the Greeks and the Persians. The confrontation between the small and divided

Greek cities and Persia, the world's largest empire, grew out of their respective patterns of expansion. A number of Greek settlements on the Anatolian seacoast, known to the Greeks as Ionia, came under Persian control as that empire extended its domination to the west. In 499 B.C.E., some of these Ionian Greek cities revolted against Persian domination and found support from Athens on the Greek mainland. Outraged by this assault from the remote and upstart Greeks, the Persians twice in ten years (490 and 480 B.C.E.) launched major military expeditions to punish the Greeks in general and Athens in particular. Against all odds and all expectations, the Greeks held them off, defeating the Persians on both land and sea.

Though no doubt embarrassing, this defeat on the far western fringes of its empire had little effect on the Persians, but it had a profound impact on the Greeks and especially on Athens, whose forces had led the way to victory. Beating the Persians in battle was a source of enormous pride for Greece. Years later, elderly Athenian men asked one another how old they had been when the Greeks triumphed in the momentous Battle of Marathon in 490 B.C.E. In their view, this victory was the product of Greek freedoms, because those freedoms had motivated men to fight with extraordinary courage for what they valued so highly. It led to a worldview in which Persia represented Asia and despotism, whereas Greece signified Europe and freedom. Thus was born the notion of an East / West divide, which has shaped European and American thinking about the world into the twenty-first century.

The Greeks' victory also radicalized Athenian democracy, for it had been men of the poorer classes who had rowed their ships to victory, and now they were in a position to insist on full citizenship. The fifty years or so after the Greco-Persian Wars were not only the high point of Athenian democracy but also the Golden Age of Greek culture. During this period, the Parthenon, that marvelous temple to the Greek goddess Athena, was built; Greek theater was born from the work of Aeschylus, Sophocles, and Euripides; and Socrates was beginning his career as a philosopher and an irritant in Athens. The great Athenian statesman Pericles celebrated the uniqueness of Athens in a famous speech, excerpted in Document 4.1 (pp. 170–72).

But Athens's Golden Age was also an era of incipient empire. In the Greco-Persian Wars, Athens had led a coalition of more than thirty Greek city-states on the basis of its naval power, but Athenian leadership in the struggle against Persian aggression had spawned an imperialism of its own. After the war, Athenian efforts to solidify Athens's dominant position among the allies led to intense resentment and finally to a bitter civil war (431–404 B.C.E.), with Sparta taking the lead in defending the traditional independence of Greek city-states. In this bloody conflict, known as the Peloponnesian War, Athens was defeated, while the Greeks exhausted themselves and magnified their distrust of one another. Thus the way was open to their eventual takeover by the growing forces of Macedonia, a frontier region on the northern fringes of the Greek world. The glory days of the Greek experiment were over, but the spread of Greek culture was just beginning.

Collision: Alexander and the Hellenistic Era

■ Connection
What changes did
Alexander's conquests
bring in their wake?

The Macedonian takeover of Greece, led by Philip II, finally accomplished by 338 B.C.E. what the Greeks themselves had been unable to achieve—the political unification of Greece, but at the cost of much of the prized independence of its various city-states. It also set in motion a second round in the collision of Greece and Persia as Philip's son, Alexander, prepared to lead a massive Greek expedition against the Persian Empire. Such a project appealed to those who sought vengeance for the earlier Persian assault on Greece, but it also served to unify the fractious Greeks in a war against their common enemy.

The story of this ten-year expedition (333–323 B.C.E.), accomplished while Alexander was still in his twenties, has become the stuff of legend (see Map 4.3). Surely it was among the greatest military feats of the classical world in that it created a Greek empire from Egypt and Anatolia in the west to Afghanistan and India in the east. In the process, the great Persian Empire was thoroughly defeated; its capital, Persepolis, was looted and burned; and Alexander was hailed as the "king of Asia." In Egypt, Alexander, then just twenty-four years old, was celebrated as a liberator from Persian domination, was anointed as pharaoh, and was declared by Egyptian priests to be the "son of the gods." Arrian, a later Greek historian, described Alexander in this way:

Map 4.3 Alexander's Empire and Successor States
Alexander's conquests, though enormous, did not long remain within a single empire, for his generals divided them into three successor states shortly after his death. This was the Hellenistic world within which Greek culture spread.

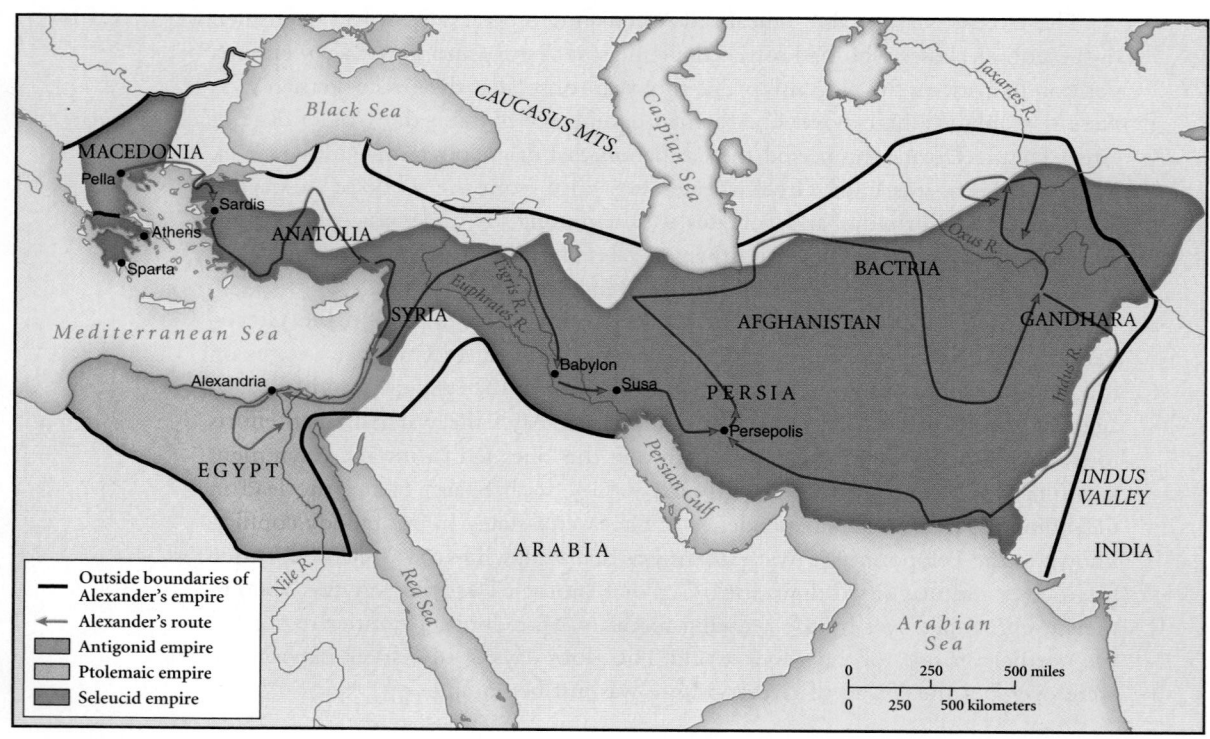

His passion was for glory only, and in that he was insatiable.... Noble indeed was his power of inspiring his men, of filling them with confidence, and in the moment of danger, of sweeping away their fear by the spectacle of his own fearlessness.[7]

Alexander died in 323 B.C.E., without returning to Greece, and his empire was soon divided into three kingdoms, ruled by leading Macedonian generals.

From the viewpoint of world history, the chief significance of Alexander's amazing conquests lay in the widespread dissemination of Greek culture during what historians call the Hellenistic era (323–30 B.C.E.). Elements of that culture, generated in a small and remote Mediterranean peninsula, now penetrated the lands of the First Civilizations—Egypt, Mesopotamia, and India—resulting in one of the great cultural encounters of the classical world.

The major avenue for the spread of Greek culture lay in the many cities that Alexander and later Hellenistic rulers established throughout the empire. Complete with Greek monuments and sculptures, Greek theaters and markets, Greek councils and assemblies, these cities attracted many thousands of Greek settlers serving as state officials, soldiers, or traders. Alexandria in Egypt—the largest of these cities, with half a million people—was an enormous cosmopolitan center where Egyptians, Greeks, Jews, Babylonians, Syrians, Persians, and many others rubbed elbows. A harbor with space for 1,200 ships facilitated long-distance commerce. Greek learning flourished thanks to a library of some 700,000 volumes and the Museum, which sponsored scholars and writers of all kinds.

From cities such as these, Greek culture spread. A simplified form of the Greek language was widely spoken from the Mediterranean to India. The Indian monarch Ashoka published some of his decrees in Greek, while an independent Greek state was established in Bactria in what is now northern Afghanistan. The attraction of many young Jews to Greek culture prompted the Pharisees to develop their own school system, as this highly conservative Jewish sect feared for the very survival of Judaism.

Cities such as Alexandria were very different from the original city-states of Greece, both in their cultural diversity and in the absence of the independence so valued by Athens and Sparta. Now they were part of large conquest states ruled by Greeks: the Ptolemaic empire in Egypt and the Seleucid empire in Persia. These were imperial states, which, in their determination to preserve order, raise taxes, and maintain the

Alexander the Great
This mosaic of Alexander on horseback comes from the Roman city of Pompeii. It depicts the Battle of Issus (333 B.C.E.), in which Greek forces, although considerably outnumbered, defeated the Persian army, led personally by Emperor Darius III. (Scala/Art Resource, NY)

authority of the monarch, resembled the much older empires of Mesopotamia, Egypt, Assyria, and Persia. Macedonians and Greeks, representing perhaps 10 percent of the population in these Hellenistic kingdoms, were clearly the elite and sought to keep themselves separate. In Egypt, different legal systems for Greeks and native Egyptians maintained this separation. An Egyptian agricultural worker complained that his supervisors despised him and refused to pay him, he said, "because I am an Egyptian."[8] Periodic rebellions expressed resentment at Greek arrogance, condescension, and exploitation.

But the separation between the Greeks and native populations was by no means complete, and a fair amount of cultural interaction and blending occurred. Alexander himself had taken several Persian princesses as his wives and actively encouraged intermarriage between his troops and Asian women. In both Egypt and Mesopotamia, Greek rulers patronized the building of temples to local gods and actively supported their priests. A growing number of native peoples were able to become Greek citizens by getting a Greek education, speaking the language, dressing appropriately, and assuming a Greek name. In India, Greeks were assimilated into the hierarchy of the caste system as members of the Kshatriya (warrior) caste, while in Bactria a substantial number of Greeks converted to Buddhism, including one of their kings, Menander. A school of Buddhist art that emerged in the early centuries of the Common Era depicted the Buddha in human form for the first time, but in Greek-like garb with a face resembling the god Apollo. Clearly, not all was conflict between the Greeks and the peoples of the East.

In the long run, much of this Greek cultural influence faded as the Hellenistic kingdoms that had promoted it weakened and vanished by the first century B.C.E. While it lasted, however, it represented a remarkable cultural encounter, born of the collision of two empires and two classical civilizations. In the western part of that Hellenistic world, Greek rule was replaced by that of the Romans, whose empire, like Alexander's, also served as a vehicle for the continued spread of Greek culture and ideas.

Comparing Empires: Roman and Chinese

While the adjacent civilizations of the Greeks and the Persians collided, two other classical empires were taking shape—the Roman Empire on the far western side of Eurasia and China's imperial state on the far eastern end. They flourished at roughly the same time (200 B.C.E.–200 C.E.); they occupied a similar area (about 1.5 million square miles); and they encompassed populations of a similar size (50 to 60 million). They were the giant empires of their time, shaping the lives of close to half of the world's population. Unlike the Greeks and the Persians, the Romans and the Chinese were only dimly aware of each other and had almost no direct contact. Historians, however, have seen them as fascinating variations on an imperial theme and have long explored their similarities and differences.

Rome: From City-State to Empire

How do empires arise? This is one of the perennial questions that historians tackle. Like the Persian Empire, that of the Romans took shape initially on the margins of the civilized world and was an unlikely rags-to-riches story. Rome began as a small and impoverished city-state on the western side of central Italy in the eighth century B.C.E., so weak, according to legend, that Romans were reduced to kidnapping neighboring women in order to reproduce. In a transformation of epic proportions, Rome became the center of an enormous imperial state that encompassed the Mediterranean basin and included parts of continental Europe, Britain, North Africa, and the Middle East.

■ **Change**
How did Rome grow from a single city to the center of a huge empire?

Originally ruled by a king, Roman aristocrats around 509 B.C.E. threw off the monarchy and established a republic in which the wealthy class, known as *patricians*, dominated. Executive authority was exercised by two consuls, who were advised by a patrician assembly, the Senate. Deepening conflict with the poorer classes, called *plebeians*, led to important changes in Roman political life. A written code of law offered plebeians some protection from abuse; a system of public assemblies provided an opportunity for lower classes to shape public policy; and a new office of *tribune*, who represented plebeians, allowed them to block unfavorable legislation. Romans took great pride in this political system, believing that they enjoyed greater freedom than did many of their more autocratic neighbors. The values of the republic—rule of law, the rights of citizens, the absence of pretension, upright moral behavior, keeping one's word—were later idealized as "the way of the ancestors."

With this political system and these values, the Romans launched their empire-building enterprise, a prolonged process that took more than 500 years (see Map 4.4). It began in the 490s B.C.E. with Roman control over its Latin neighbors in central Italy and over the next several hundred years encompassed most of the Italian peninsula. Between 264 and 146 B.C.E., victory in the Punic Wars with Carthage, a powerful empire with its capital in North Africa, extended Roman control over the western Mediterranean and made Rome a naval power. Subsequent expansion in the eastern Mediterranean brought the ancient civilizations of Greece, Egypt, and Mesopotamia under Roman domination. Rome also expanded into territories in Southern and Western Europe, including present-day Spain, France, and Britain. By early in the second century C.E., the Roman Empire had reached its maximum extent.

No overall design or blueprint drove the building of empire, nor were there any precedents to guide the Romans. What they created was something wholly new—an empire that encompassed the entire Mediterranean basin and beyond. It was a piecemeal process, which the Romans invariably saw as defensive. Each addition of territory created new vulnerabilities, which could be assuaged only by more conquests. For some, the growth of empire represented opportunity. Poor soldiers hoped for land, loot, or salaries that might lift their families out of poverty. The well-to-do or well-connected gained great estates, earned promotion, and sometimes achieved

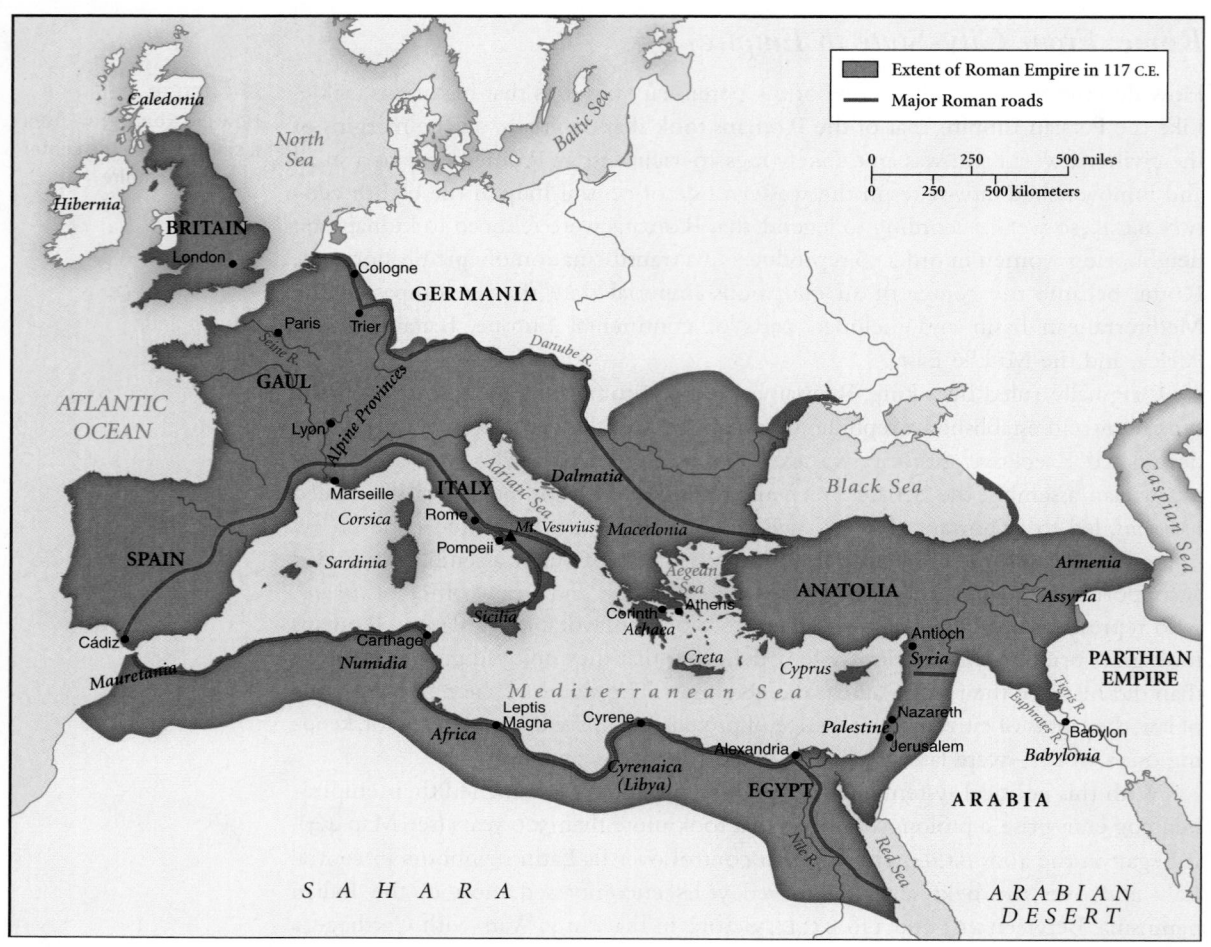

Map 4.4   The Roman Empire

At its height in the second century C.E., the Roman Empire incorporated the entire Mediterranean basin, including the lands of the Carthaginian Empire, the less developed region of Western Europe, the heartland of Greek civilization, and the ancient civilizations of Egypt and Mesopotamia.

public acclaim and high political office. The wealth of long-established societies in the eastern Mediterranean (Greece and Egypt, for example) beckoned, as did the resources and food supplies of the less developed western regions, such as Carthage and Spain. There was no shortage of motivation for the creation of the Roman Empire.

Although Rome's central location in the Mediterranean basin provided a convenient launching pad for empire, it was the army, "well-trained, well-fed, and well-rewarded," that built the empire.[9] Drawing on the growing population of Italy, that army was often brutal in war. Carthage, for example, was utterly destroyed; the city

Snapshot   Key Moments in the History of the Roman Empire

Traditional date of Rome's founding as a monarchy	753 B.C.E.
Establishment of Roman Republic	509 B.C.E.
Turmoil between patricians and plebeians ("struggle of the orders")	509–287 B.C.E.
Twelve Tables (Rome's first written law code)	450 B.C.E.
Punic Wars	264–146 B.C.E.
Civil war; Julius Caesar appointed dictator and then assassinated	49–44 B.C.E.
Reign of Caesar Augustus	27 B.C.E.–14 C.E.
Great fire in Rome; Emperor Nero blames Christians	64 C.E.
Roman citizenship extended to almost all free subjects	212 C.E.
Constantine converts to Christianity	312 C.E.
Founding of Constantinople as the "New Rome"	324 C.E.
Roman Empire split into eastern and western halves	395 C.E.
"Barbarian" invasions	4th–5th centuries C.E.
Collapse of western Roman Empire	476 C.E.

was razed to the ground, and its inhabitants were either killed or sold into slavery. Nonetheless, Roman authorities could be generous to former enemies. Some were granted Roman citizenship; others were treated as allies and allowed to maintain their local rulers. As the empire grew, so too did political forces in Rome that favored its continued expansion and were willing to commit the necessary manpower and resources.

The relentless expansion of empire raised a profound question for Rome: could republican government and values survive the acquisition of a huge empire? The wealth of empire enriched a few, enabling them to acquire large estates and slaves to work those estates, while pushing growing numbers of free farmers into the cities and poverty. Imperial riches also empowered a small group of military leaders— Marius, Sulla, Pompey, Julius Caesar—who recruited their troops directly from the ranks of the poor and whose fierce rivalries brought civil war to Rome during the first century B.C.E. Traditionalists lamented the apparent decline of republican values— simplicity, service, free farmers as the backbone of the army, the authority of the Senate—amid the self-seeking ambition of the newly rich and powerful. When the dust settled from the civil war, Rome was clearly changing, for authority was now vested primarily in an emperor, the first of whom was Octavian, later granted the title

Queen Boudica
This statue in London commemorates the resistance of the Celtic people of eastern Britain against Roman rule during a revolt in 60–61 C.E., led by Queen Boudica. A later Roman historian lamented that "all this ruin was brought upon the Romans by a woman, a fact which in itself caused them the greatest shame." (Daniel Boulet, photographer)

■ **Comparison**

How and why did the making of the Chinese empire differ from that of the Roman Empire?

of Augustus (reigned 27 B.C.E.–14 C.E.), which implied a divine status for the ruler. The republic was history; Rome was becoming an empire.

But it was an empire with an uneasy conscience, for many felt that in acquiring an empire, Rome had betrayed and abandoned its republican origins. Augustus was careful to maintain the forms of the republic—the Senate, consuls, public assemblies—and referred to himself as "first man" rather than "king" or "emperor" even as he accumulated enormous personal power. And in a bow to republican values, he spoke of the empire's conquests as reflecting the "power of the Roman people" rather than of the Roman state. Despite this rhetoric, he was emperor in practice, if not in name, for he was able to exercise sole authority, backed up by his command of a professional army. Later emperors were less reluctant to flaunt their imperial prerogatives. During the first two centuries C.E., this empire in disguise provided security, grandeur, and relative prosperity for the Mediterranean world. This was the *pax Romana*, the Roman peace, the era of imperial Rome's greatest extent and greatest authority. (See Document 4.2, pp. 172–74, for a Greek celebration of the Roman Empire.)

China: From Warring States to Empire

About the same time, on the other side of Eurasia, another huge imperial state was in the making—China. Here, however, the task was understood differently. It was not a matter of creating something new, as in the case of the Roman Empire, but of restoring something old. As one of the First Civilizations, a Chinese state had emerged as early as 2200 B.C.E. and under the Xia, Shang, and Zhou dynasties had grown progressively larger, but by 500 B.C.E. this Chinese state was in shambles. Any earlier unity vanished in an age of warring states, featuring the endless rivalries of seven competing kingdoms.

To many Chinese, this was a wholly unnatural and unacceptable condition, and rulers in various states vied to reunify China. One of them, known to history as Qin Shihuangdi (i.e., Shihuangdi from the state of Qin), succeeded brilliantly. The state of Qin had already developed an effective bureaucracy, had subordinated its aristocracy, had equipped its army with iron weapons, and enjoyed rapidly rising agricultural output and a growing population. It also had adopted a political philosophy called Legalism, which advocated clear rules and harsh punishments as a means of enforcing the authority of the state. (See Document 4.3, pp. 174–75, for a sample of Legalist thinking.) With these resources, Shihuangdi (ruled 221–210 B.C.E.) launched a military campaign to reunify China and in just ten years soundly defeated the other warring states. Believing that he had created a universal and eternal empire, he grandly named himself Shihuangdi, which means the "first emperor." Unlike Augustus, he showed little ambivalence about empire. Subsequent conquests extended China's boundaries far to the south into the northern part of Vietnam, to the northeast into Korea, and to the northwest, where the Chinese pushed back the nomadic pastoral people of the steppes. Although the boundaries fluctuated over time, Shihuangdi laid the foundations for a unified Chinese state, which has endured, with periodic interruptions, to the present (see Map 4.5).

Building on earlier precedents, the Chinese process of empire formation was far more compressed than the centuries-long Roman effort, but it was no less dependent on military force and no less brutal. Scholars who opposed Shihuangdi's policies

Map 4.5   Classical China

The brief Qin dynasty brought unity to the heartland of Chinese civilization, and the much longer Han dynasty extended its territorial reach south toward Vietnam, east to Korea, and west into Central Asia. To the north lay the military confederacy of the nomadic Xiongnu.

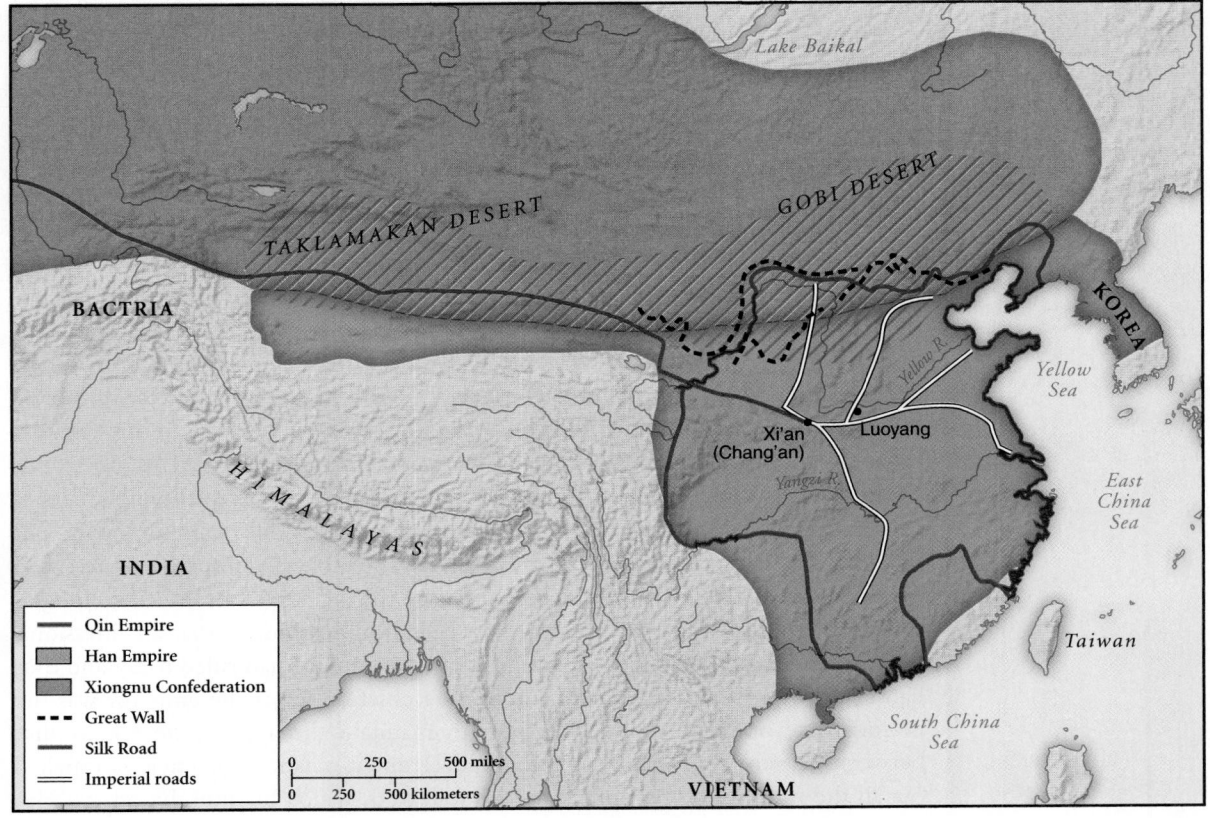

were executed and their books burned. (See Visual Source 4.1, p. 181.) Aristocrats who might oppose his centralizing policies were moved physically to the capital. Hundreds of thousands of laborers were recruited to construct the Great Wall of China, designed to keep out northern "barbarians," and to erect a monumental mausoleum as the emperor's final resting place. That enormous tomb complex is described and illustrated in Visual Sources: Qin Shihuangdi and China's Eternal Empire, pages 180–86. More positively, Shihuangdi imposed a uniform system of weights, measures, and currency and standardized the length of axles for carts and the written form of the Chinese language.

As in Rome, the creation of the Chinese empire had domestic repercussions, but they were brief and superficial compared to Rome's transition from republic to empire. The speed and brutality of Shihuangdi's policies ensured that his own Qin dynasty did not last long, and it collapsed unmourned in 206 B.C.E. The Han dynasty that followed (206 B.C.E.–220 C.E.) retained the centralized features of Shihuangdi's creation, although it moderated the harshness of his policies, adopting a milder and moralistic Confucianism in place of Legalism as the governing philosophy of the states. (See Document 5.1, pp. 217–19, for a sample of Confucius's thinking.) It was Han dynasty rulers who consolidated China's imperial state and established the political patterns that lasted into the twentieth century.

Consolidating the Roman and Chinese Empires

■ **Comparison**

In comparing the Roman and Chinese empires, which do you find more striking—their similarities or their differences?

Once established, these two huge imperial systems shared a number of common features. Both, for example, defined themselves in universal terms. The Roman writer Polybius spoke of bringing "almost the entire world" under the control of Rome,[10] while the Chinese state was said to encompass "all under heaven." Both of them invested heavily in public works—roads, bridges, aqueducts, canals, protective walls—all designed to integrate their respective domains militarily and commercially.

Furthermore, Roman and Chinese authorities both invoked supernatural sanctions to support their rule. By the first century C.E., Romans began to regard their deceased emperors as gods and established a religious cult to bolster the authority of living emperors. It was the refusal of early Christians to take part in this cult that provoked their periodic persecution by Roman authorities.

In China, a much older tradition had long linked events on earth with affairs in heaven. In this conception, heaven was neither a place nor a supreme being, but rather an impersonal moral force that regulated the universe. Emperors were called the Son of Heaven and were said to govern by the Mandate of Heaven so long as they ruled morally and with benevolence. Peasant rebellions, "barbarian" invasions, or disastrous floods were viewed as signs that the emperor had ruled badly and thus had lost the Mandate of Heaven. Among the chief duties of the emperor was the performance of various rituals thought to maintain the appropriate relationship between heaven and earth. What moral government meant in practice was spelled out in the writings of Confucius and his followers, which became the official ideology of the empire (see Chapter 5).

Both of these classical civilizations also absorbed a foreign religious tradition—Christianity in the Roman Empire and Buddhism in China—although the process unfolded somewhat differently. In the case of Rome, Christianity was born as a small sect of a small province in a remote corner of the empire. Aided by the *pax Romana* and Roman roads, the new faith spread slowly for several centuries, particularly among the poor and lower classes. Women were prominent in the leadership of the early church, as were a number of more well-to-do individuals from urban families. After suffering intermittent persecution, Christianity in the fourth century C.E. obtained state support from emperors who hoped to shore up a tottering empire with a common religion, and thereafter the religion spread quite rapidly.

In the case of China, by contrast, Buddhism came from India, far beyond the Chinese world. It was introduced to China by Central Asian traders and received little support from Han dynasty rulers. In fact, the religion spread only modestly among Chinese until after the Han dynasty collapsed (220 C.E.), when it appealed to people who felt bewildered by the loss of a predictable and stable society. Not until the Sui dynasty emperor Wendi (581–604 C.E.) reunified China did the new religion gain state support, and then only temporarily. Buddhism thus became one of several alternative cultural traditions in a complex Chinese mix, while Christianity, though divided internally, ultimately became the dominant religious tradition throughout Europe.

The Roman and Chinese empires also had a different relationship to the societies they governed. Rome's beginnings as a small city-state meant that Romans, and even Italians, were always a distinct minority within the empire. The Chinese empire, by contrast, grew out of a much larger cultural heartland, already ethnically Chinese. Furthermore, as the Chinese state expanded, especially to the south, it actively assimilated the non-Chinese or "barbarian" people. In short, they became Chinese, culturally, linguistically, through intermarriage, and in physical appearance as well. Many Chinese in modern times are in fact descended from people who at one point or another were not Chinese at all.

The Roman Empire also offered a kind of assimilation to its subject peoples. Gradually and somewhat reluctantly, the empire granted Roman citizenship to various individuals, families, or whole communities for their service to the empire or in recognition of their adoption of Roman culture. In 212 C.E., Roman citizenship was bestowed on almost all free people of the empire. Citizenship offered clear advantages—the right to hold public office, to serve in the Roman military units known as legions, to wear a toga, and more—but it conveyed a legal status, rather than cultural assimilation, and certainly did not erase other identities, such as being Greek, Egyptian, or a citizen of a particular city.

Various elements of Roman culture—its public buildings, its religious rituals, its Latin language, its style of city life—were attractive, especially in Western Europe, where urban civilization was something new. In the eastern half of the empire, however, things Greek retained tremendous prestige. Many elite Romans in fact regarded Greek culture—its literature, philosophy, and art—as superior to their own and proudly sent their sons to Athens for a Greek education. To some extent, the two blended into a mixed Greco-Roman tradition, which the empire served to disseminate throughout the realm. Other non-Roman cultural traditions—such as the cult of the Persian god Mithra or the compassionate Egyptian goddess Isis, and, most extensively, the Jewish-derived religion of Christianity—also spread throughout the empire. Nothing similar occurred in Han dynasty China, except for Buddhism, which established a modest presence, largely among foreigners. Chinese culture, widely recognized as the model to which others should conform, experienced little competition from older, venerated, or foreign traditions.

Language served these two empires in important but contrasting ways. Latin, an alphabetic language depicting sounds, gave rise to various distinct languages—Spanish, Portuguese, French, Italian, Romanian—whereas Chinese did not. Chinese characters, which represented words or ideas more than sounds, were not easily transferable to other languages, but written Chinese could be understood by all literate people, no matter which spoken dialect of the language they used. Thus Chinese, more than Latin, served as an instrument of elite assimilation. For all of these reasons, the various peoples of the Roman Empire were able to maintain their separate cultural identities far more than was the case in China.

Politically, both empires established effective centralized control over vast regions and huge populations, but the Chinese, far more than the Romans, developed an elaborate bureaucracy to hold the empire together. The Han emperor Wudi (reigned 141–87 B.C.E.) established an imperial academy for training officials for an emerging bureaucracy with a curriculum based on the writings of Confucius. This was the beginning of a civil service system, complete with examinations and selection by merit, which did much to integrate the Chinese empire and lasted into the early twentieth century. Roman administration was a somewhat ramshackle affair, rely-

Snapshot	Key Moments in Classical Chinese History	
Political fragmentation ("warring states" period)	500–221 B.C.E.	
Unification of China: Shihuangdi and Qin dynasty	221–206 B.C.E.	
Beginning of Han dynasty, with Liu Bang as its first emperor	206–195 B.C.E.	
Reign of Emperor Wudi, who established Confucian Academy for training imperial bureaucrats	141–87 B.C.E.	
Emperor Wang Mang attempts land reform, without success	9–23 C.E.	
Yellow Turban peasant revolt	184 C.E.	
Collapse of Han dynasty	220 C.E.	
Renewed political fragmentation	220–581 C.E.	
China's unity is restored (Sui dynasty)	589–618 C.E.	
Tang dynasty	618–907 C.E.	

ing more on regional aristocratic elites and the army to provide cohesion. Unlike the Chinese, however, the Romans developed an elaborate body of law, applicable equally to all people of the realm, dealing with matters of justice, property, commerce, and family life. Chinese and Roman political development thus generated different answers to the question of what made for good government. For those who inherited the Roman tradition, it was good laws, whereas for those in the Chinese tradition, it was good men.

The Collapse of Empires

Empires rise, and then, with some apparent regularity, they fall, and in doing so, they provide historians with one of their most intriguing questions: What causes the collapse of these once-mighty structures? In China, the Han dynasty empire came to an end in 220 C.E.; the traditional date for the final disintegration of the Roman Empire is 476 C.E., although a process of decline had been under way for several centuries. In the Roman case, however, only the western half of the empire collapsed, while the eastern part, subsequently known as the Byzantine Empire, maintained the tradition of imperial Rome for another thousand years.

■ **Comparison**
How did the collapse of empire play out differently in the Roman world and in China?

Despite this difference, a number of common factors have been associated with the end of these imperial states. At one level, they simply got too big, too overextended, and too expensive to be sustained by the available resources, and no fundamental technological breakthrough was available to enlarge these resources. Furthermore, the growth of large landowning families with huge estates enabled them to avoid paying taxes, turned free peasants into impoverished tenant farmers, and diminished the authority of the central government. In China, such conditions led to a major peasant revolt, known as the Yellow Turban Rebellion, in 184 C.E.

Rivalry among elite factions created instability in both empires and eroded imperial authority. In China, persistent tension between castrated court officials (*eunuchs*) loyal to the emperor and Confucian-educated scholar-bureaucrats weakened the state. In the Roman Empire between 235 and 284 C.E., some twenty-six individuals claimed the title of Roman emperor, only one of whom died of natural causes. In addition, epidemic disease ravaged both societies. The population of the Roman Empire declined by 25 percent in the two centuries following 250 C.E., a demographic disaster that meant diminished production, less revenue for the state, and fewer men available for the defense of the empire's long frontiers.

To these mounting internal problems was added a growing threat from nomadic or semi-agricultural peoples occupying the frontier regions of both empires. The Chinese had long developed various ways of dealing with the Xiongnu and other nomadic people to the north—building the Great Wall to keep them out, offering them trading opportunities at border markets, buying them off with lavish gifts, contracting marriage alliances with nomadic leaders, and conducting periodic military campaigns against them. But as the Han dynasty weakened in the second and third centuries C.E., such peoples more easily breached the frontier defenses and set

Meeting of Attila and Pope Leo I
Among the "barbarian" invaders of the Roman Empire, none were more feared than the Huns, led by the infamous Attila. In a celebrated meeting in 452 C.E., Pope Leo I persuaded Attila to spare the city of Rome and to withdraw from Italy. This painting from about 1360 C.E. records that remarkable meeting. (National Szechenyi Library, Budapest)

up a succession of "barbarian states" in north China. Culturally, however, many of these foreign rulers gradually became Chinese, encouraging intermarriage, adopting Chinese dress, and setting up their courts in Chinese fashion.

A weakening Roman Empire likewise faced serious problems from Germanic-speaking peoples living on its northern frontier. Growing numbers of these people began to enter the empire in the fourth century C.E.—some as mercenaries in Roman armies and others as refugees fleeing the invasions of the ferocious Huns, who were penetrating Europe from Central Asia. Once inside the declining empire, various Germanic groups established their own kingdoms, at first controlling Roman emperors and then displacing them altogether by 476 C.E. Unlike the nomadic groups in China, who largely assimilated Chinese culture, Germanic kingdoms in Europe developed their own ethnic identity—Visigoths, Franks, Anglo-Saxons, and others—even as they drew on Roman law and adopted Roman Christianity. Far more than in China, the fall of the Roman Empire produced a new culture, blending Latin and Germanic elements, which provided the foundation for the hybrid civilization that would arise in Western Europe.

The collapse of empire meant more than the disappearance of centralized government and endemic conflict. In both China and post-Roman Europe, it also meant the decline of urban life, a contracting population, less area under cultivation, diminishing international trade, and vast insecurity for ordinary people. It must have seemed that civilization itself was unraveling.

The most significant difference between the collapse of empire in China and that in the Mediterranean basin lay in what happened next. In China, after about 350 years of disunion, disorder, frequent warfare, and political chaos, a Chinese imperial state, similar to that of the Han dynasty, was reassembled under the Sui (589–618 C.E.), Tang (618–907), and Song (960–1279) dynasties. Once again, a single emperor ruled; a bureaucracy selected by examinations governed; and the ideas of Confucius informed the political system. Such a Chinese empire persisted into the early twentieth century, establishing one of the most continuous political traditions of any civilization in world history.

The story line of European history following the end of the Roman Empire was very different indeed. No large-scale, centralized, imperial authority encompassing all of Western Europe has ever been successfully reestablished there for any length of time. The memory of Roman imperial unity certainly persisted, and many subsequently tried unsuccessfully to re-create it. But most of Western Europe dissolved into a highly decentralized political system involving kings with little authority, nobles, knights and vassals, various city-states in Italy, and small territories ruled by princes, bishops, or the pope. From this point on, Europe would be a civilization without an encompassing imperial state.

From a Chinese point of view, Western Europe's post-Roman history must seem an enormous failure. Why were Europeans unable to reconstruct something of the unity of their classical empire, while the Chinese clearly did? Surely the greater cultural homogeneity of Chinese civilization made that task easier than it was amid the vast ethnic and linguistic diversity of Europe. The absence in the Roman legacy of a strong bureaucratic tradition also contributed to European difficulties, whereas in China the bureaucracy provided stability even as dynasties came and went. The Chinese also had in Confucianism a largely secular ideology that placed great value on political matters in the here and now. The Roman Catholic Church in Europe, however, was frequently at odds with state authorities, and its "otherworldliness" did little to support the creation of large-scale empires. Finally, Chinese agriculture was much more productive than that of Europe, and for a long time its metallurgy was more advanced.[11] These conditions gave Chinese state-builders more resources to work with than were available to their European counterparts.

Intermittent Empire: The Case of India

Among the classical civilizations of Eurasia, empire loomed large in Persian, Mediterranean, and Chinese history, but it played a rather less prominent role in India. In the Indus River valley flourished the largest of the First Civilizations, embodied in exquisitely planned cities such as Harappa but with little evidence of any central political authority. The demise of this early civilization by 1500 B.C.E. was followed over the next thousand years by the creation of a new civilization based farther east, along the Ganges River on India's northern plain. That process has occasioned considerable scholarly debate, which has focused on the role of the Aryans, a pastoral Indo-European people long thought to have invaded and destroyed the Indus Valley civilization and created the new one along the Ganges. More recent research has called this view into question. Did the Aryans invade suddenly, or did they migrate slowly into the Indus River valley, or were they already there as a part of the Indus Valley population? Was the new civilization largely the work of Aryans, or did it evolve gradually from Indus Valley culture? About all of this, scholars have yet to reach agreement.[12]

However it occurred, by 600 B.C.E. what would become the classical civilization of South Asia had begun to take shape across northern India. Politically, that civilization emerged as a fragmented collection of towns and cities, some small republics governed by public assemblies, and a number of regional states ruled by kings. An astonishing range of ethnic, cultural, and linguistic diversity also characterized this civilization, as an endless variety of peoples migrated into India from Central Asia across the mountain passes in the northwest. These features of Indian civilization— political fragmentation and vast cultural diversity—have informed much of South

■ **Comparison**
Why were centralized empires so much less prominent in India than in China?

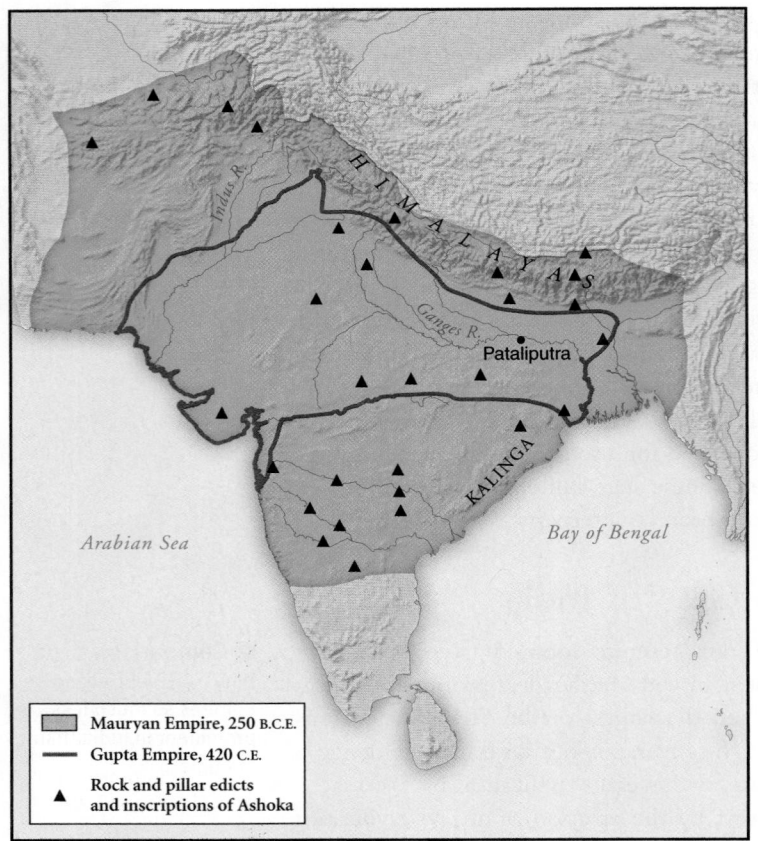

Map 4.6 Empire in South Asia

Large-scale empires in the Indian subcontinent were less frequent and less enduring than in China. Two of the largest efforts were those of the Mauryan and Gupta dynasties.

Asian history throughout many centuries, offering a sharp contrast to the pattern of development in China. What gave Indian civilization a recognizable identity and character was neither an imperial tradition nor ethnolinguistic commonality, but rather a distinctive religious tradition, known later to outsiders as Hinduism, and a unique social organization, the caste system. These features of Indian life are explored further in Chapters 5 and 6.

Nonetheless, empires and emperors were not entirely unknown in India's long history. Northwestern India had been briefly ruled by the Persian Empire and then conquered by Alexander the Great. These Persian and Greek influences helped stimulate the first and largest of India's short experiments with a large-scale political system, the Mauryan Empire (326–184 B.C.E.), which encompassed all but the southern tip of the subcontinent (see Map 4.6).

The Mauryan Empire was an impressive political structure, equivalent to the Persian, Chinese, and Roman empires, though not nearly as long-lasting. With a population of perhaps 50 million, the Mauryan Empire boasted a large military force, reported to include 600,000 infantry soldiers, 30,000 cavalry, 8,000 chariots, and 9,000 elephants. A civilian bureaucracy featured various ministries and a large contingent of spies to provide the rulers with local information. A famous treatise called the *Arthashastra* (*The Science of Worldly Wealth*) articulated a pragmatic, even amoral, political philosophy for Mauryan rulers. It was, according to one scholar, a book that showed "how the political world does work and not very often stating how it ought to work, a book that frequently discloses to a king what calculating and sometimes brutal measures he must carry out to preserve the state and the common good."[13] The state also operated many industries—spinning, weaving, mining, shipbuilding, and armaments. This complex apparatus was financed by taxes on trade, on herds of animals, and especially on land, from which the monarch claimed a quarter or more of the crop.[14]

Mauryan India is perhaps best known for one of its emperors, Ashoka (reigned 268–232 B.C.E.), who left a record of his activities and his thinking in a series of edicts carved on rocks and pillars throughout the kingdom. A sample of those edicts is contained in Document 4.4 on pp. 176–78. Ashoka's conversion to Buddhism and his moralistic approach to governance gave his reign a different tone than that of China's Shihuangdi or of Alexander the Great, who, according to legend, wept because he had no more worlds to conquer. His legacy to modern India has been that of an enlightened ruler, who sought to govern in accord with the religious values and moral teachings of Hinduism and Buddhism.

Despite their good intentions, these policies did not long preserve the empire, which broke apart soon after Ashoka's death. Several other short-lived imperial experiments, such as the Gupta Empire (320–550 C.E.), also marked India's history, but none lasted long. India's political history thus resembled that of Western Europe after the collapse of the Roman Empire far more than that of China or Persia. Neither imperial nor regional states commanded the kind of loyalty or exercised the degree of influence that they did in other classical civilizations. India's unparalleled cultural diversity surely was one reason, as was the frequency of invasions from Central Asia, which repeatedly smashed states that might have provided the nucleus for an all-India empire. Finally, India's social structure, embodied in a caste system linked to occupational groups, made for intensely local loyalties at the expense of wider identities (see Chapter 6).

Ashoka of India
This twelfth-century stone relief provides a visual image of the Mauryan dynasty's best-known ruler. (Philip Baird/ www.anthroarcheart.org)

Nonetheless, a frequently vibrant economy fostered a lively internal commerce and made India the focal point of an extensive network of trade in the Indian Ocean basin. In particular, its cotton textile industry long supplied cloth throughout the Afro-Eurasian world. Strong guilds of merchants and artisans provided political leadership in major towns and cities, and their wealth patronized lavish temples, public buildings, and religious festivals. Great creativity in religious matters generated Hindu and Buddhist traditions that later penetrated much of Asia. Indian mathematics and science, especially astronomy, also were impressive; Indian scientists plotted the movements of stars and planets and recognized quite early that the earth was round. Clearly, the absence of consistent imperial unity did not prevent the evolution of an enduring civilization.

Reflections: Classical Empires and the Twentieth Century

The classical empires discussed in this chapter have long ago passed into history, but their descendants have kept them alive in memory, for they have proved useful, even in the twentieth and early-twenty-first centuries. Those empires have provided legitimacy for contemporary states, inspiration for new imperial ventures, and abundant warnings and cautions for those seeking to criticize more recent empires. For example, in bringing communism to China in the twentieth century, the Chinese leader Mao Zedong compared himself to Shihuangdi, the unifier of China and the brutal founder of its Qin dynasty. Reflecting on his campaign against intellectuals in general and Confucianism in particular, Mao declared to a Communist Party conference: "Emperor Qin Shihuang was not that outstanding. He only buried alive 460 Confucian scholars. We buried 460 thousand Confucian scholars.... To the charge of being like Emperor Qin, of being a dictator, we plead guilty."[15]

In contrast, modern-day Indians, who have sought to present their country as a model of cultural tolerance and nonviolence, have been quick to link themselves to Ashoka and his policies of inclusiveness. When the country became independent from British colonial rule in 1947, India soon placed an image of Ashoka's Pillar on the new nation's currency.

In the West, it has been the Roman Empire that has provided a template for thinking about political life. Many in Great Britain celebrated their own global empire as a modern version of the Roman Empire. In the early twentieth century, African students in a mission school in British-ruled Kenya were asked on a history exam to list the benefits that Roman occupation brought to Britain. The implication was obvious. If the British had been "civilized" by Roman rule, then surely Africans would benefit from falling under the control of the "superior" British. Likewise, to the Italian fascist dictator Benito Mussolini, his country's territorial expansion during the 1930s and World War II represented the creation of a new Roman Empire. Most recently, of course, America's dominant role in the world has prompted the question: Are the Americans the new Romans?

Historians frequently cringe as politicians and students use (and perhaps misuse) historical analogies to make their case for particular points of view in the present. But we have little else to go on except history in making our way through the complexities of contemporary life, and historians themselves seldom agree on the "lessons" of the past. Lively debate about the continuing relevance of classical empires shows that although the past may be gone, it surely is not dead.

Second Thoughts

What's the Significance?

To assess your mastery of the material in this chapter, visit the **Student Center** at bedfordstmartins.com/strayer.

Persian Empire	Alexander the Great	Qin Shihuangdi
Athenian democracy	Hellenistic era	Han dynasty
Greco-Persian Wars	Caesar Augustus	Mauryan Empire
	pax Romana	Ashoka

Big Picture Questions

1. What common features can you identify in the empires described in this chapter?
2. In what ways did these empires differ from one another? What accounts for those differences?
3. Are you more impressed with the "greatness" of empires or with their destructive and oppressive features? Why?
4. Do you think that the classical empires hold "lessons" for the present, or are contemporary circumstances sufficiently unique as to render the distant past irrelevant?

Next Steps: For Further Study

Arthur Cotterell, *The First Emperor of China* (1988). A biography of Shihuangdi.

Christopher Kelley, *The Roman Empire: A Very Short Introduction* (2006). A brief, up-to-date, and accessible account of the Roman achievement.

Cullen Murphy, *Are We Rome? The Fall of an Empire and the Fate of America* (2007). A reflection on the usefulness and the dangers of comparing the Roman Empire to the present-day United States.

Sarah Pomeroy et al., *Ancient Greece* (1999). A highly readable survey of Greek history by a team of distinguished scholars.

Walter Scheidel, ed. *Rome and China: Comparative Perspectives on Ancient World Empires* (2009). A series of scholarly essays that systematically compare these two empires.

Romila Thapar, *Ashoka and the Decline of the Mauryas* (1961). A classic study of India's early empire builder.

Illustrated History of the Roman Empire. http://www.roman-empire.net. An interactive Web site with maps, pictures, and much information about the Roman Empire.

For Web sites and additional documents related to this chapter, see **Make History** at bedfordstmartins.com/strayer.

Documents

Considering the Evidence:
Political Authority in Classical Civilizations

States, empires, and their rulers are surely not the whole story of the human past, although historians have sometimes treated them as though they were. But they are important, because their actions shaped the lives of many millions of people. The city-states of ancient Greece, the Roman Empire, the emerging Chinese empire of the Qin dynasty, and the Indian Empire of the Mauryan dynasty—these were among the impressive political structures of the classical era in Eurasia. Rulers seeking to establish or maintain their authority mobilized a variety of ideas to give legitimacy to their regimes. Reflection on political authority was a central issue in the discourse of educated people all across classical Eurasia. In the documents that follow, four contemporary observers—two rulers and two scholars—describe some of the political institutions and ideas that operated within Mediterranean, Chinese, and Indian civilizations.

Document 4.1

In Praise of Athenian Democracy

The Greeks of Athens generated political ideas that have long been celebrated in the West, although they were exceptional even in the small world of classical Greece. (See pp. 147–50 and Map 4.2, p. 148.) The most well-known expression of praise for Athenian democracy comes from Pericles, the most prominent Athenian leader during the fifth century B.C.E. Sometimes called the "first citizen of Athens," Pericles initiated the grand building projects that still grace the Acropolis and led his city in its military struggles with archrival Sparta. To his critics, he was a populist, manipulating the masses to enhance his own power, and an Athenian imperialist whose aggressive policies ultimately ruined the city. His famous speech in praise of Athens was delivered around 431–430 B.C.E. at the end of the first year of the Peloponnesian War against Sparta. The setting was a public funeral service for Athenian citizens who had died in that conflict. Pericles' oration was recorded by the Greek historian Thucydides, who was probably present at that event.

- How does Pericles describe Athenian democracy?

- Does his argument for democracy derive from fundamental principles, such as human equality, or from the practical benefits that derive from such a system of government?

- What kind of citizens does he believe democracy produces? Keep in mind that not everyone shared this idealized view of Athenian democracy. How might critics have responded to Pericles' arguments?

- Although Pericles praised Athenian military prowess, his city lost the Peloponnesian War. In what ways does this affect your assessment of his arguments?

PERICLES

Funeral Oration

431–430 B.C.E.

Our form of government does not enter into rivalry with the institutions of others. We do not copy our neighbors, but are an example to them. It is true that we are called a democracy, for the administration is in the hands of the many and not of the few. But while the law secures equal justice to all alike in their private disputes, the claim of excellence is also recognized; and when a citizen is in any way distinguished, he is preferred to the public service, not as a matter of privilege, but as the reward of merit. Neither is poverty a bar, but a man may benefit his country whatever be the obscurity of his condition. There is no exclusiveness in our public life, and in our private intercourse we are not suspicious of one another, nor angry with our neighbor if he does what he likes.... While we are thus unconstrained in our private intercourse, a spirit of reverence pervades our public acts; we are prevented from doing wrong by respect for the authorities and for the laws....

And we have not forgotten to provide for our weary spirits many relaxations from toil; we have regular games and sacrifices throughout the year; our homes are beautiful and elegant; and the delight which we daily feel in all these things helps to banish melancholy. Because of the greatness of our city the fruits of the whole earth flow in upon us; so that we enjoy the goods of other countries as freely as of our own.

Then, again, our military training is in many respects superior to that of our adversaries. Our city is thrown open to the world, and we never expel a foreigner or prevent him from seeing or learning anything of which the secret if revealed to an enemy might profit him. We rely not upon management or trickery, but upon our own hearts and hands. And in the matter of education, whereas they from early youth are always undergoing laborious exercises which are to make them brave, we live at ease, and yet are equally ready to face the perils which they face....

For we are lovers of the beautiful, yet simple in our tastes, and we cultivate the mind without loss of manliness.... To avow poverty with us is no disgrace; the true disgrace is in doing nothing to avoid

Source: Benjamin Jowett, *Thucydides, translated into English, to which is prefixed an essay on inscriptions and a note on the geography of Thucydides*, 2nd ed. (Oxford: Clarendon Press, 1900), Book 2, para. 37–41.

it. An Athenian citizen does not neglect the state because he takes care of his own household; and even those of us who are engaged in business have a very fair idea of politics. We alone regard a man who takes no interest in public affairs, not as a harmless; but as a useless character; and if few of us are originators, we are all sound judges of a policy. The great impediment to action is, in our opinion, not discussion, but the want of that knowledge which is gained by discussion preparatory to action. For we have a peculiar power of thinking before we act and of acting too, whereas other men are courageous from ignorance but hesitate upon reflection. And they are surely to be esteemed the bravest spirits who, having the clearest sense both of the pains and pleasures of life, do not on that account shrink from danger....

To sum up: I say that Athens is the school of Hellas, and that the individual Athenian in his own person seems to have the power of adapting himself to the most varied forms of action with the utmost versatility and grace....

For we have compelled every land and every sea to open a path for our valor, and have everywhere planted eternal memorials of our friendship and of our enmity. Such is the city for whose sake these men nobly fought and died; they could not bear the thought that she might be taken from them; and every one of us who survive should gladly toil on her behalf.

Document 4.2

In Praise of the Roman Empire

By the second century C.E. the Roman Empire, now encompassing the Mediterranean basin and beyond, was in its glory days. With conquest largely completed, the *pax Romana* (Roman peace) generally prevailed and commerce flourished, as did the arts and literature. The empire enjoyed a century (96–180 C.E.) of autocratic but generally benevolent rule. In 155 C.E. a well-known scholar and orator from the city of Smyrna on the west coast of Anatolia (present-day Turkey) arrived for a visit to the imperial capital of Rome. He was Aelius Aristides (ca. 117–181 C.E.), a widely traveled Greek-speaking member of a wealthy landowning family whose members had been granted Roman citizenship several decades earlier. While in Rome, Aristides delivered to the imperial court and in front of the emperor, Antonius, a formal speech of praise and gratitude, known as a panegyric, celebrating the virtues and achievements of the Roman Empire.

- What did Aristides identify as the unique features of the Roman Empire? Which of these features in particular may have given the empire a measure of legitimacy in the eyes of its many subject peoples? What other factors, unmentioned by Aristides, may have contributed to the maintenance of Roman authority?

- What does Aristides mean by referring to the empire as a "common democracy of the world"?

- Why might Aristides, a Greek-speaking resident of a land well outside the Roman heartland, be so enamored of the empire?

■ To what extent does Aristides' oration provide evidence for the development of a composite Greco-Roman culture and sensibility within the Roman Empire?

■ How does this speech compare, in both style and content, with that of Pericles in Document 4.1?

AELIUS ARISTIDES

The Roman Oration

155 C.E.

A certain prose writer said about Asia that one man "rules all as far as is the course of the sun," untruly, since he excluded all Africa and Europe from the sun's rising and setting. [This refers to the Persian Empire.] But now it has turned out to be true that the course of the sun and your possessions are equal.... [N]or do you rule within fixed boundaries, nor does another prescribe the limits of your power....

About the [Mediterranean] sea the continents [Africa, Asia, and Europe] lie... ever supplying you with products from those regions. Here is brought from every land and sea all the crops of the seasons and the produce of each land, river and lake, as well as the arts of the Greeks and barbarians.... So many merchant ships arrive here... that the city is like a factory common to the whole earth. It is possible to see so many cargoes from India and even from [southern] Arabia.... Your farmlands are Egypt, Sicily, and all of [North] Africa which is cultivated. The arrival and departure of ships never stops....

Although your empire is so large and so great, it is much greater in its good order than in its circumference.... [Nor] are satraps° fighting against one another, as if they had no king; nor do some cities side with these and others with those.... But like the enclosure of a courtyard, cleansed of every disturbance, a circle encompasses your empire.... All everywhere are equally subjects....

°**satraps:** local authorities.

Source: Aelius Aristides, *The Complete Works*, vol. 2, translated by P. Charles A. Behr (Leiden: E. J. Brill, 1986), 73–97.

You are the only ones ever to rule over free men.... [Y]ou govern throughout the whole inhabited world as if in a single city.... You appoint governors... for the protection and care of their subjects, not to be their masters.... And here there is a great and fair equality between weak and powerful, obscure and famous, poor and rich and noble.... To excel the barbarians in wealth and power, while surpassing the Greeks in knowledge and moderation, seems to me to be an important matter....

You have divided into two parts all the men of your empire... and everywhere you have made citizens all those who are the more accomplished, noble, and powerful people, even if they retain their native affinities, while the remainder you have made subjects and the governed. And neither does the sea nor a great expanse of intervening land keep one from being a citizen, nor here are Asia and Europe distinguished. But all lies open to all men.... There has been established a common democracy of the world, under one man, the best ruler and director....

You have divided people into Romans [citizens] and non-Romans [subjects]... [M]any in each city are citizens of yours... and some of them have not even seen this city.... There is no need of garrisons..., but the most important and powerful people in each place guard their countries for you.... Yet no envy walks in your empire.... [T]here has arisen a single harmonious government which has embraced all men.

[Y]ou have established a form of government such as no one else of mankind has done.... Your government is like a mixture of all the constitutions [democracy, aristocracy, monarchy] without the inferior side of each.... Therefore whenever one considers the power of the people and how easily they attain all their wishes and requests, he will believe that it is a democracy....But when he considers the Senate deliberating and holding office, he will believe there is no more perfect aristocracy than this. But when he has considered the overseer and president of all these [the emperor], he sees in this man the possessor of the most perfect monarchy, free of the evils of the tyrant and greater than the dignity of the king....

And the whole inhabited world, as it were attending a national festival, has laid aside...the carrying of weapons and has turned...to adornments and all kinds of pleasures....Everything is full of gymnasiums, fountains, gateways, temples, handicrafts, and schools...and a boundless number of games....Now it possible for both Greek and barbarian...to travel easily wherever he wishes....[I]t is enough for his safety that he is a Roman or rather one of those under you.

Document 4.3

Governing a Chinese Empire

As the Roman Empire was taking shape in the Mediterranean basin, a powerful Chinese empire emerged in East Asia. More than in the Roman world, the political ideas and practices of classical China drew on the past. The notion of China as a unified state ruled by a single sage/emperor who mediated between heaven and the human realm had an ancient pedigree. After a long period of political fragmentation, known as the era of warring states, such a unified Chinese state took shape once again during the short-lived Qin dynasty (221–206 B.C.E.), led by its formidable ruler Shihuangdi (see pp. 158–60). That state operated under a version of Legalism (see Chapter 5, pp. 192–93), a political philosophy that found expression in the writings of Han Fei (280–233 B.C.E.) and that in large measure guided the practices of Shihuangdi and the Qin dynasty. Han Fei's Legalist thinking was discredited by the brutality and excesses of Shihuangdi's reign, and the Han dynasty that followed was sharply critical of his ideas, favoring instead the "government by morality" approach of Confucianism. Nonetheless, Han Fei's emphasis on the importance of laws and the need to enforce them influenced all succeeding Chinese dynasties.

- Why is Han Fei's approach to governing China referred to as Legalism? According to him, what is required for effective government?

- What are the "two handles"?

- To whom does Han Fei believe his measures should apply?

- What view of human nature underpins Han Fei's argument?

The Writings of Master Han Fei
Third Century B.C.E.

No country is permanently strong. Nor is any country permanently weak. If conformers to law are strong, the country is strong; if conformers to law are weak, the country is weak....

Any ruler able to expel private crookedness and uphold public law, finds the people safe and the state in order; and any ruler able to expunge private action and act on public law, finds his army strong and his enemy weak. So, find out men following the discipline of laws and regulations, and place them above the body of officials. Then the sovereign cannot be deceived by anybody with fraud and falsehood....

Therefore, the intelligent sovereign makes the law select men and makes no arbitrary promotion himself. He makes the law measure merits and makes no arbitrary regulation himself. In consequence, able men cannot be obscured, bad characters cannot be disguised; falsely praised fellows cannot be advanced, wrongly defamed people cannot be degraded. To govern the state by law is to praise the right and blame the wrong.

The law does not fawn on the noble....Whatever the law applies to, the wise cannot reject nor can the brave defy. Punishment for fault never skips ministers, reward for good never misses commoners. Therefore, to correct the faults of the high, to rebuke the vices of the low, to suppress disorders, to decide against mistakes, to subdue the arrogant, to straighten the crooked, and to unify the folkways of the masses, nothing could match the law. To warn the officials and overawe the people, to rebuke obscenity and danger, and to forbid falsehood and deceit, nothing could match penalty. If penalty is severe, the noble cannot discriminate against the humble. If law is definite, the superiors are esteemed and not violated. If the superiors are not violated, the sovereign will become strong and able to maintain the proper course of government. Such was the reason why the early kings esteemed Legalism and handed it down to posterity. Should the lord of men discard law and practice selfishness, high and low would have no distinction.

The means whereby the intelligent ruler controls his ministers are two handles only. The two handles are chastisement and commendation. What are meant by chastisement and commendation? To inflict death or torture upon culprits is called chastisement; to bestow encouragements or rewards on men of merit is called commendation.

Ministers are afraid of censure and punishment but fond of encouragement and reward. Therefore, if the lord of men uses the handles of chastisement and commendation, all ministers will dread his severity and turn to his liberality. The villainous ministers of the age are different. To men they hate they would, by securing the handle of chastisement from the sovereign, ascribe crimes; on men they love they would, by securing the handle of commendation from the sovereign, bestow rewards. Now supposing the lord of men placed the authority of punishment and the profit of reward not in his hands but let the ministers administer the affairs of reward and punishment instead; then everybody in the country would fear the ministers and slight the ruler, and turn to the ministers and away from the ruler. This is the calamity of the ruler's loss of the handles of chastisement and commendation.

Source: *The Complete Works of Han Fei Tzu*, vol. 1, translated by W. L. Liano (London: Arthur Probsthain, 1939), 40, 45–47.

Document 4.4

Governing an Indian Empire

Among the rulers of the classical era, Ashoka, of India's Mauryan dynasty (reigned 268–232 B.C.E.), surely stands out, both for the personal transformation he experienced and for the benevolent philosophy of government that he subsequently articulated (see pp. 165–67). Ashoka's career as emperor began in a familiar fashion—ruthless consolidation of his own power and vigorous expansion of the state's frontiers. A particularly bloody battle against the state of Kalinga marked a turning point in his reign. Apparently repulsed by the destruction, Ashoka converted to Buddhism and turned his attention to more peaceful and tolerant ways of governing his huge empire. His edicts and advice, inscribed on rocks and pillars throughout his realm, outlined this distinctive approach to imperial governance.

The following document provides samples of instructions from Ashoka, who is referred to as King Piyadasi, or the Beloved of the Gods. The term *dhamma*, used frequently in edicts of Ashoka, refers to the "way" or the "truth" that is embodied in religious teachings.

- How would you describe Ashoka's philosophy of state?

- How might Han Fei have responded to Ashoka's ideas?

- What specific changes did Ashoka make in state policies and practices?

- Can you think of practical reasons why he might have adopted these policies? Did he entirely abandon the use of harsher measures?

Although Ashoka's reputation as an enlightened ruler has persisted to this day, his policies ultimately were not very successful. Shortly after Ashoka's death, the Mauryan Empire broke apart into a more common Indian pattern of competing regional states that rose and fell with some regularity. Of course Shihuangdi's much harsher Legalist policies were also unsuccessful, at least in maintaining his dynasty, which lasted a mere fifteen years.

- How might this outcome affect your assessment of Ashoka?

- What does this suggest about the relationship between political philosophies and the success or longevity of political systems?

ASHOKA

The Rock Edicts

ca. 268–232 B.C.E.

Beloved-of-the-Gods, King Piyadasi, conquered the Kalingas eight years after his coronation. One hundred and fifty thousand were deported, one hundred thousand were killed, and many more died [from other causes]. After the Kalingas had been conquered, Beloved-of-the-Gods came to feel a strong inclination towards the Dhamma, a love for the Dhamma and for instruction in Dhamma. Now Beloved-of-the-Gods feels deep remorse for having conquered the Kalingas....

Now Beloved-of-the-Gods thinks that even those who do wrong should be forgiven where forgiveness is possible.

Even the forest people, who live in Beloved-of-the-Gods' domain, are entreated and reasoned with to act properly. They are told that despite his remorse Beloved-of-the-Gods has the power to punish them if necessary, so that they should be ashamed of their wrong and not be killed. Truly, Beloved-of-the-Gods desires non-injury, restraint, and impartiality to all beings, even where wrong has been done.

Now it is conquest by Dhamma that Beloved-of-the-Gods considers to be the best conquest....

I have had this Dhamma edict written so that my sons and great-grandsons may not consider making new conquests, or that if military conquests are made, that they be done with forbearance and light punishment, or better still, that they consider making conquest by Dhamma only, for that bears fruit in this world and the next. May all their intense devotion be given to this which has a result in this world and the next.

1. Here (in my domain) no living beings are to be slaughtered or offered in sacrifice.... Formerly, in the kitchen of Beloved-of-the-Gods, King Piyadasi, hundreds of thousands of animals were killed every day to make curry. But now with the writing of this Dhamma edict only three creatures, two peacocks and a deer are killed, and the deer not always. And in time, not even these three creatures will be killed.

2.... [E]verywhere has Beloved-of-the-Gods... made provision for two types of medical treatment: medical treatment for humans and medical treatment for animals. Wherever medical herbs suitable for humans or animals are not available, I have had them imported and grown.... Along roads I have had wells dug and trees planted for the benefit of humans and animals.

3. Everywhere in my domain the [royal officers] shall go on inspection tours every five years for the purpose of Dhamma instruction and also to conduct other business. Respect for mother and father is good, generosity to friends, acquaintances, relatives, Brahmans and ascetics is good, not killing living beings is good, moderation in spending and moderation in saving is good.

4. In the past, for many hundreds of years, killing or harming living beings and improper behavior toward relatives, and improper behavior toward Brahmans and ascetics has increased. But now due to Beloved-of-the-Gods' Dhamma practice, the sound of the drum [for announcing the punishment of criminals] has been replaced by the sound of the Dhamma. The sighting of heavenly cars, auspicious elephants, bodies of fire, and other divine sightings has not happened for many hundreds of years. But now because Beloved-of-the-Gods, King Piyadasi, promotes restraint in the killing and harming of living beings, proper behavior towards relatives, Brahmans and ascetics, and respect for mother, father and elders, such sightings have increased.

5. In the past there were no [officers of the Dhamma] but such officers were appointed by me

Source: *The Edicts of King Ashoka*, translated by Ven S. Dhammika (Kandy, Sri Lanka: Buddhist Publication Society, 1993).

thirteen years after my coronation. Now they work among all religions for the establishment of Dhamma....They work among soldiers, chiefs, Brahmans, householders, the poor, the aged and those devoted to Dhamma—for their welfare and happiness—so that they may be free from harassment. They...work for the proper treatment of prisoners, towards their unfettering....They are occupied everywhere....

7. Beloved-of-the-Gods, King Piyadasi, desires that all religions should reside everywhere, for all of them desire self-control and purity of heart.

8. In the past kings used to go out on pleasure tours during which there was hunting and other entertainment. But ten years after Beloved-of-the-Gods had been coronated, he went on a tour to Sambodhi° and thus instituted Dhamma tours. During these tours, the following things took place: visits and gifts to Brahmans and ascetics, visits and gifts of gold to the aged, visits to people in the countryside, instructing them in Dhamma....

12. Beloved-of-the-Gods, King Piyadasi, honors both ascetics and the householders of all religions, and he honors them with gifts and honors of various kinds....Whoever praises his own religion, due to excessive devotion, and condemns others with the thought "Let me glorify my own religion," only harms his own religion. Therefore contact [between religions] is good. One should listen to and respect the doctrines professed by others.

_____

°**Sambodhi:** the site of the Buddha's enlightenment.

Using the Evidence:
Political Authority in Classical Civilizations

1. **Making comparisons:** How would you describe the range of political thinking and practice expressed in these documents? What, if any, common elements do these writings share? Another approach to such a comparison is to take the ideas of one writer and ask how they might be viewed by several of the others. For example, how might Pericles, Aristides, and Han Fei have responded to Ashoka?

2. **Considering variation within civilizations:** You will notice that none of these civilizations practiced a single philosophy of government. Athens was governed very differently from Sparta, the practices of the Roman Empire differed substantially from those of the Republic, Legalism and Confucianism represented alternative approaches to Chinese political life, and Ashoka's ideas broke sharply with prevailing practice of Indian rulers. How can you account for these internal differences? How might you imagine an internal dialogue between each of these writers and their likely domestic critics?

3. **Comparing ancient and modern politics:** What enduring issues of political life do these documents raise? What elements of political thinking and practice during the classical era differ most sharply from those of the modern world of the last century or two? What are the points of similarity?

4. **Distinguishing "power" and "authority":** Some scholars have made a distinction between "power," the ability of rulers to coerce their subjects into some required behavior, and "authority," the ability of those rulers to persuade their subjects to obey voluntarily by convincing them that it is proper, right, or natural to do so. What appeals to "power" and "authority" can you find in these documents? How does the balance between them differ among these documents?

5. **Noticing point of view:** From what position and with what motivation did these writers compose their documents? How did this affect what they had to say?

Visual Sources

Considering the Evidence:
Qin Shihuangdi and China's Eternal Empire

In the vast saga of empire building in world history, few rulers have surpassed China's so-called First Emperor, Qin Shihuangdi (reigned 221–210 B.C.E.), in terms of imperial ambition. During his life, Shihuangdi forcefully and violently brought unity to the warring states of China with policies that were as brutal as they were effective (see pp. 158–60). That achievement gained him the respect of many Chinese in the centuries that followed. No less a figure than Mao Zedong, the twentieth-century communist revolutionary, proudly compared himself to the First Emperor. But Shihuangdi was widely hated in his own time and subject to numerous attempts at assassination, while Confucian scholars in the centuries that followed his death were also highly critical of his brutal methods of governing China.

No artistic images of Shihuangdi survive from the time of his reign, but he was the subject of many paintings in later centuries. Visual Source 4.1, dating from the eighteenth century, depicts a famous scene from his reign, when he allegedly ordered the burning of books critical of his policies and the execution of respected Confucian scholars by burying hundreds of them alive.

- What signs of imperial authority are apparent in the painting?
- What impression of the First Emperor does this painting convey? Do you think the artist sought to celebrate or criticize Shihuangdi?
- What accusations against Shihuangdi might arise from the action depicted at the bottom of Visual Source 4.1?

However his reign may have been evaluated, Shihuangdi's conception of the empire he created was grand indeed. It was to be a universal or cosmic empire. In tours throughout his vast realm, he offered sacrifices to the various spirits, bringing them, as well as the rival kingdoms of China, into a state of unity and harmony. One of the inscriptions he left behind suggested the scope of his reign: "He universally promulgated the shining laws, gave warp and woof to all under heaven."[16] Shihuangdi saw himself in the line of ancient sage kings, who had originally given order to the world.

In Shihuangdi's thinking, that empire was not only universal, encompassing the entire world known to him, but also eternal. The emperor vigorously pursued personal immortality, seeking out pills, herbs, and potions

坑儒焚書

Visual Source 4.1 An Eighteenth-Century Representation of Qin Shihuangdi (Bibliothèque nationale de France/The Art Archive)

believed to convey eternal life and sending expeditions to the mythical Isles of the Immortals, thought to lie off the east coast of China. But the most spectacular expression of the eternal character of his empire lay in a vast tomb complex constructed during his lifetime near the modern city of Xian (see Map 4.5, p. 159).

In early 1974, some Chinese peasants digging a well stumbled across a small corner of that complex, leading to what has become perhaps the most celebrated archeological discovery of the twentieth century. In subsequent and continuing excavations, archeologists have uncovered thousands of life-size ceramic statues of soldiers of various ranks, arrayed for battle and equipped with real weapons. Other statues portrayed officials, acrobats, musicians, wrestlers, horses, bronze chariots, birds, and more—all designed to accompany Shihuangdi into the afterlife.

This amazing discovery, however, was only a very small part of an immense tomb complex covering some fifty-six square kilometers and centered on the still-unexcavated burial mound of Shihuangdi. Begun in 246 B.C.E. and still incomplete when Shihuangdi died in 210 B.C.E., the construction of this gigantic complex was described by the great Chinese historian Sima Qian about a century later:

> As soon as the First Emperor became king of Qin, excavations and building had been started at Mount Li, while after he won the empire, more than 700,000 conscripts from all parts of the country worked there. They dug through three subterranean streams and poured molten copper for the outer coffin, and the tomb was filled with…palaces, pavilions, and offices as well as fine vessels, precious stones, and rarities. Artisans were ordered to fix up crossbows so that any thief breaking in would be shot. All the country's streams, the Yellow River and the Yangtze were reproduced in quicksilver [mercury] and by some mechanical means made to flow into a miniature ocean. The heavenly constellations were above and the regions of the earth below. The candles were made of whale oil to insure the burning for the longest possible time.[17]

Buried with Shihuangdi were many of the workers who had died or were killed during construction as well as sacrificed aristocrats and concubines.

This massive project was no mere monument to a deceased ruler. In a culture that believed the living and the dead formed a single community, Shihuangdi's tomb complex was a parallel society, complete with walls, palaces, cemeteries, demons, spirits, soldiers, administrators, entertainers, calendars, texts, divination records, and the luxurious objects appropriate to royalty. The tomb mound itself was like a mountain, a geographic feature that in Chinese thinking was home to gods, spirits, and immortals. From this mound, Shihuangdi would rule forever over his vast domain, although invisible to the living.

The visual sources that follow provide a small sample of the terra-cotta army that protected that underground world, as it has emerged from the excavations of the past several decades. The largest pit (Visual Source 4.2) is now covered with a canopy and conveys something of the massive size of this undertaking. Located about a mile east of Shihuangdi's burial mound, this ceramic army, replete with horses and chariots, faced the pass in the mountains from which enemies might be expected. Some six thousand terra-cotta figures have been uncovered and painstakingly pieced together in this pit alone.

■ How do you suppose Shihuangdi thought about the function of this "army" in the larger context of his tomb complex?

■ What kind of organizational effort would be required to produce such a ceramic army?

Visual Source 4.2 The Terra-Cotta Army of Shihuangdi (Dennis Cox/China Stock)

Visual Source 4.3 Terra-Cotta Infantry (Keren Su/China Span/Alamy)

Scholars have long been impressed with the apparent individuality of these terra-cotta figures, and some have argued that they were actually modeled on particular living soldiers. More recent research suggests, however, that they were "an early feat of mass production."[18] Well-organized workshops produced a limited variety of face shapes, body parts, hairstyles, and uniforms, which were then assembled in various combinations and slightly reworked to convey an impression of individuality. Visual Source 4.3 shows a group of infantrymen, located at the front of the formation, while Visual Source 4.4 represents a kneeling archer.

■ What similarities and differences can you identify between the infantrymen and the archer? Which of them do you imagine had a higher status?

■ What impressions do their postures and facial expressions convey?

■ What details help to convey a highly realistic image of these figures?

Visual Source 4.4 Terra-Cotta Archer (Museum of the Terra Cotta Army, Xian/Visual Connection Archive)

Visual Source 4.5   A Bronze Horse-Drawn Chariot (Private Collection/The Bridgeman Art Library)

Among the most delightful finds in Shihuangdi's funerary complex were two exquisitely detailed bronze carriages, each portrayed as half-sized models and pulled by four horses. Coachmen with swords provided protection on both sides. Some seven kilograms of gold and silver served to decorate the carriage and horses, which consisted of more than 3,000 separate pieces. These finds, however, were not part of the terra-cotta army and its military machine. Rather, they were found some distance away, quite close to the actual burial place of the emperor. Visual Source 4.5 shows the larger of the two carriages and features a team of horses, a driver, three windows, and a rear door. The compartment is decorated inside and out with geometric and cloud patterns, while the round roof, perhaps, represents the sun, the sky, or the heavens above.

■ Scholars differ as to the precise purpose of this carriage. Perhaps it was intended to allow the emperor to tour his realm in the afterlife much as he had done while alive. Or did it serve a one-time purpose to transport the emperor's soul into the afterlife? What line of reasoning might support either of these interpretations?

■ The carriages were found deliberately buried in a wooden coffin and facing west. What significance might you attach to these facts?

Using the Evidence:
Qin Shihuangdi and China's Eternal Empire

1. **Describing Shihuangdi:** Based on these visual sources and what you have learned about Shihuangdi's tomb complex, how would you characterize him as a ruler and as a man? In what ways did his reign reflect the views of Han Fei in Document 4.3?

2. **Evaluating Shihuangdi:** What aspects of Shihuangdi's reign might have provoked praise or criticism both during his life and later?

3. **Making comparisons:** In what ways were Shihuangdi's reign and his funerary arrangements unique, and in what respects did they fit into a larger pattern of other early rulers? Consider him in relationship to Egyptian pharaohs, Persian rulers, Alexander the Great, Augustus, or Ashoka.

CHAPTER FIVE

Eurasian Cultural Traditions

500 B.C.E.–500 C.E.

China and the Search for Order
  The Legalist Answer
  The Confucian Answer
  The Daoist Answer
Cultural Traditions of Classical India
  South Asian Religion: From Ritual Sacrifice to Philosophical Speculation
  The Buddhist Challenge
  Hinduism as a Religion of Duty and Devotion
Moving toward Monotheism: The Search for God in the Middle East
  Zoroastrianism
  Judaism
The Cultural Tradition of Classical Greece: The Search for a Rational Order
  The Greek Way of Knowing
  The Greek Legacy
Comparing Jesus and the Buddha
  The Lives of the Founders
  Establishing New Religions
  Creating Institutions
Reflections: Religion and Historians
Considering the Evidence
  Documents: The Good Life in Classical Eurasia
  Visual Sources: Representations of the Buddha

In 2004, some 180 married couples in Beijing, China, stood before a picture of their country's ancient sage, Confucius, and took an oath, pledging fidelity to each other and promising never to divorce. This was a small part of a nationwide celebration of the 2,555th anniversary of the birth of Confucius. A public memorial service was held in his hometown of Qufu, while high government officials warmly welcomed delegates attending an international symposium devoted to his teaching. What made this celebration remarkable was that it took place in a country still ruled by the Communist Party, which had long devoted enormous efforts to discrediting Confucius and his teachings. In the view of communist China's revolutionary leader, Mao Zedong, Confucianism was associated with class inequality, patriarchy, feudalism, superstition, and all things old and backward, but the country's ancient teacher and philosopher had apparently outlasted its revolutionary hero. High-ranking political leaders, all officially communist, have begun to invoke Confucius and to urge "social harmony," rather than class conflict, as China rapidly modernizes. Many anxious parents offer prayers at Confucian temples when their children are taking the national college entrance exams.

Buddhism also has experienced something of a revival in China, as thousands of temples, destroyed during the heyday of communism, have been repaired and reopened. Christianity too has grown rapidly since the death of Mao in 1976, with professing Christians numbering some 7 percent of China's huge population by the early twenty-first century. Here are reminders, in a Chinese context, of the continuing appeal of cultural traditions forged during the clas-

China's Cultural Traditions: In this idealized painting, attributed to the Chinese artist Wang Shugu (1649–1730), the Chinese teacher Confucius presents a baby Buddha to the Daoist master Laozi. The image illustrates the assimilation of a major Indian religion into China as well as the generally peaceful coexistence of these three traditions. (British Museum/The Art Archive)

sical era. Those traditions are among the most enduring legacies that second-wave civilizations have bequeathed to the modern world.

IN THE SEVERAL CENTURIES SURROUNDING 500 B.C.E., something quite remarkable happened all across Eurasia. More or less simultaneously, in China, India, the Middle East, and Greece, there emerged cultural traditions that spread widely, have persisted in various forms into the twenty-first century, and have shaped the values and outlooks of most people who have inhabited the planet over the past 2,500 years.

In China, it was the time of Kong Fuzi (Confucius) and Laozi, whose teachings gave rise to Confucianism and Daoism, respectively. In India, a series of religious writings known as the *Upanishads* gave expression to the classical philosophy of Hinduism, while a religious reformer, Siddhartha Gautama, set in motion a separate religion known later as Buddhism. In the Middle East, a distinctively monotheistic religious tradition appeared. It was expressed in Zoroastrianism, derived from the teachings of the Persian prophet Zarathustra, and in Judaism, articulated in Israel by a number of Jewish prophets such as Amos, Jeremiah, and Isaiah. Finally, in Greece, a rational and humanistic tradition found expression in the writings of Socrates, Plato, Aristotle, and many others.

These cultural traditions differed greatly. Chinese and Greek thinkers focused more on the affairs of this world and credited human rationality with the power to understand that reality. Indian, Persian, and Jewish intellectuals, who explored the realm of the divine and its relationship to human life, were much more religious. All of these traditions sought an alternative to an earlier polytheism, in which the activities of various gods and spirits explained what happened in this world. These gods and spirits had generally been seen as similar to human beings, though much more powerful. Through ritual and sacrifice, men and women might placate the gods or persuade them to do human bidding. In contrast, the new cultural traditions of the classical era sought to define a single source of order and meaning in the universe, some moral or religious realm, sharply different from and higher than the sphere of human life. The task of humankind, according to these new ways of thinking, was personal moral or spiritual transformation—often expressed as the development of compassion—by aligning ourselves with that higher order.[1] These enormously rich and varied traditions have collectively posed the great questions of human life and society that have haunted and inspired much of humankind ever since. They also defined the distinctive cultures that distinguished the various classical civilizations from one another.

Why did these traditions all emerge at roughly the same time? Here we encounter an enduring issue of historical analysis: What is the relationship between ideas and the circumstances in which they arise? Are ideas generated by particular political, social, and economic conditions? Or are they the product of creative human imagination independent of the material environment? Or do they derive from some combination of the two? In the case of the classical cultural traditions, many historians have

Snapshot Thinkers and Philosophies of the Classical Era

Person	Date	Location	Religion/Philosophy	Key Ideas
Zoroaster	7th century B.C.E. (?)	Persia (present-day Iran)	Zoroastrianism	Single High God; cosmic conflict of good and evil
Hebrew prophets (Isaiah, Amos, Jeremiah)	9th–6th centuries B.C.E.	Eastern Mediterranean/ Palestine/Israel	Judaism	Transcendent High God; covenant with chosen people; social justice
Anonymous writers of Upanishads	800–400 B.C.E.	India	Brahmanism/ Hinduism	Brahma (the single impersonal divine reality); karma; rebirth; goal of liberation (moksha)
Confucius	6th century B.C.E.	China	Confucianism	Social harmony through moral example; secular outlook; importance of education; family as model of the state
Mahavira	6th century B.C.E.	India	Jainism	All creatures have souls; purification through nonviolence; opposed to caste
Siddhartha Gautama	6th century B.C.E.	India	Buddhism	Suffering caused by desire/ attachment; end of suffering through modest and moral living and meditation practice
Laozi, Zhuangzi	6th–3rd centuries B.C.E.	China	Daoism	Withdrawal from the world into contemplation of nature; simple living; end of striving
Socrates, Plato, Aristotle	5th–4th centuries B.C.E.	Greece	Greek rationalism	Style of persistent questioning; secular explanation of nature and human life
Jesus	early 1st century C.E.	Palestine/Israel	Christianity	Supreme importance of love based on intimate relationship with God; at odds with established authorities
Saint Paul	1st century C.E.	Palestine/Israel/ eastern Roman Empire	Christianity	Christianity as a religion for all; salvation through faith in Jesus Christ

noted the tumultuous social changes that accompanied the emergence of these new teachings. An iron-age technology, available since roughly 1000 B.C.E., made possible more productive economies and more deadly warfare. Growing cities, increased trade, the prominence of merchant classes, the emergence of new states and empires, new contacts among civilizations—all of these disruptions, occurring in already-literate societies, led thinkers to question older outlooks and to come up with new solutions to fundamental questions: What is the purpose of life? How should human society be ordered? What is the relationship between human life in this world and the moral or spiritual realms that lie beyond? But precisely why various societies developed their own distinctive answers to these questions remains elusive—a tribute, perhaps, to the unpredictable genius of the human imagination.

China and the Search for Order

As one of the First Civilizations, China had a tradition of state building that historians have traced back to around 2000 B.C.E. or before. By the time the Zhou dynasty took power in 1122 B.C.E., the notion of the Mandate of Heaven had taken root, as had the idea that the normal and appropriate condition of China was one of political unity. By the eighth century B.C.E., the authority of the Zhou dynasty and its royal court had substantially weakened, and by 500 B.C.E. any unity that China had earlier enjoyed was long gone. What followed was a period (403–221 B.C.E.) of chaos, growing violence, and disharmony that became known as the "age of warring states" (see pp. 158–60). During these dreadful centuries of disorder and turmoil, a number of Chinese thinkers began to consider how order might be restored, how the apparent tranquillity of an earlier time could be realized again. From their reflections emerged classical cultural traditions of Chinese civilization.

The Legalist Answer

■ Comparison

What different answers to the problem of disorder arose in classical China?

One answer to the problem of disorder—though not the first to emerge—was a hardheaded and practical philosophy known as Legalism. To Legalist thinkers, the solution to China's problems lay in rules or laws, clearly spelled out and strictly enforced through a system of rewards and punishments. "If rewards are high," wrote Han Fei, one of the most prominent Legalist philosophers, "then what the ruler wants will be quickly effected; if punishments are heavy, what he does not want will be swiftly prevented."[2] (See Document 4.3, pp. 174–75, for an extract from the writing of Han Fei.) Legalists generally entertained a rather pessimistic view of human nature. Most people were stupid and shortsighted. Only the state and its rulers could act in their long-term interests. Doing so meant promoting farmers and soldiers, the only two groups in society who performed essential functions, while suppressing artisans, merchants, aristocrats, scholars, and other classes regarded as useless.

Legalist thinking provided inspiration and methods for the harsh reunification of China under Shihuangdi and the Qin dynasty (221–206 B.C.E.), but the brutality of that short dynasty thoroughly discredited Legalism. Although its techniques and practices played a role in subsequent Chinese statecraft, no philosopher or ruler ever again openly advocated its ideas. The Han and all subsequent dynasties drew instead on the teachings of China's greatest sage—Confucius.

The Confucian Answer

Born to an aristocratic family in the state of Lu in northern China, Confucius (551–479 B.C.E.) was both learned and ambitious. Believing that he had found the key to solving China's problem of disorder, he spent much of his adult life seeking a political position from which he might put his ideas into action. But no such opportunity came his way. Perhaps it was just as well, for it was as a thinker and a teacher that Confucius left a profound imprint on Chinese history and culture and also on other East Asian societies, such as Korea and Japan. After his death, his students collected his teachings in a short book called the *Analects*, and later scholars elaborated and commented endlessly on his ideas, creating a body of thought known as Confucianism (see Document 5.1, pp. 217–19).

The Confucian answer to the problem of China's disorder was very different from that of the Legalists. Not laws and punishments, but the moral example of superiors was the Confucian key to a restored social harmony. For Confucius, human society consisted primarily of unequal relationships: the father was superior to the son; the husband to the wife; the older brother to the younger brother; and, of course, the ruler to the subject. If the superior party in each of these relationships behaved with sincerity, benevolence, and genuine concern for others, then the inferior party would be motivated to respond with deference and obedience. Harmony then would prevail. As Confucius put it, "The relation between superiors and inferiors is like that between the wind and the grass. The grass must bend when the wind blows across it." Thus, in both family life and in political life, the cultivation of *ren*—translated as humanheartedness, benevolence, goodness, nobility of heart—was the essential ingredient of a tranquil society.

But how are these humane virtues to be nurtured? Believing that people have a capacity for improvement, Confucius emphasized education as the key to moral betterment. He prescribed a broad liberal arts education emphasizing language, literature, history, philosophy, and ethics, all applied to the practical problems of government. Ritual and ceremonies were also important, for they conveyed the rules of appropriate

■ Description
Why has Confucianism been defined as a "humanistic philosophy" rather than a supernatural religion?

Filial Piety
This Song dynasty painting served as an illustration of an ancient Chinese text in the Confucian tradition called the "Classic of Filial Piety," originally composed sometime around the fourth century B.C.E. and subsequently reissued many times. Here, a son kneels submissively in front of his parents. The long-enduring social order that Confucius advocated began at home with unquestioning obedience and the utmost respect for parents and other senior members of the family. (National Palace Museum, Taipei, Taiwan, Republic of China)

behavior in the many and varying circumstances of life. For the "superior person," or "gentleman" in Confucian terms, this process of improvement involved serious personal reflection and a willingness to strive continuously to perfect his moral character.

Such ideas left a deep mark on Chinese culture. The discrediting of Legalism during the Qin dynasty opened the door to the adoption of Confucianism as the official ideology of the Chinese state, to such an extent that Confucianism became almost synonymous with Chinese culture. As China's bureaucracy took shape during the Han dynasty and after, Confucianism became the central element of the educational system, which prepared students for the series of examinations required to gain official positions. In those examinations, candidates were required to apply the principles of Confucianism to specific situations that they might encounter once in office. Thus generation after generation of China's male elite was steeped in the ideas and values of Confucianism.

Family life had long been central to Chinese popular culture, expressed in the practice of ancestor veneration, including visiting the graves of the deceased, presenting them with offerings, and erecting commemorative tablets and shrines in their honor. In Confucian thinking, the family became a model for political life, a kind of miniature state. Filial piety, the honoring of one's ancestors and parents, was both an end in itself and a training ground for the reverence due to the emperor and state officials. Confucianism also set the tone for defining the lives of women. A somewhat later woman writer, Ban Zhao (45–116 C.E.), penned a famous work called *Lessons for Women*, which spelled out the implication of Confucian thinking for women:

> Let a woman modestly yield to others. . . . Always let her seem to tremble and to fear. . . . Then she may be said to humble herself before others. . . . To guard carefully her chastity . . . to choose her words with care . . . , to wash and scrub filth away . . . , with whole-hearted devotion to sew and to weave, to love not gossip and silly laughter, in cleanliness and order to prepare the wine and food for serving guests: [These] may be called the characteristics of womanly work.[3]

Ban Zhao called for greater attention to education for young girls, not because they were equal to boys, but so that a young woman might be better prepared to serve her husband. (See Document 6.2, pp. 263–66, for a longer selection from Ban Zhao.)

Confucianism also placed great importance on history, for the ideal good society lay in the past. Confucian ideas were reformist, perhaps even revolutionary, but they were consistently presented as an effort to restore a past golden age. Those ideas also injected a certain democratic element into Chinese elite culture, for the great sage had emphasized that "superior men" and potential government officials were those of outstanding moral character and intellectual achievement, not simply those of aristocratic background. Usually only young men from wealthy families could afford the education necessary for passing examinations, but on occasion villagers could find the resources to sponsor one of their bright sons. Thus the Confucian-based examination system provided a modest element of social mobility in an otherwise hierarchical society. Confucian values clearly justified the many inequalities of Chinese society, but they also established certain expectations for government. Emperors should keep taxes low, administer justice, and provide for the material needs of the people. Those who failed to govern by the moral norms of Confucian values forfeited the Mandate of Heaven and invited upheaval and their replacement by another dynasty.

Finally, Confucianism marked Chinese elite culture by its secular, or nonreligious, character. Confucius did not deny the reality of gods and spirits. In fact, he advised people to participate in family and state rituals "as if the spirits were present," and he believed that the universe had a moral character with which human beings should align themselves. But the thrust of Confucian teaching was distinctly this-worldly and practical, concerned with human relationships, effective government, and social harmony. Asked on one occasion about his view of death and the spirits, Confucius replied that because we do not fully understand this life, we cannot possibly know anything about the life beyond. Although members of the Chinese elite generally acknowledged that magic, the gods, and spirits were perhaps necessary for the lower orders of society, they felt that educated people would find them of little help in striving for moral improvement and in establishing a harmonious society.

The Daoist Answer

No civilization has ever painted its cultural outlook in a single color. As Confucian thinking became generally known in China, a quite different school of thought also took shape. Known as Daoism, it was associated with the legendary figure Laozi, who, according to tradition, was a sixth-century B.C.E. archivist. He is said to have penned a short poetic volume, the *Daodejing* (*The Way and Its Power*), before vanishing in the wilderness to the west of China on his water buffalo. Daoist ideas were later expressed in a more explicit fashion by the philosopher Zhuangzi (369–286 B.C.E.).

In many ways, Daoist thinking ran counter to that of Confucius, who had emphasized the importance of education and earnest striving for moral improvement and good government. The Daoists ridiculed such efforts as artificial and useless, generally making things worse. In the face of China's disorder and chaos,

Chinese Landscape Paintings
Focused largely on mountains and water, Chinese landscape paintings were much influenced by the Daoist search for harmony with nature. Thus human figures and buildings were usually eclipsed by towering peaks, waterfalls, clouds, and trees. This seventeenth-century painting entitled *Temple on a Mountain Ledge* shows a Buddhist monastery in such a setting, while the poem in the upper right refers to the artist's earlier wanderings, a metaphor for the Buddhist quest for enlightenment. (Mr. and Mrs. John D. Rockefeller 3rd Collection of Asian Art/Asia Society 179.124)

■ **Comparison**
How did the Daoist outlook differ from that of Confucianism?

they urged withdrawal into the world of nature and encouraged behavior that was spontaneous, individualistic, and natural. Whereas Confucius focused on the world of human relationships, the Daoists turned the spotlight on the immense realm of nature and its mysterious unfolding patterns. "Confucius roams within society," the Chinese have often said. "Laozi wanders beyond."

The central concept of Daoist thinking is *dao*, an elusive notion that refers to the way of nature, the underlying and unchanging principle that governs all natural phenomena. According to the *Daodejing*, the dao "moves around and around, but does not on this account suffer. All life comes from it. It wraps everything with its love as in a garment, and yet it claims no honor, for it does not demand to be lord. I do not know its name and so I call it the Dao, the Way, and I rejoice in its power."[4]

Applied to human life, Daoism invited people to withdraw from the world of political and social activism, to disengage from the public life so important to Confucius, and to align themselves with the way of nature. It meant simplicity in living, small self-sufficient communities, limited government, and the abandonment of education and active efforts at self-improvement. "Give up learning," declares the *Daodejing*, "and put an end to your troubles." The flavor of the Daoist approach to life is evident in this passage from the *Daodejing*:

> A small country has few people.
> Though there are machines that can work ten to a hundred times faster
> than man, they are not needed. . . .
> Though they have boats and carriages, no one uses them. . . .
> Men return to the knotting of ropes in place of writing.
> Their food is plain and good, their clothes fine but simple. . . .
> They are happy in their ways.
> Though they live within sight of their neighbors,
> And crowing cocks and barking dogs are heard across the way,
> Yet they leave each other in peace while they grow old and die.[5]

The Yin Yang Symbol

Despite its sharp differences with the ideas of Confucianism, the Daoist perspective was widely regarded by elite Chinese as complementing rather than contradicting Confucian values (see the chapter-opening image on p. 188). Such an outlook was facilitated by the ancient Chinese concept of *yin* and *yang*, which expressed a belief in the unity of opposites.

Thus a scholar-official might pursue the Confucian project of "government by goodness" during the day, but upon returning home in the evening or following his retirement, he might well behave in a more Daoist fashion—pursuing the simple life, reading Daoist philosophy, practicing Daoist meditation and breathing exercises, or enjoying landscape paintings in which tiny human figures are dwarfed by the vast peaks and valleys of the natural world (see image on p. 195). Daoism also shaped the culture of ordinary people as it entered popular religion. This kind of Daoism sought to tap the power of the dao for practical uses and came to include magic, fortune-telling, and the search for immortality. It also on occasion provided an ideology for peasant uprisings, such as the Yellow Turban Rebellion (184–204 C.E.), which imagined a utopian society without the oppression of governments and landlords (see Chapter 6). In its many and varied forms, Daoism, like Confucianism, became an enduring element of the Chinese cultural tradition.

Cultural Traditions of Classical India

The cultural development of Indian civilization was far different from that of China. Whereas Confucianism paid little attention to the gods, spirits, and speculation about religious matters, Indian elite culture embraced the divine and all things spiritual with enthusiasm and generated elaborate philosophical visions about the nature of ultimate reality. Still, the Indian religious tradition, known to us as Hinduism, differed from other world religions. Unlike Buddhism, Christianity, or Islam, Hinduism had no historical founder; rather, it grew up over many centuries along with Indian civilization. Although it later spread into Southeast Asia, Hinduism was not a missionary religion seeking converts, but was, like Judaism, associated with a particular people and territory.

In fact, "Hinduism" was never a single tradition at all, and the term itself derived from outsiders — Greeks, Muslims, and later the British — who sought to reduce the infinite variety of Indian cultural patterns into a recognizable system. From the inside, however, Hinduism dissolved into a vast diversity of gods, spirits, beliefs, practices, rituals, and philosophies. This endlessly variegated Hinduism served to incorporate into Indian civilization the many diverse peoples who migrated into or invaded the South Asian peninsula over many centuries and several millennia. Its ability to accommodate this diversity gave India's cultural development a distinctive quality.

South Asian Religion: From Ritual Sacrifice to Philosophical Speculation

Despite the fragmentation and variety of Indian cultural and religious patterns, an evolving set of widely recognized sacred texts provided some commonality. The earliest of these texts, known as the *Vedas*, were collections of poems, hymns, prayers, and rituals. Compiled by priests called *Brahmins*, the Vedas were for centuries transmitted orally and were reduced to writing in Sanskrit around 600 B.C.E. In the Vedas, historians have caught fleeting glimpses of classical Indian civilization in its formative centuries (1500–600 B.C.E.). Those sacred writings tell of small competing chiefdoms or kingdoms, of sacred sounds and fires, of numerous gods, rising and falling in importance over the centuries, and of the elaborate ritual sacrifices that they required. Performing these sacrifices and rituals with great precision enabled the Brahmins to acquire enormous power and wealth, sometimes exceeding even that of kings and warriors. But Brahmins also generated growing criticism, as ritual became mechanical and formal and as Brahmins required heavy fees to perform them.

From this dissatisfaction arose another body of sacred texts, the Upanishads. Composed by largely anonymous thinkers between 800 and 400 B.C.E., these were

■ **Change**
In what ways did the religious traditions of South Asia change over the centuries?

Hindu Ascetics
Hinduism called for men in the final stage of life to leave ordinary ways of living and withdraw into the forests to seek spiritual liberation, or moksha. Here, in an illustration from an early thirteenth-century Indian manuscript, a holy man explores a text with three disciples in a secluded rural setting. (Réunion des Musées Nationaux/Art Resource, NY)

mystical and highly philosophical works that sought to probe the inner meaning of the sacrifices prescribed in the Vedas. In the Upanishads, external ritual gave way to introspective thinking, which expressed in many and varied formulations the central concepts of philosophical Hinduism that have persisted into modern times. Chief among them was the idea of Brahman, the World Soul, the final and ultimate reality. Beyond the multiplicity of material objects and individual persons and beyond even the various gods themselves lay this primal unitary energy or divine reality infusing all things, similar in some ways to the Chinese notion of the dao. This alone was real; the immense diversity of existence that human beings perceived with their senses was but an illusion.

The fundamental assertion of philosophical Hinduism was that the individual human soul, or *atman*, was in fact a part of Brahman. Beyond the quest for pleasure, wealth, power, and social position, all of which were perfectly normal and quite legitimate, lay the effort to achieve the final goal of humankind—union with Brahman, an end to our illusory perception of a separate existence. This was *moksha*, or liberation, compared sometimes to a bubble in a glass of water breaking through the surface and becoming one with the surrounding atmosphere.

Achieving this exalted state was held to involve many lifetimes, as the notion of *samsara*, or rebirth/reincarnation, became a central feature of Hindu thinking. Human souls migrated from body to body over many lifetimes, depending on one's actions. This was the law of *karma*. Pure actions, appropriate to one's station in life, resulted in rebirth in a higher social position or caste. Thus the caste system of distinct and ranked groups, each with its own duties, became a register of spiritual progress. Birth in a higher caste was evidence of "good karma," based on actions in a previous life, and offered a better chance to achieve moksha, which brought with it an end to the painful cycle of rebirth.

Various ways to this final release, appropriate to people of different temperaments, were spelled out in Hindu teachings. Some might achieve moksha through knowledge or study; others by means of detached action in the world, doing one's work without regard to consequences; still others through passionate devotion to some deity or through extended meditation practice. Such ideas—carried by Brahmin priests and even more by wandering ascetics, who had withdrawn from ordinary life to pursue their spiritual development—became widely known throughout India. (See Document 5.2, pp. 219–21.)

The Buddhist Challenge

About the same time as philosophical Hinduism was taking shape, there emerged another movement that soon became a distinct and separate religious tradition—Buddhism. Unlike Hinduism, this new faith had a historical founder, Siddhartha Gautama (ca. 566–ca. 486 B.C.E.), a prince from a small north Indian state. According to Buddhist tradition, the prince had enjoyed a sheltered and delightful youth but was shocked to his core upon encountering old age, sickness, and death. Leaving family and fortune behind, he then set out on a six-year spiritual quest, finally achieving insight, or "enlightenment," at the age of thirty-five. For the rest of his life, he taught what he had learned and gathered a small but growing community whose members came to see him as the Buddha, the Enlightened One.

"I teach but one thing," the Buddha said, "suffering and the end of suffering." To the Buddha, suffering or sorrow—experiencing life as imperfect, impermanent, and unsatisfactory—was the central and universal feature of human life. Its cause was desire or craving for individual fulfillment and particularly attachment to the notion of a core self or ego that is uniquely and solidly "me." The cure for this "dis-ease" lay in living a modest and moral life combined with meditation practice. Those who followed the Buddhist path most fully could expect to achieve enlightenment, or *nirvana*, a virtually indescribable state in which individual identity would be "extinguished" along with all greed, hatred, and delusion. With the pain of unnecessary suffering finally ended, the enlightened person would experience an overwhelming serenity, even in the midst of difficulty, as well as an immense loving-kindness, or compassion, for all beings. It was a simple message, elaborated endlessly and in various forms by those who followed him.

Much of the Buddha's teaching reflected the Hindu traditions from which it sprang. The idea that ordinary life is an illusion, the concepts of karma and rebirth, the goal of overcoming the incessant demands of the ego, the practice of meditation, the hope for final release from the cycle of rebirth—all of these Hindu elements found their way into Buddhist teaching. In this respect, Buddhism was a simplified and more accessible version of Hinduism.

Other elements of Buddhist teaching, however, sharply challenged prevailing Hindu thinking. Rejecting the religious authority of the Brahmins, the Buddha ridiculed their rituals and sacrifices as irrelevant to the hard work of dealing with one's

■ **Comparison**
In what ways did Buddhism reflect Hindu traditions, and in what ways did it challenge them?

The Mahabodhi Temple Constructed on the traditional site of the Buddha's enlightenment in northern India, the Mahabodhi temple became a major pilgrimage site and was lavishly patronized by local rulers. (Alison Wright/Robert Harding World Imagery/Getty Images)

suffering. Nor was he much interested in abstract speculation about the creation of the world or the existence of God, for such questions, he declared, "are not useful in the quest for holiness; they do not lead to peace and to the direct knowledge of *nirvana*." Individuals had to take responsibility for their own spiritual development with no help from human authorities or supernatural beings. It was a religion of intense self-effort, based on personal experience. The Buddha also challenged the inequalities of a Hindu-based caste system, arguing that neither caste position nor gender was a barrier to enlightenment. The possibility of "awakening" was available to all.

When it came to establishing a formal organization of the Buddha's most devoted followers, though, the prevailing patriarchy of Indian society made itself felt. Buddhist texts recount that the Buddha's foster mother, Prajapati Gotami, sought to enter the newly created order of monks but was repeatedly refused admission by the Buddha himself. Only after the intervention of the Buddha's attendant, Ananda, did he relent and allow women to join a separate order of nuns. Even then, these nuns were subjected to a series of rules that clearly subordinated them to men. Male monks, for example, could officially admonish the nuns, but the reverse was forbidden.

Nonetheless, thousands of women flocked to join the Buddhist order of nuns, where they found a degree of freedom and independence unavailable elsewhere in Indian society. The classic Hindu text, *The Laws of Manu*, had clearly defined the position of women: "In childhood a female must be subject to her father; in youth to her husband; when her lord is dead to her sons; a woman must never be independent."[6] But Buddhist nuns delighted in the relative freedom of their order, where they largely ran their own affairs, were forbidden to do household chores, and devoted themselves wholly to the search for "awakening," which many apparently achieved. A nun named Mutta declared: "I am free from the three crooked things: mortar, pestle, and my crooked husband. I am free from birth and death and all that dragged me back."[7] (See Document 5.3, pp. 221–23, for further examples of early poetry by Indian Buddhist women.)

Gradually, Buddhist teachings found an audience in India. Buddhism's egalitarian message appealed especially to lower-caste groups and to women. The availability of its teaching in the local language of Pali, rather than the classical Sanskrit, made it accessible. Establishing monasteries and stupas containing relics of the Buddha on the site of neighborhood shrines to earth spirits or near a sacred tree linked the new religion to local traditions. The most dedicated followers joined monasteries, devoting their lives to religious practice and spreading the message among nearby people. State support during the reign of Ashoka (268–232 B.C.E.) likewise helped the new religion gain a foothold in India as a distinct tradition separate from Hinduism.

As Buddhism spread, both within and beyond India, differences in understanding soon emerged, particularly as to how nirvana could be achieved or, in a common Buddhist metaphor, how to cross the river to the far shore of enlightenment.

■ Comparison
What is the difference between the Theravada and Mahayana expressions of Buddhism?

The Buddha had taught a rather austere doctrine of intense self-effort, undertaken most actively by monks and nuns who withdrew from society to devote themselves fully to the quest. This early version of the new religion, known as Theravada (Teaching of the Elders), portrayed the Buddha as an immensely wise teacher and model, but certainly not divine. It was more psychological than religious, a set of practices rather than a set of beliefs. The gods, though never completely denied, played little role in assisting believers in their search for enlightenment. In short, individuals were on their own in crossing the river. Clearly this was not for everyone.

By the early centuries of the Common Era, a modified form of Buddhism called Mahayana (Great Vehicle) had taken root in parts of India, proclaiming that help was available for the strenuous voyage. Buddhist thinkers developed the idea of *bodhisattvas*, spiritually developed people who postponed their own entry into nirvana in order to assist those who were still suffering. The Buddha himself became something of a god, and both earlier and future Buddhas were available to offer help. Elaborate descriptions of these supernatural beings, together with various levels of heavens and hells, transformed Buddhism into a popular religion of salvation. Furthermore, religious merit, leading to salvation, might now be earned by acts of piety and devotion, such as contributing to the support of a monastery, and that merit might be transferred to others. This was the Great Vehicle, allowing far more people to make the voyage across the river. (See the Visual Sources: Representations of the Buddha, pp. 227–35, for the evolution of Buddhism reflected in images.)

Hinduism as a Religion of Duty and Devotion

Strangely enough, Buddhism as a distinct religious practice ultimately died out in the land of its birth as it was reincorporated into a broader Hindu tradition, but it spread widely and flourished, particularly in its Mahayana form, in other parts of Asia. Buddhism declined in India perhaps in part because the mounting wealth of monasteries and the economic interests of their leading figures separated them from ordinary people. Competition from Islam after 1000 C.E. also may have played a role. The most important reason for Buddhism's decline in India, however, was the growth during the first millennium C.E. of a new kind of popular Hinduism, which the masses found more accessible than the elaborate sacrifices of the Brahmins or the philosophical speculations of intellectuals. Some scholars have seen this phase of Hinduism as a response to the challenge of Buddhism. Expressed in the widely known epic poems known as the *Mahabharata* and the *Ramayana*, this revived Hinduism indicated more clearly that action in the world and the detached performance of caste duties might also provide a path to liberation.

In the much-beloved Hindu text known as the *Bhagavad Gita* (see Document 5.2, pp. 219–21), the troubled warrior-hero Arjuna is in anguish over the necessity of killing his kinsmen as a decisive battle approaches. But he is assured by his charioteer Lord Krishna, an incarnation of the god Vishnu, that performing his duty as a warrior, and doing so selflessly without regard to consequences, is an act of devotion

■ **Change**

What new emphases characterized Hinduism as it responded to the challenge of Buddhism?

that would lead to "release from the shackles of repeated rebirth." This was not an invitation to militarism, but rather an affirmation that ordinary people, not just Brahmins, could also make spiritual progress by selflessly performing the ordinary duties of their lives: "The man who, casting off all desires, lives free from attachments, who is free from egoism, and from the feeling that this or that is mine, obtains tranquillity." Withdrawal and asceticism were not the only ways to moksha.

Also becoming increasingly prominent was yet another religious path—the way of devotion to one or another of India's many gods and goddesses. Beginning in south India and moving northward, this *bhakti* (worship) movement involved the intense adoration of and identification with a particular deity through songs, prayers, and rituals associated with the many cults that emerged throughout India. By far the most popular deities were Vishnu, the protector and preserver of creation and associated with mercy and goodness, and Shiva, representing the divine in its destructive aspect, but many others also had their followers. This proliferation of gods and goddesses, and of their *bhakti* cults, occasioned very little friction or serious religious conflict. "Hinduism," writes a leading scholar, "is essentially tolerant, and would rather assimilate than rigidly exclude."[8] This capacity for assimilation extended to an already-declining Buddhism, which for many people had become yet another cult worshipping yet another god. The Buddha in fact was incorporated into the Hindu pantheon as the ninth incarnation of Vishnu. By 1000 C.E., Buddhism had largely disappeared as a separate religious tradition within India.

Thus a constantly evolving and enormously varied South Asian religious tradition had been substantially transformed. An early emphasis on ritual sacrifice gave way to that of philosophical speculation, devotional worship, and detached action in the world. In the process, that tradition had generated Buddhism, which became the first of the great universal religions of world history, and then had absorbed that new religion back into the fold of an emerging popular Hinduism.

Moving toward Monotheism: The Search for God in the Middle East

Paralleling the evolution of Chinese and Indian cultural traditions was the movement toward a distinctive monotheistic religious tradition in the Middle East, which found expression in Persian Zoroastrianism and in Judaism. Neither of these religions themselves spread very widely, but the monotheism that they nurtured became the basis for both Christianity and Islam, which have shaped so much of world history over the past 2,000 years. Amid the proliferation of gods and spirits that had long characterized religious life throughout the ancient world, monotheism—the idea of a single supreme deity, the sole source of all creation and goodness—was a radical cultural innovation. That conception created the possibility of a universal religion, open to all of humankind, but it could also mean an exclusive and intolerant faith.

Zoroastrianism

During the glory years of the powerful Persian Empire, a new religion arose to challenge the polytheism of earlier times. Tradition dates its Persian prophet, Zarathustra (Zoroaster to the Greeks), to the sixth or seventh century B.C.E., although some scholars place him hundreds of years earlier. Whenever he actually lived, his ideas took hold in Persia and received a degree of state support during the Achaemenid dynasty (558–330 B.C.E.). Appalled by the endemic violence of recurring cattle raids, Zarathustra recast the traditional Persian polytheism into a vision of a single unique god, Ahura Mazda, who ruled the world and was the source of all truth, light, and goodness. This benevolent deity was engaged in a cosmic struggle with the forces of evil, embodied in an equivalent supernatural figure, Angra Mainyu. Ultimately this struggle would be decided in favor of Ahura Mazda, aided by the arrival of a final savior who would restore the world to its earlier purity and peace. At a day of judgment, those who had aligned with Ahura Mazda would be granted new resurrected bodies and rewarded with eternal life in Paradise. Those who had sided with evil and the "Lie" were condemned to everlasting punishment. Zoroastrian teaching thus placed great emphasis on the free will of humankind and the necessity for each individual to choose between good and evil.

The Zoroastrian faith achieved widespread support within the Persian heartland, although it also found adherents in other parts of the empire, such as Egypt, Mesopotamia, and Anatolia. Because it never became an active missionary religion, it did not spread widely beyond the region. Alexander the Great's invasion of the Persian Empire and the subsequent Greek-ruled Seleucid dynasty (330–155 B.C.E.) were disastrous for Zoroastrianism, as temples were plundered, priests slaughtered, and sacred writings burned. But the new faith managed to survive this onslaught and flourished again during the Parthian (247 B.C.E.–224 C.E.) and Sassanid (224–651 C.E.) dynasties. It was the arrival of Islam and an Arab empire that occasioned the final decline of Zoroastrianism in Persia, although a few believers fled to India, where they became known as Parsis ("Persians"). The Parsis have continued their faith into present times.

Like Buddhism, the Zoroastrian faith vanished from its place of origin, but unlike Buddhism, it did not spread beyond Persia in a recognizable form. Some elements of the Zoroastrian belief system, however, did become incorporated into other religious traditions. The presence of many Jews in the Persian Empire meant that they surely became aware of Zoroastrian ideas. Many of those ideas— including the conflict of God and an evil counterpart (Satan); the notion of a last judgment and resurrected bodies; and a belief in the final defeat of evil, the arrival of a savior (Messiah), and the remaking of the world at the end of time—found a place in an evolving Judaism. Some of these teachings, especially the concepts of heaven and hell, later became prominent in those enormously

■ **Connection**

What aspects of Zoroastrianism and Judaism subsequently found a place in Christianity and Islam?

Zoroastrian Fire Altar Representing the energy of the Creator God Ahura Mazda, the fire altar became an important symbol of Zoroastrianism and was often depicted on Persian coins in association with images of Persian rulers. This particular coin dates from the third century C.E. (©AAAC/Topham/The Image Works)

influential successors to Judaism—Christianity and Islam.[9] Thus the Persian tradition of Zoroastrianism continued to echo well beyond its disappearance in the land of its birth.

Judaism

■ Description
What was distinctive about the Jewish religious tradition?

While Zoroastrianism emerged in the greatest empire of its time, Judaism, the Middle East's other ancient monotheistic tradition, was born among one of the region's smaller and, at the time, less significant peoples—the Hebrews. Their traditions, recorded in the Old Testament, tell of an early migration from Mesopotamia to Palestine under the leadership of Abraham. Those same traditions report that a portion of these people later fled to Egypt, where they were first enslaved and then miraculously escaped to rejoin their kinfolk in Palestine. There, around 1000 B.C.E., they established a small state, which soon split into two parts—a northern kingdom called Israel and a southern state called Judah.

In a region politically dominated by the large empires of Assyria, Babylon, and Persia, these tiny Hebrew communities lived a precarious existence. Israel was conquered by Assyria in 722 B.C.E., and many of its inhabitants were deported to distant regions, where they assimilated into the local culture. In 586 B.C.E., the kingdom of Judah likewise came under Babylonian control, and its elite class was shipped off to exile. In Babylon, these people, now calling themselves Jews, retained their cultural identity and later were able to return to their homeland. A large part of that identity lay in their unique religious ideas. It was in creating that religious tradition, rather than in building a powerful empire, that this small people cast a long shadow in world history.

From their unique historical experience of exodus from Egypt and exile in Babylon, the Jews evolved over many centuries a distinctive conception of God. Unlike the peoples of Mesopotamia, India, Greece, and elsewhere—all of whom populated the invisible realm with numerous gods and goddesses—the Jews found in their God, whom they called Yahweh, a powerful and jealous deity, who demanded their exclusive loyalty. "Thou shalt have no other gods before me"—this was the first of the Ten Commandments. It was a difficult requirement, for as the Jews turned from a pastoral life to agriculture, many of them were continually attracted by the fertility gods of neighboring peoples. Their neighbors' goddesses also were attractive, offering a kind of spiritual support that the primarily masculine Yahweh could not. This was not quite monotheism, for the repeated demands of the Hebrew prophets to turn away from other gods show that those deities remained real for many Jews. Over time, however, Yahweh triumphed. The Jews came to understand their relationship to him as a contract or a covenant. In return for their sole devotion and obedience, Yahweh would consider the Jews his chosen people, favoring them in battle, causing them to grow in numbers, and bringing them prosperity and blessing.

Ancient Israel

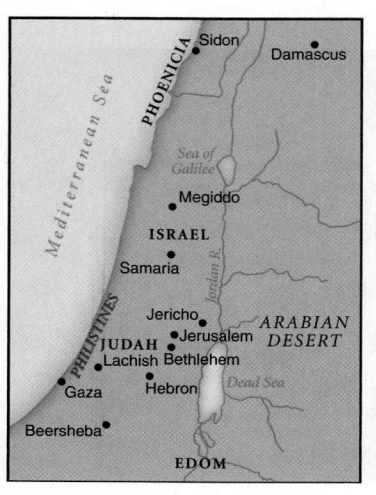

Unlike the bickering, arbitrary, polytheistic gods of Mesopotamia or ancient Greece, which were associated with the forces of nature and behaved in quite human fashion, Yahweh was increasingly seen as a lofty, transcendent deity of utter holiness and purity, set far above the world of nature, which he had created. But unlike the impersonal conceptions of ultimate reality found in Daoism and Hinduism, Yahweh was encountered as a divine person with whom people could actively communicate. He also acted within the historical process, bringing the Jews out of Egypt or using foreign empires to punish them for their disobedience.

Furthermore, Yahweh was transformed from a god of war, who ordered his people to "utterly destroy" the original inhabitants of the Promised Land, to a god of social justice and compassion for the poor and the marginalized, especially in the passionate pronouncements of Jewish prophets such as Amos and Isaiah. The prophet Isaiah describes Yahweh as rejecting the empty rituals of his chosen but sinful people: "What to me is the multitude of your sacrifices, says the Lord. . . . Wash yourselves, make yourselves clean, . . . cease to do evil, learn to do good; seek justice; correct oppression; defend the fatherless; plead for the widow."[10]

Here was a distinctive conception of the divine—singular, transcendent, personal, separate from nature, engaged in history, and demanding social justice and moral righteousness above sacrifices and rituals. This set of ideas sustained a separate Jewish identity in both ancient and modern times, and it was this understanding of God that provided the foundation on which both Christianity and Islam were built.

The Cultural Tradition of Classical Greece: The Search for a Rational Order

Unlike the Jews, the Persians, or the civilization of India, Greek thinkers of the classical era generated no lasting religious tradition of world historical importance. The religion of these city-states brought together the unpredictable, quarreling, and lustful gods of Mount Olympus, secret fertility cults, oracles predicting the future, and the ecstatic worship of Dionysus, the god of wine. The distinctive feature of the classical Greek cultural tradition was the willingness of many Greek intellectuals to abandon this mythological framework, to affirm that the world was a physical reality governed by natural laws, and to assert that human rationality could both understand these laws and work out a system of moral and ethical life. In separating science and philosophy from conventional religion, the Greeks developed a way of thinking that bore some similarity to the secularism of Confucian thought in China.

Precisely why Greek thought evolved in this direction is hard to say. Perhaps the diversity and incoherence of Greek religious mythology presented its intellectuals with a challenge to bring some order to their understanding of the world. Greece's geographic position on the margins of the great civilizations of Mesopotamia,

■ Description
What are the distinctive
features of the Greek
intellectual tradition?

Egypt, and Persia certainly provided intellectual stimulation. Furthermore, the growing role of law in the political life of Athens possibly suggested that a similar regularity also underlay the natural order.

The Greek Way of Knowing

The foundations of this Greek rationalism emerged in the three centuries between 600 and 300 B.C.E., coinciding with the flourishing of Greek city-states, especially Athens, and with the growth of its artistic, literary, and theatrical traditions. The enduring significance of Greek thinking lay not so much in the answers it provided to life's great issues, for the Greeks seldom agreed with one another, but rather in its way of asking questions. Its emphasis on argument, logic, and the relentless questioning of received wisdom; its confidence in human reason; its enthusiasm for puzzling out the world without much reference to the gods—these were the defining characteristics of the Greek cultural tradition.

The great exemplar of this approach to knowledge was Socrates (469–399 B.C.E.), an Athenian philosopher who walked about the city engaging others in conversation about the good life. He wrote nothing, and his preferred manner of teaching was not the lecture or exposition of his own ideas but rather a constant questioning of the

The Death of Socrates
Condemned to death by an Athenian jury, Socrates declined to go into exile, voluntarily drank a cup of poison hemlock, and died in 399 B.C.E. in the presence of his friends. The dramatic scene was famously described by Plato and much later was immortalized on canvas by the French painter Jacques-Louis David in 1787. (Image copyright © The Metropolitan Museum of Art/Art Resource, NY)

assumptions and logic of his students' thinking. Concerned always to puncture the pretentious, he challenged conventional ideas about the importance of wealth and power in living well, urging instead the pursuit of wisdom and virtue. He was critical of Athenian democracy and on occasion had positive things to say about Sparta, the great enemy of his own city. Such behavior brought him into conflict with city authorities, who accused him of corrupting the youth of Athens and sentenced him to death. At his trial, he defended himself as the "gadfly" of Athens, stinging its citizens into awareness. To any and all, he declared, "I shall question, and examine and cross-examine him, and if I find that he does not possess virtue, but says he does, I shall rebuke him for scorning the things that are most important and caring more for what is of less worth."[11] (See Document 5.3, pp. 221–23, for a more extensive excerpt from this famous speech.)

The earliest of the classical Greek thinkers, many of them living on the Ionian coast of Anatolia, applied this rational and questioning way of knowing to the world of nature. For example, Thales, drawing on Babylonian astronomy, predicted an eclipse of the sun and argued that the moon simply reflected the sun's light. He also was one of the first Greeks to ask about the fundamental nature of the universe and came up with the idea that water was the basic stuff from which all else derived, for it existed as solid, liquid, and gas. Others argued in favor of air or fire or some combination. Democritus suggested that atoms, tiny "uncuttable" particles, collided in various configurations to form visible matter. Pythagoras believed that beneath the chaos and complexity of the visible world lay a simple, unchanging mathematical order. What these thinkers had in common was a commitment to a rational and nonreligious explanation for the material world.

Such thinking also served to explain the functioning of the human body and its diseases. Hippocrates and his followers came to believe that the body was composed of four fluids, or "humors," which, when out of proper balance, caused various ailments. He also traced the origins of epilepsy, known to the Greeks as "the sacred disease," to simple heredity: "It is thus with regard to the disease called sacred: it appears to me to be nowise more divine nor more sacred than other diseases, but has a natural cause . . . like other afflictions."[12] The Hippocratic Oath taken by all new doctors is named for this ancient Greek scientist.

A similar approach informed Greek thinking about the ways of humankind. Herodotus, who wrote about the Greco-Persian Wars, explained his project as an effort to discover "the reason why they fought one another." This assumption that human reasons lay behind the conflict, not simply the whims of the gods, was what made Herodotus a historian in the modern sense of that word. Ethics and government also figured importantly in Greek thinking. Plato (429–348 B.C.E.) famously sketched out in *The Republic* a design for a good society. It would be ruled by a class of highly educated "guardians" led by a "philosopher-king." Such people would be able to penetrate the many illusions of the material world and to grasp the "world of forms," in which ideas such as goodness, beauty, and justice lived a real and unchanging existence. Only such people, he argued, were fit to rule.

Aristotle (384–322 B.C.E.), a student of Plato and a teacher of Alexander the Great, was perhaps the most complete expression of the Greek way of knowing, for he wrote or commented on practically everything. With an emphasis on empirical observation, he cataloged the constitutions of 158 Greek city-states, identified hundreds of species of animals, and wrote about logic, physics, astronomy, the weather, and much else besides. Famous for his reflections on ethics, he argued that "virtue" was a product of rational training and cultivated habit and could be learned. As to government, he urged a mixed system, combining the principles of monarchy, aristocracy, and democracy.

The Greek Legacy

The rationalism of the Greek tradition was clearly not the whole of Greek culture. The gods of Mount Olympus continued to be a reality for many people, and the ecstatic songs and dances that celebrated Dionysus, the god of wine, were anything but rational and reflective. The death of Socrates at the hands of an Athenian jury showed that philosophy could be a threat as well as an engaging pastime. Nonetheless, Greek rationalism, together with Greek art, literature, and theater, persisted long after the glory days of Athens were over. The Roman Empire facilitated the spread of Greek culture within the Mediterranean basin, and not a few leading Roman figures sent their children to be educated in Athens at the Academy, which Plato had founded. An emerging Christian theology was expressed in terms of Greek philosophical concepts, especially those of Plato. Even after the western Roman Empire collapsed, classical Greek texts were preserved in the eastern half, known as Byzantium (see Chapter 10).

In the West, however, direct access to Greek texts was far more difficult in the chaotic conditions of post-Roman Europe, and for centuries classical scholarship was neglected in favor of Christian writers. Much of that legacy was subsequently rediscovered after the twelfth century C.E. as European scholars gained access to classical Greek texts. From that point on, the Greek legacy has been viewed as a central element of an emerging "Western" civilization. It played a role in formulating an updated Christian theology, in fostering Europe's Scientific Revolution, and in providing a point of departure for much of European philosophy.

Long before this European rediscovery, the Greek legacy had also entered Islamic culture. Systematic translations of Greek works of science and philosophy into Arabic, together with Indian and Persian learning, stimulated Muslim thinkers and scientists, especially in the fields of medicine, astronomy, mathematics, geography, and chemistry. It was in fact largely from Arabic translations of Greek writers that Europeans became reacquainted with the legacy of classical Greece, especially during the twelfth and thirteenth centuries. Despite the many centuries that have passed since the flourishing of classical Greek culture, that tradition has remained, especially in the West, an inspiration for those who celebrate the powers of the human mind to probe the mysteries of the universe and to explore the equally challenging domain of human life.

Snapshot   Reflections on Human Love from Mediterranean Civilization

From the Jews: The Song of Solomon

My beloved speaks and says to me: "Arise my love, my fair one, and come away; for lo, the winter is past; the rain is over and gone. The flowers appear on the earth; the time of singing has come, and the voice of the turtle dove is heard in our land. The fig tree puts forth its figs; and the vines are in blossom; they give fragrance. Arise my love, my fair one, and come away."

From the Greeks: Fragments from Sappho of Lesbos

If you will come, I shall put out new pillows for you to rest on.
I was so happy. Believe me, I prayed that that night might be doubled for us.
Now I know why Eros, of all the progeny of Earth and Heaven, has been most dearly loved.

From the Romans: Ovid Giving Advice to a Young Man on the Art of Love

Add gifts of mind to bodily advantage. A frail advantage is beauty, that grows less as time draws on and is devoured by its own years. . . . O handsome youth, will soon come hoary hairs; soon will come furrows to make wrinkles in your body. Now make thee a soul that will abide, and add to it thy beauty; only that endures to the ultimate pyre. Nor let it be a slight care to cultivate your mind in the liberal arts, or to learn the two languages well. Ulysses was not comely, but he was eloquent; yet he fired two goddesses of the sea with love.

From the Christians: Saint Paul on Love: 1 Corinthians 13

Love is patient and kind; love is not jealous or boastful; it is not arrogant or rude. Love does not insist on its own way; it is not irritable or resentful; it does not rejoice at wrong, but rejoices in the right. Love bears all things, believes all things, hopes all things, endures all things. Love never ends. . . . So faith, hope and love abide, these three, but the greatest of these is love.

Comparing Jesus and the Buddha

About 500 years after the time of Confucius, the Buddha, Zarathustra, and Socrates, a young Jewish peasant/carpenter in the remote province of Judaea in the Roman Empire began a brief three-year career of teaching and miracle-working before he got in trouble with local authorities and was executed. In one of history's most unlikely stories, the teachings of that obscure man, barely noted in the historical records of the time, became the basis of the world's second great universal religion. This man, Jesus of Nazareth, and the religion of Christianity, which grew out of his life and teaching, had a dramatic impact on world history, similar to and often compared with that of India's Siddhartha Gautama, the Buddha.

■ **Comparison**

How would you compare the lives and teachings of Jesus and the Buddha? In what different ways did the two religions evolve after the deaths of their founders?

The Lives of the Founders

The family background of the two teachers could hardly have been more different. Gautama was born to royalty and luxury, whereas Jesus was a rural or small-town worker from a distinctly lower-class family. But both became spiritual seekers, mystics in their respective traditions, who claimed to have personally experienced another level of reality. Those powerful religious experiences provided the motivation for their life's work and the personal authenticity that attracted their growing band of followers.

Both were "wisdom teachers," challenging the conventional values of their time, urging the renunciation of wealth, and emphasizing the supreme importance of love or compassion as the basis for a moral life. The Buddha had instructed his followers in the practice of *metta*, or loving-kindness: "Just as a mother would protect her only child at the risk of her own life, even so, let [my followers] cultivate a boundless heart towards all beings."[13] In a similar vein during his famous Sermon on the Mount, Jesus told his followers: "You have heard that it was said 'Love your neighbor and hate your enemy,' but I tell you 'Love your enemies and pray for those who persecute you.'"[14] Both Jesus and the Buddha called for the personal transformation of their followers, through "letting go" of the grasping that causes suffering, in the Buddha's teaching, or "losing one's life in order to save it," in the language of Jesus.[15]

Despite these similarities, there were also some differences in their teachings and their life stories. Jesus inherited from his Jewish tradition an intense devotion to a single personal deity with whom he was on intimate terms, referring to him as *Abba* ("papa" or "daddy"). According to the New Testament, the miracles he performed reflected the power of God available to him as a result of that relationship. The Buddha's original message, by contrast, largely ignored the supernatural, involved no miracles, and taught a path of intense self-effort aimed at ethical living and mindfulness as a means of ending suffering. Furthermore, Jesus' teachings had a sharper social and political edge than did those of the Buddha. Jesus spoke more clearly on behalf of the poor and the oppressed, directly criticized the hypocrisies of the powerful, and deliberately associated with lepers, adulterous women, and tax collectors, all of whom were regarded as "impure." In doing so, Jesus reflected his own lower-class background, the Jewish tradition of social criticism, and the reality of Roman imperial rule over his people, none of which corresponded to the Buddha's experience. Finally, Jesus' public life was very brief, probably less than three years, compared to more than forty years for the Buddha. His teachings had so antagonized both Jewish and Roman authorities that he was crucified as a common criminal. The Buddha's message was apparently less threatening to the politically powerful, and he died a natural death at age eighty.

■ Change
In what ways was Christianity transformed in the five centuries following the death of Jesus?

Establishing New Religions

It seems likely that neither Jesus nor the Buddha had any intention of founding a new religion; rather, they sought to reform the traditions from which they had come. Nonetheless, Christianity and Buddhism soon emerged as separate religions, distinct from Judaism and Hinduism, proclaiming their messages to a much wider and more inclusive audience. In the process, both teachers were transformed by their followers into gods. According to many scholars, Jesus never claimed divine status, seeing himself as a teacher or a prophet, whose close relationship to God could be imitated by anyone.[16] The Buddha likewise viewed himself as an enlightened but fully human person, an example of what was possible for anyone who followed the path. But in Mahayana Buddhism, the Buddha became a supernatural being who could be worshipped and prayed to and was spiritually available to his followers. Jesus too soon became divine in the eyes of his followers, "the Son of God, Very God of Very God," according to one of the creeds of the early Church, while his death and resurrection made possible the forgiveness of sins and the eternal salvation of those who believed.

The transformation of Christianity from a small Jewish sect to a world religion began with Saint Paul (10–65 C.E.), an early convert whose missionary journeys in the eastern Roman Empire led to the founding of small Christian communities that included non-Jews. The Good News of Jesus, Paul argued, was for everyone, and Gentile (non-Jewish) converts need not follow Jewish laws or rituals such as circumcision. In one of his many letters to these new communities, later collected as part of the New Testament, Paul wrote, "There is neither Jew nor Greek . . . neither slave nor free . . . neither male nor female, for you are all one in Christ Jesus."[17] Despite Paul's egalitarian pronouncement, early Christianity, like Buddhism, reflected prevailing patriarchal values, even as they both offered women new opportunities. Although women apparently played leadership roles in the "house churches" of the first century C.E., Paul counseled women to "be subject to your husbands" and declared that "it is shameful for a woman to speak in church."[18]

Nonetheless, the inclusive message of early Christianity was one of the attractions of the new faith as it spread very gradually within the Roman Empire during the several centuries after Jesus' death. The earliest converts were usually lower-stratum people — artisans, traders, and a considerable number of women — mostly from towns and cities, while a scattering of wealthier, more prominent, and better-educated people subsequently joined the ranks of Christians.[19] The spread of the faith was often accompanied by reports of miracles, healings, and the casting out of demons — all of which were impressive to people thoroughly accustomed to seeing the supernatural behind the

Women in the Early Church
This third-century C.E. fresco from a Roman catacomb is called the *Fractio Panis*, "the breaking of the bread" or Holy Communion. Some scholars argue that the figures are those of women, suggesting that women held priestly office in the early Church and were only later excluded from it. (Scala/Art Resource, NY)

events of ordinary life.[20] Christian communities also attracted converts by the way their members cared for one another. In the middle of the third century C.E., the church in Rome supported 154 priests (of whom 52 were exorcists) and some 1,500 widows, orphans, and destitute people.[21] By 300 C.E., perhaps 10 percent of the Roman Empire's population (some 5 million people) identified themselves as Christians.

In the Roman world, the strangest and most offensive feature of the new faith was its exclusive monotheism and its antagonism to all other supernatural powers, particularly the cult of the emperors. Christians' denial of these other gods caused them to be tagged as "atheists" and was one reason behind the empire's intermittent persecution of Christians during the first three centuries of the Common Era. All of that ended with Emperor Constantine's conversion in the early fourth century C.E. and with growing levels of state support for the new religion in the decades that followed.

Roman rulers sought to use an increasingly popular Christianity as glue to hold together a very diverse population in a weakening imperial state. Constantine and his successors thus provided Christians with newfound security and opportunities. The emperor Theodosius (reigned 379–395 C.E.) enforced a ban on all polytheistic ritual sacrifices and ordered their temples closed. Christians by contrast received patronage for their buildings, official approval for their doctrines, suppression of their rivals, prestige from imperial recognition, and, during the late fourth century, the proclamation of Christianity as the official state religion. All of this set in motion a process by which the Roman Empire, and later all of Europe, became overwhelmingly Christian. Beyond the Roman world, the new religion also found a home in various parts of Africa, the Middle East, and Asia (see Map 5.1).

The situation in India was quite different. Even though Ashoka's support gave Buddhism a considerable boost, it was never promoted to the exclusion of other faiths. Ashoka sought harmony among India's diverse population through religious tolerance rather than uniformity. The kind of monotheistic intolerance that Christianity exhibited was quite foreign to Indian patterns of religious practice. Although Buddhism subsequently died out in India as it was absorbed into a reviving Hinduism, no renewal of Roman polytheism occurred, and Christianity became an enduring element of European civilization. Nonetheless, Christianity did adopt some elements of religious practice from the Roman world, including perhaps the cult of saints and the dating of the birth of Jesus to the winter solstice. In both cases, however, these new religions spread widely beyond their places of origin. Buddhism provided a network of cultural connections in much of Asia, and Christianity did the same for western Eurasia and parts of Africa.

Creating Institutions

As Christianity spread within the Roman Empire and beyond, it developed a hierarchical organization, with patriarchs, bishops, and priests—all men—replacing

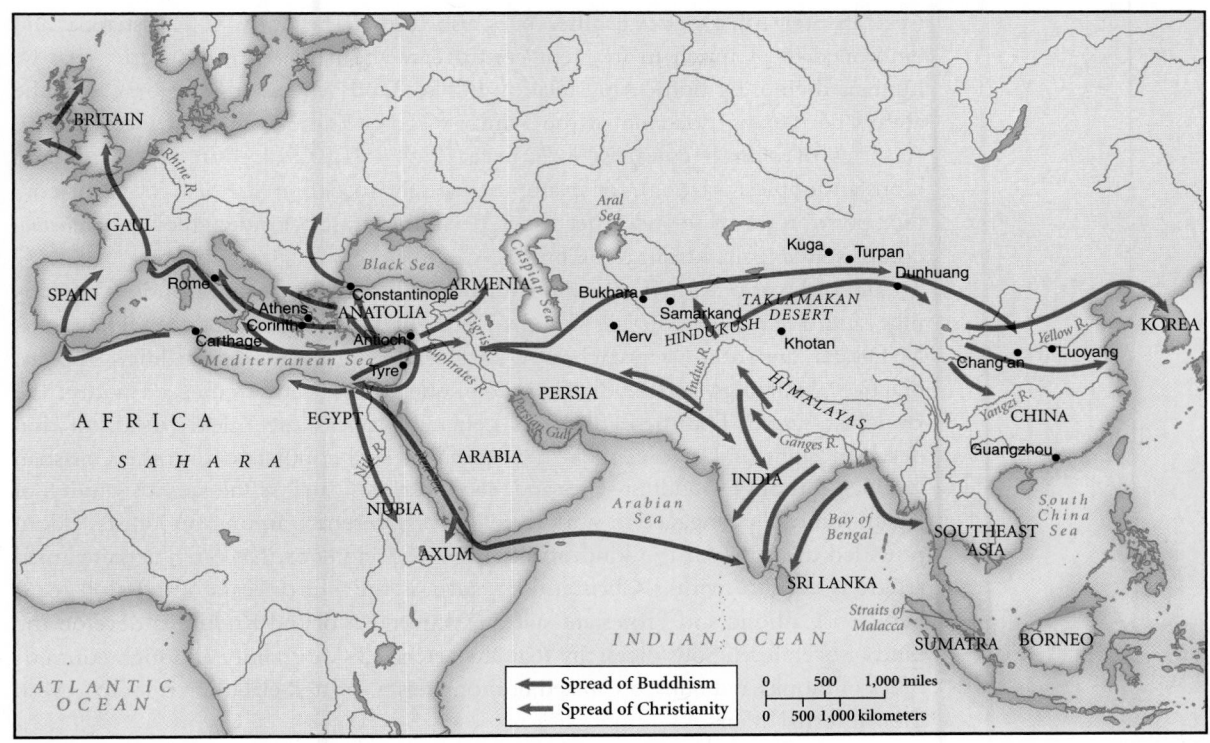

Map 5.1 The Spread of Early Christianity and Buddhism
In the five centuries after the birth of Jesus, Christianity found converts from Spain to northeast Africa, Central Asia, and India. In the Roman Empire, Axum, and Armenia, the new religion enjoyed state support as well. Subsequently Christianity took root solidly in Europe and after 1000 C.E. in Russia as well. Meanwhile, Buddhism was spreading from its South Asian homeland to various parts of Asia, even as it was weakening in India itself.

the house churches of the early years, in which women played a more prominent part. At least in some places, however, women continued to exercise leadership and even priestly roles, prompting Pope Gelasius in 494 to speak out sharply against those who encouraged women "to officiate at the sacred altars, and to take part in all matters imputed to the offices of the male sex, to which they do not belong."[22] In general, though, the exclusion of women from the priesthood established a male-dominated clergy and a patriarchal church, which has lasted into the twenty-first century.

This emerging hierarchical structure of the Church, together with its monotheistic faith, also generated a great concern for unity in matters of doctrine and practice. The bishop of Rome gradually emerged as the dominant leader, or pope, of the Church in the western half of the empire, but this role was not recognized in the east. This division contributed to the later split between Roman Catholic and Eastern Orthodox branches of Christendom, a schism that continues to the present (see Chapter 10). Doctrinal differences also tore at the unity of Christianity and embroiled the Church in frequent controversy about the nature of Jesus (was he human, divine, or both?), his relationship to God (equal or inferior?), and the always-perplexing doctrine of the Trinity (God as Father, Son, and Holy Spirit). A series of church councils—at Nicaea (325 C.E.), Chalcedon (451 C.E.), and Constantinople (553 C.E.), for example—sought to define an "orthodox," or correct, position on these and other issues, declaring those who disagreed as *anathema*, completely expelled from the Church.

Buddhists too clashed over their various interpretations of the Buddha's teachings, and a series of councils failed to prevent the division between Theravada, Mahayana, and other approaches. A considerable proliferation of different sects, practices, teachings, and meditation techniques subsequently emerged within the Buddhist world, but these divisions generally lacked the "clear-cut distinction between 'right' and 'wrong' ideas" that characterized conflicts within the Christian world.[23] Although Buddhist states and warrior classes (such as the famous samurai of Japan) sometimes engaged in warfare, religious differences among Buddhists seldom provided the basis for the kind of bitterness and violence that often accompanied religious conflict within Christendom, such as the Thirty Years' War (1618–1648) between Catholic and Protestant states in Europe. Nor did Buddhists develop the kind of overall religious hierarchy that characterized Christianity, although communities of monks and nuns, organized in monasteries, created elaborate rules to govern their internal affairs.

Reflections: Religion and Historians

To put it mildly, religion has always been a sensitive subject, and no less so for historians than for anyone else. For believers or followers of particular traditions, religion partakes of another world—that of the sacred or the divine—which is not accessible to historians or other scholars, who depend on evidence available in this world. This situation has generated various tensions or misunderstandings between historians and religious practitioners.

One of these tensions involves the question of change. Most religions present themselves as timeless, partaking of eternity or at least reflecting ancient practice. In the eyes of historians, however, the religious aspect of human life changes as much as any other. The Hindu tradition changed from a religion of ritual and sacrifice to one of devotion and worship. Buddhism became more conventionally religious, with an emphasis on the supernatural, as it evolved from Theravada to Mahayana forms. A male-dominated hierarchical Christian Church, with its pope, bishops, priests, and state support, was very different from the small house churches that suffered persecution by imperial authorities in the early Christian centuries. The implication—that religions are at least in part a human phenomenon—has been troublesome to some believers.

Historians, on the other hand, have sometimes been uncomfortable in the face of claims by believers that they have actually experienced a divine reality. Some secular scholars have been inclined to dismiss such claims as unprovable at best. Even the biographical details of the lives of the Buddha and Jesus are difficult to prove by the standards of historians. Certainly, modern historians are in no position to validate or refute the spiritual claims of these teachers, but we need to take them seriously. Although we will never know precisely what happened to the Buddha as he sat in meditation in northern India or what transpired when Jesus spent forty days in the wilderness, clearly those experiences changed the two men and motivated their subsequent actions. Later, Muhammad likewise claimed to have received revelations from God in the caves outside Mecca. Millions of the followers of these religious leaders have also acted on the basis of what they perceived to be an encounter with the divine or other levels of reality. This interior dimension of human experience, though difficult to grasp with any precision, has been a significant mover and shaper of the historical process.

Yet a third problem arises from debates within particular religious traditions about which group most accurately represents the "real" or authentic version of the faith. Historians usually refuse to take sides in such disputes. They simply notice with interest that most human cultural traditions generate conflicting views, some of which become the basis for serious conflict in their societies.

Reconciling personal religious convictions with the perspectives of modern historical scholarship is no easy task. At the very least, all of us can appreciate the immense human effort that has gone into the making of classical religious traditions, and we can acknowledge the enormous significance of these traditions in the unfolding of the human story. They have shaped the meanings that billions of people over thousands of years have attached to the world they inhabit. These religious traditions have justified the vast social inequalities and oppressive states of human civilizations, but they also have enabled human beings to endure those difficulties and on occasion have stimulated reform and rebellion. And they have guided much of humankind in our endless efforts to penetrate the mysteries of the world beyond and of the world within.

Second Thoughts

What's the Significance?

Legalism
Confucianism
Ban Zhao
Daoism
Vedas
Upanishads

Siddhartha Gautama (the Buddha)
Theravada/Mahayana
Bhagavad Gita
Zoroastrianism
Judaism

Greek rationalism
Socrates, Plato, Aristotle
Jesus of Nazareth
Saint Paul

To assess your mastery of the material in this chapter, visit the **Student Center** at bedfordstmartins.com/strayer.

Big Picture Questions

1. "Religions are fundamentally alike." Does the material in this chapter support or undermine this idea?
2. Is a secular outlook on the world an essentially modern phenomenon, or does it have precedents in the classical era?
3. "Religion is a double-edged sword, both supporting and undermining political authority and social elites." How would you support both sides of this statement?
4. How would you define the appeal of the religious/cultural traditions discussed in this chapter? To what groups were they attractive, and why?

Next Steps: For Further Study

For Web sites and additional documents related to this chapter, see **Make History** at bedfordstmartins.com/strayer.

Karen Armstrong, *The Great Transformation* (2006). A comparative and historical study of the major classical-era religions by a well-known scholar.

Peter Brown, *The Rise of Western Christendom* (2003). A history of the first 1,000 years of Christianity, cast in a global framework.

Don Johnson and Jean Johnson, *Universal Religions in World History* (2007). A comparative study of the historical development of Buddhism, Christianity, and Islam.

Huston Smith, *An Illustrated World's Religions* (1994). A sympathetic account of major world religions, beautifully illustrated, by a prominent scholar of comparative religion.

Arthur Waley, *Three Ways of Thought in Ancient China* (1983). A classic work, first published more than half a century ago, about the major philosophies of old China.

Jonathan S. Walters, *Finding Buddhists in Global History* (1998). A brief account that situates Buddhism in a world history framework.

"Religions of the World," http://www.mnsu.edu/emuseum/cultural/religion. A succinct and attractively illustrated introduction to six major world religious traditions.

Documents

Considering the Evidence:
The Good Life in Classical Eurasia

What constitutes a good life for an individual person? How can people live together in communities most effectively? These are among the central questions that have occupied human beings since the beginning of conscious thought. And they certainly played a major role in the emerging cultural traditions of the classical era all across Eurasia. The documents that follow present a sample of this thinking drawn from Confucian, Hindu, Greek, and Christian traditions.

Document 5.1

Reflections from Confucius

No one was more central to the making of classical Chinese culture than Confucius (551–479 B.C.E.). In the several generations following their master's death, his disciples recalled his teachings and his conversations, recording them in a small book called *The Analects*. This text became a touchstone for all educated people in China and across much of East Asia as well. Over the centuries, extensive commentaries and interpretations of Confucius's teachings gave rise to a body of literature known generally as Confucianism, though these ideas encompassed the thinking of many others as well.

In the translation that follows, the word "virtue" refers to the qualities of a complete or realized human being, sometimes referred to in Confucian literature as a "gentleman" or a "virtuous man."

- How would Confucius define such a person?

- How might one become this kind of person?

The terms "propriety" and "rites of propriety" point to an elaborate set of rituals or expectations that defined appropriate behavior in virtually every circumstance of life, depending on one's gender, age, or class.

- What role does propriety or ritual play in the making of a virtuous man?

- What understanding of "learning" or education comes through in this text?

- What is "filial piety" and why is it so important in Confucius's understanding of a good society?

- How do "virtue," "filial piety," and "learning" relate to the larger task of creating good government or a harmonious society?

- How does Confucius understand the role of the supernatural—gods, spirits, and ancestors for example?

CONFUCIUS

The Analects

ca. 479–221 B.C.E.

The philosopher Yu said, "They are few who, being filial and fraternal, are fond of offending against their superiors. There have been none, who, not liking to offend against their superiors, have been fond of stirring up confusion...."

The Master said, "To rule a country of a thousand chariots, there must be reverent attention to business, and sincerity; economy in expenditure, and love for men; and the employment of the people at the proper seasons."

The Master said, "A youth, when at home, should be filial, and, abroad, respectful to his elders. He should be earnest and truthful. He should overflow in love to all, and cultivate the friendship of the good. When he has time and opportunity, after the performance of these things, he should employ them in polite studies."

Tsze-hsia said, "If a man withdraws his mind from the love of [beautiful women], and applies it as sincerely to the love of the virtuous; if, in serving his parents, he can exert his utmost strength; if, in serving his prince, he can devote his life; if, in his intercourse with his friends, his words are sincere: although men say that he has not learned, I will certainly say that he has."

The philosopher Tsang said, "Let there be a careful attention to perform the funeral rites to parents, and let them be followed when long gone

with the ceremonies of sacrifice; then the virtue of the people will resume its proper excellence."

The Master said, "He who exercises government by means of his virtue may be compared to the north polar star, which keeps its place and all the stars turn toward it."

The Master said, "If the people be led by laws, and uniformity sought to be given them by punishments, they will try to avoid the punishment, but have no sense of shame. If they be led by virtue, and uniformity sought to be given them by the rules of propriety, they will have the sense of shame, and moreover will become good."

The Duke Ai asked, saying, "What should be done in order to secure the submission of the people?" Confucius replied, "Advance the upright and set aside the crooked, then the people will submit. Advance the crooked and set aside the upright, then the people will not submit."

Chi K'ang asked how to cause the people to reverence their ruler, to be faithful to him, and to go on to nerve themselves to virtue. The Master said, "Let him preside over them with gravity; then they will reverence him. Let him be final and kind to all; then they will be faithful to him. Let him advance the good and teach the incompetent; then they will eagerly seek to be virtuous."

The Master said, "If the will be set on virtue, there will be no practice of wickedness."

The Master said, "Riches and honors are what men desire. If they cannot be obtained in the proper way, they should not be held. Poverty and mean-

Source: Confucius, *The Analects*, translated by James Legge (1893).

ness are what men dislike. If they cannot be avoided in the proper way, they should not be avoided."

The Master said, "In serving his parents, a son may remonstrate with them, but gently; when he sees that they do not incline to follow his advice, he shows an increased degree of reverence, but does not abandon his purpose; and should they punish him, he does not allow himself to murmur."

Fan Ch'ih asked what constituted wisdom. The Master said, "To give one's self earnestly to the duties due to men, and, while respecting spiritual beings, to keep aloof from them, may be called wisdom."

The Master said, "The superior man, extensively studying all learning, and keeping himself under the restraint of the rules of propriety, may thus likewise not overstep what is right."

The Master's frequent themes of discourse were the Odes, the History, and the maintenance of the Rules of Propriety. On all these he frequently discoursed.

The Master was wishing to go and live among the nine wild tribes of the east. Some one said, "They are rude. How can you do such a thing?" The Master said, "If a superior man dwelt among them, what rudeness would there be?"

Chi Lu asked about serving the spirits of the dead. The Master said, "While you are not able to serve men, how can you serve their spirits?" Chi Lu added, "I venture to ask about death?" He was answered, "While you do not know life, how can you know about death?"

Yen Yuan asked about perfect virtue. The Master said, "To subdue one's self and return to propriety, is perfect virtue. If a man can for one day subdue himself and return to propriety, all under heaven will ascribe perfect virtue to him."

Chung-kung asked about perfect virtue. The Master said, "It is, when you go abroad, to behave to every one as if you were receiving a great guest; to employ the people as if you were assisting at a great sacrifice; not to do to others as you would not wish done to yourself; to have no murmuring against you in the country, and none in the family."

Chi K'ang asked Confucius about government. Confucius replied, "To govern means to rectify. If you lead on the people with correctness, who will dare not to be correct?"

Truly, if the ruler is not a ruler, the subject not a subject, the father not a father, the son not a son, then even if there be grain, would I get to eat it?

The Master said, "Of all people, girls and servants are the most difficult to behave to. If you are familiar with them, they lose their humility. If you maintain a reserve toward them, they are discontented."

Document 5.2

Reflections from the Hindu Scriptures

The flavor of Indian thinking about the good life and the good society is quite different from that of China. This distinctive outlook is reflected in these selections from the *Bhagavad Gita (The Song of the Lord)*, perhaps the most treasured of classical Hindu writings. Its dating is highly uncertain, although most scholars put it somewhere between the fifth and second centuries B.C.E. The *Bhagavad Gita* itself is an episode within the *Mahabharata*, one of the huge epic poems of India's classical tradition, which describes the struggle for power between two branches of the same family. The setting of the *Bhagavad Gita* takes places on the eve of a great battle in which the fearless warrior Arjuna is overcome with the realization that in this battle he will be required to kill some of his own kinsmen. In his distress he turns for advice to his charioteer, Lord Krishna, who is an incarnation of the great god Vishnu. Krishna's response to Arjuna's anguished questions, a part of which is reproduced here, conveys the essence of Hindu thinking about life and action in this world. A central question in the *Bhagavad Gita* is how a person can achieve spiritual fulfillment while remaining active in the world.

■ What is Krishna's answer to this dilemma?

■ What reasons does Krishna give for urging Arjuna to perform his duty as a warrior?

■ How does Krishna describe the good society?

■ What major themes of Hindu teaching can you find in this passage?

■ How does this text differ from that of *The Analects*? Are they asking the same questions? What similarities in outlook, if any, can you identify in these two texts?

Bhagavad Gita
ca. Fifth to Second Century B.C.E.

The deity said, you have grieved for those who deserve no grief. . . . Learned men grieve not for the living nor the dead. Never did I not exist, nor you, nor these rulers of men; nor will any one of us ever hereafter cease to be. As in this body, infancy and youth and old age come to the embodied self, so does the acquisition of another body; a sensible man is not deceived about that. The contacts of the senses . . . which produce cold and heat, pleasure and pain, are not permanent, they are ever coming and going. Bear them, O descendant of Bharata!

He who thinks it [a person's soul, or *atman*] to be the killer and he who thinks it to be killed, both know nothing. It kills not, [and] is not killed. It is not born, nor does it ever die, nor, having existed, does it exist no more. Unborn, everlasting, unchangeable, and primeval, it is not killed when the body is killed. . . . As a man, casting off old clothes, puts on others and new ones, so the embodied self, casting off old bodies, goes to others and new ones. . . . It is everlasting, all-pervading, stable, firm, and eternal.

It is said to be unperceived, to be unthinkable, to be unchangeable. Therefore, knowing it to be such, you ought not to grieve. . . . For to one that is born, death is certain; and to one that dies, birth is certain. . . .

Having regard to your own duty also, you ought not to falter, for there is nothing better for a Kshatriya° than a righteous battle. Happy those Kshatriyas, O son of Pritha! who can find such a battle . . . an open door to heaven! But if you will not fight this righteous battle, then you will have abandoned your own duty and your fame, and you will incur sin. . . .

Your business is with action alone, not by any means with fruit. Let not the fruit of action be your motive to action. Let not your attachment be fixed on inaction. Having recourse to devotion . . . perform actions, casting off all attachment, and being equable in success or ill-success; such equability is called devotion. . . . The wise who have obtained devotion cast off the fruit of action, and released from the shackles of repeated births, repair to that seat where there is no unhappiness. . . .

The man who, casting off all desires, lives free from attachments, who is free from egoism and from

Source: Tashinath Trimbak Teland, trans., *The Bhagavad Gita*, in Max Mueller, ed., *The Sacred Books of the East*, 50 vols. (Oxford; Clarendon Press, 1879–1910), 8:43–46, 48–49, 51–52, 126–28.

°**Kshatriya:** a member of the warrior/ruler caste.

the feeling that this or that is mine, obtains tranquility. This, O son of Pritha! is the Brahmic state. Attaining to this, one is never deluded, and remaining in it in one's last moments, one attains the Brahmic bliss [*nirvana*, or merging with the divine]....

I have passed through many births, O Arjuna! and you also. I know them all, but you...do not know them....Whensoever, O descendant of Bharata! piety languishes, and impiety is in the ascendant, I create myself. I am born age after age, for the protection of the good, for the destruction of evil-doers, and the establishment of piety....

The fourfold division of castes was created by me according to the appointment of qualities and duties....The duties of Brahmins, Kshatriyas, and Vaisyas, and of Sudras, too...are distinguished according to the qualities born of nature. Tranquillity, restraint of the senses, penance, purity, forgiveness, straightforwardness, also knowledge, experience, and belief in a future world, this is the natural duty of Brahmins. Valor, glory, courage, dexterity, not slinking away from battle, gifts, exercise of lordly power, this is the natural duty of Kshatriyas. Agriculture, tending cattle, trade, this is the natural duty of Vaisyas. And the natural duty of Sudras, too, consists in service.

Every man intent on his own respective duties obtains perfection. Listen, now, how one intent on one's own duty obtains perfection. Worshipping, by the performance of his own duty, him from whom all things proceed, and by whom all this is permeated, a man obtains perfection. One's duty, though defective, is better than another's duty well performed. Performing the duty prescribed by nature, one does not incur sin. O son of Kunti! one should not abandon a natural duty though tainted with evil; for all actions are enveloped by evil, as fire by smoke.

One who is self-restrained, whose understanding is unattached everywhere, from whom affections have departed, obtains the supreme perfection of freedom from action by renunciation. Learn from me, only in brief, O son of Kunti! how one who has obtained perfection attains the Brahman, which is the highest culmination of knowledge. A man possessed of a pure understanding, controlling his self by courage, discarding sound and other objects of sense, casting off affection and aversion, who frequents clean places, who eats little, whose speech, body, and mind are restrained, who is always intent on meditation and mental abstraction, and has recourse to unconcern, who, abandoning egoism, stubbornness, arrogance, desire, anger, and all belongings, has no thought that this or that is mine, and who is tranquil, becomes fit for assimilation with the Brahman.

Document 5.3

Reflections from Socrates

Document 5.3 comes from the tradition of Greek rationalism. The excerpt is from Socrates' famous defense of himself before a jury of 501 fellow Athenians in 399 B.C.E., as recorded by Plato, Socrates' student and disciple. Charged with impiety and corrupting the youth of the city, Socrates was narrowly condemned to death by that jury. His speech at the trial has come to be viewed as a powerful defense of intellectual freedom and the unfettered life of the mind.

■ How does Socrates respond to the charges laid against him?

■ How might Socrates define "the good life"? How does he understand "wisdom" and "virtue"? Do you think that Confucius and Socrates would agree about the nature of "virtue"?

- Why does Socrates believe he has been useful to Athens?

- What do his frequent references to God reveal about his understanding of the supernatural and its relevance to social life?

- Why did he accept the death penalty and refuse to consider a lesser sentence? (See the photo on p. 206.)

PLATO

Apology

ca. 399 B.C.E.

I will begin at the beginning, and ask what the accusation is which has given rise to this slander of me....What do the slanderers say?..."Socrates is an evil-doer, and a curious person, who searches into things under the earth and in heaven, and he makes the worse appear the better cause; and he teaches the aforesaid doctrines to others...."

I found that the men most in repute were all but the most foolish; and that some inferior men were really wiser and better....

O men of Athens,...God only is wise;...the wisdom of men is little or nothing;...And so I go my way, obedient to the god, and make inquisition into the wisdom of anyone, whether citizen or stranger, who appears to be wise; and if he is not wise, then...I show him that he is not wise; and this occupation quite absorbs me....

There is another thing: young men of the richer classes, who have not much to do, come about me of their own accord; they like to hear the pretenders examined, and they often imitate me, and examine others themselves; there are plenty of persons, as they soon enough discover, who think that they know something, but really know little or nothing: and then those who are examined by them instead of being angry with themselves are angry with me: This confounded Socrates, they say; this villainous misleader of youth!... [T]hey repeat the ready-made charges which are used against all philosophers about teaching things up in the clouds and under the earth, and having no gods, and making the worse appear the better cause; for they do not like to confess that their pretence of knowledge has been detected....

Someone will say: And are you not ashamed, Socrates, of a course of life which is likely to bring you to an untimely end? To him I may fairly answer: There you are mistaken: a man who is good for anything ought not to calculate the chance of living or dying; he ought only to consider whether in doing anything he is doing right or wrong, acting the part of a good man or of a bad....Had Achilles° any thought of death and danger? For wherever a man's place is, whether the place which he has chosen or that in which he has been placed by a commander, there he ought to remain in the hour of danger; he should not think of death or of anything, but of disgrace....

And therefore if you let me go now, and... if you say to me, Socrates, this time we will... let you off, but upon one condition, that you are not to inquire and speculate in this way any more, and that if you are caught doing this again you shall die; if this was the condition on which you let me go, I should reply: Men of Athens, I honor and love you; but I shall obey God rather than you, and while I have life and strength I shall never cease from the practice and teaching of philoso-

Source: Plato, *Apology*, translated by Benjamin Jowett (1891).

°**Achilles:** the great warrior-hero of *The Illiad*.

phy, exhorting anyone whom I meet after my manner....I interrogate and examine and cross-examine him, and if I think that he has no virtue, but only says that he has, I reproach him with undervaluing the greater, and overvaluing the less....For I do nothing but go about persuading you all, old and young alike, not to take thought for your persons and your properties, but first and chiefly to care about the greatest improvement of the soul....Wherefore, O men of Athens, I say to you...either acquit me or not; but whatever you do, know that I shall never alter my ways, not even if I have to die many times....

[I]f you kill such a one as I am, you will injure yourselves more than you will injure me....For if you kill me you will not easily find another like me, who, if I may use such a ludicrous figure of speech, am a sort of gadfly, given to the state by the God; and the state is like a great and noble steed who is tardy in his motions owing to his very size, and requires to be stirred into life. I am that gadfly which God has given the state and all day long and in all places am always fastening upon you, arousing and persuading and reproaching you....I dare say that you may feel irritated at being suddenly awakened when you are caught napping; and you may think that if you were to strike me dead..., which you easily might, then you would sleep on for the remainder of your lives....

[After the jury finds Socrates guilty, he accepts the sentence of death, rejecting the alternative punishments of prison or exile.]

There are many reasons why I am not grieved, O men of Athens, at the vote of condemnation. The difficulty, my friends, is not in avoiding death, but in avoiding unrighteousness....

I am not angry with my accusers, or my condemners....Still I have a favor to ask of them. When my sons are grown up, I would ask you, O my friends, to punish them...if they seem to care about riches, or anything, more than about virtue; or if they pretend to be something when they are really nothing, then reprove them, as I have reproved you, for not caring about that for which they ought to care, and thinking that they are something when they are really nothing. And if you do this, I and my sons will have received justice at your hands.

The hour of departure has arrived, and we go our ways—I to die, and you to live. Which is better, God only knows.

Document 5.4

Reflections from Jesus

Like Confucius, Jesus apparently never wrote anything himself. His sayings and his actions were recorded in the Gospels by his followers. The Gospel of Matthew, from which this selection is taken, was composed during the second half of the first century C.E. For Christian people, this passage, known as the Sermon on the Mount, has long been among the most beloved of biblical texts, regarded as a guide for effective living and the core of Jesus' ethical and moral teachings. In this selection, Jesus contrasts the "broad road" of conventional understanding and values with the "narrow road that leads to life."

■ In what ways does his teaching challenge or contradict the conventional outlook of his time?

■ What criticisms does he make of those referred to as hypocrites, Pharisees, and the teachers of the law?

- How would you summarize "the good life" as Jesus might have defined it?

- How might Jesus and Confucius have responded to each other's teachings?

- What is Jesus' posture toward Jewish law?

- Beyond its use as a guide for personal behavior, what are the larger social implications of the Sermon on the Mount?

The Gospel of Matthew
ca. 70–100 C.E.

Now when he [Jesus] saw the crowds, he went up on a mountainside and sat down. His disciples came to him, and he began to teach them saying:

"Blessed are the poor in spirit, for theirs is the kingdom of heaven.

"Blessed are those who mourn, for they will be comforted.

"Blessed are the meek, for they will inherit the earth.

"Blessed are those who hunger and thirst for righteousness, for they will be filled.

"Blessed are the merciful, for they will be shown mercy.

"Blessed are the pure in heart, for they will see God.

"Blessed are the peacemakers, for they will be called sons of God.

"Blessed are those who are persecuted because of righteousness, for theirs is the kingdom of heaven.

"You are the salt of the earth. But if the salt loses its saltiness, how can it be made salty again? It is no longer good for anything, except to be thrown out and trampled by men.

"You are the light of the world. A city on a hill cannot be hidden. Neither do people light a lamp and put it under a bowl. Instead they put it on its stand, and it gives light to everyone in the house. In the same way, let your light shine before men, that they may see your good deeds and praise your Father in heaven.

"Do not think that I have come to abolish the Law or the Prophets; I have not come to abolish them but to fulfill them. I tell you the truth, until heaven and earth disappear, not the smallest letter, not the least stroke of a pen, will by any means disappear from the Law until everything is accomplished. Anyone who breaks one of the least of these commandments and teaches others to do the same will be called least in the kingdom of heaven, but whoever practices and teaches these commands will be called great in the kingdom of heaven. For I tell you that unless your righteousness surpasses that of the Pharisees and the teachers of the law, you will certainly not enter the kingdom of heaven.

"You have heard that it was said to the people long ago, 'Do not murder, and anyone who murders will be subject to judgment.' But I tell you that anyone who is angry with his brother will be subject to judgment....

"Therefore, if you are offering your gift at the altar and there remember that your brother has something against you, leave your gift there in front of the altar. First go and be reconciled to your brother; then come and offer your gift.

"Settle matters quickly with your adversary who is taking you to court. Do it while you are still with him on the way, or he may hand you over to

Source: Matthew 5–7 (New International Version).

the judge, and the judge may hand you over to the officer, and you may be thrown into prison. I tell you the truth, you will not get out until you have paid the last penny.

"You have heard that it was said, 'Do not commit adultery.' But I tell you that anyone who looks at a woman lustfully has already committed adultery with her in his heart....

"You have heard that it was said, 'Eye for eye, and tooth for tooth.' But I tell you, Do not resist an evil person. If someone strikes you on the right cheek, turn to him the other also. And if someone wants to sue you and take your tunic, let him have your cloak as well. If someone forces you to go one mile, go with him two miles. Give to the one who asks you, and do not turn away from the one who wants to borrow from you.

"You have heard that it was said, 'Love your neighbor and hate your enemy.' But I tell you: Love your enemies and pray for those who persecute you, that you may be sons of your Father in heaven. He causes his sun to rise on the evil and the good, and sends rain on the righteous and the unrighteous. If you love those who love you, what reward will you get? Are not even the tax collectors doing that? And if you greet only your brothers, what are you doing more than others? Do not even pagans do that? Be perfect, therefore, as your heavenly Father is perfect.

"Be careful not to do your 'acts of righteousness' before men, to be seen by them.... So when you give to the needy, do not announce it with trumpets, as the hypocrites do in the synagogues and on the streets, to be honored by men....But when you give to the needy, do not let your left hand know what your right hand is doing, so that your giving may be in secret. Then your Father, who sees what is done in secret, will reward you.

"And when you pray, do not be like the hypocrites, for they love to pray standing in the synagogues and on the street corners to be seen by men....But when you pray, go into your room, close the door and pray to your Father, who is unseen. Then your Father, who sees what is done in secret, will reward you. And when you pray, do not keep on babbling like pagans, for they think

they will be heard because of their many words. Do not be like them, for your Father knows what you need before you ask him....

"Do not store up for yourselves treasures on earth, where moth and rust destroy, and where thieves break in and steal. But store up for yourselves treasures in heaven, where moth and rust do not destroy, and where thieves do not break in and steal. For where your treasure is, there your heart will be also....

"So do not worry, saying, 'What shall we eat?' or 'What shall we drink?' or 'What shall we wear?' For the pagans run after all these things, and your heavenly Father knows that you need them. But seek first his kingdom and his righteousness, and all these things will be given to you as well. Therefore do not worry about tomorrow, for tomorrow will worry about itself. Each day has enough trouble of its own.

"Do not judge, or you too will be judged. For in the same way you judge others, you will be judged, and with the measure you use, it will be measured to you.

"Why do you look at the speck of sawdust in your brother's eye and pay no attention to the plank in your own eye? How can you say to your brother, 'Let me take the speck out of your eye,' when all the time there is a plank in your own eye? You hypocrite, first take the plank out of your own eye, and then you will see clearly to remove the speck from your brother's eye....

"Ask and it will be given to you; seek and you will find; knock and the door will be opened to you. For everyone who asks receives; he who seeks finds; and to him who knocks, the door will be opened.

"Enter through the narrow gate. For wide is the gate and broad is the road that leads to destruction, and many enter through it. But small is the gate and narrow the road that leads to life, and only a few find it...."

When Jesus had finished saying these things, the crowds were amazed at his teaching, because he taught as one who had authority, and not as their teachers of the law.

Using the Evidence:
The Good Life in Classical Eurasia

1. **Making comparisons:** In describing the "good life" or the "good society," what commonalities do you see among these four documents? What differences are apparent? How might the authors of each text respond to the ideas of the others?

2. **Placing texts in context:** In what ways was each of these texts reacting *against* the conventional wisdom of their times? How was each shaped by the social and political circumstances in which they were composed?

3. **Relating spirituality and behavior:** What is the relationship between religion (the transcendent realm of the gods or the divine) and moral behavior on earth in each of these documents? How does the "good life" relate to politics?

4. **Defining the "good person":** How do each of these texts characterize the superior person or the fully realized human being? How do they define personal virtue?

Visual Sources

Considering the Evidence:
Representations of the Buddha

Buddhism derived from a single individual, Siddhartha Gautama, born in northern India between the sixth and fourth centuries B.C.E. Legendary accounts of his life often begin with his miraculous conception and birth, as a sacred white elephant pierced his mother's side with its trunk. The son of royalty, the young Siddhartha enjoyed a splendid but sheltered upbringing encased in luxury, and his father spared no effort to protect the child from anything painful or difficult. At the age of sixteen, he was married to a beautiful cousin, Yasodhara, who bore him a son thirteen years later. But while riding beyond the palace grounds, this curious and lively young man encountered human suffering in the form of an old man, a sick person, and a corpse. Shattered by these revelations of aging, illness, and death, Siddhartha determined to find the cause of such sufferings and a remedy for them. And so, at the age of twenty-nine and on the very day his son was born, the young prince left his luxurious life as well as his wife and child, shed his royal jewels, cut off his hair, and set off on a quest for enlightenment. This act of severing his ties to the attachments of ordinary life is known in Buddhist teaching as the Great Renunciation.

What followed were six years of spiritual experimentation that finally led Siddhartha to a particular tree in northern India, where, legend tells us, he began a forty-nine-day period of intensive meditation. There he was assailed by that figure of temptation and illusion known as Mara, who sent demons, wild beasts, and his beautiful daughters to frighten or seduce Siddhartha from his quest. But his persistence was finally rewarded with the almost indescribable experience of full enlightenment. Now he was the Buddha, the man who had awakened.

For the next forty years, he taught what he had learned, setting in motion the cultural tradition we know as Buddhism. Over many centuries, the religion evolved, as it attracted growing numbers of converts and as it intersected with various cultures throughout Asia, including China, Japan, Tibet, Korea, and Vietnam. Those changes affected not only matters of doctrine and practice but also the images that expressed the core teachings of Buddhism.

For almost five centuries after his death, which likely took place in the early fifth century B.C.E., artists represented the Buddha as an empty throne, a horse with no rider, a tree, a wheel, or in some other symbolic way, while largely shunning any depiction of him in human form. No one knows precisely why. Regarding the Buddha as a fully human teacher and guide, perhaps they sought to prevent his being perceived as a divine figure that might be worshipped. On his deathbed, after all, he had counseled his followers: "Be a lamp unto yourselves. Work out your own salvation." But it was hardly a unique form of religious representation, for some Christians and almost all Muslims likewise declined to portray their prophetic figures in human terms.

Among the most widespread of these early symbolic representations of the Buddha were images of his footprints. Found throughout Buddhist Asia, such footprints indicated the Buddha's spiritual presence and served as a focus for devotion or contemplation. They also reminded his followers that since he had passed into *nirvana*, he could not be physically present. One Buddhist text declared that those who looked upon those footprints "shall be freed from the bonds of error, and conducted upon the Way of Enlightenment."[24]

Visual Source 5.1 shows a footprint image from northwestern India dating probably from the second century C.E. and containing a number of Buddhist symbols. In the center of each footprint is a *dharmachakra*, a wheel-like structure that had long symbolized the Buddha's teaching. Here, it surrounds a lotus flower, representing the Buddha's purity. Near the heel is a three-pronged emblem known as a *triratna*. It symbolizes the three things in which Buddhists can take refuge: the Buddha himself, his teaching, and the *sangha* (the Buddhist community). This particular footprint image also includes in the bottom corners two *yakshis*, Indian female earth spirits suggesting fertility. The position of their hands conveys a respectful greeting.

- Why might the wheel serve as an effective symbol of the Buddha's message?

- What does the inclusion of the *yakshis* add to the message of this image?

- What overall religious message might this footprint convey to those who gazed upon it?

By the first century C.E., the impulse to depict the Buddha in human form had surfaced, with some of the earliest examples coming from the region of South Asia known as Gandhara in what is now northern Pakistan and eastern Afghanistan (see Map 4.3, p. 152). That area had been a part of the empire of Alexander the Great and his Hellenistic successors from about 322 B.C.E. to 50 B.C.E. and had developed commercial ties to the Roman Empire as well. These early images of the Buddha reflect this Greco-Roman influence, depicting him with a face similar to that of the Greek god Apollo, dressed in a Roman-style toga, and with curly hair characteristic of the Mediterranean region.

Visual Source 5.1 Footprints of the Buddha (Courtesy, John Eskanazi Ltd, London. Photo: A. C. Cooper N & P Ltd, London)

By the time of India's Gupta dynasty (320–550 C.E.), the Greco-Roman influence of the Gandhara style was fading, replaced by more completely Indian images of the Buddha, which became the "classic" model that spread widely across Asia. Visual Source 5.2 represents one such image, deriving from Bihar in eastern India during the sixth century C.E. Notice here the hand gestures known as *mudras*. The Buddha's right hand, for example, with palm facing the viewer, indicates reassurance, or "have no fear." The partially webbed fingers are among the *lakshanas*, or signs of a Buddha image, that denote the Buddha's unique status. So too is the knot on the top of his head, symbolizing enlightenment.

■ What might account for the emergence of human images of the Buddha?

■ What overall impression or religious meaning is this statue intended to convey?

Visual Source 5.2 A Classic Indian Buddha (Image copyright © The Metropolitan Museum of Art/Art Resource, NY)

- The elongated earlobes remind the viewer that, earlier in his life, the prince Siddhartha had worn heavy and luxurious earrings. What does their absence suggest about his transformation as the Buddha?

- Notice the partially closed and downcast eyes of the Buddha as well as his bare feet. What might these features of the image suggest?

Among the conditions favoring the proliferation of Buddha images in the early centuries of the Common Era was the growth of a new form of Buddhist belief and practice known as Mahayana (Great Vehicle). As the message of the Buddha gained a mass following in the several centuries after his death, some of its early features—rigorous and time-consuming meditation practice, a focus on monks and nuns withdrawn from ordinary life, the absence of accessible supernatural figures able to provide help and comfort—proved difficult for or beyond the reach of many converts. Expressed in various sects, practices, and schools of thought, Mahayana Buddhism offered a more accessible version of the faith, a spiritual path available to a much wider range of people beyond the monks and ascetics, who were the core group in early Buddhism.

In most expressions of Mahayana Buddhism, enlightenment (or becoming a Buddha), was available to everyone; it was possible within the context of ordinary life, rather than a monastery; and it might occur within a single life-time rather than over the course of many lives. While Buddhism had originally put a premium on spiritual wisdom, leading to liberation from rebirth and the achievement of nirvana, Mahayana expressions of the faith emphasized compassion—the ability to feel the sorrows of other people as if they were one's own. This compassionate religious ideal found expression in the notion of *bodhisattvas*, fully enlightened beings who postponed their own final liberation in order to assist a suffering humanity. They were spiritual beings, intermediaries between mortal humans and the Buddhas, whose countless images in sculpture or painting became objects of worship and sources of comfort and assistance to many Buddhists.

Across the world of Asian Mahayana Buddhism, the most widely popular of the many bodhisattva figures was that of Avalokitesvara, known in China as Guanyin and in Japan as Kannon. This Bodhisattva of Compassion, often portrayed as a woman or with distinctly feminine characteristics, was known as the "the one who hears the cries of the world." Calling upon him/her for assistance, devotees could be rescued from all kinds of danger and distress. Women might petition for a healthy child. Moral transformation too was possible. According to the *Lotus Sutra*, a major Mahayana text, "Those who act under the impulse of hatred will, after adoring the Bodhisattva Avalokitesvara, be freed from hatred."

Among the most striking of the many representation of this bodhisattva are those that portray him/her with numerous heads, with which to hear the many cries of a suffering humanity, and with multiple arms to aid them.

Visual Source 5.3 A Bodhisattva of Compassion: Kannon of 1,000 Arms (From *The Concise History of Japanese Buddhist Sculpture*, Bijutu Shuppan-sha. Photo: Lightstream)

Visual Source 5.3 provides one illustration of such a figure, the Senju Kannon, from Japan of the eighth century C.E.

- What elements of Buddhist imagery can you identify in this statue?

- To whom might such an image appeal? And why?

- Notice the lotus flower, for centuries a rich Buddhist symbol, on which the bodhisattva is resting. With its roots in the mud, the lotus emerges on the surface of the water as a pure, beautiful, and fragrant flower. Why would the artist choose to place the bodhisattva atop such a flower?

■ Some scholars have identified similarities between the Bodhisattva of Compassion and the Virgin Mary in the Christian tradition. What common elements and what differences can you identify?

Beyond numerous bodhisattvas, Mahayana Buddhism also populated the spiritual universe with various Buddhas in addition to the historical Buddha. One of these is the Maitreya Buddha or the Buddha of the future, predicted to appear when the teachings of the historical Buddha have been lost or forgotten. In China, this Buddha of the future was sometimes portrayed as the "laughing Buddha," a fat, smiling, contented figure, said to be modeled on a tenth-century monk named Budai, who wandered the country merrily spreading happiness and good cheer, while evoking contentment and abundance. Visual Source 5.4 illustrates this Chinese Maitreya Buddha together with some of his disciples in a carving, dating to the tenth through fourteenth centuries, in China's Feilai Feng caves.

Visual Source 5.4 The Chinese Maitreya Buddha (Nazima Kowail/Corbis)

■ How does this Buddha image differ, both physically and in its religious implications, from the Buddhas in Visual Sources 5.2 and 5.3?

■ Why might this image be appealing to some Buddhists, and why might others take exception to it?

■ In what ways does this figure represent an adaptation of Buddhist imagery to Chinese culture? Consider what you know about Confucian and Daoist postures to the world.

Visual Source 5.5 The Amitabha Buddha (The State Hermitage Museum, St. Petersburg. Photograph © The State Hermitage Museum)

Yet another Buddha figure within the Mahayana tradition is that of Amitabha, or Amida, the Buddha of Infinite Light, associated with the Pure Land school of China and other parts of East Asia. In this version of Buddhism, worship of the Amitabha Buddha, by sincerely chanting his name, for example, would earn devotees rebirth in the Western Paradise, or the Pure Land. Often imagined as a place of constant light, fragrant breezes, luxuriant vegetation, and abundant water, the Western Paradise was as accessible to commoners, even criminals and outcasts, as it was to monks and nuns.

Visual Source 5.5, dating from somewhere between the twelfth and the fourteenth centuries, depicts Amitabha in bright robes, accompanied by several bodhisattvas. They are shown welcoming a deceased person, represented as a naked boy in the stream of light that comes from the Amitabha's forehead, into the Pure Land, where he will be installed on the golden lotus throne, carried by the bodhisattvas. There he can continuously hear the teachings of the Buddha, while working off any remaining negative karma, before achieving complete liberation in nirvana.

- Why do you think the practice of Pure Land Buddhism became so widely popular in China by the mid-seventh century? What features of this image might help to explain its appeal?

- What details from this painting support the sacred character of the Buddha and bodhisattva figures?

- What is the significance of the small figure sitting in meditation under a tree at the bottom left of the painting?

Using the Evidence:
Representations of the Buddha

1. **Tracing change:** What transformations in Buddhist belief and practice are disclosed in these images?

2. **Identifying cultural adaptation:** What evidence do these images provide about the blending of Buddhism into a variety of cultural settings?

3. **Understanding the growth of Buddhism:** What do these images suggest about the appeal of Buddhism to growing numbers of people across Asia?

4. **Considering cultural boundaries:** To what extent are these images meaningful to people outside of the Buddhist tradition? In what ways do they speak to universal human needs or desires? What is specifically Buddhist or Asian about them?

CHAPTER SIX

Eurasian Social Hierarchies

500 B.C.E–500 C.E.

Society and the State in Classical
China
  An Elite of Officials
  The Landlord Class
  Peasants
  Merchants
Class and Caste in India
  Caste as *Varna*
  Caste as *Jati*
  The Functions of Caste
Slavery in the Classical Era: The
Case of the Roman Empire
  Slavery and Civilization
  The Making of a Slave Society: The
  Case of Rome
  Resistance and Rebellion
Comparing Patriarchies of the
Classical Era
  A Changing Patriarchy: The Case
  of China
  Contrasting Patriarchies in Athens
  and Sparta
Reflections: Arguing with Solomon
and the Buddha
Considering the Evidence
  Documents: Patriarchy and
  Women's Voices in the Classical
  Era
  Visual Sources: Pompeii as
  a Window on the Roman World

She is a twenty-six-year-old Hindu woman from Goa, on India's west coast. She speaks the Marathi language, has a high school education, is not currently employed, neither smokes nor drinks, but occasionally eats meat. Like millions of other Indians, she is seeking a partner by placing a personal ad in the newspaper or on the Internet. In addition to the personal and professional data found everywhere in such ads, in India they almost always contain another piece of information—the caste of the seeker. The young woman from Goa lists herself as a member of a "scheduled caste" known as Chambar, formerly called "untouchables," the lowest category in the hierarchy of India's ranked society. That personal ads in twenty-first-century India still refer to caste points out how deeply entrenched and enduring ancient patterns of social life can be.

THE MOST RECENT 250 YEARS OF WORLD HISTORY have called into question social structures long assumed to be natural and permanent. The French, Russian, and Chinese revolutions challenged and destroyed ancient monarchies and class hierarchies; the abolitionist movement of the nineteenth century attacked slavery, largely unquestioned for millennia; the women's movement confronted long and deeply held patriarchal assumptions about the proper relationship between women and men; and Mahatma Gandhi, during India's struggle for independence in the twentieth century, sought to raise the status of "untouchables," referring to them as Harijan, or "children of God." Nevertheless, caste, class, patriarchy, and even slavery have certainly not vanished from human society, even now.

Indian Society: A fresco from the time of India's Gupta dynasty (320–600 C.E.) shows townspeople in a royal procession. (© Benoy K. Behl)

During the era of "second-wave" civilizations in Eurasia, these patterns of inequality found expressions and generated social tensions that remain recognizable to the contemporary descendants of these classical societies.

Millions of individual people, inhabiting the classical civilizations of Eurasia, lived within a political framework of states or empires. They occupied as well a world of ideas, religions, and values that derived both from local folkways and from the teaching of the great religious or cultural traditions of their civilizations. They also lived within established societies that defined relationships between rich and poor, powerful and powerless, slaves and free people, and men and women. Those social relationships shaped the daily lives and the life chances of everyone; they provided the foundation for political authority as well as challenges to it; they were both justified and challenged by the religious and cultural traditions of these civilizations.

Like the First Civilizations, those of the classical era were sharply divided along class lines, and they too were patriarchal, with women clearly subordinated to men in most domains of life. In constructing their societies, however, the classical civilizations differed substantially from one another. Chinese, Indian, and Mediterranean civilizations provide numerous illustrations of the many and varied ways in which peoples of the classical era organized their social life. The assumptions, tensions, and conflicts accompanying these social patterns provided much of the distinctive character and texture that distinguished these diverse civilizations from one another.

Society and the State in Classical China

Chinese society was unique in the ancient world in the extent to which it was shaped by the actions of the state. Nowhere was this more apparent than in the political power and immense social prestige of Chinese state officials. For more than 2,000 years, these officials, bureaucrats acting in the name of the emperor both in the capital and in the provinces, represented the cultural and social elite of Chinese civilization. This class had its origins in the efforts of early Chinese rulers to find administrators loyal to the central state rather than to their own families or regions. Philosophers such as Confucius had long advocated selecting such officials on the basis of merit and personal morality rather than birth or wealth. As the Han dynasty established its authority in China around 200 B.C.E., its rulers required each province to send men of promise to the capital, where they were examined and chosen for official positions on the basis of their performance.

An Elite of Officials

■ Description
How would you characterize the social hierarchy of classical China?

Over time, this system of selecting administrators evolved into the world's first professional civil service. In 124 B.C.E., Emperor Wu Di established an imperial academy where potential officials were trained as scholars and immersed in Chinese classical texts dealing with history, literature, art, and mathematics, with an emphasis on Confucian teachings. By the end of the Han dynasty, it enrolled some 30,000 students, who were by then subjected to a series of written examinations to select officials of various grades. Private schools in the provinces funneled still more aspiring candidates into this examination system, which persisted until the early twentieth century. In theory open to all men, this system in practice favored those whose families were wealthy enough to provide the years of education required to pass even the lower-level exams. Proximity to the capital and family connections to the imperial court also helped in gaining a position in this highest of Chinese elites. Nonetheless, village communities or a local landowner might sponsor the education of a bright young man from a commoner family, enabling him to enter the charmed circle of officialdom. One rags-to-riches story told of a pig farmer who became an adviser to the emperor himself. Thus the examination system provided a modest measure of social mobility in an otherwise quite hierarchical society.

In later dynasties, that system grew to be even more elaborate and became an enduring and distinguishing feature of Chinese civilization. During the Tang dynasty, the famous poet and official Po Chu-I (772–846 C.E.) wrote a poem entitled "After Passing the Examination," which shows something of the fame and fortune that awaited an accomplished student as well as the continuing loyalty to family and home that ideally marked those who succeeded:

> For ten years I never left my books,
> I went up . . . and won unmerited praise.
> My high place I do not much prize;
> The joy of my parents will first make me proud.
> Fellow students, six or seven men,
> See me off as I leave the City gate.
> My covered coach is ready to drive away;
> Flutes and strings blend their parting tune.
> Hopes achieved dull the pains of parting;
> Fumes of wine shorten the long road. . . .
> Shod with wings is the horse of him who rides
> On a Spring day the road that leads to home.[1]

Those who made it into the bureaucracy entered a realm of high privilege and enormous prestige. Senior officials moved about in carriages and were bedecked with robes, ribbons, seals, and headdresses appropriate to their rank. Even lower officials who served in the provinces rather than the capital were distinguished by their polished speech, their cultural sophistication, and their urban manners as well as their political authority. Proud of their learning, they were the bearers, and often the makers, of Chinese culture. "Officials are the leaders of the populace," stated an imperial edict of 144 B.C.E., "and it is right and proper that the carriages they ride in and the robes that they wear should correspond to the degrees of their dignity."[2]

The Landlord Class

Most officials came from wealthy families, and in China wealth meant land. When the Qin dynasty unified China by 210 B.C.E., most land was held by small-scale peasant farmers. But by the first century B.C.E., the pressures of population growth, taxation, and indebtedness had generated a class of large landowners as impoverished peasants found it necessary to sell their lands to more prosperous neighbors. This accumulation of land in large estates was a persistent theme in Chinese history, and one that was persistently, though not very successfully, opposed by state authorities. Landlords of large estates often were able to avoid paying taxes, thus decreasing state revenues and increasing the tax burden for the remaining peasants. In some cases, they could also mount their own military forces that might challenge the authority of the emperor.

One of the most dramatic state efforts to counteract the growing power of large landowners is associated with Wang Mang, a high court official of the Han dynasty who usurped the emperor's throne in 8 C.E. and immediately launched a series of startling reforms. A firm believer in Confucian good government, Wang Mang saw his reforms as re-creating a golden age of long ago in which small-scale peasant farmers represented the backbone of Chinese society. Accordingly, he ordered the great private estates to be nationalized and divided up among the landless. Government loans to peasant families, limits on the amount of land a family might own, and an end to private slavery were all part of his reform program, but these measures proved impossible to enforce. Opposition from wealthy landowners, nomadic invasions, poor harvests, floods, and famines led to the collapse of Wang Mang's reforms and his assassination in 23 C.E.

Large landowning families, therefore, remained a central feature of Chinese society, although the fate of individual families rose and fell as the wheel of fortune raised them to great prominence or plunged them into poverty and disgrace. As a class, they benefited both from the wealth that their estates generated and from the power and prestige that accompanied their education and their membership in the official elite. The term "scholar-gentry" reflected their twin sources of privilege. With homes in both urban and rural areas, members of the scholar-gentry class lived luxuriously. Multistoried houses, the finest of silk clothing, gleaming carriages, private orchestras, high-stakes gambling—all of this was part of the life of China's scholar-gentry class.

Peasants

■ **Change**
What class conflicts disrupted Chinese society?

Throughout the history of China's civilization, the vast majority of its population has been peasants, living in small households representing two or three generations. Some owned enough land to support their families and perhaps even sell something on the local market. Many others could barely survive. Nature, the state, and landlords combined to make the life of most peasants extremely vulnerable. Famines, floods, droughts, hail, and pests could wreak havoc without warning. State authorities required the payment of taxes, demanded about a month's labor every year on various public projects, and conscripted young men for two years of military service. During the Han dynasty, growing numbers of impoverished and desperate peasants had to sell out to large landlords and work as tenants or sharecroppers on their estates, where rents could run as high as one-half to two-thirds of the crop. Other peasants fled, taking to a life of begging or joining a gang of bandits in a remote area.

An eighth-century C.E. Chinese poem by Li Shen reflects poignantly on the enduring hardships of peasant life:

Chinese Peasants
For many centuries, the normal activities of Chinese peasant farmers included plowing, planting, and threshing grain, as shown in this painting from China's Song dynasty (960–1279 C.E.). (*Farmers at Work*, Northern Song Dynasty, 960–1279 [wall painting]/ Mogao Caves, Dunhuang/The Bridgeman Art Library)

> The cob of corn in springtime sown
> In autumn yields a hundredfold.
> No fields are seen that fallow lie:
> And yet of hunger peasants die.
>
> As at noontide they hoe their crops,
> Sweat on the grain to earth down drops.
> How many tears, how many a groan,
> Each morsel on thy dish did mold![3]

Such conditions provoked periodic peasant rebellions, which punctuated Chinese history over the past 2,000 years. Toward the end of the second century C.E., wandering bands of peasants began to join together as floods along the Yellow River and resulting epidemics compounded the misery of landlessness and poverty. What emerged was a massive peasant uprising known as the Yellow Turban Rebellion because of the yellow scarves the peasants wore around their heads. That movement, which swelled to about 360,000 armed followers by 184 C.E., found leaders, organization, and a unifying ideology in a popular form of Daoism. Featuring supernatural healings, collective trances, and public confessions of sin, the Yellow Turban movement looked forward to the "Great Peace"—a golden age of complete equality, social harmony, and common ownership of property. Although the rebellion was suppressed by the military forces of the Han dynasty, the Yellow Turban and other peasant upheavals devastated the economy, weakened the state, and contributed to the overthrow of the dynasty a few decades later. Repeatedly in Chinese history, such peasant movements, often expressed in religious terms, registered

Yellow Turban Rebellion

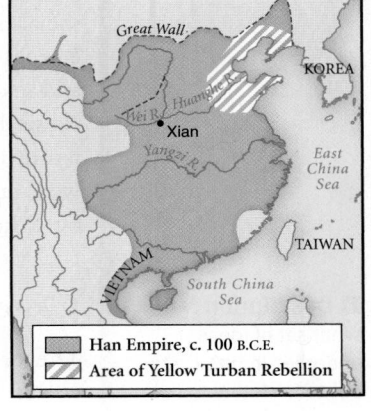

Great Wall
KOREA
Wei R.
Huang He
Xian
Yangzi R.
East China Sea
TAIWAN
VIETNAM
South China Sea

☐ Han Empire, c. 100 B.C.E.
▨ Area of Yellow Turban Rebellion

the sharp class antagonisms of Chinese society and led to the collapse of more than one ruling dynasty.

Merchants

Peasants were oppressed in China and certainly exploited, but they were also honored and celebrated in the official ideology of the state. In the eyes of the scholar-gentry, peasants were the solid productive backbone of the country, and their hard work and endurance in the face of difficulties were worthy of praise. Merchants, however, did not enjoy such a favorable reputation in the eyes of China's cultural elite. They were widely viewed as unproductive, making a shameful profit from selling the work of others. Stereotyped as greedy, luxury-loving, and materialistic, merchants stood in contrast to the alleged frugality, altruism, and cultured tastes of the scholar-gentry. They were also seen as a social threat, as their ill-gained wealth impoverished others, deprived the state of needed revenues, and fostered resentments.

Such views lay behind periodic efforts by state authorities to rein in merchant activity and to keep them under control. Early in the Han dynasty, merchants were forbidden to wear silk clothing, ride horses, or carry arms. Nor were they permitted to sit for civil service examinations or hold public office. State monopolies on profitable industries such as salt, iron, and alcohol served to limit merchant opportunities. Later dynasties sometimes forced merchants to loan large sums of money to the state. Despite this active discrimination, merchants frequently became quite wealthy. Some tried to achieve a more respectable elite status by purchasing landed estates or educating their sons for the civil service examinations. Many had backdoor relationships with state officials and landlords who found them useful and were not averse to profiting from business connections with merchants, despite their unsavory reputation.

Class and Caste in India

India's social organization shared certain broad features with that of China. In both civilizations, birth determined social status for most people; little social mobility was available for the vast majority; sharp distinctions and great inequalities characterized social life; and religious or cultural traditions defined these inequalities as natural, eternal, and ordained by the gods. Despite these similarities, the organization, flavor, and texture of ancient Indian society were distinctive compared to almost all other classical civilizations. These unique aspects of Indian society have long been embodied in what we now call the caste system, a term that comes from the Portuguese word *casta*, which means "race" or "purity of blood." That social organization emerged over thousands of years and in some respects has endured into modern times.

■ Description
What set of ideas underlies India's caste-based society?

Caste as Varna

The origins of the caste system are at best hazy. An earlier theory—that caste evolved from a racially defined encounter between light-skinned Aryan invaders and the darker-hued native peoples—has been challenged in recent years, but no clear alternative has emerged. Perhaps the best we can say at this point is that the distinctive social system of classical India grew out of the interaction of many culturally different peoples on the South Asian peninsula together with the development of economic and social differences among these peoples as the inequalities of "civilization" spread in the Ganges River valley and beyond. Notions of race, however, seem less central to the growth of the caste system than those of economic specialization and of culture.

By the beginning of the classical era, around 500 B.C.E., the idea that society was forever divided into four ranked classes known as *varna* was deeply embedded in Indian thinking. Everyone was born into and remained within one of these classes for life. At the top of this hierarchical system were the Brahmins, priests whose rituals and sacrifices alone could ensure the proper functioning of the world. They were followed by the Kshatriya class, warriors and rulers charged with protecting and governing society. Next was the Vaisya class, originally commoners who cultivated the land. These three classes came to be regarded as pure Aryans and were called the "twice-born," for they experienced not only a physical birth but also formal initiation into their respective varnas and status as people of Aryan descent. Far below these twice-born in the hierarchy of varna groups were the Sudras, native peoples incorporated into the margins of Aryan society in very subordinate positions. Regarded as servants of their social betters, they were not allowed to hear or repeat the Vedas or to take part in Aryan rituals. So little were they valued that a Brahmin who killed a Sudra was penalized as if he had killed a cat or a dog.

According to varna theory, these four classes were formed from the body of the god Purusha and were therefore eternal and changeless. Although these divisions are widely recognized in India even today, historians have noted considerable social flux in ancient Indian history. Members of the Brahmin and Kshatriya groups, for example, were frequently in conflict over which ranked highest in the varna hierarchy, and only slowly did the Brahmins emerge clearly in the top position. Both of them, although theoretically purely Aryan, absorbed various tribal peoples as classical Indian civilization expanded. Tribal medicine men or sorcerers found a place as Brahmins, while warrior groups entered the Kshatriya varna. The Vaisya varna, originally defined as cultivators, evolved into a business class with a prominent place for

India's Untouchables
Although the Indian constitution of 1950 legally abolished "untouchability," active discrimination persists against this lowest group in the caste hierarchy, now known as Dalits, or the oppressed. Sweeping is just one of many Dalit occupations; here several sweepers perform their tasks in front of an upper-caste home. (Lindsay Hebberd/Corbis)

merchants, while the Sudra varna became the domain of peasant farmers. Finally a whole new category, ranking lower even than the Sudras, emerged in the so-called untouchables, people who did the work considered most unclean and polluting, such as cremating corpses, dealing with the skins of dead animals, and serving as executioners.

Snapshot   Social Life and Duty in Classical India

Much personal behavior in classical India, at least ideally, was regulated according to caste. Each caste was associated with a particular color, with a part of the body of the god Purusha, and with a set of duties.

Caste (Varna)	Color/Symbolism	Part of Purusha	Duties
Brahmin	white/spirituality	head	priests, teachers
Kshatriya	red/courage	shoulders	warriors, rulers
Vaisya	yellow/wealth	thighs	farmers, merchants, artisans
Sudra	black/ignorance	feet	labor
Untouchables (outside of the varna system; thus no color and not associated with Purusha)	—	—	polluted labor

Beyond caste, behavior was ideally defined in terms of four stages of life, at least for the first three varna groups. Each new stage was marked by a *samskara*, a ritual initiating the person into this new phase of life.

Stage of Life	Duties
Student	Boys live with a teacher (guru); learn Sanskrit, rituals, Vedas; practice obedience, respect, celibacy, nonviolence.
Householder	Marriage and family; men practice caste-based career/occupation; women serve as wives and mothers, perform household rituals and sacrifices, actively support children and elders.
Retirement	Both husband and wife withdraw to the forests following birth of grandchildren; diminished household duties; greater focus on spiritual practice; sex permitted once a month.
Wandering ascetic	Only for men (women return to household); total rejection of ordinary existence; life as wandering hermit without shelter or possessions; caste becomes irrelevant; focus on achieving *moksha* and avoiding future rebirth.

Caste as Jati

As the varna system took shape in India, another set of social distinctions also arose, deriving largely from specific occupations. In India as elsewhere, urban-based civilization gave rise to specialized occupations, many organized in guilds that regulated their own affairs in a particular region. Over time, these occupationally based groups, known as *jatis*, blended with the varna system to create classical India's unique caste-based society.

The many thousands of jatis became the primary cell of India's social life beyond the family or household, but each of them was associated with one of the great classes (varnas). Thus Brahmins were divided into many separate jatis, or subcastes, as were each of the other varnas as well as the untouchables. In a particular region or village, each jati was ranked in a hierarchy known to all, from the highest of the Brahmins to the lowest of the untouchables. Marriage and eating together were permitted only within an individual's own jati. Each jati was associated with a particular set of duties, rules, and obligations, which defined its members' unique and separate place in the larger society. Brahmins, for example, were forbidden to eat meat, while Kshatriyas were permitted to do so. Upper-caste women, of course, covered their breasts, while some lower-caste women were forbidden to do so as a sign of their lower ranking. "It is better to do one's own duty badly than another's well"—this frequently quoted saying summed up the underlying idea of Indian society.[4]

With its many separate, distinct, and hierarchically ranked social groups, Indian society was quite different from that of China or the Greco-Roman world. It was also unique in the set of ideas that explained and justified that social system. Foremost among them was the notion of ritual purity and pollution applied to caste groups. Brahmins or other high-caste people who came in contact with members of lower castes, especially those who cleaned latrines, handled corpses, or butchered and skinned dead animals, were in great danger of being polluted, or made ritually unclean. Thus untouchables were forbidden to use the same wells or to enter the temples designated for higher-caste people. Sometimes they were required to wear a wooden clapper to warn others of their approach. A great body of Indian religious writing defined various forms of impurity and the ritual means of purification.

A further support for this idea of inherent inequality and permanent difference derived from emerging Hindu notions of *karma, dharma,* and rebirth. Being born into a particular caste was generally regarded as reflecting the good or bad deeds (karma) of a previous life. Thus an individual's own prior actions were responsible for his or her current status. Any hope for rebirth in a higher caste rested on the faithful and selfless performance of one's present caste duties (dharma) in this life. Doing so contributed to spiritual progress by subduing the relentless demands of the ego. Such teachings, like that of permanent impurity, provided powerful ideological support for the inequalities of Indian society. So too did the threat of social

■ **Comparison**
What is the difference between varna and jati as expressions of classical India's caste system?

ostracism, because each jati had the authority to expel members who violated its rules. No greater catastrophe could befall a person than this, for it meant the end of any recognized social life and the loss of all social support.

As caste restrictions tightened, it became increasingly difficult—virtually impossible—for individuals to raise their social status during their lifetimes, but another kind of upward mobility enabled entire jatis, over several generations, to raise their standing in the local hierarchy of caste groups. By acquiring land or wealth, by adopting the behaviors of higher-caste groups, by finding some previously overlooked "ancestor" of a higher caste, a particular jati might slowly be redefined in a higher category. Thus India's caste system was in practice rather more fluid and changing than the theory of caste might suggest.

■ **Comparison**
How did India's caste system differ from China's class system?

India's social system thus differed from that of China in several ways. It gave priority to religious status and ritual purity (the Brahmins), whereas China elevated political officials to the highest of elite positions. The caste system divided Indian society into vast numbers of distinct social groups; China had fewer, but broader, categories of society—scholar-gentry, landlords, peasants, merchants. Finally, India's caste society defined these social groups far more rigidly and with even less opportunity for social mobility than in China.

The Functions of Caste

A caste-based social structure shaped India's classical civilization in various ways. Because caste (jati) was a very local phenomenon, rooted in particular regions or villages, it focused the loyalties of most people on a quite restricted territory and weakened the appeal or authority of larger all-Indian states. This localization is one reason that India, unlike China, seldom experienced an empire that encompassed the entire subcontinent (see Chapter 4). Caste, together with the shared culture of Hinduism, provided a substitute for the state as an integrative mechanism for Indian civilization. It offered a distinct and socially recognized place for almost everyone. In looking after widows, orphans, and the destitute, jatis provided a modest measure of social security and support. Even the lowest-ranking jatis had the right to certain payments from the social superiors whom they served.

Furthermore, caste represented a means of accommodating the many migrating or invading peoples who entered the subcontinent. The cellular, or honeycomb, structure of caste society allowed various peoples, cultures, and traditions to find a place within a larger Indian civilization while retaining something of their unique identity. The process of assimilation was quite different in China, however; incorporation into Chinese civilization meant becoming Chinese ethnically, linguistically, and culturally. Finally, India's caste system facilitated the exploitation of the poor by the wealthy and powerful. The multitude of separate groups into which it divided the impoverished and oppressed majority of the population made class consciousness and organized resistance across caste lines much more difficult to achieve.

Slavery in the Classical Era: The Case of the Roman Empire

Beyond the inequalities of class and caste lay those of slavery, a social institution with deep roots in human history. One scholar has suggested that the early domestication of animals provided the model for enslaving people.[5] Certainly slave owners have everywhere compared their slaves to tamed animals. Aristotle, for example, observed that the ox is "the poor man's slave." War, patriarchy, and the notion of private property, all of which accompanied the First Civilizations, also contributed to the growth of slavery. Large-scale warfare generated numerous prisoners, and everywhere in the ancient world capture in war meant the possibility of enslavement. Early records suggest that women captives were the first slaves, usually raped and then enslaved as concubines, whereas male captives were killed. Patriarchal societies, in which men sharply controlled and perhaps even "owned" women, may have suggested the possibility of using other people, men as well as women, as slaves. The class inequalities of early civilizations, which were based on great differences in privately owned property, also made it possible to imagine people owning other people.

Slavery and Civilization

Whatever its precise origins, slavery generally meant ownership by a master, the possibility of being sold, working without pay, and the status of an "outsider" at the bottom of the social hierarchy. For most, it was a kind of "social death,"[6] for slaves usually lacked any rights or independent personal identity recognized by the larger society. By the time Hammurabi's law code casually referred to Mesopotamian slavery (around 1750 B.C.E.), it was already a long-established tradition in the region and in all of the First Civilizations. Likewise, virtually all subsequent civilizations—in the Americas, Africa, and Eurasia—practiced some form of slavery.

■ **Comparison**
How did the inequalities of slavery differ from those of caste?

Slave systems throughout history have varied considerably. In some times and places, such as classical Greece and Rome, a fair number of slaves might be emancipated in their own lifetimes, through the generosity or religious convictions of their owners, or to avoid caring for them in old age, or by allowing slaves to purchase their freedom with their own funds. In some societies, the children of slaves inherited the status of their parents, while in others, such as the Aztec Empire, they were considered free people. Slaves likewise varied considerably in the labor they were required to do, with some working for the state in high positions, others performing domestic duties in their owner's household, and still others toiling in fields or mines in large work gangs.

The classical civilizations of Eurasia differed considerably in the prominence and extent of slavery in their societies. In China, it was a minor element, amounting to perhaps 1 percent of the population. Convicted criminals and their families, confiscated by the government and sometimes sold to wealthy private individuals, were among the earliest slaves in Han dynasty China. In desperate circumstances, impoverished or indebted peasants might sell their children into slavery. In southern China, teenage boys of poor families could be purchased by the wealthy, for whom they served as status symbols. Chinese slavery, however, was never very widespread and did not become a major source of labor for agriculture or manufacturing.

In India as well, people could fall into slavery as criminals, debtors, or prisoners of war and served their masters largely in domestic settings, but religious writings and secular law offered, at least in theory, some protection for slaves. Owners were required to provide adequately for their slaves and were forbidden to abandon them in old age. According to one ancient text, "a man may go short himself or stint his

Snapshot   Comparing Greco-Roman and American Slavery

	Greco-Roman Slavery (500 B.C.E.–500 C.E.)	Slavery in the Americas (1500–1888)
Source of slaves	Majority were prisoners from Roman wars of conquest; victims of pirate kidnapping; obtained through networks of long-distance trade; result of natural reproduction; abandoned children	Derived almost entirely from transatlantic slave trade; many were prisoners of African wars, debtors, or criminals in African societies
Race	Not a major factor	Came to be associated with Africa and "blackness"
Manumission (granting legal freedom to slaves)	Quite common; freed slaves received citizenship in Roman Empire but not in Greece	Much less common, especially in North America; freed slaves were long feared and discriminated against in North America, but less so in Latin America
Roles/Work	No distinction between slave and wage labor; slaves worked at wide variety of jobs, from poets, physicians, scholars, and teachers to field hands and mine laborers	Majority worked as agricultural laborers on plantations producing for export; few held elite occupations
Fate of slavery	Gradual transformation from slavery to serfdom as Roman Empire collapsed; no abolitionist movements; Christianity provided general support for slavery, though some encouragement for manumission	Ended in nineteenth century as a result of slave rebellions, industrialization, and abolitionist movements, some based in Christian teaching; replaced by sharecropping or indentured labor

wife and children, but never his slave who does his dirty work for him."[7] Slaves in India could inherit and own property and earn money in their spare time. A master who raped a slave woman was required to set her free and pay compensation. The law encouraged owners to free their slaves and allowed slaves to buy their freedom. All of this suggests that Indian slavery was more restrained than that of other ancient civilizations. Nor did Indian civilization depend economically on slavery, for most work was performed by lower-caste, though free, people.

The Making of a Slave Society: The Case of Rome

In sharp contrast to other classical civilizations, slavery played an immense role in the Mediterranean, or Western, world. Although slavery was practiced in Chinese, Indian, and Persian civilizations, the Greco-Roman world can be described as a slave society. By a conservative estimate, classical Athens alone was home to perhaps 60,000 slaves, or about one-third of the total population. In Athens, ironically, the growth of democracy and status as a free person were defined and accompanied by the simultaneous growth of slavery on a mass scale. The greatest of the Greek philosophers, Aristotle, developed the notion that some people were "slaves by nature" and should be enslaved for their own good and for that of the larger society.

"The ancient Greek attitude toward slavery was simple," writes one modern scholar. "It was a terrible thing to become a slave, but a good thing to own a slave."[8] Even poor households usually had at least one or two female slaves, providing domestic work and sexual services for their owners. Although substantial numbers of Greek slaves were granted freedom by their owners, they usually did not become citizens or gain political rights. Nor could they own land or marry citizens, and particularly in Athens they had to pay a special tax. Their status remained "halfway between slavery and freedom."[9]

Practiced on an even larger scale, slavery was a defining element of Roman society. By the time of Christ, the Italian heartland of the Roman Empire had some 2 to 3 million slaves, representing 33 to 40 percent of the population.[10] Not until the modern slave societies of the Caribbean, Brazil, and the southern United States was slavery practiced again on such an enormous scale. Wealthy Romans could own many hundreds or even thousands of slaves. One woman in the fifth century C.E. freed 8,000 slaves when she withdrew into a life of Christian monastic practice.

■ **Comparison**
How did Greco-Roman slavery differ from that of other classical civilizations?

Roman Slavery
This Roman mosaic from the third century C.E. shows the slave Myro serving a drink to his master, Fructus. (Bardo Museum Tunis/Gianni Dagli Orti/The Art Archive)

Even people of modest means frequently owned two or three slaves. In doing so, they confirmed their own position as free people, demonstrated their social status, and expressed their ability to exercise power. Slaves and former slaves also might be slave owners. One freedman during the reign of Augustus owned 4,116 slaves at the time of his death. (For the role of slaves in Roman Pompeii, see Visual Sources: Pompeii as a Window on the Roman World, pp. 272–79.)

The vast majority of Roman slaves had been prisoners captured in the many wars that accompanied the creation of the empire. In 146 B.C.E., following the destruction of the North African city of Carthage, some 55,000 people were enslaved en masse. From all over the Mediterranean basin, such people were funneled into the major slave-owning regions of Italy and Sicily. Pirates also furnished slaves, kidnapping tens of thousands of people and selling them to Roman slave traders on the island of Delos. Roman merchants purchased still other slaves through networks of long-distance commerce extending to the Black Sea, the East African coast, and northwestern Europe. The supply of slaves also occurred through natural reproduction, as the children of slave mothers were regarded as slaves themselves. Such "home-born" slaves had a certain prestige and were thought to be less troublesome than those who had known freedom earlier in their lives. Finally, abandoned or exposed children could legally become the slave of anyone who rescued them.

Unlike New World slavery of later times, Roman slavery was not identified with a particular racial or ethnic group. Egyptians, Syrians, Jews, Greeks, Gauls, North Africans, and many other people found themselves alike enslaved. From within the empire and its adjacent regions, an enormous diversity of people were bought and sold at Roman slave markets.

Like slave owners everywhere, Romans regarded their slaves as "barbarians"— lazy, unreliable, immoral, prone to thieving—and came to think of certain peoples, such as Asiatic Greeks, Syrians, and Jews, as slaves by nature. Nor was there any serious criticism of slavery in principle, although on occasion owners were urged to treat their slaves in a more benevolent way. Even the triumph of Christianity within the Roman Empire did little to undermine slavery, for Christian teaching held that slaves should be "submissive to [their] masters with all fear, not only to the good and gentle, but also to the harsh."[11] In fact, Saint Paul used the metaphor of slavery to describe the relationship of believers to God, styling them as "slaves of Christ," while Saint Augustine (354–430 C.E.) described slavery as God's punishment for sin. Thus slavery was deeply embedded in the religious thinking and social outlook of elite Romans.

Similarly, slavery was entrenched throughout the Roman economy. No occupation was off-limits to slaves except military service, and no distinction existed between jobs for slaves and those for free people. Frequently they labored side by side. In rural areas, slaves provided much of the labor force on the huge estates, or *latifundia*, which produced grain, olive oil, and wine, mostly for export, much like the later plantations in the Americas. There they often worked chained together. In the cities, slaves worked in their owners' households, but also as skilled artisans, teachers, doctors, business agents, entertainers, and actors. In the empire's many mines and quarries, slaves and criminals labored under brutal conditions. Slaves in the service of the emperor provided manpower for the state bureaucracy, maintained temples and shrines, and kept Rome's water supply system functioning. Trained in special schools, they also served as gladiators in the violent spectacles of Roman public life. Thus slaves were represented among the highest and most prestigious occupations and in the lowest and most degraded.

Slave owners in the Roman Empire were supposed to provide the necessities of life to their slaves. When this occurred, slaves may have had a more secure life than was available to impoverished free people, who had to fend for themselves, but the price of this security was absolute subjection to the will of the master. Beatings, sexual abuse, and sale to another owner were constant possibilities. Lacking all rights in the law, slaves could not legally marry, although many contracted unofficial unions. Slaves often accumulated money or possessions, but such property legally belonged to their masters and could be seized at any time. If a slave murdered his master, Roman law demanded the lives of all of the victim's slaves. When one Roman official was killed by a slave in 61 C.E., every one of his 400 slaves was condemned to death. For an individual slave, the quality of life depended almost entirely on the character of the master. Brutal owners made it a living hell. Benevolent owners made life tolerable and might even grant favored slaves their freedom or permit them to buy that freedom. As in Greece, manumission of slaves was a widespread practice, and in the Roman Empire, unlike Greece, freedom was accompanied by citizenship.

Resistance and Rebellion

Roman slaves, like their counterparts in other societies, responded to enslavement in many ways. Most, no doubt, did what they had to simply to survive, but there are recorded cases of Roman prisoners of war who chose to commit mass suicide rather than face the horrors of slavery. Others, once enslaved, resorted to the "weapons of the weak"—small-scale theft, sabotage, pretending illness, working poorly, and placing curses on their masters. Fleeing to the anonymous crowds of the city or to remote rural areas prompted owners to post notices in public places, asking for information about their runaways. Catching runaway slaves became an organized private business. Occasional murders of slave owners made masters conscious of the dangers they faced. "Every slave we own is an enemy we harbor" ran one Roman saying.[12]

On several notable occasions, the slaves themselves rose in rebellion. The most famous uprising occurred in 73 B.C.E. when a slave gladiator named Spartacus led seventy other slaves from a school for gladiators in a desperate bid for freedom. The surprising initial success of their revolt attracted a growing following of rebellious slaves, numbering perhaps 120,000 at the height of the uprising. For two years, they set Italy ablaze. In a dramatic reversal of roles, they crucified some captured slave owners and set others to fighting one another in the style of gladiators. Following a series of remarkable military victories, the movement split and eventually succumbed

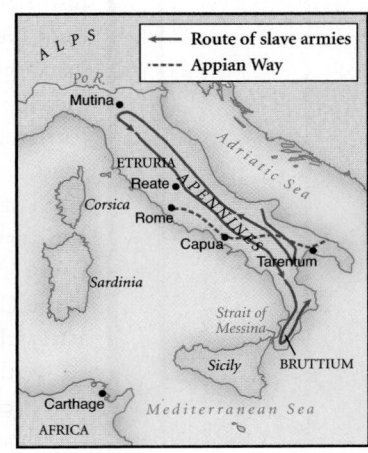

The Rebellion of Spartacus

to the vastly superior numbers of the Roman legions. A terrible vengeance followed as some 6,000 rebel slaves were nailed to crosses along the Appian Way from Rome to Capua, where the revolt had begun.

Nothing on the scale of the Spartacus rebellion occurred again in the Western world of slavery until the Haitian Revolution of the 1790s. But Haitian rebels sought the creation of a new society free of slavery altogether. None of the Roman slave rebellions, including that of Spartacus, had any such overall plan or goal. They simply wanted to escape Roman slavery themselves. Although rebellions created a perpetual fear in the minds of slave owners, the slave system itself was hardly affected.

Comparing Patriarchies of the Classical Era

No division of human society has held greater significance for the lives of individuals than that between male and female. Every human community has elaborated that basic biological difference into a gender system that sought to define masculinity and femininity and to determine the appropriate roles and positions of men and women in the larger society. At least since the emergence of the First Civilizations, those gender systems have been everywhere patriarchal, featuring the dominance of men over women in the family and in society generally. More widespread than slavery, these inequalities of gender, like those of class or caste, shaped the character of the classical civilizations.

In all of them, men were regarded as superior to women, and sons were generally preferred over daughters. Men had legal and property rights unknown to most women. Public life in general was a male domain, while women's roles—both productive and reproductive—took place mostly in domestic settings. Frequently men could marry more than one woman and claimed the right to regulate the social and sexual lives of the wives, daughters, and sisters in their families. Widely seen as weak and feared as potentially disruptive, women required the protection and control of men.

These common elements of patriarchy have been so widespread and pervasive that historians have been slow to recognize that gender systems evolved, changing over time. New agricultural technologies, the rise or decline of powerful states, the incorporation of world religions, interaction with culturally different peoples—all of these developments and more generated significant change in gender systems. Nor has patriarchy been everywhere the same. Restrictions on women were far sharper in classical civilizations than in those pastoral or agricultural societies that lay beyond the reach of urban centers and powerful empires. The degree and expression of patriarchy also varied from one civilization to another, as the discussion of Mesopotamia and Egypt in Chapter 3 illustrated. (See the Documents: Patriarchy and Women's Voices in the Classical Era, pp. 262–71, for various expressions of and reactions to patriarchy across classical Eurasia.)

Within particular civilizations, gender interacted with class to generate usually a more restricted life for upper-class women, who were largely limited to the home and the management of servants. In contrast, lower-class women often had a somewhat freer but more burdensome life, for economic necessity required them to work in the fields, to shop in the streets, or to serve in the homes of their social superiors. China provides a fascinating example of how patriarchy changed over time, while the contrasting patriarchies of Athens and Sparta illustrate clear variations even within the limited world of Greek civilization.

A Changing Patriarchy: The Case of China

Chinese Women Musicians
This tenth-century rendering by the painter Gu Hongzhong shows these upper-class women serving as musicians for a high official of a Tang dynasty emperor. It was titled *The Night Revels of Han Xizai*. The painter was apparently sent by the emperor to spy on the suspicious behavior of the minister, who in various tellings was suspected of either rebellion or undignified activity. (Werner Forman/Art Resource, NY)

As Chinese civilization took shape during the Han dynasty, elite thinking about gender issues became more explicitly patriarchal, more clearly defined, and linked to an emerging Confucian ideology (see Document 6.1, pp. 262–63, and Document 6.2, pp. 263–66). Long-established patterns of thinking in terms of pairs of opposites were now described in gendered and unequal terms. The superior principle of *yang* was viewed as masculine and related to heaven, rulers, strength, rationality, and light, whereas *yin*, the lower feminine principle, was associated with the earth, subjects, weakness, emotion, and darkness. Thus female inferiority was permanent and embedded in the workings of the universe.

■ **Change**
In what ways did the expression of Chinese patriarchy change over time, and why did it change?

What this meant more practically was spelled out repeatedly over the centuries in various Confucian texts. Two notions in particular summarized the ideal position of women, at least in the eyes of elite male writers. The adage "Men go out, women stay in" emphasized the public and political roles of men in contrast to the domestic and private domain of women. A second idea, known as the "three obediences," emphasized a woman's subordination first to her father, then to her husband, and finally to her son. "Why is it," asked one text, "that according to the rites the man takes his wife, whereas the woman leaves her house [to join her husband's family]? It is because the *yin* is lowly, and should not have the initiative; it proceeds to the *yang* in order to be completed."[13]

The Chinese woman writer and court official Ban Zhao (45–116 C.E.), whose *Lessons for Women* is excerpted in Document 6.2, pages 263–66, observed that the ancients had practiced three customs when a baby girl was born. She was placed below the bed to show that she was "lowly and weak," required always to "humble herself before others." Then she was given a piece of broken pottery to play with, signifying that "her primary duty [was] to be industrious." Finally, her birth was announced to the ancestors with an offering to indicate that she was responsible for "the continuation of [ancestor] worship in the home."[14]

Chinese Women at Work
For a long time, the spinning and weaving of cloth were part of women's domestic work in China. So too was fishing, as illustrated by the woman at the bottom right of this Chinese painting. (Palace Museum, Beijing)

Yet such notions of passivity, inferiority, and subordination were not the whole story of women's lives in classical China. A few women, particularly the wives, concubines, or widows of emperors, were able on occasion to exercise considerable political authority. In doing so, they provoked much antifemale hostility on the part of male officials, who often blamed the collapse of a dynasty or natural disasters on the "unnatural" and "disruptive" influence of women in political affairs. A number of writers, however, praised women of virtue as wise counselors to their fathers, husbands, and rulers and depicted them positively as active agents.[15]

Within her husband's family, a young woman was clearly subordinate as a wife and daughter-in-law, but as a mother of sons, she was accorded considerable honor for her role in producing the next generation of male heirs to carry on her husband's lineage. When her sons married, she was able to exercise the significant authority of a mother-in-law. Furthermore, a woman, at least in the upper classes, often brought with her a considerable dowry, which was regarded as her own property and gave her some leverage within her marriage. Women's roles in the production of textiles, often used to pay taxes or to sell commercially, made her labor quite valuable to the family economy. And a man's wife was sharply distinguished from his concubines, for the wife alone produced the legitimate heirs who could carry on the family tradition. Thus women's lives were more complex and varied than the prescriptions of Confucian orthodoxy might suggest.

Much changed in China following the collapse of the Han dynasty in the third century C.E. Centralized government vanished amid much political fragmentation and conflict. Confucianism, the main ideology of Han China, was discredited, while Daoism and Buddhism attracted a growing following. Pastoral and nomadic people invaded northern China and ruled a number of the small states that had replaced the Han government. These new conditions resulted in some loosening of the strict patriarchy of classical China over the next five or six centuries.

The cultural influence of nomadic peoples, whose women were far less restricted than those of China, was noticed, and criticized, by more Confucian-minded male observers. One of them lamented the sad deterioration of gender roles under the influence of nomadic peoples:

> In the north of the Yellow river it is usually the wife who runs the household. She will not dispense with good clothing or expensive jewelry. The husband has to settle for old horses and sickly servants. The traditional niceties between hus-

band and wife are seldom observed, and from time to time he even has to put up with her insults.[16]

Others criticized the adoption of nomadic styles of dress, makeup, and music. By the time of the Tang dynasty (618–907), writers and artists depicted elite women as capable of handling legal and business affairs on their own and on occasion riding horses and playing polo, bareheaded and wearing men's clothing. Tang legal codes even recognized a married daughter's right to inherit property from her family of birth. Such images of women were quite different from those of Han dynasty China.

A further sign of a weakening patriarchy and the cause of great distress to advocates of Confucian orthodoxy lay in the unusual reign of Empress Wu (reigned 690–705 C.E.), a former high-ranking concubine in the imperial court, who came to power amid much palace intrigue and was the only woman ever to rule China with the title of emperor. With the support of China's growing Buddhist establishment, Empress Wu governed despotically, but she also consolidated China's civil service examination system for the selection of public officials and actively patronized scholarship and the arts. Some of her actions seem deliberately designed to elevate the position of women. She commissioned the biographies of famous women, decreed that the mourning period for mothers be made equal to that for fathers, and ordered the creation of a Chinese character for "human being" that suggested the process of birth flowing from one woman without a prominent male role. Her reign was brief and unrepeated.

The growing popularity of Daoism provided new images of the feminine and new roles for women. Daoist texts referred to the *dao* as "mother" and urged the traditionally feminine virtues of yielding and passive acceptance rather than the male-oriented striving of Confucianism. Daoist sects often featured women as priests, nuns, or reclusive meditators, able to receive cosmic truth and to use it for the benefit of others. A variety of female deities from Daoist or Buddhist traditions found a place in Chinese village religion,[17] while growing numbers of women found an alternative to family life in Buddhist monasteries. None of this meant an end to patriarchy, but it does suggest some change in the tone and expression of that patriarchy.

Contrasting Patriarchies in Athens and Sparta

The patriarchies of the classical era not only fluctuated over time but also varied considerably from place to place. Nowhere is this variation more apparent than in the contrasting cases of Athens and Sparta, two of the leading city-states of classical Greek civilization (see Map 4.2, p. 148). Even within the small area of classical Greece, the opportunities available to women and the restrictions imposed on them differed substantially. Although Athens has been celebrated as a major source of Western democracy and rationalism, its posture toward women was far more negative and restrictive

■ **Comparison**

How did the patriarchies of Athens and Sparta differ from each other?

Women of Athens
This painting on a seventh-century B.C.E. ceramic vase shows Athenian women gathering water at a fountain. (Museo di Villa Giulia Rome/ Gianni Dagli Orti/The Art Archive)

than that of the highly militaristic and much less democratic Sparta.

In the several centuries between about 700 and 400 B.C.E., as the men of Athens moved toward unprecedented freedom and participation in political life, the city's women experienced growing limitations. They had no role whatsoever in the assembly, the councils, or the juries of Athens, which were increasingly the focus of life for free men. In legal matters, women had to be represented by a guardian, and court proceedings did not even refer to them by name, but only as someone's wife or mother.

Greek thinkers, especially Aristotle, provided a set of ideas that justified women's exclusion from public life and their general subordination to men. According to Aristotle, "a woman is, as it were, an infertile male. She is female in fact on account of a kind of inadequacy." That inadequacy lay in her inability to generate sperm, which contained the "form" or the "soul" of a new human being. Her role in the reproductive process was passive, providing a receptacle for the vital male contribution. Compared often to children or domesticated animals, women were associated with instinct and passion and lacked the rationality to take part in public life. "It is the best for all tame animals to be ruled by human beings," wrote Aristotle. "For this is how they are kept alive. In the same way, the relationship between the male and the female is by nature such that the male is higher, the female lower, that the male rules and the female is ruled."[18]

As in China, proper Greek women were expected to remain inside the home, except perhaps for religious festivals or funerals. Even within the home, women's space was quite separate from that of men. Although poorer women, courtesans, and prostitutes had to leave their homes to earn money, collect water, or shop, ideal behavior for upper-class women assigned these tasks to slaves or to men and involved a radical segregation of male and female space. "What causes women a bad reputation," wrote the Greek playwright Euripides in *The Trojan Women*, "is not remaining inside."

Within the domestic realm, Athenian women were generally married in their mid-teens to men ten to fifteen years older than themselves. Their main function was the management of domestic affairs and the production of sons who would become citizens. These sons were expected to become literate, while their sisters were normally limited to learning spinning, weaving, and other household tasks. The Greek writer Menander exclaimed: "Teaching a woman to read and write? What a terrible thing to do! Like feeding a vile snake on more poison." Nor did women have much economic power. Although they could own personal property obtained through dowry, gifts, or inheritance, land was passed through male heirs, with a few exceptions. By law, women were forbidden to buy or sell land and could negotiate contracts only if the sum involved was valued at less than a bushel of barley.

There were exceptions, although rare, to the restricted lives of Athenian women, the most notable of which was Aspasia (ca. 470–400 B.C.E.). She was born in the Greek city of Miletus, on the western coast of Anatolia, to a wealthy family that believed in educating its daughters. As a young woman, Aspasia found her way to Athens, where her foreign birth gave her somewhat more freedom than was normally available to the women of that city. She soon attracted the attention of Pericles, Athens's leading political figure. The two lived together as husband and wife until Pericles' death in 429 B.C.E., although they were not officially married. Treated as an equal partner by Pericles, Aspasia proved to be a learned and witty conversationalist who moved freely in the cultured circles of Athens. Her foreign birth and her apparent influence on Pericles provoked critics to suggest that she was a *hetaera,* a professional, educated, high-class entertainer and sexual companion, similar to a Japanese geisha. Although little is known about her, a number of major Athenian writers commented about her, both positively and negatively. She was, by all accounts, a rare and remarkable woman in a city that offered little opportunity for individuality or achievement to its female population.

The evolution of Sparta differed in many ways from that of Athens. Early on, Sparta solved the problem of feeding a growing population, not by creating overseas colonies as did many Greek city-states, but by conquering their immediate neighbors and reducing them to a status of permanent servitude, not far removed from slavery. Called *helots,* these dependents far outnumbered the free citizens of Sparta and represented a permanent threat of rebellion. Solving this problem shaped Spartan society decisively. Sparta's answer was a militaristic regime, constantly ready for war to keep the helots in their place. To maintain such a system, all boys were removed from their families at the age of seven to be trained by the state in military camps, where they learned the ways of war. There they remained until the age of thirty. The ideal Spartan male was a warrior, skilled in battle, able to endure hardship, and willing to die for his city. Mothers are said to have told their sons departing for battle to "come back with your shield . . . or on it." Although economic equality for men was the ideal, it was never completely realized in practice. And unlike Athens, political power was exercised primarily by a small group of wealthy men.

This militaristic and far-from-democratic system had implications for women that, strangely enough, offered them greater freedoms and fewer restrictions. Their central task was reproduction—bearing warrior sons for Sparta. To strengthen their bodies for childbearing, girls were encouraged to take part in sporting events—running, wrestling, throwing the discus and javelin, even driving chariots. At times, they competed in the nude before mixed audiences. Their education, like that of boys, was prescribed by the state, which also insisted that newly married women cut their hair short, unlike adult Greek women elsewhere. Thus Spartan women were not secluded or segregated, as were their Athenian counterparts. Furthermore,

A Girl of Sparta
This figurine portrays a young female Spartan athlete or runner. Compare her clothing with that worn by the Athenian women depicted on the vase (shown on page 256. (National Archaeological Museum, Athens/Archaeological Receipts Fund)

Spartan young women, unlike those of Athens, usually married men of their own age, about eighteen years old, thus putting the new couple on a more equal basis. Marriage often began with a trial period to make sure the new couple could produce children, with divorce and remarriage readily available if they could not. Because men were so often away at war or preparing for it, women exercised much more authority in the household than was the case in Athens.

It is little wonder that the freedom of Spartan women appalled other Greeks, who believed that it undermined good order and state authority. Aristotle complained that the more egalitarian inheritance practices of Spartans led to their women controlling some 40 percent of landed estates. In Sparta, he declared, women "live in every sort of intemperance and luxury" and "the [male] rulers are ruled by women." Plutarch, a Greek writer during the heyday of the Roman Empire, observed critically that "the men of Sparta always obeyed their wives." The clothing worn by Spartan women to give them greater freedom of movement seemed immodest to other Greeks.

Nonetheless, in another way, Sparta may have been more restrictive than Athens and other Greek city-states, particularly in its apparent prohibition of homosexuality. At least this was the assertion of the Athenian writer Xenophon (427–355 B.C.E.), who stated that Sparta's legendary founder Lycurgus "caused lovers to abstain from sexual intercourse with boys."[19] Elsewhere, however, homoerotic relationships were culturally approved and fairly common for both men and women, although this did not prevent their participants from entering heterosexual marriages as well. The ideal homosexual relationship—between an older man and a young adolescent boy—was viewed as limited in time, for it was supposed to end when the boy's beard began to grow. Unlike contemporary Western societies where sexuality is largely seen as an identity, the ancient Greeks viewed sexual choice more casually and as a matter of taste.

Sparta clearly was a patriarchy, with women serving as breeding machines for its military system and lacking any formal role in public life, but it was a lighter patriarchy than that of Athens. The joint efforts of men and women seemed necessary to maintain a huge class of helots in permanent subjugation. Death in childbirth was considered the equivalent of death in battle, for both contributed to the defense of Sparta, and both were honored alike. In Athens, on the other hand, growing freedom and democracy were associated with the strengthening of the male-dominated, property-owning household, and within that household men, the cornerstone of Athenian society, were expected to exercise authority. Doing so required increasingly severe limitations and restrictions on the lives of women. Together, the cases of Athens and Sparta illustrate how the historical record appears different when viewed through the lens of gender. Athens, so celebrated for its democracy and philosophical rationalism, offered little to its women, whereas Sparta, often condemned for its militarism and virtual enslavement of the helots, provided a somewhat wider scope for the free women of the city.

Reflections: Arguing with Solomon and the Buddha

"What has been will be again; what has been done will be done again; there is nothing new under the sun." Recorded in the Old Testament book of Ecclesiastes and generally attributed to King Solomon, this was a despairing view about the essential changelessness and futility of human life. In contrast, central to Buddhist teachings has been the concept of "impermanence"—the notion that "everything changes; nothing remains without change." These observations from classical-era thinkers were intended to point to other levels of reality that lay beyond the dreary constancy or the endless changeability of this world. For students of history, however, these comments from Solomon and the Buddha serve to focus attention on issues of change and continuity in the historical record of classical Eurasian civilizations. What is more impressive—the innovations and changes or the enduring patterns and lasting features of these civilizations?

Clearly there were some new things under the sun, even if they had roots in earlier times. The Greek conquest of the Persian Empire under the leadership of Alexander the Great was both novel and unexpected. The Roman Empire encompassed the entire Mediterranean basin in a single political system for the first time. Buddhism and Christianity emerged as new, distinct, and universal religious traditions, although both bore the marks of their origin in Hindu and Jewish religious thinking respectively. The collapse of dynasties, empires, and civilizations long thought to be solidly entrenched—the Chinese and Roman, for example—must surely have seemed to people of the time as something new under the sun. Historians therefore might take issue with Solomon's dictum, should we seek to apply it to the history of the classical era.

Students of the past might also argue a little with the Buddha and his insistence on the "impermanence" of everything. Much that was created in the classical era—particularly its social and cultural patterns—has demonstrated an impressive continuity over many centuries, even if it also changed in particular ways over time. China's scholar-gentry class retained its prominence throughout the ups and downs of changing dynasties and into the twentieth century. India's caste-based social structure still endures as a way of thinking and behaving for hundreds of millions of people on the South Asian peninsula. Although slavery gave way to serfdom in the post-Roman world, it was massively revived in Europe's American colonies after 1500 and remained an important and largely unquestioned feature of all civilizations until the nineteenth century. Patriarchy, with its assumptions of male superiority and dominance, has surely been the most fundamental, long-lasting, and taken-for-granted feature of all civilizations. Not until the twentieth century were those assumptions effectively challenged, but even then patriarchy has continued to shape the lives and the thinking of the vast majority of humankind. And many hundreds of millions of people in the twenty-first century still honor or practice religious and cultural traditions begun during the classical era.

Neither the insight of Solomon nor that of the Buddha, taken alone, offers an effective guide to the study of history, for continuity and change alike have long provided the inextricable warp and woof of historical analysis. Untangling their elusive relationship has figured prominently in the task of historians and has contributed much to the enduring fascination of historical study.

Second Thoughts

What's the Significance?

To assess your mastery of the material in this chapter, visit the **Student Center** at bedfordstmartins.com/strayer.

Wang Mang
China's scholar-gentry class
Yellow Turban Rebellion
caste as varna and jati

"ritual purity" in Indian social practice
Greek and Roman slavery
Spartacus

the "three obediences"
Empress Wu
Aspasia and Pericles
helots

Big Picture Questions

1. What is the difference between class and caste?
2. Why was slavery so much more prominent in Greco-Roman civilization than in India or China?
3. What philosophical, religious, or cultural ideas served to legitimate the class and gender inequalities of classical civilizations?
4. "Social inequality was both accepted and resisted in classical civilizations." What evidence might support this statement?
5. What changes in the patterns of social life of the classical era can you identify? What accounts for these changes?
6. "Cultural and social patterns of civilizations seem to endure longer than the political framework of states and empires." Based on Chapters 4, 5, and 6, would you agree with this statement?

Next Steps: For Further Study

For Web sites and additional documents related to this chapter, see **Make History** at bedfordstmartins.com/strayer.

Jeannine Auboyer, *Daily Life in Ancient India* (2002). A social history of classical India, with a focus on caste, ritual, religion, and art.

Sue Blundell, *Women in Ancient Greece* (1999). A well-written academic study, with occasional humorous stories and anecdotes.

Keith Bradley, *Slavery and Society at Rome* (1994). A scholarly but very readable account of slavery in the Roman Empire.

Michael Lowe, *Everyday Life in Early Imperial China* (1968). A vivid description of social life during the Han dynasty.

Bonnie Smith, ed., *Women's History in Global Perspective*, 3 volumes (2004). A collection of thoughtful essays by major scholars covering world history from ancient times to the twentieth century.

"Women in World History," http://chnm.gmu.edu/wwh/index.html. Documents, reviews, and lesson plans for learning and teaching about women's history in a global context.

Documents

Considering the Evidence:
Patriarchy and Women's Voices in the Classical Era

In American colleges and universities, courses in world history as well as those in women's history and gender history entered the curriculum at about the same time, both of them growing rapidly in the last decades of the twentieth century. During that time, world historians have increasingly sought to address on a global level the issues about gender raised by other historians within a national or local setting:

- How did patriarchy emerge? How was it expressed and experienced? How did it change over time?

- What mix of opportunities and limitations did women encounter in various societies and at various times?

- To what extent were women able to act in the arena of public life and in domestic settings?

- How did different cultural traditions define appropriate gender roles and gender identities, both feminine and masculine?

In exploring such questions, historians face a major problem: the scarcity of sources written by women themselves, especially in the pre-modern era. Furthermore, most of the female-authored sources we do have derive from elite women. As a result, scholars must sometimes make careful use of documents written by men, often "reading between the lines" to discern the perspectives of women. The documents that follow explore various expressions of patriarchy and the women's voices that emerged within them in several of the classical civilizations.

Document 6.1

A Male View of Chinese Women's Lives

In the third century C.E., Fu Xuan, a male poet, described the life of a Chinese woman. Raised as an impoverished orphan, Fu Xuan only later gained fame and wealth owing to his literary talents. Perhaps it was this early experience that allowed him to sympathize with the plight of women.

- What differences between the lives of women and men does the poem highlight?

- What is Fu Xuan's own attitude toward the women he describes?

- In what ways does this portrayal of women's lives reflect or contradict Confucian values? (See pp. 193–95 and Document 5.1, pp. 217–19.)

FU XUAN

How Sad It Is to Be a Woman
Third Century C.E.

How sad it is to be a woman!
Nothing on earth is held so cheap.
Boys stand leaning at the door
Like Gods fallen out of Heaven.
Their hearts brave the Four Oceans,
The wind and dust of a thousand miles.
No one is glad when a girl is born:
By her the family sets no store.
Then she grows up, she hides in her room
Afraid to look a man in the face.
No one cries when she leaves her home—
Sudden as clouds when the rain stops.
She bows her head and composes her face,

Her teeth are pressed on her red lips:
She bows and kneels countless times.
She must humble herself even to the servants.
His love is distant as the stars in Heaven,
Yet the sunflower bends toward the sun.
Their hearts more sundered than water and fire—
A hundred evils are heaped upon her.
Her face will follow the years' changes:
Her lord will find new pleasures.
They that were once like substance and shadow
Are now as far as Hu from Ch'in.°
Yet Hu and Ch'in shall sooner meet
Than they whose parting is like Ts'an and Ch'en.°

Source: Fu Xuan, "How Sad It Is to Be a Woman," in Arthur Waley, *Translations from the Chinese* (New York: Alfred A. Knopf, 1941), 72–73.

°**Hu from Ch'in:** two distant places.

°**Ts'an and Ch'en:** two distant stars.

Document 6.2

A Chinese Woman's Instructions to Her Daughters

Confucius himself apparently said little about women, perhaps reflecting his assumptions about their limited importance in Chinese society. Nonetheless, Confucianism as a social philosophy, formulated by the sage's later followers, had profound implications for the lives of women. Those sentiments found expression in the work of Ban Zhao (45–116 C.E.), a remarkable woman born into an elite family with connections to the imperial court. Although she received a fine literary education, she was married at the age of fourteen, gave birth to several children, and was widowed early in life. Although she never remarried, Ban Zhao had a significant career as a court historian and as an adviser to the empress-dowager (the widow of a deceased emperor). Her most famous work, *Lessons for Women*, was an effort to apply the principles of Confucianism to the lives and behavior of women.

- Why do you think Ban Zhao began her work in such a self-deprecating manner?

- In what ways does *Lessons for Women* reflect Confucian attitudes (see Document 5.1, pp. 217–19)? Why do you think *The Analects* itself seldom referred directly to women?

- How would Ban Zhao define an ideal woman? An ideal man? An ideal marriage?

- In what ways is she critical of existing attitudes and practices regarding women?

- How does she understand the purposes of education for boys and for girls?

- Does *Lessons for Women* support or undermine the view of women's lives that appears in Fu Xuan's poem?

Ban Zhao

Lessons for Women

Late First Century C.E.

I, the unworthy writer, am unsophisticated, unenlightened, and by nature unintelligent, but I am fortunate both to have received not a little favor from my scholarly Father, and to have had a cultured mother and instructresses upon whom to rely for a literary education as well as for training in good manners. More than forty years have passed since at the age of fourteen I took up the dustpan and the broom in the Cao family [the family into which she married]. During this time with trembling heart I feared constantly that I might disgrace my parents, and that I might multiply difficulties for both the women and the men of my husband's family. Day and night I was distressed in heart, but I labored without confessing weariness. Now and

hereafter, however, I know how to escape from such fears.

Being careless, and by nature stupid, I taught and trained my children without system.... I do grieve that you, my daughters, just now at the age for marriage, have not... learned the proper customs for married women. I fear that by failure in good manners in other families you will humiliate both your ancestors and your clan.... At hours of leisure I have composed... these instructions under the title, *Lessons for Women*.

Humility

On the third day after the birth of a girl the ancients observed three customs: first to place the baby below the bed; second to give her a potsherd° with which to play; and third to announce her birth

Source: Nancy Lee Swann, trans., *Pan Chao: Foremost Woman Scholar of China*, (New York: Century, 1932), 82–90.

°**potsherd:** a piece of a broken pot.

to her ancestors by an offering. Now to lay the baby below the bed plainly indicated that she is lowly and weak, and should regard it as her primary duty to humble herself before others. To give her potsherds with which to play indubitably signified that she should practice labor and consider it her primary duty to be industrious. To announce her birth before her ancestors clearly meant that she ought to esteem as her primary duty the continuation of the observance of worship in the home.

These three ancient customs epitomize woman's ordinary way of life and the teachings of the traditional ceremonial rites and regulations. Let a woman modestly yield to others; let her respect others; let her put others first, herself last.... Always let her seem to tremble and to fear. When a woman follows such maxims as these then she may be said to humble herself before others....

Let a woman retire late to bed, but rise early to duties; let her nor dread tasks by day or by night.... When a woman follows such rules as these, then she may be said to be industrious.

Let a woman be correct in manner and upright in character in order to serve her husband.... Let her love not gossip and silly laughter. Let her cleanse and purify and arrange in order the wine and the food for the offerings to the ancestors. When a woman observes such principles as these, then she may be said to continue ancestral worship.

No woman who observes these three fundamentals of life has ever had a bad reputation or has fallen into disgrace. If a woman fails to observe them, how can her name be honored; how can she but bring disgrace upon herself?

Husband and Wife

The Way of husband and wife is intimately connected with Yin and Yang and relates the individual to gods and ancestors. Truly it is the great principle of Heaven and Earth, and the great basis of human relationships....

If a husband be unworthy, then he possesses nothing by which to control his wife. If a wife be unworthy, then she possesses nothing with which to serve her husband. If a husband does not control his wife, then the rules of conduct manifesting his

authority are abandoned and broken. If a wife does not serve her husband, then the proper relationship between men and women and the natural order of things are neglected and destroyed. As a matter of fact the purpose of these two is the same.

Now examine the gentlemen of the present age. They only know that wives must be controlled, and that the husband's rules of conduct manifesting his authority must be established. They therefore teach their boys to read books and study histories. But they do not in the least understand that husbands and masters must also be served, and that the proper relationship and the rites should be maintained. Yet only to teach men and not to teach women—is that not ignoring the essential relation between them? According to the "Rites" [a classic text], it is the rule to begin to teach children to read at the age of eight years, and by the age of fifteen years they ought then to be ready for cultural training. Only why should it not be that girls' education as well as boys' be according to this principle?

Respect and Caution

As Yin and Yang are not of the same nature, so man and woman have different characteristics. The distinctive quality of the Yang is rigidity; the function of the Yin is yielding. Man is honored for strength; a woman is beautiful on account of her gentleness. Hence there arose the common saying: "A man though born like a wolf may, it is feared, become a weak monstrosity; a woman though born like a mouse may, it is feared, become a tiger."

Now for self-culture nothing equals respect for others.... Consequently it can be said that the Way of respect and acquiescence is woman's most important principle of conduct.... Those who are steadfast in devotion know that they should stay in their proper places....

If husband and wife have the habit of staying together, never leaving one another, and following each other around within the limited space of their own rooms, then they will lust after and take liberties with one another. From such action improper language will arise between the two. This kind of discussion may lead to licentiousness. But of licentiousness will be born a heart of disrespect to the husband. Such a result comes from not knowing that one should stay in one's proper place....

If wives suppress not contempt for husbands, then it follows that such wives rebuke and scold their husbands. If husbands stop not short of anger, then they are certain to beat their wives. The correct relationship between husband and wife is based upon harmony and intimacy, and conjugal love is grounded in proper union. Should actual blows be dealt, how could matrimonial relationship be preserved? Should sharp words be spoken, how could conjugal love exist? If love and proper relationship both be destroyed, then husband and wife are divided.

Womanly Qualifications

A woman ought to have four qualifications: (1) womanly virtue; (2) womanly words; (3) womanly bearing; and (4) womanly work. Now what is called womanly virtue need not be brilliant ability, exceptionally different from others. Womanly words need be neither clever in debate nor keen in conversation. Womanly appearance requires neither a pretty nor a perfect face and form. Womanly work need not be work done more skillfully than that of others.

To guard carefully her chastity; to control circumspectly her behavior; in every motion to exhibit modesty; and to model each act on the best usage, this is womanly virtue.

To choose her words with care; to avoid vulgar language; to speak at appropriate times; and nor to weary others with much conversation, may be called the characteristics of womanly words.

To wash and scrub filth away; to keep clothes and ornaments fresh and clean; to wash the head and bathe the body regularly, and to keep the person free from disgraceful filth, may be called the characteristics of womanly bearing.

With whole-hearted devotion to sew and to weave; to love not gossip and silly laughter; in cleanliness and order to prepare the wine and food for serving guests, may be called the characteristics of womanly work....

Implicit Obedience

Whenever the mother-in-law says, "Do not do that," and if what she says is right, unquestionably the daughter-in-law obeys. Whenever the mother-in-law says, "Do that," even if what she says is wrong, still the daughter-in-law submits unfailingly to the command. Let a woman not act contrary to the wishes and the opinions of parents-in-law about right and wrong; let her not dispute with them what is straight and what is crooked. Such docility may be called obedience which sacrifices personal opinion. Therefore the ancient book, *A Pattern for Women*, says: "If a daughter-in-law who follows the wishes of her parents-in-law is like an echo and shadow, how could she not be praised?"

Document 6.3

An Alternative to Patriarchy in India

About the same time that Ban Zhao was applying the principles of Confucianism to women in China, *The Laws of Manu* was being compiled in India. A core text of classical Indian civilization, those laws defined and sharply circumscribed the behavioral expectations appropriate for women. According to one passage, "In childhood a female must be subject to her father, in youth to her husband, when her lord is dead to her sons; a woman must never be independent."

One path of release for women from such conditions of Indian patriarchy lay in becoming a Buddhist nun and entering a monastery where women were relatively less restricted and could exercise more authority than in ordinary life. Known as *bikkhunis*, such women composed hundreds of poems in the early centuries of Indian Buddhism. They were long recited and transmitted in an oral form and brought together in a collection known as the *Psalms of the Sisters*, which was set to writing probably during the first century B.C.E. These poems became part of the officially recognized Buddhist scriptures, known as the Pali Canon. As such, they represent the only early text in any of the world's major religions that was written by women and about the religious experience of women. A selection of those poems follows here.

- What kinds of women were attracted to Buddhist monastic life? What aspects of life as a *bikkhuni* appealed to them?

- What views of the world, of sensuality, and of human fulfillment are apparent in these poems?

- In what ways might these poems represent a criticism of Hindu patriarchy?

- What criticism of these women would you anticipate? How might advocates of Hindu patriarchy view the renunciation that these nuns practiced?

- How do these poems reflect core Buddhist teachings?

Psalms of the Sisters
First Century B.C.E.

Sumangala's Mother

O woman well set free! how free am I,
How throughly free from kitchen drudgery!
Me stained and squalid 'mong my cooking-pots
My brutal husband ranked as even less
Than the sunshades he sits and weaves alway.
Purged now of all my former lust and hate,
I dwell, musing at ease beneath the shade
Of spreading boughs—O, but 'tis well with me!

A Former Courtesan

How was I once puff'd up, incens'd with the
    bloom of my beauty,

Vain of my perfect form, my fame and success
    'midst the people,
Fill'd with the pride of my youth, unknowing the
    Truth and unheeding!
Lo! I made my body, bravely arrayed, deftly
    painted,
Speak for me to the lads, whilst I at the door of
    the harlot
Stood, like a crafty hunter, weaving his snares,
    ever watchful.
Yea, I bared without shame my body and wealth
    of adorning;
Manifold wiles I wrought, devouring the virtue
    of many.
To-day with shaven head, wrapt in my robe,
I go forth on my daily round for food; ...
Now all the evil bonds that fetter gods
And men are wholly rent and cut away. ...
Calm and content I know Nibbana's
    Peace.

Source: *Psalms of the Sisters*, Vol. I, in *Psalms of the Early Buddhists*, translated by Mrs. Rhys Davids (London: Henry Frowde, Oxford University Press Warehouse, Amen Corner, E.C., 1909), poems 21, 39, 49, 54, 70.

The Daughter of a Poor Brahmin

Fallen on evil days was I of yore.
No husband had I, nor no child, no friends
Or kin—whence could I food or raiment find?
As beggars go, I took my bowl and staff,
And sought me alms, begging from house to
     house,
Sunburnt, frost-bitten, seven weary years.
Then came I where a woman Mendicant
Shared with me food, and drink, and welcomed me,
And said: "Come forth into our homeless life!"...
I heard her and I marked, and did her will.

The Daughter of a Wealthy Treasurer

Daughter of Treas'rer Majjha's famous house,
Rich, beautiful and prosperous, I was born
To vast possessions and to lofty rank.
Nor lacked I suitors—many came and wooed;
The sons of Kings and merchant princes came
With costly gifts, all eager for my hand....
But I had seen th' Enlightened, Chief o' the
     World, The One Supreme. [the Buddha]
And [I] knew this world should see me ne'er
     return.

Then cutting off the glory of my hair,
I entered on the homeless ways of life.
'Tis now the seventh night since first all sense
Of craving drièd up within my heart.

The Goldsmith's Daughter

A maiden I, all clad in white, once heard
The Norm,° and hearkened eager, earnestly,
So in me rose discernment of the Truths.
Thereat all worldly pleasures irked me sore,
For I could see the perils that beset
This reborn compound, 'personality,'
And to renounce it was my sole desire.
So I forsook my world—my kinsfolk all,
My slaves, my hirelings, and my villages,
And the rich fields and meadows spread around,
Things fair and making for the joy of life—
All these I left, and sought the Sisterhood,
Turning my back upon no mean estate....
See now this Subhā, standing on the Norm,
Child of a craftsman in the art of gold!
Behold! she hath attained to utter calm....

———————————

°**Norm:** Buddhist teaching.

Document 6.4

Roman Women in Protest

On occasion women not only wrote but also acted in the public arena. A particularly well-known example of such action took place in Rome in the wake of the Second Punic War with Carthage in North Africa. In 218 B.C.E. the Carthaginian commander Hannibal had invaded the Italian peninsula and threatened Rome itself. In those desperate circumstances Roman authorities passed the Oppian Laws (215 B.C.E.), which restricted women's use of luxury goods so as to preserve resources for the war effort. Twenty years later (195 B.C.E.), with Rome now secure and prosperous, Roman women demanded the repeal of those laws and in the process triggered a major debate among Roman officials. That debate and the women's protest that accompanied it were chronicled early in the first century C.E. by Livy, a famous Roman historian.

■ How did Roman women make their views known? Do you think the protesters represented all Roman women or those of a particular class?

■ How might you summarize the arguments against repeal (Cato) and those favoring repeal (Lucius Valerius)? To what extent did the two men actually differ in their views of women?

■ How might one of the Roman women involved in the protest have made her own case?

■ What can we learn from Livy's account about the social position of Roman women and the attitudes of Roman men?

■ This document was written by a male historian and records the speeches of two other male officials. How might this affect the ability of historians to use it for understanding Roman women?

LIVY

History of Rome

Late First Century B.C.E. to Early First Century C.E.

The law said that no woman might own more than half an ounce of gold nor wear a multicolored dress nor ride in a carriage in the city or in a town within a mile of it, unless there was a religious festival.... [A] crowd of men, both supporters and opponents [of repeal], filled the Capitoline Hill. The matrons, whom neither counsel nor shame nor their husbands' orders could keep at home, blockaded every street in the city and every entrance to the Forum. As the men came down to the Forum, the matrons besought them to let them, too, have back the luxuries they had enjoyed before, giving as their reason that the republic was thriving and that everyone's private wealth was increasing with every day. This crowd of women was growing daily, for now they were even gathering from the towns and villages. Before long they dared go up and solicit the consuls, praetors, and other magistrates; but one of the consuls could not be moved in the least, Marcus Porcius Cato, who spoke in favor of the law:

"If each man of us, fellow citizens, had established that the right and authority of the husband should be held over the mother of his own family,

we should have less difficulty with women in general; now, at home our freedom is conquered by female fury, here in the Forum it is bruised and trampled upon, and, because we have not contained the individuals, we fear the lot....

"Indeed, I blushed when, a short while ago, I walked through the midst of a band of women. Had not respect for the dignity and modesty of certain ones (not them all!) restrained me....I should have said, 'What kind of behavior is this? Running around in public, blocking streets, and speaking to other women's husbands! Could you not have asked your own husbands the same thing at home? Are you more charming in public with others' husbands than at home with your own? And yet, it is not fitting even at home... for you to concern yourselves with what laws are passed or repealed here.' Our ancestors did not want women to conduct any— not even private—business without a guardian; they wanted them to be under the authority of parents, brothers, or husbands; we (the gods help us!) even now let them snatch at the government and meddle in the Forum and our assemblies. What are they doing now on the streets and crossroads, if they are not persuading the tribunes to vote for repeal? Give the reins to their unbridled nature and this unmastered creature....They want freedom, nay license... in all things. If they are victorious now, what will

Source: Livy, "History of Rome" in *Women's Life in Greece and Rome*, 2nd ed., edited by Mary R. Lefkowitz and translated by Maureen B. Fant (Baltimore: Johns Hopkins Press, 1982), 143–47.

they not attempt?... As soon as they begin to be your equals, they will have become your superiors....

"What honest excuse is offered, pray, for this womanish rebellion? 'That we might shine with gold and purple,' says one of them, 'that we might ride through the city in coaches on holidays and working-days.'...

"The woman who can spend her own money will do so; the one who cannot will ask her husband. Pity that husband—the one who gives in and the one who stands firm! What he refuses, he will see given by another man. Now they publicly solicit other women's husbands, and, what is worse, they ask for a law and votes, and certain men give them what they want.... Fellow citizens, do not imagine that the state which existed before the law was passed will return..., as when wild animals are first chafed by their chains and then released."

After this... Lucius Valerius spoke on behalf of the motion....

"[Cato]... has called this assemblage 'secession' and sometimes 'womanish rebellion,' because the matrons have publicly asked you, in peacetime when the state is happy and prosperous, to repeal a law passed against them during the straits of war....

'What, may I ask, are the women doing that is new, having gathered and come forth publicly in a case which concerns them directly? Have they never appeared in public before this?... Listen to how often they have done so—always for the public good. From the very beginning—the reign of Romulus— when the Capitoline had been taken by the Sabines and there was fighting in the middle of the Forum, was not the battle halted by the women's intervention between the two lines?... When Rome was in the hands of the Gauls, who ransomed it? Indeed the matrons agreed unanimously to turn their gold over to the public need.... Indeed, as no one is amazed that they acted in situations affecting men and women alike, why should we wonder that they have taken action in a case which concerns themselves?... We have proud ears indeed, if, while masters do not scorn the appeals of slaves, we are angry when honorable women ask something of us....

"Who then does not know that this is a recent law, passed twenty years ago? Since our matrons

lived for so long by the highest standards of behavior without any law, what risk is there that, once it is repealed, they will yield to luxury?...

"Shall it be our wives alone to whom the fruits of peace and tranquility of the state do not come?... Shall we forbid only women to wear purple? When you, a man, may use purple on your clothes, will you not allow the mother of your family to have a purple cloak, and will your horse be more beautifully saddled than your wife is garbed?...

"[Cato] has said that, if none of them had anything, there would be no rivalry among individual women. By Hercules! All are unhappy and indignant when they see the finery denied them permitted to the wives of the Latin allies, when they see them adorned with gold and purple, when those other women ride through the city and they follow on foot, as though the power belonged to the other women's cities, not to their own. This could wound the spirits of men; what do you think it could do the spirits of women, whom even little things disturb? They cannot partake of magistracies, priesthoods, triumphs, badges of office, gifts, or spoils of war; elegance, finery, and beautiful clothes are women's badges, in these they find joy and take pride, this our forebears called the women's world. When they are in mourning, what, other than purple and gold, do they take off? What do they put on again when they have completed the period of mourning? What do they add for public prayer and thanksgiving other than still greater ornament? Of course, if you repeal the Oppian law, you will not have the power to prohibit that which the law now forbids; daughters, wives, even some men's sisters will be less under your authority—never, while her men are well, is a woman's slavery cast off; and even they hate the freedom created by widowhood and orphanage. They prefer their adornment to be subject to your judgment, not the law's; and you ought to hold them in marital power and guardianship, not slavery; you should prefer to be called fathers and husbands to masters. The consul just now used odious terms when he said 'womanish rebellion' and 'secession'. For there is danger—he would have us believe— that they will seize the Sacred Hill as once the angry plebeians did.... It is for the weaker sex to submit to whatever you advise. The more power you possess, all the more moderately should you exercise your authority."

When these speeches for and against the law had been made, a considerably larger crowd of women poured forth in public the next day; as a single body they besieged the doors of the Brutuses, who were vetoing their colleagues' motion, and they did not stop until the tribunes took back their veto.... Twenty years after it was passed, the law was repealed.

Using the Evidence:
Patriarchy and Women's Voices in the Classical Era

1. **Comparing gender systems:** Based on these documents, how might you compare the gender systems of China, India, and the Roman Empire? What common features of patriarchy did they share? In what ways did they differ?

2. **Evaluating the possibilities of action for women:** In what ways were women able to challenge at least some elements of their classical-era patriarchal societies? Is there evidence in these documents of anything similar to the feminist thinking or action of our own times?

3. **Internalizing social values:** To what extent did women in the classical era civilizations internalize or accept the patriarchal values of their societies? Why might they have done so?

4. **Making judgments:** If you were a woman living in the classical era, which of these civilizations would you prefer to live in and why? Do you think this kind of question—judging the past by the standards of the present—is a valid approach to historical inquiry?

Visual Sources

Considering the Evidence:
Pompeii as a Window on the Roman World

You could hear the shrieks of women, the wailing of infants, and the shouting of men; some were calling their parents, others their children or their wives, trying to recognize them by their voices. People bewailed their own fate or that of their relatives, and there were some who prayed for death in their terror of dying. Many besought the aid of the gods, but still more imagined there were no gods left, and that the universe was plunged into eternal darkness for evermore."[20]

Written by a prominent Roman known as Pliny the Younger, this eye-witness account details reactions to the volcanic eruption of Mount Vesuvius, located on the southwestern side of the Italian peninsula, on August 24, 79 C.E. That eruption buried the nearby Roman city of Pompeii, but it also preserved the city, frozen in time, until archaeologists began to uncover it in the mid-eighteenth century (see Map 4.4, p. 156). Now substantially excavated, Pompeii is an archaeological and historical treasure, offering a unique window into life in the Roman Empire during the first century C.E.

As this city of perhaps 20,000 people emerged from layers of ash, it stood revealed as a small but prosperous center of commerce and agriculture, serving as a point of entry for goods coming to the southern Italian peninsula by sea. Pompeii also hosted numerous vineyards, production facilities for wine and olive oil, and a fisheries industry. In addition, the city was a tourist destination for well-to-do Romans. The houses of the wealthy were elegant structures, often built around a central courtyard, and decorated with lovely murals displaying still-life images, landscapes, and scenes from Greek and Roman mythology. An inscription found on the threshold of one house expressed the entrepreneurial spirit of the town: "Gain is pure joy."[21]

Laid out in a grid pattern with straight streets, the city's numerous public facilities included a central bathing/swimming pool, some twenty-five street fountains, various public bathhouses, and a large food market as well as many bars and small restaurants. More than thirty brothels, often featuring explicit erotic art, offered sexual services at relatively inexpensive prices. One inscription, apparently aimed at local tourists, declared: "If anyone is looking for some tender love in this town, keep in mind that here all the girls are very

Visual Source 6.1 Terentius Neo and His Wife (Scala/Art Resource, NY)

Visual Source 6.2 A Pompeii Banquet (Museo Archeologico Nazionale, Naples/Roger-Viollet/The Bridgeman Art Library)

friendly." Graffiti too abounded, much of it clearly sexual. Here are three of the milder examples: "Atimetus got me pregnant"; "Sarra, you are not being very nice, leaving me all alone like this"; and "If anyone does not believe in Venus, they should gaze at my girlfriend."[22]

The preserved art of Pompeii, especially the wall paintings, provides a glimpse into the social life of that city. Most of that art, of course, catered to and reflected the life of the more prosperous classes. Visual Source 6.1 shows a portrait of Terentius Neo, a prominent businessman and magistrate (an elected public official), and his wife. He is wearing a toga and holding a papyrus scroll, while she wears a tunic and is holding to her lips a stylus, used for writing on the wax-covered wooden tablet that she carries. Her hair is styled in a fashion popular in the mid-first century.

■ What do you think the artist is trying to convey by highlighting the literacy of both people?

■ What overall impression of these two people and their relationship to each other does this painting suggest?

Terentius Neo and his wife were no doubt served by slaves in their home, as slave owning was common in the Roman world, particularly among the upper classes. In the streets and homes of urban areas, slaves and free people mingled quite openly. Roman slavery was not distinguished by race, and the outward signs of urban slavery were few, especially for those practicing professions. Such a couple no doubt gave and attended banquets similar to the one depicted in Visual Source 6.2, where well-to-do guests reclined on padded couches while slaves served them food and drink. Dancers, acrobats, and singers often provided entertainment at such events, which provided an occasion for elites to impress others with their lavish display of wealth and generosity.

■ What signs of social status are evident in this painting?

■ How are slaves, shown here in the foreground, portrayed?

The lives of the less exalted appear infrequently in the art of Pompeii, but the images in Visual Source 6.3 provide some entrée into their world. These are frescoes painted on the wall of a *caupona*, an inn or tavern catering to the lower classes. This particular caupona was located at the intersection of two busy streets where it might easily attract customers. The first image shows Myrtale, a prostitute, kissing a man, while the caption above reads: "I don't want to, with Myrtale." In the second image a female barmaid serves two

Visual Source 6.3 Scenes in a Pompeii Tavern (©Ministero per I Beni e le Attivita Culturali— Soprintendenza archeologica di Napoli)

customers with a large jug and a cup, while they compete for her attention. In the third image, two men playing dice are arguing.

- Why do you think a tavern owner might have such paintings in his place of business?

- What might we learn about tavern life from these images?

- What roles did women play in the tavern?

- What differences do you notice between these paintings and those depicting the lives of the upper classes?

The excavated ruins of Pompeii have much to tell us about the religious as well as the social life of the Roman world in the first century C.E., before Christianity had spread widely. Based on ritual observance rather than doctrine or theology, Roman religious practice sought to obtain the favor of the gods as a way of promoting success, prosperity, and good fortune. A core expression of the diverse and eclectic world of Roman religion was the imperial cult. In Pompeii, a number of temples were dedicated to one or another of the deified emperors, employing together a large cadre of priests and priestesses. Linked to the imperial cult were temples devoted to the traditional Greco-Roman gods such as Apollo, Venus, and Jupiter.

Probably more important to ordinary people were their *lararia* (household shrines), often a niche in the wall that housed paintings or sculptures of *lares* (guardian spirits or deities believed to provide protection within the home). Families offered gifts of fruit, cakes, and wine to these spirits, and the lararia were the focal point for various sacrifices and rituals associated with birth, marriage, and death. Visual Source 6.4 shows one of these shrines, uncovered in the home of a well-to-do freedman (former slave) named Vetti. Protecting the family from external danger were two lares, standing on either side of the lararium and holding their drinking horns. In the center was the *genius*, the spirit of the male head of household. Dressed in a toga and offering a sacrifice, this spirit embodied the character of the man, especially his procreative powers, and so guaranteed many children for the household. The snake at the bottom represented still other benevolent guardian spirits of the family in a fashion very different from Christian symbolism of the snake.

- Why might such a shrine and the spirits it accommodated be more meaningful for many people than the state-approved cults?

- What significance might you find in the temple-like shape of the lararium?

Visual Source 6.4 A Domestic Shrine (Alinari/Art Resource, NY)

In addition to the official cults and the worship of household gods, by the first century C.E. a number of newer traditions, often called "mystery religions," were spreading widely in the Roman Empire. Deriving from the eastern realm of the empire and beyond (Greece, Egypt, and Persia, for example), these mystery religions illustrate the kinds of cultural exchange that took place within the Empire. They offered an alternative to the official cults, for they were more personal, emotional, and intimate, usually featuring a ritual initiation into sacred mysteries, codes of moral behavior, and the promise of an afterlife. Among the most popular of these mystery cults in Pompeii was that of Isis, an Egyptian goddess who restored her husband/brother, Osiris, to life and was worshipped as a compassionate protector of the downtrodden.

Visual Source 6.5 Mystery Religions: The Cult of Dionysus (Werner Forman/Corbis)

Another mystery cult, this one of Greek origin, was associated with Dionysus, a god of wine, ecstasy, and poetic inspiration and especially popular with women. Often associated with drunkenness, trance states, wild dancing, and unrestrained sexuality, the cult of Dionysus encouraged at least the temporary abandonment of conventional inhibitions and social restrictions as initiates sought union with Dionysus. A series of wall paintings on a Pompeii building known as the Villa of Mysteries depicts the process of initiation into the cult of Dionysus, perhaps in preparation for marriage. Visual Source 6.5 shows a particularly dramatic phase of that initiation in which a woman is ritually whipped, while a naked devotee dances ecstatically with a pair of cymbals above her head and a companion holds a rod of phallic symbolism that is sacred to Dionysus. In any such process of religious initiation, the initiate undergoes a series of trials or purifications in which he or she "dies" symbolically, achieves mystical union with the god, and is "reborn" into the new community of the cult.

- What aspects of the initiation process are visible in this image?

- How might you understand the role of whipping in the initiation process? How would you interpret the relationship of the initiate and the woman on whose lap she is resting her head?

- In what way is sexual union, symbolized by the rod, significant in the initiation?

- Why do you think Roman authorities took action against these mystery religions, even as they did against Christianity?

- What did the mystery cults of Isis or Dionysus provide that neither the state cults nor household gods might offer?

Using the Evidence:
Pompeii as a Window on the Roman World

1. **Characterizing Pompeii:** What does the art of Pompeii, as reflected in these visual sources, tell us about the social and religious life of this small Roman city in the first century C.E.? To what extent, if at all, should historians generalize from Pompeii to the Roman Empire as a whole?

2. **Noticing class differences:** What class or social distinctions are apparent in these visual sources?

3. **Identifying gender roles:** What do these visual sources suggest about the varied lives and social roles of women and men in Pompeii?

CHAPTER SEVEN

Classical Era Variations

Africa and the Americas

500 B.C.E.—1200 C.E.

The African Northeast
  Meroë: Continuing a Nile Valley
    Civilization
  Axum: The Making of a Christian
    Kingdom
Along the Niger River: Cities without
  States
South of the Equator: The World of
  Bantu Africa
  Cultural Encounters
  Society and Religion
Civilizations of Mesoamerica
  The Maya: Writing and Warfare
  Teotihuacán: The Americas'
    Greatest City
Civilizations of the Andes
  Chavín: A Pan-Andean Religious
    Movement
  Moche: A Regional Andean
    Civilization
North America in the Classical Era:
  From Chaco to Cahokia
  Pit Houses and Great Houses: The
    Ancestral Pueblo
  The Mound Builders of the Eastern
    Woodlands
Reflections: Deciding What's
  Important: Balance in World History
Considering the Evidence
  Documents: Axum and the World
  Visual Sources: Art and the
    Maya Elite

"In a [Maya] community called Xolep, there was no paper or pencils where I taught. I started by drawing figures in the dirt. We then taught letters by forming them with sticks. One day students brought flower petals to shape the letters. . . . When we were able to gather enough money for notebooks, we gave them to the students and asked them to report the next day to the tree where we were holding school. . . . They proudly filed under the teaching tree, notebooks tucked under their arms, feeling that they were now officially students."[1]

This incident, reported in 1999 by a participant in an independent schools movement among the Maya of southern Mexico, was a tiny part of an ongoing revival of Maya culture. Despite the collapse of their famous classical civilization more than a thousand years ago, Maya language and folkways have persisted among some 6 million people currently living in Mexico, Belize, Guatemala, and Honduras. And despite five centuries of repression, exploitation, and neglect at the hands of Spanish colonizers and the independent governments that followed, they were now in the midst of what one writer called "a new time of the Maya."[2] They were writing their own histories, celebrating their own culture, creating their own organizations, and teaching their children to read. The most dramatic expression of this recent Maya revival was an armed uprising, begun in early 1994 and led by the Zapatista Army of National Liberation. Growing out of long-term social and economic grievances against local landowners and an unresponsive government, that rebellion stunned Mexico and focused global attention on the poverty and misery of the country's indigenous Maya people. Once

The Maya Temple of the Great Jaguar in Tikal: Located in the Maya city of Tikal in present-day Guatemala, this temple was constructed in the eighth century C.E. and excavated by archeologists in the late nineteenth century. It served as the tomb of the Tikal ruler Jasaw Chan K'awiil I (682–734). Some 144 feet tall, it was topped by a three-room temple complex and a huge roofcomb showing the ruler on his throne. Carved on a wooden beam inside the temple is an image of the ruler protected by a huge jaguar along with illustrations of his military victories. (Peter M. Wilson/Alamy)

again, some 1,500 years after the high point of their classical civilization, the Maya were making history.

FOR MANY PEOPLE, THE CLASSICAL ERA EVOKES most vividly the civilizations of Eurasia—especially the Greeks and the Romans, the Persians and the Chinese, and the Indians of South Asia—yet those were not the only classical-era civilizations. During this period, the Mesoamerican Maya and the Peruvian Moche thrived, as did several civilizations in Africa, including Meroë, Axum, and the Niger River valley. Furthermore, those peoples who did not organize themselves around cities or states likewise had histories of note and alternative ways of constructing their societies, although they are often neglected in favor of civilizations. This chapter explores the histories of the varied peoples of Africa and the Americas during the classical era. On occasion, those histories will extend some centuries beyond the chronological boundaries of the classical age in Eurasia, because patterns of historical development around the world did not always coincide precisely.

At the broadest level, however, human cultures evolved in quite similar fashion around the world. All, of course, were part of that grand process of human migration that initially peopled the planet. Beginning in Africa, that vast movement of humankind subsequently encompassed Eurasia, Australia, the Americas, and Oceania. Almost everywhere, gathering and hunting long remained the sole basis for sustaining life and society. Then, on the three supercontinents—Eurasia, Africa, and the Americas—the momentous turn of the Agricultural Revolution took place independently and in several distinct areas of each landmass. That revolutionary transformation of human life subsequently generated, in particularly rich agricultural environments of all three regions, those more complex societies that we know as civilizations, which featured cities, states, monumental architecture, and great social inequality. In these ways, the historical trajectory of the human journey on the earth has a certain unity and similarity across quite distinct continental regions. At the beginning of the Common Era, that trajectory had generated a total world population of about 250 million people, substantially less than the current population of the United States alone. By contemporary standards, it was still a sparsely populated planet.

The world's human population was distributed very unevenly across the three giant continents, as the Snapshot indicates. If these estimates are even reasonably accurate, then during the classical era Eurasia was home to more than 80 percent of the world's people, Africa about 11 percent, and the Americas between 5 and 7 percent. That unevenness in population distribution is part of the reason why world historians focus more attention on Eurasia than on Africa or the Americas. Here lies one of the major differences among the continents.

There were other differences as well. The absence of most animals capable of domestication meant that no pastoral societies developed in the Americas, and no draft animals were available to pull plows or carts or to carry heavy loads for long distances. Africa lacked wild sheep, goats, chickens, horses, and camels, but its proximity to Eurasia meant that these animals, once domesticated, became widely available

Snapshot   **Continental Population in the Classical Era**[3]

(Note: Population figures for such early times are merely estimates and are often controversial among scholars. Percentages do not always total 100 percent due to rounding.)

	Eurasia	Africa	North America	Central/South America	Australia/ Oceania	Total World
Area (in square miles and as percentage of world total)						
	21,049,000 (41%)	11,608,000 (22%)	9,365,000 (18%)	6,880,000 (13%)	2,968,000 (6%)	51,870,000
Population (in millions and as percentage of world total)						
400 B.C.E.	127 (83%)	17 (11%)	1 (0.7%)	7 (5%)	1 (0.7%)	153
10 C.E.	213 (85%)	26 (10%)	2 (0.8%)	10 (4%)	1 (0.4%)	252
200 C.E.	215 (84%)	30 (12%)	2 (0.8%)	9 (4%)	1 (0.4%)	257
600 C.E.	167 (80%)	24 (12%)	2 (1%)	14 (7%)	1 (0.5%)	208
1000 C.E.	195 (77%)	39 (15%)	2 (0.8%)	16 (6%)	1 (0.4%)	253

to African peoples. Metallurgy in the Americas was likewise far less developed than in the Eastern Hemisphere, where iron tools and weapons played such an important role in economic and military life. In the Americas, writing was limited to the Mesoamerican region and was most highly developed among the Maya, whereas in Africa it was confined to the northern and northeastern parts of the continent during the classical era. In Eurasia, by contrast, writing emerged elaborately in many regions. Classical-era civilizations in Africa and the Americas were fewer in number and generally smaller than those of Eurasia, and larger numbers of their people lived in communities that did not feature cities and states.

To illustrate the historical developments of the classical era beyond Eurasia, this chapter focuses on three regions in Africa and three in the Americas. To what extent did these histories parallel those of Eurasia? In what ways did they forge new or different paths?

The African Northeast

When historians refer to Africa during the classical era, they are speaking generally of a geographic concept, a continental landmass, and not a cultural identity. Certainly no one living on the continent at that time thought of himself or herself as an African. Like Eurasia or the Americas, Africa hosted numerous separate societies, cultures, and civilizations with vast differences among them as well as some interaction between them.

Many of these differences grew out of the continent's environmental variations. Small regions of Mediterranean climate in the northern and southern extremes, large deserts (the Sahara and the Kalahari), even larger regions of savanna grasslands, tropical rain forest in the continent's center, highlands and mountains in eastern Africa—all of these features, combined with the continent's enormous size, ensured variation and difference among Africa's many peoples. Africa did, however, have one distinctive environmental feature: bisected by the equator, it was the most tropical of the world's three supercontinents. Persistent warm temperatures caused the rapid decomposition of vegetable matter called humus, resulting in poorer and less fertile soils and a less productive agriculture than in the more temperate Eurasia. Those climatic conditions also spawned numerous disease-carrying insects and parasites, which have long created serious health problems in many parts of the continent. It was within these environmental constraints that African peoples made their histories.

A further geographic feature shaped African history—its proximity to Eurasia, which allowed parts of Africa to interact with Eurasian civilizations. During the classical era, North Africa was incorporated into the Roman Empire and used to produce wheat and olives on large estates with slave labor. Christianity spread widely, giving rise to some of the early Church's most famous martyrs and to one of its most important theologians, Saint Augustine (354–430 C.E.). The Christian faith found an even more permanent foothold in the lands now known as Ethiopia.

Arabia was another point of contact with the larger world for African peoples. The arrival of the domesticated camel, probably from Arabia, generated a nomadic pastoral way of life among some of the Berber peoples of the western Sahara during the first three centuries C.E. A little later, camels also made possible trans-Saharan commerce, which linked interior West Africa to the world of Mediterranean civilization. Over many centuries, the East African coast was a port of call for Egyptian, Roman, and Arab merchants, and that region subsequently became an integral part of Indian Ocean trading networks.

Both the external connections and, more important, the internal development of African societies generated various patterns of historical change during the classical era. Three regions—northeastern Africa, the Niger River basin in West Africa, and the vast world of Bantu-speaking Africa south of the equator—serve to illustrate these differences and the many social and cultural experiments spawned by the peoples of this continent.

Meroë: Continuing a Nile Valley Civilization

■ Connection
How did the history of Meroë and Axum reflect interaction with neighboring civilizations?

In the Nile Valley south of Egypt lay the lands of Nubian civilization, almost as old as Egypt itself. Over many centuries, Nubians both traded and fought with Egypt, alternately conquering and being conquered by their northern neighbor. While borrowing heavily from Egypt, Nubia remained a distinct and separate civilization

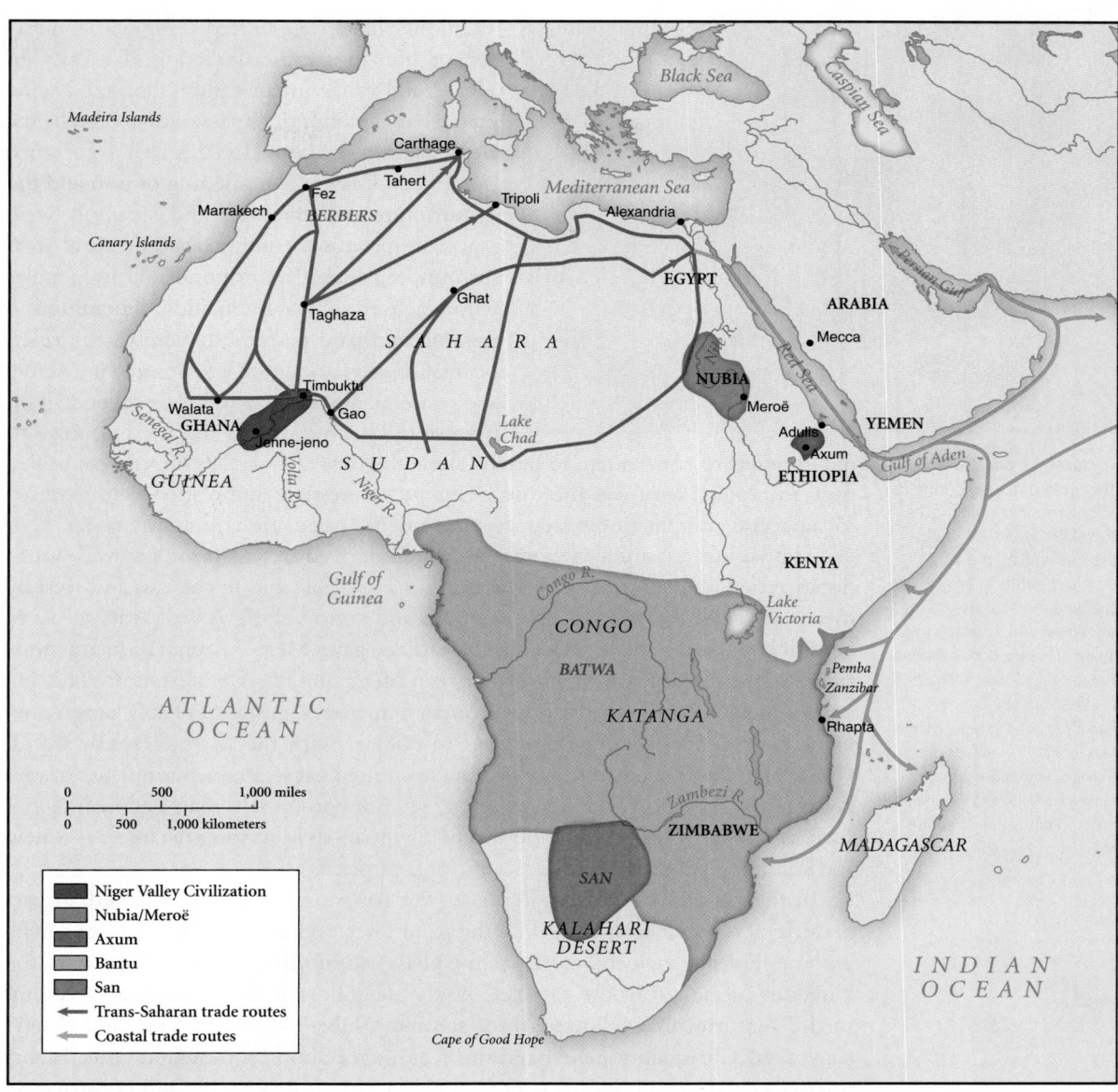

Map 7.1   Africa in the Classical Era
During the classical era, older African civilizations such as Egypt and Nubia persisted and changed, while new civilizations emerged in Axum and the Niger River valley. South of the equator, Bantu-speaking peoples spread rapidly, creating many new societies and identities.

(see Chapter 3). By the classical era, as Egypt fell under foreign control, Nubian civilization came to center on the southern city of Meroë, where it flourished between 300 B.C.E. and 100 C.E. (see Map 7.1).

Politically, the Kingdom of Meroë was governed by an all-powerful and sacred monarch, a position occasionally conferred on women. In accordance with ancient

A Bracelet from Meroë
This gold bracelet, dating to about 100 B.C.E., illustrates the skill of Meroë's craftsmen as well as the kingdom's reputation as one of the wealthiest states of the ancient world. (Bracelet with image of Hathor, Nubian, Meroitic Period, about 100 B.C.E. Object Place: Sudan, Nubia, Gebel Barkal, Pyramid 8, Gold, enamel. Museum of Fine Arts, Boston, Harvard University–Boston Museum of Fine Arts Expedition, 20.333. Photograph © 2008 Museum of Fine Arts, Boston)

traditions, rulers were buried along with a number of human sacrificial victims. The city of Meroë and other urban centers housed a wide variety of economic specialties—merchants, weavers, potters, and masons, as well as servants, laborers, and slaves. The smelting of iron and the manufacture of iron tools and weapons were especially prominent industries. The rural areas surrounding Meroë were populated by peoples who practiced some combination of herding and farming and paid periodic tribute to the ruler. Rainfall-based agriculture was possible in Meroë, and consequently farmers were less dependent on irrigation. This meant that the rural population did not need to concentrate so heavily along the Nile and was less directly controlled from the capital than was the case in Egypt, where state authorities were required to supervise an irrigation system serving a dense population along the river.

The wealth and military power of Meroë derived in part from extensive long-distance trading connections, to the north via the Nile and to the east and west by means of camel caravans. Its iron weapons and cotton cloth, as well as its access to gold, ivory, tortoiseshells, and ostrich feathers, gave Meroë a reputation for great riches in the classical world of northeastern Africa and the Mediterranean. The discovery in Meroë of a statue of the Roman emperor Augustus, probably seized during a raid on Roman Egypt, testifies to contact with the Mediterranean world. Culturally, Meroë seemed to move away from the heavy Egyptian influence of earlier times. A local lion god, Apedemek, grew more prominent than Egyptian deities such as Isis and Osiris, while the use of Egyptian-style writing declined as a new and still undeciphered Meroitic script took its place.

In the centuries following 100 C.E., the Kingdom of Meroë declined, in part because of deforestation caused by the need for wood to make charcoal for smelting iron. The effective end of the Meroë phase of Nubian civilization came with the kingdom's conquest in the 340s C.E. by the neighboring and rising state of Axum. In the centuries that followed, three separate Nubian states emerged, and Coptic (Egyptian) Christianity penetrated the region. For almost a thousand years, Nubia was a Christian civilization, using Greek as a liturgical language and constructing churches in Coptic or Byzantine fashion. After 1300 or so, political division, Arab immigration, and the penetration of Islam eroded this Christian civilization, and Nubia became part of the growing world of Islam.

Axum: The Making of a Christian Kingdom

If Meroë and Nubia represented the continuation of an old African civilization, Axum marked the emergence of a new one. (For various accounts about or from

Axum, see Documents: Axum and the World, pp. 307–15.) Axum lay in the Horn of Africa, in what is now Eritrea and northern Ethiopia (see Map 7.1). Its economic foundation was a highly productive agriculture that used a plow-based farming system, unlike most of the rest of Africa, which relied on the hoe or digging stick. Axum's agriculture generated substantial amounts of wheat, barley, millet, and teff, a highly nutritious grain unique to that region. By 50 C.E. or so, a substantial state had emerged, stimulated by its participation in Red Sea and Indian Ocean commerce. At Adulis, then the largest port on the East African coast, a wide range of merchants sought the products of the African interior—animal hides, rhinoceros horn, ivory, obsidian, tortoiseshells, and slaves. Taxes on this trade provided a major source of revenue for the Axumite state and the complex society that grew up within it.

The interior capital city, also known as Axum, was a center of monumental building and royal patronage for the arts. The most famous buildings were huge stone obelisks, which most likely marked royal graves. Some of them were more than 100 feet tall and at the time were the largest structures in the world hewn from a single piece of rock. The language used at court, in the towns, and for commerce was Geez, written in a script derived from South Arabia. The Axumite state exercised a measure of control over the mostly Agaw-speaking people of the country through a loose administrative structure focusing on the collection of tribute payments. To the Romans, Axum was the third major empire within the world they knew, following their own and the Persian Empire.

Through its connections to Red Sea trade and the Roman world, particularly Egypt, Axum was introduced to Christianity in the fourth century C.E. Its monarch at the time, King Ezana, adopted the new religion about the same time as Constantine did in the Roman Empire. Supported by royal authority, Christianity took root in Axum, linking that kingdom religiously to Egypt, where a distinctive Christian church known as Coptic was already well established. Although Egypt subsequently became largely Islamic, reducing its Christian community to a small minority, Christianity maintained a dominant position in the mountainous terrain of highland Ethiopia and in the early twenty-first century still represents the faith of perhaps half of the country's population.

During the fourth through the sixth century C.E., Axum mounted a campaign of imperial expansion that took its forces into the Kingdom of Meroë and across the Red Sea into Yemen in South Arabia. By 571, the traditional date for the birth of Muhammad, an Axumite army, including a number of African war elephants, had reached the gates of Mecca, but it was a fairly short-lived imperial

The Columns of Axum Dating to the time when Axum first encountered Christianity (300–500 C.E.), this column, measuring some seventy-nine feet tall, probably served as a funeral monument for the kingdom's ancient rulers. (Antonello Langellotto/TIPS Images)

venture. The next several centuries were ones of decline for the Axumite state, owing partly to environmental changes, such as soil exhaustion, erosion, and deforestation, brought about by intensive farming. Equally important was the rise of Islam, which altered trade routes and diminished the revenue available to the Axumite state. Its last coins were struck in the early seventh century. When the state revived several centuries later, it was centered farther south on the Ethiopian plateau. There emerged the Christian church and the state that present-day Ethiopia has inherited, but the link to ancient Axum was long remembered and revered.

With their long-distance trading connections, urban centers, centralized states, complex societies, monumental architecture, written languages, and imperial ambitions, both Meroë and Axum paralleled on a smaller scale the major features of the classical civilizations of Eurasia. Furthermore, both were in direct contact with the world of Mediterranean civilizations. Elsewhere in Africa during the classical era, quite different histories unfolded.

Along the Niger River: Cities without States

In the middle stretches of the Niger River in West Africa, the classical era witnessed the emergence of a remarkable urbanization (see Map 7.1). A prolonged dry period during the five centuries after 500 B.C.E. brought growing numbers of people from the southern Sahara into the fertile floodplain of the middle Niger in search of more reliable access to water. Accompanying them were their domesticated cattle, sheep, and goats; their agricultural skills; and their ironworking technology. Over the centuries of the classical era and beyond (roughly 300 B.C.E.–900 C.E.), the peoples of this region created a distinctive city-based civilization. The most fully studied of the urban clusters that grew up along the middle Niger was the city of Jenne-jeno, which at its high point probably housed more than 40,000 people.

Among the most distinctive features of the Niger Valley civilization was the apparent absence of a corresponding state structure. Unlike the cities of Egypt, China, the Roman Empire, or Axum, these middle Niger urban centers were not encompassed within some larger imperial system. Nor were they like the city-states of ancient Mesopotamia, in which each city had its own centralized political structure, embodied in a monarch and his accompanying bureaucracy. According to a leading historian of the region, they were "cities without citadels," complex urban centers that apparently operated without the coercive authority of a state, for archeologists have found in their remains few signs of despotic power, widespread warfare, or deep social inequalities.[4] In this respect, these urban centers resemble the early cities of the Indus Valley civilization, where likewise little archeological evidence of centralized state structures has been found (see Chapter 3).

In place of such hierarchical organization, Jenne-jeno and other cities of the region emerged as clusters of economically specialized settlements surrounding a larger central town. The earliest and most prestigious of these specialized occupations

■ Description
How does the experience of the Niger Valley challenge conventional notions of "civilization"?

was iron smithing. Working with fire and earth (ore) to produce this highly useful metal, the smiths of the Niger Valley were both feared and revered. Archeologist Roderick McIntosh, a leading figure in the excavation of Jenne-jeno, argued that "their knowledge of the transforming arts—earth to metal, insubstantial fire to the mass of iron—was the key to a secret, occult realm of immense power and immense danger."[5]

Other specializations followed. Villages of cotton weavers, potters, leather workers, and griots (praise-singers who preserved and recited the oral traditions of their societies) grew up around the central towns. Gradually these urban artisan communities became occupational castes, whose members passed their jobs and skills to their children and could marry only within their own group. In the surrounding rural areas, as in all urban-based civilizations, farmers tilled the soil and raised their animals, but specialization also occurred in farming as various ethnic groups focused on fishing, rice cultivation, or some other agricultural pursuit. At least for a time, these middle Niger cities represented an African alternative to an oppressive state, which in many parts of the world accompanied an increasingly complex urban economy and society. A series of distinct and specialized economic groups shared authority and voluntarily used the services of one another, while maintaining their own identities through physical separation.

Accompanying this unique urbanization, and no doubt stimulating it, was a growing network of indigenous West African commerce. The middle Niger flood-plain supported a rich agriculture and had clay for pottery, but it lacked stone, iron ore, salt, and fuel. This scarcity of resources was the basis for long-distance commerce, which operated by boat along the Niger River and overland by donkey to the north and south. Iron ore from more than 50 miles away, copper from mines 200 miles distant, gold from even more distant sources, stones and salt from the Sahara—all of these items have been found in Jenne-jeno, in return no doubt for grain, fish, smoked meats, iron implements, and other staples. Jenne-jeno itself was an important transshipment point in this commerce, in which goods were transferred from boat to donkey or vice versa. By the 500s C.E., there is evidence of an even wider commerce and at least indirect contact, from Mauritania in the west to present-day Mali and Burkina-Faso in the east.

In the second millennium C.E., new historical patterns developed in West Africa (see Chapter 8). A number of large-scale states or empires emerged in the region— Ghana, Mali, and Songhay, among the most well known. At least partially responsible for this development was the flourishing of a camel-borne trans-Saharan commerce, previously but a trickle across the great desert. As West Africa became more firmly connected to North Africa and the Mediterranean, Islam penetrated the region, marking a gradual but major cultural transformation. All of this awaited West Africa in the postclassical era, submerging, but not completely eliminating, the decentralized city life of the Niger Valley.

South of the Equator: The World of Bantu Africa

Farther south on the African continent, patterns of historical change differed from those that gave rise to the small civilizations of Nubia/Meroë, Axum, and the Niger River valley. In this vast region, and particularly south of the equator, the most significant development of the classical era involved the accelerating movement of Bantu-speaking peoples into the enormous subcontinent. It was a process that had begun many centuries earlier from a homeland region in what is now southeastern Nigeria and the Cameroons. In the long run, that movement of peoples generated some 400 distinct but closely related languages, known collectively as Bantu. By the first century C.E., agricultural peoples speaking Bantu languages had largely occupied the forest regions of equatorial Africa, and at least a few of them had probably reached the East African coast. In the several centuries that followed, they established themselves quite rapidly in most of eastern and southern Africa (see Map 7.1), introducing immense economic and cultural changes to a huge region of the continent.

Bantu expansion was not a conquest or invasion such as that of Alexander the Great; nor was it a massive and self-conscious migration like that of Europeans to the Americas. Rather, it was a slow movement of peoples, perhaps a few extended families at a time, but taken as a whole, it brought to Africa south of the equator a measure of cultural and linguistic commonality, marking it as a distinct region of the continent.

Cultural Encounters

■ Connection

In what ways did the arrival of Bantu-speaking peoples stimulate cross-cultural interaction?

That movement of peoples also generated numerous cross-cultural encounters, as the Bantu-speaking newcomers interacted with already-established societies, changing both of them in the process. Among those encounters, none was more significant than that between the agricultural Bantu and the gathering and hunting peoples who earlier occupied Africa south of the equator. This was part of a long-term global phenomenon in which farmers largely replaced foragers as the dominant people on the planet (see Chapter 2).

In this encounter, Bantu-speaking farmers had various advantages. One was numerical, as agriculture generated a more productive economy, enabling larger numbers to live in a smaller area than was possible with a gathering and hunting way of life. Another advantage was disease, for the farmers brought with them both parasitic and infectious diseases—malaria, for example—to which foraging people had little immunity. A third advantage was iron, so useful for tools and weapons, which Bantu migrants brought to many of their interactions with peoples still operating with stone-age technology. Thus, during the classical era, gathering and hunting peoples were displaced, absorbed, or largely eliminated in most parts of Africa south of the equator—but not everywhere.

In the Kalahari region of southwestern Africa and a few places in East Africa, gathering and hunting peoples such as the San (see Chapter 1) survived into modern times. Furthermore, many of the Bantu languages of southern Africa retain to this day the distinctive "clicks" that they borrowed from the now-vanished gathering and hunting peoples who long preceded them in the region.

In the rain forest region of Central Africa, the foraging Batwa (Pygmy) people, at least some of them, became "forest specialists" who produced honey, wild game, elephant products, animal skins, and medicinal barks and plants, all of which entered regional trading networks in exchange for the agricultural products of their Bantu neighbors. They also adopted Bantu languages, while maintaining a nonagricultural lifestyle and a separate identity. For their part, the Bantu farmers regarded their Batwa

Khoikhoi of South Africa The Khoikhoi people of South Africa, several of whom are shown here in an 1886 photograph, were originally gatherers and hunters who adopted cattle and sheep raising from outsiders, perhaps from early Bantu-speaking immigrants to the region, but did not practice agriculture. Living in southern Africa for most of the last two millennia, they illustrate the interaction and selective cultural borrowing that took place among the various peoples of the region. (Hulton-Deutsch Collection/Corbis)

neighbors as first-comers to the region and therefore closest to the ancestral and territorial spirits that determined the fertility of the land and people. Thus, as forest-dwelling and Bantu-speaking farmers grew in numbers and created chiefdoms, those chiefs appropriated the Batwa title of "owners of the land" for themselves, claimed Batwa ancestry, and portrayed the Batwa as the original "civilizers" of the earth.[6]

In other ways as well, Bantu cultures changed as they encountered different peoples. In the drier environment of East Africa, the yam-based agriculture of the West African Bantu homeland was unable to support their growing numbers, so Bantu farmers increasingly adopted grains as well as domesticated sheep and cattle from the already-established people of the region. Their agriculture also was enriched by acquiring a variety of food crops from Southeast Asia—coconuts, sugarcane, and especially bananas—which were brought to East Africa by Indonesian sailors and immigrants early in the first millennium C.E. Bantu farmers then spread this agricultural package and their acquired ironworking technology throughout the vast area of eastern and southern Africa, probably reaching present-day South Africa by 400 C.E. They also brought a common set of cultural and social practices, which diffused widely across Bantu Africa. One prominent historian described these practices as encompassing,

> in religion, the centrality of ancestor observances; in philosophy, the problem of evil understood as the consequence of individual malice or of the failure to honor one's ancestors; in music, an emphasis on polyrhythmic performance with drums as the key instrument; in dance, a new form of expression in which a variety of prescribed body movements took preference over footwork; and in agriculture, the pre-eminence of women as the workers and innovators.[7]

All of this became part of the common culture of Bantu-speaking Africa.

Society and Religion

In the thousand years or so (500–1500 C.E.) that followed their initial colonization of Africa south of the equator, agricultural Bantu-speaking peoples also created a wide variety of quite distinct societies and cultures. Some—in present-day Kenya, for example—organized themselves without any formal political specialists at all. Instead they made decisions, resolved conflicts, and maintained order by using kinship structures or lineage principles supplemented by age grades, which joined men of a particular generation together across various lineages (see Document 2.2, pp. 309–10). Elsewhere, lineage heads who acquired a measure of personal wealth or who proved skillful at mediating between the local spirits and the people might evolve into chiefs with a modest political authority. In several areas, such as the region around Lake Victoria or present-day Zimbabwe, larger and more substantial kingdoms evolved. Along the East African coast after 1000 C.E., dozens of rival city-states linked the African interior with the commerce of the Indian Ocean basin (see Chapter 8). The kind of society that developed in any particular area depended on a host of local factors, including population density, trading opportunities, and interaction among culturally different peoples.

In terms of religion, Bantu practice in general placed less emphasis on a High or Creator God, who was viewed as remote and largely uninvolved in ordinary life, and focused instead on ancestral or nature spirits. The power of dead ancestors might be accessed through rituals of sacrifice, especially that of cattle. Supernatural power deriving from ancient heroes, ancestors, or nature spirits also resided in charms, which could be activated by proper rituals and used to control the rains, defend the village, achieve success in hunting, or identify witches. Belief in witches was widespread, reflecting the idea that evil or misfortune was the work of malicious people. Diviners, skilled in penetrating the world of the supernatural, used dreams, visions, charms, or trances to identify the source of misfortune and to prescribe remedies. Was a particular illness the product of broken taboos, a dishonored ancestor, an unhappy nature spirit, or a witch? Was a remedy to be found in a cleansing ceremony, a sacrifice to an ancestor, the activation of a charm, or the elimination of a witch?[8] Such issues constantly confronted the people of Bantu Africa.

Unlike the major monotheistic religions, with their "once and for all" revelations from God through the Christian Bible or the Muslim Quran, Bantu religious practice was predicated on the notion of "continuous revelation"—the possibility of constantly receiving new messages from the world beyond. Moreover, unlike Buddhism, Christianity, or Islam, Bantu religions were geographically confined, intended to explain, predict, and control local affairs, with no missionary impulse or inclination toward universality.

Civilizations of Mesoamerica

Westward across the Atlantic Ocean lay the altogether separate world of the Americas. Although geography permitted some interaction between African and Eurasian peoples, the Atlantic and Pacific oceans ensured that the cultures and societies of the Western Hemisphere had long operated in a world apart from their Afro-Eurasian counterparts. Nor were the cultures of the Americas stimulated by the kind of fruitful interaction among their own peoples that played such an important role in the Eastern Hemisphere. Nothing similar to the contact between Egypt and Mesopotamia, or Persia and the Greeks, or the extensive communication along the Silk Road trading network enriched the two major centers of civilization in the Americas—Mesoamerica and the Andes—which had little if any direct contact with each other. Furthermore, the remarkable achievements of early American civilizations and cultures occurred without the large domesticated animals or ironworking technologies that were so important throughout the Eastern Hemisphere.

Accounts of pre-Columbian American societies often focus primarily on the Aztec and Inca empires (see Chapter 13), yet these impressive creations, flourishing in the fifteenth and early sixteenth centuries, were but the latest in a long line of civilizations that preceded them in Mesoamerica and the Andes respectively. Although these two regions housed the vast majority of the population of the Americas, the peoples of North America, the Amazon River basin, and elsewhere were the centers of their own worlds and made their own histories. It is the period preceding the Aztecs and Incas that represents the classical era in the history of the Americas.

Stretching from central Mexico to northern Central America, the area known as Mesoamerica was, geographically speaking, one of "extraordinary diversity compressed into a relatively small space."[9] That environment ranged from steamy lowland rain forests to cold and windy highland plateaus, cut by numerous mountains and valleys and generating many microclimates. Such conditions contributed to substantial linguistic and ethnic diversity and to many distinct and competing cities, chiefdoms, and states.

Despite this diversity, Mesoamerica, like Bantu Africa, was also a distinct region, bound together by elements of a common culture. Its many peoples shared an intensive agricultural technology devoted to raising maize, beans, chili peppers, and squash; they prepared maize in a distinctive and highly nutritious fashion; they based their economies on market exchange; they practiced religions featuring a similar pantheon of deities, belief in a cosmic cycle of creation and destruction, human sacrifice, and monumental ceremonial centers; they employed a common ritual calendar of 260 days and hieroglyphic writing; and they interacted frequently among themselves. During the first millennium B.C.E., for example, the various small states and chiefdoms of the region, particularly the Olmec, exchanged a number of luxury goods used to display social status and for ritual purposes—jade, serpentine, obsidian tools, ceramic pottery, shell ornaments, stingray spines, and turtle shells. As a result, aspects of Olmec culture, such as artistic styles, temple pyramids, the calendar system, and rituals involving human sacrifice, spread widely throughout Mesoamerica and influenced many of the civilizations that followed.

Classical Civilizations of Mesoamerica

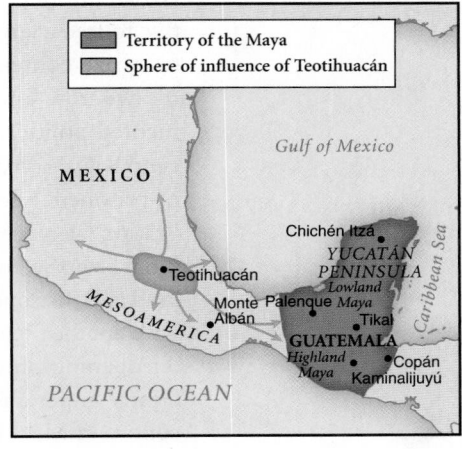

The Maya: Writing and Warfare

■ Comparison
With what Eurasian
civilizations might the
Maya be compared?

Among the Mesoamerican civilizations, none has attracted more attention than that of the Maya, the major classical civilization of Mesoamerica. Scholars have traced the beginnings of the Maya people to ceremonial centers constructed as early as 2000 B.C.E. in present-day Guatemala and the Yucatán region of Mexico, but it was during the classical phase of Maya civilization, between 250 and 900 C.E., that their most notable cultural achievements emerged. Their intellectuals, probably priests, developed a mathematical system that included the concept of zero and place notation and was capable of complex calculations. They combined this mathematical ability with careful observation of the night skies to plot the cycles of planets, to predict eclipses of the sun and the moon, to construct elaborate calendars, and to calculate accurately the length of the solar year. The distinctive art of the Maya elite, featured in Visual Sources: Art and the Maya Elite, pages 216–23, was likewise impressive to later observers.

Accompanying these intellectual and artistic achievements was the creation of the most elaborate writing system in the Americas, which used both pictographs and phonetic or syllabic elements. Carved on stone and written on bark paper or deerskin books, Mayan writing recorded historical events, masses of astronomical data, and religious or mythological texts. Temples, pyramids, palaces, and public plazas abounded, graced with painted murals and endless stone carving. It is not surprising that early scholars viewed Maya civilization as a peaceful society led by gentle stargazing priest-kings devoted to temple building and intellectual pursuits.

The economic foundations for these cultural achievements were embedded in an "almost totally engineered landscape."[10] The Maya drained swamps, terraced hillsides, flattened ridgetops, and constructed an elaborate water management system. Much of this underpinned a flourishing agriculture, which supported a very rapidly growing and dense population by 750 C.E. This agriculture sustained substantial elite classes of nobles, priests, merchants, architects, and sculptors, as well as specialized artisans producing pottery, tools, and cotton textiles. And it was sufficiently productive to free a large labor force for work on the many public structures that continue to amaze contemporary visitors.

We now know that these many achievements took place within a highly fragmented political system of city-states, local lords, and regional kingdoms with no central authority, with frequent warfare, and with the extensive capture and sacrifice of prisoners (see Visual Source 7.2, p. 319). The larger political units of Maya civilization were densely populated urban and ceremonial centers, ruled by powerful kings, who were divine rulers or "state shamans" able to mediate between humankind and the supernatural. One of these cities, Tikal, contained perhaps 50,000 people, with another 50,000 or so in the surrounding countryside, by 750 C.E.[11] (See the chapter opening photo, p. 280, of a temple from Tikal.) Some of these city-states were clearly imperialistic, but none succeeded in creating a unified Maya empire. Various centers of Maya civilization rose and fell; fluctuating alliances among them alternated with periods of sporadic warfare; ruling families intermarried; the elite classes sought luxury goods from far away—jade, gold, shells, feathers from exotic birds, cacao—to bolster their authority and status. In its political dimensions, classical Maya civilization more closely resembled the competing city-states of ancient Mesopotamia or classical Greece than the imperial structures of Rome, Persia, or China.

But that imposing civilization collapsed with a completeness and rapidity rare in world history. In less than a century following the onset of a long-term drought in 840, the population of the low-lying southern heartland of the Maya dropped by 85 percent or more as famine, epidemic, and fratricidal warfare reaped a horrific toll. It was a catastrophe from which there was no recovery. Elements of Maya culture survived in scattered settlements, but the great cities were deserted, and large-scale construction and artistic work ceased. The last date inscribed in stone corresponds to 909 C.E. As a complex civilization, the Maya had passed into history.

Explaining this remarkable demise has long kept scholars guessing. It seems clear that neither foreign invasion nor internal rebellion played a major role, as they had in the collapse of the Roman and Chinese empires. One recent account focuses on ecological and political factors.[12] Extremely rapid population growth after 600 C.E. pushed total Maya numbers to perhaps 5 million or more and soon outstripped available resources, resulting in deforestation and the erosion of hillsides. Under such conditions, climate change in the form of prolonged droughts in the 800s may well have triggered the collapse, while political disunity and endemic rivalries prevented a coordinated and effective response to the emerging catastrophe. Maya warfare in fact became more frequent as competition for increasingly scarce land for cultivation became sharper. Whatever the precise explanation, the Maya collapse, like that of the Romans and others, illustrates the fragility of civilizations, whether they are embodied in large empires or organized in a more decentralized fashion.

Teotihuacán: The Americas' Greatest City

At roughly the same time as the Maya flourished in the southern regions of Mesoamerica, the giant city of Teotihuacán, to the north in the Valley of Mexico, was also thriving. Begun around 150 B.C.E. and apparently built to a plan rather than evolving haphazardly, the city came to occupy about eight square miles and by 550 C.E. had a population variously estimated between 100,000 and 200,000. It was by far the largest urban complex in the Americas at the time and one of the six largest in the world. Beyond this, much about Teotihuacán is unknown, such as its original name, the language of its people, the kind of government that ordered its life, and the precise function of its many deities.

Physically, the city was enormously impressive, replete with broad avenues, spacious plazas, huge marketplaces, temples, palaces, apartment complexes, slums, waterways, reservoirs, drainage systems, and colorful murals. Along the main north/south boulevard, now known as the Street of the Dead, were the grand homes of the elite, the headquarters of state authorities, many temples, and two giant pyramids. One of them, the Pyramid of the Sun, had been constructed over an ancient tunnel leading to a cave and may well have been regarded as the site of creation itself, the birthplace

■ **Connection**
In what ways did Teotihuacán shape the history of Mesoamerica?

of the sun and the moon. At the Temple of the Feathered Serpent, archeologists have found the remains of some 200 people, their hands and arms tied behind them; they were the apparently unwilling sacrificial victims meant to accompany into the afterlife the high-ranking persons buried there.

Off the main avenues in a gridlike pattern of streets lay thousands of residential apartment compounds, home to the city's commoners, each with its own kitchen area, sleeping quarters, courtyards, and shrines. In these compounds, perhaps in groups of related families or lineages, lived many of the farmers who tilled the lands outside the city. Thousands of Maya specialists—masons, leather workers, potters, construction laborers, merchants, civil servants—also made their homes in these apartments. So too did skilled makers of obsidian blades, who plied their trade in hundreds of separate workshops, generating products that were in great demand throughout Mesoamerica. At least two small sections of the city were reserved exclusively for foreigners.

Buildings, both public and private, were decorated with mural paintings, sculptures, and carvings. Many of these works of art display abstract geometric and stylized images. Others depict gods and goddesses, arrayed in various forms—feathered serpents, starfish, jaguars, flowers, and warriors. One set of murals shows happy people cavorting in a paradise of irrigated fields, playing games, singing, and chasing butterflies, which were thought to represent the souls of the dead. Another portrays dancing warriors carrying elaborate curved knives, to which were attached bleeding human hearts.

The art of Teotihuacán, unlike that of the Maya, has revealed few images of self-glorifying rulers or individuals. Nor did the city have a tradition of written public inscriptions as the Maya did, although a number of glyphs or characters suggest at least a limited form of writing. One scholar has suggested that "the rulers of Teotihuacán might have intentionally avoided the personality cult of the dynastic art and writing" so characteristic of the Maya.[13] Some have argued that those rulers may have constituted an oligarchy or council of high-ranking elites rather than a single monarch.

However it was governed, Teotihuacán cast a huge shadow over Mesoamerica, particularly from 300 to 600 C.E., although scholars disagree as to precisely how its power and influence were exercised. A core region of perhaps 10,000 square miles was administered directly from the city itself, while

A Mural of Teotihuacán
This mural depicts the paradise of Tlaloc, the god of the rain, which was available only to those who had died through drowning, storms, or lightning. Fish and human figures swim and play in the river, while others cavort on the land in what seems to be a fertile and happy place. The dating of such murals is uncertain, but most were apparently created between 450 and 650 C.E. (Richard Seaman)

tribute was no doubt exacted from other areas within its broader sphere of influence. At a greater distance, the power of Teotihuacán's armies gave it a presence in the Maya heartland more than 600 miles to the east. At least one Maya city, Kaminalijuyu in the southern highlands, was completely taken over by the Teotihuacán military and organized as a colony. In Tikal, a major lowland Maya city, in the year 378 C.E., agents of Teotihuacán apparently engineered a coup that placed a collaborator on the throne and turned the city for a time into an ally or a satellite. Elsewhere—in the Zapotec capital of Monte Alban, for example—murals show unarmed persons from Teotihuacán engaged in what seems to be more equal diplomatic relationships.

At least some of this political and military activity was no doubt designed to obtain, either by trade or by tribute, valued commodities from afar—food products, cacao beans, tropical bird feathers, honey, salt, medicinal herbs. The presence in Teotihuacán of foreigners, perhaps merchants, from the Gulf Coast and Maya lowlands, as well as much pottery from those regions, provides further evidence of long-distance trade. Moreover, the sheer size and prestige of Teotihuacán surely persuaded many, all across Mesoamerica, to imitate the architectural and artistic styles of the city. Thus, according to a leading scholar, "Teotihuacán meant something of surpassing importance far beyond its core area."[14] Almost a thousand years after its still-mysterious collapse around 650 C.E., the peoples of the Aztec Empire dubbed the great metropolis as Teotihuacán, the "city of the gods."

Civilizations of the Andes

Yet another center of civilization in the Americas lay in the dramatic landscape of the Andes. Bleak deserts along the coast supported human habitation only because they were cut by dozens of rivers flowing down from the mountains, offering the possibility of irrigation and cultivation. The offshore waters of the Pacific Ocean also provided an enormously rich marine environment with an endless supply of seabirds and fish. The Andes themselves, a towering mountain chain with many highland valleys, afforded numerous distinct ecological niches, depending on altitude. On its steep slopes, people carved out huge staircase terrace systems, which remain impressive in the twenty-first century.

Classical Civilizations of the Andes

The most well known of the civilizations to take shape in this environment was that of the Incas, which encompassed practically the entire region, some 2,500 miles in length, in the fifteenth century. Yet the Incas represented only the most recent and the largest in a long history of civilizations in the area.

The coastal region of central Peru had in fact generated one of the world's First Civilizations, known as Norte Chico, dating back to around 3000 B.C.E. (see Chapter 3). The classical era in Andean civilization, roughly 1000 B.C.E. to 1000 C.E., provides an opportunity to look briefly at several of the cultures that followed Norte Chico and preceded the Inca civilization. Because none of them had developed writing, historians are largely dependent on archeology for an understanding of these civilizations.

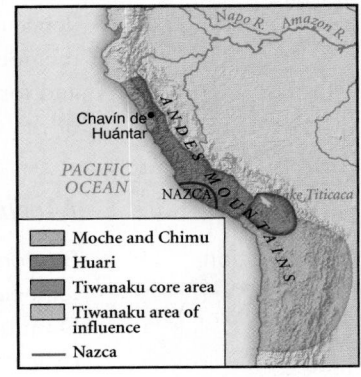

Chavín de Huántar

PACIFIC OCEAN

NAZCA

ANDES MOUNTAINS

Lake Titicaca

Napo R. Amazon R.

Moche and Chimu
Huari
Tiwanaku core area
Tiwanaku area of influence
Nazca

Chavín: A Pan-Andean Religious Movement

■ Connection
What kind of influence
did Chavín exert in the
Andes region?

In both the coastal and highland regions of Peru, archeologists have uncovered numerous local ceremonial centers or temple complexes, dating to between 2000 and 1000 B.C.E. Often constructed in a characteristic U shape, they were associated with small-scale irrigation projects and suggest the growing authority of religious leaders. Human trophy heads indicate raiding, warfare, and violence among these local centers. Then around 900 B.C.E., one of them, located in the Andean highlands at a village called Chavín de Huántar, became the focus of a religious movement that soon swept through both coastal and highland Peru.

Chavín de Huántar enjoyed a strategic location, high in the Andes and situated on trade routes to both the coastal region to the west and the Amazon rain forest to the east. By perhaps 750 B.C.E., it had become a small town of 2,000 to 3,000 people, with clear distinctions between an elite class, who lived in stone houses, and ordinary people, with adobe dwellings. An elaborate temple complex included numerous galleries, hidden passageways, staircases, ventilation shafts, drainage canals, and distinctive carvings. Little is known about the rituals or beliefs that animated Chavín's religious practice, but the artwork suggests that it drew on ideas from both the desert coastal region and the rain forests. Major deities were represented as jaguars, crocodiles, and snakes, all of them native to the Amazon basin. Shamans or priests likely made use of the San Pedro cactus, native to the Andes Mountains, employing its hallucinogenic properties to penetrate the supernatural world. Some of the fantastic artwork of this civilization—its jaguar-human images, for example—may well reflect the visions of these religious leaders.

Over the next several centuries, this blended religious movement proved attractive across much of Peru and beyond, as Chavín-style architecture, sculpture, pottery, religious images, and painted textiles were widely imitated within the region. Chavín itself became a pilgrimage site and perhaps a training center for initiates from distant centers. At locations three weeks or more away by llama caravan, temples were remodeled to resemble that of Chavín, although in many cases with locally inspired variations.[15] Much of the spread of Chavín religious imagery and practice paralleled the trade routes that linked highland and coastal Peru. Although there is some evidence for violence and warfare, no Chavín "empire" emerged. Instead, a widespread religious cult, traveling on the back of a trading network, provided for the first time and for several centuries a measure of economic and cultural integration to much of the Peruvian Andes.

Moche: A Regional Andean Civilization

■ Description
What features of Moche
life characterize it as a
civilization?

By 200 B.C.E., the pan-Andes Chavín cult had faded, replaced by a number of regional civilizations. Among them, the Moche civilization clearly stands out. Dominating a 250-mile stretch of Peru's northern coast and incorporating thirteen river valleys, the Moche people flourished between about 100 and 800 C.E. Their economy was rooted in a complex irrigation system, requiring constant maintenance, which funneled runoff from the Andes into fields of maize, beans, and squash and acres of cotton, all fertilized by rich bird droppings called guano. Moche fishermen also harvested millions of anchovies from the bountiful Pacific.

Politically, Moche was governed by warrior-priests, some of whom lived atop huge pyramids. The largest of these structures, dubbed the Pyramid of the Sun, had been constructed from 143 million sun-dried bricks. There shaman-rulers, often under the influence of hallucinogenic drugs, conducted ancient rituals that mediated between the world of humankind and that of the gods. They also presided over the ritual sacrifice of human victims, drawn from their many prisoners of war, which became central to the politico-religious life of the Moche. Images on Moche pottery show a ruler attired in a magnificent feather headdress and seated on a pyramid, while a parade of naked prisoners marches past him. Other scenes of decapitation and dismemberment indicate the fate that awaited those destined for sacrifice. For these rulers, the Moche world was apparently one of war, ritual, and diplomacy.

The immense wealth of this warrior-priest elite and the exquisite artistry of Moche craftsmen are reflected in the elaborate burials accorded the rulers. At one site, Peruvian archeologists uncovered the final resting place of three such individuals, whom they named the Lords of Sipan. Laid in adobe burial chambers, one above the other, each was decked out in his ceremonial regalia—elaborate gold masks, necklaces, and headdresses; turquoise and gold bead bracelets; cotton tunics covered with copper plates; a gold rattle showing a Moche warrior smashing a prisoner with his war club; and a copper knife. In 2005, in another remarkable discovery dating to about 450 C.E., archeologists found the burial place of a very high-status woman, who was in her late twenties and heavily tattooed. She had been laid to rest with hundreds of funeral objects, including gold sewing needles; weaving tools; much gold, silver, and copper jewelry; and a female sacrificial victim lying beside her. Even more suggestive were two elaborate war clubs and twenty-three spear throwers. Was she perhaps a warrior, a priest, or a ruler?

The most accessible aspect of Moche life and much of what scholars know about the Moche world derive from the superb skill of their craftspeople, such as metalworkers, potters, weavers, and painters. Face masks, figures of animals, small earrings, and other jewelry items, many plated in gold, display amazing technical abilities and a striking artistic sensibility. On their ceramic pottery are naturalistic portraits of noble lords and rulers and images from the life of common people, including the blind and the sick. Battle scenes show warriors confronting their enemies with raised clubs. Erotic encounters between men and women and gods making love to humans likewise represent common themes, as do grotesque images of their many gods and goddesses. Much of this, of course, reflects the culture of the Moche elite. We know much less about the daily life of the farmers, fishermen, weavers, traders, construction workers, and servants whose labor made that elite culture possible.

These cultural achievements, however, rested on fragile environmental foundations, for the region was subject to drought, earthquakes, and occasional torrential

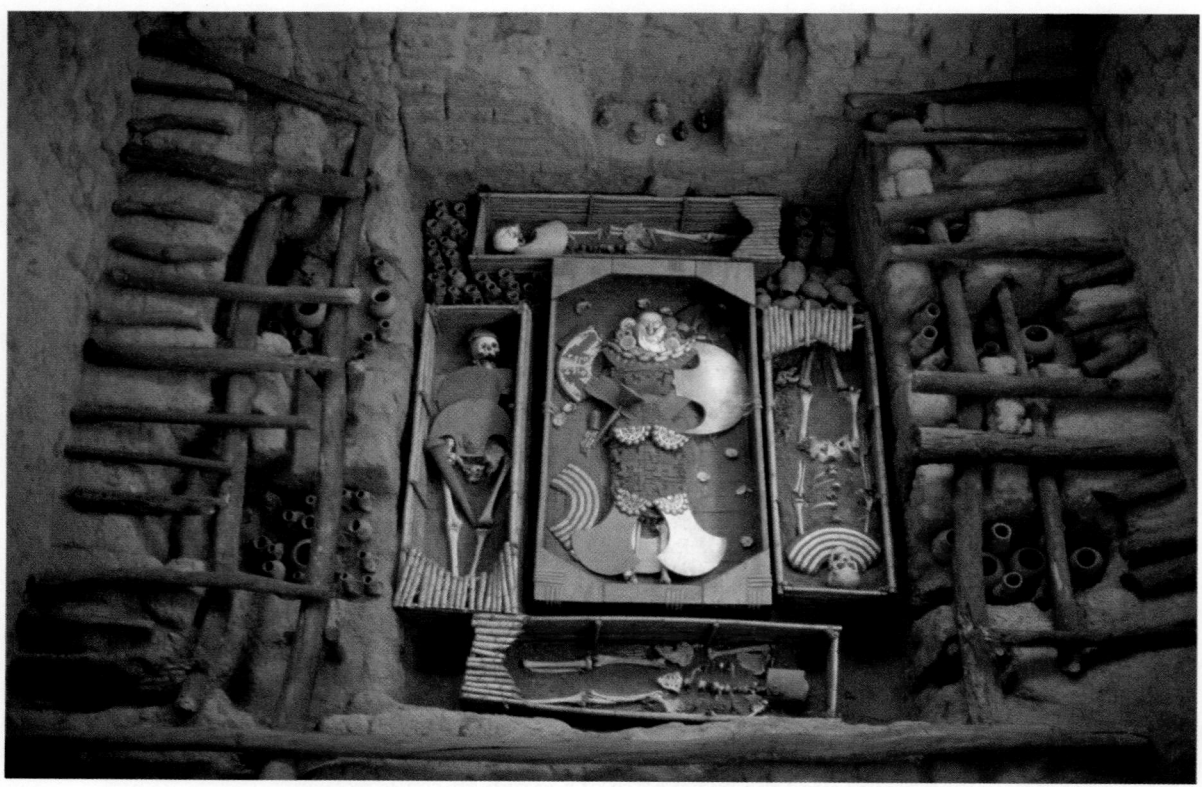

The Lord of Sipan
The Moche ruler in the center of the grave, dating to about 290 C.E., was about forty years old when he died and, at five feet five inches, was quite tall for the time. Except for early signs of arthritis, he was in good health and seems to have performed little physical labor during his life. Accompanying him in death were the four individuals shown here, plus three young women, a priest, a guard, a dog, and considerable food and drink. (Kevin Schafter/Corbis)

rains associated with El Niño episodes (dramatic changes in weather patterns caused by periodic warming of Pacific Ocean currents). Scholars believe that during the sixth century C.E. some combination of these forces caused extended ecological disruption, which seriously undermined Moche civilization. In these circumstances, the Moche were vulnerable to aggressive neighbors and possibly to internal social tensions as well. By the end of the eighth century C.E., that civilization had passed into history.[16]

The Chavín and Moche civilizations were but two of the many that grew up in the Andes region before the Incas consolidated the entire area into a single empire. The Nazca, for example, on the arid southern coast of Peru, have become famous for their underground irrigation canals, polychrome pottery, and textiles, but especially for their gigantic and mysterious lines in the desert in the form of monkeys, birds, spiders, whales, and various abstract designs. In the interior, a series of larger states emerged. One of them was centered on Tiwanaku, a city of monumental buildings and perhaps 40,000 to 50,000 people that flourished during much of the first millennium C.E. The Huari and Chimu kingdoms were further examples of this Andean civilization, to which the Incas gave a final and spectacular expression before all of the Americas was swallowed up in European empires from across the sea.

North America in the Classical Era: From Chaco to Cahokia

The peoples of the Americas in the pre-Columbian era might be divided into three large groupings. The most prominent and well known are those of the Mesoamerican and Andean regions, where cities, states, and dense populations created civilizations broadly similar to those of classical Eurasia. Elsewhere, gathering and hunting peoples carried on the most ancient of human adaptations to the environment. Arctic and subarctic cultures; the bison hunters of the Great Plains; the complex and settled communities of the Pacific coast, such as the Chumash (see Chapter 1); nomadic bands living in the arid regions of southern South America—all of these represent the persistence of gathering and hunting peoples in substantial regions of the Americas.

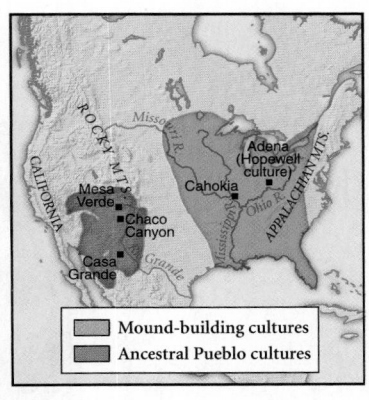

North America in the Classical Era

Even larger areas—the eastern woodlands of the United States, Central America, the Amazon basin, the Caribbean islands—were populated by peoples sometimes defined as "semi-sedentary."[17] These were agricultural societies, although less intensive and productive than those of Mesoamerica or the Andes and supporting usually much smaller populations. Nor did they generate large urban centers or inclusive empires.

These peoples who lived beyond the direct reach of the major civilizations also made their own histories, changing in response to their unique environments, their interactions with outsiders, and their own visions of the world. The Anasazi of the southwestern United States, now called the Ancestral Pueblo, and the mound-building cultures of the eastern woodlands provide two illustrations from North America during the classical era.

Pit Houses and Great Houses: The Ancestral Pueblo

The southwestern region of North America, an arid land cut by mountain ranges and large basins, first acquired maize from its place of origin in Mesoamerica during the second millennium B.C.E., but it took roughly 2,000 years for that crop, later supplemented by beans and squash, to become the basis of a settled agricultural way of living. In a desert region, farming was risky, and maize had to be gradually adapted to the local environment. Not until around 600 to 800 C.E. did permanent village life take hold widely. People then lived in pit houses with floors sunk several feet below ground level. Some settlements had only a few such homes, whereas others contained twenty-five or more. By 900 C.E., many of these villages also included kivas, much larger pit structures used for ceremonial purposes, which symbolized the widespread belief that humankind emerged into this world from another world below. Individual settlements were linked to one another in local trading networks and sometimes in wider webs of exchange that brought them buffalo hides, copper, turquoise, seashells, macaw feathers, and coiled baskets from quite distant locations.

■ **Comparison**

In what ways were the histories of the Ancestral Pueblo and the Mound Builders similar to each other, and how did they differ?

Pueblo Bonito
Called Pueblo Bonito ("pretty village") by the Spanish, this great house of the Ancestral Pueblo people was at its high point in the eleventh century C.E. The circular structures, known as kivas, were probably ceremonial sites. Their prominence, and the absence of major trash collections, have persuaded some scholars that Pueblo Bonito was more of a ritual center than a residential town. (Courtesy, Chaco Canyon National Historic Park)

These processes of change—growing dependence on agriculture, increasing population, more intensive patterns of exchange—gave rise to larger settlements and adjacent aboveground structures known as pueblos. The most spectacular of these took shape in Chaco canyon in what is now northwestern New Mexico. There, between 860 and 1130 C.E., five major pueblos emerged. This Chaco Phenomenon encompassed 25,000 square miles and linked some seventy outlying settlements to the main centers. The population was not large, perhaps as few as 5,000 people, although experts continue to debate the issue. The largest of these towns, or "great houses," Pueblo Bonito, stood five stories high and contained more than 600 rooms and many kivas. Hundreds of miles of roads, up to forty feet wide, radiated out from Chaco, likewise prompting much debate among scholars. Without wheeled carts or large domesticated animals, such an elaborate road system seems unnecessary for ordinary trade or travel. Did the roads represent, as some scholars speculate, a "sacred landscape which gave order to the world," joining its outlying communities to a "Middle Place," an entrance perhaps to the underworld?[18]

Among the Chaco elite were highly skilled astronomers, who constructed an observatory of three large rock slabs situated so as to throw a beam of light across a spiral rock carving behind it at the summer solstice. By the eleventh century, Chaco also had become a dominant center for the production of turquoise ornaments, which became a major item of regional commerce, extending as far south as Mesoamerica. Not all was sweetness and light, however. Warfare, internal conflict, and occasional cannibalism (a matter of much controversy among scholars) apparently increased in frequency as an extended period of drought in the half century following 1130 brought this flourishing culture to a rather abrupt end. By 1200, the great houses had been abandoned and their inhabitants scattered in small communities that later became the Pueblo peoples of more recent times.

The Mound Builders of the Eastern Woodlands

Unlike the Chaco region in the southwest, the eastern woodlands of North America and especially the Mississippi River valley hosted an independent Agricultural Revolution. By 2000 B.C.E., many of its peoples had domesticated local plant species, including sunflowers, sumpweed, goosefoot, some gourds and squashes, and a form of artichoke. These few plants, however, were not sufficient to support a fully settled agricultural village life; rather they supplemented diets derived from gathering and hunting without fundamentally changing that ancient way of life. Such peoples created societies distinguished by arrays of large earthen mounds, found all over the United States east of the Mississippi, prompting archeologists to dub them the Mound Builders.[19] The earliest of them date to around 2000 B.C.E., but the most elaborate and widespread of these mound-building cultures took shape between 200 B.C.E. and 400 C.E. and is known to scholars as the Hopewell culture, after an archeological site in Ohio.

Several features of the Hopewell culture have intrigued archeologists. Particularly significant are the striking burial mounds and geometric earthworks, sometimes covering areas equivalent to several city blocks, and the wide variety of artifacts found within them—smoking pipes, human figurines, mica mirrors, flint blades, fabrics, and jewelry of all kinds. The mounds themselves were no doubt the focus of elaborate burial rituals, but some of them were aligned with the moon with such precision as to allow the prediction of lunar eclipses. Developed most elaborately in the Ohio River valley, Hopewell-style earthworks, artifacts, and ceremonial pottery have also been found throughout the eastern woodlands region of North America. Hopewell centers in Ohio contained mica from the Appalachian Mountains, volcanic glass from Yellowstone, conch shells and sharks' teeth from the Gulf of Mexico, and copper from the Great Lakes. All of this suggests an enormous "Hopewell Interaction Sphere," linking this huge region in a loose network of exchange, as well as a measure of cultural borrowing of religious ideas and practices within this immense area.[20]

The next and most spectacular phase in the history of these mound-building peoples took shape as corn-based agriculture, derived ultimately but indirectly from Mexico, gained ground in the Mississippi valley after 800 C.E., allowing larger populations and more complex societies to emerge. The dominant center was Cahokia, near present-day St. Louis, Missouri, which flourished from about 900 to 1250 C.E. Its central mound, a terraced pyramid of four levels, measured 1,000 feet long by 700 feet wide, rose more than 100 feet above the ground, and occupied fifteen acres. It was the largest structure north of Mexico, the focal point of a community numbering 10,000 or more people, and the center of a widespread trading network (see an artist's reconstruction of Cahokia on p. 66).

Cahokia emerged and flourished at about the same time as did the great houses of Chaco canyon, but its urban presence was far larger than that of its southwestern counterpart. Both were made possible by the arrival of corn-based agriculture, originating in Mesoamerica, though direct contact with Mexico is much more apparent in Chaco. Finally, Cahokia emerged as the climax of a long history of mound-building cultures in the eastern woodlands, whereas Chaco was more of a "start-up" culture, emerging quite quickly "with a relatively shallow history."[21]

Evidence from burials and from later Spanish observers suggests that Cahokia and other centers of this Mississippi culture were stratified societies with a clear elite and with rulers able to mobilize the labor required to build such enormous structures. One high-status male was buried on a platform of 20,000 shell beads, accompanied by 800 arrowheads, sheets of copper and mica, and a number of sacrificed men and women nearby.[22] Well after Cahokia had declined and was abandoned, sixteenth-century Spanish and French explorers encountered another such chiefdom among the Natchez people, located in southwestern Mississippi. Paramount chiefs, known as Great Suns, dressed in knee-length fur coats and lived luxuriously in deerskin-covered homes. An elite class of "principal men" or "honored peoples" clearly occupied a different status from commoners, sometimes referred to as "stinkards." These sharp class distinctions were blunted by the requirement that upperclass people, including the Great Suns, had to marry "stinkards."

The military capacity of these Mississippi chiefdoms greatly impressed European observers, as this Spanish account indicates:

> The next day the cacique [paramount chief] arrived with 200 canoes filled with men, having weapons... the warriors standing erect from bow to stern, holding bows and arrows.... [F]rom under the canopy where the chief man was, the course was directed and orders issued to the rest.... [W]hat with the awnings, the plumes, the shields, the pennons, and the number of people in the fleet, it appeared like a famous armada of galleys.[23]

Here then in the eastern woodlands of North America were peoples who independently generated a modest Agricultural Revolution, assimilated corn and beans from distant sources, developed increasingly complex societies, and created monumental structures, new technologies, and artistic traditions. In doing so, they gave rise to a regional cultural complex that enveloped much of the United States east of the Mississippi in a network of ceremonial, economic, and cultural exchange.

Reflections: Deciding What's Important: Balance in World History

Among the perennial problems that teachers and writers of world history confront is sorting through the vast record of times past and choosing what to include and what to leave out. A related issue involves the extent to which particular peoples or civilizations will be treated. Should the Persians get as much space as the Greeks? Does Africa merit equal treatment with Eurasia? Where do the Americas fit in the larger human story? What, in short, are the criteria for deciding what is important in telling the story of the human venture?

One standard might be duration. Should ways of living that have endured for longer periods of time receive greater attention than those of lesser length? If historians followed only this criterion, then the Paleolithic era of gathering and hunting should occupy 90 percent or more of any world history text. On the other hand, perhaps change is more important than continuity. If so, then something new merits more space than something old. Thus we pay attention to both agriculture and civilizations because they represent significant turning points in human experience. Population provides yet another principle for determining inclusion. That, of course, is the reason that Eurasia, with about 80 percent of the world's population during the classical era, is addressed in three chapters of this book, whereas Africa and the Americas together receive only one chapter. There is also the related issue of influence. Buddhism, Christianity, and Islam spread more widely and shaped the lives of more people than did the religions of the Maya or the Bantu-speaking peoples of Africa. Do the major religions therefore deserve more extended treatment? Still another factor involves the availability of evidence. In this respect, classical-era Eurasia generated far more written records than either Africa or the Americas did, and therefore its history has been investigated far more thoroughly.

A final possible criterion involves the location of the historian and his or her audience. The recent development of world history as a field of study has sought vigorously to counteract a Eurocentric telling of the human story. Still, is there anything inherently wrong with an account of world history that is centered on one's own people? When I taught history in an Ethiopian high school in the mid-1960s, I was guided by an Afrocentric curriculum, which focused first on Ethiopian history, then on Africa as a whole, and finally on the larger world. Might a world historian from the Middle East, for example, legitimately strike a somewhat different balance in the treatment of various civilizations than someone writing for a largely Western audience or for Chinese readers?

Any account of the world's past will mix and match these criteria in various and contested ways. Among scholars, there exists neither a consensus about this question nor any formula to ensure a "proper" balance. You may want to consider whether the balance struck in this chapter, this section, and the book as a whole is appropriate or somehow out of line.

Second Thoughts

What's the Significance?

To assess your mastery of the material in this chapter, visit the **Student Center** at bedfordstmartins.com/strayer.

Meroë	Maya civilization	Chaco Phenomenon
Axum	Teotihuacán	Mound Builders/Cahokia
Niger Valley civilization	Chavín	
Bantu expansion	Moche	

Big Picture Questions

1. "The histories of Africa and the Americas during the classical era largely resemble those of Eurasia." Do you agree with this statement? Explain why or why not.
2. "The particular cultures and societies of Africa and of the Americas discussed in this chapter developed largely in isolation from one another." What evidence would support this statement, and what might challenge it?
3. What generated change in the histories of Africa and the Americas during the classical era?

Next Steps: For Further Study

For Web sites and additional documents related to this chapter, see **Make History** at bedfordstmartins.com/strayer.

Richard E. W. Adams, *Ancient Civilizations of the New World* (1997). A broad survey based on current scholarship of the Americas before Columbus.

Christopher Ehret, *The Civilizations of Africa* (2002). A recent overview of African history before 1800 by a prominent scholar.

Brian M. Fagan, *Ancient North America* (2005). A prominent archeologist's account of North American history.

Eric Gilbert and Jonathan T. Reynolds, *Africa in World History* (2004). An accessible account of African history set in a global context.

Guy Gugliotta, "The Maya: Glory and Ruin," *National Geographic* (August 2007). A beautifully illustrated account of the rise and fall of Maya civilization.

Kairn A. Klieman, *"The Pygmies Were Our Compass": Bantu and Batwa in the History of West Central Africa, Early Times to c. 1900 C.E.* (2003). A scholarly examination of the Pygmies (Batwa) of the Congo River basin and their interaction with Bantu-speaking peoples.

Charles Mann, *1491* (2005). A thoughtful journalist's account, delightfully written, of the controversies surrounding the history of the Americas before 1492.

"Ancient Africa's Black Kingdoms," http://www.homestead.com/wysinger/ancientafrica.html. A Web site exploring the history of Nubia.

"Maya Adventures," http://www.smm.org/sln/ma. A collection of text and pictures about the Maya, past and present.

Documents

Considering the Evidence:
Axum and the World

In the world of ancient African history, Axum has occupied a unique position in several ways. (See Map 7.1, p. 285, and pp. 286–88.) It is one of the few places in Africa, outside of Egypt, for which considerable documentary evidence exists. Some of the written sources—royal inscriptions and coins, for example—derive from within Axum itself, while others come from Greco-Roman and Christian visitors. Furthermore, after the rise of Islam, Axum—and its Ethiopian successor state—was the major surviving outpost of a Christian tradition, which had earlier spread widely across north and northeast Africa. Finally, Axum demonstrated an impressive cultural and religious continuity. Even after the decline of the Axumite empire by the eighth century C.E., the city of Axum remained a major pilgrimage site for Christians, while Ethiopian kings into the twentieth century were crowned there.[24] The documents that follow offer a series of windows on this classical-era African kingdom.

Document 7.1

A Guidebook to
the World of Indian Ocean Commerce

The earliest documentary reference to Axum was composed during the first century C.E. in an anonymous text known as *The Periplus of the Erythraean Sea.* Likely written by a sea captain from Roman-controlled Egypt, the *Periplus* offers a guide to the places and conditions that merchants might encounter as they traversed the Red Sea and the East African coast while on their way to India.

- According to this text, why is the Axumite port of Adulis significant?

- What evidence does the *Periplus* provide about Axum's cultural and economic ties to the larger world?

- Based on the list of imports and exports, how would you describe Axum's role in the international commerce of the first century C.E.?

- How might Axum's participation in long-distance trade have stimulated and sustained its growth as an empire?

The Periplus of the Erythraean Sea
First Century C.E.

Below Ptolemais of the Hunts°... there is Adulis, a port established by law, lying at the inner end of a bay that runs in toward the south. Before the harbor lies the so-called Mountain Island, about two hundred stadia° sea-ward from the very head of the bay, with the shores of the mainland close to it on both sides. Ships bound for this port now anchor here because of attacks from the land. They used formerly to anchor at the very head of the bay, by an island called Diodorus, close to the shore, which could be reached on foot from the land; by which means the barbarous natives attacked the island. Opposite Mountain Island, on the mainland twenty stadia from shore, lies Adulis, a fair-sized village, from which there is a three-days' journey to Coloe, an inland town and the first market for ivory. From that place to the city of the people called Axumites there is a five days' journey more; to that place all the ivory is brought from the country beyond the Nile through the district called Cyeneum, and thence to Adulis. Practically the whole number of elephants and rhinoceros that are killed live in the places inland, although at rare intervals they are hunted on the seacoast even near Adulis. Before the harbor of that market-town, out at sea on the right hand, there lie a great many little sandy islands called Alalaei, yielding tortoise-shell, which is brought to market there by the Fish-Eaters.

And about eight hundred stadia beyond there is another very deep bay, with a great mound of sand piled up at the right of the entrance; at the bottom of which the opsian° stone is found, and this is the only place where it is produced. These places... are governed by Zoscales,° who is miserly in his ways and always striving for more, but otherwise upright, and acquainted with Greek literature.

There are imported into these places undressed cloth made in Egypt for the Berbers; robes from Arsinoe; cloaks of poor quality dyed in colors; double-fringed linen mantles; many articles of flint glass, and others of murrhine, made in Diospolis;° and brass, which is used for ornament and in cut pieces instead of coin; sheets of soft copper, used for cooking utensils and cut up for bracelets and anklets for the women; iron, which is made into spears used against the elephants and other wild beasts, and in their wars. Besides these, small axes are imported, and adzes and swords; copper drinking-cups, round and large; a little coin° for those coming to the market [probably foreign merchants living in Adulis]; wine of Laodicea and Italy, not much; olive oil, not much; for the king, gold and silver plate made after the fashion of the country, and for clothing, military cloaks, and thin coats of skin, of no great value. Likewise from the district of Ariaca° across this sea, there are imported Indian iron, and steel, and Indian cotton cloth; the broad cloth called *monache* and that called *sagimtogene*, and girdles, and coats of skin and mallow-colored cloth, and a few muslins, and colored lac.° There are exported from these places ivory, and tortoise-shell and rhinoceros-horn. The most from Egypt is brought to this market from the month of January, to September, that is, from Tybi to Thoth; but seasonably they put to sea about the month of September.

°**Ptolemais of the Hunts:** near modern Port Sudan on the Red Sea.

°**stadia:** 1 stadium = ⅛ mile.

°**opsian:** obsidian.

Source: Wilfred H. Schoff, *The Periplus of the Erythraean Sea* (New York: Longman, Green and Co., 1912), Sections 4–6.

°**Zoscales:** an Axumite ruler.

°**Diospolis:** Thebes.

°**coin:** Roman money.

°**Ariaca:** an area in western India.

°**lac:** a resinous secretion of an insect, used in the form of shellac.

Document 7.2

The Making of an Axumite Empire

At its high point in the mid-fourth century C.E., Axum ruled an empire stretching from Meroë in the upper Nile Valley, across most of what is now Eritrea and Ethiopia, and incorporating parts of southern Arabia on the opposite side of the Red Sea. Document 7.2 comes from an Axumite inscription written in Greek on a stone throne adorned with figures of the Greek gods Hercules and Mercury. Commissioned by an unknown Axumite monarch, the inscription dates probably from the second or third century C.E. It was copied and then published in the sixth century by Cosmas, a Greek merchant born in Alexandria, Egypt, who had become a monk. This text describes some of the conquests that generated the Axumite Empire.

- What internal evidence from the document itself dates it prior to Axum's acceptance of Christianity?

- How would you describe the point of view from which the document was written?

- What techniques of imperial control does the document reveal?

- How might you account for the obvious Greek influence that is apparent in the inscription?

- How would you describe the religious or ideological underpinnings of this empire? Why might the Axumite ruler who commissioned this inscription single out Ares, Zeus, and Poseidon for special attention?

Inscription on a Stone Throne
Second or Third Century C.E.

Having after this with a strong hand compelled the nations bordering on my kingdom to live in peace, I made war upon the following nations, and by force of arms reduced them to subjection. I warred first with the nation of Gaze [Axum, probably in an internal struggle for power], then with Agame and Sigye, and having conquered them, I exacted the half of all that they possessed. I next reduced Aua and Tiamo, called Tziam, and the Gambela, and the tribes near them, and Zingabene and Angabe and Tiama and Athagaus and Kalaa, and the Semenoi—a people who lived beyond the Nile on mountains difficult of access and covered with snow, where the year is all winter with hailstorms, frosts and snows into which a man sinks knee-deep. I passed the river to attack these nations, and reduced them. I next subdued Lazine and Zaa and Gabala, tribes which inhabit mountains with steep declivities abounding with hot springs, the Atalmo and Bega, and all the tribes in the same quarter along with them.°

Source: J. W. McCrindle, trans. and ed., *The Christian Topography of Cosmas, an Egyptian Monk* (London: The Hakluyt Society, 1897), 59–66.

°(Note that scholars are often unable to precisely locate the people or places mentioned in the text.)

I proceeded next against the Tangaltae, who adjoin the borders of Egypt; and having reduced them I made a footpath giving access by land into Egypt from that part of my dominions. Next I reduced Annine and Metine—tribes inhabiting precipitous mountains. My arms were next directed against the Sesea nation. These had retired to a high mountain difficult of access; but I blockaded the mountain on every side, and compelled them to come down and surrender. I then selected for myself the best of their young men and their women, with their sons and daughters and all besides that they possessed. The tribes of Rhausi I next brought to submission: a barbarous race spread over wide waterless plains in the interior of the frankincense country. [Advancing thence toward the sea,] I encountered the Solate, whom I subdued, and left with instructions to guard the coast.

All these nations, protected though they were by mountains all but impregnable, I conquered, after engagements in which I was myself present. Upon their submission I restored their territories to them, subject to the payment of tribute. Many other tribes besides these submitted of their own accord, and became likewise tributary. And I sent a fleet and land forces against the Arabitae and Cinaedocolpitae who dwelt on the other side of the Red Sea [southern Arabia], and having reduced the sovereigns of both, I imposed on them a land tribute and charged them to make traveling safe both by sea and by land. I thus subdued the whole coast from Leuce Come to the country of the Sabaeans.

I first and alone of the kings of my race made these conquests. For this success I now offer my thanks to my mighty god, Ares,° who begat me, and by whose aid I reduced all the nations bordering on my own country, on the east to the country of frankincense, and on the west to Ethiopia and Sasu. Of these expeditions, some were conducted by myself in person, and ended in victory, and the others I entrusted to my officers. Having thus brought all the world under my authority to peace, I came down to Adulis and offered sacrifice to Zeus,° and to Ares, and to Poseidon,° whom I entreated to befriend all who go down to the sea in ships.° Here also I reunited all my forces, and setting down this Chair [throne] in this place, I consecrated it to Ares in the twenty-seventh year of my reign.

°**Ares:** the Greek god of warfare and slaughter.

°**Zeus:** the chief god of the Greek pantheon.

°**Poseidon:** the Greek god of the sea.

°(Note that many Axumite deities derived from southern Arabia but came to be identified with the gods of the Greek pantheon.)

Document 7.3

The Coming of Christianity to Axum

The introduction of Christianity in the mid-fourth century represented a major change in the cultural history of Axum. It meant that Axum would be more closely aligned to Christian Egypt and Byzantium than to South Arabia, from which many of its earlier cultural traditions had derived. Document 7.3 relates the story of the coming of Christianity to Axum. It was written by Rufinus (345–410 C.E.), a Christian monk and writer who was born in Italy but spent much of his life in Jerusalem, where he heard this story from those who had taken part in it. Note that Greco-Roman writers of this time used "India" to refer vaguely to East Africa and Southern Arabia as well as the south Asian peninsula.

■ According to this document, by what means was Christianity introduced to Axum? What do you think was the relative importance of Frumentius and Aedesius, as opposed to Roman merchants living in Axum?

■ Why do you think the Axumite royal family was so receptive to this foreign religion? How might the story differ if told from the ruling family's perspective?

■ How does the fact that this document was written by outsiders shape the emphasis of the story?

RUFINUS

On the Evangelization of Abyssinia
Late Fourth Century C.E.

One Metrodorus, a philosopher, is said to have penetrated to further India [the Red Sea area including Axum] in order to view places and see the world. Inspired by his example, one Meropius, a philosopher [and a Christian merchant] of Tyre,° wished to visit India with a similar object, taking with him two small boys who were related to him and whom he was educating in humane studies. The younger of these was called Aedesius, the other Frumentius. When, having seen and taken note of what his soul fed upon, the philosopher had begun to return, the ship on which he traveled put in for water or some other necessary at a certain port. It is the custom of the barbarians of these parts that, if ever the neighboring tribes report that their treaty with the Romans is broken, all Romans found among them should be massacred. The philosopher's ship was boarded; all with himself were put to the sword.

The boys were found studying under a tree and preparing their lessons, and, preserved by the mercy of the barbarians, were taken to the king [of Axum]. He made one of them, Aedesius, his cupbearer.

°**Tyre:** a city in Lebanon.

Source: Quoted in A. H. M. Jones and Elizabeth Monroe, *A History of Abyssinia* (Oxford: Oxford University Press, 1935), 26–27.

Frumentius, whom he had perceived to be sagacious and prudent, he made his treasurer and secretary. Thereafter they were held in great honor and affection by the king. The king died, leaving his wife with an infant son [Ezana] as heir of the bereaved kingdom. He gave the young men liberty to do what they pleased but the queen besought them with tears, since she had no more faithful subjects in the whole kingdom, to share with her the cares of governing the kingdom until her son should grow up, especially Frumentius, whose ability was equal to guiding the kingdom, for the other, though loyal and honest of heart, was simple.

While they lived there and Frumentius held the reins of government in his hands, God stirred up his heart and he began to search out with care those of the Roman merchants who were Christians and to give them great influence and to urge them to establish in various places conventicles to which they might resort for prayer in the Roman manner. He himself, moreover, did the same and so encouraged the others, attracting them with his favor and his benefits, providing them with whatever was needed, supplying sites for buildings and other necessaries, and in every way promoting the growth of the seed of Christianity in the country. When the prince [Ezana] for whom they exercised the regency had grown up, they completed and faithfully delivered over their trust, and, though the queen and her son sought greatly to detain them and begged them to remain, returned to the Roman Empire.

Aedesius hastened to Tyre to revisit his parents and relatives. Frumentius went to Alexandria, saying that it was not right to hide the work of God. He laid the whole affair before the bishop and urged him to look for some worthy man to send as bishop over the many Christians already congregated and the churches built on barbarian soil. Then Athanasius (for he had recently assumed the episcopate), having carefully weighed and considered Frumentius' words and deeds, declared in a council of the priests: "What other man shall we find in whom the Spirit of God is as in thee, who can accomplish these things?" And he consecrated him and bade him return in the grace of God whence he had come. And when he had arrived in India [Axum] as bishop, such grace is said to have been given to him by God that apostolic miracles were wrought by him and a countless number of barbarians were converted by him to the faith. From which time Christian peoples and churches have been created in the parts of India, and the priesthood has begun. These facts I know not from vulgar report but from the mouth of Aedesius himself, who had been Frumentius' companion and was later made a priest in Tyre.

Document 7.4

A Byzantine View of an Axumite Monarch

In the sixth century, Axum became embroiled in the larger conflict between the Byzantine and Persian empires, then the superpowers of the region. In this epic struggle the Persians found an ally in the Himyarite kingdom of Arabia, several of whose leaders had converted to Judaism and were actively persecuting Christians. In 530–531, the Byzantine emperor Justinian sent an emissary to King Kaleb of Axum, appealing for his aid in attacking this threat to their common Christian faith. That emissary, named Julian, subsequently made a report to Justinian that contained a description of the court of the Axumite ruler and his now Christian court.

■ Why do you think King Kaleb was so eager join Byzantium in its struggle against Persia and its Arab Himyarite ally? Consider both religious and strategic reasons.

■ What evidence in the document suggests that the Byzantine authorities considered King Kaleb an equal? What evidence might suggest that they saw him as a subordinate?

■ What did Julian find especially striking about King Kaleb's appearance and behavior?

JULIAN

Report to the Byzantine Emperor on Axum

530-531

In the same year, the Romans and Persians broke their peace. The Persian war was renewed because of the embassy of the…Himyarite Arabs to the Romans. The Romans sent the Magistrianos Julian from Alexandria down the Nile River and through the Indian Ocean with sacral letters to [Kaleb], the king of the Ethiopans. King [Kaleb] received him with great joy, since [Kaleb] longed after the Roman Emperor's friendship.

On his return (to Constantinople), this same Julian reported that King [Kaleb] was naked when he received him but had round his kidneys a loin-cloth of linen and gold thread. On his belly he wore linen with precious pearls; his bracelets had five spikes, and he wore gold armlets by his hands. He had a linen-and-gold cloth turban round his head, with four cords hanging down from both its straps.

He stood on (a carriage drawn by) four standing elephants which had a yoke and four wheels. Like any stately carriage, it was ornamented with golden petals, just as are the carriages of provincial governors. While he stood upon it, he held in his hands a small gilded shield and two gold javelins. His counselors were all armed, and sang musical tunes.

When the Roman ambassador was brought in and had performed the prostration, he was ordered to rise by the king and was led before him. [Kaleb] accepted the Emperor's sacral letters and tenderly kissed the seal which had the Emperor's image. He also accepted Julian's gifts and greatly rejoiced.

When he read the letter, he found that it was urgent for him to arm himself against the Persian king, devastate Persian territory near him [in South Arabia], and in the future no longer make covenants with the Persian. Rather, the letter arranged that the land of the [Himyarites] would conduct its business with Egyptian Alexandria by way of the Nile River.

In the sight of the envoy, King [Kaleb] immediately began to campaign: he set war in motion against the Persians and sent out his Saracens [Arabs]. He himself also went off against Persian territory and pillaged all of it in that area. After conquering, King [Kaleb] gave Julian a kiss of peace on the head and sent him off with a large retinue and many gifts.

Source: Theophanes, *Chronographia*, Annus mundi 6064. Unpublished translation by Dr. Harry Turtledove. In *Ancient African Civilizations: Kush and Axum*, edited by Stanley Burstein (Princeton: Markus Weiner, 1998), 125–26.

Document 7.5

Axum and the Gold Trade

The foundations of the Axumite state lay not only in its military conquests and its adoption of a new religion but also in its economic ties to the larger world. Among these ties was its reputation as a major source of gold for the Roman Empire. Document 7.5 describes the distinctive fashion in which Axumite traders obtained the gold from the African peoples living on the margins of the Axumite state. The author, Cosmas (see Document 7.2, pp. 309–10), was involved in this trade.

- How would you define the pattern of exchange described in this document? Was it state-directed trade, private enterprise, or both? To what problems of cross-cultural interaction was it a response?

- Who, if anyone, had the upper hand in this trade? Was it conducted between politically equal parties?

- What purposes did this trade serve for the people who mined and "sold" the gold?

- Beyond the peaceful trade for gold described here, what other purposes did this region serve for Axum?

COSMAS

The Christian Topography

Sixth Century C.E.

The country known as that of Sasu is itself near the ocean, just as the ocean is near the frankincense country,° in which there are many gold mines. The King of the Axumites accordingly, every other year, through the governor of Agau, sends thither special agents to bargain for the gold, and these are accompanied by many other traders—upwards, say, of five hundred—bound on the same errand as themselves. They take along with them to the mining district oxen, lumps of salt, and iron, and when they reach its neighborhood, they make a halt at a certain spot and form an encampment, which they fence round with a great hedge of thorns. Within this they live, and having slaughtered the oxen, cut them in pieces, and lay the pieces on the top of the thorns, along with the lumps of salt and the iron. Then come the natives bringing gold in nuggets like peas, and lay one or two or more of these upon what pleases them—the pieces of flesh or the salt or the iron, and then they retire to some distance off. Then the owner of the meat approaches, and if he is satisfied he takes the gold away, and upon seeing this, its owner comes and takes the flesh or the salt or the iron. If, however, he is not satisfied, he leaves the gold, when the native, seeing that he has not taken it, comes and either puts down more gold,

or takes up what he had laid down, and goes away. Such is the mode in which business is transacted with the people of that country, because their language is different and interpreters are hardly to be found.

The time they stay in that country is five days more or less, according as the natives, more or less readily coming forward, buy up all their wares. On the journey homeward they all agree to travel well-armed, since some of the tribes through whose country they must pass might threaten to attack them from a desire to rob them of their gold. The space of six months is taken up with this trading expedition, including both the going and the returning. In going they march very slowly, chiefly because of the cattle, but in returning they quicken their pace lest on the way they should be overtaken by winter and its rains. For the sources of the river Nile lie somewhere in these parts, and in winter, on account of the heavy rains, the numerous rivers which they generate obstruct the path of the traveler. The people there have their winter at the time we have our summer... and during the three months the rain falls in torrents, and makes a multitude of rivers all of which flow into the Nile.

The facts which I have just recorded fell partly under my own observation and partly were told me by traders who had been to those parts....

For most of the slaves which are now found in the hands of merchants who resort to these parts are taken from the tribes of which we speak. As for the Semenai, where...there are snows and ice, it is to that country the King of the Axumites expatriates anyone whom he has sentenced to be banished.

°**frankincense country:** probably what is now Somalia.

Source: J. W. McCrindle, trans. and ed., *The Christian Topography of Cosmas, an Egyptian Monk* (London: The Hakluyt Society, 1897), 52–54, 67.

Using the Evidence:
Axum and the World

1. **Assessing sources:** How does each of these documents reflect the distinctive perspective of its author? What different perspectives can you notice between those documents written from within Axum and those written by outsiders? How did the particular social role that each author represents (missionary, monarch, merchant) affect his view of Axum?

2. **Considering external influences:** Based on these documents, how would you describe Axum's various relationships with the world beyond its borders? How did its geographical location shape those relationships? (See Map 7.1, p. 285.) In what ways did those external connections influence Axum's historical development? From another perspective, how did Axum actively assimilate foreign influences or deliberately take advantage of opportunities that came from outside?

3. **Explaining the rise and significance of Axum:** How might you account for the flourishing of Axum during its classical era? What was the religious and military significance of Axum within the region?

4. **Comparing civilizations:** In what ways might Axum be viewed as a smaller-scale version of the classical civilizations of Eurasia? In what ways did it differ from them?

5. **Seeking further evidence:** What else would you like to know about Axum? If you could uncover one additional document, what would you want it to reveal?

Visual Sources

Considering the Evidence:
Art and the Maya Elite

The ancient Maya world," writes a major scholar of the region, "was a world of Maya art."[25] In magnificent architecture, carvings, pottery, ceramic figures, wall paintings, and illustrated books, Maya culture was suffused by a distinctive style of artistic expression, more complex, subtle, extensive, and innovative than any other in the Americas. Commissioned by Maya rulers, that art centered on life at court, depicting kings, nobles, warriors, and wealthy merchants together with the women, musicians, and artists who served them as well as the many deities who populated the Maya universe. Far more than in China, India, or Europe, historians rely on art and archeology for their insights into Maya civilization. While the Maya had writing, their literature was less extensive than that of classical-era Eurasian cultures and much of it was tragically destroyed during the early decades of Spanish rule. The images that follow provide a window into the life of the Maya elite during its classical era (see the map on p. 293).

Visual Source 7.1 shows a royal couple from the Maya city of Yaxchilan in the year 724 C.E. with the king Shield Jaguar, on the left, and his primary wife, Lady Xok, on the right. In helping him dress for a war-related ceremony or sacrifice, Lady Xok offers her husband his helmet, the head of a jaguar, an animal that was widely associated with strength, bravery, aggression, warfare, and high social status. The T-shaped frame at the center top, which contains a number of Maya glyphs (written symbols), indicates a doorway and thus sets the action in an interior space. The king is wearing cotton body armor and carrying a knife, while his wife is clad in a *huipil*, a blouse similar to those still worn by Maya women in southern Mexico.

■ What elements of their dress and decoration serve to mark their high status?

■ What aspects of the physical appearance of this couple might represent ideal male and female characteristics in Maya culture? Pay attention to their hair, foreheads, and noses, as well as to the attitude suggested by their faces.

■ What might you infer about the relationship of Shield Jaguar and Lady Xok from this carving? Notice the relatively equal size of the two figures and the gesture that Shield Jaguar makes with his left hand. Keep in mind that the carving comes from a temple in Yaxchilan dedicated to Lady Xok.

Visual Source 7.1 Shield Jaguar and Lady Xok: A Royal Couple of Yaxchilan (Museo Nacional de Antropologia—INAH, Mexico)

Warfare was frequent among Maya cities and thus a common theme in their court art. Fought with spear throwers, lances, clubs, axes, swords, and shields, Maya wars were depicted as chaotic affairs aimed at the capture of individual prisoners, who were destined for sacrifice or slavery. Those prisoners were often named in the glyphs that accompanied the portrayal of battles along with the inscription "He is seized/roped."

Visual Source 7.2, a reconstructed image, comes from a Maya archeological site in southern Mexico called Bonampak, well known for its vivid murals. Depicting events that took place in 792 C.E., this mural shows King Chan Muwan of Bonampak (in the center) holding a staff and receiving nine prisoners of war from his victorious noble warriors. To the king's right are two allies from the nearby city of Yaxchilan, followed by the king's wife, his mother, and a servant-musician playing a conch. To the king's left are six more high-ranking warriors from Bonampak, while lower-level warriors guard each side of the door at the bottom.

The prisoners hold center stage in the mural. Notice in particular the dead captive sprawling below the king's staff as a severed head lies on a bed of leaves below him. The four small images at the top indicate constellations, showing the favorable position of the sky for this occasion. The turtle on the far right, for example, depicts the constellation Gemini, while the three stars on its back represent what we know as Orion's belt.

- What can you infer about Maya warfare and court practice from this mural?

- What do the various postures of the captives suggest?

- Notice that a number of the captives have blood dripping from their fingers. What does this indicate? What might be happening to the prisoner at the far left?

- What status distinctions can you observe among the figures in the mural? Notice the jaguar skins worn by the king and three other warriors.

- What meaning might you attach to the presence of the king's wife and mother at this event?

The bleeding and ultimately the sacrifice of the captives in Visual Source 7.2 was only part of a more pervasive practice of bloodletting that permeated Maya religious and court life. Significant occasions—giving birth, getting married, dying, planting crops, dedicating buildings, and many more—were sanctified with human blood, the most valued and holy substance in the world. Behind this practice lay the Maya belief in the mutual relationship of humans and their gods. Two of the major scholars in this field explain: "The earth and its creatures were created through a sacrificial act of the gods, and human beings, in turn, were required to strengthen and nourish the gods."[26] The means of

Visual Source 7.2 The Presentation of Captives (Peabody Museum, Harvard University, Cambridge, MA, USA/The Bridgeman Art Library)

doing so was blood. The massive loss of blood often triggered a trancelike state that the Maya experienced as mystical union with their gods or ancestors. The lancets used to draw blood—usually from the tongue in women and often from the penis in men—were invested with sacred power.

Kings and their wives were central to this bloodletting ritual, as Visual Source 7.3 so vividly shows.   Here we meet again Shield Jaguar and Lady Xok, depicted also in Visual Source 7.1. The date of this carving is October 28,

Visual Source 7.3 A Bloodletting Ritual
(© Justin Kerr, K2887)

709 C.E. The king is holding a large torch, suggesting that the ritual occurs at night, while his kneeling wife draws a thorn-studded rope through her perforated tongue. The rope falls into a basket of bloody paper, which will later be burned with the resulting smoke nourishing the gods. Shield Jaguar too will soon let his own blood flow, for the glyphs accompanying this carving declare that "he is letting blood" and "she is letting blood."

- What details can you notice in the exquisitely carved work?

- What significance might you attribute to the fact that the couple is performing this ritual together?

- Why do you think Lady Xok is kneeling?

- Notice the shrunken head in Shield Jaguar's headdress. How would you assess its significance? How might it enhance his status?

- To what extent is this pervasive bloodletting a uniquely mesoamerican religious practice? What roles do blood and sacrifice play in other religious traditions?

Among the most well-known and intriguing features of Maya life was a ball game in which teams of players, often two on a side, sought to control a rubber ball, using only their thighs, torsos, and upper arms to make it hit a marker or ring. Deeply rooted in Maya mythology, the game was played both before and after the classical Maya era on ball courts found throughout the Maya territory as well as elsewhere in Mesoamerica. On one level, the game was sport, often played simply for entertainment and recreation. But it also reflected and symbolized the prevalence of warfare among Maya cities. As one recent account put it: "[T]he game re-enacted the paradigms for war and sacrifice, where the skillful and blessed triumph and the weak and undeserving are vanquished."[27] The ball game was yet another occasion for the shedding of blood, as losing players, often war captives, were killed, sometimes bound in ball-like fashion and rolled down the steps of the court to their death. Thus the larger mythic context of the ball game was the eternal struggle of life and death, so central to Maya religious thinking.

Visual Source 7.4, a rollout of a vase dating from the seventh or eighth century C.E., depicts the ball game in action. The two players on each side echo the Hero Twins of Maya mythology, famous ball players who triumphed over the lords of the underworld in an extended game and who were later transformed triumphantly into the sun and moon. The glyphs accompanying this image named two kings of adjacent cities, suggesting that the game may have been played on occasion as a substitute for warfare between rival cities.

■ What might the elaborate dress of the players suggest about the function of the game and the status of its players?

Visual Source 7.4 The Ball Game (© Justin Kerr, K2803)

■ Notice the deer headdress on the player at the far left and the vulture image on the corresponding player at the far right. What do the headdresses suggest about the larger mythic context in which the game was understood?

■ Notice the heavy protective padding around the waist as well as the wrappings around one knee, foot, and upper arm of the two lead players. What was the purpose of such padding? Keep in mind that the rubber ball, shown here in an exaggerated form, was roughly the size of a modern volleyball but weighed perhaps seven or eight pounds.

Visual Source 7.5 An Embracing Couple (© Dumbarton Oaks, Pre-Columbian Collection, Washington, D.C.)

■ How might you compare this ancient Maya ball game to contemporary athletic contests? Consider the larger social meaning of the game as well as its more obvious features.

Certainly not all was war, sacrifice, and bloodletting among the Maya. Visual Source 7.5, a ceramic figurine from the late classical era, illustrates a more playful and explicitly sexual side to Maya art.

■ How might you describe what is transpiring between this older man and the much younger woman? Notice the position of their hands, the woman's knee, and the expression of their faces.

As was frequently the case among the Maya, artistic expression had a mythic significance. Here the young woman probably represents the moon goddess, associated with sexuality, fertility, night, death, and frequent change of lovers, reflecting the changing cycles of the moon. In an effort to spy out her infidelities, her husband/lover, the aged sun god in Maya mythology, took on the form of a deer as represented in his headdress.

■ What might this image and its mythological context tell us about Maya views of sexuality?

Using the Evidence:
Art and the Maya Elite

1. **Considering art as evidence:** What can you learn from these visual sources about the values, preoccupations, and outlook of the Maya elite? What are the strengths and limitations of art as a source of evidence? What other kinds of evidence would you want to discover to further your understanding of the Maya elite?

2. **Assessing gender roles:** In what ways are women and men depicted in these visual sources? What might this suggest about their respective roles in the elite circles of Maya society?

3. **Making comparisons:** How might you compare the life of the Maya elite depicted in these visual sources with that of the Roman elite of Pompeii shown in the Visual Sources section of Chapter 6 (pp. 272–79)? For a second comparison, consider the similarities and differences of Maya and Axumite civilizations.

4. **Considering the values of the historian:** What feelings or judgments do these visual sources evoke in you? Which of your values might get in the way of a sympathetic understanding of the Maya elite?

PART THREE

An Age of Accelerating Connections

500–1500

Contents

Chapter 8. Commerce and Culture, 500–1500

Chapter 9. China and the World: East Asian Connections, 500–1300

Chapter 10. The Worlds of European Christendom: Connected and Divided, 500–1300

Chapter 11. The Worlds of Islam: Afro-Eurasian Connections, 600–1500

Chapter 12. Pastoral Peoples on the Global Stage: The Mongol Moment, 1200–1500

Chapter 13. The Worlds of the Fifteenth Century

Defining a Millennium

History seldom turns sharp corners, and historians often have difficulty deciding just when one phase of the human story ends and another begins. Between roughly 200 and 850 C.E., many of the classical states and civilizations of the world (Han dynasty China, the Roman Empire, Gupta India, Meroë, Axum, Maya, Teotihuacán, Moche) experienced severe disruption, decline, or collapse. For many historians, this marks the end of the classical era and the start of some new period of world history. Furthermore, almost everyone agrees that the transatlantic voyages of Columbus around 1500 represent yet another new departure in world history. This coupling of the Eastern and Western hemispheres set in motion historical processes that transformed most of the world and signaled the beginning of the modern era.

But how are we to understand the thousand years (roughly 500 to 1500) between the end of the classical era and the beginning of modern world history? Historians, frankly, have had some difficulty in defining a distinct identity for this millennium, and this problem is reflected in the vague terms used to describe it. Many textbooks, including this one on occasion, refer to this 1,000-year period simply as the "postclassical" age, but that, of course, merely indicates that it came after the classical era. Others have termed it "medieval," a middle or intermediate age, something in between the classical and modern eras. Many historians feel uncomfortable with this term because it derives specifically from European history and thus runs the risk of appearing Eurocentric. It also seems to suggest that this millennium was merely a run-up to modernity, rather than something of significance in its own right. This book sometimes uses the concept of "third-wave civilizations," distinguishing, at least chronologically, those that emerged after 500 C.E. from both the First Civilizations and those of the classical era (the second-wave civilizations). At best, these terms indicate where this period falls in the larger time frame of world history, but none of them are very descriptive.

Third-Wave Civilizations: Something New, Something Old, Something Blended

A large part of the problem lies in the rather different trajectories of various regions of the world during this postclassical era. It is not easy to identify clearly defined features that encompass all the major civilizations during this period and distinguish them from what went before, but we can point to several distinct patterns of development among these third-wave societies of the postclassical era.

In some areas, for example, wholly new but smaller civilizations arose where none had existed before. Along the East African coast, Swahili civilization emerged in a string of thirty or more city-states, very much engaged in the commercial life of the Indian Ocean basin. In the area now encompassed by Ukraine and western Russia, another new civilization, known as Kievan Rus, likewise took shape with a good deal of cultural borrowing from Mediterranean civilization. East and Southeast Asia also witnessed new centers of civilization. Those in Japan, Korea, and Vietnam were strongly influenced by China, while Srivijaya on the Indonesian island of Sumatra and later the Angkor kingdom, centered in present-day Cambodia, drew on the Hindu and Buddhist traditions of India.

All of these represent a continuation of a well-established pattern in world history—the globalization of civilization. It began with the First Civilizations of Mesopotamia, Egypt, and elsewhere about 3000 B.C.E. and then took new and larger forms in the classical era (500 B.C.E.–500 C.E.), when Greco-Roman, Persian, Indian, and Chinese civilizations flourished across Eurasia. Each of the new third-wave civilizations was, of course, culturally unique, but like their predecessors, they too featured states, cities, specialized economic roles, sharp class and gender inequalities, and other elements of "civilized" life. They were certainly distinctive, but not fundamentally different from earlier civilizations. As newcomers to the growing number of civilizations, all of them borrowed heavily from larger or more established centers.

The largest, most expansive, and most widely influential of the new third-wave civilizations was surely that of Islam. It began in Arabia in the seventh century C.E., projecting the Arab peoples into a prominent role as builders of an enormous empire while offering a new, vigorous, and attractive religion. Viewed as a new civilization defined by its religion, the world of Islam came to encompass many other centers of civilization, including Egypt, Mesopotamia, Persia, India, the interior of West Africa and the coast of East Africa, Spain, southeastern Europe, and more. Here was a uniquely cosmopolitan or "umbrella" civilization that, according to one leading scholar, "came closer than any had ever come to uniting all mankind under its ideals."[1]

Yet another, and quite different, historical pattern during the postclassical millennium involved older or classical civilizations that persisted or were reconstructed. The Byzantine Empire, embracing the eastern half of the old Roman Empire, continued the patterns of Mediterranean Christian civilization and persisted until 1453, when it was overrun by the Ottoman Turks. In China, following almost four centuries of fragmentation, the Sui, Tang, and Song dynasties (589–1279) restored China's imperial unity and reasserted its Confucian tradition. Indian civilization retained its ancient patterns of caste and Hinduism amid vast cultural diversity, even as parts of India fell under the control of Muslim rulers. The West African savanna kingdoms of Ghana, Mali, and Songhay, stimulated and sustained by long-distance trade across the Sahara, built upon the earlier Niger Valley civilization.

Variations on this theme of continuing or renewing older traditions took shape in the Western Hemisphere, where two centers of civilization—in Mesoamerica and in the Andes—had been long established. In Mesoamerica, the collapse of classical Maya civilization and of the great city-state of Teotihuacán by about 900 C.E. opened the way for other peoples to give new shape to this ancient civilization. The most well known of these efforts was associated with the Mexica or Aztec people, who created a powerful and impressive state in the fifteenth century. About the same time, on the western rim of South America, a Quechua-speaking people, now known as the Inca, incorporated various centers of Andean civilization into a huge bureaucratic empire. Both the Aztecs and the Incas gave a new political expression to much older patterns of civilized life.

Yet another pattern took shape in Western Europe following the collapse of the Roman Empire. There would-be kings and church leaders alike sought to maintain links with the older Greco-Roman-Christian traditions of classical Mediterranean civilization. In the absence of empire, though, new and far more decentralized societies emerged, led now by Germanic peoples and centered in Northern and Western Europe, considerably removed from the older centers of Rome and Athens. It was a hybrid civilization, combining old and new, classical and Germanic elements, in a unique blending. For five centuries or more, this region was a relative backwater, compared to the more vibrant, prosperous, and powerful civilizations of the Islamic world and of China. During the centuries after 1000 C.E., however, Western European civilization emerged as a rapidly growing and expansive set of competitive states, willing, like other new civilizations, to borrow quite extensively from their more developed neighbors.

The Ties That Bind: Transregional Interaction in the Postclassical Era

These quite different patterns of development within particular civilizations of the postclassical millennium have made it difficult to define that era in a single, all-encompassing fashion. In another way, though, a common theme emerges, for during this time, the world's various regions, cultures, and peoples interacted with one another far more extensively. More than before, change in human societies was the product of contact with strangers, or at least with their ideas, armies, goods, or diseases. In a variety of places—island Southeast Asia, coastal East Africa, Central Asian cities, parts of Western Europe, the Islamic Middle East, and the Inca Empire—local cosmopolitan regions emerged in which trade, migration, or empire had brought peoples of different cultures together in a restricted space. These "mini-globalizations," both larger and more common than in the classical era, became a distinctive feature of third-wave civilizations.

"No man is an island, entire of itself," wrote the seventeenth-century English poet John Donne. "Every man is a piece of the continent, a part of the main." Much the same might be said of every civilization, culture, or region. None of them were wholly isolated or separate from their neighbors, although the range and intensity of cross-cultural interaction certainly varied over time. In limited ways, that was the case for the First Civilizations as well as their classical successors. Both Egyptian and Mesopotamian cultural influence spread well beyond the core regions of those civilizations. Horseback-riding skills and chariot technology diffused widely across Eurasia. The encounter of the Greeks and Persians changed both of those classical civilizations. Cross-cultural mixing in northern India gave rise to the caste system, while the Silk Road trading networks across Eurasia provided some modest contact among the distant empires of Rome, China, and India.

The scale and pace of such interaction accelerated considerably during the era of third-wave, or postclassical, civilizations. Much of Part Three highlights these intersections and spells out their many and varied consequences. Three major mechanisms of cross-cultural interaction, which we will meet in the chapters that follow, were of particular significance for transforming the lives and societies of those who took part in them.

One such mechanism was trade. The exchange of goods has been everywhere one of the primary means of cross-cultural interaction, and virtually every human society has engaged in it at some level. Although most trade in the premodern world occurred locally among nearby communities, world historians have focused attention especially on long-distance trade, commercial relationships that linked distant human communities. This kind of commerce grew considerably during the postclassical era—along the Silk Roads of Eurasia, within the Indian Ocean basin, across the Sahara, and along the Mississippi and other rivers. Everywhere it acted as an agent of change for all of its participants. In places where long-distance trade was practiced extensively, it required that more people devote their energies to producing for a distant market rather than for the consumption of their own communities. Those who controlled this kind of trade often became extremely wealthy, exciting envy or outrage among those less fortunate. Many societies learned about new products via these trade routes. Europe's knowledge of pepper and other spices, for example, derived from Roman seaborne trade with India beginning in the first century C.E. Many centuries later, Europeans' desire for Asian spices played a part in propelling Western commercial and military expansion into the Indian Ocean.

Such trade also had political consequences as many new states or empires were established on the basis of resources derived from long-distance commerce. The West African kingdoms of Ghana and Mali, the Swahili cities of the East African coast, the early eastern Slavic state known as Rus, and the Indonesian state of Srivijaya are four such examples. Furthermore, far more than goods traveled the trade routes that linked various third-wave civilizations with one another. Religious ideas, technologies, and germs also made their ways along those paths of commerce, bringing significant change to their participants.

Yet another mechanism of cross-cultural interaction lay in large empires. Not only did they incorporate many distinct cultures within a single political system, but their size and stability also provided the security that encouraged travelers and traders to journey long distances from their homelands. Empires, of course, were nothing new in world history, but many of those associated with third-wave civilizations were distinctive. In the first place, they were larger. The Arab Empire, which accompanied the initial spread of Islam, stretched from Spain to India. Even more extensive was the Mongol Empire of the thirteenth and fourteenth centuries. In the Western Hemisphere, the Inca Empire encompassed dozens of distinct peoples in a huge state that ran some 2,500 miles along the spine of the Andes Mountains.

Furthermore, the largest of these empires were the creation of nomadic or pastoral peoples. Classical empires in the Mediterranean basin, China, India, and Persia had been the work of settled farming societies. But now, in the thousand years between

500 and 1500, peoples with a recent history of a nomadic or herding way of life entered the stage of world history as empire builders—Arabs, Turks, Mongols, Aztecs—ruling over agricultural peoples and established civilizations. These empires changed those who created them as well as those who were forcibly incorporated within them. They also did much to foster cross-cultural interaction. Marco Polo, for example, made his way from Italy to China and back in the thirteenth century, thanks largely to the security provided by the Mongol Empire.

Together, large-scale empires and long-distance trade facilitated the spread of ideas, technologies, food crops, and germs far beyond their points of origin. Buddhism spread from India to much of Asia; Christianity encompassed Europe and took root in distant Russia as well as in northeastern Africa, southern India, and western China. Hinduism attracted followers in Southeast Asia; and more than any of the other world religions, Islam became an Afro-Eurasian phenomenon with an enormous reach. Beyond the connections born of commerce and conquest, those of culture and religion generated lasting ties among many peoples of the Eastern Hemisphere.

Technologies, too, were diffused widely. Until the sixth century C.E., China maintained a monopoly on the manufacture of raw silk. Then this technology spread beyond East Asia, allowing the development of a silk industry in the eastern Mediterranean and later in Italy. India too contributed much to the larger world— crystallized sugar, a system of numerals and the concept of zero, techniques for making cotton textiles, and many food crops. Arabs, who were responsible for spreading many of these Indian innovations, found India a "place of marvels."[2] In the Americas, corn gradually diffused from Mesoamerica, where it was initially domesticated, to North America, where it stimulated population growth and the development of more complex societies. Disease also linked distant communities. The plague, or Black Death, decimated many parts of Eurasia and North Africa as it made its deadly way from east to west in the fourteenth century.

A focus on these accelerating connections across cultural boundaries puts the historical spotlight on merchants, travelers, missionaries, migrants, soldiers, and administrators—people who traveled abroad rather than those who stayed at home. Frequently, they stimulated cultural change in the lands they visited, and of course they themselves often were changed by the experience. More than a few of the Christian Crusaders who invaded the Middle East to rescue the holy places from Islamic control wound up as Muslims themselves.

This cross-cultural emphasis in world history also raises provocative questions about what happens when cultures interact or when strangers meet. How did external stimuli operate to produce change within particular societies? How did individuals or societies decide what to accept and what to reject when confronted with new ideas or practices? Were they free to decide such questions, or were they acting under pressure or constraints that limited the possibilities of real choice? In what ways did they alter foreign customs or traditions to better meet their own needs and correspond to their own values? These are some of the questions that will arise as we consider the accelerating connections associated with third-wave civilizations.

Landmarks in the Era of Accelerating Connections, 500–1500

500	600	700	800	900

East Asia

589–618
Sui dynasty;
reunification of China

688
Withdrawal of
Chinese military
forces from Korea

845
Suppression
of Buddhism
in China

939
Vietnam establishes
independence
from China

604
Seventeen Article
Constitution
in Japan

868
First printed
book in China

Islamic World

570–632
Life of
Muhammad

650s
Quran compiled

750–900 High point
of Abbasid dynasty

912–961 Reign of
Abd al-Rahman III
in Spain

656
Emergence of
Shia Islam

800–1000 Emergence of Sufism

The World of Christendom

726–843 Iconoclasm in Byzantium

476
End of western
Roman Empire

988
Conversion
of Kievan
Rus to
Christianity

527–565
Justinian rules
Byzantine Empire

800
Charlemagne crowned as
new "Roman emperor"

Africa

7th–8th centuries Introduction of Islam and
Arab culture in North Africa

900s Kings of Ghana
convert to Islam

300–500
Beginnings of
trans-Saharan trade

869–883
African slave
rebellion
in Iraq

The Americas

600–1150 Anasazi culture, Ancestral Pueblo

500 Flourishing
of Teotihuacán

900–1250 Cahokia

950–1150
Flourishing
of Toltec
civilization

850 Collapse of
Maya civilization

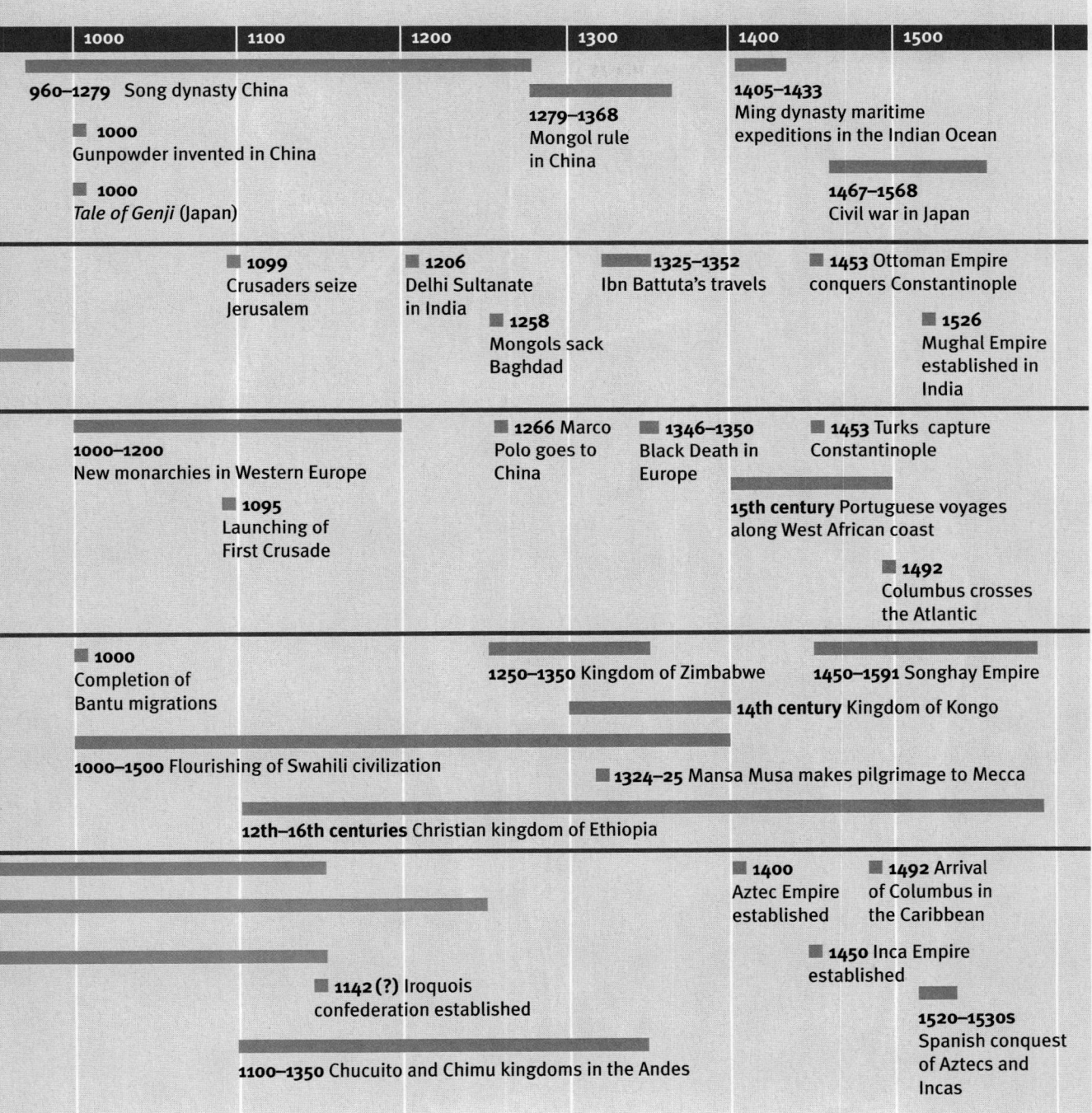

1000 | 1100 | 1200 | 1300 | 1400 | 1500

960–1279 Song dynasty China

■ **1000**
Gunpowder invented in China

■ **1000**
Tale of Genji (Japan)

1279–1368
Mongol rule
in China

1405–1433
Ming dynasty maritime
expeditions in the Indian Ocean

1467–1568
Civil war in Japan

■ **1099**
Crusaders seize
Jerusalem

■ **1206**
Delhi Sultanate
in India

■ **1258**
Mongols sack
Baghdad

■ **1325–1352**
Ibn Battuta's travels

■ **1453** Ottoman Empire
conquers Constantinople

■ **1526**
Mughal Empire
established in
India

1000–1200
New monarchies in Western Europe

■ **1095**
Launching of
First Crusade

■ **1266** Marco
Polo goes to
China

■ **1346–1350**
Black Death in
Europe

■ **1453** Turks capture
Constantinople

15th century Portuguese voyages
along West African coast

■ **1492**
Columbus crosses
the Atlantic

■ **1000**
Completion of
Bantu migrations

1250–1350 Kingdom of Zimbabwe

1450–1591 Songhay Empire

14th century Kingdom of Kongo

1000–1500 Flourishing of Swahili civilization

■ **1324–25** Mansa Musa makes pilgrimage to Mecca

12th–16th centuries Christian kingdom of Ethiopia

■ **1400**
Aztec Empire
established

■ **1492** Arrival
of Columbus in
the Caribbean

■ **1450** Inca Empire
established

■ **1142 (?)** Iroquois
confederation established

■ **1520–1530s**
Spanish conquest
of Aztecs and
Incas

1100–1350 Chucuito and Chimu kingdoms in the Andes

CHAPTER EIGHT

Commerce and Culture

500–1500

Silk Roads: Exchange across
Eurasia
  The Growth of the Silk Roads
  Goods in Transit
  Cultures in Transit
  Disease in Transit
Sea Roads: Exchange across the
Indian Ocean
  Weaving the Web of an Indian
  Ocean World
  Sea Roads as a Catalyst for
  Change: Southeast Asia and
  Srivijaya
  Sea Roads as a Catalyst for
  Change: East Africa and Swahili
  Civilization
Sand Roads: Exchange across the
Sahara
  Commercial Beginnings in West
  Africa
  Gold, Salt, and Slaves: Trade and
  Empire in West Africa
An American Network: Commerce
and Connection in the Western
Hemisphere
Reflections: Economic
Globalization—Ancient and
Modern
Considering the Evidence
  Documents: Travelers' Tales and
  Observations
  Visual Sources: Art, Religion, and
  Cultural Exchange in Central Asia

"Forget compass readings, camel caravans, and disorienting, potentially deadly Jeep journeys through the world's most fabled and forbidding desert. Soon it will be possible to take a leisurely drive along a paved two-lane highway from the spot where Europe kisses the tip of this continent into the heart of sub-Saharan Africa. That's the idea, anyway."[1] So wrote a journalist for the *New York Times* in late 2003, describing international plans for a modern highway across the Sahara, linking Europe and North Africa with the vast interior of West Africa. Such a road, its advocates hoped, would not only promote tourism, trade, and economic growth but also provide an alternative route for West African Muslims making the pilgrimage to Mecca. At the same time, in early 2004, some twenty-three nations signed an agreement to build a network of highways all across Asia, ultimately linking Tokyo with Istanbul and enabling a number of landlocked countries of Central Asia to participate more fully in the world economy.

THESE TWO AMBITIOUS PROJECTS OF THE EARLY TWENTY-FIRST CENTURY were part of the accumulating infrastructure of contemporary globalization. But they also evoked much older patterns of global commerce, the famous Silk Road network across Eurasia and the trans-Saharan trade routes, both of which flourished in the postclassical era. Here is a reminder, from the viewpoint of world history, that exchange among distant peoples is not altogether new and that the roots of economic globalization lie deep in the past.

Travels on the Silk Road: This Chinese ceramic figurine from the Tang dynasty (618–907 C.E.) shows a group of musicians riding on a camel along the famous Silk Road commercial network that long linked the civilizations of western and eastern Eurasia. The bearded figures represent Central Asian merchants, while the others depict Chinese. (©Asian Art & Archaeology, Inc./Corbis)

The exchange of goods among communities occupying different ecological zones has long been a prominent feature of human history. Coastlands and highlands, steppes and farmlands, islands and mainlands, valleys and mountains, deserts and forests—each generates different products desired by others. Furthermore, some societies have been able to monopolize, at least temporarily, the production of particular products, such as silk in China or certain spices in Southeast Asia, which others have found valuable. This uneven distribution of goods and resources, whether natural or resulting from human activity, has long motivated exchange, not only within particular civilizations or regions but among them as well. In the world of 500–1500, long-distance trade became more important than ever before in linking and shaping distant societies and peoples. For the most part, it was indirect, a chain of separate transactions in which goods traveled farther than individual merchants. Nonetheless, a network of exchange and communication extending all across the Afro-Eurasian world, and separately in parts of the Americas as well, slowly came into being.

In what ways was trade significant? How did it generate change within the societies that it connected? Economically speaking, it often altered consumption, enabling West Africans, for example, to import scarce salt, necessary for human diets and useful for seasoning and preserving food, from distant mines in the Sahara in exchange for the gold of their region. Trade also affected the day-to-day working lives of many people, encouraging them to specialize in producing particular products for sale in distant markets rather than for use in their own communities. Trade, in short, diminished the economic self-sufficiency of local societies.

Trade shaped the structure of those societies as well. Traders often became a distinct social group, viewed with suspicion by others because of their impulse to accumulate wealth without actually producing anything themselves. In some societies, trade became a means of social mobility, as Chinese merchants, for example, were able to purchase landed estates and establish themselves within the gentry class. Long-distance trade also enabled elite groups in society to distinguish themselves from commoners by acquiring prestigious goods from a distance—silk, tortoiseshells, rhinoceros horn, or particular feathers, for example. The association with faraway or powerful societies, signaled by the possession of their luxury goods, often conveyed status in communities more remote from major civilizations.

Political life also was sometimes transformed by trade. The wealth available from controlling and taxing trade motivated the creation of states in various parts of the world and sustained those states once they had been constructed. Furthermore, commerce posed a set of problems to governments everywhere. Should trade be left in private hands, as in the Aztec Empire, or should it be controlled by the state, as in the Inca Empire? How should state authorities deal with men of commerce, who were both economically useful and potentially disruptive?

Moreover, the saddlebags of camel caravans or the cargo holds of merchant vessels carried more than goods. Trade became the vehicle for the spread of religious ideas, technological innovations, disease-bearing germs, and plants and animals to regions far from their places of origin. In just this fashion, Buddhism made its way from India to Central and East Asia, and Islam crossed the Sahara into West Africa. So did the pathogens that devastated much of Eurasia during the Black Death. These immense cultural and biological transformations were among the most significant outcomes of the increasingly dense network of long-distance commerce during the era of third-wave civilizations.

Silk Roads: Exchange across Eurasia

The Eurasian landmass has long been home to the majority of humankind as well as to the world's most productive agriculture, largest civilizations, and greatest concentration of pastoral peoples. Beyond its many separate societies and cultures, Eurasia also gave rise to one of the world's most extensive and sustained networks of exchange among its diverse peoples. Known to scholars as the Silk Roads, a reference to their most famous product, these land-based trade routes linked pastoral and agricultural peoples as well as the large civilizations on the continent's outer rim (see Map 8.1). None of its numerous participants knew the full extent of this network's reach, for it was largely a "relay trade" in which goods were passed down the line, changing hands many times before reaching their final destination. Nonetheless, the Silk Roads provide a certain unity and coherence to Eurasian history alongside the distinct stories of its separate civilizations and peoples.

Map 8.1 The Silk Roads
For 2,000 years, goods, ideas, technologies, and diseases made their way across Eurasia on the several routes of the Silk Roads.

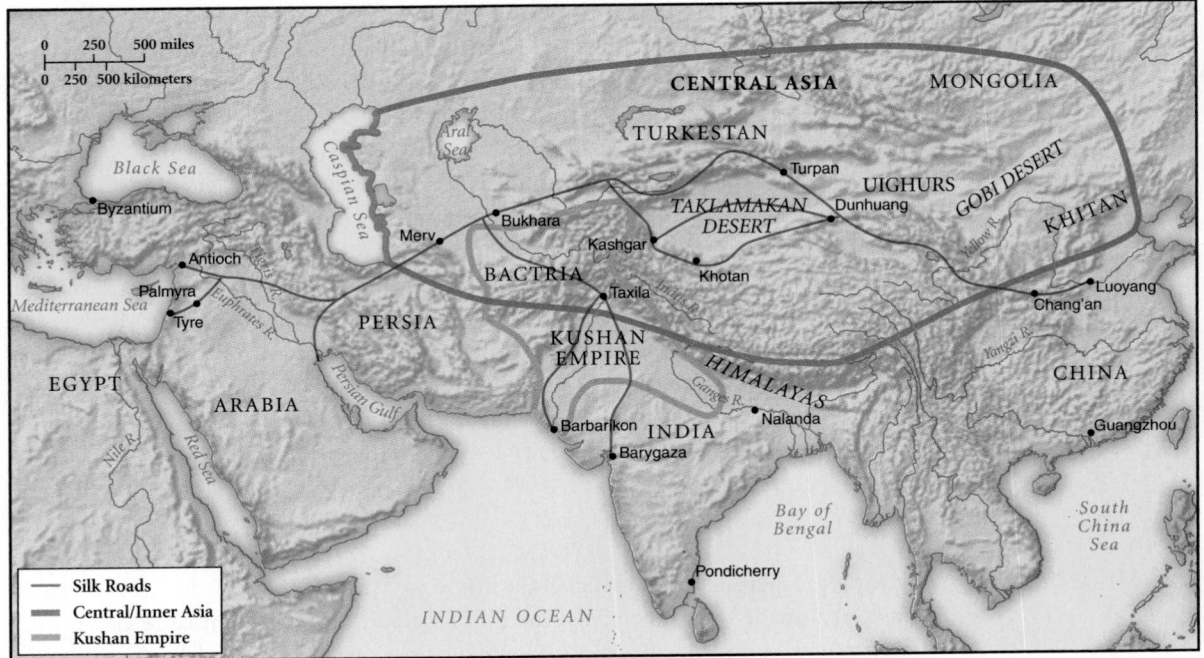

The Growth of the Silk Roads

■ Change
What lay behind the emergence of Silk Road commerce, and what kept it going for so many centuries?

The beginnings of the Silk Roads lay in both geography and history. As a geographic unit, Eurasia is often divided into inner and outer zones that represent quite different environments. Outer Eurasia consists of relatively warm, well-watered areas, suitable for agriculture, which provided the setting for the great civilizations of China, India, the Middle East, and the Mediterranean. Inner Eurasia—the lands of eastern Russia and Central Asia—lies farther north and has a harsher and drier climate, much of it not conducive to agriculture. Herding their animals from horseback, the pastoral people of this region had for centuries traded with and raided their agricultural neighbors to the south. Products of the forest and of semi-arid northern grasslands known as the steppes—such as hides, furs, livestock, wool, and amber—were exchanged for the agricultural products and manufactured goods of adjacent civilizations. The movement of pastoral peoples for thousands of years also served to diffuse Indo-European languages, bronze metallurgy, horse-based technologies, and more all across Eurasia.

The construction of the classical civilizations and their imperial states during the last five centuries B.C.E. added another element to these earlier Eurasian connections. From the south, the Persian Empire invaded the territory of pastoral peoples in present-day Turkmenistan and Uzbekistan. From the west, Alexander the Great's empire stretched well into Central Asia. From the east, China's Han dynasty extended its authority westward, seeking to control the nomadic Xiongnu and to gain access to the powerful "heavenly horses" that were so important to Chinese military forces. By the early centuries of the Common Era, indirect trading connections, often brokered by pastoral peoples, linked the classical civilizations in a network of transcontinental exchange. (For the role of Central Asian pastoral peoples in the exchange of the Silk Roads, see Visual Sources: Art, Religion, and Cultural Exchange in Central Asia, pp. 367–77.)

Silk Road trading networks prospered most when large and powerful states provided security for merchants and travelers. Such conditions prevailed during the classical era when the Roman and Chinese empires anchored long-distance commerce at the western and eastern ends of Eurasia. Silk Road trade flourished again during the seventh and eighth centuries C.E. as the Byzantine Empire, the Muslim Abbasid dynasty, and Tang dynasty China created an almost continuous belt of strong states across Eurasia. In the thirteenth and fourteenth centuries, the Mongol Empire briefly encompassed almost the entire route of the Silk Roads in a single state, giving a renewed vitality to long-distance trade.

Goods in Transit

During prosperous times especially, a vast array of goods (detailed in the Snapshot on p. 337) made their way across the Silk Roads, often carried in large camel caravans that traversed the harsh and dangerous steppes, deserts, and oases of Central Asia. In high demand and hard to find, most of these goods were luxury products,

Snapshot   Economic Exchange along the Silk Roads

Region	Products Contributed to Silk Road Commerce
China	silk, bamboo, mirrors, gunpowder, paper, rhubarb, ginger, lacquerware, chrysanthemums
Forest lands of Siberia and grasslands of Central Asia	furs, walrus tusks, amber, livestock, horses, falcons, hides, copper vessels, tents, saddles, slaves
India	cotton textiles, herbal medicine, precious stones, spices
Middle East	dates, nuts, almonds, dried fruit, dyes, lapis lazuli, swords
Mediterranean basin	gold coins, glassware, glazes, grapevines, jewelry, artworks, perfume, wool and linen textiles, olive oil

destined for an elite and wealthy market, rather than staple goods, for only readily moved commodities of great value could compensate for the high costs of transportation across such long and forbidding distances.

Of all these luxury goods, it was silk that came to symbolize this Eurasian exchange system. When China held a monopoly on silk-producing technology, this precious fabric moved generally from east to west. The demand for silk as well as cotton textiles from India was so great in the Roman Empire that various Roman writers were appalled at the drain of resources that it represented. They also were outraged at the moral impact of wearing revealing silk garments. "I can see clothes of silk," lamented Seneca the Younger in the first century C.E., "if materials that do not hide the body, nor even one's decency, can be called clothes.... Wretched flocks of maids labour so that the adulteress may be visible through her thin dress, so that her husband has no more acquaintance than any outsider or foreigner with his wife's body."[2]

By the sixth century C.E., however, the knowledge and technology for producing raw silk had spread beyond China. An old Chinese story attributes it to a Chinese princess who smuggled out silkworms in her turban when she was married off to a Central Asian ruler. In a European version of the tale, Christian monks living in China did the deed by hiding some silkworms in a bamboo cane, an act of industrial espionage that allowed an independent silk-producing and silk-weaving industry to take hold in the Byzantine Empire. However it happened, Koreans, Japanese, Indians, and Persians likewise learned how to produce this precious fabric.

As the supply of silk increased, its many varieties circulated even more extensively across Eurasian trade routes. In Central Asia, silk was used as currency and as a means of accumulating wealth. In both China and the Byzantine Empire, silk became a symbol of high status, and governments passed laws that restricted silk clothing to members of the elite. Furthermore, silk became associated with the sacred in the expanding world religions of Buddhism and Christianity. Chinese Buddhist pilgrims who made their way to India seeking religious texts and relics took with them large quantities of silk as gifts to the monasteries they visited (see

■ Significance
What made silk such a highly desired commodity across Eurasia?

Visual Source 8.2, p. 370). Buddhist monks in China received purple silk robes from Tang dynasty emperors as a sign of high honor. In the world of Christendom, silk wall hangings, altar covers, and vestments became highly prestigious signs of devotion and piety. Because no independent silk industry developed in Western Europe until the twelfth century C.E., a considerable market developed for silks imported from the Islamic world. Ironically, the splendor of Christian churches depended in part on Islamic trading networks and on silks manufactured in the Muslim world. Some of those silks were even inscribed with passages in Arabic from the Quran, unbeknownst to their European buyers.[3]

■ **Connection**

What were the major economic, social, and cultural consequences of Silk Road commerce?

Compared to contemporary global commerce, the volume of trade on the Silk Roads was small, and its focus on luxury goods limited its direct impact on most people. Nonetheless, it had important economic and social consequences. Peasants in the Yangzi River delta of southern China sometimes gave up the cultivation of food crops, choosing to focus instead on producing silk, paper, porcelain, lacquerware, or iron tools, much of which was destined for the markets of the Silk Roads. In this way, the impact of long-distance trade trickled down to affect the lives of ordinary farmers. Furthermore, favorably placed individuals could benefit immensely from long-distance trade. The twelfth-century Persian merchant Ramisht made a personal fortune from his long-distance trading business and with his profits purchased an enormously expensive silk covering for the Kaaba, the central shrine of Islam in Mecca.[4]

Cultures in Transit

■ **Change**

What accounted for the spread of Buddhism along the Silk Roads?

More important even than the economic impact of the Silk Roads was their role as a conduit of culture. Buddhism in particular, a cultural product of Indian civilization, spread widely throughout Central and East Asia, owing much to the activities of merchants along the Silk Roads. From its beginnings in India during the sixth century B.C.E., Buddhism had appealed to merchants, who preferred its universal message to that of a Brahmin-dominated Hinduism that privileged the higher castes. Indian traders and Buddhist monks, sometimes supported by rulers such as Ashoka, brought the new religion to the trans-Eurasian trade routes. To the west, Persian Zoroastrianism largely blocked the spread of Buddhism, but in the oasis cities of Central Asia, such as Merv, Samarkand, Khotan, and Dunhuang, Buddhism quickly took hold. By the first century B.C.E., many of the inhabitants of these towns had converted to Buddhism, and foreign merchant communities soon introduced it to northern China as well.[5] (See Visual Sources 8.1 and 8.2, pp. 369 and 370, as well as Document 8.1, pp. 356–59.)

Conversion to Buddhism in the oasis cities was a voluntary process, without the pressure of conquest or foreign rule. Dependent on long-distance trade, the inhabitants and rulers of those sophisticated and prosperous cities found in Buddhism a link to the larger, wealthy, and prestigious civilization of India. Well-to-do Buddhist merchants could earn religious merit by building monasteries and supporting monks. The monasteries in turn provided convenient and culturally familiar places of rest and resupply for merchants making the long and arduous trek across Central Asia. Many of these cities became cosmopolitan centers of learning and commerce. Scholars have found thousands of Buddhist texts in the city of Dunhuang, where several branches of the Silk Roads joined to enter western China, together with hundreds of cave temples, lavishly decorated with murals and statues.

Outside of the oasis communities, Buddhism progressed only slowly among pastoral peoples of Central Asia. The absence of a written language was an obstacle to the penetration of a highly literate religion, and their nomadic ways made the founding of monasteries, so important to Buddhism, quite difficult. But as pastoralists became involved in long-distance trade or came to rule settled agricultural peoples, Buddhism seemed more attractive. The nomadic Jie people, who controlled much of northern China after the collapse of the Han dynasty, are a case in point. Their ruler in the early fourth century C.E., Shi Le, became acquainted with a Buddhist monk called Fotudeng, who had traveled widely on the Silk Roads. The monk's reputation as a miracle worker, a rainmaker, and a fortune-teller and his skills as a military strategist cemented a personal relationship with Shi Le and led to the conversions of thousands and the construction of hundreds of Buddhist temples. In China itself, Buddhism remained for many centuries a religion of foreign merchants or foreign rulers. Only slowly did it become popular among the Chinese themselves, a process examined more closely in Chapter 9.

As Buddhism spread across the Silk Roads from India to Central Asia, China, and beyond, it also changed. The original faith had shunned the material world, but Buddhist monasteries in the rich oasis towns of the Silk Roads found themselves very much involved in secular affairs. Some of them became quite wealthy, receiving gifts from well-to-do merchants, artisans, and local rulers. The begging bowls of the monks became a symbol rather than a daily activity. Sculptures and murals in the monasteries depicted musicians and acrobats, women applying makeup, and even drinking parties.[6]

Doctrines changed as well. It was the more devotional Mahayana form of Buddhism (see Chapter 5)—featuring the Buddha as a deity, numerous bodhisattvas, an emphasis on compassion, and the possibility of earning merit—that flourished on the Silk Roads, rather than the more austere psychological teachings of the original Buddha. Moreover, Buddhism picked up elements of other cultures while in transit on the Silk Roads. In the area northwest of India that had been

Dunhuang
Located in western China at a critical junction of the Silk Road trading network, Dunhuang was also a center of Buddhist learning, painting, and sculpture as that religion made its way from India to China and beyond. In some 492 caves, a remarkable gallery of Buddhist art has been preserved. These images of Buddhist deities and heavenly beings date from the sixth century C.E. (© Benoy K. Behl)

influenced by the invasions of Alexander the Great, statues of the Buddha reveal distinctly Greek influences. The Greco-Roman mythological figure of Herakles, the son of Zeus and associated with great strength, courage, masculinity, and sexual prowess, was used to represent Vajrapani, one of the divine protectors of the Buddha (see Visual Source 8.1, p. 369). In a similar way, the gods of many peoples along the Silk Roads were incorporated into Buddhist practice as bodhisattvas.

Disease in Transit

■ Connection

What was the impact of disease along the Silk Roads?

Beyond goods and cultures, diseases too traveled the trade routes of Eurasia, and with devastating consequences.[7] Each of the major population centers of the Afro-Eurasian world had developed characteristic disease patterns, mechanisms for dealing with them, and in some cases immunity to them. But when contact among human communities occurred, people were exposed to unfamiliar diseases for which they had little immunity or few effective methods of coping. An early example involved Athens, which in 430–429 B.C.E. was suddenly afflicted by a new and still unidentified infectious disease that had entered Greece via seaborne trade from Egypt, killing perhaps 25 percent of its army and permanently weakening the city-state.

Even more widespread diseases affected the Roman Empire and Han dynasty China during the classical era as the Silk Roads promoted contact all across Eurasia. Smallpox and measles devastated the populations of both empires, contributing to their political collapse. Paradoxically, these disasters may well have strengthened the appeal of Christianity in Europe and Buddhism in China, for both of them offered compassion in the face of immense suffering.

Again in the period between 534 and 750 C.E., intermittent outbreaks of bubonic plague ravaged the coastal areas of the Mediterranean Sea as the black rats that carried the disease arrived via the seaborne trade with India, where they originally lived. What followed was catastrophic. Constantinople, the capital city of the Byzantine Empire, lost some 10,000 people per day during a forty-day period in 534 C.E., according to a contemporary historian. Disease played an important role in preventing Byzantium from reintegrating Italy into its version of a renewed Roman Empire encompassing the Mediterranean basin. The repeated recurrence of the disease over the next several centuries also weakened the ability of Christendom to resist the Muslim armies that poured out of Arabia in the seventh century C.E.

The most well-known dissemination of disease was associated with the Mongol Empire, which briefly unified much of the Eurasian landmass during the thirteenth and fourteenth centuries C.E. (see Chapter 12). That era of intensified interaction facilitated the spread of the Black Death—identified variously with the bubonic plague, anthrax, or a package of epidemic diseases—from China to Europe. Its consequences were enormous. Between 1346 and 1350, one-third or more of the population of Europe perished from the plague. "A dead man," wrote the Italian writer Boccaccio, "was then of no more account than a dead goat."[8] Despite the terrible human toll, some among the living benefited. Tenant farmers and urban workers, now in short supply, could demand higher wages or better terms. Some landowning nobles, on the other hand, were badly hurt as the price of their grains dropped and the demands of their dependents grew.

A similar death toll afflicted China and parts of the Islamic world. The Central Asian steppes, home to many nomadic peoples including the Mongols, also suffered terribly, undermining Mongol rule and permanently altering the balance between pastoral and agricultural peoples to the advantage of settled farmers. In these and many other ways, disease carried by long-distance trade shaped the lives of millions and altered their historical development.

In the long run of world history, the exchange of diseases gave Europeans a certain advantage when they confronted the peoples of the Western Hemisphere after 1500. Exposure over time had provided them with some degree of immunity to Eurasian diseases. In the Americas, however, the absence of domesticated animals, the less intense interaction among major centers of population, and their isolation from the Eastern Hemisphere ensured that native peoples had little defense against the diseases of Europe and Africa. Thus, when their societies were suddenly confronted by Europeans and Africans from across the Atlantic, they perished in appalling numbers. Such was the long-term outcome of the very different histories of the two hemispheres.

Sea Roads: Exchange across the Indian Ocean

If the Silk Roads linked Eurasian societies by land, sea-based trade routes likewise connected distant peoples all across the Eastern Hemisphere. Since the days of the Phoenicians, Greeks, and Romans, the Mediterranean Sea had been an avenue of maritime commerce throughout the region, a pattern that continued during the postclassical era. The Italian city of Venice, for example, emerged by 1000 C.E. as a major center of commerce, with its ships and merchants active in the Mediterranean and Black seas as well as on the Atlantic coast. Much of its wealth derived from control of expensive and profitable imported goods from Asia, many of which came up the Red Sea through the Egyptian port of Alexandria. There Venetian merchants picked up those goods and resold them throughout the Mediterranean basin. This type of transregional exchange linked the maritime commerce of the Mediterranean Sea to the much larger and more extensive network of seaborne trade in the Indian Ocean basin.

Until the creation of a genuinely global oceanic system of trade after 1500, the Indian Ocean represented the world's largest sea-based system of communication and exchange, stretching from southern China to eastern Africa (see Map 8.2). Like the Silk Roads, oceanic trade also grew out of the vast environmental and cultural diversities of the region. The desire for various goods not available at home—such as porcelain from China, spices from the islands of Southeast Asia, cotton goods and pepper from India, ivory and gold from the African coast—provided incentives for Indian Ocean commerce. Transportation costs were lower on the Sea

■ **Comparison**

How did the operation of the Indian Ocean trading network differ from that of the Silk Roads?

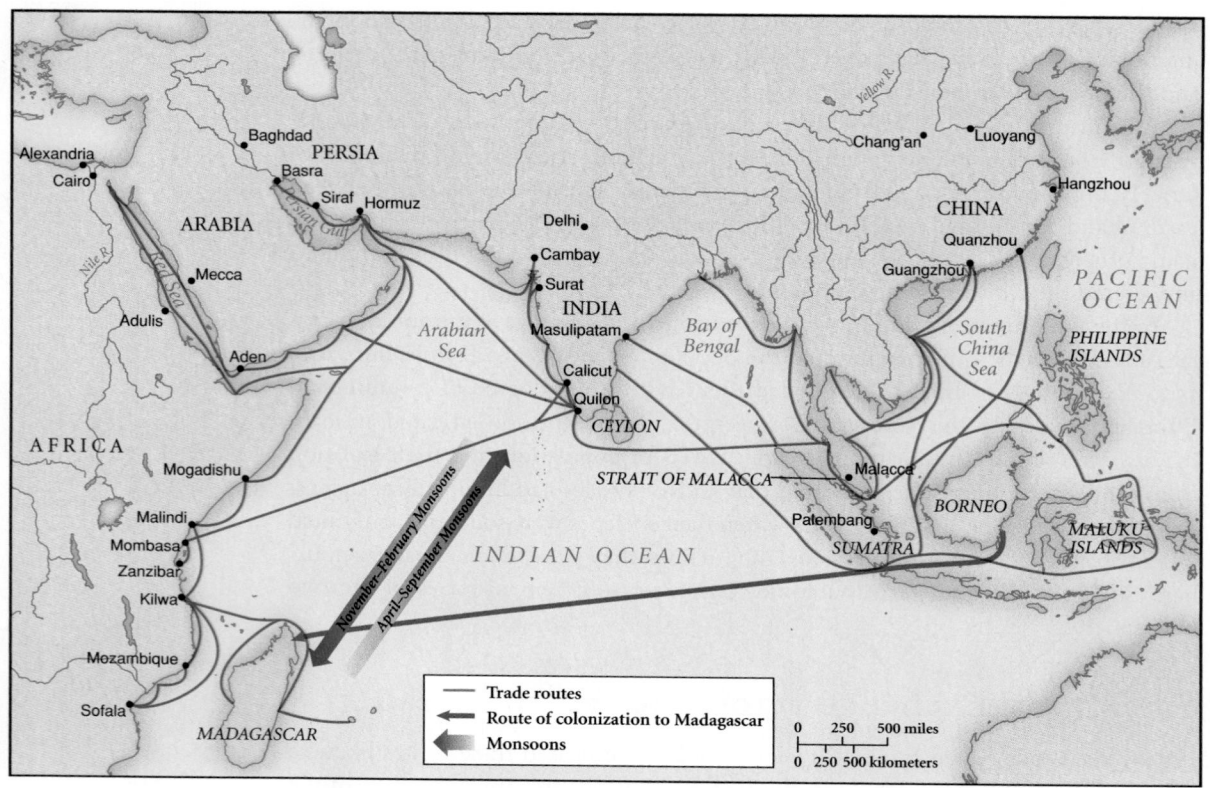

Map 8.2   The Sea Roads
Paralleling the Silk Road trading network, a sea-based commerce in the Indian Ocean basin connected the many peoples between China and East Africa.

Roads than on the Silk Roads, because ships could accommodate larger and heavier cargoes than camels. This meant that the Sea Roads could eventually carry more bulk goods and products destined for a mass market—textiles, pepper, timber, rice, sugar, wheat—whereas the Silk Roads were limited largely to luxury goods for the few.

What made Indian Ocean commerce possible were the monsoons, alternating wind currents that blew predictably eastward during the summer months and westward during the winter. An understanding of monsoons and a gradually accumulating technology of shipbuilding and oceanic navigation drew on the ingenuity of many peoples—Chinese, Malays, Indians, Arabs, Swahilis, and others. Collectively they made "an interlocked human world joined by the common highway of the Indian Ocean."[9]

But this world of Indian Ocean commerce did not occur between entire regions and certainly not between "countries," even though historians sometimes write about India, Indonesia, Southeast Asia, or East Africa as a matter of shorthand or convenience. It operated rather across an "archipelago of towns" whose merchants often had more in common with one another than with the people of their own hinterlands.[10] It was these urban centers, strung out around the entire Indian Ocean basin, that provided the nodes of this widespread commercial network.

Weaving the Web of an Indian Ocean World

The world of Indian Ocean commerce was long in the making, dating back to the time of the First Civilizations. Seaborne trade via the Persian Gulf between ancient Mesopotamia and the Indus Valley civilization is reflected in archeological finds in both places. Some scholars believe that the still-undeciphered Indian writing system may have been stimulated by Sumerian cuneiform. The ancient Egyptians, and later the Phoenicians, likewise traded down the Red Sea, exchanging their manufactured goods for gold, ivory, frankincense, and slaves from the coasts of Ethiopia, Somalia, and southern Arabia. These ventures mostly hugged the coast and took place over short distances. An exception was Malay sailors; speaking Austronesian languages, they jumped off from the islands of present-day Indonesia during the first millennium B.C.E. and made their way in double-outrigger canoes across thousands of miles of open ocean to the East African island of Madagascar. There they introduced their language and their crops. Those food crops—bananas, coconuts, and cocoyams—soon spread to the mainland, where they greatly enriched the diets of African peoples. Also spread to the mainland was a Malayo-Polynesian xylophone, which is still played in parts of Africa today.

The tempo of Indian Ocean commerce picked up in the era of classical civilizations during the early centuries of the Common Era, as mariners learned how to ride the monsoons. Merchants from the Roman Empire, mostly Greeks, Syrians, and Jews, established settlements in southern India and along the East African coast. The introduction of Christianity into both Ethiopia and Kerala (in southern India) testifies to the long-term cultural impact of that trade. In the eastern Indian Ocean and the South China Sea, Chinese and Southeast Asian merchants likewise generated a growing commerce, and by 100 C.E. Chinese traders had reached India.

The fulcrum of this growing commercial network lay in India itself. Its ports bulged with goods from both west and east, as illustrated in the Snapshot. Its merchants were in touch with Southeast Asia by the first century C.E., and settled communities of Indian traders appeared throughout the Indian Ocean basin and as far away as

Snapshot **Economic Exchange in the Indian Ocean Basin**

Region	Products Contributed to Indian Ocean Commerce
Mediterranean basin	ceramics, glassware, wine, gold, olive oil
East Africa	ivory, gold, iron goods, slaves, tortoiseshells, quartz, leopard skins
Arabia	frankincense, myrrh, perfumes
India	grain, ivory, precious stones, cotton textiles, spices, timber, tortoiseshells
Southeast Asia	tin, sandalwood, cloves, nutmeg, mace
China	silks, porcelain, tea

Alexandria in Egypt. Indian cultural practices, such as Hinduism and Buddhism, as well as South Asian political ideas began to take root in Southeast Asia.

In the era of third-wave civilizations between 500 and 1500, two major processes changed the landscape of the Afro-Eurasian world and wove the web of Indian Ocean exchange even more densely than before. One was the economic and political revival of China, some four centuries after the collapse of the Han dynasty. Especially during the Tang and Song dynasties (618–1279), China reestablished an effective and unified state, which actively encouraged maritime trade. Furthermore, the impressive growth of the Chinese economy sent Chinese products pouring into the circuits of Indian Ocean commerce, while providing a vast and attractive market for Indian and Southeast Asian goods. Chinese technological innovations, such as larger ships and the magnetic compass, likewise added to the momentum of commercial growth.

A second transformation in the world of Indian Ocean commerce involved the sudden rise of Islam in the seventh century C.E. and its subsequent spread across much of the Afro-Eurasian world (see Chapter 11). Unlike Confucian culture, which was quite suspicious of merchants, Islam was friendly to commercial life; the Prophet Muhammad himself had been a trader. The creation of an Arab Empire, stretching from the Atlantic Ocean through the Mediterranean basin and all the way to India, brought together in a single political system an immense range of economies and cultural traditions and provided a vast arena for the energies of Muslim traders.

Those energies greatly intensified commercial activity in the Indian Ocean basin in many ways. Middle Eastern gold and silver flowed into southern India to purchase pepper, pearls, textiles, and gemstones. Muslim merchants and sailors, as well as Jews and Christians living within the Islamic world, established communities of traders from East Africa to the southern China coast. Efforts to reclaim wasteland in Mesopotamia to produce sugar and dates for export stimulated a slave trade from East Africa, which landed thousands of Africans in southern Iraq to work on plantations and in salt mines under horrendous conditions. A massive fifteen-year revolt (868–883) among these slaves badly disrupted the Islamic Abbasid Empire before it was brutally crushed.[11]

Beyond these specific outcomes, the expansion of Islam gave rise to an international maritime culture by 1000, shared by individuals living in the widely separated port cities around the Indian Ocean. The immense prestige, power, and prosperity of the Islamic world stimulated widespread conversion, which in turn facilitated commercial transactions. Even those who did not convert to Islam, such as Buddhist rulers in Burma, nonetheless regarded it as commercially useful to assume Muslim names.[12] Thus was created "a maritime Silk Road . . . a commercial and informational network of unparalleled proportions."[13] After 1000, the culture of this network was increasingly Islamic.

Sea Roads as a Catalyst for Change: Southeast Asia and Srivijaya

Oceanic commerce transformed all of its participants in one way or another, but nowhere more so than in Southeast Asia and East Africa, at opposite ends of the Indian Ocean network. In both regions, trade stimulated political change as ambitious

---

■ Change

What lay behind the flourishing of Indian Ocean commerce in the postclassical millennium?

■ Connection

What is the relationship between the rise of Srivijaya and the world of Indian Ocean commerce?

or aspiring rulers used the wealth derived from commerce to construct larger and more centrally governed states or cities. Both areas likewise experienced cultural change as local people were attracted to foreign religious ideas from Hindu, Buddhist, or Islamic sources. As on the Silk Roads, trade was a conduit for culture.

Located between the major civilizations of China and India, Southeast Asia was situated by geography to play an important role in the evolving world of Indian Ocean commerce. When Malay sailors, long active in the waters around Southeast Asia, opened an all-sea route between India and China through the Straits of Malacca around 350 C.E., the many small ports along the Malay Peninsula and the coast of Sumatra began to compete intensely to attract the growing number of traders and travelers making their way through the straits. From this competition emerged the Malay kingdom of Srivijaya, which dominated this critical choke point of Indian Ocean trade from 670 to 1025. A number of factors—Srivijaya's plentiful supply of gold; its access to the source of highly sought-after spices, such as cloves, nutmeg, and mace; and the taxes levied on passing ships—provided resources to attract supporters, to fund an embryonic bureaucracy, and to create the military and naval forces that brought some security to the area.

Srivijaya monarchs drew upon local beliefs that chiefs possessed magical powers and were responsible for the prosperity of their people, but they also made use of imported Indian political ideas and Buddhist religious concepts, which had been brought to the area by a multitude of Indian merchants and teachers. Some Indians were employed as advisers, clerks, or officials to Srivijaya rulers, who began to assign Sanskrit titles to their subordinates. The capital city of Palembang was a cosmopolitan place, where even the parrots were said to speak four languages. Buddhism in particular provided a "higher level of magic" for rulers as well as the prestige of association with Indian civilization.[14] These rulers sponsored the creation of images of the Buddha and various bodhisattvas whose faces resembled those of deceased kings and were inscribed with traditional curses against anyone who would destroy them. Srivijaya grew into a major center of Buddhist observance and teaching, attracting thousands of monks and students from throughout the Buddhist world. The seventh-century Chinese monk Yi Jing was so impressed that he advised Buddhist monks headed for India to study first in Srivijaya for several years.[15]

Srivijaya was not the only part of Southeast Asia to be influenced by Indian culture. The Sailendra kingdom in central Java, an agriculturally rich region closely allied with Srivijaya, mounted a massive building program between the eighth and tenth centuries featuring Hindu temples and Buddhist monuments. The most famous, known as Borobudur, is an enormous mountain-shaped structure of ten levels, with a three-mile walkway and elaborate carvings illustrating the spiritual journey from ignorance and illusion to full enlightenment. The largest Buddhist monument anywhere in the world, it is nonetheless a distinctly Javanese creation, whose carved figures have Javanese features and whose scenes are clearly set in Java, not India. Its shape resonated with an ancient Southeast Asian veneration of mountains as

Southeast Asia ca. 1200 C.E.

Borobudur

This huge Buddhist monument, constructed probably in the ninth century C.E., was subsequently abandoned and covered with layers of volcanic ash and vegetation as Java came under Islamic influence. It was rediscovered by British colonial authorities in the early nineteenth century and has undergone several restorations over the past two centuries. Although Indonesia is a largely Muslim country, its Buddhist minority (about 1 percent of the country's population) still celebrates the Buddha's birthday at Borobudur. (Robert Harding World Imagery/Alamy)

sacred places and the abode of ancestral spirits. Borobudur represents the process of Buddhism becoming culturally grounded in a new place.

Temple complexes such as Borobudur and others constructed in Burma, in the Khmer state of Angkor, and elsewhere illustrate vividly the penetration of Indian culture—in both Hindu and Buddhist forms—throughout mainland and island Southeast Asia. Some scholars have spoken of the "Indianization" of the region, similar perhaps to the earlier spread of Greek culture within the empires of Alexander the Great and Rome. In the case of Southeast Asia, however, no imperial control accompanied Indian cultural influence. It was a matter of voluntary borrowing by independent societies that found Hindu or Buddhist ideas useful and were free to adapt those ideas to their own needs and cultures. Somewhat later, but in much the same way, Islam too began to penetrate Southeast Asia, as the world of Indian Ocean commerce brought yet another religious tradition to the region.

■ Connection

What was the role of Swahili civilization in the world of Indian Ocean commerce?

Sea Roads as a Catalyst for Change: East Africa and Swahili Civilization

On the other side of the Indian Ocean, the transformative processes of long-distance trade were likewise at work, giving rise to an East African civilization known as

Swahili. Emerging in the eighth century C.E., this civilization took shape as a set of commercial city-states stretching all along the East African coast, from present-day Somalia to Mozambique.

The earlier ancestors of the Swahili lived in small farming and fishing communities, spoke Bantu languages, and traded with the Arabian, Greek, and Roman merchants who occasionally visited the coast during the classical era. But what stimulated the growth of Swahili cities was the far more extensive commercial life of the western Indian Ocean following the rise of Islam. As in Southeast Asia, local people and aspiring rulers found opportunity for wealth and power in the growing demand for East African products associated with an expanding Indian Ocean commerce. Gold, ivory, quartz, leopard skins, and sometimes slaves acquired from interior societies, as well as iron and processed timber manufactured along the coast, found a ready market in Arabia, Persia, India, and beyond. In response to such opportunities, an African merchant class developed, villages turned into sizable towns, and clan chiefs became kings. A new civilization was in the making.

Between 1000 and 1500, that civilization flourished along the coast, and it was a very different kind of society than the farming and pastoral cultures of the East African interior. It was thoroughly urban, centered in cities of 15,000 to 18,000 people, such as Lamu, Mombasa, Kilwa, Sofala, and many others. Like the city-states of ancient Greece, each Swahili city was politically independent, generally governed by its own king, and in sharp competition with other cities. No imperial system or larger territorial states unified the world of Swahili civilization. Nor did any of them control a critical choke point of trade, as Srivijaya did for the Straits of Malacca. Swahili cities were commercial centers that accumulated goods from the interior and exchanged them for the products of distant civilizations, such as Chinese porcelain and silk, Persian rugs, and Indian cottons. While the transoceanic journeys occurred largely in Arab vessels, Swahili craft navigated the coastal waterways, concentrating goods for shipment abroad. Swahili cities were class-stratified societies with sharp distinctions between a mercantile elite and commoners.

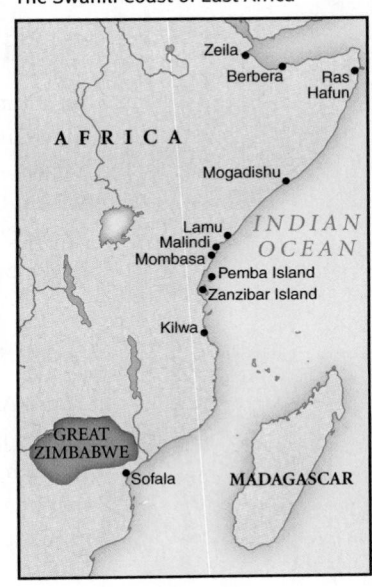

The Swahili Coast of East Africa

Culturally as well as economically, Swahili civilization participated in the larger Indian Ocean world. Arab, Indian, and perhaps Persian merchants were welcome visitors, and some settled permanently. Many ruling families of Swahili cities claimed Arab or Persian origins as a way of bolstering their prestige, even while they dined off Chinese porcelain and dressed in Indian cottons. The Swahili language, widely spoken in East Africa today, was grammatically an African tongue within the larger Bantu family of languages, but it was written in Arabic script and contained a number of Arabic loan words. A small bronze lion found in the Swahili city of Shanga and dating to about 1100 illustrates the distinctly cosmopolitan character of Swahili culture. It depicted a clearly African lion, but it was created in a distinctly Indian artistic style and was made from melted-down Chinese copper coins.[16]

Most important, however, Swahili civilization rapidly became Islamic. Introduced by Arab traders, Islam was voluntarily and widely adopted within the Swahili world. Like Buddhism in Southeast Asia, Islam linked Swahili cities to the larger Indian Ocean world. These East African cities were soon dotted with substantial mosques. When Ibn Battuta, a widely traveled Arab scholar, merchant, and public official, visited the Swahili coast in the early fourteenth century, he found altogether Muslim societies in which religious leaders often spoke Arabic, and all were eager to welcome a learned visitor from the heartland of Islam. But these were African Muslims, not colonies of transplanted Arabs. "The rulers, scholars, officials, and big merchants as well as the port workers, farmers, craftsmen, and slaves, were dark-skinned people speaking African tongues in everyday life."[17]

Islam sharply divided the Swahili cities from their African neighbors to the west, for neither the new religion nor Swahili culture penetrated much beyond the coast until the nineteenth century. Economically, however, the coastal cities acted as intermediaries between the interior producers of valued goods and the Arab merchants who carried them to distant markets. Particularly in the southern reaches of the Swahili world, this relationship extended the impact of Indian Ocean trade well into the African interior. Hundreds of miles inland, between the Zambezi and Limpopo rivers, lay rich sources of gold, much in demand on the Swahili coast. The emergence of a powerful state, known as Great Zimbabwe, seems clearly connected to the growing trade in gold to the coast as well as to the wealth embodied in its large herds of cattle. At its peak between 1250 and 1350, Great Zimbabwe had the resources and the labor power to construct huge stone enclosures entirely without mortar, with walls sixteen feet thick and thirty-two feet tall. "[It] must have been an astonishing sight," writes a recent scholar, "for the subordinate chiefs and kings who would have come there to seek favors at court."[18] Here in the interior of southeastern Africa lay yet another example of the reach and transforming power of Indian Ocean commerce.

Sand Roads: Exchange across the Sahara

In addition to the Silk Roads and the Sea Roads, another important pattern of long-distance trade—this one across the vast reaches of the Sahara—linked North Africa and the Mediterranean world with the land and peoples of interior West Africa. Like the others, these Sand Road commercial networks had a transforming impact, stimulating and enriching West African civilization and connecting it to larger patterns of world history during the postclassical era.

Commercial Beginnings in West Africa

Trans-African trade, like the commerce of the Silk Roads and the Sea Roads, was rooted in environmental variation. The North African coastal regions, long part of Roman or later Arab empires, generated cloth, glassware, weapons, books, and other manufactured goods. The great Sahara held deposits of copper and especially salt, while its oases produced sweet and nutritious dates. Although the sparse populations of the desert were largely pastoral and nomadic, farther south lived agricultural peoples who grew a variety of crops, produced their own textiles and metal products, and mined a considerable amount of gold. The agricultural regions of sub-Saharan Africa are normally divided into two ecological zones: the savanna grasslands immediately south of the Sahara, which produced grain crops such as millet and sorghum; and the forest areas farther south, where root and tree crops such as yams and kola nuts predominated. These quite varied environments provided the economic incentive for the exchange of goods.

The earliest long-distance trade within this huge region was not across the Sahara at all, but largely among the agricultural peoples themselves in the area later known to Arabs as the Sudan, or "the land of black people." During the first millennium B.C.E., the peoples of Sudanic West Africa began to exchange metal goods, cotton textiles, gold, and various food products across considerable distances using boats along the Niger River and donkeys overland. On the basis of this trade, a number of independent urban clusters emerged by the early centuries of the Common Era. The most well known was Jenne-jeno, which was located at a crucial point on the Niger River where goods were transshipped from boat to donkey or vice versa.[19] This was the Niger Valley civilization, described in Chapter 7.

Gold, Salt, and Slaves: Trade and Empire in West Africa

A major turning point in African commercial life occurred with the introduction of the camel to North Africa and the Sahara in the early centuries of the Common Era. This remarkable animal, which could go for ten days without water, finally made possible the long trek across the Sahara. It was camel-owning dwellers of desert oases who initiated regular trans-Saharan commerce by 300 to 400 C.E. Several centuries later, North African Arabs, now bearing the new religion of Islam, also organized caravans across the desert.

■ Connections
What changes did trans-Saharan trade bring to West Africa?

What they sought, above all else, was gold, which was found in some abundance in the border areas straddling the grasslands and the forests of West Africa. From its source, it was transported by donkey to transshipment points on the southern edge of the Sahara and then transferred to camels for the long journey north across the desert. African ivory, kola nuts, and slaves were likewise in considerable demand in the desert, the Mediterranean basin, and beyond. In return, the peoples of the Sudan received horses, cloth, dates, various manufactured goods, and especially salt from the rich deposits in the Sahara.

Thus the Sahara was no longer simply a barrier to commerce and cross-cultural interaction; it quickly became a major international trade route that fostered new relationships among distant peoples. The caravans that made the desert crossing could be huge, with as many as 5,000 camels and hundreds of people. Traveling mostly at night to avoid the daytime heat, the journey might take up to seventy days, covering fifteen to twenty-five miles per day. For well over 1,000 years, such caravans traversed the desert, linking the interior of West Africa with lands and people far to the north.

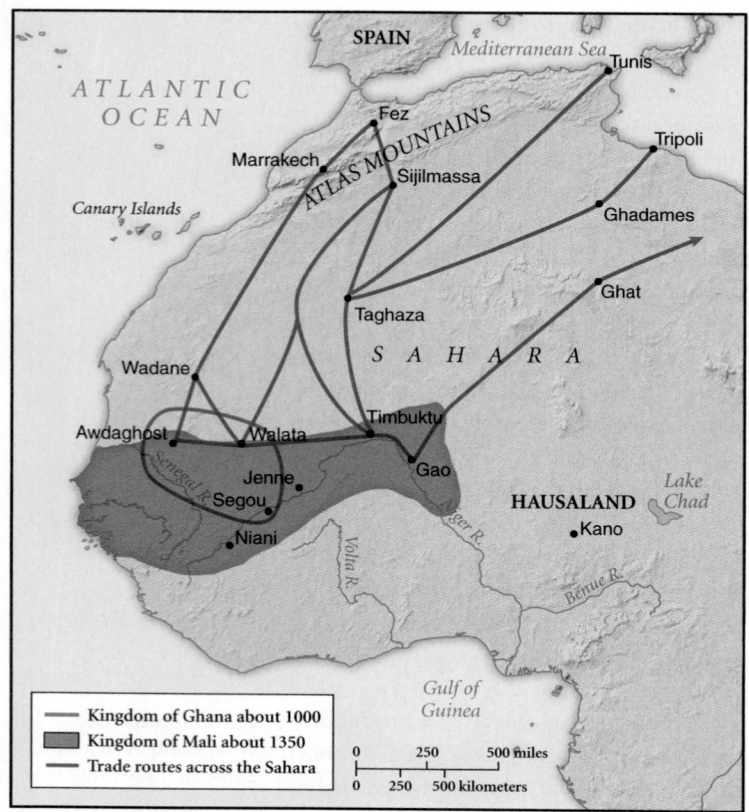

Map 8.3 The Sand Roads

For a thousand years or more, the Sahara was an ocean of sand that linked the interior of West Africa with the world of North Africa and the Mediterranean but separated them as well.

As in Southeast Asia and East Africa, long-distance trade across the Sahara provided both incentive and resources for the construction of new and larger political structures. It was the peoples of the western and central Sudan, living between the forests and the desert, who were in the best position to take advantage of these new opportunities. Between roughly 500 and 1600, they constructed a series of states, empires, and city-states that reached from the Atlantic coast to Lake Chad, including Ghana, Mali, Songhay, Kanem, and the city-states of the Hausa people (see Map 8.3).

All of them were monarchies with elaborate court life and varying degrees of administrative complexity and military forces at their disposal. All drew upon the wealth of trans-Saharan trade, taxing the merchants who conducted it. In the wider world, these states soon acquired a reputation for great riches. An Arab traveler in the tenth century C.E. described the ruler of Ghana as "the wealthiest king on the face of the earth because of his treasures and stocks of gold."[20] At its high point in the fourteenth century, Mali's rulers monopolized the import of strategic goods such as horses and metals; levied duties on salt, copper, and other merchandise; and reserved large nuggets of gold for themselves while permitting the free export of gold dust.

As in all civilizations, slavery found a place in West Africa. Early on, most slaves had been women, working as domestic servants and concubines. As West African civilization crystallized, however, male slaves were put to work as state officials, porters, craftsmen, miners harvesting salt from desert deposits, and especially agricultural laborers producing for the royal granaries on large estates or plantations. Most came from non-Islamic and stateless societies farther south, which were raided during the dry season by cavalry-based forces of West African states, though some white slave women from the eastern Mediterranean also made an appearance in Mali. A song in honor of one eleventh-century ruler of Kanem boasted of his slave-raiding achievements.

The best you took (and sent home) as the first fruits of battle. The children crying on their mothers you snatched away from their mothers. You took the slave wife from a slave, and set them in lands far removed from one another.[21]

Most of these slaves were used within this emerging West African civilization, but a trade in slaves also developed across the Sahara. Between 1100 and 1400, perhaps 5,500 slaves per year made the perilous trek across the desert. When the famous Muslim traveler Ibn Battuta visited Mali in the fourteenth century, he returned home to Morocco with a caravan that included 600 female slaves, who walked across the burning desert, while he rode a camel. Most such slaves were put to work in the homes of the wealthy in Islamic North Africa, but a small number were sold in Europe. Those who arrived in Ireland, for example, were termed "blue men." Far more significant in Europe were slaves from the Slavic-speaking regions along the northern coast of the Black Sea. They were so numerous that the word "slave" in many European languages derives from the term "Slav." Not until the Atlantic slave trade developed after the 1440s did Africans become the major source of slaves for Europeans.

The Gold of Mali
This detail from the *Catalan Atlas*, a series of maps issued in Spain in 1375, illustrates Mali's reputation in Europe for its great wealth in gold. This reputation later propelled Portuguese voyages down the west coast of Africa in search of direct access to that wealth. (Bibliothèque nationale de France)

These states of Sudanic Africa developed substantial urban and commercial centers—such as Koumbi-Saleh, Jenne, Timbuktu, Gao, Gobir, and Kano—where traders congregated and goods were exchanged. Some of these cities also became centers of manufacturing, creating finely wrought beads, iron tools, or cotton textiles, some of which entered the circuits of commerce. Visitors described them as cosmopolitan places where court officials, artisans, scholars, students, and local and foreign merchants all rubbed elbows. As in East Africa, Islam accompanied trade and became an important element in the urban culture of West Africa (see Document 8.3, pp. 362–65). The growth of long-distance trade had stimulated the development of an African civilization, which was linked to the wider networks of exchange in the Eastern Hemisphere.

An American Network: Commerce and Connection in the Western Hemisphere

Before the voyages of Columbus, the world of the Americas developed quite separately from that of the Eastern Hemisphere. Despite intriguing hints of occasional contacts, no sustained interaction between the peoples of these two great landmasses took place. But if the Silk, Sea, and Sand Roads linked the diverse peoples of the Afro-Eurasian world, did a similar network of interaction join and transform the various societies of the Western Hemisphere?

Clearly, direct connections among the various civilizations and cultures of the Americas were less densely woven than in the Afro-Eurasian region. The llama and the potato, both domesticated in the Andes, never reached Mesoamerica; nor did the writing system of the Maya diffuse to Andean civilizations. The Aztecs and the Incas, contemporary civilizations in the fifteenth century, had little if any direct contact with each other. The limits of these interactions owed something to the

■ **Comparison**
In what ways did networks of interaction in the Western Hemisphere differ from those in the Eastern Hemisphere?

absence of horses, donkeys, camels, wheeled vehicles, and large oceangoing vessels, all of which facilitated long-distance trade and travel in Afro-Eurasia.

Geographic or environmental differences added further obstacles. The narrow bottleneck of Panama, largely covered by dense rain forests, surely inhibited contact between South and North America. Furthermore, the north/south orientation of the Americas—which required agricultural practices to move through, and adapt to, quite distinct climatic and vegetation zones—slowed the spread of agricultural products. By contrast, the east/west axis of Eurasia meant that agricultural innovations could diffuse more rapidly because they were entering roughly similar environments. Thus nothing equivalent to the long-distance trade of the Silk, Sea, or Sand Roads of the Eastern Hemisphere arose in the Americas, even though local and regional commerce flourished in many places. Nor did distinct cultural traditions such as Buddhism, Christianity, and Islam spread so widely to integrate distant peoples.

Nonetheless, scholars have discerned "a loosely interactive web stretching from the North American Great Lakes and upper Mississippi south to the Andes."[22] (See Map 8.4.) Partly, it was a matter of slowly spreading cultural elements, such as the gradual diffusion of maize from its Mesoamerican place of origin to the southwestern United States and then on to much of eastern North America as well as to much of South America in the other direction. A game played with rubber balls on an outdoor court has left traces in the Caribbean, Mexico, and northern South America. Construction in the Tantoc region of northeastern Mexico resembled the earlier building styles of Cahokia, suggesting the possibility of some interaction between the two regions.[23] The spread of particular pottery styles and architectural conventions likewise suggests at least indirect contact over wide distances.

Commerce too played an important role in the making of this "American web." A major North American chief-

Map 8.4 **The American Web**
Transcontinental interactions within the American web were more modest than those of the Afro-Eurasian hemisphere. The most intense areas of exchange and communication occurred within the Mississippi valley, Mesoamerican, and Andean regions.

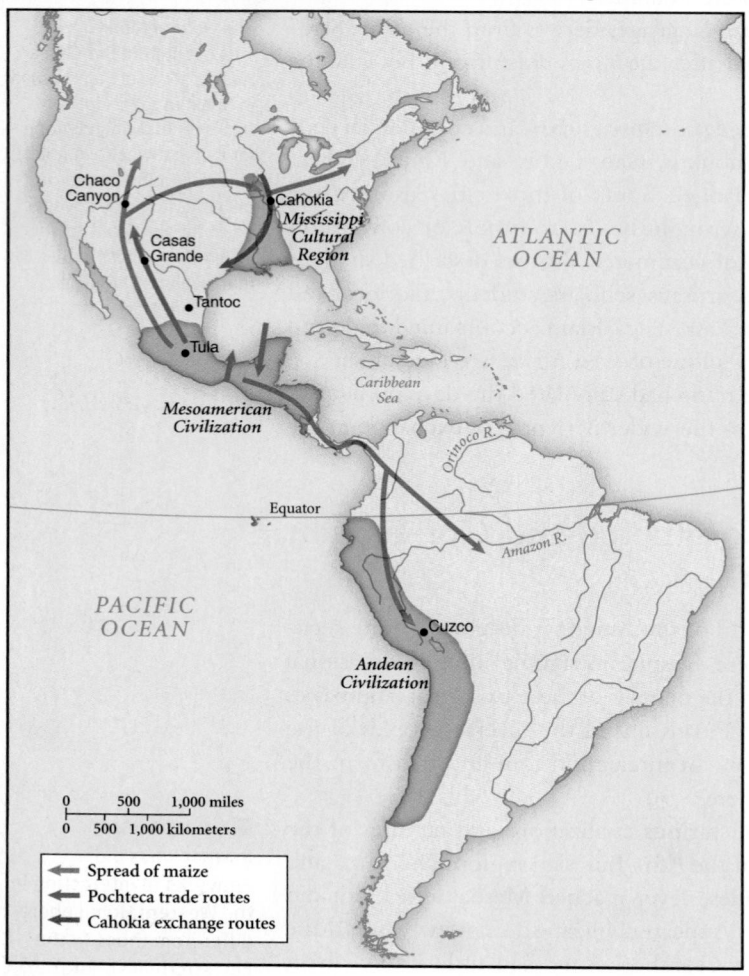

dom at Cahokia, near present-day St. Louis, flourished from about 900 to 1250 at the confluence of the Mississippi, Illinois, and Missouri rivers (see pp. 303–04). Cahokia lay at the center of a widespread trading network that brought it shells from the Atlantic coast, copper from the Lake Superior region, buffalo hides from the Great Plains, obsidian from the Rocky Mountains, and mica from the southern Appalachian Mountains. Sturdy dugout canoes plied the rivers of the eastern woodlands, connecting their diverse but related societies. Early European explorers and travelers along the Amazon and Orinoco rivers of South America reported active networks of exchange that may well have operated for many centuries. Caribbean peoples using large oceangoing canoes had long conducted an inter-island trade, and the Chincha people undertook ocean-based exchange in copper, beads, and shells along the Pacific coasts of Peru and Ecuador in large seagoing rafts.[24] Another regional commercial network, centered in Mesoamerica, extended north to what is now the southwestern United States and south to Ecuador and Colombia. Many items from Mesoamerica—copper bells, macaw feathers, tons of shells—have been found in the Chaco region of New Mexico. Residents of Chaco also drank liquid chocolate, using jars of Mayan origin and cacao beans imported from Mesoamerica, where the practice began.[25] Turquoise, mined and worked among the Ancestral Pueblo (see pp. 301–03) flowed in the other direction.

But the most active and dense networks of communication and exchange in the Americas lay within, rather than between, the regions that housed the two great civilizations of the Western Hemisphere—Mesoamerica and the Andes. During the classical era of Mesoamerican civilization (200–900 C.E.), both the Maya cities in the Yucatán area of Mexico and Guatemala and the huge city-state of Teotihuacán in central Mexico maintained commercial relationships with one another and throughout the region. In addition to this land-based trade, the Maya conducted a seaborne commerce, using large dugout canoes holding forty to fifty people, along both the Atlantic and Pacific coasts.[26] Although most of this trade was in luxury goods rather than basic necessities, it was critical to upholding the position and privileges of royal and noble families. Items such as cotton clothing, precious jewels, and feathers from particular birds marked the status of elite groups and served to attract followers. Controlling access to such high-prestige goods was an important motive for war among Mesoamerican states.[27] Among the Aztecs of the fifteenth century, professional merchants, known as *pochteca*, undertook large-scale trading expeditions both within and well beyond the borders of

Inca Roads
Used for transporting goods by pack animal or sending messages by foot, the Inca road network included some 2,000 inns where travelers might find food and shelter. Messengers, operating in relay, could cover as many as 150 miles a day. Here a modern-day citizen of Peru walks along an old Inca trail road. (Loren McIntyre/lorenmcintyre.com)

their empire, sometimes as agents for the state or for members of the nobility, but more often acting on their own as private businessmen.

Unlike the Aztec Empire, in which private traders largely handled the distribution of goods, economic exchange in the Andean Inca Empire during the fifteenth century was a state-run operation, and no merchant group similar to the Aztec *pochteca* emerged there. Instead, great state storehouses bulged with immense quantities of food, clothing, military supplies, blankets, construction materials, and more, all carefully recorded on *quipus* (knotted cords used to record numerical data) by a highly trained class of accountants. From these state centers, goods were transported as needed by caravans of human porters and llamas across the numerous roads and bridges of the empire. Totaling some 20,000 miles, Inca roads traversed the coastal plain and the high Andes in a north/south direction, while lateral roads linked these diverse environments and extended into the eastern rain forests and plains as well. Despite the general absence of private trade, local exchange took place at highland fairs and along the borders of the empire with groups outside the Inca state.

Reflections: Economic Globalization— Ancient and Modern

The densely connected world of the modern era, linked by ties of commerce and culture around the planet, certainly has roots in much earlier patterns. Particularly in the era of third-wave civilizations from 500 to 1500, the Silk, Sea, and Sand roads of the Afro-Eurasian world and the looser networks of the American web linked distant peoples both economically and culturally, prompted the emergence of new states, and sustained elite privileges in many ancient civilizations. In those ways, they resembled the globalized world of modern times.

In other respects, though, the networks and webs of the premodern millennium differed sharply from those of more recent centuries. Most people still produced primarily for their own consumption rather than for the market, and a much smaller range of goods was exchanged in the marketplaces of the world. Far fewer people then were required to sell their own labor for wages, an almost universal practice in modern economies. Because of transportation costs and technological limitations, most trade was in luxury goods rather than in necessities. In addition, the circuits of commerce were rather more limited than the truly global patterns of exchange that emerged after 1500.

Furthermore, the world economy of the modern era increasingly had a single center—industrialized Western European countries—which came to dominate much of the world both economically and politically during the nineteenth century. Though never completely equal, the economic relationships of earlier times occurred among much more equivalent units. For example, no one region dominated the complex pattern of Indian Ocean exchange, although India and China generally offered manufactured goods, while Southeast Asia and East Africa contributed agricultural products or raw materials. And with the exception of the brief Mongol control of the Silk Roads and the Inca domination of the Andes for a century, no single power exercised political control over the other major networks of world commerce.

The world of third-wave civilizations, in short, was a more balanced, multicentered world than that of the modern era. Although massive inequalities occurred within particular regions or societies, relationships among the major civilizations operated on a rather more equal basis than in the globalized world of the past several centuries. With the rise of China and India as major players in the world economy of the twenty-first century, are we perhaps returning to that earlier pattern?

Second Thoughts

What's the Significance?

Silk Roads	Srivijaya	Sand Roads
Black Death	Borobudur	Ghana, Mali, Songhay
Indian Ocean trading network	Swahili civilization	trans-Saharan slave trade
	Great Zimbabwe	American web

To assess your mastery of the material in this chapter, visit the **Student Center** at bedfordstmartins.com/strayer.

Big Picture Questions

1. What motivated and sustained the long-distance commerce of the Silk Roads, Sea Roads, and Sand Roads?
2. Why did the Eastern Hemisphere develop long-distance trade more extensively than did the societies of the Western Hemisphere?
3. In what ways did commercial exchange foster other changes?
4. In what ways was Afro-Eurasia a single interacting zone, and in what respects was it a vast region of separate cultures and civilizations?

Next Steps: For Further Study

Jerry Bentley, *Old World Encounters* (1993). A wonderfully succinct and engaging history of cross-cultural interaction all across Afro-Eurasia before 1500.

E. W. Bovill, *The Golden Trade of the Moors* (1970). A classic account of the trans-Saharan trade.

Rainer Buschmann, *Oceans in World History* (2007). A brief study of communication and exchange across the world's oceans.

K. N. Chaudhuri, *Trade and Civilization in the Indian Ocean* (1985). A well-regarded study that treats the Indian Ocean basin as a single region linked by both commerce and culture during the postclassical era.

Philip Curtin, *Cross-Cultural Trade in World History* (1984). Explores long-distance trade as a generator of social change on a global level.

Liu Xinru and Lynda Shaffer, *Connections across Eurasia* (2007). A brief, accessible, and up-to-date account by two major scholars of the Silk Road trading network.

Bridging World History, http://www.learner.org/channel/courses/worldhistory. Units 9 and 10 of this Web-based guide to world history provide an illustrated examination of global trade in the postclassical millennium.

For Web sites and additional documents related to this chapter, see **Make History** at bedfordstmartins.com/strayer.

Documents

Considering the Evidence:
Travelers' Tales and Observations

Historians generally prefer to rely on "insiders" for understanding the so-cieties and cultures they study. Documents, artifacts, and images created by people actually living in those times and places have an authenticity that accounts by foreigners may lack. Nonetheless, scholars often find it helpful—even necessary—to make use of records written by outsiders as well. During the postclassical millennium, as long-distance trade flourished and large trans-regional empires grew, opportunities for individuals to travel far beyond their homelands increased. Their accounts have provided historians with invaluable information about particular regions and cultures, as well as about interactions among disparate peoples. The authors of these accounts, perhaps inadvertently, also reveal much about themselves and about the perceptions and mispercep-tions generated by cross-cultural encounters. The selections that follow provide three examples of intrepid long-distance travelers and their impressions of the societies they encountered on their arduous journeys.

Document 8.1

A Chinese Buddhist in India

During the seventh century, Xuanzang (600–664 C.E.), a highly educated Buddhist monk from China, made a long and difficult journey to India through some of the world's most daunting deserts and mountain ranges, returning home in 645 C.E. after sixteen years abroad (see Visual Source 8.2, p. 370). His motives, like those of many other Buddhist travelers to India, were essentially religious. "I regretted that the teachings of [Buddhism] were not complete and the scriptures deficient in my own country," he wrote. "I have doubts and have puzzled in my mind, but I could find no one to solve them. That was why I decided to travel to the West...."[28] In India, the homeland of Buddhism, he hoped to find the teachers and the sacred texts that would answer his ques-tions, enrich Buddhist practice in China, and resolve the many disputes that had created serious divisions within the Buddhist community of his own country.

During a ten-year stay in India, Xuanzang visited many of the holy sites associated with the Buddha's life and studied with leading Buddhist teachers, particularly those at Nalanda University, a huge monastic complex dedicated to Buddhist scholarship (see Map 8.1, p. 335). He traveled widely within India and established a personal relationship with Harsha, the ruler of the state which then encompassed much of northern India. On his return journey to China, he carried hundreds of manuscripts, at least seven statues of the Buddha, and even some relics. Warmly greeted by the Chinese emperor, Xuanzang spent the last two decades of his life translating the texts he had collected into Chinese. He also wrote an account of his travels, known as the *Record of the Western Regions,* and shared his recollections with a fellow monk and translator named Huili, who subsequently wrote a biography of Xuanzang.[29] The selections that follow derive from these two accounts and convey something of Xuanzang's impressions of Indian civilization in the seventh century C.E.

■ What do you think surprised or impressed Xuanzang on his visit to India? What features of Indian life might seem most strange to a Chinese visitor?

■ How might these selections serve to illustrate or to contradict the descriptions of classical Indian civilization in Chapters 4–6?

■ What can this document contribute to our understanding of Buddhist practice in India?

HUILI

A Biography of the Tripitaka Master
Seventh Century C.E.

[Certainly the emotional highlight of Xuanzang's travels in India was his visit to the site of the Buddha's enlightenment under the famous Bodhi tree. The great traveler's biographer, Huili, recorded his Master's response.]

Upon his arrival there, the Master worshipped the Bodhi tree and the image of the Buddha attaining enlightenment made by Maitreya Bodhisattva. After having looked at the image with deep sincerity, he prostrated himself before it and deplored sadly, saying with self-reproach, "I do not know where I was born in the course of transmigration at the time

Source: Li Rongxi (trans.), *A Biography of the Tripitaka Master of the Great Ci'en Monastery of the Great Tang Dynasty* (Berkeley: Numata Center for Buddhist Translation, 1995), 89–90, 94–95.

when the Buddha attained enlightenment. I could only come here at this time....It makes me think that my karmic hindrances must have been very heavy!" While he was saying so, his eyes brimmed with sorrowful tears. As that was the time when the monks dismissed the summer retreat, several thousand people forgathered from far and near. Those who saw the Master were choked by sobs in sympathy with him.

[The great Buddhist monastery/university at Nalanda was likewise a major destination of Xuanzang's journey. It must have been a place of wonder and delight to the Chinese monk, as he described it to Huili.]

Ten thousand monks always lived there, both hosts and guests. They studied Mahayana teachings and the doctrines of the eighteen schools, as well as wordly books such as the Vedas. They also learned about works on logic, grammar, medicine, and divination.... Lectures were given at more than a hundred places in the monastery every day, and the students studied diligently without wasting a single moment. As all the monks who lived there were men of virtue, the atmosphere in the monastery was naturally solemn and dignified. For more than seven hundred years since its establishment, none of the monks had committed any offence. Out of

respect for them, the king gave more than a hundred villages for their sustenance. Each village had two hundred families, who daily provided several hundred *shi* of polished nonglutinous rice, butter, and milk. Thus the students could enjoy sufficient supplies of the four requisites without the trouble of going to beg for them. It was because of this effort of their supporters that the scholars could gain achievements in learning.

XUANZANG

Record of the Western Region
Seventh Century C.E.

[Selections from Xuanzang's more general description of Indian civilization follow here drawn from his own account.]

On Towns and Villages

The towns and villages have inner gates; the walls are wide and high; the streets and lanes are tortuous, and the roads winding. The thoroughfares are dirty and the stalls arranged on both sides of the road with appropriate signs. Butchers, fishers, dancers, executioners, and scavengers, and so on [untouchables], have their abodes without [outside] the city. In coming and going these persons are bound to keep on the left side of the road till they arrive at their homes. Their houses are surrounded by low walls and form the suburbs. The earth being soft and muddy, the walls of the towns are mostly built of brick or tiles....

On Buddhist Studies

The different schools are constantly at variance, and their contending utterances rise like the angry waves of the sea. The different sects have their separate masters....

There are eighteen schools, each claiming pre-

eminence. The partisans of the Great and Little Vehicle are content to dwell apart. There are some who give themselves up to quiet contemplation, and devote themselves, whether walking or standing still or sitting down, to the acquirement of wisdom and insight; others, on the contrary, differ from these in raising noisy contentions about their faith. According to their fraternity, they are governed by distinctive rules and regulations....

The *Vinaya* discourses [rules governing monastic life] are equally Buddhist books. He who can entirely explain one class of these books is exempted from the control of the *karmadâna*°. If he can explain two classes, he receives in addition the equipments of an upper seat (*room*); he who can explain three classes has allotted to him different servants to attend to and obey him; he who can explain four classes has "pure men" allotted to him as attendants; he who can explain five classes of books is then allowed an elephant carriage; he who can explain six classes of books is allowed a surrounding escort. When a man's renown has reached to a high distinction, then at different times he convokes an assembly for discussion. He judges of the superior or inferior talent of those who take part in it; he distinguishes their good or bad points; he praises the clever and reproves the faulty; if one of the assembly distinguishes himself by refined language, subtle

Source: Samuel Beal (trans.), *Su-Yu-Ki: Buddhist Records of the Western World* (London: K. Paul, Trench, Trubner & Co., 1906), vol. I, book 2, 73–74, 77, 79–84.

°*karmadâna:* a high monastic official.

investigation, deep penetration, and severe logic, then he is mounted on an elephant covered with precious ornaments, and conducted by a numerous suite to the gates of the convent.

If, on the contrary, one of the members breaks down in his argument, or uses poor and inelegant phrases, or if he violates a rule in logic and adapts his words accordingly, they proceed to disfigure his face with red and white, and cover his body with dirt and dust, and then carry him off to some deserted spot or leave him in a ditch. Thus they distinguish between the meritorious and the worthless, between the wise and the foolish.

On Caste and Marriage

With respect to the division of families, there are four classifications. The first is called the Brâhman, men of pure conduct. They guard themselves in religion, live purely, and observe the most correct principles. The second is called Kshattriya, the royal caste. For ages they have been the governing class: they apply themselves to virtue and kindness. The third is called Vaiśyas, the merchant class: they engage in commercial exchange, and they follow profit at home and abroad. The fourth is called Sûdra, the agricultural class: they labor in plowing and tillage. In these four classes purity or impurity of caste assigns to every one his place. When they marry they rise or fall in position according to their new relationship. They do not allow promiscuous marriages between relations. A woman once married can never take another husband. Besides these there are other classes of many kinds that intermarry according to their several callings.

On Manners and Justice

With respect to the ordinary people, although they are naturally light-minded, yet they are upright and honorable. In money matters they are without craft, and in administering justice they are considerate. They dread the retribution of another state of existence, and make light of the things of the present world. They are not deceitful or treacherous in their conduct, and are faithful to their oaths and promises. In their rules of government there is remarkable rectitude, whilst in their behavior there is much gentleness and sweetness. With respect to criminals or rebels, these are few in number, and only occasionally troublesome. When the laws are broken or the power of the ruler violated, then the matter is clearly sifted and the offenders imprisoned. There is no infliction of corporal punishment; they are simply left to live or die, and are not counted among men. When the rules of propriety or justice are violated, or when a man fails in fidelity or filial piety, then they cut his nose or his ears off, or his hands and feet, or expel him from the country or drive him out into the desert wilds. For other faults, except these, a small payment of money will redeem the punishment. In the investigation of criminal cases there is no use of rod or staff to obtain proofs (*of guilt*).

Document 8.2

A European Christian in China

Of all the travelers along the Silk Road network, the most well-known and celebrated, at least in the West, was Marco Polo (1254–1324). Born and raised in the prosperous commercial city-state of Venice in what is now northern Italy, Marco Polo was a member of a family prominent in the long-distance trade of the Mediterranean and Black sea regions. At the age of seventeen, Marco accompanied his father and an uncle on an immense journey across Eurasia which by 1275 brought the Polos to China, recently conquered by the Mongols. It was, in fact, the relative peace which the Mongols had created in their huge transcontinental empire that facilitated the Polos' journey (see Map 12.1, p. 530). For the next seventeen years, they lived in China, where they were employed in minor administrative positions by Khublai Khan, the country's Mongol ruler. During these years, Marco Polo apparently traveled widely within China where he gathered material for the book about his travels, which he dictated to a friend after returning home in 1295.

Marco Polo's journey and the book that described it, generally known as *The Travels of Marco Polo*, were important elements of the larger process by which an emerging West European civilization reached out to and became aware of the older civilizations of the East. Christopher Columbus carried a marked-up copy of the book on his transatlantic journeys, believing that he was seeking by sea the places Marco Polo had visited by land. Some modern scholars are skeptical about parts of Marco Polo's report, and a few even question whether he ever got to China at all, largely because he omitted any mention of certain prominent features of Chinese life, for example, foot binding, the Great Wall, and tea drinking. Most historians, however, accept the basic outlines of Marco Polo's account, even as they notice exaggerations as well as an inflated perception of his own role within China. The selection that follows conveys Marco Polo's description of the city of Hangzhou, which he referred to as Kinsay. At the time of Marco Polo's visit, it was among the largest cities in the world.

- How would you describe Marco Polo's impressions of the city? What did he notice? What surprised him?

- Why did Marco Polo describe the city as "the finest and the noblest in the world"?

- What marks his account of the city as that of a foreigner and a Christian?

- What evidence of China's engagement with a wider world does this account offer?

MARCO POLO
The Travels of Marco Polo
1299

The city is beyond dispute the finest and the noblest in the world. In this we shall speak

Source: *The Book of Sir Marco Polo the Venetian Concerning the Kingdoms and Marvels of the East*, 3rd ed., translated and edited by Henry Yule, revised by Henri Cordier (London: John Murray, 1903), vol. 2:185–206.

according to the written statement which the Queen of this Realm sent to Bayan, the [Mongol] conqueror of the country for transmission to the Great Kaan, in order that he might be aware of the surpassing grandeur of the city and might be moved to save it from destruction or injury. I will tell you all the truth as it was set down in that document. For truth it was, as the said Messer Marco Polo at a later date was able to witness with his own eyes....

First and foremost, then, the document stated the city of Kinsay to be so great that it hath an hundred miles of compass. And there are in it 12,000 bridges of stone....[Most scholars consider these figures a considerable exaggeration.] And though the bridges be so high, the approaches are so well contrived that carts and horses do cross them.

The document aforesaid also went on to state that there were in this city twelve guilds of the different crafts, and that each guild had 12,000 houses in the occupation of its workmen. Each of these houses contains at least twelve men, whilst some contain twenty and some forty.... And yet all these craftsmen had full occupation, for many other cities of the kingdom are supplied from this city with what they require.

The document aforesaid also stated that the number and wealth of the merchants, and the amount of goods that passed through their hands, were so enormous that no man could form a just estimate thereof. And I should have told you with regard to those masters of the different crafts who are at the head of such houses as I have mentioned, that neither they nor their wives ever touch a piece of work with their own hands, but live as nicely and delicately as if they were kings and queens. The wives indeed are most dainty and angelical creatures! Moreover it was an ordinance laid down by the King that every man should follow his father's business and no other, no matter if he possessed 100,000 bezants.°

Inside the city there is a Lake . . . and all round it are erected beautiful palaces and mansions, of the richest and most exquisite structure that you can imagine, belonging to the nobles of the city. There are also on its shores many abbeys and churches of the Idolaters [Buddhists]. In the middle of the Lake are two Islands, on each of which stands a rich, beautiful, and spacious edifice, furnished in such style as to seem fit for the palace of an Emperor. And when any one of the citizens desired to hold a marriage feast, or to give any other entertainment, it used to

be done at one of these palaces. And everything would be found there ready to order, such as silver plate, trenchers, and dishes, napkins and table-cloths, and whatever else was needful.... Sometimes there would be at these palaces an hundred different parties; some holding a banquet, others celebrating a wedding...in so well-ordered a manner that one party was never in the way of another....

Both men and women are fair and comely, and for the most part clothe themselves in silk, so vast is the supply of that material, both from the whole district of Kinsay, and from the imports by traders from other provinces. And you must know they eat every kind of flesh, even that of dogs and other unclean beasts, which nothing would induce a Christian to eat....

You must know also that the city of Kinsay has some 3,000 baths, the water of which is supplied by springs. They are hot baths, and the people take great delight in them, frequenting them several times a month, for they are very cleanly in their persons. They are the finest and largest baths in the world....

And the Ocean Sea comes within twenty-five miles of the city at a place called Ganfu, where there is a town and an excellent haven, with a vast amount of shipping which is engaged in the traffic to and from India and other foreign parts, exporting and importing many kinds of wares, by which the city benefits....

I repeat that everything appertaining to this city is on so vast a scale, and the Great Kaan's yearly revenues therefrom are so immense, that it is not easy even to put it in writing....

In this part are the ten principal markets, though besides these there are a vast number of others in the different parts of the town.... [T]oward the [market] squares are built great houses of stone, in which the merchants from India and other foreign parts store their wares, to be handy for the markets. In each of the squares is held a market three days in the week, frequented by 40,000 or 50,000 persons, who bring thither for sale every possible necessary of life, so that there is always an ample supply of every kind of meat and game....

Those markets make a daily display of every kind of vegetables and fruits.... [V]ery good raisins are

----

°**bezant:** a Byzantine gold coin.

brought from abroad, and wine likewise.... From the Ocean Sea also come daily supplies of fish in great quantity, brought twenty-five miles up the river.... All the ten market places are encompassed by lofty houses, and below these are shops where all sorts of crafts are carried on, and all sorts of wares are on sale, including spices and jewels and pearls. Some of these shops are entirely devoted to the sale of wine made from rice and spices, which is constantly made fresh, and is sold very cheap. Certain of the streets are occupied by the women of the town, who are in such a number that I dare not say what it is. They are found not only in the vicinity of the market places, where usually a quarter is assigned to them, but all over the city. They exhibit themselves splendidly attired and abundantly perfumed, in finely garnished houses, with trains of waiting-women. These women are extremely accomplished in all the arts of allurement, and readily adapt their conversation to all sorts of persons, insomuch that strangers who have once tasted their attractions seem to get bewitched, and are so taken with their blandishments and their fascinating ways that they never can get these out of their heads....

Other streets are occupied by the Physicians, and by the Astrologers, who are also teachers of reading and writing; and an infinity of other professions have their places round about those squares. In each of the squares there are two great palaces facing one another, in which are established the officers appointed by the King to decide differences arising between merchants, or other inhabitants of the quarter....

The crowd of people that you meet here at all hours ... is so vast that no one would believe it possible that victuals enough could be provided for their consumption, unless they should see how, on every market-day, all those squares are thronged and crammed with purchasers, and with the traders who have brought in stores of provisions by land or water; and everything they bring in is disposed of....

The natives of the city are men of peaceful character, both from education and from the example of their kings, whose disposition was the same. They know nothing of handling arms, and keep none in their houses. You hear of no feuds or noisy quarrels or dissensions of any kind among them. Both in their commercial dealings and in their manufactures they are thoroughly honest and truthful, and there is such a degree of good will and neighborly attachment among both men and women that you would take the people who live in the same street to be all one family.

And this familiar intimacy is free from all jealousy or suspicion of the conduct of their women. These they treat with the greatest respect, and a man who should presume to make loose proposals to a married woman would be regarded as an infamous rascal. They also treat the foreigners who visit them for the sake of trade with great cordiality and entertain them in the most winning manner, affording them every help and advice on their business. But on the other hand they hate to see soldiers, and not least those of the Great Kaan's garrisons, regarding them as the cause of their having lost their native kings and lords.

Document 8.3

An Arab Muslim in West Africa

For most of the postclassical millennium, the world of Islam was far more extensive than that of Christendom. Nothing more effectively conveys both the extent and the cultural unity of the Islamic world than the travels of Ibn Battuta (1304–1368). Born in Morocco, this learned Arab scholar traversed nearly 75,000 miles during his extraordinary journeys, which took him to Spain, Anatolia, West and East Africa, Arabia, Iraq, Persia, Central and Southeast Asia, India, and China. He traveled at various times as a pilgrim, as a religious seeker, as a legal scholar, and frequently in the company of Muslim merchants. Remarkably, almost all of his extensive travels occurred within the realm of Islam, where he moved among people who shared his faith and often his Arabic language. Marco Polo, by contrast, had felt himself constantly an outsider, "a stranger in a strange land," for he was traveling almost everywhere beyond the borders of Christendom. But as a visitor from a more-established Islamic society, Ibn Battuta was often highly critical of the quality of Islamic observance in the frontier regions of the faith.

One such frontier region was West Africa, where a new civilization was taking shape, characterized by large empires such as Mali, a deep involvement in trans-Saharan commerce, and the gradual assimilation of Islam (see Map 8.3, p. 350, and pp. 348–51 and 492–94). The new faith had been introduced by North African Muslim traders and had found a growing acceptance, particularly in the urban centers, merchant communities, and ruling classes of West African kingdoms. On the last of his many journeys, Ibn Battuta crossed the Sahara Desert with a traders' caravan to visit Mali in 1352. Upon returning home the following year, he dictated his recollections and experiences to a scribe, producing a valuable account of this West African civilization in the fourteenth century.

■ How would you describe Ibn Battuta's impression of Mali? What surprised or shocked him? What did he appreciate?

■ What does Ibn Battuta's description of his visit to Mali reveal about his own attitudes and his image of himself?

■ What might historians learn from this document about the nature and extent of Islam's penetration in this West African empire? What elements of older and continuing West African cultural traditions are evident in the document?

■ What specifically does Ibn Battuta find shocking about the women he encounters on his travels in West Africa?

■ What indications of Mali's economic involvement with a wider world are evident in the document?

IBN BATTUTA

Travels in Asia and Africa

1354

Thus we reached the town of Iwalatan° after a journey from Sijilmasa of two months to a day. Iwalatan is the northernmost province of the blacks.... The garments of its inhabitants, most of whom belong to the Massufa tribe, are of fine Egyptian fabrics.

°**Iwalatan:** Walata.

Source: Ibn Battuta, *Travels in Asia and Africa 1325–1354,* translated and edited by H. A. R. Gibb (London: Broadway House, 1929), 319–34.

Their women are of surpassing beauty, and are shown more respect than the men. The state of affairs amongst these people is indeed extraordinary. Their men show no signs of jealousy whatever; no one claims descent from his father, but on the contrary from his mother's brother. A person's heirs are his sister's sons, not his own sons. This is a thing which I have seen nowhere in the world except among the Indians of Malabar. But those are heathens; these people are Muslims, punctilious in observing the hours of prayer, studying books of law, and memorizing the Koran. Yet their women show no bashfulness before men and do not veil themselves, though they are assiduous in attending the prayers.

The women there have "friends" and "companions" amongst the men outside their own families, and the men in the same way have "companions" amongst the women of other families. A man may go into his house and find his wife entertaining her "companion," but he takes no objection to it. One day at Iwalatan I went into the qadi's° house, after asking his permission to enter, and found with him a young woman of remarkable beauty. When I saw her I was shocked and turned to go out, but she laughed at me, instead of being overcome by shame, and the qadi said to me "Why are you going out? She is my companion." I was amazed at their conduct, for he was a theologian and a pilgrim [to Mecca] to boot....

When I decided to make the journey to Malli,° which is reached in twenty-four days from Iwalatan if the traveler pushes on rapidly, I hired a guide from the Massufa—for there is no necessity to travel in a company on account of the safety of that road—and set out with three of my companions....

A traveler in this country carries no provisions, whether plain food or seasonings, and neither gold nor silver. He takes nothing but pieces of salt and glass ornaments, which the people call beads, and some aromatic goods. When he comes to a village the womenfolk of the blacks bring out millet, milk, chickens, pulped lotus fruit, rice,

"funi" (a grain resembling mustard seed, from which "kuskusu"° and gruel are made), and pounded haricot beans....

Thus I reached the city of Malli, the capital of the king of the blacks. I stopped at the cemetery and went to the quarter occupied by the whites, where I asked for Muhammad ibn al-Faqih. I found that he had hired a house for me and went there....I met the qadi of Malli, 'Abd ar-Rahman, who came to see me; he is a black, a pilgrim [to Mecca], and a man of fine character. I met also the interpreter Dugha, who is one of the principal men among the blacks. All these persons sent me hospitality gifts of food and treated me with the utmost generosity....

The sultan° of Malli is Mansa Sulayman....He is a miserly king, not a man from whom one might hope for a rich present. It happened that I spent these two months without seeing him, on account of my illness. Later on he held a banquet...to which the commanders, doctors, qadi, and preacher were invited, and I went along with them. Reading-desks were brought in, and the Koran was read through, then they prayed for our master Abu'l-Hasan° and also for Mansa Sulayman.

When the ceremony was over I went forward and saluted Mansa Sulayman....When I withdrew, the [sultan's] hospitality gift was sent to me....I stood up thinking . . . that it consisted of robes of honor and money, and lo!, it was three cakes of bread, and a piece of beef fried in native oil, and a calabash of sour curds. When I saw this I burst out laughing, and thought it a most amazing thing that they could be so foolish and make so much of such a paltry matter.

On certain days the sultan holds audiences in the palace yard, where there is a platform under a tree, with three steps; this they call the "pempi." It is carpeted with silk and has cushions placed on it. [Over it] is raised the umbrella, which is a sort of pavilion made of silk, surmounted by a bird in gold, about the size of a falcon. The sultan comes out of a door in a corner of the palace, carrying a bow in his hand and a quiver on his back. On his head he has a golden

---

°**qadi:** judge.

°**Malli:** the city of Mali.

°**kuskusu:** couscous.

°**sultan:** ruler.

°**Abu'l-Hasan:** the sultan of Morocco.

skullcap, bound with a gold band which has narrow ends shaped like knives, more than a span in length. His usual dress is a velvety red tunic, made of the European fabrics called "mutanfas." The sultan is preceded by his musicians, who carry gold and silver guimbris°, and behind him come three hundred armed slaves. He walks in a leisurely fashion, affecting a very slow movement, and even stops from time to time. On reaching the pempi he stops and looks round the assembly, then ascends it in the sedate manner of a preacher ascending a mosque-pulpit. As he takes his seat the drums, trumpets, and bugles are sounded. Three slaves go out at a run to summon the sovereign's deputy and the military commanders, who enter and sit down. Two saddled and bridled horses are brought, along with two goats, which they hold to serve as a protection against the evil eye....

The blacks are of all people the most submissive to their king and the most abject in their behavior before him.... If he summons any of them while he is holding an audience in his pavilion, the person summoned takes off his clothes and puts on worn garments, removes his turban and dons a dirty skullcap, and enters with his garments and trousers raised knee-high. He goes forward in an attitude of humility and dejection and knocks the ground hard with his elbows, then stands with bowed head and bent back listening to what he says. If anyone addresses the king and receives a reply from him, he uncovers his back and throws dust over his head and back, for all the world like a bather splashing himself with water....

On feast-days ..., the poets come in. Each of them is inside a figure resembling a thrush, made of feathers, and provided with a wooden head with a red beak, to look like a thrush's head. They stand in front of the sultan in this ridiculous makeup and recite their poems. I was told that their poetry is a kind of sermonizing in which they say to the sultan: "This pempi which you occupy was that whereon sat this king and that king, and such and such were this one's noble actions and such and such the other's. So do you too do good deeds whose memory will

outlive you."... I was told that this practice is a very old custom amongst them, prior to the introduction of Islam, and that they have kept it up.

The blacks possess some admirable qualities. They are seldom unjust, and have a greater abhorrence of injustice than any other people. Their sultan shows no mercy to anyone who is guilty of the least act of it. There is complete security in their country. Neither traveler nor inhabitant in it has anything to fear from robbers or men of violence. They do not confiscate the property of any white man who dies in their country, even if it be uncounted wealth. On the contrary, they give it into the charge of some trustworthy person among the whites, until the rightful heir takes possession of it. They are careful to observe the hours of prayer, and assiduous in attending them in congregations, and in bringing up their children to them.

On Fridays, if a man does not go early to the mosque, he cannot find a corner to pray in, on account of the crowd. It is a custom of theirs to send each man his boy [to the mosque] with his prayer-mat; the boy spreads it out for his master in a place befitting him [and remains on it] until he comes to the mosque....

Another of their good qualities is their habit of wearing clean white garments on Fridays. Even if a man has nothing but an old worn shirt, he washes it and cleans it, and wears it to the Friday service. Yet another is their zeal for learning the Koran by heart.... I visited the qadi in his house on the day of the festival. His children were chained up, so I said to him, "Will you not let them loose?" He replied, "I shall not do so until they learn the Koran by heart."

Among their bad qualities are the following. The women servants, slave-girls, and young girls go about in front of everyone naked, without a stitch of clothing on them. Women go into the sultan's presence naked and without coverings, and his daughters also go about naked. Then there is their custom of putting dust and ashes on their heads, as a mark of respect, and the grotesque ceremonies we have described when the poets recite their verses. Another reprehensible practice among many of them is the eating of carrion, dogs, and asses.

°**guimbris:** two-stringed guitars.

I went on…to Gawgaw°, which is a large city on the Nile°, and one of the finest towns in the

°**Gawgaw:** Gogo.

°**Nile:** Niger. The Niger River was long regarded by outsiders as a tributary of The Nile.

land of the blacks. It is also one of their biggest and best-provisioned towns, with rice in plenty, milk, and fish.…The buying and selling of its inhabitants is done with cowry shells, and the same is the case at Malli. I stayed there about a month.

Using the Evidence:
Travelers' Tales and Observations

1. **Describing a foreign culture:** Each of these documents was written by an outsider to the people or society he is describing. What different postures toward these foreign cultures are evident in the sources? How did the travelers' various religions shape their perception of places they visited? How did they view the women of their host societies? Were these travelers more impressed by the similarities or by the differences between their home cultures and the ones they visited?

2. **Defining the self-perception of authors:** What can we learn from these documents about the men who wrote them? What motivated them? How did they define themselves in relationship to the societies they observed?

3. **Assessing the credibility of sources:** What information in these sources would be most valuable for historians seeking to understand India, China, and West Africa in the postclassical era? What statements in these sources might be viewed with the most skepticism? You will want to consider the authors' purposes and their intended audiences in evaluating their writings.

4. **Considering outsiders' accounts:** What are the advantages and limitations for historians in drawing on the writings of foreign observers?

Visual Sources

Considering the Evidence:
Art, Religion, and Cultural Exchange in Central Asia

The huge region between the Caspian Sea and western China is known to scholars as Central Asia, or sometimes as Inner Asia (see Map 8.1, p. 335). Its geography features rugged mountains, vast deserts, extensive grasslands, and a generally arid climate, all of which made settled farming difficult or impossible, except in scattered oases. As a result, most of Central Asia's peoples pursued a pastoral and nomadic way of life, dependent on their horses, camels, sheep, goats, or cattle. Linguistically and culturally, the majority were of Turkic or Mongol background. These features have long given Central Asia a distinctive character, despite the diversity of its many disparate peoples.

In recent centuries, Central Asia gained a reputation as a remote and backward region, far removed from the major centers of global trade and development. During the postclassical millennium, however, that region functioned as a vital Eurasian crossroad. Perhaps most obviously, it was a commercial crossroads, as the Silk Roads traversed its territory, while many of its peoples participated actively in that network of exchange. Central Asia was also a cultural and religious crossroads: Buddhism, Judaism, Christianity, Islam, Manichaeism, elements of Greek and Chinese culture—all of these traditions, born in the outer rim of Eurasian civilizations, found a place among the peoples of Central Asia, frequently carried there by merchants. Finally, Central Asia was an imperial crossroads, for there the empires or military federations periodically established by pastoral societies clashed with the established civilizations and states of China, India, the Middle East, and Europe to the south and west. Thus Central Asia was for many centuries a vast arena of intense cross-cultural interaction. The images that follow provide a brief introduction to a few of its many peoples and to the mingling of their cultures with those of a wider world.

The Kushans were a pastoral nomadic people from the area around Dunhuang at the far western edge of China. In the early centuries B.C.E., they had migrated to the region that now makes up northwestern India, Pakistan, Afghanistan, and Tajikistan, where they established a sizable and prosperous empire linked to the Silk Road trading network. It was a remarkably cosmopolitan place, and it flourished until the third or fourth century C.E. That empire, according to one recent account, "created stable conditions at the heart of Central Asia, allowing for the great flowering of trans-Eurasian mercantile and cultural exchange that occurred along the Silk Roads."[30]

Since parts of this empire had earlier been ruled by Alexander the Great and his Greek successors (see pp. 152–54), classical Mediterranean culture was a prominent element of Kushan culture. The Kushans used the Greek alphabet to write their official language, which was derived from India. The greatest of the Kushan rulers, Kanishka (ruled ca. 127–153 C.E.), styled himself "Great King, King of Kings, Son of God," a title that had both Persian and Chinese precedents. Hindu devotional cults as well as Buddhism flourished, and the Kushan Empire became a launching pad for the spread of Buddhism into Central Asia and ultimately into China and Japan (see pp. 338–40). It was here that the earliest human representations of the Buddha were sculpted, and often with distinctly Greek features. Despite multiple Eurasian influences, Kushan artists depicted their rulers in typical steppe nomadic style: on horseback, wearing loose trousers, heavy boots, and knee-length robes.[31]

In Visual Source 8.1, a Kushan pendant dating to the fourth century C.E. provides an illustration of the cultural blending so characteristic of the region. The medallion features Hariti, originally a fearsome Hindu goddess who abducted and killed children, feeding their flesh to her own offspring. But in an encounter with the Buddha, Hariti repented and was transformed into a compassionate protector of children. Here she is depicted holding in her right hand a lotus blossom, a prominent Buddhist symbol; her left hand holds another lotus flower supporting a flask or cornucopia overflowing with pomegranates (symbolizing food and abundance). According to local mythology, the Buddha had offered Hariti pomegranates (often said to resemble human flesh) as a substitute for the children she was devouring.

While the content of this pendant is thoroughly Indian and Buddhist, scholars believe that this representation of Hariti was probably modeled after the Greek goddess Tyche, also portrayed holding a cornucopia. Furthermore, her short tunic worn with a belt was likewise of Greek or Hellenistic origin. A further cultural influence is found in the decorations that surround the image, for the border of pearls and stylized flowers derives from Persia.

■ Why do you think the Kushan artist who created this image chose to weave together so many distinct cultural strands?

■ What does the story of Hariti's transformation tell us about the impact of Buddhism in the region?

■ Why might the Greek goddess Tyche been used as a model for Hariti? (Hint: you might want to do a little research on Tyche before answering this question.)

Visual Source 8.1 Greek Culture, Buddhism, and the Kushans (V&A Images, Victoria and Albert Museum)

If the Kushan state was a major point of departure for the spread of Buddhism beyond India, that faith soon took hold in many of the Central Asian oasis cities along the Silk Road network, reaching China in the early centuries C.E. (see pp. 335–41). In addition to merchants, Buddhist monks traversed the Silk Roads, some of them headed for India in search of holy texts and sacred relics (see Document 8.1), while others traveled from town to town teaching the message of the Buddha. Thus at least until the rise of Islam (see Chapter 11), Buddhism was a common feature in the experience of many Central Asian peoples and a point of contact with the civilizations of India and China. Visual Source 8.2, a tenth-century Chinese painting, shows a traveling monk on the Silk Road. It derives from the Magao Caves, located near Dunhuang, a major center of Buddhist art and an important stop on the Silk Roads. (See Map 8.1, p. 335, and the photo on p. 339.) Notice that the monk is leading a tiger, long a symbol of protection and courage and a messenger between heaven and the human world (see the photo on p. 91). It also recalls a much-told story of the Buddha, in an earlier life, compassionately offering his blood and body to feed some starving tiger cubs and their mother.

■ What function does the small Buddha sitting on a cloud at the upper left play in this painting?

■ On his back the monk is carrying a heavy load of Buddhist texts, or *sutras*. Why do you think Buddhist monks were so eager to acquire and to disseminate such texts? (See also Document 8.1, pp. 356–59.)

■ At the end of the monk's staff hangs what is probably a container for relics, perhaps a bone or a tuft of hair from the Buddha himself. Why might such relics have had such an appeal for the faithful? Can you identify a similar veneration of relics in other religious traditions?

Visual Source 8.2 Buddhist Monks on the Silk Road (British Museum/The Bridgeman Art Library)

Another central Asian people with extensive involvement in trans-Eurasian commerce were the Uighurs, Turkic-speaking nomads living north of the Gobi Desert (see Map 8.1, p. 335). By the eighth century C.E., they had established a powerful state that endured for about a century (744–840). Controlling a critical passage of the Silk Road network, Uighurs traded extensively with China, exchanging horses, camels, yaks, and hides for enormous quantities of Chinese silk. In fact, Uighur military forces saved the Chinese Tang dynasty from an internal rebellion between 755 and 763 and gained even greater access to Chinese wealth as they looted Chinese cities. A Chinese dynastic history bemoaned the unequal relationship that followed for a time: "The barbarians acquired silk insatiably and we were given useless horses."[32] The Uighur court likewise gained a series of Chinese princesses and considerable Chinese cultural influence.

They also acquired a new religion in China—Manichaeism. This was a faith of Persian origin, whose prophet, Mani (216–274 C.E.), saw himself in a long line of prophets including Zoroaster, the Buddha, and Jesus. Drawing on all of these traditions, Mani fashioned a religion that understood the world as an arena of intense conflict between the forces of Light (the soul) and the Dark (the material world). It spread widely within the Roman Empire and along the Silk Road network into China, where it was soon subject to intense persecution at the hands of Buddhists. From there the invading Uighurs picked it up and made it the official faith of their empire. No one knows precisely why Uighur rulers chose to convert to this Persian-based religion. Perhaps it linked the Uighurs to the larger world of agrarian civilizations, while reducing their cultural dependence on China. In any event, it represents another remarkable example of cultural interchange along the crossroads of Central Asia.

Visual Source 8.3 comes from a page in a Manichaean book dated variously between the eighth and eleventh centuries and found in the Uighur region of Khocho. It shows a number of Manichaean priests, wearing their characteristic tall white hats and writing at their desks. The fragmentary text in the middle, written in a Uighur script, warns against those who "believe in a wrong and contrary law" and "pray false prayers." As if to symbolize the corrupt and inverted world of Darkness, the image presents the priests writing left-handed and the script running from bottom to top instead of the normal top-down fashion.[33]

■ How would you read the overall religious message of the painting? What might suggest the ultimate triumph of the Light? Consider the role of the trees, bearing the flowers and fruits of good deeds.

■ What does the presence of this Persian-based religion among a distant Central Asian people suggest about the postclassical Eurasian world?

Visual Source 8.3 Manichaean Scribes (Bildarchiv Preussischer Kulturbesitz/Art Resource, NY)

Clearly the most well-known of Central Asian peoples were the Mongols, described more fully in Chapter 12. Under the leadership of Chinggis Khan, a number of quite distinct and rival pastoral tribes in what is now Mongolia had been brought together in a powerful military confederation by the early thirteenth century. That newly created Mongol state then embarked on an enormous effort of conquest that gave rise to the world's largest empire. That empire encompassed the civilizations of China, Persia, and Russia as well as many of the other nomadic peoples of Central Asia, and it threatened Japan, Southeast Asia, central Europe, and Egypt (see Map 12.1, p. 530.). Its presence loomed all across Eurasia in the thirteenth and fourteenth centuries, generating numerous cross-cultural encounters and interactions.

None of these was of greater significance than the Mongol conquest of China fully accomplished by 1279. While the Mongols ruled China in a largely Chinese fashion, they also sought to preserve much of their own culture. Thus they undertook an annual ritual of scattering mare's milk, employed Mongol shamans at the ruler's court, continued to wear native costumes of leather and fur, and rode to the hunt in traditional Mongol fashion. Mongol women living in China generally gave birth in a traditional felt-covered dwelling rather than in a Chinese-style home.

Visual Source 8.4 illustrates the Mongol effort to maintain their own identity even as they were immersed in the sophisticated culture of China, which had proved so attractive to many neighboring peoples. The painting (ca. 1280) is by the Chinese court artist Liu Guandao and was commissioned by Khubilai Khan, grandson of Chinggis Khan and the Mongol ruler of China from 1264 to 1294. Titled *Khubilai Khan on a Hunt*, it shows the Mongol ruler on a dark horse, wearing a distinctive fur-rimmed white robe that covers his Chinese royal garments, and accompanied by a female consort and a number of servants and officials. The figure in blue in the lower group of hunters carries a hawk, often used by Central Asian peoples during a hunt, while a trained wildcat sits on the horse below.

- Why do you think Khubilai Khan commissioned such a painting? What impression of himself did he seek to convey?

- What features of the landscape and depictions of people and animals illustrate the world of pastoral peoples from which the Mongols had come?

- What elements of Central Asian history are suggested by the camel train in the upper right?

- How might traditional Chinese officials respond to this painting? How might they react to the inclusion of women in a royal hunt?

Visual Source 8.4 The Mongols in China (National Palace Museum, Taipei, Taiwan)

Among the peoples of Central Asia, none had a longer-lasting impact on world history than the Turks, a term that refers to a variety of groups speaking related Turkic languages. Originating as pastoral nomads in what is now Mongolia, Turkic peoples gradually migrated westward, occupying much of Central Asia, sometimes creating sizeable empires and settling down as farmers. But the greatest transformation of Turkic culture occurred with the Turkic peoples' conversion to Islam. That process took place between the tenth and fourteenth centuries, as Muslim armies penetrated Central Asia and Muslim merchants became prominent traders on the Silk Road.

Also very important in the Turks' conversion to Islam were Muslim holy men known as dervishes. Operating within the Sufi tradition of Islam, dervishes were spiritual seekers who sought a direct personal experience of the Divine Reality and developed reputations for good works, personal kindness, and sometimes magic or religious powers. A Turkic tale from the fourteenth century tells the story of one such holy man, Baba Tukles, sent by God to convert a ruler named Ozbek Khan. To overcome the opposition of the khan's traditional shamans, Baba Tukles invited one of the shamans to enter a fiery-hot oven pit with him. The shaman was instantly incinerated, while the Muslim holy man emerged unscathed from that test of religious power.[34] Such tales of the supernatural and the conversion of rulers contributed to the attractiveness of Islam among Turkic peoples and have been a common feature in the spread of all of the major world religions.

Visual Source 8.5, a painting dating from the sixteenth century, shows a number of Turkish dervishes performing the turning or whirling dance associated with the Sufi religious order established in the thirteenth century by the great mystical poet Rumi. Intended to bring participants into direct contact with the Divine, the whirling dance itself drew upon the ideas and practices of an ancient Central Asian religious life in which practitioners, known as shamans, entered into an ecstatic state of consciousness and connection to the spirit world. "Especially in Central Asia, the Caucasus and Anatolia," writes one scholar, "the mystical ecstasy [of the whirling dance] was understood in the spirit of the shamanic tradition."[35] This blending of two religious traditions—mystical or Sufi Islam and shamanism—represents yet another example of the cultural interactions that washed across Central Asia in the postclassical millennium.

- What image of these dervishes was the artist trying to convey?

- Why might such holy men have been effective missionaries of Islam in Central Asia?

- Notice the musical instruments that accompany the turning dance—sticks on the left, a flutelike instrument known as a *ney* in the center, and drums on the right. What do you think this music and dance contributed to the religious experience of the participants?

Visual Source 8.5 Islam, Shamanism, and the Turks (Topkapi Library Istanbul/Gianni Dagli Orti/The Art Archive)

Using the Evidence:
Art, Religion, and Cultural Exchange in Central Asia

1. **Considering cross-cultural interactions:** The pastoral peoples of Central Asia and the settled agricultural civilizations adjacent to them did not live in closed or separate worlds. What evidence contained in these visual sources supports or challenges this assertion?

2. **Defining change and continuity:** In what ways do these visual sources indicate that the peoples of Central Asia were changed by their interactions with surrounding civilizations? In what respects did they retain elements of their earlier cultures?

3. **Explaining cultural change:** What aspects of these visual sources indicate that the various peoples of Central Asia were receptive to the religious and cultural traditions of neighboring civilizations?

智多星吳用

東溪村の人
にて字は學究道
号を加亮先生とふ
陳汾八孔明太公望よ
不方陰謀死蟲
梁山泊乃
軍師ふり
勝まり

CHAPTER NINE

China and the World

East Asian Connections

500–1300

The Reemergence of a Unified China
  A "Golden Age" of Chinese
    Achievement
  Women in the Song Dynasty
China and the Northern Nomads: A
  Chinese World Order in the Making
  The Tribute System in Theory
  The Tribute System in Practice
  Cultural Influence across an
    Ecological Frontier
Coping with China: Comparing
  Korea, Vietnam, and Japan
  Korea and China
  Vietnam and China
  Japan and China
China and the Eurasian World
  Economy
  Spillovers: China's Impact on Eurasia
  On the Receiving End: China as
    Economic Beneficiary
China and Buddhism
  Making Buddhism Chinese
  Losing State Support: The Crisis of
    Chinese Buddhism
Reflections: Why Do Things Change?
Considering the Evidence
  Documents: The Making of
    Japanese Civilization
  Visual Sources: The Leisure Life of
    China's Elites

"China will be the next superpower."[1] That was the frank assertion of an article in the British newspaper *The Guardian* in June 2006. Nor was it alone in that assessment. As the new millennium dawned, headlines with this message appeared with increasing frequency in public lectures, in newspaper and magazine articles, and in book titles all across the world. China's huge population, its booming economy, its massive trade surplus with the United States, its entry into world oil markets, its military potential, and its growing presence in global political affairs—all of this suggested that China was headed for a major role, perhaps even a dominant role, in the world of the twenty-first century. Few of these authors, however, paused to recall that China's prominence on the world stage was hardly something new or that its nineteenth- and twentieth-century position as a "backward," weak, or dependent country was distinctly out of keeping with its long history. Is China perhaps poised to resume in the twenty-first century a much older and more powerful role in world affairs?

IN THE WORLD OF THIRD-WAVE CIVILIZATIONS, even more than during the classical era that preceded it, China cast a long shadow. Its massive and powerful civilization, widely imitated by adjacent peoples, gave rise to a China-centered "world order" encompassing most of eastern Asia.[2] China extended its borders deep into Central Asia, while its wealthy and cosmopolitan culture attracted visitors from all over Eurasia. None of its many neighbors—whether

Chinese Astronomy: During classical and postclassical times, the impressive achievements of Chinese astronomy included the observation of sunspots, supernovae, and solar and lunar eclipses as well as the construction of elaborate star maps and astronomical devices such as those shown here. The print itself is of Japanese origin and shows a figure wearing the dragon robes of a Chinese official. It illustrates the immense cultural influence of China on its smaller Japanese neighbor. (Courtesy of the Trustees of the British Museum)

nomadic peoples to the north and west or smaller peripheral states such as Tibet, Korea, Japan, and Vietnam—could escape its gravitational pull. All of them had to deal with China. Far beyond these near neighbors, China's booming economy and many technological innovations had ripple effects all across Eurasia.

Even as China so often influenced the world, it too was changed by its many interactions with non-Chinese peoples. Northern nomads—"barbarians" to the Chinese—frequently posed a military threat and on occasion even conquered and ruled parts of China. The country's growing involvement in international trade stimulated important social, cultural, and economic changes within China itself. Buddhism, a religion of Indian origin, took root in China, and, to a lesser extent, so did Christianity and Islam. In short, China's engagement with the wider world became a very significant element in a global era of accelerating connections.

The Reemergence of a Unified China

The collapse of the Han dynasty around 220 C.E. ushered in more than three centuries of political fragmentation in China and signaled the rise of powerful and locally entrenched aristocratic families. It also meant the incursion of northern nomads, many of whom learned Chinese, dressed like Chinese, married into Chinese families, and governed northern regions of the country in a Chinese fashion. Such conditions of disunity, unnatural in the eyes of many thoughtful Chinese, discredited Confucianism and opened the door to a greater acceptance of Buddhism and Daoism among the elite.

Those centuries also witnessed the beginning of Chinese migration southward toward the Yangzi River valley, a movement of people that gave southern China some 60 percent of the country's population by 1000. That movement of Chinese people, accompanied by their intensive agriculture, set in motion a vast environmental transformation, marked by the destruction of the old-growth forests that once covered much of the country and the retreat of the elephants that had inhabited those lands. Around 800 C.E., the Chinese official and writer Liu Zongyuan lamented what was happening.

> A tumbled confusion of lumber as flames on the hillside crackle
> Not even the last remaining shrubs are safeguarded from destruction
> Where once mountain torrents leapt—nothing but rutted gullies.[3]

A "Golden Age" of Chinese Achievement

■ Change
Why are the centuries of the Tang and Song dynasties in China sometimes referred to as a "golden age"?

Unlike the fall of the western Roman Empire, where political fragmentation proved to be a permanent condition, China regained its unity under the Sui dynasty (589–618). Its emperors solidified that unity by a vast extension of the country's canal system, stretching some 1,200 miles in length and described by one scholar as "an engineering feat without parallel in the world of its time."[4] Those canals linked northern and southern China economically and contributed much to the prosperity that followed. But the ruthlessness of Sui emperors and a futile military campaign to conquer Korea exhausted the state's resources, alienated many people, and prompted the overthrow of the dynasty.

This dynastic collapse, however, witnessed no prolonged disintegration of the Chinese state. The two dynasties that followed—the Tang (618–907) and the Song (960–1279)—built on the Sui foundations of renewed unity (see Map 9.1). Together they established patterns of Chinese life that endured into the twentieth century, despite a fifty-year period of disunity between the two dynasties. Culturally, this era

Map 9.1 Tang and Song Dynasty China

During the postclassical millennium, China interacted extensively with its neighbors. The Tang dynasty extended Chinese control deep into Central Asia, while the Song dynasty witnessed incursions by the nomadic Jurchen people, who created the Jin Empire, which ruled parts of northern China.

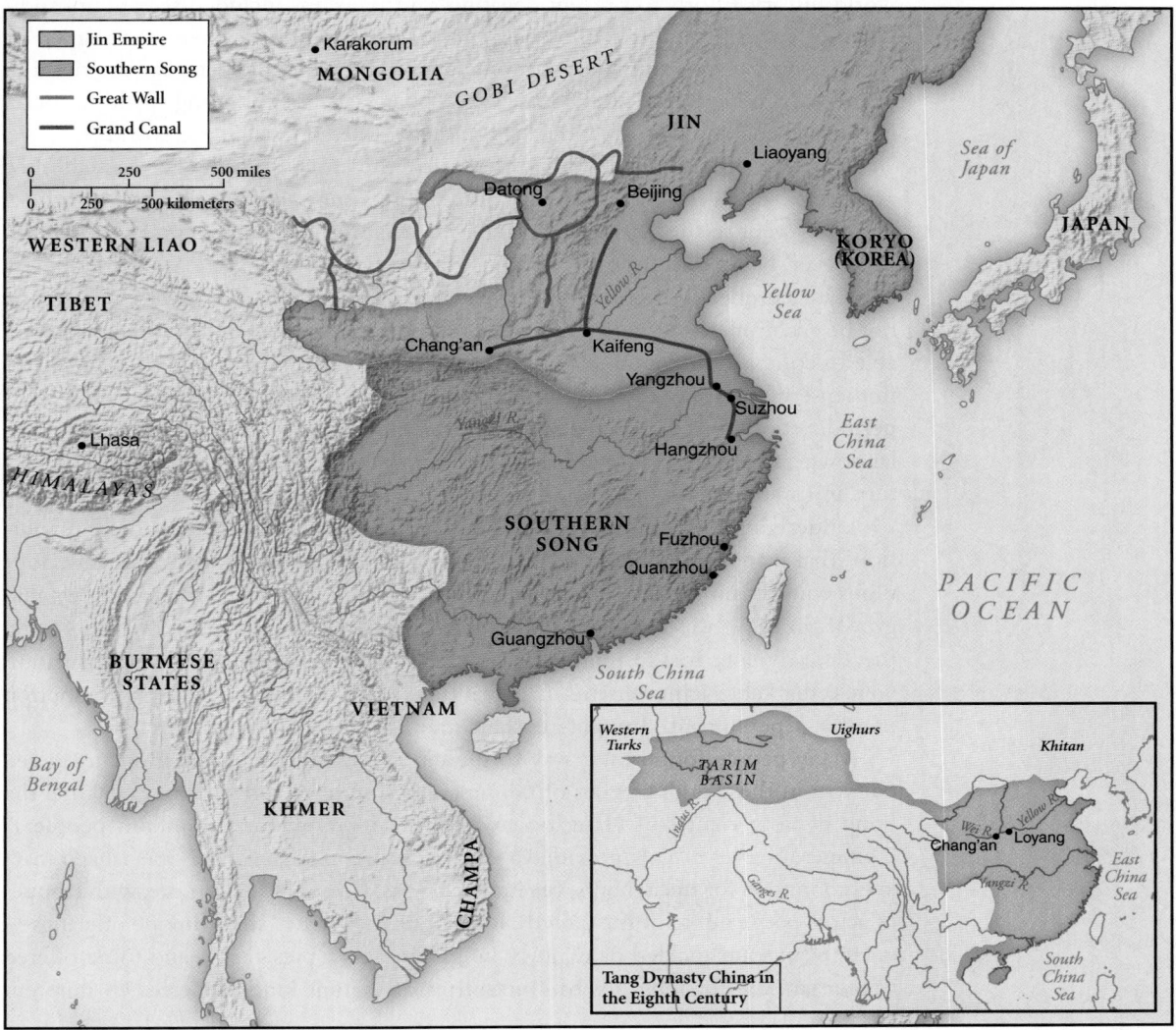

has long been regarded as a "golden age" of arts and literature, setting standards of excellence in poetry, landscape painting, and ceramics. (See Visual Sources: The Leisure Life of Chinese Elites, pp. 417–23, for Chinese painting during this time.) Particularly during the Song dynasty, an explosion of scholarship gave rise to Neo-Confucianism, an effort to revive Confucian thinking while incorporating into it some of the insights of Buddhism and Daoism.

Politically, the Tang and Song dynasties built a state structure that endured for a thousand years. Six major ministries—personnel, finance, rites, army, justice, and public works—were accompanied by the Censorate, an agency that exercised surveillance over the rest of the government, checking on the character and competence of public officials. To staff this bureaucracy, the examination system was revived and made more elaborate, encouraged by the ability to print books for the first time in world history. Efforts to prevent cheating on the exams included searching candidates entering the examination hall and placing numbers rather than names on their papers. Schools and colleges proliferated to prepare candidates for the rigorous exams, which became a central feature of upper-class life. A leading world historian has described Tang dynasty China as "the best ordered state in the world."[5]

Selecting officials on the basis of merit represented a challenge to established aristocratic families' hold on public office. Still, a substantial percentage of official positions went to the sons of the privileged, even if they had not passed the exams. Moreover, because education and the examination system grew far more rapidly than the number of official positions, many who passed lower-level exams could not be accommodated with a bureaucratic appointment. Often, however, they were able to combine landowning and success in the examination system to maintain an immense cultural prestige and prominence in their local areas. Despite the state's periodic efforts to redistribute land in favor of the peasantry, the great families of large landowners continued to encroach on peasant plots. This has been a recurring pattern in rural China from classical times to the present.

Underlying these cultural and political achievements was an "economic revolution" that made Song dynasty China "by far the richest, most skilled, and most populous country on earth."[6] The most obvious sign of China's prosperity was its rapid growth in population, which jumped from about 50 million or 60 million during the Tang dynasty to 120 million by 1200. Behind this doubling of the population were remarkable achievements in agricultural production, particularly the adoption of a fast-ripening and drought-resistant strain of rice from Vietnam.

Many people found their way to the cities, making China the most urbanized country in the world. Dozens of Chinese cities numbered over 100,000, while the Song dynasty capital of Hangzhou was home to more than a million people. A Chinese observer in 1235 provided a vivid description of that city.[7] Specialized markets abounded for meat, herbs, vegetables, books, rice, and much more, with troupes of actors performing for the crowds. Restaurants advertised their unique offerings— sweet bean soup, pickled dates, juicy lungs, meat pies, pigs' feet—and some offered vegetarian fare for religious banquets. Inns of various kinds appealed to different

Kaifeng
This detail comes from a huge watercolor scroll, titled *Upper River during Qing Ming Festival*, originally painted during the Song dynasty. It illustrates the urban sophistication of Kaifeng and other Chinese cities at that time and has been frequently imitated and copied since then. (Palace Museum, Beijing)

groups. Those that served only wine, a practice known as "hitting the cup," were regarded as "unfit for polite company." "Luxuriant inns," marked by red lanterns, featured prostitutes, and "the wine chambers [were] equipped with beds." Specialized agencies managed elaborate dinner parties for the wealthy, complete with a Perfume and Medicine Office to "help sober up the guests." Schools for musicians offered thirteen different courses. Numerous clubs provided companionship for poets, fishermen, Buddhists, physical fitness enthusiasts, antiques collectors, horse lovers, and many other groups. No wonder that the Italian visitor Marco Polo described Hangzhou later in the thirteenth century as "beyond dispute the finest and noblest [city] in the world."[8] (See Document 8.2, pp. 359–62, for a fuller description of Marco Polo's impressions of Hangzhou.)

Supplying these cities with food was made possible by an immense network of internal waterways—canals, rivers, and lakes—stretching perhaps 30,000 miles. They provided a cheap transportation system that bound the country together economically and created the "world's most populous trading area."[9]

Industrial production likewise soared. In both large-scale enterprises employing hundreds of workers and in smaller backyard furnaces, China's iron industry increased its output dramatically. By the eleventh century, it was providing the government with 32,000 suits of armor and 16 million iron arrowheads annually, in addition to supplying metal for coins, tools, construction, and bells in Buddhist monasteries. Technological innovation in other fields also flourished. Inventions in printing, both woodblock and movable type, generated the world's first printed books, and by 1000 relatively cheap books on religious, agricultural, mathematical, and medical topics became widely available in China. Its navigational and shipbuilding technologies led the world. The Chinese invention of gunpowder created within a few centuries a revolution in military affairs that had global dimensions.

Most remarkably, perhaps, all of this occurred within the world's most highly commercialized society, in which producing for the market, rather than for local consumption, became a very widespread phenomenon. Cheap transportation allowed peasants to grow specialized crops for sale, while they bought rice or other staples on the market. In addition, government demands for taxes paid in cash rather than in kind required peasants to sell something in order to meet their obligations. The growing use of paper money as well as financial instruments such as letters of credit and promissory notes further contributed to the commercialization of Chinese society. Two prominent scholars have described the outcome: "Output increased, population grew, skills multiplied, and a burst of inventiveness made Song China far wealthier than ever before—or than any of its contemporaries."[10]

Women in the Song Dynasty

■ **Change**
In what ways did women's lives change during the Tang and Song dynasties?

The "golden age" of Song dynasty China was perhaps less than "golden" for many of the country's women, for that era marked yet another turning point in the history of Chinese patriarchy. Under the influence of steppe nomads, whose women led less restricted lives, elite Chinese women of the Tang dynasty era, at least in the north, had participated in social life with greater freedom than in classical times. Paintings and statues from that time show aristocratic women riding horses, while the Queen Mother of the West, a Daoist deity, was widely worshipped by female Daoist priests and practitioners (see p. 255 and Visual Sources 9.2 and 9.5, pp. 419 and 422). By the Song dynasty, however, a reviving Confucianism and rapid economic growth seemed to tighten patriarchal restrictions on women and to restore some of the earlier Han dynasty images of female submission and passivity.

Once again Confucian writers highlighted the subordination of women to men and the need to keep males and females separate in every domain of life. The Song dynasty historian and scholar Sima Guang (1019–1086) summed up the prevailing view: "The boy leads the girl, the girl follows the boy; the duty of husbands to be resolute and wives to be docile begins with this."[11] Women were also frequently viewed as a distraction to men's pursuit of a contemplative and introspective life. The remarriage of widows, though legally permissible, was increasingly condemned, for "to walk through two courtyards is a source of shame for a woman."[12]

The most compelling expression of a tightening patriarchy lay in foot binding. Apparently beginning among dancers and courtesans in the tenth or eleventh century C.E., this practice involved the tight wrapping of young girls' feet, usually breaking the bones of the foot and causing intense pain. During the Tang dynasty, foot binding spread widely among elite families and later became even more widespread in Chinese society. It was associated with new images of female beauty and eroticism that emphasized small size, delicacy, and reticence, all of which were necessarily produced by foot binding. It certainly served to keep women restricted to the "inner quarters," where Confucian tradition asserted that they belonged. Many mothers imposed this painful procedure on their daughters, perhaps to enhance their marriage prospects and to assist them in competing with concubines for the attention of their husbands.[13]

Furthermore, a rapidly commercializing economy undermined the position of women in the textile industry. Urban workshops and state factories, run by men, increasingly took over the skilled tasks of weaving textiles, especially silk, which had previously been the work of rural women. But as their economic role in textile production declined, other opportunities beckoned in an increasingly prosperous Song China. In the cities, women operated restaurants, sold fish and vegetables, and worked as maids, cooks, and dressmakers. The growing prosperity of elite families funneled increasing numbers of women into roles as concubines, entertainers, courtesans, and prostitutes. Their ready availability surely reduced the ability of wives to negotiate as equals with their husbands, setting women against one another and creating endless household jealousies.

In other ways, the Song dynasty witnessed more positive trends in the lives of women. Their property rights expanded, in terms of both controlling their own dowries and inheriting property from their families. "Neither in earlier nor in later periods," writes one scholar, "did as much property pass through women's hands" as during the Song dynasty.[14] Furthermore, lower-ranking but ambitious officials strongly urged the education of women, so that they might more effectively raise their sons and increase the family's fortune. Song dynasty China, in short, offered a mixture of tightening restrictions and new opportunities to its women.

Foot Binding
The two young women pictured in this late-nineteenth-century photograph have bound feet, while the boy standing between them does not. A girl of a similar age would likely have begun this painful process already. The practice, dating back to around 1000 C.E., lasted into the twentieth century, when it was largely eliminated by reformist and Communist governments. (Photograph courtesy Peabody Essex Museum; image #A9392)

China and the Northern Nomads: A Chinese World Order in the Making

Chinese history has been subjected to two enduring misconceptions in popular thinking, if not in scholarly writing. First, it was often viewed as the story of an impressive but largely static civilization. In fact, however, China changed substantially over the centuries as its state structures evolved, as its various cultural traditions mixed and blended, as its economy expanded, as its population grew and migrated to the south, and as its patriarchy altered in tone and emphasis. A second misconception has portrayed China as a self-contained civilization. The balance of this chapter challenges this impression by showing how China's many interactions with

Snapshot   Key Moments in the History of Postclassical China

Collapse of Han dynasty; end of classical era	220
Political fragmentation of China; incursion of nomads in the north; Buddhism takes root	220–581
Sui dynasty; reunification of China	589–618
Reign of Emperor Wendi; state support for Buddhism	581–604
Tang dynasty; golden age of Chinese culture; expansion into Central Asia; high point of Chinese influence in Japan	618–907
Withdrawal of Chinese military forces from Korea	688
Reign of Empress Wu, China's only female emperor	690–705
State action against Buddhism	9th century
Political breakdown between dynasties	907–960
Vietnam establishes independence from China	939
Song dynasty; China's economic revolution; northern China ruled by peoples of nomadic background (Khitan, Jurchen)	960–1279
Yuan dynasty; Mongol rule of China	1271–1368
Ming dynasty; Chinese rule resumed	1368–1644
Maritime expeditions in the Indian Ocean	1405–1433

a larger Eurasian world shaped both China's own development and that of classical and postclassical world history more generally.

■ **Connection**

How did the Chinese and their nomadic neighbors to the north view each other?

From early times to the nineteenth century, China's most enduring and intense interaction with foreigners lay to the north, involving the many nomadic pastoral or semi-agricultural peoples of the steppes. Living in areas unable to sustain Chinese-style farming, the northern nomads had long focused their economies around the raising of livestock (sheep, cattle, goats) and the mastery of horse riding. Organized locally in small, mobile, kinship-based groups, sometimes called tribes, these peoples also periodically created much larger and powerful states or confederations that could draw upon the impressive horsemanship and military skills of virtually the entire male population of their societies. Such specialized pastoral societies needed grain and other agricultural products from China, and their leaders developed a taste for Chinese manufactured and luxury goods—wine and silk, for example—with which they could attract and reward followers. Thus the nomads were drawn like a magnet toward China, trading, raiding, and extorting in order to obtain the resources so vital to their way of life. For 2,000 years or more, pressure from the steppes and the intrusion of nomadic peoples were constant factors in China's historical development.

From the nomads' point of view, the threat often came from the Chinese, who periodically directed their own military forces deep into the steppes, built the Great Wall to keep the nomads out, and often proved unwilling to allow pastoral peoples easy access to trading opportunities within China.[15] And yet the Chinese needed the nomads. Their lands were the source of horses, so essential for the Chinese military. Other products of the steppes and the forests beyond, such as skins, furs, hides, and amber, were also of value in China. Furthermore, pastoral nomads controlled much of the Silk Road trading network, which funneled goods from the West into China. The continuing interaction between China and the northern nomads brought together peoples occupying different environments, practicing different economies, governing themselves with different institutions, and thinking about the world in quite different ways.

The Tribute System in Theory

An enduring outcome of this cross-cultural encounter was a particular view the Chinese held of themselves and of their neighbors, fully articulated by the time of the Han dynasty (200 B.C.E.–200 C.E.) and lasting for more than two millennia. That understanding cast China as the "middle kingdom," the center of the world, infinitely superior to the "barbarian" peoples beyond its borders. With its long history, great cities, refined tastes, sophisticated intellectual and artistic achievements, bureaucratic state, literate elite, and prosperous economy, China represented "civilization." All of this, in Chinese thinking, was in sharp contrast to the rude cultures and primitive life of the northern nomads, who continually moved about "like beasts and birds," lived in tents, ate mostly meat and milk, and practically lived on their horses, while making war on everyone within reach. Educated Chinese saw their own society as self-sufficient, requiring little from the outside world, while barbarians, quite understandably, sought access to China's wealth and wisdom. Furthermore, China was willing to permit that access under controlled conditions, for its sense of superiority did not preclude the possibility that barbarians could become civilized Chinese. China was a "radiating civilization," graciously shedding its light most fully to nearby barbarians and with diminished intensity to those farther away.[16]

Such was the general understanding of literate Chinese about their own civilization in relation to northern nomads and other non-Chinese peoples. That worldview also took shape as a practical system for managing China's relationship with these people. Known to us as the "tribute system," it was a set of practices that required non-Chinese authorities to acknowledge Chinese superiority and their own subordinate place in a Chinese-centered world order. Foreigners seeking access to China had to send a delegation to the Chinese court, where they would perform the kowtow, a series of ritual bowings and prostrations, and present their tribute—produce of value from their countries—to the Chinese emperor. In return for these expressions of submission, he would grant permission for foreigners to trade in China's rich markets and would provide them with gifts or "bestowals," often worth far

■ **Connection**
What assumptions underlay the tribute system?

The Tribute System
This Qing dynasty painting shows an idealized Chinese version of the tribute system. The Chinese emperor receives barbarian envoys, who perform rituals of subordination and present tribute in the form of a horse. (Réunion des Musées Nationaux/Art Resource, NY)

more than the tribute they had offered. This was the mechanism by which successive Chinese dynasties attempted to regulate their relationships with northern nomads; with neighboring states such as Korea, Vietnam, Tibet, and Japan; and, after 1500, with those European barbarians from across the sea.

Often, this system seemed to work. Over the centuries, countless foreign delegations proved willing to present their tribute, say the required words, and perform the necessary rituals in order to gain access to the material goods of China. Aspiring non-Chinese rulers also gained prestige as they basked in the reflected glory of even this subordinate association with the great Chinese civilization. The official titles, seals of office, and ceremonial robes they received from China proved useful in their local struggles for power.

The Tribute System in Practice

■ **Connection**

How did the tribute system in practice differ from the ideal Chinese understanding of its operation?

But the tribute system also disguised some realities that contradicted its assumptions. Frequently, China was confronting not separate and small-scale barbarian societies, but large and powerful nomadic empires able to deal with China on at least equal terms. An early nomadic confederacy was that of the Xiongnu, established about the same time as the Han dynasty and eventually reaching from Manchuria to Central Asia (see Map 4.5, p. 159). Devastating Xiongnu raids into northern China persuaded the Chinese emperor to negotiate an arrangement that recognized the nomadic state as a political equal, promised its leader a princess in marriage, and, most important, agreed to supply him annually with large quantities of grain, wine, and silk. Although these goods were officially termed "gifts," granted in accord with the tribute system, they were in fact tribute in reverse or even protection money. In return for these goods, so critical for the functioning of the nomadic state, the Xiongnu agreed to refrain from military incursions into China. The basic realities of the situation were summed up in this warning to the Han dynasty in the first century B.C.E.:

> Just make sure that the silks and grain stuffs you bring the Xiongnu are the right measure and quality, that's all. What's the need for talking? If the goods you deliver are up to measure and good quality, all right. But if there is any deficiency or the

quality is no good, then when the autumn harvest comes, we will take our horses and trample all over your crops.[17]

Something similar occurred during the Tang dynasty as a series of Turkic empires arose in Mongolia. Like the Xiongnu, they too extorted large "gifts" from the Chinese. One of these peoples, the Uighurs, actually rescued the Tang dynasty from a serious internal revolt in the 750s. In return, the Uighur leader gained one of the Chinese emperor's daughters as a wife and arranged a highly favorable exchange of poor-quality horses for high-quality silk that brought half a million rolls of the precious fabric annually into the Uighur lands. Despite the rhetoric of the tribute system, the Chinese were clearly not always able to dictate the terms of their relationship with the northern nomads.

Steppe nomads were generally not much interested in actually conquering and ruling China. It was easier and more profitable to extort goods from a functioning Chinese state. On occasion, though, that state broke down, and various nomadic groups moved in to "pick up the pieces," conquering and governing parts of China. Such a process took place following the fall of the Han dynasty and again after the collapse of the Tang dynasty, when the Khitan (907–1125) and then the Jin or Jurchen (1115–1234) peoples established states that encompassed parts of northern China as well as major areas of the steppes to the north. Both of them required the Chinese Song dynasty, located farther south, to deliver annually huge quantities of silk, silver, and tea, some of which found its way into the Silk Road trading network. The practice of "bestowing gifts on barbarians," long a part of the tribute system, allowed the proud Chinese to imagine that they were still in control of the situation even as they were paying heavily for protection from nomadic incursion. Those gifts, in turn, provided vital economic resources to nomadic states.

Cultural Influence across an Ecological Frontier

When nomadic peoples actually ruled parts of China, some of them adopted Chinese ways, employing Chinese advisers, governing according to Chinese practice, and, at least for the elite, immersing themselves in Chinese culture and learning. This process of "becoming Chinese" went furthest among the Jurchen, many of whom lived in northern China and learned to speak Chinese, wore Chinese clothing, married Chinese husbands and wives, and practiced Buddhism or Daoism. On the whole, however, Chinese culture had only a modest impact on the nomadic people of the northern steppes. Unlike the native peoples of southern China, who were gradually absorbed into Chinese culture, the pastoral societies north of the Great Wall generally retained their own cultural patterns. Few of them were incorporated, at least not for long, within a Chinese state, and most lived in areas where Chinese-style agriculture was simply impossible. Under these conditions, there were few incentives for adopting Chinese culture wholesale. But various modes of interaction—peaceful trade, military conflict, political negotiations, economic extortion, some cultural

■ Connection
In what ways did China and the nomads influence each other?

influence—continued across the ecological frontier that divided two quite distinct and separate ways of life. Each was necessary for the other. (See Visual Sources 8.2, 8.3, and 8.4, pp. 370–74, for another example of Chinese/nomadic interaction.)

On the Chinese side, elements of steppe culture had some influence in those parts of northern China that were periodically conquered and ruled by nomadic peoples. The founders of the Sui and Tang dynasties were in fact of mixed nomad and Chinese ancestry and came from the borderland region where a blended Chinese/Turkic culture had evolved. High-ranking members of the imperial family personally led their troops in battle in the style of Turkic warriors. Furthermore, Tang dynasty China was awash with foreign visitors from all over Asia—delegations bearing tribute, merchants carrying exotic goods, bands of clerics or religious pilgrims bringing new religions such as Christianity, Islam, Buddhism, and Manichaeism. For a time in the Tang dynasty, almost anything associated with "western barbarians"—Central Asians, Persians, Indians, Arabs—had great appeal among northern Chinese elites. Their music, dancing, clothing, foods, games, and artistic styles found favor among the upper classes. The more traditional southern Chinese, feeling themselves heir to the legacy of the Han dynasty, were sharply critical of their northern counterparts for allowing women too much freedom, for drinking yogurt rather than tea, for listening to "western" music, all of which they attributed to barbarian influence. Around 800 C.E., the poet Yuan Chen gave voice to a growing backlash against this too easy acceptance of things "western":

> Ever since the Western horsemen began raising smut and dust,
> Fur and fleece, rank and rancid, have filled Hsien and Lo [two Chinese cities].
> Women make themselves Western matrons by the study of Western makeup.
> Entertainers present Western tunes, in their devotion to Western music.[18]

Coping with China: Comparing Korea, Vietnam, and Japan

Also involved in tributary relationships with China during the postclassical era were the newly emerging states and civilizations of Korea, Vietnam, and Japan. Unlike the northern nomads, these societies were thoroughly agricultural and sedentary. During the first millennium C.E., they were part of a larger process—the globalization of civilization—which produced new city- and state-based societies in various parts of the world. Proximity to their giant Chinese neighbor decisively shaped the histories of these new East Asian civilizations, for all of them borrowed major elements of Chinese culture. But unlike the native peoples of southern China, who largely became Chinese, the peoples of Korea, Vietnam, and Japan did not. They retained distinctive identities, which have lasted into modern times. While resisting Chinese political domination, they also appreciated Chinese culture and sought the source of Chinese wealth and power. In such ways, these smaller East Asian civilizations resembled the "developing" Afro-Asian societies of the twentieth century, which embraced "modernity" and elements of Western culture, while trying to maintain their political and cultural independence from the European and American centers of that modern way of life. Korea, Vietnam, and Japan, however, encountered China and responded to it in quite different ways.

■ Comparison

In what different ways did Korea, Vietnam, and Japan experience and respond to Chinese influence?

Korea and China

Immediately adjacent to northeastern China, the Korean peninsula and its people have long lived in the shadow of their imposing neighbor. Temporary Chinese conquest of northern Korea during the Han dynasty and some colonization by Chinese settlers provided an initial channel for Chinese cultural influence, particularly in the form of Buddhism. Early Korean states, which emerged in the fourth through seventh centuries C.E., all referred to their rulers with the Chinese term *wang* (king). Bitter rivals with one another, these states strenuously resisted Chinese political control, except when they found it advantageous to join with China against a local enemy. In the seventh century, one of these states—the Silla kingdom—allied with Tang dynasty China to bring some political unity to the peninsula for the first time. But Chinese efforts to set up puppet regimes and to assimilate Koreans to Chinese culture provoked sharp military resistance, persuading the Chinese to withdraw their military forces in 688 and to establish a tributary relationship with a largely independent Korea.

Under a succession of dynasties—the Silla (688–900), Koryo (918–1392), and Yi (1392–1910)—Korea generally maintained its political independence while participating in China's tribute system. Its leaders actively embraced the connection with China and, especially during the Silla dynasty, sought to turn their small state into a miniature version of Tang China.

Tribute missions to China provided legitimacy for Korean rulers and knowledge of Chinese court life and administrative techniques, which they sought to replicate back home. A new capital city of Kumsong was modeled directly on the Chinese capital of Chang'an. Tribute missions also enabled both official and private trade, mostly in luxury goods such as ceremonial clothing, silks, fancy teas, Confucian and Buddhist texts, and artwork—all of which enriched the lives of a Korean aristocracy that was becoming increasingly Chinese in culture. Thousands of Korean students were sent to China, where they studied primarily Confucianism but also natural sciences and the arts. Buddhist monks visited centers of learning and pilgrimage in China and brought back popular forms of Chinese Buddhism, which quickly took root in Korea. Schools for the study of Confucianism, using texts in the Chinese language, were established in Korea. In these ways, Korea became a part of the expanding world of Chinese culture, and refugees from the peninsula's many wars carried Chinese culture to Japan as well.

These efforts to plant Confucian values and Chinese culture in Korea had what one scholar has called an "overwhelmingly negative" impact on

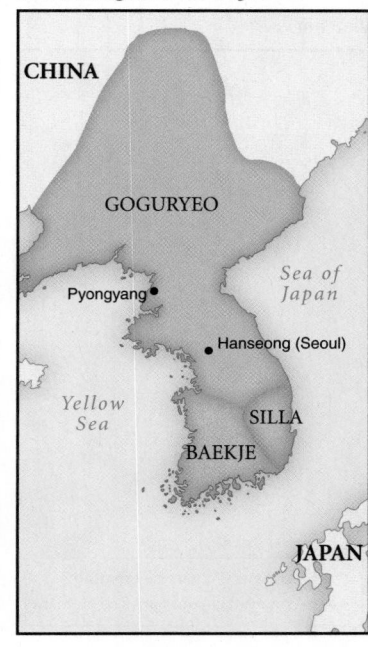

Korean Kingdoms about 500 C.E.

CHINA

GOGURYEO

Pyongyang●

● Hanseong (Seoul)

Sea of Japan

Yellow Sea

SILLA

BAEKJE

JAPAN

Korean women, particularly after 1300.[19] Early Chinese observers noticed, and strongly disapproved of, "free choice" marriages in Korea as well as the practice of women singing and dancing together late at night. With the support of the Korean court, Chinese models of family life and female behavior, especially among the elite, gradually replaced the more flexible Korean patterns. Earlier a Korean woman had generally given birth and raised her young children in her parents' home, where she was often joined by her husband. This was now strongly discouraged, for it was deeply offensive to Confucian orthodoxy, which held that a married woman belonged to her husband's family. Some Korean customs—funeral rites in which a husband was buried in the sacred plot of his wife's family, the remarriage of widowed or divorced women, and female inheritance of property—eroded under the pressure of Confucian orthodoxy. So too did the practice of plural marriages for men. In 1413, a legal distinction between primary and secondary wives required men to identify one of their wives as primary. Because she and her children now had special privileges and status, sharp new tensions emerged within families. Korean restrictions on elite women, especially widows, came to exceed even those in China itself.

Still, Korea remained Korean. After 688, the country's political independence, though periodically threatened, was largely intact. Chinese cultural influence, except for Buddhism, had little impact beyond the aristocracy and certainly did not penetrate the lives of Korea's serf-like peasants. Nor did it register among Korea's many slaves, amounting to about one-third of the country's population by 1100 C.E. A Chinese-style examination system to recruit government officials, though encouraged by some Korean rulers, never assumed the prominence that it gained in Tang and Song dynasty China. Korea's aristocratic class was able to maintain an even stronger monopoly on bureaucratic office than their Chinese counterparts. And in the 1400s, Korea moved toward greater cultural independence by developing a phonetic alphabet, known as *hangul*, for writing the Korean language. Although resisted by male conservative elites, who were long accustomed to using the more prestigious Chinese characters to write Korean, this new form of writing gradually took hold, especially in private correspondence, in popular fiction, and among women. Clearly part of the Chinese world order, Korea nonetheless retained a distinctive culture as well as a separate political existence.

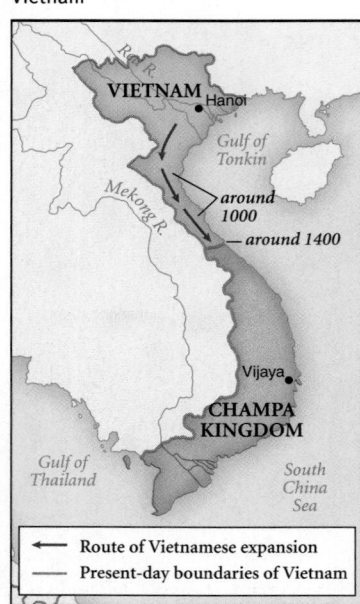

Vietnam

Route of Vietnamese expansion
Present-day boundaries of Vietnam

Vietnam and China

At the southern fringe of the Chinese cultural world, the people who eventually came to be called Vietnamese had a broadly similar historical encounter with China. As in Korea, the elite culture of Vietnam borrowed heavily from China—adopting Confucianism, Daoism, Buddhism, administrative techniques, the examination system, artistic and literary styles—even as its popular culture remained distinctive. And, like Korea, Vietnam achieved political independence, while participating fully in the tribute system as a vassal state.

But there were differences as well. The cultural heartland of Vietnam in the Red River valley was fully incorporated into the Chinese state for more than a thousand years (111 B.C.E.–939 C.E.), far longer than corresponding parts of Korea. Regarded by the Chinese as "southern barbarians," the Vietnamese were ruled by Chinese officials who expected to fully assimilate this rich rice-growing region into China culturally as well as politically. To these officials, it was simply a further extension of the southward expansion of Chinese civilization. Thus Chinese-style irrigated agriculture was introduced; Vietnamese elites were brought into the local bureaucracy and educated in Confucian-based schools; Chinese replaced the local language in official business; Chinese clothing and hairstyles became mandatory; and large numbers of Chinese, some fleeing internal conflicts at home, flooded into the relative security of what they referred to as "the pacified south," while often despising the local people.[20]

The heavy pressure of the Chinese presence generated not only a Vietnamese elite thoroughly schooled in Chinese culture but also periodic rebellions. In 39 C.E., a short-lived but long-remembered uprising was launched by two sisters, daughters of a local leader deposed by the Chinese. One of them, Trung Trac, whose husband had been executed, famously addressed some 30,000 soldiers, while dressed in full military regalia:

> Foremost I will avenge my country.
> Second I will restore the Hung lineage.
> Third I will avenge the death of my husband.
> Lastly I vow that these goals will be accomplished.[21]

When the rebellion was crushed several years later, the Trung sisters committed suicide rather than surrender to the Chinese, but in literature, monuments, and public memory, they long remained powerful symbols of Vietnamese resistance to Chinese aggression.

The weakening of the Tang dynasty in the early tenth century C.E. finally enabled a particularly large rebellion to establish Vietnam as a separate state, though one that carefully maintained its tributary role, sending repeated missions to do homage at the Chinese court. Nonetheless, successive Vietnamese dynasties found the Chinese approach to government useful, styling their rulers as emperors, claiming the Mandate of Heaven, and making use of Chinese court rituals, while expanding their state

The Trung Sisters
Although it occurred nearly 2,000 years ago, the revolt of the Trung sisters against Chinese occupation remains a national symbol of Vietnam's independence, as illustrated by this modern Vietnamese painting of the two women, astride war elephants, leading their followers into battle against the Chinese invaders. (From William J. Duiker, *Sacred War: Nationalism and Revolution in a Divided Vietnam* [New York: The McGraw-Hill Companies, 1995])

steadily southward. More so than in Korea, a Chinese-based examination system in Vietnam functioned to undermine an established aristocracy, to provide some measure of social mobility for commoners, and to create a merit-based scholar-gentry class to staff the bureaucracy. Furthermore, the Vietnamese elite class remained deeply committed to Chinese culture, viewing their own country less as a separate nation than as a southern extension of a universal civilization, the only one they knew.[22]

Beyond the elite, however, there remained much that was uniquely Vietnamese, such as a distinctive language, a fondness for cockfighting, the habit of chewing betel nuts, and a greater role for women in social and economic life. Female nature deities and even a "female Buddha" continued to be part of Vietnamese popular religion, even as Confucian-based ideas took root among the elite. These features of Vietnamese life reflected larger patterns of Southeast Asian culture that distinguished it from China. And like Korea, the Vietnamese developed a variation of Chinese writing called *chu nom* ("southern script"), which provided the basis for an independent national literature.

Japan and China

Unlike Korea and Vietnam, the Japanese islands were physically separated from China by 100 miles or more of ocean and were never successfully invaded or conquered by their giant mainland neighbor. Thus Japan's very extensive borrowing from Chinese civilization was wholly voluntary, rather than occurring under conditions of direct military threat or outright occupation. The high point of that borrowing took place during the seventh to the ninth centuries C.E., as the first more or less unified Japanese state began to emerge from dozens of small clan-based aristocratic chiefdoms. That state found much that was useful in Tang dynasty China and set out, deliberately and systematically, to transform Japan into a centralized bureaucratic state on the Chinese model. (See Documents: The Making of Japanese Civilization, pp. 406–16.)

The initial leader of this effort was Shotoku Taishi (572–622), a prominent aristocrat from one of the major clans. He launched a series of large-scale missions to China, which took hundreds of Japanese monks, scholars, artists, and students to the mainland, and when they returned, they put into practice what they had learned. He issued the Seventeen Article Constitution, proclaiming the Japanese ruler as a Chinese-style emperor and encouraging both Buddhism and Confucianism. In good Confucian fashion, that document emphasized the moral quality of rulers as a foundation for social harmony (see Document 9.1, pp. 406–08). In the decades that followed, Japanese authorities adopted Chinese-style court rituals and a system of court rankings for officials as well as the Chinese calendar. Subsequently, they likewise established Chinese-based taxation systems, law codes, government ministries, and provincial administration, at least on paper. Two capital cities, first Nara and then Heian (Kyoto), arose, both modeled on the Chinese capital of Chang'an.

Japan

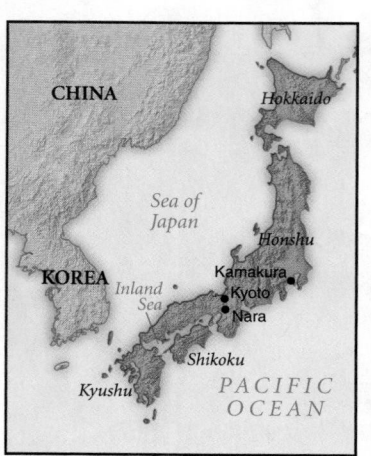

Chinese culture, no less than its political practices, also found favor in Japan. Various schools of Chinese Buddhism took root, first among the educated and literate classes and later more broadly in Japanese society, affecting, according to one scholar, "nearly every aspect of Japanese life" (see Document 9.2, pp. 408–10). Art, architecture, education, medicine, views of the afterlife, attitudes toward suffering and the impermanence of life—all of this and more reflected the influence of Buddhist culture in Japan.[23] The Chinese writing system—and with it an interest in historical writing, calligraphy, and poetry—likewise proved attractive among the elite.

The absence of any compelling threat from China made it possible for the Japanese to be selective in their borrowing. By the tenth century, deliberate efforts to absorb additional elements of Chinese culture diminished, and formal tribute missions to China stopped, although private traders and Buddhist monks continued to make the difficult journey to the mainland. Over many centuries, the Japanese combined what they had assimilated from China with elements of their own tradition into a distinctive Japanese civilization, which differed from Chinese culture in many ways.

In the political realm, for example, the Japanese never succeeded in creating an effective centralized and bureaucratic state to match that of China. Although the court and the emperor retained an important ceremonial and cultural role, their real political authority over the country gradually diminished in favor of competing aristocratic families, both at court and in the provinces. A Chinese-style university trained officials, but rather than serving as a mechanism for recruiting talented commoners into the political elite, it enrolled students who were largely the sons of court aristocrats.

As political power became increasingly decentralized, local authorities developed their own military forces, the famous *samurai* warrior class of Japanese society. Bearing their exquisite curved swords, the samurai developed a distinctive set of values featuring great skill in martial arts, bravery, loyalty, endurance, honor, and a preference for death over surrender. This was *bushido*, the way of the warrior, illustrated in Document 9.5, pages 414–16. Japan's celebration of the samurai and of military virtues contrasted sharply with China's emphasis on intellectual achievements and political officeholding, which were accorded higher prestige than bearing arms. "The educated men of the land," wrote a Chinese minister in the eleventh century, "regard the carrying of arms as a disgrace."[24] The Japanese, clearly, did not agree.

Religiously as well, Japan remained distinctive. Although Buddhism in many forms took hold in the country, it never completely replaced the native beliefs and practices, which focused attention on numerous *kami*, sacred spirits associated with human ancestors and various natural phenomena. Much later referred to as Shinto, this tradition provided legitimacy to the imperial family, based on claims of descent from the sun goddess, as illustrated in Document 9.3, pages 410–12. Because veneration of the kami lacked an elaborate philosophy or ritual, it conflicted very little with Buddhism. In fact, numerous kami were assimilated into Japanese Buddhism as local expressions of Buddhist deities or principles.

The Samurai of Japan
This twelfth-century painting depicts the famous naval battle of Dan-no-ura (1185), in which the samurai warriors of two rival clans fought to the death. Many of the defeated Taira warriors, along with some of their women, plunged into the sea rather than surrender to their Minamoto rivals. The prominence of martial values in Japanese culture was one of the ways in which Japan differed from its Chinese neighbor, despite much borrowing. (Tokyo National Museum. Image: TNM Images Archives. Source: http://TnmArchives.jp/)

■ **Comparison**
In what different ways did Japanese and Korean women experience the pressures of Confucian orthodoxy?

Japanese literary and artistic culture likewise evolved in distinctive ways, despite much borrowing from China. As in Korea and Vietnam, there emerged a unique writing system that combined Chinese characters with a series of phonetic symbols. A highly stylized Japanese poetic form, known as *tanka*, developed early and has remained a favored means of expression ever since. Particularly during the Heian period of Japanese history (794–1192), a highly refined esthetic culture found expression at the imperial court, even as the court's real political authority melted away. Court aristocrats and their ladies lived in splendor, composed poems, arranged flowers, and conducted their love affairs. "What counted," wrote one scholar, "was the proper costume, the right ceremonial act, the successful turn of phrase in a poem, and the appropriate expression of refined taste."[25] Much of our knowledge of this courtly culture comes from the work of women writers, who composed their diaries and novels in the vernacular Japanese script, rather than in the classical Chinese used by elite men. *The Tale of Genji*, a Japanese novel written by the woman author Murasaki Shikibu around 1000, provides an intimate picture of the intrigues and romances of court life. So too does Sei Shonagon's *Pillow Book*, excerpted in Document 9.4, pages 412–14.

At this level of society, Japan's women, unlike those in Korea, largely escaped the more oppressive features of Chinese Confucian culture, such as the prohibition of remarriage for widows, seclusion within the home, and foot binding. Perhaps this is because the most powerful Chinese influence on Japan occurred during the Tang dynasty, when Chinese elite women enjoyed considerable freedom. Japanese women continued to inherit property; Japanese married couples often lived apart or with the wife's family; and marriages were made and broken easily. None of this corresponded to Confucian values. When Japanese women did begin to lose status in the twelfth century and later, it had less to do with Confucian pressures than with the rise of a warrior culture. As the personal relationships of samurai warriors to their lords replaced marriage alliances as a political strategy, the influence of women in political life was reduced, but this was an internal Japanese phenomenon, not a reflection of Chinese influence.

Japan's ability to borrow extensively from China while developing its own distinctive civilization perhaps provided a model for its encounter with the West in the nineteenth century. Then, as before, Japan borrowed selectively from a foreign culture without losing either its political independence or its cultural uniqueness.

China and the Eurasian World Economy

Beyond China's central role in East Asia was its economic interaction with the wider world of Eurasia generally. On the one hand, China's remarkable economic growth, taking place during the Tang and Song dynasties, could hardly be contained within China's borders and clearly had a major impact throughout Eurasia. On the other hand, China was recipient as well as donor in the economic interactions of the postclassical era, and its own economic achievements owed something to the stimulus of contact with the larger world.

Spillovers: China's Impact on Eurasia

One of the outcomes of China's economic revolution lay in the diffusion of its many technological innovations to peoples and places far from East Asia as the movements of traders, soldiers, slaves, and pilgrims conveyed Chinese achievements abroad. Chinese techniques for producing salt by solar evaporation spread to the Islamic world and later to Christian Europe. Papermaking, known in China since the Han dynasty, spread to Korea and Vietnam by the fourth century C.E., to Japan and India by the seventh, to the Islamic world by the eighth, to Muslim Spain by 1150, to France and Germany in the 1300s, and to England in the 1490s. Printing, likewise a Chinese invention, rapidly reached Korea, where movable type became a highly developed technique, and Japan as well. Both technologies were heavily influenced by Buddhism, which accorded religious merit to the act of reproducing sacred texts. The Islamic world, however, valued handwritten calligraphy highly and generally resisted printing as impious until the nineteenth century. The adoption of printing in Europe was likewise delayed because of the absence of paper until the fourteenth century. Then movable type was reinvented by Johannes Gutenberg in the fifteenth century, although it is unclear whether he was aware of Chinese and Korean precedents. With implications for mass literacy, bureaucracy, scholarship, the spread of

■ **Connection**
In what ways did China participate in the world of Eurasian commerce and exchange, and with what outcomes?

religion, and the exchange of information, papermaking and printing were Chinese innovations of revolutionary and global dimensions.

Chinese technologies were seldom simply transferred from one place to another. More often a particular Chinese technique or product stimulated innovations in more distant lands in accordance with local needs.[26] For example, as the Chinese formula for gunpowder, invented around 1000, became available in Europe, together with some early and simple firearms, these innovations triggered the development of cannons in the early fourteenth century. Soon cannons appeared in the Islamic world and by 1356 in China itself, which first used cast iron rather than bronze in their construction. But the highly competitive European state system drove the "gunpowder revolution" much further and more rapidly than in China's imperial state. Chinese textile, metallurgical, and naval technologies likewise stimulated imitation and innovation all across Eurasia. An example is the magnetic compass, a Chinese invention eagerly embraced by mariners of many cultural backgrounds as they traversed the Indian Ocean.

In addition to its technological influence, China's prosperity during the Song dynasty greatly stimulated commercial life and market-based behavior all across the Eurasian trading world. China's products—silk, porcelain, lacquerware—found eager buyers from Japan to East Africa, and everywhere in between. The immense size and wealth of China's domestic economy also provided a ready market for hundreds of commodities from afar. For example, the lives of many thousands of people in the spice-producing islands of what is now Indonesia were transformed as they came to depend on Chinese consumers' demand for their products. "[O]ne hundred million [Chinese] people," wrote historian William McNeill, "increasingly caught up within a commercial network, buying and selling to supplement every day's livelihood, made a significant difference to the way other human beings made their livings throughout a large part of the civilized world."[27] Such was the ripple effect of China's economic revolution.

On the Receiving End: China as Economic Beneficiary

Chinese economic growth and technological achievements significantly shaped the Eurasian world of the postclassical era, but that pattern of interaction was surely not a one-way street, for China too was changed by its engagement with a wider world. During this period, for example, China had learned about the cultivation and processing of both cotton and sugar from India. From Vietnam, around 1000, China gained access to the new, fast-ripening, and drought-resistant strains of rice that made a highly productive rice-based agriculture possible in the drier and more rugged regions of southern China. This marked a major turning point in Chinese history as the frontier region south of the Yangzi River grew rapidly in population, overtaking the traditional centers of Chinese civilization in the north.

Technologically as well, China's extraordinary burst of creativity owed something to the stimulus of cross-cultural contact. Awareness of Persian windmills, for example, spurred the development of a distinct but related device in China. Printing arose from China's growing involvement with the world of Buddhism, which put a spiritual premium on the reproduction of the Buddha's image and of short religious texts that were carried as charms. It was in Buddhist monasteries during the Tang dynasty that the long-established practice of printing with seals was elaborated by Chinese monks into woodblock printing. The first printed book, in 868 C.E., was a famous Buddhist text, the *Diamond Sutra*. Gunpowder too seems to have had an Indian and Buddhist connection. An Indian Buddhist monk traveling in China in 644 C.E. identified soils that contained saltpeter and showed that they produced a purple flame when put into a fire. This was the beginning of Chinese experiments, which finally led to a reliable recipe for gunpowder.

A further transforming impact of China's involvement with a wider world derived from its growing participation in Indian Ocean trade. By the Tang dynasty, thousands of ships annually visited the ports of southern China, and settled communities of foreign merchants—Arabs, Persians, Indians, Southeast Asians—turned some of these cities into cosmopolitan centers. Buddhist temples, Muslim mosques and cemeteries, and Hindu phallic sculptures graced the skyline of Quanzhou, a coastal city in southern China. Occasionally the tensions of cultural diversity erupted in violence, such as the massacre of tens of thousands of foreigners in Canton during the 870s when Chinese rebel forces sacked the city. Indian Ocean commerce also contributed much to the transformation of southern China from a subsistence economy to one more heavily based on producing for export. In the process, merchants achieved a degree of social acceptance not known before, including their frequent appointment to high-ranking bureaucratic positions. Finally, much-beloved stories of the monkey god, widely popular even in contemporary China, derived from Indian sources transmitted by Indian Ocean commerce.[28]

China and Buddhism

By far the most important gift that China received from India was neither cotton, nor sugar, nor the knowledge of saltpeter, but a religion, Buddhism. The gradual assimilation of this South Asian religious tradition into Chinese culture illustrates the process of cultural encounter and adaptation and invites comparison with the spread of Christianity into Europe. Until the adoption of Marxism in the twentieth century, Buddhism was the only large-scale cultural borrowing in Chinese history. It also made China into a launching pad for Buddhism's dispersion to Korea and from there to Japan as well. Thus, as Buddhism faded in the land of its birth, it became solidly rooted in much of East Asia, providing an element of cultural commonality for a vast region (see Map 9.2).

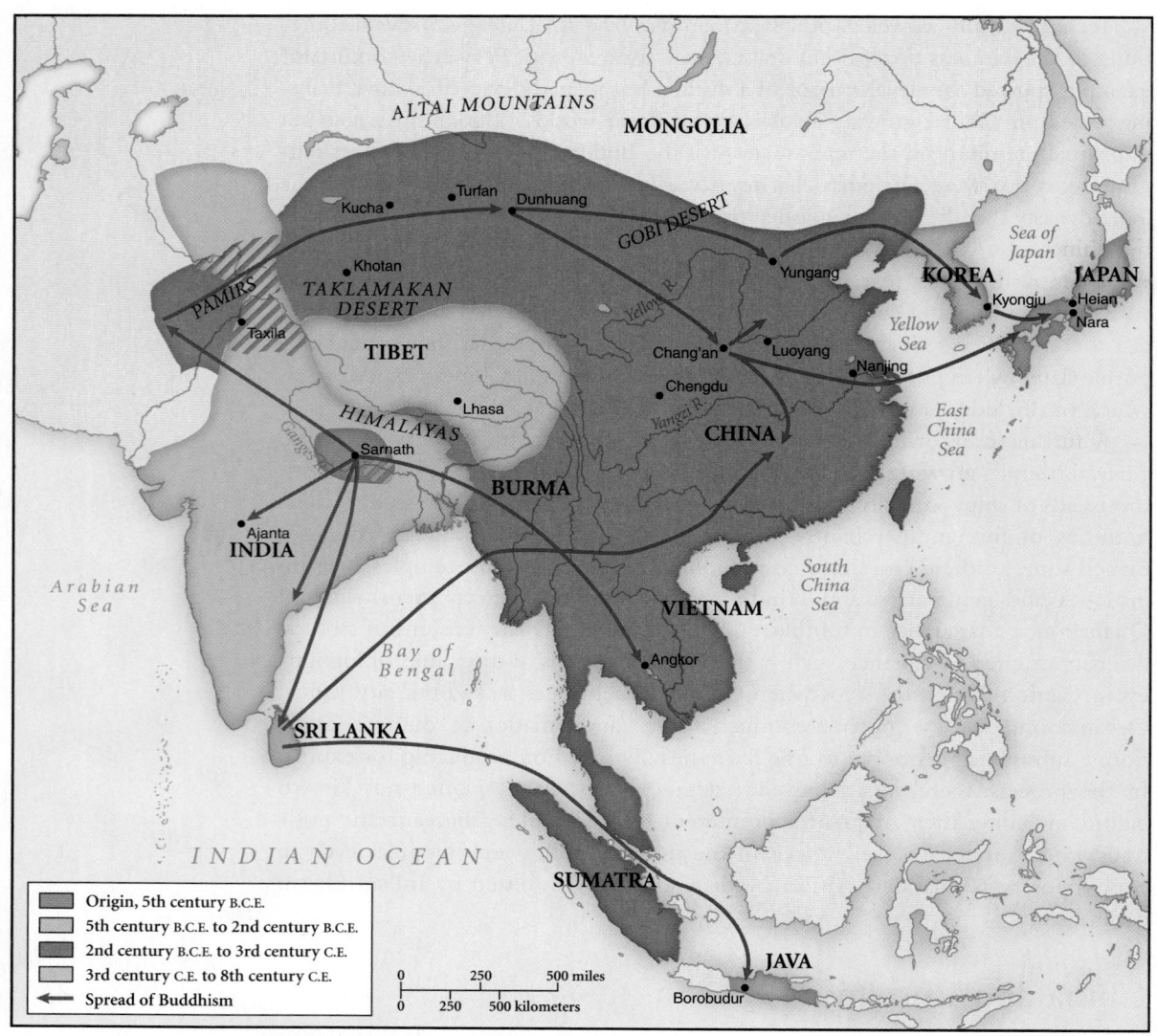

Map 9.2   The World of Asian Buddhism
Born in India, Buddhism later spread widely throughout much of Asia to provide a measure of cultural or religious commonality across this vast region.

Making Buddhism Chinese

■ **Change**
What facilitated the rooting of Buddhism within China?

Buddhism initially entered China via the Silk Road trading network during the first and second centuries C.E. The stability and prosperity of the Han dynasty, then at its height, ensured that the new "barbarian" religion held little appeal for native Chinese. Furthermore, the Indian culture from which Buddhism sprang was at odds with Chinese understandings of the world in many ways. Buddhism's commitment to a secluded and monastic life for monks and nuns seemed to dishonor Chinese family values, and its concern for individual salvation or enlightenment appeared selfish, contradicting the social orientation of Confucian thinking. Its abstract philosophy ran counter to the more concrete, "this-worldly" concerns of Chinese thinkers; and the Buddhist concept of infinite eons of time, endlessly repeating themselves, was quite a stretch for the Chinese, who normally thought in terms of finite family generations or dynastic cycles. No wonder that for the first several centuries C.E., Buddhism was largely the preserve of foreign merchants and monks living in China.

In the half millennium between roughly 300 and 800 C.E., however, Buddhism took solid root in China within both elite and popular culture, becoming a permanent, though fluctuating, presence in Chinese life. How did this remarkable transformation unfold? It began, arguably, with the collapse of the Han dynasty around 200 C.E. The chaotic, violent, and politically fragmented centuries that followed seriously discredited Confucianism and opened the door to alternative understandings of the world. Nomadic rulers, now governing much of northern China, found Buddhism useful in part because it was foreign. "We were born out of the marches," declared one of them, "and though we are unworthy, we have complied with our appointed destiny and govern the Chinese as their prince.... Buddha being a barbarian god is the very one we should worship."[29] Rulers and elite families provided money and land that enabled the building of many Buddhist monasteries, temples, and works of art. In southern China, where many northern aristocrats had fled following the disastrous decline of the Han dynasty, Buddhism provided some comfort in the face of a collapsing society. Its emphasis on ritual, morality, and contemplation represented an intellectually and esthetically satisfying response to times that were so clearly out of joint.

Meanwhile, Buddhist monasteries increasingly provided an array of social services for ordinary people. In them, travelers found accommodation; those fleeing from China's many upheavals discovered a place of refuge; desperate people received charity; farmers borrowed seed for the next planting; the sick were treated; children learned to read. And for many, Buddhism was associated with access to magical powers as reports of miracles abounded. Battles were won, rain descended on drought-ridden areas, diseases were cured, and guilt was relieved—all through the magical ministrations of charismatic monks.

Accompanying all of this was a serious effort by monks, scholars, and translators to present this Indian religion in terms that Chinese could relate to. Thus the Buddhist term *dharma*, referring to the Buddha's teaching, was translated as *dao*, or "the way," a notion long familiar in both Daoist and Confucian thinking (see Chapter 5). The Buddhist notion of "morality" was translated with the Confucian term that referred to "filial submission and obedience." Some Indian concepts were modified in the process of translation. For example, the idea that "husband supports wife," which reflected a considerable respect for women and mothers in early Indian Buddhism, became in translation "husband controls wife."[30]

As Buddhism took hold in China, it was primarily in its broader Mahayana form—complete with numerous deities, the veneration of relics, many heavens and hells, and bodhisattvas to aid the believer—rather than the more psychological and individualistic Theravada Buddhism (see Chapter 5 and Visual Source 5.4, p. 233). One of the most popular forms of Buddhism in China was the Pure Land School, in which faithfully repeating the name of an earlier Buddha, the Amitabha, was sufficient to ensure rebirth in a beautifully described heavenly realm, the Pure Land. In its emphasis on salvation by faith, without arduous study or intensive meditation, Pure Land Buddhism became a highly popular and authentically Chinese version of the Indian faith (see Visual Source 5.5, p. 234).

China's reunification under the Sui and early Tang dynasties witnessed growing state support for Buddhism. The Sui emperor Wendi (reigned 581–604 C.E.) had monasteries constructed at the base of China's five sacred mountains, further identifying the imported religion with traditional Chinese culture. He even used Buddhism to justify his military campaigns. "With a hundred victories in a hundred battles," he declared, "we promote the practice of the ten Buddhist virtues."[31] With state support and growing popular acceptance, monasteries became centers of great wealth, largely exempt from taxation, owning large estates; running businesses such as oil presses, water mills, and pawn shops; collecting gems, gold, and lavish works of art; and even employing slaves. But Buddhism, while solidly entrenched in Chinese life by the early Tang dynasty, never achieved the independence from state authorities that the Christian church acquired in Europe. The examinations for becoming a monk were supervised by the state, and education in the monasteries included the required study of the Confucian classics. In the mid-ninth century, the state showed quite dramatically just how much control it could exercise over the Buddhist establishment.

Losing State Support: The Crisis of Chinese Buddhism

■ Change
What were the major sources of opposition to Buddhism within China?

The impressive growth of Chinese Buddhism was accompanied by a persistent undercurrent of resistance and criticism. Some saw the Buddhist establishment, at least potentially, as a "state within a state" and a challenge to imperial authority. More important was a deepening resentment of its enormous wealth. One fifth-century critic, referring to monks, put the issue squarely: "Why is it that their ideals are noble and far-reaching and their activities still are base and common? [They] become merchants and engage in barter, wrangling with the masses for profit."[32] When state treasuries were short of funds, government officials cast a covetous eye on wealthy and tax-exempt monasteries. Furthermore, Buddhism was clearly of foreign origin and offensive for that reason to some Confucian and Daoist thinkers. The celibacy of the monks and their withdrawal from society, the critics argued, undermined the Confucian-based family system of Chinese tradition.

Such criticisms took on new meaning in the changed environment of China after about 800 C.E. Following centuries of considerable foreign influence in China, a growing resentment against foreign culture, particularly among the literate classes, increasingly took hold. The turning point may well have been the An Lushan rebellion (755–763), in which a general of foreign origin led a major revolt against the Tang dynasty. Whatever its origins, an increasingly xenophobic reaction set in among the upper classes, reflected in a desire to return to an imagined "purity" of earlier times.[33] In this setting, the old criticisms of Buddhism became more sharply focused. In 819, Han Yu, a leading figure in the Confucian counterattack on Buddhism, wrote a scathing memorial to the emperor, criticizing his willingness to honor a relic of the Buddha's finger.

> Now the Buddha was of barbarian origin. His language differed from Chinese speech; his clothes were of a different cut; his mouth did not pronounce the prescribed words of the Former Kings.... He did not recognize the relationship between prince and subject, nor the sentiments of father and son.... I pray that Your Majesty will turn this bone over to the officials that it may be cast into water or fire.[34]

Several decades later, the Chinese state took direct action against the Buddhist establishment as well as against other foreign religions. A series of imperial decrees between 841 and 845 ordered some 260,000 monks and nuns to return to normal life as tax-paying citizens. Thousands of monasteries, temples, and shrines were either destroyed or turned to public use, while the state confiscated the lands, money, metals, and serfs belonging to monasteries. Buddhists were now forbidden to use gold, silver, copper, iron, and gems in constructing their images. These actions dealt a serious blow to Chinese Buddhism. Its scholars and monks were scattered, its creativity diminished, and its institutions came even more firmly under state control.

Despite this persecution, Buddhism did not vanish from China. At the level of elite culture, its philosophical ideas played a role in the reformulation of Confucian thinking that took place during the Song dynasty. At the village level, Buddhism became one element of Chinese popular religion, which also included the veneration of ancestors, the honoring of Confucius, and Daoist shrines and rituals. Temples frequently included statues of Confucius, Laozi, and the Buddha, with little sense of any incompatibility among them. "Every black-haired son of Han," the Chinese have long said, "wears a Confucian thinking cap, a Daoist robe, and Buddhist sandals." Unlike Europe, where an immigrant religion triumphed over and excluded all other faiths, Buddhism in China became assimilated into Chinese culture alongside its other traditions.

Reflections: Why Do Things Change?

The rapidity of change in modern societies is among the most distinctive features of recent history, but change and transformation, though at various rates, have been constants in the human story since the very beginning. Explaining how and why human societies change is perhaps the central issue that historians confront, no matter which societies or periods of time they study. Those who specialize in the history of some particular culture or civilization often emphasize sources of change operating within those societies, although there is intense disagreement as to which are most significant. The ideas of great thinkers, the policies of leaders, struggles for power, the conflict of classes, the impact of new technologies, the growth or decline in population, variations in local climate or weather—all of these and more have their advocates as the primary motor of historical transformation.

Of course, it is not necessary to choose among them. The history of classical and postclassical China illustrates the range of internal factors that have driven change in that civilization. The political conflicts of the "era of warring states" provided the setting and the motivation for the emergence of Confucianism and Daoism, which in turn have certainly shaped the character and texture of Chinese civilization over many centuries. The personal qualities and brutal policies of Shihuangdi surely played a role in China's unification and in the brief duration of the Qin dynasty. The subsequent creation of a widespread network of canals and waterways as well as the country's technological achievements served to maintain that unity over very long periods of time. But the massive inequalities of Chinese society generated the peasant upheavals, which periodically shattered that unity and led to new ruling dynasties. Sometimes natural events, such as droughts and floods, triggered those rebellions.

World historians, more than those who study particular civilizations or nations, have been inclined to find the primary source of change in contact with strangers, in external connections and interactions, whether direct or indirect. The history of China and East Asia provide plenty of examples for this point of view as well. Conceptions of China as the "middle kingdom," infinitely superior to all surrounding societies, grew out of centuries of involvement with its neighbors. Some of those neighbors became Chinese as China's imperial reach grew, especially to the south. Even those that did not, such as Korea, Vietnam, and Japan, were decisively transformed by proximity to the "radiating civilization" of China. China's own cuisine, so distinctive in recent centuries, may well be a quite recent invention, drawing heavily on Indian and Southeast Asian cooking. Buddhism, of course, is an obvious borrowing from abroad, although its incorporation into Chinese civilization and its ups and downs within China owed much to internal cultural and political realities.

In the end, clear distinctions between internal and external sources of change in China's history—or that of any other society—are perhaps misleading. The boundary between "inside" and "outside" is itself a constantly changing line. Should the borderlands of northern China, where Chinese and Turkic peoples met and mingled, be regarded as internal or external to China itself? And, as the histories of Chinese Buddhism and of Japanese culture so clearly indicate, what comes from beyond is always transformed by what it encounters within.

Second Thoughts

What's the Significance?

Sui dynasty

Tang dynasty

Song dynasty economic
   revolution

Hangzhou

foot binding

tribute system

Xiongnu

Khitan/Jurchen people

Silla dynasty (Korea)

hangul

chu nom

Trung sisters

Shotoku Taishi

bushido

Chinese Buddhism

Emperor Wendi

To assess your mastery of the
material in this chapter, visit
the **Student Center** at
bedfordstmartins.com/strayer.

Big Picture Questions

1. In what ways did Tang and Song dynasty China resemble the classical Han dynasty period, and in what ways had China changed?

2. Based on this chapter, how would you respond to the idea that China was a self-contained or isolated civilization?

3. In what different ways did nearby peoples experience their giant Chinese neighbor, and how did they respond to it?

4. How can you explain the changing fortunes of Buddhism in China?

5. How did China influence the world beyond East Asia? How was China itself transformed by its encounters with a wider world?

Next Steps: For Further Study

Samuel Adshead, *Tang China: The Rise of the East in World History* (2004). Explores the role of China within the larger world.

Patricia Ebrey, *The Inner Quarters* (1993). A balanced account of the gains and losses experienced by Chinese women during the changes of the Song dynasty.

Mark Elvin, *The Pattern of the Chinese Past* (1973). A classic account of the Chinese economic revolution.

Edward Shaffer, *The Golden Peaches of Samarkand* (1985). Examines the interaction between China and Central Asia during the Tang dynasty.

Murasaki Shikibu, *The Tale of Genji,* translated by Royall Tyler (2002). Written around 1000, this saga of Japanese court life is sometimes called the world's first novel.

Arthur F. Wright, *Buddhism in Chinese History* (1959). An older account filled with wonderful stories and anecdotes.

Upper River during the Qing Ming Festival, http://www.ibiblio.org/ulysses/gec/painting/qingming/full.htm. A scrolling reproduction of a huge Chinese painting, showing in detail the Song dynasty city of Kaifeng.

For Web sites and additional
documents related to this
chapter, see **Make History** at
bedfordstmartins.com/strayer.

Documents

Considering the Evidence:
The Making of Japanese Civilization

Japan's historical development during the postclassical era places it among the third-wave civilizations—Russian, Swahili, Srivijaya, west European, Islamic—that took shape between 500 and 1500. Each of them was distinctive in particular ways, but all of them followed the general patterns of earlier civilizations in the creation of cities, states, stratified societies, patriarchies, written languages, and more. Furthermore, many of them borrowed extensively from nearby and older civilizations. In the case of Japan, that borrowing was primarily from China, its towering neighbor to the west. The documents that follow provide glimpses of a distinctive Japanese civilization in the making, even as that civilization selectively incorporated elements of Chinese thinking and practice (see pp. 394–97).

Document 9.1

Japanese Political Ideals

As an early Japanese state gradually took shape in the sixth and seventh centuries, it was confronted by serious internal divisions of clan, faction, and religion. Externally, Japanese forces had been expelled from their footholds in Korea, while Japan also faced the immense power and attractiveness of a reunified China under the Sui and Tang dynasties (see pp. 380–85). In these circumstances, Japanese authorities sought to strengthen their own emerging state by adopting a range of Chinese political values and practices. This Chinese influence in Japanese political thinking was particularly apparent in the so-called Seventeen Article Constitution issued by Shotoku, which was a set of general guidelines for court officials.

■ What elements of Buddhist, Confucian, or Legalist thinking are reflected in this document? (Review pp. 192–95 and 199–201 and Documents 4.3, pp. 174–75, and 5.1, pp. 217–19.)

■ What can you infer about the internal problems that Japanese rulers faced?

■ How might Shotoku define an ideal Japanese state?

■ Why do you think Shotoku omitted any mention of traditional Japanese gods or spirits or the Japanese claim that their emperor was descended from the sun goddess Amaterasu?

Despite this apparent embrace of all things Chinese, Shotoku's attitude toward China itself is less clear. In various letters that he sent to the Chinese Sui dynasty ruler, Shotoku inscribed them as follows: "The Son of Heaven of the Land of the Rising Sun to the Son of Heaven of the Land of the Setting Sun." Another read: "The Eastern Emperor Greets the Western Emperor."[35] Considering their country as the Middle Kingdom, greatly superior to all its neighbors, Chinese court officials were incensed at these apparent assertions of equality. It is not clear whether Shotoku was deliberately claiming equivalence with China or if he was simply unaware of how such language might be viewed in China.

SHOTOKU

The Seventeen Article Constitution

604

1. Harmony is to be valued, and an avoidance of wanton opposition to be honored. All men are influenced by class feelings, and there are few who are intelligent. Hence there are some who disobey their lords and fathers, or who maintain feuds with the neighboring villages. But when those above are harmonious and those below are friendly, and there is concord in the discussion of business, right views of things spontaneously gain acceptance....

2. Sincerely reverence the three treasures... the Buddha, the Law [teachings], and the Priesthood [community of monks]....

3. When you receive the Imperial commands, fail not scrupulously to obey them. The lord is Heaven, the vassal is Earth. Heaven overspreads, and Earth upbears.... [W]hen the superior acts, the inferior yields compliance.

4. The Ministers and functionaries should make decorous behavior their leading principle.... If the superiors do not behave with decorum, the inferiors are disorderly....

5. Ceasing from gluttony and abandoning covetous desires, deal impartially with the [legal] suits which are submitted to you....

6. Chastise that which is evil and encourage that which is good. This was the excellent rule of antiquity....

7. Let every man have his own charge, and let not the spheres of duty be confused. When wise men are entrusted with office, the sound of praise arises. If unprincipled men hold office, disasters and tumults are multiplied. In this world, few are born with knowledge: wisdom is the product of earnest meditation. In all things, whether great or small, find the right man, and they will surely be well managed....

Source: W. G. Aston, trans., *Nihongi: Chronicles of Japan from the Earliest Times to A.D. 697* (London: Paul, Trench, Truebner, 1896), 2:129–33.

10. Let us cease from wrath, and refrain from angry looks. Nor let us be resentful when others differ from us. For all men have hearts, and each heart has its own leanings.... [All] of us are simply ordinary men....

11. Give clear appreciation to merit and demerit, and deal out to each its sure reward or punishment. In these days, reward does not attend upon merit, nor punishment upon crime. You high functionaries, who have charge of public affairs, let it be your task to make clear rewards and punishments....

12. Let not the provincial authorities or the [local nobles] levy exactions on the people. In a country, there are not two lords.... The sovereign is the master of the people of the whole country....

15. To turn away from that which is private, and to set our faces toward that which is public—this is the path of a Minister....

16. Let the people be employed [in forced labor] at seasonable times. This is an ancient and excellent rule. Let them be employed, therefore, in the winter months, when they are at leisure. But from spring to autumn, when they are engaged in agriculture or with the mulberry trees, the people should not be so employed. For if they do not attend to agriculture, what will they have to eat? If they do not attend the mulberry trees, what will they do for clothing?

17. Decisions on important matters should not be made by one person alone. They should be discussed with many.

Document 9.2

Buddhism in Japan: The Zen Tradition

Buddhism was perhaps Japan's most significant cultural borrowing. Although the religion had begun in India and entered Japan from Korea in the mid-sixth century, it was widely viewed as a Chinese import, conveying, according to one historian, a "Chinese-style dignity and civilization" for an emerging Japanese state. To the rulers of that new state, Buddhism was politically useful, for it provided a potentially unifying religious tradition for a divided society and support for the imperial regime.[36] Yet Buddhism in Japan was never a single tradition, for a great variety of Buddhist sects, practices, and schools of thought, most of them of Chinese origin, took root in Japan. Frequently they were at odds with one another and with the Japanese state as well.

The Pure Land school of Buddhist practice achieved widespread popularity in Japan beginning in the twelfth century and represented a democratization of a religion that had earlier given special prominence to monks and to elites in aristocratic circles. Its goal was no longer *nirvana*, the enlightenment gained in this life by the strenuous personal effort of a few individuals, but rather rebirth in the Pure Land of the Western Paradise, a heavenly place of beauty and delight where full awakening was virtually guaranteed (see Visual Source 5.5, p. 234). That possibility was now open to many simply by calling repeatedly on the name of Amida, a compassionate Buddha figure from ages past and an earlier incarnation of the historical Buddha. *Nama Amida Butsu* (Praise be to Amida Buddha)—that was the invocation, known as *nembutsu*, that offered divine assistance to all struggling seekers, ordinary people as well as monks, women as well as men, and even outcasts and the impure.

Zen Buddhism, often known as Chan in China, was introduced to Japan about the same time that Pure Land was taking root. Both were concerned with making Buddhism available to the widest possible audience, for all persons possessed a Buddha nature and could potentially achieve awakening. But the Zen tradition decisively rejected the idea of relying on an external divine source, such as the Amida Buddha. Rather, serious practitioners should look within themselves through a highly disciplined form of meditation known as *zazen*. This meant much less emphasis on religious texts and philosophical discussion than in some other expressions of Buddhism. Furthermore, Zen valued very highly the transmission of teachings from master to disciple in an unbroken line of succession from the historical Buddha himself. Document 9.2 presents extracts from the writings of Dogen (1200–1253), among the first and most well-known of those Japanese monks who introduced Zen to their homeland, after extensive study in China.

■ What was distinctive about Zen practice?

■ Why do you think Zen was particularly attractive for Japan's warlords and its *samurai* warrior class?

■ What distinguished Zen from Pure Land Buddhism in Japan?

■ What understandings lie behind the strict discipline of Zen? How might Buddhist critics of this approach take issue with Dogen?

DOGEN
Writings on Zen Buddhism
Thirteenth Century

We teach: For all the Buddha dharma–preserving Zen ancestors and Buddhas, sitting upright in the practice of self-actualizing *samādhi* [concentration] is the true path of awakening. Both in India and in China, all who have attained awakening did so in this way. Because in every generation each teacher and each disciple intimately and correctly transmitted this marvelous art, I learned the genuine initiation.

In the correctly transmitted Zen lineage we teach: This directly transmitted, authoritative Buddha dharma is the best of the best. Once you start studying under a good teacher, there is no need for lighting incense, worshipful prostrations, recalling the Buddha (*nembutsu*), repentance, or chanting scripture. Just sit and slough off body-mind....

★　★　★

When I stayed at T'ien-t'ung monastery [in China], the venerable Ching used to stay up sitting until the small hours of the morning and then after only a little rest would rise early to start sitting again. In the meditation hall he went on sitting with the other elders, without letting up for even a single night. Meanwhile many of the monks went off to sleep. The elder would go around among them and hit the sleepers with his fist or a slipper, yelling at them to wake up. If their sleepiness persisted, he would go out to the hallway and ring the bell to summon the

Source: William Theodore de Bary et al., *Sources of Japanese Tradition*, 1:321; William Theodore de Bary, *The Buddhist Tradition in India, China and Japan* (New York: Vintage Books, 1969), 372–73.

monks to a room apart, where he would lecture to them by the light of a candle.

"What use is there in your assembling together in the hall only to go to sleep? Is this all that you left the world and joined holy orders for?... Great is the problem of birth and death; fleeting indeed is our transitory existence. Upon these truths both the scriptural and meditation schools agree. What sort of illness awaits us tonight, what sort of death tomorrow? While we have life, not to practice Buddha's Law but to spend the time in sleep is the height of foolishness. Because of such foolishness Buddhism today is in a state of decline....

Upon another occasion his attendants said to him, "The monks are getting overtired or falling ill, and some are thinking of leaving the monastery, all because they are required to sit too long in medita-tion. Shouldn't the length of the sitting period be shortened?" The master became highly indignant. "That would be quite wrong. A monk who is not really devoted to the religious life may very well fall asleep in a half hour or an hour. But one truly devoted to it who has resolved to persevere in his religious discipline will eventually come to enjoy the practice of sitting, no matter how long it lasts. When I was young I used to visit the heads of various mon-asteries, and one of them explained to me, 'Formerly I used to hit sleeping monks so hard that my fist just about broke. Now I am old and weak, so I can't hit them hard enough. Therefore it is difficult to pro-duce good monks. In many monasteries today the superiors do not emphasize sitting strongly enough, and so Buddhism is declining. The more you hit them the better,' he advised me."

Document 9.3

The Uniqueness of Japan

Despite Japan's extensive cultural borrowing from abroad, or perhaps because of that borrowing, Japanese writers often stressed the unique and superior fea-tures of their own country. Nowhere is this theme echoed more clearly than in *The Chronicle of the Direct Descent of Gods and Sovereigns*, written by Kitabatake Chikafusa (1293–1354). A longtime court official and member of one branch of Japan's imperial family, Kitabatake wrote at a time of declining imperial authority in Japan, when two court centers competed in an extended "war of the courts." As an advocate for the southern court, Kitabatake sought to prove that the emperor he served was legitimate because he had descended in unbro-ken line from the Age of the Gods. In making this argument, he was also a spokesman for the revival of Japan's earlier religious tradition of numerous gods and spirits, known later as Shintoism.

- In Kitabatake's view, what was distinctive about Japan in comparison to China and India?

- How might the use of Japan's indigenous religious tradition, especially the Sun Goddess, serve to legitimize the imperial rule of Kitabatake's family?

- How did Kitabatake understand the place of Confucianism and Buddhism in Japan and their relationship to Shinto beliefs?

KITABATAKE CHIKAFUSA

The Chronicle of the Direct Descent of Gods and Sovereigns

1339

Japan is the divine country. The heavenly ancestor it was who first laid its foundations, and the Sun Goddess left her descendants to reign over it forever and ever. This is true only of our country, and nothing similar may be found in foreign lands. That is why it is called the divine country.

In the age of the gods, Japan was known as the "ever-fruitful land of reed-covered plains and luxuriant ricefields." This name has existed since the creation of heaven and earth.... [I]t may thus be considered the prime name of Japan. It is also called the country of the great eight islands. This name was given because eight islands were produced when the Male Deity and the Female Deity begot Japan.... Japan is the land of the Sun Goddess [Amaterasu]. Or it may have thus been called because it is near the place where the sun rises.... Thus, since Japan is a separate continent, distinct from both India and China and lying in a great ocean, it is the country where the divine illustrious imperial line has been transmitted.

The creation of heaven and earth must everywhere have been the same, for it occurred within the same universe, but the Indian, Chinese, and Japanese traditions are each different....

In China, nothing positive is stated concerning the creation of the world, even though China is a country which accords special importance to the keeping of records....

The beginnings of Japan in some ways resemble the Indian descriptions, telling as it does of the world's creation from the seed of the heavenly gods. However, whereas in our country the succession to the throne has followed a single undeviating line since the first divine ancestor, nothing of the kind has existed in India. After their first ruler, King People's Lord, had been chosen and raised to power by the populace, his dynasty succeeded, but in later times most of his descendants perished, and men of inferior genealogy who had powerful forces became the rulers, some of them even controlling the whole of India. China is also a country of notorious disorders. Even in ancient times, when life was simple and conduct was proper, the throne was offered to wise men, and no single lineage was established. Later, in times of disorder, men fought for control of the country. Thus some of the rulers rose from the ranks of the plebians, and there were even some of barbarian origin who usurped power. Or some families after generations of service as ministers surpassed their princes and eventually supplanted them. There have already been thirty-six changes of dynasty since Fuxi, and unspeakable disorders have occurred.

Only in our country has the succession remained inviolate from the beginning of heaven and earth to the present. It has been maintained within a single lineage, and even when, as inevitably has happened, the succession has been transmitted collaterally, it has returned to the true line. This is due to the ever-renewed Divine Oath and makes Japan unlike all other countries....

Then the Great Sun Goddess...sent her grandchild to the world below. Eighty million deities obeyed the divine decree to accompany and serve him. Among them were thirty-two principal deities.... Two of these deities...received a divine decree specially instructing them to aid and protect the divine grandchild. [The Sun Goddess] uttered these words of command: "Thou, my illustrious grandchild, proceed thither and govern the land. Go, and may prosperity attend thy dynasty, and may it, like Heaven and Earth, endure forever."...

Because our Great Goddess is the spirit of the sun, she illuminates with a bright virtue which is incomprehensible in all its aspects but dependable alike in the realm of the visible and invisible. All

Source: William Theodore de Bary et al., *Sources of Japanese Tradition* (New York: Columbia University Press, 2001), 1:358–63.

sovereigns and ministers have inherited the bright seeds of the divine light, or they are descendants of the deities who received personal instruction from the Great Goddess. Who would not stand in reverence before this fact? The highest object of all teachings, Buddhist and Confucian included, consists in realizing this fact and obeying in perfect consonance its principles. It has been the power of the dissemination of the Buddhist and Confucian texts which has spread these principles.... Since the reign of the Emperor Ōjin, the Confucian writings have been disseminated, and since Prince Shōtoku's time Buddhism has flourished in Japan. Both these men were sages incarnate, and it must have been their intention to spread a knowledge of the way of our country, in accordance with the wishes of the Great Sun Goddess.

Document 9.4

Social Life at Court

For many centuries, high culture in Japan—art, music, poetry, and literature— found a home in the imperial court, where men and women of the royal family and nobility, together with various attendants, mixed and mingled. That aristocratic culture reached its high point between the ninth and twelfth centuries, but, according to one prominent scholar, it "has shaped the aesthetic and emotional life of the entire Japanese people for a millennium."[37] Women played a prominent role in that culture, both creating it and describing it. Among them was Sei Shonagon (966–1017), a lady-in-waiting to the Empress Sadako. In her *Pillow Book*, a series of brief and often witty observations, Sei Shonagon described court life as well as her own likes and dislikes.

- What impression does Sei Shonagon convey about the relationship of men and women at court?

- How would you describe her posture toward men, toward women, and toward ordinary people? What insight can you gain about class differences from her writing?

- In what ways does court life, as Sei Shonagon describes it, reflect Buddhist and Confucian influences, and in what ways does it depart from, and even challenge, those traditions?

SEI SHONAGON

Pillow Book

ca. 1000

That parents should bring up some beloved son of theirs to be a priest is really distressing. No doubt it is an auspicious thing to do; but unfortunately most people are convinced that a priest is as unimportant as a piece of wood, and they treat him accordingly. A priest lives poorly on meager food, and cannot even sleep without being criticized. While he is young, it is only natural that he should be

Source: Ivan Morris, trans. and ed., *The Pillow Book of Sei Shonagon* (New York: Columbia University Press, 1991), 25–26, 39, 44–45, 47, 49–50, 53, 254–55.

curious about all sorts of things, and, if there are women about, he will probably peep in their direction (though, to be sure, with a look of aversion on his face). What is wrong about that? Yet people immediately find fault with him for even so small a lapse....

A preacher ought to be good-looking. For, if we are properly to understand his worthy sentiments, we must keep our eyes on him while he speaks; should we look away, we may forget to listen. Accordingly an ugly preacher may well be the source of sin....

When I make myself imagine what it is like to be one of those women who live at home, faithfully serving their husbands—women who have not a single exciting prospect in life yet who believe that they are perfectly happy—I am filled with scorn....

I cannot bear men who believe that women serving in the Palace are bound to be frivolous and wicked. Yet I suppose their prejudice is understandable. After all, women at Court do not spend their time hiding modestly behind fans and screens, but walk about, looking openly at people they chance to meet. Yes, they see everyone face to face, not only ladies-in-waiting like themselves, but even Their Imperial Majesties (whose august names I hardly dare mention), High Court Nobles, senior courtiers, and other gentlemen of high rank. In the presence of such exalted personages the women in the Palace are all equally brazen, whether they be the maids of ladies-in-waiting, or the relations of Court ladies who have come to visit them, or housekeepers, or latrine-cleaners, or women who are of no more value than a roof-tile or a pebble. Small wonder that the young men regard them as immodest! Yet are the gentlemen themselves any less so? They are not exactly bashful when it comes to looking at the great people in the Palace. No, everyone at Court is much the same in this respect....

Hateful Things

...A man who has nothing in particular to recommend him discusses all sorts of subjects at random as though he knew everything....

An admirer has come on a clandestine visit, but a dog catches sight of him and starts barking. One feels like killing the beast.

One has been foolish enough to invite a man to spend the night in an unsuitable place—and then he starts snoring.

A gentleman has visited one secretly. Though he is wearing a tall, lacquered hat, he nevertheless wants no one to see him. He is so flurried, in fact, that upon leaving he bangs into something with his hat. Most hateful! ...

A man with whom one is having an affair keeps singing the praises of some woman he used to know. Even if it is a thing of the past, this can be very annoying. How much more so if he is still seeing the woman! ...

A good lover will behave as elegantly at dawn as at any other time. He drags himself out of bed with a look of dismay on his face. The lady urges him on: "Come, my friend, it's getting light. You don't want anyone to find you here." He gives a deep sigh, as if to say that the night has not been nearly long enough and that it is agony to leave. Once up, he does not instantly pull on his trousers. Instead he comes close to the lady and whispers whatever was left unsaid during the night. Even when he is dressed, he still lingers, vaguely pretending to be fastening his sash....

Indeed, one's attachment to a man depends largely on the elegance of his leave-taking. When he jumps out of bed, scurries about the room, tightly fastens his trouser-sash, rolls up the sleeves of his Court cloak, over-robe, or hunting costume, stuffs his belongings into the breast of his robe and then briskly secures the outer sash—one really begins to hate him....

It is very annoying, when one has visited Hase Temple and has retired into one's enclosure, to be disturbed by a herd of common people who come and sit outside in a row, crowded so close together that the tails of their robes fall over each other in utter disarray. I remember that once I was overcome by a great desire to go on a pilgrimage. Having made my way up the log steps, deafened by the fearful roar of the river, I hurried into my enclosure, longing to gaze upon the sacred countenance of Buddha. To my dismay I found that a throng of commoners had settled themselves directly in front of me, where they were incessantly standing up, prostrating themselves, and squatting down again. They looked like so many basket-worms as they crowded together in their hideous clothes, leaving hardly an inch of space between themselves and me. I really felt like pushing them all over sideways.

Document 9.5

The Way of the Warrior

As the Japanese imperial court gradually lost power to military authorities in the countryside, a further distinctive feature of Japanese civilization emerged in the celebration of martial virtues and the warrior class—the *samurai*—that embodied those values. From the twelfth through the mid-nineteenth century, public life and government in Japan was dominated by the samurai, while their culture and values, known as *bushido*, expressed the highest ideals of political leadership and of personal conduct. At least in the West, the samurai are perhaps best known for preferring death over dishonor, a posture expressed in *seppuku* (ritual suicide). But there was much more to bushido than this, for the samurai served not only as warriors but also as bureaucrats—magistrates, land managers, and provincial governors—acting on behalf of their lords (*daimyo*) or in service to military rulers known as *shoguns*. Furthermore, although bushido remained a distinctively Japanese cultural expression, it absorbed both Confucian and Buddhist values as well as those of the indigenous Shinto tradition.

The two selections that follow reflect major themes of an emerging bushido culture, the way of the warrior. The first excerpt comes from the writings of Shiba Yoshimasa (1349–1410), a feudal lord, general, and administrator as well as a noted poet, who wrote a manual of advice for the young warriors of his own lineage. Probably the man who most closely approximated in his own life the emerging ideal of a cultivated warrior was Imagawa Ryoshun (1325–1420), famous as a poet, a military commander, and a devout Buddhist. The second excerpt contains passages from a famous and highly critical letter Imagawa wrote to his adopted son (who was also his younger brother). The letter was published and republished hundreds of times and used for centuries as a primer or school text for the instruction of young samurai.

- Based on these accounts, how would you define the ideal samurai?

- What elements of Confucian, Buddhist, or Shinto thinking can you find in these selections? How do these writers reconcile the peaceful emphasis of Confucian and Buddhist teachings with the military dimension of bushido?

- What does the Imagawa letter suggest about the problems facing the military rulers of Japan in the fourteenth century?

Shiba Yosimasa
Advice to Young Samurai
ca. 1400

Wielders of bow and arrow should behave in a manner considerate not only of their own honor, of course, but also of the honor of their descendants. They should not bring on eternal disgrace by solicitude for their limited lives.

That being said, nevertheless to regard your one and only life as like dust or ashes and die when you shouldn't is to acquire a worthless reputation. A genuine motive would be, for example, to give up your life for the sake of the sole sovereign, or serving under the commander of the military in a time of need; these would convey an exalted name to children and descendants. Something like a strategy of the moment, whether good or bad, cannot raise the family reputation much.

Warriors should never be thoughtless or absentminded but handle all things with forethought....

It is said that good warriors and good Buddhists are similarly circumspect. Whatever the matter, it is vexing for the mind not to be calm. Putting others' minds at ease too is something found only in the considerate....

Source: Thomas Cleary, trans. and ed., *Training the Samurai Mind* (Boston: Shambhala, 2008), 18–20.

When you begin to think of yourself, you'll get irritated at your parents' concern and defy their instructions. Even if your parents may be stupid, if you obey their instructions, at least you won't be violating the principle of nature. What is more, eighty to ninety percent of the time what parents say makes sense for their children. It builds up in oneself to become obvious. The words of our parents we defied in irritation long ago are all essential. You should emulate even a bad parent rather than a good stranger; that's how a family culture is transmitted and comes to be known as a person's legacy....

Even if one doesn't perform any religious exercises and never makes a visit to a shrine, neither deities nor buddhas will disregard a person whose mind is honest and compassionate. In particular, the Great Goddess of Ise,° the great bodhisattva Hachiman,° and the deity of Kitano° will dwell in the heads of people whose minds are honest, clean, and good.

°**Great Goddess of Ise:** Amaterasu, the sun goddess.

°**Hachiman:** a Japanese deity who came to be seen as a Buddhist bodhisattva.

°**Kitano:** patron god of learning.

Imagawa Ryoshun
The Imagawa Letter
1412

As you do not understand the Arts of Peace° your skill in the Arts of War° will not, in the end, achieve victory.

°**Arts of Peace:** literary skills including poetry, history, philosophy, and ritual.

°**Arts of War:** horsemanship, archery, swordsmanship.

You like to roam about, hawking and cormorant fishing, relishing the purposelessness of taking life.

You live in luxury by fleecing the people and plundering the shrines.

Source: From Carl Steenstrup, trans., "The Imagawa Letter," *Monumenta Nipponica* 28, no. 3 (Autumn 1973), 295–316.

To build your own dwelling you razed the pagoda and other buildings of the memorial temple of our ancestors.

You do not distinguish between good and bad behavior of your retainers, but reward or punish them without justice.

You permit yourself to forget the kindness that our lord and father showed us; thus you destroy the principles of loyalty and filial piety.

You do not understand the difference in status between yourself and others; sometimes you make too much of other people, sometimes too little.

You disregard other people's viewpoints; you bully them and rely on force.

You excel at drinking bouts, amusements, and gambling, but you forget the business of our clan.

You provide yourself lavishly with clothes and weapons, but your retainers are poorly equipped.

You ought to show utmost respect to Buddhist monks and priests and carry out ceremonies properly.

You impede the flow of travelers by erecting barriers everywhere in your territory.

Whether you are in charge of anything—such as a province or a district—or not, it will be difficult to put your abilities to any use if you have not won the sympathy and respect of ordinary people.

Just as the Buddhist scriptures tell us that the Buddha incessantly strives to save mankind, in the same way you should exert your mind to the utmost in all your activities, be they civil or military, and never fall into negligence.

It should be regarded as dangerous if the ruler of the people in a province is deficient even in a single [one] of the cardinal virtues of human-heartedness, righteousness, propriety, wisdom, and good faith.

You were born to be a warrior, but you mismanage your territory, do not maintain the army, and are not ashamed although people laugh at you. It is, indeed, a mortifying situation for you and our whole clan.

Using the Evidence:
The Making of Japanese Civilization

1. **Considering cultural borrowing and assimilation:** What evidence of cultural borrowing can you identify in these documents? To what extent did those borrowed elements come to be regarded as Japanese?

2. **Looking for continuities:** What older patterns of Japanese thought and practice persisted despite much cultural borrowing from China?

3. **Noticing inconsistencies and change:** No national culture develops as a single set of ideas and practices. What inconsistencies, tensions, or differences in emphasis can you identify in these documents? What changes over time can you identify in these selections?

4. **Considering Japanese Buddhism:** In what different ways did Buddhism play a role in Japan during the postclassical era? How did Buddhism change Japan, and how did Japan change Buddhism?

Visual Sources

Considering the Evidence:
The Leisure Life of China's Elites

From the earliest centuries of Chinese civilization, that country's artists have painted—on pottery, paper, wood, and silk; in tombs, on coffins, and on walls; in albums and on scrolls. Relying largely on ink rather than oils, their brushes depicted human figures, landscapes, religious themes, and images of ordinary life. While Chinese painting evolved over many centuries, both in terms of subject matter and technique, by most accounts it reached a high point of artistic brilliance during the Tang and Song dynasties.

Here, however, we are less interested in the aesthetic achievements of Chinese painting than in what those works can show us about the life of China's elite class—those men who had passed the highest-level examinations and held high office in the state bureaucracy and those women who lived within the circles of the imperial court. While they represented only a tiny fraction of China's huge population, such elite groups established the tone and set the standards of behavior for Chinese civilization. For such people, leisure was a positive value, a time for nurturing relationships and cultivating one's character in good Confucian or Daoist fashion. According to the Tang dynasty writer and scholar Duan Chengshi,

> Leisure is good.
> Dusty affairs don't entangle the mind.
> I sit facing the tree outside the window
> And watch its shadow change direction three times.[38]

Action and work, in the Chinese view of things, need to be balanced by self-reflection and leisure. In the visual sources that follow, we can catch a glimpse of how the Chinese elite lived and interacted with one another, particularly in their leisure time.

Leading court officials and scholar-bureaucrats must have been greatly honored to be invited to an elegant banquet, hosted by the emperor himself, such as that shown in Visual Source 9.1. Usually attributed to the emperor Huizong (1082–1135)—who was himself a noted painter, poet, calligrapher, and collector—the painting shows a refined dinner gathering of high officials drinking tea and wine with the emperor presiding at the left.[39] This emperor's great attention to the arts rather than to affairs of state gained him a reputation as a negligent and dissolute ruler. His reign ended in disgrace as China suffered a humiliating defeat at the hands of northern nomadic Jin people, who took the emperor captive.

■ What features of this painting contribute to the impression of imperial elegance?

■ What mood does this painting evoke?

■ What social distinction among the figures in the painting can you discern?

■ How is the emperor depicted in this painting in comparison to that on page 388? How would you explain the difference?

■ How might you imagine the conversation around this table?

Visual Source 9.1 A Banquet with the Emperor (National Palace Museum, Taipei, Taiwan)

Visual Source 9.2 At Table with the Empress (National Palace Museum, Taipei, Taiwan)

Elite women of the court likewise gathered to eat, drink, and talk, as illustrated in Visual Source 9.2, an anonymous Tang dynasty painting on silk. Hosting the event is the empress, shown seated upright in the middle of the left side of the table, holding a fan and wearing a distinctive headdress. Her guests and paid professional musicians sit around the table.

- How does this gathering of elite women differ from that of the men in Visual Source 9.1? How might their conversation differ from that of the men?

- To what extent are the emperor and empress in Visual Sources 9.1 and 9.2 distinguished from their guests? How do you think the emperor and empress viewed their roles at these functions? Were they acting as private persons among friends or in an official capacity?

- What differences in status among these women can you identify?

- What view of these women does the artist seek to convey?

- What does the posture of the women suggest about the event?

Visual Source 9.3 A Literary Gathering (Palace Museum, Beijing)

Confucian cultural ideals gave great prominence to literature, poetry, and scholarly pursuits as leisure activities appropriate for "gentlemen" (see pp. 193–95). Confucius himself had declared that "gentlemen make friends through literature, and through friendship increase their benevolence." Thus literary gatherings of scholars and officials, often in garden settings, were common themes in Tang and Song dynasty paintings. Visual Source 9.3, by the tenth-century painter Zhou Wenju, provides an illustration of such a gathering.

- What marks these figures as cultivated men of literary or scholarly inclination?

- What meaning might you attribute to the outdoor garden setting of this image and that of Visual Source 9.1?

- Notice the various gazes of the four figures. What do they suggest about the character of this gathering and the interpersonal relationships among its participants?

- Do you think the artist was seeking to convey an idealized image of what a gathering of officials ought to be or a realistic portrayal of an actual event? What elements of the painting support your answer?

Chinese scholars and bureaucrats are often shown, in their leisure hours, as solitary contemplatives, immersing themselves in nature. The famous Song dynasty painter Ma Yuan (1160–1225) depicted such an image in his masterpiece entitled *On a Mountain Path in Spring*. In Visual Source 9.4, a scholar walks in the countryside watching several birds, while his servant trails behind carrying his master's *qin* (lute). A short poem in the upper right reads:

Brushed by his sleeves, wild flowers dance in the wind;
Fleeing from him, the hidden birds cut short their songs.[40]

- How would you define the mood of this painting? What techniques did Ma Yuan use to evoke this mood?

- How might this painting reflect the perspectives of Daoism (see pp. 195–97)? How does it differ from the more Confucian tone of Visual Source 9.3?

- What relationship with nature does this painting convey?

- During Ma Yuan's lifetime, the northern part of China was coming under the control of the feared Mongols. How might an awareness of this situation affect our understanding of this painting?

Visual Source 9.4 Solitary Reflection (National Palace Museum, Taipei, Taiwan)

Visual Source 9.5 An Elite Night Party (Palace Museum, Beijing)

Not all was poetry and contemplation of nature in the leisure-time activities of China's elite. Nor were men and women always so strictly segregated as the preceding visual sources may suggest. Visual Source 9.5 illustrates another side of Chinese elite life. These images are part of a long tenth-century scroll painting entitled *The Night Revels of Han Xizai*. Apparently, the Tang dynasty emperor Li Yu became suspicious that one of his ministers, Han Xizai, was overindulging in suspicious night-long parties in his own home. He therefore commissioned the artist Gu Hongzhong to attend these parties secretly and to record the events in a painting, which he hoped would shame his wayward but talented official into more appropriate and dignified behavior. The entire scroll shows men and women together, sometimes in flirtatious situations, while open sleeping areas suggest sexual activity.

- What kinds of entertainment were featured at this gathering?

- What aspects of these parties shown in the scroll paintings might have caused the emperor some concern? Refer back to the "singsong girls," shown on page 253. In what respects might these kinds of gatherings run counter to Confucian values?

- How are women portrayed in these images? In what ways are they relating to the men in the paintings?

Using the Evidence:
The Leisure Life of China's Elites

1. **Describing elite society:** Based on these visual sources, write a brief description of the social life of Chinese elites during the Tang and Song dynasties.

2. **Defining the self-image of an elite:** What do these visual sources suggest about how members of the elite ideally viewed themselves? In what ways do those self-portraits draw upon Confucian, Daoist, or Buddhist teachings?

3. **Noticing differences in the depiction of women:** In what different ways are women represented in these paintings? Keep in mind that all of the artists were men. How might this affect the way women were depicted? How might female artists have portrayed them differently?

4. **Using images to illustrate change:** Reread the sections on Chinese women (pp. 253–55 and 384–85). How might these images be used to illustrate the changes in women's lives that are described in those pages?

5. **Seeking additional sources:** What other kinds of visual sources might provide further insight into the lives of Chinese elites?

CHAPTER TEN

The Worlds of European Christendom

Connected and Divided

500–1300

Eastern Christendom: Building on the Roman Past
  The Byzantine State
  The Byzantine Church and Christian Divergence
  Byzantium and the World
  The Conversion of Russia
Western Christendom: Rebuilding in the Wake of Roman Collapse
  Political Life in Western Europe, 500–1000
  Society and the Church, 500–1000
  Accelerating Change in the West, 1000–1300
  Europe Outward Bound: The Crusading Tradition
The West in Comparative Perspective
  Catching Up
  Pluralism in Politics
  Reason and Faith
Reflections: Remembering and Forgetting: Continuity and Surprise in the Worlds of Christendom
Considering the Evidence
  Documents: The Making of Christian Europe . . . and a Chinese Counterpoint
  Visual Sources: Reading Byzantine Icons

"We embraced each other once, then again and again. We were like brothers meeting after a long separation."[1] That is how the Eastern Orthodox patriarch Athenagoras described his historic meeting with Roman Catholic Pope Paul VI in early 1964 near the Mount of Olives in Jerusalem, the very site where Jesus had spent the night before his arrest. Not for more than 500 years had the heads of these two ancient branches of Christianity personally met. Now they held each other and exchanged gifts, including a representation of two of Christ's disciples embracing. Then they lifted mutual decrees of excommunication that representatives of their respective churches had imposed almost a thousand years earlier. It was a small step in a still very incomplete process of overcoming this deep rift within Christianity, which had been in the making for well over a millennium. How had the world of Christendom come to be so sharply divided, religiously, politically, and in terms of the larger historical trajectories of its eastern and western halves?

DURING THE POSTCLASSICAL ERA, CHRISTIANITY PROVIDED a measure of cultural commonality for the diverse societies of western Eurasia, much as Chinese civilization and Buddhism did for East Asia. By 1300, almost all of these societies—from Spain and England in the west to Russia in the east—had embraced in some form the teachings of the Jewish carpenter called Jesus, but the world of European Christendom was deeply divided in a way that the Chinese world was not. Its eastern half, known as the Byzantine

Charlemagne: This fifteenth-century manuscript painting depicts Charlemagne, King of the Franks, who was crowned Emperor by the pope in 800 C.E. His reign illustrates the close and sometimes conflicted relationship of political and religious authorities in postclassical Europe. It also represents the futile desire of many in Western Europe to revive the old Roman Empire, even as a substantially new civilization was taking shape in the aftermath of the Roman collapse several centuries earlier. (Victoria & Albert Museum, London, UK/The Bridgeman Art Library)

Empire or Byzantium, encompassed much of the eastern Mediterranean basin while continuing the traditions of the Roman Empire, though on a smaller scale, until its conquest by the Muslim Ottoman Empire in 1453. Centered on the magnificent city of Constantinople, Byzantium gradually evolved a distinctive civilization, all the while claiming to be Roman and seeking to preserve the heritage of the classical Mediterranean. With a particular form of Christianity known as Eastern Orthodoxy, the Byzantine Empire housed one of the major third-wave civilizations.

In Western or Latin Christendom, encompassing what we now know as Western Europe, political and religious leaders also tried to maintain links to the classical world, as illustrated by the spread of Christianity, the use of Latin in elite circles, and various efforts to revive or imitate the Roman Empire. The setting, however, was far different. In the West, the Roman imperial order had largely vanished by 500 C.E., accompanied by the weakening of many features of Roman civilization. Roads fell into disrepair, cities decayed, and long-distance trade shriveled. What replaced the old Roman order was a highly localized society—fragmented, decentralized, and competitive—in sharp contrast to the unified state of Byzantium. Like Byzantium, the Latin West ultimately became thoroughly Christian, but it was a gradual process lasting centuries, and its Roman Catholic Church, increasingly centered on the pope, had an independence from political authorities that the Eastern Orthodox Church did not. Moreover, the western church in particular and its society in general were far more rural than Byzantium and certainly had nothing to compare to the splendor of Constantinople. However, slowly at first and then with increasing speed after 1000, Western Europe emerged as an especially dynamic, expansive, and innovative third-wave civilization, combining elements of its classical past with the culture of Germanic and Celtic peoples to produce a distinctive hybrid, or blended, civilization.

Europe eventually became the global center of Christianity, but that destiny was far from clear in 500 C.E. At that time, only about one-third of the world's Christians lived in Europe, while the rest found their homes in various parts of Africa, the Middle East, and Asia.[2] There they often followed alternate forms of Christianity, such as Nestorianism, which was regarded as heretical in Europe for its distinctive understanding of the nature of Christ. In Egypt, India, and Persia, remnants of these earlier and larger Christian communities have survived as tolerated minorities into the present. By contrast, in early Armenia and Ethiopia (Axum), Christianity became the faith of the majority and has continued to express the national identity of peoples long cut off from contact with other Christian societies. (See Document 7.3, pp. 310–12 for the coming of Christianity to Axum in East Africa.) Finally, the early Christian communities of North Africa, Nubia, Central Asia, and western China largely vanished as these regions subsequently embraced alternative religious traditions, such as Islam, Buddhism, or Confucianism. (See Document 10.6, pp. 462–64, on the brief flourishing of Nestorian Christianity in China.) In this chapter, however, the historical spotlight falls on those regions that became the center of the Christian world—Byzantium and Western Europe.

Eastern Christendom: Building on the Roman Past

Unlike most empires, Byzantium has no clear starting point. Its own leaders, as well as its neighbors and enemies, viewed it as simply a continuation of the Roman Empire. Some historians date its beginning to 330 C.E., when the Roman emperor Constantine, who became a Christian during his reign, established a new capital, Constantinople, on the site of an ancient Greek city called Byzantium. At the end of that century, the Roman Empire was formally divided into eastern and western halves, thus launching a division of Christendom that has lasted into the twenty-first century. Although the western Roman Empire collapsed during the fifth century, the eastern half persisted for another thousand years. Housing the ancient civilizations of Egypt, Greece, Syria, and Anatolia, the eastern Roman Empire (Byzantium) was far wealthier, more urbanized, and more cosmopolitan than its western counterpart; it possessed a much more defensible capital in the heavily walled city of Constantinople; and it had a shorter frontier to guard. Byzantium also enjoyed access to the Black Sea and command of the eastern Mediterranean. With a stronger army, navy, and merchant marine as well as clever diplomacy, its leaders were able to deflect the Germanic and Hun invaders who had overwhelmed the western Roman Empire.

Much that was late Roman—its roads, taxation system, military structures, centralized administration, imperial court, laws, Christian church—persisted in the east for many centuries. Like Tang dynasty China seeking to restore the glory of the Han era, Byzantium consciously sought to preserve the legacy of classical civilization and the Roman Empire. Constantinople was to be a "New Rome," and Byzantines referred to themselves as "Romans." Fearing contamination by "barbarian" customs, emperors forbade the residents of Constantinople from wearing boots, trousers, clothing made from animal skins, and long hairstyles, all of which were associated with

■ Continuity and Change
In what respects did Byzantium continue the patterns of the classical Roman Empire? In what ways did it diverge from those patterns?

in their form of government and also they way they dress and in much of the country's infostructure. taxation methods and military stocture

Snapshot Key Moments in Byzantine History	
Founding of Constantinople	330
Final division of Roman Empire into eastern and western halves	ca. 395
Reign of Justinian; attempted reconquest of western empire	527–565
Loss of Syria/Palestine, Egypt, and North Africa to Arab forces	7th century
Iconoclastic controversy	726–843
Conversion of Vladimir, prince of Kiev, to Christianity	988
Mutual excommunication of pope and patriarch	1054
Crusaders sack Constantinople	1204
Ottomans seize Constantinople; end of Byzantine Empire	1453

Germanic peoples, and insisted instead on Roman-style robes and sandals. But much changed as well over the centuries, marking the Byzantine Empire as the home of a distinctive civilization.

The Byzantine State

Perhaps the most obvious change was one of scale, as the Byzantine Empire never approximated the size of its Roman predecessor (see Map 10.1). The western Roman Empire was permanently lost to Byzantium, despite Emperor Justinian's (reigned 527–565) impressive but short-lived attempt to reconquer the Mediterranean basin. The rapid Arab/Islamic expansion in the seventh century resulted in the loss of Syria/Palestine, Egypt, and North Africa. Nonetheless, until roughly 1200, a more compact Byzantine Empire remained a major force in the eastern Mediterranean, controlling Greece, much of the Balkans (southeastern Europe), and Anatolia. A reformed administrative system gave appointed generals civil authority in the empire's

Map 10.1   The Byzantine Empire
The Byzantine Empire reached its greatest extent under Emperor Justinian in the mid-sixth century C.E. It subsequently lost considerable territory to various Christian European powers as well as to Muslim Arab and Turkic invaders.

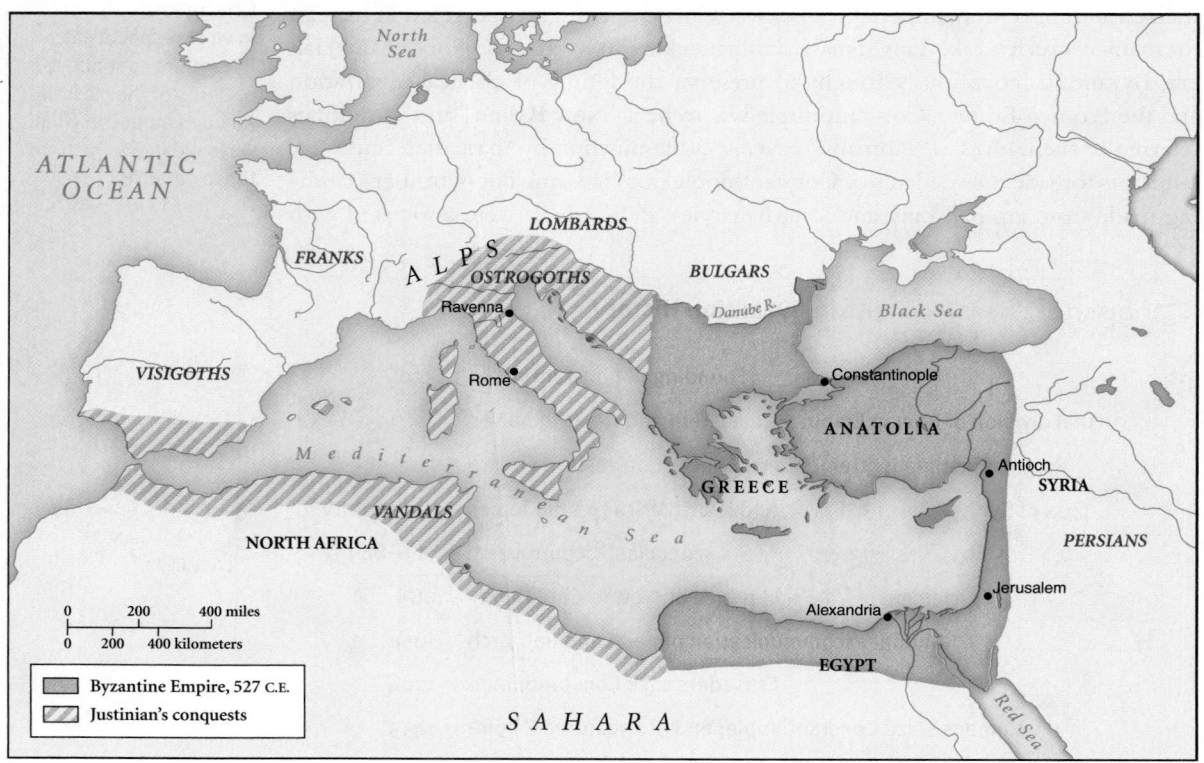

provinces and allowed them to raise armies from the landowning peasants of the region. From that territorial base, the empire's naval and merchant vessels were active in both the Mediterranean and Black seas.

In its heyday, the Byzantine state was an impressive creation. Political authority remained tightly centralized in Constantinople, where the emperor claimed to govern all creation as God's worldly representative, styling himself the "peer of the Apostles" and the "sole ruler of the world." The imperial court tried to imitate the awesome grandeur of what they thought was God's heavenly court, but in fact it resembled ancient Persian imperial splendor. Aristocrats trained in classical Greek rhetoric and literature took jobs in the administration in order to participate in court ceremonies that maintained their elite status. Parades of these silk-clad administrators added splendor to the imperial court, which also included mechanical lions that roared, birds that sang, and an immense throne that quickly elevated the emperor high above his presumably awestruck visitors. Nonetheless, this centralized state touched only lightly on the lives of most people, as it focused primarily on collecting taxes, maintaining order, and suppressing revolts. "Personal freedom in the provinces was constrained more by neighbors and rival households," concluded one historian, "than by the imperial government."[3]

After 1085, Byzantine territory shrank, owing to incursions by aggressive Western European powers, by Catholic Crusaders, and later by Turkic Muslim invaders. The end came in 1453 when the Turkic Ottoman Empire, then known as the "sword of Islam," finally took Constantinople. One eyewitness to the event wrote a moving lament to his fallen city:

> And the entire city was to be seen in the tents of the [Turkish] camp, the city deserted, lying lifeless, naked, soundless, without either form or beauty. O city, head of all cities, center of the four corners of the world, pride of the Romans, civilizer of the barbarians.... Where is your beauty, O paradise...? Where are the bodies of the Apostle of my Lord...? Where are the relics of the saints, those of the martyrs? Where are the remains of Constantine the Great and the other emperors?... Oh, what a loss![4]

The Byzantine Church and Christian Divergence

Intimately tied to the state was the Church, a relationship that became known as caesaropapism. Unlike Western Europe, where the Roman Catholic Church maintained some degree of independence from political authorities, in Byzantium the emperor assumed something of the role of both "caesar," as head of state, and the pope, as head of the Church. Thus he appointed the patriarch, or leader, of the Orthodox Church; sometimes made decisions about doctrine; called church councils into session; and generally treated the Church as a government department. "The [Empire] and the church have a great unity and community," declared a twelfth-century patriarch. "Indeed they cannot be separated."[5] A dense network of bishops and priests brought the message of the Church to every corner of the empire, while numerous

■ **Comparison**
How did Eastern Orthodox Christianity differ from Roman Catholicism?

monasteries accommodated holy men, whose piety, self-denial, and good works made them highly influential among both elite and ordinary people.

Eastern Orthodox Christianity had a pervasive influence on every aspect of Byzantine life. It legitimated the supreme and absolute rule of the emperor, for he was a God-anointed ruler, a reflection of the glory of God on earth. It also provided a cultural identity for the empire's subjects. Even more than being "Roman," they were orthodox, or "right-thinking," Christians for whom the empire and the Church were equally essential to achieving eternal salvation. Constantinople was filled with churches and the relics of numerous saints. And the churches were filled with icons—religious paintings of Jesus, Mary, and the other saints—some of them artistic masterpieces, that many believed conveyed the divine presence to believers. (For more on icons, see Visual Sources: Reading Byzantine Icons, pp. 466–71.) Complex theological issues about the Trinity and especially about the relationship of God and Jesus engaged the attention of ordinary people. One fourth-century bishop complained: "I wish to know the price of bread; one answers 'The Father is greater than the Son.' I inquire whether my bath is ready; one answers 'The Son has been made out of nothing.' "[6] Partisans of competing chariot-racing teams, known as the Greens and the Blues, vigorously debated theological issues as well as the merits of their favorite drivers.

St. Mark's Basilica Consecrated in 1094, this ornate cathedral, although located in Venice, Italy, is a classic example of Byzantine architecture. Such churches represented perhaps the greatest achievement of Byzantine art and were certainly the most monumental expressions of Byzantine culture. (Erich Lessing/Art Resource, NY)

In its early centuries and beyond, the Christian movement was rent by theological controversy and political division. Followers of Arius, an Egyptian priest, held that Jesus had been created by God the Father rather than living eternally with Him. Nestorius, the fifth-century bishop of Constantinople, argued that Mary had given birth only to the human Jesus, who then became the "temple" of God. This view, defined as heretical in the western Christian world, predominated in a separate Persian church, which spread its views to India, China, and Arabia.

But the most lasting and deepest division within the Christian world occurred as Eastern Orthodoxy came to define itself against an emerging Latin Christianity centered on papal Rome. Both had derived, of course, from the growth of Christianity in the Roman Empire and therefore had much in common—the teachings of Jesus; the Bible; the sacraments; a church hierarchy of patriarchs, bishops, and priests; a missionary impulse; and intolerance toward other religions. Despite these shared features, any sense of a single widespread Christian community was increasingly replaced by an awareness of difference, competition, and outright hostility that even a common fear of Islam could not overcome. In part, this growing religious divergence reflected the political separation and rivalry between the Byzantine Empire and the emerging kingdoms of Western Europe. As the growth of Islam in the seventh century (described more fully in Chapter 11) submerged earlier centers of Christianity in the Middle East and North Africa, Constantinople and Rome alone remained as alternative hubs of the Church. But they were now in different states that competed with each other for territory and for the right to claim the legacy of imperial Rome.

Beyond such political differences were those of language and culture. Although Latin remained the language of the Church and of elite communication in the West, it was abandoned in the Byzantine Empire in favor of Greek, which remained the basis for Byzantine education. More than in the West, Byzantine thinkers sought to formulate Christian doctrine in terms of Greek philosophical concepts.

Differences in theology and church practice likewise widened the gulf between Orthodoxy and Catholicism, despite agreement on fundamental doctrines. Disagreements about the nature of the Trinity, the source of the Holy Spirit, original sin, and the relative importance of faith and reason gave rise to much controversy. So too for a time did the Byzantine efforts to prohibit the use of icons, popular paintings of saints and biblical scenes, usually painted on small wooden panels. (See Visual Sources: Reading Byzantine Icons, pp. 466–71.) Other more modest differences also occasioned mutual misunderstanding and disdain. Priests in the West shaved and, after 1050 or so, were supposed to remain celibate, while those in Byzantium allowed their beards to grow long and were permitted to marry. Orthodox ritual called for using bread leavened with yeast in the Communion, but Catholics used unleavened bread. Far more significant was the question of authority. Eastern Orthodox leaders sharply rejected the growing claims of Roman popes to be the sole and final authority for all Christians everywhere.

The rift in the world of Christendom grew gradually from the seventh century on, punctuated by various efforts to bridge the mounting divide between the western and eastern branches of the Church. A sign of this continuing deterioration occurred in 1054 when representatives of both churches mutually excommunicated each other, declaring in effect that those in the opposing tradition were not true Christians. The Crusades, launched in 1095 by the Catholic pope against the forces of Islam, made things worse. Western Crusaders, passing through the Byzantine Empire on their way to the Middle East, engaged in frequent conflict with local people and thus deepened the distrust between them. From the western viewpoint, Orthodox practices were "blasphemous, even heretical." One western observer of the Second Crusade noted that the Greeks "were judged not to be Christians and the Franks [French] considered killing them a matter of no importance."[7] During the Fourth Crusade in 1204, western forces seized and looted Constantinople and ruled Byzantium for the next half century. Their brutality only confirmed Byzantine views of their Roman Catholic despoilers as nothing more than barbarians. According to one Byzantine account, "they sacked the sacred places and trampled on divine things . . . they tore children from their mothers . . . and they defiled virgins in the holy chapels, fearing neither God's anger nor man's vengeance."[8] After this, the rupture in the world of Christendom proved irreparable.

Byzantium and the World

■ Connection

In what ways was the Byzantine Empire linked to a wider world?

Beyond its tense relationship with Western Europe, the Byzantine Empire, located astride Europe and Asia, also interacted intensively with its other neighbors. On a political and military level, Byzantium continued the long-term Roman struggle with the Persian Empire. That persisting conflict weakened both of them and was one factor in the remarkable success of Arab armies as they poured out of Arabia in the seventh century. Although Persia quickly became part of the Islamic world, Byzantium held out, even as it lost considerable territory to the Arabs. A Byzantine military innovation, known as "Greek fire"—a potent and flammable combination of oil, sulfur, and lime that was launched from bronze tubes—helped to hold off the Arabs. It operated something like a flamethrower and subsequently passed into Arab and Chinese arsenals as well. Byzantium's ability to defend its core regions delayed for many centuries the Islamic advance into southeastern Europe, which finally occurred at the hands of the Turkish Ottoman Empire in the fifteenth and sixteenth centuries.

Economically, the Byzantine Empire was a central player in the long-distance trade of Eurasia, with commercial links to Western Europe, Russia, Central Asia, the Islamic world, and China. Its gold coin, the bezant, was a widely used currency in the Mediterranean basin for more than 500 years, and wearing such coins as pendants was a high-status symbol in the less developed kingdoms of Western Europe.[9] The luxurious products of Byzantine craftspeople—jewelry, gemstones, silver and gold work, linen and woolen textiles, purple dyes—were much in demand. Its silk industry, based on Chinese technology, supplied much of the Mediterranean basin with this precious fabric.

The cultural influence of Byzantium was likewise significant. Preserving much of ancient Greek learning, the Byzantine Empire transmitted this classical heritage to the Islamic world as well as to the Christian West. In both places, it had an immensely stimulating impact among scientists, philosophers, theologians, and other intellectuals. Some saw it as an aid to faith and to an understanding of the world, while others feared it as impious and distracting. (See the section "Reason and Faith" later in this chapter.)

Byzantine religious culture also spread widely among Slavic-speaking peoples in the Balkans and Russia. As lands to the south and the east were overtaken by Islam, Byzantium looked to the north. By the early eleventh century, steady military pressure had brought many of the Balkan Slavic peoples, especially the Bulgars, under Byzantine control. Christianity and literacy accompanied this Byzantine offensive. Already in the ninth century, two Byzantine missionaries, Cyril and Methodius, had developed an alphabet, based on Greek letters, with which Slavic languages could be written. This Cyrillic script made it possible to translate the Bible and other religious literature into these languages and greatly aided the process of conversion.

The Conversion of Russia

The most significant expansion of Orthodox Christianity occurred among the Slavic peoples of what is now Ukraine and western Russia. In this culturally diverse region, which also included Finnic and Baltic peoples as well as Viking traders, a modest state known as Kievan Rus—named after the most prominent city, Kiev—emerged in the ninth century C.E. Like many of the new third-wave civilizations, the development of Rus was stimulated by trade, in this case along the Dnieper River, linking Scandinavia and Byzantium. Loosely led by various princes, especially the prince of Kiev, Rus was a society of slaves and freemen, privileged people and commoners, dominant men and subordinate women. This stratification marked it as a third-wave civilization in the making (see Map 10.3 on page 439).

Religion reflected the region's cultural diversity, with the gods and practices of many peoples much in evidence. Ancestral spirits, household deities, and various gods related to the forces of nature were in evidence with Perun, the god of thunder, perhaps the most prominent. Small numbers of Christians, Muslims, and Jews were likewise part of the mix. Then, in the late tenth century, a decisive turning point occurred. The growing interaction of Rus with the larger world prompted Prince Vladimir of Kiev to affiliate with one of the major religions of the area. He was searching for a faith that would unify the diverse peoples of his region, while linking Rus into wider networks of communication and exchange. According to ancient chronicles, he actively considered Judaism, Islam, Roman Catholicism, and Greek Orthodoxy before finally deciding on the religion of Byzantium. He rejected Islam, the chronicles tell us, because it prohibited alcoholic drink and "drinking is the joy of the Russes." The splendor of Constantinople's Orthodox churches apparently captured the imagination of Rus's envoys, for there, they reported, "[W]e knew not whether we were in heaven or on earth."[10] Political and commercial considerations no doubt also played a role in Vladimir's decision, and he acquired a sister of the Byzantine emperor as his bride, along with numerous Byzantine priests and advisers. Whatever the precise process, it was a freely made decision. Eastern Orthodox Christianity thus came to Rus without the pressure of foreign military defeat or occupation. Eventually, it took deep root among the Russian people.

It was a fateful choice with long-term implications for Russian history, for it brought this fledgling civilization firmly into the world of Orthodox Christianity, separating it from both the realm of Islam and the Roman Catholic West. Like many new civilizations, Rus borrowed extensively from its older and more sophisticated neighbor. Among these borrowings were Byzantine architectural styles, the Cyrillic alphabet, the extensive use of icons, a monastic tradition stressing prayer and service, and political ideals of imperial control of the Church, all of which became part of a

■ **Connection**

How did links to Byzantium transform the new civilization of Kievan Rus?

transformed Rus. Orthodoxy also provided a more unified identity for this emerging civilization and religious legitimacy for its rulers. Centuries later, when Byzantium had fallen to the Turks, a few Russian church leaders proclaimed the doctrine of a "third Rome." The original Rome had betrayed the faith, and the second Rome, Constantinople, had succumbed to Muslim infidels. Moscow was now the third Rome, the final protector and defender of Orthodox Christianity. Though not widely proclaimed in Russia itself, such a notion reflected the "Russification" of Eastern Orthodoxy and its growing role as an element of Russian national identity. It was also a reminder of the enduring legacy of a thousand years of Byzantine history, long after the empire itself had vanished.

Western Christendom: Rebuilding in the Wake of Roman Collapse

The western half of the Christian world followed a rather different path than that of the Byzantine Empire. For much of the postclassical millennium, it was distinctly on the margins of world history, partly because of its geographic location at the far western end of the Eurasian landmass. Thus it was far removed from the growing routes of world trade—by sea in the Indian Ocean and by land across the Silk Roads to China and the Sand Roads to West Africa. Not until the Eastern and Western hemispheres were joined after 1500 did Western Europe occupy a geographically central position in the global network. Internally, Europe's geography made political unity difficult. It was a region in which population centers were divided by mountain ranges and dense forests as well as by five major peninsulas

Founding Constantinople 330 CE/AD
Final division of the Roman Empire 395 AD/CE

Snapshot Key Moments in the Evolution of Western Civilization

End of the western Roman Empire	476
Papacy of Gregory I	590–604
Muslim conquest of Spain	711
Charlemagne crowned as emperor	800
Otto I crowned as Holy Roman Emperor	962
Viking colony in Newfoundland	1000
Investiture conflict	1059–1152
Crusades begin	1095
Translations of Greek and Arab works available in Europe	12th–13th centuries
Thomas Aquinas	1225–1274
Marco Polo visits China	1271–1295

and two large islands (Britain and Ireland). However, its extensive coastlines and interior river systems facilitated exchange within Europe, while a moderate climate, plentiful rainfall, and fertile soils enabled a productive agriculture that could support a growing population.

Political Life in Western Europe, 500–1000

In the early centuries of the postclassical era, history must have seemed more significant than geography, for the Roman Empire, long a fixture of the western Mediterranean region, had collapsed. The traditional date marking the fall of Rome is 476, when the German general Odoacer overthrew the last Roman emperor in the West. In itself not very important, this event has come to symbolize a major turning point in the West, for much that had characterized Roman civilization also weakened, declined, or disappeared in the several centuries before and after 476. Any semblance of large-scale centralized rule vanished. Disease and warfare reduced Western Europe's population by more than 25 percent. Land under cultivation contracted, while forests, marshland, and wasteland expanded. Urban life too diminished sharply, as Europe reverted to a largely rural existence. Rome at its height was a city of 1 million people, but by the tenth century it numbered perhaps 10,000. Public buildings crumbled from lack of care. Outside Italy, long-distance trade dried up as Roman roads deteriorated, and money exchange gave way to barter in many places. Literacy lost ground as well. Germanic peoples, whom the Romans had viewed as barbarians—Goths, Visigoths, Franks, Lombards, Angles, Saxons—now emerged as the dominant peoples of Western Europe. In the process, Europe's center of gravity moved away from the Mediterranean toward the north and west.

Yet much that was classical or Roman persisted, even as a new order emerged in Europe. On the political front, a series of regional kingdoms—led by Visigoths in Spain, Franks in France, Lombards in Italy, and Angles and Saxons in England— arose to replace Roman authority, but many of these Germanic peoples, originally organized in small kinship-based tribes with strong warrior values, had already been substantially Romanized. Contact with the Roman Empire in the first several centuries C.E. had generated more distinct ethnic identities among them, militarized their societies, and gave greater prominence to Woden, their god of war. As Germanic peoples migrated into or invaded Roman lands, many were deeply influenced by Roman culture, especially if they served in the Roman army. On the funeral monument of one such person was the telling inscription: "I am a Frank by nationality, but a Roman soldier under arms."[11]

The prestige of things Roman remained high, even after the empire itself had collapsed. Now as leaders of their own kingdoms, the Germanic rulers actively embraced written Roman law, using fines and penalties to provide order and justice in their new states in place of feuds and vendettas. One Visigoth ruler named Athaulf (reigned 410–415), who had married a Roman noblewoman, gave voice to the continuing attraction of Roman culture and its empire.

■ **Comparison**

How did the historical development of the European West differ from that of Byzantium in the postclassical era?

They could interact with the far eastern world mainly because of the geographical disposition but they could exchange goods and interact politically and militarily with the rest of Western Europe cause of it coast lines and rivers

■ **Change**

What replaced the Roman order in Western Europe?

At first I wanted to erase the Roman name and convert all Roman territory into a Gothic empire. . . . But long experience has taught me that . . . without law a state is not a state. Therefore I have more prudently chosen the different glory of reviving the Roman name with Gothic vigour, and I hope to be acknowledged by posterity as the initiator of a Roman restoration.[12]

Several of the larger, though relatively short-lived, Germanic kingdoms also had aspirations to re-create something of the unity of the Roman Empire. Charlemagne (reigned 768–814), ruler of the Carolingian Empire, occupying what is now France, Belgium, the Netherlands, and parts of Germany and Italy, erected an embryonic imperial bureaucracy, standardized weights and measures, and began to act like an imperial ruler (see Document 10.3, pp. 458–60). On Christmas Day of the year 800, he was crowned as a new Roman emperor by the pope, although his realm splintered shortly after his death (see Map 10.2). Later Otto I of Saxony (reigned 936–973) gathered much of Germany under his control, saw himself as renewing Roman rule, and was likewise invested with the title of emperor by the pope. Otto's realm, subsequently known as the Holy Roman Empire, was largely limited to Germany and soon proved little more than a collection of quarreling principalities. Though unsuccessful in reviving anything approaching Roman imperial authority, these efforts testify to the continuing appeal of the classical world, even as a new political system of rival kingdoms blended Roman and Germanic elements.

Map 10.2 Western Europe in the Ninth Century Charlemagne's Carolingian Empire brought a temporary unity to parts of Western Europe, but it was subsequently divided among his three sons, who waged war on one another.

The Carolingian Empire in the Ninth Century C.E.

- ■ Kingdom of Charles the Bald
- ■ Kingdom of Louis the German
- ■ Kingdom of Lothar
- —— Charlemagne's territory

NORWAY
SWEDEN
NORTHUMBRIA
DENMARK
North Sea
Baltic Sea
SAXONY
ATLANTIC OCEAN
Aachen
NORMANDY
Rhine R.
MAGYARS
Danube R.
UMAYYAD CALIPHATE OF SPAIN
Ebro R.
PAPAL STATES
Adriatic Sea
DUCHY OF BENEVENTO
Mediterranean Sea
BYZANTINE EMPIRE
MUSLIM-RULED NORTH AFRICA

0   150   300 miles
0   150   300 kilometers

Society and the Church, 500–1000

Within these new kingdoms, a highly fragmented and decentralized society widely known as feudalism emerged with great local variation. In thousands of independent, self-sufficient, and largely isolated landed estates or manors, power—political, economic, and social—was exercised by a warrior elite of landowning lords. In the constant competition of these centuries, lesser lords and knights swore allegiance to greater lords or kings and thus became their vassals, frequently receiving lands and plunder in return for military service.

Such reciprocal ties between superior and subordinate were also apparent at the bottom of the social hierarchy, as Roman-style slavery gradually gave way to serfdom. Unlike slaves, serfs were not the personal property of their masters, could not be arbitrarily thrown off their land, and were allowed to live in families. However, they were bound to their masters' estates as peasant laborers and owed various payments and services to the lord of the manor. One family on a manor near Paris in the ninth century owed four silver coins, wine, wood, three hens, and fifteen eggs per year. Women generally were required to weave cloth and make clothing for the lord, while men labored in the lord's fields. In return, the serf family received a small farm and such protection as the lord could provide. In a violent and insecure world adjusting to the absence of Roman authority, the only security available to many individuals or families lay in these communities, where the ties to kin, manor, and lord constituted the primary human loyalties. It was a world apart from the stability of life in imperial Rome or its continuation in Byzantium.

Also filling the vacuum left by the collapse of empire was the Church, later known as Roman Catholic, yet another link to the now defunct Roman world. Its hierarchical organization of popes, bishops, priests, and monasteries was modeled on that of the Roman Empire and took over some of its political, administrative, educational, and welfare functions. Latin continued as the language of the Church even as it gave way to various vernacular languages in common speech. In fact literacy in the classical languages of Greek and Latin remained the hallmark of educated people in the West well into the twentieth century.

Like the Buddhist establishment in China, the Church subsequently became extremely wealthy, with reformers often accusing it of forgetting its central spiritual mission. It also provided a springboard for the conversion of Europe's many "pagan" peoples. Numerous missionaries, commissioned by the pope, monasteries, or already converted rulers, fanned out across Europe, generally pursuing a "top-down" strategy. Frequently it worked, as local kings and warlords found status and legitimacy in association with a literate and "civilized" religion that still bore something of the grandeur of Rome. With "the wealth and protection of the powerful," ordinary people followed their rulers into the fold of the Church.[13] This process was similar to Buddhism's appeal for the nomadic rulers of northern and western China following the collapse of the Han dynasty. Christianity, like Buddhism, also bore the promise of superior supernatural powers, and its spread was frequently associated with reported miracles of healing, rainfall, fertility, and victory in battle.

But it was not an easy sell. Outright coercion was sometimes part of the process, as Document 10.3 (pp. 458–60) clearly shows. More often, however, softer methods prevailed. The Church proved willing to accommodate a considerable range of earlier cultural practices, absorbing them into an emerging Christian tradition. For example, amulets and charms to ward off evil became medals with the image of Jesus or the Virgin Mary, traditionally sacred wells and springs became the sites of churches, and festivals honoring ancient gods became Christian holy days. December 25 was selected as the birthday of Jesus, for it was associated with the winter solstice, the coming of more light, and the birth or rebirth of various deities in pre-Christian European traditions. By 1100, most of Europe had embraced Christianity. Even so, priests and bishops had to warn their congregations against the worship of rivers, trees, and mountains, and for many people, ancient gods, monsters, trolls, and spirits still inhabited the land. The spreading Christian faith, like the new political framework of European civilization, was a blend of many elements. (For more on the rooting of Christianity in Western Europe, see Documents 10.1–10.5, pp. 455–61.)

Church authorities and the nobles/warriors who exercised political influence reinforced each other. Rulers provided protection for the papacy and strong encouragement for the faith. In return, the Church offered religious legitimacy for the powerful and the prosperous. "It is the will of the Creator," declared the teaching of the Church, "that the higher shall always rule over the lower. Each individual and class should stay in its place [and] perform its tasks."[14] But Church and nobility competed as well as cooperated, for they were rival centers of power in post-Roman Europe. Particularly controversial was the right to appoint bishops and the pope himself; this issue, known as the investiture conflict, was especially prominent in the eleventh and twelfth centuries. Was the right to make appointments the responsibility of the Church alone, or did kings and emperors also have a role? In the compromise that ended the conflict, the Church won the right to appoint its own officials, while secular rulers retained an informal and symbolic role in the process.

Accelerating Change in the West, 1000–1300

The pace of change in this emerging civilization picked up considerably in the several centuries after 1000. For the preceding 300 years, Europe had been subject to repeated invasions from every direction. Muslim armies had conquered Spain and threatened the rest of Europe. Magyar (Hungarian) invasions from the east and Viking incursions from the north likewise disrupted and threatened post-Roman Europe (see Map 10.3). But by the year 1000, these invasions had been checked and the invaders absorbed into settled society. The greater security and stability that came with relative peace arguably opened the way to an accelerating tempo of change. The climate also seemed to cooperate. A generally warming trend after 750 reached its peak in the eleventh and twelfth centuries, enhancing agricultural production.

■ Change

In what ways was European civilization changing after 1000?

Whatever may have launched this new phase of European civilization, commonly called the High Middle Ages (1000–1300), the signs of expansion and growth were widely evident. The population of Europe grew from perhaps 35 million in 1000 to about 80 million in 1340. With more people, many new lands were opened for cultivation in a process paralleling that of China's expansion to the south at the same time. Great lords, bishops, and religious orders organized new villages on what had recently been forest or wasteland. Marshes were drained; land was reclaimed from the sea in the Netherlands; everywhere trees were felled. By 1300, the forest cover of Europe had been reduced to about 20 percent of the land area. "I believe

Map 10.3 Europe in the High Middle Ages

By the eleventh century, the national monarchies—of France, Spain, England, Poland, and Germany—that would organize European political life had begun to take shape. The earlier external attacks on Europe from Vikings, Magyars, and Muslims had largely ceased, although it was clear that European civilization was developing in the shadow of the Islamic world.

that the forest . . . covers the land to no purpose," declared a German abbot, "and hold this to be an unbearable harm."[15]

The increased production associated with this agricultural expansion stimulated a considerable growth in long-distance trade, much of which had dried up in the aftermath of the Roman collapse. One center of commercial activity lay in Northern

Europe from England to the Baltic coast and involved the exchange of wood, beeswax, furs, rye, wheat, salt, cloth, and wine. The other major trading network centered on northern Italian towns such as Florence, Genoa, and Venice. Their trading partners were the more established civilizations of Islam and Byzantium, and the primary objects of trade included the silks, drugs, precious stones, and spices from Asia. At great trading fairs, particularly those in the Champagne area of France near Paris, merchants from Northern and Southern Europe met to exchange the products of their respective areas, such as northern woolens for Mediterranean spices. Thus the self-sufficient communities of earlier centuries increasingly forged commercial bonds among themselves and with more distant peoples.

The population of towns and cities likewise grew on the sites of older Roman towns, at trading crossroads and fortifications, and around cathedrals all over Europe. Some had only a few hundred people, but others became much larger. In the early 1300s, London had about 40,000 people, Paris had approximately 80,000, and Venice by the end of the fourteenth century could boast perhaps 150,000. To keep these figures in perspective, Constantinople housed some 400,000 people in 1000, Córdoba in Muslim Spain about 500,000, the Song dynasty capital of Hangzhou more than 1 million in the thirteenth century, and the Aztec capital of Tenochtitlán perhaps 200,000 by 1500. Nonetheless, urbanization was proceeding apace in Europe. These towns gave rise to and attracted new groups of people, particularly merchants, bankers, artisans, and university-trained professionals such as lawyers, doctors, and scholars. Many of these groups, including university professors and students, organized themselves into guilds (associations of people pursuing the same line of work) in order to regulate their respective professions. In doing so, they introduced a new and more productive division of labor into European society.

Between the eleventh and thirteenth centuries, economic growth and urbanization offered European women substantial new opportunities. Women were active in a number of urban professions, such as weaving, brewing, milling grain, midwifery, small-scale retailing, laundering, spinning, and prostitution. In twelfth-century Paris, for example, a list of 100 occupations identified 86 as involving women workers, of which 6 were exclusively female. In England, women worked as silk weavers, hatmakers, tailors, brewers, and leather processors and were entitled to train female apprentices in some of these trades. In Frankfurt, about one-third of the crafts and trades were entirely female, another 40 percent were dominated by men, and the rest were open to both. Widows of great merchants sometimes continued their husbands' businesses, and one of them, Rose Burford, lent a large sum of money to the king of England to finance a war against Scotland in 1318.

By the fifteenth century, such opportunities were declining. Most women's guilds were gone, and women were restricted or banned from many others. Even brothels were run by men. Technological progress may have been one reason for this change. Water- and animal-powered grain mills replaced the hand-grinding previously undertaken by women, and larger looms making heavier cloth replaced the

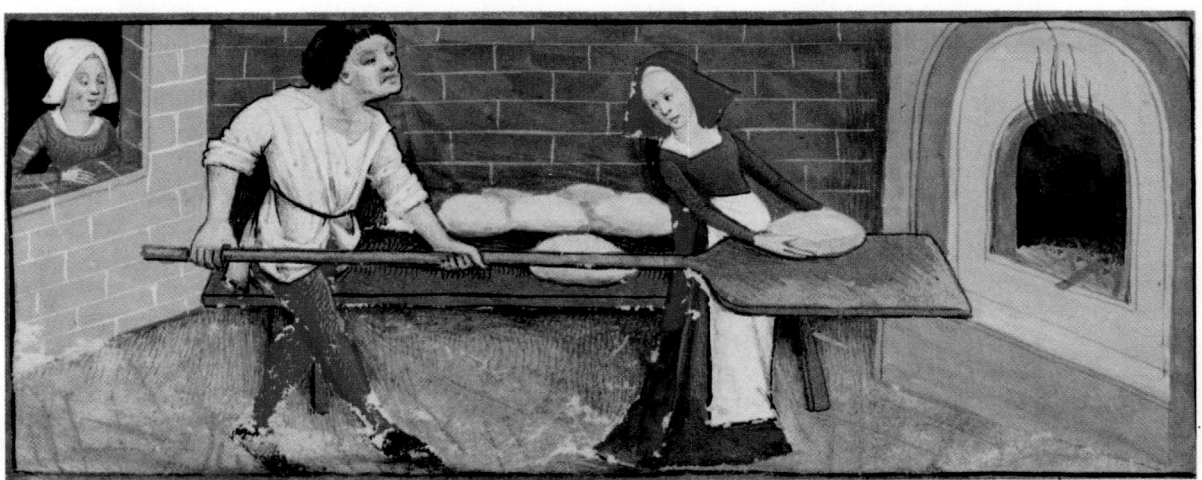

lighter looms that women had worked. Men increasingly took over these profes-sions and trained their sons as apprentices, making it more difficult for women to remain active in these fields.

European Women at Work This manuscript painting from the Middle Ages shows women and men cooperating in the baking of bread, long a staple of European diets. (Bibliothèque nationale de France)

If urban work roles were diminishing for women, religious life provided other possibilities. As in Buddhist lands, substantial numbers of women, particularly from aristocratic families, were attracted to the secluded life of poverty, chastity, and obedience within a nunnery for the relative freedom from male control that it offered. Here was one of the few places where some women could exercise authority and obtain a measure of education. Operating outside of monastic life, the Beguines were groups of laywomen, often from poorer families in Northern Europe, who lived together, practiced celibacy, and devoted themselves to weav-ing and to working with the sick, the old, and the poor. Another religious role was that of anchoress, a woman who withdrew to a locked cell, usually attached to a church, where she devoted herself to prayer and fasting. Some of them gained reputations for great holiness and were much sought after for spiritual guidance. For a few women—the nun Hildegard of Bingen and the anchoress Julian of Norwich, for example—religious life brought considerable public prominence and spiritual influence.

A further sign of accelerating change in the West lay in the growth of territo-rial states with more effective institutions of government commanding the loyalty, or at least the obedience, of their subjects. Since the disintegration of the Roman Empire, Europeans' loyalties had focused on the family, the manor, or the religious community, but seldom on the state. Great lords may have been recognized as kings, but their authority was extremely limited and was exercised through a complex and decentralized network of feudal relationships with earls, counts, barons, and knights, who often felt little obligation to do the king's bidding. But in the eleventh through the thirteenth century, the nominal monarchs of Europe gradually and painfully began to consolidate their authority, and the outlines of French, English, Spanish, Scandinavian, and other states began to appear, each with its own distinct language and culture (see Map 10.3). Royal courts and embryonic bureaucracies were established, and groups of professional administrators appeared. Territorial kingdoms were not universal, however. In Italy, city-states flourished as urban areas grew wealthy and powerful, whereas the Germans remained loyal to a large number of small principalities within the Holy Roman Empire.

Europe Outward Bound: The Crusading Tradition

■ **Change**
What was the impact of the Crusades in world history?

Accompanying the growth of European civilization after 1000 were efforts to engage more actively with both near and more distant neighbors. This "medieval expansion" of Western Christendom took place as the Byzantine world was contracting under pressure from the West, from Arab invasion, and later from Turkish conquest. The western half of Christendom was on the rise, while the eastern part was in decline. It was a sharp reversal of their earlier trajectories.

Expansion, of course, has been characteristic of virtually every civilization and has taken a variety of forms—territorial conquest, empire building, settlement of new lands, vigorous trading initiatives, and missionary activity. European civilization was no exception. As population mounted, settlers cleared new land, much of it on the eastern fringes of Europe. The Vikings of Scandinavia, having raided much of Europe, set off on a maritime transatlantic venture around 1000 that briefly established a colony in Newfoundland in North America, and more durably in Greenland and Iceland. As Western economies grew, merchants, travelers, diplomats, and missionaries brought European society into more intensive contact with more distant peoples and with Eurasian commercial networks. By the thirteenth and fourteenth centuries, Europeans had direct, though limited, contact with India, China, and Mongolia. Europe clearly was outward bound.

Nothing more dramatically revealed European expansiveness and the religious passions that informed it than the Crusades, a series of "holy wars" that captured the imagination of Western Christendom for more than four centuries, beginning in 1095. In European thinking and practice, the Crusades were wars undertaken at God's command and authorized by the pope as the Vicar of Christ on earth. They required participants to swear a vow and in return offered an indulgence, which removed the penalties for any confessed sins, as well as various material benefits, such as immunity from lawsuits and a moratorium on the repayment of debts. Any number of political, economic, and social motives underlay the Crusades, but at their core they were religious wars. Within Europe, the amazing support for the Crusades reflected an understanding of them "as providing security against mortal enemies threatening the spiritual health of all Christendom and all Christians."[16] Crusading drew upon both Christian piety and the warrior values of the elite, with little sense of contradiction between these impulses.

The most famous Crusades were those aimed at wresting Jerusalem and the holy places associated with the life of Jesus from Islamic control and returning them to Christendom (see Map 10.4). Beginning in 1095, wave after wave of Crusaders from all walks of life and many countries flocked to the eastern Mediterranean, where they temporarily carved out four small Christian states, the last of which was recaptured by Muslim forces in 1291. Led or supported by an assortment of kings, popes, bishops, monks, lords, nobles, and merchants, the Crusades demonstrated a growing European capacity for organization, finance, transportation, and recruitment, made all the more impressive by the absence of any centralized direction for the project. They also demonstrated considerable cruelty. The seizure of Jerusalem in 1099 was accompanied by the slaughter of many Muslims and Jews as the Crusaders made their way, according to perhaps exaggerated reports, through streets littered with corpses and ankle deep in blood to the tomb of Christ.

Map 10.4   The Crusades

Western Europe's crusading tradition reflected the expansive energy and religious impulses of an emerging civilization. It was directed against Muslims in the Middle East, Sicily, and Spain as well as the Eastern Orthodox Christians of the Byzantine Empire. The Crusades also involved attacks on Jewish communities, probably the first organized mass pogroms against Jews in Europe's history.

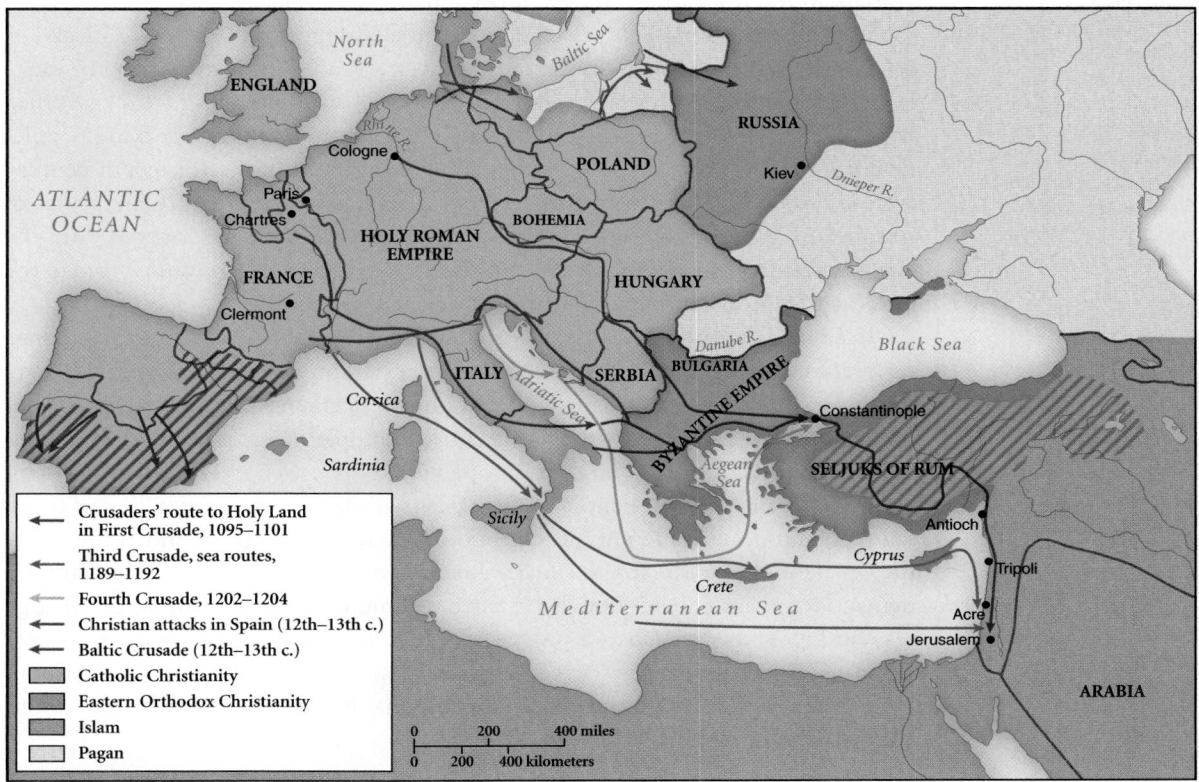

Christians and Muslims
This fourteenth-century painting illustrates the Christian seizure of Jerusalem during the First Crusade in 1099. The crowned figure in the center is Godefroi de Bouillon, a French knight and nobleman who played a prominent role in the attack and was briefly known as the king of Jerusalem. (Snark/Art Resource, NY)

Crusading was not limited to targets in the Islamic Middle East, however. Those Christians who waged war for centuries to reclaim the Iberian Peninsula from Muslim hands were likewise declared "crusaders," with a similar set of spiritual and material benefits. So too were Scandinavian and German warriors who took part in wars to conquer, settle, and convert lands along the Baltic Sea. The Byzantine Empire and Russia, both of which followed Eastern Orthodox Christianity, were also on the receiving end of Western crusading, as were Christian heretics and various enemies of the pope in Europe itself. Crusading, in short, was a pervasive feature of European expansion, which persisted as Europeans began their oceanic voyages in the fifteenth century and beyond.

Surprisingly perhaps, the Crusades had little lasting impact, either politically or religiously, in the Middle East. European power was not sufficiently strong or long-lasting to induce much conversion, and the small European footholds there had come under Muslim control by 1300. The penetration of Turkic-speaking peoples from Central Asia and the devastating Mongol invasions of the thirteenth century were far more significant in Islamic history than were the temporary incursions of European Christians. In fact, Muslims largely forgot about the Crusades until the late nineteenth and early twentieth centuries, when their memory was revived in the context of a growing struggle against European imperialism.

In Europe, however, interaction with the Islamic world had very significant long-term consequences. Spain, Sicily, and the Baltic region were brought permanently into the world of Western Christendom, while a declining Byzantium was further weakened by the Crusader sacking of Constantinople in 1204 and left even more vulnerable to Turkish conquest. In Europe itself, popes strengthened their position, at least for a time, in their continuing struggles with secular authorities. Tens of thousands of Europeans came into personal contact with the Islamic world, from which they picked up a taste for the many luxury goods available there, stimulating a demand for Asian goods. They also learned techniques for producing sugar on large plantations using slave labor, a process that had incalculable consequences in later centuries as Europeans transferred the plantation system to the Americas. Muslim scholarship, together with the Greek learning that it incorporated, also flowed into Europe, largely through Spain and Sicily.

If the cross-cultural contacts born of crusading opened channels of trade, technology transfer, and intellectual exchange, they also hardened cultural barriers between peoples. The rift between Eastern Orthodoxy and Roman Catholicism deepened further and remains to this day a fundamental divide in the Christian world. Christian anti-Semitism was both expressed and exacerbated as Crusaders on their way to Jerusalem found time to massacre Jews in a number of European cities. European empire building, especially in the Americas, continued the crusading notion that "God wills it." And more recently, over the past two centuries, as the world of the Christian West and that of Islam collided, both sides found many occasions in which images of the Crusades, however distorted, proved politically or ideologically useful.[17]

The West in Comparative Perspective

At one level, the making of Western civilization in the postclassical era was unremarkable. Civilizations had risen, fallen, renewed themselves, and evolved at many times and in many places. The European case has received extraordinary scrutiny, not so much because of its special significance at the time, but because of its later role as a globally dominant region. Historians have sometimes sought to account for Western Europe's global influence after 1500 in terms of some unique feature of its earlier history. However we might explain Europe's later rise to prominence on the world stage, its development in the several centuries after 1000 made only modest ripples beyond its own region. In some respects, Europe was surely distinctive, but it was not yet a major player in the global arena. Comparisons, particularly with China, help to place European developments in a world history context.

Catching Up

As the civilization of the West evolved, it was clearly less developed in comparison to Byzantium, China, India, and the Islamic world. European cities were smaller, its political authorities weaker, its economy less commercialized, its technology inferior to the more established civilizations. Muslim observers who encountered Europeans saw them as barbarians. An Arab geographer of the tenth century commented as follows: "Their bodies are large, their manners harsh, their understanding dull, and their tongues heavy. . . . Those of them who are farthest to the north are the most subject to stupidity, grossness and brutishness."[18] Muslim travelers over the next several centuries saw more to be praised in West African kingdoms, where Islam was practiced and gold was plentiful.

Furthermore, thoughtful Europeans who directly encountered other peoples often acknowledged their own comparative backwardness. "In our time," wrote a twelfth-century European scholar, "it is in Toledo [a Spanish city long under Muslim rule] that the teaching of the Arabs . . . is offered to the crowds. I hastened there to listen to the teaching of the wisest philosophers of this world."[19] The Italian traveler Marco Polo in the thirteenth century proclaimed Hangzhou in China "the finest and noblest [city] in the world." In the sixteenth century, Spanish invaders of Mexico were stunned at the size and wealth of the Aztec capital, especially its huge market, claiming that "we had never seen such a thing before."[20]

■ Change
In what ways did borrowing from abroad shape European civilization after 1000?

Curious about the rest of the world, Europeans proved quite willing to engage with and borrow from the more advanced civilizations to the east. Growing European economies, especially in the northwest, reconnected with the Eurasian trading system, with which they had lost contact after the fall of Rome. Now European elites eagerly sought spices, silks, porcelain, sugar, and much else that was available on the world market. Despite their belief in Christianity as the "one true religion," Europeans embraced scientific treatises and business practices from the Arabs, philosophical and artistic ideas from the pagan Greeks, and mathematical concepts from India. It was China, however, that was the most significant source of European borrowing, although often indirectly. From that East Asian civilization, Europeans learned about the compass, papermaking, gunpowder, nautical technology, iron casting, a public postal service, and more. When the road to China opened in the thirteenth and fourteenth centuries, many Europeans, including the merchant-traveler Marco Polo, were more than willing to make the long and difficult journey, returning with amazing tales of splendor and abundance far beyond what was available in Europe. When Europeans took to the oceans in the fifteenth and sixteenth centuries, they were seeking out the sources of African and Asian wealth. Thus the accelerating growth of European civilization was accompanied by its reintegration into the larger Afro-Eurasian networks of exchange and communication.

In this willingness to borrow, Europe resembled several other third-wave civilizations of the time. Japan, for example, took much from China; West Africa drew heavily on Islamic civilization; and Russia actively imitated Byzantium. All of them were then developing civilizations, in a position similar to the developing countries of the third world in the twentieth century. The whole process was then rather less deliberate and self-conscious than it became in the last century.

Technological borrowing required adaptation to the unique conditions of Europe and was accompanied by considerable independent invention as well. Together these processes generated a significant tradition of technological innovation that allowed Europe by 1500 to catch up with, and in some areas perhaps to surpass, China and the Islamic world. That achievement bears comparison with the economic revolution of Tang and Song dynasty China, although Europe began at a lower level and depended more on borrowing than did its Chinese counterpart (see Chapter 9). But in the several centuries surrounding 1000 at both ends of Eurasia, major processes of technological innovation were under way.

In Europe, technological breakthroughs first became apparent in agriculture as Europeans adapted to the very different environmental conditions north of the Alps in the several centuries following 500 C.E. They developed a heavy wheeled plow that could handle the dense soils of Northern Europe far better than the light or "scratch" plow used in Mediterranean agriculture. To pull the plow, Europeans began to rely increasingly on horses rather than oxen and to use iron horseshoes and a more efficient collar, which probably originated in China or Central Asia and could support much heavier loads. In addition, Europeans developed a new three-field system of crop rotation, which allowed considerably more land to be planted at any one time. These were the technological foundations for a more productive agriculture that could support the growing population of European civilization, and especially its urban centers, far more securely than before.

Beyond agriculture, Europeans began to tap nonanimal sources of energy in a major way, particularly after 1000. A new type of windmill, very different from an earlier Persian version, was widely used in Europe by the twelfth and thirteenth centuries. The water-driven mill was even more important. The Romans had used such mills largely to grind grain, but their development was limited, given that few streams flowed all year and many slaves were available to do the work. By the ninth century, however, water mills were rapidly becoming more evident in Europe. In the early fourteenth century, a concentration of sixty-eight mills dotted a one-mile stretch of the Seine River near Paris. In addition to grinding grain, these mills provided power for sieving flour, tanning hides, making beer, sawing wood, manufacturing iron, and making paper. Devices such as cranks, flywheels, camshafts, and complex gearing

European Technology
Europeans' fascination with technology and their religious motivation for investigating the world are apparent in this thirteenth-century portrayal of God as a divine engineer, laying out the world with a huge compass. (Erich Lessing/Art Resource, NY)

mechanisms, when combined with water or wind power, enabled Europeans of the High Middle Ages to revolutionize production in a number of industries and to break with the ancient tradition of depending almost wholly on animal or human muscle as sources of energy. So intense was the interest of European artisans and engineers in tapping mechanical sources of energy that a number of them experimented with perpetual-motion machines, an idea borrowed from Indian philosophers.

Technological borrowing also was evident in the arts of war. Gunpowder was invented in China, but Europeans were probably the first to use it in cannons, in the early fourteenth century, and by 1500 they had the most advanced arsenals in the world. In 1517, one Chinese official, upon first encountering European ships and weapons, remarked with surprise, "The westerns are extremely dangerous because of their artillery. No weapon ever made since memorable antiquity is superior to their cannon."[21] Advances in shipbuilding and navigational techniques—including the magnetic compass and sternpost rudder from China and adaptations of the Mediterranean or Arab lateen sail, which enabled vessels to sail against the wind—provided the foundation for European mastery of the seas.

Europe's passion for technology was reflected in its culture and ideas as well as in its machines. About 1260, the English scholar and Franciscan friar Roger Bacon wrote of the possibilities he foresaw, and in doing so, he expressed the confident spirit of the age:

> Machines of navigation can be constructed, without rowers...which are borne under the guidance of one man at a greater speed than if they were full of men. Also a chariot can be constructed, that will move with incalculable speed without any draught animal.... Also flying machines may be constructed so that a man may sit in the midst of the machine turning a certain instrument by means of which wings artificially constructed would beat the air after the manner of a bird flying...and there are countless other things that can be constructed.[22]

Pluralism in Politics

■ Comparison

Why was Europe unable to achieve the kind of political unity that China experienced? What impact did this have on the subsequent history of Europe?

Unlike the large centralized states of Byzantium, the Islamic world, and China, post-Roman European civilization never regained the unity it had under Roman rule. Rather, political life gradually crystallized into a system of competing states (France, Spain, England, Sweden, Prussia, the Netherlands, and Poland, among others) that has persisted into the twenty-first century and that the European Union still confronts. Geographic barriers, ethnic and linguistic diversity, and the shifting balances of power among its many states prevented the emergence of a single European empire, despite periodic efforts to re-create something resembling the still-remembered unity of the Roman Empire.

This multicentered political system shaped the emerging civilization of the West in many ways. It gave rise to frequent wars, enhanced the role and status of military men, and drove the "gunpowder revolution." Thus European society and values were militarized far more than in China, which gave greater prominence to scholars and bureaucrats. Intense interstate rivalry, combined with a willingness to borrow, also stimulated European technological development. By 1500, Europeans had gone a long way toward catching up with their more advanced Asian counterparts in agriculture, industry, war, and sailing.

But endemic warfare did not halt European economic growth. Capital, labor, and goods found their way around political barriers, while the common assumptions of Christian culture and the use of Latin and later French by the literate elite fostered communication across political borders. Europe's multistate system thus provided enough competition to be stimulating but also sufficient order and unity to allow economic endeavors to prosper.

The states within this emerging European civilization also differed from those to the east. Their rulers generally were weaker and had to contend with competing sources of power. Unlike the Orthodox Church in Byzantium, with its practice of caesaropapism, the Roman Catholic Church in the West maintained a degree of independence from state authority that served to check the power of kings and lords. European vassals had certain rights in return for loyalty to their lords and kings. By the thirteenth century, this meant that high-ranking nobles, acting through formal councils, had the right to advise their rulers and to approve new taxes.

This three-way struggle for power among kings, warrior aristocrats, and church leaders, all of them from the nobility, enabled urban-based merchants in Europe to achieve an unusual independence from political authority. Many cities, where wealthy merchants exercised local power, won the right to make and enforce their own laws and appoint their own officials. Some of them—Venice, Genoa, Pisa, and Milan, for example—became almost completely independent city-states. In the case of other cities, kings granted charters that allowed them to have their own courts, laws, and governments, while paying their own kind of taxes to the king instead of feudal dues. Powerful, independent cities were a distinctive feature of European life after 1100 or so. By contrast, Chinese cities, which were far larger than those of Europe, were simply part of the empire and enjoyed few special privileges. Although commerce was far more extensive in China than in an emerging European civilization, the powerful Chinese state favored the landowners over merchants, monopolized the salt and iron industries, and actively controlled and limited merchant activity far more than the new and weaker royal authorities of Europe were able to do.

The relative weakness of Europe's rulers allowed urban merchants more leeway and, according to some historians, paved the way to a more thorough development of capitalism in later centuries. It also led to the development of representative institutions or parliaments through which the views and interests of these contending forces could be expressed and accommodated. Intended to strengthen royal authority by consulting with major social groups, these embryonic parliaments did not represent the "people" or the "nation" but instead embodied the three great "estates of the realm"—the clergy (the first estate), the landowning nobility (the second estate), and urban merchants (the third estate).

Reason and Faith

A further feature of this emerging European civilization was a distinctive intellectual tension between the claims of human reason and those of faith. Christianity, of course, had developed in a classical world suffused with Greek rationalism. Some early Christian thinkers sought to maintain a clear separation between the new religion and the ideas of Plato and Aristotle. "What indeed has Athens to do with Jerusalem?" asked Tertullian (150–225 C.E.), an early church leader from North Africa. More common, however, was the notion that Greek philosophy could serve as a "handmaiden" to faith, more fully disclosing the truths of Christianity. In the reduced circumstances of Western Europe after the collapse of the Roman Empire,

■ **Comparison**

In what different ways did classical Greek philosophy and science have an impact in the West, in Byzantium, and in the Islamic world?

European University Life in the Middle Ages
This fourteenth-century manuscript painting shows a classroom scene from the University of Bologna in Italy. Note the sleeping and disruptive students. Some things apparently never change. (Bildarchiv Preussischer Kulturbesitz/Art Resource, NY)

the Church had little direct access to the writings of the Greeks, although some Latin translations and commentaries provided a continuing link to the world of classical thought.

But intellectual life in Europe changed dramatically in the several centuries after 1000, amid a rising population, a quickening commercial life, emerging towns and cities, and the Church's growing independence from royal or noble authorities. Moreover, the West was developing a legal system that guaranteed a measure of independence for a variety of institutions—towns and cities, guilds, professional associations, and especially universities. An outgrowth of earlier cathedral schools, these European universities—in Paris, Bologna, Oxford, Cambridge, Salamanca—became "zones of intellectual autonomy" in which scholars could pursue their studies with some freedom from the dictates of religious or political authorities, although that freedom was never complete and was frequently contested.[23]

This was the setting in which European Christian thinkers, a small group of literate churchmen, began to emphasize, quite self-consciously, the ability of human reason to penetrate divine mysteries and to grasp the operation of the natural order. An early indication of this new emphasis occurred in the late eleventh century when students in a monastic school in France asked their teacher, Anselm, to provide them a proof for the existence of God based solely on reason, without using the Bible or other sources of divine revelation.

The new interest in rational thought was applied first and foremost to theology, the "queen of the sciences" to European thinkers. Here was an effort to provide a rational foundation for faith, not to replace faith or to rebel against it. Logic, philosophy, and rationality would operate in service to Christ. Of course, some people opposed this new emphasis on human reason. Bernard of Clairvaux, a twelfth-century French abbot, declared, "Faith believes. It does not dispute."[24] His contemporary and intellectual opponent, the French scholar William of Conches, lashed out: "You poor fools. God can make a cow out of a tree, but has he ever done so? Therefore show some reason why a thing is so or cease to hold that it is so."[25]

European intellectuals also applied their newly discovered confidence in human reason to law, medicine, and the world of nature, exploring optics, magnetism, astronomy, and alchemy. Slowly and never completely, the scientific study of nature, known as "natural philosophy," began to separate itself from theology. In European universities, natural philosophy was studied in the faculty of arts, which was separate from the faculty of theology, although many scholars contributed to both fields.

This mounting enthusiasm for rational inquiry stimulated European scholars to seek out original Greek texts, particularly those of Aristotle. They found them in the Greek-speaking world of Byzantium and in the Arab world, where they had long ago been translated into Arabic. In the twelfth and thirteenth centuries, an explosion of translations from Greek and Arabic into Latin gave European scholars direct access to the works of ancient Greeks and to the remarkable results of Arab scholarship in astronomy, optics, medicine, pharmacology, and more. Much of this Arab science was now translated into Latin and provided a boost to Europe's changing intellectual life, centered in the new universities. One of these translators, Adelard of Bath (1080–1142), remarked that he had learned, "under the guidance of reason from Arabic teachers," not to trust established authority.[26]

It was the works of the prolific Aristotle, with his logical approach and "scientific temperament," that made the deepest impression. His writings became the basis for university education and largely dominated the thought of Western Europe in the five centuries after 1200. In the work of the thirteenth-century theologian Thomas Aquinas, Aristotle's ideas were thoroughly integrated into a logical and systematic presentation of Christian doctrine. In this growing emphasis on human rationality, at least partially separate from divine revelation, lay one of the foundations of the later Scientific Revolution and the secularization of European intellectual life.

Surprisingly, nothing comparable occurred in the Byzantine Empire, where knowledge of the Greek language was widespread and access to Greek texts was easy. Although Byzantine scholars kept the classical tradition alive, their primary interest lay in the humanities (literature, philosophy, history) and theology rather than in the natural sciences or medicine. Furthermore, both state and church had serious reservations about classical Greek learning. In 529, the emperor Justinian closed Plato's Academy in Athens, claiming that it was an outpost of paganism. Its scholars dispersed into lands that soon became Islamic, carrying Greek learning into the Islamic world. Church authorities as well were suspicious of classical Greek thought, sometimes persecuting scholars who were too enamored with the ancients. Even those who did study the Greek writers did so in a conservative spirit, concerned to preserve and transmit the classical heritage rather than using it as a springboard for creating new knowledge. "The great men of the past," declared the fourteenth-century Byzantine scholar and statesman Theodore Metochites, "have said everything so perfectly that they have left nothing for us to say."[27]

In the Islamic world, classical Greek thought was embraced "with far more enthusiasm and creativity" than in Byzantium.[28] A massive translation project in the ninth and tenth centuries made Aristotle and many other Greek writers available in Arabic. That work contributed to a flowering of Arab scholarship, especially in the sciences and natural philosophy, between roughly 800 and 1200 (see Chapter 11), but it also stimulated a debate about faith and reason among Muslim thinkers, many of whom greatly admired Greek philosophical, scientific, and medical texts. As in the Christian world, the issue was whether secular Greek thought was an aid or a threat to the faith. Western European church authorities after the thirteenth century had come to regard natural philosophy as a wholly legitimate enterprise and had thoroughly incorporated Aristotle into university education, but learned opinion in the Islamic world swung the other way. Though never completely disappearing from Islamic scholarship, the ideas of Plato and Aristotle receded after the thirteenth century in favor of teachings that drew more directly from the Quran or from mystical experience. Nor was natural philosophy a central concern of Islamic higher education as it was in the West. The integration of political and religious life in the Islamic world, as in Byzantium, contrasted with their separation in the West, where there was more space for the independent pursuit of scientific subjects.

Reflections: Remembering and Forgetting: Continuity and Surprise in the Worlds of Christendom

Many of the characteristic features of Christendom, which emerged during the era of third-wave civilizations, have had a long life, extending well into the modern era. The crusading element of European expansion was prominent among the motives of Spanish and Portuguese explorers. Europe's grudging freedom for merchant activity and its eagerness to borrow foreign technology arguably contributed to the growth of capitalism and industrialization in later centuries. The endemic military conflicts of European states, unable to recover the unity of the Roman Empire, found terrible expression in the world wars of the twentieth century. The controversy about reason and faith resonates still, at least in the United States, in debates about the authority of the Bible in secular and scientific matters. The rift between Eastern Orthodoxy and Roman Catholicism remains one of the major divides in the Christian world. Modern universities and the separation of religious and political authority likewise have their origins in the European Middle Ages. Such a perspective, linking the past with what came later, represents one of the great contributions that the study of history makes to human understanding.

Yet that very strength of historical study can be misleading, particularly if it suggests a kind of inevitability, in which the past determines the future. Some historians have argued, looking backward from the present, that Europe's industrial transformation and global domination in the nineteenth century grew inexorably out of its unique character as a changing civilization after 1000. This kind of thinking, however, misses the great surprise of Europe's more recent historical trajectory, and it minimizes the way people at the time understood their world.

Surely in 1000, few people would have predicted the startling reversal of roles between the Eastern and Western wings of Christendom, which the next several centuries witnessed. At that time, the many small, rural, unsophisticated, and endlessly quarreling warrior-based societies of Western Europe would hardly have borne comparison with the powerful Byzantine Empire and its magnificent capital of Constantinople. Even in 1500, when Europe had begun to catch up with China and the Islamic world in various ways, there was little to predict its remarkable transformation over the next several centuries and the dramatic change in the global balance of power that this transformation produced. To recapture the unexpectedness of the historical process and to allow ourselves to be surprised, it may be useful on occasion to forget the future and to see the world as contemporaries viewed it.

Second Thoughts

What's the Significance?

Byzantine Empire
Constantinople
Justinian
caesaropapism
Eastern Orthodox
    Christianity
icons

Kievan Rus
Prince Vladimir of Kiev
Charlemagne
Holy Roman Empire
Roman Catholic Church
Western Christendom

Crusades
European cities
system of competing
    states
Aristotle and classical
    Greek learning

To assess your mastery of the material in this chapter, visit the **Student Center** at bedfordstmartins.com/strayer.

Big Picture Questions

1. How did the histories of the Byzantine Empire and Western Europe differ during the era of third-wave civilizations?
2. What accounts for the different historical trajectories of these two expressions of Christendom?
3. How did Byzantium and Western Europe interact with each other and with the larger world of the postclassical era?
4. Was the civilization of the Latin West distinctive and unique, or was it broadly comparable to other third-wave civilizations?
5. How does the history of the Christian world in the postclassical era compare with that of Tang and Song dynasty China?

Next Steps: For Further Study

Renate Bridenthal et al., eds., *Becoming Visible: Women in European History* (1998). A series of essays that reflects recent scholarship on women.

Edward Grant, *Science and Religion from Aristotle to Copernicus* (2004). Demonstrates the impact of Greek philosophy and science in Europe, with comparisons to Byzantium and the Islamic world.

For Web sites and additional documents related to this chapter, see **Make History** at bedfordstmartins.com/strayer.

Barbara A. Hanawalt, *The Middle Ages: An Illustrated History* (1999). A brief and beautifully illustrated introduction to the Middle Ages in European history.

Rowena Loverance, *Byzantium* (2004). A lavishly illustrated history of the Byzantine Empire, drawing on the rich collection of artifacts in the British Museum.

Christopher Tyerman, *Fighting for Christendom: Holy Wars and the Crusades* (2005). A very well-written, up-to-date history of the Crusades designed for nonspecialists.

Mark Whittow, *The Making of Byzantium, 600–1025* (1996). An engaging account of Byzantium at its height, with an emphasis on its external connections.

"Middle Ages," http://www.learner.org/exhibits/middleages. An interactive Web site with text and images relating to life in Europe after the collapse of the Roman Empire.

Documents

Considering the Evidence:
The Making of Christian Europe . . .
and a Chinese Counterpoint

Like Buddhism, Christianity became a universal religion, taking root well beyond its place of origin. During the classical era, this new faith, born in a Jewish context in Roman Palestine, spread throughout the Roman Empire, where it received state support during the fourth century C.E. In the centuries that followed the collapse of the western Roman Empire, Christianity also took hold among the peoples of Western Europe in what are now England, France, Germany, and Scandinavia. While we often think about this region as solidly Christian, Western Europe in the period between 500 and 1000 C.E. was very much on the frontier of an expanding Christian world. During those centuries, a number of emerging monarchs of post-Roman Europe found the Christian faith and the Church useful in consolidating their new and fragile states by linking them to the legacy of the Roman Empire. Although the religion of Jesus ultimately became widely accepted, the making of Christian Europe was a prolonged and tentative process, filled with setbacks, resistance, and struggles among variant versions of the faith as well as growing acceptance and cultural compromise. An interesting counterpoint to the story of Christianity in Western Europe lies in its spread to China at about the same time. There, however, it did not take root in any permanent fashion, although it briefly generated a fascinating expression of the Christian faith.

Document 10.1

The Conversion of Clovis

Among the Germanic peoples of post-Roman Western Europe, none were of greater significance than the Franks, occupying the region of present-day France (see Map 10.1, p. 428). By the early sixth century, a more or less unified Frankish kingdom had emerged under the leadership of Clovis (reigned 485–511), whose Merovingian dynasty ruled the area until 751. Clovis's conversion to Christianity was described about a century later by a well-known bishop and writer, Gregory of Tours (538–594). It was an important step in the triumph of Christianity over Frankish "paganism." It also marked the victory of what would later become Roman Catholicism, based on the idea of the Trinity, over a rival form of the Christian faith, known as Arianism, which held that Jesus was a created divine being subordinate to God the Father.

- According to Gregory, what led to the conversion of Clovis?

- What issues are evident in the religious discussions of Clovis and his wife, Clotilda?

- Notice how Gregory modeled his picture of Clovis on that of Constantine, the famous Roman emperor whose conversion to Christianity in the fourth century gave official legitimacy and state support to the faith (see Chapter 5). What message did Gregory seek to convey in making this implied comparison?

- How might a modern secular historian use this document to help explain the spread of Christianity among the Franks?

GREGORY OF TOURS

History of the Franks
Late Sixth Century

[Clovis] had a first-born son by queen Clotilda, and as his wife wished to consecrate him in baptism, she tried unceasingly to persuade her husband, saying: "The gods you worship are nothing, and they will be unable to help themselves or any one else. For they are graven out of stone or wood or some metal.... They are endowed rather with the magic arts than with the power of the divine name. But he [God] ought rather to be worshipped who created by his word heaven and earth, the sea and all that in them is out of a state of nothingness... [and] by whose hand mankind was created...."

But though the queen said this, the spirit of the king was by no means moved to belief, and he said: "It was at the command of our gods that all things were created and came forth, and it is plain that your God has no power and, what is more, he is proven

not to belong to the family of the gods." Meantime the faithful queen made her son ready for baptism; she gave command to adorn the church with hangings and curtains, in order that he who could not moved by persuasion might be urged to belief by this mystery. The boy, whom they named Ingomer, died after being baptized, still wearing the white garments in which he became regenerate. At this the king was violently angry, and reproached the queen harshly, saying: "If the boy had been dedicated in the name of my gods he would certainly have lived; but as it is, since he was baptized in the name of your God, he could not live at all." To this the queen said: "I give thanks to the omnipotent God, creator of all, who has judged me not wholly unworthy, that he should deign to take to his kingdom one born from my womb. My soul is not stricken with grief for his sake, because I know that, summoned from this world as he was in his baptismal garments, he will be fed by the vision of God...."

The queen did not cease to urge him to recognize the true God and cease worshipping idols. But he could not be influenced in any way to this belief,

Source: Gregory Bishop of Tours, *History of the Franks*, translated by Ernest Brehaut (New York: Columbia University Press, 1916; copyright renewed 1944), Book 2, selections from Sections 27, 29, 30, 31, 36–41.

until at last a war arose with the Alamanni,° in which he was driven by necessity to confess what before he had of his free will denied. It came about that as the two armies were fighting fiercely, there was much slaughter, and Clovis's army began to be in danger of destruction. He saw it and raised his eyes to heaven, and with remorse in his heart he burst into tears and cried: "Jesus Christ, whom Clotilda asserts to be the son of the living God..., I beseech the glory of thy aid, with the vow that if thou wilt grant me victory over these enemies..., I will believe in thee and be baptized in thy name. For I have invoked my own gods but, as I find, they have withdrawn from aiding me; and therefore I believe that

---

°**Alamanni:** a Germanic people.

they possess no power, since they do not help those who obey them...." And when he said thus, the Alamanni turned their backs, and began to disperse in flight. And when they saw that their king was killed, they submitted to the dominion of Clovis, saying: "Let not the people perish further, we pray; we are yours now." And he stopped the fighting, and after encouraging his men, retired in peace and told the queen how he had had merit to win the victory by calling on the name of Christ. This happened in the fifteenth year of his reign....

And so the king confessed all-powerful God in the Trinity, and was baptized in the name of the Father, Son and Holy Spirit, and was anointed with the holy ointment with the sign of the cross of Christ. And of his army more than 3,000 were baptized.

Document 10.2

Advice on Dealing with "Pagans"

In their dealings with the "pagan," or non-Christian, peoples and kings of Western Europe, church authorities such as missionaries, bishops, and the pope himself sometimes advocated compromise with existing cultural traditions rather than overt hostility to them. Here Pope Gregory (reigned 590–604) urges the bishop of England to adopt a strategy of accommodation with the prevailing religious practices of the Anglo-Saxon peoples of the island. It was contained in a famous work about the early Christian history of England, composed by a Benedictine monk known as The Venerable Bede and completed about 731.

■ What can we learn about the religious practices of the Anglo-Saxons from Bede's account?

■ In what specific ways did the pope urge toleration? And why did he advocate accommodation or compromise with existing religious practices? Keep in mind that the political authorities in England at the time had not yet become thoroughly Christian.

■ What implication might Gregory's policies have for the beliefs and practices of English converts?

POPE GREGORY
Advice to the English Church
601

[T]he temples of the idols in that nation [England] ought not to be destroyed; but let the idols that are in them be destroyed; let holy water be made and sprinkled in the said temples, let altars be erected, and relics placed. For if those temples are well built, it is requisite that they be converted from the worship of devils to the service of the true God; that the nation, seeing that their temples are not destroyed, may remove error from their hearts, and knowing and adoring the true God, may the more familiarly resort to the places to which they have been accustomed.

And because they have been used to slaughter many oxen in the sacrifices to devils, some solemnity must be exchanged for them on this account, as that on the day of the dedication, or the nativities of the holy martyrs, whose relics are there deposited, they may build themselves huts of the boughs of trees, about those churches which have been turned

Source: The Venerable Bede, *The Ecclesiastical History of the English Nation*, edited by Ernest Rhys (London: J. M. Dent and Sons; New York: E. P. Dutton and Co., 1910), 52–53.

to that use from temples, and celebrate the solemnity with religious feasting, and no more offer beasts to the Devil, but kill cattle to the praise of God in their eating, and return thanks to the Giver of all things for their sustenance; to the end that, while some gratifications are outwardly permitted them, they may the more easily consent to the inward consolations of the grace of God. For there is no doubt that it is impossible to efface everything at once from their obdurate minds; because he who endeavors to ascend to the highest place, rises by degrees or steps, and not by leaps.

Thus the Lord made Himself known to the people of Israel in Egypt; and yet He allowed them the use of the sacrifices which they were wont to offer to the Devil, in his own worship; so as to command them in his sacrifice to kill beasts, to the end that, changing their hearts, they might lay aside one part of the sacrifice, while they retained another; that while they offered the same beasts which they were wont to offer, they should offer them to God, and not to idols; and thus they would no longer be the same sacrifices.

Document 10.3

Charlemagne and the Saxons

The policies of peaceful conversion and accommodation described in Document 10.2 did not prevail everywhere, as Charlemagne's dealings with the Saxons reveals. During late eighth and early ninth centuries C.E., Charlemagne (reigned 768–814) was the powerful king of the Franks. He turned his Frankish kingdom into a Christian empire that briefly incorporated much of continental Europe, and he was crowned as a renewed Roman emperor by the pope. In the course of almost constant wars of expansion, Charlemagne struggled for over thirty years (772–804) to subdue the Saxons, a "pagan" Germanic people who inhabited a region on the northeastern frontier of Charlemagne's growing empire (see Map 10.2, p. 436). The document known as the *Capitulary on Saxony* outlines a series of laws, regulations, and punishments (known collectively as a capitulary) regarding religious practice of the Saxons. This document reveals both the coercive policies of Charlemagne and the vigorous resistance of the Saxons to their forcible incorporation into his Christian domain.

- What does this document reveal about the kind of resistance that the Saxons mounted against their enforced conversion?
- How did Charlemagne seek to counteract that resistance?
- What does this document suggest about Charlemagne's views of his duties as ruler?

CHARLEMAGNE

Capitulary on Saxony

785

1. It was pleasing to all that the churches of Christ, which are now being built in Saxony and consecrated to God, should not have less, but greater and more illustrious honor, than the fanes° of the idols had had....

3. If any one shall have entered a church by violence and shall have carried off anything in it by force or theft, or shall have burned the church itself, let him be punished by death.

4. If any one, out of contempt for Christianity, shall have despised the holy Lenten fast and shall have eaten flesh, let him be punished by death. But, nevertheless, let it be taken into consideration by a priest, lest perchance any one from necessity has been led to eat flesh.

5. If any one shall have killed a bishop or priest or deacon, let him likewise be punished capitally.

6. If any one deceived by the devil shall have believed, after the manner of the pagans, that any man or woman is a witch and eats men, and on this account shall have burned the person, or shall have given the person's flesh to others to eat, or shall have

eaten it himself, let him be punished by a capital sentence.

7. If any one, in accordance with pagan rites, shall have caused the body of a dead man to be burned and shall have reduced his bones to ashes, let him be punished capitally....

9. If any one shall have sacrificed a man to the devil, and after the manner of the pagans shall have presented him as a victim to the demons, let him be punished by death.

10. If any one shall have formed a conspiracy with the pagans against the Christians, or shall have wished to join with them in opposition to the Christians, let him be punished by death; and whoever shall have consented to this same fraudulently against the king and the Christian people, let him be punished by death....

17. Likewise, in accordance with the mandate of God, we command that all shall give a tithe of their property and labor to the churches and priests;

18. That on the Lord's day no meetings and public judicial assemblages shall be held, unless perchance in a case of great necessity or when war compels it, but all shall go to the church to hear the word of God, and shall be free for prayers or good works. Likewise, also, on the especial festivals they shall devote themselves to God and to the services of the church, and shall refrain from secular assemblies.

°**fanes:** temples.

Source: D. C. Munro, trans., *Translations and Reprints from the Original Sources of European History*, vol. 6, no. 5, *Selections from the Laws of Charles the Great* (Philadelphia: University of Pennsylvania Press, 1900), 2–4.

19. Likewise,...all infants shall be baptized within a year....

21. If any one shall have made a vow at springs or trees or groves, or shall have made any offerings after the manner of the heathen and shall have partaken of a repast in honor of the demons, if he shall be a noble, [he must pay a fine of] 60 solidi,° if a freeman 30, if a litus° 15.

°**solidi:** gold coins.

°**litus:** neither a slave nor a free person.

Documents 10.4 and 10.5

The Persistence of Tradition

Conversion to Christianity in Western Europe was neither easy nor simple. Peoples thought to have been solidly converted to the new faith continued to engage in earlier practices. Others blended older traditions with Christian rituals. The two documents that follow illustrate both patterns. Document 10.4 describes the encounter between Saint Boniface (672–754), a leading missionary to the Germans, and the Hessians during the eighth century. It was written by one of Boniface's devoted followers, Willibald, who subsequently composed a biography of the missionary. Document 10.5 comes from a tenth-century Anglo-Saxon manuscript known as the *Leechbook*, a medical text that describes cures for various problems caused by "elves and nightgoers."

- What practices of the Hessians conflicted with Boniface's understanding of Christianity? How did he confront the persistence of these practices?

- What do these documents reveal about the process of conversion to Christianity?

- How might Pope Gregory (Document 10.2), Charlemagne (Document 10.3), and Boniface (Document 10.4) have responded to the cures and preventions described in the *Leechbook*?

WILLIBALD

Life of Boniface

ca. 760 C.E.

Now many of the Hessians who at that time had acknowledged the Catholic faith were confirmed by the grace of the Holy Spirit and received the laying-on of hands. But others, not yet strong in the spirit, refused to accept the pure teachings of the church in their entirety. Moreover, some continued secretly, others openly, to offer sacrifices to trees and springs, to inspect the entrails of victims; some practiced divination, legerdemain, and incantations; some turned their attention to auguries, auspices, and other sacrificial rites; while others, of a more

---

Source: Willibald, "Life of Boniface," in *The Anglo-Saxon Missionaries in Germany*, translated by C. H. Talbot (London: Sheed and Ward, 1954), 45–46.

reasonable character, forsook all the profane practices of the [heathens] and committed none of these crimes.

With the counsel and advice of the latter persons, Boniface in their presence attempted to cut down...a certain oak of extraordinary size, called in the old tongue of the pagans the Oak of Jupiter. Taking his courage in his hands (for a great crowd of pagans stood by watching and bitterly cursing in their hearts the enemy of the gods), he cut the first notch. But when he had made a superficial cut, suddenly, the oak's vast bulk, shaken by a mighty blast of wind from above crashed to the ground shivering its topmost branches into fragments in its fall. As if by the express will of God (for the brethren present had done nothing to cause it) the oak burst asunder into four parts, each part having a trunk of equal length.

At the sight of this extraordinary spectacle the heathens who had been cursing ceased to revile and began, on the contrary, to believe and bless the Lord. Thereupon the holy bishop took counsel with the brethren, built an oratory° from the timber of the oak and dedicated it to Saint Peter the Apostle. He then set out on a journey to Thuringia.... Arrived there, he addressed the elders and the chiefs of the people, calling on them to put aside their blind ignorance and to return to the Christian religion that they had formerly embraced.

°**oratory:** a place of prayer.

The Leechbook
Tenth Century

Work a salve against elfkind and nightgoers,... and the people with whom the Devil has intercourse. Take eowohumelan, wormwood, bishopwort, lupin, ashthroat, henbane, harewort, haransprecl, heathberry plants, cropleek, garlic, hedgerife grains, githrife, fennel. Put these herbs into one cup, set under the altar, sing over them nine masses; boil in butter and in sheep's grease, add much holy salt, strain through a cloth; throw the herbs in running water. If any evil temptation, or an elf or nightgoers, happen to a man, smear his forehead with this salve, and put on his eyes, and where his body is sore, and cense him [with incense], and sign [the cross] often. His condition will soon be better.

...Against elf disease...Take bishopwort, fennel, lupin, the lower part of *ælfthone*, and lichen from the holy sign of Christ [cross], and incense; a handful of each. Bind all the herbs in a cloth, dip in hallowed font water thrice. Let three masses be sung over it, one "Omnibus sanctis [For all the saints]," a second "Contra tribulationem [Against tribulation]," a third "Pro infirmis [For the sick]." Put then coals in a coal pan, and lay the herbs on it. Smoke the man with the herbs before... [9 A.M.] and at night; and sing a litany, the Creed [Nicene], and the Pater noster [Our Father]; and write on him Christ's mark on each limb. And take a little handful of the same kind of herbs, similarly sanctified, and boil in milk; drip holy water in it thrice. And let him sip it before his meal. It will soon be well with him.

Against the Devil and against madness,...a strong drink. Put in ale hassock, lupin roots, fennel, ontre, betony, hind heolothe, marche, rue, wormwood, nepeta (catmint), helenium, *ælfthone*, wolfs comb. Sing twelve masses over the drink; and let him drink. It will soon be well with him.

A drink against the Devil's temptations: thefanthorn, cropleek, lupin, ontre, bishopwort, fennel, hassock, betony. Sanctify these herbs; put into ale holy water. And let the drink be there in where the sick man is. And continually before he drinks sing thrice over the drink,... "God, in your name make me whole (save me)."

Source: Karen Louise Jolly, *Popular Religion in Late Saxon England: Elf Charms in Context* (Chapel Hill: University of North Carolina Press, 1996), 159–67.

Document 10.6

The Jesus Sutras in China

In 635 C.E. the Tang dynasty emperor Taizon welcomed a Persian Christian monk named Alopen and some two dozen of his associates to the Chinese capital of Chang'an (now Xian, see Map 5.1, p. 213). The Chinese court at this time was unusually open to a variety of foreign cultural traditions, including Buddhism, Islam, and Zoroastrianism in addition to Christianity. The version of Christianity that Alopen brought to China was known as Nestorianism (see p. 426). Regarded as heretics in the West and much persecuted, Nestorians had found refuge in Persia and from there introduced the faith into India, Mongolia, and China.

In sharp contrast to its success in Europe, Christianity did not establish a widespread or lasting presence in China. Isolation from the Persian heartland of Nestorian Christianity, opposition from Buddhists, and state persecution of all foreign religions in the ninth century reduced the Nestorian presence to near extinction. But for several centuries, under more favorable political conditions, a number of small Christian communities had flourished, generating a remarkable set of writings known as the "Jesus sutras." (A sutra is a Buddhist religious text.)

Some were carved on large stone slabs, while others were written on scrolls discovered early in the twentieth century in the caves of Dunhuang in northwestern China. What has fascinated scholars about these writings is the extent to which they cast the Christian message in distinctively Chinese terms, making use particularly of Buddhist and Daoist concepts long familiar in China. For example, at the top of a large stone tablet known as the Nestorian Monument is a Christian cross arising out of a white cloud (a characteristic Daoist symbol) and a lotus flower (an enduring Buddhist image). The written texts themselves, which refer to Christianity as the "Religion of Light from the West" or the "Luminous Religion," describe its arrival in China and outline its message within the framework of Chinese culture.

- What was the role of the emperor in establishing Christianity in China? How does this compare with the religious role of European monarchs such as Clovis or Charlemagne in Europe?

- How do the sutras depict the life, death, and teachings of Jesus?

- In what ways are Daoist or Buddhist concepts used to express the Christian message? (See pp. 195–97 and 199–201.)

- How does this Persian/Chinese version of Christianity differ from that of Catholic Europe?

The Jesus Sutras
635–1005

On the Coming of Christianity to China

The Emperor Taizong was a champion of culture. He created prosperity and encouraged illustrious sages to bestow their wisdom on the people....

In... 638 C.E., ... the Emperor issued a proclamation saying:

"There is no single name for the Way.

Sages do not come in a single form.

These Teachings embrace everyone and can be adopted in any land.

A Sage of great virtue, Aleben, has brought these scriptures... and offered them to us in the Capital.

We have studied these scriptures and found them otherwordly, profound and full of mystery....

These teachings will save all creatures and benefit mankind, and it is only proper that they be practiced throughout the world."

Following the Emperor's orders, the Greater Qin Monastery was built.... Twenty-one ordained monks of the Luminous Religion were allowed to live there....

Imperial officers were ordered to paint a portrait of the Emperor on the wall of the monastery.... This auspicious symbol of the imperial presence added brilliance and bestowed favor upon the religion....

The Luminous Religion spread throughout all ten provinces, the Empire prospered and peace prevailed. Temples were built in 100 cities and countless families received the blessings of the Luminous Religion.

On the Story of Jesus

The Lord of Heaven sent the Cool Wind to a girl named Mo Yen. It entered her womb and at that moment she conceived....

Source: Martin Palmer, *The Jesus Sutras* (New York: Random House, 2001), 62–65, 68–69, 80–83, 90, 91, 103, 106, 107, 115–19.

Mo Yen became pregnant and gave birth to a son named Jesus, whose father is the Cool Wind....

When Jesus Messiah was born, the world saw clear signs in heaven and earth. A new star that could be seen everywhere appeared in heaven above....

From the time the Messiah was 12 until he was 32 years old, he sought out people with bad karma and directed them to turn around and create good karma by following a wholesome path. After the Messiah had gathered 12 disciples, he concerned himself with the suffering of others. Those who had died were made to live. The blind were made to see. The deformed were healed and the sick were cured. The possessed were freed of their demons and the crippled were made to walk. People with all kinds of illnesses drew near to the Messiah to touch his ragged robe and be healed....

The scribes who drank liquor and ate meat and served other gods brought false testimony against him. They waited for an opportunity to kill him. But many people had come to have faith in his teaching and so the scribes could not kill the Messiah. Eventually these people, whose karma was unwholesome, formed a conspiracy against him....

When the Messiah was 32 years old, his enemies came before the Great King Pilate and accused him by saying, The Messiah has committed a capital offense. The Great King should condemn him....

For the sake of all living beings and to show us that a human life is as frail as a candle flame, the Messiah gave his body to these people of unwholesome karma. For the sake of the living in this world, he gave up his life....

On the Four Laws of Dharma

The first law is no desire. Your heart seeks one thing after another, creating a multitude of problems. You must not allow them to flare up.... Desire can sap wholesome energy from the four limbs and the body's openings, turning it into unwholesome activity. This cuts us off from the roots of Peace and Joy. That is why you must practice the law of no desire.

The second law is no action. Doing things for mundane reasons is not part of your true being. You have to cast aside vain endeavors and avoid shallow experiences. Otherwise you are deceiving yourself.... We live our lives veering this way and that: We do things for the sake of progress and material gain, neglecting what is truly important and losing sight of the Way. That is why you must distance yourself from the material world and practice the law of no action.

The third law is no virtue. Don't try to find pleasure by making a name for yourself through good deeds. Practice instead universal loving kindness that is directed toward everyone. Never seek praise for what you do.... But do it without acclaim. This is the law of no virtue.

The fourth law is no truth. Don't be concerned with facts, forget about right and wrong, sinking or rising, winning or losing. Be like a mirror.... It reflects everything as it is, without judging. Those who have awakened to the Way, who have attained the mind of Peace and Joy, who can see all karmic conditions and who share their enlightenment with others, reflect the world like a mirror, leaving no trace of themselves.

On God, Humankind and the Sutras

Heaven and earth are the creation of the One God. The power and will of God pass like the wind over everything. His is not a body of flesh, but a divine consciousness, completely unseen to human eyes....

People can live only by dwelling in the living breath of God. Only in this way can they be at peace and realize their aspirations. From sunrise to sunset, they dwell in the living breath of God; every sight and thought is part of that breath. God provides a place for them filled with clarity and bliss and stillness. All the Buddhas are moved by this wind, which blows everywhere in the world. God resides permanently in this still, blissful place; no karma is done without God....

Do what you have to do here on earth and your actions will determine your place in the next world. We are not born to live forever in the world, but are here to plant wholesome seeds that will produce good fruit in the world beyond this one. Everyone who seeks the other world will attain it if they plant good seeds before departing....

Anyone who crosses the ocean must have a boat before taking on the wind and waves. But a broken boat won't reach the far shore. It is the Sutras of the Luminous Religion that enable us to cross the sea of birth and death to the other shore, a land fragrant with the treasured aroma of Peace and Joy.

Using the Evidence:
The Making of Christian Europe . . .
and a Chinese Counterpoint

1. **Describing cultural encounters:** Consider the spread of Christianity in Europe and China from the viewpoint of those seeking to introduce the new religion. What obstacles did they encounter? What strategies did they employ? What successes and failures did they experience?

2. **Describing cultural encounters . . . from another point of view:** Consider the same process from the viewpoint of new adherents to Christianity. What were the motives for or the advantages of conversion for both political elites and ordinary people? To what extent was it possible to combine prevailing practices and beliefs with the teachings of the new religion?

3. **Making comparisons:** How did the spread of Christianity to China differ from its introduction to Western Europe? How might you describe and explain the very different outcomes of those two processes?

4. **Defining a concept:** The notion of "conversion" often suggests a quite rapid and complete transformation of religious commitments based on sincere inner conviction. In what ways do these documents support or challenge this understanding of religious change?

5. **Noticing point of view and assessing credibility:** From what point of view is each of the documents written? Which statements in each document might historians find unreliable and which would they find most useful?

Visual Sources

Considering the Evidence:
Reading Byzantine Icons

Within the world of Byzantine or Eastern Orthodox Christianity, the icon—a Greek word meaning image, likeness, or picture—came to have a prominent role in both public worship and private devotion. Since Christianity had emerged in a Roman world filled with images—statues of the emperor, busts of ancestors and famous authors, frescoes, and murals—it is hardly surprising that Christians felt a need to represent their faith in some concrete fashion. Icons fulfilled that need.

The creation of icons took off in earnest as Christianity became the official religion of the Roman Empire in the fourth century C.E. Usually painted by monks, icons depicted Jesus, the Virgin Mary, saints, scenes from biblical stories, church feasts, and more. To Byzantine believers, such images were "windows on heaven," an aid to worship that conveyed the very presence of God, bestowing divine grace on the world. They were also frequently associated with miracles, and on occasion people scraped paint off an icon, mixing it with water to produce a "holy medicine" that could remedy a variety of ailments. Icons also served a teaching function for a largely illiterate audience. As Pope Gregory II in the eighth century explained:

> What books are to those who can read, that is a picture to the ignorant who look at it; in a picture even the unlearned may see what example they should follow; in a picture they who know no letters may yet read. Hence, for Barbarians especially a picture takes the place of a book.[29]

Icons were deliberately created—or "written"—as flat, two-dimensional images, lacking the perspective of depth. This nonrepresentational, nonrealistic portrayal of human figures was intended to suggest another world and to evoke the mysteries of faith that believers would encounter as they knelt before the image, crossed themselves, and kissed it. The images themselves were full of religious symbolism. The posture of the body, the position of the hand, and the fold of the clothing were all rich with meaning: a saint touching his hand to his cheek conveyed sorrow; a halo surrounding the head of a human figure reflected divinity or sacredness. Likewise, colors were symbolic: red stood for either love or the blood of martyrs; blue suggested faith, humility, or heaven; and purple indicated royalty. Those who painted icons were bound by strict traditions derived from the distant past. Lacking what we might consider "artistic freedom," they sought to faithfully replicate earlier models.

In Judaism, Christianity, and Islam alike, the artistic representation of God occasioned heated debates. After all, the Ten Commandments declared, "You shall not make for yourselves a graven image or any likeness of anything that is in heaven above." Almost since the beginning of Christian art, an undercurrent of opposition had criticized efforts to represent the divine in artistic form. Between 726 and 843, Byzantine emperors took the offensive against the use of icons in worship, arguing that they too easily became "idols," distracting believers from the adoration of God himself. Some scholars suggest that this effort, known as iconoclasm (icon breaking), also reflected a concern of religious and political authorities in Byzantium about the growing power of monks, who both created icons and ardently supported their use in worship. It may also have owed something to a desire to avoid offending a rapidly expanding Islamic world, which itself largely prohibited the representation of the human form.[30] Icons were collected from both homes and churches and burned in public square. Thousands of monks fled, and active supporters of icon use were subject to severe punishment. Some critics accused the emperor of sympathy with Islam. But by 843 this controversy was resolved in favor of icon use, an event still commemorated every year in Orthodox churches as the Triumph of Orthodoxy. Thereafter, the creation and use of icons flourished in the Byzantine Empire and subsequently in Russia, where Eastern Christianity began to take root in the late tenth century.

The three icons reproduced here provide an opportunity for you to "read" these visual sources and to imagine what religious meaning they may have conveyed to the faithful of Byzantine Christianity.

Visual Source 10.1, among the oldest icons in existence, dates from the sixth century and survived the destruction of icons during the century of iconoclasm. In contrast to many images of the suffering Jesus on the cross, this icon belongs to a tradition of icon painting that depicts Jesus as Christ Pantokrator. *Pantokrator* derives from a Greek term translated as "Almighty," "Ruler of All," or "Sustainer of the World." Wearing a dark purple robe and surrounded by a halo of light, Jesus holds a copy of the gospels in his left hand. Notice that Jesus' right hand is raised in blessing with the three fingers together representing the trinity and the two remaining fingers symbolizing the dual nature of Christ, both human and divine. Many observers have suggested that this important theological statement of Christ's divine and human nature is also conveyed in the asymmetrical character of the image.

Visual Source 10.1 Christ Pantokrator
(Ancient Art & Architecture Collection)

- What differences can you notice in the two sides of Christ's face? (Pay attention to the eyebrows, the irises and pupils, the hair, the mustache, and the cheeks. Notice also the difference in color between the face and the hands.)

- How does this image portray Jesus as an all-powerful ruler?

- How does this depiction of Jesus differ from others you may have seen?

- Which features of this image suggest Christ's humanity and which might portray his divinity?

Icons frequently portrayed important stories from the Bible, none of which was more significant than that of the nativity. Visual Source 10.2, from fifteenth-century Russia, graphically depicts the story of Jesus' birth for the faithful. The central person in the image is not Jesus but his mother, Mary, who in Orthodox theology was known as the God-bearer.

- Why do you think Mary is pictured as facing outward toward the viewer rather than focusing on her child?

- Notice the three rays from heaven, symbolizing the trinity—God the Father, the Son, and the Holy Spirit—represented by the three figures at the top. What other elements of the biblical story of Jesus' birth can you identify in the image?

- The figure in the bottom left is that of a contemplative and perhaps troubled Joseph, Mary's husband-to-be. What do you imagine that Joseph is thinking? Why might he be troubled?

- Facing Joseph is an elderly person, said by some to represent Satan and by others to be a shepherd comforting Joseph. What thinking might lie behind each of these interpretations?

Visual Source 10.2 The Nativity (Private Collection/The Bridgeman Art Library)

Visual Source 10.3 Ladder of Divine Ascent (Roger Wood/Corbis)

Visual Source 10.3 is a twelfth-century Byzantine painting intended to illustrate an instructional book for monks, written in the sixth century by Saint John Climacus. Both the book and the icon are known as the *Ladder of Divine Ascent*. Written by an ascetic monk with a reputation for great piety and wisdom, the book advised monks to renounce the world with its many temptations and vices and to ascend step by step toward union with God in heaven. The icon served as a visual illustration of that process. The monks are climbing the ladder of the spiritual journey toward God but are beset by winged demons representing various sins—lust, anger, and pride, for example—which are described in Climacus's book. Some have fallen off the ladder into the mouth of a dragon, which represents hell.

■ How does this icon portray the spiritual journey?

■ What sources of help are available for the monks on the ladder? Notice the figures in the upper left and lower right.

■ What message might beginning monks have taken from this image?

Using the Evidence:
Reading Byzantine Icons

1. **Viewing icons from opposing perspectives:** How might supporters and opponents of icons have responded to these visual sources?

2. **Identifying religious ideas in art:** What elements of religious thought or practice can you identify in these icons? In what ways were these religious ideas represented artistically?

3. **Comparing images of Jesus:** In what different ways is Jesus portrayed in the three icons? What similarities can you identify?

4. **Comparing religious art cross-culturally:** How might you compare these icons to the Buddha images in Chapter 5? Consider their purposes, their religious content, and their modes of artistic representation.

وكـادَ يُنَزِّعُ الجِمَالَ الشَّمَرُ والنَّشَدَ

مَا الحَجُّ سَيْرُكَ تَأْوِيبًا وإِدْلَاجَا وَلَا اعْتِيَامُكَ جِمَالًا وأَحْدَاجَا

الحَجُّ أَنْ تَقْصِدَ البَيْتَ الحَرَامَ عَلَى تَحْرِيكِكَ الحَجَّ لَا تَبْغِي بِهِ حَاجَا

وتَمْطِيَ كَأَهْلِ الإِنْصَافِ مُتَّخِذًا رَدْعَ الهَوَى هَادِيًا والحَقَّ مِنْهَاجَا

CHAPTER ELEVEN

The Worlds of Islam

Afro-Eurasian Connections

600–1500

The Birth of a New Religion
  The Homeland of Islam
  The Messenger and the Message
  The Transformation of
    Arabia
The Making of an Arab Empire
  War and Conquest
  Conversion to Islam
  Divisions and Controversies
  Women and Men in Early Islam
Islam and Cultural Encounter:
  A Four-Way Comparison
  The Case of India
  The Case of Anatolia
  The Case of West Africa
  The Case of Spain
The World of Islam as a New
  Civilization
  Networks of Faith
  Networks of Exchange
Reflections: Past and Present:
  Choosing Our History
Considering the Evidence
  Documents: Voices of Islam
  Visual Sources: Islamic Civilization
    in Persian Miniature Paintings

"There were tens of thousands of pilgrims, from all over the world. They were of all colors, from blue-eyed blondes to black-skinned Africans. But we were all participating in the same ritual, displaying a spirit of unity and brotherhood that my experiences in America had led me to believe never could exist between the white and non-white. . . . I have never before seen sincere and true brotherhood practiced by all colors together, irrespective of their color."[1] So said Malcolm X, the American black radical leader and convert to Islam, following his participation in 1964 in the hajj, or pilgrimage, to Mecca. That experience persuaded him to abandon his earlier commitment to militant black separatism, for he was now convinced that racial barriers could indeed be overcome within the context of Islam.

As the twenty-first century dawned, Islam had acquired a noticeable presence in the United States, with more than 1,200 mosques and an estimated 8 million Muslims, of whom some 2 million were African Americans. Here was but one sign of the growing international influence of the Islamic world. Independence from colonial rule, the Iranian Revolution of 1979, repeated wars between Israel and its Arab neighbors, the rising price of oil—all of this focused global attention on the Islamic world in the second half of the twentieth century. Osama bin Laden and the September 11, 2001, attacks on the United States, U.S. military action in Afghanistan and Iraq, and the increasing assertiveness of Muslims in Europe likewise signaled the growing role of Islam in world affairs in the first decade of the new millennium.

The Hajj: The pilgrimage to Mecca, known as the *hajj*, has long been a central religious ritual in Islamic practice. It also embodies the cosmopolitan character of Islam as pilgrims from all over the vast Islamic realm assemble in the city where the faith was born. This painting shows a group of joyful pilgrims, led by a band, on their way to Mecca. (Bibliothèque nationale de France)

PROMINENCE ON THE WORLD STAGE, OF COURSE, was nothing new for Muslim societies. For a thousand years (roughly 600–1600), peoples claiming allegiance to Islam represented a highly successful, prosperous, and expansive civilization, encompassing parts of Africa, Europe, the Middle East, and Asia. While Chinese culture and Buddhism provided the cultural anchor for East Asia during the postclassical millennium and Christianity did the same for western Eurasia, the realm of Islam touched on both of them and decisively shaped the history of the entire Afro-Eurasian world.

The significance of a burgeoning Islamic world was enormous. It thrust the previously marginal and largely nomadic Arabs into a central role in world history, for it was among them and in their language that the newest of the world's major religions was born. The sudden emergence and rapid spread of that religion in the seventh century C.E. was accompanied by the creation of a huge empire that stretched from Spain to India. Both within that empire and beyond it, a new and innovative civilization took shape, drawing on Arab, Persian, Turkish, Greco-Roman, South Asian, and African cultures. It was clearly the largest and most influential of the new third-wave civilizations. Finally, the broad reach of Islam generated many of the great cultural encounters of this age of accelerating connections, as Islamic civilization challenged and provoked Christendom, penetrated and was transformed by African cultures, and also took root in India, Central Asia, and Southeast Asia. The spread of Islam continued in the modern era so that by the beginning of the twenty-first century, perhaps 1.2 billion people, or 22 percent of the world's population, identified as Muslims. It was second only to Christianity as the world's most widely practiced religion, and it extended far beyond the Arab lands where it had originated.

The Birth of a New Religion

Most of the major religious or cultural traditions of the classical era had emerged from the core of established civilizations—Confucianism and Daoism from China, Hinduism and Buddhism from India, Greek philosophy from the Mediterranean world, and Zoroastrianism from Persia. Christianity and Islam, by contrast, emerged more from the margins of Mediterranean and Middle Eastern civilizations. The former, of course, appeared among a small Middle Eastern people, the Jews, in a remote province of the Roman Empire, while Islam took hold in the cities and deserts of the Arabian Peninsula.

The Homeland of Islam

■ Description
In what ways did the early history of Islam reflect its Arabian origins?

The central region of the Arabian Peninsula had long been inhabited by nomadic Arabs, known as Bedouins, who herded their sheep and camels in seasonal migrations. These peoples lived in fiercely independent clans and tribes, which often engaged in bitter blood feuds with one another. They recognized a variety of gods, ancestors, and nature spirits; valued personal bravery, group loyalty, and hospitality; and greatly treasured their highly expressive oral poetry. But there was more to Arabia than camel-herding nomads. Scattered oases, the highlands of Yemen, and interior mountains supported sedentary village-based agriculture, and in the north-ern and southern regions of Arabia, small kingdoms had flourished in ear-lier times. Arabia also sat astride increasingly important trade routes that connected the Indian Ocean world with that of the Mediterranean Sea and gave rise to more cosmopolitan commercial cities, whose values and prac-tices were often in conflict with those of traditional Arab tribes.

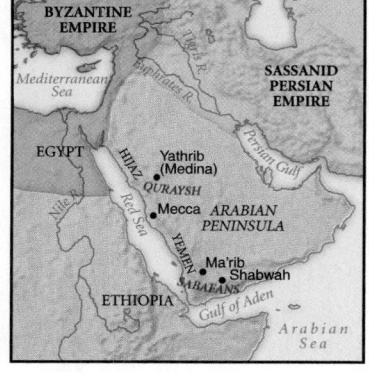

Arabia at the Time of Muhammad

One of those cities, Mecca, came to occupy a distinctive role in Arabia. Though somewhat off the major long-distance trade routes, Mecca was the site of the Kaaba, the most prominent religious shrine in Arabia, which housed representations of some 360 deities and was the destination for many pilgrims. Mecca's dominant tribe, the Quraysh, had come to control access to the Kaaba and grew wealthy by taxing the local trade that accompanied the annual pilgrimage season. By the sixth century C.E., Mecca was home to people from various tribes and clans as well as an assortment of individual outlaws, exiles, refugees, and foreign merchants, but much of its growing wealth was concentrated in the hands of a few ruling Quraysh families.

Furthermore, Arabia was located on the periphery of two established and rival civilizations of that time—the Byzantine Empire, heir to the Roman world, and the Sassanid Empire, heir to the imperial traditions of old Persia. This location, coupled with long-distance trade, ensured some familiarity with the larger world, particularly in the cities and settled farming regions of the peninsula. Many Jews and Christians as well as some Zoroastrians lived among the Arabs, and their monotheistic ideas became widely known. By the time of Muhammad, most of the settled Arabs had acknowl-edged the preeminent position of Allah, the supreme god of the Arab pantheon, although they usually found the lesser gods, including the three daughters of Allah, far more accessible. Moreover, they increasingly identified Allah with Yahweh, the Jewish High God, and regarded themselves too as "children of Abraham." A few Arabs were beginning to explore the possibility that Allah/Yahweh was the only God and that the many others, residing in the Kaaba and in shrines across the peninsula, were nothing more than "helpless and harmless idols."[2]

To an outside observer around 600, it might well have seemed that Arabs were moving toward Judaism religiously or that Christianity, the most rapidly growing reli-gion in western Asia, would encompass Arabia as well. Any such expectations, how-ever, were thoroughly confounded by the dramatic events of the seventh century.

The Messenger and the Message

The catalyst for those events and for the birth of this new religion was a single indi-vidual, Muhammad Ibn Abdullah (570–632 C.E.), who was born in Mecca to a Quraysh family. As a young boy, Muhammad lost his parents, came under the care of an uncle, and worked as a shepherd to pay his keep. Later he became a trader and traveled as far north as Syria. At the age of twenty-five, he married a wealthy widow, Khadija, herself a prosperous merchant, with whom he fathered six children. A highly

■ Comparison

How does the core message of Islam compare with that of Judaism and Christianity?

$\mathcal{S}$napshot   **Key Moments in the Early History of Islam**

Birth of Muhammad	570
Beginning of Muhammad's revelations	610
Hijra (the emigration from Mecca to Medina)	622
Muhammad returns to Mecca in triumph	630
Death of Muhammad	632
Rightly Guided Caliphs	632–661
Arab victories against Byzantine and Persian forces	636–637
Conquest of Egypt	640
Compilation of the Quran	650s
Umayyad caliphate	661–750
Conquest of Spain	711–718
Abbasid caliphate	750–1258
Battle of Talas River	751

reflective man deeply troubled by the religious corruption and social inequalities of Mecca, he often undertook periods of withdrawal and meditation in the arid mountains outside the city. There, like the Buddha and Jesus, Muhammad had a powerful, overwhelming religious experience that left him convinced, albeit reluctantly, that he was Allah's messenger to the Arabs, commissioned to bring to them a scripture in their own language.

According to Muslim tradition, the revelations began in 610 and continued periodically over the next twenty-two years. Those revelations, recorded in the Quran, became the sacred scriptures of Islam, which to this day Muslims everywhere regard as the very words of God and the core of their faith. Intended to be recited rather than simply read for information, the Quran, Muslims claim, when heard in its original Arabic, conveys nothing less than the very presence of the divine. Its unmatched poetic beauty, miraculous to Muslims, convinced many that it was indeed a revelation from God. One of the earliest converts testified to its power: "When I heard the Quran, my heart was softened and I wept and Islam entered into me."[3] (See Document 11.1, pp. 502–04 for selections from the Quran.)

In its Arabian setting, the Quran's message, delivered through Muhammad, was revolutionary. Religiously, it was radically monotheistic, presenting Allah as the only God, the all-powerful Creator, good, just, and merciful. It rejected as utterly false and useless the many gods housed in the Kaaba and scorned the Christian notion of the Trinity. Allah was the "Lord sustainer of the worlds, the Compassionate, the Caring, master of the day of reckoning."[4] Here was an exalted conception of the Deity that drew heavily on traditions of Jewish and Christian monotheism. As "the Messenger of

God," Muhammad presented himself in the line of earlier prophets—Abraham, Moses, Jesus, and many others. He was the last, "the seal of the prophets," bearing God's final revelation to humankind. It was not so much a call to a new faith as an invitation to return to the old and pure religion of Abraham from which Arabs, Jews, and Christians alike had deviated.

Submission to Allah ("Muslim" means "one who submits") was the primary obligation of believers and the means of achieving a place in paradise

Muslims, Jews, and Christians
The close relationship of three Middle Eastern monotheistic traditions is illustrated in this fifteenth-century Persian painting, which portrays Muhammad leading Moses, Abraham, and Jesus in prayer. The fire surrounding the prophet's head represents his religious fervor. The painting reflects the Islamic belief that the revelations granted to Muhammad built upon and completed those given earlier to Jews and Christians. (Bibliothèque nationale de France)

after death. According to the Quran, however, submission was not merely an individual or spiritual act, for it involved the creation of a whole new society. Over and again, the Quran denounced the prevailing social practices of an increasingly prosperous Mecca: the hoarding of wealth, the exploitation of the poor, the charging of high rates of interest on loans, corrupt business deals, the abuse of women, and the neglect of the widows and orphans. Like the Jewish prophets of the Old Testament, the Quran demanded social justice and laid out a prescription for its implementation. It sought a return to the older values of Arab tribal life—solidarity, equality, concern for the poor—which had been undermined, particularly in Mecca, by growing wealth and commercialism.

The message of the Quran challenged not only the ancient polytheism of Arab religion and the social injustices of Mecca but also the entire tribal and clan structure of Arab society, which was so prone to war, feuding, and violence. The just and moral society of Islam was the *umma*, the community of all believers, replacing tribal, ethnic, or racial identities. Such a society would be a "witness over the nations," for according to the Quran, "You are the best community evolved for mankind, enjoining what is right and forbidding what is wrong."[5] In this community, women too had an honored and spiritually equal place. "The believers, men and women, are protectors of one another," declared the Quran.[6] The umma, then, was to be a new and just community, bound by a common belief, rather than by territory, language, or tribe.

The core message of the Quran—surrendering to the divine—was effectively summarized as a set of five requirements for believers, known as the Pillars of Islam. The first pillar expressed the heart of the Islamic message: "There is no god but Allah, and Muhammad is the messenger of God." The second pillar was prayer, to be performed five times a day while facing in the direction of Mecca. The accompanying rituals, including cleansing, bowing, kneeling, and prostration, expressed believers' submission to Allah and provided a frequent reminder, amid the busyness of daily life, that they were living in the presence of the divine. The third pillar, almsgiving, reflected the Quran's repeated demands for social justice by requiring believers to give generously to support the poor and needy of the community. The fourth pillar established a month of fasting during Ramadan, which meant abstaining from food, drink, and sexual relations from the first light of dawn to sundown. It provided an occasion for self-purification and a reminder of the needs of the hungry. The fifth pillar encouraged a pilgrimage to Mecca, known as the *hajj*, where believers from all over the Islamic world assembled once a year and put on identical simple white clothing as they performed together rituals reminding them of key events in Islamic history. For at least the few days of the hajj, the many worlds of Islam must surely have seemed a single realm.

A further requirement for believers, sometimes called the sixth pillar, was "struggle," or *jihad* in Arabic. Its more general meaning, which Muhammad referred to as the "greater jihad," was an interior personal effort of each Muslim against greed and selfishness, a spiritual striving toward living a God-conscious life. In its "lesser" form, the "jihad of the sword," the Quran authorized armed struggle against the forces of unbelief and evil as a means of establishing Muslim rule and of defending the umma from the threats of infidel aggressors. The understanding and use of the jihad concept has varied widely over the many centuries of Islamic history and remains a matter of controversy among Muslims in the twenty-first century.

The Transformation of Arabia

■ Change

In what ways was the rise of Islam revolutionary, both in theory and in practice?

As the revelations granted to Muhammad became known in Mecca, they attracted a small following of some close relatives, a few prominent Meccan leaders, and an assortment of lower-class dependents, freed slaves, and members of poorer clans. Those teachings also soon attracted the vociferous opposition of Mecca's elite families, particularly those of Muhammad's own tribe, the Quraysh. Muhammad's claim to be a "messenger of Allah," his unyielding monotheism, his call for social reform, his condemnation of Mecca's business practices, and his apparent disloyalty to his own tribe enraged the wealthy and ruling families of Mecca. So great had this opposition become that in 622 Muhammad and his small band of followers emigrated to the more welcoming town of Yathrib, soon to be called Medina, the city of the Prophet. This agricultural settlement of mixed Arab and Jewish population had invited Muhammad to serve as an arbitrator of their intractable conflicts. The emigration to Yathrib, known in Arabic as the *hijra*, was a momentous turning point in the early history of Islam and thereafter marked the beginning of a new Islamic calendar.

The Islamic community, or umma, that took shape in Medina was a kind of "supertribe," but very different from the traditional tribes of Arab society. Membership was a matter of belief rather than birth, allowing the community to expand rapidly. Furthermore, all authority, both political and religious, was concentrated in the hands of Muhammad, who proceeded to introduce radical changes. Usury was outlawed, tax-free marketplaces were established, and a mandatory payment to support the poor was imposed.

In Medina, Muhammad not only began to create a new society but also declared Islam's independence from its earlier affiliation with Judaism. In the early years, he had anticipated a warm response from Jews and Christians, based on a common mono-theism and prophetic tradition, and had directed his followers to pray facing Jerusalem. But when some Jewish groups allied with his enemies, Muhammad acted harshly to suppress them, exiling some and enslaving or killing others. This was not, however, a general suppression of Jews, since others among them remained loyal to Muhammad's new state. But the prophet now redirected Muslims' prayer toward Mecca, essentially declaring Islam an Arab religion, though one with a universal message.

From its base in Medina, the Islamic community rapidly extended its reach throughout Arabia. Early military successes against Muhammad's Meccan opponents convinced other Arab tribes that the Muslims and their God were on the rise, and they sought to negotiate alliances with the new power. Growing numbers, though not all, converted. The religious appeal of the new faith, its promise of material gain, the end of incessant warfare among feuding tribes, periodic military actions skillfully led by Muhammad, and the Prophet's willingness to enter into marriage alliances with leading tribes—all of this contributed to the consolidation of Islamic control through-out Arabia. In 630, Muhammad triumphantly and peacefully entered Mecca itself, purging the Kaaba of its idols and declaring it a shrine to the one God, Allah. By the time Muhammad died in 632, most of Arabia had come under the control of this new Islamic state, and many had embraced the new faith.

Thus the birth of Islam differed sharply from that of Christianity. Jesus' teach-ing about "giving to Caesar what is Caesar's and to God what is God's" reflected the minority and subordinate status of the Jews within the Roman Empire. Early Christians found themselves periodically persecuted by Roman authorities for more than three centuries, requiring them to work out some means of dealing with an often hostile state. The answer lay in the development of a separate church hierar-chy and the concept of two coexisting authorities, one religious and one political, an arrangement that persisted even after the state became Christian.

The young Islamic community, by contrast, found itself constituted as a state, and soon a huge empire, at the very beginning of its history. Muhammad was not only a religious figure but also, unlike Jesus or the Buddha, a political and military leader able to implement his vision of an ideal Islamic society. Nor did Islam give rise to a separate religious organization, although tension between religious and polit-ical goals frequently generated conflict. No professional clergy mediating between God and humankind emerged within Islam. Teachers, religious scholars, prayer lead-ers, and judges within an Islamic legal system did not have the religious role that priests held within Christianity. No distinction between religious law and civil law, so important in the Christian world, existed within the realm of Islam. One law, known as the *sharia*, regulated every aspect of life. The sharia (literally, a path to water, which is the source of life) evolved over the several centuries following the birth of this new religion and found expression in a number of separate schools of Islamic legal practice.

In little more than twenty years (610–632), a profound transformation had occurred in the Arabian Peninsula. A new religion had been born, though one that had roots in earlier Jewish, Christian, and Zoroastrian traditions. A new and vigorous state had emerged, bringing peace to the warring tribes of Arabia. Within that state, a distinctive society had begun to take shape, one that served ever after as a model for Islamic communities everywhere. In his farewell sermon, Muhammad described the outlines of this community:

> All mankind is from Adam and Eve, an Arab has no superiority over a non-Arab nor a non-Arab has any superiority over an Arab; also a white has no superiority over a black nor a black has any superiority over a white—except by piety and good action. Learn that every Muslim is a brother to every Muslim and that the Muslims constitute one brotherhood.[7]

The Making of an Arab Empire

It did not take long for the immense transformations occurring in Arabia to have an impact beyond the peninsula. In the centuries that followed, the energies born of those vast changes profoundly transformed much of the Afro-Eurasian world. The new Arab state became a huge empire, encompassing all or part of Egyptian, Roman/Byzantine, Persian, Mesopotamian, and Indian civilizations. The Islamic faith spread widely within and outside that empire. So too did the culture and language of Arabia, as many Arabs migrated far beyond their original homeland and many others found it advantageous to learn Arabic. From the mixing and blending of these many peoples emerged the new and distinctive third-wave civilization of Islam, bound by the ties of a common faith but divided by differences of culture, class, politics, gender, and religious understanding. These enormously consequential processes—the making of a new religion, a new empire, and a new civilization—were central to world history during the postclassical millennium.

War and Conquest

■ **Change**
Why were Arabs able to construct such a huge empire so quickly?

Within a few years of Muhammad's death in 632, Arab armies engaged the Byzantine and Persian Sassanid empires, the great powers of the region. It was the beginning of a process that rapidly gave rise to an Islamic/Arab empire that stretched from Spain to India, penetrating both Europe and China and governing most of the lands between them (see Map 11.1). In creating that empire, Arabs were continuing a long pattern of tribal raids into surrounding civilizations, but now the Arabs were newly organized in a state of their own with a central command able to mobilize the military potential of the entire Arab population. The Byzantine and Persian empires, weakened by decades of war with each other and by internal revolts, continued to view the Arabs as a mere nuisance rather than a serious threat. But the Sassanid Empire was defeated by Arab forces during the 650s, while Byzantium soon lost the southern half of its territories. Beyond these victories, Arab forces, operating on both land and sea, swept westward across North Africa, conquered Spain in the early 700s, and attacked southern France. To the east, Arab

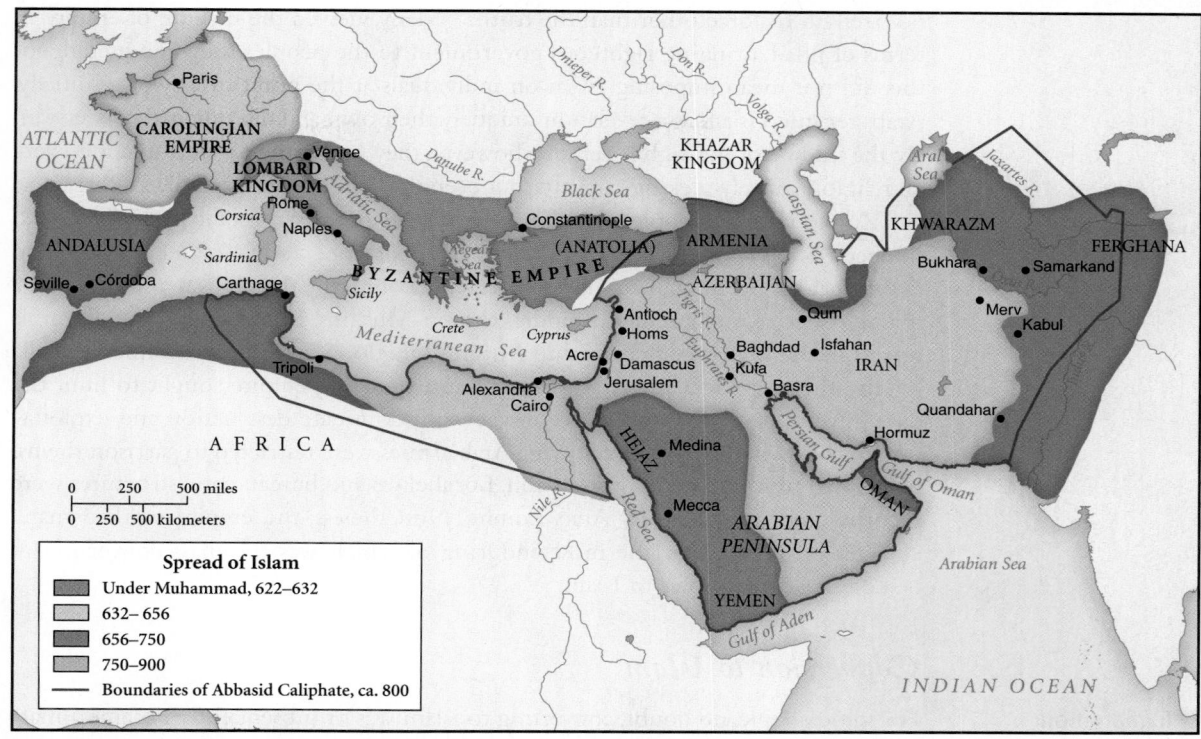

Map 11.1   The Arab Empire and the Initial Expansion of Islam, 622–900 c.e.
Far more so than with Buddhism or Christianity, the initial spread of Islam was both rapid and extensive.
And unlike the other two world religions, Islam gave rise to a huge empire, ruled by Muslim Arabs, which
encompassed many of the older civilizations of the region.

forces reached the Indus River and seized some of the major oases towns of Central
Asia. In 751, Arab armies inflicted a crushing defeat on Chinese forces in the Battle
of Talas River, which had lasting consequences for the cultural evolution of Asia,
for it checked the further expansion of China to the west and made possible the
conversion to Islam of Central Asia's Turkic-speaking people.

The motives driving the creation of the Arab Empire were in many ways similar to those of other empires. The merchant leaders of the new Islamic community
wanted to capture profitable trade routes and wealthy agricultural regions. Individual
Arabs found in military expansion a route to wealth and social promotion. The need
to harness the immense energies of the Arabian transformation was also important.
The fragile unity of the umma threatened to come apart after Muhammad's death,
and external expansion provided a common task for the community.

Also apparent in the making of the Arab Empire was a distinctly religious dimension. To the Arabs themselves, the only possible explanation for their amazing, indeed
miraculous, success was that "God gave us the victory over them, allowing us to take
their countries and to settle in their lands, their homes, and their property, we having

no strength or force other than the truth."[8] Many viewed the mission of empire in terms of jihad, bringing righteous government to the peoples they conquered, but this did not mean imposing Islam on individuals at the point of a sword. Initially, Arabs regarded Islam as a revelation uniquely their own and discouraged conversion. By the middle of the eighth century, however, they had come to view it as a universal religion actively seeking converts, but even then they recognized Jews, Christians, and Zoroastrians as "people of the book," giving them the status of *dhimmis* (protected subjects). Such people were permitted to freely practice their own religion, so long as they paid a special tax known as the *jizya*. Theoretically the tax was a substitute for military service, supposedly forbidden to non-Muslims. In practice, many dhimmis served in the highest offices within Muslim kingdoms and in their armies as well.

In other ways too, the Arab rulers of an expanding empire sought to limit the disruptive impact of conquest. To prevent indiscriminate destruction and exploitation of conquered peoples, occupying Arab armies were restricted to garrison towns, segregated from the native population. Local elites and bureaucratic structures were incorporated into the new Arab Empire. Nonetheless, the empire worked many changes on its subjects, the most enduring of which was the mass conversion of Middle Eastern peoples to Islam.

Conversion to Islam

■ Explanation
What accounts for the widespread conversion to Islam?

For some people, no doubt, converting to Islam was or subsequently became a matter of profound spiritual or psychological transformation, but far more often, at least initially, it was "social conversion," defined as "movement from one religiously defined social community to another."[9] It happened at various rates and in different ways, but in the four centuries or so after the death of Muhammad, millions of individuals and many whole societies within the Arab Empire found their cultural identity bound up with a belief in Allah and the message of his prophet. They had become Muslims. How had this immense cultural change occurred?

In some ways, perhaps, the change was not so dramatic, as major elements of Islam—monotheism; ritual prayer and cleansing ceremonies; fasting; divine revelation; the ideas of heaven, hell, and final judgment—were quite familiar to Jews, Christians, and Zoroastrians. Furthermore, Islam was from the beginning associated with the sponsorship of a powerful state, quite unlike the experience of early Buddhism or Christianity. Conquest called into question the power of old gods, while the growing prestige of the Arab Empire attracted many to Allah. Although deliberately forced conversion was rare, living in an Islamic-governed state provided a variety of incentives for claiming Muslim identity.[10] Slaves and prisoners of war were among the early converts, particularly in Persia. Converts could also avoid the jizya, the tax imposed on non-Muslims. In Islam, merchants found a religion friendly to commerce, and in the Arab Empire they enjoyed a huge and secure arena for trade. People aspiring to official positions found conversion to Islam an aid to social mobility.

Conversion was not an automatic or easy process. Vigorous resistance delayed conversion for centuries among the Berbers of North Africa; a small group of zealous Spanish Christians in the ninth century provoked their own martyrdom by publicly insulting the Prophet; and some Persian Zoroastrians fled to avoid Muslim rule. More generally, though, a remarkable and lasting religious transformation occurred throughout the Arab Empire. In Persia, for example, between 750 and 900, about 80 percent of the population had made the transition to a Muslim religious identity, while retaining their own ancient language.[11] In places where large-scale Arab migration had occurred, such as Egypt, North Africa, and Iraq, Arabic culture and language, as well as the religion of Islam, took hold. Such areas are today both Muslim and Arab, while Iran, Turkey, and Pakistan, for example, have "Islamized" without "Arabizing."

Divisions and Controversies

The ideal of a unified Muslim community, so important to Muhammad, proved difficult to realize as conquest and conversion vastly enlarged the Islamic umma. A central problem was that of leadership and authority in the absence of Muhammad's towering presence. Who should hold the role of caliph, the successor to Muhammad as the political leader of the umma, the protector and defender of the faith? That issue crystallized a variety of emerging conflicts within the Islamic world—between early and later converts, among various Arab tribes and factions, between Arabs and non-Arabs, between privileged and wealthy rulers and their far less fortunate subjects. Many of these political and social conflicts found expression in religious terms as various understandings of the Quran and of Muhammad's life and teachings took shape within the growing Islamic community.

The first four caliphs, known among most Muslims as the Rightly Guided Caliphs (632–661), were close "companions of the Prophet," selected by the Muslim elders of Medina. Division surfaced almost immediately as a series of Arab tribal rebellions and new "prophets" persuaded the first caliph, Abu Bakr, to suppress them forcibly. The third and fourth caliphs, Uthman and Ali, were both assassinated, and by 656, less than twenty-five years after Muhammad's death, civil war pitted Muslim against Muslim.

■ **Comparison**
What is the difference between Sunni and Shia Islam?

Out of that conflict emerged one of the deepest and most enduring rifts within the Islamic world. On one side were the Sunni Muslims, who held that the caliphs were rightful political and military leaders, selected by the Islamic community. On the other side of this sharp divide was the Shia (an Arabic word meaning "party" or "faction") branch of Islam. Its adherents felt strongly that leadership in the Islamic world should derive from the line of Ali and his son Husayn, blood relatives of Muhammad, both of whom died at the hands of their political or religious enemies.

In the beginning, therefore, this divide was simply a political conflict without serious theological or religious meaning, but over time the Sunni/Shia split acquired deeper significance. For Sunni Muslims, religious authority in general emerged

The Kaaba
Located in Mecca, this stone structure covered with a black cloth and known as the Kaaba was originally home to the numerous deities of pre-Islamic Arabia. Cleansed by Muhammad, it became the sacred shrine of Islam and the destination of countless pilgrims undertaking the hajj. Part of that ritual involves circling the Kaaba seven times, as shown here in a photograph from 2004. (Dan Mohiuddin, photographer)

from the larger community, particularly from the religious scholars known as *ulama*. Shia Muslims, on the other hand, invested their leaders, known as *imams*, with a religious authority that the caliphs lacked, allowing them to infallibly interpret divine revelation and law. For much of early Islamic history, Shia Muslims saw themselves as the minority opposition within Islam. They felt that history had taken a wrong turn and that they were "the defenders of the oppressed, the critics and opponents of privilege and power," while the Sunnis were the advocates of the established order.[12] Various armed revolts by Shias over the centuries, most of which failed, led to a distinctive conception of martyrdom and to the expectation that their defeated leaders were merely in hiding and not really dead and that they would return in the fullness of time. Thus a messianic element entered Shia Islam. The Sunni/Shia schism was a lasting division in the Islamic world, reflected in conflicts among various Islamic states, and was exacerbated by further splits among the Shia. Those divisions echo still in the twenty-first century.

As the Arab Empire grew, its caliphs were transformed from modest Arab chiefs into absolute monarchs of the Byzantine or Persian variety, complete with elaborate court rituals, a complex bureaucracy, a standing army, and centralized systems of taxation and coinage. They were also subject to the dynastic rivalries and succession disputes common to other empires. The first dynasty, following the era of the Rightly Guided Caliphs, came from the Umayyad family (ruled 661–750). Under its rule, the Arab Empire expanded greatly, caliphs became hereditary rulers, and the capital moved from Medina to the cosmopolitan Roman/Byzantine city of Damascus in Syria. Its ruling class was an Arab military aristocracy, drawn from various tribes. But Umayyad rule provoked growing criticism and unrest. The Shia viewed the Umayyad caliphs as illegitimate usurpers, and non-Arab Muslims resented their second-class citizenship in the empire. Many Arabs protested the luxurious living and impiety of their rulers. The Umayyads, they charged, "made God's servants slaves, God's property something to be taken by turns among the rich, and God's religion a cause of corruption."[13]

Such grievances lay behind the overthrow of the Umayyads in 750 and their replacement by a new Arab dynasty, the Abbasids. With a splendid new capital in Baghdad, the Abbasid caliphs presided over a flourishing and prosperous Islamic civilization in which non-Arabs, especially Persians, now played a prominent role. Persian influence was reflected in a new title for the caliph, "the shadow of God on earth." Persian became the language of elite culture in the eastern Islamic lands; Persian poetry, painting, architecture, and court rituals were widely imitated. (See Visual Sources: Islamic Civilization in Persian Miniature Paintings, pp. 512–19, for examples of Persian miniature painting.) But the political unity of the Abbasid Empire did not last long. Beginning in the mid-ninth century, many local governors or military commanders effectively asserted the autonomy of their regions, while still giving formal allegiance to the caliph in Baghdad. Long before Mongol conquest put an official end to the Abbasid Empire in 1258, the Islamic world had fractured politically into a series of "sultanates," many ruled by Persian or Turkish military dynasties.

A further tension within the world of Islam, though seldom a violent conflict, lay in different answers to the central question: What does it mean to be a Muslim, to submit wholly to Allah? That question took on added urgency as the expanding Arab Empire incorporated various peoples and cultures that had been unknown during Muhammad's lifetime. One answer lay in the development of the sharia (see Document 11.3, pp. 506–09), the body of Islamic law developed by religious scholars, the ulama, primarily in the eighth and ninth centuries.

■ Comparison
In what ways were Sufi Muslims critical of mainstream Islam?

Based on the Quran, the life and teachings of Muhammad, deductive reasoning, and the consensus of scholars, the emerging sharia addressed in great detail practically every aspect of religious and social life. It was a blueprint for an authentic Islamic society, providing detailed guidance for prayer and ritual cleansing; marriage, divorce, and inheritance; business and commercial relationships; the treatment of slaves; political life; and much more. Debates among the ulama led to the creation of four schools of law among Sunni Muslims and still others in the lands of Shia Islam. To the ulama and their followers, living as a Muslim meant following the sharia and thus participating in the creation of an Islamic society.

A second and quite different understanding of the faith emerged among those who saw the worldly success of Islamic civilization as a distraction and deviation from the purer spirituality of Muhammad's time. Known as Sufis, they represented Islam's mystical dimension, in that they sought a direct and personal experience of the divine. Through renunciation of the material world, meditation on the words of the Quran, chanting the names of God, the use of music and dance, the veneration of Muhammad and various "saints," Sufis pursued the taming of the ego and spiritual union with Allah. To describe that inexpressible experience, they often resorted to metaphors of drunkenness or the embrace of lovers. "Stain your prayer rug with wine," urged the famous Sufi poet Hafiz, referring to the intoxication of the believer with the divine presence. Rabia, an eighth-century woman and Sufi master, conveyed something of the fervor of early Sufi devotion in her famous prayer:

> O my Lord, if I worship Thee from fear of Hell, burn me in Hell; and if I worship Thee from hope of Paradise, exclude me thence; but if I worship Thee for Thine own sake, then withhold not from me Thine Eternal Beauty.[14]

(See Document 11.4, pp. 509–10, for another expression of Sufi religious sensibility from the thirteenth-century poet Rumi.)

This mystical tendency in Islamic practice, which became widely popular by the ninth and tenth centuries, was sharply critical of the more scholarly and legalistic practitioners of the sharia. To Sufis, establishment teachings about the law and correct behavior, while useful for daily living, did little to bring the believer into the presence of God. For some, even the Quran had its limits. Why spend time reading a love letter (the Quran), asked one Sufi master, when one might be in the very presence of the Beloved who wrote it?[15] Furthermore, they felt that many of the ulama had been compromised by their association with worldly and corrupt governments. Sufis therefore often charted their own course to God, implicitly challenging the religious authority of the ulama. For these orthodox religious scholars, Sufi ideas and practice verged on heresy, as Sufis claimed to be one with God, to receive new revelations, or to incorporate religious practices from outside the Islamic world.

Despite their differences, the legalistic emphasis of the ulama and Sufi spirituality never became irreconcilable versions of Islam. A major Islamic thinker, al-Ghazali (1058–1111), himself both a legal scholar and a Sufi practitioner, in fact worked out an intellectual accommodation among different strands of Islamic thought. Rational philosophy alone could never enable believers to know Allah, he argued. Nor were revelation and the law sufficient, for Muslims must know God in their hearts, through direct personal encounter with Allah. Thus al-Ghazali incorporated Sufism into mainstream Islamic thinking. Nonetheless, differences in emphasis remained an element of tension and sometimes discord within the world of Islam.

Women and Men in Early Islam

■ **Change**
How did the rise of Islam change the lives of women?

What did the rise of Islam and the making of the Arab Empire mean for the daily lives of women and their relationship with men? Virtually every aspect of this question has been and remains highly controversial. The debates begin with the Quran itself. Did its teachings release women from earlier restrictions, or did they impose new limitations? At the level of spiritual life, the Quran was quite clear and explicit: men and women were equal.

> Those who surrender themselves to Allah and accept the true faith; who are devout, sincere, patient, humble, charitable, and chaste; who fast and are ever mindful of Allah — on these, both men and women, Allah will bestow forgiveness and rich reward.[16]

But in social terms, and especially within marriage, the Quran, like the written texts of almost all civilizations, viewed women as inferior and subordinate:

> Men have authority over women because Allah has made the one superior to the other, and because they spend their wealth to maintain them. Good women are obedient. They guard their unseen parts because Allah has guarded them. As for those from whom you fear disobedience, admonish them and send them to beds apart and beat them. Then if they obey you, take no further action against them.[17]

More specifically, the Quran provided a mix of rights, restrictions, and protections for women. The earlier Arab practice of female infanticide, for example, was forbidden. Women were given control over their own property, particularly their dowries, and were granted rights of inheritance, but at half the rate of their male counterparts. Marriage was considered a contract between consenting parties, thus making marriage by capture illegitimate. Within marriage, women were expected to enjoy sexual satisfaction and could sue for divorce if they had not had sexual relations for more than four months. Divorce was thus possible for both parties, although it was far more readily available for men. The practice of taking multiple husbands, which operated in some pre-Islamic Arab tribes, was prohibited, while polygyny (the practice of having multiple wives) was permitted, though more clearly regulated than before. Men were limited to four wives and required to treat each of them equally. The difficulty of doing so has been interpreted by some as virtually requiring monogamy. Men were, however, permitted to have sexual relations with female slaves, but any children born of those unions were free, as was the mother once her owner died. Furthermore, men were strongly encouraged to marry orphans, widows, and slaves.

Such Quranic prescriptions were but one factor shaping the lives of women and men. At least as important were the long-established practices of the societies into which Islam spread and the growing sophistication, prosperity, and urbanization of Islamic civilization. As had been the case in Athens and China during their "golden ages," women, particularly in the upper classes, experienced growing restrictions as Islamic civilization flourished culturally and economically in the Abbasid era. In early Islamic times, a number of women played visible public roles, particularly Muhammad's youngest wife, Aisha. Women prayed in the mosques, although separately, standing beside the men. Nor were women generally veiled or secluded. As the Arab empire grew in size and splendor, however, the position of women became more limited. The second caliph, Umar, asked women to offer prayers at home. Now veiling and the seclusion of women became standard practice among the upper and ruling classes, removing them from public life. Separate quarters within the homes of the wealthy were the domain of women, from which they could emerge only completely veiled. The caliph Mansur (ruled 754–775) carried this separation of the sexes even further when he ordered a separate bridge for women to be built over the Euphrates in the new capital of Baghdad. Such seclusion was less possible for lower-class women, who lacked the servants of the rich and had to leave the home for shopping or work.

Such practices derived far more from established traditions of Middle Eastern cultures than from the Quran itself, but they soon gained an Islamic rationale in the

Men and Women at Worship
This sixteenth-century Persian painting of a mosque service shows older men with beards toward the front, younger men behind them, and veiled women and children in a separate area. (Bodleian Library, University of Oxford, Ms. Ouseley. Add 24, fol. 55v)

writings of Muslim thinkers. The famous philosopher and religious scholar al-Ghazali clearly saw a relationship between Muslim piety and the separation of the sexes:

> It is not permissible for a stranger to hear the sound of a pestle being pounded by a woman he does not know. If he knocks at the door, it is not proper for the woman to answer him softly and easily because men's hearts can be drawn to [women] for the most trifling [reason].... However, if the woman has to answer the knock, she should stick her finger in her mouth so that her voice sounds like that of an old woman.[18]

Other signs of a tightening patriarchy—such as "honor killing" of women by their male relatives for violating sexual taboos and, in some places, clitorectomy (female genital cutting)—likewise derived from local cultures, with no sanction in the Quran or Islamic law. Where they were practiced, such customs often came to be seen as Islamic, but they were certainly not limited to the Islamic world. In many cultures, concern with family honor, linked to women's sexuality, dictated harsh punishments for women who violated sexual taboos.

Negative views of women, presenting them variously as weak, deficient, and a sexually charged threat to men and social stability, emerged in the *hadiths*, traditions about the sayings or actions of Muhammad, which became an important source of Islamic law. (See Document 11.2, pp. 505–06, for examples of hadiths.) A changing interpretation of the Adam and Eve story illustrates the point. In the Quran, equal blame attaches to both of them for yielding to the temptation of Satan, and both alike ask for and receive God's forgiveness. Nothing suggests that Eve tempted or seduced Adam into sin. In later centuries, however, several hadiths and other writings took up Judeo-Christian versions of the story that blamed Eve, and thus women in general, for Adam's sin and for the punishment that followed, including expulsion from the garden and pain in childbirth.[19]

Even as women faced growing restrictions in society generally, Islam, like Buddhism and Christianity, also offered new outlets for them in religious life. The Sufi practice of mystical union with Allah allowed a greater role for women than did mainstream Islam. Some Sufi orders had parallel groups for women, and a few welcomed women as equal members. Within the world of Shia Islam, women teachers of the faith were termed *mullahs*, the same as their male counterparts. Islamic education, either in the home or in Quranic schools, allowed some to become literate and a few to achieve higher levels of learning. Visits to the tombs of major Islamic figures as well as the ritual of the public bath provided some opportunity for women to interact with other women beyond their own family circle.

Islam and Cultural Encounter: A Four-Way Comparison

In its earliest centuries, the rapid spread of Islam had been accompanied by the creation of an immense Arab Empire, very much in the tradition of earlier Mediterranean and Middle Eastern empires. By the tenth century, however, little political unity

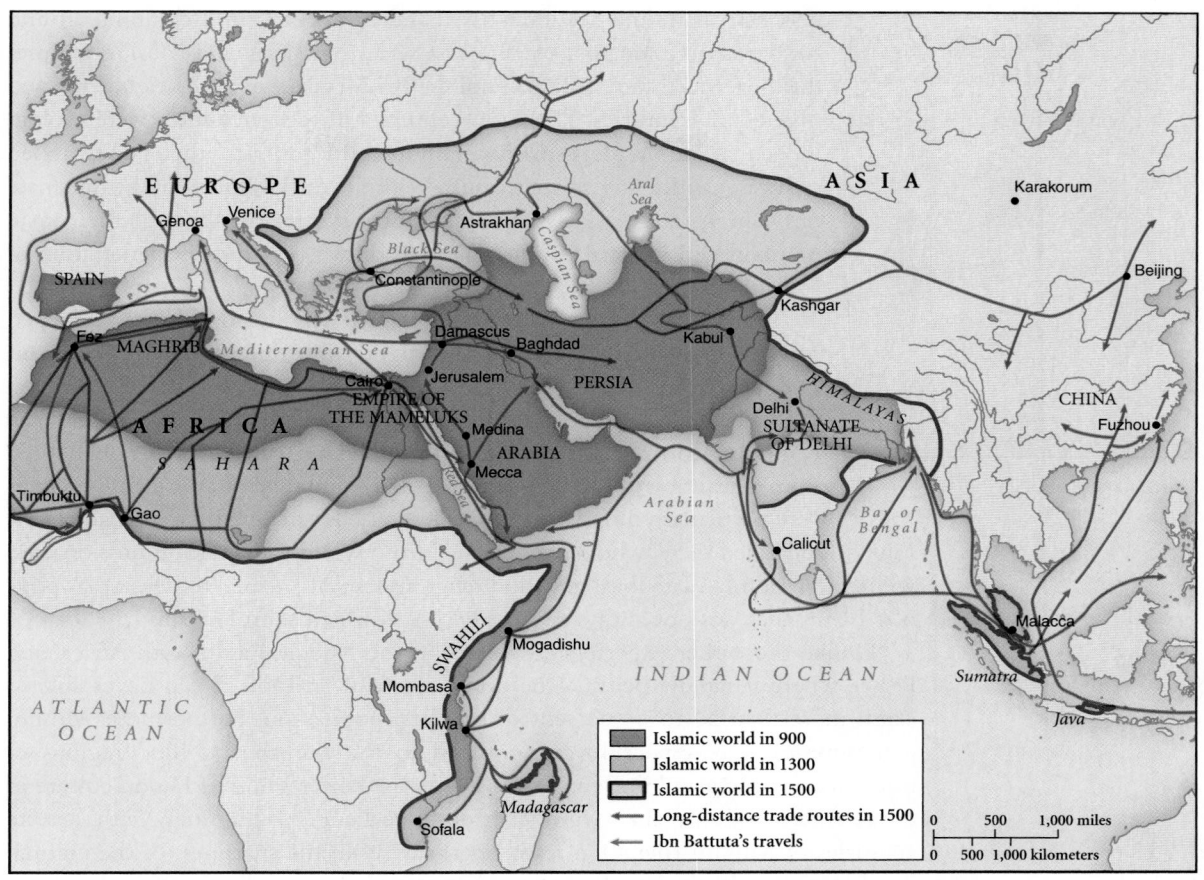

Map 11.2 The Growing World of Islam (900–1500) Islam as a religion, a civilization, and an arena of commerce continued to grow even as the Arab Empire fragmented.

remained, and in 1258 even the powerless symbol of that earlier unity vanished as Mongol forces sacked Baghdad and killed the last Abbasid caliph. But even as the empire disintegrated, the civilization that was born within it grew and flourished. Perhaps the most significant sign of a flourishing Islamic civilization was the continued spread of the religion both within and beyond the boundaries of a vanishing Arab Empire (see Map 11.2), although that process differed considerably from place to place. The examples of India, Anatolia, West Africa, and Spain illustrate the various ways that Islam penetrated these societies as well as the rather different outcomes of these epic cultural encounters.

The Case of India

In South Asia, Islam found a permanent place in a long-established civilization as invasions by Turkic-speaking warrior groups from Central Asia, recently converted to Islam, brought the faith to India. Thus the Turks became the third major carrier of Islam, after the Arabs and Persians, as their conquests initiated an enduring encounter

■ **Comparison**

What similarities and differences can you identify in the spread of Islam to India, Anatolia, West Africa, and Spain?

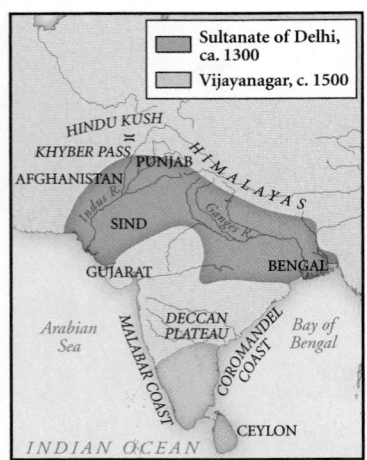

The Sultanate of Delhi

between Islam and a Hindu-based Indian civilization. Beginning around 1000, those conquests gave rise to a series of Turkic and Muslim regimes that governed much of India until the British takeover in the eighteenth and nineteenth centuries. The early centuries of this encounter were violent indeed, as the invaders smashed Hindu and Buddhist temples and carried off vast quantities of Indian treasure. With the establishment of the Sultanate of Delhi in 1206, Turkic rule became more systematic, although their small numbers and internal conflicts allowed only a very modest penetration of Indian society.

In the centuries that followed, substantial Muslim communities emerged in India, particularly in regions less tightly integrated into the dominant Hindu culture. Disillusioned Buddhists as well as low-caste Hindus and untouchables found the more egalitarian Islam attractive. So did peoples just beginning to make the transition to settled agriculture. Others benefited from converting to Islam by avoiding the tax imposed on non-Muslims. Sufis were particularly important in facilitating conversion, for India had always valued "god-filled men" who were detached from worldly affairs. Sufi missionaries, willing to accommodate local gods and religious festivals, helped to develop a "popular Islam" that was not always so sharply distinguished from Hinduism.

Unlike the earlier experience of Islam in the Middle East, North Africa, and Persia, where it rapidly became the dominant faith, in India it was never able to claim more than 20 to 25 percent of the total population. Furthermore, Muslim communities were especially concentrated in the Punjab and Sind regions of northwestern India and in Bengal to the east. The core regions of Hindu culture in the northern Indian plain were not seriously challenged by the new faith, despite centuries of Muslim rule. One reason perhaps lay in the sharpness of the cultural divide between Islam and Hinduism. Islam was the most radically monotheistic of the world's religions, forbidding any representation of Allah, while Hinduism was surely among the most prolifically polytheistic, generating endless statues and images of the divine in many forms. The Muslim notion of the equality of all believers contrasted sharply with the hierarchical assumptions of the caste system. The sexual modesty of Muslims was deeply offended by the open eroticism of some Hindu religious art.

Although such differences may have limited the appeal of Islam in India, they also may have prevented it from being absorbed into the tolerant and inclusive embrace of Hinduism as had so many other religious ideas, practices, and communities. The religious exclusivity of Islam, born of its firm monotheistic belief and the idea of a unique revelation, set a boundary that the great sponge of Hinduism could not completely absorb.

Certainly not all was conflict across that boundary. Many prominent Hindus willingly served in the political and military structures of a Muslim-ruled India. Mystical seekers after the divine blurred the distinction between Hindu and Muslim, suggesting that God was to be found "neither in temple nor in mosque." "Look within your heart," wrote the great fifteenth-century mystic poet Kabir, "for there you will find both [Allah] and Ram [a famous Hindu deity]."[20] In fact, during the early sixteenth century, a new and distinct religious tradition emerged in India, known as Sikhism, which blended elements of Islam, such as devotion to one universal God, with Hindu concepts, such as karma and rebirth. "There is no Hindu and no Muslim. All are children of God," declared Guru Nanak (1469–1539), the founder of Sikhism.

Nonetheless, Muslims usually lived quite separately, remaining a distinctive minority within an ancient Indian civilization, which they now largely governed but which they proved unable to completely transform.

The Case of Anatolia

At the same time that India was being subjected to Turkic invasion, so too was Anatolia (now modern Turkey), where the largely Christian and Greek-speaking population was then governed by the Byzantine Empire (see Maps 11.1 and 11.3). Here, as in India, the invaders initially wreaked havoc as Byzantine authority melted away in the eleventh century. Sufi missionaries likewise played a major role in the process of conversion. The outcome, however, was a far more profound cultural transformation than in India. By 1500, the population was 90 percent Muslim and largely Turkic-speaking, and Anatolia was the heartland of the powerful Turkish Ottoman Empire that had overrun Christian Byzantium. Why did the Turkic intrusion into Anatolia generate a much more thorough Islamization than in India?

One factor clearly lies in a very different demographic balance. The population of Anatolia—perhaps 8 million—was far smaller than India's roughly 48 million people, but far more Turkic-speaking peoples settled in Anatolia, giving them a much greater cultural weight than the smaller colonizing force in India. Furthermore, the disruption of Anatolian society was much more extensive. Massacres, enslavement, famine, and flight led to a sharp drop in the native population. The Byzantine state had been fatally weakened. Church properties were confiscated, and monasteries were destroyed or deserted. Priests and bishops were sometimes unable to serve their congregations. Christians, though seldom forced to convert, suffered many discriminations. They had to wear special clothing and pay special taxes, and they were forbidden to ride saddled horses or carry swords. Not a few Christians came to believe that these disasters represented proof that Islam was the true religion.[21] Thus Byzantine civilization in Anatolia, focused on the centralized institutions of church and state, was rendered leaderless and dispirited, whereas India's decentralized civilization, lacking a unified political or religious establishment, was better able to absorb the shock of external invasion while retaining its core values and identity.

The Turkish rulers of Anatolia built a new society that welcomed converts and granted them material rewards and opportunity for high office. Moreover, the cultural barriers to conversion were arguably less severe than in India. The common monotheism of Islam and Christianity, and Muslim respect for Jesus and the Christian

■ **Comparison**
Why was Anatolia so much more thoroughly Islamized than India?

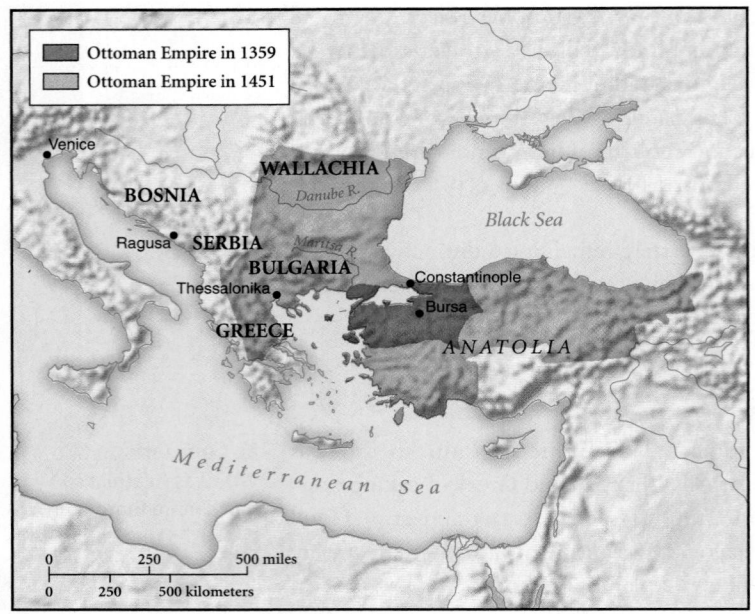

Map 11.3 **The Ottoman Empire by the Mid-Fifteenth Century**
As Turkic-speaking migrants bearing the religion of Islam penetrated Anatolia, the Ottoman Empire took shape, reaching into southeastern Europe and finally displacing the Christian Byzantine Empire. Subsequently, it came to control much of the Middle East and North Africa as well.

scriptures, made conversion easier than crossing the great gulf between Islam and Hinduism. Such similarities lent support to the suggestion of some Sufi teachers that the two religions were but different versions of the same faith. Sufis also established schools, mills, orchards, hospices, and rest places for travelers and thus replaced the destroyed or decaying institutions of Christian Anatolia.[22] All of this contributed to the thorough religious transformation of Anatolia and laid a foundation for the Ottoman Empire, which by 1500 became the most impressive and powerful state within the Islamic world (see Map 11.3).

But the Islamization of Anatolia occurred within a distinctly Turkish context. A Turkish language, not Arabic, predominated. Some Sufi religious practices, such as ecstatic turning dances, derived from Central Asian Turkic shamanism (see Visual Source 8.5, p. 376). And Turkic traditions offering a freer, more gender-equal life for women, common among pastoral people, persisted well after conversion to Islam, much to the distress of the Arab Moroccan visitor Ibn Battuta during his travels among them in the fourteenth century: "A remarkable thing that I saw... was the respect shown to women by the Turks, for they hold a more dignified position than the men.... The windows of the tent are open and her face is visible, for the Turkish women do not veil themselves."[23] He was not pleased.

The Case of West Africa

Still another pattern prevailed in West Africa. Here Islam accompanied Muslim traders across the Sahara rather than being brought by invading Arab or Turkic armies. Its acceptance in the emerging civilization of West African states in the centuries after 1000 was largely peaceful and voluntary, lacking the incentives associated elsewhere with foreign conquest. Introduced by Muslim merchants from an already Islamized North Africa, the new faith was accepted primarily in the urban centers of the West African empires—Ghana, Mali, Songhay, Kanem-Bornu, and others (see Map 11.4). For African merchant communities, Islam provided an important link to Muslim trading partners, much as Buddhism had done in Southeast Asia. For the monarchs and their courts, it offered a source of literate officials to assist in state administration as well as religious legitimacy, particularly for those who gained the prestige conferred by a pilgrimage to Mecca. Islam was a world religion with a single Creator-God, able to comfort and protect people whose political and

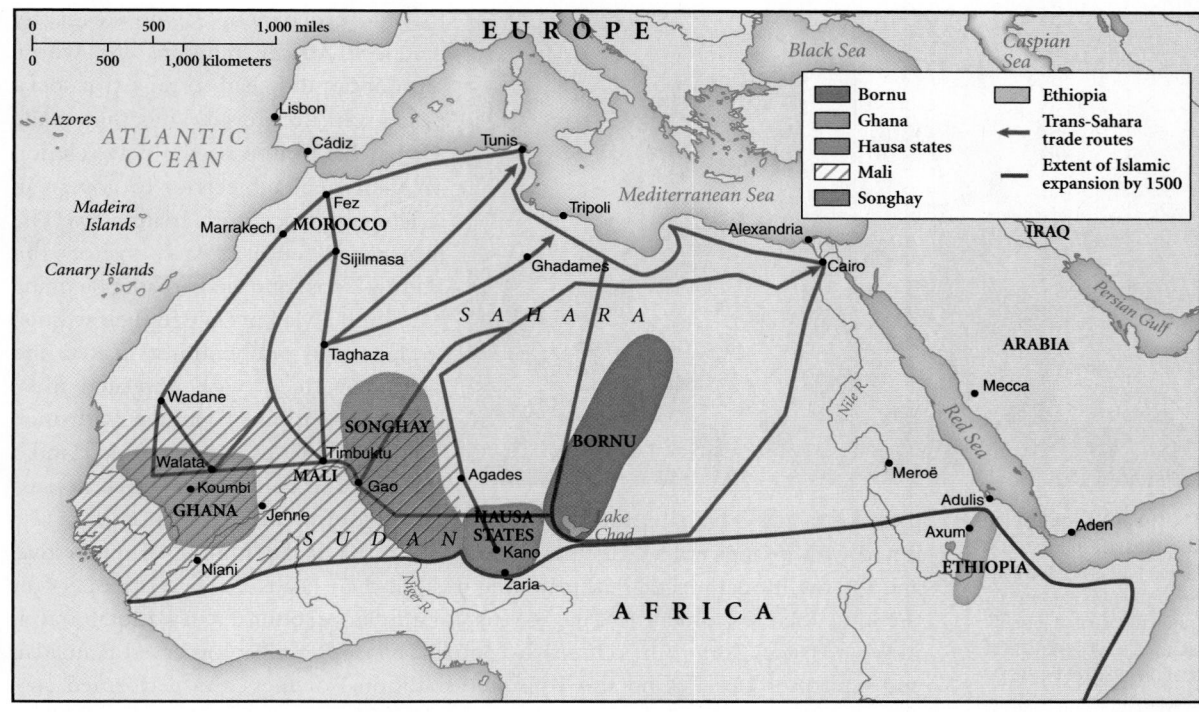

Map 11.4 West Africa and the World of Islam
Both trans-Saharan commerce and Islam linked the civilization of West Africa to the larger Muslim world.

economic horizons had expanded well beyond the local realm where ancestral spirits and traditional deities might be effective. It had a religious appeal for societies that were now participating in a wider world.

By the sixteenth century, a number of West African cities had become major centers of Islamic religious and intellectual life, attracting scholars from throughout the Muslim world. Timbuktu boasted more than 150 lower-level Quranic schools and several major centers of higher education with thousands of students from all over West Africa and beyond. Libraries held tens of thousands of books and scholarly manuscripts. Monarchs subsidized the construction of mosques as West Africa became an integral part of a larger Islamic world. Arabic became an important language of religion, education, administration, and trade, but it did not become the dominant language of daily life. Nor did West Africa experience the massive migration of Arab peoples that had promoted the Arabization of North Africa and the Middle East. Moreover, in contrast to India and Anatolia, Sufi holy men played little role until at least the eighteenth century. Scholars, merchants, and rulers, rather than mystic preachers, initially established Islam in West Africa.

Islam remained the culture of urban elites and spread little into the rural areas of West Africa until the nineteenth century. No thorough religious transformation occurred in West Africa as it had in Anatolia. Although many rulers adopted Islam,

The Great Mosque at Jenne
This mosque in the city of Jenne, initially constructed in the thirteenth century, illustrates the assimilation of Islam into West African civilization. (Bildagentur/TIPS Images)

they governed people who steadfastly practiced African religions and whose sensibilities they had to respect if social peace were to prevail. Thus they made few efforts to impose the new religion on their rural subjects or to govern in strict accordance with Islamic law. The fourteenth-century Arab visitor Ibn Battuta was appalled that practicing Muslims in Mali permitted their women to appear in public almost naked and to mingle freely with unrelated men. "The association of women with men is agreeable to us," he was told, "and a part of good conduct to which no suspicion attaches. They are not like the women of your country."[24] Ibn Battuta also noted with disapproval a "dance of the masks" on the occasion of an Islamic festival and the traditional practice of sprinkling dust on their heads as a sign of respect for the king. (See Document 8.3, pp. 362–65, for a fuller account if Ibn Battuta's travels in West Africa.) Sonni Ali, a fifteenth-century ruler of Songhay, observed Ramadan and built mosques, but he also consulted traditional diviners and performed customary sacrifices. In such ways, Islam became Africanized even as parts of Africa became Islamized.

The Case of Spain

The chief site of Islamic encounter with Catholic Europe occurred in Spain (called al-Andalus by Muslims), which was conquered by Arab and Berber forces in the early eighth century during the first wave of Islamic expansion. But there, Islam did not overwhelm Christianity as it did later in Anatolia. In fact, Muslim Spain in the several centuries that followed conquest has often been portrayed as a vibrant civilization characterized by harmony and tolerance between its Muslim rulers and its Christian and Jewish subjects.

Certainly Spain's agricultural economy was the most prosperous in Europe during the ninth and tenth centuries, and at that time its capital of Córdoba was among the largest and most splendid cities in the world. Muslims, Christians, and Jews alike contributed to a brilliant high culture in which astronomy, medicine, the arts, architecture, and literature flourished. It was largely from Spain that the rich heritage of Islamic learning became available to Christian Europe.

Furthermore, social relationships among upper-class members of different faiths were easy and frequent. More than a few Christians converted to Islam, and many others, known as Mozarabs (would-be Arabs), learned Arabic, veiled their women, stopped eating pork, appreciated Arabic music and poetry, and sometimes married

Muslims. One Christian bishop complained that Spanish Christians knew the rules of Arabic grammar better than those of Latin. During the reign of Abd al-Rahman III (912–961), freedom of worship was declared as well as the opportunity for all to rise in the bureaucracy of the state.

Even assimilated or Arabized Christians, however, remained infidels in the eyes of their Muslim counterparts, and by the late tenth century the era of toleration began to erode. Warfare with the remaining Christian states in northern Spain picked up in the tenth and eleventh centuries, and more puritanical and rigid forms of Islam entered Spain from North Africa. In these circumstances, the golden age of religious harmony faded. Under the rule of Abu Amir al-Mansur (981–1002), an official policy of tolerance turned to one of overt persecution against Christians, which now included the plundering of churches. Social life also changed. Devout Muslims avoided contact with Christians; Christian homes had to be built lower than those of Muslims; priests were forbidden to carry a cross or a Bible, lest they offend Muslim sensibilities; and Mozarabs were permitted to live only in particular places. Thus, writes one scholar, "the era of harmonious interaction between Muslim and Christian in Spain came to an end, replaced by intolerance, prejudice, and mutual suspicion."[25]

That intolerance was perpetuated as the Christian reconquest of Spain gained ground after 1200. Many Muslims were then forced out of Spain, while those who remained could no longer give the call to prayer, go on pilgrimage, or publicly practice their faith. When the reconquest was completed in 1492, all Jews, some 200,000 of them, were likewise expelled from the country. Thus, as Christianity was displaced by Islam in Anatolia, the opposite process was taking place in Spain, though with far less tolerance for other religions.

The World of Islam as a New Civilization

As the religion spread and the Abbasid dynasty declined, the civilization of Islam, like Western Christendom and the Hindu world, operated without a single political center, bound more by a shared religious culture than by a shared state. Unlike the other civilizations, however, the Islamic world by 1500 embraced at least parts of virtually every other civilization in the Afro-Eurasian hemisphere. It was in that sense "history's first truly global civilization," although the Americas, of course, were not involved.[26] What held the Islamic world together? What enabled many people to feel themselves part of a single civilization despite its political fragmentation, religious controversies, and cultural and regional diversity?

Networks of Faith

At the core of that vast civilization was a common commitment to Islam. No group was more important in the transmission of those beliefs and practices than the ulama. These learned scholars were not "priests" in the Christian sense, for in Islam, at least theoretically, no person could stand between the believer and Allah. Rather

■ **Description**
What makes it possible to speak of the Islamic world as a distinct and coherent civilization?

they served as judges, interpreters, administrators, prayer leaders, and reciters of the Quran, but especially as preservers and teachers of the sharia. Supported mostly by their local communities, some also received the patronage of *sultans*, or rulers, and were therefore subject to criticism for corruption and undue submission to state authority. In their homes, mosques, shrines, and Quranic schools, the ulama passed on the core teachings of the faith. Beginning in the eleventh century, formal colleges called *madrassas* offered more advanced instruction in the Quran and the sayings of Muhammad; grammar and rhetoric; sometimes philosophy, theology, mathematics, and medicine; and, above all else, law. Teaching was informal, mostly oral, and involved much memorization of texts. It was also largely conservative, seeking to preserve an established body of Islamic learning.

The ulama were an "international elite," and the system of education they created served to bind together an immense and diverse civilization. Common texts were shared widely across the world of Islam. Students and teachers alike traveled great distances in search of the most learned scholars. From Indonesia to West Africa, educated Muslims inhabited a "shared world of debate and reference."[27]

Paralleling the educational network of the ulama were the emerging religious orders of the Sufis. By the tenth century, particular Sufi *shaykhs*, or teachers, began to attract groups of disciples who were eager to learn their unique devotional practices and ways of achieving union with Allah. The disciples usually swore eternal allegiance to their teacher and valued highly the chain of transmission by which those teachings and practices had come down from earlier masters. In the twelfth and thirteenth centuries, Sufis began to organize in a variety of larger associations, some limited to particular regions and others with chapters throughout the Islamic world. The Qadiriya order, for example, began in Baghdad but spread widely throughout the Arab world and into sub-Saharan Africa. Sufi orders were especially significant in the frontier regions of Islam because they followed conquering armies or traders into Central and Southeast Asia, India, Anatolia, West Africa, and elsewhere. Their devotional teachings, modest ways of living, and reputation for supernatural powers gained a hearing for the new faith. Their emphasis on personal experience of the divine, rather than on the law, allowed the Sufis to accommodate elements of local belief and practice and encouraged the growth of a popular or blended Islam. But that flexibility also often earned them the enmity of the ulama, who were sharply critical of such deviations from the sharia.

Like the madrassas and the sharia, Sufi religious ideas and institutions spanned the Islamic world and were yet another thread in the cosmopolitan web of Islamic civilization. Particular devotional teachings and practices spread widely, as did the writings of such famous Sufi poets as Hafiz and Rumi. (For the poetry of Rumi, see Document 11.4, pp. 509–10.) Devotees made pilgrimages to the distant tombs of famous teachers, who, they often believed, might intercede with God on their behalf. Wandering Sufis, in search of the wisdom of renowned shaykhs, found fellow seekers and welcome shelter in the compounds of these religious orders.

In addition to the networks of the Sufis and the ulama, many thousands of people, from kings to peasants, made the grand pilgrimage to Mecca—the hajj—each year, no doubt gaining some sense of the umma. There men and women together, hailing from all over the Islamic world, joined as one people to rehearse the central elements of their faith. The claims of local identities based on family, clan, tribe, ethnicity, or state never disappeared, but now overarching them all was the inclusive unity of the Muslim community.

Networks of Exchange

The world of Islamic civilization cohered not only as a network of faith but also as an immense arena of exchange in which goods, technologies, food products, and ideas circulated widely. It rapidly became a vast trading zone of hemispheric dimensions. In part, this was due to its central location in the Afro-Eurasian world and the breaking down of earlier political barriers between the Byzantine and Persian empires. Furthermore, commerce was valued positively within Islamic teaching, for Muhammad himself had been a trader, and the pilgrimage to Mecca likewise fostered commerce. The extraordinary spurt of urbanization that accompanied the growth of Islamic civilization also promoted trade. (See Visual Source 11.2, p. 516, for a sixteenth-century image of an Islamic city.) Baghdad, established in 756 as the capital of the Abbasid Empire, soon grew into a magnificent city of half a million people. The appetite of urban elites for luxury goods stimulated both craft production and the desire for foreign products.

> ■ **Connection**
> In what ways was the world of Islam a "cosmopolitan civilization"?

Thus Muslim merchants, Arabs and Persians in particular, quickly became prominent and sometimes dominant players in all of the major Afro-Eurasian trade routes of the postclassical era—in the Mediterranean Sea, along the revived Silk Roads, across the Sahara, and throughout the Indian Ocean basin (see Chapter 8). By the eighth century, Arab and Persian traders had established a commercial colony in Canton in southern China, thus linking the Islamic heartland with Asia's other giant and flourishing economy. Various forms of banking, partnerships, business contracts, and instruments for granting credit facilitated these long-distance economic relationships and generated a prosperous, sophisticated, and highly commercialized economy that spanned the Old World.[28]

The vast expanses of Islamic civilization also contributed to the diffusion of agricultural products and practices from one region to another, a process already under way in the earlier Roman and Persian empires. The Muslim conquest of northwestern India opened the Middle East to a veritable treasure trove of crops that had been domesticated long before in South and Southeast Asia, including rice, sugarcane, new strains of sorghum, hard wheat, bananas, lemons, limes, watermelons, coconut palms, spinach, artichokes, and cotton. Some of these subsequently found their way into the Middle East and Africa and by the thirteenth century to Europe as well.[29] Both cotton and sugarcane, associated with complex production processes and slave labor, came to play central roles in the formation of the modern global system after 1500. These new crops and the development of the intensified agricultural techniques that often accompanied them contributed to increased food production, population growth, urbanization, and industrial development characteristic of the Muslim Middle East in early Abbasid times.

Technology too diffused widely within the Islamic world. Ancient Persian techniques for obtaining water by drilling into the sides of hills now spread across North Africa as far west as Morocco. Muslim technicians made improvements on rockets, first developed in China, by developing one that carried a small warhead and another used to attack ships.[30] Papermaking techniques entered the Abbasid Empire from China in the eighth century, with paper mills soon operating in Persia, Iraq, and Egypt. This revolutionary technology, which everywhere served to strengthen bureaucratic governments, spread from the Middle East into India and Europe over the following centuries.

Ideas likewise circulated across the Islamic world. The religion itself drew heavily and quite openly on Jewish and Christian precedents. Persia also contributed much in the way of bureaucratic practice, court ritual, and poetry, with Persian becoming a major literary language in elite circles. Scientific, medical, and philosophical texts, especially from ancient Greece, the Hellenistic world, and India, were systematically

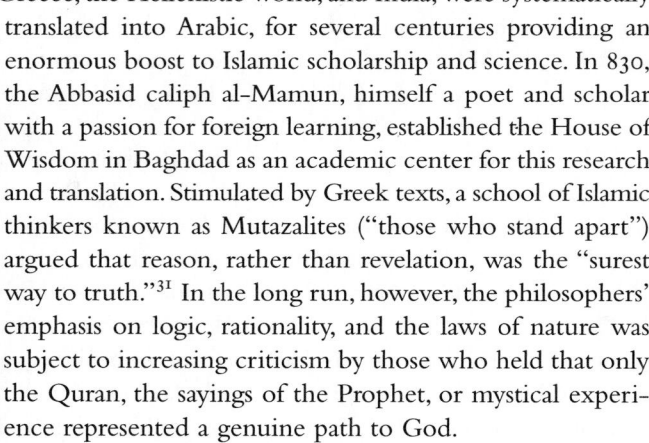

translated into Arabic, for several centuries providing an enormous boost to Islamic scholarship and science. In 830, the Abbasid caliph al-Mamun, himself a poet and scholar with a passion for foreign learning, established the House of Wisdom in Baghdad as an academic center for this research and translation. Stimulated by Greek texts, a school of Islamic thinkers known as Mutazalites ("those who stand apart") argued that reason, rather than revelation, was the "surest way to truth."[31] In the long run, however, the philosophers' emphasis on logic, rationality, and the laws of nature was subject to increasing criticism by those who held that only the Quran, the sayings of the Prophet, or mystical experience represented a genuine path to God.

But the realm of Islam was much more than a museum of ancient achievements from the civilizations that it encompassed. Those traditions mixed and blended to generate a distinctive Islamic civilization with many new contributions to the world of learning.[32] (See the Snapshot on p. 499.) Using Indian numerical notation, for example, Arab scholars developed algebra as a novel mathematical discipline. They also undertook much original work in astronomy and optics. They built upon earlier Greek and Indian practice to create a remarkable tradition in medicine and pharmacology. Arab physicians such as al-Razi and Ibn Sina accurately

A Muslim Astronomical Observatory
Drawing initially on Greek, Indian, and Persian astronomy, the Islamic world after 1000 developed its own distinctive tradition of astronomical observation and prediction, reflected in this Turkish observatory constructed in 1557. Muslim astronomy subsequently exercised considerable influence in both China and Europe. (University Library, Istanbul, Turkey/The Bridgeman Art Library)

Snapshot   **Key Achievements in Islamic Science and Scholarship**

Person/Dates	Achievement
al-Khwarazim (790–840)	Mathematician; spread use of Arabic numerals in Islamic world; wrote first book on algebra
al-Razi (865–925)	Discovered sulfuric acid; wrote a vast encyclopedia of medicine drawing on Greek, Syrian, Indian, and Persian work and his own clinical observation
al-Biruni (973–1048)	Mathematician, astronomer, cartographer; calculated the radius of the earth with great accuracy; worked out numerous mathematical innovations; developed a technique for displaying a hemisphere on a plane
Ibn Sina (Avicenna) (980–1037)	Prolific writer in almost all fields of science and philosophy; especially known for *Canon of Medicine*, a fourteen-volume work that set standards for medical practice in Islamic and Christian worlds for centuries
Omar Khayyam (1048–1131)	Mathematician; critic of Euclid's geometry; measured the solar year with great accuracy; Sufi poet; author of *The Rubaiyat*
Ibn Rushd (Averroës) (1126–1198)	Translated and commented widely on Aristotle; rationalist philosopher; made major contributions in law, mathematics, and medicine
Nasir al-Din Tusi (1201–1274)	Founder of the famous Maragha observatory in Persia (data from Maragha probably influenced Copernicus); mapped the motion of stars and planets
Ibn Khaldun (1332–1406)	Greatest Arab historian; identified trends and structures in world history over long periods of time

diagnosed many diseases, such as hay fever, measles, smallpox, diphtheria, rabies, and diabetes. In addition, treatments such as using a mercury ointment for scabies, cataract and hernia operations, and filling teeth with gold emerged from Arab doctors. The first hospitals, traveling clinics, and examinations for physicians and pharmacologists also were developed within the Islamic world. In the eleventh and twelfth centuries, this enormous body of Arab medical scholarship entered Europe via Spain, and it remained at the core of European medical practice for many centuries.[33]

⊥⊤ Reflections: Past and Present: Choosing Our History

Prominent among the many uses of history is the perspective it provides on the present. Although historians sometimes worry that an excessive "present-mindedness" may distort our perception of the past, all of us look to history, almost instinctively, to comprehend the world we now inhabit. Given the obvious importance of the Islamic world in the international arena of the twenty-first century, how might some grasp of the early development of Islamic civilization assist us in understanding our present circumstances?

First, that history reminds us of the central role that Islam played in the Afro-Eurasian world for a thousand years or more. From 600 to 1600 or later, it was a proud, cosmopolitan, often prosperous, and frequently powerful civilization that spanned Africa, Europe, the Middle East, and Asia. What followed were several centuries of European or Western imperialism that many Muslims found humiliating, even if some were attracted by elements of modern Western culture. In their recent efforts to overcome those centuries of subordination and exploitation, Muslims have found encouragement and inspiration in reflecting on the more distant and perhaps more glorious past. But they have not all chosen to emphasize the same past. Those labeled as "fundamentalists" have often viewed the early Islamic community associated with Medina, Mecca, and Muhammad as a model for Islamic renewal in the present. Others, often known as Islamic modernizers, have looked to the somewhat later achievements of Islamic science and scholarship as a foundation for a more open engagement with the West and the modern world.

The history of Islam also reveals to us a world of great diversity and debate. Sharp religious differences between Sunni and Shia understandings of the faith; differences in emphasis between advocates of the sharia and of Sufi spirituality; political conflicts among various groups and regions within the larger Islamic world; different postures toward women in Arab lands and in West Africa—all of this and more divided the umma and divide it still. Recalling that diversity is a useful reminder for any who would tag all Muslims with a single label.

A further dimension of that diversity lies in the many cultural encounters that the spread of Islam has spawned. Sometimes great conflict and violence have accompanied those encounters as in the Crusades and in Turkic invasions of India and Anatolia. At other times and places, Muslims and non-Muslims have lived together in relative tranquillity and tolerance—in Spain, in West Africa, in India, and in the Ottoman Empire. Some commentaries on the current interaction of Islam and the West seem to assume an eternal hostility or an inevitable clash of civilizations. The record of the past, however, shows considerable variation in the interaction of Muslims and others. While the past certainly shapes and conditions what happens next, the future, as always, remains open. Within limits, we can choose the history on which we seek to build.

Second Thoughts

What's the Significance?

Quran	ulama	Ibn Battuta
umma	Umayyad caliphate	Timbuktu
Pillars of Islam	Abbasid caliphate	al-Andalus
hijra	al-Ghazali	madrassas
sharia	Sikhism	House of Wisdom
jizya	Anatolia	Ibn Sina

To assess your mastery of the material in this chapter, visit the **Student Center** at bedfordstmartins.com/strayer.

Big Picture Questions

1. What distinguished the first centuries of Islamic history from the early history of Christianity and Buddhism? What similarities and differences characterized their religious outlooks?
2. How might you account for the immense religious and political/military success of Islam in its early centuries?
3. In what ways might Islamic civilization be described as cosmopolitan, international, or global?
4. "Islam was simultaneously both a single world of shared meaning and interaction and a series of separate and distinct communities, often in conflict with one another." What evidence could you provide to support both sides of this argument?
5. What changes did Islamic expansion generate in those societies that encountered it, and how was Islam itself transformed by those encounters?

Next Steps: For Further Study

Reza Aslan, *No God but God* (2005). A well-written and popular history of Islam by an Iranian immigrant to the United States.

Richard Bulliet, *Conversion to Islam in the Medieval Period* (1979). A scholarly study of the meaning and process of conversion in the early history of Islam and in several distinct places.

Richard Eaton, *Islamic History as Global History* (1990). A short account by a major scholar that examines Islam in a global framework.

John Esposito, ed., *The Oxford History of Islam* (1999). Up-to-date essays on various periods and themes in Islamic history. Beautifully illustrated.

Francis Robinson, ed., *Cambridge Illustrated History of the Islamic World* (1996). A series of essays by major scholars, with lovely pictures and maps.

Judith Tucker, *Gender and Islamic History* (1994). A brief overview of the changing lives of Islamic women.

"The Travels of Ibn Battuta: A Virtual Tour with the Fourteenth Century Traveler," http://www.sfusd.k12.ca.us/schwww/sch618/Ibn_Battuta/Battuta's_Trip_Twelve.html. A beautifully illustrated journey across the Islamic world in the early 1300s.

For Web sites and additional documents related to this chapter, see **Make History** at bedfordstmartins.com/strayer.

Documents

Considering the Evidence:
Voices of Islam

Like every other great religious tradition, Islam found expression in various forms. Its primary text, the Quran, claimed to represent the voice of the divine, God's final revelation to humankind. Other early Islamic writings, known as *hadith*, recorded the sayings and deeds of the Prophet Muhammad. Still others reflected the growing body of Islamic law, the *sharia*, which sought to construct a social order aligned with basic religious teachings. Devotional practices and expressions of adoration for Allah represented yet another body of Islamic literature. All of this gave rise to differing interpretations and contending views, generating for Islam a rich and complex literary tradition that has been the source of inspiration and debate for almost 1,400 years. From this immense body of work, we present just a few samples of the voices of Islam.

Document 11.1

The Voice of Allah

To Muslims, the Quran contains the very words of God. The term *quran* itself means "recitation" in Arabic, and the faithful believe that the angel Gabriel spoke God's words to Muhammad, who then recited them. Often called "noble" or "glorious," the Quran, compiled into an established text within thirty years of the Prophet's death, was regarded as a book without equal, written in the most sublime Arabic. Copying it was an act of piety, memorizing it was the starting point for Muslim education, and reciting it was both an art form and a high honor. Organized in 114 Surahs (chapters), the Quran was revealed to Muhammad over a period of some twenty-two years. Often the revelations came in response to particular problems that the young Islamic community and the Prophet were facing. The selections that follow convey something of the Quran's understanding of God, of humankind, of the social life prescribed for believers, of relations with non-Muslims, and much more.

- What are the chief characteristics of Allah, to Muslims the single source of all life and being?

- What religious practices are prescribed for Muslims in these passages? What are their purposes in the life of believers?

- What specific prescriptions for social life do these selections contain? Notice in particular those directed toward the weakest members of society. How would you describe the Quran's view of a good society?

- What attitude toward Jews, Christians, and other non-Muslim peoples do these passages suggest?

- What circumstances surrounding the birth of Islam might help to explain the references in the Quran to fighting and warfare?

- The sacred texts of all religious traditions provide ample room for conflicting understandings and interpretations. What debates or controversies might arise from these passages? Consider in particular views of women, of religious practice, of warfare, and of relationships with Jews and Christians.

The Quran
Seventh Century C.E.

Surah 1

In the name of God, the Most Gracious and the Dispenser of Grace. All praise is due to God alone, the sustainer of all the worlds... Lord of the Day of Judgment. Thee alone do we worship; and unto Thee alone do we turn for aid. Guide us in the straight way, the way of those upon whom Thou hast bestowed Thy blessing, not of those who have been condemned, nor those who go astray.

Surah 2

This divine writ [the Quran]— let there be no doubt about it— is [meant to be] a guidance for all the God-conscious who believe in [the existence of] that which is beyond the reach of human perception, and are constant in prayer, and spend on others out of what We provide for them as sustenance; and who believe in that which has been bestowed from on high upon thee, [O Prophet,] as well as in that which was bestowed before thy time....

Verily, those who have attained to faith, as well as those who follow the Jewish faith, and the Christians...—all who believe in God and the Last Day and do righteous deeds— shall have their reward with their Sustainer; and no fear need they have, and neither shall they grieve....

And they say, "Be Jews"—or, "Christians"—"and you shall be on the right path." Say: "Nay, but [ours is] the creed of Abraham, who turned away from all that is false, and was not of those who ascribe divinity to aught beside God." Say: "We believe in God, and in that which has been bestowed from on high upon us, and that which has been bestowed upon Abraham and Ishmael and Isaac and Jacob, and their descendants, and that which has been vouchsafed to Moses and Jesus; and that which has been vouchsafed to all the [other] prophets by their Sustainer: we make no distinction between any of them...."

Verily, in the creation of the heavens and of the earth, and the succession of night and day: and in the ships that speed through the sea with what is useful to man: and in the waters which God sends down from the sky, giving life thereby to the earth after it had been lifeless, and causing all manner of living creatures to multiply thereon: and in the change of the winds, and the clouds that run their appointed courses between sky and earth: [in all this] there are messages indeed for people who use their reason....

Source: Muhammad Asad, *The Message of the Qur'ān* (Bristol: The Book Foundation, 2003), Surahs 1, 2, 4, 5.

True piety does not consist in turning your faces toward the east or the west, but truly pious is he who believes in God, and the Last Day; and the angels, and revelation, and the prophets; and spends his substance—however much he himself may cherish it—upon his near of kin, and the orphans, and the needy, and the wayfarer, and the beggars, and for the freeing of human beings from bondage....

Fasting is ordained for you as it was ordained for those before you, so that you might remain conscious of God....

And fight in God's cause against those who wage war against you, but do not commit aggression, for verily, God does not love aggressors. And slay them wherever you may come upon them, and drive them away from wherever they drove you away, for oppression is even worse than killing. And fight not against them near the Inviolable House of Worship° unless they fight against you there first; but if they fight against you, slay them: such shall be the recompense of those who deny the truth. But if they desist, behold, God is much-forgiving, a dispenser of grace. Hence, fight against them until there is no more oppression and all worship is devoted to God alone; but if they desist, then all hostility shall cease, save against those who [willfully] do wrong....

And perform the pilgrimage...[to Mecca] in honor of God; and if you are held back, give instead whatever offering you can easily afford....

There shall be no coercion in matters of faith....

Do not deprive your charitable deeds of all worth by stressing your own benevolence and hurting [the feelings of the needy], as does he who spends his wealth only to be seen and praised by men....

God has made buying and selling lawful and usury° unlawful. Hence, whoever...desists [from

_____

°**Inviolable House of Worship:** a mosque.

°**usury:** the lending of money to be paid back with interest.

usury], may keep his past gains, and it will be for God to judge him; but as for those who return to it they are destined for the fire.... God deprives usurious gains of all blessing, whereas He blesses charitable deeds with manifold increase.

Surah 4

[R]ender unto the orphans their possessions...and do not consume their possessions together with your own: this, verily, is a great crime....

Men shall have a share in what parents and kinsfolk leave behind, and women shall have a share in what parents and kinsfolk leave behind, whether it be little or much....

And as for those of your women who become guilty of immoral conduct, call upon four from among you who have witnessed their guilt; and if these bear witness thereto, confine the guilty women to their houses until death takes them away or God opens for them a way [through repentance]. And punish [thus] both of the guilty parties; but if they both repent and mend their ways, leave them alone: for, behold, God is an acceptor of repentance, a dispenser of grace....

And it will not be within your power to treat your wives with equal fairness, however much you may desire it; and so, do not allow yourselves to incline toward one to the exclusion of the other, leaving her in a state, as it were, of having and not having a husband.

Surah 5

Do not take the Jews and Christians for your allies: they are but allies of one another—and whoever of you allies himself with them becomes, verily, one of them.

Document 11.2

The Voice of the Prophet Muhammad

As an expression of Islam, the sayings and deeds of Muhammad, known as the *hadiths,* are second in importance only to the Quran. In various collections of hadiths, Muslims hear the voice and witness the actions of their prophet. While they do not have the authority of divine revelation, these statements have served to guide and inspire Muslims to this day.

In the several centuries following his death, an enormous number of stories about Muhammad circulated within the Islamic community. Scholars gradually developed methods of authentication designed to discover which of these stories most reliably represented the Prophet's words and actions. Considerable controversy accompanied this process, and no single collection of hadiths has ever achieved universal acceptance. One of the earliest and most highly respected of these collections was the work the Persian scholar al-Bukhari (810–870). Traveling extensively throughout the Islamic world, al-Bukhari is said to have collected some 600,000 stories, memorized 200,000 of them, and finally authenticated and published 7,275. The selections that follow suggest something of the range and variety of the hadiths.

- What portrait of Muhammad emerges from this record of his sayings and actions?

- How do these hadiths reflect or build on the teaching of the Quran in Document 11.1?

- What religious and social values do these hadiths highlight?

- In what ways do these hadiths reflect common themes in many of the world's "wisdom traditions," and in what respects are they distinctly Islamic?

The Hadith
Eighth and Ninth Centuries

The Apostle of Allah . . . was asked which [good] work was the most excellent, and he answered: "Belief in Allah and in His Apostle." He was asked: "And then which?" He replied: "Jihād in the way of Allah." He was again asked: "And then what?" and he replied: "An acceptable pilgrimage." . . .

If a slave serves honestly his [earthly] master and worships earnestly his [heavenly] Lord, he will have a double recompense.

He who shows concern for the widows and the unfortunate [ranks as high] as one who goes on Jihād in the way of Allah, or one who fasts by day and who rises at night [for prayer].

A [true] believer views his sins as though he were sitting beneath a mountain which he fears may fall

Source: Arthur Jeffery, ed. and trans., *A Reader on Islam* (The Hague: Mouton, 1962), 81–86.

on him, but as evil-doer views his sins as a fly that moves across his nose.

In this world be as a stranger, or as one who is just passing along the road.

In two things an old man's heart never ceases to be that of a youth, in love of this world and in hoping long....

To look at a woman is forbidden, even if it is a look without desire, so how much the more is touching her.

Said he—upon whom be Allah's blessing and peace—"Avoid seven pernicious things." [His Companions] said: "And what are they, O Apostle of Allah?" He answered: "Associating anything with Allah, sorcery, depriving anyone of life where Allah has forbidden that save for just cause, taking usury, devouring the property of orphans, turning the back on the day of battle, and slandering chaste believing women even though they may be acting carelessly."

No one who enters Paradise will ever want to return to this world, even could he possess the earth and all that is on it, save the martyrs who desire to return to this world and be killed ten times so great is the regard in which they find themselves held.

To be stationed on the frontier for one day during Holy War is better than (to possess) this world and all that is on it. A place in Paradise the size of one of your whip-lashes is better than this world and all that is on it....

If a man sees something in [the conduct of] his ruler which he dislikes let him put up with it patiently, for there is no one who separates himself even a span from the community and dies [in that separation], but dies a pagan death....

Said the Prophet...: "I had a look into Paradise and I saw that the poor made up most of its inhabitants, and I had a look into Hell and saw that most of its inhabitants were women....

Treat women-folk kindly for woman was created of a rib. The crookedest part of a rib is its upper part. If you go to straighten it out you will break it, and if you leave it alone it will continue crooked. So treat women in kindly fashion....

Said the Apostle of Allah...: "O band of youths, let him among you who is able to make a home get married, and let him who is not able betake himself to fasting for he will find in that a quencher [of his passions]."

The worst of foods is that of a feast to which the rich have been invited and the poor overlooked....

Said the Apostle of Allah—upon whom be Allah's blessing and peace—: "Do not wear silks and satins, and do not drink from gold and silver vessels nor eat from dishes made thereof, for these things are theirs in this world but ours in the world to come."...

Said the Prophet—upon whom be Allah's blessing and peace—: "He who drinks wine in this world and repents not of it will be forbidden it in the world to come."...

Al-Aqra' said: "I have ten sons but never have I kissed any one of them." The Apostle of Allah—upon whom be Allah's blessing and peace—looked at him, and then said: "He who does not show tenderness will not have tenderness shown him."

Document 11.3

The Voice of the Law

While Christian scholarship emphasized theology and correct belief, learned Muslims gave more attention to law and correct behavior. That law was known as the sharia, an Arabic term that referred to a path toward water, which is the source of life. To many Muslims, that was the role of law—to construct the good society within which an authentic religious life could find expression.

The sharia emerged as the early Islamic community confronted the practical problems of an expanding empire with a very diverse population. But no single legal framework developed. Rather, four major schools of Islamic law crystallized, agreeing on fundamentals but differing in emphasis. How much weight should be given to the hadiths and which of them were most reliably authentic? What scope should reason and judgment have in applying religious principles to particular circumstances? Despite disagreement on such questions, each of the four approaches to legal interpretation sought to be all-embracing, providing highly detailed guidance on ritual performance, personal behavior, marriage and family matters, crime and punishment, economic transactions, and political action. The selections that follow, drawn from various legal traditions, illustrate this comprehensive nature of Islamic law and its centrality in an evolving Islamic civilization.

- What do you find most striking about the legal prescriptions in these passages?

- In what ways do these selections draw on and apply the teachings of the Quran and the hadiths?

- How does the role of law in early Islamic civilization differ from that of modern Western society?

- Why do you think the role of law was so central, so highly detailed, and so comprehensive in Islamic civilization?

- What do this document and Document 11.2 suggest about the problems that the early Islamic community confronted?

The Sharia
Ninth Century

On Prayer

The five prayers are obligatory for every Muslim who has reached the age of puberty and has the use of reason, except for women who are menstruating or recovering from childbirth.

If Muslims deny the necessity of prayer through ignorance, one must instruct them; if they deny it willfully, they have apostatized....

If Muslims abstain from saying the prayers from negligence, one should ask them three times to repent; if they repent, it is well, and if they refuse, it is lawful to put them to death.

On *Zakat*°

The obligation pertains only to a free Muslim who has complete ownership of the property on which it is due.... *Zakat* is due only on animals, agricultural products, precious metals, objects intended for sale, the products of mines, and treasure troves.

Whoever has the obligation to pay *zakat* and is able must pay it; if not, they commit a fault for which they must answer. If anyone refuses to pay it and denies its obligatory character they have committed apostasy and may be put to death. If they refuse it from avarice, they shall have the amount taken from them and be given a sentence at the judge's discretion.

Source: John Alden Williams, trans. and ed., *The Word of Islam* (Austin: University of Texas Press, 1994), 71, 80–82, 88–89, 94–95, 98–101, 104–5.

°***Zakat:*** alms for the poor.

On Marriage

[Marriage] is contracted by means of declaration and consent. When both parties are Muslims, it must be contracted in the presence of two male or one male and two female Muslim witnesses who are free, sane, and adult....

It is not lawful for a man to marry two women who are sisters or to cohabit with two sisters who are his slaves....

A man may not marry his slave-girl unless he sets her free first, and a woman may not marry her slave, since marriage has as its object that the children belong equally to both parents, and ownership and slavery are not equal states.

Similarly, marriage with an idolatress is forbidden, until she accepts Islam or a religion of the Book.

It is not lawful for a man already married to a free woman to marry a slave.... However, a man may lawfully marry a free woman after a slave.

A free man may marry four women, free or slave, but no more. It is unlawful for a slave to marry more than two women....

On Government

There are ten things a Caliph° must do in public affairs:

1) Maintain religion according to its established principles.
2) Apply legal judgments for litigants so that equity reigns without aiding the oppressor or weakening the oppressed.
3) Protect the flock...so that people may gain their living and move from place to place securely.
4) Apply the *hudud*, or punishments of the Law, so as to secure God's prohibitions from violation.
5) Fortify the marches so that the enemy will not appear due to neglect, shedding the blood of any Muslim or protected person.
6) Wage *jihad* against those who reject Islam so that they become either Muslims or protected people.
7) Collect the *zakat* and taxes on conquered territory...without fear or oppression.
8) Administer treasury expenditures.
9) Delegate loyal and trustworthy people.
10) Directly oversee matters and not delegate his authority seeking to occupy himself with either pleasure or devotion....

It is necessary therefore to cause the masses to act in accord with divine laws in all the affairs, both in this world and in the world to come. The authority to do so was possessed by the prophets and after them by their successors.

On Things Disliked in the Law

It is not permitted to men or women to eat or drink or keep unguents° in vessels of gold or silver....

It is not permitted for a man to wear silk, but it is permitted for a woman....

It is not permitted for a man to wear gold or silver, except for silver on a ring, or on a weapon.

It is not permitted for a man to look at a strange woman.°... A woman frequently needs to bare her hands and face in transactions with men. Abu Hanifa said it was also permitted to look at her feet and Abu Yusuf said it was permitted to look at her forearms as well.... However, if a man is not secure from feeling lust, he should not look needlessly even at the face or hands, to avoid sin. He is not allowed to touch her face or hands even if he is free from lust, whether he be young or old.

On the Economy

It is disliked to corner the market in food for humans or animals if it occurs in a town where this may prove harmful to the people. It is disliked to sell weapons in a time of trouble.

°**Caliph:** successor to Muhammad as political leader of the Islamic community.

°**unguents:** ointments.

°**strange woman:** a woman from outside one's immediate family.

There is no harm in selling fruit juice to someone who will make wine of it, since the transgression is not in the juice but in the wine after it has been changed....

Earning a living by changing money is a great danger to the religion of the one who practices it.... It is the duty of the *muhtasib*° to search out the money changers' places of business and spy on them,

---

°**Muhtasib:** an inspector of the markets.

and if he finds one of them practicing usury or doing something illegal... he must punish that person....

Owners of ships and boats must be prevented from loading their vessels above the usual load, for fear of sinking.... If they carry women on the same boat with men, there must be a partition between them.

Sellers of [pottery] are not to overlay any that are pierced or cracked with gypsum... and then sell them as sound.

Document 11.4

The Voice of the Sufis

Alongside the law, there ran a very different current of Islamic thinking and expression known as Sufism. The Sufis, sometimes called the "friends of God," were the mystics of Islam, those for whom the direct, personal, and intoxicating experience of the divine source was of far greater importance than the laws, regulations, and judgments of the sharia (see pp. 485–86, 496). Organized in hundreds of separate orders, or "brotherhoods," the Sufis constituted one of the transregional networks that linked the far-flung domains of the Islamic world. Often they were the missionaries of Islam, introducing the faith to Anatolia, India, Central Asia, and elsewhere.

Among the most prominent exemplars of Sufi sensibility was Rumi (1207–1273), born in what is now Afghanistan and raised in a Persian cultural tradition. Rumi's family later migrated to Anatolia, and Rumi lived most of his adult life in the city of Konya, where he is buried. There he wrote extensively, including a six-volume work of rhymed couplets known as the *Mathnawi*. Following Rumi's death, his son established the Mevlevi Sufi order, based on Rumi's teachings and known in the West as the "whirling dervishes," on account of the turning dances that became a part of their practice (see Visual Source 8.5 on p. 376).

Rumi's poetry has remained a sublime expression of the mystical dimension of Islamic spiritual seeking and has provided inspiration and direction for millions, both within and beyond the Islamic world. In the early twenty-first century, Rumi was the best-selling poet in the United States. The selections that follow provide a brief sample of the Sufi approach to religious life.

■ How would you define the religious sensibility of Rumi's poetry?

■ How does it differ from the approach to Islam reflected in the sharia?

■ What criticisms might the orthodox legal scholars (ulama) have made regarding the Sufi understanding of Islam?

Inscription in Rumi's Tomb
Thirteenth Century

Come, come, whoever you are,
Wanderer, worshipper, lover of leaving.

It doesn't matter.
Ours is not a caravan of despair.
Come, even if you have broken your vow a
    thousand times,
Come, yet again, come, come.

Source: A frequently quoted inscription hanging inside
the tomb of Rumi and generally, though not universally,
attributed to him; translator unknown.

RUMI

Poem
Thirteenth Century

I searched for God among the Christians and on
    the Cross and therein I found Him not.
I went into the ancient temples of idolatry; no
    trace of Him was there.

I entered the mountain cave of Hira and then went
    as far as Qandhar but God I found not....
Then I directed my search to the Kaaba, the resort
    of old and young; God was not there even.
Turning to philosophy I inquired about him from
    ibn Sina but found Him not within his range....
Finally, I looked into my own heart and there I
    saw Him; He was nowhere else.

Source: M. M. Sharif, *A History of Muslim Philosophy*,
(Wiesbaden: Harrassowitz, 1966), 2:838.

RUMI

"Drowned in God," Mathnawi
Thirteenth Century

Dam the torrent of ecstacy when it runs in
    flood,
So that it won't bring shame and ruin.
But why should I fear ruin?
Under the ruin waits a treasure.
He that is drowned in God wishes to be more
    drowned.
While his spirit is tossed up and down by the
    waves of the sea,

He asks, "Is the bottom of the sea more delightful
    or the top?"
Is the Beloved's arrow more fascinating, or the
    shield?
O heart, if you recognize any difference between
    joy and sorrow,
These lies will tear you apart.
Although your desire tastes sweet,
Doesn't the Beloved desire you to be desireless?
The life of lovers is in death:
You will not win the Beloved's heart unless you
    lose your own.

Source: From Kabir Helminski, ed., *The Pocket Rumi
Reader* (Boston: Shambhala, 2001), 89.

Using the Evidence:
Voices of Islam

1. **Defining differences within Islam:** In what different ways do the various voices of Islam represented in these documents understand and express the common religious tradition of which they are all a part? What grounds for debate or controversy can you identify within or among them?

2. **Comparing religious traditions:** How would you compare Islamic religious ideas and practices with those of other traditions such as Hinduism, Buddhism, and Christianity?

3. **Considering gender and Islam:** How do these documents represent the roles of men and women in Islamic society? Pay particular attention to differences in emphasis.

4. **Seeking additional sources:** Notice that all of these documents derive from literate elites, and each of them suggests or prescribes appropriate behavior. What additional documents would you need if you were to assess the impact of these prescriptions on the lives of ordinary people? What specific questions might you want to pose to such documents?

Visual Sources

Considering the Evidence:
Islamic Civilization in Persian
Miniature Paintings

I ran, homeland of the ancient Persian Empire and its successors, entered the world of Islam rather differently than did Iraq, Syria, Egypt, and North Africa. In the latter regions, converts to Islam gradually abandoned their native languages, adopted Arabic, and came to be seen as Arabs. In Iran or Persia, by contrast, Arab conquest did not involve the cultural Arabization of the region, despite some initial efforts to impose the Arabic language (see Map 11.1, p. 481). By the tenth century, the vast majority of Persians were Muslims, but the Persian language, Farsi (still spoken in modern Iran), flourished, enriched now by a number of Arabic loan words and written in an Arabic script. In 1010, that language received its classic literary expression when the Persian poet Ferdowsi completed his epic work, the *Shahnama* (*The Book of Kings*). A huge text of some 60,000 rhyming couplets, it recorded the mythical and pre-Islamic history of Iran and gave an enduring expression to a distinctly Persian cultural identity.

That culture had an enormous influence within the world of Islam. Many religious ideas of Persian Zoroastrianism—an evil satanic power, final judgment, heaven and hell, paradise—found their way into Islam, often indirectly via Jewish or Christian precedents. In Iran, Central Asia, India, and later in the Ottoman Empire, Persian influences were pervasive. Persian administrative and bureaucratic techniques; Persian court practices with their palaces, gardens, and splendid garments; Persian architecture, poetry, music, and painting—all of this decisively shaped the high culture of these eastern Islamic lands. One of the Abbasid caliphs, himself an Arab, observed: "The Persians ruled for a thousand years and did not need us Arabs even for a day. We have been ruling them for one or two centuries and cannot do without them for an hour."[34]

Prominent among the artistic achievements of Persian culture were miniature paintings—small, colorful, and exquisitely detailed works often used to illustrate books or manuscripts. One art historian described them as "little festivals of color in images separated from each other by pages of text."[35] This artistic style flourished especially from the thirteenth through the sixteenth centuries, when Persia was invaded and ruled by a succession of Mongol or Turkic dynasties. These invasions, especially that of the Mongols in the thirteenth century, were highly destructive. Great cities were devastated, libraries burned, and artists forced to flee. But the new rulers also proved to be generous patrons of the arts and served as carriers of Buddhist and Chinese artistic forms that enriched Persian painting.

During these centuries, the artists who created these Persian miniatures drew heavily on Persian mythology, poetry, and history as subjects for their paintings. Landscapes, influenced by Chinese techniques, also appeared in Persian miniatures. Scenes from the life of the Prophet Muhammad were likewise among the themes explored by Persian artists, although explicitly Islamic subject matter was represented in only a small proportion of these paintings. Particularly helpful to historians, images of daily life also found a place in Persian miniature painting, providing glimpses into social life in the Arab or Persian centers of Islamic civilization.

Visual Sources 11.1 and 11.2, dating from the early to mid-sixteenth century and measuring about eight by eleven inches, illustrate this focus within Persian miniature painting. Visual sources such as these are often most revealing in their detail, as artists depicted elements of daily life not often recorded elsewhere. Both of them, however, are idealized images that reflect enduring values within the Islamic world rather than referring to specific times or places.

Visual Source 11.1 offers a window on the life of desert pastoral nomads of Arabia.[36] The style of both clothing and tents indicate that this is an Arab nomadic encampment. The image focuses the viewer's attention on the two older men seated inside the elaborately decorated blue tent in the lower left. Seven cups are lined up in front of the men at the bottom, together with their lids, perhaps to keep the beverage warm or the bugs out. The red tent at the left is decorated with a *simurgh*, a legendary Persian winged creature with the head of a dog and the claws of a lion, said to have lived so long that it had acquired universal knowledge. Outside the tent of the woman at the right of the painting are her slippers, and above her another woman tenderly feeds her child. In perhaps the only directly Islamic reference in the painting, the old man approaching the washerwoman holds prayer beads in his right hand. Notice also some apparent Chinese influence in the painting. The presentation of rocks, clouds, and twisted trees reflects features of Chinese landscape painting, while the blue-and-white ceramic bowl near the woman washing clothes suggests some trade with China.

According to some art historians, this image has yet another level of meaning, for it may have served to illustrate the well-known and ancient Arab love story of Layla and Majnun, tragic star-crossed lovers prevented (like Romeo and Juliet) from marrying by a family feud and united only in death. The young man tending the fire at the upper right may represent Majnun, driven mad and into the wilderness by his unfulfilled love. The woman in the beautiful green

Visual Source 11.1 An Arab Camp Scene (Harvard Art Museum, Arthur M. Sackler Museum, Gift of John Goelet)

gown sitting in the doorway of the red tent on the left side of the painting may be Layla. In this interpretation of the image, the meeting of the two older men represents an incident in the story in which Majnun's father, together with his relatives, asks for Layla's hand in marriage from her father.

- What specific features and activities of nomadic life does the painting portray? What marks this image as an idealized version of an Arab camp? What features of nomadic life may have been omitted?

- Do the writing implements at the very bottom left of the painting—books, a pencase, an inkwell—offer a clue to the discussion that the two men may be having?

- What social distinctions are revealed in this painting?

- What differences in the lives of men and women are suggested in this image?

- What other details do you notice as you study this miniature painting?

Unlike the rural scene of Visual Source 11.1, the urban landscape of Visual Source 11.2 corresponds to no identifiable story or narrative. Also a sixteenth-century painting, it reflects the urban bustle and commercial sophistication of Islamic civilization. Here buildings replace tents as the major structures in the painting. Nine separate sources of light—lamps, candles, and torches—mark this as a nighttime scene, but in Persian painting, unlike in European art, light does not reflect on people or objects and does not cast shadows.

Three distinct sections of the painting illustrate various elements of city life. On the left and bottom of the image, a young prince holds court in his court pavilion attended by various turbaned courtiers. Above and to the right of the court scene, characteristic urban activities unfold along a city street. Finally, in the upper left a woman lounges on the balcony of an urban dwelling, while another woman speaks to an older turbaned man. Notice also the mosque in the upper right corner, inscribed with a well-known saying of Muhammad: "He who builds a mosque for God, God will build for him a dwelling in Paradise." There is also an inscription above the building in the lower right from the fourteenth-century Persian Sufi poet Hafiz: "The pupil of my eye is your nesting place; be kind, alight, for it is your home." As in Visual Source 11.1, intriguing details abound: the garden seen through the window in the arched pavilion; various types of musical instruments; the headscarves on women and the henna decorations on their hands; the elaborate geometric designs on buildings; the prayer beads in the hand of the young boy in front of the mosque.

Visual Source 11.2 City Life in Islamic Persia (Harvard Art Museum, Arthur M. Sackler Museum, Gift of John Goelet)

■ What might a historian interested in daily urban life in the Islamic world notice in this painting? What different social groups can you identify?

■ What in particular seems to be going on in the court scene? What products and transactions can you find in or around the several shops that line the street?

■ How would you define the roles of women as depicted here? Notice in particular the three young women above the court pavilion, seeking to observe the excitement below, from which they were presumably excluded.

■ In what ways are the activities shown in the painting idealized?

■ How might you understand the inscriptions of Muhammad and Hafiz in the context of this painting?

■ What details do you find most striking in Visual Source 11.2?

The Persian miniature painting in Visual Source 11.3 moves from ordinary life to religious imagination. While explicitly religious themes appear only infrequently in these paintings, the most common religious subject by far was that of the Prophet Muhammad's Night Journey, said to have taken place in 619 or 620. The Quran refers briefly to God taking the prophet "from the sacred place of worship to the far distant place of worship." This passage became the basis for a story, much embellished over the centuries, of rich and deep meaning for Muslims. In this religious narrative, Muhammad was led one night by the angel Gabriel from Mecca to Jerusalem. For the journey he was given a *buraq*, a mythical winged creature with the body of a mule or donkey and the face of a woman. Upon arriving in Jerusalem, he led prayers for an assembly of earlier prophets including Abraham, Moses, and Jesus. (See p. 477 for another illustration of Muhammad's relationship with earlier Jewish and Christian prophets.) Then, accompanied by many angels, Muhammad made his way through seven heavens into the presence of God, where, according to the Quran, "he did see some of the most profound of his Sustainer's symbols." There too Allah spoke to Muhammad about the importance of regular prayer, commanding fifty prayers a day, a figure later reduced to five on the advice of Moses.

From the beginning, Muslims have been divided on how to interpret this journey of the Prophet. For most, perhaps, it was taken quite literally as a miraculous event. Some, however, viewed it as a dream or a vision, while others understood it as the journey of Muhammad's soul but not his body. The Prophet's youngest wife, Aisha, for example, reported that "his body did not leave its place." Visual Source 11.3, dating from the early sixteenth century, is one of many representations of the Night Journey that emerged within Persian miniature painting.

Visual Source 11.3 The Night Journey of Muhammad (© British Library Board)

■ How do you understand the halo of fire that surrounds the Prophet's image in the center of the painting? Notice also that a similar halo envelops the head of the angel Gabriel (in blue dress), who is leading Muhammad heavenward.

■ What significance might attach to the female head of the buraq?

- What are the accompanying angels offering to the Prophet during his journey?

- What meaning might the artist seek to convey by the image of the world below and slightly to the right of the buraq?

- The willingness of Persian artists to represent Muhammad bodily contrasts sharply with a general Arab unwillingness to do so. Nonetheless, the Prophet's face is not shown. Why do you think Muslim artists have often been reluctant to represent the Prophet in human form? How might veiling his face address these concerns? Do you see any similarity with the controversy over icons in the Christian tradition? (See pp. 466–71.)

- Consider finally the larger meaning of the Night Journey within Islam. What is the significance of Muhammad's encounter with earlier prophets such as Abraham, Moses, and Jesus? How does the story explain the second of the five pillars of Islam, the requirement to pray five times a day?

- Review the discussion of the Sufi tradition of Islam on pages 485–86. How might Sufis have understood the Night Journey? How might it serve as a metaphor for the spiritual journey?

Using the Evidence:
Islamic Civilization in Persian Miniature Paintings

1. **Noticing point of view:** Consider these three visual sources together with the six other photos within the chapter (pp. 475, 477, 484, 487, 494, and 498). What general impression of the Islamic world emerges? What point of view, if any, is reflected in the selection of visual sources? Do they convey a positive, negative, or neutral impression of Islamic civilization? Explain your answer with specific references to the various images.

2. **Making comparisons:** Compare these visual sources to the icons in the Visual Sources section in Chapter 10 (pp. 466–71) in terms of purpose, artistic style, and themes. In particular, how does Visual Source 11.3 and the story of the Night Journey compare to the *Ladder of Divine Ascent* (Visual Source 10.3, p. 470) as artistic representations of the spiritual quest?

3. **Using images as evidence:** In what ways can historians use these visual sources? What insights about Islamic civilization can we derive from them? How should consideration of artist/author, audience, and purpose affect historians' assessment of these paintings?

CHAPTER TWELVE

Pastoral Peoples on the Global Stage

The Mongol Moment

1200—1500

Looking Back and Looking Around:
 The Long History of Pastoral
 Nomads
 The World of Pastoral Societies
 The Xiongnu: An Early
 Nomadic Empire
 The Arabs and the Turks
 The Masai of East Africa
Breakout: The Mongol Empire
 From Temujin to Chinggis Khan:
 The Rise of the Mongol Empire
 Explaining the Mongol Moment
Encountering the Mongols:
 Comparing Three Cases
 China and the Mongols
 Persia and the Mongols
 Russia and the Mongols
The Mongol Empire as a
 Eurasian Network
 Toward a World Economy
 Diplomacy on a Eurasian Scale
 Cultural Exchange in the
 Mongol Realm
 The Plague: A Eurasian Pandemic
Reflections: Changing Images of
 Nomadic Peoples
Considering the Evidence
 Documents: Perspectives on
 the Mongols
 Visual Sources: The Black Death
 and Religion in Western Europe

In 1937, the great Mongol warrior Chinggis Khan lost his soul, some seven centuries after his death. According to Mongol tradition, a warrior's soul was contained in his spirit banner, consisting of strands of hair from his best horses attached to a spear. For many centuries, Chinggis Khan's spirit banner had been housed in a Buddhist monastery in central Mongolia, where lamas (religious teachers) had tended it.[1] But in the 1930s, Mongolia, then under communist control and heavily dominated by Stalin's Soviet Union, launched a brutal antireligious campaign that destroyed many monasteries and executed some 2,000 monks. In the confusion that ensued, Chinggis Khan's spirit banner, and thus his soul, disappeared.

By the end of the twentieth century, as communism faded away, the memory of Chinggis Khan, if not his spirit banner, made a remarkable comeback in the land of his birth. Vodka, cigarettes, a chocolate bar, two brands of beer, the country's best rock band, and the central square of the capital city all bore his name, while his picture appeared on Mongolia's stamps and money. Rural young people on horseback sang songs in his honor, and their counterparts in urban Internet cafés constructed Web sites to celebrate his achievements. The country organized elaborate celebrations in 2006 to mark the 800th anniversary of his founding of the Mongol Empire.

ALL OF THIS IS A REMINDER OF THE ENORMOUS AND SURPRISING role that the Mongols played in the Eurasian world of the thirteenth and fourteenth centuries and of the continuing echoes of that long-vanished empire. More generally, the story of the Mongols serves as

Chinggis Khan at Prayer: This sixteenth-century Indian painting shows Chinggis Khan at prayer in the midst of battle. He is perhaps praying to Tengri, the great sky god, on whom the Mongol conqueror based his power. (Werner Forman/Art Resource, NY)

a useful corrective to the almost exclusive focus that historians often devote to agricultural peoples and their civilizations, for the Mongols, and many other such peoples, were pastoral nomads who disdained farming while centering their economic lives around their herds of animals. Normally they did not construct elaborate cities, enduring empires, or monumental works of art, architecture, and written literature. Nonetheless, they left an indelible mark on the historical development of the entire Afro-Eurasian hemisphere, and particularly on the agricultural civilizations with which they so often interacted.

Looking Back and Looking Around: The Long History of Pastoral Nomads

The "revolution of domestication," beginning around 11,500 years ago, involved both plants and animals. People living in more favored environments were able to combine farming with animal husbandry and on this economic foundation generated powerful and impressive civilizations with substantial populations. But on the arid margins of agricultural lands, where productive farming was difficult or impossible, an alternative kind of food-producing economy emerged around 4000 B.C.E., focused on the raising of livestock. Peoples practicing such an economy learned to use the milk, blood, wool, hides, and meat of their animals to occupy lands that could not support agricultural societies. Some of those animals also provided new baggage and transportation possibilities. Horses, camels, goats, sheep, cattle, yaks, and reindeer were the primary animals that separately, or in some combination, enabled the construction of pastoral or herding societies. Such societies took shape in the vast grasslands of inner Eurasia and sub-Saharan Africa, in the Arabian and Saharan deserts, in the subarctic regions of the Northern Hemisphere, and in the high plateau of Tibet. Pastoralism emerged only in the Afro-Eurasian world, for in the Americas the absence of large animals that could be domesticated precluded a herding economy. But where such animals existed, their domestication shaped unique societies adapted to diverse environments.

The World of Pastoral Societies

■ **Comparison**

In what ways did pastoral societies differ from their agricultural counterparts?

Despite their many differences, pastoral societies shared several important features that distinguished them from settled agricultural communities and civilizations. Pastoral societies' generally less productive economies and their need for large grazing areas meant that they supported far smaller populations than did agricultural societies. People generally lived in small and widely scattered encampments of related kinfolk rather than in the villages, towns, and cities characteristic of agrarian civilizations. Beyond the family unit, pastoral peoples organized themselves in kinship-based groups or clans that claimed a common ancestry, usually through the male line. Related clans might on occasion come together as a tribe, which could also absorb unrelated people into the community. Although their values stressed equality and individual achievement, in some pastoral societies clans were ranked as noble or commoner,

Snapshot **Varieties of Pastoral Societies[2]**

Region and Peoples	Primary Animals	Features
Inner Eurasian steppes (Xiongnu, Yuezhi, Turks, Uighurs, Mongols, Huns, Kipchaks)	Horses; also sheep, goats, cattle, Bactrian (two-humped) camel	Domestication of horse by 4000 B.C.E.; horseback riding by 1000 B.C.E.; site of largest nomadic empires
Southwestern and Central Asia (Seljuks, Ghaznavids, Mongol Il-khans, Uzbeks, Ottomans)	Sheep and goats; used horses, camels, and donkeys for transport	Close economic relationship with neighboring towns; provided meat, wool, milk products, and hides in exchange for grain and manufactured goods
Arabian and Saharan deserts (Bedouin Arabs, Berbers, Tuareg)	Dromedary (one-humped) camel; sometimes sheep	Camel caravans made possible long-distance trade; camel-mounted warriors central to early Arab/Islamic expansion
Grasslands of sub-Saharan Africa (Fulbe, Nuer, Turkana, Masai)	Cattle; also sheep and goats	Cattle were a chief form of wealth and central to ritual life; little interaction with wider world until nineteenth century
Subarctic Eurasia (Lapps)	Reindeer	Reindeer domesticated only since 1500 C.E.; little impact on world history
Tibetan plateau (Tibetans)	Yaks; also sheep, cashmere goats, some cattle	Tibetans supplied yaks as baggage animal for overland caravan trade; exchanged wool, skins, and milk with valley villagers and received barley in return

and considerable differences emerged between wealthy aristocrats owning large flocks of animals and poor herders. Many pastoral societies held slaves as well.

Furthermore, nomadic societies generally offered women a higher status, fewer restrictions, and a greater role in public life than their sisters in agricultural civilizations enjoyed. Everywhere women were involved in productive labor as well as having domestic responsibility for food and children. The care of smaller animals such as sheep and goats usually fell to women, although only rarely did women own or control their own livestock. Among the Mongols, the remarriage of widows carried none of the negative connotations that it did among the Chinese, and women could initiate divorce. Mongol women frequently served as political advisers and were active in military affairs as well. A thirteenth-century European visitor, the Franciscan friar Giovanni DiPlano Carpini, recorded his impressions of Mongol women:

> Girls and women ride and gallop as skillfully as men. We even saw them carrying quivers and bows, and the women can ride horses for as long as the men; they have shorter stirrups, handle horses very well, and mind all the property. [Mongol] women make everything: skin clothes, shoes, leggings, and everything made of leather. They drive carts and repair them, they load camels, and are quick and vigorous in all their tasks. They all wear trousers, and some of them shoot just like men.[3]

(See Document 12.5, pp. 557–59, for more on Mongol women.)

■ Connection
In what ways did pastoral societies interact with their agricultural neighbors?

Certainly literate observers from adjacent civilizations noticed and clearly disapproved of the freedom granted to pastoral women. Ancient Greek writers thought that the pastoralists with whom they were familiar were "women governed." To Han Kuan, a Chinese Confucian scholar in the first century B.C.E., China's northern nomadic neighbors "[made] no distinction between men and women."[4]

The most characteristic feature of pastoral societies was their mobility. As people frequently on the move, they are often referred to as nomads because they shifted their herds in regular patterns. These movements were far from aimless wanderings, as popular images often portray them, but rather sought to systematically follow the seasonal changes in vegetation and water supply. It was a life largely dictated by local environmental conditions and based on turning grass, which people cannot eat, into usable food and energy. Nor were nomads homeless; they took their homes, often elaborate felt tents, with them. According to a prominent scholar of pastoral life, "They know where they are going and why."[5]

Even though nomadic pastoralists represented an alternative to the agricultural way of life that they disdained, they were almost always deeply connected to, and often dependent on, their agricultural neighbors. Few nomadic peoples could live solely from the products of their animals, and most of them actively sought access to

The Scythians
An ancient horse-riding nomadic people during the classical era, the Scythians occupied a region in present-day Kazakhstan and southern Russia. Their pastoral way of life is apparent in this detail from an exquisite gold necklace from the fourth century B.C.E. (Private Collection/Photo Boltin Picture Library/The Bridgeman Art Library)

the foodstuffs, manufactured goods, and luxury items available from the urban workshops and farming communities of nearby civilizations. Particularly among the nomadic peoples of inner Eurasia, this desire for the fruits of civilization periodically stimulated the creation of tribal confederations or nomadic states that could more effectively deal with the powerful agricultural societies on their borders. The Mongol Empire of the thirteenth century was but the most recent and largest in a long line of such efforts, dating back to the first millennium B.C.E.

Constructing a large state among nomadic pastoralists was no easy task. Such societies generally lacked the wealth needed to pay for the professional armies and bureaucracies that everywhere sustained the states and empires of agricultural civilizations. And the fierce independence of widely dispersed pastoral clans and tribes as well as their internal rivalries made any enduring political unity difficult to achieve. Nonetheless, charismatic leaders, such as Chinggis Khan, were periodically able to weld together a series of tribal alliances that for a time became powerful states. In doing so, they often employed the device of "fictive kinship," designating allies as blood relatives and treating them with a corresponding respect.

Despite their limited populations, such states had certain military advantages in confronting larger and more densely populated civilizations. They could draw upon the horseback-riding and hunting skills of virtually the entire male population and some women as well. Easily transferred to the role of warrior, these skills, which were practiced from early childhood, were an integral part of pastoral life. But what sustained nomadic states was their ability to extract wealth, through raiding, trading, or extortion, from agricultural civilizations such as China, Persia, and Byzantium. As long as that wealth flowed into pastoral states, rulers could maintain the fragile alliances among fractious clans and tribes. When it was interrupted, however, those states often fragmented.

Pastoral nomads interacted with their agricultural neighbors not only economically and militarily but also culturally as they "became acquainted with and tried on for size all the world and universal religions."[6] At one time or another, Judaism, Buddhism, Islam, and several forms of Christianity all found a home somewhere among the nomadic peoples of inner Eurasia. So did Manichaeism, a religious tradition born in third-century Persia and combining elements of Zoroastrian, Christian, and Buddhist practice. (See Visual Sources: Art, Religion, and Cultural Exchange in Central Asia, pp. 367–77 in Chapter 8, for cultural exchanges involving Central Asian nomadic peoples.) Usually conversion was a top-down process as nomadic elites and rulers adopted a foreign religion for political purposes, sometimes changing religious allegiance as circumstances altered. Nomadic peoples, in short, did not inhabit a world totally apart from their agricultural and civilized neighbors.

Surely the most fundamental contribution of pastoralists to the larger human story was their mastery of environments unsuitable for agriculture. Through the creative use of their animals, they brought a version of the food-producing revolution and a substantial human presence to the arid grasslands and desert regions of Afro-Eurasia. As the pastoral peoples of the Inner Asian steppes learned the art of horseback riding, by roughly 1000 B.C.E., their societies changed dramatically. Now they could accumulate and tend larger herds of horses, sheep, and goats and move more rapidly over a much wider territory. New technologies, invented or adapted by pastoral societies, added to the mastery of their environment and spread widely across the Eurasian steppes, creating something of a common culture in this vast region. These innovations included complex horse harnesses, saddles with iron stirrups, a small compound bow that could be fired from horseback, various forms of armor, and new kinds of swords. Agricultural peoples were amazed at the centrality of the

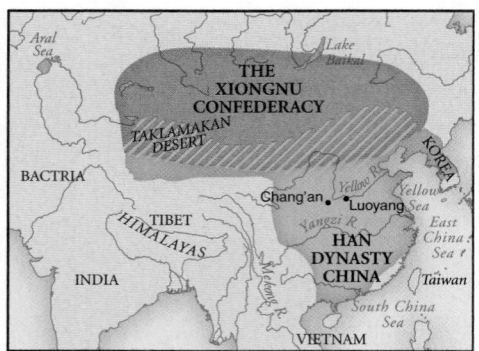

The Xiongnu Confederacy

■ **Significance**

In what ways did the Xiongnu, Arabs, and Turks make an impact on world history?

horse in pastoral life. As one observer noted, "From their horses, by day and night every one of that [nomadic] nation buys and sells, eats and drinks, and bowed over the narrow neck of the animal relaxes in a sleep so deep as to be accompanied by many dreams."[7]

The Xiongnu: An Early Nomadic Empire

What enabled pastoral peoples to make their most visible entry onto the stage of world history was the military potential of horseback riding, and of camel riding somewhat later. Their mastery of mounted warfare made possible a long but intermittent series of nomadic empires across the steppes of inner Eurasia and elsewhere. For 2,000 years, those states played a major role in Eurasian history and represented a standing challenge to and influence upon the agrarian civilizations on their borders.

During the classical era, one such large-scale nomadic empire was associated with the people known as the Xiongnu, who lived in the Mongolian steppes north of China (see Chapter 9). Provoked by Chinese penetration of their territory, the Xiongnu in the third and second centuries B.C.E. created a huge military confederacy that stretched from Manchuria deep into Central Asia. Under the charismatic leadership of Modun (reigned 210–174 B.C.E.), the Xiongnu Empire effected a revolution in nomadic life. Earlier fragmented and egalitarian societies were now transformed into a far more centralized and hierarchical political system in which power was concentrated in a divinely sanctioned ruler and differences between "junior" and "senior" clans became more prominent. "All the people who draw the bow have now become one family," declared Modun. Tribute, exacted from other nomadic peoples and from China itself, sustained the Xiongnu Empire and forced the Han dynasty emperor Wen to acknowledge, unhappily, the equality of people he regarded as barbarians. "Our two great nations," he declared, no doubt reluctantly, "the Han and the Xiongnu, stand side by side."[8]

Although it subsequently disintegrated under sustained Chinese counterattacks, the Xiongnu Empire created a model that later Turkic and Mongol empires emulated. Even without a powerful state, various nomadic or seminomadic peoples played a role in the collapse of already weakened classical Chinese and Roman empires and the subsequent rebuilding of those civilizations (see Chapter 4).

The Arabs and the Turks

It was during the era of third-wave civilizations (500–1500 C.E.) that nomadic peoples made their most significant mark on the larger canvas of world history. Arabs, Berbers, Turks, and Mongols—all of them of nomadic origin—created the largest and most influential empires of that postclassical millennium. The most expansive religious tradition of the era, Islam, derived from a largely nomadic people, the Arabs, and was carried to new regions by another nomadic people, the Turks. In that millennium, most of the great civilizations of outer Eurasia—Byzantium, Persia, India, and China—had come under the control of previously nomadic people, at least for a time. But as pastoral nomads entered and shaped the arena of world history, they too were transformed by the experience.

The first and most dramatic of these nomadic incursions came from Arabs. In the Arabian Peninsula, the development of a reliable camel saddle somewhere between 500 and 100 B.C.E. enabled nomadic Bedouin (desert-dwelling) Arabs to fight effectively from atop their enormous beasts. With this new military advantage, they came to control the rich trade routes in incense running through Arabia. Even more important, these camel nomads served as the shock troops of Islamic expansion, providing many of the new religion's earliest followers and much of the military force that carved out the Arab Empire. Although intellectual and political leadership came from urban merchants and settled farming communities, the Arab Empire was in some respects a nomadic creation that subsequently became the foundation of a new and distinctive civilization.

Even as the pastoral Arabs encroached on the world of Eurasian civilizations from the south, Turkic-speaking nomads were making inroads from the north. Never a single people, various Turkic-speaking clans and tribes migrated from their homeland in Mongolia and southern Siberia generally westward and entered the historical record as creators of a series of nomadic empires between 552 and 965 C.E., most of them lasting little more than a century. Like the Xiongnu Empire, they were fragile alliances of various tribes headed by a supreme ruler known as a *kaghan*, who was supported by a faithful corps of soldiers called "wolves," for the wolf was the mythical ancestor of Turkic peoples. From their base in the steppes, these Turkic states confronted the great civilizations to their south—China, Persia, Byzantium— alternately raiding them, allying with them against common enemies, trading with them, and extorting tribute payments from them. Turkic language and culture spread widely over much of Inner Asia, and elements of that culture entered the agrarian civilizations. In the courts of northern China, for example, yogurt thinned with water, a drink derived from the Turks, replaced for a time the traditional beverage of tea, and at least one Chinese poet wrote joyfully about the delights of snowy evenings in a felt tent.[9]

A major turning point in the history of the Turks occurred with their conversion to Islam between the tenth and fourteenth centuries. This extended process represented a major expansion of the faith and launched the Turks into a new role as the third major carrier of Islam, following the Arabs and the Persians. It also brought the Turks into an increasingly important position within the heartland of an established Islamic civilization as they migrated southward into the Middle East. There they served first as slave soldiers within the Abbasid caliphate, and then, as the caliphate declined, they increasingly took political and military power themselves. In the Seljuk Turkic Empire of the eleventh and twelfth centuries, centered in Persia and present-day Iraq, Turkic rulers began to claim the Muslim title of *sultan* (ruler) rather than the Turkic *kaghan*. Although the Abbasid caliph remained the formal ruler, real power was exercised by Turkic sultans.

Not only did Turkic peoples become Muslims themselves, but they carried Islam to new areas as well. Their invasions of northern India solidly planted Islam in that ancient civilization. In Anatolia, formerly ruled by Christian Byzantium, they brought both Islam and a massive infusion of Turkic culture, language, and people, even as they created the Ottoman Empire, which by 1500 became one of the great powers of Eurasia (see pp. 584–86). In both places, Turkic dynasties governed and would continue to do so well into the modern era. Thus Turkic people, many of them at least, had transformed themselves from pastoral nomads to sedentary farmers, from creators of steppe empires to rulers of agrarian civilizations, and from polytheistic worshippers of their ancestors and various gods to followers and carriers of a monotheistic Islam.

The Masai of East Africa

■ **Comparison**

Did the history and society of the East African Masai people parallel that of Asian nomads?

In East African history as well, the relationship between nomads and settled farmers worked itself out over many centuries, although solid historical information in this case largely dates to after 1500. Unlike Inner Asia, no large states or chiefdoms developed among either agricultural or pastoral peoples in present-day Kenya and Tanzania. Instead the nomadic cattle-keeping Masai and their settled agricultural neighbors found another way to bind their people together beyond the ties of village and clan. Adolescent boys from a variety of villages or lineages were initiated together in a ritual that often included circumcision, an experience that produced a profound bond among them. This ceremony created an "age-set," which then moved through a series of "age-grades" or ranks, from warrior through elder, during their lives. Such a system provided an alternative to the state as a means of mobilizing young men for military purposes, for integrating outsiders into the community, and for establishing a larger social identity. (See Document 2.2, pp. 71–73).

The Masai of East Africa

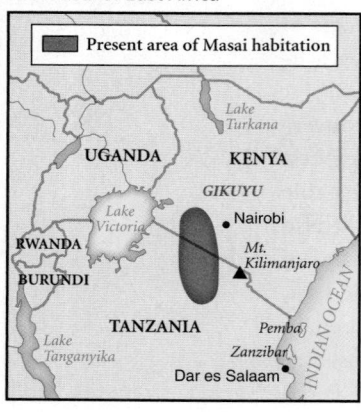

Sharp distinctions and strong views separated people practicing agricultural and pastoral ways of living. From the viewpoint of the Masai, who composed songs and poems in honor of their cattle, pastoralism was a vastly superior way of life, whereas farming was seen as demeaning and as destroying land that could be much better used for grazing. Farmers were fit only to provide beer, wives, and occasionally food for herding peoples. Conversely, agricultural peoples often saw the Masai as arrogant, aggressive, and lazy, stubbornly unwilling to engage in the hard work of cultivation or even to eat the products of the land.[10] Such views paralleled those that the Chinese and Xionghu held of one another.

But ways of life were hardly static in East Africa. Earlier in their history, the proudly pastoral Masai had in fact raised sorghum and millet, fully abandoning cultivation only in the eighteenth and nineteenth centuries as they migrated southward from the upper Nile Valley into the more arid regions of central Kenya. Later several Masai groups returned to agriculture after bitter conflicts in the mid-nineteenth century drove them to the periphery of Masai territory. Furthermore, the Masai, while trumpeting the superiority of their culture, were altogether willing to admit others into its charmed circle, much like the Chinese in relation to surrounding barbarians. Outsiders could become Masai, and many did so by obtaining a herd of cattle, by joining a Masai age-set, by learning the language, or by giving a woman in marriage to a Masai man and receiving "bride-wealth" in cattle in return.

The Masai
This contemporary Masai woman from Tanzania is milking goats while carrying a child on her back, in much the same fashion as her ancestors have done for centuries. (The Africa Image Library, photographersdirect .com. Photographer: Ariadne Van Zandbergen)

The Masai were also dependent on those practicing other ways of life. Although they despised hunters as "poor people without cattle," the Masai relied on them for animal skins, bows and arrows, shields, and, most of all, honey, which was required in their ritual ceremonies. They were even more involved with neighboring agricultural peoples. Despite a great deal of mutual raiding and warfare, that relationship also involved substantial economic exchange as women conducted frequent trade to supplement the diet of milk, meat, and blood derived from their cattle. Elaborate peace negotiations after periods of conflict, frequent intermarriage, and occasional military alliances against a common enemy also brought the Masai into close contact with nearby farmers, such as the Gikuyu. And in times of desperation owing to drought or disease, the Masai might find refuge with hunters or farmers with whom they had long-established relationships.[11]

The prestige and the military success of the Masai encouraged those agricultural societies to borrow elements of Masai culture, such as hairstyles, shield decorations, terms referring to cattle, and the name for their high god. Farming societies also adopted elements of Masai military organization, the long Masai spear, and the practice of drinking cow's milk before battle.[12] Peaceful interaction and mutual dependence as well as conflict and hostility characterized the relationship of nomadic herders and settled farmers in East Africa, much as it did in Eurasia.

Breakout: The Mongol Empire

Of all the pastoral peoples who took a turn on the stage of world history, the Mongols made the most stunning entry. Their thirteenth-century breakout from Mongolia gave rise to the largest land-based empire in all of human history, stretching from the Pacific coast of Asia to Eastern Europe (see Map 12.1). This empire joined

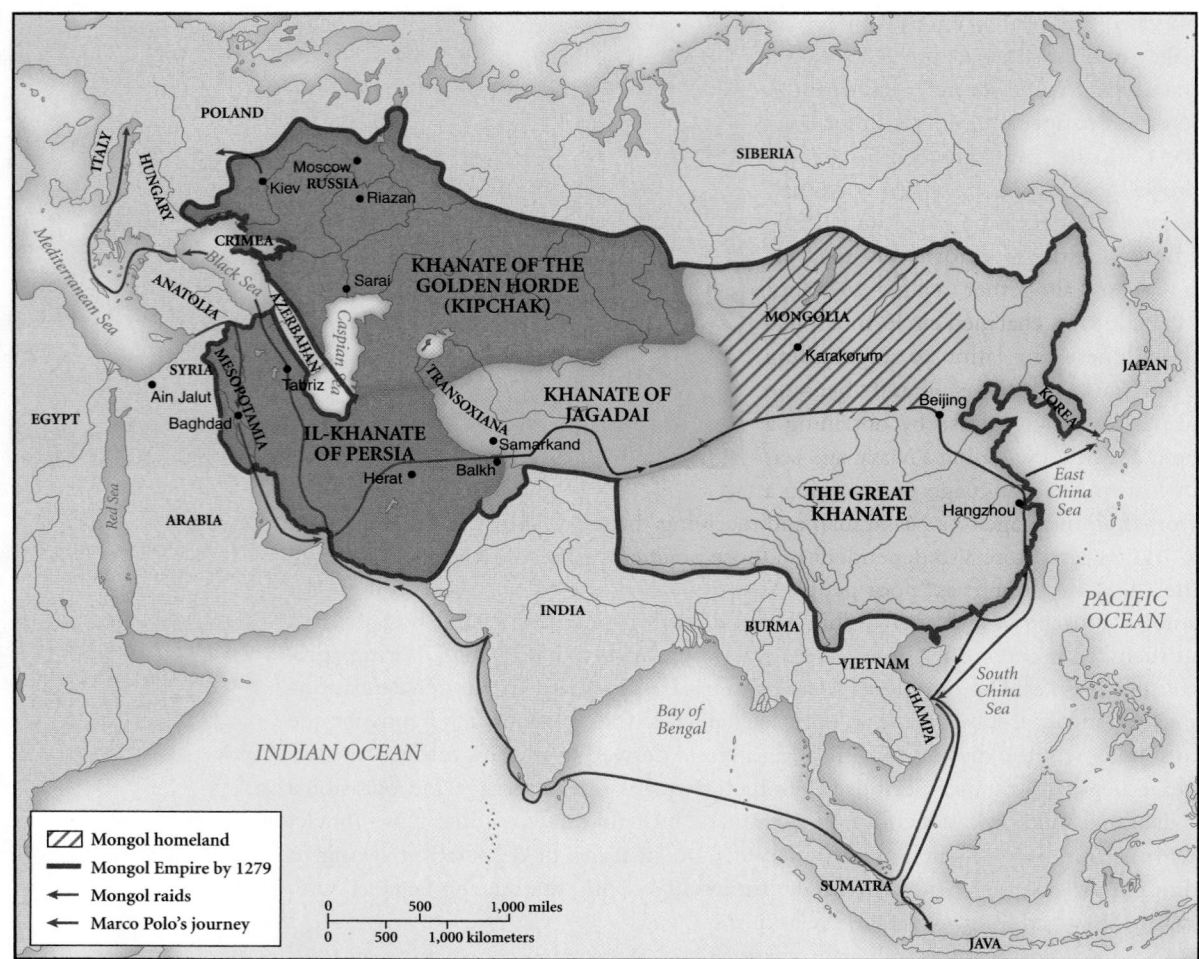

Map 12.1   The Mongol Empire

Encompassing much of Eurasia, the Mongol Empire was divided into four khanates after the death of Chinggis Khan.

the nomadic peoples of the inner Eurasian steppes with the settled agricultural civilizations of outer Eurasia more extensively and more intimately than ever before. It also brought the major civilizations of Eurasia—Europe, China, and the Islamic world—into far more direct contact than in earlier times. Both the enormous destructiveness of the process and the networks of exchange and communication that it spawned were the work of the Mongols, numbering only about 700,000 people. It was another of history's unlikely twists.

For all of its size and fearsome reputation, the Mongol Empire left a surprisingly modest cultural imprint on the world it had briefly governed. Unlike the Arabs, the Mongols bequeathed to the world no new religion or civilization. Whereas the Islamic community offered a common religious home for all converts—conquerors and conquered alike—the Mongols never tried to spread their own faith among subject peoples. At the level of family life, that religion centered on rituals invoking the ancestors, which were performed around the hearth. Rulers sometimes consulted religious specialists, known as *shamans*, who might predict the future, offer sacrifices, and communicate with the spirit world, and particularly with Tengri, the supreme sky god of the Mongols. There was little in this tradition to attract outsiders, and in any event the Mongols proved uninterested in religious imperialism.

The Mongols offered the majority of those they conquered little more than the status of defeated, subordinate, and exploited people, although people with skills were put to work in ways useful to Mongol authorities. Unlike the Turks, whose languages and culture flourish today in many places far from the Turkic homeland, Mongol culture remains confined largely to Mongolia. Furthermore, the Mongol Empire, following in the tradition of Xiongnu and Turkic state building, proved to be "the last, spectacular bloom of pastoral power in Inner Eurasia."[13] Some Mongols themselves became absorbed into the settled societies they conquered. After the decline and disintegration of the Mongol Empire, the tide turned against the pastoralists of inner Eurasia, who were increasingly swallowed up in the expanding Russian or Chinese empires. Nonetheless, while it lasted and for a few centuries thereafter, the Mongol Empire exercised an enormous impact throughout the entire Eurasian world.

Snapshot   Key Moments in Mongol History

Birth of Temujin	1162
Temujin gains title of Chinggis Khan ("universal ruler")	1206
Reign of Chinggis Khan	1206–1227
Beginning of Mongol conquests	1209
Conquest of China	1209–1279
Initial assault on Persia	1219–1221
Conquest of Russia	1237–1240
Attacks in Eastern Europe; then withdrawal	1241–1242
Mongol seizure of Baghdad	1258
Khubilai Khan as ruler of China	1271–1294
Failed Mongol attacks on Japan	1274, 1281
Conversion of Il-khan Ghazan to Islam	1295
High point of plague in Europe	1348–1350
Ming dynasty established; end of Mongol rule in China	1368
End of "Mongol yoke" in Russia; Moscow emerges as center of a Russian state	1480

From Temujin to Chinggis Khan: The Rise of the Mongol Empire

■ **Description**

Identify the major steps in the rise of the Mongol Empire.

World historians are prone to focus attention on large-scale and long-term processes of change in explaining "what happened in history," but in understanding the rise of the Mongol Empire, most scholars have found themselves forced to look closely at the role of a single individual—Temujin (1162–1227), later known as Chinggis Khan (universal ruler). The twelfth-century world into which he was born found the Mongols an unstable and fractious collection of tribes and clans, much reduced from a somewhat earlier and more powerful position in the shifting nomadic alliances in what is now Mongolia. "Everyone was feuding," declared a leading Mongol shaman. "Rather than sleep, they robbed each other of their possessions.... There was no respite, only battle. There was no affection, only mutual slaughter."[14]

The early life of Temujin showed few signs of a prominent future. The boy's father had been a minor chieftain of a noble clan, but he was murdered by tribal rivals before Temujin turned ten, and the family was soon deserted by other members of the clan. As social outcasts, Temujin's small family, headed by his resourceful mother, was forced to live by hunting, fishing, and gathering wild foods. Without livestock, they had fallen to the lowest level of nomadic life. In these desperate circumstances, Temujin's remarkable character came into play. His personal magnetism and courage and his inclination to rely on trusted friends rather than ties of kinship allowed him to build up a small following and to ally with a more powerful tribal leader. This alliance received a boost from Chinese patrons, who were always eager to keep the nomads divided. Military victory over a rival tribe resulted in Temujin's recognition as a chief in his own right with a growing band of followers.

Temujin's rise to power amid the complex tribal politics of Mongolia was a surprise to everyone. It took place among shifting alliances and betrayals, a mounting string of military victories, the indecisiveness of his enemies, a reputation as a leader generous to friends and ruthless to enemies, and the incorporation of warriors from defeated tribes into his own forces. In 1206, a Mongol tribal assembly recognized Temujin as Chinggis Khan, supreme leader of a now unified Great Mongol Nation (see Document 12.1, pp. 550–52). It was a remarkable achievement, but one little noticed beyond the highland steppes of Mongolia. That would soon change.

The unification of the Mongol tribes raised an obvious question: What was Chinggis Khan to do with the powerful army he had assembled? Without a common task, the new and fragile unity of the Mongols would surely dissolve into quarrels and chaos; and without external resources to reward his followers, Chinggis Khan would be hard-pressed to maintain his supreme position. Both considerations pointed in a single direction—expansion, particularly toward China, long a source of great wealth for nomadic peoples.[15]

In 1209, the first major attack on the settled agricultural societies south of Mongolia set in motion half a century of a Mongol world war, a series of military campaigns, massive killing, and empire building without precedent in world history. In the process, Chinggis Khan, followed by his sons and grandsons (Ogodei, Mongke, and Khubilai), constructed an empire that contained China, Korea, Central Asia, Russia, much of the Islamic Middle East, and parts of Eastern Europe (see Map 12.1). "In a flash," wrote a recent scholar, "the Mongol warriors would defeat every army, capture every fort, and bring down the walls of every city they encountered. Christians, Muslims, Buddhists, and Hindus would soon kneel before the dusty boots of illiterate young Mongol horsemen."[16]

Various setbacks—the Mongols' withdrawal from Eastern Europe (1242), their defeat at Ain Jalut in Palestine at the hands of Egyptian forces (1260), the failure of their invasion of Japan owing to two typhoons (1274, 1281), and the difficulty of penetrating the tropical jungles of Southeast Asia—marked the outer limits of the Mongol Empire. But what an empire it was! How could a Mongol confederation, with a total population of less than 1 million people and few resources beyond their livestock, assemble an imperial structure of such staggering transcontinental dimensions?

Explaining the Mongol Moment

Like the Roman Empire but far more rapidly, the Mongol Empire grew of its own momentum without any grand scheme or blueprint for world conquest. Each fresh victory brought new resources for making war and new threats or insecurities that seemed to require further expansion. As the empire took shape and certainly by the end of his life, Chinggis Khan had come to see his career in terms of a universal mission. "I have accomplished a great work," he declared, "uniting the whole world in one empire."[17] Thus the Mongol Empire acquired an ideology in the course of its construction.

What made this "great work" possible? The odds seemed overwhelming, for China alone, after all, outnumbered the Mongols 100 to 1 and possessed incomparably greater resources. Nor did the Mongols enjoy any technological superiority over their many adversaries. They did, however, enjoy the luck of good timing, for China was divided, having already lost control of its northern territory to the nomadic Jurchen people, while the decrepit Abbasid caliphate, once the center of the Islamic world, had shrunk to a fraction of its earlier size. But clearly, the key to the Mongols' success lay in their army. According to one scholar, "Mongol armies were simply better led, organized, and disciplined than those of their opponents."[18] In an effort to diminish a divisive tribalism, Chinggis Khan reorganized the entire social structure of the Mongols into military units of 10, 100, 1,000, and 10,000 warriors, an arrangement that allowed for effective command and control. Conquered tribes especially were broken up and their members scattered among these new units, which enrolled virtually all nomadic men and supplied the cavalry forces of Mongol armies. A highly prestigious imperial guard, also recruited across tribal lines, marked the further decline of the old tribalism as a social revolution, imposed from above by Chinggis Khan, reshaped Mongol society.

An impressive discipline and loyalty to their leaders characterized Mongol military forces, and discpline was reinforced by the provision that should any members of a unit desert in battle, all were subject to the death penalty. More positively, loyalty

■ **Explanation**
What accounts for the political and military success of the Mongols?

was cemented by the leaders' willingness to share the hardships of their men. "I eat the same food and am dressed in the same rags as my humble herdsmen," wrote Chinggis Khan. "I am always in the forefront, and in battle I am never at the rear."[19] (See Document 12.2, pp. 553–54.) Such discipline and loyalty made possible the elaborate tactics of encirclement, retreat, and deception that proved decisive in many a battle. Furthermore, the enormous flow of wealth from conquered civilizations benefited all Mongols, though not equally. Even ordinary Mongols could now dress in linens and silks rather than hides and felt, could own slaves derived from the many prisoners of war, and had far greater opportunities to improve their social position in a constantly expanding empire.

To compensate for their own small population, the Mongols incorporated huge numbers of conquered peoples into their military forces. "People who lived in felt tents"—mostly Mongol and Turkic nomads—were conscripted en masse into the cavalry units of the Mongol army, while settled agricultural peoples supplied the infantry and artillery forces. As the Mongols penetrated major civilizations, with their walled cities and elaborate fortifications, they quickly acquired Chinese techniques and technology of siege warfare. Some 1,000 Chinese artillery crews, for example, took part in the Mongol invasion of distant Persia. Beyond military recruitment, Mongols demanded that their conquered people serve as laborers, building roads and bridges and ferrying supplies over long distances. Artisans, craftsmen, and skilled people generally were carefully identified, spared from massacre, and often sent to distant regions of the empire where their services were required.

A Mongol Warrior
Horseback-riding skills, honed in herding animals and adapted to military purposes, were central to Mongol conquests, as illustrated in this Ming-dynasty Chinese painting of a mounted Mongol archer. (Victoria and Albert Museum, London/V&A Images)

A French goldsmith, captured by Mongol forces in Hungary, wound up as a slave in the Mongol capital of Karakorum, where he constructed an elaborate silver fountain that dispensed wine and other intoxicating drinks.

A further element in the military effectiveness of Mongol forces lay in a growing reputation for a ruthless brutality and utter destructiveness. Chinggis Khan's policy was clear: "whoever submits shall be spared, but those who resist, they shall be destroyed with their wives, children and dependents . . . so that the others who hear and see should fear and not act the same."[20] The Central Asian kingdom of Khwarizm, whose ruler had greatly offended Chinggis Khan by murdering and mutilating Mongol envoys and merchants, was among the first, but by no means the last, to feel the full

effects of Mongol terror. City after city was utterly destroyed, and enemy soldiers were passed out in lots to Mongol troops for execution, while women and skilled craftsmen were enslaved. Unskilled civilians served as human shields for attacks on the next city or were used as human fill in the moats surrounding those cities.

One scholar explained such policies in this way: "Extremely conscious of their small numbers and fearful of rebellion, Chinggis often chose to annihilate a region's entire population, if it appeared too troublesome to govern."[21] These policies also served as a form of psychological warfare, a practical inducement to surrender for those who knew of the Mongol terror. Historians continue to debate the extent and uniqueness of the Mongols' brutality, but their reputation for unwavering harshness proved a military asset.

Underlying the purely military dimensions of the Mongols' success was an impressive ability to mobilize both the human and material resources of their growing empire. Elaborate census taking allowed Mongol leaders to know what was available to them and made possible the systematic taxation of conquered people. An effective system of relay stations, about a day's ride apart, provided rapid communication across the empire and fostered trade as well. Marco Polo, the Venetian trader who traveled through Mongol domains in the thirteenth century, claimed that the Mongols maintained some 10,000 such stations, together with 200,000 horses available to authorized users. The beginnings of a centralized bureaucracy with various specialized offices took shape in the new capital of Karakorum. There scribes translated official decrees into the various languages of the empire, such as Persian, Uighur, Chinese, and Tibetan.

Other policies appealed to various groups among the conquered peoples of the empire. Interested in fostering commerce, Mongol rulers often offered merchants 10 percent or more above their asking price and allowed them the free use of the relay stations for transporting their goods. In administering the conquered regions, Mongols held the highest decision-making posts, but Chinese and Muslim officials held many advisory and lower-level positions in China and Persia respectively. In religious matters, the Mongols welcomed and supported many religious traditions—Buddhist, Christian, Muslim, Daoist—as long as they did not become the focus of political opposition. This policy of religious toleration allowed Muslims to seek converts among Mongol troops and afforded Christians much greater freedom than they had enjoyed under Muslim rule.[22] Toward the end of his life and apparently feeling his approaching death, Chinggis Khan himself summoned a famous Daoist master from China and begged him to "communicate to me the means of preserving life." One of his successors, Mongke, arranged a debate among representatives of several religious faiths, after which he concluded: "Just as God gave different fingers to the hand, so has He given different ways to men."[23] Such economic, administrative, and religious policies provided some benefits and a place within the empire—albeit subordinate—for many of its conquered peoples.

Encountering the Mongols: Comparing Three Cases

The Mongol moment in world history represented an enormous cultural encounter between nomadic pastoralists and the settled civilizations of Eurasia. Differences among those civilizations—Confucian China, Muslim Persia, Christian Russia—ensured considerable diversity as this encounter unfolded across a vast realm. The process of conquest, the length and nature of Mongol rule, the impact on local people, and the extent of Mongol assimilation into the cultures of the conquered—all this and more varied considerably across the Eurasian domains of the empire. The experiences of China, Persia, and Russia provide brief glimpses into several expressions of this massive clash of cultures.

China and the Mongols

■ Change

How did Mongol rule change China? In what ways were the Mongols changed by China?

Long the primary target for nomadic steppe-dwellers in search of agrarian wealth, China proved the most difficult and extended of the Mongols' many conquests, lasting some seventy years, from 1209 to 1279. The invasion began in northern China, which had been ruled for several centuries by various dynasties of nomadic origin, and was characterized by destruction and plunder on a massive scale. Southern China, under the control of the native Song dynasty, was a different story, for there the Mongols were far less violent and more concerned to accommodate the local population. Landowners, for example, were guaranteed their estates in exchange for their support or at least their neutrality. By whatever methods, the outcome was the unification of a divided China, a treasured ideal among educated Chinese. This achievement persuaded many of them that the Mongols had indeed been granted the Mandate of Heaven and, despite their foreign origins, were legitimate rulers. (See Document 12.4, pp. 555–57, for a positive Chinese view of their Mongol rulers.)

Having acquired China, what were the Mongols to do with it? One possibility, apparently considered by the Great Khan Ogodei in the 1230s, was to exterminate everyone in northern China and turn the country into pastureland for Mongol herds. That suggestion, fortunately, was rejected in favor of extracting as much wealth as possible from the country's advanced civilization. Doing so meant some accommodation to Chinese culture and ways of governing, for the Mongols had no experience with the operation of a complex agrarian society.

That accommodation took many forms. The Mongols made use of Chinese administrative practices, techniques of taxation, and their postal system. They gave themselves a Chinese dynastic title, the Yuan, suggesting a new beginning in Chinese history. They transferred their capital from Karakorum in Mongolia to what is now Beijing, building a wholly new capital city there known as Khanbalik, the "city of the khan." Thus the Mongols were now rooting themselves solidly on the soil of a highly sophisticated civilization, well removed from their homeland on the steppes.

Marco Polo and Khubilai Khan

In ruling China, the Mongols employed in high positions a number of Muslims and a few Europeans, such as Marco Polo, shown here kneeling before Khubilai Khan in a painting from the fifteenth century. (Ms 2810 f.5. Nicolo and Marco Polo before the Great Khan [vellum], Boucicaut Master, [fl. 1390–1430, and workshop]/Bibliothèque nationale de France, Paris, France/The Bridgeman Art Library)

Khubilai Khan, the grandson of Chinggis Khan and China's Mongol ruler from 1271 to 1294, ordered a set of Chinese-style ancestral tablets to honor his ancestors and posthumously awarded them Chinese names. Many of his policies evoked the values of a benevolent Chinese emperor as he improved roads, built canals, lowered some taxes, patronized scholars and artists, limited the death penalty and torture, supported peasant agriculture, and prohibited Mongols from grazing their animals on peasants' farmland. Mongol khans also made use of traditional Confucian rituals, supported the building of some Daoist temples, and were particularly attracted to a Tibetan form of Buddhism, which returned the favor with strong political support for the invaders.

Despite these accommodations, Mongol rule was still harsh, exploitative, foreign, and resented. The Mongols did not become Chinese, nor did they accommodate every aspect of Chinese culture. Deep inside the new capital, the royal family and court could continue to experience something of steppe life. There, animals roamed freely in large open areas, planted with steppe grass. Many of the Mongol elite much preferred to live, eat, sleep, and give birth in the traditional tents that sprouted everywhere. In administering the country, the Mongols largely ignored the traditional Chinese examination system and relied heavily on foreigners, particularly Muslims from Central Asia and the Middle East, to serve as officials, while keeping the top decision-making posts for themselves. Few Mongols learned Chinese, and Mongol law discriminated against the Chinese, reserving for them the most severe punishments. In social life, the Mongols forbade intermarriage and prohibited Chinese scholars from learning the Mongol script. Mongol women never adopted foot binding and scandalized the Chinese by mixing freely with men at official gatherings and riding to the hunt with their husbands. Furthermore, the Mongols honored and supported merchants and artisans far more than Confucian bureaucrats had been inclined to do.

However one assesses Mongol rule in China, it was brief, lasting little more than a century. By the mid-fourteenth century, intense factionalism among the Mongols, rapidly rising prices, furious epidemics of the plague, and growing peasant rebellions combined to force the Mongols out of China. By 1368, rebel forces had triumphed, and thousands of Mongols returned to their homeland in the steppes. For several centuries, they remained a periodic threat to China, but during the Ming dynasty that followed, the memory of their often brutal and alien rule stimulated a renewed commitment to Confucian values and practices and an effort to wipe out all traces of the Mongols' impact.

Persia and the Mongols

■ Comparison
How was Mongol rule in Persia different from that in China?

A second great civilization conquered by the Mongols was that of an Islamic Persia. There the Mongol takeover was far more abrupt than the extended process of conquest in China. A first invasion (1219–1221), led by Chinggis Khan himself, was followed thirty years later by a second assault (1251–1258) under his grandson Hulegu, who became the first il-khan (subordinate khan) of Persia. More destructive than the conquest of Song dynasty China, the Mongol offensive against Persia and Iraq had no precedent in their history, although Persia had been repeatedly attacked, from the invasion of Alexander the Great to that of the Arabs. The most recent incursion had featured Turkic peoples, but they had been Muslims, recently converted, small in number, and seeking only acceptance within the Islamic world. The Mongols, however, were infidels in Muslim eyes, and their stunning victory was a profound shock to people accustomed to viewing history as the progressive expansion of Islamic rule. Furthermore, Mongol military victory brought in its wake a degree of ferocity and slaughter that simply had no parallel in Persian experience. The Persian historian Juwayni described it in fearful terms:

> Every town and every village has been several times subjected to pillage and massacre and has suffered this confusion for years so that even though there be generation and increase until the Resurrection the population will not attain to a tenth part of what it was before.[24]

The sacking of Baghdad in 1258, which put an end to the Abbasid caliphate, was accompanied by the massacre of more than 200,000 people, according to Hulegu himself.

Beyond this human catastrophe lay the damage to Persian and Iraqi agriculture and to those who tilled the soil. Heavy taxes, sometimes collected twenty or thirty times a year and often under torture or whipping, pushed large numbers of peasants off their land. Furthermore, the in-migration of nomadic Mongols, together with their immense herds of sheep and goats, turned much agricultural land into pasture and sometimes into desert. In both cases, a fragile system of underground water channels that provided irrigation to the fields was neglected, and much good agricultural land was reduced to waste. Some sectors of the Persian economy gained, however. Wine production increased because the Mongols were fond of alcohol, and the Persian silk industry benefited from close contact with a Mongol-ruled China. In general, though, even more so than in China, Mongol rule in Persia represented "disaster on a grand and unparalleled scale."[25]

Nonetheless, the Mongols in Persia were themselves transformed far more than their counterparts in China. They made extensive use of the sophisticated Persian bureaucracy, leaving the greater part of government operations in Persian hands. During the reign of Ghazan (1295–1304), they made some efforts to repair the damage caused by earlier policies of ruthless exploitation, by rebuilding damaged cities and repairing neglected irrigation works. Most important, the Mongols who conquered Persia became Muslims, following the lead of Ghazan, who converted to Islam in 1295. No such widespread conversion to the culture of the conquered occurred in China or in Christian Russia. Members of the court and Mongol elites learned at least some Persian, unlike most of their counterparts in China. A number of Mongols also turned to farming, abandoning their nomadic ways, while some married local people. When the Mongol dynasty of Hulegu's descendants collapsed in the 1330s for lack of a suitable heir, the Mongols were not driven out of Persia as they had been from China. Rather they and their Turkic allies simply disappeared, assimilated into Persian society. From a Persian point of view, the barbarians had been civilized.

Russia and the Mongols

When the Mongol military machine rolled over Russia between 1237 and 1240, it encountered a relatively new third-wave civilization, located on the far eastern fringe of Christendom (see Chapter 10). Whatever political unity this new civilization of Kievan Rus had earlier enjoyed was now gone, and various independent princes proved unable to unite even in the face of the Mongol onslaught. Although they had interacted extensively with nomadic people of the steppes north of the Black Sea, nothing had prepared them for the Mongols.

■ **Comparison**
What was distinctive about the Russian experience of Mongol rule?

The devastation wrought by the Mongol assault matched or exceeded anything experienced by the Persians or the Chinese. City after city fell to Mongol forces, which were now armed with the catapults and battering rams adopted from Chinese or Muslim sources. The slaughter that sometimes followed was described in horrific terms by Russian chroniclers, although twentieth-century historians often regard such

Mongol Russia
This sixteenth-century painting depicts the Mongol burning of the Russian city of Ryazan in 1237. Similar destruction awaited many Russian towns that resisted the invaders. (Sovfoto/Eastfoto)

accounts as exaggerated. (See Document 12.3, pp. 554–55, for one such account.) From the survivors and the cities that surrendered early, laborers and skilled craftsmen were deported to other Mongol lands or sold into slavery. A number of Russian crafts were so depleted of their workers that they did not recover for a century or more.

If the ferocity of initial conquest bore similarities to the experiences of Persia, Russia's incorporation into the Mongol Empire was very different. To the Mongols, it was the Kipchak Khanate, named after the Kipchak Turkic-speaking peoples north of the Caspian and Black seas, among whom the Mongols had settled. To the Russians, it was the "Khanate of the Golden Horde." By whatever name, the Mongols had conquered Russia, but they did not occupy it as they had China and Persia. Because there were no garrisoned cities, permanently stationed administrators, or Mongol settlement, the Russian experience of Mongol rule was quite different than elsewhere. From the Mongol point of view, Russia had little to offer. Its economy was not nearly as developed as that of more established civilizations; nor was it located on major international trade routes. It was simply not worth the expense of occupying. Furthermore, the availability of extensive steppe lands for pasturing their flocks north of the Black and Caspian seas meant that the Mongols could maintain their preferred nomadic way of life, while remaining in easy reach of Russian cities when the need arose to send further military expeditions. They could dominate and exploit Russia from the steppes.

And exploit they certainly did. Russian princes received appointment from the khan and were required to send substantial tribute to the Mongol capital at Sarai, located on the lower Volga River. A variety of additional taxes created a heavy burden, especially on the peasantry, while continuing border raids sent tens of thousands of Russians into slavery. The Mongol impact was highly uneven, however. Some Russian princes benefited considerably because they were able to manipulate their role as tribute collectors to grow wealthy. The Russian Orthodox Church likewise flourished under the Mongol policy of religious toleration, for it received exemption from many taxes. Nobles who participated in Mongol raids earned a share of the loot. Some cities, such as Kiev, resisted the Mongols and were devastated, while others collaborated and were left undamaged. Moscow in particular emerged as the primary collector of tribute for the Mongols, and its princes parlayed this position into a leading role as the nucleus of a renewed Russian state when Mongol domination receded in the fifteenth century.

The absence of direct Mongol rule had implications for the Mongols themselves, for they were far less influenced by or assimilated within Russian cultures than their counterparts in China and Persia had been. The Mongols in China had turned themselves into a Chinese dynasty, with the khan as a Chinese emperor. Some learned calligraphy, and a few came to appreciate Chinese poetry. In Persia, the Mongols had converted to Islam, with some becoming farmers. Not so in Russia. There "the Mongols of the Golden Horde were still spending their days in the saddle and their nights in tents."[26] They could dominate Russia from the adjacent steppes without in any way adopting Russian culture. Even though they remained culturally separate from Russia, eventually the Mongols assimilated to the culture and the Islamic faith of the Kipchak people of the steppes, and in the process they lost their distinct identity and became Kipchaks.

Despite this domination from a distance, "the impact of the Mongols on Russia was, if anything, greater than on China and Iran [Persia]," according to a leading scholar.[27] Russian princes, who were more or less left alone if they paid the required tribute and taxes, found it useful to adopt the Mongols' weapons, diplomatic rituals, court practices, taxation system, and military draft. Mongol policies facilitated, although not intentionally, the rise of Moscow as the core of a new Russian state, and that state made good use of the famous Mongol mounted courier service, which Marco Polo had praised so highly. Mongol policies also strengthened the hold of the Russian Orthodox Church and enabled it to penetrate the rural areas more fully than before. Some Russians, seeking to explain their country's economic backwardness and political autocracy in modern times, have held the Mongols responsible for both conditions, though most historians consider such views vastly exaggerated.

Divisions among the Mongols and the growing strength of the Russian state, centered now on the city of Moscow, enabled the Russians to break the Mongols' hold by the end of the fifteenth century. With the earlier demise of Mongol rule in China and Persia, and now in Russia, the Mongols had retreated from their brief but spectacular incursion into the civilizations of outer Eurasia. Nonetheless, they continued to periodically threaten these civilizations for several centuries, until their homelands were absorbed into the expanding Russian and Chinese empires. But the Mongol moment in world history was over.

The Mongol Empire as a Eurasian Network

During the postclassical millennium, Chinese culture and Buddhism provided a measure of integration among the peoples of East Asia; Christianity did the same for Europe, while the realm of Islam connected most of the lands in between. But it was the Mongol Empire, during the thirteenth and fourteenth centuries, that brought all of these regions into a single interacting network. It was a unique moment in world history and an important step toward the global integration of the modern era.

Toward a World Economy

■ Connection
In what ways did the Mongol Empire contribute to the globalization of the Eurasian world?

The Mongols themselves produced little of value for distant markets, nor were they active traders. Nonetheless, they consistently promoted international commerce, largely so that they could tax it and thus extract wealth from more developed civilizations. The Great Khan Ogodei, for example, often paid well over the asking price in order to attract merchants to his capital of Karakorum. The Mongols also provided financial backing for caravans, introduced standardized weights and measures, and gave tax breaks to merchants.

In providing a relatively secure environment for merchants making the long and arduous journey across Central Asia between Europe and China, the Mongol Empire brought the two ends of the Eurasian world into closer contact than ever before and launched a new phase in the history of the Silk Roads. Marco Polo was only the most famous of many European merchants, mostly from Italian cities, who made their way to China through the Mongol Empire. So many traders attempted the journey that guidebooks were published with much useful advice about the trip. Merchants returned with tales of rich lands and prosperous commercial opportunities, but what they described were long-established trading networks of which Europeans had been largely ignorant.

The Mongol trading circuit was a central element in an even larger commercial network that linked much of the Afro-Eurasian world in the thirteenth century (see Map 12.2). Mongol-ruled China was the fulcrum of this vast system, connecting the overland route through the Mongol Empire with the oceanic routes through the South China Sea and Indian Ocean. Here, some historians have argued, lay the beginnings of those international economic relationships that have played such a major role in the making of the modern world.

Diplomacy on a Eurasian Scale

Not only did the Mongol Empire facilitate long-distance commerce, but it also prompted diplomatic relationships from one end of Eurasia to the other. As their invasion of Russia spilled over into Eastern Europe, Mongol armies destroyed Polish, German, and Hungarian forces in 1241–1242 and seemed poised to march on Central and Western Europe. But the death of the Great Khan Ogodei required Mongol leaders to return to Mongolia, and Western Europe lacked adequate pasture for Mongol herds. Thus Western Europe was spared the trauma of conquest, but fearing the possible return of the Mongols, both the pope and European rulers dispatched delegations to the Mongol capital, mostly led by Franciscan friars. They hoped to

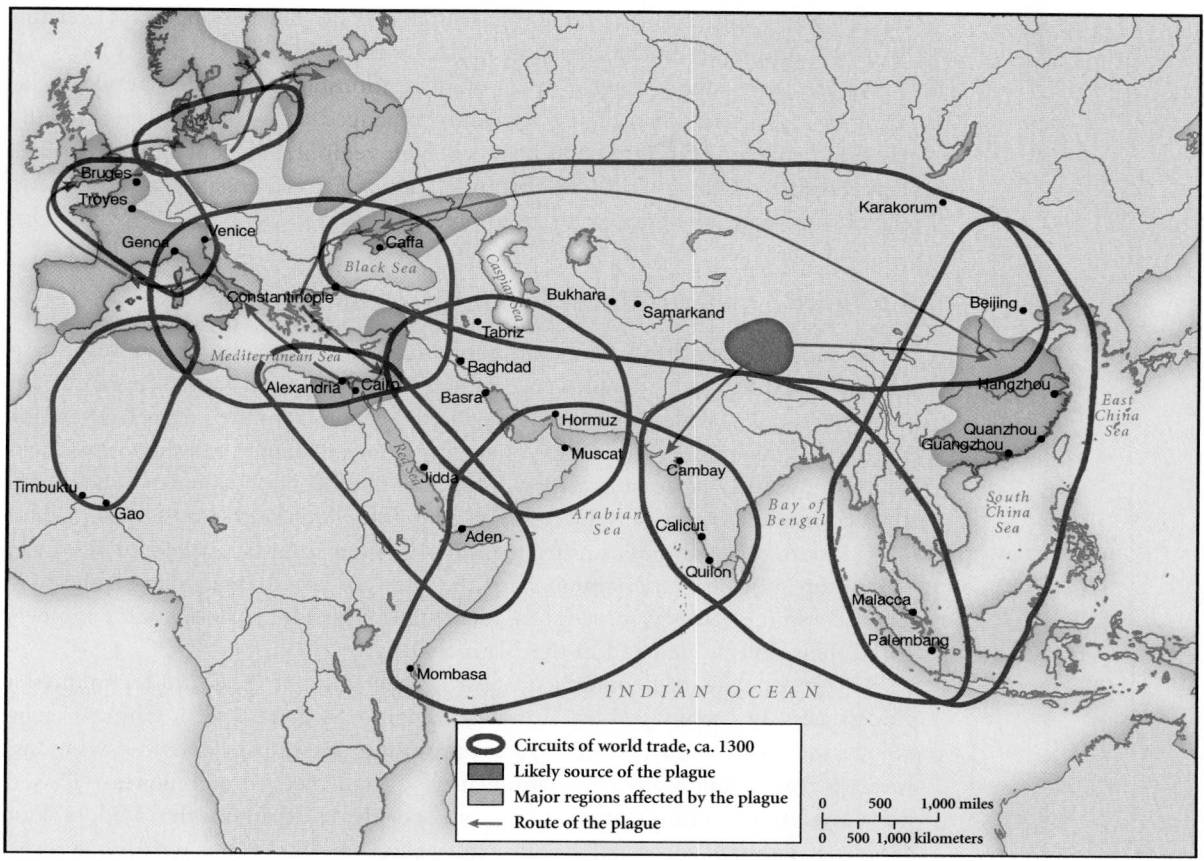

Map 12.2 Trade and Disease in the Fourteenth Century

The Mongol Empire played a major role in the commercial integration of the Eurasian world as well as in the spread of the plague across this vast area.

learn something about Mongol intentions, to secure Mongol aid in the Christian crusade against Islam, and, if possible, to convert Mongols to Christianity.

These efforts were largely in vain, for no alliance or widespread conversion occurred. In fact, one of these missions came back with a letter for the pope from the Great Khan Guyuk, demanding that Europeans submit to him. "But if you should not believe our letters and the command of God nor hearken to our counsel," he warned, "then we shall know for certain that you wish to have war. After that we do not know what will happen."[28] Perhaps the most important outcome of these diplomatic probings was the useful information about lands to the east that European missions brought back. Those reports contributed to a dawning European awareness of a wider world, and they have certainly provided later historians with much useful information about the Mongols (see Document 12.5, pp. 557–59). Somewhat later, in 1287, the il-khanate of Persia sought an alliance with European powers to take Jerusalem and crush the forces of Islam, but the Persian Mongols' conversion to Islam soon put an end to any such anti–Muslim coalition.

Within the Mongol Empire itself, close relationships developed between the courts of Persia and China. They regularly exchanged ambassadors, shared intelligence information, fostered trade between their regions, and sent skilled workers back and forth. Thus political authorities all across Eurasia engaged in diplomatic relationships with one another to an unprecedented degree.

Cultural Exchange in the Mongol Realm

Accompanying these transcontinental economic and diplomatic relationships was a substantial exchange of peoples and cultures. Mongol policy forcibly transferred many thousands of skilled craftsmen and educated people from their homelands to distant parts of the empire, while the Mongols' religious tolerance and support of merchants drew missionaries and traders from afar. The Mongol capital at Karakorum was a cosmopolitan city with places of worship for Buddhists, Daoists, Muslims, and Christians. Actors and musicians from China, wrestlers from Persia, and a jester from Byzantium provided entertainment for the Mongol court. Persian and Arab doctors and administrators were sent to China, while Chinese physicians and engineers found their skills in demand in the Islamic world.

This movement of people facilitated the exchange of ideas and techniques, a process actively encouraged by Mongol authorities. A great deal of Chinese technology and artistic conventions—such as painting, printing, gunpowder weapons, compass navigation, high-temperature furnaces, and medical techniques—flowed westward. Acupuncture, for example, was poorly received in the Middle East because it required too much bodily contact for Muslim taste, but Chinese techniques for diagnosing illness by taking the pulse of patients proved quite popular, as they involved minimal body contact. Muslim astronomers brought their skills and knowledge to China because Mongol authorities wanted "second opinions on the reading of heavenly signs and portents" and assistance in constructing accurate calendars, so necessary for ritual purposes.[29] Plants and crops likewise circulated within the Mongol domain. Lemons and carrots from the Middle East found a welcome reception in China, while the Persian Il-Khan Ghazan sent envoys to India, China, and elsewhere to seek "seeds of things which are unique in that land."[30]

Europeans arguably gained more than most from these exchanges, for they had long been cut off from the fruitful interchange with Asia, and in comparison to the Islamic and Chinese worlds, they were less technologically developed. Now they could reap the benefits of much new technology, new crops, and new knowledge of a wider world. And almost alone among the peoples of Eurasia, they could do so without having suffered the devastating consequences of Mongol conquest. In these circumstances, some historians have argued, lay the roots of Europe's remarkable rise to global prominence in the centuries that followed.

The Plague: A Eurasian Pandemic

Any benefits derived from participation in Mongol networks of communication and exchange must be measured alongside the Eurasian catastrophe known as the "plague" or the "pestilence" and later called the Black Death. Originating most likely in Central Asia, the bacteria responsible for the disease spread across the trade routes of the vast Mongol Empire in the early fourteenth century (see Map 12.2). Carried by rodents and transmitted by fleas to humans, the plague erupted initially in 1331 in northeastern China and had reached the Middle East and Western Europe by 1347. One lurid but quite uncertain story has the Mongols using catapults to hurl corpses infected with the plague into the Genoese city of Caffa in the Crimea.

■ **Change**
Disease changes societies. How might this argument apply to the plague?

The disease itself was associated with swelling of the lymph nodes, most often in the groin; terrible headaches; high fever; and internal bleeding just below the skin. Infected people generally died within a few days. In the densely populated civilizations of China, the Islamic world, and Europe as well as in the steppe lands of the nomads, the plague claimed enormous numbers of human victims, causing a sharp contraction in Eurasian population for a century or more. Chroniclers reported rates of death that ranged from 50 to 90 percent of the affected population, depending on the time and place. A recent study suggests that about half of Europe's people perished during the initial outbreak of 1348–1350.[31] A fifteenth-century Egyptian historian wrote that within a month of the plague's arrival in 1349, "Cairo had become an abandoned desert.... Everywhere one heard lamentations and one could not pass by any house without being overwhelmed by the howling."[32] The Middle East generally had lost perhaps one-third of its population by the early fifteenth century.[33] The intense first wave of the plague was followed by periodic visitations over the next several centuries, although India and sub-Saharan Africa were much less affected than other regions of the eastern hemisphere.

The Plague
This illustration depicts a European doctor visiting a patient with the plague. Notice that the doctor and others around the bedside cover their noses to prevent infection. During the Black Death, doctors were often criticized for refusing to treat dying patients, as they feared for their own lives. (The Granger Collection, New York)

But in those places where it struck, the plague left thoughtful people grasping for language with which to describe a horror of such unprecedented dimensions. One Italian man, who had buried all five of his children with his own hands, wrote in 1348 that "so many have died that everyone believes it is the end of the world."[34] Another Italian, the Renaissance scholar Francesco Petrarch, was equally stunned by the impact of the Black Death; he wrote to a friend in 1349:

> When at any time has such a thing been seen or spoken of? Has what happened in these years ever been read about: empty houses, derelict cities, ruined estates, fields strewn with cadavers, a horrible and vast solitude encompassing the whole world? Consult historians, they are silent; ask physicians, they are stupefied; seek the answers from philosophers, they shrug their shoulders, furrow their brows, and with fingers pressed against their lips, bid you be silent. Will posterity believe these things, when we who have seen it can scarcely believe it…?[35]

In the Islamic world, the famous historian Ibn Khaldun, who had lost both of his parents to the plague, also wrote about it in apocalyptic terms:

> Civilization in both the East and the West was visited by a destructive plague which devastated nations and caused populations to vanish. It swallowed up many of the good things of civilization and wiped them out.… It was as if the voice of existence had called out for oblivion and restriction, and the world responded to its call.[36]

(See Visual Sources: The Black Death and Religion in Western Europe, pp. 560–67, for more on religious response to the plague in Europe.)

Beyond its immediate devastation, the Black Death worked longer-term changes in European society, the region where the plague's impact has been most thoroughly studied. Labor shortages following the initial outburst provoked sharp conflict between scarce workers, who sought higher wages or better conditions, and the rich, who resisted those demands. A series of peasant revolts in the fourteenth century reflected this tension, which also undermined the practice of serfdom. That labor shortage also may have fostered a greater interest in technological innovation and created, at least for a time, more employment opportunities for women. Thus a resilient European civilization survived a cataclysm that had the power to destroy it. In a strange way, that catastrophe may have actually fostered its future growth.

Whatever its impact in particular places, the plague also had larger consequences. Ironically, that human disaster, born of the Mongol network, was a primary reason for the demise of that network in the fourteenth and fifteenth centuries. Population contracted, cities declined, and the volume of trade diminished all across the Mongol world. By 1350, the Mongol Empire itself was in disarray, and within a century the Mongols had lost control of Chinese, Persian, and Russian civilizations. The Central Asian trade route, so critical to the entire Afro-Eurasian world economy, largely closed.

This disruption of the Mongol-based land routes to the east, coupled with a desire to avoid Muslim intermediaries, provided incentives for Europeans to take to the sea in their continuing efforts to reach the riches of Asia. Their naval technology gave them military advantages on the seas, much as the Mongols' skill with the bow and their mobility on horseback gave these nomads a decisive edge in land battles.

As Europeans penetrated Asian waters in the sixteenth century, they took on, in some ways, the role of the Mongols in organizing and fostering world trade and in creating a network of communication and exchange over an even larger area. Like the Mongols, Europeans were people on the periphery of the major established civilizations: they too were economically less developed in comparison to Chinese and Islamic civilizations, and both were prone to forcibly plundering the wealthier civilizations they encountered.[37] Europeans, of course, brought far more of their own culture and many more of their own people to the societies they conquered, as Christianity, European languages, settler societies, and western science and technology took root within their empires. Although their imperial presence lasted far longer and operated on a much larger scale, European actions at the beginning of their global expansion bore some resemblance to those of their Mongol predecessors. They were, as one historian put it, "the Mongols of the seas."[38]

Reflections: Changing Images of Nomadic Peoples

Until recently, nomads generally received bad press in history books. Normally they entered the story only when they were threatening or destroying established civilizations. In presenting a largely negative image of pastoral peoples, historians were reflecting the long-held attitudes of literate elites in the civilizations of Eurasia. Fearing and usually despising nomadic peoples, educated observers in China, the Middle East, and Europe often described them as bloodthirsty savages or barbarians, bringing only chaos and destruction in their wake. Han Kuan, a Chinese scholar of the first century B.C.E., described the Xiongnu people as "abandoned by Heaven . . . in foodless desert wastes, without proper houses, clothed in animal hides, eating their meat uncooked and drinking blood."[39] To the Christian Saint Jerome (340–420 C.E.), the nomadic Huns "filled the whole earth with slaughter and panic alike as they flitted hither and thither on their swift horses."[40] Almost a thousand years later, the famous Arab historian Ibn Khaldun described nomads in a very similar fashion: "It is their nature to plunder whatever other people possess."[41]

Because nomadic peoples generally did not have written languages, the sources available to historians came from less-than-unbiased observers in adjacent agricultural civilizations. Furthermore, in the long-running conflict across the farming/pastoral frontier, agricultural civilizations ultimately triumphed. Over the centuries, some nomadic or barbarian peoples, such as the Germanic tribes of Europe and the Arabs, created new civilizations. Others, such as the Turkic and Mongol peoples, took over existing civilizations or were encompassed within established agrarian empires. By the early twentieth century, and in most places much earlier, nomadic peoples everywhere had lost their former independence and had often shed their nomadic life as well. Since "winners" usually write history, the negative views of nomads held by agrarian civilizations normally prevailed.

Reflecting more inclusive contemporary values, historians in recent decades have sought to present a more balanced picture of nomads' role in world history, emphasizing what they created as well as what they destroyed. These historians have highlighted the achievements of nomadic peoples, such as their adaptation to inhospitable environments; their technological innovations; their development of horse-, camel-, or cattle-based cultures; their role in fostering cross-cultural exchange; and their state-building efforts.

A less critical or judgmental posture toward the Mongols may also owe something to the "total wars" and genocides of the twentieth century, in which the mass slaughter of civilians became a strategy to induce enemy surrender. During the cold war, the United States and the Soviet Union were prepared, apparently, to obliterate each other's entire population with nuclear weapons in response to an attack. In light of this recent history, Mongol massacres may appear a little less unique. Historians living in the glass houses of contemporary societies are perhaps more reluctant to cast stones at the Mongols. In understanding the Mongols, as in so much else, historians are shaped by the times and circumstances of their own lives as much as by "what really happened" in the past.

Second Thoughts

What's the Significance?

To assess your mastery of the material in this chapter, visit the **Student Center** at bedfordstmartins.com/strayer.

pastoralism	Temujin/Chinggis Khan	Kipchak Khanate/Golden
Xiongnu	the Mongol world war	Horde
Modun	Yuan dynasty China	Black Death/plague
Turks	Khubilai Khan	
Masai	Hulegu	

Big Picture Questions

1. Prior to the rise of the Mongols, in what ways had pastoral peoples been significant in world history?

2. What accounts for the often negative attitudes of settled societies toward the pastoral peoples living on their borders? Why have historians often neglected pastoral peoples' role in world history?

3. In what ways did the Mongol Empire resemble other empires, and in what ways did it differ from them? Why did it last a relatively short time?

4. In what different ways did Mongol rule affect the Islamic world, Russia, China, and Europe?

5. How would you define both the immediate and the long-term significance of the Mongols in world history?

6. How would you assess the perspective of this chapter toward the Mongols? Does it strike you as negative and critical of the Mongols, as bending over backward to portray them in a positive light, or as a balanced presentation?

Next Steps: For Further Study

John Aberth, *The First Horseman: Disease in Human History* (2007). A global study of the history of disease, with a fine chapter on the Black Death.

Thomas Allsen, *Culture and Conquest in Mongol Eurasia* (2001). A history of cultural exchange within the Mongol realm, particularly between China and the Islamic world.

Thomas J. Barfield, *The Nomadic Alternative* (1993). An anthropological and historical survey of pastoral peoples on a global basis.

Carter Finley, *The Turks in World History* (2005). The evolution of Turkic-speaking people, from their nomadic origins to the twentieth century.

Jack Weatherford, *Genghis Khan and the Making of the Modern World* (2004). A lively, well-written, and balanced account of the world the Mongols made and the legacy they left for the future.

"The Mongols in World History," http://afe.easia.columbia.edu/mongols. A wonderful resource on the Mongols generally, with a particular focus on their impact in China.

For Web sites and additional documents related to this chapter, see **Make History** at bedfordstmartins.com/strayer.

Documents

Considering the Evidence: Perspectives on the Mongols

How did the Mongols understand themselves and the enormous empire they had created? How did the peoples who were forcibly incorporated within that empire or threatened by it view the Mongols? In studying the Mongol phenomenon, historians use documents that reflect both the Mongols' perception of themselves and the perspectives of outsiders. The first two documents derive from Mongol sources, while the final three represent views from Russian, Chinese, and Western European observers (see Map 12.1, p. 530).

Sorting through these various perceptions of the Mongols raises questions about the kinds of understandings—or misunderstandings—that arise as culturally different peoples meet, especially under conditions of conquest. These documents also require reflection on the relative usefulness of sources that come from the Mongols themselves as well as those that derive from the victims of Mongol aggression.

Document 12.1

Mongol History from a Mongol Source

The major literary work to emerge from the Mongols themselves, widely known as *The Secret History of the Mongols*, was written a decade or two after the death in 1227 of Chinggis Khan. The unknown author of this work was clearly a contemporary of the Great Khan and likely a member of the royal household. The first selection discusses the Mongol practice of *anda*, a very close relationship between two unrelated men. Although they later broke with one another, the anda relationship of Temujin, the future Chinggis Khan, and his friend Jamugha was important in Temujin's rise to power. The second selection from the *Secret History* describes the process by which Temujin was elevated to the rank of Chinggis Khan, the ruler of a united Mongol nation, while the third recounts the reflections of Ogodei, Chinggis Khan's son and successor, probably toward the end of his reign, which lasted from 1229 to 1241.

- How would you describe the anda relationship?

- What does the *Secret History* suggest about the nature of political authority and political relationships among the Mongols?

- What did Ogodei regard as his greatest achievements and his most notable mistakes?

- What evidence do the selections from the *Secret History* provide that the author was an insider?

The Secret History of the Mongols
ca. 1240

Anda: Temujin and Jamugha

Temujin and Jamugha pitched their tents in the Khorkonagh Valley.
With their people united in one great camp,
the two leaders decided they should renew their friendship,
their pledge of anda.
They remembered when they'd first made that pledge,
and said, " We should love one another again."
That first time they'd met Temujin was eleven years old....
So Temujin and Jamugha said to each other:
"We've heard the elders say,
'When two men become anda their lives become one.
One will never desert the other and will always defend him.'
This is the way we'll act from now on.
We'll renew our old pledge and love each other forever."
Temujin took the golden belt he'd received
in the spoils from Toghtoga's defeat
and placed it around Anda Jamugha's waist.
Then he led out the Merkid chief's warhorse,
a light yellow mare with black mane and tail,
and gave it to Anda Jamugha to ride.
Jamugha took the golden belt he'd received
in the spoils from Dayir Usun's defeat
and placed it around the waist of Anda Temujin.
Then he led out the whitish-tan warhorse of Dayir Usun

and had Anda Temujin ride on it.
Before the cliffs of Khuldaghar
in the Khorkhonagh Valley,
beneath the Great Branching Tree of the Mongol,
they pledged their friendship and promised to love one another.
They held a feast on the spot
and there was great celebration.
Temujin and Jamugha spent that night alone,
sharing one blanket to cover them both.

Temujin and Jamugha loved each other for one year,
and when half of the second year had passed
they agreed it was time to move camp....

Temujin Becomes Chinggis Khan

Then they moved the whole camp
to the shores of Blue Lake in the Gurelgu Mountains.
Altan, Khuchar, and Sacha Beki conferred with each other there,
and then said to Temujin:
"We want you to be khan.
Temujin, if you'll be our khan
we'll search through the spoils
for the beautiful women and virgins,
for the great palace tents,
for the young virgins and loveliest women,
for the finest geldings and mares.
We'll gather all these and bring them to you.
When we go off to hunt for wild game
we'll go out first to drive them together for you to kill.
We'll drive the wild animals of the steppe together so that their bellies are touching.

Source: Paul Kahn, *The Secret History of the Mongols: The Origin of Chingis Khan* (San Francisco: North Point Press, 1984), 44–45, 48–49, 192–93.

We'll drive the wild game of the mountains together
    so that they stand leg to leg.
If we disobey your command during battle
take away our possessions, our children, and wives.
Leave us behind in the dust,
cutting off our heads where we stand and letting
    them fall to the ground.
If we disobey your counsel in peacetime
take away our tents and our goods, our wives, and
    our children.
Leave us behind when you move,
abandoned in the desert without a protector."
Having given their word,
having taken this oath,
they proclaimed Temujin khan of the Mongol
and gave him the name Chingis Khan....

Reflections of Ogodei

Then Ogodei Khan spoke these words:
"Since my father the Khan passed away
and I came to sit on his great throne,
what have I done?
I went to war against the people of Cathay° and I
    destroyed them.
For my second accomplishment
I established a network of post stations
so that my words are carried across the land with
    great speed.
Another of my accomplishments has been
to have my commanders dig wells in the desert
so that there would be pasture and water for the
    people there.
Lastly I placed spies and agents among all the
    people of the cities.
In all directions I've brought peace to the Nation
    and the people,
making them place their feet on the ground;
making them place their hands on the earth.
Since the time of my father the Khan
I added these four accomplishments to all that
    he did.

°**Cathay:** China.

But also since my father passed away
and I came to sit on his great throne
with the burden of all the numerous people on
    my shoulders
I allowed myself to be conquered by wine.
This was one of my mistakes.
Another of my mistakes was to listen to a woman
    with no principles
and because of her
take away the daughters who belonged to my
    Uncle Odchigin.
Even though I'm the Khan,
the Lord of the Nation,
I have no right to go against established principle,
so this was my mistake.
Another mistake was to secretly harm Dokholkhu.
If you ask, 'Why was this wrong?'
I would say that to secretly harm Dokholkhu,
a man who had served his proper lord, my father
    the Khan,
performing heroic deeds in his service, was a
    mistake.
Now that I've done this
who'll perform heroic deeds in my service?
So now I admit that I was wrong and didn't
    understand.
I secretly harmed a man who had served my
    father the Khan,
someone who deserved my protection.
Then my last mistake was to desire too much,
to say to myself,
'I'm afraid that all the wild game born under
    Heaven
will run off toward the land of my brothers.'
So I ordered earthen walls to be built
to keep the wild game from running away,
but even as these walls were being built
I heard my brothers speaking badly of me.
I admit that I was wrong to do this.
Since the time of my father the Khan
I've added four accomplishments to all that
    he'd done
and I've done four things which I admit were
    wrong."

Document 12.2

A Letter from Chingghis Khan

Document 12.2 comes from a remarkable letter that Chinggis Khan sent to an elderly Chinese Daoist master named Changchun in 1219, requesting a personal meeting with the teacher. Changchun in fact made the arduous journey to the camp of Chinggis Khan, then located in Afghanistan, where he stayed with the Mongol ruler for almost a year, before returning to China.

- Why did Chinggis Khan seek a meeting with Changchun?

- How does Chinggis Khan define his life's work? What is his image of himself?

- How would you describe the tone of Chinggis Khan's letter to Changchun? What does the letter suggest about Mongol attitudes toward the belief systems of conquered peoples?

- How do Documents 12.1 and 12.2 help explain the success of the Mongols' empire-building efforts?

- What core Mongol values do these documents suggest?

CHINGGIS KHAN

Letter to Changchun

1219

Heaven has abandoned China owing to its haughtiness and extravagant luxury. But I, living in the northern wilderness, have not inordinate passions. I hate luxury and exercise moderation. I have only one coat and one food. I eat the same food and am dressed in the same tatters as my humble herdsmen. I consider the people my children, and take an interest in talented men as if they were my brothers.... At military exercises I am always in the front, and in time of battle am never behind. In the space of seven years I have succeeded in accomplishing a great work, and uniting the whole world into one empire. I have not myself distinguished qualities. But the government of the [Chinese] is inconstant, and

therefore Heaven assists me to obtain the throne.... All together have acknowledged my supremacy. It seems to me that since the remote time...such an empire has not been seen.... Since the time I came to the throne I have always taken to heart the ruling of my people; but I could not find worthy men to occupy [high offices]....With respect to these circumstances I inquired, and heard that thou, master, hast penetrated the truth....For a long time thou has lived in the caverns of the rocks, and hast retired from the world; but to thee the people who have acquired sanctity repair, like clouds on the paths of the immortals, in innumerable multitudes....But what shall I do? We are separated by mountains and plains of great extent, and I cannot meet thee. I can only descend from the throne and stand by the side. I have fasted and washed. I have ordered my adjutant...to prepare an escort and a cart for thee.

Source: E. Bretschneider, *Mediaeval Researches from Eastern Asiatic Sources* (London, 1875), 37–39.

Do not be afraid of the thousand *li.*° I implore thee to move thy sainted steps. Do not think of the extent of the sandy desert. Commiserate the people

—————————

°*li:* a great distance.

in the present situation of affairs, or have pity upon me, and communicate to me the means of preserving life. I shall serve thee myself. I hope that at least thou wilt leave me a trifle of thy wisdom. Say only one word to me and I shall be happy.

Document 12.3

A Russian View of the Mongols

The initial impression of the Mongol impact in many places was one of utter devastation, destruction, and brutality. Document 12.3 offers a Russian commentary from that perspective drawn from the *Chronicle of Novgorod*, one of the major sources for the history of early Russia.

- How did the Russian writer of the *Chronicle* account for what he saw as the disaster of the Mongol invasion?

- Can you infer from the document any additional reasons for the Mongol success?

- Beyond the conquest itself, what other aspects of Mongol rule offended the Russians?

- To what extent was the Mongol conquest of Russia also a clash of cultures?

The Chronicle of Novgorod
1238

That same year [1238] foreigners called Tartars° came in countless numbers, like locusts, into the land of Ryazan, and on first coming they halted at the river Nukhla, and took it, and halted in camp there. And thence they sent their emissaries to the *Knyazes*° of Ryazan, a sorceress and two men with her, demanding from them one-tenth of everything: of men and *Knyazes* and horses—of everything

—————————

°**Tartars:** Mongols.

°*Knyazes:* Princes.

Source: Robert Mitchell and Nevill Forbes, trans., *The Chronicle of Novgorod, 1016–1471* (New York: AMS Press, 1970; repr. from the edition of 1914, London), 81–83, 88.

one-tenth. And the *Knyazes* of Ryazan, Gyurgi, Ingvor's brother, Oleg, Roman Ingvorevich, and those of Murom and Pronsk, without letting them into their towns, went out to meet them to Voronazh. And the *Knyazes* said to them: "Only when none of us remain then all will be yours."... And the *Knyazes* of Ryazan sent to Yuri of Volodimir asking for help, or himself to come. But Yuri neither went himself nor listened to the request of the *Knyazes* of Ryazan, but he himself wished to make war separately. But it was too late to oppose the wrath of God.... Thus also did God before these men take from us our strength and put into us perplexity and thunder and dread and trembling for our sins. And then the pagan foreigners surrounded Ryazan and fenced it in with a stockade.... And the Tartars took the town on

December 21, and they had advanced against it on the 16th of the same month. They likewise killed the *Knyaz* and *Knyaginya*, and men, women, and children, monks, nuns and priests, some by fire, some by the sword, and violated nuns, priests' wives, good women and girls in the presence of their mothers and sisters. But God saved the Bishop, for he had departed the same moment when the troops invested the town. And who, brethren, would not lament over this, among those of us left alive when they suffered this bitter and violent death? And we, indeed, having seen it, were terrified and wept with sighing day and night over our sins, while we sigh every day and night, taking thought for our possessions and for the hatred of brothers.

...The pagan and godless Tartars, then, having taken Ryazan, went to Volodimir.... And when the lawless ones had already come near and set up battering rams, and took the town and fired it on Friday before Sexagesima Sunday, the *Knyaz* and *Knyaginya* and *Vladyka*, seeing that the town was on fire and that the people were already perishing, some by fire and others by the sword, took refuge in the Church of the Holy Mother of God and shut themselves in the Sacristy. The pagans breaking down the doors, piled up wood and set fire to the sacred church; and slew all, thus they perished, giving up their souls to God.... And Rostov and Suzhdal went each its own way. And the accursed ones having come thence took Moscow, Pereyaslavi, Yurev, Dmitrov, *Volok*, and Tver; there also they killed the son of Yaroslav. And thence the lawless ones came and invested Torzhok on the festival of the first Sunday in Lent. They fenced it all round with a fence as they had taken other towns, and here the accursed ones fought with battering rams for two weeks. And the people in the town were exhausted and from Novgorod there was no help for them; but already every man began to be in perplexity and terror. And so the pagans took the town, and slew all from the male sex even to the female, all the priests and the monks, and all stripped and reviled gave up their souls to the Lord in a bitter and a wretched death, on March 5...Wednesday in Easter week.

Document 12.4

Chinese Perceptions of the Mongols

Chinese responses to Mongol rule varied considerably. To some, of course, the Mongols were simply foreign conquerors and therefore illegitimate as Chinese rulers. Marco Polo, who was in China at the time, reported that some Mongol officials or their Muslim intermediaries treated Chinese "just like slaves," demanding bribes for services, ordering arbitrary executions, and seizing women at will—all of which generated outrage and hostility. Document 12.4 illustrates another side to Chinese perception of the Mongols. It comes from a short biography of a Mongol official named Menggu, which was written by a well-educated Chinese scholar on the occasion of Menggu's death. Intended to be inscribed on stone and buried with the Mongol officer, it emphasizes the ways in which Menggu conformed to Chinese ways of governing. Such obituaries were an established form of Chinese historical writing, usually commissioned by the children of the deceased.

■ Why might Menggu's children have requested such a document and asked a Chinese scholar to compose it? What does this suggest about Mongol attitudes to Chinese culture?

- What features of Menggu's governship did this Chinese author appreciate? In what ways did Menggu's actions and behavior reflect Confucian values? What might the writer have omitted from his account?

- What might inspire a highly educated Chinese scholar to compose such a flattering public tribute to a Mongol official?

- Why might historians be a bit skeptical about this document? Which statements might be most suspect?

Epitaph for the Honorable Menggu
1274

Emperor Taizu [Chinggis Khan] received the mandate of Heaven and subjugated all regions. When Emperor Taizong [Ogodei Khan] succeeded, he revitalized the bureaucratic system and made it more efficient and organized. At court, one minister supervised all the officials and helped the emperor rule. In the provinces, commanderies and counties received instructions from above and saw that they got carried out. Prefects and magistrates were as a rule appointed only after submitting [to the Mongols]. Still one Mongol, called the governor, was selected to supervise them. The prefects and magistrates all had to obey his orders....

In the fourth month of 1236, the court deemed Menggu capable of handling Zhangde, so promoted him... to be its governor.... Because regulations were lax, the soldiers took advantage of their victory to plunder. Even in cities and marketplaces, some people kept their doors closed in the daytime. As soon as Menggu arrived, he took charge. Knowing the people's grievances, he issued an order, "Those who oppress the people will be dealt with according to the law. Craftsmen, merchants, and shopkeepers, you must each go about your work with your doors open, peaceably attending to your business without fear. Farmers, you must be content with your lands and exert yourselves diligently according to the seasons. I will instruct or punish those who mistreat

you." After this order was issued, the violent became obedient and no one any longer dared violate the laws. Farmers in the fields and travelers on the roads felt safe, and people began to enjoy life.

In the second month of 1238, Wang Rong, prefect of Huaizhou, rebelled. The grand preceptor and prince ordered Menggu to put down this rebellion, telling him to slaughter everyone. Menggu responded, "When the royal army suppresses rebels, those who were coerced into joining them ought to be pardoned, not to mention those who are entirely innocent." The prince approved his advice and followed it. When Wang Rong surrendered, he was executed but the region was spared. The residents, with jugs of wine and burning incense, saw Menggu off tearfully, unable to bear his leaving. Forty years later when he was put in charge of Henei, the common people were delighted with the news, saying, "We will all survive—our parents and relatives through marriage all served him before."

In 1239 locusts destroyed all the vegetation in Xiang and Wei, so the people were short of food. Menggu reported this to the great minister Quduqu, who issued five thousand piculs of army rations to save the starving. As a consequence no one had to flee or starve....

At that time [1247] the harvest failed for several years in a row, yet taxes and labor services were still exacted. Consequently, three or four of every ten houses was vacant. Menggu ordered the officials to travel around announcing that those who returned to their property would be exempt from

Source: Patricia Buckley Ebrey, ed. and trans., *Chinese Civilization: A Sourcebook* (New York: Free Press, 1991), 192–94.

taxes and services for three years. That year seventeen thousand households returned in response to his summons....

When there was a drought in 1263, Menggu prayed for rain and it rained. That year he was given the title Brilliant and August General and made governor of Zhongshan prefecture. In 1270 he was transferred and became governor of Hezhong prefecture. In the spring of 1274 he was allowed to wear the golden tiger tablet in recognition of his long and excellent service, his incorruptibility, and the repute in which he was held where he had served....

The house where Menggu lived when he governed Zhangde nearly forty years ago, and the fields from which he obtained food then, were just adequate to keep out the wind and rain and supply enough to eat. When he died there were no estates or leftover wealth to leave his sons or grandsons. Therefore they had to model themselves on him and concentrate on governing in a way that would bring peace and safety, show love for the people, and benefit all. They have no need to be ashamed even if compared to the model officials of the Han and Tang dynasties.

Document 12.5

Mongol Women through European Eyes

Document 12.5 provides some insight into the roles of Mongol women and men through the eyes of a European observer, William of Rubruck (1220–1293). A Flemish Franciscan friar, William was one of several emissaries sent to the Mongol court by the pope and the king of France. They hoped that these diplomatic missions might lead to the conversion of the Mongols to Christianity, perhaps an alliance with the Mongols against Islam, or at least some useful intelligence about Mongol intentions. While no agreements with the Mongols came from these missions, William of Rubruck left a detailed account of Mongol life in the mid-thirteenth century, which included observations about the domestic roles of men and women.

■ How does William of Rubruck portray the lives of Mongol women? What was the class background of the Mongol women he describes?

■ What do you think he would have found most upsetting about the position of women in Mongol society?

■ Based on this account, how might you compare the life of Mongol women to that of women in more established civilizations, such as China, Europe, or the Islamic world?

WILLIAM OF RUBRUCK
Journey to the Land of the Mongols
ca. 1255

The matrons° make for themselves most beautiful (luggage) carts.... A single rich Mo'al or Tartar° has quite one hundred or two hundred such carts with coffers. Baatu° has twenty-six wives, each of whom has a large dwelling, exclusive of the other little ones which they set up after the big one, and which are like closets, in which the sewing girls live, and to each of these (large) dwellings are attached quite two hundred carts. And when they set up their houses, the first wife places her dwelling on the extreme west side, and after her the others according to their rank, so that the last wife will be in the extreme east; and there will be the distance of a stone's throw between the yurt of one wife and that of another. The ordu° of a rich Mo'al seems like a large town, though there will be very few men in it.

When they have fixed their dwelling, the door turned to the south, they set up the couch of the master on the north side. The side for the women is always the east side... on the left of the house of the master, he sitting on his couch his face turned to the south. The side for the men is the west side... on the right. Men coming into the house would never hang up their bows on the side of the woman.

It is the duty of the women to drive the carts, get the dwellings on and off them, milk the cows, make butter and gruit,° and to dress and sew skins, which they do with a thread made of tendons. They divide the tendons into fine shreds, and then twist them into one long thread. They also sew the boots, the socks, and the clothing. They never wash clothes, for they say that God would be angered, and that it would thunder if they hung them up to dry. They will even beat those they find washing [their clothes]. Thunder they fear extraordinarily; and when it thunders they will turn out of their dwellings all strangers, wrap themselves in black felt, and thus hide themselves till it has passed away. Furthermore, they never wash their bowls, but when the meat is cooked they rinse out the dish in which they are about to put it with some of the boiling broth from the kettle, which they pour back into it. They [the women] also make the felt and cover the houses.

The men make bows and arrows, manufacture stirrups and bits, make saddles, do the carpentering on their dwellings and the carts; they take care of the horses, milk the mares, churn the cosmos or mare's milk, make the skins in which it is put; they also look after the camels and load them. Both sexes look after the sheep and goats, sometimes the men, other times the women, milking them.

They dress skins with a thick mixture of sour ewe's milk and salt. When they want to wash their hands or head, they fill their mouths with water, which they let trickle onto their hands, and in this way they also wet their hair and wash their heads.

As to their marriages, you must know that no one among them has a wife unless he buys her; so it sometimes happens that girls are well past marriageable age before they marry, for their parents always keep them until they sell them.... Among them no widow marries, for the following reason: they believe that all who serve them in this life shall serve them in the next, so as regards a widow they believe that she will always return to her first husband after death. Hence this shameful custom prevails among them, that sometimes a son takes to wife all his father's wives, except his own mother; for the ordu of the father and mother always belongs to the youngest son, so it is he who must provide for all his

---

°**matrons:** married women.

°**Mo'al or Tartar:** Mongol.

°**Baatu:** grandson of Chinggis Khan.

°**ordu:** residence.

°**gruit:** sour curd.

Source: *The Journey of William of Rubruck*..., translated from the Latin and edited, with an introductory notice, by William Woodville Rockhill (London: Hakluyt Society, 1900), chaps 2, 7.

father's wives... and if he wishes it, he uses them as wives, for he esteems not himself injured if they return to his father after death. When then anyone has made a bargain with another to take his daughter, the father of the girl gives a feast, and the girl flees to her relatives and hides there. Then the father says: "Here, my daughter is yours: take her wheresoever you find her." Then he searches for her with his friends till he finds her, and he must take her by force and carry her off with a semblance of violence to his house.

Using the Evidence:
Perspectives on the Mongols

1. **Assessing sources:** What are the strengths and limitations of these documents for understanding the Mongols? Taking the position of their authors into account, what exaggerations, biases, or misunderstandings can you identify in these sources? What information seems credible and what should be viewed more skeptically?

2. **Characterizing the Mongols:** Based on these documents and on the text of Chapter 12, write an essay assessing the Mongol moment in world history. How might you counteract the view of many that the Mongols were simply destructive barbarians? How do your own values affect your understanding of the Mongol moment?

3. **Considering self-perception and practice:** How would you describe the core values of Mongol culture? (Consider their leaders' goals, attitudes toward conquered peoples, duties of rulers, views of political authority, role of women.) To what extent were these values put into practice in acquiring and ruling their huge empire? And in what ways were those values undermined or eroded as that empire took shape?

Visual Sources

Considering the Evidence:
The Black Death and Religion
in Western Europe

Among the most far-reaching outcomes of the Mongol moment in world history was the spread all across Eurasia and North Africa of that deadly disease known as the plague or the Black Death. While the Mongols certainly did not cause the plague, their empire facilitated the movement not only of goods and people but also of the microorganisms responsible for this pestilence (see Map 12.2, p. 543 and pp. 545–47). The impact of the Black Death was catastrophic almost everywhere it struck, but it is from Western Europe that our most detailed accounts and illustrations have survived about how people responded to that calamity.

Religion permeated the cultural world of Western Europe in the fourteenth century. The rituals of the Roman Catholic Church attended the great passages of life such as birth, marriage, and death, while the major themes of Christian teaching—sin and repentance, salvation and heaven, the comfort available through Jesus, Mary, and the saints—shaped most people's outlook on life and the world. It is hardly surprising, then, that many people would turn to religion in their efforts to understand and cope with a catastrophe of such immense proportions.

Seeking the aid of parish priests, invoking the intercession of the Virgin Mary, participating in religious processions and pilgrimages, attending mass regularly, increasing attention to private devotion—these were among the ways that beleaguered people sought to tap the resources of faith to alleviate the devastating impact of the plague. From Church leaders, the faithful heard a message of the plague as God's punishment for sins. An Italian layman reflected this understanding when he wrote *A History of the Plague* in 1348. There he pictured God witnessing the world "sinking and sliding into all kinds of wickedness." In response, "the quivering spear of the Almighty, in the form of the plague, was sent down to infect the whole human race."[42]

Accompanying such ideas were religiously based attacks on prostitutes, homosexuals, and Jews, people whose allegedly immoral behavior or alien beliefs had invited God's retribution. In Florence alone, some 17,000 men were accused of sodomy during the fifteenth century. Jews, who were sometimes held responsible for deliberately spreading the disease, were subject to terrible persecution, including the destruction of synagogues, massacres, burnings, expulsion, and seizure of property. Although several popes and kings defended them, many Jews fled to Poland, where authorities welcomed their urban and commercial skills, leading to a flourishing Jewish culture there in the several centuries that followed.

The most well-known movement reflecting an understanding of the plague as God's judgment on a sinful world was that of the flagellants, whose name derived from the Latin word *flagella*, "whips." The practice of flagellation, whipping oneself or allowing oneself to be whipped, had a long tradition within the Christian world and elsewhere as well. Flagellation served as a penance for sin and as a means of identifying with Christ, who was himself whipped prior to his crucifixion. It reemerged as a fairly widespread practice, especially in Germany, between 1348 and 1350 in response to the initial outbreak of the plague. Its adherents believed that perhaps the terrible wrath of God could be averted by performing this extraordinary act of atonement or penance. Groups of flagellants moved from city to city, where they called for repentance, confessed their sins, sang hymns, and participated in ritual dances, which climaxed in whipping themselves with knotted cords sometimes embedded with iron points. Visual Source 12.1 is a contemporary representation of the flagellants in the town of Doornik in the Netherlands in 1349. The text at the bottom reads in part:

> In [1349] it came to pass that on the day of the Assumption of the Blessed Virgin (Aug. 15) some 200 persons came here from Bruges about noon.... [I]mmediately the whole town was filled with curiosity as to why these folk had come.... Meantime the folk from Bruges prepared to perform their ceremonies which they called "penance." The inhabitants of both sexes, who had never before seen any such thing, began to imitate the actions of the strangers, to torment themselves also by the penitential exercises and to thank God for this means of penance which seemed to them most effectual.

■ Flagellation was but one form of penance. What other forms of self-inflicted punishment for sin are suggested in the image?

■ What is the significance of the Christ on the cross that precedes the flagellants?

■ Does the procession seem spontaneous or organized? Do Church authorities appear to have instigated or approved this procession?

■ How might the flagellants have understood their own actions?

■ Church authorities generally opposed the flagellant movement. Why do you think they did so?

A caditt anno predito q̃ m die
a cũmptionis uirginis glori
ose venerunt a villa buugen
ũ arater. CC. hominũ: quali hora

ceperũt compati psonis ẽt
penitenne condolere et deo gra
tias redrere super tanta peni
renta quam grauillimam re

Visual Source 12.1 The Flagellants (Private Collection/The Bridgeman Art Library)

While many people certainly turned to religion for solace in the face of the unimaginable disaster of the Black Death, others found traditional Christian rituals and teachings of little use or difficult to reconcile with the overwhelming realities of the disease. For some the plague prompted an orgy of hedonism, perhaps to affirm life in the face of endless death or simply to live to the full in what time remained to them. A contemporary Italian observer noted, "As they wallowed in idleness, their dissolution led them into the sin of gluttony, into banquets, taverns, delicate foods, and gambling. The rushed headlong into lust."[43] In 1394 a representative of the pope threatened excommunication for those who practiced debauchery in the graveyards.

Among the deepest traumas inflicted by the plague was its interference with proper Christian rituals surrounding death and dying, practices that were believed to assist the dead to achieve eternal rest and the living to accept their loss and find hope for reunion in heaven. Priests were scarce and sometimes refused to administer last rites, fearing contact with the dying. The sheer numbers of dead were overwhelming. City authorities at times ordered quick burials in mass graves to avoid the spread of the disease. A French observer in 1348 wrote, "No relatives, no friends showed concern for what might be happening. No priest came to hear the confessions of the dying, or to administer the sacraments

Visual Source 12.2 Burying the Dead (Bibliothèque Royale de Belgique, Brussels, Belgium/The Bridgeman Art Library)

to them."[44] The fourteenth-century Italian poet Boccaccio echoed those sentiments: "[T]here were no tears or candles or mourners to honor the dead; in fact no more respect was accorded to dead people than would nowadays be shown toward dead goats."[45] Visual Source 12.2, published in 1352, illustrates a burial of plague victims of 1349 in the city of Tournai in what is now Belgium.

- How does this visual source support or contradict the written accounts excerpted above?

- How would you characterize the burial scene in this visual source?

- How does it differ from what an image of a proper Christian burial might contain? How might survivors of the plague have regarded such a burial?

The initial and subsequent outbreaks of the plague in Western Europe generated an understandable preoccupation with death, which was reflected in the art of the time. A stained-glass window in a church in Norwich, England, from about 1500 personified Death as a chess player contesting with a high Church official. A type of tomb called a cadaver tomb included a sculpture of the deceased as a rotting cadaver, sometimes with flesh-eating worms emerging from the body. An inscription on one such tomb in the Canterbury Cathedral in England explained the purpose of the image:

> Whoever you be who will pass by, I ask you to remember,
> You will be like me after you die,
> For all [to see]: horrible, dust, worms, vile flesh.[46]

Visual Source 12.3 A Culture of Death (St. Nicolair's Church, Tallinn, now the Niguliste Museum. Photo: Visual Connection Archive)

This intense awareness of the inevitability of death and its apparent indiscriminate occurrence was also expressed in the Dance of Death, which began in France in 1348 as a ritual intended to prevent the plague or to cure the afflicted. During the performance people would periodically fall to the ground, allowing others to trample on them. By 1400 such performances took place in a number of parish churches and subsequently in more secular settings. The Dance of Death also received artistic expression in a variety of poems, paintings, and sketches. The earliest of the paintings dates from 1425 and depicts dozens of people—from an emperor, king, pope, and bishop to a merchant, peasant, and an infant—each dancing with skeletal figures enticing them toward death. Visual Source 12.3 reproduces a portion of one of these Dance of Death paintings, originally created by the German artist Berndt Notke in 1463 and subsequently restored and reproduced many times.

In the inscriptions at the bottom of the painting, each living character addresses a skeletal figure, who in turn makes a reply. Here is the exchange between the empress (shown in a red dress at the far right of the image) and Death. First, the empress speaks:

> I know, Death means me!
> I was never terrified so greatly!
> I thought he was not in his right mind,
> after all, I am young and also an empress.
> I thought I had a lot of power,
> I had not thought of him
> or that anybody could do something against me.
> Oh, let me live on, this I implore you!

And then Death replies:

> Empress, highly presumptuous,
> I think, you have forgotten me.
> Fall in! It is now time.
> You thought I should let you off?
> No way! And were you ever so much,
> You must participate in this play,
> And you others, everybody—
> Hold on! Follow me, Mr Cardinal![47]

■ How is the status of each of the various living figures—from left to right: the pope, the emperor, the empress—depicted?

■ What does the white sheet around each of the death images represent? What do their expressions suggest about their attitude toward the living?

■ Notice that the living figures face outward toward the viewer rather than toward the entreating death figures on either side of them. What might this mean?

■ Does the portrayal of death pictured here reflect Christian views of death or does it challenge them?

■ How is the exchange between the empress and Death reflected in the painting?

The horrific experience of the Black Death also caused some people to question fundamental Christian teachings about the mercy and benevolence of God or even of his power to affect the outcome of the plague. A late-fourteenth-century clergyman in England expressed the dismay that many must have felt:

> For God is deaf nowadays and will not hear us
> And for our guilt, he grinds good men to dust.[48]

In a similar vein, the fourteenth-century Italian Renaissance scholar Francesco Petrarch questioned why God's vengeance had fallen so hard on the people of his own time: "While all have sinned alike, we alone bear the lash." He asked whether it was possible "that God does not care for mortal men." In the end, Petrarch dismissed that idea but still found God's judgments "inscrutable and inaccessible to human senses."[49] Thus the Black Death eroded more optimistic thirteenth-century Christian views, based on the ideas of the ancient Greek philosopher Aristotle, that human rationality could penetrate the mind of God.

Efforts to interpret Visual Source 12.4, a fifteenth-century English painting, raise similar issues to those expressed by Petrarch.

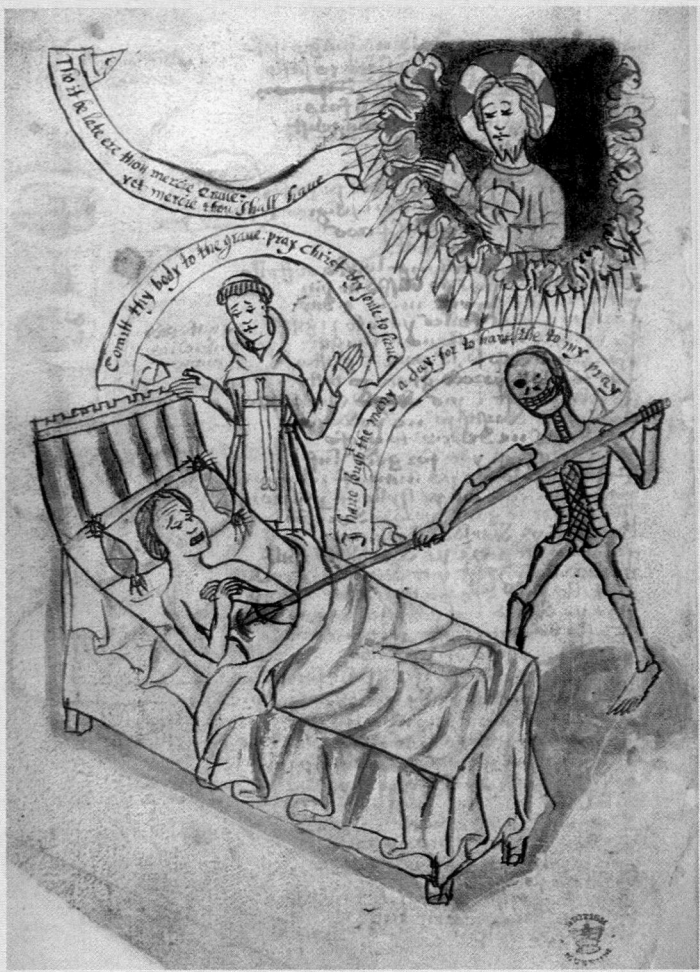

Visual Source 12.4 In the Face of Catastrophe—Questioning or Affirming the Faith (HIP/Art Resource, New York)

- Why is the death figure smiling?

- How does this skeletal figure differ from the ones in Visual Source 12.3?

- How are the priest and the Christ figure depicted? What possible interpretations of their gestures can you imagine?

- Notice that the death figure spears the dying person in the side, an action that evokes the biblical account of Jesus being speared in his side during his crucifixion. What might the artist have sought to convey by such a reference?

- The captions, from top to bottom, read: Christ figure: "Tho it be late ere thou mercie came: yet mercie thou shalt have." Priest figure: "Commit thy body to the grave: pray Christ thy soul to save." Death figure: "I have sought thee many a day: for to have thee to my pray." How do these captions influence your understanding of the painting?

- Would you characterize the overall message of this painting as one of hopefulness, despair, or something else? What elements in the painting might support each of these conclusions?

Using the Evidence:
The Black Death and Religion
in Western Europe

1. **Assessing motives:** Do you think the artists who created these visual sources sought to reinforce traditional Christian teachings or to challenge them?

2. **Using art as evidence:** What do these visual sources tell you about the impact of and responses to the plague in fourteenth- and fifteenth-century Western Europe?

3. **Connecting past and present:** Considering the various ways that people sought to avert, cope with, or explain the plague in these visual sources, what parallels to the human responses to crises or catastrophes in more recent centuries or in our own time can you identify?

CHAPTER THIRTEEN

The Worlds of the Fifteenth Century

The Shapes of Human Communities
  Paleolithic Persistence
  Agricultural Village Societies
  Herding Peoples
Civilizations of the Fifteenth Century:
  Comparing China and Europe
  Ming Dynasty China
  European Comparisons: State
    Building and Cultural Renewal
  European Comparisons:
    Maritime Voyaging
Civilizations of the Fifteenth
  Century: The Islamic World
  In the Islamic Heartland: The
    Ottoman and Safavid Empires
  On the Frontiers of Islam: The
    Songhay and Mughal Empires
Civilizations of the Fifteenth
  Century: The Americas
  The Aztec Empire
  The Inca Empire
Webs of Connection
A Preview of Coming Attractions:
  Looking Ahead to the Modern Era,
  1500–2010
Reflections: What If? Chance and
  Contingency in World History
Considering the Evidence
  Documents: The Aztecs and the
    Incas through Spanish Eyes
  Visual Sources: Sacred Places in the
    World of the Fifteenth Century

During 2005, Chinese authorities marked the 600th anniversary of the initial launching of their country's massive maritime expeditions in 1405. Some eighty-seven years before Columbus sailed across the Atlantic with three small ships and a crew of about ninety men, the Chinese admiral Zheng He had captained a fleet of more than 300 ships and a crew numbering some 27,000 people, which brought a Chinese naval presence into the South China Sea and the Indian Ocean as far as the East African coast. Now in 2005, China was celebrating. Public ceremonies, books, magazine articles, two television documentaries, an international symposium, a stamp in honor of Zheng He—all of this and more was part of a yearlong remembrance of these remarkable voyages.

Given China's recent engagement with the larger world, Chinese authorities sought to use Zheng He as a symbol of their country's expanding, but peaceful, role on the international stage. Until recently, however, his achievement was barely noticed in China's collective memory, and for six centuries Zheng He had been largely forgotten or ignored. Columbus, on the other hand, had long been highly visible in the West, celebrated as a cultural hero and more recently harshly criticized as an imperialist, but certainly remembered. The voyages of both of these fifteenth-century mariners were pregnant with meaning for world history. Why were they remembered so differently in the countries of their origin?

THE FIFTEENTH CENTURY, DURING WHICH BOTH ZHENG HE and Columbus undertook their momentous expeditions, proved in

The Meeting of Two Worlds: This famous sixteenth-century engraving by the Flemish artist Theodore de Bry shows Columbus landing in Hispaniola (Haiti), where the Taino people bring him presents, while the Europeans claim the island for God and queen. In light of its long-range consequences, this voyage was arguably the most important single event of the fifteenth century. (Bildarchiv Preussischer Kulturbesitz/Art Resource, NY)

$Snapshot$ **Major Developments around the World in the Fifteenth Century**

Region	Major Developments
Central, East, and Southeast Asia	Ming dynasty China, 1368–1644 Conquests of Timur, 1370–1406 Zheng He's maritime voyages, 1405–1433 Spread of Islam into Southeast Asia Rise of Malacca Civil war among competing warlords in Japan
South Asia/India	Timur's invasion of India, 1398 Various Muslim sultanates in northern India Rise of Hindu state of Vijayanagar in southern India Founding of Mughal Empire, 1526
Middle East	Expansion of Ottoman Empire Ottoman seizure of Constantinople, 1453 Founding of Safavid Empire in Persia, 1501 Ottoman siege of Vienna, 1529
Christendom/Europe	European Renaissance Portuguese voyages of exploration along West African coast Completion of reconquest of Spain, ending Muslim control End of the Byzantine Empire, 1453 End of Mongol rule in Russia; reign of Ivan the Great, 1462–1505
Africa	Songhay Empire in West Africa, 1464–1591 Kingdom of the Kongo in West Central Africa Expansion of Ethiopian state in East Africa Kingdom of Zimbabwe/Mwene Mutapa in southern Africa
The Americas/Western Hemisphere	Aztec Empire in Mesoamerica, 1345–1521 Inca Empire along the Andes, 1438–1533 Iroquois confederacy (New York State) "Complex" Paleolithic societies along west coast of North America
Pacific Oceania	Paleolithic persistence in Australia Chiefdoms and stratified societies on Pacific islands Yap as center of oceanic trading network with Guam and Palau

retrospect to mark a major turning point in the human story. At the time, of course, no one was aware of it. No one knew in 1405 that the huge armada under Zheng He's command would be recalled in 1433, never to sail again. And no one knew in 1492 that Columbus's minuscule fleet of three ships would utterly transform the world, bringing the people of two "old worlds" and two hemispheres permanently together, with enduring consequences for them all. The outcome of the processes set in motion by those three small ships included the Atlantic slave trade, the decimation of the native population of the Americas, the massive growth of world population, the Industrial Revolution, and the growing prominence of Europeans on the world stage. But none of these developments were even remotely foreseeable in 1492.

Thus the fifteenth century, as a hinge of major historical change, provides an occasion for a bird's-eye view of the world through a kind of global tour. This excursion around the world will serve to briefly review the human saga thus far and to establish a baseline from which the transformations of the modern era might be measured. How then might we describe the world, and the worlds, of the fifteenth century?

The Shapes of Human Communities

One way to describe the world of the fifteenth century is to identify the various types of societies that it contained. Bands of hunters and gatherers, villages of agricultural peoples, newly emerging chiefdoms or small states, nomadic/pastoral communities, established civilizations and empires—all of these social or political forms would have been apparent to a widely traveled visitor in the fifteenth century. They represented alternative ways of organizing human communities and responded to differences in the environment, in the historical development of various regions, and in the choices made by particular peoples. All of them were long established by the fifteenth century, but the balance among these distinctive kinds of societies at the end of the post-classical millennium (1500) was quite different than it had been at the beginning (500).

Paleolithic Persistence

Despite millennia of agricultural advance, substantial areas of the world still hosted gathering and hunting societies, known to scholars as Paleolithic (old stone-age) peoples. All of Australia, much of Siberia, the arctic coastlands, and parts of Africa and the Americas fell into this category. These peoples were not simply relics of a bygone age, however. They too had changed over time, though more slowly than their agricultural counterparts, and they too interacted with their neighbors. In short, they had a history, although most history books largely ignore them after the age of agriculture arrived. Nonetheless, this most ancient way of life still had a sizable and variable presence in the world of the fifteenth century.

Consider, for example, Australia. That continent's many separate groups, some 250 of them, still practiced a gathering and hunting way of life in the fifteenth century, a pattern that continued well after Europeans arrived in the late eighteenth century.

■ **Comparison**

In what ways did the gathering and hunting people of Australia differ from those of the northwest coast of North America?

Over many thousands of years, these people had assimilated various material items or cultural practices from outsiders—outrigger canoes, fish hooks, complex netting techniques, artistic styles, rituals, and mythological ideas—but despite the presence of farmers in nearby New Guinea, no agricultural practices penetrated the Australian mainland. Was it because large areas of Australia were unsuited for the kind of agriculture practiced in New Guinea? Or did the peoples of Australia, enjoying an environment of sufficient resources, simply see no need to change their way of life?

Despite the absence of agriculture, Australia's peoples had mastered and manipulated their environment, in part through the practice of "firestick farming," a pattern of deliberately set fires, which they described as "cleaning up the country." These controlled burns served to clear the underbrush, thus making hunting easier and encouraging the growth of certain plant and animal species. In addition, native Australians exchanged goods among themselves over distances of hundreds of miles, created elaborate mythologies and ritual practices, and developed sophisticated traditions of sculpture and rock painting. They accomplished all of this on the basis of an economy and technology rooted in the distant Paleolithic past.

A very different kind of gathering and hunting society flourished in the fifteenth century along the northwest coast of North America among the Chinookan, Tulalip, Skagit, and other peoples. With some 300 edible animal species and an abundance of salmon and other fish, this extraordinarily bounteous environment provided the foundation for what scholars sometimes call "complex" or "affluent" gathering and hunting cultures. What distinguished the northwest coast peoples from those of Australia were permanent village settlements with large and sturdy houses, considerable economic specialization, ranked societies that sometimes included slavery, chiefdoms dominated by powerful clan leaders or "big men," and extensive storage of food.

Although these and other gathering and hunting peoples persisted still in the fifteenth century, both their numbers and the area they inhabited had contracted greatly as the Agricultural Revolution unfolded across the planet. That relentless advance of the farming frontier continued in the centuries ahead as the Russian, Chinese, and European empires encompassed the lands of the remaining Paleolithic peoples. By the early twenty-first century, what was once the only human way of life had been reduced to minuscule pockets of people whose cultures seemed doomed to a final extinction.

Agricultural Village Societies

■ Change
What kinds of changes were transforming West African agricultural village societies and those of the Iroquois as the fifteenth century dawned?

Far more numerous than hunters and gatherers were those many peoples who, though fully agricultural, had avoided incorporation into larger empires or civilizations and had not developed their own city- or state-based societies. Living usually in small village-based communities and organized in terms of kinship relations, such people predominated during the fifteenth century in much of North America and in parts of the Amazon River basin, Southeast Asia, and Africa south of the equator. They had created societies largely without the oppressive political authority, class inequalities, and seclusion of women that were so common in civilizations. Historians have largely relegated such societies to the periphery of world history, marginal to their overwhelming focus on large-scale civilizations. Viewed from within their own circles, though, these societies were of course at the center of things, each with its own history of migration, cultural transformation, social conflict, incorporation of new people, political rise and fall, and interaction with strangers. In short, they too changed as their histories unfolded.

In the forested region of what is now southern Nigeria in West Africa, for example, three quite different patterns of change emerged in the centuries between 1000 and 1500 (see Map 13.3, p. 582). Each of them began from a base of farming village societies whose productivity was generating larger populations.

Among the Yoruba-speaking people, a series of rival city-states emerged, each within a walled town and ruled by an *oba*, or "king" (some of whom were women), who performed both religious and political functions. As in ancient Mesopotamia or classical Greece, no single state or empire encompassed all of Yorubaland. Nearby lay the kingdom of Benin, a small, highly centralized territorial state that emerged by the fifteenth century and was ruled by a warrior king named Ewuare, said to have conquered 201 towns and villages in the process of founding the new state. His administrative chiefs replaced the heads of kinship groups as major political authorities, while the ruler sponsored extensive trading missions and patronized artists who created the remarkable brass sculptures for which Benin is so famous.

East of the Niger River lay the lands of the Igbo peoples, where dense population and extensive trading networks might well have given rise to states, but the deliberate Igbo preference was to reject the kingship and state-building efforts of their neighbors, boasting on occasion that "the Igbo have no kings." Instead they relied on other institutions—title societies in which wealthy men received a series of prestigious ranks, women's associations, hereditary ritual experts serving as mediators, a balance of power among kinship groups—to maintain social cohesion beyond the level of the village. It was a "stateless society," famously described in Chinua Achebe's *Things Fall Apart*, the most widely read novel to emerge from twentieth-century Africa.

The Yoruba, Bini, and Igbo peoples did not live in isolated, self-contained societies, however. They traded actively among themselves and with more distant peoples, such as the large African kingdom of Songhay far to the north. Cotton cloth, fish, copper and iron goods, decorative objects, and more drew neighboring peoples into networks of exchange. Common artistic traditions reflected a measure of cultural unity in a politically fragmented region, and all of these peoples seem to have changed from a matrilineal to a patrilineal system of tracing their descent. Little of this registered in the larger civilizations of the Afro-Eurasian world, but to the peoples of the West African forest during the fifteenth century, these processes were central to their history and their daily lives. Soon, however, all of them would be caught up in the transatlantic slave trade and would be changed substantially in the process.

Benin Bronzes
With the patronage of the royal court, Benin's artists produced an array of wood, ivory, and most famously exquisite brass or bronze sculptures, most of which celebrated the royal family and decorated their palaces. Here is a sixteenth-century representation of the Queen Mother of Benin. (National Museum, Lagos, Nigeria/The Bridgeman Art Library)

Across the Atlantic in what is now central New York State, other agricultural village societies were also in the process of substantial change during the several centuries preceding their incorporation into European trading networks and empires. The Iroquois-speaking peoples of that region had only recently become fully agricultural, adopting maize- and bean-farming techniques that had originated long ago in Mesoamerica. As this productive agriculture took hold by 1300 or so, the population grew, the size of settlements increased, and distinct peoples emerged, such as the Onondaga, Seneca, Cayuga, Oneida, and Mohawk. Frequent warfare also erupted among them. Some scholars have speculated that as agriculture, largely seen as women's work, became the primary economic activity, "warfare replaced successful food getting as the avenue to male prestige."[1]

Whatever caused it, this increased level of conflict among Iroquois peoples triggered a remarkable political innovation—a loose alliance or confederation among five Iroquois peoples based on an agreement known as the Great Law of Peace (see Map 13.5, p. 589). It was an agreement to settle their differences peacefully through a confederation council of clan leaders, some fifty of them altogether, who had the authority to adjudicate disputes and set reparation payments. Operating by consensus, the Iroquois League of Five Nations effectively suppressed the blood feuds and tribal conflicts that had only recently been so widespread. It also coordinated their peoples' relationship with outsiders, including the Europeans, who arrived in growing numbers in the centuries after 1500.

The Iroquois League also gave expression to values of limited government, social equality, and personal freedom, concepts that some European colonists found highly attractive. One British colonial administrator declared in 1749 that the Iroquois had "such absolute Notions of Liberty that they allow no Kind of Superiority of one over another, and banish all Servitude from their Territories."[2] Such equality extended to gender relationships, for among the Iroquois, descent was matrilineal (reckoned through the woman's line), married couples lived with the wife's family, and women controlled agriculture. While men were hunters, warriors, and the primary political officeholders, women selected and could depose those leaders.

Wherever they lived in 1500, over the next several centuries independent agricultural peoples such as the Iroquois, Yoruba, and Igbo were increasingly encompassed in expanding economic networks and conquest empires based in Western Europe, Russia, China, or India. In this respect, they repeated the experience of many other village-based farming communities that had much earlier found themselves forcibly included in the powerful embrace of Egyptian, Mesopotamian, Roman, Indian, Chinese, and other civilizations.

Herding Peoples

■ Significance
What role did Central Asian and West African pastoralists play in their respective regions?

Nomadic pastoral peoples impinged more directly and dramatically on civilizations than did hunting and gathering or agricultural village societies. The Mongol incursion, along with the enormous empire to which it gave rise, was one in a long series of challenges from the steppes, but it was not the last. As the Mongol Empire disintegrated, a brief attempt to restore it occurred in the late fourteenth and early fifteenth centuries under the leadership of a Turkic warrior named Timur, born in what is now Uzbekistan and known in the West as Tamerlane (see Map 13.1, p. 576).

With a ferocity that matched or exceeded that of his model, Chinggis Khan, Timur's army of nomads brought immense devastation yet again to Russia, Persia, and India. Timur himself died in 1405, while preparing for an invasion of China. Conflicts among his successors prevented any lasting empire, although his descendants retained control of the area between Persia and Afghanistan for the rest of the fifteenth century. That state hosted a sophisticated elite culture, combining Turkic and Persian elements, particularly at its splendid capital of Samarkand, as its rulers patronized artists, poets, traders, and craftsmen. Timur's conquest proved to be the last great military success of nomadic peoples from Central Asia. In the centuries that followed, their homelands were swallowed up in the expanding Russian and Chinese empires, as the balance of power between steppe nomads of inner Eurasia and the civilizations of outer Eurasia turned decisively in favor of the latter.

In Africa, pastoral peoples stayed independent of established empires several centuries longer than the nomads of Inner Asia, for not until the late nineteenth century were they incorporated into European colonial states. The experience of the Fulbe, West Africa's largest pastoral society, provides a useful example of an African herding people with a highly significant role in the fifteenth century and beyond. From their homeland in the western fringe of the Sahara along the upper Senegal River, the Fulbe migrated gradually eastward in the centuries after 1000 C.E. (see Map 13.3, p. 582). Unlike the pastoral peoples of Inner Asia, they generally lived in small communities among agricultural peoples and paid various grazing fees and taxes for the privilege of pasturing their cattle. Relations with their farming hosts often were tense because the Fulbe resented their subordination to agricultural peoples, whose way of life they despised. That sense of cultural superiority became even more pronounced as the Fulbe, in the course of their eastward movement, slowly adopted Islam. Some of them in fact dropped out of a pastoral life and settled in towns, where they became highly respected religious leaders. In the eighteenth and nineteenth centuries, the Fulbe were at the center of a wave of religiously based uprisings, or jihads, that greatly expanded the practice of Islam and gave rise to a series of new states, ruled by the Fulbe themselves.

Civilizations of the Fifteenth Century: Comparing China and Europe

Beyond the foraging, farming, and herding societies of the fifteenth-century world were its civilizations, those city-centered and state-based societies that were far larger and more densely populated, more powerful and innovative, and much more unequal in terms of class and gender than other forms of human community. Since the First Civilizations had emerged between 3500 and 1000 B.C.E., both the geographic space they encompassed and the number of people they embraced had grown substantially. By the fifteenth century, a considerable majority of the world's population lived within one or another of these civilizations, although most of these people no doubt identified more with local communities than with a larger civilization. What might an imaginary global traveler notice about the world's major civilizations in the fifteenth century?

Ming Dynasty China

■ **Description**
How would you define the major achievements of Ming dynasty China?

Such a traveler might well begin his or her journey in China, heir to a long tradition of effective governance, Confucian and Daoist philosophy, a major Buddhist presence, sophisticated artistic achievements, and a highly productive economy. That civilization, however, had been greatly disrupted by a century of Mongol rule, and its population had been sharply reduced by the plague. During the Ming dynasty (1368–1644), however, China recovered (see Map 13.1). The early decades of that dynasty witnessed an effort to eliminate all signs of foreign rule, discouraging the use

Map 13.1   Asia in the Fifteenth Century
The fifteenth century in Asia witnessed the massive Ming dynasty voyages into the Indian Ocean, the last major eruption of nomadic power in Timur's empire, and the flourishing of the maritime city of Malacca.

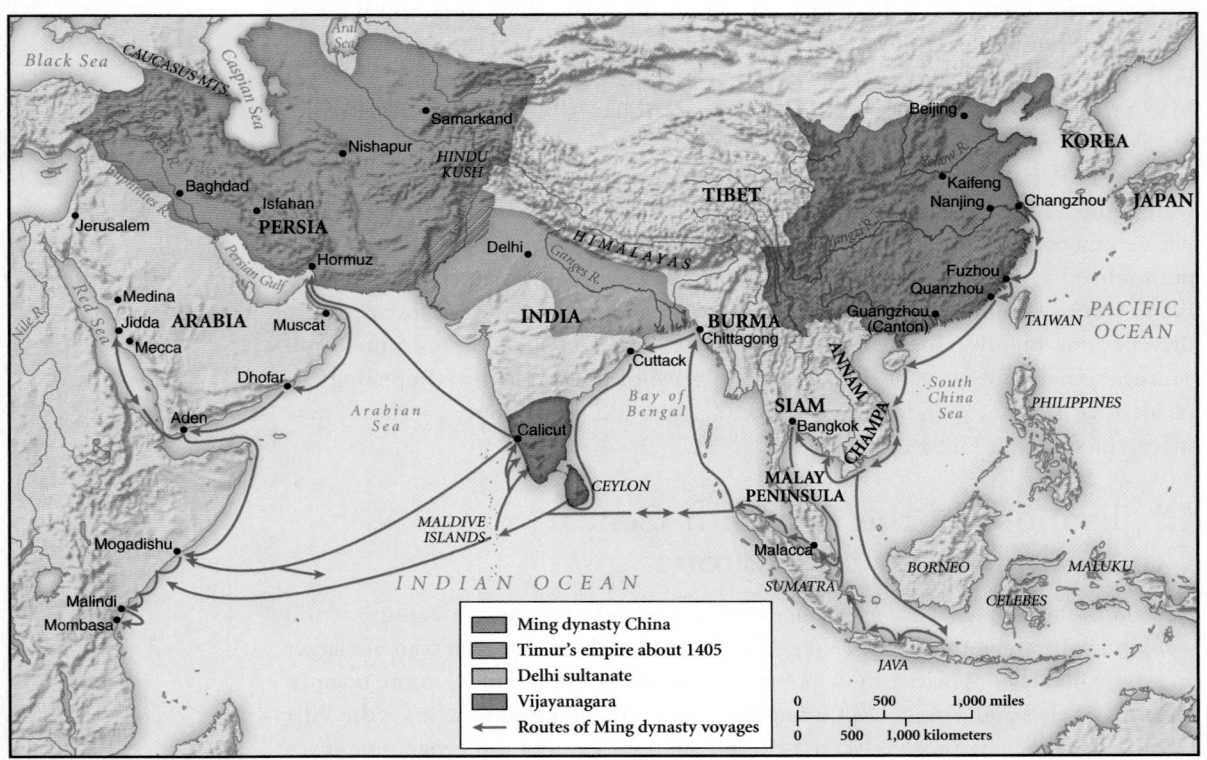

of Mongol names and dress, while promoting Confucian learning based on earlier models from the Han, Tang, and Song dynasties. Emperor Yongle (reigned 1402–1422) sponsored an enormous *Encyclopedia* of some 11,000 volumes. With contributions from more than 2,000 scholars, this work sought to summarize or compile all previous writing on history, geography, ethics, government, and more. Yongle also relocated the capital to Beijing, ordered the building of a magnificent imperial residence known as the Forbidden City, and constructed the Temple of Heaven, where subsequent rulers performed Confucian-based rituals to ensure the well-being of Chinese society (see Visual Source 13.1, p. 610). Culturally speaking, China was looking to its past.

Politically, the Ming dynasty reestablished the civil service examination system that had been neglected under Mongol rule and went on to create a highly centralized government. Power was concentrated in the hands of the emperor himself, while a cadre of eunuchs (castrated men) personally loyal to the emperor exercised great authority, much to the dismay of the official bureaucrats. The state acted vigorously to repair the damage of the Mongol years by restoring millions of acres to cultivation; rebuilding canals, reservoirs, and irrigation works; and planting, according to some estimates, a billion trees in an effort to reforest China. As a result, the economy rebounded, both international and domestic trade flourished, and the population grew. During the fifteenth century, China had recovered and was perhaps the best-governed and most prosperous of the world's major civilizations.

China also undertook the largest and most impressive maritime expeditions the world had ever seen. Since the eleventh century, Chinese sailors and traders had been a major presence in the South China Sea and in Southeast Asian port cities, with much of this activity in private hands. But now, after decades of preparation, an enormous fleet, commissioned by Emperor Yongle himself, was launched in 1405, followed over the next twenty-eight years by six more such expeditions. On board more than 300 ships of the first voyage was a crew of some 27,000, including 180 physicians, hundreds of government officials, 5 astrologers, 7 high-ranking or grand eunuchs, carpenters, tailors, accountants, merchants, translators, cooks, and thousands of soldiers and sailors. Visiting many ports in Southeast Asia, Indonesia, India, Arabia, and East Africa, these fleets, captained by the Muslim eunuch Zheng He, sought to enroll distant peoples and states in the Chinese tribute system (see Map 13.1). Dozens of rulers accompanied the fleets back to China, where they presented tribute, performed the required rituals of submission, and received in return abundant gifts, titles, and trading opportunities. Chinese officials were amused by some of the exotic products to be found abroad—ostriches, zebras, and giraffes, for

Comparing Chinese and European Ships Among the largest vessels in Zheng He's early-fifteenth-century fleet were "treasure ships" such as this vessel measuring more than 400 feet long and carrying a crew of perhaps 1,000 men. The figure at the bottom right represents one of Columbus's ships. (© Dugald Stermer)

example. Officially described as "bringing order to the world," Zheng He's expeditions served to establish Chinese power and prestige in the Indian Ocean and to exert Chinese control over foreign trade in the region. The Chinese, however, did not seek to conquer new territories, establish Chinese settlements, or spread their culture, though they did intervene in a number of local disputes. On one of the voyages, Zheng He erected on the island of Ceylon (Sri Lanka) a tablet honoring alike the Buddha, Allah, and a Hindu deity.

The most surprising feature of these voyages was how abruptly and deliberately they were ended. After 1433, Chinese authorities simply stopped such expeditions and allowed this enormous and expensive fleet to deteriorate in port. "In less than a hundred years," wrote a recent historian of these voyages, "the greatest navy the world had ever known had ordered itself into extinction."[3] Part of the reason involved the death of the emperor Yongle, who had been the chief patron of the enterprise. Many high-ranking officials had long seen the expeditions as a waste of resources because China, they believed, was the self-sufficient "middle kingdom," requiring little from the outside world. In their eyes, the real danger to China came from the north, where nomadic barbarians constantly threatened. Finally, they viewed the voyages as the project of the court eunuchs, whom these officials despised. Even as these voices of Chinese officialdom prevailed, private Chinese merchants and craftsmen continued to settle and trade in Japan, the Philippines, Taiwan, and Southeast Asia, but they did so without the support of their government. The Chinese state quite deliberately turned its back on what was surely within its reach—a large-scale maritime empire in the Indian Ocean basin.

European Comparisons: State Building and Cultural Renewal

■ Comparison
What political and cultural differences stand out in the histories of fifteenth-century China and Western Europe? What similarities are apparent?

At the other end of the Eurasian continent, similar processes of demographic recovery, political consolidation, cultural flowering, and overseas expansion were under way. Western Europe, having escaped Mongol conquest but devastated by the plague, began to regrow its population during the second half of the fifteenth century. As in China, the infrastructure of civilization proved a durable foundation for demographic and economic revival.

Politically too Europe joined China in continuing earlier patterns of state building. In China, however, this meant a unitary and centralized government that encompassed almost the whole of its civilization, while in Europe a decidedly fragmented system of many separate, independent, and highly competitive states made for a sharply divided Christendom (see Map 13.2). Many of these states—Spain, Portugal, France, England, the city-states of Italy (Milan, Venice, and Florence), various German principalities—learned to tax their citizens more efficiently, to create more effective administrative structures, and to raise standing armies. A small Russian state centered on the city of Moscow also emerged in the fifteenth century as Mongol rule faded away. Much of this state building was driven by the needs of war, a frequent occurrence in such a fragmented and competitive political environment. England and

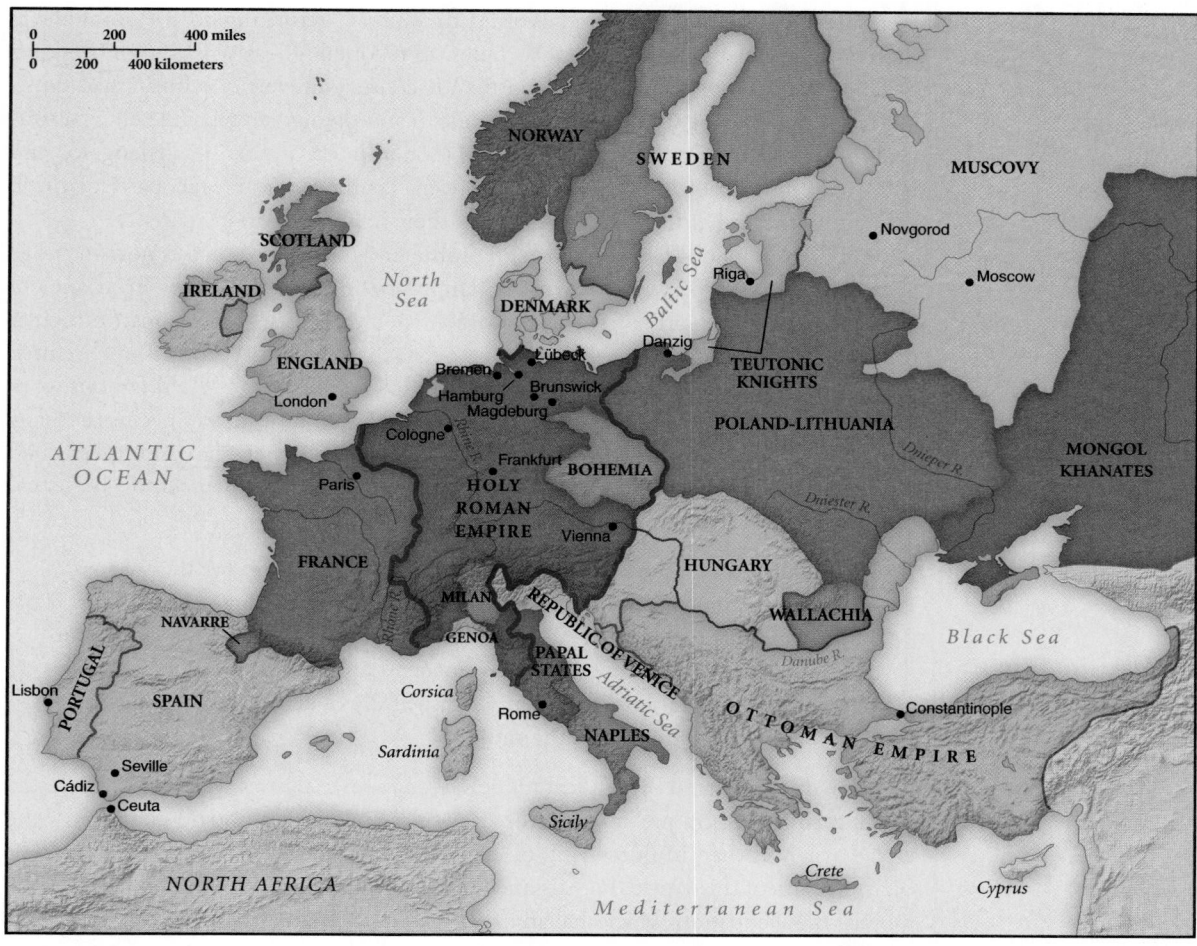

Map 13.2   Europe in 1500
By the end of the fifteenth century, Christian Europe had assumed its early modern political shape as a system of competing states threatened by an expanding Muslim Ottoman Empire.

France, for example, fought intermittently for more than a century in the Hundred Years' War (1337–1453) over rival claims to territory in France. Nothing remotely similar disturbed the internal life of Ming dynasty China.

A renewed cultural blossoming, known in European history as the Renaissance, likewise paralleled the revival of all things Confucian in Ming dynasty China. In Europe, however, that blossoming celebrated and reclaimed a classical Greek tradition that earlier had been obscured or viewed through the lens of Arabic or Latin translations. Beginning in the vibrant commercial cities of Italy between roughly 1350 and 1500, the Renaissance reflected the belief of the wealthy elite that they were living in a wholly new era, far removed from the confined religious world of feudal Europe. Educated citizens of these cities sought inspiration in the art and literature of ancient Greece and Rome; they were "returning to the sources," as they put it. Their purpose was not so much to reconcile these works with the ideas of Christianity, as the twelfth- and thirteenth-century university scholars had done, but to use them as a cultural standard to imitate and then to surpass. The elite patronized great Renaissance artists such as Leonardo da Vinci, Michelangelo, and Raphael, whose paintings and sculptures were far more naturalistic, particularly in portraying the human body, than those of their medieval counterparts.

Although religious themes remained prominent, Renaissance artists now included portraits and busts of well-known contemporary figures and scenes from ancient mythology. In the work of scholars, known as "humanists," reflections on secular topics such as grammar, history, politics, poetry, rhetoric, and ethics complemented more religious matters. For example, Niccolò Machiavelli's (1469-1527) famous work *The Prince* was a prescription for political success based on the way politics actually operated in a highly competitive Italy of rival city-states rather than on idealistic and religiously based principles. To the question of whether a prince should be feared or loved, Machiavelli replied:

> One ought to be both feared and loved, but as it is difficult for the two to go together, it is much safer to be feared than loved.... For it may be said of men in general that they are ungrateful, voluble, dissemblers, anxious to avoid danger, and covetous of gain.... Fear is maintained by dread of punishment which never fails.... In the actions of men, and especially of princes, from which there is no appeal, the end justifies the means.[4]

Heavily influenced by classical models, Renaissance figures were more interested in capturing the unique qualities of particular individuals and in describing the world as it was than in portraying or exploring eternal religious truths. In its focus on the affairs of this world, Renaissance culture reflected the urban bustle and commercial preoccupations of the Italian cities. Its secular elements challenged the otherworldliness of Christian culture, and its individualism signaled the dawning of a more capitalist economy of private entrepreneurs. A new Europe was in the making, rather more different from its own recent past than Ming dynasty China was from its pre-Mongol glory.

European Comparisons: Maritime Voyaging

■ Comparison

In what ways did European maritime voyaging in the fifteenth century differ from that of China? What accounts for these differences?

A global traveler during the fifteenth century might be surprised to find that Europeans, like the Chinese, were also launching outward-bound maritime expeditions. Initiated in 1415 by the small country of Portugal, those voyages sailed ever farther down the west coast of Africa, supported by the state and blessed by the pope (see Map 13.3). As the century ended, two expeditions marked major breakthroughs, although few suspected it at the time. In 1492, Christopher Columbus, funded by Spain, Portugal's neighbor and rival, made his way west across the Atlantic hoping to arrive in the East and, in one of history's most consequential mistakes, ran into the Americas. Five years later, in 1497, Vasco da Gama launched a voyage that took him

Snapshot   **Key Moments in European Maritime Voyaging**

Portuguese seize Ceuta in Morocco	1415
Prince Henry the Navigator launches Portuguese exploration of the West African coast	1420
Portuguese settle the Azores	1430s
Chinese fleets withdrawn from Indian Ocean	1433
Portuguese reach the Senegal River; beginning of Atlantic slave trade	1440s
Portuguese contact with Kongo; royal family converts to Christianity	1480s
Sugar production begins in Atlantic islands (Canaries, São Tomé)	1480s
Establishment of trading station at Elmina (in present-day Ghana)	1480s
First transatlantic voyage of Columbus	1492
John Cabot sails across North Atlantic to North America	1496
Vasco da Gama enters Indian Ocean and reaches India	1497–1498
Portuguese attacks on various Swahili cities; establishment of Fort Jesus at Mombasa; Portuguese contacts with Christian Ethiopia	1497–1520s
Magellan's voyage to Asia via the Americas; first circumnavigation of the globe	1520–1523

around the tip of South Africa, along the East African coast, and, with the help of a Muslim pilot, across the Indian Ocean to Calicut in southern India.

The differences between the Chinese and European oceangoing ventures were striking, most notably perhaps in terms of size. Columbus captained three ships and a crew of about 90, while da Gama had four ships, manned by perhaps 170 sailors. These were minuscule fleets compared to Zheng He's hundreds of ships and a crew in the many thousands. "All the ships of Columbus and da Gama combined," according to a recent account, "could have been stored on a single deck of a single vessel in the fleet that set sail under Zheng He."[5]

Motivation as well as size differentiated the two ventures. Europeans were seeking the wealth of Africa and Asia—gold, spices, silk, and more. They also were in search of Christian converts and of possible Christian allies with whom to continue their long crusading struggle against threatening Muslim powers. China, by contrast, faced no equivalent power, needed no military allies in the Indian Ocean basin, and required little that these regions produced. Nor did China possess an impulse to convert foreigners to Chinese culture or religion as the Europeans surely did. Furthermore, the confident and overwhelmingly powerful Chinese fleet sought neither conquests nor colonies, while the Europeans soon tried to monopolize by force the commerce of the Indian Ocean and violently carved out huge empires in the Americas.

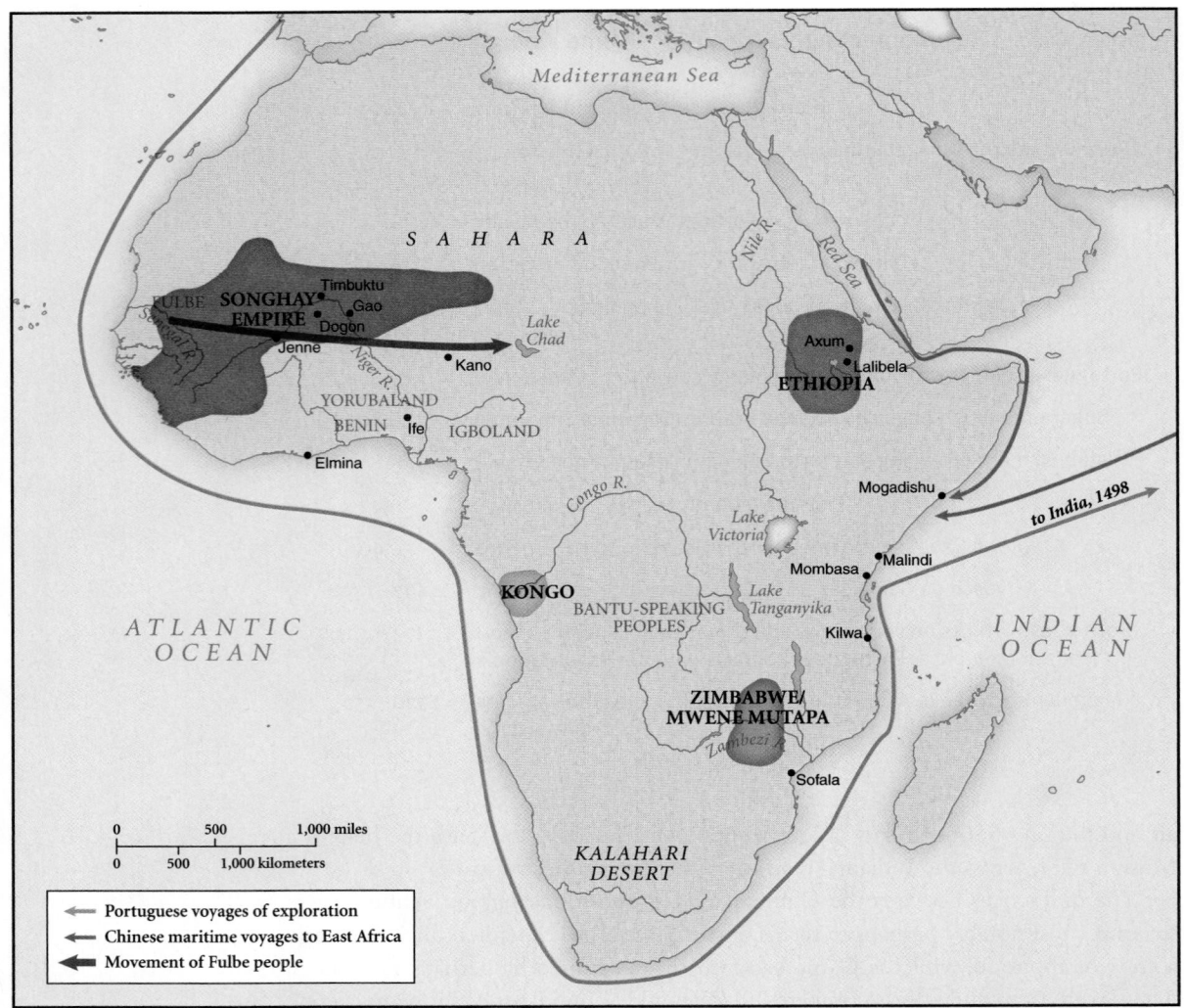

Map 13.3   Africa in the Fifteenth Century

By the 1400s, Africa was a virtual museum of political and cultural diversity, encompassing large empires, such as Songhay; smaller kingdoms, such as Kongo; city-states among the Yoruba, Hausa, and Swahili peoples; village-based societies without states at all, as among the Igbo; and nomadic pastoral peoples, such as the Fulbe. Both European and Chinese maritime expeditions touched on Africa during that century, even as Islam continued to find acceptance in the northern half of the continent.

The most striking difference in these two cases lay in the sharp contrast between China's decisive ending of its voyages and the continuing, indeed escalating, European effort, which soon brought the world's oceans and growing numbers of the world's people under its control. This is the reason that Zheng He's voyages were so long neglected in China's historical memory. They led nowhere, whereas the initial European expeditions, so much smaller and less promising, were but the first steps on a journey to world power. But why did the Europeans continue a process that the Chinese had deliberately abandoned?

In the first place, of course, Europe had no unified political authority with the power to order an end to its maritime outreach. Its system of competing states, so unlike China's single unified empire, ensured that once begun, rivalry alone would drive the Europeans to the ends of the earth. Beyond this, much of Europe's elite had an interest in overseas expansion. Its budding merchant communities saw opportunity for profit; its competing monarchs eyed the revenue that could come from taxing overseas trade or from seizing overseas resources; the Church foresaw the possibility of widespread conversion; impoverished nobles might imagine fame and fortune abroad. In China, by contrast, support for Zheng He's voyages was very shallow in official circles, and when the emperor Yongle passed from the scene, those opposed to the voyages prevailed within the politics of the court.

Finally, the Chinese were very much aware of their own antiquity, believed strongly in the absolute superiority of their culture, and felt with good reason that, should they desire something from abroad, others would bring it to them. Europeans too believed themselves unique, particularly in religious terms as the possessors of Christianity, the "one true religion." In material terms, though, they were seeking out the greater riches of the East, and they were highly conscious that Muslim power blocked easy access to these treasures and posed a military and religious threat to Europe itself. All of this propelled continuing European expansion in the centuries that followed.

The Waldseemüller Map of 1507
Just fifteen years after Columbus landed in the Western Hemisphere, this map, which was created by the German cartographer Martin Waldseemüller, reflected a dawning European awareness of the planet's global dimensions and location of the world's major landmasses. (Bildarchiv Preussischer Kulturbesitz/Art Resource, NY)

The Chinese withdrawal from the Indian Ocean actually facilitated the European entry. It cleared the way for the Portuguese to enter the region, where they faced only the eventual naval power of the Ottomans. Had Vasco da Gama encountered Zheng He's massive fleet as his four small ships sailed into Asian waters in 1498, world history may well have taken quite a different turn. As it was, however, China's abandonment of oceanic voyaging and Europe's embrace of the seas marked different responses to a common problem that both civilizations shared—growing populations and land shortage. In the centuries that followed, China's rice-based agriculture was able to expand production internally by more intensive use of the land, while the country's territorial expansion was inland toward Central Asia. By contrast, Europe's agriculture, based on wheat and livestock, expanded primarily by acquiring new lands in overseas possessions, which were gained as a consequence of a commitment to oceanic expansion.

Civilizations of the Fifteenth Century: The Islamic World

■ Comparison
What differences can you identify among the four major empires in the Islamic world of the fifteenth and sixteenth centuries?

Beyond the domains of Chinese and European civilization, our fifteenth-century global traveler would surely have been impressed with the transformations of the Islamic world. Stretching across much of Afro-Eurasia, the enormous realm of Islam experienced a set of remarkable changes during the fifteenth and early sixteenth centuries, as well as the continuation of earlier patterns. The most notable change lay in the political realm, for an Islamic civilization that had been severely fragmented since at least 900 now crystallized into four major states or empires (see Map 13.4). At the same time, a long-term process of conversion to Islam continued the cultural transformation of Afro-Eurasian societies both within and beyond these new states.

In the Islamic Heartland: The Ottoman and Safavid Empires

The most impressive and enduring of the new Islamic states was the Ottoman Empire, which lasted in one form or another from the fourteenth to the early twentieth century. It was the creation of one of the many Turkic warrior groups that had earlier migrated into Anatolia. By the mid-fifteenth century, these Ottoman Turks had already carved out a state that encompassed much of the Anatolian peninsula and had pushed deep into southeastern Europe (the Balkans), acquiring in the process a substantial Christian population. In the two centuries that followed, the Ottoman Empire extended its control to much of the Middle East, coastal North Africa, the lands surrounding the Black Sea, and even farther into Eastern Europe.

The Ottoman Empire was a state of enormous significance in the world of the fifteenth century and beyond. In its huge territory, long duration, incorporation of many diverse peoples, and economic and cultural sophistication, it was

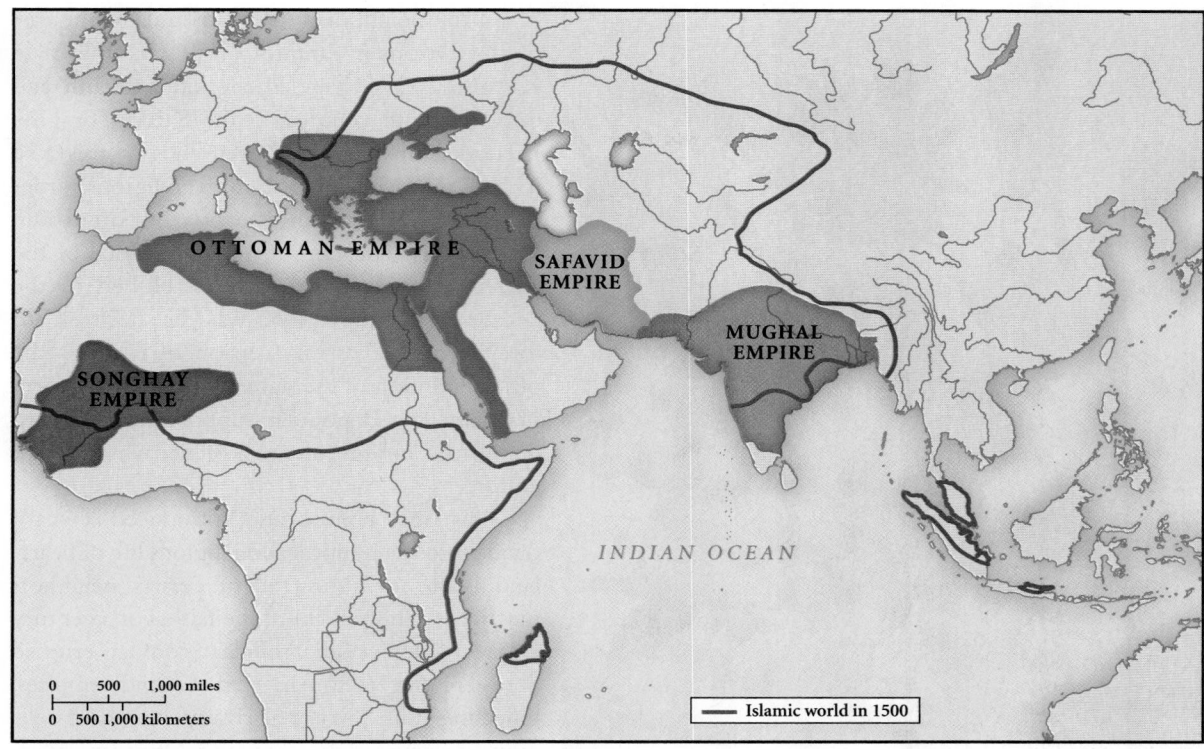

Map 13.4   Empires of the Islamic World

The most prominent political features of the vast Islamic world in the fifteenth and sixteenth centuries were four large states: the Songhay, Ottoman, Safavid, and Mughal empires.

one of the great empires of world history. In the fifteenth century, only Ming dynasty China and the Incas matched it in terms of wealth, power, and splendor. The empire represented the emergence of the Turks as the dominant people of the Islamic world, ruling now over many Arabs, who had initiated this new faith more than 800 years before. In adding "caliph" (successor to the Prophet) to their other titles, Ottoman sultans claimed the legacy of the earlier Abbasid Empire. They sought to bring a renewed unity to the Islamic world, while also serving as protector of the faith, the "strong sword of Islam."

The Ottoman Empire also represented a new phase in the long encounter between Christendom and the world of Islam. In the Crusades, Europeans had taken the aggressive initiative in that encounter, but the rise of the Ottoman Empire reversed their roles. The seizure of Constantinople in 1453 marked the final demise of Christian Byzantium and allowed Ottoman rulers to see themselves as successors to the Roman Empire. In 1529, a rapidly expanding Ottoman Empire laid siege to Vienna in the heart of Central Europe. The political and military expansion of Islam, at the expense of Christendom, seemed clearly under way. Many Europeans spoke fearfully of the "terror of the Turk."

Des obristen kamerling Vnd Früchles

Ottoman Janissaries
Originating in the fourteenth century, the Janissaries became the elite infantry force of the Ottoman Empire. Complete with uniforms, cash salaries, and marching music, they were the first standing army in the region since the days of the Roman Empire. When gunpowder technology became available, Janissary forces soon were armed with muskets, grenades, and handheld cannon. This image dates from the seventeenth century. (Austrian National Library, picture archive, Vienna: Cod. 8626, fol. 15r)

In the neighboring Persian lands to the east of the Ottoman Empire, another Islamic state was also taking shape in the late fifteenth and early sixteenth centuries—the Safavid Empire. Its leadership was also Turkic, but in this case it had emerged from a Sufi religious order founded several centuries earlier by Safi al-Din (1252–1334). The long-term significance of the Safavid Empire, which was established in the decade following 1500, was its decision to forcibly impose a Shia version of Islam as the official religion of the state. Over time, this form of Islam gained popular support and came to define the unique identity of Persian (Iranian) culture.

This Shia empire also introduced a sharp divide into the political and religious life of heartland Islam, for almost all of Persia's neighbors practiced a Sunni form of the faith. For a century (1534–1639), periodic military conflict erupted between the Ottoman and Safavid empires, reflecting both territorial rivalry and sharp religious differences. In 1514, the Ottoman sultan wrote to the Safavid ruler in the most bitter of terms:

You have denied the sanctity of divine law…you have deserted the path of salvation and the sacred commandments…you have opened to Muslims the gates of tyranny and oppression…you have raised the standard of irreligion and heresy.…[Therefore] the *ulama* and our doctors have pronounced a sentence of death against you, perjurer and blasphemer.[6]

This Sunni/Shia hostility has continued to divide the Islamic world into the twenty-first century.

On the Frontiers of Islam: The Songhay and Mughal Empires

While the Ottoman and Safavid empires brought both a new political unity and a sharp division to the heartland of Islam, two other states performed a similar role on the expanding African and Asian frontiers of the faith. In the West African savannas, the Songhay Empire rose in the second half of the fifteenth century. It was the most recent and the largest in a series of impressive states that operated at a crucial intersection of the trans-Saharan trade routes and that derived much of their revenue from taxing that commerce. Islam was a growing faith in Songhay but was limited largely to urban elites. This cultural divide within Songhay largely accounts for the religious behavior of its fifteenth-century monarch Sonni Ali (reigned 1465–1492), who gave alms and fasted during Ramadan in proper Islamic style but also enjoyed a reputation as a magician and possessed a charm thought to render his soldiers invisible to their enemies. Nonetheless, Songhay had become a major center of Islamic learning and commerce by the early sixteenth century. A North African traveler known as Leo Africanus remarked on the city of Timbuktu:

> Here are great numbers of [Muslim] religious teachers, judges, scholars, and other learned persons who are bountifully maintained at the king's expense. Here too are brought various manuscripts or written books from Barbary [North Africa] which are sold for more money than any other merchandise.... Here are very rich merchants and to here journey continually large numbers of negroes who purchase here cloth from Barbary and Europe.... It is a wonder to see the quality of merchandise that is daily brought here and how costly and sumptuous everything is.[7]

Sonni Ali's successor made the pilgrimage to Mecca and asked to be given the title "Caliph of the Land of the Blacks." Songhay then represented a substantial Islamic state on the African frontier of a still-expanding Muslim world.

The Mughal Empire in India bore similarities to Songhay, for both governed largely non-Muslim populations. Much as the Ottoman Empire initiated a new phase in the interaction of Islam and Christendom, so too did the Mughal Empire continue an ongoing encounter between Islamic and Hindu civilizations. Established in the early sixteenth century, the Mughal Empire was the creation of yet another Islamized Turkic group, which invaded India in 1526. Over the next century, the Mughals (a Persian term for Mongols) established unified control over most of the Indian peninsula, giving it a rare period of political unity and laying the foundation for subsequent British colonial rule. During its first several centuries, the Mughal Empire, a land of great wealth and imperial splendor, was the location of a remarkable effort to blend many Hindu groups and a variety of Muslims into an effective partnership. The inclusive policies of the early Mughal emperors showed that Muslim rulers could accommodate their overwhelmingly Hindu subjects in somewhat the same fashion as Ottoman authorities provided religious autonomy for their Christian peoples. In southernmost India, however, the distinctly Hindu kingdom of Vijayanagara flourished in the fifteenth century, even as it borrowed architectural styles from the Muslim states of northern India and sometimes employed Muslim mercenaries in its military forces.

Together these four Muslim empires—Ottoman, Safavid, Songhay, and Mughal—brought to the Islamic world a greater measure of political coherence, military power, economic prosperity, and cultural brilliance than it had known since the early centuries of Islam. This new energy, sometimes called a "second flowering of Islam," impelled the continuing spread of the faith to yet new regions. The most prominent of these was oceanic Southeast Asia, which for centuries had been intimately bound up in the world of Indian Ocean commerce. By the fifteenth century, that trading network was largely in Muslim hands, and the demand for Southeast Asian spices was mounting as the Eurasian world recovered from the devastation of Mongol conquest and the plague. Growing numbers of Muslim traders, many of them from India, settled in Java and Sumatra, bringing their faith with them. Thus, unlike the Middle East and India, where Islam was established in the wake of Arab or Turkic conquest, in Southeast Asia, as in West Africa, it was introduced by traveling merchants and solidified through the activities of Sufi holy men.

The rise of Malacca, strategically located on the waterway between Sumatra and Malaya, was a sign of the times (see Map 13.1, p. 576). During the fifteenth century, it was transformed from a small fishing village to a major Muslim port city. A Portuguese visitor in 1512 observed that Malacca had "no equal in the world.... Commerce between different nations for a thousand leagues on every hand must come to Malacca."[8] That city also became a springboard for the spread of Islam throughout the region. The Islam of Malacca, however, demonstrated much blending with local and Hindu/Buddhist traditions, while the city itself, like many port towns, had a reputation for "rough behavior." An Arab Muslim pilot in the 1480s commented critically:

> They have no culture at all.... You do not know whether they are Muslim or not.... They are thieves, for theft is rife among them and they do not mind.... They appear liars and deceivers in trade and labor.[9]

Nonetheless, Malacca, like Timbuktu, became a center for Islamic learning, and students from elsewhere in Southeast Asia were studying there in the fifteenth century. As the more central regions of Islam were consolidating politically, the frontier of the faith continued to move steadily outward.

Civilizations of the Fifteenth Century: The Americas

■ **Comparison**
What distinguished the Aztec and Inca empires from each other?

Across the Atlantic, centers of civilization had long flourished in Mesoamerica and in the Andes. The fifteenth century witnessed new, larger, and more politically unified expressions of those civilizations in the Aztec and Inca empires. Both were the work of previously marginal peoples who had forcibly taken over and absorbed older cultures, giving them new energy, and both were decimated in the sixteenth century at the hands of Spanish conquistadores and their diseases. To conclude this global tour of world civilizations, we will send our weary traveler to the Western Hemisphere for a brief look at these American civilizations (see Map 13.5).

The Aztec Empire

The empire known to history as the Aztec state was largely the work of the Mexica people, a seminomadic group from northern Mexico who had migrated southward and by 1325 had established themselves on a small island in Lake Texcoco. Over the

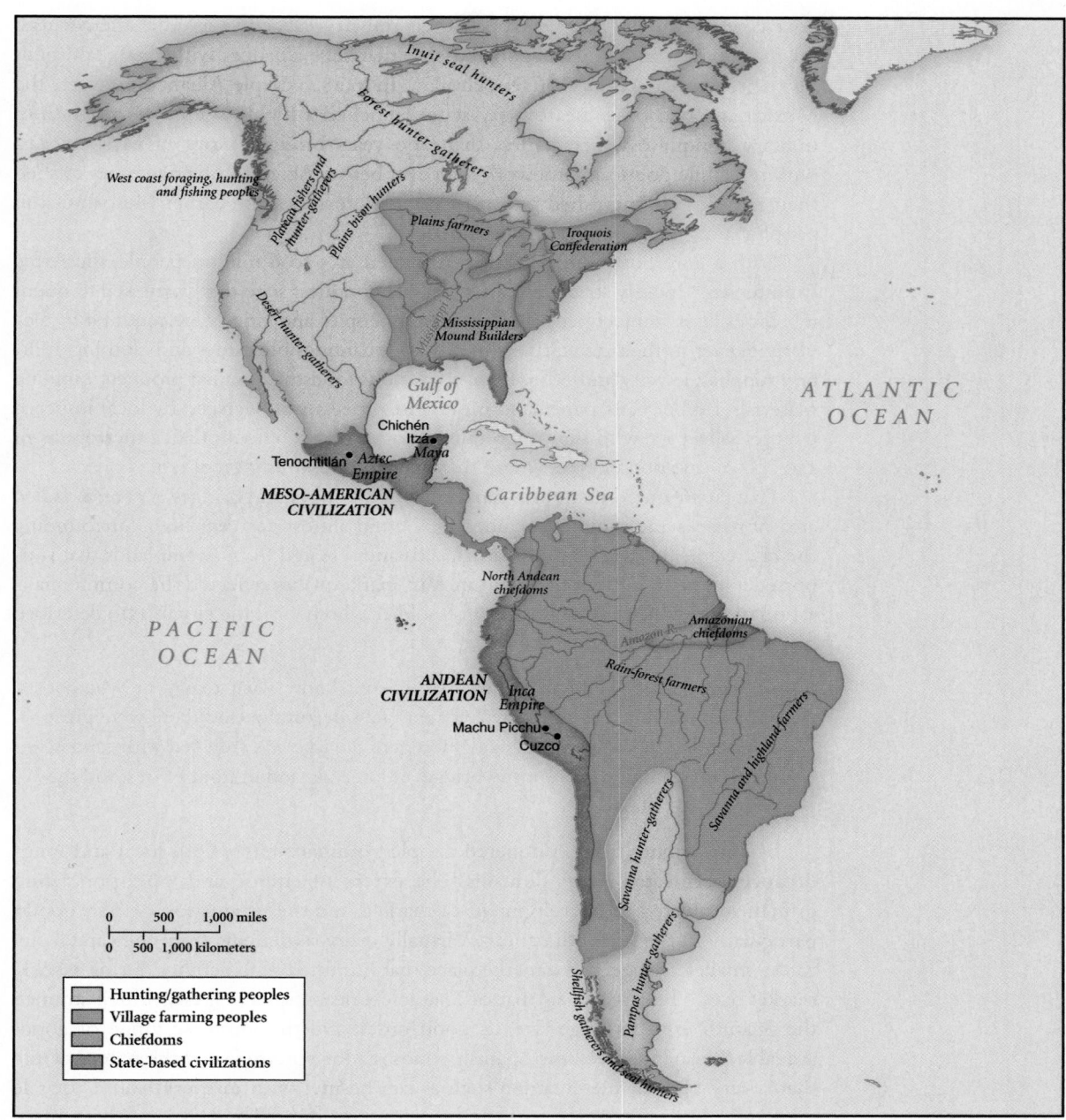

Map 13.5 **The Americas in the Fifteenth Century**
The Americas before Columbus represented a world almost completely separate from Afro-Eurasia. It featured similar kinds of societies, though with a different balance among them, but it completely lacked the pastoral economies that were so important in the Eastern Hemisphere.

Map labels:
- Inuit seal hunters
- Forest hunter-gatherers
- West coast foraging, hunting and fishing peoples
- Plateau fishers and hunter-gatherers
- Plains bison hunters
- Plains farmers
- Iroquois Confederation
- Desert hunter-gatherers
- Mississippian Mound Builders
- Gulf of Mexico
- Chichén Itzá
- Maya
- Tenochtitlán
- Aztec Empire
- MESO-AMERICAN CIVILIZATION
- ATLANTIC OCEAN
- Caribbean Sea
- North Andean chiefdoms
- Amazonian chiefdoms
- PACIFIC OCEAN
- Rainforest farmers
- ANDEAN CIVILIZATION
- Inca Empire
- Machu Picchu
- Cuzco
- Savanna and highland farmers
- Savanna hunter-gatherers
- Pampas hunter-gatherers
- Shellfish gatherers and seal hunters

Scale:
0   500   1,000 miles
0   500   1,000 kilometers

Legend:
- Hunting/gathering peoples
- Village farming peoples
- Chiefdoms
- State-based civilizations

next century, the Mexica developed their military capacity, served as mercenaries for more powerful people, negotiated elite marriage alliances with them, and built up their own capital city of Tenochtitlán. In 1428, a Triple Alliance between the Mexica and two other nearby city-states launched a highly aggressive program of military conquest, which in less than 100 years brought more of Mesoamerica within a single political framework than ever before. Aztec authorities, eager to shed their rather undistinguished past, now claimed descent from earlier Mesoamerican peoples such as the Toltecs and Teotihuacán.

With a core population recently estimated at 5 to 6 million people, the Aztec Empire was a loosely structured and unstable conquest state that witnessed frequent rebellions by its subject peoples. Conquered peoples and cities were required to regularly deliver to their Aztec rulers impressive quantities of textiles and clothing, military supplies, jewelry and other luxuries, various foodstuffs, animal products, building materials, rubber balls, paper, and more. The process was overseen by local imperial tribute collectors, who sent the required goods on to Tenochtitlán, a metropolis of 150,000 to 200,000 people, where they were meticulously recorded.

That city featured numerous canals, dikes, causeways, and bridges. A central walled area of palaces and temples included a pyramid almost 200 feet high. Surrounding the city were "floating gardens," artificial islands created from swamplands that supported a highly productive agriculture. Vast marketplaces reflected the commercialization of the economy. A young Spanish soldier who beheld the city in 1519 described his reaction:

> Gazing on such wonderful sights, we did not know what to say, or whether what appeared before us was real, for on one side, on the land there were great cities, and in the lake ever so many more, and the lake was crowded with canoes, and in the causeway were many bridges at intervals, and in front of us stood the great city of Mexico.[10]

Beyond tribute from conquered peoples, ordinary trade, both local and long-distance, permeated Aztec domains. The extent of empire and rapid population growth stimulated the development of markets and the production of craft goods, particularly in the fifteenth century. Virtually every settlement, from the capital city to the smallest village, had a marketplace that hummed with activity during weekly market days. The largest was that of Tlatelolco, near the capital city, which stunned the Spanish with its huge size, its good order, and the immense range of goods available. Hernán Cortés, the Spanish conquistador who defeated the Aztecs, wrote that "every kind of merchandise such as can be met with in every land is for sale there, whether of food and victuals, or ornaments of gold and silver, or lead, brass, copper, tin, precious stones, bones, shells, snails and feathers."[11] Professional merchants, known as *pochteca*, were legally commoners, but their wealth, often exceeding that of the nobility, allowed them to rise in society and become "magnates of the land." (See Document 13.1, pp. 601–04, for another Spanish view of the Aztec realm.)

■ **Description**
How did Aztec religious thinking support the empire?

Among the "goods" that the pochteca obtained were slaves, many of whom were destined for sacrifice in the bloody rituals so central to Aztec religious life. Long a part of Mesoamerican and many other world cultures, human sacrifice assumed an unusually prominent role in Aztec public life and thought during the fifteenth century. Tlacaelel (1398–1480), who was for more than half a century a prominent official of the Aztec Empire, is often credited with crystallizing the ideology of state that gave human sacrifice such great importance.

In that cyclical understanding of the world, the sun, central to all of life and identified with the Aztec patron deity Huitzilopochtli, tended to lose its energy in a constant battle against encroaching darkness. Thus the Aztec world hovered always on the edge of catastrophe. To replenish its energy and thus postpone the descent into endless darkness, the sun required the life-giving force found in human blood. Because the gods had shed their blood ages ago in creating humankind, it was wholly proper for people to offer their own blood to nourish the gods in the present. The high calling of the Aztec state was to supply this blood, largely through its wars of expansion and from prisoners of war, who were destined for sacrifice. The victims were "those who have died for the god." The growth of the Aztec Empire therefore became the means for maintaining cosmic order and avoiding utter catastrophe. This ideology also shaped the techniques of Aztec warfare, which put a premium on capturing prisoners rather than on killing the enemy. As the empire grew, priests and rulers became mutually dependent, and "human sacrifices were carried out in the service of politics."[12] Massive sacrificial rituals, together with a display of great wealth, served to impress enemies, allies, and subjects alike with the immense power of the Aztecs and their gods.

Alongside these sacrificial rituals was a philosophical and poetic tradition of great beauty, much of which mused on the fragility and brevity of human life. Such an outlook characterized the work of Nezahualcoyotl (1402–1472), a poet and king of the city-state of Texcoco, which was part of the Aztec Empire:

Aztec Women
Within the home, Aztec women cooked, cleaned, spun and wove cloth, raised their children, and undertook ritual activities. Outside the home, they served as officials in palaces, priestesses in temples, traders in markets, teachers in schools, and members of craft workers' organizations. This domestic image comes from the sixteenth-century Florentine Codex, which was compiled by the Spanish but illustrated by Aztec artists. (Templo Mayor Library Mexico/Gianni Dagli Orti/The Art Archive)

Truly do we live on Earth?
Not forever on earth; only a little while here.
Be it jade, it shatters.
Be it gold, it breaks.
Be it a quetzal feather, it tears apart.
Not forever on earth; only a little while here.

Like a painting, we will be erased.
Like a flower, we will dry up here on earth.
Like plumed vestments of the precious bird,
That precious bird with an agile neck,
We will come to an end.[13]

The Inca Empire

While the Mexica were constructing an empire in Mesoamerica, a relatively small community of Quechua-speaking people, known to us as the Inca, was building the Western Hemisphere's largest imperial state along the spine of the Andes Mountains, which run almost the entire length of the west coast of South America. Much as the Aztecs drew upon the traditions of the Toltecs and Teotihuacán, the Incas incorporated the lands and cultures of earlier Andean civilizations: the Chavín, Moche, Nazca, and Chimu. The Inca Empire, however, was much larger than the Aztec state; it stretched some 2,500 miles along the Andes and contained perhaps 10 million subjects. Although the Aztec Empire controlled only part of the Mesoamerican cultural region, the Inca state encompassed practically the whole of Andean civilization during its short life in the fifteenth and early sixteenth centuries.

Both the Aztec and Inca empires represent rags-to-riches stories in which quite modest and remotely located people very quickly created by military conquest the largest states ever witnessed in their respective regions, but the empires themselves were quite different. In the Aztec realm, the Mexica rulers largely left their conquered people alone, if the required tribute was forthcoming. No elaborate administrative system arose to integrate the conquered territories or to assimilate their people to Aztec culture.

The Incas, on the other hand, erected a rather more bureaucratic empire, though with many accommodations for local circumstances. At the top reigned the emperor, an absolute ruler regarded as divine, a descendant of the creator god Viracocha and the son of the sun god Inti. In theory, the state owned all land and resources, and each of the some eighty provinces in the empire had an Inca governor. At least in the central regions of the empire, subjects were grouped into hierarchical units of 10, 50, 100, 500, 1,000, 5,000, and 10,000 people, each headed by local officials, who were appointed and supervised by an Inca governor or the emperor. A separate set of "inspectors" provided the imperial center with an independent check on provincial

■ **Description**
In what ways did Inca authorities seek to integrate their vast domains?

officials. Births, deaths, marriages, and other population data were carefully recorded on *quipus*, the knotted cords that served as an accounting device. A resettlement program moved one-quarter or more of the population to new locations, in part to disperse conquered and no doubt resentful people.

Efforts at cultural integration required the leaders of conquered peoples to learn Quechua. Their sons were removed to the capital of Cuzco for instruction in Inca culture and language. Even now, millions of people from Ecuador to Chile still speak Quechua, and it is the official second language of Peru after Spanish. While the Incas required their subject peoples to acknowledge major Inca deities, these peoples were then largely free to carry on their own religious traditions. Human sacrifice took place on great public occasions or at times of special difficulty, but nothing remotely on the scale of the Aztec practice.

Like the Aztec Empire, the Inca state represented an especially dense and extended network of economic relationships within the "American web," but these relationships took shape in quite a different fashion. Inca demands on their conquered people were expressed, not so much in terms of tribute, but as labor service, known as *mita*, which was required periodically of every household.[14] What people produced at home usually stayed at home, but almost everyone also had to work for the state. Some labored on large state farms or on "sun farms," which supported temples and religious institutions; others herded, mined, served in the military, or toiled on state-directed construction projects. Those with particular skills were put to work manufacturing textiles, metal goods, ceramics, and stonework. The most well known of these specialists were the "chosen women," who were removed from their homes as young girls, trained in Inca ideology, and set to producing corn beer and cloth at state centers. Later they were given as wives to men of distinction or sent to serve as priestesses in various temples, where they were known as "wives of the Sun." In return for such labor services, Inca ideology, expressed in terms of family relationships, required the state to provide elaborate feasts at which large quantities of food and drink were consumed. Thus the authority of the state penetrated and directed the Incas' society and economy far more than did that of the Aztecs. (See Document 13.2, pp. 605–07, for an early Spanish account of Inca governing practices.)

If the Inca and Aztec civilizations differed sharply in their political and economic arrangements, they resembled each other more closely in their gender

Machu Picchu
Machu Picchu, high in the Andes Mountains, was constructed by the Incas in the 1400s on a spot long held sacred by local people. Its 200 buildings stand at some 8,000 feet above sea level, making it truly a "city in the sky." According to scholars, it was probably a royal retreat or religious center, rather than serving administrative, commercial, or military purposes. The outside world became aware of Machu Picchu only in 1911, when it was discovered by a Yale University archeologist. (Crispin Rodwell/Alamy)

systems. Both societies practiced what scholars call "gender parallelism," in which "women and men operate in two separate but equivalent spheres, each gender enjoying autonomy in its own sphere."[15]

In both Mesoamerican and Andean societies, such systems had emerged long before their incorporation into the Aztec and Inca empires. In the Andes, men reckoned their descent from their fathers and women from their mothers, while Mesoamericans had long viewed children as belonging equally to their mothers and fathers. Parallel religious cults for women and men likewise flourished in both societies. Inca men venerated the sun, while women worshipped the moon, with matching religious officials. In Aztec temples, both male and female priests presided over rituals dedicated to deities of both sexes. Particularly among the Incas, parallel hierarchies of male and female political officials governed the empire, while in Aztec society, women officials exercised local authority under a title that meant "female person in charge of people." Social roles were clearly defined and different for men and women, but the domestic concerns of women—childbirth, cooking, weaving, cleaning—were not regarded as inferior to the activities of men. Among the Aztec, for example, sweeping was a powerful and sacred act with symbolic significance as "an act of purification and a preventative against evil elements penetrating the center of the Aztec universe, the home."[16] In the Andes, men broke the ground, women sowed, and both took part in the harvest.

None of this meant gender equality. Men occupied the top positions in both political and religious life, and male infidelity was treated more lightly than was women's unfaithfulness. As the Inca and Aztec empires expanded, military life, limited to men, grew in prestige, perhaps skewing an earlier gender parallelism. In other ways, the new Aztec and Inca rulers adapted to the gender systems of the people they had conquered. Among the Aztecs, the tools of women's work, the broom and the weaving spindle, were ritualized as weapons; sweeping the home was believed to assist men at war; and childbirth for women was regarded as "our kind of war."[17] Inca rulers did not challenge the gender parallelism of their subjects but instead replicated it at a higher level, as the *sapay Inca* (the Inca ruler) and the *coya* (his female consort) governed jointly, claiming descent respectively from the sun and the moon.

Webs of Connection

■ Connection
In what different ways did the peoples of the fifteenth century interact with one another?

Few people in the fifteenth century lived in entirely separate and self-contained communities. Almost all were caught up, to one degree or another, in various and overlapping webs of influence, communication, and exchange. Such interactions represent, of course, one of the major concerns of world history. What kinds of webs or networks linked the various societies and civilizations of the fifteenth century?[18]

Perhaps most obvious were the webs of empire, large-scale political systems that brought together a variety of culturally different people. Christians and Muslims encountered each other directly in the Ottoman Empire, as did Hindus and Muslims in the Mughal Empire. No empire tried more diligently to integrate its diverse peoples than the fifteenth-century Incas.

Religion too linked far-flung peoples, and divided them as well. Christianity provided a common religious culture for peoples from England to Russia, although the great divide between Roman Catholicism and Eastern Orthodoxy endured, and in the sixteenth century the Protestant Reformation would shatter permanently the Christian unity of the Latin West. Although Buddhism had largely vanished from its South Asian homeland, it remained a link among China, Korea, Tibet, Japan, and parts of Southeast Asia, even as it splintered into a variety of sects and practices. More than either of these, Islam actively brought together its many peoples. In the hajj, the pilgrimage to Mecca, Africans, Arabs, Persians, Turks, Indians, and many others joined as one people as they rehearsed together the events that gave birth to their common faith. And yet divisions and conflicts persisted within the vast realm of Islam, as the violent hostility between the Sunni Ottoman Empire and the Shia Safavid Empire so vividly illustrates.

Long-established patterns of trade among peoples occupying different environments and producing different goods were certainly much in evidence during the fifteenth century, as they had been for millennia. Hunting societies of Siberia funneled furs and other products of the forest into the Silk Road trading network traversing the civilizations of Eurasia. In the fifteenth century, some of the agricultural peoples in southern Nigeria were receiving horses brought overland from the drier regions to the north, where those animals flourished better. The Mississippi River in North America and the Orinoco and Amazon rivers in South America facilitated a canoe-borne commerce along those waterways. Coastal shipping in large seagoing canoes operated in the Caribbean and along the Pacific coast between Mexico and Peru. In the Pacific, the Micronesian island of Yap by the fifteenth century was the center of an oceanic trading network, which included the distant islands of Guam and Palau and used large stone disks as money. Likewise the people of Tonga, Samoa, and Fiji intermarried and exchanged a range of goods, including mats and canoes.

The great long-distance trading patterns of the Afro-Eurasian world, in operation for a thousand years or more, likewise continued in the fifteenth century, although the balance among them was changing (see Map 13.6). The Silk Road overland network, which had flourished under Mongol control in the thirteenth and fourteenth centuries, contracted in the fifteenth century as the Mongol Empire broke up and the devastation of the plague reduced demand for its products. The rise of the Ottoman Empire also blocked direct commercial contact between Europe and China, but oceanic trade from Japan, Korea, and China through the islands of Southeast Asia and across the Indian Ocean picked up considerably. Larger ships made it possible to trade in bulk goods such as grain as well as luxury products, while more sophisticated partnerships and credit mechanisms greased the wheels of commerce. A common Islamic culture over much of this vast region likewise smoothed the passage of goods among very different peoples, as it also did for the trans-Saharan trade.

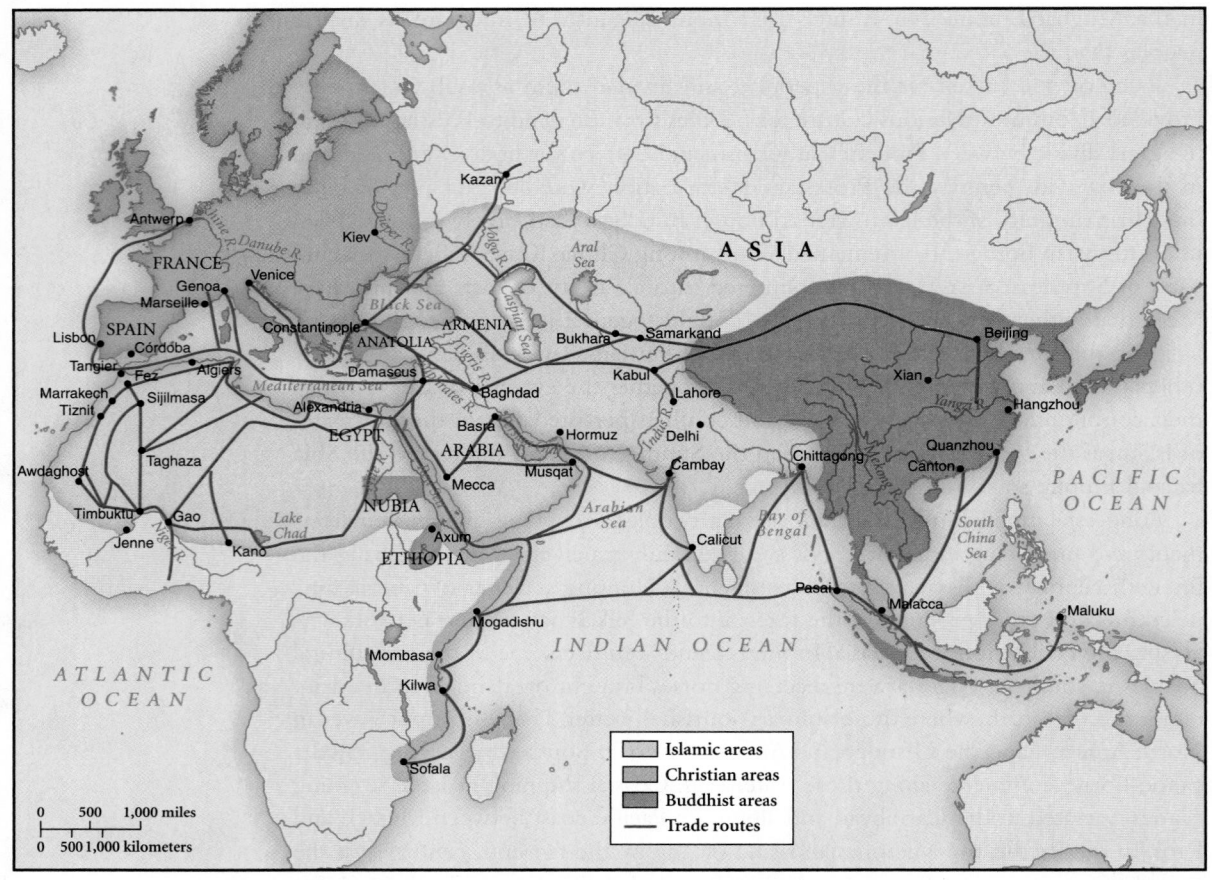

Map 13.6   Religion and Commerce in the Afro-Eurasian World

By the fifteenth century, the many distinct peoples and societies of the Eastern Hemisphere were linked to one another by ties of religion and commerce. Of course, not everyone was involved in long-distance trade, and many people in areas shown as Buddhist or Islamic on the map practiced other religions.

A Preview of Coming Attractions: Looking Ahead to the Modern Era, 1500–2010

While ties of empire, culture, and commerce surely linked many of the peoples in the world of the fifteenth century, none of those connections operated on a genuinely global scale. Although the densest webs of connection had been woven within the Afro-Eurasian zone of interaction, this huge region had no sustained ties with the Americas, and neither of them had meaningful contact with the peoples of Pacific Oceania. That situation was about to change as Europeans in the sixteenth century and beyond forged a set of genuinely global relationships that generated sustained interaction among all of these regions. That huge process and the many outcomes that flowed from it marked the beginning of what historians commonly call the modern age—the more than five centuries that followed the voyages of Columbus starting in 1492.

Over those five centuries, the previously separate worlds of Afro-Eurasia, the Americas, and Pacific Oceania became inextricably linked, with enormous consequences for everyone involved. Global empires, a global economy, global cultural exchanges, global migrations, global disease, global wars, and global environmental changes have made the past 500 years a unique phase in the human journey. Those webs of communication and exchange have progressively deepened, so much so that by the end of the twentieth century few people in the world lived beyond the cultural influences, economic ties, or political relationships of a globalized world.

A second distinctive feature of the past five centuries involves the emergence of a radically new kind of human society, also called "modern," which took shape first in Europe during the nineteenth century and then in various forms elsewhere in the world. The core feature of such societies was industrialization, rooted in a sustained growth of technological innovation. The human ability to create wealth made an enormous leap forward in a very short period of time, at least by world history standards. Accompanying this economic or industrial revolution was an equally distinctive and unprecedented jump in human numbers, a phenomenon that has affected not only human beings but also many other living species and the earth itself (see the Snapshot).

Moreover, these modern societies were far more urbanized and much more commercialized than ever before, as more and more people began to work for wages, to produce for the market, and to buy the requirements of daily life rather than

Snapshot   **World Population Growth, 1000–2000**[19]

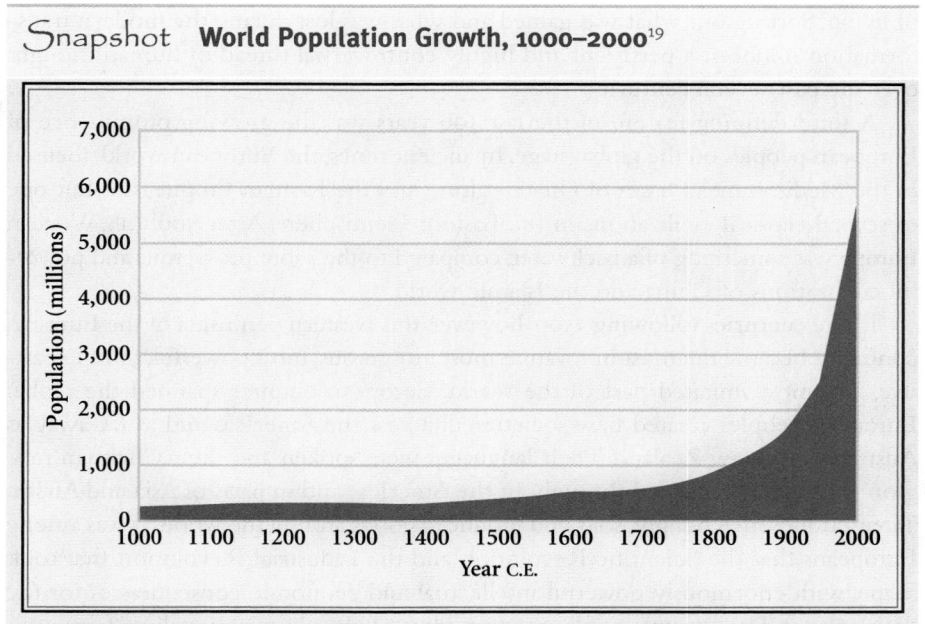

growing or making those products for their own use. These societies gave prominence and power to holders of urban wealth—merchants, bankers, industrialists, educated professionals—at the expense of rural landowning elites, while simultaneously generating a substantial factory working class and diminishing the role of peasants and handicraft artisans.

Modern societies were generally governed by states that were more powerful and intrusive than earlier states and empires had been, and they offered more of their people an opportunity to play an active role in public and political life. Literacy in modern societies was far more widespread than ever before, while new national identities became increasingly prominent, competing with more local loyalties. To the mix of established religious ideas and folk traditions were now added the challenging outlook and values of modern science, with its secular emphasis on the ability of human rationality to know and manipulate the world. Modernity has usually meant a self-conscious awareness of living and thinking in new ways that deliberately departed from tradition.

This revolution of modernity, comparable in its pervasive consequences only to the Agricultural Revolution of some 10,000 years ago, introduced new divisions and new conflicts into the experience of humankind. The ancient tensions between rich and poor within particular societies were now paralleled by new economic inequalities among entire regions and civilizations and a much-altered global balance of power. The first societies to experience the modern transformation—those in Western Europe and North America—became both a threat and a source of envy to much of the rest of the world. As modern societies emerged and spread, they were enormously destructive of older patterns of human life, even as they gave rise to many new ways of living. Sorting out what was gained and what was lost during the modern transformation has been a persistent and highly controversial thread of human thought over the past several centuries.

A third defining feature of the last 500 years was the growing prominence of European peoples on the global stage. In ancient times, the European world, focused in the Mediterranean basin of Greek culture and the Roman Empire, was but one of several classical civilizations in the Eastern Hemisphere. After 500 C.E., Western Europe was something of a backwater, compared to the more prosperous and powerful civilizations of China and the Islamic world.

In the centuries following 1500, however, this western peninsula of the Eurasian continent became the most innovative, most prosperous, most powerful, most expansive, and most imitated part of the world. European empires spanned the globe. European peoples created new societies all across the Americas and as far away as Australia and New Zealand. Their languages were spoken and their Christian religion was widely practiced throughout the Americas and in parts of Asia and Africa. Their businessmen bought, sold, and produced goods around the world. It was among Europeans that the Scientific Revolution and the Industrial Revolution first took shape, with enormously powerful intellectual and economic consequences for the entire planet. The quintessentially modern ideas of liberalism, nationalism, feminism, and socialism all bore the imprint of their European origin. By the beginning of the twentieth century, Europeans or peoples of European descent exercised unprecedented influence and control over the earth's many other peoples, a wholly novel experience in human history.

For the rest of the world, growing European dominance posed a common task. Despite their many differences, the peoples of Asia, Africa, the Middle East, the Americas, and Pacific Oceania all found themselves confronted by powerful and intrusive Europeans. The impact of this intrusion and how various peoples responded to it—resistance, submission, acceptance, imitation, adaptation—represent critically important threads in the world history of the past five centuries.

Reflections: What If? Chance and Contingency in World History

Seeking meaning in the stories they tell, historians are inclined to look for deeply rooted or underlying causes for the events they recount. And yet, is it possible that, at least on occasion, history turns less on profound and long-term causes than on coincidence, chance, or the decisions of a few that might well have gone another way?

Consider, for example, the problem of explaining the rise of Europe to a position of global power in the modern era. What if the Great Khan Ogodei had not died in 1241, requiring the forces then poised for an assault on Germany to return to Mongolia? It is surely possible that Central and Western Europe might have been overrun by Mongol armies as so many other civilizations had been, a prospect that could have drastically altered the trajectory of European history. Or what if the Chinese had decided in 1433 to continue their huge maritime expeditions, creating an empire in the Indian Ocean basin and perhaps moving on to "discover" the Americas and Europe? Such a scenario suggests a wholly different future for world history than the one that in fact occurred. Or what if the forces of the Ottoman Empire had taken the besieged city of Vienna in 1529? Might they then have incorporated even larger parts of Europe into their expanding domain, requiring a halt to Europe's overseas empire-building enterprise?

None of this necessarily means that the rise of Europe was merely a fluke or an accident of history, but it does raise the issue of "contingency," the role of unforeseen or small events in the unfolding of the human story. An occasional "what if" approach to history reminds us that alternative possibilities existed in the past and that the only certainty about the future is that we will be surprised.

Second Thoughts

What's the Significance?

Paleolithic persistence	Iroquois	Ming dynasty China
Benin	Timur	Zheng He
Igbo	Fulbe	European Renaissance

To assess your mastery of the material in this chapter, visit the **Student Center** at bedfordstmartins.com/strayer.

Ottoman Empire	Songhay Empire	Aztec Empire
seizure of Constantinople	Timbuktu	Inca Empire
(1453)	Mughal Empire	
Safavid Empire	Malacca	

Big Picture Questions

1. Assume for the moment that the Chinese had *not* ended their maritime voyages in 1433. How might the subsequent development of world history have been different? What value is there in asking this kind of "what if" or counterfactual question?

2. How does this chapter distinguish among the various kinds of societies that comprised the world of the fifteenth century? What other ways of categorizing the world's peoples might work as well or better?

3. What would surprise a knowledgeable observer from 500 C.E., were he or she to make a global tour in the fifteenth century? What features of that earlier world might still be recognizable?

4. What predictions about the future might a global traveler of the fifteenth century reasonably have made? To what extent would it depend on precisely when and where those predictions were made?

Next Steps: For Further Study

For Web sites and additional documents related to this chapter, see **Make History** at bedfordstmartins.com/strayer.

Terence N. D'Altroy, *The Incas* (2002). A history of the Inca Empire that draws on recent archeological and historical research.

Edward L. Dreyer, *Zheng He: China and the Oceans in the Early Ming Dynasty* (2006). The most recent scholarly account of the Ming dynasty voyages.

Halil Inalcik and Donald Quataert, *An Economic and Social History of the Ottoman Empire, 1300–1914* (1994). A classic study of the Ottoman Empire.

Robin Kirkpatrick, *The European Renaissance, 1400–1600* (2002). A beautifully illustrated history of Renaissance culture as well as the social and economic life of the period.

Charles Mann, *1491: New Revelations of the Americas before Columbus* (2005). A review of Western Hemisphere societies and academic debates about their pre-Columbian history.

J. R. McNeill and William H. McNeill, *The Human Web* (2003). A succinct account of the evolving webs or relationships among human societies in world history.

Michael Smith, *The Aztecs* (2003). A history of the Aztec Empire, with an emphasis on the lives of ordinary people.

"Ming Dynasty," http://www.metmuseum.org/toah/hd/ming/hd_ming.htm. A sample of Chinese art from the Ming dynasty from the collection of the Metropolitan Museum of Art.

"Renaissance Art in Italy," http://witcombe.sbc.edu/ARTHrenaissanceitaly.html. An extensive collection of painting and sculpture from the Italian Renaissance.

Documents

Considering the Evidence:
The Aztecs and the Incas
through Spanish Eyes

During the fifteenth century, the Western Hemisphere hosted human communities of many kinds—gathering and hunting peoples, agricultural village societies, chiefdoms, and two major state-based agrarian civilizations. Most of the population of the Americas was concentrated in those two societies—the Aztec and Inca empires (see Map 13.5, p. 589). Since neither had an extensive literary tradition, historians seeking to understand their history and culture have depended heavily on the records and observations of the Spanish who conquered them in the sixteenth century. This raises obvious questions about the credibility of such accounts. Can writers from a conquering power and a completely different culture accurately describe the life and history of those they have recently defeated? At least some of those Spanish observers were able to draw on the local knowledge and experience of native peoples. What follows are accounts of the Aztec and Inca empires as seen through the eyes of two remarkable Spanish observers, both of whom at least tried to understand the people of these American civilizations.

Document 13.1

Diego Duran on the Aztecs

Coming to Mexico with his family as a young boy, Diego Duran (1537–1588) subsequently became a Dominican friar, learned to speak fluently the native Nahuatl language of the Aztecs, and began a lifelong enterprise of studying their history and culture. His research often involved extensive interviewing of local people in the rural areas where he worked and resulted in three books published between 1574 and 1581. The first excerpt records a series of laws or decrees, which Duran attributes to the Aztec ruler Moctezuma I, who governed the empire between 1440 and 1469. They reveal something of the court practices and social hierarchy of the Aztec realm as the empire was establishing itself in the middle decades of the fifteenth century. The second excerpt touches on various aspects of Aztec culture—religion, human sacrifice, social mobility, commercial markets, and slavery.

■ What do Moctezuma's laws tell us about the social and moral values of the Aztecs?

■ Based on these two excerpts, how would you describe Aztec society? What distinct social groups or classes can you identify? How were they distinguished from one another? What opportunities for social mobility were available? How might people fall into slavery?

■ What impressed Duran about the markets operating within the Aztec Empire?

■ How was human sacrifice related to war, to market activity, to slavery, and to religious belief and practice?

■ Duran's accounts of Aztec life and history were written more than fifty years after the Spanish conquest of the Aztec Empire. To what extent do you think this compromises his efforts to describe preconquest Aztec society?

KING MOCTEZUMA I
Laws, Ordinances, and Regulations
ca. 1450

The following laws were decreed:

1. The king must never appear in public except when the occasion is extremely important and unavoidable.

2. Only the king may wear a golden diadem in the city, though in war all the great lords and brave captains may wear this (but on no other occasion)....

3. Only the king and the prime minister Tlacaelel may wear sandals within the palace.... [N]oblemen are the only ones to be allowed to wear sandals in the city and no one else, also under pain of death, with the exception of men who have performed some great feat in war....

4. Only the king is to wear the final mantles of cotton brocaded with designs and threads of different colors and adorned with featherwork....

5. The great lords, who are twelve, may wear special mantles of certain make and design, and the minor lords, according to their valor and accomplishments, may wear others.

6. The common soldiers are permitted to wear only the simplest type of mantle. They are prohibited from using any special designs that might set them off from the rest....

7. The commoners will not be allowed to wear cotton clothing, under pain of death, but can use only garments of maguey fiber....

8. Only the great noblemen and valiant warriors are given license to build a house with a second story; for disobeying this law a person receives the death penalty....

9. Only the great lords are to wear labrets, ear plugs, and nose plugs of gold and precious stones, except for commoners who are strong men, brave captains, and soldiers, but their labrets, ear plugs, and nose plugs must be of bone, wood, or other inferior material of little value....

Source: Fray Diego Duran, *The History of the Indies of New Spain*, translated by Doris Heyden (Norman: University of Oklahoma Press, 1994), 208–10.

11. In the royal palace there are to be diverse rooms where different classes of people are to be received, and under pain of death no one is to enter that of the great lords or to mix with those men [unless of that class himself]....

12. An order of judges is to be established, beginning with the judges of the supreme council. After these would come regular court judges, municipal judges, district officials, constables, and councilmen, although none of them may give the death sentence without notifying the king. Only the sovereign can sentence someone to death or pardon him....

13. All the barrios will possess schools or monasteries for young men where they will learn religion and correct comportment. They are to do penance, lead hard lives, live with strict morality, practice for warfare, do physical work, fast, endure disciplinary

measures, draw blood from different parts of the body, and keep watch at night. There are to be teachers and old men to correct them and chastise them and lead them in their exercises and take care that they are not idle, do not lose their time. All of these youth must observe chastity in the strictest way, under pain of death.

14. There is to be a rigorous law regarding adulterers. They are to be stoned and thrown into the rivers or to the buzzards.

15. Thieves will be sold for the price of their theft, unless the theft be grave, having been committed many times. Such thieves will be punished by death.

16. Great privileges and exemptions are to be given those who dedicate themselves to religion, to the temples and the gods. Priests will be awarded great distinction, reverence, and authority.

DIEGO DURAN
Book of the Gods and Rites
1574–1576

I wish to tell of the way in which the natives sacrificed....

So ended the ceremony of the blessing of the pieces of dough in the form of the bones and the flesh of the god. They were revered and honored in the name of Huitzilopochtli with all the respectful veneration that we ourselves hold for the Divine Sacrament of the Altar. To exalt the occasion further, the sacrificers of men were also present....

Smeared with black, the six sacrificers appeared.... Seeing them come out with their ghastly aspect filled all the people with dread and terrible fear! The high priest carried in one hand a large stone knife, sharp and wide. Another carried a wooden yoke carved in the form of a snake. They humbled themselves before the idol and then stood

in order next to a pointed stone, which stood in front of the door of the idol's chamber....

All the prisoners of war who were to be sacrificed upon this feast were then brought forth.... They seized the victims one by one, one by one foot, another by the other, one priest by one hand, another by the other hand. The victim was thrown on his back, upon the pointed stone, where the wretch was grabbed by the fifth priest, who placed the yoke upon his throat. The high priest then opened the chest and with amazing swiftness tore out the heart, ripping it out with his own hands. Thus steaming, the heart was lifted toward the sun, and the fumes were offered up to the sun. The priest then turned toward the idol and cast the heart in its face. After the heart had been extracted, the body was allowed to roll down the steps of the pyramid....

All the prisoners and captives of war brought from the towns we have mentioned were sacrificed in this manner, until none were left. After they had been slain and cast down, their owners—those who

Source: Fray Diego Duran, *Book of the Gods and Rites and the Ancient Calendar*, translated by Fernando Horcasitas and Doris Heyden (Norman: University of Oklahoma Press, 1971), 90–92, 137–38, 273–76, 279, 281–82.

had captured them—retrieved the bodies. They were carried away, distributed, and eaten, in order to celebrate the feast. There were at least forty or fifty captives, depending upon the skill which the men had shown in seizing and capturing men in war....

[M]any strove, in every possible way, to lift their names on high, to obtain glory, to procure greater honors, to found lineages and titles, and [to gain] good fame for their persons. There were three established and honored ways in all the nations [for obtaining these rewards]. The first and principal path which the kings designated was soldiery—to make oneself known in war through valiant feats, to be outstanding in killing, taking prisoners, to destroy armies and squadrons, to have directed these things. These [warriors] were given great honors, rewards, weapons, and insignia which were proof of their splendid deeds and valor....

The second way in which men rose was through religion, entering the priesthood. After having served in the temples in a virtuous, penitential, and cloistered way of life, in their old age they were sent out to high and honorable posts.... They were present when the government councils were held, their opinions and advice were listened to, and they were part of the ruling boards and juntas. Without their council and opinion kings did not dare act....

The third and least glorious manner of [rising in the world] was that of becoming a merchant or trader, that of buying and selling, going forth to all the markets of the land, bartering cloth for jewels, jewels for feathers, feathers for stones, and stones for slaves, always dealing in things of importance, of renown, and of high value. These [men] strengthened their social position with their wealth.... They acquired wealth and obtained slaves to sacrifice to this their god [Quetzalcoatl]. And so they were considered among the magnates of the land, just as the valorious soldier brought sacrificial captives from war, gaining fame as a brave....

[I]n olden times there was a god of markets and fairs....

The gods of these market places threatened terrible ills and made evil omens and auguries to the neighboring villages which did not attend their market places....

The markets were so inviting, pleasurable, appealing, and gratifying to these people that great crowds attended, and still attend, them, especially during the big fairs, as is well known to all....

The markets in this land were all enclosed by walls and stood either in front of the temples of the gods or to one side. Market day in each town was considered a main feast in that town or city. And thus in that small shrine where the idol of the market stood were offered ears of corn, chili, tomatoes, fruit, and other vegetables, seeds, and breads—in sum, everything sold in the *tianguiz*....

Furthermore, a law was established by the republic prohibiting the selling of goods outside the market place. Not only were there laws and penalties connected with this, but there was a fear of the supernatural, of misfortune, and of the ire and wrath of the god of the market. No one ventured, therefore, to trade outside [the market limits]....

There were many ways of becoming a slave within the law of the Indian nations....

First, he who stole the number of pieces of cloth or ears of corn, jewels, or turkeys which the laws of the republic had determined and set a penalty for was himself sold for the same amount in order to satisfy the owner of the purloined goods....

Second, another way in which a native could become a slave was that of the gambler who risked all his possessions on the dice or in any other game which the natives played....

Third, if the father of a family had many sons and daughters and among them was one [who was] incorrigible, disobedient, shameless, dissolute, incapable of receiving counsel or advice, the law... permitted [the father] to sell him in the public market place as an example and lesson to bad sons and daughters....

Fourth, one became a slave if he borrowed valuable things, such as cloth, jewels, featherwork, and did not return them on the appointed date....

In times of famine a man and wife could agree to a way of satisfying their needs and rise from their wretched state. They could sell one another, and thus husband sold wife and wife sold husband, or they sold one of their children.

Document 13.2

Pedro de Cieza de Léon on the Incas

Like Duran, Pedro de Cieza de Léon (1520–1554), a Spanish chronicler of the Inca Empire, came to the Americas as a boy. But unlike Duran, he came alone at the age of thirteen, and he followed a very different career. For the next seventeen years Cieza took part as a soldier in a number of expeditions that established Spanish rule in various parts of South America. Along the way, he collected a great deal of information, especially about the Inca Empire, which he began to publish upon his return to Spain in 1550. Despite a very limited education, Cieza wrote a series of works that have become a major source for historians about the workings of the Inca Empire and about the Spanish conquest of that land. The selection that follows focuses on the techniques that the Inca used to govern their huge empire.

■ How would you describe Cieza's posture toward the Inca Empire? What in particular did he seem to appreciate about it?

■ Based on this account, what difficulties did the Inca rulers face in governing their large and diverse realm?

■ What policies or practices did the Inca authorities follow in seeking to integrate their empire? How do these compare with other empires that you have studied?

■ Some modern observers have described the Inca Empire as "totalitarian" or "socialist." Do such terms seem appropriate? How else might you describe the Inca state?

PEDRO DE CIEZA DE LÉON

Chronicles of the Incas

ca. 1550

The Incas had the seat of their empire in the city of Cuzco, where the laws were given and the captains set out to make war.... As soon as one of these large provinces was conquered, ten or twelve thousand of the men and their wives, or six thousand, or the number decided upon, were ordered to leave and remove themselves from it. These were transfered to another town or province of the same climate and nature as that which they left.... And they had another device to keep the natives from hating them, and this was that they never divested the natural chieftains of their power. If it so happened that one of them committed a crime or in some way deserved to be stripped of his power, it was vested in his sons or brothers, and all were ordered to obey them....

★ ★ ★

Source: *The Incas of Pedro de Cieza de Leon*, translated by Harriet de Onis (Norman: University of Oklahoma Press, 1959), 56–57, 158–60, 165–73, 177–78.

One of the things most to be envied these rulers is how well they knew to conquer such vast lands....

[T]hey entered many lands without war, and the soldiers who accompanied the Inca were ordered to do no damage or harm, robbery or violence. If there was a shortage of food in the province, he ordered supplies brought in from other regions so that those newly won to his service would not find his rule and acquaintance irksome....

In many others, where they entered by war and force of arms, they ordered that the crops and houses of the enemy be spared.... But in the end the Incas always came out victorious, and when they had vanquished the others, they did not do them further harm, but released those they had taken prisoner, if there were any, and restored the booty, and put them back in possession of their property and rule, exhorting them not to be foolish and try to compete with his royal majesty nor abandon his friendship, but to be his friends as their neighbors were. And saying this, he gave them a number of beautiful women and fine pieces of wool or gold....

They never deprived the native chieftains of their rule. They were all ordered to worship the sun as God, but they were not prohibited from observing their own religions and customs....

It is told for a fact of the rulers of this kingdom that in the days of their rule they had their representatives in the capitals of all the provinces.... They served as head of the provinces or regions, and from every so many leagues around the tributes were brought to one of these capitals, and from so many others, to another. This was so well organized that there was not a village that did not know where it was to send its tribute. In all these capitals the Incas had temples of the sun, mints, and many silversmiths who did nothing but work rich pieces of gold or fair vessels of silver.... The tribute paid by each of these districts where the capital was situated, and that turned over by the natives, whether gold, silver, clothing, arms, and all else they gave, was entered in the accounts of the [*quipu-*] *camayocs*, who kept the quipus and did everything ordered by the governor in the matter of finding the soldiers or supplying whomever the

Inca ordered, or making delivery to Cuzco; but when they came from the city of Cuzco to go over the accounts, or they were ordered to go to Cuzco to give an accounting, the accountants themselves gave it by the quipus, or went to give it where there could be no fraud, but everything had to come out right. Few years went by in which an accounting of all these things was not made....

When the Incas set out to visit their kingdom, it is told that they traveled with great pomp, riding in rich litters set upon smooth, long poles of the finest wood and adorned with gold and silver....

So many people came to see his passing that all the hills and slopes seemed covered with them, and all called down blessings upon him....

He [the Inca] traveled four leagues each day, or as much as he wished; he stopped wherever he liked to inquire into the state of his kingdom; he willingly listened to those who came to him with complaints, righting wrongs and punishing those who had committed an injustice....

[T]hese rulers, as the best measure, ordered and decreed, with severe punishment for failure to obey, that all the natives of their empire should know and understand the language of Cuzco, both they and their women.... This was carried out so faithfully that in the space of a very few years a single tongue was known and used in an extension of more than 1,200 leagues; yet, even though this language was employed, they all spoke their own [languages], which were so numerous that if I were to list them it would not be credited....

[The Inca] appointed those whose duty it was to punish wrongdoers, and to this end they were always traveling about the country. The Incas took such care to see that justice was meted out that nobody ventured to commit a felony or theft. This was to deal with thieves, ravishers of women, or conspirators against the Inca; however, there were many provinces that warred on one another, and the Incas were not wholly able to prevent this.

By the river [Huatanay] that runs through Cuzco justice was executed on those who were caught or brought in as prisoners from some other place.

There they had their heads cut off, or were put to death in some other manner which they chose. Mutiny and conspiracy were severely punished, and, above all, those who were thieves and known as such; even their wives and chidren were despised and considered to be tarred with the same brush....

[I]n each of the many provinces there were many storehouses filled with supplies and other needful things; thus, in times of war, wherever the armies went they draw upon the contents of these store-houses, without ever touching the supplies of their confederates or laying a finger on what they had in their settlements. And when there was no war, all this stock of supplies and food was divided up among the poor and the widows. These poor were the aged, or the lame, crippled, or paralyzed, or those afflicted with some other diseases.... If there came a lean year, the storehouses were opened and the provinces were lent what they needed in the way of supplies; then, in a year of abundance, they paid back all they had received.

Using the Evidence:
The Aztecs and the Incas
through Spanish Eyes

1. **Assessing documents:** Both Duran and Cieza were outsiders to the societies they described, and they were part of the conquering Spanish forces. In what ways did these conditions affect their descriptions of the Aztec and Inca empires?

2. **Considering the subtext of documents:** In what ways might these authors have been using their observation of Aztec or Inca society to praise or to criticize their own European homeland?

3. **Evaluating the credibility of documents:** Which statements in these documents do you find most credible and which ones might you be inclined to question or challenge? What criteria might you use to assess the evidence in these documents?

4. **Relating primary documents and text narrative:** How might you use the information in these documents to support the descriptions of the Aztec and Inca empires that are contained in this chapter? Are there ways the documents might challenge statements in the text?

5. **Making comparisons:** What similarities and differences between Aztec and Inca societies can you glean from these documents?

6. **Seeking more data:** What additional primary sources about the Aztec and Inca empires of the fifteenth century would you like to have? What other perspectives on those states would be useful for historians?

Visual Sources

Considering the Evidence:
Sacred Places in the World
of the Fifteenth Century

Virtually every human community throughout history has designated certain places and certain structures as particularly sacred or holy, even if they understand all of creation to partake in that sacredness. Such sites represent intersections between the ordinary world and the world beyond. Many such places were private—the Chinese family altars displaying ancestral tablets and the "house churches" of early Christians, for example—but the most visible and prominent were public spaces such as shrines, cathedrals, temples, and mosques.

Sometimes the holiness of such sites derived from the burial of a highly respected figure, such as the tomb of Abraham in Israel, sacred to Jews and Muslims alike, or Lenin's tomb in Moscow, virtually a shrine to faithful communists. Particular historical or religious events, such as the birth of Jesus or the enlightenment of the Buddha, have contributed to the sacred status of structures erected in those places. Formal rites of consecration, the presence of relics, and rituals of devotion such as the Muslim pilgrimage to Mecca add to the extraordinary character of particular buildings. So too did distinctive architectural styles as well as the sensory stimulus of bells, calls to prayer, and the burning of incense or candles.[20] Still other buildings acquired a sacred character because they were gathering places for prayer or worship.

Such sacred sites, however, did not function exclusively in the spiritual realm; they often operated as well in the more secular domains of commerce and politics. The New Testament records that Jesus angrily drove the money changers from the temple in Jerusalem, while Buddhist monasteries on the Silk Road and elsewhere often became wealthy centers of trade. Furthermore, sacred places played important political roles as rulers sought the blessing and support of religious leaders and the aura of legitimacy that derived from some association with the realm of the holy. State authorities and wealthy elites often patronized the construction of sacred buildings and contributed to their upkeep. Sacred sites have sometimes spawned violence as rivalries erupted among competing sects or between political and religious authorities.

The four sacred sites shown in this section might well have been on the itinerary of an imaginary global traveler in the fifteenth century. Together they illustrate something of the diversity of such places in terms of their physical setting and architectural styles, the sources of their sacredness, their intended function, and their relationship to those who exercised political power. Yet they also bore similarities to one another. All of them were deliberately set apart from the profane or ordinary world, were linked to a wider sacred geography, and were commissioned and funded by a ruler.

Perhaps not surprisingly, the largest sacred site in the world of the fifteenth century lay in China. Known as the Temple of Heaven, it was constructed during the early fifteenth century in the Ming dynasty capital of Beijing by the ambitious emperor Yongle (reigned 1402–1424), who likewise ordered the building of the magnificent imperial residence of the Forbidden City. (He also sent Zheng He on his immense maritime voyages in the Indian Ocean; see pp. 577–78.)

Set in a forest of more than 650 acres, the Temple of Heaven was, in Chinese thinking, the primary place where Heaven and earth met. From his residence in the Forbidden City, the Chinese emperor led a procession of thousands twice a year to this sacred site, where he offered sacrifices, implored the gods for a good harvest, and performed those rituals that maintained the cosmic balance. These sacred ceremonies, from which commoners were barred even from watching, demonstrated the emperor's respect for the age-old source of his imperial authority, the Mandate of Heaven, from which Chinese emperors derived their legitimate right to rule. As the emperor bowed to Heaven, he was modeling in good Confucian fashion the respect required of all subordinates to their social superiors and especially to the emperor himself.

The temple complex was laced with ancient symbolism. The southern part of the wall that enclosed the complex was square, symbolizing the earth, while the northern wall was rounded or semicircular, suggesting Heaven in Daoist thinking. Major buildings were likewise built in the round while being situated within a square enclosure, also symbolizing the intersection of Heaven and earth. The most prominent building was the Hall of Prayer for Good Harvest (Visual Source 13.1), constructed by 1420. There the emperor prayed and conducted rituals to ensure a successful agricultural season on which the country's well-being and his own legitimacy depended. The emperor and others approached the hall from the south on a gradually ascending 360-meter walkway symbolizing progression from earth to Heaven. The walkway divides into three parallel paths: the center one for the gods; the left for the emperor; and the right for the empress and court officials. Originally the three roofs of the structure were of different colors: the top was blue, suggesting Heaven; the middle was yellow, the color of the emperor; and the lowest was green, indicating commoners or the earth. Later all three roofs were painted blue.

Visual Source 13.1 The Hall of Prayer for Good Harvest at the Temple of Heaven, Beijing, China (AP Images)

- Which symbolic features can you identify in Visual Source 13.1?

- What did the original color scheme of the roofs suggest?

- What was the role of the emperor within the Temple of Heaven and in the larger religious or cosmological framework of Chinese thinking?

- What impressions or understandings might those who observed the ceremonies or learned about them take away from that experience?

About the same time as the Temple of Heaven was taking shape in China, another sacred site was under construction in Kyoto, Japan: a Buddhist temple known as Kinkakuji, or the "Temple of the Golden Pavilion" (Visual Source 13.2). Like the Chinese structure, Kinkakuji was a project of the Japanese ruler of the time, the *shogun* (military leader) Yoshimitsu Ashikaga (1358–1408), rather than the emperor. Unlike his Chinese counterpart, the Japanese emperor functioned more as a symbol of Japan's historical tradition rather than its effective ruler. Initially, Kinkakuji was constructed as part of a villa to which Yoshimitsu retired when he gave up his formal political role in 1394 to devote himself to Buddhist practice and the arts. After his death it was converted into a Zen Buddhist temple, as he had wished.

The building itself reflects the strong influence of Chinese culture on Japan. Yoshimitsu, well known as a lover of all things Chinese, modeled Kinkakuji on the lakeside villas of earlier Chinese emperors and collected in the Golden Pavilion thousands of Chinese paintings. He also accepted the title "King of Japan" from a Ming dynasty emperor and reopened trade relations with China.

As a Buddhist temple, Kinkakuji is situated in a garden setting at the edge of a "mirror lake," suggesting, some have said, a position between heaven and earth. The lake contained a series of rocks and small islands representing the eight oceans and nine mountains of the Buddhist creation story. Inside were statues of the Amida Buddha, the benevolent bodhisattva of compassion known as Kannon, and dozens of other sacred figures. It also became known as one of the few Buddhist temples housing relics of the historical Buddha himself.

While Buddhism has a reputation as a religion of peace and tranquillity, in Japan from the tenth century on, various Buddhist sects organized private armies, fought among themselves, and contested both imperial and samurai authorities. Kinkakuji itself was burned several times in the fifteenth century amid the wars that racked Japan and left Kyoto in ruins.

- How might you compare the purposes that Kinkakuji served with those of the Temple of Heaven?

Visual Source 13.2 Kinkakuji: A Buddhist Temple in Japan (© Craig Lovell/Corbis)

■ What elements of Kinkakuji and its surroundings contribute to its sacredness?

■ What emotions do you think Kinkakuji was intended to evoke?

■ In what ways did Kinkakuji have a political as well as a religious significance?

In the Islamic world of the fifteenth century, the structure known as the Dome of the Rock in Jerusalem (Visual Source 13.3) was second only to Mecca as a pilgrimage site for Muslims. When expanding Muslim forces took control of Jerusalem in 638 and subsequently constructed the Dome of the Rock (687–691), that precise location had long been regarded as sacred. To Jews, it contained the rock on which Abraham prepared to offer his son Isaac as a sacrifice to God, and it was the site of the first two Jewish temples. To Christians, it was a place that Jesus had visited as a youngster to converse with learned teachers and later to drive out the moneychangers.

Thus, when the Umayyad caliph (successor to the prophet) Abd al-Malik ordered the construction of the Dome of the Rock on that site, he was appropriating for Islam both Jewish and Christian legacies. But he was also demonstrating the victorious arrival of a new faith and announcing to Christians that "the Islamic state was here to stay."[21] The architecture and decoration of the Dome of the Rock drew heavily on Roman, Byzantine, and Persian precedents as if to show that "'unbelievers' had been defeated and brought into the fold of the true faith."[22] The domed rotunda had long been used in the Christian Byzantine Empire to denote holy sites, often the burial place of a martyr, saint, or prophet. The Muslim structure, designed and built by Christian architects and artisans, closely resembled the nearby Church of the Holy Sepulcher. Interior decorations featured crowns, jewels, breastplates, and flowers of Persian origins.

Nonetheless, the Dome of the Rock was distinctly Islamic, as its many mosaics lacked any representations of animals or humans, while multiple inscriptions from the Quran emphasized Islamic monotheism, presenting Jesus as an honored prophet but not as the divine son of God. Furthermore, the Dome of the Rock was soon thought to cover the stone from which Muhammad had made his famous Night Journey into the presence of God as suggested

Visual Source 13.3 The Dome of the Rock, Jerusalem (© Aaron Horowitz/Corbis)

in the Quran and embellished in popular mythology. Some claimed to see an indentation in that stone, which lies uncovered in the center of the dome, as the footprint of the prophet himself.

Over many centuries, and even to the present, the Dome of the Rock has been an enormously contested site. When Christian crusaders seized Jerusalem in 1099, they did not destroy the Muslim shrine but converted it into a Christian sacred place—the Temple of the Lord—and erected a huge golden cross on its dome. Likewise, when Muslim forces retook Jerusalem in 1187, they removed that cross, replaced it with a Muslim crescent, and then cleansed the Dome of the Rock three times with rose water. In the fifteenth century, the Dome was under the control and protection of a Turkic dynasty, known as Mamluks, based in Egypt. In 1517 it fell within the domains of the Ottoman Empire.

- The Dome of the Rock was never intended as a mosque for regular worship but rather as a pilgrimage site. How might you imagine the reaction of a Muslim pilgrim encountering it for the first time during the fifteenth century? How would that pilgrim's place of origin (Arabia, Africa, India, or Europe, for example) have made a difference in how he or she responded to it?

- What contributed to the sacred character of the Dome of the Rock?

- How might you compare the intended purpose of the Dome of the Rock to that of the Temple of Heaven in China?

- You might do a little research on the current disputes about the Dome of the Rock. What role does it play in the contemporary Israeli/Palestinian conflict?

In seeking sacred sites within the Christian world of the fifteenth century, our imaginary global traveler would have had a wide range of choices. He or she might well have visited one of the many Renaissance cathedrals of Italy or chosen from among the dozens of impressive Christian churches scattered across Europe. The newly reconstructed Kremlin in Moscow might also have been of interest, for in that fortified enclosure lay an elaborate palace for Grand Prince Ivan III as well as a number of churches, demonstrating the close relationship of religious and political authority in the emerging Russian state. But in the highlands of Ethiopia, amid some of the most remarkable Christian architecture of the time, the rock churches of Lalibela provide a useful reminder that the Christian world of the fifteenth century was not limited to Europe.

With its origins in the ancient civilization of Axum well before the birth of Christ, Ethiopia by the fifteenth century had hosted a Christian culture for more than a thousand years. By then, the center of that civilization had moved southward to the region later known as Lalibela. There, in the twelfth

Visual Source 13.4 The Church of St. George, Lalibela, Ethiopia (Heltler/Robert Harding World Imagery/Corbis)

century, a local prince had seized the throne and initiated the Zagwe dynasty. Zagwe rulers, in particular King Lalibela (ruled early thirteenth century), for whom the region was subsequently named, sponsored the creation of eleven remarkable underground churches, carved from the soft volcanic rock of the region. This enormous and sacred project served to legitimate the rule of these upstart Zagwe monarchs over this ancient Christian kingdom and provided an alternative to the older political and religious center of Ethiopian civilization in Axum to the north.

A further motivation for the construction of these churches lay perhaps in Ethiopia's long relationship with Jerusalem. Ancient stories linked its monarchy to the union of King Solomon and the Queen of Sheba, said to be an Ethiopian monarch. Local legends held that King Lalibela had been mysteriously transported to Jerusalem, where he received divine instructions about building the churches. Certainly, Ethiopian Christians had long made pilgrimages to the Holy City. When Muslim forces reconquered Jerusalem from the Christian crusaders in 1187, Ethiopia's Zagwe monarchs apparently determined to create a New Jerusalem in their kingdom. The churches of Lalibela, many of them named for famous sites in Jerusalem, were the outcome of that project.

Thus, while the Dome of the Rock physically occupied an already sacred site in Jerusalem, the rock churches of Lalibela sought to symbolically re-create the Holy City in the highlands of Ethiopia. They have been both a monastic site and a pilgrimage destination ever since.

These belowground churches represent an enormously impressive architectural achievement, said by local people to have been assisted by angels. But well before the coming of Christianity, the local Agaw-speaking people had long incorporated rock shrines into their religious practice. And the architecture of the churches shows a clear connection to earlier Axumite styles.

While this sacred site clearly had indigenous roots, these churches were certainly distinctive as Christian structures. Unlike almost all other religious architecture—Christian or otherwise—they were virtually invisible from a distance, becoming apparent only when the observer was looking down on them from ground level. In fact these eleven churches were not really constructed at all, but rather excavated, using only hammers and chisels. Underground, they were connected to one another by a series of "hidden tunnels, dark twisting passages, and secret chambers," while the whole complex abounded with "columns and arches, shafts and galleries, courts and terraces."[23] The first European observer to see them, the Portuguese priest Francisco Alvarez in the 1520s, was stunned. "I weary of writing more about these buildings," he declared, "because it seems to me that I shall not be believed if I write more."[24] Visual Source 13.4 shows one of these structures, the Church of St. George, the patron saint of Ethiopia.

- How might our imaginary traveler, a pilgrim who had toured the grand Christian cathedrals of Europe, have responded to these Ethiopian churches? How might he or she understand their belowground construction? What might strike such a traveler as distinctive about Lalibela as a sacred site in comparison to the others presented here?

- What do these churches disclose about the outlook of the Zagwe monarchs who ordered their creation?

- What might you infer about the labor and social organization required to create these churches?

Using the Evidence:
Sacred Places in the World of the Fifteenth Century

1. **Comparing experiences of the sacred:** What do these visual sources and the documents for this chapter (see pp. 601–07) suggest about the experience of the sacred? What common features and what differences

characterize that experience? In particular, how might our global traveler have responded to sacred places among the Aztecs after visiting the various sites shown here?

2. **Considering the construction of the sacred:** What historical circumstances and what motivations contributed to the creation of each site? What factors rendered them holy in the eyes of believers? What evidence of cultural borrowing can you see in these sites?

3. **Defining purpose:** How would you compare the purposes for which each of these sacred places was intended?

4. **Thinking about religion and politics:** In what ways were these sacred sites embedded in the political circumstances of their societies? How might people of the fifteenth century have understood the connection between the religious and the political as evidenced in these images? To what extent did those understandings differ from more modern views?

PART FOUR
The Early Modern World
1450–1750

Contents

Chapter 14. Empires and Encounters, 1450–1750
Chapter 15. Global Commerce, 1450–1750
Chapter 16. Religion and Science, 1450–1750

Debating the Character of an Era

For the sake of clarity and coherence, historians often characterize a particular period of time in a brief phrase—the age of First Civilizations, the classical era, the age of empires, the era of revolutions, and so on. Though useful and even necessary, such capsule descriptions leave a lot out and vastly oversimplify what actually happened. Historical reality is always more messy, more complicated, and more uncertain than any shorthand label can convey. Such is surely the case when we examine the three centuries spanning the years from roughly 1450 to 1750.

An Early Modern Era?

Those three centuries, which are addressed in Chapters 14 through 16, are conventionally labeled as "the early modern era." In using this term, historians are suggesting that during these three centuries we can find signs or markers of the modern era, such as those described at the end of Chapter 13: the beginnings of genuine globalization, elements of distinctly modern societies, and a growing European presence in world affairs.

The most obvious expression of globalization, of course, lay in the oceanic journeys of European explorers and the European conquest and colonial settlement of the Americas. The Atlantic slave trade linked Africa permanently to the Western Hemisphere, while the global silver trade allowed Europeans to use New World precious metals to buy their way into ancient Asian trade routes. The massive transfer of plants, animals, diseases, and people, known to scholars as the Columbian exchange, created wholly new networks of interaction across both the Atlantic and Pacific oceans, with enormous global implications. Missionaries carried Christianity far beyond Europe, allowing it to become a genuinely world religion, with a presence in the Americas, China, Japan, the Philippines, and south-central Africa. Other threads in the emerging global web were also woven as Russians marched across Siberia to the Pacific, as China expanded deep into Inner Asia, and as the Ottoman Empire encompassed much of the Middle East, North Africa, and southeastern Europe (see Chapter 14).

Scattered signs of what later generations thought of as "modernity" appeared in various places around the world. China, Japan, India, and Europe experienced the beginnings of modern population growth as the foods of the Americas—corn and potatoes, for example—provided nutrition to support larger numbers. World population more than doubled between 1400 and 1800 (from about 374 million to 968 million), even as the globalization of disease produced a demographic catastrophe in the

Americas and the slave trade limited African population growth. More highly commercialized economies centered in large cities developed in various parts of Eurasia and the Americas. By the early eighteenth century, for example, Japan was one of the most urbanized societies in the world, with Edo (Tokyo) housing more than a million inhabitants and ranking as the world's largest city. In China, Southeast Asia, India, and across the Atlantic basin, more and more people found themselves, sometimes willingly and at other times involuntarily, producing for distant markets rather than for the use of their local communities.

Stronger and more cohesive states also emerged in various places, incorporating many local societies into larger units that were both able and willing to actively promote trade, manufacturing, and a common culture within their borders. France, the Dutch Republic, Russia, Morocco, the Mughal Empire, Vietnam, Burma, Siam, and Japan all represent this kind of state.[1] Their military power likewise soared as the "gunpowder revolution" kicked in around the world. Large-scale empires proliferated, and various European powers carved out new domains in the Americas. The most obviously modern cultural development took place in Europe, where the Scientific Revolution transformed, at least for members of a small educated elite, their view of the world, their approach to knowledge, and their understanding of traditional Christianity.

A Late Agrarian Era?

All of these developments give some validity to the notion of an early modern era. But this is far from the whole story, and it may be misleading if it suggests that European world domination and more fully modern societies were a sure thing, an inevitable outgrowth of early modern developments. In fact, that future was far from clear in 1750.

Although Europeans ruled the Americas and controlled the world's sea routes, their political and military power in mainland Asia and Africa was very limited. Eighteenth-century China and Japan strictly controlled the European missionaries and merchants who operated in their societies, and African authorities frequently set the terms under which the slave trade was conducted. Islam, not Christianity, was the most rapidly spreading faith in much of Asia and Africa, and in 1750 Europe, India, and China were roughly comparable in their manufacturing output. In short, it was not obvious that Europeans would soon dominate the planet. Moreover, populations and economies had surged at various points in the past, only to fall back again in a cyclical pattern. Nothing guaranteed that the early modern surge would be any more lasting than the others.

Nor was there much to suggest that anything approaching modern industrial society was on the horizon. Animal and human muscles, wind, and water still provided almost all of the energy that powered human economies. Handicraft techniques of manufacturing had nowhere been displaced by factory-based production or steam power. Long-established elites, not middle-class upstarts, everywhere provided leadership and enjoyed the greatest privileges, while rural peasants, not urban workers, represented the primary social group in the lower classes. Kings and nobles, not parliaments and parties, governed. Male dominance was assumed to be natural almost everywhere. Modern society, with its promise of liberation from ancient inequalities and the end of poverty for most, hardly seemed around the corner.

Most of the world's peoples, in fact, continued to live in long-established ways, and their societies operated according to traditional principles. Kings ruled most of Europe, and landowning aristocrats remained at the top of the social hierarchy. Another change in ruling dynasties occurred in China, while that huge country affirmed Confucian values and a social structure that privileged landowning and officeholding elites. Most Indians practiced some form of Hinduism and owed their most fundamental loyalty to local castes, even as South Asia continued its centuries-long incorporation into the Islamic world. The realm of Islam maintained its central role in the Eastern Hemisphere as the Ottoman Empire revived the political fortunes of Islam and the religion sustained its long-term expansion into Africa and Southeast Asia.

In short, for the majority of humankind, the three centuries between 1450 and 1750 marked less an entry into the modern era than the continuing development of older agrarian societies. It was as much a late agrarian era as an early modern age. Persistent patterns rooted in the past characterized that period, along with new departures and sprouts of modernity. Nor was change always in the direction of what we now regard as "modern." In European, Islamic, and Chinese societies alike, some people urged a return to earlier ways of living and thinking rather than embracing what was new and untried. Although Europeans were increasingly prominent on the world stage, they certainly did not hold all of the leading roles in the global drama of these three centuries.

From this mixture of what was new and what was old during the early modern era, the three chapters that follow highlight the changes. Chapter 14 turns the spotlight on the new empires of those three centuries—European, Middle Eastern, and Asian. New global patterns of long-distance trade in spices, sugar, silver, fur, and slaves represent the themes of Chapter 15. New cultural trends—both within the major religious traditions of the world and in the emergence of modern science—come together in Chapter 16. With the benefit of hindsight, we may see many of these developments as harbingers of a modern world to come, but from the viewpoint of 1700 or so, the future was open and uncertain, as it almost always is.

Landmarks in the Early Modern Era, 1450–1750

1400	1450	1500	1550

Europe

1492 Columbus's first voyage to the Americas

1543 Copernicus publishes heliocentric view of the universe

1400–1600 Renaissance

1400s Portuguese maritime voyages

1517 Beginnings of Protestant Reformation

Africa

1441 Beginnings of Atlantic slave trade

1464–1591 Songhay Empire (West Africa)

1505 Portuguese attacks on Swahili cities

1516 Benin begins to restrict slave trade

1506–1542 Reign of King Afonso (Kongo)

1500–1530 Christian-Muslim conflict in Ethiopia

The Americas

1494 Treaty of Tordesillas divides New World between Spain and Portugal

1541 Discovery of silver near Potosí

1530s First Portuguese plantations in Brazil

1532–1540 Spanish conquest of Inca Empire

1519–1521 Spanish conquest of Aztec Empire

Islamic World

1453 Ottoman conquest of Constantinople

1501–1722 Safavid Empire in Persia

1534–1639 Conflict between Ottoman and Safavid empires

1526–1707 Flourishing of Mughal Empire

1556–1605 Reign of Mughal emperor Akbar

1520–1566 Reign of Ottoman emperor Suleiman

1529 Ottoman siege of Vienna

Asia

1433 Withdrawal of Chinese fleet from Indian Ocean

1498 Vasco da Gama arrives in India

1550 Russian expansion across Siberia begins

1582 Jesuit missionary Matteo Ricci arrives in China

1565 Spanish takeover of Philippines begins

1600	1650	1700	1750

1642–1727 Life of Isaac Newton

1700s European Enlightenment

1618–1648
Thirty Years' War

1682–1725 Peter the Great begins
Westernization of Russia

1620s
Establishment
of kingdom of
Dahomey

1670–1820s Wars of Islamic renewal in West Africa

1652
Establishment of
Dutch settlement
in South Africa

1700s Atlantic slave trade peaks

1607 Jamestown,
VA, established as
first permanent
English settlement in
North America

1690 High point of
Palmares, Brazil's largest
runaway slave community

1775–1783
American
Revolution

1608 French
colony in Quebec
established

1700s High point of plantation system and slave trade

1742 Ottoman printing
press closed as impious

1683
Second Ottoman siege of Vienna

1631–1648
Taj Mahal constructed

1707–1800 Fragmentation of Mughal empire

1600–1602 British and Dutch East India
companies begin operations in Asia

early 1600s
European missionaries expelled from Japan

1750–1760 Chinese
territorial expansion
in Inner Asia

1603 Tokugawa shogunate
established in Japan

1644 Ming/Qing transition in China

CHAPTER FOURTEEN

Empires and Encounters

1450-1750

European Empires in the Americas
  The European Advantage
  The Great Dying
  The Columbian Exchange
Comparing Colonial Societies in
  the Americas
  In the Lands of the Aztecs and
    the Incas
  Colonies of Sugar
  Settler Colonies in North America
The Steppes and Siberia:
  The Making of a Russian Empire
  Experiencing the Russian Empire
  Russians and Empire
Asian Empires
  Making China an Empire
  Muslims and Hindus in the
    Mughal Empire
  Muslims, Christians, and the
    Ottoman Empire
Reflections: Countering
  Eurocentrism . . . or Reflecting It?
Considering the Evidence
  Documents: State Building in the
    Early Modern Era
  Visual Sources: The Conquest
    of Mexico Through Aztec Eyes

"We will not yield to the Chinese authorities, no matter what brutal means they will take against us. We are preparing our fight."[1] So stated Muhammet Tursun, a forty-year-old Uighur businessman from the far western province of China known as Xinjiang, in 1999. A Central Asian Muslim Turkic-speaking people, the Uighurs had been brought under Chinese control in the early eighteenth century as part of a huge expansion of China's imperial state. Now in the late twentieth and early twenty-first centuries, some Uighurs were seeking independence from what they regarded as centuries of Chinese colonial rule. Clashes in mid-2009 between Uighurs and immigrant Han Chinese left scores of people dead.

Nor was this the only echo of early modern empire building to find expression in recent times. The breakup of the Soviet Union in 1991 represented the partial end of the Russian Empire, which was initially constructed in the sixteenth and seventeenth centuries. In 1992, many Native Americans strenuously objected to any celebration of the 500th anniversary of Columbus's arrival in the Americas. Winona LaDuke, president of the Indigenous Women's Network, declared: "Columbus was a perpetrator of genocide . . . , a slave trader, a thief, a pirate, and most certainly not a hero. To celebrate Columbus is to congratulate the process and history of the invasion."[2]

IN CHINA, RUSSIA, AND THE UNITED STATES ALIKE, the legacy of early modern empire building continued to provoke both debate and action as a new millennium dawned. Of those empires, none

---

The Mughal Empire: Among the most magnificent of the early modern empires was that of the Mughals in India. In this painting by an unknown Mughal artist, the seventeenth-century emperor Shah Jahan is holding a *durbar*, or ceremonial assembly, in the audience hall of his palace. The overall material splendor of the setting shows the immense wealth of the court, while the halo around Shah Jahan's head indicates the special spiritual grace or enlightenment associated with emperors. (© British Library Board, Add or 385)

were more significant than the European colonies—Spanish, Portuguese, British, French, and Dutch—constructed all across the Western Hemisphere. Within those empires, vast transformations took place, old societies were destroyed, and new societies arose as Native Americans, Europeans, and Africans came into sustained contact with one another for the first time in world history. It was a revolutionary encounter with implications that extended far beyond the Americas themselves.

But European empires in the Americas were not alone on the imperial stage of the early modern era. Across the immense expanse of Siberia, the Russians constructed what was then the world's largest territorial empire, making Russia an Asian as well as a European power. Qing dynasty China penetrated deep into Inner Asia, doubling the size of the country while incorporating millions of non-Chinese people who practiced Islam, Buddhism, or animistic religions. On the South Asian peninsula, the Islamic Mughal Empire brought Hindus and Muslims into a closer relationship than ever before, sometimes quite peacefully and at other times with great conflict. In the Middle East, the Turkish Ottoman Empire reestablished something of the earlier political unity of heartland Islam and posed an ominous military and religious threat to European Christendom.

Thus the early modern era was an age of empire. Within their borders, those empires mixed and mingled diverse peoples in a wide variety of ways. Those relationships represented a new stage in the globalization process and new arenas of cross-cultural encounter. The transformations they set in motion echo still in the twenty-first century.

European Empires in the Americas

Among the early modern empires, those of Western Europe were distinctive because the conquered territories lay an ocean away from the imperial heartland, rather than adjacent to it. Following the breakthrough voyages of Columbus, the Spanish focused their empire-building efforts in the Caribbean and then in the early sixteenth century turned to the mainland, with stunning conquests of the powerful Aztec and Inca empires. Meanwhile the Portuguese established themselves along the coast of present-day Brazil. In the early seventeenth century, the British, French, and Dutch launched colonial settlements along the eastern coast of North America. From these beginnings, Europeans extended their empires to encompass most of the Americas, at least nominally, by the mid-eighteenth century (see Map 14.1). It was a remarkable achievement. What had made it possible?

The European Advantage

■ Connection
What enabled Europeans to carve out huge empires an ocean away from their homelands?

Geography provides a starting point for explaining Europe's American empires. It was countries on the Atlantic rim of Europe (Portugal, Spain, Britain, and France) that led the way to empire in the Western Hemisphere. They were simply closer to the Americas than was any possible Asian competitor. Furthermore, the fixed winds

Map 14.1 European Colonial Empires in the Americas

By the beginning of the eighteenth century, European powers had laid claim to most of the Western Hemisphere. Their wars and rivalries during that century led to an expansion of Spanish and English claims, at the expense of the French.

of the Atlantic blew steadily in the same direction. Once these air currents were understood and mastered, they provided a far different environment than the alternating monsoon winds of the Indian Ocean, in which Asian maritime powers had long operated. The enormously rich markets of the Indian Ocean world provided little incentive for its Chinese, Indian, or Muslim participants to venture much beyond their own waters.

Europeans, however, were powerfully motivated to do so. After 1200 or so, Europeans were increasingly aware of their marginal position in the world of Eurasian commerce and were determined to gain access to that world. Rulers were driven by the enduring rivalries of competing states. The growing and relatively independent merchant class in a rapidly commercializing Europe sought direct access to Asian wealth in order to avoid the reliance on Muslim intermediaries that they found so distasteful. Impoverished nobles and commoners alike found opportunity for gaining wealth and status in the colonies. Missionaries and others were inspired by crusading zeal to enlarge the realm of Christendom. Persecuted minorities were in search of a new start in life. All of these compelling motives drove the relentlessly expanding imperial frontier in the Americas. They were aptly summarized by one Spanish conquistador: "We came here to serve God and the King, and also to get rich."[3]

In carving out these empires, often against great odds and with great difficulty, Europeans nonetheless bore certain advantages, despite their distance from home. Their states and trading companies enabled the effective mobilization of both human and material resources. (See Documents 14.4 and 14.5, pp. 659–62, for French state-building efforts.) Their seafaring technology, built on Chinese and Islamic precedents, allowed them to cross the Atlantic with growing ease, transporting people and supplies across great distances. Their ironworking technology, gunpowder weapons, and horses initially had no parallel in the Americas, although many peoples subsequently acquired them.

Divisions within and between local societies provided allies for the determined European invaders. Various subject peoples of the Aztec Empire, for example, resented Mexican domination and willingly joined Hernán Cortés in the Spanish assault on that empire (see Visual Sources: The Conquest of Mexico Through Aztec Eyes, pp. 664–71). Much of the Inca elite, according to a recent study, "actually welcomed the Spanish invaders as liberators and willingly settled down with them to share rule of Andean farmers and miners."[4] A violent dispute between two rival contenders for the Inca throne, the brothers Atahualpa and Huáscar, certainly helped the European invaders. Perhaps the most significant of European advantages lay in their germs and diseases, to which Native Americans had no immunities. Those diseases decimated society after society, sometimes in advance of the Europeans' actual arrival. In particular regions such as the Caribbean, Virginia, and New England, the rapid buildup of immigrant populations, coupled with the sharply diminished native numbers, allowed Europeans to actually outnumber local peoples within a few decades.

The Great Dying

Whatever combination of factors explains the European acquisition of their empires in the Americas, there is no doubting their global significance. Chief among those consequences was the demographic collapse of Native American societies, a phenomenon that one prominent scholar described as "surely the greatest tragedy in the history of the human species."[5] Although precise figures remain the subject of much debate, scholars generally agree that the pre-Columbian population of the Western Hemisphere was substantial, on the order of that of Europe, perhaps 60 to 80 million. The greatest concentrations of people lived in the Mesoamerican and Andean zones, which were dominated by the Aztec and Inca empires. Long isolation from the Afro-Eurasian world and the lack of most domesticated animals meant the absence of acquired immunities to Old World diseases, such as smallpox, measles, typhus, influenza, malaria, and yellow fever.

> ■ **Change**
> What large-scale transformations did European empires generate?

Therefore, when they came into contact with these European and African diseases, Native American peoples died in appalling numbers, in many cases up to 90 percent of the population. The densely settled peoples of Caribbean islands virtually vanished within fifty years of Columbus's arrival. Central Mexico, with a population estimated at some 10 to 20 million, declined to about 1 million by 1650. A native Nahuatl account depicted the social breakdown that accompanied the smallpox pandemic: "A great many died from this plague, and many others died of hunger. They could not get up to search for food, and everyone else was too sick to care for them, so they starved to death in their beds"[6] (see Visual Source 14.5, p. 670).

The situation was similar in North America. A Dutch observer in New Netherland (later New York) reported in 1656 that "the Indians ... affirm that before the arrival of the Christians, and before the small pox broke out amongst them, they were ten times as numerous as they are now, and that their population had been melted down by this disease, whereof nine-tenths of them have died."[7] To Governor Bradford of Plymouth colony (in present-day Massachusetts), such conditions represented the "good hand of God" at work, "sweeping away great multitudes of the natives ... that he might make room for us."[8] Not until the late seventeenth century did native numbers begin to recuperate somewhat from this catastrophe, and even then not everywhere.

The Columbian Exchange

In sharply diminishing the population of the Americas, the "great dying" created an acute labor shortage and certainly did make room for immigrant newcomers, both colonizing Europeans and enslaved Africans. Over the several centuries of the colonial era and beyond, various combinations of indigenous, European, and African peoples created entirely new societies in the Americas, largely replacing the many and varied cultures that had flourished before 1492. To those colonial societies,

Europeans and Africans brought not only their germs and their people but also their plants and animals. Wheat, rice, sugarcane, grapes, and many garden vegetables and fruits, as well as numerous weeds, took hold in the Americas, where they transformed the landscape and made possible a recognizably European diet and way of life. Even more revolutionary were their animals—horses, pigs, cattle, goats, sheep—all of which were new to the Americas and multiplied spectacularly in an environment largely free of natural predators. These domesticated animals made possible the ranching economies, the cowboy cultures, and the transformation of many Native American societies that were seen in both North and South America. Environmentally speaking, it was nothing less than revolutionary.

In the other direction, American food crops such as corn, potatoes, and cassava spread widely in the Eastern Hemisphere, where they provided the nutritional foundation for the immense population growth that became everywhere a hallmark of the modern era. In Europe, calories derived from corn and potatoes helped push human numbers from some 60 million in 1400 to 390 million in 1900. Those Amerindian crops later provided cheap and reasonably nutritious food for millions of industrial workers. Potatoes especially allowed Ireland's population to grow enormously and then condemned many of them to starvation or emigration when an airborne fungus, also from the Americas, destroyed the crop in the mid-nineteenth century. In China, corn, peanuts, and especially sweet potatoes supplemented the traditional rice and wheat to sustain China's modern population explosion. By the early twentieth century, American food plants represented about 20 percent of total Chinese food production. In Africa, corn took hold quickly and was used as a cheap food for the human cargoes of the transatlantic trade. Scholars have speculated that corn, together with peanuts and cassava, underwrote some of Africa's population growth and partially offset the population drain of the slave trade. Never

Plants and Animals of the Columbian Exchange
This eighteenth-century Peruvian painting illustrates two of the many biological species that crossed the Atlantic. Cattle from Europe flourished in the Americas, while cassava (also known as manioc), shown in the bottom of the picture, was native to South America but spread widely in Asia, and especially in Africa, where its edible root provided a major source of carbohydrates. (Martinez Campañon, Trujillo del Peru, v. II, courtesy of the Biblioteca del Palacio Real/Oronoz Archives)

before in human history had such a large-scale and consequential exchange of plants and animals operated to remake the biological environment of the planet.

Furthermore, the societies that developed within the American colonies drove the processes of globalization and reshaped the world economy of the early modern era (see Chapter 15 for a more extended treatment). The silver mines of Mexico and Peru fueled both transatlantic and transpacific commerce, encouraged Spain's unsuccessful effort to dominate Europe, and enabled Europeans to buy the Chinese tea, silk, and porcelain that they valued so highly. The plantation owners of the tropical lowland regions needed workers and found them by the millions in Africa. The slave trade, which brought these workers to the colonies, and the sugar and cotton trade, which distributed the fruits of their labor abroad, created a lasting link among Africa, Europe, and the Americas, while scattering peoples of African origin throughout the Western Hemisphere.

This enormous network of communication, migration, trade, the spread of disease, and the transfer of plants and animals, all generated by European colonial empires in the Americas, has been dubbed the "Columbian exchange." It gave rise to something wholly new in world history: an interacting Atlantic world connecting four continents. Millions of years ago, the Eastern and Western hemispheres had physically drifted apart, and, ecologically speaking, they had remained largely apart. Now these two "old worlds" were joined, increasingly creating a single biological regime, a "new world" of global dimensions.

The long-term benefits of this Atlantic network were very unequally distributed. Western Europeans were clearly the dominant players in the Atlantic world, and their societies reaped the greatest rewards. Mountains of new information flooded into Europe, shaking up conventional understandings of the world and contributing to a revolutionary new way of thinking known as the Scientific Revolution. The wealth of the colonies—precious metals, natural resources, new food crops, slave labor, financial profits, colonial markets—provided one of the foundations on which Europe's Industrial Revolution was built. The colonies also provided an outlet for the rapidly growing population of European societies and represented an enormous extension of European civilization. In short, the colonial empires of the Americas greatly facilitated a changing global balance of power, which now thrust the previously marginal Western Europeans into an increasingly central and commanding role on the world stage. "[W]ithout a New World to deliver economic balance in the Old," concluded a prominent world historian, "Europe would have remained inferior, as ever, in wealth and power, to the great civilizations of Asia."[9]

Comparing Colonial Societies in the Americas

What the Europeans had discovered across the Atlantic was a second "old world," but their actions surely gave rise to a "new world" in the Americas. Their colonial empires did not simply conquer and govern established societies, but rather generated wholly new societies. In at least one respect, these various colonial empires—Spanish, Portuguese, British, and French—had something in common. Each of them was viewed through the lens of the prevailing economic theory known as mercantilism. This view held that European governments served their countries' economic interests best by encouraging exports and accumulating bullion (precious metals such as silver and gold), which were believed to be the source of national prosperity. Colonies, in this scheme of things, provided closed markets for the manufactured goods of the "mother country" and, if they were lucky, supplied great quantities of bullion as well. Mercantilist thinking thus fueled European wars and colonial rivalries around the world in the early modern era.

Beyond this shared mercantilism, though, the various colonial societies that grew up in the Americas differed sharply from one another, varying with the cultures and policies of the colonizing power. The character of the Native American cultures— the more densely populated and urbanized Mesoamerican and Andean civilizations versus the more sparsely populated rural villages of North America, for example— also shaped the new colonial societies. The kind of economy established in particular regions—settler-dominated agriculture, slave-based plantations, ranching, or mining—likewise influenced their development. Three examples indicate the differences among these new colonial societies.

In the Lands of the Aztecs and the Incas

■ **Change**
What was the economic foundation of colonial rule in Mexico and Peru? How did it shape the kinds of societies that arose there?

The Spanish conquest of the Aztec and Inca empires in the early sixteenth century gave Spain access to the most wealthy, urbanized, and densely populated regions of the Western Hemisphere. Within a century and well before the British had even begun their colonizing efforts in North America, the Spanish in Mexico and Peru had established nearly a dozen major cities; several impressive universities; hundreds of cathedrals, churches, and missions; an elaborate administrative bureaucracy; and a network of regulated international commerce. The economic foundation for this emerging colonial society lay in commercial agriculture, much of it on large rural estates, and in silver and gold mining. In both cases, native peoples, rather than African slaves or European workers, provided the labor, despite their much-diminished numbers. Almost everywhere it was forced labor, often directly required by colonial authorities. The loss of land to European settlers represented another incentive for wage labor, as did the growing need to repay debts to employers.

On this economic base, a distinctive social order grew up, replicating something of the Spanish class hierarchy while accommodating the racially and culturally different Indians and Africans as well as growing numbers of racially mixed people. At the top of this colonial society were the Spanish settlers, who were politically and economically dominant and seeking to become a landed aristocracy. One Spanish official commented in 1619: "The Spaniards, from the able and rich to the humble and poor, all hold themselves to be lords and will not serve [do manual labor]."[10] Politically, they increasingly saw themselves, not as colonials, but as residents of a Spanish kingdom, subject to the Spanish monarch, yet separate and distinct from Spain itself and deserving of a large measure of self-government. Therefore, they chafed under the heavy bureaucratic restrictions imposed by the Crown. "I obey but I do not enforce" was a slogan that reflected local authorities' resistance to orders from Spain.

But the Spanish minority, never more than 20 percent of the population, was itself a divided community. Descendants of the original conquistadores sought to protect their privileges against immigrant newcomers; Spaniards born in the Americas (*creoles*) resented the pretensions to superiority of those born in Spain (*peninsulares*); landowning Spaniards felt threatened by the growing wealth of commercial and mercantile groups practicing less prestigious occupations. Spanish missionaries and church authorities were often sharply critical of how these settlers treated native peoples. "By what right ... do you keep these Indians in such a cruel and horrible servitude?" demanded a Dominican priest in 1511 to a Spanish audience in Santo Domingo that included the son of Columbus himself. "Why do you keep those who survive so oppressed and weary, not giving them enough to eat, not caring for them in their illness?"[11]

The most distinctive feature of these new colonial societies in Mexico and Peru was the emergence of a *mestizo*, or mixed-race, population, initially the product of unions between Spanish men and Indian women. Rooted in the sexual imbalance among Spanish immigrants (seven men to one woman in early colonial Peru, for example), the emergence of a mestizo population was facilitated by the desire of many surviving Indian women for the relative security of life in a Spanish household, where their children would not be subject to the abuse and harsh demands made on native peoples. The Spanish Crown encouraged settlers to marry into elite Indian families, and Cortés, the conqueror of Mexico, fathered children with two of Moctezuma's daughters. Over the 300 years of the colonial era, mestizo numbers grew substantially, becoming the majority of the population in Mexico sometime during the nineteenth century.

Racial Mixing in Colonial Mexico
This eighteenth-century painting by the famous Zapotec artist Miguel Cabrera shows a Spanish man, a *mestiza* woman, and their child, who was labeled as *castiza*. By the twentieth century, such mixed-race people represented the majority of the population of Mexico, and cultural blending had become a central feature of the country's identity. (Scala/Art Resource, NY)

Mestizos were largely Hispanic in culture, but Spaniards looked down on them during much of the colonial era, regarding them as illegitimate, for many were not born of "proper" marriages. Despite this attitude, their growing numbers and their economic usefulness as artisans, clerks, supervisors of labor gangs, and lower-level officials in both church and state bureaucracies led to their recognition as a distinct social group. Particularly in Mexico, mestizo identity blurred the sense of sharp racial difference between Spanish and Indian peoples and became a major element in the identity of modern Mexico.

At the bottom of Mexican and Peruvian colonial societies were the indigenous peoples, known to Europeans as "Indians." Traumatized by "the great dying," they were subject to gross abuse and exploitation as the primary labor force for the mines and estates of the Spanish Empire and were required to render tribute payments to their Spanish overlords. Their empires dismantled by Spanish conquest, their religions attacked by Spanish missionaries, and their diminished numbers forcibly relocated into larger settlements, many Indians gravitated toward the world of their conquerors. Many learned Spanish; converted to Christianity; moved to cities to work for wages; ate the meat of cows, chickens, and pigs; used plows and draft animals rather than traditional digging sticks; and took their many grievances to Spanish courts.

But much that was native persisted. At the local level, Indian authorities retained a measure of autonomy, and traditional markets operated regularly. Maize, beans, and squash continued as the major elements of Indian diets in Mexico. Christian saints in many places blended easily with specialized indigenous gods, while belief in magic, folk medicine, and communion with the dead remained strong (see pp. 728–30). Memories of the past also persisted, and the Tupac Amaru revolt in Peru during 1780–1781 was made in the name of the last independent Inca emperor.

Thus Spaniards, mestizos, and Indians represented the major social groups in the colonial lands of what had been the Inca and Aztec empires, while African slaves and freemen were far less numerous than elsewhere in the Americas. Despite the sharp divisions among these groups, some movement was possible. Indians who acquired an education, wealth, and some European culture might "pass" as mestizo. Likewise more fortunate mestizo families might be accepted as Spaniards over time. Colonial Spanish America was a vast laboratory of ethnic mixing and cultural change. It was dominated by Europeans to be sure, but with a rather more fluid and culturally blended society than in the racially rigid colonies of North America.

Colonies of Sugar

■ **Comparison**

How did the plantation societies of Brazil and the Caribbean differ from those of southern colonies in British North America?

A second and quite different kind of colonial society emerged in the lowland areas of Brazil, ruled by Portugal, and in the Spanish, British, French, and Dutch colonies in the Caribbean. These regions lacked the great civilizations of Mexico and Peru. Nor did they provide much mineral wealth until the Brazilian gold rush of the 1690s and the discovery of diamonds a little later. Still, Europeans found a very profitable substitute in sugar, which was much in demand in Europe, where it was used as a medicine, a spice, a sweetener, a preservative, and in sculptured forms as a decoration that indicated high status. Although commercial agriculture in the Spanish Empire served a domestic market in its towns and mining camps, these sugar-based colonies produced almost exclusively for export, while importing their food and other necessities.

Large-scale sugar production had been pioneered by Arabs, who introduced it into the Mediterranean. Europeans learned the technique and transferred it to their Atlantic island possessions and then to the Americas. For a century (1570–1670), Portuguese planters along the northeast coast of Brazil dominated the world market for sugar. Then the British, French, and Dutch turned their Caribbean territories into highly productive sugar-producing colonies, breaking the Portuguese and Brazilian monopoly.

Sugar decisively transformed Brazil and the Caribbean. Its production, which involved both growing the sugarcane and processing it into usable sugar, was very labor intensive and could most profitably occur in a large-scale, almost industrial setting. It was perhaps the first modern industry in that it produced for an international and mass market, using capital and expertise from Europe, with production

Plantation Life in the Caribbean
This painting from 1823 shows the use of slave labor on a plantation in Antigua, a British-ruled island in the Caribbean. Notice the overseer with a whip supervising the tilling and planting of the field. (British Library/HIP/Art Resource, NY)

Snapshot   **Ethnic Composition of Colonial Societies in Latin America (1825)[12]**

	Highland Spanish America	Portuguese America (Brazil)
Europeans	18.2 percent	23.4 percent
Mixed-race	28.3 percent	17.8 percent
Africans	11.9 percent	49.8 percent
Native Americans	41.7 percent	9.1 percent

facilities located in the Americas. However, its most characteristic feature—the massive use of slave labor—was an ancient practice. In the absence of a Native American population, which had been almost totally wiped out in the Caribbean or had fled inland in Brazil, European sugarcane planters turned to Africa and the Atlantic slave trade for an alternative workforce. The vast majority of the African captives transported across the Atlantic, some 80 percent or more, ended up in Brazil and the Caribbean. (See Chapter 15 for a more extensive description of the Atlantic slave trade.)

Slaves worked on sugar-producing estates in horrendous conditions. The heat and fire from the cauldrons, which turned raw sugarcane into crystallized sugar, reminded many visitors of scenes from hell. These conditions, combined with disease, generated a high death rate, perhaps 5 to 10 percent per year, which required plantation owners to constantly import fresh slaves. A Jesuit observer in 1580 aptly summarized the situation: "The work is great and many die."[13]

The extensive use of African slave labor gave these plantation colonies a very different ethnic and racial makeup than that of highland Spanish America, as the Snapshot indicates. Thus, after three centuries of colonial rule, a substantial majority of Brazil's population was either partially or wholly of African descent. In the French Caribbean colony of Haiti in 1790, the corresponding figure was 93 percent.

As in Spanish America, a considerable amount of racial mixing took place in Brazil. Cross-racial unions accounted for only about 10 percent of all marriages in Brazil, but the use of concubines and informal liaisons among Indians, Africans, and Portuguese produced a substantial mixed-race population. From their ranks derived much of the urban skilled workforce and supervisors in the sugar industry. *Mulattoes*, the product of Portuguese-African unions, predominated, but as many as forty separate and named groups, each indicating a different racial mixture, emerged in colonial Brazil.

The plantation complex of the Americas, based on African slavery, extended beyond the Caribbean and Brazil to encompass the southern colonies of British North America, where tobacco, cotton, rice, and indigo were major crops, but the social outcomes of these plantation colonies were quite different from those farther south. Because European women had joined the colonial migration to North America at an early date, these colonies experienced less racial mixing and certainly demonstrated less willingness to recognize the offspring of such unions and accord them a place in society. A sharply defined racial system (with black Africans, "red" Native Americans, and white Europeans) evolved in North America, whereas both Portuguese and Spanish colonies acknowledged a wide variety of mixed-race groups.

Slavery too was different, being perhaps somewhat less harsh in North America than in the sugar colonies. By 1750 or so, slaves in the United States proved able to reproduce themselves, and by the time of the Civil War almost all North American slaves had been born in the New World. That was never the case in Latin America, where large-scale importation of new slaves continued well into the nineteenth century. Nonetheless, many more slaves were voluntarily set free by their owners in Brazil than in North America, and free blacks and mulattoes in Brazil had more economic opportunities than did their counterparts in the United States. At least a few among them found positions as political leaders, scholars, musicians, writers, and artists. Some were even hired as slave catchers.

Does this mean then that racism was absent in colonial Brazil? Certainly not, but it was different from racism in North America. For one thing, in North America, any African ancestry, no matter how small or distant, made a person "black"; in Brazil, a person of African and non-African ancestry was considered not black, but some other mixed-race category. Racial prejudice surely persisted, for white characteristics and features were prized more highly than those of blacks, and people regarded as white had enormously greater privileges and opportunities than others. Nevertheless, skin color in Brazil, and in Latin America generally, was only one criterion of class status, and the perception of color changed with the educational or economic standing of individuals. A light-skinned mulatto who had acquired some wealth or education might well pass as a white. One curious visitor to Brazil was surprised to find a darker-skinned man serving as a local official. "Isn't the governor a mulatto?" inquired the visitor. "He was, but he isn't any more," was the reply. "How can a governor be a mulatto?"[14]

Settler Colonies in North America

A third and distinctive type of colonial society emerged in the northern British colonies of New England, New York, and Pennsylvania. Because the British were the last of the European powers to establish a colonial presence in the Americas, a full century after Spain, they found that "only the dregs were left."[15] The lands they acquired were widely regarded in Europe as the unpromising leftovers of the New World, lacking the obvious wealth and sophisticated cultures of the Spanish possessions. Until at least the eighteenth century, these British colonies remained far less prominent on the world stage than those of Spain or Portugal.

■ **Comparison**
What distinguished the British settler colonies of North America from their counterparts in Latin America?

The British settlers came from a more rapidly changing society than did those from an ardently Catholic, semifeudal, authoritarian Spain. When Britain launched its colonial ventures in the seventeenth century, it had already experienced considerable conflict between Catholics and Protestants, the rise of a merchant capitalist class distinct from the nobility, and the emergence of parliament as a check on the authority of kings. Although they brought much of their English culture with them, many of the British settlers—Puritans in Massachusetts and Quakers in Pennsylvania, for example—sought to escape aspects of an old European society rather than to re-create it, as was the case for most Spanish and Portuguese colonists. The easy availability of land and the outsider status of many British settlers made it even more difficult to follow the Spanish or Portuguese colonial pattern of sharp class hierarchies, large rural estates, and dependent laborers.

The British settlers also were far more numerous. By 1750, they outnumbered Spanish settlers by five to one. This disparity was the most obvious distinguishing feature of the New England and middle Atlantic colonies. By the time of the American Revolution, some 90 percent or more of these colonies' populations were Europeans. Devastating diseases and a highly aggressive military policy had largely cleared the colonies of Native Americans, and their numbers did not rebound in subsequent centuries as they did in the lands of the Aztecs and the Incas. Moreover, slaves were not needed in an agricultural economy dominated by numerous small-scale independent farmers working their own land, although elite families, especially in urban areas, sometimes employed household slaves. These were almost pure settler colonies, without the racial mixing that was so prominent in Spanish and Portuguese territories.

Other differences likewise emerged. A largely Protestant England was far less interested in spreading Christianity among the remaining native peoples than were the large and well-funded missionary societies of Catholic Spain. Although religion loomed large in the North American colonies, the church and colonial state were not so intimately connected as they were in Latin America. The Protestant emphasis on reading the Bible for oneself led to a much greater mass literacy than in Latin America, where three centuries of church education still left some 95 percent of the population illiterate at independence. Furthermore, far more so than in Latin America, British settler colonies evolved traditions of local self-government. Preferring to rely on joint stock companies or wealthy individuals operating under a royal charter, Britain had nothing resembling the elaborate bureaucracy that governed Spanish colonies. For much of the seventeenth century, a prolonged power struggle between the English king and parliament meant that the British government paid little attention to the internal affairs of the colonies. Therefore, elected colonial assemblies, seeing themselves as little parliaments defending "the rights of Englishmen," vigorously contested the prerogatives of royal governors sent to administer their affairs.

The grand irony of the modern history of the Americas lay in the reversal of long-established relationships between the northern and southern continents. For thousands of years, the major centers of wealth, power, commerce, and innovation lay in Mesoamerica and the Andes. That pattern continued for much of the colonial era, as the Spanish and Portuguese colonies seemed far more prosperous and successful than their British or French counterparts. In the nineteenth and twentieth centuries, however, the balance shifted. What had once been the "dregs" of the colonial world became the United States, which was more politically stable, more democratic, more economically successful, and more internationally powerful than a divided, unstable, and economically less developed Latin America.

The Steppes and Siberia: The Making of a Russian Empire

At the same time as Western Europeans were building their empires in the Americas, the Russian Empire, which subsequently became the world's largest state, was beginning to take shape. When Columbus crossed the Atlantic, a small Russian state centered on the city of Moscow was emerging from two centuries of Mongol rule. That state soon conquered a number of neighboring Russian-speaking cities and incorporated them into its expanding territory. Located on the remote, cold, and heavily forested eastern fringe of Christendom, it was perhaps an unlikely candidate for constructing one of the great empires of the modern era. And yet, over the next three centuries, it did precisely that, extending Russian domination over the vast tundra, forests, and grasslands of northern Asia that lay to the south and east of Moscow. Furthermore, Russian expansion westward brought numerous Poles, Germans, Ukrainians, Belorussians, and Baltic peoples into the Russian Empire.

■ **Description**
What motivated Russian empire building?

Russian attention was drawn first to the grasslands south and east of the Russian heartland, an area long inhabited by various nomadic pastoral peoples, who were organized into feuding tribes and clans and adjusting to the recent disappearance of the Mongol Empire. From the viewpoint of the emerging Russian state, the problem was security because these pastoral peoples, like the Mongols before them, frequently raided their agricultural Russian neighbors and sold many of them into slavery. To the east across the vast expanse of Siberia, Russian motives were quite different, for the scattered peoples of its endless forests and tundra posed no threat to Russia. Numbering only some 220,000 in the seventeenth century and speaking more than 100 languages, they were mostly hunting, gathering, and herding people, living in small-scale societies and largely without access to gunpowder weapons. What drew the Russians across Siberia was opportunity—primarily the "soft gold" of fur-bearing animals, whose pelts were in great demand on the world market.

Whatever motives drove it, the enormous Russian Empire, stretching to the Pacific, took shape in the three centuries between 1500 and 1800 (see Map 14.2). A growing line of wooden forts offered protection to frontier towns and trading centers as well as to mounting numbers of Russian farmers. Empire building was an extended process, involving the Russian state and its officials as well as a variety of private interests—merchants, hunters, peasant agricultural settlers, churchmen,

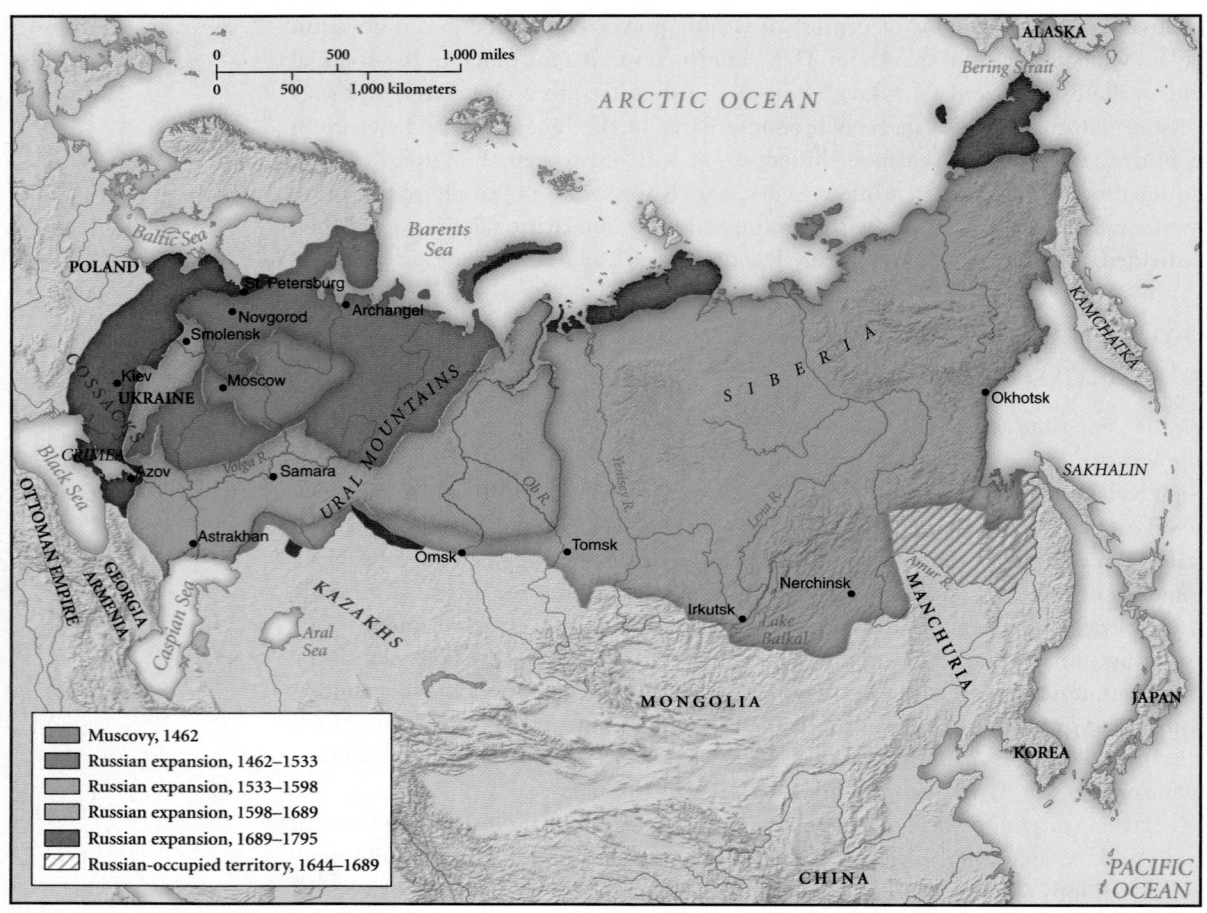

Map 14.2 The Russian Empire
From its beginnings as a small principality under Mongol control, Moscow became the center of a vast Russian Empire during the early modern era.

exiles, criminals, and adventurers. For the Russian migrants to these new lands, the empire offered "economic and social improvements over what they had known at home—from more and better land to fewer lords and officials."[16] Political leaders and educated Russians generally defined the empire in grander terms: defending Russian frontiers; enhancing the power of the Russian state; and bringing Christianity, civilization, and enlightenment to savages. But what did that empire mean to those on its receiving end?

Experiencing the Russian Empire

■ **Change**

How did the Russian Empire transform the life of its conquered people and of the Russian homeland itself?

First, of course, creating an empire meant conquest. Although resistance was frequent, especially from nomadic peoples, in the long run Russian military might, based in modern weaponry and the organizational capacity of a powerful state, brought both the steppes and Siberia under Russian control. Everywhere Russian authorities demanded an oath of allegiance by which native peoples swore "eternal submission to the grand tsar," the monarch of the Russian Empire. They also demanded *yasak*, or "tribute," paid in cash or in kind. In Siberia, this meant enormous quantities of furs, especially the extremely valuable sable, which Siberian peoples were compelled to produce. As in the Americas, devastating epidemics accompanied conquest, particularly in the more remote regions of Siberia, where local people had little immunity to smallpox or measles. Also accompanying conquest was an intermittent pressure to convert to Christianity. Tax breaks, exemptions from paying tribute, and the promise of land or cash provided incentives for conversion, while the destruction of many mosques and the forced resettlement of Muslims added to the pressures. Yet the Russian state did not pursue conversion with the single-minded intensity that Spanish authorities exercised in Latin America, particularly if missionary activity threatened political and social stability. The empress Catherine the Great, for example, established religious tolerance for Muslims in the late eighteenth century and created a state agency to oversee Muslim affairs.

The most profoundly transforming feature of the Russian Empire was the influx of Russian settlers, whose numbers by the end of the eighteenth century overwhelmed native peoples, thus giving their lands a distinctively Russian character. By 1720, some 700,000 Russians lived in Siberia, thus reducing the native Siberians to 30 percent of the total population, a figure that dropped to 14 percent in the nineteenth century. The loss of hunting grounds and pasturelands to Russian agricultural settlers undermined long-standing economies and rendered local people dependent on Russian markets for grain, sugar, tea, tobacco, and alcohol. Pressures to encourage pastoralists to abandon their nomadic ways included the requirement to pay fees and to obtain permission to cross agricultural lands. Kazakh herders responded with outrage: "The grass and the water belong to Heaven, and why should we pay any fees?"[17] Intermarriage, prostitution, and sexual abuse resulted in some mixed-race offspring, but these were generally absorbed as Russians rather than identified as distinctive communities, as in Latin America.

Over the course of three centuries, both Siberia and the steppes were incorporated into the Russian state. Their native peoples were not driven into reservations or eradicated as in the

A Cossack Jail
In the vanguard of Russian expansion across Siberia were the Cossacks, bands of fiercely independent warriors consisting of peasants who had escaped serfdom as well as criminals and other adventurers. This seventeenth-century jail was part of an early Cossack settlement on the Kamchatka Peninsula at the easternmost end of Siberia. It illustrates Russian wooden architecture. (Sovfoto/Eastfoto)

Americas. Many of them, though, were Russified, adopting the Russian language and converting to Christianity, even as their traditional ways of life—hunting and herding—were much disrupted. The Russian Empire represented the final triumph of an agrarian civilization over the hunting societies of Siberia and over the pastoral peoples of the grasslands.

Russians and Empire

If the empire transformed the conquered peoples, it also fundamentally changed Russia itself. As it became a multiethnic empire, Russians diminished as a proportion of the overall population, although they remained politically dominant. Among the growing number of non-Russians in the empire, Slavic-speaking Ukrainians and Belorussians predominated, while the vast territories of Siberia and the steppes housed numerous separate peoples, but with quite small populations.[18] The wealth of empire—rich agricultural lands, valuable furs, mineral deposits—played a major role in making Russia one of the great powers of Europe by the eighteenth century, and it has enjoyed that position ever since. This European and Christian state also became an Asian power, bumping up against China, India, Persia, and the Ottoman Empire. It was on the front lines of the encounter between Christendom and the world of Islam.

This straddling of Asia and Europe was the source of a long-standing identity problem that has troubled educated Russians for 300 years. Was Russia a backward European country, destined to follow the lead of more highly developed Western European societies? Or was it different, uniquely Slavic or even Asian, shaped by its Mongol legacy and its status as an Asian power? It is a question that Russians have not completely answered even in the twenty-first century. Either way, the very size of that empire, bordering on virtually all of the great agrarian civilizations of outer Eurasia, turned Russia, like many empires before it, into a highly militarized state, "a society organized for continuous war," according to one scholar.[19] It also reinforced the highly autocratic character of the Russian Empire because such a huge state arguably required a powerful monarchy to hold its vast domains and highly diverse peoples together.

Clearly the Russians had created an empire, similar to those of Western Europe in terms of conquest, settlement, exploitation, religious conversion, and feelings of superiority. Nonetheless, the Russians had acquired their empire under different circumstances than did the Western Europeans. The Spanish and the British had conquered and colonized the New World, an ocean away and wholly unknown to them before 1492. They acquired those empires only after establishing themselves as distinct European states. The Russians, on the other hand, entered adjacent territories with which they had long interacted, and they did so *at the same time* that a modern Russian state was taking shape. "The British had an empire," wrote historian Geoffrey Hosking. "Russia *was* an empire."[20] Perhaps this helps explain the unique longevity of the Russian Empire. Whereas the Spanish, Portuguese, and British colonies in the Americas long ago achieved independence, the Russian Empire remained intact until the collapse of the Soviet Union in 1991. So thorough was Russian colonization that Siberia and much of the steppes remain still an integral part of the Russian state. But many internal administrative regions, which exercise a measure of autonomy, reflect the continuing presence of some 160 non-Russian peoples who were earlier incorporated into the Russian Empire.

Asian Empires

Even as Europeans were building their empires in the Americas and across Siberia, other imperial projects were likewise under way. The Chinese pushed deep into central Eurasia; Turko-Mongol invaders from Central Asia created the Mughal Empire, bringing much of Hindu South Asia within a single Muslim-ruled political system; and the Ottoman Empire brought Muslim rule to a largely Christian population in southeastern Europe and Turkish rule to largely Arab populations in North Africa and the Middle East. None of these empires had the global reach or worldwide impact of Europe's American colonies; they were regional rather than global in scope. Nor did they have the same devastating and transforming impact on their conquered peoples, for those peoples were not being exposed to new diseases. Nothing remotely approaching the catastrophic population collapse of Native American peoples occurred in these Asian empires. Moreover, the process of building these empires did not transform the imperial homeland as fundamentally as did the wealth of the Americas and to a lesser extent Siberia for European imperial powers. Nonetheless, these expanding Asian empires reflected the energies and vitality of their respective civilizations in the early modern era, and they gave rise to profoundly important cross-cultural encounters, with legacies that echoed for many centuries.

Making China an Empire

In the fifteenth century, China had declined an opportunity to construct a maritime empire in the Indian Ocean, as Zheng He's massive fleet was withdrawn and left to wither away (see pp. 580–84). In the seventeenth and eighteenth centuries, however, China built another kind of empire on its northern and western frontiers that vastly enlarged the territorial size of the country and incorporated a number of non-Chinese peoples. Undertaking this enormous project of imperial expansion was China's Qing, or Manchu, dynasty (1644–1912). (See Document 14.1, pp. 653–54, for Chinese state building during the Qing dynasty.) Strangely enough, the Qing dynasty was itself of foreign and nomadic origin, hailing from Manchuria, north of the Great Wall. Having conquered China, the Qing rulers sought to maintain their ethnic distinctiveness by forbidding intermarriage between themselves and Chinese. Nonetheless, their ruling elites also mastered the Chinese language and Confucian teachings and used Chinese bureaucratic techniques to govern the empire.

For many centuries, the Chinese had interacted with the nomadic peoples, who inhabited the dry and lightly populated regions now known as Mongolia, Xinjiang, and Tibet. Trade, tribute, and warfare ensured that these ecologically and culturally

■ **Description**
What were the major features of Chinese empire building in the early modern era?

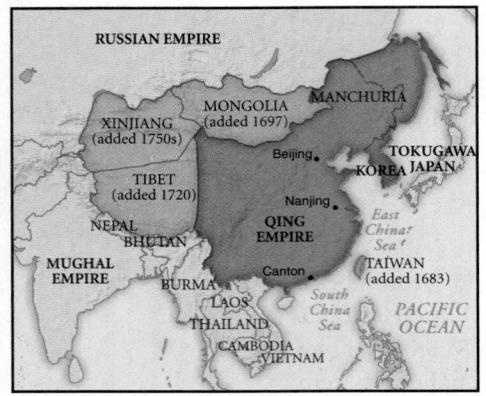

China's Qing Dynasty Empire

different worlds were well known to each other, quite unlike the New World "discoveries" of the Europeans. Chinese authority in the area had been intermittent and actively resisted. Then, in the early modern era, Qing dynasty China undertook an eighty-year military effort (1680–1760) that brought these huge regions solidly under Chinese control. It was largely security concerns that motivated this aggressive posture. During the late seventeenth century, the creation of a substantial state among the western Mongols, known as the Zunghars, revived Chinese memories of an earlier Mongol conquest. As in so many other cases, Chinese expansion was viewed as a defensive necessity. The eastward movement of the Russian Empire likewise appeared potentially threatening, but this danger was resolved diplomatically, rather than militarily, in the Treaty of Nerchinsk (1689), which marked the boundary between Russia and China.

Although undertaken by the non-Chinese Manchus, the Qing dynasty campaigns against the Mongols marked the evolution of China into a Central Asian empire. The Chinese, however, have seldom thought of themselves as an imperialist power. Rather they spoke of the "unification" of the peoples of central Eurasia within a Chinese state. Nonetheless, historians have seen many similarities between Chinese expansion and other cases of early modern empire building, while noting some clear differences as well.

Clearly the Qing dynasty takeover of central Eurasia was a conquest, making use of China's more powerful military technology and greater resources. Furthermore, the area was ruled separately from the rest of China through a new office called the Court of Colonial Affairs. Like other colonial powers, the Chinese made active use of local notables—Mongol aristocrats, Muslim officials, Buddhist leaders—as they attempted to govern the region as inexpensively as possible. Sometimes these native officials abused their authority, demanding extra taxes or labor service from local people and thus earning their hostility. In places, those officials imitated Chinese ways by wearing peacock feathers, decorating their hats with gold buttons, or adopting a Manchu hairstyle that was much resented by many Chinese who were forced to wear it.

More generally, however, Chinese or Qing officials did not seek to assimilate local people into Chinese culture and showed considerable respect for the Mongolian, Tibetan, and Muslim cultures of the region. People of noble rank, Buddhist monks, and those associated with monasteries were excused from the taxes and labor service required of ordinary people. Nor was the area flooded with Chinese settlers. In parts of Mongolia, for example, Qing authorities sharply restricted the entry of Chinese merchants and other immigrants in an effort to preserve the area as a source of recruitment for the Chinese military. They feared that the "soft" and civilized Chinese ways might erode the fighting spirit of the Mongols.

The long-term significance of this new Chinese imperial state was tremendous. It greatly expanded the territory of China and added a small but important minority of non-Chinese people to the empire's vast population. The borders of contemporary China are essentially those created during the Qing dynasty. Some of those peoples, particularly those in Tibet and Xinjiang, have retained their older identities and in recent decades have actively sought greater autonomy or even independence from China.

Even more important, Chinese conquests, together with the expansion of the Russian Empire, utterly transformed Central Asia. For centuries, that region had been the cosmopolitan crossroads of Eurasia, hosting the Silk Road trading network, welcoming all of the major world religions, and generating an enduring encounter between the nomads of the steppes and the farmers of settled agricultural regions. Now under Russian or Chinese rule, it became the backward and impoverished region known to nineteenth- and twentieth-century observers. Land-based commerce across Eurasia increasingly took a backseat to oceanic trade. Indebted Mongolian nobles lost their land to Chinese merchants, while nomads, no longer able to herd their animals freely, fled to urban areas, where many were reduced to begging. The incorporation of the heartland of Eurasian nomads into the Russian and Chinese empires "eliminated permanently as a major actor on the historical stage the nomadic pastoralists, who had been the strongest alternative to settled agricultural society since the second millennium B.C.E."[21] It was the end of a long era.

Muslims and Hindus in the Mughal Empire

If the creation of a Chinese imperial state in the early modern era provoked a final clash of nomadic pastoralists and settled farmers, India's Mughal Empire hosted a different kind of encounter—a further phase in the long interaction of Islamic and Hindu cultures in South Asia. That empire was the product of Central Asian warriors, who were Muslims in religion and Turkic in culture and who claimed descent from Chinggis Khan and Timur (see pp. 587–88). Their brutal conquests in the sixteenth century provided India with a rare period of relative political unity (1526–1707), as Mughal emperors exercised a fragile control over a diverse and fragmented subcontinent, which had long been divided into a bewildering variety of small states, principalities, tribes, castes, sects, and ethnolinguistic groups.

The central division within Mughal India was religious. The ruling dynasty and perhaps 20 percent of the population were Muslims; most of the rest practiced some form of Hinduism. Mughal India's most famous emperor, Akbar (ruled 1556–1605), clearly recognized this fundamental reality and acted deliberately to accommodate the Hindu majority. After conquering the warrior-based and Hindu Rajputs of northwestern India, Akbar married several of their princesses but did not require them to convert to Islam. He incorporated a substantial number of Hindus into the political-military elite of the empire and supported the building of Hindu temples as well as mosques, palaces, and forts. (See Document 14.2, pp. 655–57, for Mughal state-building under Akbar and his son Jahangir.)

■ **Change**

How did Mughal attitudes and policies toward Hindus change from the time of Akbar to that of Aurangzeb?

The Mughal Empire

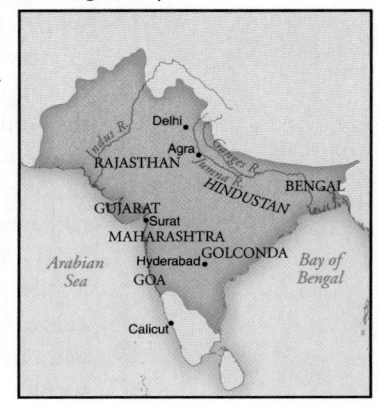

In directly religious matters, Akbar imposed a policy of toleration, deliberately restraining the more militantly Islamic ulama (religious scholars) and removing the special tax (jizya) on non-Muslims. He constructed a special House of Worship where he presided over intellectual discussion with representatives of many religions—Muslim, Hindu, Christian, Buddhist, Jewish, Jain, and Zoroastrian. His son Jahangir wrote proudly of his father: "He associated with the good of every race and creed and persuasion.... The professors of various faiths had room in the broad expanse of his incomparable sway."[22] Akbar went so far as to create his own state cult, a religious faith aimed at the Mughal elite. This cult drew on Islam, Hinduism, and Zoroastrianism and emphasized loyalty to the emperor himself. The overall style of the Mughal Empire was that of a blended elite culture in which both Hindus and various Muslim groups could feel comfortable. Thus Persian artists and writers were welcomed into the empire, and the Hindu epic *Ramayana* was translated into Persian, while various Persian classics appeared in Hindi and Sanskrit. In short, Akbar and his immediate successors downplayed a distinctly Islamic identity for the Mughal Empire in favor of a cosmopolitan and hybrid Indian-Persian-Turkic culture.

Such policies fostered sharp opposition among some Muslims. The philosopher Shayk Ahmad Sirhindi (1564–1624), claiming to be a "renewer" of authentic Islam in his time, strongly objected to this cultural synthesis. The worship of saints, the sacrifice of animals, and support for Hindu religious festivals all represented impure intrusions of Sufi Islam or Hinduism that needed to be rooted out. It was the duty of Muslim rulers to impose the sharia (Islamic law), to enforce the jizya, and to remove non-Muslims from high office. This strain of Muslim thinking found a champion in the emperor Aurangzeb (1658–1707), who reversed Akbar's policy of accommodation and sought to impose Islamic supremacy. He forbade the Hindu practice of *sati*, in which a widow followed her husband to death by throwing herself on his funeral pyre. Music and dance were now banned at court, and previously tolerated vices such as gambling, drinking, prostitution, and narcotics were actively suppressed. Some Hindu temples were destroyed, and the jizya was reimposed. "Censors of public morals," posted to large cities, enforced Islamic law.

Aurangzeb's religious policies, combined with intolerable demands for taxes to support his many wars of expansion, antagonized Hindus and prompted various movements of opposition to the Mughals. "Your subjects are trampled underfoot," wrote one anonymous protester. "Every province of your empire is impoverished.... God is the God of all mankind, not the God of Mussalmans [Muslims] alone."[23] These opposition movements, some of them self-consciously Hindu, fatally fractured the Mughal Empire, especially after Aurangzeb's death in 1707, and opened the way for a British takeover in the second half of the eighteenth century.

Thus the Mughal Empire was the site of a highly significant encounter between two of the world's great religious traditions. It began with an experiment in multicultural empire building and ended in growing antagonism between Hindus and Muslims. In the centuries that followed, both elements of the Mughal experience would be repeated.

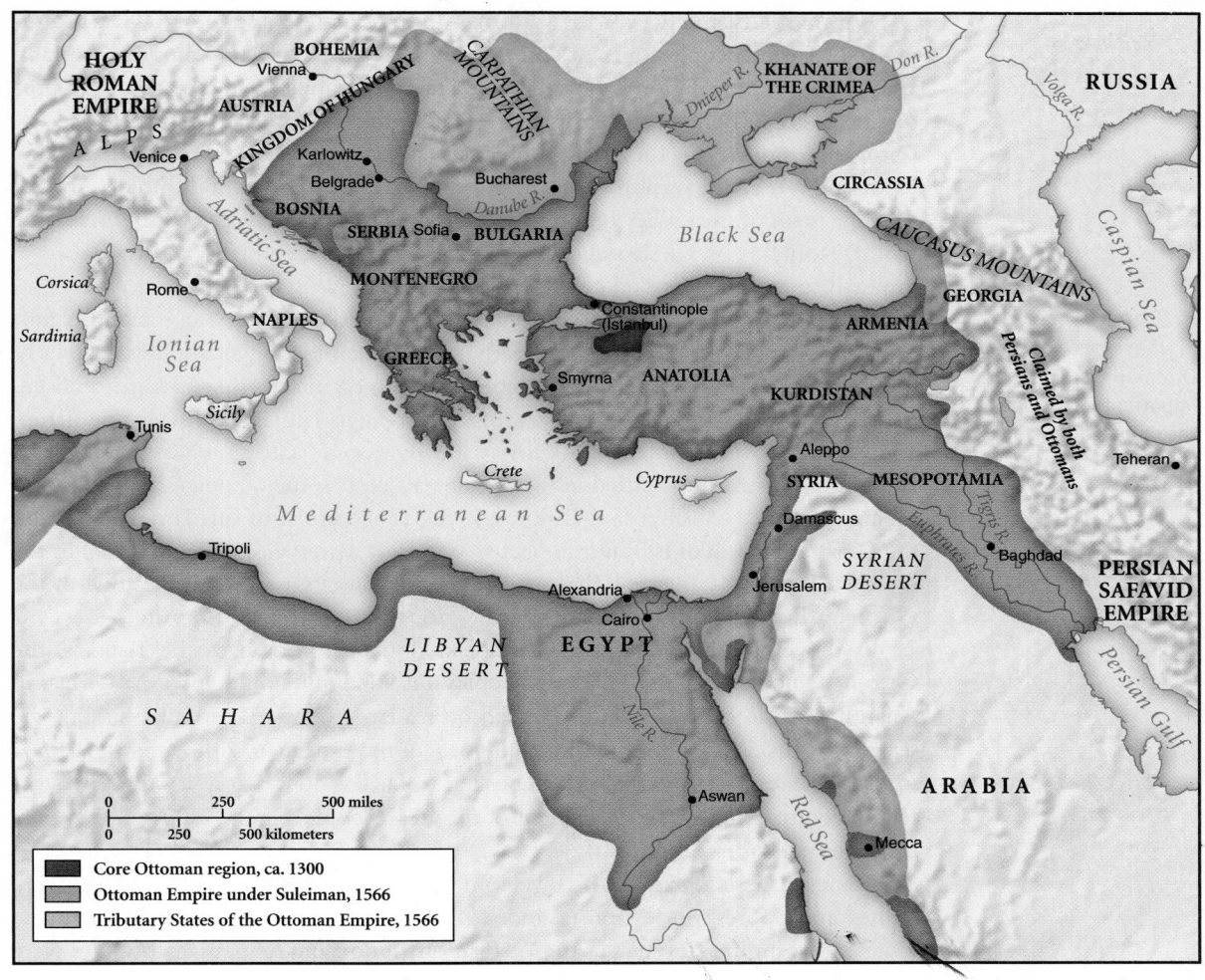

Map 14.3 The Ottoman Empire

At its high point in the mid-sixteenth century, the Ottoman Empire encompassed a vast diversity of peoples; straddled Europe, Africa, and Asia; and battled both the Austrian and Safavid empires.

Muslims, Christians, and the Ottoman Empire

Like the Mughal state, the Ottoman Empire was also the creation of Turkic warrior groups, whose aggressive raiding of agricultural civilization was now legitimized in Islamic terms. Beginning around 1300 from a base area in northwestern Anatolia, these Ottoman Turks over the next three centuries swept over much of the Middle East, North Africa, and southeastern Europe to create the Islamic world's most significant empire (see Map 14.3). During those centuries, the Ottoman state was transformed from a small frontier principality to a prosperous, powerful, cosmopolitan empire, heir to both the Byzantine Empire and to leadership within the Islamic world. Its sultan combined the roles of a Turkic warrior prince, a Muslim caliph, and a conquering emperor, bearing the "strong sword of Islam" and serving as chief defender of the faith.

Within the Islamic world, the Ottoman Empire represented the growing prominence of Turkic people, for their empire now incorporated a large number of Arabs, among whom the religion had been born. The responsibility and the prestige of protecting Mecca, Medina, and Jerusalem—the holy cities of Islam—now fell to the Ottoman Empire. A century-long conflict (1534–1639) between the Ottoman Empire, espousing the Sunni version of Islam, and the Persian Safavid Empire, holding fast to the Shia form of the faith, expressed a deep and enduring division within the Islamic world. Nonetheless, Persian culture, especially its poetry, painting, and traditions of imperial splendor, occupied a prominent position among the Ottoman elite.

■ Significance
In what ways was the Ottoman Empire important for Europe in the early modern era?

The Ottoman Empire, like its Mughal counterpart, was the site of a highly significant cross-cultural encounter in the early modern era, adding yet another chapter to the long-running story of interaction between the Islamic world and Christendom. As the Ottoman Empire expanded across Anatolia, its largely Christian population converted in large numbers to Islam as the Byzantine state visibly weakened and large numbers of Turks settled in the region. By 1500, some 90 percent of Anatolia's inhabitants were Muslims and Turkic speakers. The climax of this Turkic assault on the Christian world of Byzantium occurred in 1453, when Constantinople fell to the invaders. Renamed Istanbul, that splendid Christian city became the capital of the Ottoman Empire. Byzantium, heir to the glory of Rome, was no more.

In the empire's southeastern European domains, known as the Balkans, the Ottoman encounter with Christian peoples unfolded quite differently than it had in Anatolia. In the Balkans, Muslims ruled over a large Christian population, but the scarcity of Turkish settlers and the willingness of the Ottoman authorities to accommodate the region's Christian churches led to far less conversion. By the early sixteenth century, only about 19 percent of the area's people were Muslims, and 81 percent were Christians.

Many of these Christians had welcomed Ottoman conquest because taxes were lighter and oppression less pronounced than under their former Christian rulers. Christian communities such as the Eastern Orthodox and Armenian churches were granted considerable autonomy in regulating their internal social, religious, educational, and charitable affairs. A substantial number of these Christians—Balkan landlords, Greek merchants, government officials, and high-ranking clergy—became part of the Ottoman elite, without converting to Islam. Jewish refugees, fleeing Christian persecution in a Spain recently "liberated" from Islamic rule, likewise found greater opportunity in the Ottoman Empire, where they became prominent in trade and banking circles. In these ways, Ottoman dealings with the Christian and Jewish populations of their empire broadly resembled Akbar's policies toward the Hindu majority of Mughal India.

In another way, however, Turkish rule bore heavily on Christians. Through a process known as the *devshirme* (the collecting or gathering), Balkan Christian communities were required to hand over a quota of young boys, who were then removed from their families, required to learn Turkish, usually converted to Islam, and trained for either civil administration or military service in elite Janissary units. Although it was a terrible blow for families who lost their children, the *devshirme* also represented a means of upward mobility within the Ottoman Empire. Nonetheless, this social gain occurred at a high price.

Even though Ottoman authorities were relatively tolerant toward Christians within their borders, the empire itself represented an enormous threat to Christendom generally. The seizure of Constantinople, the conquest of the Balkans, Ottoman naval power in the Mediterranean, and the siege of Vienna in 1529 and again in 1683 raised anew "the specter of a Muslim takeover of all of Europe."[24] (See Document 14.3, pp. 657–59.) One European ambassador reported fearfully in 1555 from the court of the Turkish ruler Suleiman:

> He tramples the soil of Hungary with 200,000 horses, he is at the very gates of Austria, threatens the rest of Germany, and brings in his train all the nations that extend from our borders to those of Persia.[25]

Indeed, the "terror of the Turk" inspired fear across much of Europe and placed Christendom on the defensive, even as Europeans were expanding aggressively across the Atlantic and into the Indian Ocean.

The Ottoman encounter with Christian Europe spawned admiration and cooperation as well as fear and trembling. The sixteenth-century French philosopher Jean

The Ottoman Siege of Vienna, 1683
In this late-seventeenth-century painting by artist Frans Geffels, the last Ottoman incursion into the Austrian Empire was pushed back with French and Polish help, marking the end of a serious Muslim threat to Christian Europe. (Historisches Museum der Stadt Wien/Gianni Dagli Orti/The Art Archive)

Bodin praised the religious tolerance of the Ottoman sultan in contrast to Christian intolerance: "The King of the Turks who rules over a great part of Europe safeguards the rites of religion as well as any prince in this world. Yet he constrains no-one, but on the contrary permits everyone to live as his conscience dictates."[26] The French government on occasion found it useful to ally with the Ottoman Empire against their common enemy of Habsburg Austria, while European merchants willingly violated a papal ban on selling firearms to the Turks. In the early eighteenth century, the wife of an English diplomat posted to Istanbul praised the morality of Ottoman women as well as their relative freedom: "It is easy to see they have more liberty than we do."[27] Cultural encounter involved more than conflict.

Reflections: Countering Eurocentrism... or Reflecting It?

With an emphasis on empires and cross-cultural encounters, this chapter deliberately places the more familiar account of European colonization in the Americas alongside the less well-known stories of Russian, Chinese, Mughal, and Ottoman empire building. The chief purpose in doing so is to counteract a Eurocentric understanding of the early modern age, in which European initiatives dominate our view of this era. It reminds us that Western Europe was not the only center of vitality and expansion and that the interaction of culturally different peoples, so characteristic of the modern age, derived from multiple sources. How often do we notice that a European Christendom creating empires across the Atlantic was also the victim of Ottoman imperial expansion in the Balkans?

A critic of this chapter, however, might well argue that it is nonetheless a Eurocentric narrative, for it allots rather more space to the Western European empires than to the others, and it tells the European story first. What led to such an ordering of this material?

Underlying the organization of this chapter is the notion that Western European empires in the Americas were in some ways both different from and more significant than the others. They represented something wholly new in human history, an interacting Atlantic world, while the Russian, Chinese, Mughal, and Ottoman empires continued older patterns of historical development. Furthermore, the European empires had a far heavier impact on the peoples they incorporated than did the others. After all, the great tragedies of the early modern era—the population collapse of Native American societies and the Atlantic slave trade—both grew out of these European empires. Moreover, they had, arguably, a far wider impact on the world as a whole, as they extended European civilization to the vast areas of the Americas, laid the nutritional foundation for the global population explosion of modern times, and contributed to both the Scientific Revolution and the Industrial Revolution.

Counteracting Eurocentrism, while acknowledging the unique role of Europe, continues to generate controversy among both scholars and students of modern world history. It is an issue that will recur repeatedly in the chapters that follow.

Second Thoughts

What's the Significance?

the great dying

Columbian exchange

peninsulares

mestizo

mulattoes

plantation complex

settler colonies

Siberia

yasak

Qing dynasty empire

Mughal Empire

Akbar

Aurangzeb

Ottoman Empire

Constantinople, 1453

devshirme

To assess your mastery of the material in this chapter, visit the **Student Center** at bedfordstmartins.com/strayer.

Big Picture Questions

1. In comparing the European empires in the Americas with the Russian, Chinese, Mughal, and Ottoman empires, should world historians emphasize the similarities or the differences? What are the implications of each approach?

2. In what different ways was European colonial rule expressed and experienced in the Americas?

3. Why did the European empires in the Americas have such an enormously greater impact on the conquered people than did the Chinese, Mughal, and Ottoman empires?

4. In what ways did the empires of the early modern era continue patterns of earlier empires? In what ways did they depart from those patterns?

Next Steps: For Further Study

Jorge Canizares-Esguerra and Erik R. Seeman, eds., *The Atlantic in Global History* (2007). A collection of essays that treats the Atlantic basin as a single interacting region.

Alfred W. Crosby, *The Columbian Voyages, the Columbian Exchange, and Their Historians* (1987). A brief and classic account of changing understandings of Columbus and his global impact.

John Kicza, *Resilient Cultures: America's Native Peoples Confront European Colonization, 1500–1800* (2003). An account of European colonization in the Americas that casts the native peoples as active agents rather than passive victims.

Peter Perdue, *China Marches West: The Qing Conquest of Central Eurasia* (2005). Describes the process of China becoming an empire as it incorporated the non-Chinese people of Central Asia.

John F. Richards, *The Mughal Empire* (1996). A well-regarded summary by a major scholar in the field.

David R. Ringrose, *Expansion and Global Interaction, 1200–1700* (2001). A world history perspective on empire building that bridges the postclassical and early modern eras.

Willard Sutherland, *Taming the Wild Fields: Colonization and Empire on the Russian Steppe* (2004). An up-to-date account of Russian expansion in the steppes.

"1492: An Ongoing Voyage," http://www.ibiblio.org/expo/1492.exhibit/Intro.html. An interactive Web site based on an exhibit from the Library of Congress that provides a rich context for exploring the meaning of Columbus and his voyages.

For Web sites and additional documents related to this chapter, see **Make History** at bedfordstmartins.com/strayer.

Documents

Considering the Evidence:
State Building in the Early Modern Era

The empires of the early modern era were the projects of states, though these states often made use of various private groups—missionaries, settlers, merchants, mercenaries—to achieve the goals of empire. Such imperial states, Qing-dynasty China, Mughal India, the Ottoman Empire, and France, for example, were invariably headed by monarchs—kings or emperors who were the source of ultimate political authority in their lands. Each of those rulers sought to govern societies divided by religion, region, ethnicity, or class.

During the three centuries between 1450 and 1750, all of these states, and a number of non-imperial states as well, moved toward greater political integration and centralization. In all of them, more effective central bureaucracies curtailed, though never eliminated, entrenched local interests; royal courts became more elaborate; and the role of monarchs grew more prominent. The growth of empire accompanied this process of political integration, and perhaps helped to cause it. However, the process of state building differed considerably across the early modern world, depending on variations in historical backgrounds, the particular problems and circumstances that each state faced, the cultural basis of political authority, and the policies that individual leaders followed.

The documents that follow allow us to examine this state-building effort in several distinct settings through the writings of monarchs, the edicts they issued, or outsiders who observed them. Pay attention to both the similarities and the variations in this process of state building as you study the documents. You may also want to consider how these early modern states differed from the states of later centuries. To what extent was government personal rather than institutional? In what ways was power exercised—through coercion and violence, through accommodation with established elites, through the operation of new bureaucratic structures, or by persuading people that the central authority was in fact legitimate?

Document 14.1

The "Self-Portrait" of a Chinese Emperor

Of all the early modern states, China had the longest tradition of centralized rule and political integration. By the time the Qing dynasty came to power in 1644, China could look back on many centuries of effective unity. Although interrupted periodically by peasant upheaval, external invasion, or changes in dynasties, cultural expectations nonetheless defined a unified state, headed by an emperor, as the norm. The Qing dynasty, although of Manchurian origin and proud of its military skills, generally accepted Chinese conceptions of statecraft, based on literary learning and a long-established system of civil service examinations designed to recruit scholar-officials into official positions. During the long reign of Kangxi (reigned 1661–1722), that dynasty initiated a vast imperial project extending Chinese control deep into inner Asia. (See the map on p. 644, and see pp. 643–45.) Document 14.1 contains a number of Kangxi's personal reflections on the management of this huge imperial state and its bureaucracy. Drawn from his own writings, this "self-portrait" of the Chinese emperor was compiled by the highly regarded historian Jonathan Spence.

- What major challenges to the effective exercise of state authority does Kangxi identify in this document?

- How would you describe Kangxi's style of governance or his posture toward imperial rule?

- Look carefully at the second paragraph of the document. Why did Kangxi impose a harsher penalty on Hu Chien-ching than the one originally given?

- What does this document suggest about the sources of Kangxi's authority?

The Emperor Kangxi
Reflections
1671–1722

Giving life to people and killing people—those are the powers that the emperor has.... He knows that sometimes people have to be persuaded into morality by the example of an execution....

Hu Chien-ching was a subdirector of the Court of Sacrificial Worship whose family terrorized their native area in Kiangsu, seizing people's lands and wives and daughters, and murdering people after falsely accusing them of being thieves. When a commoner finally managed to impeach him, the Governor was slow to hear the case and the Board of Punishment recommended that Hu be dismissed

Source: Jonathan D. Spence, *Emperor of China* (New York: Alfred A. Knopf, 1974), 29–58.

and sent into exile for three years. I ordered instead that he be executed with his family, and in his native place, so that all the local gentry might learn how I regarded such behavior....

I have been merciful where possible. For the ruler must always check carefully before executions and leave room for the hope that men will get better if they are given the time....

Of all the things that I find distasteful, none is more so than giving a final verdict on the death sentences that are sent to me for ratification.... Each year we went through the lists, sparing sixteen out of sixty-three at one session, eighteen out of fifty-seven at another....

There are too many men who claim to be *ju*—pure scholars—and yet are stupid and arrogant; we'd be better off with less talk of moral principles and more practice of it.... This is one of the worst habits of the great officials, that if they are not recommending their teachers or their friends for high office, then they recommend their relatives....

There is no way the emperor can know every official in the country, so he has to rely on the officials themselves for evaluation, or on censors to impeach the wicked. But when they are in cliques, he has to make his own inquiries as well; for no censor impeached the corrupt army officers Cho-ts'e and Hsu-sheng until I heard how they were hated by their troops and people and had them dismissed....

The emperor can get extra information in audience, on tours, and in palace memorials. From the beginning of my reign, I sought ways to guarantee that discussion among the great officials be kept confidential. The palace memorials were read by me in person, and I wrote rescripts on them myself.... [R]egular audiences are crucial with military men, especially when they have held power for a long time. There might have been no rebellion if Wu San-kuei, Keng Ching-chung, and Shang Chih-hsin had been summoned for regular audiences and made properly fearful. And army officers on the frontiers tend to obey only their own commander, acknowledging him as the ruler....

On tours I learned about the common people's grievances by talking with them, or by accepting their petitions. I asked peasants about their officials, looked at their houses and discussed their crops. I heard pleas from a woman whose husband had been wrongfully enslaved, from a traveling trader complaining about high customs dues, from a monk whose temple was falling down, and from a man who was robbed on his way to town....

In 1694 I noted that we were losing talent because of the way the exams were being conducted: even in the military *chin-shih* exams, most of the successful candidates were from Cheikiang and Chiangnan, while there was only one from Honan and one from Shansi. The successful ones had often done no more than memorize old examination books, whereas the best should be selected on the basis of riding and archery....

Even among the examiners, there are those who are corrupt, those who do not understand basic works, those who ask detailed questions about practical matters of which they know nothing, those who insist entirely on memorization of the *Classics*... those who put candidates from their own geographical area at the top of the list....

My divines have often been tempted to pass over bad auguries, but I have double-checked their calculations and warned them not to distort the truth: the Bureau of Astronomy once reported that a benevolent southeast wind was blowing, but I myself calculated the wind's direction with the palace instruments and found it to be, in fact, an inauspicious northeast wind; I told the Bureau that ours was not a dynasty that shunned bad omens; I also warned the Bureau not to guess or exaggerate in interpreting the omens that they observed, but simply to state their findings.... And being precise about forecasting the motions of the sun, moon, and planets, the winter and summer festivals, the eclipses of the sun and moon—all that is relevant to regulating spring planting, summer weeding, and autumn harvest....

I have never tired of the *Book of Changes*, and have use it in fortune-telling and as a source of moral principles; the only thing you must not do, I told my court lecturers, is to make this book appear simple, for there are meanings here that lie beyond words.

Document 14.2

The Memoirs of Emperor Jahangir

The peoples of India, unlike those of China, had only rarely experienced a political system that encompassed most of the subcontinent. Its vast ethnic and cultural diversity and the division between its Hindu and Muslim peoples usually generated a fragmented political order of many competing states and principalities. But in the early modern era, the Mughal Empire gave to South Asia a rare period of substantial political unity. Document 14.2 offer excerpts from the memoirs of Jahangir, who ruled the Mughal state from 1605 to 1627, following the reign of his more famous father Akbar (see pp. 645–46). Written in Persian, the literary language of the eastern Islamic world, Jahangir's account of his reign followed the tradition of earlier Mughal emperors in noting major events of his lifetime, but it departed from that tradition in reflecting personally on art, politics, family life, and more.

- Why do you think Jahangir mounted such an elaborate coronation celebration for himself?

- In what ways did Jahangir seek to ensure the effective authority of the state he led?

- In what ways was Jahangir a distinctly Muslim ruler? In what respects did he and his father depart from Islamic principles?

- How would you compare the problems Jahangir faced with those of Kangxi? Notice, among other things, that each of them had to adjust to a long-established cultural tradition—Kangxi to Chinese Confucianism and Jahangir to Hinduism. In what ways did they do so?

JAHANGIR
Memoirs
1605–1627

At the age of thirty-eight, I became Emperor, and under auspices the most felicitous, took my seat on the throne of my wishes....

As at the very instant that I seated myself on the throne, the sun rose from the horizon; I accepted this as the omen of victory, and as indicating a reign of unvarying prosperity. Hence I assumed the titles of... the world-subduing emperor, the world-subduing king. I ordained that the following legend should be stamped on the coinage of the empire: "Stricken at Agrah by that... safeguard of the world, the sovereign splendor of the faith, Jahangir, son of the imperial Akbar."

On this occasion I made use of the throne prepared by my father, and enriched at an expense without parallel for the celebration of the festival of the

Source: *The Memoirs of the Emperor Jahangir*, translated from the Persian by Major David Price (London: Oriental Translation Committee, 1829), 1–3, 5–8, 15.

new year.... Having thus seated myself on the throne of my expectations and wishes, I caused also the imperial crown, which my father had caused to be made after the manner of that which was worn by the great kings of Persia, to be brought before me, and then, in the presence of the whole assembled Emirs, having placed it on my brows, as an omen auspicious to the stability and happiness of my reign, kept it there for the space of a full astronomical hour....

For forty days and forty nights I caused the... great imperial state drum, to strike up, without ceasing, the strains of joy and triumph; and... around my throne, the ground was spread by my directions with the most costly brocades and gold embroidered carpets. Censers° of gold and silver were disposed in different directions for the purpose of burning odoriferous drugs, and nearly three thousand camphorated wax lights... illuminated the scene from night till morning. Numbers of blooming youths, beautiful as young Joseph in the pavilions of Egypt, clad in dresses of the most costly materials... awaited my commands, rank after rank, and in attitude most respectful. And finally, the Emirs of the empire... covered from head to foot in gold and jewels, and shoulder to shoulder, stood round in brilliant array, also waiting for the commands of their sovereign. For forty days and forty nights did I keep open to the world these scenes of festivity and splendor, furnishing altogether an example of imperial magnificence seldom paralleled in this stage of earthly existence....

I instituted... special regulations... as rules of conduct, never to be deviated from in their respective stations.

1. I remitted [canceled] altogether to my subjects three sources of revenue taxes or duties....

2. I directed, when the district lay waste or destitute of inhabitants, that towns should be built.... I charged the Jaguir-daurs,° or feudatories of the empire, in such deserted places to erect mosques and substantial... stations for the accommodation of travelers, in order to render the district once more an inhabited country, and that wayfaring men might again be able to pass and repass in safety.

3. Merchants traveling through the country were not to have their bales or packages of any kind opened without their consent. But when they were perfectly willing to dispose of any article of merchandise, purchasers were permitted to deal with them, without, however, offering any species of molestation....

5. No person was permitted either to make or sell either wine or any other kind of intoxicating liquor. I undertook to institute this regulation, although it is sufficiently notorious that I have myself the strongest inclination for wine, in which from the age of sixteen I have liberally indulged....

6. No person [official] was permitted to take up his abode obtrusively in the dwelling of any subject of my realm....

7. No person was to suffer, for any offense, the loss of a nose or ear. If the crime were theft, the offender was to be scourged with thorns, or deterred from further transgression by an attestation on the Koran.

8. [High officials] were prohibited from possessing themselves by violence of the lands of the subject, or from cultivating them on their own account....

10. The governors in all the principal cities were directed to establish infirmaries or hospitals, with competent medical aid for the relief of the sick....

11. During the month of my birth... the use of all animal food was prohibited both in town and country; and at equidistant periods throughout the year a day was set apart, on which all slaughtering of animals was strictly forbidden.

[H]aving on one occasion asked my father [Akbar] the reason why he had forbidden any one to prevent or interfere with the building of these haunts of idolatry [Hindu temples], his reply was in the following terms: "My dear child," said he, "I find myself a powerful monarch, the shadow of God upon earth. I have seen that he bestows the blessings of his gracious providence upon all his creatures without distinction. Ill should I discharge the duties of my exalted station, were I to withhold my compas-

---

°**Censers:** containers for burning incense.

°**Jaguir-daurs:** local rulers granted a certain territory by the Emperor.

sion and indulgence from any of those entrusted to my charge. With all of the human race, with all of God's creatures, I am at peace: why then should I permit myself, under any consideration, to be the cause of molestation or aggression to any one? Besides, are not five parts in six of mankind either Hindus or aliens to the faith; and were I to be governed by motives of the kind suggested in your inquiry, what alternative can I have but to put them all to death! I have thought it therefore my wisest plan to let these men alone. Neither is it to be forgotten, that the class of whom we are speaking… are usefully engaged, either in the pursuits of science or the arts, or of improvements for the benefit of mankind, and have in numerous instances arrived at the highest distinctions in the state, there being, indeed, to be found in this city men of every description, and of every religion on the face of the earth."

Document 14.3

An Outsider's View of Suleiman I

Under Suleiman I (1520–1566), the Ottoman Empire reached its greatest territorial extent and perhaps its "golden age" in terms of culture and economy (see Map 14.3, p. 647). A helpful window into the life of this most powerful of Muslim states comes from the writings of Ogier Ghiselin de Busbecq, a Flemish nobleman who served as a diplomat for the Austrian Empire, which then felt under great threat from Ottoman expansion into central Europe. For six years in the mid-sixteenth century, Busbecq represented Austria in the Ottoman Empire, from which he sent a stream of letters to a friend. The excerpts in Document 14.3 present his view of the Ottoman court and his reflections on Ottoman military power.

- How do you think Busbecq's outsider status shaped his perceptions of Ottoman political and military life? To what extent does his role as a foreigner enhance or undermine the usefulness of his account for historians?

- How did he define the differences between Ottoman Empire and Austria? What do you think he hoped to accomplish by highlighting these differences?

- What sources of Ottoman political authority are apparent in Busbecq's account?

- What potential problems of the Ottoman Empire does this document imply or state?

OGIER GHISELIN DE BUSBECQ

The Turkish Letters

1555–1562

On his [Suleiman's] arrival we were admitted to an audience; but the manner and spirit in which he listened to our address, our arguments, and our message, was by no means favorable. The Sultan was seated on a very low ottoman, not more than a foot from the ground, which was covered with a quantity of costly rugs and cushions of exquisite workmanship; near him lay his bow and arrows. His air, as I said, was by no means gracious, and his face wore a stern, though dignified, expression. On entering we were separately conducted into the royal presence by the chamberlains, who grasped our arms. This has been the Turkish fashion of admitting people to the Sovereign ever since a Croat, in order to avenge the death of his master... asked Amurath [an earlier Sultan] for an audience, and took advantage of it to slay him. After having gone through a pretense of kissing his hand, we were conducted backward to the wall opposite his seat, care being taken that we should never turn our backs on him....

The Sultan's hall was crowded with people, among whom were several officers of high rank. Besides these there were all the troopers of the Imperial guard and a large force of Janissaries; but there was not in all that great assembly a single man who owed his position to aught save his valor and his merit. No distinction is attached to birth among the Turks.... In making his appointments the Sultan pays no regard to any pretensions on the score of wealth or rank, nor does he take into consideration recommendations or popularity.... It is by merit that men rise in the service, a system which ensures that posts should only be assigned to the competent.... Those who receive the highest offices from the Sultan are for the most part the sons of shepherds or herdsmen, and so far from being ashamed of their parentage, they

actually glory in it, and consider it a matter of boasting that they owe nothing to the accident of birth....

Among the Turks, therefore, honors, high posts, and judgeships are the rewards of great ability and good service. If a man be dishonest, or lazy, or careless, he remains at the bottom of the ladder, an object of contempt; for such qualities there are no honors in Turkey! This is the reason that they are successful in their undertakings, that they lord it over others, and are daily extending the bounds of their empire. These are not our ideas, with us [Europeans] there is no opening left for merit; birth is the standard for everything; the prestige of birth is the sole key to advancement in the public service....

[T]ake your stand by my side, and look at the sea of turbaned heads, each wrapped in twisted folds of the whitest silk; look at those marvelously handsome dresses of every kind and every color; time would fail me to tell how all around is glittering with gold, with silver, with purple, with silk, and with velvet; words cannot convey an adequate idea of that strange and wondrous sight: it was the most beautiful spectacle I ever saw.

With all this luxury, great simplicity and economy are combined; every man's dress, whatever his position may be, is of the same pattern; no fringes or useless points are sewn on, as is the case with us, appendages which cost a great deal of money, and are worn out in three days.... I was greatly struck with the silence and order that prevailed in this great crowd. There were no cries, no hum of voices, the usual accompaniments of a motley gathering, neither was there any jostling; without the slightest disturbance each man took his proper place according to his rank....

On leaving the assembly we had a fresh treat in the sight of the household cavalry returning to their quarters; the men were mounted on splendid horses, excellently groomed, and gorgeously accoutred. And so we left the royal presence, taking with us but little hope of a successful issue to our embassy.

Source: Charles Thornton Forester and F. H. Blackburne Daniell, *The Life and Letters of Ogier Ghiselin de Busbecq* (London: C. Kegan Paul and Co., 1881), 114–15, 152–56, 219–22.

The Turkish monarch going to war takes with him over 40,000 camels and nearly as many baggage mules, of which a great part, when he is invading Persia, are loaded with rice and other kinds of grain.... The invading army carefully abstains from encroaching on its magazines° at the outset.... The Sultan's magazines are opened, and a ration just sufficient to sustain life is daily weighed out to the Janissaries and other troops of the royal household.

From this you will see that it is the patience, self-denial, and thrift of the Turkish soldier that enable him to face the most trying circumstances.... What a contrast to our men! Christian soldiers on a campaign refuse to put up with their ordinary food, and call for thrushes, beccaficos,° and such like dainty dishes! If these are not supplied they grow mutinous and work their own ruin; and, if they are supplied, they are ruined all the same. For each man is his own worst enemy, and has no foe more deadly than his own intemperance, which is sure to kill him, if the enemy be not quick.

It makes me shudder to think of what the result of a struggle between such different systems must be; one of us must prevail and the other be destroyed.... On their side is the vast wealth of their empire, unimpaired resources, experience and practice in arms, a veteran soldiery, an uninterrupted series of victories, readiness to endure hardships, union, order, discipline, thrift, and watchfulness. On ours are found an empty exchequer, luxurious habits, exhausted resources, broken spirits, a raw and insubordinate soldiery, and greedy generals; there is no regard for discipline, license runs riot, the men indulge in drunkenness and debauchery, and, worst of all, the enemy are accustomed to victory, we, to defeat. Can we doubt what the result must be? The only obstacle is Persia, whose position on his rear forces the invader to take precautions. The fear of Persia gives us a respite, but it is only for a time. When he has secured himself in that quarter, he will fall upon us with all the resources of the East. How ill prepared we are to meet such an attack it is not for me to say.

[In the following passage, Busbeq reflects on a major problem of the Ottoman state, succession to the throne.]

The sons of Turkish Sultans are in the most wretched position in the world, for, as soon as one of them succeeds his father, the rest are doomed to certain death. The Turk can endure no rival to the throne, and, indeed, the conduct of the Janissaries renders it impossible for the new Sultan to spare his brothers; for if one of them survives, the Janissaries are forever asking largesses. If these are refused, forthwith the cry is heard, "Long live the brother!" "God preserve the brother!"—a tolerably broad hint that they intend to place him on the throne. So that the Turkish Sultans are compelled to celebrate their succession by imbruing their hands in the blood of their nearest relatives.

_____

°**magazines:** supplies.

°**beccafico:** a small bird.

Documents 14.4 and 14.5

French State Building and Louis XIV

Like their counterparts in the Middle East and Asia, a number of European states in the early modern era also pursued the twin projects of imperial expansion abroad and political integration at home. But consolidating central authority was a long and difficult task. Obstacles to the ambitions of kings in Europe were many—the absence of an effective transportation and communication infrastructure; the difficulty of acquiring information about the population and resources; the entrenched interests of privileged groups such as the nobility, church, town councils, and guilds; and the division between Catholics and Protestants.

Perhaps the most well-known example of such European state-building efforts is that of France under the rule of Louis XIV (reigned 1643–1715). Louis and other European monarchs, such as those in Spain and Russia, operated under a set of assumptions known as "absolutism," which held that kings ruled by "divine right" and could legitimately claim sole and uncontested power in their realms. Louis's famous dictum *"L'etat, c'est moi"* ("I am the state") summed up the absolutist ideal. Documents 14.4 and 14.5 illustrate several ways in which Louis attempted to realize this ideal.

Document 14.4, written by Louis himself, focuses on the importance of "spectacle" and public display in solidifying the exalted role of the monarch. The "carousel" described in the document was an extravagant pageant, held in Paris in June of 1662. It featured various exotic animals, slaves, princes, and nobles arrayed in fantastic costumes representing distant lands, together with much equestrian competition. Unifying this disparate assembly was King Louis himself, dressed as a Roman emperor, while on the shields of the nobles was that grand symbol of the monarchy, the sun.

■ What posture does Louis take toward his subjects in this document?

■ How does he understand the role of spectacle in general and the carousel in particular?

■ What does the choice of the sun as a royal symbol suggest about Louis's conception of his role in the French state and empire?

Document 14.5 explores yet another effort at French state building, expanding the power of *intendants*, royal officials appointed by the king. They differed from other officials in that they were not native to the regions they administered and did not own the offices they held. Thus they were instruments of royal authority and more centralized control. Document 14.5, written in 1680 by Jean-Baptiste Colbert, Louis's famous minister of finance, instructs these intendants on their duties.

■ What was the main purpose of the intendants according to this document?

■ What kind of opposition do you expect the intendants experienced?

Louis XIV
Memoirs
1670

It was necessary to conserve and cultivate with care all that which, without diminishing the authority and the respect due to me, linked me by bonds of affection to my peoples and above all to the people of rank, so as to make them see by this very means that it was neither aversion for them nor affected severity, nor harshness of spirit, but simply reason and duty, that made me more reserved and more exact toward them in other matters. That sharing of pleasures, which gives people at court a respectable familiarity with us, touches them and charms them more than can be expressed. The common people, on the other hand, are delighted by shows in which, at bottom, we always have the aim of pleasing them; and all our subjects, in general, are delighted to see that we like what they like, or what they excel in. By this means we hold on to their hearts and their minds, sometimes more strongly perhaps than by recompenses and gifts; and with regard to foreigners, in a state they see flourishing and well ordered, that which is spent on expenses and which could be called superfluous, makes a very favorable impression on them, of magnificence, of power, of grandeur. . . .

The carousel, which has furnished me the subject of these reflections, had only been conceived at first as a light amusement; but little by little, we were carried away, and it became a spectacle that was fairly grand and magnificent, both in the number of exercises, and by the novelty of the costumes and the variety of the [heraldic] devices. It was then that I began to employ the one that I have always kept since and which you see in so many places. I believed that, without limiting itself to something precise and lessening, it ought to represent in some way the duties of a prince, and constantly encourage me to fulfill them. For the device they chose the sun, which, according to the rules of this art, is the most noble of all, and which, by its quality of being unique, by the brilliance that surrounds it, by the light that it communicates to the other stars which form for it a kind of court, by the just and equal share that the different climates of the world receive of this light, by the good it does in all places, ceaselessly producing as it does, in every sphere of life, joy and activity, by its unhindered movement, in which it nevertheless always appears calm, by its constant and invariable course, from which it never departs nor wavers, is the most striking and beautiful image of a great monarch.

Those who saw me governing with a good deal of ease and without being confused by anything, in all the numerous attentions that royalty demands, persuaded me to add the earth's globe, and for motto, *nec pluribus impar* (not unequal to many things): by which they meant something that flattered the aspirations of a young king, namely that, being sufficient to so many things, I would doubtless be capable of governing other empires, just as the sun was capable of lighting up other worlds if they were exposed to its rays.

Source: Robert Campbell, *Louis XIV* (London: Longmans, 1993), 117–18.

Jean-Baptiste Colbert
Instructions for Intendants
1680

The King has instructed me to repeat most strongly to you the orders which His Majesty has given you, in every preceding year, about the inspection of the generality in which you serve. He wants you to apply yourself to this task even more vigorously than you have in the past, because he wishes there to be equality in the allocation of taxes and a reduction in all kinds of abuses and expenses, thus bringing further relief to his peoples in addition to that which they have received from the lowering of taxation.

The King intends that, as soon as you have read this letter, you should begin your visit to each of the elections in your generality:

That, during this tour, you should examine with the utmost care the extent of landed wealth, the quality of livestock, the state of industries and in fact everything in each election [district] which helps to attract money there; that you should seek out, with the same diligence, anything which might help to increase animal foodstuffs, to expand industrial production or even to establish new manufactures. At the same time, His Majesty wants you to journey to three or four of the main towns in each election, excluding those which you have chosen in earlier years, and in these places to call before you a large number of the tax-collectors and leading inhabitants from the surrounding parishes; to take pains to find out all that has taken place concerning the receipt of the King's orders, the nomination of collectors, and the allocation and payment of the *taille*;° to ferret out all the malpractices in these procedures; try to remedy them yourself; and, in case you find some which can be treated

only by a royal judgment or decree, to send me a report in order that I may inform His Majesty....

Listen to all the complaints which are brought to you about inequalities in allocation on the rolls of the *tailles*, and do everything which you consider appropriate to stamp out these iniquities and to make the allocation as fair as possible. Examine with the same thoroughness the expenses which are incurred, both by the receivers in relation to the collectors and by the collectors in relation to the taxpayers.... One of the most effective methods which His Majesty wishes you to use in repressing these abuses is to suspend the receiver of the *tailles* who seems the most culpable in your generality, and to entrust his duties to someone else for the next year. This punishment will assuredly cause the disappearance of many of these evil practices. His Majesty will also offer a reward to the receiver who has run his election the most effectively, and who has incurred the least expenses.

His Majesty likewise requires that you should report every three months, without fail, on the number of prisoners who have been arrested concerning the *taille* or the various indirect taxes....

You must also inspect in each election the amount of the taxes collected to date, both for last year and for this, giving all the necessary orders for hurrying up the whole process....

He also requires you to keep watch over everything involving the coinage throughout your generality, which is to say that only coins authorized by royal edict and decree may be in circulation. On this same subject, His Majesty wants you continually to ascertain that there are no mints producing false coins; and, if you should find one, to send word immediately, so that His Majesty may issue the necessary orders for bringing the culprits to trial without delay, because there is no crime which is more prejudicial to the interests of the people than this one.

°**taille:** land tax.

Source: Roger R. Mettan, *Government and Society in Louis XIV's France* (Basingstoke: Macmillan, 1977), 18–21.

Using the Evidence:
State Building in the Early Modern Era

1. **Making comparisons:** To what extent did these four early modern states face similar problems and devise similar solutions? How did they differ? In particular, how did the rulers of these states deal with subordinates? How did they use violence? What challenges to imperial authority did they face?

2. **Assessing spectacle:** In what different ways was spectacle, royal splendor, or public display evident in the documents? How would you define the purpose of such display? How effective do you think spectacle has been in consolidating state authority?

3. **Distinguishing power and authority:** Some scholars have made a distinction between "power," the ability of a state to coerce its subjects into some required behavior, and "authority," the ability of a state to persuade its subjects to do its bidding voluntarily by convincing them that it is proper, right, or natural to do so. What examples of power and authority can you find in these documents? How were they related? What are the advantages and disadvantages of each, from the viewpoint of ambitious rulers?

4. **Comparing past and present:** It is important to recognize that early modern states differed in many ways from twentieth or twenty-first century states. How would you define those differences? Consider, among other things, the personal role of the ruler, the use of violence, the means of establishing authority, and the extent to which the state could shape the lives of its citizens.

Visual Sources

Considering the Evidence:
The Conquest of Mexico
Through Aztec Eyes

Among the sagas of early modern empire building, few have been more dramatic, more tragic, or better documented than the Spanish conquest of Mexico during the early sixteenth century (see Map 14.1, p. 627). In recounting this story, historians are fortunate in having considerable evidence—both documentary and visual—from the Aztec side of the encounter.

The peoples of central Mexico had long used a type of book called a codex to record their history. Codices included drawings and symbols (glyphs) painted by carefully trained high-status persons known as *tlacuilo* (artist-scribes). Although Spanish invaders destroyed most of these codices, the codex tradition continued in a modified form in the century following conquest. These new codices, often assembled under the supervision of European missionaries, were largely composed by native peoples, many of them new converts to Christianity and some of them literate in both Spanish and Latin. These codices included numerous paintings by local artists as well as written texts in a variety of Mesoamerican languages using the Roman alphabet.

The *Florentine Codex*, for example, was compiled under the leadership of Fray Bernardino de Sahagun, a Franciscan missionary who felt that an understanding of Aztec culture was essential to the task of conversion. Because Sahagun relied on Aztec informants and artists, many scholars believe that the Florentine and other codices represent indigenous understandings of the conquest. However, they require a critical reading. They date from several decades after the events they describe. Many contributors to the codices had been influenced by the Christian and European culture of their missionary mentors, and they were writing in a society thoroughly dominated by Spanish colonial rule. Furthermore, the codices reflect the ethnic and regional diversity of Mesoamerica rather than a single Aztec perspective. Despite such limitations, these codices represent a unique window into Mesoamerican understandings of the conquest.

In the Aztec telling of the Spanish conquest, accounts of earlier warnings or omens of disaster abound. One of these was described as follows in the *Florentine Codex*: "Ten years before the arrival of the Spaniards an omen first

Visual Source 14.1 Disaster Foretold (Biblioteca Nacional Madrid/Gianni Dagli Orti/The Art Archive)

appeared in the sky like a flame or tongue of fire.... For a full year it showed itself.... People were taken aback, they lamented."[28] That ominous appearance was illustrated in the *Duran Codex*, presented here in Visual Source 14.1 showing the Aztec ruler Moctezuma observing this omen of death from the rooftop of his palace. Some scholars suggest that such stories reflect a postconquest understanding of the traumatic defeat the Aztecs suffered, for other evidence indicates that the Aztecs were not initially alarmed by the coming of the Spanish and that, instead, they viewed the Europeans as "simply another group of powerful and dangerous outsiders who needed to be controlled or accommodated."[29]

■ Why might Aztec contributors to the codices have included accounts of such supernatural events preceding the arrival of the Spanish?

■ Why do you think the Spanish frequently incorporated such accounts into their own descriptions of the conquest?

■ Why might the artist have chosen to show Moctezuma alone rather than in the company of his supposedly fearful people?

Visual Source 14.2 Moctezuma and Cortés (The Granger Collection, New York)

In February of 1519 Hernán Cortés, accompanied by some 350 Spanish soldiers, set off from Cuba with a fleet of eleven ships, stopping at several places along the Gulf of Mexico before proceeding to march inland toward Tenochtitlán, the capital of the Aztec Empire. Along the way, he learned something about the fabulous wealth of this empire and about the fragility of its political structure. Through a combination of force and astute diplomacy, Cortés was able to negotiate alliances with a number of the Aztecs' restive subject peoples and with the Aztecs' many rivals or enemies, especially the Tlaxcala. With his modest forces thus greatly reinforced, Cortés arrived in Tenochtitlán on November 8, 1519, where he met with Moctezuma. Visual Source 14.2 presents an image of that epic encounter, drawn from the Lienzo de Tlaxcala, a series of paintings completed by 1560. They reflect generally the viewpoint of the Tlaxcala people.

■ How does this painting present the relationship between Cortés and Moctezuma? Are they meeting as equals, as enemies, as allies, as ruler and subject? Notice that both sit on European-style chairs, which had come to suggest authority in the decades following Spanish conquest.

■ What do the items at the bottom of the image represent?

■ Does this image support or challenge the perception that the Aztecs viewed the Spanish newcomers, at least initially, in religious terms as gods?

■ What might the painter have tried to convey by placing three attendants behind Moctezuma, while Cortés appears alone, except for his translator?

The woman standing behind Cortés in Visual Source 14.2 is Doña Marina (sometimes called La Malinche), a Nahuatl-speaking woman who had been a slave in Maya territory and was given as a gift to Cortés's forces in April 1519. She subsequently became an interpreter for the Spanish, as well as Cortés's mistress. Doña Marina appears frequently and prominently in many of the paintings of the era. Cortés himself wrote that "after God we owe this conquest of New Spain to Doña Marina." But in Mexico, some have condemned her as a traitor to her people, while others have praised her as the beginning of European and Native American cooperation and mixing.

■ What impression of Doña Marina does this image suggest?

Whatever the character of their initial meeting, the relationship of the Spanish and Aztecs soon deteriorated amid mutual suspicion. Within a week, Cortés had seized Moctezuma, holding him under a kind of house arrest in his own palaces. For reasons not entirely clear, this hostile act did not immediately trigger a violent Aztec response. Perhaps Aztec authorities were concerned for the life of their ruler, or perhaps their factional divisions inhibited coordinated resistance.

But in May 1520, while Cortés was temporarily away at the coast, an incident occurred that set in motion the most violent phase of the encounter. During a religious ceremony in honor of Huitzilopochtli, the Aztec patron deity of Tenochtitlán, the local Spanish commander, apparently fearing an uprising, launched a surprise attack on the unarmed participants in the celebration, killing hundreds of the leading warriors and nobles. An Aztec account from the *Florentine Codex* described the scene:

Visual Source 14.3   The Massacre of the Nobles (Bridgeman-Giraudon/Art Resource, NY)

[W]hen the dance was loveliest and when song was linked to song, the Spaniards were seized with an urge to kill the celebrants. They all ran forward, armed as if for battle. They closed the entrances and passageways...then [they] rushed into the Sacred Patio to slaughter the inhabitants....They attacked the man who was drumming and cut off his arms. Then they cut off his head, and it rolled across the floor. They attacked all the celebrants stabbing them, spearing them, striking them with swords....Others they beheaded...or split their heads to pieces....The blood of the warriors flowed like water and gathered into pools...[T]hey invaded every room, hunting and killing.[30]

Visual Source 14.3 shows a vivid depiction of this "massacre of the nobles," drawn from the *Codex Duran*, first published in 1581.

■ What elements of the description above are reflected in this painting?

■ What image of the Spanish does this painting reflect?

■ What do the drums in the center of the image represent?

The massacre of the nobles prompted a citywide uprising against the hated Spanish, who were forced to flee Tenochtitlán on June 30, 1520, across a causeway in Lake Texcoco amid ferocious fighting. Some 600 Spaniards and several thousand of their Tlaxcala allies perished in the escape, many of them laden with gold they had collected in Tenochtitlán. For the Spaniards it was La Noche Triste (the night of sorrow), while for the Aztecs it was no doubt a fitting revenge and a great triumph. Visual Source 14.4, from a Tlaxcala codex, depicts the scene. Cortés and his Tlaxcala allies to the left of the image are shown on the causeway, while many others are drowning in the lake, pursued by Aztec warriors in canoes.

- Whose perspective do you think is represented in this image—that of the Spanish, their Tlaxcala allies, or the Aztecs? How might each of them have understood this retreat differently?

- In neither Visual Source 14.3 or 14.4 are the Spanish portrayed with their firearms. How might you understand this omission?

- Notice the blending of artistic styles in this image. The water, the boats, and shields of the warriors are shown in traditional Mesoamerican fashion, while the Spanish are portrayed in European stereotypes. What does this blending suggest about the cultural processes at work in the codices?

Visual Source 14.4 The Spanish Retreat from Tenochtitlán (The Rout of La Noche Triste [June 30, 1520], Lienzo de Tlaxcala, Pl 18. Library of Congress)

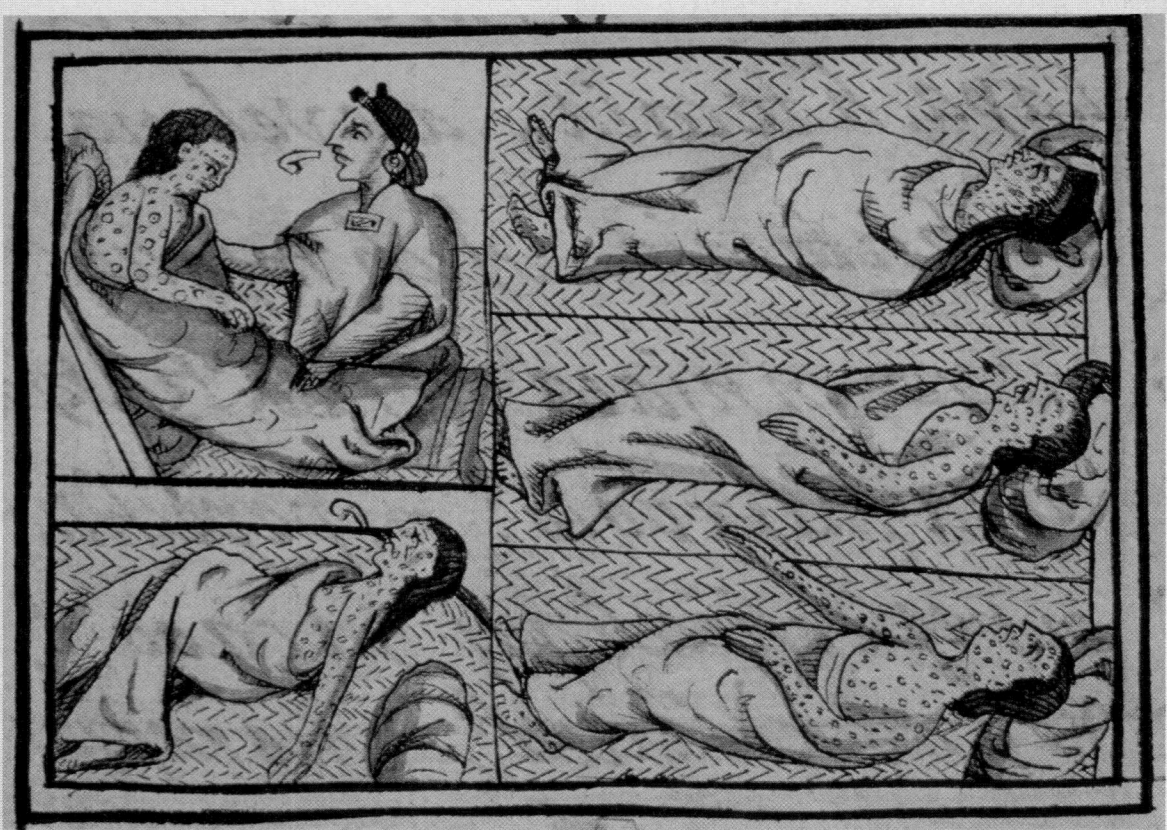

Visual Source 14.5 Smallpox: Disease and Defeat (Biblioteca Medicea Laurenziana, Florence)

While the Aztecs may well have thought themselves permanently rid of the Spanish, La Noche Triste offered only a temporary respite from the European invaders. Cortés and his now diminished forces found refuge among their Tlaxcala allies, where they regrouped and planned for yet another assault on Tenochtitlán. Meanwhile, smallpox had begun to ravage the Aztec population, which lacked any immunity to this Old World disease. The *Florentine Codex* described the situation: "[A]n epidemic broke out, a sickness of pustules. . . . [The disease] brought great desolation; a great many died of it. They could no longer walk about . . . no longer able to move or stir. . . . Starvation reigned, and no one took care of others any longer. . . . And when things were in this state, the Spaniards came." Visual Source 14.5, likewise from the *Florentine Codex*, is an Aztec portrayal of the disease.

In mid-1521, Cortés returned, strengthened with yet more Mesoamerican allies, and laid siege to the Aztec capital. Bitter fighting ensued, often in the form of house-to-house combat, ending with the surrender of the last Aztec emperor on August 13, 1521. In Tenochtitlán, all was sorrow and lamentation, as reflected in some of the poetry of the time:

> Nothing but flowers and songs of sorrow are left in Mexico and Tlateloco
> where once we saw warriors and wise men....
> We wander here and there in our desolate poverty.
> We are mortal men.
> We have seen bloodshed and pain where once we saw beauty and valor.
> We are crushed to the ground; we lie in ruins....
> Have you grown weary of your servants?
> Are you angry with your servants, O giver of Life?[31]

■ How does Visual Source 14.5 represent the impact of the smallpox epidemic and Aztec response to it?

Using the Evidence:
The Conquest of Mexico through Aztec Eyes

1. **Evaluating images as evidence:** What are the strengths and the limitations of these images as sources for understanding the colonial conquest of Mexico? How well did the native artists who created them understand the Spanish?

2. **Analyzing perspectives:** How might you define the perspective from which these visual sources approach their subjects? Keep in mind that they were drawn by native artists who had been clearly influenced by Spanish culture and religion. In what ways are they criticizing the Spanish conquest, celebrating it, or simply describing it?

3. **Portraying the Spanish:** In what ways do these visual sources portray the Spanish? How might the Spanish themselves present a different account of the conquest?

4. **Describing the conquest:** Based on the information in this section, write a brief description of the conquest from the Aztec point of view.

Global Commerce

1450–1750

Europeans and Asian Commerce
  A Portuguese Empire of Commerce
  Spain and the Philippines
  The East India Companies
  Asian Commerce
Silver and Global Commerce
The "World Hunt": Fur in
  Global Commerce
Commerce in People: The Atlantic
  Slave Trade
  The Slave Trade in Context
  The Slave Trade in Practice
  Comparing Consequences: The
    Impact of the Slave Trade in Africa
Reflections: Economic
  Globalization—Then and Now
Considering the Evidence
  Documents: Voices from the
    Slave Trade
  Visual Sources: Exchange and
    Status in the Early Modern World

"I have come full circle back to my destiny: from Africa to America and back to Africa. I could hear the cries and wails of my ancestors. I weep with them and for them."[1] This is what an African American woman from Atlanta wrote in 2002 in the guest book of the Cape Coast Castle, one of the many ports of embarkation for slaves located along the coast of Ghana in West Africa. There she no doubt saw the whips and leg irons used to discipline the captured Africans as well as the windowless dungeons in which hundreds of them were crammed while waiting for the ships that would carry them across the Atlantic to the Americas. Almost certainly she also caught sight of the infamous "gate of no return," through which the captives departed to their new life as slaves.

THIS VISITOR'S EMOTIONAL ENCOUNTER WITH THE LEGACY OF THE ATLANTIC SLAVE TRADE reminds us of the enormous significance of this commerce in human beings for the early modern world and of its continuing echoes even at the beginning of the twenty-first century. The slave trade, however, was only one component of those international trading networks that shaped human interactions during the centuries between 1450 and 1750. Europeans now smashed their way into the ancient spice trade of the Indian Ocean, developing new relationships with Asian societies as a result. Silver, obtained from mines in Spanish America, enriched Western Europe, even as much of it made its way to China, where it allowed Europeans

The Atlantic Slave Trade: Among the threads of global commerce during the early modern era, none has resonated more loudly in historical memory than the Atlantic slave trade. This eighteenth-century French painting shows the sale of slaves at Goree, a major slave trading port in what is now Dakar in Senegal. A European merchant and an African authority figure negotiate the arrangement, while the shackled victims themselves wait for their fate to be decided. (Bibliothèque des Arts Décoratifs, Paris/Archives Charmet/The Bridgeman Art Library)

to participate more fully in the rich commerce of East Asia. Furs from North America and Siberia found a ready market in Europe and China, while the hunting and trapping of those fur-bearing animals transformed both natural environments and human societies. Despite their growing prominence in long-distance exchange, Europeans were far from the only active traders. Southeast Asians, Chinese, Indians, Armenians, Arabs, and Africans likewise played major roles in the making of the world economy of the early modern era.

Thus commerce joined empire as the twin drivers of globalization during these centuries. Together they created new relationships, disrupted old patterns, brought distant peoples into contact with one another, enriched some, and impoverished or enslaved others. From the various "old worlds" of the premodern era, a single "new world" emerged—slowly, with great pain, and accompanied by growing inequalities. What was gained and what was lost in the transformations born of global commerce have been the subject of great controversy ever since.

Europeans and Asian Commerce

Schoolchildren everywhere know that European empires in the Western Hemisphere grew out of an accident—Columbus's unknowing encounter with the Americas—and that new colonial societies and new commercial connections across the Atlantic were the result. In Asia, it was a very different story. The voyage (1497–1499) of the Portuguese mariner Vasco da Gama, in which Europeans sailed to India for the first time, was certainly no accident. It was the outcome of a deliberate, systematic, century-long Portuguese effort to explore a sea route to the East, by creeping slowly down the West African coast, around the tip of South Africa, up the East African coast, and finally to Calicut in southern India in 1498. There Europeans encountered an ancient and rich network of commerce that stretched from East Africa to China. They were certainly aware of the wealth of that commercial network, but largely ignorant of its workings.

■ **Causation**
What drove European involvement in the world of Asian commerce?

The most immediate motivation for this massive effort was the desire for tropical spices—cinnamon, nutmeg, mace, cloves, and, above all, pepper—which were widely used as condiments and preservatives and were sometimes regarded as aphrodisiacs. Other products of the East, such as Chinese silk, Indian cottons, rhubarb for medicinal purposes, emeralds, rubies, and sapphires, also were in great demand.

Underlying this growing interest in Asia was the more general recovery of European civilization following the disaster of the Black Death in the early fourteenth century. During the fifteenth century, Europe's population was growing again, and its national monarchies—in Spain, Portugal, England, and France—were learning how to tax their subjects more effectively and to build substantial military forces equipped with gunpowder weapons. Its cities were growing too. Some of them—in England, the Netherlands, and northern Italy, for example—were becoming centers of international commerce, giving birth to a more capitalist economy based on market exchange, private ownership, and the accumulation of capital for further investment.

For many centuries, Eastern goods had trickled into the Mediterranean through the Middle East from the Indian Ocean commercial network. From the viewpoint of an increasingly dynamic Europe, several major problems accompanied this pattern of commerce. First, of course, the source of supply for these much-desired goods lay solidly in Muslim hands. Most immediately, Muslim Egypt was the primary point of transfer into the Mediterranean basin and its European customers. The Italian commercial city of Venice largely monopolized the European trade in Eastern goods, annually sending convoys of ships to Alexandria in Egypt. Venetians resented the Muslim monopoly on Indian Ocean trade, and other European powers disliked relying on Venice as well as on Muslims. Circumventing these monopolies was yet another impetus—both religious and political—for the Portuguese to attempt a sea route to India that bypassed both Venetian and Muslim middlemen. In addition, many Europeans of the time were persuaded that a mysterious Christian monarch, known as Prester John, ruled somewhere in Asia or Africa. Joining with his mythical kingdom to continue the Crusades and combat a common Islamic enemy was likewise a goal of the Portuguese voyages.

A final problem lay in paying for Eastern goods. Few products of an economically less developed Europe were attractive in Eastern markets. Thus Europeans were required to pay cash—gold or silver—for Asian spices or textiles. This persistent trade deficit contributed much to the intense desire for precious metals that attracted early modern European explorers, traders, and conquerors. Portuguese voyages along the West African coast, for example, were seeking direct access to African goldfields. The enormously rich silver deposits of Mexico and Bolivia provided at least a temporary solution to this persistent European problem.

First the Portuguese and then the Spanish, French, Dutch, and British found their way into the ancient Asian world of Indian Ocean commerce (see Map 15.1). How they behaved in that world and what they created there differed considerably among the various European countries, but collectively they contributed much to the new regime of globalized trade.

A Portuguese Empire of Commerce

The arena of Indian Ocean commerce into which Vasco da Gama and his Portuguese successors sailed was a world away from anything they had known. It was a vast world, both in geographic extent and in the diversity of those who participated in it. East Africans, Arabs, Persians, Indians, Malays, Chinese, and others traded freely. Most of them were Muslims, though hailing from many separate communities, but Hindus, Christians, Jews, and Chinese likewise had a role in this commercial network. Had the Portuguese sought simply to participate in peaceful trading, they certainly could have done so, but it was quickly apparent that European trade goods were crude and unattractive in Asian markets and that Europeans would be unable to compete effectively. Moreover, the Portuguese soon learned that most Indian Ocean merchant ships were not heavily armed and certainly lacked the onboard cannons that Portuguese ships carried. Since the withdrawal of the Chinese fleet from the Indian

■ **Connection**
To what extent did the Portuguese realize their own goals in the Indian Ocean?

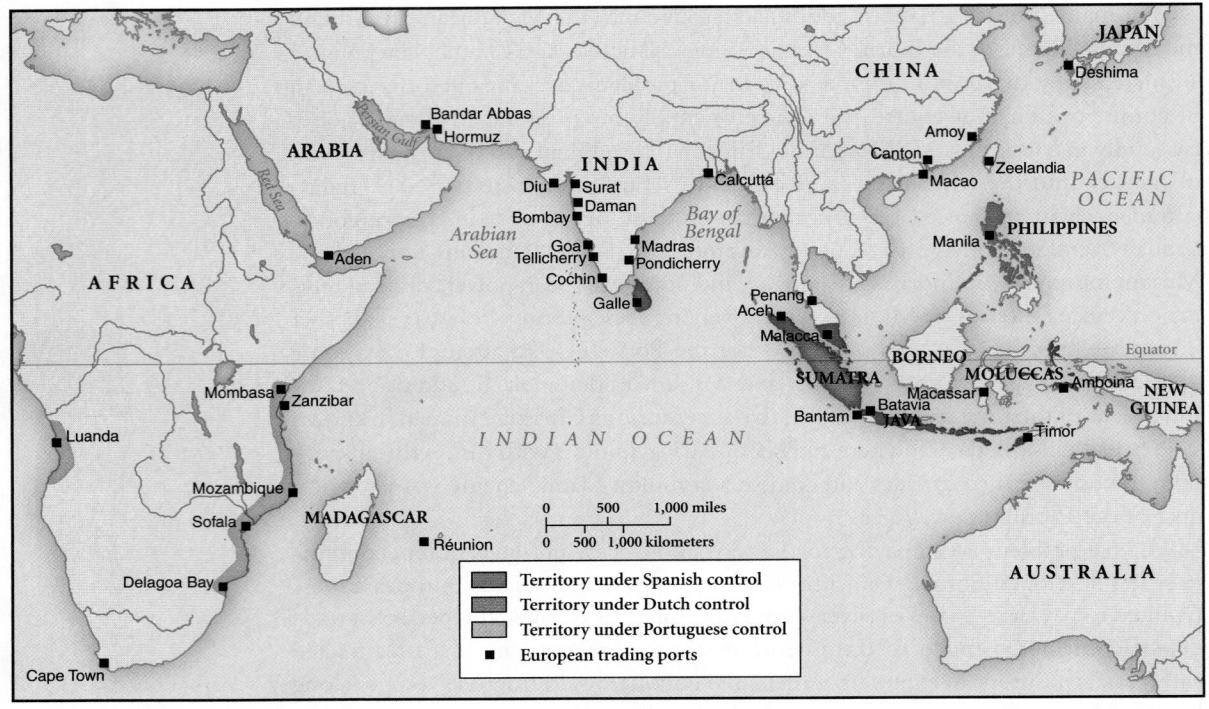

Map 15.1 Europeans in Asia in the Early Modern Era
The early modern era witnessed only very limited territorial control by Europeans in Asia. Trade, rather than empire, was the chief concern of the Western newcomers, who were not, in any event, a serious military threat to major Asian states.

Ocean early in the fifteenth century, no major power was in a position to dominate the sea-lanes, and the many smaller-scale merchants generally traded openly, although piracy was sometimes a problem.

Given these conditions, the Portuguese saw an opening, for their ships could outgun and outmaneuver competing naval forces, while their onboard cannons could devastate coastal fortifications. Although their overall economy lagged behind that of Asian producers, Europeans had more than caught up in the critical area of naval technology and naval warfare. This military advantage enabled the Portuguese to quickly establish fortified bases at several key locations within the Indian Ocean world—Mombasa in East Africa, Hormuz at the entrance to the Persian Gulf, Goa on the west coast of India, Malacca in Southeast Asia, and Macao on the south coast of China. With the exception of Macao, which had been obtained through bribery and negotiations with Chinese authorities, these Portuguese bases were obtained forcibly against small and weak states. In Mombasa, for example, the commander of a Portuguese fleet responded to local resistance in 1505 by burning and sacking the city, killing some 1,500 people, and seizing large quantities of cotton and silk textiles and carpets. The king of Mombasa wrote a warning to a neighboring city:

This is to inform you that a great lord has passed through the town, burning it and laying it waste. He came to the town in such strength and was of such a cruelty that he spared neither man nor woman, or old nor young—nay, not even the smallest child. . . . Nor can I ascertain nor estimate what wealth they have taken from the town.[2]

What the Portuguese created in the Indian Ocean is commonly known as a "trading post empire," for they aimed to control commerce, not large territories or populations, and to do so by force of arms rather than by economic competition. Seeking to monopolize the spice trade, the Portuguese king grandly titled himself "Lord of the Conquest, Navigation, and Commerce of Ethiopia, Arabia, Persia, and India." Portuguese authorities in the East tried to require all merchant vessels to purchase a *cartaz*, or pass, and to pay duties of 6 to 10 percent on their cargoes. They partially blocked the traditional Red Sea route to the Mediterranean and for a century or so monopolized the highly profitable route around Africa to Europe. Even so, they never succeeded in controlling much more than half of the spice trade to Europe.[3]

Failing to dominate Indian Ocean commerce as they had hoped, the Portuguese gradually assimilated themselves to its ancient patterns. They became heavily involved in carrying Asian goods to Asian ports, selling their shipping services because they were largely unable to sell their goods. Even in their major settlements, the Portuguese were outnumbered by Asian traders, and many married Asian women. Hundreds of Portuguese escaped the control of their government altogether and settled in Asian or African ports, where they learned local languages, sometimes converted to Islam, and became simply one more group in the diverse trading culture of the East.

By 1600, the Portuguese trading post empire was in steep decline. This small European country was overextended, and rising Asian states such as Japan, Burma, Mughal India, Persia, and the sultanate of Oman actively resisted Portuguese commercial control. Unwilling to accept a dominant Portuguese role in the Indian Ocean, other European countries also gradually contested Portugal's efforts to monopolize the rich spice trade to Europe.

The Spice Trade
For thousands of years, spices were a major trade item in the Indian Ocean commercial network, as this fifteenth-century French depiction of the gathering of pepper in southern India illustrates. In the early modern era, Europeans gained direct access to this ancient network for the first time. (Bibliothèque nationale de France)

Spain and the Philippines

Spain was the first to challenge Portugal's position. As precious and profitable spices began to arrive in Europe on Portuguese ships in the early sixteenth century, the Spanish soon realized that they were behind in the race to gain access to the riches of the East. In an effort to catch up, they established themselves on what became the Philippine Islands, named after the Spanish king Philip II. The Spanish first

■ **Comparison**
How did the Portuguese, Spanish, Dutch, and British initiatives in Asia differ from one another?

$\mathcal{S}$napshot   **Key Moments in the European Encounter with Asia**

Vasco da Gama's arrival in India	1498
Portuguese trading post empire established	early 1500s
Spanish takeover of Philippines begins	1565
China establishes taxes payable in silver	1570s
Beginning of silver shipments from Mexico to Manila	1570s
British and Dutch East India companies begin operation in Asia	1601–1602
Missionaries expelled from Japan	early 1600s
Dutch conquest of nutmeg-producing Banda Islands	1620
French East India Company established	1664
British begin military conquest of India	1750s

encountered the region during the famous round-the-world voyage (1519–1521) of Ferdinand Magellan, a Portuguese mariner sailing on behalf of the Spanish Crown. There they found an archipelago of islands, thousands of them, occupied by culturally diverse peoples and organized in small and highly competitive chiefdoms. One of the local chiefs later told the Spanish: "There is no king and no sole authority in this land; but everyone holds his own view and opinion, and does as he prefers."[4] Some were involved in tribute trade with China, and a small number of Chinese settlers lived in the port towns. Nonetheless, the region was of little interest to the governments of China and Japan, the major powers in the area.

These conditions—proximity to China and the spice islands, small and militarily weak societies, the absence of competing claims—encouraged the Spanish to establish outright colonial rule on the islands, rather than to imitate a Portuguese-style trading post empire. Small-scale military operations, gunpowder weapons, local alliances, gifts and favors to chiefs, and the pageantry of Catholic ritual all contributed to a relatively easy and often bloodless Spanish takeover of the islands in the century or so after 1565. They remained a Spanish colonial territory until the end of the nineteenth century, when the United States assumed control following the Spanish–American War of 1898.

Accompanying Spanish rule was a major missionary effort, which turned Filipino society into the only major outpost of Christianity in Asia. That effort also opened up a new front in the long encounter of Christendom and Islam, for on the southern island of Mindanao, Islam was gaining strength and provided an ideology of resistance to Spanish encroachment for 300 years. Indeed Mindanao remains a contested part of the Philippines into the twenty-first century.

Beyond the missionary enterprise, other features of Spanish colonial practice in the Americas found expression in the Philippines. People living in scattered settlements were persuaded or forced to relocate into more concentrated Christian communities. Tribute, taxes, and unpaid labor became part of ordinary life. Large landed estates emerged, owned by Spanish settlers, Catholic religious orders, or prominent Filipinos. Women who had played a major role as ritual specialists, healers, and midwives were now displaced by male Spanish priests, and their ceremonial instruments were deliberately defiled and disgraced. Short-lived revolts and flight to interior mountains were among the Filipino responses to colonial oppression.

Yet others fled to Manila, the new capital of the colonial Philippines. By 1600, it had become a flourishing and culturally diverse city of more than 40,000 inhabitants and was home to many Spanish settlers and officials and growing numbers of Filipino migrants. Its rising prosperity also attracted some 3,000 Japanese and more than 20,000 Chinese. Serving as traders, artisans, and sailors, the Chinese in particular became an essential element in the Spanish colony's growing economic relationship with China; however, their economic prominence and their resistance to conversion earned them Spanish hostility and clearly discriminatory treatment. Periodic Chinese revolts, followed by expulsions and massacres, were the result. On one occasion in 1603, the Spanish killed about 20,000 people, nearly the entire Chinese population of the island.

The East India Companies

Far more important than the Spanish as European competitors for the spice trade were the Dutch and English, both of whom entered Indian Ocean commerce in the early seventeenth century. Together they quickly overtook and displaced the Portuguese, often by force, even as they competed vigorously with each other as well. These rising Northern European powers were both militarily and economically stronger than the Portuguese. For example, during the sixteenth century, the Dutch had become a highly commercialized and urbanized society, and their business skills and maritime shipping operations were the envy of Europe. Around 1600, both the British and the Dutch, unlike the Portuguese, organized their Indian Ocean ventures through private trading companies, which were able to raise money and share risks among a substantial number of merchant investors. The British East India Company and the Dutch East India Company received charters from their respective governments granting them trading monopolies and the power to make war and to govern conquered peoples. Thus they established their own parallel and competing trading post empires, with the Dutch focused on the islands of Indonesia and the English on India. Somewhat later, a French company also established settlements in the Indian Ocean basin.

Operating in a region of fragmented and weak political authority, the Dutch acted to control not only the shipping but also the production of cloves, cinnamon, nutmeg, and mace. With much bloodshed, the Dutch seized control of a number of small spice-producing islands, forcing their people to sell only to the Dutch and destroying the crops of those who refused. On the Banda Islands, famous for their

■ Change
To what extent did the British and Dutch trading companies change the societies they encountered in Asia?

A European View of Asian Commerce
The various East India companies (British, French, and Dutch) represented the major vehicle for European commerce in Asia during the early modern era. This wall painting, dating from 1778 and titled *The East Offering Its Riches to Britannia*, hung in the main offices of the British East India Company. (© British Library Board)

nutmeg, the Dutch killed, enslaved, or left to starve virtually the entire population of some 15,000 people and then replaced them with Dutch planters, using a slave labor force to produce the nutmeg crop. For a time in the seventeenth century, the Dutch were able to monopolize the trade in nutmeg, mace, and cloves and to sell these spices in Europe and India at fourteen to seventeen times the price they paid in Indonesia.[5] While Dutch profits soared, the local economy of the Spice Islands was shattered, and their people were impoverished.

The British East India Company operated differently than its Dutch counterpart. Less well financed and less commercially sophisticated, the British were largely excluded from the rich Spice Islands by the Dutch monopoly. Thus they fell back on India, where they established three major trading settlements during the seventeenth century: Bombay, on India's west coast, and Calcutta and Madras, on the east coast. Although British naval forces soon gained control of the Arabian Sea and the Persian Gulf, largely replacing the Portuguese, on land they were no match for the powerful Mughal Empire, which ruled most of the Indian subcontinent. Therefore, the British were unable to practice "trade by warfare," as the Dutch did in Indonesia.[6] Rather they secured their trading bases with the permission of Mughal authorities or local rulers, with substantial payments and bribes as the price of admission to the Indian market. When some independent English traders plundered a Mughal ship in 1636, local authorities detained British East India Company officials for two months and forced them to pay a whopping fine. Although pepper and other spices remained important in British trade, British merchants came to focus much more heavily on Indian cotton textiles, which were becoming widely popular in England and its American colonies. Hundreds of villages in the interior of southern India became specialized producers for this British market.

Like the Portuguese before them, both the Dutch and English became heavily involved in trade within Asia. The profits from this "carrying trade" enabled them to purchase Asian goods without paying for them in gold or silver from Europe. Dutch and English traders also began to deal in bulk goods for a mass market—pepper, textiles, and later tea and coffee—rather than just luxury goods for an elite market. In the second half of the eighteenth century, both the Dutch and British trading post empires slowly evolved into a more conventional form of colonial domination, in which the British came to rule India and the Dutch controlled Indonesia.

Asian Commerce

Although European commerce in the Indian Ocean and the South China Sea created new linkages between East and West, historians have sometimes exaggerated their impact on Asian societies during the early modern era. Certainly the European presence was far less significant in Asia than it was in the Americas or Africa during these centuries. European political control was limited to the Philippines and a few of the Spice Islands. To the great powers of South and East Asia—Mughal India, China, and Japan—Europeans represented no real military threat and played minor roles in their large and prosperous economies. Japan provides a fascinating case study in the ability of major Asian powers to control the European intruders.

When Portuguese traders and missionaries first arrived on that island nation in the mid-sixteenth century, soon followed by Spanish, Dutch, and English merchants, Japan was plagued by endemic conflict among numerous feudal lords, known as *daimyo*, each with his own cadre of *samurai* warriors. In these circumstances, the European newcomers found a hospitable welcome, for their military technology, shipbuilding skills, geographic knowledge, commercial opportunities, and even religious ideas proved useful or attractive to various elements in Japan's fractious and competitive society. The second half of the sixteenth century, for example, witnessed the growth of a substantial Christian movement, with some 300,000 converts and a Japanese-led church.

By the early seventeenth century, however, a series of remarkable military figures had unified Japan politically, under the leadership of a supreme military commander known as the *shogun*, who hailed from the Tokugawa clan. With the end of Japan's civil wars, successive shoguns came to view Europeans as a threat to the country's newly established unity rather than an opportunity. They therefore expelled Christian missionaries and violently suppressed the practice of Christianity. This policy included the execution, often under torture, of some sixty-two missionaries and thousands of Japanese converts. Shogunate authorities also forbade Japanese from traveling abroad and banned most European traders altogether, permitting only the Dutch, who appeared less interested in spreading Christianity, to trade at a single site. Thus, for two centuries (1650–1850), Japanese authorities of the Tokugawa shogunate largely closed their country off from the emerging world of European commerce, although they maintained their trading ties to China and Korea.

Despite the European naval dominance in Asian waters, Asian merchants did not disappear. Arab, Chinese, Javanese, Malay, and other traders benefited from the upsurge in seaborne commerce. Chinese merchants, for example, continued to carry most of the spice trade from Southeast Asia to China. Overland trade within Asia remained wholly in Asian hands and grew considerably. Christian merchants from Armenia were particularly active in the overland commerce linking Europe, the Middle East, and Central Asia. Tens of thousands of Indian merchants and moneylenders, mostly Hindus representing sophisticated family firms, lived throughout Central Asia, Persia, and Russia, thus connecting this vast region to markets in India. These commercial networks, equivalent in their sophistication to those of Europe, continued to operate successfully even as Europeans militarized the seaborne commerce of the Indian Ocean.

Silver and Global Commerce

■ **Significance**
What was the world historical importance of the silver trade?

Even more than the spice trade of Eurasia, it was the silver trade that gave birth to a genuinely global network of exchange (see Map 15.2). As one historian put it, silver "went round the world and made the world go round."[7] The mid-sixteenth-century discovery of enormously rich silver deposits in Bolivia, and simultaneously in Japan, suddenly provided a vastly increased supply of that precious metal. Spanish America alone produced perhaps 85 percent of the world's silver during the early modern era. Spain's sole Asian colony, the Philippines, provided a critical link in this emerging network of global commerce. Manila, the colonial capital of the Philippines, was the destination of annual Spanish shipments of silver, which were drawn from the rich mines of Bolivia, transported initially to Acapulco in Mexico, and from there shipped across the Pacific to the Philippines. This trade was the first direct and sustained link between the Americas and Asia, and it initiated a web of Pacific commerce that grew steadily over the centuries.

Map 15.2   The Global Silver Trade
Silver was one of the first major commodities to be exchanged on a genuinely global scale.

At the heart of that Pacific web, and of early modern global commerce generally, was China's huge economy, and especially its growing demand for silver. In the

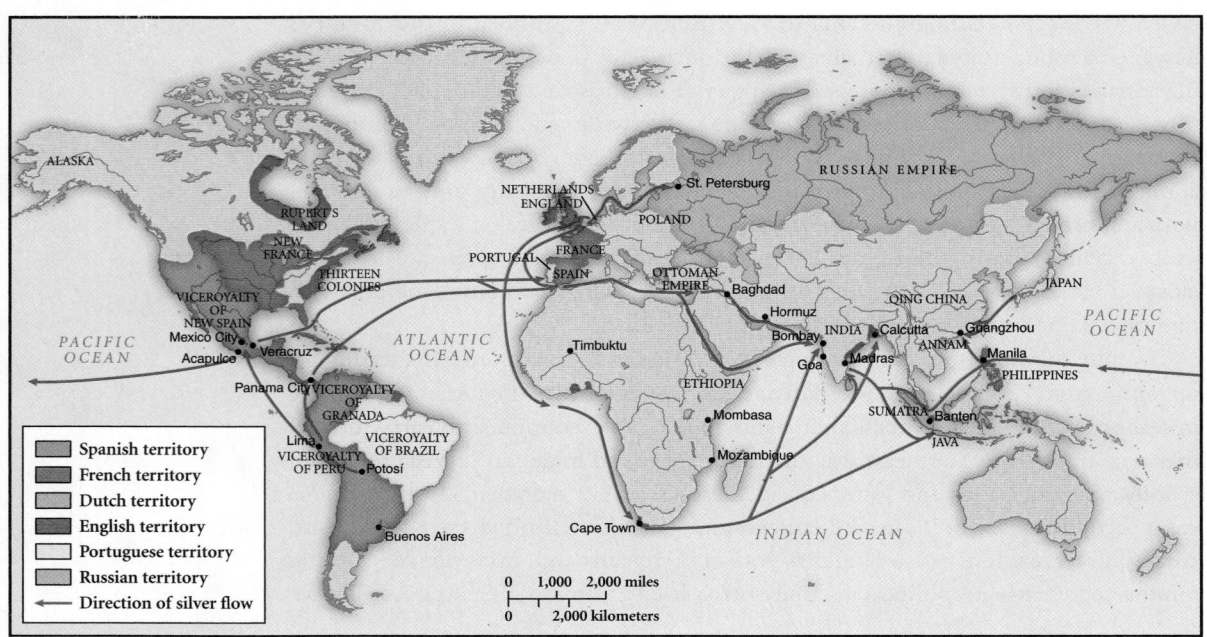

1570s, Chinese authorities consolidated a variety of tax levies into a single tax, which its huge population was now required to pay in silver. This sudden new demand for the white metal caused its value to skyrocket. It meant that foreigners with silver could now purchase far more of China's silks and porcelains than before.

This demand set silver in motion around the world, with the bulk of the world's silver supply winding up in China and much of the rest elsewhere in Asia. The routes by which this "silver drain" operated were numerous. Chinese, Portuguese, and Dutch traders flocked to Manila to sell Chinese goods in exchange for silver. European ships carried Japanese silver to China. Much of the silver shipped across the Atlantic to Spain was spent in Europe generally and then used to pay for the Asian goods that the French, British, and Dutch so greatly desired. Silver paid for some African slaves and for spices in Southeast Asia. The standard Spanish silver coin, known as a "piece of eight," was used by merchants in North America, Europe, India, Russia, and West Africa as a medium of exchange. By 1600, it circulated widely in southern China. A Portuguese merchant in 1621 noted that silver "wanders throughout all the world... before flocking to China, where it remains as if at its natural center."[8]

In its global journeys, silver transformed much that it touched. At the world's largest silver mine in what is now Bolivia, the city of Potosí arose from a barren landscape high in the Andes, a ten-week mule trip away from Lima. "New people arrive by the hour, attracted by the smell of silver," commented a Spanish observer in the 1570s. With 160,000 people, Potosí became the largest city in the Americas and equivalent in size to London, Amsterdam, or Seville. Its wealthy European elite lived in luxury, with all the goods of Europe and Asia at their disposal. Meanwhile, the city's Native American miners worked in conditions so horrendous that some families held funeral services for men drafted to work the mines. One Spanish priest referred to Potosí as a "portrait of hell."[9]

In Spain itself, which was the initial destination for much of Latin America's silver, the precious metal vastly enriched the Crown, making Spain the envy of its European rivals during the sixteenth century. Spanish rulers could now pursue military and political ambitions in both Europe and the Americas far beyond the country's own resource base. "New World mines," concluded one scholar, "supported the Spanish empire."[10] Nonetheless, this vast infusion of wealth did not fundamentally transform the Spanish economy, because it generated more inflation of prices than real economic

Potosí
This colonial-era painting shows the enormously rich silver mines of Potosí, then a major global source of the precious metal and the largest city in the Americas. Brutally hard work and poisonous exposure to mercury, which was used in the refining process, led to the deaths of many thousands of workers, even as the silver itself contributed to European splendor in the early modern era. (Courtesy, The Hispanic Society of America)

growth. A rigid economy laced with monopolies and regulations, an aristocratic class that preferred leisure to enterprise, and a crusading insistence on religious uniformity all prevented the Spanish from using their silver windfall in a productive fashion. When the value of silver dropped in the early seventeenth century, Spain lost its earlier position as the dominant Western European power.

Japan, another major source of silver production in the sixteenth century, did better. Its military rulers, the Tokugawa shoguns, used silver-generated profits to defeat hundreds of rival feudal lords and unify the country. Unlike their Spanish counterparts, the shoguns allied with the country's vigorous merchant class to develop a market-based economy and to invest heavily in agricultural and industrial enterprises. Japanese state and local authorities alike acted vigorously to protect and renew Japan's dwindling forests, while millions of families in the eighteenth century took steps to have fewer children by practicing late marriages, contraception, abortion, and infanticide. The outcome was the dramatic slowing of Japan's population growth, the easing of an impending ecological crisis, and a flourishing, highly commercialized economy. These were the foundations for Japan's remarkable nineteenth-century Industrial Revolution.

In China, silver deepened the already substantial commercialization of the country's economy. In order to obtain the silver needed to pay their taxes, more and more people had to sell something—either their labor or their products. Communities that devoted themselves to growing mulberry trees, on which silkworms fed, had to buy their rice from other regions. Thus the Chinese economy became more regionally specialized. Particularly in southern China, this surging economic growth resulted in the loss of about half the area's forest cover as more and more land was devoted to cash crops. No Japanese-style conservation program emerged to address this growing problem. An eighteenth-century Chinese poet, Wang Dayue, gave voice to the fears that this ecological transformation wrought:

> Rarer, too, their timber grew, and rarer still and rarer
> As the hills resembled heads now shaven clean of hair.
> For the first time, too, moreover, they felt an anxious mood
> That all their daily logging might not furnish them with fuel.[11]

China's role in the silver trade is a useful reminder of Asian centrality in the world economy of the early modern era. Its large and prosperous population, increasingly operating within a silver-based economy, fueled global commerce, vastly increasing the quantity of goods exchanged and the geographic range of world trade. Despite their obvious physical presence in the Americas, Africa, and Asia, economically speaking Europeans were essentially middlemen, funneling American silver to Asia and competing with one another for a place in the rich markets of the East. The productivity of the Chinese economy was evident in Spanish America, where cheap and well-made Chinese goods easily outsold those of Spain. In 1594, the Spanish viceroy of Peru observed that "a man can clothe his wife in Chinese silks for [25 pesos], whereas he could not provide her with clothing of Spanish silks with 200 pesos."[12] Indian cotton textiles likewise outsold European woolen or linen textiles in the seventeenth century to such an extent that French laws in 1717 prohibited the wearing of Indian cotton or Chinese silk clothing as a means of protecting French industry.

The "World Hunt": Fur in Global Commerce[13]

In the early modern era, furs joined silver, textiles, and spices as major items of global commerce. Their production had an important environmental impact as well as serious implications for the human societies that generated and consumed them. Furs, of course, had long provided warmth and conveyed status in colder regions of the world, but the integration of North America and of northern Asia (Siberia) into a larger world economy vastly increased their significance in global trade.

■ Change
Describe the impact of the fur trade on North American native societies.

By 1500, European population growth and agricultural expansion had sharply diminished the supply of fur-bearing animals, such as beaver, rabbits, sable, marten, and deer. Furthermore, much of the early modern era witnessed a period of cooling temperatures and harsh winters, known as the Little Ice Age, which may well have increased the demand for furs. "The weather is bitterly cold and everyone is in furs although we are almost in July," observed a surprised visitor from Venice while in London in 1604.[14] These conditions pushed prices higher. The cost of a good-quality beaver pelt, for example, quadrupled in France between 1558 and 1611. This translated into strong economic incentives for European traders to tap the immense wealth of fur-bearing animals found in North America.

Like other aspects of imperial expansion, the fur trade was a highly competitive enterprise. The French were most prominent in the St. Lawrence valley, around the Great Lakes, and later along the Mississippi River; British traders pushed into the Hudson Bay region; and the Dutch focused their attention along the Hudson River in what is now New York. They were frequently rivals for the great prize of North American furs. In the southern colonies of British North America, deerskins by the hundreds of thousands found a ready market in England's leather industry (see Map 15.3).

Only a few Europeans directly engaged in commercial trapping or hunting. They usually waited for Indians to bring the furs or skins initially to their coastal settlements and later to their fortified trading posts in the interior of North America. European merchants paid for the furs with a variety of trade goods, including guns, blankets, metal tools, rum, and brandy, amid much ceremony, haggling over prices, and ritualized gift-giving. Native Americans represented a cheap labor force in this international commercial effort, but they were not a directly coerced labor force.

Over the three centuries of the early modern era, enormous quantities of furs and deerskins found their way to Europe, where they considerably enhanced the standard of living in those cold climates. The environmental price was paid in the

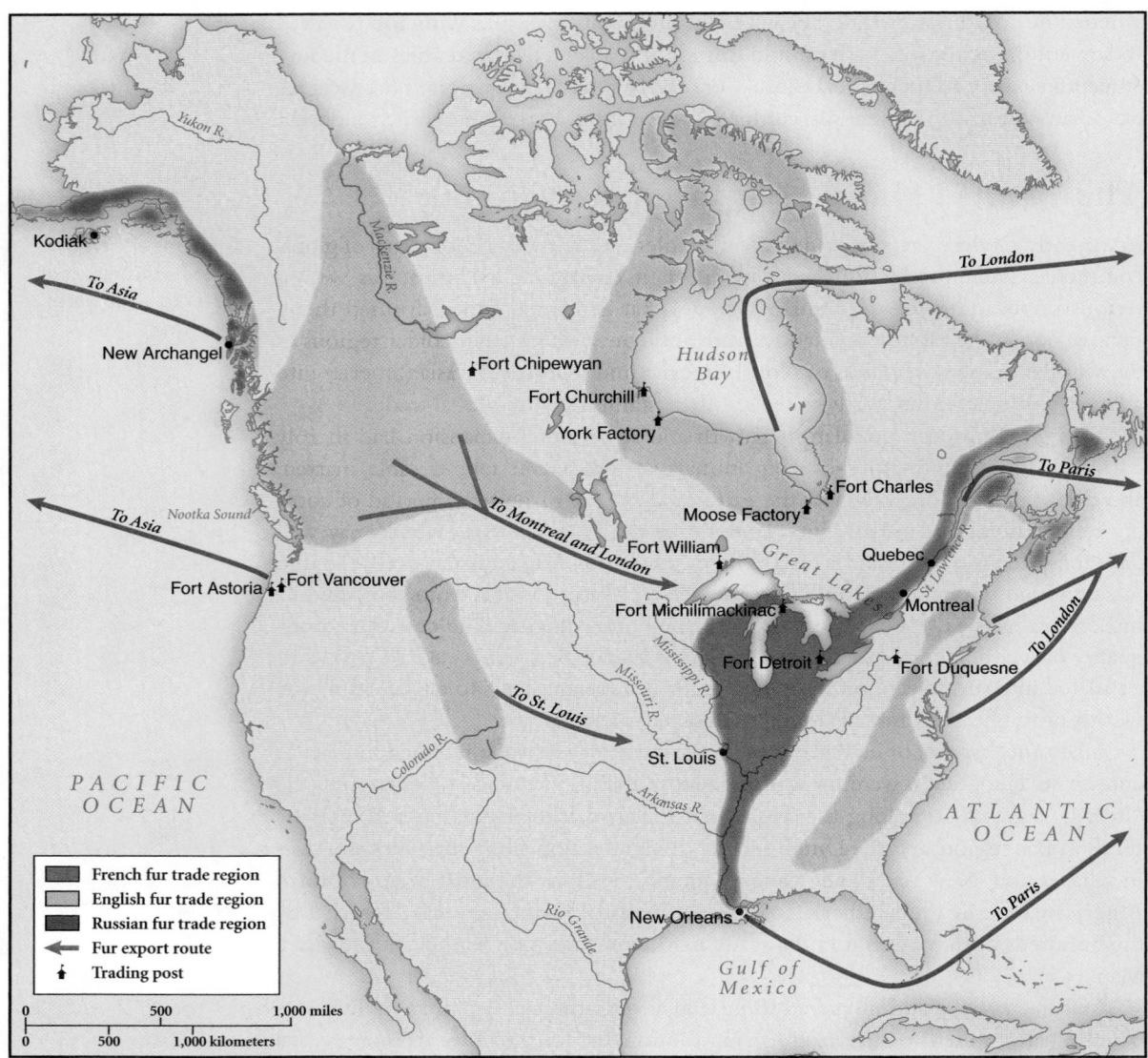

Map 15.3   The North American Fur Trade
North America, as well as Russian Siberia, funneled an apparently endless supply of furs into the circuits of global trade during the early modern era.

Americas, and it was high. A consistent demand for beaver hats led to the near extinction of that industrious animal in much of North America by the early nineteenth century. Many other fur-bearing species were seriously depleted as the trade moved inexorably westward. By the 1760s, hunters in southeastern British colonies took about 500,000 deer every year, seriously diminishing the deer population of the region.

For the Native American peoples who hunted, trapped, processed, and transported these products, the fur trade bore various benefits, particularly at the beginning. The Hurons, for example, who lived on the northern shores of Lakes Erie and Ontario in the early seventeenth century, annually exchanged some 20,000 to 30,000 pelts, mostly beaver, and in return received copper pots, metal axes, knives, cloth, firearms, and alcohol. Many of these items were of real value, which strengthened the Hurons in their relationship with neighboring peoples. These goods also enhanced the authority of Huron chiefs by providing them with gifts to distribute among their followers. At least initially, competition among Europeans ensured that Native American leaders could negotiate reasonable prices for their goods. Furthermore, their important role in the lucrative fur trade protected them for a time from the kind of extermination, enslavement, or displacement that was the fate of native peoples in Portuguese Brazil.

Nothing, however, protected them against the diseases carried by Europeans. In the 1630s and 1640s, to cite only one example of many, about half of the Hurons perished from influenza, smallpox, and other European-borne diseases. Furthermore, the fur trade generated warfare beyond anything previously known. Competition among Native American societies became more intense as the economic stakes grew higher. Catastrophic population declines owing to disease stimulated "mourning wars," designed to capture people who could be assimilated into much-diminished societies. A century of French-British rivalry for North America (1664–1763) forced Native American societies to take sides, to fight, and to die in these European imperial conflicts. Firearms, of course, made warfare far more deadly than before.

As many Native American peoples became enmeshed in commercial relationships with Europeans, they grew dependent on European trade goods. Among the Algonquians, for example, iron tools and cooking pots replaced those of stone, wood, or bone; gunpowder weapons took the place of bows and arrows; European textiles proved more attractive than traditional beaver and deerskin clothing; flint and steel were more effective for starting fires than wooden drills. A wide range of traditional crafts were thus lost, without the native peoples gaining a corresponding ability to manufacture the new items for themselves. Enthusiasm for these imported goods and continued European demands for furs and skins frequently eroded the customary restraint that characterized traditional hunting practices, resulting in the depletion of many species. One European observer wrote of the Creek Indians: "[They] wage eternal war against deer and bear...which is indeed carried to an unreasonable and perhaps criminal excess, since the white people have dazzled their senses with foreign superfluities."[15]

Beyond germs and guns, the most destructive of the imported goods was surely alcohol—rum and brandy, in particular. Whiskey, a locally produced grain-based alcohol, only added to the problem. With no prior experience of alcohol and little time to adjust to its easy availability, these drinks "hit Indian societies with explosive force."[16] Binge drinking, violence among young men, promiscuity, and addiction followed in many places. In 1753, Iroquois leaders complained bitterly to European authorities in Pennsylvania: "These wicked Whiskey Sellers, when they have once got the Indians in liquor, make them sell their very clothes from their backs.... If this practice be continued, we must be inevitably ruined."[17] In short, it was not so much the fur trade itself that decimated Native American societies, but all that accompanied it—disease, dependence, guns, alcohol, and the growing encroachment of European colonial empires.

Much the same could be said about the other fur trade that was simultaneously taking shape within a rapidly expanding Russian Empire. As a new Russian state emerged from Mongol rule around the city of Moscow in the late fifteenth century, it became a major source of furs for both Western Europe and the Ottoman Empire. The profitability of that trade in furs was the chief incentive for Russia's rapid expansion during the sixteenth and seventeenth centuries across Siberia, where the "soft gold" of fur-bearing animals was abundant. With growing markets in both China and Europe, the fur trade greatly enriched the Russian state as well as many private merchants, trappers, and hunters. Here the silver trade and the fur trade intersected, as Europeans paid for Russian furs largely with American gold and silver.

The consequences for native Siberians were similar to those in North America as disease took its toll, as indigenous people became dependent on Russian goods, as the settler frontier encroached on native lands, and as many species of fur-bearing mammals were seriously depleted. In several ways, however, the Russian fur trade was unique. Whereas several European nations competed in North America and generally obtained their furs through commercial negotiations with Indian societies, no such competition accompanied Russian expansion across Siberia. Russian authorities imposed a tax or tribute, payable in furs, on every able-bodied Siberian male between eighteen and fifty years of age. To enforce the payment, they took hostages from Siberian societies, with death as a possible outcome if the required furs were not forthcoming. A further difference lay in the large-scale presence of private Russian hunters and trappers, who competed directly with their Siberian counterparts.

■ Comparison
How did the North American and Siberian fur trades differ from each other? What did they have in common?

Fur and the Russians
This colored engraving shows a sixteenth-century Russian ambassador and his contingent arriving at the court of the Holy Roman Emperor and bearing gifts of animal pelts, the richest fruit of the expanding Russian Empire. (RIA Novosti)

Commerce in People: The Atlantic Slave Trade

Of all the commercial ties that linked the early modern world into a global network of exchange, none had more profound or enduring human consequences than the Atlantic slave trade. Between 1500 and 1866, this trade in humankind took an estimated 12.5 million people from African societies, shipped them across the Atlantic in the infamous Middle Passage, and deposited some 10.7 million of them in the Americas, where they lived out their often brief lives as slaves. About 1.8 million (14.4 percent) died during the transatlantic crossing, while countless millions more perished in the process of capture and transport to the African coast.[18] (See Map 15.4 and Documents: Voices of the Slave Trade, pp. 700–09, for various perspectives from the slave trade.)

Beyond the multitude of individual tragedies that it spawned—capture and sale, displacement from home cultures, forced labor, beatings and brandings, broken families—the Atlantic slave trade transformed the societies of all of its participants. Within Africa itself, some societies were thoroughly disrupted, others were strengthened, and many were corrupted. Elites were often enriched, while the slaves themselves, of course, were victimized beyond imagination.

Map 15.4   The Atlantic Slave Trade
Stimulated by the plantation complex of the Americas, the Atlantic slave trade represented an enormous extension of the ancient practice of people owning and selling other people.

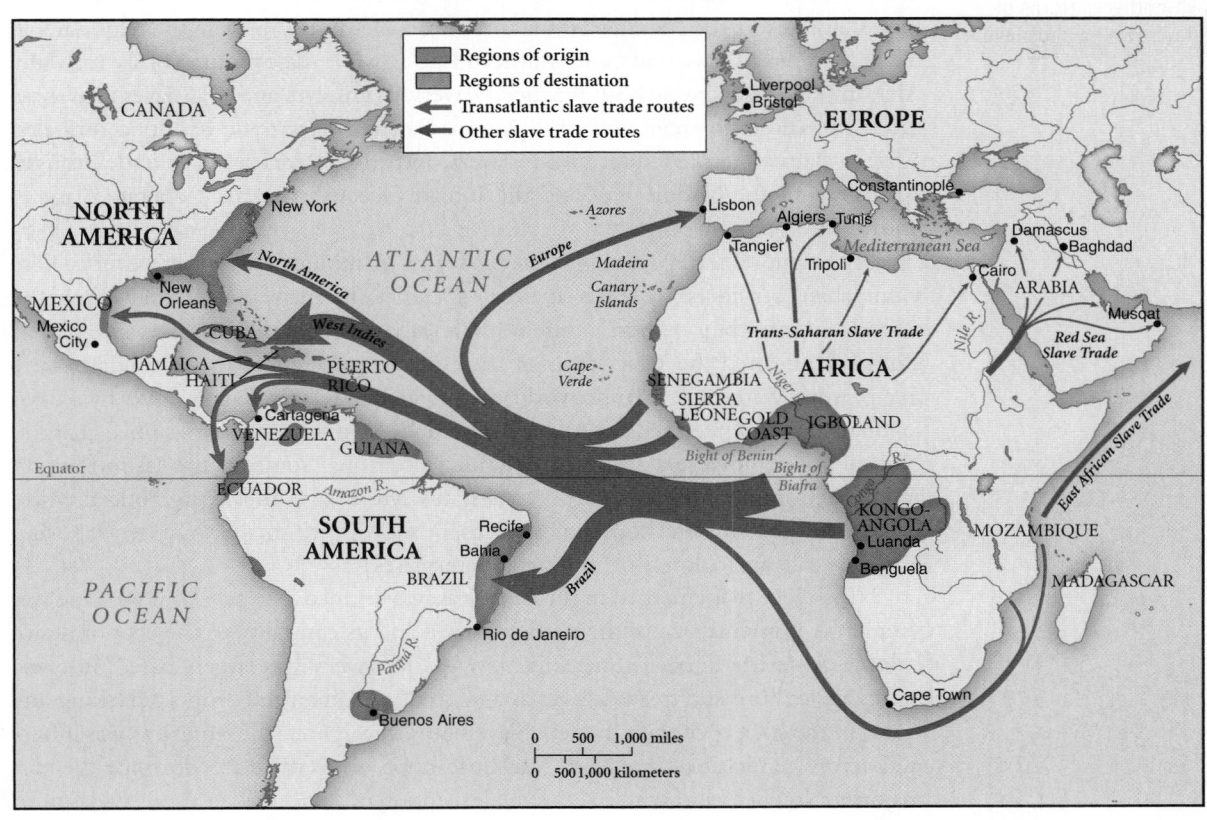

In the Americas, the slave trade added a substantial African presence to the mix of European and Native American peoples. This African diaspora (the transatlantic spread of African peoples) injected into these new societies issues of race that endure still in the twenty-first century. It also introduced elements of African culture, such as religious ideas, musical and artistic traditions, and cuisine, into the making of American cultures. The profits from the slave trade and the forced labor of African slaves certainly enriched European and Euro-American societies, even as the practice of slavery contributed much to the racial thinking of European peoples. Finally, slavery became a metaphor for many kinds of social oppression, quite different from plantation slavery, in the centuries that followed. Workers protested the slavery of wage labor, colonized people rejected the slavery of imperial domination, and feminists sometimes defined patriarchy as a form of slavery.

The Slave Trade in Context

■ Comparison
What was distinctive about the Atlantic slave trade? What did it share with other patterns of slave owning and slave trading?

The Atlantic slave trade and slavery in the Americas represented the most recent large-scale expression of an almost universal human practice—the owning and exchange of human beings. With origins in the earliest civilizations, slavery was widely accepted as a perfectly normal human enterprise and was closely linked to warfare and capture. Before 1500, the Mediterranean and Indian Ocean basins were the major arenas of the Old World slave trade, and southern Russia was a major source of slaves. Many African societies likewise both practiced slavery themselves and sold slaves into these international commercial networks. A trans-Saharan slave trade had long funneled African captives into Mediterranean slavery, and an East African slave trade brought Africans into the Middle East and the Indian Ocean basin. Both operated largely within the Islamic world.

Furthermore, slavery came in many forms. Although slaves were everywhere vulnerable "outsiders" to their masters' societies, in many places they could be assimilated into their owners' households, lineages, or communities. In some places, children inherited the slave status of their parents; elsewhere those children were free persons. Within the Islamic world, the preference was for female slaves by a two-to-one margin, while the later Atlantic slave trade favored males by a similar margin. Not all slaves, however, occupied degraded positions. Some in the Islamic world acquired prominent military or political status. Most slaves in the premodern world worked in their owners' households, farms, or shops, with smaller numbers laboring in large-scale agricultural or industrial enterprises.

The slavery that emerged in the Americas was distinctive in several ways. One was simply the immense size of the traffic in slaves and its centrality to the economies of colonial America. Furthermore, this New World slavery was largely based on plantation agriculture and treated slaves as a form of dehumanized property, lacking any rights in the society of their owners. Slave status throughout the Americas was inherited across generations, and there was little hope of eventual freedom for the vast majority. Nowhere else, with the possible exception of ancient Greece, was widespread slavery associated with societies affirming values of human freedom and equality.

Perhaps most distinctive was the racial dimension: Atlantic slavery came to be identified wholly with Africa and with "blackness." How did this exceptional form of slavery emerge?

The origins of Atlantic slavery clearly lie in the Mediterranean world and with that now common sweetener known as sugar. Until the Crusades, Europeans knew nothing of sugar and relied on honey and fruits to sweeten their bland diets. However, as they learned from the Arabs about sugarcane and the laborious techniques for producing usable sugar, Europeans established sugar-producing plantations within the Mediterranean and later on various islands off the coast of West Africa. It was a "modern" industry, perhaps the first one, in that it required huge capital investment, substantial technology, an almost factory-like discipline among workers, and a mass market of consumers. The immense difficulty and danger of the work, the limitations attached to serf labor, and the general absence of wage workers all pointed to slavery as a source of labor for sugar plantations.

Initially, Slavic-speaking peoples from the Black Sea region furnished the bulk of the slaves for Mediterranean plantations, so much so that "Slav" became the basis for the word "slave" in many European languages. In 1453, however, when the Ottoman Turks seized Constantinople, the supply of Slavic slaves was effectively cut off. At the same time, Portuguese mariners were exploring the coast of West Africa; they were looking primarily for gold, but they also found there an alternative source of slaves available for sale. Thus, when sugar, and later tobacco and cotton, plantations took hold in the Americas, Europeans had already established links to a West African source of supply.

Largely through a process of elimination, Africa became the primary source of slave labor for the plantation economies of the Americas. Slavic peoples were no longer available; Native Americans quickly perished from European diseases; marginal Europeans were Christians and therefore supposedly exempt from slavery; and European indentured servants were expensive and temporary. Africans, on the other hand, were skilled farmers; they had some immunity to both tropical and European diseases; they were not Christians; they were, relatively speaking, close at hand; and they were readily available in substantial numbers through African-operated commercial networks.

Moreover, Africans were black. The precise relationship between slavery and European

■ **Causation**
What explains the rise of the Atlantic slave trade?

The Middle Passage
This mid-nineteenth-century painting of slaves held below deck on a Spanish slave ship illustrates the horrendous conditions of the transatlantic voyage, a journey experienced by many millions of captured Africans. (The Art Archive)

racism has long been a much-debated subject. Historian David Brion Davis has suggested the controversial view that "racial stereotypes were transmitted, along with black slavery itself, from Muslims to Christians."[19] For many centuries, Muslims had drawn on sub-Saharan Africa as one source of slaves and in the process had developed a form of racism. The fourteenth-century Tunisian scholar Ibn Khaldun wrote that black people were "submissive to slavery, because Negroes have little that is essentially human and have attributes that are quite similar to those of dumb animals."[20]

Other scholars find the origins of racism within European culture itself. For the English, argues historian Audrey Smedley, the process of conquering Ireland had generated by the sixteenth century a view of the Irish as "rude, beastly, ignorant, cruel, and unruly infidels," perceptions that were then transferred to Africans enslaved on English sugar plantations of the West Indies.[21] Whether Europeans borrowed such images of Africans from their Muslim neighbors or developed them independently, slavery and racism soon went hand in hand. "Europeans were better able to tolerate their brutal exploitation of Africans," writes a prominent world historian, "by imagining that these Africans were an inferior race, or better still, not even human."[22]

The Slave Trade in Practice

■ Connection

What roles did Europeans and Africans play in the unfolding of the Atlantic slave trade?

The European demand for slaves was clearly the chief cause of this tragic commerce, and from the point of sale on the African coast to the massive use of slave labor on American plantations, the entire enterprise was in European hands. Within Africa itself, however, a different picture emerges, for over the four centuries of the Atlantic slave trade, European demand elicited an African supply. A few early efforts by the Portuguese at slave raiding along the West African coast convinced Europeans that such efforts were unnecessary and unwise, for African societies were quite capable of defending themselves against European intrusion, and many were willing to sell their slaves peacefully. Furthermore, Europeans died like flies when they entered the interior because they lacked immunities to common tropical diseases. Thus the slave trade quickly came to operate largely with Europeans waiting on the coast, either on their ships or in fortified settlements, to purchase slaves from African merchants and political elites. Certainly Europeans tried to exploit African rivalries to obtain slaves at the lowest possible cost, and the firearms they funneled into West Africa may well have increased the warfare from which so many slaves were derived. But from the point of initial capture to sale on the coast, the entire enterprise was normally in African hands. Almost nowhere did Europeans attempt outright military conquest; instead they generally dealt as equals with local African authorities.

An arrogant agent of the British Royal Africa Company in the 1680s learned the hard way who was in control when he spoke improperly to the king of Niumi, a small state in what is now Gambia. The company's records describe what happened next:

> [O]ne of the grandees [of the king], by name Sambalama, taught him better manners by reaching him a box on the ears, which beat off his hat, and a few thumps

on the back, and seizing him, disarmed him together with the rest of his attendance, among which was Benedict Stafford, commander of the *Margaret*... (who
made his escape and ran like a lusty fellow to his ship) and several others, who
together with the agent were taken and put into the king's pound and stayed
there three or four days till their ransom was brought, value five hundred bars.[23]

In exchange for slaves, African sellers sought both European and Indian textiles,
cowrie shells (widely used as money in West Africa), European metal goods, firearms
and gunpowder, tobacco and alcohol, and various decorative items such as beads.
Europeans purchased some of these items—cowrie shells and Indian textiles, for
example—with silver mined in the Americas. Thus the slave trade connected with
commerce in silver and textiles as it became part of an emerging worldwide network
of exchange. Issues about the precise mix of goods African authorities desired, about
the number and quality of slaves to be purchased, and always about the price of everything were settled in endless negotiation (see Document 15.2, pp. 703–05). In most
places most of the time, a leading scholar concluded, the slave trade took place "not
unlike international trade anywhere in the world of the period."[24]

If African authorities and elite classes in many places controlled their side of
the slave trade, on occasion they were almost overwhelmed by it. Many small-scale
kinship-based societies, lacking the protection of a strong state, were thoroughly disrupted by raids from more powerful neighbors. Even some sizable states were desta-
bilized. In the early sixteenth century, the kingdom of Kongo, located mostly in
present-day Angola, was badly damaged by the commerce in slaves and the authority of its ruler severely undermined (see Document 15.3, pp. 705–07).

Whatever the relationship between European buyers and African sellers, for the
slaves themselves—who were seized in the interior, often sold several times on the har-
rowing journey to the coast, sometimes branded, and held in squalid slave dungeons
while awaiting transportation to the New World—it was anything but a normal commercial transaction (see Document 15.1, pp. 700–03). One European engaged in the
trade noted that "the negroes are so willful and loath to leave their own country, that
they have often leap'd out of the canoes, boat, and ship, into the sea, and kept under
water till they were drowned, to avoid being taken up and saved by our boats."[25]

Over the four centuries of the slave trade, millions of Africans underwent some
such experience, but their numbers varied considerably over time. During the sixteenth century, slave exports from Africa averaged under 3,000 annually. In those
years, the Portuguese were at least as much interested in African gold, spices, and
textiles. Furthermore, as in Asia, they became involved in transporting African
goods, including slaves, from one African port to another, thus becoming the "truck
drivers" of coastal West African commerce.[26] In the seventeenth century, the pace
picked up as the slave trade became highly competitive, with the British, Dutch, and
French contesting the earlier Portuguese monopoly. The century and a half between
1700 and 1850 marked the high point of the slave trade as the plantation economies
of the Americas boomed (see the Snapshot on p. 694).

Snapshot   **The Slave Trade in Numbers (1501–1866)[27]**

The Rise and Decline of the Slave Trade

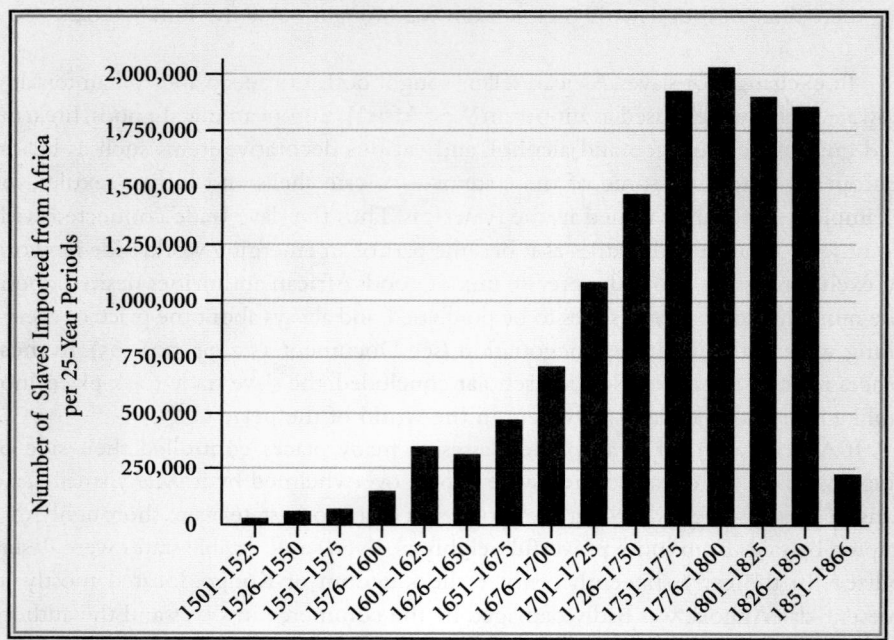

The Destinations of Slaves

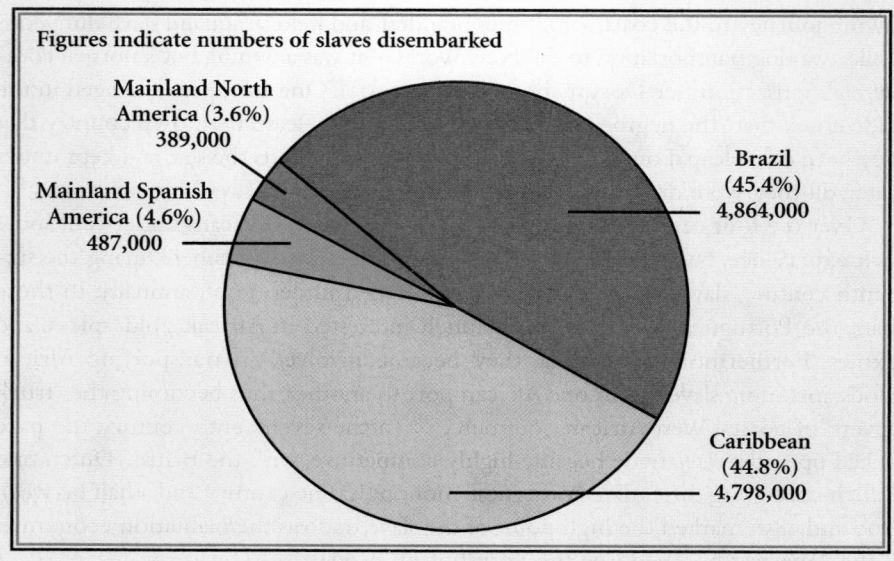

Where did these Africans come from, and where did they go? Geographically, the slave trade drew mainly on the societies of West Africa, from present-day Mauritania in the north to Angola in the south. Initially focused on the coastal regions, the slave trade progressively penetrated into the interior as the demand for slaves picked up. Socially, slaves were mostly drawn from various marginal groups in African societies—prisoners of war, criminals, debtors, people who had been "pawned" during times of difficulty. Thus Africans did not generally sell "their own people" into slavery. Divided into hundreds of separate, usually small-scale, and often rival communities—cities, kingdoms, microstates, clans, and villages—the various peoples of West Africa had no concept of an "African" identity. Those whom they captured and sold were normally outsiders, vulnerable people who lacked the protection of membership in an established community. When short-term economic or political advantage could be gained, such people were sold. In this respect, the Atlantic slave trade was little different from the experience of enslavement elsewhere in the world.

The destination of enslaved Africans, half a world away in the Americas, was very different. The vast majority wound up in Brazil or the Caribbean, where the labor demands of the plantation economy were most intense. Smaller numbers found themselves in North America, mainland Spanish America or in Europe itself. The journey across the Atlantic was horrendous almost beyond description, with the Middle Passage having an overall mortality rate of more than 14 percent (see Document 15.1, pp. 700–03). About 10 percent of the transatlantic voyages experienced a major rebellion by the desperate captives.

Comparing Consequences: The Impact of the Slave Trade in Africa

From the viewpoint of world history, the chief outcome of the slave trade lay in the new transregional linkages that it generated. Both commercially and demographically, Africa became a permanent part of an interacting Atlantic world. Millions of its people were now compelled to make their lives in the Americas. West African economies were increasingly connected to an emerging European-centered world economy. These vast processes set in motion a chain of consequences that have transformed the lives and societies of people on both sides of the Atlantic.

■ Change
In what different ways did the Atlantic slave trade transform African societies?

Although the slave trade did not result in the kind of population collapse that occurred in the Americas, it certainly slowed Africa's growth at a time when Europe, China, and other regions were expanding demographically. Scholars have estimated that sub-Saharan Africa represented about 18 percent of the world's population in 1600, but only 6 percent in 1900.[28] A portion of that difference reflects the slave trade's impact on Africa's population history.

That impact derived not only from the loss of millions of people over four centuries but also from the economic stagnation and political disruption that the slave trade generated. Economically, the slave trade stimulated little positive change in Africa because those Africans who benefited most from the traffic in people were not investing in the productive capacities of African societies. Although European imports generally did not displace traditional artisan manufacturing, no technological breakthroughs in agriculture or industry increased the wealth available to these societies. Maize and manioc (cassava), introduced from the Americas, added a new source of calories to African diets, but the international demand was for Africa's people, not its agricultural products.

Within particular African societies, the impact of the slave trade differed considerably from place to place and over time. Particularly in small-scale societies that were frequently subjected to slave raiding and that had little centralized authority, insecurity was pervasive. Oral traditions in southern Ghana, for example, reported that "there was no rest in the land," that people went about in groups rather than alone, and that mothers kept their children inside when European ships appeared.[29] Some larger kingdoms such as Kongo and Oyo slowly disintegrated as access to trading opportunities and firearms enabled outlying regions to establish their independence. However, African authorities also sought to take advantage of the new commercial opportunities and to manage the slave trade in their own interests, as the contrasting experience of the neighboring kingdoms of Benin and Dahomey illustrates.[30]

The kingdom of Benin, in the forest area of present-day Nigeria, was one of the oldest and most highly developed states in the coastal hinterland of West Africa, dating perhaps to the eleventh century C.E. Its capital was a large walled city with wide avenues, a lavish court, a wealthy elite, and a powerful monarch, or *oba*, who strictly controlled the country's trade. Benin's uniqueness lay in its relatively successful efforts to avoid a deep involvement in the slave trade and to diversify the exports with which it purchased European firearms and other goods. As early as 1516, the oba began to restrict the slave trade and soon forbade the export of male slaves altogether, a ban that lasted until the early eighteenth century. By then, the oba's authority over outlying areas had declined, and the country's major exports of pepper and cotton cloth had lost out to Asian and then European competition. In these circumstances, Benin felt compelled to resume limited participation in the slave trade. But even at the height of the trade, in the late eighteenth century, Benin exported fewer than 1,000 slaves a year.

Among the Aja-speaking peoples to the west of Benin, the situation was very different. There the slave trade had thoroughly disrupted a series of small and weak states along the coast. Some distance inland, the kingdom of Dahomey arose in the early eighteenth century, at least in part as an effort to contain the constant raiding and havoc occasioned by the coastal trade. It was a unique and highly authoritarian state in which commoners and chiefs alike were responsible directly to the king and in which the power of lineages and secret societies was considerably weakened. For a time, Dahomey tried to limit the external slave trade, to import European craftsmen, and to develop plantation agriculture within the kingdom, but all this failed. In view of hostile relations with the neighboring kingdom of Oyo and others, Dahomey instead turned to a vigorous involvement in the slave trade, under strict royal control.

The army conducted annual slave raids, and the government soon came to depend on the trade for its essential revenues. Unlike in Benin, the slave trade in Dahomey became the chief business of the state and remained so until well into the nineteenth century.

Reflections: Economic Globalization— Then and Now

The study of history reminds us of two quite contradictory truths. One is that our lives in the present bear remarkable similarities to those of people long ago. We are perhaps not so unique as we might think. The other is that our lives are very different from theirs and that things have changed substantially. This chapter about global commerce—long-distance trade in spices and textiles, silver and gold, beaver pelts and deerskins, slaves and sugar—provides both perspectives.

If we are accustomed to thinking about globalization as a product of the late twentieth century, early modern world history provides a corrective. Those three centuries reveal much that is familiar to people of the twenty-first century—the global circulation of goods; an international currency; production for a world market; the growing economic role of the West on the global stage; private enterprise, such as the British and Dutch East India companies, operating on a world scale; national governments eager to support their merchants in a highly competitive environment. By the eighteenth century, many Europeans dined from Chinese porcelain dishes called "china," wore Indian-made cotton textiles, and drank chocolate from Mexico, tea from China, and coffee from Yemen while sweetening these beverages with sugar from the Caribbean or Brazil. The millions who worked to produce these goods, whether slave or free, were operating in a world economy. Some industries were thoroughly international. New England rum producers, for example, depended on molasses imported from the Caribbean, while the West Indian sugar industry used African labor and European equipment to produce for a global market.

Nonetheless, early modern economic globalization was a far cry from that of the twentieth century. Most obvious perhaps were scale and speed. By 2000, immensely more goods circulated internationally and far more people produced for and depended on the world market than was the case even in 1750. Back-and-forth communications between England and India that took eighteen months in the eighteenth century could be accomplished in an hour by telegraph in the late nineteenth century and almost instantaneously via the Internet in the late twentieth century. Moreover, by 1900 globalization was firmly centered in the economies of Europe and North America. In the early modern era, by contrast, Asia in general and China in particular remained major engines of the world economy, despite the emerging presence of Europeans around the world. By the end of the twentieth century, the booming economies of India and China suggested at least a partial return to that earlier pattern.

Early modern globalization differed in still other ways from that of the contemporary world. Economic life then was primarily preindustrial, still powered by human and animal muscles, wind, and water and lacking the enormous productive capacity that accompanied the later technological breakthrough of the steam engine and the Industrial Revolution. Finally, the dawning of a genuinely global economy in the early modern era was tied unapologetically to empire building and to slavery, both of which had been discredited by the late twentieth century. Slavery lost its legitimacy during the nineteenth century, and formal territorial empires largely disappeared in the twentieth. Most people during the early modern era would have been surprised to learn that a global economy, as it turned out, could function effectively without either of these long-standing practices.

Second Thoughts

What's the Significance?

Indian Ocean commercial network	British/Dutch East India companies	Potosí
trading post empire	Tokugawa shogunate	"soft gold"
Philippines (Spanish)	"silver drain"	African diaspora
		Benin/Dahomey

Big Picture Questions

1. In what specific ways did trade foster change in the world of the early modern era?
2. To what extent did Europeans transform earlier patterns of commerce, and in what ways did they assimilate into those older patterns?
3. Describe and account for the differing outcomes of European expansion in the Americas (see Chapter 14), Africa, and Asia.
4. How should we distribute the moral responsibility for the Atlantic slave trade? Is this a task appropriate for historians?
5. What lasting legacies of early modern globalization are evident in the early twenty-first century? Pay particular attention to the legacies of the slave trade.

Next Steps: For Further Study

Glenn J. Ames, *The Globe Encompassed: The Age of European Discovery, 1500–1700* (2007). An up-to-date survey of European expansion in the early modern era.

Andre Gunder Frank, *ReOrient: Global Economy in the Asian Age* (1998). An account of the early modern world economy that highlights the centrality of Asia.

Erik Gilbert and Jonathan Reynolds, *Trading Tastes: Commodity and Cultural Exchange to 1750* (2006). A world historical perspective on transcontinental and transoceanic commerce.

David Northrup, ed., *The Atlantic Slave Trade* (2002). A fine collection of essays about the origins, practice, impact, and abolition of Atlantic slavery.

John Richards, *The Endless Frontier* (2003). Explores the ecological consequences of early modern commerce.

John Thornton, *Africa and Africans in the Making of the Atlantic World* (1998). A well-regarded but somewhat controversial account of the slave trade, with an emphasis on African authorities as active and independent players in the process.

"Atlantic Slave Trade and Slave Life in the Americas: A Visual Record," http://hitchcock.itc.virginia .edu/Slavery/index.php. An immense collection of maps and images illustrating the slave trade and the life of slaves in the Americas.

Documents

Considering the Evidence: Voices from the Slave Trade

By any measure the Atlantic slave trade was an enormous enterprise and enormously significant in modern world history: its geographical scope encompassed four continents, it endured for over four centuries, its victims numbered in the many millions, its commercial operation was complex and highly competitive, and its consequences echo still in both public and private life (see pp. 689–97). The four documents that follow allow us to hear several individual voices from this vast historical process and to sample the evidence available to historians as they seek to understand this tragic chapter of the human story.

Document 15.1

The Journey to Slavery

We begin with the voice of an individual victim of the slave trade—Olaudah Equiano. Born in what is now the Igbo-speaking region of Nigeria around 1745, Equiano was seized from his home at the age of eleven and sold into the Atlantic slave trade at the high point of that infamous commerce (see Map 15.4, p. 689). In service to three different owners, his experience as a slave in the Americas was quite unusual. He learned to read and write, traveled extensively as a seaman aboard one of his masters' ships, and was allowed to buy his freedom in 1766. Settling in England, he became a prominent voice in the emerging abolitionist movement of the late eighteenth century and wrote a widely read account of his life, addressed largely to European Christians: "O, ye nominal Christians! Might not an African ask you, Learned you this from your God, who says unto you, Do unto all men as you would men should do unto you?" His book was published in 1789 as abolitionism was gaining wider acceptance.

Despite some controversy about his birthplace and birth date, most historians accept Equiano's autobiography as broadly accurate. Document 15.1 presents Equiano's account of his capture, his journey to the coast, his experience on a slave ship, and his arrival in the Americas. It was a journey forcibly undertaken by millions of others as well.

- How does Equiano describe the kind of slavery he knew in Africa itself? How does it compare with the plantation slavery of the Americas?

- What part did Africans play in the slave trade, according to this account?

- What aspects of the shipboard experience contributed to the slaves' despair?

OLAUDAH EQUIANO

The Interesting Narrative of the Life of Olaudah Equiano

1789

As we live in a country where nature is prodigal of her favours, our wants are few and easily supplied; of course we have few manufactures. They consist for the most part of calicoes, earthen ware, ornaments, and instruments of war and husbandry.... We have also markets, at which I have been frequently with my mother. These are sometimes visited by stout mahogany-coloured men from the south west of us:...They generally bring us fire-arms, gunpowder, hats, beads, and dried fish....They always carry slaves through our land;...Sometimes indeed we sold slaves to them, but they were only prisoners of war, or such among us as had been convicted of kidnapping or adultery, and some other crimes, which we esteemed heinous....

My father, besides many slaves, had a numerous family, of which seven lived to grow up, including myself and a sister, who was the only daughter....I was trained up from my earliest years in the art of war; my daily exercise was shooting and throwing javelins; and my mother adorned me with emblems, after the manner of our greatest warriors. In this way I grew up till I was turned the age of eleven, when an end was put to my happiness in the following manner....

One day, when all our people were gone out to their works as usual, and only I and my dear sister were left to mind the house, two men and a woman got over our walls and in a moment seized us both, and, without giving us time to cry out, or make resistance, they stopped our mouths, and ran off with us into the nearest wood. Here they tied our hands, and continued to carry us as far as they could, till night came on....The next morning we left the house, and continued travelling all the day. For a long time we had kept the woods, but at last we came into a road which I believed I knew. I had now some hopes of being delivered; for we had advanced but a little way before I discovered some people at a distance, on which I began to cry out for their assistance: but my cries had no other effect than to make them tie me faster and stop my mouth, and then they put me into a large sack....

The next day proved a day of greater sorrow than I had yet experienced; for my sister and I were then separated, while we lay clasped in each other's arms. It was in vain that we besought them not to part us; she was torn from me, and immediately carried away....

At length, after many days traveling, during which I had often changed masters, I got into the hands of a chieftain, in a very pleasant country. This man had two wives and some children, and they all used me extremely well, and did all they could to

Source: Olaudah Equiano, *The Interesting Narrative of the Life of Olaudah Equiano, or Gustavus Vassa, the African*, vol. 1 (London, 1789), chaps. 1, 2.

comfort me; particularly the first wife, who was something like my mother. Although I was a great many days journey from my father's house, yet these people spoke exactly the same language with us....

[After about a month], I was again sold. I was now carried to the left of the sun's rising, through many different countries, and a number of large woods. The people I was sold to used to carry me very often, when I was tired, either on their shoulders or on their backs. I saw many convenient well-built sheds along the roads, at proper distances, to accommodate the merchants and travelers, who lay in those buildings along with their wives, who often accompany them; and they always go well armed.

I was again sold, and carried through a number of places, till, after traveling a considerable time, I came to a town called Tinmah, in the most beautiful country I had yet seen in Africa.... Their money consisted of little white shells, the size of the finger nail. I was sold here for one hundred and seventy-two of them by a merchant who lived and brought me there. I had been about two or three days at his house, when a wealthy widow, a neighbor of his, came there one evening, and brought with her an only son, a young gentleman about my own age and size. Here they saw me; and, having taken a fancy to me, I was bought of the merchant, and went home with them.... The next day I was washed and perfumed, and when meal-time came I was led into the presence of my mistress, and ate and drank before her with her son. This filled me with astonishment; and I could scarce help expressing my surprise that the young gentleman should suffer me, who was bound, to eat with him who was free; and not only so, but that he would not at any time either eat or drink till I had taken first, because I was the eldest, which was agreeable to our custom. Indeed everything here, and all their treatment of me, made me forget that I was a slave. The language of these people resembled ours so nearly, that we understood each other perfectly,... In this resemblance to my former happy state I passed about two months; and I now began to think I was to be adopted into the family, and was beginning to be reconciled to my situation, and to forget by degrees my misfortunes when all at once the delusion vanished; for, without the least previous knowledge, one morning early, while my dear master and companion was still asleep, I was wakened out of my reverie to fresh sorrow, and hurried away....

Thus I continued to travel, sometimes by land, sometimes by water, through different countries and various nations, till, at the end of six or seven months after I had been kidnapped, I arrived at the sea coast.... The first object which saluted my eyes when I arrived on the coast was the sea, and a slave ship, which was then riding at anchor, and waiting for its cargo. These filled me with astonishment, which was soon converted into terror when I was carried on board. I was immediately handled and tossed up to see if I were sound by some of the crew; and I was now persuaded that I had gotten into a world of bad spirits, and that they were going to kill me. Their complexions too differing so much from ours, their long hair, and the language they spoke... united to confirm me in this belief.... When I looked round the ship too and saw a large furnace or copper boiling, and a multitude of black people of every description chained together, every one of their countenances expressing dejection and sorrow, I no longer doubted of my fate; and quite overpowered with horror and anguish, I fell motionless on the deck and fainted....

I was soon put down under the decks, and there I received such a salutation in my nostrils as I had never experienced in my life: so that, with the loathsomeness of the stench and crying together, I became so sick and low that I was not able to eat, nor had I the least desire to taste anything. I now wished for the last friend, death, to relieve me; but soon, to my grief, two of the white men offered me eatables; and on my refusing to eat, one of them held me fast by the hands, and laid me across I think the windlass and tied my feet, while the other flogged me severely....

I had never seen among any people such instances of brutal cruelty; and this not only shewn towards us blacks, but also to some of the whites themselves. One white man in particular I saw, when we were permitted to be on deck, flogged so unmercifully with a large rope near the foremast that he died in consequence of it; and they tossed him over the side as they would have done a brute....

The closeness of the place, and the heat of the climate, added to the number in the ship, which was so crowded that each had scarcely room to turn himself, almost suffocated us. This produced copious perspirations, so that the air soon became unfit for respiration, from a variety of loathsome smells, and brought on a sickness among the slaves, of which many died, thus falling victims to the improvident avarice, as I may call it, of their purchasers. This wretched situation was again aggravated by the galling of the chains, now become insupportable; and the filth of the necessary tubs, into which the children often fell, and were almost suffocated. The shrieks of the women, and the groans of the dying, rendered the whole a scene of horror almost inconceivable....

At last we came in sight of the island of Barbados, at which the whites on board gave a great shout, and made many signs of joy to us.... Many merchants and planters now came on board, though it was in the evening. They put us in separate parcels, and examined us attentively. They also made us jump, and pointed to the land, signifying we were to go there. We thought by this we should be eaten by those ugly men, as they appeared to us;... at last the white people got some old slaves from the land to pacify us. They told us we were not to be eaten, but to work, and were soon to go on land, where we should see many of our country people. This report eased us much; and sure enough, soon after we were landed, there came to us Africans of all languages. We were conducted immediately to the merchant's yard, where we were all pent up together like so many sheep in a fold, without regard to sex or age.

Document 15.2

The Business of the Slave Trade

For its African victims like Equiano, the slave trade was a horror beyond their imagination; for kings and merchants—both European and African—it was a business. Document 15.2 shows how that business was conducted. It comes from the journal of an English merchant, Thomas Phillips, who undertook a voyage to the kingdom of Whydah in what is now the West African country of Benin in 1693–1694.

- How would you describe the economic transactions described in the document? To what extent were they conducted between equal parties? Who, if anyone, held the upper hand in these dealings?

- What obstacles did European merchants confront in negotiating with African authorities?

- How might an African merchant have described the same transaction? How might Equiano describe it?

- Notice the outcomes of Phillips's voyage to Barbados in the last two paragraphs. What does this tell you about European preferences for slaves, about the Middle Passage, and about the profitability of the enterprise?

THOMAS PHILLIPS

A Journal of a Voyage Made in the Hannibal of London

1694

As soon as the king understood of our landing, he sent two of his cappasheirs, or noblemen, to compliment us at our factory, where we design'd to continue that night, and pay our [respects] to his majesty next day...whereupon he sent two more of his grandees to invite us there that night, saying he waited for us, and that all former captains used to attend him the first night: whereupon being unwilling to infringe the custom, or give his majesty any offence, we took our hamocks, and Mr. Peirson, myself, Capt. Clay, our surgeons, pursers, and about 12 men, arm'd for our guard, were carry'd to the king's town, which contains about 50 houses....

We returned him thanks by his interpreter, and assur'd him how great affection our masters, the royal African company of England, bore to him, for his civility and fair and just dealings with their captains; and that notwithstanding there were many other places, more plenty of negro slaves that begg'd their custom, yet they had rejected all the advantageous offers made them out of their good will to him, and therefore had sent us to trade with him, to support his country with necessaries, and that we hop'd he would endeavour to continue their favour by his kind usage and fair dealing with us in our trade, that we may have our slaves with all expedition.... He answer'd that we should be fairly dealt with, and not impos'd upon; But he did not prove as good as his word...so after having examin'd us about our cargoe, what sort of goods we had, and what quantity of slaves we wanted, etc., we took our leaves and return'd to the factory....

According to promise we attended his majesty with samples of our goods, and made our agree-ment about the prices, tho' not without much difficulty;... next day we paid our customs to the king and cappasheirs,... then the bell was order'd to go about to give notice to all people to bring their slaves to the trunk to sell us....

Capt. Clay and I had agreed to go to the trunk to buy the slaves by turns, each his day, that we might have no distractions or disagreement in our trade, as often happens when there are here more ships than one, and...their disagreements create animosities, underminings, and out-bidding each other, whereby they enhance the prices to their general loss and detriment, the blacks well knowing how to make the best use of such opportunities, and as we found make it their business, and endeavour to create and foment misunderstandings and jealousies between commanders, it turning to their great account in the disposal of their slaves.

When we were at the trunk, the king's slaves, if he had any, were the first offer'd to sale,... and we must not refuse them, tho' as I observ'd they were generally the worst slaves in the trunk, and we paid more for them than any others, which we could not remedy, it being one of his majesty's perogatives: then the cappasheirs each brought out his slaves according to his degree and quality, the greatest first, etc. and our surgeon examin'd them well in all kinds, to see that they were sound wind and limb, making them jump, stretch out their arms swiftly, looking in their mouths to judge of their age; for the cappasheirs are so cunning, that they shave them all close before we see them, so that let them be never so old we can see no grey hairs in their heads or beards; and then having liquor'd them well and sleek with palm oil, 'tis no easy matter to know an old one from a middle-age one....

When we had selected from the rest such as we liked, we agreed in what goods to pay for them, the prices being already stated before the king, how much of each sort of merchandize we were to give for a

Source: Thomas Phillips, "A Journal of a Voyage Made in the Hannibal of London in 1694," in *Documents Illustrative of the History of the Slave Trade to America*, edited by Elizabeth Donnan (Washington DC: Carnegie Institute, 1930), 399–405, 408, 410.

man, woman, and child, which gave us much ease, and saved abundance of disputes and wranglings.... [T]hen we mark'd the slaves we had bought in the breast, or shoulder, with a hot iron, having the letter of the ship's name on it, the place being before anointed with a little palm oil, which caus'd but little pain, the mark being usually well in four or five days, appearing very plain and white after....

After we are come to an agreement for the prices of our slaves,...we are oblig'd to pay our customs to the king and cappasheirs for leave to trade, protection and justice; which for every ship are as follow, *viz.*

To the king six slaves value in cowries, or what other goods we can perswade him to take, but cowries are most esteem'd and desir'd; all which are measur'd in his presence, and he would wrangle with us stoutly about heaping up the measure.

To the cappasheirs in all two slaves value, as above....

The best goods to purchase slaves here are cowries, the smaller the more esteem'd....

The next in demand are brass neptunes or basons, very large, thin, and flat; for after they have bought them they cut them in pieces to make...bracelets, and collars for their arms legs and necks....

[I]f they can discover that you have good store of cowries and brass aboard, then no other goods will serve their turn, till they have got as much as you have; and after, for the rest of the goods they will be indifferent, and make you come to their own terms, or else lie a long time for your slaves, so that those you have on board are dying while you are buying others ashore; therefore every man that comes here, ought to be very cautious in making his report to the king at first, of what sorts and quantities of goods he has, and be sure to say his cargo consists mostly in iron, coral, rangoes, chints, etc. so that he may dispose of those goods as soon as he can, and at last his cowries and brass will bring him slaves as fast as he can buy them; but this is to be understood of a single ship: or more, if the captains agree, which seldom happens; for where there are divers ships, and of separate interests, about buying the same commodity they commonly undermine, betray, and out-bid one the other; and the Guiney commanders words and promises are the least to be depended upon of any I know use the sea; for they would deceive their fathers in their trade if they could....

Having bought my compliment of 700 slaves, *viz.* 480 men and 220 women, and finish'd all my business at Whidaw, I took my leave of the old king, and his cappasheirs, and parted, with many affectionate expressions on both sides, being forced to promise him that I would return again the next year, with several things he desired me to bring him from England; and having sign'd bills of lading...for the negroes aboard, I set sail the 27th of July in the morning....

I deliver'd alive at Barbadoes to the company's factors 372, which being sold, came out at about nineteen pounds per head.

Document 15.3

The Slave Trade and the Kingdom of Kongo

While African elites often eagerly facilitated the traffic in slaves and benefited from doing so, in one well-known case, quite early in the slave trade era, an African ruler sought to curtail it. This occurred in the kingdom of Kongo, in what is now Angola (see Map 15.4, p. 689). That state had welcomed Portuguese traders as early as the 1480s, as its rulers imagined that an alliance with Portugal could strengthen their regime. The royal family converted to Christianity and encouraged the importation of European guns, cattle, and horses. Several Kongolese were sent to Portugal for education, while Portuguese priests, artisans, merchants, and soldiers found a place in the kingdom. None of this worked as planned, however, and by the early sixteenth century, Kongo was in disarray and the authority of its ruler greatly undermined. This was the context in which its monarch Nzinga Mbemba, whose Christian name was Affonso I, wrote a series of letters to King Jao of Portugal in 1526, two of which are presented here.

- ■ According to King Affonso, how had the Portuguese connection in general and the slave trade in particular transformed his state?

- ■ How did the operation of the slave trade in Kongo differ from that of Whydah as described in Document 15.2? How did the rulers of these two states differ in their relationship to Europeans?

- ■ To what extent did Affonso seek the end of the slave trade? What was the basis for his opposition to it? Do you think he was opposed to slavery itself?

- ■ What did Affonso seek from Portugal? What kind of relationship did he envisage with the Portuguese?

KING AFFONSO I
Letters to King Jao of Portugal
1526

Sir, Your Highness [of Portugal] should know how our Kingdom is being lost in so many ways that it is convenient to provide for the necessary remedy, since this is caused by the excessive freedom given by your factors and officials to the men and merchants who are allowed to come to this Kingdom to set up shops with goods and many things which have been prohibited by us, and which they spread throughout our Kingdoms and Domains in such an abundance that many of our vassals, whom we had in obedience, do not comply because they have the things in greater abundance than we ourselves; and it was with these things that we had them content and subjected under our vassalage and jurisdiction, so it is doing a great harm not only to the service of God, but to the security and peace of our Kingdoms and State as well.

And we cannot reckon how great the damage is, since the mentioned merchants are taking every day our natives, sons of the land and the sons of our noblemen and vassals and our relatives, because the thieves and men of bad conscience grab them wishing to have the things and wares of this Kingdom which they are ambitious of; they grab them and get them to be sold; and so great, Sir, is the corruption and licentiousness that our country is being completely depopulated, and Your Highness should not agree with this nor accept it as in your service. And to avoid it we need from those [your] Kingdoms no more than some priests and a few people to teach in schools, and no other goods except wine and flour for the holy sacrament. That is why we beg of Your Highness to help and assist us in this matter, commanding your factors that they should not send here either merchants or wares, because it is *our will that in these Kingdoms there should not be any trade of slaves nor outlet for them.* Concerning what is referred

Source: Basil Davidson, *The African Past* (Boston: Little Brown, 1964), 191–94.

above, again we beg of Your Highness to agree with it, since otherwise we cannot remedy such an obvious damage. Pray Our Lord in His mercy to have Your Highness under His guard and let you do for ever the things of His service. I kiss your hands many times.

At our town of Congo, written on the sixth day of July.

João Teixeira did it in 1526.

The King. Dom Affonso.

[On the back of this letter the following can be read:

To the most powerful and excellent prince Dom João, King our Brother.]

Moreover, Sir, in our Kingdoms there is another great inconvenience which is of little service to God, and this is that many of our people, keenly desirous as they are of the wares and things of your Kingdoms, which are brought here by your people, and in order to satisfy their voracious appetite, seize many of our people, freed and exempt men; and very often it happens that they kidnap even noblemen and the sons of noblemen, and our relatives, and take them to be sold to the white men who are in our Kingdoms; and for this purpose thay have concealed them; and others are brought during the night so that they might not be recognized.

And as soon as they are taken by the white men they are immediately ironed and branded with fire, and when they are carried to be embarked, if they are caught by our guards' men the whites allege that they have bought them but they cannot say from whom, so that it is our duty to do justice and to restore to the freemen their freedom, but it cannot be done if your subjects feel offended, as they claim to be.

And to avoid such a great evil we passed a law so that any white man living in our Kingdoms and wanting to purchase goods in any way should first inform three of our noblemen and officials of our court whom we rely upon in this matter, and these are Dom Pedro Manipanza and Dom Manuel Manissaba, our chief usher, and Gonçalo Pires our chief freighter, who should investigate if the men-

tioned goods are captives or free men, and if cleared by them there will be no further doubt nor embargo for them to be taken and embarked. But if the white men do not comply with it they will lose the aforementioned goods. And if we do them this favor and concession it is for the part Your Highness has in it, since we know that it is in your service too that these goods are taken from our Kingdom, otherwise we should not consent to this....

Sir, Your Highness has been kind enough to write to us saying that we should ask in our letters for anything we need, and that we shall be provided with everything, and as the peace and the health of our Kingdom depend on us, and as there are among us old folks and people who have lived for many days, it happens that we have continuously many and different diseases which put us very often in such a weakness that we reach almost the last extreme; and the same happens to our children, relatives, and natives owing to the lack in this country of physicians and surgeons who might know how to cure properly such diseases. And as we have got neither dispensaries nor drugs which might help us in this forlornness, many of those who had been already confirmed and instructed in the holy faith of Our Lord Jesus Christ perish and die; and the rest of the people in their majority cure themselves with herbs and breads and other ancient methods, so that they put all their faith in the mentioned herbs and ceremonies if they live, and believe that they are saved if they die; and this is not much in the service of God.

And to avoid such a great error and inconvenience, since it is from God in the first place and then from your Kingdoms and from Your Highness that all the goods and drugs and medicines have come to save us, we beg of you to be agreeable and kind enough to send us two physicians and two apothecaries and one surgeon, so that they may come with their drugstores and all the necessary things to stay in our kingdoms, because we are in extreme need of them all and each of them. We shall do them all good and shall benefit them by all means, since they are sent by Your Highness, whom we thank for your work in their coming. We beg of Your Highness as a great favor to do this for us, because besides being good in itself it is in the service of God as we have said above.

Document 15.4

The Slave Trade and the Kingdom of Asante

Elsewhere in Africa, the slave trade did not have such politically destabilizing effects as it did in Kongo. In the region known as the Gold Coast (now the modern state of Ghana), the kingdom of Asante arose in the eighteenth century, occupying perhaps 100,000 square miles and incorporating some 3 million people (see Map 15.4, p. 689). It was a powerful conquest state, heavily invested in the slave trade, from which much of its wealth derived. Many slaves from its wars of expansion and from the tribute of its subject people were funneled into Atlantic commerce, while still others were used as labor in the gold mines and on the plantations within Asante itself. No wonder, then, that the ruler (or Asantehene) Osei Bonsu was dismayed in the early nineteenth century when, in reaction to the expanding abolitionist movement, the British stopped buying slaves. A conversation between Osei Bonsu and a British diplomat in 1820 highlights the role of the slave trade in Asante and in the thinking of its monarch.

■ How did Osei Bonsu understand the slave trade and its significance for his kingdom?

■ Some scholars have argued that the slave trade increased the incidence of warfare in West Africa as various states deliberately sought captives whom they could exchange for desired goods from Europe. How might Osei Bonsu respond to that idea? What was his understanding of the relationship between war and the slave trade?

■ In what ways did Osei Bonsu compare Muslim traders from the north with European merchants from the sea?

OSEI BONSU

Conversation with Joseph Dupuis

1820

"Now," said the king, after a pause, "I have another palaver, and you must help me to talk it. A long time ago the great king [of England] liked plenty of trade, more than now; then many ships came, and they bought ivory, gold, and slaves; but now he will not let the ships come as before, and the people buy gold and ivory only. This is what I have in my head, so now tell me truly, like a friend, why does the king do so?" "His majesty's question," I replied, "was connected with a great palaver, which my instructions did not authorise me to discuss. I had nothing to say regarding the slave trade." "I know that too," retorted the king; "because, if my master liked that trade, you would have told me so before. I only want to hear what you think as a friend: this is not like

Source: Osei Bonsu, *The Slave Trade and the Kingdom of Asante* (London: Henry Colburn, 1824), 162–64.

the other palavers." I was confessedly at a loss for an argument that might pass as a satisfactory reason, and the sequel proved that my doubts were not groundless. The king did not deem it plausible, that this obnoxious traffic should have been abolished from motives of humanity alone; neither would he admit that it lessened the number either of domestic or foreign wars.

Taking up one of my observations, he remarked, "[T]he white men who go to council with your master, and pray to the great God for him, do not understand my country, or they would not say the slave trade was bad. But if they think it bad now, why did they think it good before. Is not your law an old law, the same as the Crammo° law? Do you not both serve the same God, only you have different fashions and customs? Crammos are strong people in fetische,° and they say the law is good, because the great God made the book [Quran]; so they buy slaves, and teach them good things, which they knew not before. This makes every body love the Crammos, and they go every where up and down, and the people give them food when they want it. Then these men come all the way from the great water [Niger River], and from Manding, and Dagomba, and Killinga; they stop and trade for slaves, and then go home. If the great king would like to restore this trade, it would be good for the white men and for me too, because Ashantee is a country for war, and the people are strong; so if you talk that palaver for me properly, in the white country, if you go there, I will give you plenty of gold, and I will make you richer than all the white men."

°**Crammo:** Muslim.

°**fetische:** magical powers.

I urged the impossibility of the king's request, promising, however, to record his sentiments faithfully. "Well then," said the king, "you must put down in my master's book all I shall say, and then he will look to it, now he is my friend. And when he sees what is true, he will surely restore that trade. I cannot make war to catch slaves in the bush, like a thief. My ancestors never did so. But if I fight a king, and kill him when he is insolent, then certainly I must have his gold, and his slaves, and the people are mine too. Do not the white kings act like this? Because I hear the old men say, that before I conquered Fantee and killed the Braffoes and the kings, that white men came in great ships, and fought and killed many people; and then they took the gold and slaves to the white country: and sometimes they fought together. That is all the same as these black countries. The great God and the fetische made war for strong men every where, because then they can pay plenty of gold and proper sacrifice. When I fought Gaman, I did not make war for slaves, but because Dinkera (the king) sent me an arrogant message and killed my people, and refused to pay me gold as his father did. Then my fetische made me strong like my ancestors, and I killed Dinkera, and took his gold, and brought more than 20,000 slaves to Coomassy. Some of these people being bad men, I washed my stool in their blood for the fetische. But then some were good people, and these I sold or gave to my captains: many, moreover, died, because this country does not grow too much corn like Sarem, and what can I do? Unless I kill or sell them, they will grow strong and kill my people. Now you must tell my master that these slaves can work for him, and if he wants 10,000 he can have them. And if he wants fine handsome girls and women to give his captains, I can send him great numbers."

Using the Evidence:
Voices from the Slave Trade

1. **Highlighting differences:** What different experiences of the slave trade are reflected in these documents? How can you account for those differences?

2. **Noticing what's missing:** What perspectives are missing that might add other dimensions to our understanding of this commerce in people?

3. **Integrating documents and the text narrative:** In what ways do these documents support, illustrate, or contradict this chapter's narrative discussion of the slave trade?

4. **Assessing historical responsibility:** What light do these documents shed on the much-debated question about who should be held responsible for the tragedy of the Atlantic slave trade?

Visual Sources

Considering the Evidence:
Exchange and Status in the
Early Modern World

In many cultures across many centuries, the possession of scarce foreign goods has served not only to meet practical needs and desires but also to convey status. For centuries Chinese silk signified rank, position, or prestige across much of Eurasia. Pepper and other spices from South and Southeast Asia likewise appealed to elite Romans and Chinese, eager to demonstrate their elevated position in society. In the late twentieth century, American blue jeans were much in demand among Soviet young people who sought to display their independence from an oppressive communist regime, while Americans who could afford a German Porsche or an Italian Ferrari acquired an image of sophistication or glamour, setting them apart from others.

As global commerce expanded in the early modern era, so too did the exchange of foods, fashions, finery, and more. Already in 1500, according to a recent study, "it would be possible for a person in the Persian Gulf to wear cotton cloth from India while eating a bowl of rice also from India while sitting under a roof made of timber imported from East Africa. As he finished the rice he would see a Chinese character—the bowl itself came from China."[31] In the centuries that followed, growing numbers of people all across the world, particularly in elite social circles, had access to luxury goods from far away with which they could display, and perhaps enhance, their status. Some of these goods—sugar, pepper, tobacco, tea, and Indian cotton textiles, for example—gradually dropped in price, becoming more widely available. The images that follow illustrate this relationship between global trade and the display of status during the several centuries after 1500.

More than the peoples of other major civilizations, Europeans in the early modern era embraced the goods of the world. They had long been fascinated by and impressed with the wealth and splendor of Asia, which Marco Polo had described in the early fourteenth century after returning from his famous sojourn in China. Now in the early modern era, Western Europe was increasingly at the hub of a growing network of global commerce with access to products from around the world. Tea, porcelain, and silk from China; cotton textiles and spices from India and Southeast Asia; sugar, chocolate, and tobacco from the Americas; coffee from the Middle East—all of this and much more flooded into Europe. By the eighteenth century, a fascination for things Chinese had seized the elite classes of Europe—Chinese textiles, porcelains, tea, wallpaper, furniture, gardens, and artistic styles. The son of King George II of England built a "Mandarin yacht" resembling a Chinese pleasure boat to sail on a large artificial lake near London.

Visual Source 15.1, which shows a German painting from the early eighteenth century, illustrates the growing popularity of tea as a beverage of choice in Europe. Long popular in China and Japan, tea made its entry in Europe in the sixteenth century aboard Portuguese ships. Initially, it was extremely expensive and limited to the very wealthy, but the price dropped as the supply increased, and by the eighteenth century, it was widely consumed in Europe. Chinese teacups without handles also became popular and arrived via European merchant vessels packed in tea or rice. Like many other porcelains, these teacups had been created by Chinese artisans specifically for a European market. Those sitting on the table in front of the painting were manufactured in China between 1662 and 1722. Notice the practice of pouring the tea into the saucer to cool it.

- What foreign trade items can you identify in this painting?

- Note the European house on the teacup at the bottom left. What does this indicate about Chinese willingness to cater to the tastes of European customers?

- From what social class do you think the woman in the image comes?

- How might you explain the great European interest in Chinese products and styles during the eighteenth century? Why might their possession have suggested status?

Like tea from China and coffee from Ethiopia, chocolate from Mesoamerica also became an elite beverage and an indictor of high status in Europe during the early modern era. It was the Olmecs, the Maya, and the Aztecs who first discovered how to process the seeds of the cacao tree into a chocolate drink. After the Spanish conquest of the Aztec Empire, that drink was introduced into Spain, where it became highly fashionable in court and aristocratic circles. And from Spain it spread to much of the rest of Europe, also limited to the elite social classes, who could afford to purchase this expensive import. Not until the Industrial Revolution made it possible to produce solid chocolate candy for mass consumption did this Mesoamerican acquisition become more widely available. Unlike tobacco and coffee, however, chocolate did not take hold in the Islamic world or China until more recent times.

A part of the larger Columbian exchange, chocolate in Europe lost the religious or ritual associations with which the Aztecs had invested it, becoming a medicine, sometimes an aphrodisiac, and in general a recreational bever-

Visual Source 15.1 Tea and Porcelain in Europe (Erich Lessing/Art Resource, NY)

age. Cortés, the Spanish conqueror of the Aztecs, described chocolate as "the divine drink which builds up resistance and fights fatigue. A cup of this precious drink permits a man to walk for a whole day without food."[32] After some debate, the Church approved it as a nutritional substitute during times of fasting, when taking solid food was forbidden. Europeans also innovated with the beverage, adding sugar, cinnamon, and other spices, and later milk. With ingredients from the Americas and Asia, some of them produced by African slave labor, chocolate illustrated the process by which Europe was becoming the center of an emerging world economy.

Visual Source 15.2, a painted tile panel from the early eighteenth century, shows a *chocolatada*, or "chocolate party," in Valencia, Spain. Notice the saucer, or *mancerina*, also a European innovation for drinking chocolate without spilling it.

Visual Source 15.2 A Chocolate Party in Spain (Courtesy Museu de Cerámica, Barcelona. Photo: Guillem Fernandez-Huerta)

- What marks this event as an upper-class occasion?

- What steps in the preparation of the chocolate drink can you observe in the image?

- Why do you think Europeans embraced a practice of people they regarded as uncivilized, bloodthirsty, and savage? What does this suggest about the process of cultural borrowing?

Europeans, of course, were not the only people to embrace foreign tastes newly available in the early modern era. Tobacco and coffee, like tea, soon found a growing range of consumers all across Eurasia. Originating in the Americas, tobacco smoking spread quickly to Europe and Asia. Well before 1700 it had become perhaps the first global recreation. In the Ottoman Empire, as elsewhere, it provoked strenuous opposition on the grounds that it was an intoxicant, like wine, and was associated with unwholesome and promiscuous behavior. It was also associated with coffee, which had entered the Ottoman

Empire in the sixteenth century from its place of origin in Ethiopia and Yemen. Coffee too encountered considerable opposition, partly because it was consumed in the new social arena of the coffeehouse. To moralists and other critics, the coffeehouse was a "refuge of Satan," which drew people away from the mosques even as it drew together all different classes. Authorities suspected that coffeehouses were places of political intrigue. None of this stopped the spread of either tobacco or coffee, and the coffeehouse, in the Ottoman Empire and in Europe, came to embody a new "public culture of fun" as it wore away at earlier religious restrictions on the enjoyment of life.[33]

Visual Source 15.3 is a sixteenth-century miniature painting depicting a Turkish coffeehouse in the Ottoman Empire.

- What activities can you identify in the painting?

- Would you read this painting as critical of the coffeehouse, as celebrating it, or as a neutral description? Notice that the musicians and those playing board games at the bottom were engaged in activities considered rather disreputable. How would you describe the general demeanor of the men in the coffeehouse?

- Notice the cups that the patrons are using and those stacked in the upper right. Do they look similar to those shown in Visual Source 15.1? Certainly Ottoman elites by the sixteenth century preferred Chinese porcelain to that manufactured within their own empire.[34]

The emerging colonial societies of Spanish and Portuguese America gave rise to a wide variety of recognized mixed-race groups known as *castas*, or "castes," and defined in terms of the precise mixture of Native American, European, and African ancestry that an individual possessed. While this system slotted people into a hierarchical social order defined by race and heritage, it did allow for some social mobility. If individuals managed to acquire some education, land, or money, they might gain in social prestige and even pass as members of a more highly favored category (see pp. 636–37). Adopting the dress and lifestyle of higher-ranking groups could facilitate this process.

Visual Source 15.4 shows a woman of Indian ancestry and a man of African/ Indian descent as well as their child, who is categorized as a *loba*, or "wolf." It comes from a series of "casta paintings" created in eighteenth-century Mexico by the well-known Zapotec artist Miguel Cabrera to depict some eighteen or more mixed-race couples and their children, each with a distinct designation. The woman in this image is wearing a lovely *huipil*, a traditional Maya tunic or blouse, while the man is dressed in a European-style waistcoat, vest, and lace shirt as well as a black tricornered hat, widely popular in Europe during the seventeenth and eighteenth centuries. The popularity of such paintings reflected both a Spanish fascination with race and a more general European interest in classification, which was characteristic of eighteenth-century scientific thinking.

Visual Source 15.3 An Ottoman Coffeehouse (Chester Beatty Library, Dublin, Ms 439, folio 9)

De Chino cambujo y dIndia; Loba

Visual Source 15.4 Clothing and Status in Colonial Mexico (Oronoz)

■ What indications of status ambition or upward mobility can you identify in this image? Keep in mind that status here is associated with race and gender as well as the possession of foreign products.

■ Why do you think the woman is shown in more traditional costume, while the man is portrayed in European dress?

■ Notice the porcelain items at the bottom right. Where might they have come from?

■ In what cultural tradition do you think this couple raised their daughter? What problems might they have experienced in the process?

As West Africa became integrated into a European-centered Atlantic economy via the slave trade, its peoples gained access to a variety of goods and products from around the world: corn and tobacco from the Americas; metal goods, alcohol, textiles, decorative items, and gunpowder weapons from Europe; cowrie shells (used for money) and Indian cotton textiles from Asia. Many of these items were economically or militarily valuable, and some of them were also useful for purposes of display.

Visual Source 15.5 Procession and Display in the Kingdom of Dahomey (Private Collection/The Stapleton Collection/The Bridgeman Art Library)

Visual Source 15.5, an illustration entitled "Public Procession of the King's Women," is taken from a book by a British official stationed in West Africa during the late eighteenth century. It shows an elaborate ceremony in the kingdom of Dahomey, held in the presence of its powerful monarch. Several Europeans, perhaps slave merchants or officials, are depicted as guests of the king sitting behind the table in the bottom left. At the time, Dahomey was heavily involved in the slave trade, while keeping it under strict royal control (see pp. 695–97).

- What material evidence of international trade can you find in this image?

- What do you imagine was the purpose of this procession?

- Why might the women be clad in European-style dresses?

Using the Evidence:
Exchange and Status in the Early Modern World

1. **Analyzing the display of status:** In what different ways did the possession of foreign objects convey status in the early modern world? Toward whom were these various claims of status directed? Notice the difference between the display of status in public and private settings.

2. **Noticing gender differences:** In what ways are men and women portrayed in these visual sources? Why might women be absent in Visual Sources 15.2 and 15.3?

3. **Exploring the functions of trade:** How might you use these visual sources to support the idea that "trade served more than economic needs"?

4. **Raising questions about cultural borrowing:** What issues about cross-cultural borrowing do these visual sources suggest?

5. **Evaluating images as evidence:** What are the strengths and limitations of visual sources as a means of understanding the relationship of trade and status in the early modern era? What other kinds of sources would be useful for pursuing this theme?

CHAPTER SIXTEEN

Religion and Science

1450–1750

The Globalization of Christianity
 Western Christendom Fragmented:
  The Protestant Reformation
 Christianity Outward Bound
 Conversion and Adaptation in
  Spanish America
 An Asian Comparison: China and
  the Jesuits
Persistence and Change in Afro-
 Asian Cultural Traditions
 Expansion and Renewal in the
  Islamic World
 China: New Directions in an
  Old Tradition
 India: Bridging the Hindu/
  Muslim Divide
A New Way of Thinking: The Birth of
 Modern Science
 The Question of Origins: Why Europe?
 Science as Cultural Revolution
 Science and Enlightenment
 Looking Ahead: Science in the
  Nineteenth Century
 European Science beyond the West
Reflections: Cultural Borrowing and
 Its Hazards
Considering the Evidence
 Documents: Cultural Change in the
  Early Modern World
 Visual Sources: Global Christianity
  in the Early Modern World

Nigerian pastor Daniel Ajayi-Adeniran is a missionary... to the United States.... with his mission field in the Bronx. The church he represents, the Redeemed Christian Church of God, began in Nigeria in 1952. It has acquired millions of members in Nigeria and boasts a missionary network with a presence in 100 countries. According to its leader, the church was "made in heaven, assembled in Nigeria, exported to the world." And the Redeemed Church of God is not alone. As secularism and materialism born of the Scientific Revolution and modern life have eroded religious faith in the West, many believers in Asia, Africa, and Latin America have felt called to reinvigorate Christianity in Europe and North America. In a remarkable reversal of an earlier pattern, they now seek to "reevangelize" the West, from which they originally received the faith. After all, more than 60 percent of the world's professing Christians now live outside Europe and North America, and, within the United States, one in six Catholic diocesan priests and one in three seminary students are foreign-born. For example, hundreds of Filipino priests, nuns, and lay workers now serve churches in the West. "We couldn't just throw up our hands and see these churches turned into nightclubs or mosques," declared Tokunboh Adeyemo, another Nigerian church leader seeking to minister to an "increasingly godless West."[1]

THE EARLY MODERN ERA OF WORLD HISTORY gave birth to two intersecting and perhaps contradictory trends that continue to play out in the twenty-first century. The first was the spread of

---

The Virgin of Guadalupe: According to Mexican tradition, a dark-skinned Virgin Mary appeared to an indigenous peasant named Juan Diego in 1531, an apparition reflected in this Mexican painting from 1720. Belief in the Virgin of Guadalupe represented the incorporation of Catholicism into the emerging culture and identity of Mexico.
(National Palace Mexico City/Gianni Dagli Orti/The Art Archive)

Christianity to Asians, Africans, and Native Americans, some of whom now seem to be returning the favor. The second lay in the emergence of a modern scientific outlook, which sharply challenged Western Christianity even as it too acquired a global presence.

And so, alongside new empires and new patterns of commerce, the early modern centuries also witnessed novel cultural transformations that likewise connected distant peoples. Riding the currents of European empire building and commercial expansion, Christianity was established solidly in the Americas and the Philippines; far more modestly in Siberia, China, Japan, and India; and hardly at all within the vast and still growing domains of Islam. A cultural tradition largely limited to Europe now became a genuine world religion, spawning a multitude of cultural encounters. While this ancient faith was spreading, a new understanding of the universe and a new approach to knowledge were taking shape among European thinkers of the Scientific Revolution, giving rise to another kind of cultural encounter—that between science and religion. In some ways, science was a new and competing worldview, and for some it was almost a new religion. In time, it became a defining feature of global modernity, achieving a worldwide acceptance that exceeded that of Christianity or any other religious tradition.

Although Europeans were central players in the globalization of Christianity and the emergence of modern science, they did not act alone in the cultural transformations of the early modern era. Asian, African, and Native American peoples largely determined how Christianity would be accepted, rejected, or transformed as it entered new cultural environments. Science emerged within an international and not simply a European context, and it met varying receptions in different parts of the world. Islam continued a long pattern of religious expansion and renewal, even as Christianity began to compete with it as a world religion. Buddhism maintained its hold in much of East Asia, as did Hinduism in South Asia and numerous smaller-scale religious traditions in Africa. And Europeans themselves were certainly affected by the many "new worlds" that they now encountered. The cultural interactions of the early modern era, in short, did not take place on a one-way street.

The Globalization of Christianity

Despite its Middle Eastern origins, Christianity was largely limited to Europe at the beginning of the early modern era. In 1500, the world of Christendom stretched from Spain and England in the west to Russia in the east, with small and beleaguered communities of various kinds in Egypt, Ethiopia, southern India, and Central Asia. Internally, Christianity was seriously divided between the Roman Catholics of Western and Central Europe and the Eastern Orthodox of Eastern Europe and Russia. Externally, it was very much on the defensive against an expansive Islam. Muslims had ousted Christian Crusaders from their toeholds in the Holy Land by 1300, and with the Ottoman seizure of Constantinople in 1453, they had captured the prestigious capital of Eastern Orthodoxy. The Ottoman siege of Vienna in 1529 marked a

Muslim advance into the heart of Central Europe. Except in Spain, which had recently been reclaimed for Christendom after centuries of Muslim rule, the future, it must have seemed, lay with Islam rather than Christianity.

Western Christendom Fragmented: The Protestant Reformation

As if these were not troubles enough, in the early sixteenth century the Protestant Reformation shattered the unity of Roman Catholic Christianity, which for the previous 1,000 years had provided the cultural and organizational foundation of Western European civilization. The Reformation began in 1517 when a German priest, Martin Luther (1483–1546), publicly invited debate about various abuses within the Roman Catholic Church by issuing a document, known as the Ninety-five Theses, allegedly nailing it to the door of a church in Wittenberg. In itself, this was nothing new, for many people were critical of the luxurious life of the popes, the corruption and immorality of some clergy, the Church's selling of indulgences (said to remove the penalties for sin), and other aspects of church life and practice.

What made Luther's protest potentially revolutionary, however, was its theological basis. A troubled and brooding man who was anxious about his relationship with God, Luther recently had come to a new understanding of salvation, which held that it came through faith alone. Neither the good works of the sinner nor the sacraments of the Church had any bearing on the eternal destiny of the soul, for faith was a free gift of God, graciously granted to his needy and undeserving people. To Luther, the source of these beliefs, and of religious authority in general, was not the teaching of the Church, but the Bible alone, interpreted according to the individual's conscience. (See Document 16.1, pp. 749–51, for more of Luther's thinking.) All of this challenged the authority of the Church and called into question the special position of the clerical hierarchy and of the pope in particular. In sixteenth-century Europe, this was the stuff of revolution.

Contrary to Luther's original intentions, his ideas ultimately provoked a massive schism within the world of Catholic Christendom, for they came to express a variety of political, economic, and social tensions as well as religious differences. Some kings and princes, many of whom had long disputed the political authority of the pope, found in these ideas a justification for their own independence and an opportunity to gain the

■ **Change**

In what ways did the Protestant Reformation transform European society, culture, and politics?

The Protestant Reformation This sixteenth-century painting by the well-known German artist Lucas Cranach the Elder shows Martin Luther and his supporters using a giant quill to write their demands for religious reform on a church door. It memorializes the posting of the Ninety-five Theses in 1517, which launched the Protestant Reformation. (Dr. Henning Schleifenbaum, Siegen, Germany/Visual Connection Archive)

Snapshot **Catholic/Protestant Differences in the Sixteenth Century**

	Catholic	Protestant
Religious authority	Pope and church hierarchy	The Bible, as interpreted by individual Christians
Role of the pope	Ultimate authority in faith and doctrine	Denied the authority of the pope
Ordination of clergy	Apostolic succession: direct line between original apostles and all subsequently ordained clergy	Apostolic succession denied; ordination by individual congregations or denominations
Salvation	Importance of church sacraments as channels of God's grace	By faith alone; God's grace is freely and directly granted to believers
Status of Mary	Highly prominent, ranking just below Jesus; provides constant intercession for believers	Less prominent; denied Mary's intercession on behalf of the faithful
Prayer	To God, but often through or with Mary and saints	To God alone; no role for Mary and saints
Holy Communion	Transubstantiation: bread and wine become the actual body and blood of Christ	Denied transubstantiation; bread and wine have a spiritual or symbolic significance
Role of clergy	Generally celibate; sharp distinction between priests and laypeople; mediators between God and humankind	Ministers may marry; priesthood of all believers; clergy have different functions (to preach, administer sacraments) but no distinct spiritual status

lands and taxes previously held by the Church. In the Protestant idea that all vocations were of equal merit, middle-class urban dwellers found a new religious legitimacy for their growing role in society, since the Roman Catholic Church was associated in their eyes with the rural and feudal world of aristocratic privilege. For common people, who were offended by the corruption and luxurious living of some bishops, abbots, and popes, the new religious ideas served to express their opposition to the entire social order, particularly in a series of German peasant revolts in the 1520s. (See Visual Sources 16.1 and 16.2, pp. 762 and 763, for contrasting images of Protestant and Catholic churches.)

Although large numbers of women were attracted to Protestantism, Reformation teachings and practices did not offer them a substantially greater role in the church or society. In Protestant-dominated areas, the veneration of Mary and female saints ended, leaving the male Christ figure as the sole object of worship. Protestant opposition to celibacy and monastic life closed the convents, which had offered some women an alternative to marriage. Nor were Protestants (except the Quakers) any more willing than Catholics to offer women an official role within their churches. The importance that Protestants gave to reading the Bible for oneself stimulated education and literacy for women, but given the emphasis on women as wives and mothers subject to male supervision, they had little opportunity to use that education outside of the family.

Reformation thinking spread quickly both within and beyond Germany, thanks in large measure to the recent invention of the printing press. Luther's many pamphlets and his translation of the New Testament into German were soon widely available. "God has appointed the [printing] Press to preach, whose voice the pope is never able to stop," declared one Reformation leader.[2] As the movement spread to France, Switzerland, England, and elsewhere, it also splintered, amoeba-like, into a variety of competing Protestant churches—Lutheran, Calvinist, Anglican, Quaker, Anabaptist—many of which subsequently subdivided, producing a bewildering array of Protestant denominations. Each was distinctive, but none gave allegiance to Rome or the pope.

Thus to the divided societies and the fractured political system of Europe was now added the potent brew of religious difference, operating both within and between states (see Map 16.1). For more than thirty years (1562–1598), French society was torn by violence between Catholics and the Protestant minority known as Huguenots. On a single day, August 24, 1572, Catholic mobs in Paris massacred some 3,000 Huguenots, and thousands more perished in provincial towns in the weeks that followed. Finally, a war-weary monarch, Henry IV, issued the Edict of Nantes (1598), which granted a substantial measure of religious toleration to French Protestants, though with the intention that they would soon return to the Catholic Church. The culmination of European religious conflict took shape in the Thirty Years' War (1618–1648), a Catholic–Protestant struggle that began in the Holy Roman Empire but eventually engulfed most of Europe. It was a horrendously destructive war, during which, scholars estimate, between 15 and 30 percent of the German population perished from violence, famine, or disease. Finally, the Peace of Westphalia (1648) brought the conflict to an end, with some reshuffling of boundaries and an agreement that each state was sovereign, authorized to control religious affairs within its own territory. Whatever religious unity Catholic Europe had once enjoyed was now permanently broken.

The Protestant breakaway, combined with reformist tendencies within the Catholic Church itself, provoked a Catholic Counter-Reformation. In the Council of Trent (1545–1563), Catholics clarified and reaffirmed their unique doctrines and practices, such as the authority of the pope, priestly celibacy, the veneration of saints and relics, and the importance of church tradition and good works, all of which Protestants had rejected. Moreover, they set about correcting the abuses and corruption that had

Map 16.1 Reformation Europe in the Sixteenth Century

The rise of Protestantism added yet another set of religious divisions, both within and between states, to European Christendom, which was already sharply divided between the Roman Catholic Church and the Eastern Orthodox Church.

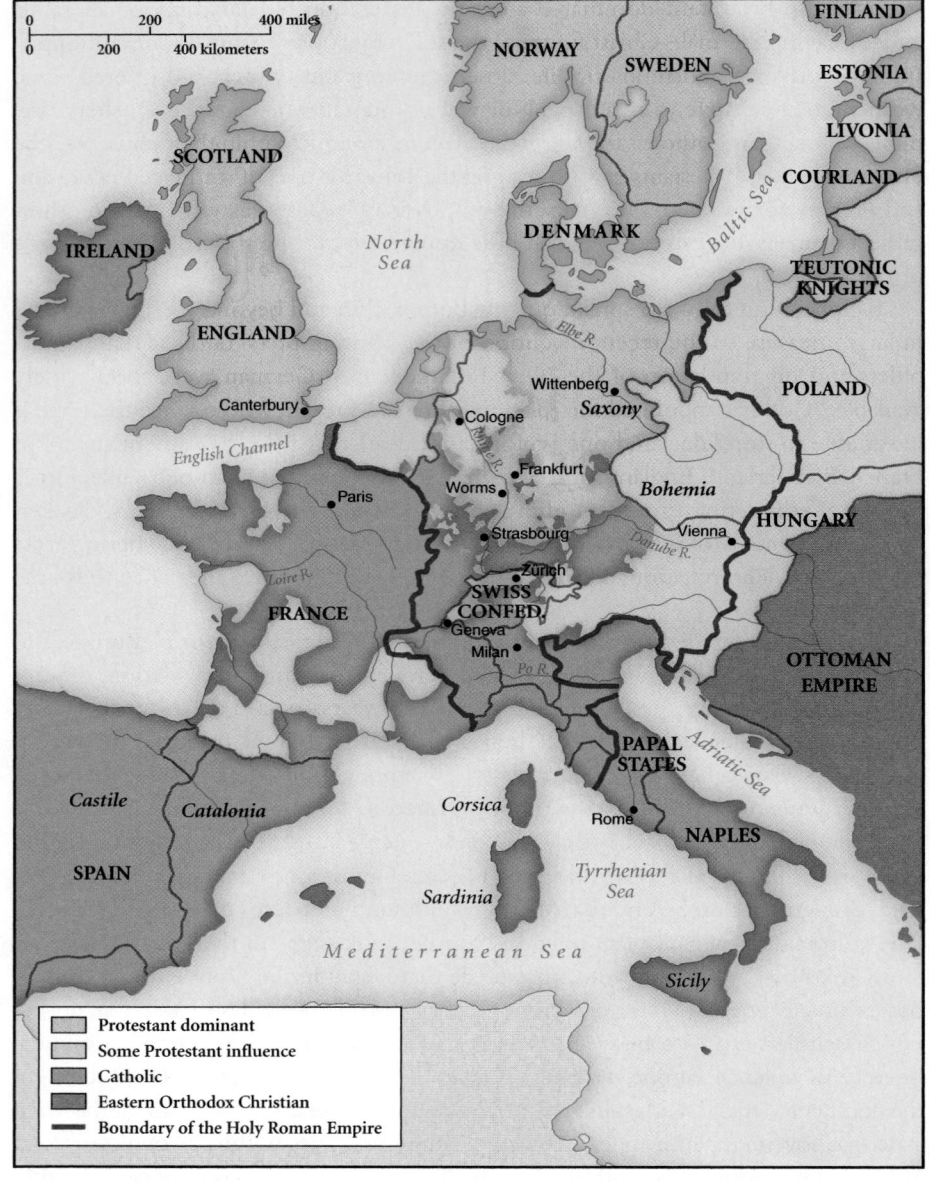

stimulated the Protestant movement by placing a new emphasis on the education of priests and their supervision by bishops. A crackdown on dissidents included the censorship of books, fines, exile, penitence, and occasionally the burning of heretics. Renewed attention was given to individual spirituality and personal piety. New religious orders, such as the Society of Jesus (Jesuits), provided a dedicated brotherhood of priests committed to the renewal of the Catholic Church and its extension abroad.

Although the Reformation was profoundly religious, it encouraged a skeptical attitude toward authority and tradition, for it had, after all, successfully challenged the immense prestige and power of the pope and the established Church. Protestant reformers fostered religious individualism as people were now encouraged to read and interpret the scriptures for themselves and to seek salvation without the mediation of the Church. In the centuries that followed, some people turned that skepticism and the habit of thinking independently against all revealed religion. Thus the Protestant Reformation opened some space for new directions in European intellectual life.

In short, it was a more highly fragmented but also a renewed and revitalized Christianity that established itself around the world in the several centuries after 1500.

Christianity Outward Bound

Christianity motivated European political and economic expansion and also benefited from it. The resolutely Catholic Spanish and Portuguese both viewed their movement overseas as a continuation of a long crusading tradition, which only recently had completed the liberation of their countries from Muslim control. When Vasco da Gama's small fleet landed in India in 1498, local authorities understandably asked, "What brought you hither?" The reply: they had come "in search of Christians and of spices."[3] Likewise, Columbus, upon arriving in the Americas, expressed the no doubt sincere hope that the people "might become Christians," even as he promised his Spanish patrons an abundant harvest of gold, spice, cotton, aloe wood, and slaves.[4] Neither man sensed any contradiction or hypocrisy in this blending of religious and material concerns.

■ **Connection**
How was European imperial expansion related to the spread of Christianity?

If religion drove and justified European ventures abroad, it is difficult to imagine the globalization of Christianity without the support of empire. Colonial settlers and traders, of course, brought their faith with them and sought to replicate it in their newly conquered homelands. New England Puritans, for example, planted a distinctive Protestant version of Christianity in North America, with an emphasis on education, moral purity, personal conversion, civic responsibility, and little tolerance for competing expressions of the faith. They did not show much interest in converting native peoples but sought rather to push them out of their ancestral territories. It was missionaries, mostly Catholic, who actively spread the Christian message beyond European communities. Organized in missionary orders such as the Dominicans, Franciscans, and Jesuits, Portuguese missionaries took the lead in Africa and Asia, while Spanish and French missionaries were most prominent in the Americas. Missionaries of the Russian Orthodox Church likewise accompanied the expansion of the Russian Empire across Siberia, where priests and monks ministered to Russian settlers and trappers, who often donated their first sable furs to a church or monastery.

Missionaries had their greatest success in Spanish America and in the Philippines, areas that shared two critical elements beyond their colonization by Spain. Most

Japanese Christian Martyrs
Christianity was beginning to take root in sixteenth-century Japan, but intensive persecution by Japanese authorities in the early seventeenth century largely ended that process. This monument was later erected in memory of twenty-six martyrs, Japanese and European alike, who were executed during this suppression of Christianity. (Photo Agency MH Martin Hladik, Photographer)

■ **Connection**

In what ways was European Christianity assimilated into the Native American cultures of Spanish America?

important, perhaps, was an overwhelming European presence, experienced variously as military conquest, colonial settlement, missionary activity, forced labor, social disruption, and disease. Surely it must have seemed as if the old gods had been bested and that any possible future lay with the powerful religion of the European invaders. A second common factor was the absence of a literate world religion in these two regions. Throughout the modern era, peoples solidly rooted in Confucian, Buddhist, Hindu, or Islamic traditions proved far more resistant to the Christian message than those who practiced more localized, small-scale, orally based polytheistic religions.

Conversion and Adaptation in Spanish America

Spanish America and China illustrate the difference between those societies in which Christianity became widely practiced and those that largely rejected it. Both cases, however, represent major cultural encounters of a kind that was becoming more frequent as European expansion brought the Christian faith to distant peoples with very different cultural traditions.

The decisive conquest of the Aztec and Inca empires and all that followed from it—disease, population collapse, loss of land to Europeans, forced labor, resettlement into more compact villages—created a setting in which the religion of the victors took hold in Spanish American colonies. Europeans saw their political and military success as a demonstration of the power of the Christian God. Native American peoples generally agreed, and by 1700 or earlier the vast majority had been baptized and saw themselves in some respects as Christians. After all, other conquerors such as the Aztecs and the Incas had always imposed their gods in some fashion on defeated peoples. It made sense, both practically and spiritually, to affiliate with the Europeans' God, saints, rites, and rituals. Many millions accepted baptism, contributed to the construction of village churches, attended services, and embraced images of Mary and other saints.

Earlier conquerors, however, had made no attempt to eradicate local deities and religious practices. The flexibility and inclusiveness of Mesoamerican and Andean religions had made it possible for subject people to accommodate the gods of their new rulers while maintaining their own traditions. But Europeans were different. They claimed an exclusive religious truth and sought the utter destruction of local gods and everything associated with them. Operating within a Spanish colonial regime that actively encouraged conversion, missionaries often proceeded by persuasion and patient teaching. At times, though, their frustration with the persistence of "idolatry, superstition, and error" boiled over into violent campaigns designed to uproot old religions once and for all. In 1535, the bishop of Mexico proudly claimed that he had destroyed 500 pagan shrines and 20,000 idols. During the seventeenth and early eighteenth centuries, church authorities in the Andean region periodically launched movements of "extirpation," designed to fatally undermine native religion. They destroyed religious images and ritual objects, publicly urinated on native "idols," desecrated the remains of ancestors, held religious trials and "processions of shame" aimed at humiliating offenders, and flogged "idolaters."[5]

Occasionally, overt resistance erupted. One such example was the religious revivalist movement in central Peru in the 1560s, known as Taki Onqoy (dancing sickness). Possessed by the spirits of local gods, or *huacas*, traveling dancers and teachers predicted that an alliance of Andean deities would soon overcome the Christian God, inflict the intruding Europeans with the same diseases that they had brought to the Americas, and restore the world of the Andes to an imagined earlier harmony. They called on native peoples to cut off all contact with the Spanish, to reject Christian worship, and to return to traditional practices. "The world has turned about," one member declared, "and this time God and the Spaniards [will be] defeated and all the Spaniards killed and their cities drowned; and the sea will rise and overwhelm them, so that there will remain no memory of them."[6]

More common than such frontal attacks on Christianity, which were quickly smashed by colonial authorities, were efforts at blending two religious traditions, reinterpreting Christian practices within an Andean framework, and incorporating local elements into an emerging Andean Christianity. Even female dancers in the Taki Onqoy movement sometimes took the names of Christian saints, seeking to appropriate for themselves the religious power of Christian figures. Within Andean Christian communities, people might offer the blood of a llama to strengthen a village church or make a cloth covering for the Virgin Mary and a shirt for an image of a huaca with the same material. Although the state cults of the Incas faded away, missionary attacks did not succeed in eliminating the influence of local huacas. Images and holy sites might be destroyed, but the souls of the huacas remained, and their representatives gained prestige. One resilient Andean resident inquired of a Jesuit missionary: "Father, are you tired of taking our idols from us? Take away that mountain if you can, since that is the God I worship."[7] (See Visual Source 16.3, p. 765, for an illustration of the blending of Andean religious symbols and the new Christian message.)

In Mexico as well, an immigrant Christianity was assimilated into patterns of local culture. Parishes were organized largely around precolonial towns or regions. Churches built on or near the sites of old temples became the focus of community identity. *Cofradias*, church-based associations of laypeople, organized community processions and festivals and made provision for a proper funeral and burial for their members. Central to an emerging Mexican Christianity were the saints who closely paralleled the functions of precolonial gods. Saints were imagined as parents of the local community and the true owners of its land, and their images were paraded through the streets on the occasion of great feasts and were collected by individual households. Although parish priests were almost always Spanish, the *fiscal*, or leader of the church staff, was a native Christian of great local prestige, who carried on the traditions and role of earlier religious specialists.

Throughout the colonial period and beyond, many Mexican Christians also took part in rituals derived from the past, with little sense that this was incompatible with Christian practice. Incantations to various gods for good fortune in hunting, farming, or healing; sacrifices of self-bleeding; offerings to the sun; divination; the use of hallucinogenic drugs—all of these rituals provided spiritual assistance in those areas of everyday life not directly addressed by Christian rites. Conversely, these practices also showed signs of Christian influence. Wax candles, normally used in Christian services, might now appear in front of a stone image of a precolonial god. The anger of a neglected saint, rather than that of a traditional god, might explain someone's illness and require offerings, celebration, or a new covering to regain his or her favor.[8] In such ways did Christianity take root in the new cultural environments of Spanish America, but it was a distinctly Andean or Mexican Christianity, not merely a copy of the Spanish version.

An Asian Comparison: China and the Jesuits

■ Comparison

Why were missionary efforts to spread Christianity so much less successful in China than in Spanish America?

The Chinese encounter with Christianity was very different from that of Native Americans in Spain's New World empire. The most obvious difference was the political context. The peoples of Spanish America had been defeated, their societies thoroughly disrupted, and their cultural confidence sorely shaken. China, on the other hand, encountered European Christianity between the sixteenth and eighteenth centuries during the powerful and prosperous Ming (1368–1644) and Qing (1644–1912) dynasties. Although the transition between these two dynasties occasioned several decades of internal conflict, at no point was China's political independence or cultural integrity threatened by the handful of European missionaries and traders working there.

The reality of a strong, independent, confident China required a different missionary strategy, for Europeans needed the permission of Chinese authorities to operate in the country. Whereas Spanish missionaries working in a colonial setting sought primarily to convert the masses, the leading missionary order in China, the Jesuits, took deliberate aim at the official Chinese elite. Following the lead of their most famous missionary, Matteo Ricci (in China 1582–1610), many Jesuits learned Chinese, became thoroughly acquainted with classical Confucian texts, and dressed like Chinese scholars. Initially, they downplayed their mission to convert and instead emphasized their interest in exchanging ideas and learning from China's ancient culture. As highly educated men, the Jesuits carried the recent secular knowledge of Europe—science, technology, geography, mapmaking—to an audience of curious Chinese scholars. In presenting Christian teachings, Jesuits were at pains to be respectful of Chinese culture, pointing out parallels between Confucianism and Christianity rather than portraying it as something new and foreign. They chose to define Chinese rituals honoring the emperor or venerating ancestors as secular or civil observances rather than as religious practices that had to be abandoned. Such efforts to accommodate Chinese culture contrast sharply with the frontal attacks on Native American religions in the Spanish Empire (see Visual Source 16.4, p. 767).

The religious and cultural outcomes of the missionary enterprise likewise differed greatly in the two regions. Nothing approaching the mass conversion to Christianity of Native American peoples took place in China. During the sixteenth and seventeenth centuries, a modest number of Chinese scholars and officials—who were attracted by the personal lives of the missionaries, by their interest in Western science, and by the moral certainty that Christianity offered—did become Christians. Jesuit missionaries found favor for a time at the Chinese imperial court, where their mathematical, astronomical, technological, and mapmaking skills rendered them useful. For more than a century, they were appointed to head the Chinese Bureau of Astronomy. Among ordinary people, Christianity spread very modestly amid tales of miracles attributed to the Christian God, while missionary teachings about "eternal life" sounded to some like Daoist prescriptions for immortality. At most, though, missionary efforts over the course of some 250 years (1550–1800) resulted in 200,000 to 300,000 converts, a minuscule number in a Chinese population approaching 300 million by 1800. What explains the very limited acceptance of Christianity in early modern China?

Fundamentally, the missionaries offered little that the Chinese really needed. Confucianism for the elites and Buddhism, Daoism, and a multitude of Chinese gods and spirits at the local level adequately supplied the spiritual needs of most Chinese. Furthermore, it became increasingly clear that Christianity was an all-or-nothing faith that required converts to abandon much of traditional Chinese culture. Christian monogamy, for example, seemed to require Chinese men to put away their concubines. What would happen to these deserted women?

Jesuits in China
In this seventeenth-century Dutch engraving, two Jesuit missionaries hold a map of China. Their mapmaking skills were among the reasons that the Jesuits were initially welcomed among the educated elite of that country. (Frontispiece to *China Illustrated* by Athanasius Kircher [1601–1680] 1667 [engraving], Dutch School, [17th century]/Private Collection, The Stapleton Collection/The Bridgeman Art Library)

By the early eighteenth century, the papacy and competing missionary orders came to oppose the Jesuit policy of accommodation. The pope claimed authority over Chinese Christians and declared that sacrifices to Confucius and the veneration of ancestors were "idolatry" and thus forbidden to Christians. The pope's pronouncements represented an unacceptable challenge to the authority of the emperor and an affront to Chinese culture. In 1715, an outraged Emperor Kangxi wrote:

> I ask myself how these uncultivated Westerners dare to speak of the great precepts of China.... [T]heir doctrine is of the same kind as the little heresies of the Buddhist and Taoist monks.... These are the greatest absurdities that have ever been seen. As from now I forbid the Westerners to spread their doctrine in China; that will spare us a lot of trouble.[9]

This represented a major turning point in the relationship of Christian missionaries and Chinese society. Many were subsequently expelled, and missionaries lost favor at court.

In other ways as well, missionaries played into the hands of their Chinese opponents. Their willingness to work under the Manchurian Qing dynasty, which came to power in 1644, discredited them with those Chinese scholars who viewed the Qing as uncivilized foreigners and their rule in China as disgraceful and illegitimate. Missionaries' reputation as miracle workers further damaged their standing as men of science and rationality, for elite Chinese often regarded miracles and supernatural religion as superstitions, fit only for the uneducated masses. Some viewed the Christian ritual of Holy Communion as a kind of cannibalism. Others came to see missionaries as potentially subversive, for various Christian groups met in secret, and such religious sects had often provided the basis for peasant rebellion. Nor did it escape Chinese notice that European Christians had taken over the Philippines and that their warships were active in the Indian Ocean. Perhaps the missionaries, with their great interest in maps, were spies for these aggressive foreigners. All of this contributed to the general failure of Christianity to secure a prominent presence in China.

Persistence and Change in Afro-Asian Cultural Traditions

Although Europeans were central players in the globalization of Christianity, theirs was not the only expanding or transformed culture of the early modern era. African religious ideas and practices, for example, accompanied slaves to the Americas. Common African forms of religious revelation—divination, dream interpretation, visions, spirit possession—found a place in the Africanized versions of Christianity that emerged in the New World. Europeans frequently perceived these practices as evidence of sorcery, witchcraft, or even devil worship and tried to suppress them. Nonetheless, syncretic (blended) religions such as Vodou in Haiti, Santeria in Cuba, and Candomble and Macumba in Brazil persisted. They derived from various West

African traditions and featured drumming, ritual dancing, animal sacrifice, and spirit possession. Over time, they incorporated Christian beliefs and practices such as church attendance, the search for salvation, and the use of candles and crucifixes and often identified their various spirits or deities with Catholic saints.

Expansion and Renewal in the Islamic World

The early modern era likewise witnessed the continuation of the "long march of Islam" across the Afro-Asian world. In sub-Saharan Africa, in the eastern and western wings of India, and in Central and Southeast Asia, the expansion of the Islamic frontier, a process already almost 1,000 years in the making, extended farther still. Conversion to Islam generally did not mean a sudden abandonment of old religious practices in favor of the new. Rather it was more often a matter of "assimilating Islamic rituals, cosmologies, and literatures into...local religious systems."[10]

Continued Islamization usually was not the product of conquering armies and expanding empires. It depended instead on wandering Muslim holy men, Islamic scholars, and itinerant traders, none of whom posed a threat to local rulers. In fact, such people often were useful to those rulers and their village communities. They offered literacy in Arabic, established informal schools, provided protective charms containing passages from the Quran, served as advisers to local authorities and healers to the sick, often intermarried with local people, and generally did not insist that new converts give up their older practices. What they offered, in short, was connection to the wider, prestigious, prosperous world of Islam. Islamization extended modestly even to the Americas, where enslaved African Muslims planted their faith, particularly in Brazil. There Muslims led a number of slave revolts in the early nineteenth century.

To more orthodox Muslims, this religious syncretism, which accompanied Islamization almost everywhere, became increasingly offensive, even heretical. Such sentiments played an important role in movements of religious renewal and reform that emerged throughout the vast Islamic world of the eighteenth century. The leaders of such movements sharply criticized those practices that departed from earlier patterns established by Muhammad and from the authority of the Quran. For example, in India, which was governed by the Muslim Mughal Empire, religious resistance to official policies that accommodated Hindus found concrete expression during the reign of the emperor Aurangzeb (1658–1707) (see p. 646). A series of religious wars in West Africa during the eighteenth and early nineteenth centuries took aim at corrupt Islamic practices and the rulers, Muslim and non-Muslim alike, who permitted them. In Southeast and Central Asia, tension grew between practitioners of localized and blended versions of Islam and those who sought to purify such practices in the name of a more authentic and universal faith.

The most well-known and widely visible of these Islamic renewal movements took place during the mid-eighteenth century in Arabia itself, where the religion had been born more than 1,000 years earlier. It originated in the teachings of the

■ **Explanation**
What accounts for the continued spread of Islam in the early modern era and for the emergence of reform or renewal movements within the Islamic world?

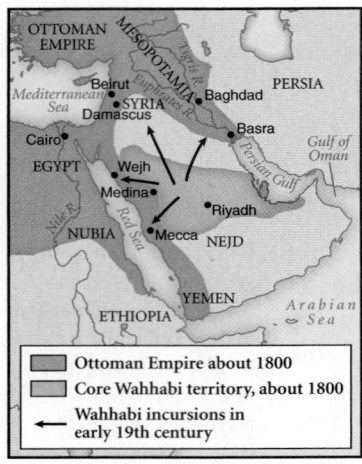

The Expansion of Wahhabi Islam

Islamic scholar Muhammad ibn Abd al-Wahhab (1703–1792). The growing difficulties of the Islamic world, such as the weakening of the Ottoman Empire, were directly related, he argued, to deviations from the pure faith of early Islam. Al-Wahhab was particularly upset by common religious practices in central Arabia that seemed to him idolatry—the widespread veneration of Sufi saints and their tombs, the adoration of natural sites, and even the respect paid to Muhammad's tomb at Mecca. All of this was a dilution of the absolute monotheism of authentic Islam.

The Wahhabi movement took a new turn in the 1740s when it received the political backing of Muhammad Ibn Saud, a local ruler who found al-Wahhab's ideas compelling. With Ibn Saud's support, the religious movement became an expansive state in central Arabia. Within that state, offending tombs were razed; "idols" were eliminated; books on logic were destroyed; the use of tobacco, hashish, and musical instruments was forbidden; and certain taxes not authorized by religious teaching were abolished. Likewise, male control of women was strengthened in strict accordance with the law, but al-Wahhab was also concerned about lack of attention to widows and orphans, about sexual immorality, and about women who had not received a proper share of their families' inheritance. By the early nineteenth century, this new reformist state encompassed much of central Arabia, with Mecca itself coming under Wahhabi control in 1803. Although an Egyptian army broke the power of the Wahhabis in 1818, the movement's influence continued to spread across the Islamic world. (See Document 16.4, pp. 756–57, for a statement of the Wahhabi outlook.)

Together with the ongoing expansion of the religion, these movements of reform and renewal signaled the continuing cultural vitality of the "abode of Islam," even as the European presence on the world stage assumed larger dimensions. In the nineteenth and twentieth centuries, such movements persisted and became associated with resistance to the political, military, and cultural intrusion of the European West into the affairs of the Islamic world.

China: New Directions in an Old Tradition

■ **Comparison**

In what ways did Asian cultural changes in the early modern era parallel those of Europe, and in what ways were they different?

Neither China nor India experienced cultural or religious change as dramatic as that of the Reformation in Europe, nor did Confucian or Hindu cultures during the early modern era spread widely, as did Christianity and Islam. Nonetheless, neither of these traditions remained static. As in Christian Europe, challenges to established orthodoxies in China and India emerged as commercial and urban life, as well as political change, fostered new thinking.

China during the Ming and Qing dynasties continued to operate broadly within a Confucian framework, enriched now by the insights of Buddhism and Daoism to generate a system of thought called Neo-Confucianism. Chinese Ming dynasty rulers, in their aversion to the despised Mongols, embraced and actively supported this native Confucian tradition, whereas the foreign Manchu or Qing rulers did so in order to woo Chinese intellectuals to support the new dynasty. Within this context, a considerable amount of controversy, debate, and new thinking emerged during the early modern era.

During late Ming times, for example, the influential thinker Wang Yangming (1472–1529) argued that truth and moral knowledge were innate to the human person. (See Document 16.3, pp. 754–55, for a selection from the writings of Wang Yangming.) Thus anyone could achieve a virtuous life by introspection and contemplation, without the extended education, study of the classical texts, and constant striving for improvement that traditional Confucianism prescribed for an elite class of "gentlemen." Such ideas figured prominently among Confucian scholars of the sixteenth century, although critics later contended that such thinking promoted an excessive individualism. They also argued that Wang Yangming's ideas had undermined the Ming dynasty and contributed to China's conquest by the foreign Manchus. Some Chinese Buddhists as well sought to make their religion more accessible to ordinary people, by suggesting that laypeople at home could undertake practices similar to those performed by monks in monasteries. Withdrawal from the world was not necessary for enlightenment. This kind of moral or religious individualism bore some similarity to the thinking of Martin Luther, who argued that individuals could seek salvation by "faith alone," without the assistance of a priestly hierarchy.

Another new direction in Chinese elite culture took shape in a movement known as *kaozheng*, or "research based on evidence." Intended to "seek truth from facts," kaozheng was critical of the unfounded speculation of conventional Confucian philosophy and instead emphasized the importance of verification, precision, accuracy, and rigorous analysis in all fields of inquiry. During the late Ming years, this emphasis generated works dealing with agriculture, medicine, pharmacology, botany, craft techniques, and more. In the Qing era, kaozheng was associated with a recovery and critical analysis of ancient historical documents, which sometimes led to sharp criticism of Neo-Confucian orthodoxy. It was a genuinely scientific approach to knowledge, but it was applied more to the study of the past than to the natural world of astronomy, physics, or anatomy, as in the West.

While such matters occupied the intellectual elite of China, in the cities a lively popular culture emerged among the less well educated. For city-dwellers, plays, paintings, short stories, and especially novels provided diversion and entertainment that were a step up from what could be found in teahouses and wine shops. Numerous "how-to" painting manuals allowed a larger public to participate in this favorite Chinese art form. Even though Confucian scholars disdained popular fiction, a vigorous printing industry responded to the growing demand for exciting novels. The most famous was Cao Xueqin's mid-eighteenth-century novel *The Dream of the Red Chamber*, a huge book that contained 120 chapters and some 400 characters, most of them women. It explored the social life of an eighteenth-century elite family with connections to the Chinese court.

India: Bridging the Hindu/Muslim Divide

Guru Nanak
In this early-eighteenth-century manuscript painting, Guru Nanak, the founder of Sikhism, and his constant companion Mardana (with a musical instrument) encounter a robber (the man with a sword) along the road. According to the story accompanying the painting, that experience persuaded the robber to abandon his wicked ways and become a follower of the Sikh path.
(© British Library Board)

In a largely Hindu India, ruled by the Muslim Mughal Empire, several significant cultural departures took shape in the early modern era that brought Hindus and Muslims together in new forms of religious expression. One was the flourishing of a devotional form of Hinduism known as *bhakti.* Through songs, prayers, dances, poetry, and rituals, devotees sought to achieve union with one or another of India's many deities. Appealing especially to women, the bhakti movement provided an avenue for social criticism. Its practitioners often set aside caste distinctions and disregarded the detailed rituals of the Brahmin priests in favor of direct contact with the divine. This emphasis had much in common with the mystical Sufi form of Islam and helped blur the distinction between these two traditions in India (see Document 16.5, pp. 758–59).

Among the most beloved of bhakti poets was Mirabai (1498–1547), a high-caste woman from northern India who abandoned her upper-class family and conventional Hindu practice. Upon her husband's death, tradition asserts, she declined to burn herself on his funeral pyre (a practice known as *sati*). She further offended caste restrictions by taking as her guru (religious teacher) an old untouchable shoemaker. To visit him, she apparently tied her saris together and climbed down the castle walls at night. Then she would wash his aged feet and drink the water from these ablutions. Much of her poetry deals with her yearning for union with Krishna, a Hindu deity she regarded as her husband, lover, and lord.

> What I paid was my social body, my town body, my family body, and all my inherited jewels.
> Mirabai says: The Dark One [Krishna] is my husband now.[11]

Yet another major cultural change that blended Islam and Hinduism emerged with the growth of Sikhism as a new and distinctive religious tradition in the Punjab region of northern India. Its founder, Guru Nanak (1469–1539), had been involved in the bhakti movement but came to believe that "there is no Hindu; there is no Muslim; only God." His teachings and those of subsequent gurus also generally ignored caste distinctions and untouchability and ended the seclusion of women, while proclaiming the "brotherhood of all mankind" as well as the essential equality of men and women. Drawing converts from Punjabi peasants and merchants, both Muslim and Hindu, the Sikhs gradually became a separate religious community. They developed their own sacred book, known as the Guru Granth (teacher book); created a central place of worship and pilgrimage in the Golden Temple of Amritsar; and prescribed certain dress requirements for men, including keeping hair and beards uncut, wearing a turban, and carrying a short sword. During the seventeenth century, Sikhs encountered hostility from both the Mughal Empire and some of their Hindu neighbors. In response, Sikhism evolved from a peaceful religious movement, blending Hindu and Muslim elements, into a militant community whose military skills were highly valued by the British when they took over India in the late eighteenth century.

A New Way of Thinking: The Birth of Modern Science

While some Europeans were actively attempting to spread the Christian faith to distant corners of the world, others were nurturing an understanding of the cosmos very much at odds with traditional Christian teaching. These were the makers of Europe's Scientific Revolution, a vast intellectual and cultural transformation that took place between the mid-sixteenth and early eighteenth centuries. These men of science would no longer rely on the external authority of the Bible, the Church, the speculations of ancient philosophers, or the received wisdom of cultural tradition. For them, knowledge would be acquired through a combination of careful observations, controlled experiments, and the formulation of general laws, expressed in mathematical terms. Those who created this revolution—Copernicus from Poland, Galileo from Italy, Descartes from France, Newton from England, and many others—saw themselves as departing radically from older ways of thinking. "The old rubbish must be thrown away," wrote a seventeenth-century English scientist. "These are the days that must lay a new Foundation of a more magnificent Philosophy."[12]

The long-term significance of the Scientific Revolution can hardly be overestimated. Within early modern Europe, it fundamentally altered ideas about the place of humankind within the cosmos and sharply challenged both the teachings and the authority of the Church. Over the past several centuries, it has substantially eroded religious belief and practice in the West, particularly among the well educated. When applied to the affairs of human society, scientific ways of thinking challenged ancient social hierarchies and political systems and played a role in the revolutionary upheavals of the modern era. But science also was used to legitimize racial and gender inequalities, by defining people of color and women as inferior by nature. When married to the technological innovations of the Industrial Revolution, science fostered both the marvels of modern production and the horrors of modern means of destruction. By the twentieth century, science had become so widespread that it largely lost its association with European culture and became the chief symbol of global modernity. Like Buddhism, Christianity, and Islam, modern science became a universal worldview, open to all who could accept its premises and its techniques.

The Question of Origins: Why Europe?

■ Comparison
Why did the Scientific Revolution occur in Europe rather than in China or the Islamic world?

Why did the breakthrough of the Scientific Revolution occur first in Europe and during the early modern era? The realm of Islam, after all, had generated the most advanced science in the world during the centuries between 800 and 1400. Arab scholars could boast of remarkable achievements in mathematics, astronomy, optics, and medicine, and their libraries far exceeded those of Europe.[13] And what of China? Its elite culture of Confucianism was both sophisticated and secular, less burdened by religious dogma than in the Christian or Islamic worlds; its technological accomplishments and economic growth were unmatched anywhere in the several centuries after 1000. In neither civilization, however, did these achievements lead to the kind of intellectual innovation that occurred in Europe.

Europe's historical development as a reinvigorated and fragmented civilization (see Chapter 10) arguably gave rise to conditions uniquely favorable to the scientific enterprise. By the twelfth and thirteenth centuries, Europeans had evolved a legal system that guaranteed a measure of independence for a variety of institutions— the Church, towns and cities, guilds, professional associations, and universities. This legal revolution was based on the idea of a "corporation," a collective group of people that was treated as a unit, a legal person, with certain rights to regulate and control its own members.

Most important for the development of science in the West was the autonomy of its emerging universities. By 1215, the University of Paris was recognized as a "corporation of masters and scholars," which could admit and expel students, establish courses of instruction, and grant a "license to teach" to its faculty. Such universities—for example, in Paris, Bologna, Oxford, Cambridge, and Salamanca—became "neutral zones of intellectual autonomy" in which scholars could pursue their studies in relative freedom from the dictates of church or state authorities. Within them, the study of the natural order began to slowly separate itself from philosophy and theology and to gain a distinct identity. Their curricula featured "a basically scientific core of readings and lectures" that drew heavily on the writings of the Greek thinker Aristotle, which had only recently become available to Western Europeans. Most of the major figures in the Scientific Revolution had been trained in and were affiliated with these universities.

In the Islamic world, by contrast, science was patronized by a variety of local authorities, but it occurred largely outside the formal system of higher education. Within colleges known as madrassas, Quranic studies and religious law held the central place, whereas philosophy and natural science were viewed with great suspicion. To religious scholars, the Quran held all wisdom, and scientific thinking might well challenge it. An earlier openness to free inquiry and religious toleration was increasingly replaced by a disdain for scientific and philosophical inquiry, for it seemed to lead only to uncertainty and confusion. "May God protect us from useless knowledge" was a saying that reflected this outlook. Nor did Chinese authorities permit independent institutions of higher learning in which scholars could conduct their studies in relative freedom. Instead Chinese education focused on preparing for a rigidly defined set of civil service examinations and emphasized the humanistic and moral texts of classical Confucianism. "The pursuit of scientific subjects," one recent historian concluded, "was thereby relegated to the margins of Chinese society."[14]

Beyond its distinctive institutional development, Western Europe was in a position to draw extensively upon the knowledge of other cultures, especially that of the Islamic world. Arab medical texts, astronomical research, and translations of Greek classics played a major role in the birth of European natural philosophy (as science was then called) between 1000 and 1500. In constructing his proofs for a sun-centered solar system, Copernicus in the sixteenth century likely drew upon astronomical work and mathematical formulations undertaken 200 to 300 years earlier in the Islamic world, particularly at the famous Muslim observatory of Maragha in present-day Iran.

In the sixteenth through the eighteenth centuries, Europeans found themselves at the center of a massive new exchange of information as they became aware of lands, peoples, plants, animals, societies, and religions from around the world. This tidal wave of new knowledge, uniquely available to Europeans, clearly shook up older ways of thinking and opened the way to new conceptions of the world. The sixteenth-century Italian doctor, mathematician, and writer Girolamo Cardano (1501–1576) clearly expressed this sense of wonderment: "The most unusual [circumstance of my life] is that I was born in this century in which the whole world became known; whereas the ancients were familiar with but a little more than a third part of it." He worried, however, that amid this explosion of knowledge, "certainties will be exchanged for uncertainties."[15] It was precisely those uncertainties—skepticism about established views—that provided such a fertile cultural ground for the emergence of modern science.

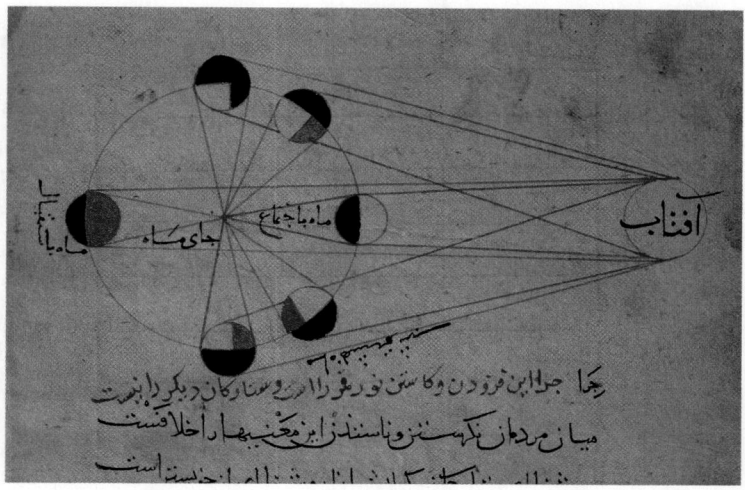

Muslim Astronomy and the Scientific Revolution This diagram of the eclipses of the moon by the eleventh-century Muslim mathematician and astronomer al-Biruni is a reminder of Muslim scientific achievements, some of which stimulated European scientific thinking. (Roland and Sabrina Michaud/Rapho/Eyedea)

Science as Cultural Revolution

Before the Scientific Revolution, educated Europeans held a view of the world that derived from Aristotle, perhaps the greatest of the ancient Greek philosophers, and from Ptolemy, a Greco-Egyptian mathematician and astronomer who lived in Alexandria during the second century C.E. To medieval European thinkers, the earth

■ **Change**
What was revolutionary about the Scientific Revolution?

Snapshot **Major Thinkers and Achievements of the Scientific Revolution**

Thinker/Scientist	Achievements
Nicolaus Copernicus (Polish; 1473–1543)	Posited that sun is at the center of solar system, earth rotates on its axis, and earth and planets revolve around the sun
Andreas Vesalius (Flemish; 1514–1564)	"Father of anatomy"; made detailed drawings of human body based on dissection
Francis Bacon (English; 1561–1626)	Emphasized observation and experimentation as the key to modern science
Galileo Galilei (Italian; 1564–1642)	Developed an improved telescope; discovered sunspots, mountains on the moon, and Jupiter's moons; performed experimental work on the velocity of falling objects
Johannes Kepler (German; 1571–1630)	Posited that planets follow elliptical, not circular, orbits; described laws of planetary motion
William Harvey (English; 1578–1657)	Described the circulation of the blood and the function of the heart
René Descartes (French; 1596–1650)	Emphasized the importance of mathematics and logical deduction in understanding the physical world; invented analytical geometry
Isaac Newton (English; 1642–1727)	Synthesized earlier findings around the concept of universal gravitation; invented calculus; formulated concept of inertia and laws of motion

was stationary and at the center of the universe, and around it revolved the sun, moon, and stars embedded in ten spheres of transparent crystal. This understanding coincided well with the religious outlook of the Catholic Church because the attention of the entire universe was centered on the earth and its human inhabitants, among whom God's plan for salvation unfolded. It was a universe of divine purpose, with angels guiding the hierarchically arranged heavenly bodies along their way while God watched over the whole from his realm beyond the spheres. The Scientific Revolution was revolutionary because it fundamentally challenged this understanding of the universe.

The initial breakthrough came from the Polish mathematician and astronomer Nicolaus Copernicus, whose famous book *On the Revolutions of the Heavenly Spheres* was published in the year of his death, 1543. Its essential argument was that "at the middle of all things lies the sun" and that the earth, like the other planets, revolved around it. Thus the earth was no longer unique or at the obvious center of God's attention.

Other European scientists built on Copernicus's central insight, and some even argued that other inhabited worlds and other kinds of humans existed. Less speculatively, in the early seventeenth century Johannes Kepler, a German mathematician, showed that the planets followed elliptical orbits, undermining the ancient belief that they moved in perfect circles. The Italian Galileo Galilei developed an improved telescope, with which he observed sunspots, or blemishes, moving across the face of the sun. This called into question the traditional notion that no change or imperfection marred the heavenly bodies. His discovery of the moons of Jupiter and many new stars suggested a cosmos far larger than the finite universe of traditional astronomy. Some thinkers began to discuss the notion of an unlimited universe in which humankind occupied a mere speck of dust in an unimaginable vastness. The French mathematician and philosopher Blaise Pascal (1623–1662) perhaps spoke for many when he wrote: "The eternal silence of infinite space frightens me."[16]

The culmination of the Scientific Revolution came in the work of Sir Isaac Newton, the Englishman who formulated the modern laws of motion and mechanics, which remained unchallenged until the twentieth century. At the core of Newton's thinking was the concept of universal gravitation. "All bodies whatsoever," Newton declared, "are endowed with a principle of mutual gravitation."[17] Here was the grand unifying idea of early modern science. The radical implication of this view was that the heavens and the earth, long regarded as separate and distinct spheres, were not so different after all, for the motion of a cannonball on earth or the falling of an apple from a tree obeyed the same natural laws that governed the orbiting planets.

By the time Newton died, a revolutionary new understanding of the physical universe had emerged among educated Europeans. That universe was no longer propelled by supernatural forces but functioned on its own according to scientific principles that could be described mathematically. In Kepler's view, "the machine of the universe is not similar to a divine animated being but similar to a clock."[18] Furthermore, it was a machine that regulated itself, requiring neither God nor angels to account for its normal operation. Knowledge of that universe could be obtained through human reason alone—by observation, deduction, and experimentation—without the aid of ancient authorities or divine revelation. The French philosopher René Descartes resolved "to seek no other knowledge than that which I might find within myself, or perhaps in the book of nature."[19]

Like the physical universe, the human body also lost some of its mystery. The careful dissections of cadavers and animals enabled doctors and scientists to describe the human body with much greater accuracy and to understand the circulation of the blood throughout the body. The heart was no longer the mysterious center of the body's heat and the seat of its passions; instead it was just another machine, a complex muscle that functioned as a pump.

Much of this thinking developed in the face of strenuous opposition from the Catholic Church, for both its teachings and its authority were under attack. The Italian philosopher Giordano Bruno, proclaiming an infinite universe and many worlds, was burned at the stake in 1600, and Galileo was compelled by the Church to publicly renounce his belief that the earth moved around an orbit and rotated on its axis.

But not all was conflict between the Church and an emerging science. None of the early scientists rejected Christianity. Galileo himself proclaimed the compatibility of science and faith when he wrote that "God is no less excellently revealed in Nature's actions than in the sacred statements of the Bible."[20] Newton was a serious biblical scholar and saw no necessary contradiction between his ideas and belief in God. "This most beautiful system of the sun, planets, and comets," he declared, "could only proceed from the counsel and dominion of an intelligent Being."[21] The Church gradually accommodated as well as resisted the new ideas, largely by compartmentalizing them. Science might prevail in its limited sphere of describing the physical universe, but religion was still the arbiter of truth about those ultimate questions concerning human salvation, righteous behavior, and the larger purposes of life.

Science and Enlightenment

■ Change
In what ways did the Enlightenment challenge older patterns of European thinking?

Initially limited to a small handful of scholars, the ideas of the Scientific Revolution spread to a wider European public during the eighteenth century. That process was aided by novel techniques of printing and book-making, by a popular press, and by a host of scientific societies. Moreover, the new approach to knowledge—rooted in human reason, skeptical of authority, expressed in natural laws—was now applied to human affairs, not just to the physical universe. The Scottish professor Adam Smith (1723–1790), for example, formulated laws that accounted for the operation of the economy and that, if followed, he believed, would generate inevitably favorable results for society. Growing numbers of people believed that the long-term outcome of scientific development would be "enlightenment," a term that has come to define the eighteenth century in European history. If human reason could discover the laws that governed the universe, surely it could uncover ways in which humankind might govern itself more effectively.

"What is Enlightenment?" asked the prominent German intellectual Immanuel Kant (1724–1804). "It is man's emergence from his self-imposed…inability to use one's own understanding without another's guidance….Dare to know! 'Have the courage to use your own understanding' is therefore the motto of the enlightenment."[22] Although they often disagreed sharply with one another, European Enlightenment thinkers shared this belief in the power of knowledge to transform human society. They also shared a satirical, critical style, a commitment to open-mindedness and inquiry, and in various degrees a hostility to established political and religious authority.

Many took aim at arbitrary governments, the "divine right of kings," and the aristocratic privileges of European society. The English philosopher John Locke (1632–1704) offered principles for constructing a constitutional government, a contract between rulers and ruled that was created by human ingenuity rather than divinely prescribed. Any number of writers, including many women, advocated education for women as a means of raising their status in society.

Much of Enlightenment thinking was directed against the superstition, ignorance, and corruption of established religion. In his *Treatise on Toleration*, the French writer Voltaire (1694–1778) reflected the outlook of the Scientific Revolution as he commented sarcastically on religious intolerance:

> This little globe, nothing more than a point, rolls in space like so many other globes; we are lost in its immensity. Man, some five feet tall, is surely a very small part of the universe. One of these imperceptible beings says to some of his neighbors in Arabia or Africa: "Listen to me, for the God of all these worlds has enlightened me; there are nine hundred million little ants like us on the earth, but only my anthill is beloved of God; He will hold all others in horror through all eternity; only mine will be blessed, the others will be eternally wretched."[23]

Voltaire's own faith, like many others among the "enlightened," was deism. Deists believed in a rather abstract and remote Deity, sometimes compared to a clockmaker, who had created the world, but not in a personal God who intervened in history or tampered with natural law. Others became *pantheists*, who believed that God and nature were identical. Here was a conception of religion shaped by the outlook of science. Sometimes called "natural religion," it was devoid of mystery, revelation, ritual, and spiritual practice, while proclaiming a God that could be "proven" by human rationality, logic, and the techniques of scientific inquiry. In this view, all else was superstition. Among the most radical of such thinkers were the several Dutchmen who wrote the *Treatise of Three Imposters*, which claimed that Moses, Jesus, and Muhammad were fraudulent imposters who based their teachings on "the ignorance of Peoples [and] resolved to keep them in it."[24]

Though solidly rooted in Europe, Enlightenment thought was influenced by the growing global awareness of its major thinkers. Voltaire, for example, idealized China as an empire governed by an elite of secular scholars selected for their talent, which stood in sharp contrast to continental Europe, where aristocratic birth and military prowess were far more important. The example of Confucianism—supposedly secular, moral, rational, and tolerant—encouraged Enlightenment thinkers to imagine a future for European civilization without the kind of supernatural religion that they found so offensive in the Christian West. (See Visual Source 15.1, p. 712, for European fascination with things Chinese.)

The central theme of the Enlightenment—and what made it potentially revolutionary—was the idea of progress. Human society was not fixed by tradition or divine command but could be changed, and improved, by human action guided by reason. No one expressed this soaring confidence in the unending perfectability of humankind more clearly than the French thinker the Marquis de Condorcet (1743–1794), whose views are excerpted in Document 16.2 on pages 752–54. Belief in

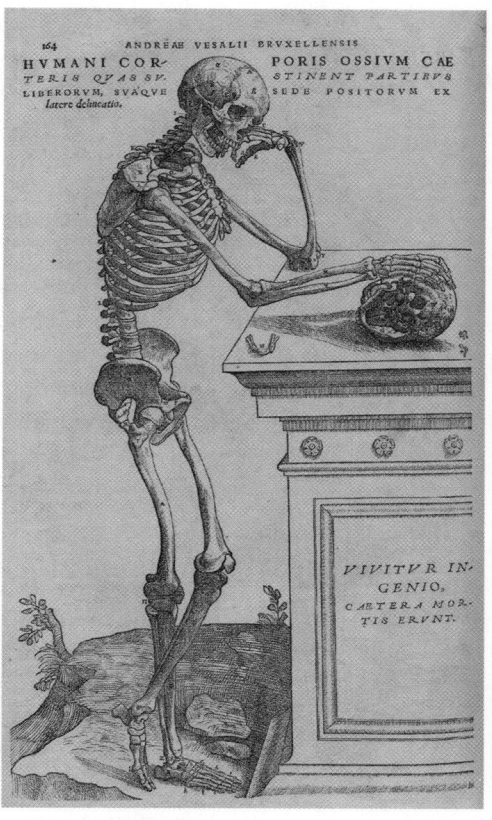

Uncovering the Human Skeleton
This drawing by the sixteenth-century Flemish anatomist Andreas Vesalius suggests a rational and philosophical approach to life, even as it presents the human skeleton with scientific precision. (Courtesy, National Library of Medicine)

progress was a sharp departure from much of premodern social thinking, and it inspired those who later made the American, French, Haitian, and Latin American revolutions. Born of the Scientific Revolution, that was the faith of the Enlightenment. For some, it was virtually a new religion.

The age of the Enlightenment, however, also witnessed a reaction against too much reliance on human reason. Jean-Jacques Rousseau (1712–1778) minimized the importance of book learning for the education of children and prescribed instead an immersion in nature, which taught self-reliance and generosity rather than the greed and envy fostered by "civilization." The Romantic movement in art and literature appealed to emotion, intuition, passion, and imagination rather than cold reason and scientific learning. Religious awakenings—complete with fiery sermons, public repentance, and intense personal experience of sin and redemption—shook Protestant Europe and North America. Science and the Enlightenment surely challenged religion, and for some they eroded religious belief and practice. Just as surely, though, religion persisted, adapted, and revived for many others.

Looking Ahead: Science in the Nineteenth Century

■ **Change**
How did nineteenth-century developments in the sciences challenge the faith of the Enlightenment?

The perspectives of the Enlightenment were challenged not only by romanticism and religious "enthusiasm" but also by the continued development of science itself. This remarkable phenomenon justifies a brief look ahead at several scientific developments in the nineteenth century.

Modern science was a cumulative and self-critical enterprise, which in the nineteenth century and after was applied to new domains of human inquiry in ways that undermined some of the assumptions of the Enlightenment. In the realm of biology, for example, Charles Darwin (1809–1882) laid out a complex argument that all of life was in flux, that an endless and competitive struggle for survival over millions of years constantly generated new species of plants and animals, while casting others into extinction. Human beings were not excluded from this vast process, for they too were the work of evolution operating through natural selection. Darwin's famous books *The Origin of Species* (1859) and *The Descent of Man* (1871) were as shattering to traditional religious views as Copernicus's ideas about a sun-centered universe had been several centuries earlier.

At the same time, Karl Marx (1818–1883) articulated a view of human history that likewise emphasized change and struggle. Conflicting social classes—slave owners and slaves, nobles and peasants, capitalists and workers—successively drove the process of historical transformation. Although he was describing the evolution of human civilization, Marx saw himself as a scientist. He based his theories on extensive historical research; like Newton and Darwin, he sought to formulate general laws that would explain events in a rational way. Nor did he believe in heavenly intervention, chance, or the divinely endowed powers of kings. The coming of socialism, in this view, was not simply a good idea; it was inscribed in the laws of historical development (see Document 18.1, pp. 856–59).

Like the intellectuals of the Enlightenment, Darwin and Marx believed strongly in progress, but in their thinking, conflict and struggle rather than reason and education were the motors of progress. The Enlightenment image of the thoughtful, rational, and independent individual was fading. Individuals—plant, animal, and human alike—were now viewed as enmeshed in vast systems of biological, economic, and social conflict.

The work of the Viennese doctor Sigmund Freud (1856–1939) applied scientific techniques to the operation of the human mind and emotions and in doing so cast further doubt on Enlightenment conceptions of human rationality. At the core of each person, Freud argued, lay primal impulses toward sexuality and aggression, which were only barely held in check by the thin veneer of social conscience derived from civilization. Our neuroses arose from the ceaseless struggle between our irrational drives and the claims of conscience. This too was a far cry from the Enlightenment conception of the human condition.

European Science beyond the West

In the long run, the achievements of the Scientific Revolution spread globally, becoming the most widely sought-after product of European culture and far more desired than Christianity, democracy, socialism, or Western literature. In the early modern era, however, the level of interest in European scientific thinking within major Asian societies was both modest and selective.

■ **Connection**
In what ways was European science received in the major civilizations of Asia in the early modern era?

In China, for example, Qing dynasty emperors and scholars were most interested in European astronomy and mathematics, derived largely from Jesuit missionaries, because those disciplines proved useful in predicting eclipses, reforming the calendar, and making accurate maps of the empire. European medicine, however, held little interest for Chinese physicians before the nineteenth century. But the reputation of the Jesuits suffered when it became apparent in the 1760s that for two centuries the missionaries had withheld information about Copernican views of a sun-centered solar system because those ideas had been condemned by the Church. Nonetheless, European science had a substantial impact on a number of Chinese scholars as it interacted with the data-based kaozheng movement, described by one participant as "an ant-like accumulation of facts."[25] European mathematics was of particular interest to kaozheng researchers who were exploring the history of Chinese mathematics. To convince their skeptical colleagues that the barbarian Europeans had something to offer in this field, some Chinese scholars argued that European mathematics had in fact grown out of much earlier Chinese ideas and could therefore be adopted with comfort.[26] In such ways, early modern Chinese thinkers selectively assimilated Western science very much on their own terms.[27]

Although Japanese authorities largely closed their country off from the West in the early seventeenth century (see Chapter 15), one window remained open. Alone among Europeans, the Dutch were permitted to trade in Japan at a single location near Nagasaki, but not until 1720 did the Japanese lift the ban on importing Western books. Then a number of European texts in medicine, astronomy, geography, mathematics, and other disciplines were translated and studied by a small group of Japanese scholars. They were especially impressed with Western anatomical studies, for in Japan dissection was work fit only for outcasts. Returning from an autopsy conducted by Dutch physicians, several Japanese observers reflected on their experience: "We remarked to each other how amazing the autopsy had been, and how inexcusable it had been for us to be ignorant of the anatomical structure of the human body."[28] Nonetheless, this small center of "Dutch learning," as it was called, remained isolated amid a pervasive Confucian-based culture. Not until the mid-nineteenth century, when Japan was forcibly opened to Western penetration, would European science assume a prominent place in Japanese culture.

Like China and Japan, the Ottoman Empire in the sixteenth and seventeenth centuries was an independent, powerful, successful society whose intellectual elites saw no need for a wholesale embrace of things European. Ottoman scholars were conscious of the rich tradition of Muslim astronomy and chose not to translate the works of major European scientists such as Copernicus, Kepler, or Newton, although they were broadly aware of European scientific achievements by 1650. Insofar as they were interested in these developments, it was for their practical usefulness in making maps and calendars rather than for their larger philosophical implications. In any event, the notion of a sun-centered solar system did not cause the kind of upset that it did in Europe.[29]

More broadly, theoretical science of any kind—Muslim or European—faced an uphill struggle in the face of a conservative Islamic educational system. In 1580, for example, a highly sophisticated astronomical observatory was dismantled under pressure from conservative religious scholars and teachers, who interpreted an outbreak of the plague as God's disapproval with those who sought to understand his secrets. As in Japan, the systematic embrace of Western science would have to await the nineteenth century, when the Ottoman Empire was under far more intense European pressure and reform seemed more necessary.

⊨ Reflections: Cultural Borrowing and Its Hazards

Ideas are important in human history. They shape the mental or cultural worlds that people everywhere inhabit, and they often influence behavior as well. Many of the ideas developed or introduced during the early modern era have had enormous and continuing significance in the centuries that followed. The Western Hemisphere was solidly incorporated into Christendom. A Wahhabi version of Islam remains the official faith of Saudi Arabia into the twenty-first century and has influenced many contemporary Islamic revival movements, including al-Qaeda. Modern science and the associated notions of progress have become for many people something approaching a new religion.

Accompanying the development of these ideas has been a great deal of cultural borrowing. Filipinos, Siberians, and many Native American peoples borrowed elements of Christianity from Europeans. Numerous Asian and African peoples borrowed Islam from the Arabs. Northern Indian Sikhs drew upon both Hindu and Muslim teachings. Europeans borrowed scientific ideas from the Islamic world.

In virtually every case, though, that borrowing was selective rather than wholesale, even when it took place under conditions of foreign domination or colonial rule. Many peoples who appropriated Christianity or Islam certainly did not accept the rigid exclusivity and ardent monotheism of those faiths. Elite Chinese were far more interested in European astronomy and mathematics than in Western medicine, while Japanese scholars became fascinated with the anatomical work of the Dutch. Neither, however, adopted Christianity in a widespread manner.

Borrowing was frequently the occasion for serious conflict. Some objected to much borrowing at all, particularly when it occurred under conditions of foreign domination or foreign threat. Thus members of the Taki Onqoy movement in Peru sought to wipe out Spanish influence and control, while Chinese and Japanese authorities clamped down firmly on European missionaries, even as they maintained some interest in European technological and scientific skills. Another kind of conflict derived from the efforts to control the terms of cultural borrowing. For example, European missionaries and Muslim reformers alike sought to root out "idolatry" among native converts.

To ease the tensions of cultural borrowing, efforts to "domesticate" foreign ideas and practices proliferated. Thus the Jesuits in China tried to point out similarities between Christianity and Confucianism, and Native American converts identified Christian saints with their own gods and spirits. By the late seventeenth century, some local churches in central Mexico had come to associate Catholicism less with the Spanish than with ancient pre-Aztec communities and beliefs that were now, supposedly, restored to their rightful position.

The pace of global cultural borrowing and its associated tensions stepped up even more as Europe's modern transformation unfolded in the nineteenth century and as its imperial reach extended and deepened around the world.

Second Thoughts

What's the Significance?

Protestant Reformation
Catholic Counter-Reformation
Taki Onqoy
Jesuits in China
Wahhabi Islam

Wang Yangmin
kaozheng
Mirabai
Sikhism
Copernicus

Newton
European Enlightenment
Voltaire
Condorcet and the idea of
  progress

To assess your mastery of the material in this chapter, visit the **Student Center** at bedfordstmartins.com/strayer.

Big Picture Questions

1. Why did Christianity take hold in some places more than in others?
2. In what ways was the missionary message of Christianity shaped by the cultures of Asian and American peoples?
3. Compare the processes by which Christianity and Islam became world religions.
4. In what ways did the spread of Christianity, Islam, and modern science give rise to culturally based conflicts?
5. Based on Chapters 13 through 16, how does the history of Islam in the early modern era challenge a Eurocentric understanding of those centuries?

Next Steps: For Further Study

For Web sites and additional documents related to this chapter, see **Make History** at bedfordstmartins.com/strayer.

Natana J. Delong-Bas, *Wahhabi Islam: From Revival and Reform to Global Jihad* (2004). A careful study of the origins of Wahhabi Islam and its subsequent development.

Patricia B. Ebrey et al., *East Asia: A Cultural, Social, and Political History* (2005). A broad survey by major scholars in the field.

Geoffrey C. Gunn, *First Globalization: The Eurasian Exchange, 1500–1800* (2003). Explores the two-way exchange of ideas between Europe and Asia in the early modern era.

Toby E. Huff, *The Rise of Early Modern Science* (2003). A fascinating and controversial explanation as to why modern science arose in the West rather than in China or the Islamic world.

Steven Shapin, *The Scientific Revolution* (1996). A brief, accessible, and scholarly account of the emergence of modern science.

Paul R. Spickard and Kevin M. Cragg, *A Global History of Christians* (1994). A broad-brush account of the global spread of Christianity and its various expressions in different cultures.

Internet Modern History Sourcebook, "The Scientific Revolution," http://www.fordham.edu/halsall/mod/modsbook09.html. A collection of primary-source documents dealing with the breakthrough to modern science in Europe.

Documents

Considering the Evidence:
Cultural Change in the Early Modern World

Cultural and religious traditions change over time in various ways and for various reasons. Some of those changes occur as a result of internal tensions or criticisms within those traditions or in response to social and economic transformations in the larger society. The Protestant Reformation, for example, grew out of deep disaffection with prevailing teachings and practices of the Roman Catholic Church and drew support from a growing middle class and a disaffected peasantry. At other times, cultural change occurred by incorporating or reacting against new ideas drawn from contact with outsiders. Chinese Confucianism took on a distinctive tone and flavor as it drew upon the insights of Buddhism, and a new South Asian religion called Sikhism sought to combine elements of Hindu and Muslim belief. Whatever the stimulus for cultural change, departures from accepted ways of thinking have sometimes been represented as a return to a purer and more authentic past, even if that past is largely imaginary. In other cases, however, change was presented as a necessary break from an outmoded past even if many elements from earlier times were retained.

All across the Eurasian world of the early modern era—in Western Europe, China, India, and the Middle East—important cultural changes were brewing. In each of the documents that follow, we are listening in on just one side of extended debates or controversies, focusing on those who sought some change from established ways of thinking. To what extent were these changes moving in the same direction? How did they differ? What were the sources of these changes and how were they expressed? How might those who opposed these changes respond?

Document 16.1

Luther's Protest

Europe was home to perhaps the most substantial cultural transformations of the early modern centuries. There the Protestant Reformation sharply challenged both the doctrines and the authority of the Roman Catholic Church, ending the religious monopoly that the Church had exercised in Western Europe for many centuries and introducing a bitter and often violent divide into the religious and political life of the region. Then the practitioners of the Scientific Revolution, and the Enlightenment that followed from it, introduced a revolutionary new understanding of both the physical world and human society and constructed novel means of obtaining knowledge.

The Protestant Reformation and the Scientific Revolution/Enlightenment shared a common hostility to established authority, and they both represented a clear departure from previous patterns of thought and behavior. But they differed sharply in how they represented the changes they sought. Reformation leaders looked to the past, seeking to restore or renew what they believed was an earlier and more genuine version of Christianity. Leaders of the Scientific Revolution and the Enlightenment, on the other hand, foresaw and embraced an altogether new world in the making. They were the "moderns" combating the "ancients."

The most prominent figure in the Protestant Reformation was Martin Luther (1483–1546), a German monk, priest, and theologian (see pp. 723–27). A prolific writer, Luther composed theological treatises, translations of the Bible into German, and many hymns. The excerpts in Document 16.1, however, come from conversations with his students, friends, and colleagues, which they carefully recorded. After Luther's death, these recollections of the reformer's thoughts were collected and published under the title *Table Talk*.

- Based on this document, what issues drove the Protestant Reformation?

- What theological questions are addressed in these excerpts? How does Luther understand the concepts of law, good works, grace, and faith?

- In what ways is Luther critical of the papacy, monks, and the monastic orders of the Catholic Church?

- Why might Catholic authorities challenge Luther's singular emphasis on the Bible? In what other ways might thoughtful Catholics respond to Luther's charges? (See pp. 725–27 on the Catholic Counter-Reformation.)

MARTIN LUTHER
Table Talk
Early Sixteenth Century

On the Bible

Let us not lose the Bible, but with diligence, in fear and invocation of God, read and preach it.

No greater mischief can happen to a Christian people, than to have God's Word taken from them, or falsified, so that they no longer have it pure and clear. The ungodly papists prefer the authority of the church far above God's Word; a blasphemy abominable and not to be endured; wherewith, void of all shame and piety, they spit in God's face.

Pope, cardinals, bishops, not a soul of them has read the Bible; 'tis a book unknown to them. They

Source: William Hazlitt, ed. and trans., *The Table Talk of Martin Luther* (London: H. G. Bohn, 1857).

are a pack of guzzling, stuffing wretches, rich, wallowing in wealth and laziness, resting secure in their power, and never, for a moment, thinking of accomplishing God's will.

On Salvation

He that goes from the gospel to the law, thinking to be saved by good works, falls as uneasily as he who falls from the true service of God to idolatry; for, without Christ, all is idolatry and fictitious imaginings of God, whether of the Turkish Koran, of the pope's decrees, or Moses' law.

The Gospel preaches nothing of the merit of works; he that says the Gospel requires works for salvation, I say, flat and plain, is a liar. Nothing that is properly good proceeds out of the works of the law, unless grace be present; for what we are forced to do, goes not from the heart, nor is acceptable.

But a true Christian says: I am justified and saved only by faith in Christ, without any works or merits of my own....

Prayer in popedom is mere tongue-threshing...; not prayer but a work of obedience.

On the Pope and the Church Hierarchy

The great prelates, the puffed-up saints, the rich usurers, the ox drovers that seek unconscionable gain, etc., these are not God's servants....

Our dealing and proceeding against the pope is altogether excommunication, which is simply the public declaration that a person is disobedient to Christ's Word. Now we affirm in public, that the pope and his retinue believe not; therefore we conclude that he shall not be saved, but be damned....

Antichrist is the pope and the Turk together; a beast full of life must have a body and soul; the spirit or soul of antichrist is the pope, his flesh or body the Turk.... Kings and princes coin money only out of metals, but the pope coins money out of every thing—indulgences, ceremonies, dispensations, pardons; 'tis all fish comes to his net....

The pope and his crew are mere worshippers of idols, and servants of the devil.... He pretends great holiness, under color of the outward service of God, for he has instituted orders with hoods, with shavings, fasting, eating of fish, saying mass, and such like.... [F]or his doctrine he gets money and wealth, honor and power, and is so great a monarch, that he can bring emperors under his girdle.

The chief cause that I fell out with the pope was this: the pope boasted that he was the head of the church, and condemned all that would not be under his power and authority....

If the pope were the head of the Christian church, then the church were a monster with two heads, seeing that St. Paul says that Christ is her head. The pope may well be, and is, the head of the false church.

The fasting of the friars is more easy to them than our eating to us. For one day of fasting there are three of feasting. Every friar for his supper has two quarts of beer, a quart of wine, and spice-cakes, or bread prepared with spice and salt, the better to relish their drink. Thus go on these poor fasting brethren; getting so pale and wan, they are like the fiery angels.

The state of celibacy is great hypocrisy and wickedness.... Christ with one sentence confutes all their arguments: God created them male and female.... Now eating, drinking, marrying, etc., are of God's making, therefore they are good.

[T]hey [the Catholic Church] must make full restitution of that which, with their lies and deceit, they have got and stolen from emperors, kings, princes, nobility, and other people.

A Christian's worshipping is not the external, hypocritical mask that our spiritual friars wear, when they chastise their bodies, torment and make themselves faint, with ostentatious fasting, watching, singing, wearing hair shirts, scourging themselves, etc. Such worshipping God desires not.

Document 16.2

Progress and Enlightenment

If the Protestant Reformation represented a major change within the framework of the Christian faith, the Scientific Revolution and the European Enlightenment (see pp. 737–44) came to be seen by many as a challenge to all Christian understandings of the world. After all, those two movements celebrated the powers of human reason to unlock the mysteries of the universe and proclaimed the possibility of a new human society shaped by human hands. Among the most prominent spokesmen for the Enlightenment was the Marquis de Condorcet (1743–1794), a French mathematician, philosopher, and active participant in the French Revolution. In his *Sketch of the Progress of the Human Mind*, Condorcet described ten stages of human development. Document 16.2 contains excerpts from "The Ninth Epoch," whose title refers to the era in which Cordorcet was living, and the "The Tenth Epoch," referring to the age to come. Condorcet's optimism about that future was not borne out in his own life, for he fell afoul of the radicalism of the French Revolution and died in prison in 1794.

■ What is Condorcet's view of the relationship between the Scientific Revolution and the Enlightenment?

■ How, precisely, does Condorcet imagine the future of humankind?

■ How might Martin Luther respond to Condorcet's vision of the future? How do their understandings of human potential differ?

■ To what extent have Condorcet's predictions come to fruition in the two centuries since his death?

Marquis de Condorcet
Sketch of the Progress of the Human Mind
1793–1794

The Ninth Epoch: From Descartes to the Formation of the French Republic

[T]he progress of philosophy...destroyed within the general mass of people the prejudices that have af-

Source: Marquis de Condorcet, *Sketch of the Progress of the Human Mind* (Paris: Firmin Didot Frères, 1847), Epoch IX and Epoch X.

flicted and corrupted the human race for so long a time.

Humanity was finally permitted to boldly proclaim the long ignored right to submit every opinion to reason, that is to utilize the only instrument given to us for grasping and recognizing the truth. Each human learned with a sort of pride that nature had never destined him to believe the word of others. The superstitions of antiquity and the abasement of reason before the madness of supernatural religion disappeared from society just as they had disappeared from philosophy....

If we were to limit ourselves to showing the benefits derived from the immediate applications of the sciences, or in their applications to man-made devices for the well-being of individuals and the prosperity of nations, we would be making known only a slim part of their benefits. The most important, perhaps, is having destroyed prejudices, and reestablished human intelligence, which until then had been forced to bend down to false instructions instilled in it by absurd beliefs passed on to the children of each generation by the terrors of superstition and the fear of tyranny....

The advances of scientific knowledge are all the more deadly to these errors because they destroy them without appearing to attack them, while lavishing on those who stubbornly defend them the degrading taunt of ignorance....

Finally this progress of scientific knowledge... results in a belief that not birth, professional status, or social standing gives anyone the right to judge something he does not understand. This unstoppable progress cannot be observed without having enlightened men search unceasingly for ways to make the other branches of learning follow the same path....

The Tenth Epoch: The Future Progress of the Human Mind

Our hopes for the future of the human species may be reduced to three important points: the destruction of inequality among nations; the progress of equality within nations themselves; and finally, the real improvement of humanity. Should not all the nations of the world approach one day the state of civilization reached by the most enlightened peoples such as the French and the Anglo-Americans? Will not the slavery of nations subjected to kings, the barbarity of African tribes, and the ignorance of savages gradually disappear?...

If we cast an eye at the existing state of the globe, we will see right away that in Europe the principles of the French constitution are already those of all enlightened men. We will see that they are too widely disseminated and too openly professed for the efforts

of tyrants and priests to prevent them from penetrating into the hovels of their slaves....

Can it be doubted that either wisdom or the senseless feuds of the European nations themselves, working with the slow but certain effects of progress in their colonies, will not soon produce the independence of the new world; and that then the European population, spreading rapidly across that immense land, must either civilize or make disappear the savage peoples that now inhabit these vast continents?...

Thus the day will come when the sun will shine only on free men born knowing no other master but their reason; where tyrants and their slaves, priests and their ignorant, hypocritical writings will exist only in the history books and theaters; where we will only be occupied with mourning their victims and their dupes; when we will maintain an active vigilance by remembering their horrors; when we will learn to recognize and stifle by the force of reason the first seeds of superstition and tyranny, if ever they dare to appear!...

If we consider the human creations based on scientific theories, we shall see that their progress can have no limits;... that new tools, machines, and looms will add every day to the capabilities and skill of humans; they will improve and perfect the precision of their products while decreasing the amount of time and labor needed to produce them....

A smaller piece of land will be able to produce commodities of greater usefulness and value than before; greater benefits will be obtained with less waste; the production of the same industrial product will result in less destruction of raw materials and greater durability.... [E]ach individual will work less but more productively and will be able to better satisfy his needs....

Among the advances of the human mind we should reckon as most important for the general welfare is the complete destruction of those prejudices that have established an inequality of rights between the sexes, and inequality damaging even to the party it favors....

The most enlightened people...will slowly come to perceive war as the deadliest plague and the most monstrous of crimes....They will understand that they cannot become conquerors without losing their liberty; that perpetual alliances are the only way to preserve independence; and that they should seek their security, not power....

We may conclude then that the perfectibility of humanity is indefinite.

Finally, can we not also extend the same hopes to the intellectual and moral faculties?... Is it not also probable that education, while perfecting these qualities, will also influence, modify, and improve that bodily nature itself?...

Document 16.3

Debating Confucianism

Cultural change in early modern China was not as dramatic as in Europe. But Confucianism, which had long provided the framework for elite thinking and the basis for China's famous civil service examinations, was surely not a monolithic tradition. The version of Confucianism that prevailed in Ming dynasty China (1368–1644) emphasized strenuous educational efforts ("investigation of things") leading to moral self-improvement and appropriate action. In practice, this often amounted to the rote memorization of texts in order to pass the examinations, which in turn led to official positions and great social prestige for the elite few. Wang Yangming (1472–1529), a prominent Chinese philosopher, state official, and general, contested this kind of Confucianism. His was a more individualistic, inner-directed Confucianism, allowing ordinary people, not just the well-educated few, to achieve sagehood. Although he explicitly rejected both Buddhism and Daoism, he drew on the interior emphasis of both traditions. It is not surprising, therefore, that Wang Yangming's ideas stirred considerable controversy in elite circles (see p. 735). The selections that follow are presented as conversations between Wang Yangming and his followers.

- In what ways were Wang Yangming's ideas at odds with the prevailing Confucianism of his time?

- Why might his ideas have been subject to severe criticism by more established Confucian thinkers?

- What similarities might you find in the ideas of Martin Luther and Wang Yangming? What differences are apparent? Consider their views of human nature, the ability of individuals to achieve moral improvement, and their relationship to established authority.

WANG YANGMING

Conversations

Early Sixteenth Century

In 1520 I went to Qianzhou and saw Wang Yangming again. I told him that recently, although I was making a little headway in my studies, I was finding it hard to feel secure or happy. He responded, "The problem is that you go to your mind to seek Heavenly principles, a practice called obscuration by principle. There is a trick for what you want to do."

"Please tell me what it is."

"It is simply the extension of knowledge."

"How does one do it?" I asked.

"Take your intuitive moral knowledge as your personal standard. If you think about something, you will know it is right if it is right, wrong if it is wrong. You cannot conceal anything from your intuitive moral knowledge. Just don't try to deceive it. Honestly follow it in whatever you do. That way you will keep what is good and get rid of what is bad. . . .

Once when Wang Yuzhong, Zou Shouyi, and I were attending him, Wang Yangming said, "Each person has a sage inside of him or her, which he or she suppresses because of lack of confidence." He then looked at Wang Yuzhong and said, "You have been a sage from the start." Yuzhong rose and politely demurred. The teacher added, "This is something everyone has. Why should you demur?"

"I do not deserve your praise."

"Everyone has this, so naturally you do. Why be so polite? Politeness is not appropriate here." Yuzhong then accepted with a smile.

Wang Yangming carried the discussion further. "Intuitive moral knowledge exists in people. No mat-

ter what they do, they cannot destroy it. Even robbers know that they should not rob. If you call them robbers they are embarrassed."

Wang Yuzhong said, "Material desires can obscure the intuitive moral knowledge in a person, but not make it disappear. It is like the clouds obscuring the sun. The sun is not lost."

Wang Yangming said, "You are so smart. No one else sees it."

A lower-ranking official, who had for a long time been listening to discussions of our teacher's doctrines, once said, "His doctrines are excellent, but because I am so busy keeping records and taking care of legal cases, I cannot study them further."

When Wang Yangming heard of his remark, he said to him, "When did I say you should abandon your records and legal cases to take up study? Since you have official duties, you should use them as a basis for your study. That is the true investigation of things. For instance, if you are questioning a plaintiff, you should not get angry because his answers are impolite or become pleased because he uses ingratiating language. You should not hate him for his efforts to go around you and purposely punish him. Nor should you bend your principles and forgive someone because he implores you. You should not dispose of a case quickly because your own affairs are too pressing, nor let other people's criticisms or praise or plots influence your decision. These ways of responding are all selfish. All you need to know is in yourself. Carefully check for any sign that you are biased, for that would confuse your recognition of right and wrong. This is how to investigate things and extend knowledge. Real learning is to be found in every aspect of record keeping and legal cases. What is empty is study that is detached from things."

Source: Patricia Buckley Ebrey, ed. and trans., *Chinese Civilization: A Sourcebook* (New York: Free Press, 1993), 257–58.

Document 16.4

The Wahhabi Perspective on Islam

Within the Islamic world, the major cultural movements of the early modern era were those of religious renewal. Such movements sought to eliminate the "deviations" that had crept into Islamic practice over the centuries and to return to a purer version of the faith that presumably had prevailed during the early years of the religion in the seventh century. The most influential of these movements was associated with Muhammad ibn Abd al-Wahhab (1703–1791), whose revivalist movement spread widely in Arabia during the second half of the eighteenth century (see pp. 733–34). Document 16.3, written by the grandson of al-Wahhab shortly after the capture of Mecca in 1803, provides a window into the outlook of Wahhabi Islam.

- What specific objections did the Wahhabis have to the prevailing practice of Islam in eighteenth-century Arabia?

- How did Wahhabis put their ideas into practice once they had seized control of Mecca?

- What similarities do you see between the outlook of the Wahhabis and that of Martin Luther? What differences can you identify?

- How might you compare eighteenth-century Wahhabi Islam with movements of Islamic renewal, or "fundamentalism," in the late twentieth and early twenty-first centuries? (See Chapter 24.)

ABDULLAH WAHHAB
History and Doctrines of the Wahhabis
1803

Now I was engaged in the holy war, carried on by those who truly believe in the Unity of God, when God, praised be He, graciously permitted us to enter Mecca.... Now, though we were more numerous, better armed and disciplined than the people of Mecca, yet we did not cut down their trees, neither did we hunt, nor shed any blood except the blood of victims, and of those four-footed beasts which the Lord has made lawful by his commands.

When our pilgrimage was over... our leader, whom the Lord saves, explained to the divines what we required of the people,... namely, a pure belief in the Unity of God Almighty. He pointed out to them that there was no dispute between us and them except on two points, and that one of these was a sincere belief in the Unity of God, and a knowledge of the different kinds of prayer....

They then acknowledged our belief, and there was not one among them who doubted.... And they swore a binding oath, although we had not asked them, that their hearts had been opened and their doubts removed, and that they were convinced who-

Source: J. O'Kinealy, "Translation of an Arabic Pamphlet on the History and Doctrines of the Wahhabis," *Journal of the Asiatic Society of Bengal* 43 (1874): 68–82.

ever said, "Oh prophet of God!" or "Oh Ibn 'Abbes!" or "Oh 'Abdul Qadir!" or called on any other created being, thus entreating him to turn away evil or grant what is good (where the power belongs to God alone), such as recovery from sickness, or victory over enemies, or protection from temptation, etc.; he is a *Mushrik*, guilty of the most heinous form of shirk,° his blood shall be shed and property confiscated.... Again, the tombs which had been erected over the remains of the pious, had become in these times as it were idols where the people went to pray for what they required; they humbled themselves before them, and called upon those lying in them, in their distress, just as did those who were in darkness before the coming of Muhammad....

We razed all the large tombs in the city which the people generally worshipped and believed in, and by which they hoped to obtain benefits or ward off evil, so that there did not remain an idol to be adored in that pure city, for which God be praised. Then the taxes and customs we abolished, all the different kinds of instruments for using tobacco we destroyed, and tobacco itself we proclaimed forbidden. Next we burned the dwellings of those selling *hashish*, and living in open wickedness, and issued a proclamation, directing the people to constantly exercise themselves in prayer. They were not to pray in separate groups..., but all were directed to arrange themselves at each time of prayer behind any Imam who is a follower of any of the four Imams.°... For in this way the Lord would be worshiped by as it were one voice, the faithful of all sects would become friendly disposed towards each other, and all dissensions would cease....

[W]e do not reject anyone who follows any of the four Imams, as do the Shias, the Zaidiyyahs, and the Imamiyyahs, &c. Nor do we admit them in any way to act openly according to their vicious creeds; on the contrary, we compelled them to follow one of the four Imams. We do not claim to exercise our reason in all matters of religion, and of our faith, save that we follow our judgment where a point is clearly demonstrated to us in either the Quran or the Sunnah.°... We do not command the destruction of any writings except such as tend to cast people into infidelity to injure their faith, such as those on Logic, which have been prohibited by all Divines. But we are not very exacting with regard to books or documents of this nature, if they appear to assist our opponents, we destroy them.... We do not consider it proper to make Arabs prisoners of war, nor have we done so, neither do we fight with other nations. Finally, we do not consider it lawful to kill women or children....

We consider pilgrimage is supported by legal custom, but it should not be undertaken except to a mosque, and for the purpose of praying in it. Therefore, whoever performs pilgrimage for this purpose, is not wrong, and doubtless those who spend the precious moments of their existence in invoking the Prophet, shall... obtain happiness in this world and the next.... We do not deny miraculous powers to the saints, but on the contrary allow them.... But whether alive or dead, they must not be made the object of any form of worship....

We prohibit those forms of Bidah° that affect religion or pious works. Thus drinking coffee, reciting poetry, praising kings, do not affect religion or pious works and are not prohibited....

All games are lawful. Our prophet allowed play in his mosque. So it is lawful to chide and punish persons in various ways; to train them in the use of different weapons; or to use anything which tends to encourage warriors in battle, such as a war-drum. But it must not be accompanied with musical instruments. These are forbidden, and indeed the difference between them and a war drum is clear.

°**shirk:** unbelief.

°**the four Imams:** founders of the four major schools of Islamic law.

°**Sunnah:** traditions of Muhammad's actions.

°**Bidah:** improper or erroneous behavior.

Document 16.5

The Poetry of Kabir

Early modern India was a place of much religious creativity and the interaction of various traditions. The majority of India's people practiced one or another of the many forms of Hinduism, while its Mughal rulers and perhaps 20 percent of the population were Muslims. And a new religion—Sikhism—took shape in the sixteenth century as well (see pp. 736–37). Certainly there was tension and sometimes conflict among these religious communities, but not all was hostility across religious boundaries. In the writings of Kabir (1440–1518), perhaps India's most beloved poet, the sectarian differences among these religions dissolved into a mystical and transcendent love of the divine in all of its many forms. Born into a family of Muslim weavers, Kabir as a young man became a student of a famous Hindu ascetic, Ramananda. Kabir's own poetry was and remains revered among Hindus, Muslims, and Sikhs alike. Document 16.5 contains selections from his poetry, translated by the famous Indian writer Rabindranath Tagore in the early twentieth century.

■ In what ways was Kabir critical of conventional religious practice—both Muslim and Hindu?

■ How would you describe Kabir's religious vision?

■ How might more orthodox Hindus and Muslims respond to Kabir? How would the Wahhabis in particular take issue with Kabir's religious outlook?

Kabîr

Poetry

ca. Late Fifteenth Century

O servant, where dost thou seek Me? Lo! I am beside thee.
I am neither in temple nor in mosque: I am neither in Kaaba° nor in Kailash:°
Neither am I in rites and ceremonies, nor in Yoga and renunciation.

If thou art a true seeker, thou shalt at once see Me:…
Kabir says, "O Sadhu!° God is the breath of all breath."

It is needless to ask of a saint the caste to which he belongs;
For the priest, the warrior, the tradesman, and all the thirty-six castes, alike are seeking for God.…

°**Kaaba:** the central shrine of Islam in Mecca.

°**Kailash:** a mountain sacred to Hindus.

Source: Rabindranath Tagore, trans., *The Songs of Kabir* (New York: The Macmillan Company, 1915).

°**Sadhu:** a Hindu spiritual seeker who has abandoned ordinary life.

The barber has sought God, the washerwoman,
  and the carpenter—
Even Raidas° was a seeker after God.
The Rishi Swapacha was a tanner by caste [an
  untouchable].
Hindus and Moslems alike have achieved that End,
  where remains no mark of distinction.

Within this earthen vessel° are bowers and groves,
  and within it is the Creator:
Within this vessel are the seven oceans and the
  unnumbered stars.
The touchstone and the jewel-appraiser are
  within;
And within this vessel the Eternal soundeth, and
  the spring wells up.
Kabir says: "Listen to me, my Friend! My beloved
  Lord is within."

Your Lord is near: yet you are climbing the palm-
  tree to seek Him.
The Brâhman priest goes from house to house and
  initiates people into faith:
Alas! the true fountain of life is beside you, and
  you have set up a stone to worship.
Kabir says: "I may never express how sweet my
  Lord is.

Yoga and the telling of beads, virtue and vice—
  these are naught to Him."

I do not ring the temple bell:
I do not set the idol on its throne:
I do not worship the image with flowers.
It is not the austerities that mortify the flesh which
  are pleasing to the Lord,
When you leave off your clothes and kill your
  senses, you do not please the Lord.
The man who is kind and who practices righteousness, who remains passive amidst the
  affairs of the world, who considers all creatures
  on earth as his own self,
He attains the Immortal Being, the true God is
  ever with him.

There is nothing but water at the holy bathing places;
And I know that they are useless, for I have
  bathed in them.
The images are all lifeless, they cannot speak;
  I know, for I have cried aloud to them.
The Purana° and the Koran are mere words; lifting
  up the curtain, I have seen.
Kabir gives utterance to the words of experience;
  and he knows very well that all other things
  are untrue.

_____
°**Raidas:** a Hindu poet from a low-ranking Sudra
caste.

°**earthen vessel:** the human body.

_____
°**Purana:** Hindu religious texts.

Using the Evidence:
Cultural Change in the Early Modern World

1. **Identifying the object of protest:** Each of these documents is protesting
   or criticizing something. How might you compare the ideas, practices, or
   authorities against which they are reacting? What historical circumstances
   generated these protests?

2. **Comparing views of human potential:** In what different ways might
   each of these authors understand human potential? What do they believe is
   necessary to realize or fulfill that potential?

3. **Comparing religious reformers:** Consider the religious outlook of Luther, al-Wahhab, and Kabir. What similarities and differences can you identify? Do you think Wang Yangming should be included in this category of religious reformers?

4. **Imagining a conversation:** Construct an imaginary debate or conversation between Condorcet and one or more of the religious or spiritually inclined authors of these documents.

Visual Sources

Considering the Evidence:
Global Christianity in the Early Modern Era

During the early modern centuries, the world of Christendom, long divided between its Roman Catholic and Eastern Orthodox branches, underwent two major transformations. First, the Reformation sharply divided western Christendom into bitterly hostile Protestant and Catholic halves. And while that process was unfolding in Europe, missionaries—mostly Roman Catholic—rode the tide of European expansion to establish the faith in the Americas and parts of Asia. In those places, native converts sometimes imitated European patterns and at other times adapted the new religion to their own cultural traditions. Furthermore, smaller but ancient Christian communities persisted in Ethiopia, Armenia, Egypt, southern India, and elsewhere. Thus the Christian world of the early modern era was far more globalized and much more varied than ever before. That variety found expression in both art and architecture, as the visual sources that follow illustrate.

Some of the differences between Protestant and Catholic Christianity become apparent in the interiors of their churches. To Martin Luther, the founder of Protestant Christianity, elaborate church interiors, with their many sculptures and paintings, represented a spiritual danger, for he feared that the wealthy few who endowed such images would come to believe that they were buying their way into heaven rather than relying on God's grace. "It would be better," he wrote, "if we gave less to the churches and altars,...and more to the needy."[30] John Calvin, the prominent French-born Protestant theologian, went even further, declaring that "God forbade...the making of any images representing him."[31]

Behind such statements lay different understandings of the church building. While Roman Catholics generally saw a church as a temple or "house of God," sacred because it is where God dwells on earth, Protestants viewed churches more as meetinghouses, gathering places for a congregation. They were not sacred in themselves as places, but only on account of the worship that occurred within them.[32] Furthermore, to Protestants, images of the saints were an invitation to idolatry. Acting on such ideas, Protestants in various places stripped older churches of the offending images, decapitated statues, and sometimes ritually burned statues and paintings at the stake. The new churches they created were often quite different from their Catholic counterparts. Visual Source 16.1, a

Visual Source 16.1 Pieter Saenredam, *Interior of a Dutch Reformed Church* (Rijksmuseum Museum)

painting by Dutch artist Pieter Saenredam from about 1645, portrays the interior of a typical Dutch Reformed (Protestant) Church.

Roman Catholic response to the Reformation took shape in the Catholic Counter-Reformation (see pp. 725–27). That vigorous movement found expression in a style of church architecture known as Baroque, which emerged powerfully in Catholic Europe as well as in the Spanish and Portuguese colonies of Latin America during the seventeenth and eighteenth centuries. The interiors of such churches were ornately adorned with paintings, ceiling frescoes, and statues, depicting Jesus on the cross, the Virgin and child, numerous saints, and biblical stories. The exuberant art of these church interiors appealed to the senses, seeking to provoke an emotional response of mystery, awe, and grandeur while kindling the faith of the worshippers and binding them firmly to the Catholic Church in the face of Protestant competition. Visual Source 16.2 is a photograph of the interior of the Pilgrimage Church of Mariazell, located in present-day Austria. A church site since the twelfth century, the building was enlarged and refurbished in Baroque style in the seventeenth century.

■ What obvious differences do you notice between these two church interiors? What kind of emotional responses would each of them have evoked?

Visual Source 16.2 Catholic Baroque: Interior of Pilgrimage Church, Mariazell, Austria (Erich Lessing/Art Resource, NY)

■ In what ways do these church interiors reflect differences between Protestant and Catholic theology? (See Snapshot, p. 724.) Why does the Protestant congregation face toward the pulpit, from which the minister presents his sermon, while the Catholic worshippers look toward the altar, where Holy Communion takes place? Pay attention as well to the kind of geometric shapes apparent in each church and to the role of preaching.

■ How might Protestants and Catholics have reacted upon entering each other's churches?

■ Keep in mind that Visual Source 16.1 is a painting. Why do you think the artist showed the people disproportionately small?

Throughout Latin America, Christianity was established in the context of conquest and colonial rule (see pp. 728–30). As the new faith took hold across the region, it incorporated much that was of European origin as the construction of many large and ornate Baroque churches illustrates. But local communities also sought to blend this European Catholic Christianity with religious symbols and concepts drawn from their own traditions in a process that historians call syncretism. In the Andes, for example, Inca religion featured a supreme creator god (Viracocha); a sun god (Inti), regarded as the creator of the Inca people; a moon goddess (Killa), who was the wife of Inti and was attended by an order of priestesses; and an earth mother goddess (Pachamama), associated with mountain peaks and fertility. Those religious figures found their way into Andean understanding of Christianity, as Visual Source 16.3 illustrates.

Painted around 1740 by an unknown artist, this striking image shows the Virgin Mary placed within the "rich mountain" of Potosí in Bolivia, from which the Spanish had extracted so much silver (see p. 683). A number of smaller figures within the mountain represent the native miners whose labor had enriched their colonial rulers. A somewhat larger figure at the bottom of the mountain is an Inca ruler dressed in royal garb receiving tribute from his people. At the bottom left are the pope and a cardinal, while on the right stands the Habsburg emperor Charles V and perhaps his wife.

■ What is Mary's relationship to the heavenly beings standing above her as well as to the miners at work in the mountain? What is the significance of the crown above her head and her outstretched arms?

■ The European figures at the bottom are shown in a posture of prayer or thanksgiving. What might the artist have been trying to convey? How would you interpret the relative size of the European and Andean figures?

■ Why do you think the artist placed Mary actually inside the mountain rather than on it, while depicting her dress in a mountain-like form?

Visual Source 16.3 Cultural Blending in Andean Christianity (Nick Buxton, photographer)

■ What marks this painting as an example of syncretism?

■ Do you read this image as subversive of the colonial order or as supportive of it? Do you think the artist was a European or a Native American Christian?

In China, unlike Latin America, Christian missionaries operated in a setting wholly outside of European political control, bringing their faith to a powerful and proud civilization, long dominant in eastern Asia, where Confucianism, Daoism, and Buddhism had for many centuries mixed and mingled. The outcome of those missionary efforts was far more modest and much less successful than in the Americas (see pp. 000–00). Nonetheless, in China too the tendency toward syncretism was evident. Jesuit missionaries themselves sought to present the Christian message within a Chinese cultural context to the intellectual and political elites who were their primary target audience. And Chinese Christians often transposed the new religion into more familiar cultural concepts. European critics of the Jesuit approach, however, feared that syncretism watered down the Christian message and risked losing its distinctive character.

Visual Source 16.4 provides an example of Christianity becoming Chinese.[33] In the early seventeenth century, the Jesuits published several books in the Chinese language describing the life of Christ and illustrated them with a series of woodblock prints created by Chinese artists affiliated with the Jesuits. Although they were clearly modeled on European images, those prints cast Christian figures into an altogether Chinese setting. The woodblock print in Visual Source 16.4 portrays the familiar biblical story of the annunciation, when an angel informs Mary that she will be the mother of Christ. The house and furniture shown in the print suggest the dwelling of a wealthy Chinese scholar. The reading table in front of Mary was a common item in the homes of the literary elite of the time. The view from the window shows a seascape, mountains in the distance, a lone tree, and a "scholar's rock"—all of which were common features in Chinese landscape painting. The clouds that appear at the angel's feet and around the shaft of light shining on Mary are identical to those associated with sacred Buddhist and Daoist figures. To Chinese eyes, the angel might well appear as a Buddhist boddhisatva, while Mary may resemble a Ming dynasty noblewoman or perhaps Kuanyin, the Chinese Buddhist goddess of mercy and compassion.

■ What specifically Chinese elements can you identify in this image?

■ To whom might this image have been directed?

■ How might educated Chinese have responded to this image?

■ The European engraving on which this Chinese print was modeled included in the background the scene of Jesus' crucifixion. Why might the Chinese artist have chosen to omit that scene from his image?

Visual Source 16.4 Making Christianity Chinese (Courtesy, Archivum Romanum Societatis Iesu, Rome)

■ How would European critics of the Jesuits' approach to missionary work have reacted to this image? To what extent has the basic message of Catholic Christianity been retained or changed in this Chinese cultural setting?

As Chinese emperors welcomed Jesuit missionaries at court, so too did the rulers of Mughal India during the time of Akbar and Jahangir (1556–1627). But while Chinese elite circles received the Jesuits for their scientific skills, especially in astronomy, the Mughal court seemed more interested in the religious and artistic achievements of European civilization. Akbar invited the Jesuits to take part in cross-religious discussions that included Muslim, Hindu, Jain, and Zoroastrian scholars. Furthermore, the Mughal emperors eagerly embraced the art of late Renaissance Europe, which the Jesuits provided to them, much

Visual Source 16.5 Christian Art at the Mughal Court
(Rare Book Department, The Free Library of Philadelphia)

of it devotional and distinctly Christian. Mughal artists quickly learned to paint in the European style, and soon murals featuring Jesus, Mary, and Christian saints appeared on the walls of palaces, garden pavilions, and harems of the Mughal court, while miniature paintings adorned books, albums, and jewelry.

In religious terms, however, the Jesuit efforts were "a fantastic and extravagant failure,"[34] for these Muslim rulers of India were not in the least interested in abandoning Islam for the Christian faith, and few conversions of any kind occurred. Akbar and Jahangir, however, were cosmopolitan connoisseurs of art, which they collected, reproduced, and displayed. European religious art also had propaganda value in enhancing their status. Jesus and Mary, after all, had a prominent place within Islam. Jesus was seen both as an earlier prophet and as mystical figure, similar to the Sufi masters who were so important in Indian Islam. Mughal paintings, pairing the adult Jesus and Mary side by side, were placed above the imperial throne as well as on the emperor's jewelry and his official seal, suggesting an identification of Jesus and a semidivine emperor. That the mothers of both Akbar and Jahangir were named Mary only added to the appeal. Thus Akbar and Jahangir sought to incorporate European-style Christian art into their efforts to create a blended and tolerant religious culture for the elites of their vast and diverse realm. It was a culture that drew on Islam, Hinduism, Zoroastrianism, and Christianity.

But as Catholic devotional art was reworked by Mughal artists, it was also subtly changed. Visual Source 16.5 shows an early-seventeenth-century depiction of the Holy Family painted by an Indian artist.

- Why do you think that this Mughal painter portrayed Mary and Joseph as rather distinguished and educated persons rather than as the humble carpenter and his peasant wife, as in so many European images?

- Similarly, why might he have placed the family in rather palatial surroundings instead of a stable?

- How do you imagine European missionaries responded to this representation of the Holy Family?

- How might more orthodox Muslims have reacted to the larger project of creating a blended religion making use of elements from many traditions? Consider the possible reactions of the Wahhabis (Document 16.4, pp. 756–57) and Kabir (Document 16.5, pp. 758–59).

- What similarities can you identify between this Indian image and the Chinese print in Visual Source 16.4? Pay attention to the setting, the clothing, and the class status of the human figures, and the scenes outside the windows.

Using the Evidence:
Global Christianity in the Early Modern Era

1. **Making comparisons:** What common elements of Christianity can you identify in these visual sources? What differences in the expression of Christianity can you define?

2. **Considering Mary:** The Catholic Christian tradition as it developed in Latin America, China, and India as well as Europe provided a very important place for representations of the Virgin Mary. Why might this feature of the Christian message have been so widely appealing? But in what ways does the image of the Holy Mother differ in Visual Sources 16.3, 16.4, and 16.5? In what ways were those images adapted to the distinctive cultures in which they were created?

3. **Pondering syncretism:** From a missionary viewpoint, develop arguments for and against religious syncretism using these visual sources as points of reference.

4. **Considering visual sources as evidence:** What are the strengths and limitations of these visual sources, as opposed to texts, as historians seek to understand the globalization of Christianity in the early modern era? What other visual sources might be useful?

PART FIVE

The European Moment in World History

1750–1914

Contents

Chapter 17. Atlantic Revolutions and Their Echoes, 1750–1914
Chapter 18. Revolutions of Industrialization, 1750–1914
Chapter 19. Internal Troubles, External Threats: China, the Ottoman
Empire, and Japan, 1800–1914
Chapter 20. Colonial Encounters, 1750–1914

European Centrality and the Problem of Eurocentrism

During the century and a half between 1750 and 1914, sometimes referred to as the "long nineteenth century," two new and related phenomena held center stage in the global history of humankind and represent the major themes of the four chapters that follow. The first of these, explored in Chapters 17 and 18, was the creation of a new kind of human society, commonly called "modern," which was the outgrowth of the Scientific, French, and Industrial revolutions, all of which took shape in Western Europe. Those societies generated many of the ideas that have guided human behavior over the past several centuries—notions of progress, constitutional government, political democracy, socialism, nationalism, feminism, and opposition to slavery.

The second theme of this long nineteenth century, which is addressed in Chapters 19 and 20, was the growing ability of these modern societies to exercise enormous power and influence over the rest of humankind. In some places, this occurred within growing European empires, such as those that governed India, Southeast Asia, and Africa. Elsewhere, it took place through less formal means—economic penetration, military intervention, diplomatic pressure, missionary activity—in states that remained officially independent, such as China, Japan, the Ottoman Empire, and various countries in Latin America.

Together, these two phenomena thrust Western Europe, and to a lesser extent North America, into a new and far more prominent role in world history than ever before. While various regions had experienced sprouts of modernity during the "early modern" centuries, it was in Western European societies that these novel ways of living emerged most fully. Those societies, and their North American offspring, also came to exercise a wholly unprecedented role in world affairs, as they achieved, collectively, something approaching global dominance by the early twentieth century.

Eurocentric Geography and History

That unprecedented power included the ability to rewrite geography and history in ways that centered the human story on Europe and to impose those views on other people. Thus maps placed Europe at the center of the world, while dividing Asia in half. Europe was granted continental status, even though it was more accurately only the western peninsula of Asia, much as India was its southern peninsula. Other regions of the world, such as the Far East or the Near (Middle) East, were defined in terms of their distance from Europe. The entire world came to measure

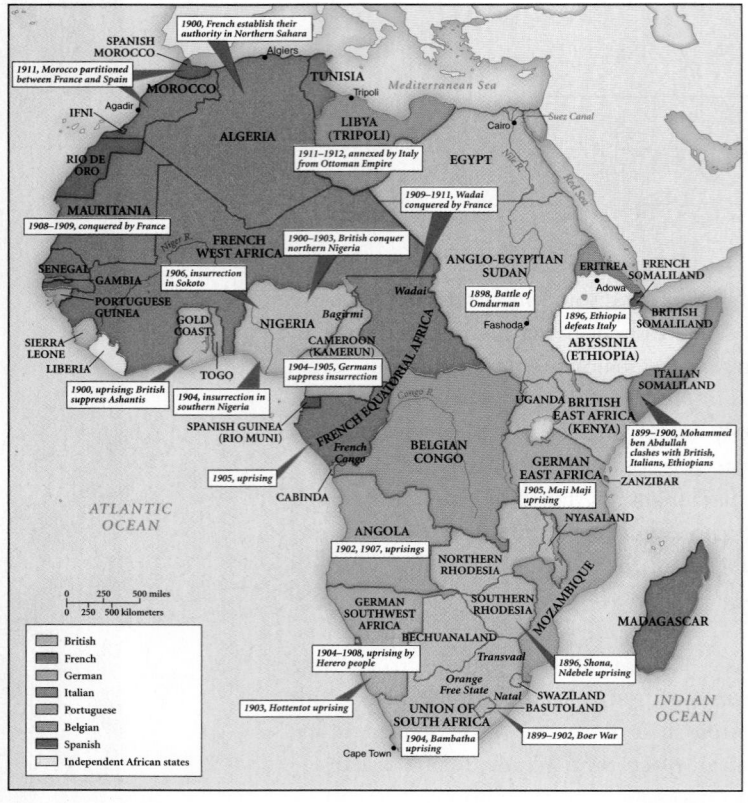

Conquest and Resistance in Colonial Africa (p. 927)

longitude from a line, known as the prime meridian, that passes through the Royal Astronomical Observatory in Greenwich, England.

History textbooks as well often reflected a Europe-centered outlook, sometimes blatantly. In 1874, the American author William O. Swinton wrote *An Outline of the World's History*, a book intended for use in high school and college classes, in which he flatly declared that "the race to which we belong, the Aryan, has always played the leading part in the great drama of the world's progress."[1] Other peoples and civilizations, by contrast, were long believed to be static and unchanging, thus largely lacking any real history. Most Europeans assumed that these "backward" peoples and regions must either imitate the Western model or face further decline and possible extinction. Until the mid-twentieth century, such ideas went largely unchallenged in the Western world. They implied that history was a race toward the finish line of modernity. That Europeans arrived there first seemed to suggest something unique, special, or superior about them or their culture, while everyone else struggled to overcome their inadequacy and catch up.

As the discipline of world history took shape in the decades after World War II, scholars and teachers actively sought to counteract such a Eurocentric understanding of the past, but they faced a special problem in dealing with recent centuries. How can we avoid an inappropriate Eurocentrism when dealing with a phase of world history in which Europeans were in fact central? The long nineteenth century, after all, was "the European moment," a time when Europeans were clearly the most powerful, most innovative, most prosperous, most expansive, and most widely imitated people on the planet.

Countering Eurocentrism

At least five answers to this dilemma are reflected in the chapters that follow. You may want to look for examples of them as you read. The first is simply to remind ourselves how recent and perhaps how brief the European moment in world history has been. Other peoples too had times of "cultural flowering" that granted them a period of primacy or influence—for example, the Greeks (500 B.C.E.–200 C.E.), Indians of South Asia (200–600 C.E.), Arabs (600–1000), Chinese (1000–1500), Mongols (1200–1350), Incas and Aztecs (fifteenth century)—but all of these were limited to particular regions of Afro-Eurasia or the Americas.[2] Even though the European moment operated on a genuinely global scale, Western peoples have enjoyed their worldwide primacy for at most two centuries. Some scholars have suggested that the events of the late twentieth and early twenty-first centuries—the end of colonial empires,

Railroads (p. 832)

the rise of India and especially China, and the assertion of Islam—mark the end, or at least the erosion, of the age of Europe.

Second, we need to remember that the rise of Europe occurred within an international context. It was the withdrawal of the Chinese naval fleet that allowed Europeans to dominate the Indian Ocean in the sixteenth century, while Native Americans' lack of immunity to European diseases and their own divisions and conflicts greatly assisted the European takeover. Europe's Scientific Revolution drew upon earlier Islamic science and was stimulated by the massive amounts of new information pouring in from around the world. The Industrial Revolution, explored in Chapter 18, likewise benefited from New World resources and markets and from the stimulus of superior Asian textile and pottery production. Chapters 19 and 20 make clear that European control of other regions everywhere depended on the cooperation of local elites. None of this diminishes the remarkable—indeed revolutionary—transformations of the European moment in world history. Rather it suggests that they did not derive wholly from some special European genius or long-term advantage but emerged from a unique intersection of European historical development with that of other peoples, regions, and cultures.

A third reminder is that the rise of Europe to a position of global dominance was not an easy or automatic process. Frequently it occurred in the face of ferocious resistance and rebellion, which often required Europeans to modify their policies and practices. The so-called Indian mutiny in mid-nineteenth-century South Asia, a massive uprising against British colonial rule, did not end British control, but it substantially transformed the character of the colonial experience. In

Africa, fear of offending Muslim sensibilities persuaded the British to keep European missionaries and mission schools out of northern Nigeria during the colonial era. Even when Europeans exercised political power, they could not do so precisely as they pleased. Empire, formal and informal alike, was always in some ways a negotiated arrangement.

Fourth, peoples the world over made active use of Europeans and European ideas for their own purposes, seeking to gain advantage over local rivals or to benefit themselves in light of new conditions. In Southeast Asia, for example, a number of highland minority groups, long oppressed by the dominant lowland Vietnamese, viewed the French invaders as liberators and assisted in their takeover of Vietnam. Hindus in India used the railroads, which had been introduced by the British, to go on pilgrimages to holy sites more easily, while the printing press made possible the more widespread distribution of their sacred texts. During the Haitian Revolution, examined in Chapter 17, enslaved Africans made use of radical French ideas about "the rights of man" in ways that most Europeans never intended. The leaders of a massive Chinese peasant upheaval in the mid-nineteenth century adopted a unique form of Christianity to legitimate their revolutionary assault on an ancient social order. Recognizing that Asian and African peoples remained active agents, pursuing their own interests even in oppressive conditions, is another way of countering residual Eurocentrism.

What was borrowed from Europe was always adapted to local circumstances. Thus Japanese or Russian industrial development did not wholly follow the pattern of England's Industrial Revolution. The Christianity that took root in the Americas or later in Africa evolved in culturally distinctive ways. Ideas of nationalism, born in Europe, were used to oppose European imperialism throughout Asia and Africa. Chinese socialism in the twentieth century departed in many ways from the vision of Karl Marx. The most interesting stories of modern world history are not simply those of European triumph or the imposition of Western ideas and practices but of encounters, though highly unequal, among culturally different peoples. It was from these encounters, not just from the intentions and actions of Europeans, that the dramatic global changes of the modern era arose.

A fifth and final antidote to Eurocentrism in an age of European centrality lies in the recognition that although Europeans gained an unprecedented prominence on the world stage, they were not the only game in town, nor were they the sole preoccupation of Asian, African, and Middle Eastern peoples. While China confronted Western aggression in the nineteenth century, it was also absorbing a huge population increase and experiencing massive peasant rebellions that grew out of distinctly Chinese conditions. The long relationship of Muslim and Hindu cultures in India continued to evolve under British colonial rule as it had for centuries under other political systems. West African societies in the nineteenth century experienced a wave of religious wars that created new states and extended and transformed the practice of Islam, and that faith continued its centuries-long spread on the continent even under European colonial rule. A further wave of wars and state formation in southern Africa transformed the political and ethnic landscape, even as European penetration picked up speed.

None of this diminishes the significance of the European moment in world history, but it sets that moment in a larger context of continuing patterns of historical development and of interaction and exchange with other peoples.

Landmarks of the European Moment in World History, 1750–1914

1750	1775	1800	1825	

Europe

1780s Beginnings of British Industrial Revolution

1799–1814 Reign of Napoleon

1848 Publication of Karl Marx's *Communist Manifesto*

1789–1799 French Revolution

1780s Beginnings of antislavery movement

North America

1775–1783 American Revolution

1787 U.S. Constitutional Convention

1803 Louisiana Purchase

1845–1848 Mexican-American War

1848 Women's Rights Convention, Seneca Falls, New York

1849 California gold rush

Latin America

1783–1830 Life of Simón Bolívar

1791–1803 Haitian Revolution

1810–1825 Latin American wars of independence

1810 Hidalgo-Morelos rebellion in Mexico

Africa

1798 Napoleon's invasion of Egypt

1815–1840 Rise of Zulu kingdom in South Africa

1804–1817 Fulbe wars and establishment of Sokoto caliphate in West Africa

1805–1848 Reign of Muhammad Ali in Egypt

1830 French invasion of Algeria

East Asia

1793 Chinese rejection of British request for open trade

1830s Famines and rebellions in Japan

1838–1842 First Opium War

South, Southwest, and Southeast Asia

1839–1876 Tanzimat reforms in Ottoman Empire

1740s–1818 Wahhabi movement of Islamic renewal in Arabia

1750s Beginnings of British takeover in India

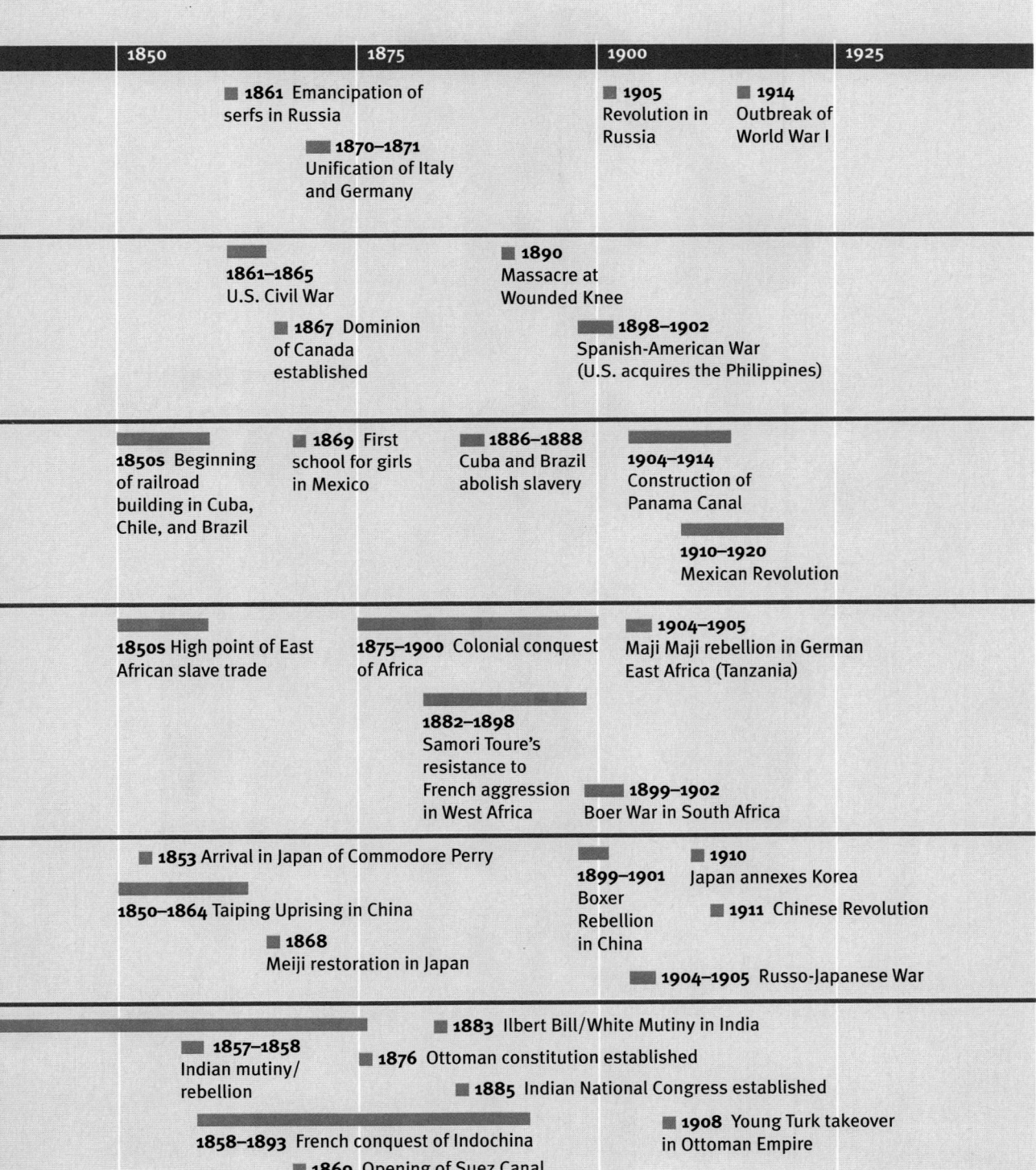

1850	1875	1900	1925

■ **1861** Emancipation of serfs in Russia

■ **1870–1871** Unification of Italy and Germany

■ **1905** Revolution in Russia

■ **1914** Outbreak of World War I

1861–1865 U.S. Civil War

■ **1867** Dominion of Canada established

■ **1890** Massacre at Wounded Knee

■ **1898–1902** Spanish-American War (U.S. acquires the Philippines)

1850s Beginning of railroad building in Cuba, Chile, and Brazil

■ **1869** First school for girls in Mexico

■ **1886–1888** Cuba and Brazil abolish slavery

1904–1914 Construction of Panama Canal

1910–1920 Mexican Revolution

1850s High point of East African slave trade

1875–1900 Colonial conquest of Africa

■ **1904–1905** Maji Maji rebellion in German East Africa (Tanzania)

1882–1898 Samori Toure's resistance to French aggression in West Africa

■ **1899–1902** Boer War in South Africa

■ **1853** Arrival in Japan of Commodore Perry

1850–1864 Taiping Uprising in China

■ **1868** Meiji restoration in Japan

1899–1901 Boxer Rebellion in China

■ **1910** Japan annexes Korea

■ **1911** Chinese Revolution

■ **1904–1905** Russo-Japanese War

■ **1883** Ilbert Bill/White Mutiny in India

1857–1858 Indian mutiny/ rebellion

■ **1876** Ottoman constitution established

■ **1885** Indian National Congress established

■ **1908** Young Turk takeover in Ottoman Empire

1858–1893 French conquest of Indochina

■ **1869** Opening of Suez Canal

Atlantic Revolutions
and Their Echoes

1750–1914

Comparing Atlantic Revolutions
  The North American Revolution,
  1775–1787
  The French Revolution, 1789–1815
  The Haitian Revolution, 1791–1804
  Spanish American Revolutions,
  1810–1825
Echoes of Revolution
  The Abolition of Slavery
  Nations and Nationalism
  Feminist Beginnings
Reflections: Revolutions Pro
  and Con
Considering the Evidence
  Documents: Claiming Rights
  Visual Sources: Representing the
  French Revolution

On July 14, 1989, France celebrated the bicentennial of its famous revolution with a huge parade in Paris. At the head of that parade, strangely enough, were a number of Chinese students, pushing empty bicycles. Just a few weeks earlier, those students had been part of massive demonstrations in Beijing's Tiananmen Square, demanding from their communist government the kind of democratic political rights that the French Revolution had inspired two centuries before. In the process, they had created a thirty-foot-tall papier-mâché Goddess of Democracy, which resembled the U.S. Statue of Liberty. Chinese authorities had violently crushed those demonstrations, and now a few students who had escaped to France were paying tribute to the ideals that the French Revolution had unleashed. Their empty bicycles symbolized thousands of their colleagues who had been killed or jailed during the Chinese struggle for democracy. Thus the reverberations of the French Revolution of 1789 echoed still two centuries later and half a world away.

ESSENTIAL AS IT WAS TO THE HISTORY OF EUROPE, the French Revolution holds an even larger significance as the centerpiece of a more extensive revolutionary process that unfolded all around the Atlantic world in the century or so following 1775. The upheaval in France, of course, was preceded by the American Revolution, which gave birth to the United States. It was followed by the Haitian Revolution, the first successful slave revolt in history, and by the Latin American revolutions, in which Spanish and Portuguese colonial rule

---

The Three Estates of Old-Regime France: This satirical eighteenth-century illustration represents the three estates of prerevolutionary French society as women, with the peasant woman carrying a nun and an aristocratic lady on her back. Such social tensions contributed much to the making of the French Revolution. (Réunion des Musées Nationaux/Art Resource, NY)

was ended and the modern states of Latin America emerged. Further revolutionary outbreaks shook various European societies in 1830, 1848, and 1870.

These upheavals also had an impact well beyond the Atlantic world. The armies of revolutionary France, for example, invaded Egypt, Germany, Poland, and Russia, carrying seeds of change. The ideals that animated these Atlantic revolutions inspired efforts in many countries to abolish slavery, to extend the right to vote, and to secure greater equality for women. Nationalism, perhaps the most potent ideology of the modern era, was nurtured in the Atlantic revolutions and shaped much of nineteenth- and twentieth-century world history. The ideas of equality that were articulated in these revolutions later found expression in socialist and communist movements. And the Universal Declaration of Human Rights, adopted by the United Nations in 1948, echoed and amplified those principles while providing the basis for any number of subsequent protests against oppression, tyranny, and deprivation. The Atlantic revolutions had a long reach.

Comparing Atlantic Revolutions

■ **Causation**
In what ways did the ideas of the Enlightenment contribute to the Atlantic revolutions?

Writing to a friend in 1772, before any of the Atlantic revolutions had occurred, the French intellectual Voltaire asked, "My dear philosopher, doesn't this appear to you to be the century of revolutions?"[1] He was certainly on target: in the century that followed, revolutionary outbreaks punctuated the histories of three continents, with influences and echoes even farther afield. Nor were these various revolutions—in North America, France, Haiti, and Latin America—entirely separate and distinct events, for they clearly influenced one another. The American revolutionary leader Thomas Jefferson was the U.S. ambassador to France on the eve of the French Revolution, and while there he provided advice and encouragement to French reformers and revolutionaries. Simón Bolívar, a leading figure in Spanish American struggles for independence, twice visited Haiti, where he received military aid from the first black government in the Americas.

Beyond such direct connections, the various Atlantic revolutionaries shared a set of common ideas. The Atlantic basin had become a world of intellectual and cultural exchange as well as one of commercial and biological interaction. The ideas that animated the Atlantic revolutions derived from the European Enlightenment and were shared across the ocean in newspapers, books, and pamphlets. At the heart of these ideas was the radical notion that human political and social arrangements could be engineered, and improved, by human action. Thus conventional and long-established ways of living and thinking—the divine right of kings, state control of trade, aristocratic privilege, the authority of a single church—were no longer sacrosanct and came under repeated attack. New ideas of liberty, equality, free trade, religious tolerance, republicanism, and human rationality were in the air. Politically, the core notion was "popular sovereignty," which meant that the authority to govern derived from the people rather than from God or from established tradition. As the Englishman John Locke (1632–1704) had argued, the "social contract" between ruler and ruled

Snapshot   **Key Moments in the History of Atlantic Revolutions**

American Declaration of Independence	1776
British recognition of American independence	1783
U.S. Constitutional Convention	1787
Tupac Amaru revolt in Peru	1780s
Outbreak of French Revolution	1789
Haitian Revolution	1791–1804
French Terror, execution of Louis XVI	1793–1794
Napoleon's rise to power	1799
High point of Napoleon's empire	1810–1811
Hidalgo-Morelos rebellion in Mexico	1810–1813
Wars of Spanish American independence	1810–1825
Final defeat of Napoleon	1815
Independence of Brazil from Portugal	1822

should last only as long as it served the people well. In short, it was both possible and desirable to start over in the construction of human communities.

Such ideas generated endless controversy. Were liberty and equality compatible? What kind of government—unitary and centralized or federal and decentralized—best ensured freedom? And how far should liberty be extended? Except in Haiti, the chief beneficiaries of these revolutions were propertied white men of the "middling classes." Although women, slaves, Native Americans, and men without property did not gain much from these revolutions, the ideas that accompanied those upheavals gave them ammunition for the future. Because their overall thrust was to extend political rights further than ever before, these Atlantic movements have often been referred to as "democratic revolutions."

Beneath a common political vocabulary and a broadly democratic character, the Atlantic revolutions differed substantially from one another. They were triggered by different circumstances, expressed quite different social and political tensions, and varied considerably in their outcomes. Liberty, noted Simón Bolívar, "is a succulent morsel, but one difficult to digest."[2] "Digesting liberty" occurred in quite distinct ways in the various sites of the Atlantic revolutions.

The North American Revolution, 1775–1787

Every schoolchild in the United States learns early that the American Revolution was a struggle for independence from oppressive British rule. That struggle was

■ **Change**
What was revolutionary about the American Revolution, and what was not?

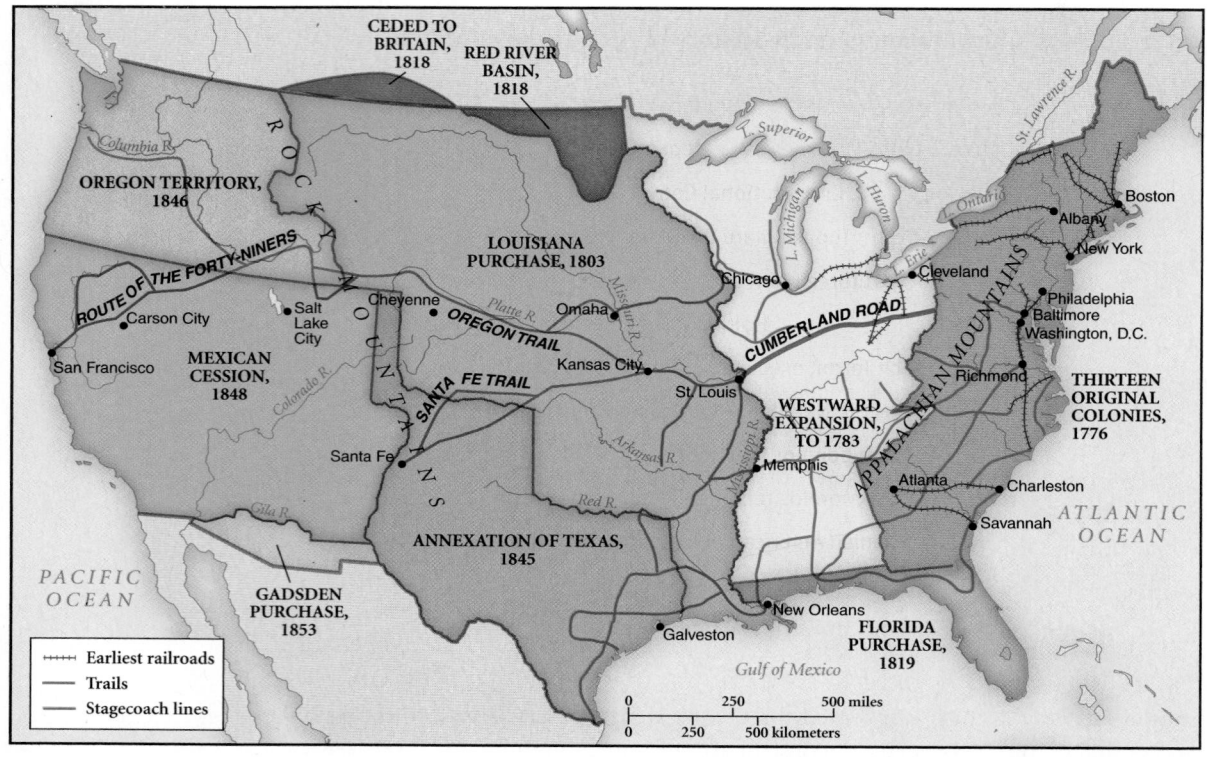

Map 17.1   The Expansion of the United States
The union of the thirteen British colonies in North America provided the foundation for the westward and transcontinental expansion of the United States during the nineteenth century, a process that turned the country into a global power by the early twentieth century.

launched with the Declaration of Independence in 1776, resulted in an unlikely military victory by 1781, and generated a federal constitution in 1787, joining thirteen formerly separate colonies into a new nation (see Map 17.1). It was the first in a series of upheavals that rocked the Atlantic world and beyond in the century that followed. But was it a genuine revolution? What, precisely, did it change?

In its break with Britain, the American Revolution marked a decisive political change, but in other ways it was, strangely enough, a <u>conservative movement</u>, because it originated in an effort to preserve the existing liberties of the colonies rather than to create new ones. For much of the seventeenth and eighteenth centuries, the British colonies in North America enjoyed a considerable degree of local autonomy as the British government was embroiled in its own internal conflicts and various European wars. Furthermore, Britain's West Indian colonies seemed more profitable and of greater significance than those of North America. In these circumstances, local elected assemblies in North America, dominated by the wealthier property-owning settlers, achieved something close to self-government. Colonists came to regard such autonomy as a birthright and part of their English heritage. Thus, until the mid-eighteenth century, almost no one in the colonies thought of breaking away from England because participation in the British Empire provided many advantages— protection in war, access to British markets, and confirmation of their continuing identity as "Englishmen"—and few drawbacks.

Within these colonies, English settlers had developed societies described by a leading historian as "the most radical in the contemporary Western world." Certainly class distinctions were real and visible, and a small class of wealthy "gentlemen"—the Adamses, Washingtons, Jeffersons, and Hancocks—wore powdered wigs, imitated the latest European styles, were prominent in political life, and were generally deferred to by ordinary people. But the ready availability of land following the elimination of Native Americans, the scarcity of people, and the absence of both a titled nobility and a single established church meant that social life was far more open than in Europe. No legal distinctions differentiated clergy, aristocracy, and commoners, as they did in France. All free men enjoyed the same status before the law, a situation that excluded black slaves and, in some ways, white women as well. These conditions made for less poverty, more economic opportunity, fewer social differences, and easier relationships among the classes than in Europe. The famous economist Adam Smith observed that British colonists were "republican in their manners...and their government" well before their independence from England.[3]

Thus the American Revolution did not grow out of social tensions within the colonies, but from a rather sudden and unexpected effort by the British government to tighten its control over the colonies and to extract more revenue from them. As Britain's global struggle with France drained its treasury and ran up its national debt, British authorities, beginning in the 1760s, looked to America to make good these losses. Abandoning its neglectful oversight of the colonies, Britain began to act like a genuine imperial power, imposing a variety of new taxes and tariffs on the colonies without their consent, for they were not represented in the British parliament. By challenging their economic interests, their established traditions of local autonomy, and their identity as true Englishmen, such measures infuriated many of the colonists. Armed with the ideas of the Enlightenment—popular sovereignty, natural rights, the consent of the governed—they went to war, and by 1781 they had prevailed, with considerable aid from the French.

What was revolutionary about the American experience was not so much the revolution itself but the kind of society that had already emerged within the colonies. Independence from Britain was not accompanied by any wholesale social transformation. Rather the revolution accelerated the established democratic tendencies of the colonial societies. Political authority remained largely in the hands of existing elites who had led the revolution, although property requirements for voting were lowered and more white men of modest means, such as small farmers and urban artisans, were elected to state legislatures.

This widening of political participation gradually eroded the power of traditional gentlemen, but no women or people of color shared in these gains. Land was not seized from its owners, except in the case of pro-British loyalists who had fled the country. Although slavery was gradually abolished in the northern states, where it counted for little, it remained firmly entrenched in the southern states, where it counted for much. Chief Justice John Marshall later gave voice to this conservative understanding of the American Revolution: "All contracts and rights, respecting property, remained unchanged by the Revolution."[4] In the century that followed independence, the United States did become the world's most democratic country, but it was less the direct product of the revolution and more the gradual working out in a reformist fashion of earlier practices and the principles of equality announced in the Declaration of Independence.

Nonetheless, many American patriots felt passionately that they were creating "a new order for the ages." James Madison in the *Federalist Papers* made the point clearly: "We pursued a new and more noble course...and accomplished a revolution that has no parallel in the annals of human society." Supporters abroad agreed. On the eve of the French Revolution, a Paris newspaper proclaimed that the United States was "the hope and model of the human race."[5] In both cases, they were referring primarily to the political ideas and practices of the new country. The American Revolution, after all, initiated the political dismantling of Europe's New World empires. The "right to revolution," proclaimed in the Declaration of Independence and made effective only in a great struggle, inspired revolutionaries and nationalists from Simón Bolívar in nineteenth-century Latin America to Ho Chi Minh in twentieth-century Vietnam. Moreover, the new U.S. Constitution—with its Bill of Rights, checks and balances, separation of church and state, and federalism—was one of the first sustained efforts to put the political ideas of the Enlightenment into practice. That document, and the ideas that it embraced, echoed repeatedly in the political upheavals of the century that followed.

The French Revolution, 1789–1815

■ Comparison
How did the French Revolution differ from the American Revolution?

Act Two in the drama of the Atlantic revolutions took place in France, beginning in 1789, although it was closely connected to Act One in North America. Thousands of French soldiers had provided assistance to the American colonists and now returned home full of republican enthusiasm. Thomas Jefferson, the U.S. ambassador in Paris, reported that France "has been awakened by our revolution."[6] More immediately, the French government, which had generously aided the Americans in an effort to undermine its British rivals, was teetering on the brink of bankruptcy and had long sought reforms that would modernize the tax system and make it more equitable. In a desperate effort to raise taxes against the opposition of the privileged classes, the French king, Louis XVI, had called into session an ancient representative body, the Estates General. It consisted of representatives of the three "estates," or legal orders, of prerevolutionary France: the clergy, the nobility, and the commoners. The first two estates comprised about 2 percent of the population, and the third estate included everyone else. When that body convened in 1789, representatives of the third estate soon organized themselves as the National Assembly, claiming the sole authority to make laws for the country. A few weeks later they drew up the Declaration of the Rights of Man and Citizen, which forthrightly declared that "men are born and remain free and equal in rights" (see Document 17.1, pp. 806–08). These actions, unprecedented and illegal in the *ancien régime* (the old regime), launched the French Revolution and radicalized many of the participants in the National Assembly.

That revolution was quite different from its North American predecessor. Whereas the American Revolution expressed the tensions of a colonial relationship with a distant imperial power, the French insurrection was driven by sharp conflicts within French society. Members of the titled nobility—privileged, prestigious, and wealthy—resented and resisted the monarchy's efforts to subject them to new taxes. Educated middle-class groups, such as doctors, lawyers, lower-level officials, and merchants, were growing in numbers and sometimes in wealth and were offended by the remaining privileges of the aristocracy, from which they were excluded. Ordinary urban residents, many of whose incomes had declined for a generation, were particularly hard-hit in the late 1780s by the rapidly rising price of bread and widespread unemployment. Peasants in the countryside, though largely free of serfdom, were subject to a variety of hated dues imposed by their landlords, taxes from the state, obligations to the Church, and the requirement to work without pay on public roads. As Enlightenment ideas penetrated French society, more and more people, mostly in the third estate but including some priests and nobles, found a language with which to articulate these grievances. The famous French writer Jean-Jacques Rousseau had told them that it was "manifestly contrary to the law of nature . . . that a handful of people should gorge themselves with superfluities while the hungry multitude goes in want of necessities."[7]

These social conflicts gave the French Revolution, especially during its first five years, a much more violent, far-reaching, and radical character than its American counterpart. It was a profound social upheaval, more comparable to the revolutions of Russia and China in the twentieth century than to the earlier American Revolution. Initial efforts to establish a constitutional monarchy and promote harmony among the classes (see Visual Source 17.1, p. 818) gave way to more radical measures, as internal resistance and foreign opposition produced a fear that the revolution might be overturned. In the process, urban crowds organized insurrections. Some peasants attacked the castles of their lords, burning the documents that recorded their dues and payments. The National Assembly decreed the end of all legal privileges and ended what remained of feudalism in France. Even slavery was abolished, albeit briefly. Church lands were sold to raise revenue, and priests were put under government authority. (See Visual Sources 17.2 and 17.3, pp. 819 and 820, for images reflecting this more radical phase of the revolution.)

In 1793, King Louis XVI and his queen, Marie Antoinette, were executed, an act of regicide that shocked traditionalists all across Europe and marked a new stage in revolutionary violence (see Visual Source 17.4, p. 821). What followed was the Terror of 1793–1794. Under the leadership of Maximilien Robespierre and his Committee of Public Safety, tens of thousands deemed enemies of the revolution lost their lives on the guillotine. Shortly thereafter, Robespierre himself was arrested and guillotined, accused of leading France into tyranny and dictatorship. "The revolution," remarked one of its victims, "was devouring its own children."

Accompanying attacks on the old order were efforts to create a wholly new society, symbolized by a new calendar with the Year 1 in 1792, marking a fresh start

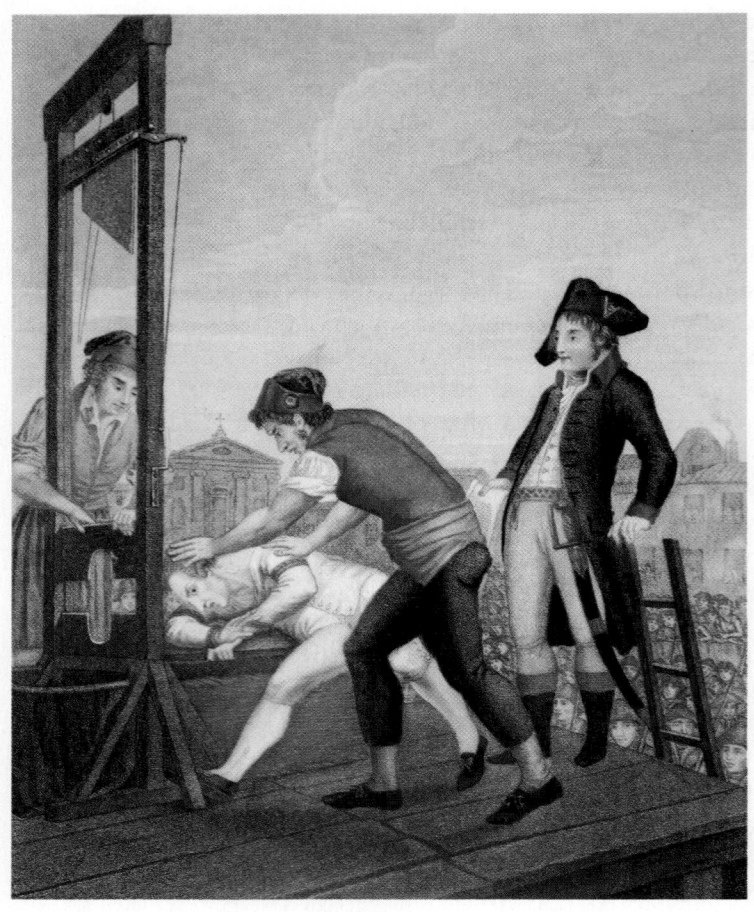

The Execution of Robespierre
The beheading of the radical leader Robespierre, who had himself brought thousands of others to the guillotine, marked a decisive turning point in the unfolding of the French Revolution and the end of its most violent phase. (Musée de la Revolution Française, Vizille, France/ Bridgeman Art Library)

for France. Unlike the Americans, who sought to restore or build upon earlier freedoms, French revolutionaries perceived themselves to be starting from scratch and looked to the future. For the first time in its history, the country became a republic and briefly passed universal male suffrage, although it was never implemented. The old administrative system was rationalized into eighty-three territorial departments, each with a new name. As revolutionary France prepared for war against its threatened and threatening neighbors, it created the world's largest army, with some 800,000 men, and all adult males were required to serve. Led by officers from the middle and even lower classes, this was an army of citizens representing the nation.

The impact of the revolution was felt in many ways. Streets got new names; monuments to the royal family were destroyed; titles vanished; people referred to one another as "citizen so-and-so." Real politics in the public sphere emerged for the first time as many people joined political clubs, took part in marches and demonstrations, served on local committees, and ran for public office. Common people, who had identified primarily with their local community, now began to think of themselves as belonging to a nation. The state replaced the Catholic Church as the place for registering births, marriages, and deaths, and revolutionary festivals substituted for church holidays.

More radical revolutionary leaders deliberately sought to convey a sense of new beginnings. A Festival of Unity held in 1793 to mark the first anniversary of the end of monarchy burned the crowns and scepters of the royal family in a huge bonfire while releasing a cloud of 3,000 white doves. The Cathedral of Notre Dame was temporarily turned into the Temple of Reason, while the "Hymn to Liberty" combined traditional church music with the explicit message of the Enlightenment:

Oh Liberty, sacred Liberty
Goddess of an enlightened people
Rule today within these walls.
Through you this temple is purified.
Liberty! Before you reason chases out deception,

Error flees, fanaticism is beaten down.
Our gospel is nature
And our cult is virtue.
To love one's country and one's brothers,
To serve the Sovereign People—
These are the sacred tenets
And pledge of a Republican.[8]

The French Revolution differed from the American Revolution also in the way its influence spread. At least until the United States became a world power at the end of the nineteenth century, what inspired others was primarily the example of its revolution and its constitution. French influence, by contrast, spread through conquest, largely under the leadership of Napoleon Bonaparte (ruled 1799–1814). A highly successful general who seized power in 1799, Napoleon is often credited with taming the revolution in the face of growing disenchantment with its more radical features and with the social conflicts it generated. He preserved many of its more moderate elements, such as civil equality, a secular law code, religious freedom, and promotion by merit, while reconciling with the Catholic Church and suppressing the revolution's more democratic elements in a military dictatorship. In short, Napoleon kept the revolution's emphasis on social equality but dispensed with liberty.

Like many of the revolution's ardent supporters, Napoleon was intent on spreading its benefits far and wide. In a series of brilliant military campaigns, his forces subdued most of Europe, thus creating the continent's largest empire since the days of the Romans (see Map 17.2). Within that empire, Napoleon imposed such revolutionary practices as ending feudalism, proclaiming equality of rights, insisting on religious toleration, codifying the laws, and rationalizing government administration. In many places, these reforms were welcomed, and seeds of further change were planted. But French domination was also resented and resisted, stimulating national consciousness throughout Europe. (See Visual Source 17.5, p. 822, for a German caricature of Napoleon.) That too was a seed that bore fruit in the century that followed. More immediately, national resistance, particularly from Russia and Britain, brought down Napoleon and his amazing empire by 1815 and marked an end to the era of the French Revolution, though not to the potency of its ideas.

The Haitian Revolution, 1791–1804

Nowhere did the example of the French Revolution echo more loudly than in the French Caribbean colony of Saint Domingue, later renamed Haiti (see Map 17.3, p. 791). Widely regarded as the richest colony in the world, Saint Domingue boasted 8,000 plantations, which in the late eighteenth century produced some 40 percent of the world's sugar and perhaps half of its coffee. A slave labor force of about 500,000 people made up the vast majority of the colony's population. Whites numbered about 40,000, sharply divided between very well-to-do plantation owners, merchants, and lawyers and those known as *petits blancs*, or poor whites. A third

■ **Comparison**

What was distinctive about the Haitian Revolution, both in world history generally and in the history of Atlantic revolutions?

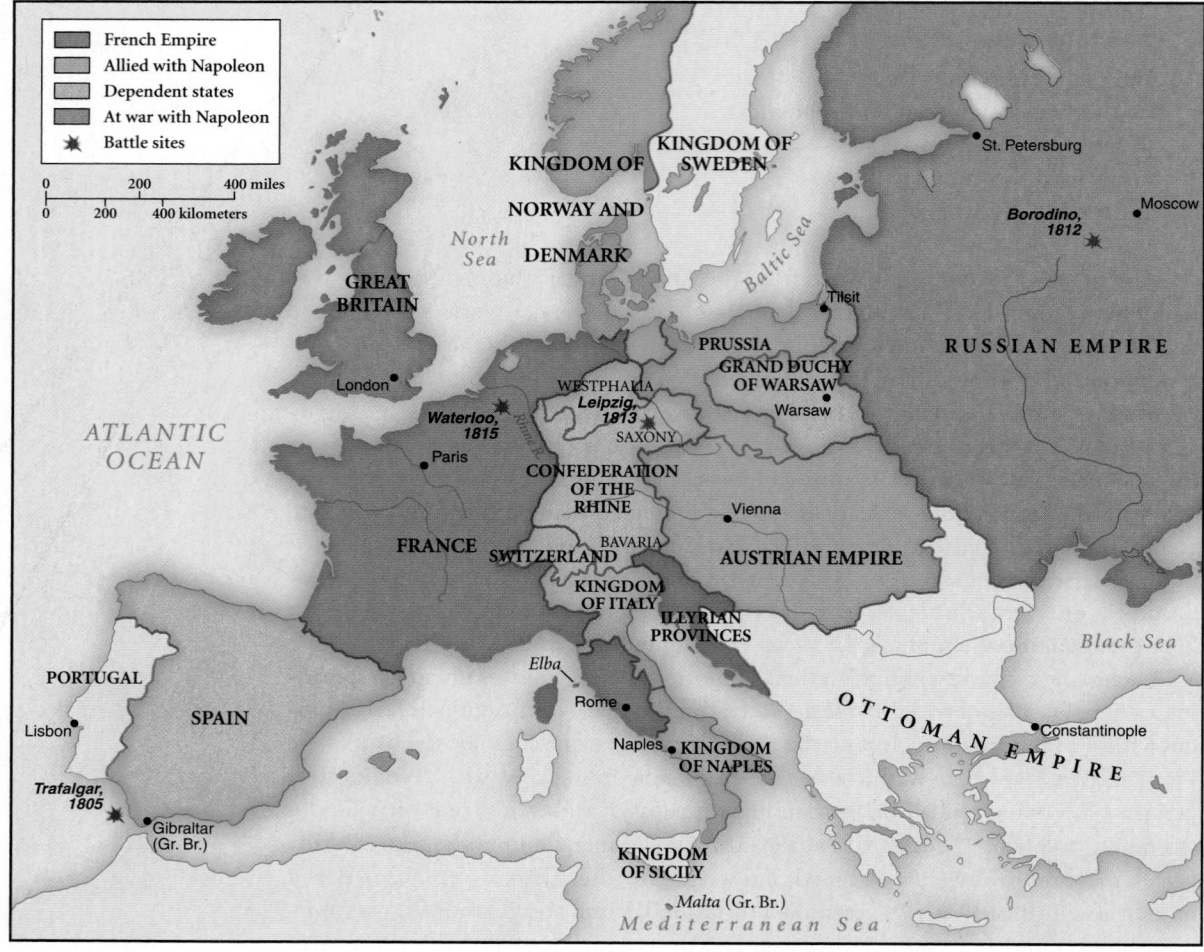

Map 17.2 Napoleon's European Empire
The French Revolution spawned a French empire, under Napoleon's leadership, that encompassed most of Europe and served to spread the principles of the revolution.

social group consisted of some 30,000 *gens de couleur libres* (free people of color), many of them of mixed-race background. Saint Domingue was a colonial society very different from the New England colonies or even the southern colonies of British North America. Given its enormous inequalities and its rampant exploitation, this Caribbean colony was primed for explosion.

In such a volatile setting, the ideas and example of the French Revolution lit several fuses and set in motion a spiral of violence that engulfed the colony for more than a decade. The principles of the revolution, however, meant different things to different people. To the *grands blancs*—the rich white landowners—it suggested greater autonomy for the colony and fewer economic restrictions on trade, but they resented the demands of the *petits blancs*, who sought equality of citizenship for all whites. Both white groups were adamantly opposed to the insistence of free people of color that the "rights of man" meant equal treatment for all free people regardless of race. To the slaves, the promise of the French Revolution was a personal freedom that threatened the entire slave labor system. In a massive revolt beginning in 1791, triggered by rumors that the French king had already declared an end to slavery, slaves burned 1,000 plantations and killed hundreds of whites as well as mixed-race people.

Soon warring factions of slaves, whites, and free people of color battled one another. Spanish and British forces, seeking to enlarge their own empires at the expense of the French, only added to the turmoil. Amid the confusion, brutality, and massacres of the 1790s, power gravitated toward the slaves, now led by the astute Toussaint Louverture, himself a former slave. He and his successor overcame internal resistance, outmaneuvered the foreign powers, and even defeated an attempt by Napoleon to reestablish French control.

When the dust settled in the early years of the nineteenth century, it was clear that something remarkable and unprecedented had taken place, a revolution unique in the Atlantic world and in world history. Socially, the last had become first. In the only completely successful slave revolt in recorded history, "the lowest order of the society—slaves—became equal, free, and independent citizens."[9] Politically, they had thrown off French colonial rule, becoming the second independent republic in the Americas and the first non-European state to emerge from Western colonialism. They renamed their country Haiti, a term meaning "mountainous" or "rugged" in the language of the original Taino people. It was a symbolic break with Europe and represented an effort to connect with the long-deceased native inhabitants of the land. Some, in fact, referred to themselves as "Incas." At the formal declaration of Haiti's independence on January 1, 1804, Jean-Jacques Dessalines, the new country's first head of state, declared: "I have given the French cannibals blood for blood; I have avenged America."[10] In defining all Haitians as "black," Haiti directly confronted an emerging racism, even as they declared all citizens legally equal regardless of race, color, or class. Economically, the country's plantation system, oriented wholly toward the export of sugar and coffee, had been largely destroyed. As whites fled or were killed, both private and state lands were redistributed among former slaves and free blacks, and Haiti became a nation of small-scale farmers producing mostly for their own needs, with a much smaller export sector.

PL. VII.

Wraak door het leger der zwarten genomen van de wreedheden, hun door de Franschen aangedaan.

The Haitian Revolution
This early-nineteenth-century engraving, entitled *Revenge Taken by the Black Army*, shows black Haitian soldiers hanging a large number of French soldiers, thus illustrating both the violence and the racial dimension of the upheaval in Haiti. (Schomburg Center, NY/Art Resource, NY)

The destructiveness of the Haitian Revolution, its bitter internal divisions of race and class, and continuing external opposition contributed much to Haiti's abiding poverty as well as to its authoritarian and unstable politics. In the early nineteenth century, however, it was a source of enormous hope and of great fear. Within weeks of the Haitian slave uprising in 1791, Jamaican slaves had composed songs in its honor, and it was not long before slave owners in the Caribbean and North America observed a new "insolence" in their slaves. Certainly its example inspired other slave rebellions, gave a boost to the dawning abolitionist movement, and has been a source of pride for people of African descent ever since.

To whites throughout the hemisphere, the cautionary saying "Remember Haiti" reflected a sense of horror at what had occurred there and a determination not to allow political change to reproduce that fearful outcome again. Particularly in Latin America, it injected a deep caution and social conservatism in the elites that led their countries to independence in the early nineteenth century. Ironically, though, the Haitian Revolution also led to a temporary expansion of slavery elsewhere. Cuban plantations and their slave workers considerably increased their production of sugar as that of Haiti declined. Moreover, Napoleon's defeat in Haiti persuaded him to sell to the United States the French territories known as the Louisiana Purchase, from which a number of "slave states" were carved out. In such contradictory ways did the echoes of the Haitian Revolution reverberate in the Atlantic world.

Spanish American Revolutions, 1810–1825

■ Connection
How were the Spanish American revolutions shaped by the American, French, and Haitian revolutions that happened earlier?

The final act in a half century of Atlantic revolutionary upheaval took place in the Spanish and Portuguese colonies of mainland Latin America (see Map 17.3). Their revolutions were shaped by preceding events in North America, France, and Haiti as well as by their own distinctive societies and historical experience. As in British North America, native-born elites in the Spanish colonies (known as *creoles*) were offended and insulted by the Spanish monarchy's efforts during the eighteenth century to exercise greater power over its colonies and to subject them to heavier taxes and tariffs. Creole intellectuals also had become familiar with ideas of popular sovereignty, republican government, and personal liberty derived from the European Enlightenment. But these conditions, similar to those in North America, led initially only to scattered and uncoordinated protests rather than to outrage, declarations of independence, war, and unity, as had occurred in the British colonies. Why did Spanish American struggles for independence occur decades later than those of British North America?

The settlers in the Spanish colonies had little tradition of local self-government such as had developed in North America, and their societies were far more authoritarian and divided by class. In addition, whites throughout Latin America were vastly outnumbered by Native Americans, people of African ancestry, and those of mixed race. All of this inhibited the growth of a movement for independence, despite the example of North America and similar provocations.

Despite their growing disenchantment with Spanish rule, creole elites did not so much generate a revolution as have one thrust upon them by events in Europe. In 1808, Napoleon invaded Spain and Portugal, deposing the Spanish king Ferdinand VII and forcing the Portuguese royal family into exile in Brazil. With legitimate royal authority now in disarray, Latin Americans were forced to take action. The outcome, ultimately, was independence for the various states of Latin America, established almost everywhere by 1826. But the way in which it occurred and the kind of societies it generated differed greatly from the experience of both North America and Haiti.

The process lasted more than twice as long as it did in North America, partly because Latin American societies were so conflicted and divided by class, race, and region. In North America, violence was directed almost entirely against the British and seldom spilled over into domestic disputes, except for

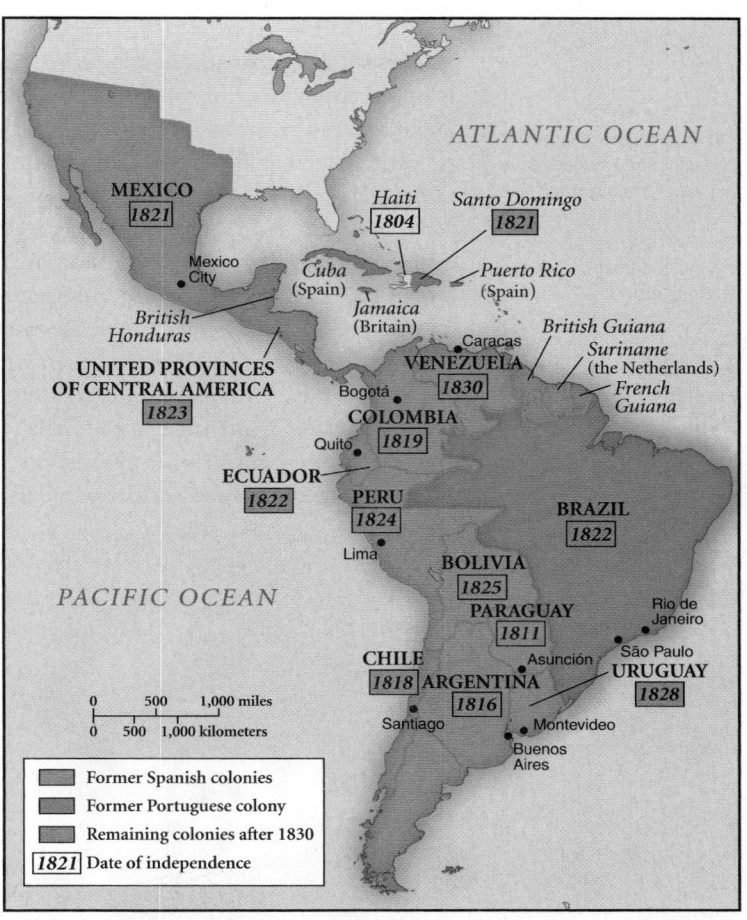

Map 17.3 Latin American Independence
With the exception of Haiti, Latin American revolutions brought independence to new states but offered little social change or political opportunity for the vast majority of people.

some bloody skirmishes with loyalists. Even then, little lasting hostility occurred, and some loyalists were able to reenter U.S. society after independence was achieved. In Mexico, by contrast, the move toward independence began in 1810 in a peasant insurrection, driven by hunger for land and by high food prices and led successively by two priests, Miguel Hidalgo and José Morelos. Alarmed by the social radicalism of the Hidalgo–Morelos rebellion, creole landowners, with the support of the Church, raised an army and crushed the insurgency. Later that alliance of clergy and creole elites brought Mexico to a more socially controlled independence in 1821. Such violent conflict among Latin Americans, along lines of race, class, and ideology, accompanied the struggle against Spain in many places.

The entire independence movement in Latin America took place under the shadow of a great fear—the dread of social rebellion from below—that had little counterpart in North America. The great violence of the French and Haitian revolutions was a lesson to Latin American elites that political change could easily get out of hand and was fraught with danger to themselves. An abortive rebellion of

Native Americans in Peru in the early 1780s, made in the name of the last Inca emperor, Tupac Amaru, as well as the Hidalgo-Morelos rebellion in Mexico, reminded whites that they sat atop a potentially explosive society, most of whose members were exploited and oppressed people of color.

And yet the creole sponsors of independence movements, both regional military leaders such as Simón Bolívar and José de San Martín and their civilian counterparts, required the support of "the people," or at least some of them, if they were to prevail against Spanish forces. The answer to this dilemma was found in nativism, which cast all of those born in the Americas—creoles, Indians, mixed-race people, free blacks—as *Americanos*, while the enemy was defined as those born in Spain or Portugal.[11] This was no easy task, because many creole whites and mestizos saw themselves as Spanish and because great differences of race, culture, and wealth separated the Americanos. Nonetheless, nationalist leaders made efforts to mobilize people of color into the struggle with promises of freedom, the end of legal restrictions, and social advancement. Many of these leaders were genuine liberals, who had been influenced by the ideals of the Enlightenment, the French Revolution and Spanish liberalism. In the long run, however, few of those promises were kept. Certainly the lower classes, Native Americans, and slaves benefited little from independence. "The imperial state was destroyed in Spanish America," concluded one historian, "but colonial society was preserved."[12]

A further difference in the Latin American situation lay in the apparent impossibility of uniting the various Spanish colonies, despite several failed efforts to do so. Thus no United States of Latin America emerged. Distances among the colonies and geographic obstacles to effective communication were certainly greater than in the eastern seaboard colonies of North America, and their longer colonial experience had given rise to distinct and deeply rooted regional identities. Shortly before his death in 1830, the "great liberator" Bolívar, who so admired George Washington and had so ardently hoped for greater unity, wrote in despair to a friend: "[Latin] America is ungovernable. Those who serve the revolution plough the sea."[13] (See Document 17.3, pp. 810–11, for Bolívar's views on the struggle for independence.)

Simón Bolívar
Among the heroic figures of Spanish American independence movements, none was more significant than Simón Bolívar (1783–1830), shown here in a moment of triumph entering his hometown of Caracas in present-day Venezuela. But Bolívar was immensely disappointed in the outcomes of independence as his dream of a unified South America perished amid the rivalries of separate countries. (akg-images)

The aftermath of independence in Latin America marked a reversal in the earlier relationship of the two American continents. The United States, which began its history as the leftover "dregs" of the New World, grew increasingly wealthy, industrialized, democratic, internationally influential, and generally stable, with the major exception of the Civil War. The Spanish colonies, which took shape in the wealthiest areas and among the most sophisticated cultures of the Americas, were widely regarded as the more promising region compared to the backwater reputation of England's North American territories. But in the nineteenth century, as newly independent countries in both regions launched a new phase of their histories, those in Latin America became relatively underdeveloped, impoverished, undemocratic, politically unstable, and dependent on foreign technology and investment (see pp. 846–48). Begun in broadly similar circumstances, the Latin American and North American revolutions occurred in very different societies and gave rise to very different historical trajectories.

Echoes of Revolution

The core values of the Atlantic revolutions continued to reverberate well after those upheavals had been concluded. Within Europe, which was generally dominated by conservative governments following Napoleon's final defeat, smaller revolutions erupted in 1830, more widely in 1848, and in Paris in 1870. They expressed ideas of republicanism, greater social equality, and national liberation from foreign rule. Such ideas and social pressures pushed the major states of Western Europe, the United States, and Argentina to enlarge their voting publics, generally granting universal male suffrage by 1914. An abortive attempt to establish a constitutional regime even broke out in autocratic Russia in 1825. It was led by military officers who had been influenced by ideals of the Enlightenment and the French Revolution while campaigning in Europe against Napoleon.

Beyond this limited extension of political democracy, three movements arose to challenge continuing patterns of oppression or exclusion. Abolitionists sought the end of slavery; nationalists hoped to do away with disunity and foreign rule; and feminists tried to end, or at least mitigate, male dominance. Each of these movements bore the marks of the Atlantic revolutions, and although they took root first in Europe, each came to have a global significance in the centuries that followed.

The Abolition of Slavery

In little more than a century, from roughly 1780 to 1890, a remarkable transformation occurred in human affairs as slavery, widely practiced and little condemned since the beginning of civilization, lost its legitimacy and was largely ended. In this amazing process, the ideas and practices of the Atlantic revolutions played an important role.

Enlightenment thinkers in eighteenth-century Europe had become increasingly critical of slavery as a violation of the natural rights of every person, and the public

■ **Change**

What accounts for the end of Atlantic slavery during the nineteenth century?

pronouncements of the American and French revolutions about liberty and equality likewise focused attention on this obvious breach of those principles. To this secular antislavery thinking was added an increasingly vociferous religious voice, expressed first by Quakers and then Protestant evangelicals in Britain and the United States. To them slavery was "repugnant to our religion" and a "crime in the sight of God."[14] What made these moral arguments more widely acceptable was the growing belief that, contrary to much earlier thinking, slavery was not essential for economic progress. After all, England and New England were among the most prosperous regions of the Western world in the early nineteenth century, and both were based on free labor. Slavery in this view was out of date, unnecessary in the new era of industrial technology and capitalism. Thus moral virtue and economic success were joined. It was an attractive argument. (See Document 17.4, pp. 811–13, for the views of the U.S. abolitionist Fredrick Douglass.)

The actions of slaves themselves likewise hastened the end of slavery. The dramatically successful Haitian Revolution was followed by three major rebellions in the British West Indies, all of which were harshly crushed, in the early nineteenth century. They demonstrated clearly that slaves were hardly "contented," and the brutality with which the revolts were suppressed appalled British public opinion. Growing numbers of the British public came to feel that slavery was "not only morally wrong and economically inefficient, but also politically unwise."[15]

These various strands of thinking—secular, religious, economic, and political— came together in abolitionist movements, most powerfully in Britain, which brought growing pressure on governments to close down the trade in slaves and then to ban slavery itself. In the late eighteenth century, such a movement gained wide support among middle- and working-class people in Britain. Its techniques included pamphlets with heartrending descriptions of slavery, numerous petitions to parliament, lawsuits, boycotts of slave-produced sugar, and frequent public meetings, some of which dramatically featured the testimony of Africans who had experienced the horrors of slavery firsthand. In 1807, Britain forbade the sale of slaves within its empire and in 1834 emancipated those who remained enslaved. Over the next half century, other nations followed suit, responding to growing international pressure, particularly from Britain, then the world's leading economic and military power. British naval vessels patrolled the Atlantic, intercepted illegal slave ships, and freed their human cargoes in a small West African settlement called Freetown, in present-day Sierra Leone. Following their independence, most Latin American countries abolished slavery by the 1850s. Brazil, in 1888, was the last to do so, bringing more than four centuries of Atlantic slavery to an end. A roughly similar set of conditions—fear of rebellion, economic inefficiency, and moral concerns—persuaded the Russian tsar to free the many serfs of that huge country in 1861, although there it occurred by fiat from above rather than from growing public pressure.

None of this happened easily. Slave economies continued to flourish well into the nineteenth century, and plantation owners vigorously resisted the onslaught of abolitionists. So did slave traders, both European and African, who together shipped

Abolitionism
This antislavery medallion was commissioned in the late eighteenth century by English Quakers, who were among the earliest participants in the abolitionist movement. Its famous motto, "Am I not a man and a brother," reflected both Enlightenment and Christian values of human equality. (The Art Archive)

millions of additional captives, mostly to Cuba and Brazil, long after the trade had been declared illegal. Osei Bonsu, the powerful king of the West African state of Asante, was puzzled as to why the British would no longer buy his slaves. "If they think it bad now," he asked a local British representative in 1820, "why did they think it good before?"[16] (See Document 15.4, pp. 708–09.) Nowhere was the persistence of slavery more evident and resistance to abolition more intense than in the southern states of the United States. It was the only slaveholding society in which the end of slavery occurred through such a bitter, prolonged, and highly destructive civil war (1861–1865).

The end of Atlantic slavery during the nineteenth century surely marked a major and quite rapid turn in the world's social history and in the moral thinking of humankind. Nonetheless, the outcomes of that process were often surprising and far from the expectations of abolitionists or the newly freed slaves. In most cases, the economic lives of the former slaves did not improve dramatically. Nowhere in the Atlantic world, except Haiti, did a redistribution of land follow the end of slavery. But freedmen everywhere desperately sought economic autonomy on their own land, and in parts of the Caribbean such as Jamaica, where unoccupied land was available, independent peasant agriculture proved possible for some. Elsewhere, as in the southern United States, various forms of legally free but highly dependent labor, such as sharecropping, emerged to replace slavery and to provide low-paid and often indebted workers for planters. The understandable reluctance of former slaves to continue working in plantation agriculture created labor shortages and set in motion a huge new wave of global migration. Large numbers of indentured servants from India and China were imported into the Caribbean, Peru, South Africa, Hawaii, Malaya, and elsewhere to work in mines, on sugar plantations, and in construction projects. There they often toiled in conditions not far removed from slavery itself.

Newly freed people did not achieve anything close to political equality, except in Haiti. White planters, farmers, and mine owners retained local authority in the Caribbean. In the southern United States, a brief period of "radical reconstruction," during which newly freed blacks did enjoy full political rights and some power, was followed by harsh segregation laws, denial of voting rights, a wave of lynching, and a virulent racism that lasted well into the twentieth century. For most former slaves, emancipation usually meant, in the words of a well-known historian, "nothing but freedom."[17]

Unlike the situation in the Americas, the end of serfdom in Russia transferred to the peasants a considerable portion of the nobles' land, but the need to pay for this land with "redemption dues" and the rapid growth of Russia's rural population ensured that most peasants remained impoverished and politically volatile. In both West and East Africa, the closing of the external slave trade decreased the price of slaves and increased their use within African societies to produce the export crops that the world economy now sought. Thus, as Europeans imposed colonial rule on Africa in the late nineteenth century, one of their justifications for doing so was the need to emancipate enslaved Africans. Europeans proclaiming the need to end slavery in

■ **Change**
How did the end of slavery affect the lives of the former slaves?

a continent from which they had extracted slaves for more than four centuries was surely among the more ironic outcomes of the abolitionist process.

Nations and Nationalism

■ Explanation
What accounts for the growth of nationalism as a powerful political and personal identity in the nineteenth century?

In addition to contributing to the end of slavery, the Atlantic revolutions also gave new prominence to a relatively recent kind of human community—the nation. By the end of the twentieth century, the idea that humankind was divided into separate nations, each with a distinct culture and territory and deserving an independent political life, was so widespread as to seem natural and timeless. And yet for most of human experience, states did not usually coincide with the culture of a particular people, for all of the great empires and many smaller states governed culturally diverse societies. Few people considered rule by foreigners itself a terrible offense because the most important identities and loyalties were local, limited to clan, village, or region, with only modest connection to the larger state or empire that governed them. People might on occasion consider themselves part of larger religious communities (such as Christians or Muslims) or ethnolinguistic groupings such as Greek, Arab, or Mayan, but such identities rarely provided the basis for enduring states.

All of that began to change during the era of Atlantic revolutions. Independence movements in both North and South America were made in the name of new nations. The French Revolution declared that sovereignty lay with "the people," and its leaders mobilized this people to defend the "French nation" against its many external enemies. In 1793, the revolutionary government of France declared a mass conscription (*levée en masse*) with this stirring call to service:

> Henceforth, until the enemies have been driven from the territory of the Republic, all the French are in permanent requisition for army service. The young men shall go to battle; the married men shall forge arms and transport provisions; the women shall make tents and clothes, and shall serve in the hospitals; the children shall turn old linen into lint; the old men shall repair to the public places, to stimulate the courage of the warriors and preach the unity of the Republic and the hatred of kings.[18]

Moreover, Napoleon's conquests likewise stimulated national resistance in many parts of Europe. European states had long competed and fought with one another, but increasingly in the nineteenth century, those states were inhabited by people who felt themselves to be citizens of a nation, deeply bound to their fellows by ties of blood, culture, or common experience, not simply common subjects of a ruling dynasty. It was a novel form of political community.

Europe's modern transformation also facilitated nationalism, even as older identities and loyalties eroded. Science weakened the hold of religion on some. Migration to industrial cities or abroad diminished allegiance to local communities. At the same time, printing and the publishing industry standardized a variety of dialects

Snapshot   **Key Moments in the Growth of Nationalism**

Independence of colonies in the Americas	1776–1825
Mass conscription to defend the French Revolution	1793
Wars of resistance to Napoleonic empire	1800–1815
Greek independence from Ottoman Empire	1830
Polish insurrections against Russian rule	1830, 1863
Young Ireland movement begins	1842
First Ukrainian nationalist organization established	1846
Hungarian national uprising against Austrian Habsburg rule	1848
Unification of Italy and Germany	1870, 1871
Egyptian revolt against British and French imperialism	1880
Founding of Indian National Congress	1885
Political Zionism emerges, seeking a homeland in Palestine for Jews	1890s

into a smaller number of European languages, a process that allowed a growing reading public to think of themselves as members of a common linguistic group or nation. All of this encouraged political and cultural leaders to articulate an appealing idea of their particular nations and ensured a growing circle of people receptive to such ideas. Thus the idea of the "nation" was constructed or even invented, but it was often presented as a reawakening of older linguistic or cultural identities, and it certainly drew upon the songs, dances, folktales, historical experiences, and collective memories of earlier cultures (see Map 17.4).

Whatever its precise origins, nationalism proved to be an infinitely flexible and enormously powerful idea in the nineteenth-century Atlantic world and beyond. It inspired the political unification of both Germany and Italy, gathering their previously fragmented peoples into new states by 1871. It encouraged Greeks and Serbs to assert their independence from the Ottoman Empire; Czechs and Hungarians to demand more autonomy within the Austrian Empire; Poles and Ukrainians to become more aware of their oppression within the Russian Empire; and the Irish to seek "home rule" and separation from Great Britain. By the end of the nineteenth century, a small Zionist movement, seeking a homeland in Palestine, had emerged among Europe's frequently persecuted Jews. Popular nationalism made the normal rivalry among European states even more acute and fueled a highly competitive drive for colonies in Asia and Africa. The immensity of the suffering and sacrifice that nationalism generated in Europe was vividly disclosed during the horrors of World War I.

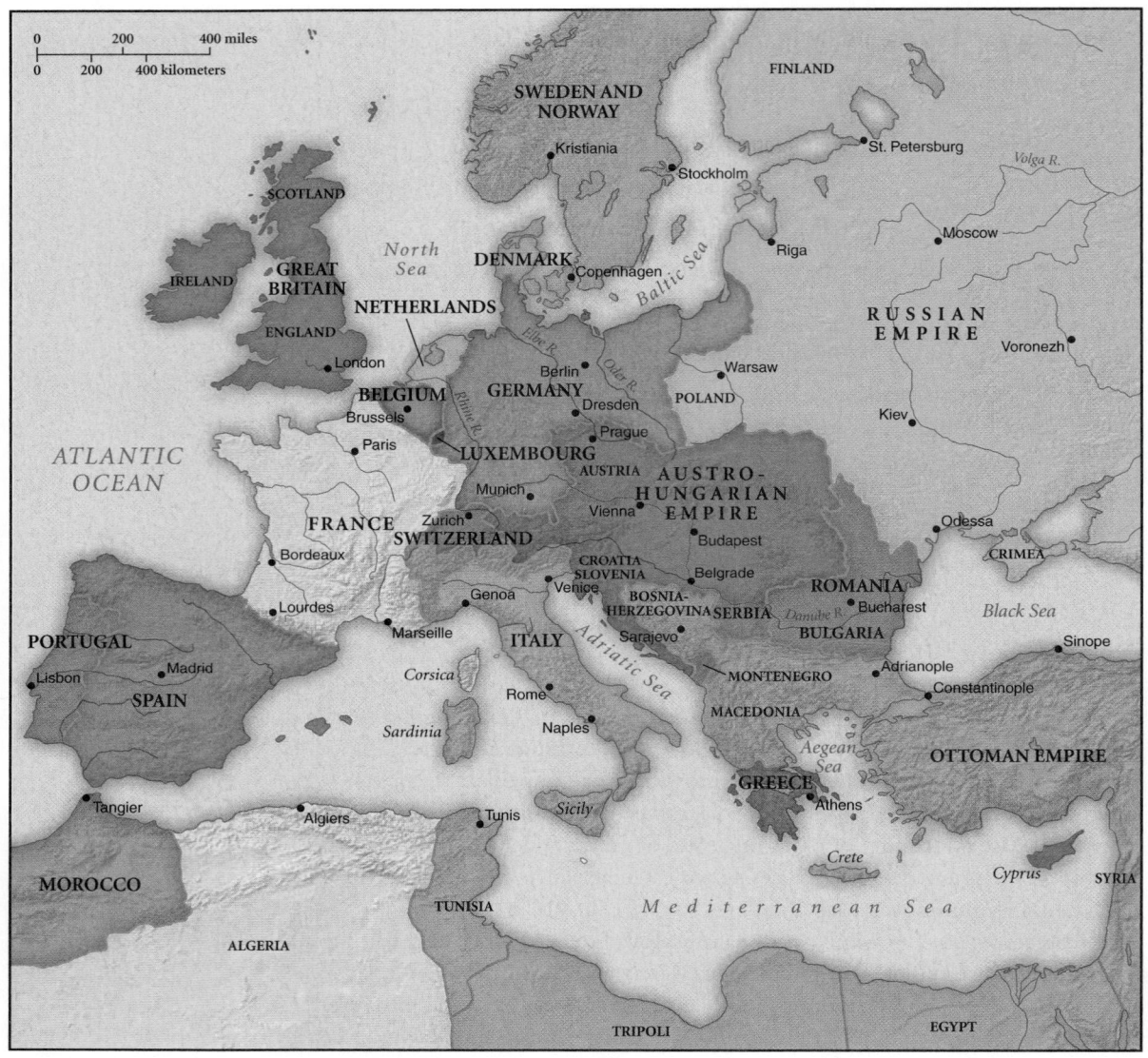

Map 17.4 The Nations and Empires of Europe, ca. 1880

By the end of the nineteenth century, the national principle had substantially reshaped the map of Europe, especially in the unification of Germany and Italy. However, several major empires (Russian, Austro-Hungarian, and Ottoman) remained, each with numerous subject peoples who likewise sought national independence.

Governments throughout the Western world claimed now to act on behalf of their nations and deliberately sought to instill national loyalties in their citizens through schools, public rituals, the mass media, and military service. Russian authorities, for example, imposed the use of the Russian language, even in parts of the country where it was not widely spoken. They succeeded, however, only in producing a greater awareness of Ukrainian, Polish, and Finnish nationalism.

As it became more prominent in the nineteenth century, nationalism took on a variety of political ideologies. Some supporters of liberal democracy and representative government, as in France or the United States, saw nationalism, with its emphasis on "the people," as an aid to their aspirations toward wider involvement in political life. Often called "civic nationalism," such a view identified the nation with a particular territory and maintained that people of various cultural backgrounds could assimilate into the dominant culture, as in the process of "becoming American." Other versions of nationalism, in Germany for example, sometimes defined the nation in racial terms, which excluded those who did not share a common ancestry, such as Jews. In the hands of conservatives, nationalism could be used to combat socialism and feminism, for those movements only divided the nation along class or gender lines. Thus nationalism generated endless controversy because it provided no clear answer to the questions of who belonged to the nation or who should speak for it.

Nor was nationalism limited to the Euro-American world in the nineteenth century. An "Egypt for the Egyptians" movement arose in the 1870s as British and French intervention in Egyptian affairs deepened. When Japan likewise confronted European aggression in the second half of the nineteenth century, its long sense of itself as a distinct culture was readily transformed into an assertive modern nationalism.

Nationalism in Poland
In the eighteenth century, Poland had been divided among Prussia, Austria, and Russia and disappeared as a separate and independent state. Polish nationalism found expression in the nineteenth century in a series of revolts, among which was a massive uprising in 1863, directed against Poland's Russian occupiers. This famous painting by Polish artist Jan Matejko shows a crowd of Polish prisoners awaiting transportation to imprisonment in Siberia, while Russian military officers supervise a blacksmith, who fastens fetters on a woman representing Poland. (Courtesy, Czartoryski Museum, Cracow)

Small groups of Western-educated men in British-ruled India began to think of their enormously diverse country as a single nation. The Indian National Congress, established in 1885, gave expression to this idea. The notion of the Ottoman Empire as a Turkish national state rather than a Muslim or dynastic empire took hold among a few people. By the end of the nineteenth century, some Chinese intellectuals began to think in terms of a Chinese nation beset both by a foreign ruling dynasty and by predatory Europeans. Along the West African coast, the idea of an "African nation" stirred among a handful of freed slaves and missionary-educated men. Although Egyptian and Japanese nationalism gained broad support, elsewhere in Asia and Africa such movements would have to wait until the twentieth century, when they exploded with enormous power on the stage of world history.

Feminist Beginnings

■ Significance
What were the achievements and limitations of nineteenth-century feminism?

A third echo of the Atlantic revolutions lay in the emergence of a feminist movement. Although scattered voices had earlier challenged patriarchy, never before had an organized and substantial group of women called into question this most fundamental and accepted feature of all preindustrial civilizations—the subordination of women to men. But in the century following the French Revolution, such a challenge took shape, especially in Europe and North America. Then, in the twentieth century, feminist thinking transformed "the way in which women and men work, play, think, dress, worship, vote, reproduce, make love and make war."[19] How did this extraordinary process get launched in the nineteenth century?

Thinkers of the European Enlightenment had challenged many ancient traditions, including on occasion that of women's intrinsic inferiority. The French writer Condorcet, for example, called for "the complete destruction of those prejudices that have established an inequality of rights between the sexes." The French Revolution then raised the possibility of re-creating human societies on new foundations. Many women participated in these events, and a few insisted, unsuccessfully, that the revolutionary ideals of liberty and equality must include women. In neighboring England, the French Revolution stimulated the writer Mary Wollstonecraft to pen her famous *Vindication of the Rights of Woman*, one of the earliest expressions of a feminist consciousness (see Document 17.2, pp. 808–09).

Within the growing middle classes of industrializing societies, more women found both educational opportunities and some freedom from household drudgery. Such women increasingly took part in temperance movements, charities, abolitionism, and missionary work, as well as socialist and pacifist organizations. Some of their working-class sisters became active trade unionists. On both sides of the Atlantic, small numbers of these women began to develop a feminist consciousness that viewed women as individuals with rights equal to those of men.[20] Others, particularly in France, based their claims less on abstract notions of equality and more on the distinctive role of women as mothers. "It is above all this holy function of motherhood...," wrote one advocate of "maternal feminism," "which requires that women watch over the futures of their children and gives women the right to intervene not only in all acts of civil life, but also in all acts of political life."[21] The first organized expression of this new feminism took place at a women's rights conference in Seneca Falls, New York, in 1848. At that meeting, Elizabeth Cady Stanton drafted a statement that began by paraphrasing the Declaration of Independence: "We hold these truths to be self-evident, that all men and women are created equal."

From the beginning, feminism was a transatlantic movement in which European and American women attended the same conferences, corresponded regularly, and read one another's work. Access to schools, universities, and the professions were among their major concerns as growing numbers of women sought these previously unavailable opportunities. The more radical among them refused to take their husbands' surname or wore trousers under their skirts. Elizabeth Cady Stanton published a Women's Bible, eliminating the parts she found offensive. As heirs to the French Revolution, feminists ardently believed in progress and insisted that it must now include a radical transformation of the position of women.

By the 1870s, feminist movements in the West were focusing primarily on the issue of suffrage and were gaining a growing constituency. Now many ordinary middle-class housewives and working-class mothers joined their better-educated sisters in the movement. By 1914, some 100,000 women took part in French feminist organizations, while the National American Woman Suffrage Association claimed 2 million members. Most operated through peaceful protest and persuasion, but the British Women's Social and Political Union organized a campaign of violence that included blowing up railroad stations, slashing works of art, and smashing department store windows. One British activist, Emily Davison, threw herself in front of the king's horse during a race in Britain in 1913 and was trampled to death. By the beginning of the twentieth century in the most highly industrialized countries of the West, the women's movement had become a mass movement.

That movement had some effect. By 1900, upper- and middle-class women had gained entrance to universities, though in small numbers, and women's literacy rates were growing steadily. In the United States, a number of states passed legislation allowing women to manage and control their own property and wages, separate from their husbands. Divorce laws were liberalized in some places. Professions such as medicine opened to a few, and teaching beckoned to many more. In Britain, Florence Nightingale professionalized nursing and attracted thousands of women into it, while Jane Addams in the United States virtually invented social work, which also became a female-dominated profession. Progress was slower in the political domain. In 1893, New Zealand became the first country to give the vote to all adult women; Finland followed in 1906. Elsewhere widespread voting rights for women in national elections were not achieved until after World War I and in France not until 1945.

Beyond these concrete accomplishments, the movement prompted an unprecedented discussion about the role of women in modern society. In Henrik Ibsen's play *A Doll's House* (1879), the heroine, Nora, finding herself in a loveless and oppressive marriage, leaves both her husband and her children. European audiences were

Women's Suffrage
What began as a few isolated voices of feminist protest in the early nineteenth century had become by the end of the century a mass movement in the United States and Western Europe. Here, in a photograph of an American suffrage parade in 1912, is an illustration of that movement in action. (The Granger Collection, New York)

riveted, and many were outraged. Writers, doctors, and journalists addressed previously taboo sexual topics, including homosexuality and birth control. Socialists too found themselves divided about women's issues. Did the women's movement distract from the class solidarity that Marxism proclaimed, or did it provide added energy to the workers' cause? Feminists themselves disagreed about the proper basis for women's rights. Some took their stand on the modern idea of human equality: "Whatever is right for a man is right for a woman." Others argued that women's traditional role as mothers, the guardians of family life and social virtue, provided the stronger case for women's rights.

Not surprisingly, feminism provoked bitter opposition. Some academic and medical experts argued that the strains of education and life in the world outside the home would cause serious reproductive damage and as a consequence depopulate the nation. Thus feminists were viewed as selfish, willing to sacrifice the family or even the nation while pursuing their individual goals. Some saw suffragists, like Jews and socialists, as "a foreign body in our national life." Never before in any society had such a passionate and public debate about the position of women erupted. It was a novel feature of Western historical experience in the aftermath of the Atlantic revolutions.

Like nationalism, a concern with women's rights spread beyond Western Europe and the United States, though less widely. An overtly feminist newspaper was established in Brazil in 1852, and an independent school for girls was founded in Mexico in 1869. A handful of Japanese women and men, including the empress Haruko, raised issues about marriage, family planning, and especially education as the country began its modernizing process after 1868, but the state soon cracked down firmly, forbidding women from joining political parties or even attending political meetings. In Russia, the most radical feminist activists operated within socialist or anarchist circles, targeting the oppressive tsarist regime. Within the Islamic world and in China, some modernists came to feel that education and a higher status for women strengthened the nation in its struggles for development and independence and therefore deserved support. (See Document 17.5, pp. 814–16, for an example from the Dutch East Indies.) Huda Sharawi, founder of the first feminist organization in Egypt, returned to Cairo in 1923 from an international conference in Italy and threw her veil into the sea. Many upper-class Egyptian women soon followed her example.

Nowhere did nineteenth-century feminism have thoroughly revolutionary consequences. But as an outgrowth of the French and Industrial revolutions, it raised issues that echoed repeatedly and more loudly in the century that followed.

Reflections: Revolutions Pro and Con

Not long before he died in 1976, the Chinese revolutionary and communist leader Zhou Enlai was asked what he thought about the French Revolution. His famous reply—"It's too early to say"—highlights the endless controversies that revolutions everywhere have spawned. Long after the dust had settled from these Atlantic upheavals, their legacies have continued to provoke controversy. Were these revolutions necessary? Did they really promote the freedoms that they advertised? Did their benefits outweigh their costs in blood and treasure?

To the people who made these revolutions, benefited from them, or subsequently supported them, they represented an opening to new worlds of human possibility, while sweeping away old worlds of oppression, exploitation, and privilege. Modern revolutionaries acted on the basis of Enlightenment ideas, believing that the structure of human societies was not forever ordained by God or tradition and that it was both possible and necessary to reconstruct those societies. They also saw themselves as correcting ancient and enduring injustices. To those who complained about the violence of revolutions, supporters pointed to the violence that maintained the status quo and the unwillingness of privileged classes to accommodate changes that threatened those privileges. It was persistent injustice that made revolution necessary and perhaps inevitable.

To their victims, critics, and opponents, revolutions appeared quite different. Conservatives generally viewed human societies, not as machines whose parts could be easily rearranged, but as organisms that evolved slowly. Efforts at radical and sudden change only invited disaster, as the unrestrained violence of the French Revolution at its height demonstrated. The brutality and bitterness of the Haitian Revolution arguably contributed much to the unhappy future of that country. Furthermore, critics charged that revolutions were largely unnecessary, since societies were in fact changing. France was becoming a modern society and feudalism was largely gone well before the revolution exploded. Slavery was ended peacefully in many places, and democratic reform proceeded gradually throughout the nineteenth century. Was this not a preferable alternative to that of revolutionary upheaval?

Historians too struggle with the passions of revolution—both pro and con—as they seek to understand the origins and consequences of these momentous events. Were revolutions the product of misery, injustice, and oppression? Or did they reflect the growing weakness of established authorities, the arrival of new ideas, or the presence of small groups of radical activists able to fan the little fires of ordinary discontent into revolutionary conflagrations? The outcomes of revolutions have been as contentious as their beginnings. Did the American Revolution enable the growth of the United States as an economic and political "great power"? Did the Haitian Revolution stimulate the later end of slavery elsewhere in the Atlantic world? Did the French Revolution and the threat of subsequent revolutions encourage the democratic reforms that followed in the nineteenth century? Such questions have been central to an understanding of eighteenth-century revolutions as well as to those that followed in Russia, China, and elsewhere in the twentieth century.

Second Thoughts

What's the Significance?

To assess your mastery of the material in this chapter, visit the **Student Center** at bedfordstmartins.com/strayer.

North American Revolution
French Revolution
Declaration of the Rights of Man and Citizen
Napoleon Bonaparte

Haitian Revolution
Spanish American revolutions
abolitionist movement
nationalism

Vindication of the Rights of Woman
maternal feminism
Elizabeth Cady Stanton

Big Picture Questions

1. Make a chart comparing the North American, French, Haitian, and Spanish American revolutions. What categories of comparison would be most appropriate to include?
2. Do revolutions originate in oppression and injustice, in the weakening of political authorities, in new ideas, or in the activities of small groups of determined activists?
3. "The influence of revolutions endured long after they ended." To what extent does this chapter support or undermine this idea?
4. In what ways did the Atlantic revolutions and their echoes give a new and distinctive shape to the emerging societies of nineteenth-century Europe and the Americas?

Next Steps: For Further Study

Benedict Anderson, *Imagined Communities: Reflections on the Origins and Spread of Nationalism* (1991). A now-classic though controversial examination of the process by which national identities were created.

Bonnie S. Anderson, *Joyous Greetings: The First International Women's Movement, 1830–1860* (2000). Describes the beginnings of transatlantic feminism.

Laurent Dubois and John Garrigus, *Slave Revolution in the Caribbean, 1789–1804* (2006). A brief and up-to-date summary of the Haitian Revolution, combined with a number of documents.

Susan Dunn, *Sister Revolutions* (1999). A stimulating comparative study of the American and French revolutions.

Eric Hobsbawm, *The Age of Revolution, 1789–1848* (1999). A highly respected survey by a well-known British historian.

Lynn Hunt, ed., *The French Revolution and Human Rights* (1996). A collection of documents, with a fine introduction by a prominent scholar.

"Liberty, Equality, Fraternity: Exploring the French Revolution," http://chnm.gmu.edu/revolution/browse/images/#. A collection of cartoons, paintings, and artifacts illustrating the French Revolution.

For Web sites and additional documents related to this chapter, see **Make History** at bedfordstmartins.com/strayer.

Documents

Considering the Evidence:
Claiming Rights

In the discourse of the age of revolution, no idea had a more enduring resonance than that of "rights"—natural rights, political and civic rights, and "the rights of man" or, in a more recent expression, "human rights." However those rights were defined, they were understood as both natural and universal. They were considered inherent in the human condition rather than granted by some authority, and they were envisioned as being the same for everyone rather than depending on a person's birth, rank, or status in society. Growing out of the European Enlightenment (see pp. 742–44), this understanding of "rights" was genuinely revolutionary, challenging almost all notions of government and society prior to the late eighteenth century. But even among supporters, the idea of human rights was highly controversial. What precisely were these rights? Did they support or contradict one another? Did they really apply equally to all persons? How should they be established and maintained? Such questions were central to this age of revolution and have informed much of the world's political history ever since.[22]

Document 17.1

The French Revolution and the "Rights of Man"

The most prominent example of the language of rights found expression during the French Revolution in the Declaration of the Rights of Man and Citizen. It was a document hammered out in the French National Assembly early in that revolutionary upheaval and adopted at the end of August 1789 (see pp. 784–87). Ever since, it has been viewed as the philosophical core of the French Revolution.

Clearly the French document bears similarities to the language of the U.S. Declaration of Independence, for both drew upon the ideas of the European Enlightenment. Furthermore, Thomas Jefferson, who largely wrote the U.S. Declaration, served as the ambassador to France at this time and was in close contact with Marquis de Lafayette, the principal author of the French

Declaration. And Lafayette in turn had earlier served with the American revolutionary forces seeking independence from England.

- What purposes did the writers of the Declaration expect it to fulfill?

- What specific rights are spelled out in this document? What rights does it omit?

- What was revolutionary about the Declaration? What grievances against the old regime did the declaration reflect?

- What grounds for debate or controversy can you indentify within the Declaration?

The Declaration of the Rights of Man and Citizen
1789

The representatives of the French people, constituted as a National Assembly, and considering that ignorance, neglect, or contempt of the rights of man are the sole causes of public misfortunes and governmental corruption, have resolved to set forth in a solemn declaration the natural, inalienable and sacred rights of man....

1. Men are born and remain free and equal in rights. Social distinctions may be based only on common utility.

2. The purpose of all political association is the preservation of the natural and imprescriptible rights of man. These rights are liberty, property, security, and resistance to oppression.

3. The principle of all sovereignty rests essentially in the nation. No body and no individual may exercise authority which does not emanate expressly from the nation.

4. Liberty consists in the ability to do whatever does not harm another; hence the exercise of the natural rights of each man has no other limits than those which assure to other members of society the enjoyment of the same rights. These limits can only be determined by the law.

5. The law only has the right to prohibit those actions which are injurious to society. No hindrance should be put in the way of anything not prohibited by the law, nor may any one be forced to do what the law does not require.

6. The law is the expression of the general will. All citizens have the right to take part, in person or by their representatives, in its formation. It must be the same for everyone whether it protects or penalizes. All citizens being equal in its eyes are equally admissible to all public dignities, offices, and employments, according to their ability, and with no other distinction than that of their virtues and talents.

7. No man may be indicted, arrested, or detained except in cases determined by the law and according to the forms which it has prescribed....

9. Every man being presumed innocent until judged guilty, if it is deemed indispensable to arrest him, all rigor unnecessary to securing his person should be severely repressed by the law.

10. No one should be disturbed for his opinions, even in religion, provided that their manifestation does not trouble public order as established by law.

11. The free communication of thoughts and opinions is one of the most precious of the rights of man. Every citizen may therefore speak, write, and print freely, if he accepts his own responsibility for any abuse of this liberty in the cases set by the law.

Source: Lynn Hunt, ed., *The French Revolution and Human Rights* (Boston: Bedford/St. Martin's, 1996), 77–79.

12. The safeguard of the rights of man and the citizen requires public powers. These powers are therefore instituted for the advantage of all, and not for the private benefit of those to whom they are entrusted.

13. For maintenance of public authority and for expenses of administration, common taxation is indispensable. It should be apportioned equally among all the citizens according to their capacity to pay....

17. Property being an inviolable and sacred right, no one may be deprived of it except when public necessity, certified by law, obviously requires it, and on the condition of a just compensation in advance.

Document 17.2

The Rights of Women

But did the "rights of man" include women? Although none of the legislative assemblies that arose during the French Revolution seriously considered granting women the right to vote or hold office, the question of women's rights was sharply debated. Just two years after the famous French Declaration, the French playwright and journalist Olympe de Gouges sought to apply those rights to women when she crafted her *Declaration of the Rights of Woman and the Female Citizen.* "Woman, wake up," she wrote, "the tocsin [warning bell] of reason is being heard throughout the whole universe; discover your rights."[23] Most men, however, even ardent revolutionaries, agreed with the French lawyer Jean-Denis Lanjuinais that "the physique of women, their goal in life [marriage and motherhood], and their position distance them from the exercise of a great number of political rights and duties."[24]

Debates about the "rights of women" were hardly limited to France. During the nineteenth century, they echoed loudly throughout Europe, North America, and beyond and gave rise to the world's first women's rights movement. Among the earliest expressions of that debate was a treatise titled *A Vindication of the Rights of Woman* (1792) by Mary Wollstonecraft, a British writer whose thinking about women's rights had been clearly stimulated by events in France. She wrote the book as a response to French diplomat Charles Talleyrand, who had recently advocated a very limited and domestic education for women.

■ On what basis does Wollstonecraft argue for the rights of women? To what extent were her arguments based on the principles of the French Declaration?

■ In what kind of rights does she seem most interested? What problems does the denial of those rights generate?

■ Should Wollstonecraft be considered a feminist in the contemporary sense of insisting on the complete equality of women and men in every sphere of life? Keep in mind that the term "feminism" itself was not in use when she wrote in 1792.

MARY WOLLSTONECRAFT

A Vindication of the Rights of Woman

1792

Contending for the rights of woman, my main argument is built on this simple principle, that if she be not prepared by education to become the companion of man, she will stop the progress of knowledge and virtue;...but the education and situation of woman at present shuts her out from such investigations....

Consider, sir, dispassionately these observations, for a glimpse of this truth seemed to open before you when you observed, "that to see one-half of the human race excluded by the other from all participation of government was a political phenomenon that, according to abstract principles, it was impossible to explain." If so, on what does your constitution rest?...

Consider—I address you as a legislator—whether, when men contend for their freedom, and to be allowed to judge for themselves respecting their own happiness, it be not inconsistent and unjust to subjugate women, even though you firmly believe that you are acting in the manner best calculated to promote their happiness? Who made man the exclusive judge, if woman partake with him of the gift of reason?

In this style argue tyrants of every denomination, from the weak king to the weak father of a family; they are all eager to crush reason, yet always assert that they usurp its throne only to be useful. Do you not act a similar part when you force all women, by denying them civil and political rights, to remain immured in their families groping in the dark?... They may be convenient slaves, but slavery will have its constant effect, degrading the master and the abject dependent....

I have repeatedly asserted...that women cannot by force be confined to domestic concerns; for they will, however ignorant, intermeddle with more weighty affairs, neglecting private duties only to disturb, by cunning tricks, the orderly plans of reason which rise above their comprehension....

Let there be then no coercion established in society, and the common law of gravity prevailing, the sexes will fall into their proper places. And now that more equitable laws are forming your citizens, marriage may become more sacred; your young men may choose wives from motives of affection, and your maidens allow love to root out vanity.

The father of a family will not then weaken his constitution and debase his sentiments by visiting the harlot, nor forget, in obeying the call of appetite, the purpose for which it was implanted. And the mother will not neglect her children to practise the arts of coquetry, when sense and modesty secure her the friendship of her husband.

But, till men become attentive to the duty of a father, it is vain to expect women to spend that time in their nursery which they,...choose to spend at their glass [mirror]; for this exertion of cunning is only an instinct of nature to enable them to obtain indirectly a little of that power of which they are unjustly denied a share; for, if women are not permitted to enjoy legitimate rights, they will render both men and themselves vicious to obtain illicit privileges.

I wish, sir, to set some investigations of this kind afloat in France; and should they lead to a confirmation of my principles when your constitution is revised, the Rights of Woman may be respected, if it be fully proved that reason calls for this respect, and loudly demands JUSTICE for one-half of the human race.

Source: Mary Wollstonecraft, *A Vindication of the Rights of Woman* (New York: W. W. Norton, 1967), Dedication.

Document 17.3

Rights and National Independence

The "rights of man" could be mobilized not only in the struggles of women but also on behalf of colonial subjects, as the American Declaration of Independence illustrated. Some thirty-five years after the outbreak of the North American revolution, Spain's American colonies were likewise in revolt. Among the most prominent political and military leaders of that struggle was Simón Bolívar, often regarded as the George Washington of Latin America. Born in Caracas, Venezuela, Bolívar hailed from an old, wealthy, and aristocratic family. Although his struggles were successful in ending Spanish colonial rule, they manifestly failed to achieve his lifelong dream of a federation, like that of North America, among the various newly independent republics of Latin America. In a well-known letter, written in 1815, Bolívar made the case for the independence of his continent.

■   What understanding of "rights" informed Bolívar's demand for independence?

■   What were his chief objections to Spanish rule?

■   What difficulties did Bolívar foresee in achieving the kind of stable and unified independence that he so much desired?

■   What might you infer from Bolívar's statements, or his silences, about his willingness to apply human rights thinking to people of Native American, African, or mixed-race ancestry?

SIMÓN BOLÍVAR

The Jamaica Letter

1815

Success will crown our efforts because the destiny of [Latin] America is irrevocably fixed; the tie that bound her to Spain is severed.... The hatred we feel for the Peninsula is greater than the sea separating us from it; it would be easier to bring the two continents together than to reconcile the spirits and the minds of the two countries. The habit of obedience, a commerce of shared interests, knowledge, and religion; mutual goodwill; a tender concern for the birthland and glory of our ancestors; in brief everything that constituted our hopes came to us from Spain.... Today the opposite is true: death, dishonor, everything harmful threatens us and makes us fearful. That wicked stepmother is the source of all our sufferings.... The chains have been broken, we've been liberated, and now our enemies want to make us slaves. That is why America fights with such defiance, and it would be rare should such desperate intensity not bring victory in its wake....

Source: David Bushnell, ed., *El Libertador: Writings of Simón Bolívar*, translated by Frederick H. Fornoff (Oxford: Oxford University Press, 2003), 13–14, 18–20, 27–28, 30.

[W]e are moreover neither Indians nor Europeans, but a race halfway between the legitimate owners of the land and the Spanish usurpers—in short, being Americans by birth and endowed with rights from Europe—find ourselves forced to defend these rights against the natives while maintaining our position in the land against the intrusion of the invaders. Thus we find ourselves in the most extraordinary and complicated situation....

The posture of those who dwell in the American hemisphere has been over the centuries purely passive. We are at a level even lower than servitude, and by that very reason hindered from elevating ourselves to the enjoyment of freedom.... From the beginning we were plagued by a practice that in addition to depriving us of the rights to which we were entitled left us in a kind of permanent infancy with respect to public affairs....

The Americans... occupy no other place in society than that of servants suited for work or, at best, that of simple consumers, and even this is limited by appalling restrictions: for instance the prohibition against the cultivation of European crops or the sale of products monopolized by the king, the restriction against the construction of factories that don't even exist on the peninsula, exclusive privileges for engaging in commerce even of items that are basic necessities, the barrier between American provinces, preventing them from establishing contact, or communicating, or doing business with one another. In short, would you like to know the extent of our destiny? Fields for the cultivation of indigo, grain, coffee, sugar cane, cacao, and cotton, empty prairies for raising cattle, wilderness for hunting ferocious beasts, the bowels of the earth for excavating gold that will never satisfy the lusts of that greedy nation.... Is this not an outrage and a violation of the rights of humanity?

We were... absent from the universe in all things relative to the science of government and the administration of the state. We were never viceroys, never governors, except in extraordinary circumstances; hardly ever bishops or archbishops; never diplomats; soldiers only in lower ranks; nobles, but without royal privileges. In short, we were never leaders, never financiers, hardly ever merchants....

From the foregoing, we can deduce certain consequences: The American provinces are involved in a struggle for emancipation, which will eventually succeed.... The idea of merging the entire New World into a single nation with a single unifying principle to provide coherence to the parts and to the whole is both grandiose and impractical. Because it has a common origin, a common language, similar customs, and one religion, we might conclude that it should be possible for a single government to oversee a federation of different states eventually to emerge. However, this is not possible, because America is divided by remote climates, diverse geographies, conflicting interests, and dissimilar characteristics.... Such a corporation might conceivably emerge at some felicitous moment in our regeneration....

When we are at last strong, under the auspices of a liberal nation that lends us its protection, then we will cultivate in harmony the virtues and talents that lead to glory; then we will follow the majestic path toward abundant prosperity marked out by destiny for South America; then the arts and sciences that were born in the Orient and that brought enlightenment to Europe will fly to a free Columbia, which will nourish and shelter them.

Document 17.4

Rights and Slavery

The language of "rights" resonated not only with women seeking equality and colonial subjects seeking independence but also with slaves demanding freedom. Clearly, the ideas and events of the French Revolution had sparked the massive slave uprising in Haiti in 1791 (see pp. 787–90). In the United States the language of the Declaration of Independence with its affirmation that "all men are created equal" stood in glaring contrast to the brutal realities of slavery. That great contradiction in the new American nation was forcefully highlighted in a famous speech by Frederick Douglass. Born a slave in 1818, Douglass had escaped from bondage to become a leading abolitionist, writer, newspaper publisher, and African American spokesperson. He was invited to address an antislavery meeting in Rochester, New York, on July 4, 1852.

- On what basis does Douglass demand the end of slavery? How do his arguments relate to the ideology of the American Revolution?

- How would you describe the rhetorical strategy of his speech?

- What does Douglass mean when he says "it is not light that is needed, but fire"?

- In what ways does he argue that slavery has poisoned American life?

- Why, in the end, can Douglass claim "I do not despair of this country"? How would you evaluate the following assertion in the last paragraph: "There are forces in operation, which must inevitably work the downfall of slavery"? What forces was he referring to?

FREDERICK DOUGLASS

What to the Slave Is the Fourth of July?

1852

Fellow-citizens, pardon me, allow me to ask, why am I called upon to speak here to-day? What have I, or those I represent, to do with your national independence? Are the great principles of political freedom and of natural justice, embodied in that Declaration of Independence, extended to us? and am I, therefore, called upon to bring our humble offering to the national altar, and to confess the benefits and express devout gratitude for the blessings resulting from your independence to us?

Would to God, both for your sakes and ours, that an affirmative answer could be truthfully returned to these questions!...

But, such is not the state of the case. I say it with a sad sense of the disparity between us. I am not

included within the pale of this glorious anniversary! Your high independence only reveals the immeasurable distance between us.... The sunlight that brought life and healing to you, has brought stripes and death to me. This Fourth [of] July is yours, not mine. You may rejoice, I must mourn. To drag a man in fetters into the grand illuminated temple of liberty, and call upon him to join you in joyous anthems, were inhuman mockery and sacrilegious irony. Do you mean, citizens, to mock me, by asking me to speak to-day?...

Fellow-citizens; above your national, tumultuous joy, I hear the mournful wail of millions!... I shall see, this day... from the slave's point of view.... I do not hesitate to declare, with all my soul, that the character and conduct of this nation never looked blacker to me than on this 4th of July!... Standing with God and the crushed and bleeding slave on this occasion, I will... dare to call in question and to denounce, with all the emphasis I can command, everything

Source: Frederick Douglass, "What to the Slave Is the Fourth of July?" http://www.trinicenter.com/historicalviews/4thjuly.htm.

that serves to perpetuate slavery—the great sin and shame of America!

For the present, it is enough to affirm the equal manhood of the Negro race. Is it not astonishing that... while we are engaged in all manner of enterprises common to other men..., we are called upon to prove that we are men!

Would you have me argue that man is entitled to liberty? that he is the rightful owner of his own body? You have already declared it. Must I argue the wrongfulness of slavery? Is that a question for Republicans?...

At a time like this, scorching irony, not convincing argument, is needed.... For it is not light that is needed, but fire.... [T]he conscience of the nation must be roused;... the hypocrisy of the nation must be exposed; and its crimes against God and man must be proclaimed and denounced.

What, to the American slave, is your 4th of July? I answer: a day that reveals to him, more than all other days in the year, the gross injustice and cruelty to which he is the constant victim. To him, your celebration is a sham; your boasted liberty, an unholy license; your national greatness, swelling vanity; your sounds of rejoicing are empty and heartless; your denunciations of tyrants, brass-fronted impudence; your shouts of liberty and equality, hollow mockery; your prayers and hymns, your sermons and thanksgivings, with all your religious parade, and solemnity, are, to him, mere bombast, fraud, deception, impiety, and hypocrisy—a thin veil to cover up crimes which would disgrace a nation of savages. There is not a nation on the earth guilty of practices, more shocking and bloody, than are the people of these United States, at this very hour....

Fellow-citizens! I will not enlarge further on your national inconsistencies. The existence of slavery in this country brands your republicanism as a sham, your humanity as a base pretence, and your Christianity as a lie. It destroys your moral power abroad; it corrupts your politicians at home. It saps the foundation of religion; it makes your name a hissing, and a byword to a mocking earth. It is the antagonistic force in your government, the only thing that seriously disturbs and endangers your Union. It fetters your progress; it is the enemy of improvement, the deadly foe of education; it fosters pride; it breeds insolence; it promotes vice; it shelters crime; it is a curse to the earth that supports it; and yet, you cling to it, as if it were the sheet anchor of all your hopes. Oh! be warned! be warned! a horrible reptile is coiled up in your nation's bosom; the venomous creature is nursing at the tender breast of your youthful republic; for the love of God, tear away, and fling from you the hideous monster, and let the weight of twenty millions crush and destroy it forever!...

Allow me to say, in conclusion..., I do not despair of this country. There are forces in operation, which must inevitably work the downfall of slavery.... While drawing encouragement from the Declaration of Independence, the great principles it contains, and the genius of American Institutions, my spirit is also cheered by the obvious tendencies of the age. Nations do not now stand in the same relation to each other that they did ages ago. No nation can now shut itself up from the surrounding world, and trot round in the same old path of its fathers without interference.... But a change has now come over the affairs of mankind. Walled cities and empires have become unfashionable. The arm of commerce has borne away the gates of the strong city. Intelligence is penetrating the darkest corners of the globe. It makes its pathway over and under the sea, as well as on the earth. Wind, steam, and lightning are its chartered agents. Oceans no longer divide, but link nations together. From Boston to London is now a holiday excursion. Space is comparatively annihilated. Thoughts expressed on one side of the Atlantic are distinctly heard on the other. The far off and almost fabulous Pacific rolls in grandeur at our feet. The Celestial Empire, the mystery of ages, is being solved. The fiat of the Almighty, "Let there be Light," has not yet spent its force.

Document 17.5

Rights in the Colonial World

The idea of rights did not long remain limited to the Atlantic world of Europe and the Americas. Much as that idea proved revolutionary in the colonial world of the Americas, so too did it have an impact in the new European colonial empires that took shape during the nineteenth century. As Western colonialism embraced much of Asia and Africa, such ideas gradually became familiar to at least a few people in those colonial societies. One example was Raden Adjeng Kartini, a young Javanese woman from an aristocratic family who had become fluent in Dutch, the language of the Netherlands, the colonial power that ruled her country. In 1899, at the age of twenty, she wrote a letter to a Dutch friend, describing the impact of European thinking on her own outlook and her own life.

- Although Kartini did not directly use the language of "rights," what evidence in the letter suggests that she might have been influenced by the idea of human rights?

- What elements of European thinking are most compelling to Kartini?

- In what ways does her encounter with European thinking generate conflict or dissatisfaction with her own society? What else provokes her desire for change?

- Some Indonesians have celebrated Kartini as a pioneer of both feminism and nationalism. To what extent does this letter support that view?

- How would you compare Kartini's thinking about women's emancipation with that of Wollstonecraft?

RADEN ADJENG KARTINI
Letter to a Friend
1899

I have longed to make the acquaintance of a "modern girl," that proud, independent girl who has all my sympathy!... I do not belong to the Indian world, but to that of my pale sisters who are struggling forward in the distant West.

If the laws of my land permitted it, there is nothing that I had rather do than give myself wholly to the working and striving of the new woman in Europe; but age-long traditions that cannot be broken hold us fast cloistered in their unyielding arms. Some day those arms will loosen and let us go, but that time lies as yet far from us, infinitely far. It will come, that I know; it may be three, four generations after us. Oh, you do not know what it is to love this young, this new age with heart and soul, and yet to

Source: Raden Adjeng Kartini, *Letters of a Javanese Princess*, translated by Agnes Louise Symmers (Oxford: Oxford University Press, 1976), 3–7.

be bound hand and foot, chained by all the laws, customs, and conventions of one's land. All our institutions are directly opposed to the progress for which I so long for the sake of our people. Day and night I wonder by what means our ancient traditions could be overcome. For myself, I could find a way to shake them off, to break them, were it not that another bond, stronger than any age-old tradition could ever be, binds me to my world; and that is the love which I bear for those to whom I owe my life, and whom I must thank for everything. Have I the right to break the hearts of those who have given me nothing but love and kindness my whole life long, and who have surrounded me with the tenderest care?

But it was not the voices alone which reached me from that distant, that bright, that new-born Europe, which made me long for a change in existing conditions. Even in my childhood, the word "emancipation" enchanted my ears; it had a significance that nothing else had, a meaning that was far beyond my comprehension, and awakened in me an evergrowing longing for freedom and independence—a longing to stand alone. Conditions both in my own surroundings and in those of others around me broke my heart, and made me long with a nameless sorrow for the awakening of my country.

Then the voices which penetrated from distant lands grew clearer and clearer, till they reached me, and to the satisfaction of some who loved me, but to the deep grief of others, brought seed which entered my heart, took root, and grew strong and vigorous.

And now I must tell you something of myself so that you can make my acquaintance.

I am the eldest of the three unmarried daughters of the Regent of Japara, and have six brothers and sisters. What a world, eh? My grandfather...was a great leader in the progressive movement of his day, and the first regent of middle Java to unlatch his door to that guest from over the sea—Western civilization. All of his children had European educations....We girls, so far as education goes, fettered by our ancient traditions and conventions, have profited but little by these advantages. It was a great crime against the customs of our land that we should be taught at all, and especially that we should leave the house every day to go to school. For the customs of our country forbade girls in the strongest manner ever to go outside of the house. We were never allowed to go anywhere, however, save to the school, and the only place of instruction of which our city could boast, which was open to us, was a free grammar school for Europeans.

When I reached the age of twelve, I was kept at home—I must go into the "box." I was locked up, and cut off from all communication with the outside world, toward which I might never turn again save at the side of a bridegroom, a stranger, an unknown man whom my parents would choose for me, and to whom I should be betrothed without my own knowledge....I went into my prison. Four long years I spent between thick walls, without once seeing the outside world.

How I passed through that time, I do not know....But there was one great happiness left me: the reading of Dutch books and correspondence with Dutch friends was not forbidden. This—the only gleam of light in that empty, sombre time, was my all....

At last in my sixteenth year, I saw the outside world again. Thank God! Thank God! I could leave my prison as a free human being and not chained to an unwelcome bridegroom....

In the following year, at the time of the investiture of our young Princess [Queen Wilhelmina of the Netherlands], our parents presented us "officially" with our freedom. For the first time in our lives we were allowed to leave our native town, and to go to the city where the festivities were held in honour of the occasion. What a great and priceless victory it was! That young girls of our position should show themselves in public was here an unheard-of occurrence. The "world" stood aghast; tongues were set wagging at the unprecedented crime. Our European friends rejoiced, and as for ourselves, no queen was so rich as we. But I am far from satisfied. I would go still further, always further. I do not desire to go out to feasts, and little frivolous amusements. That has never been the cause of my longing for freedom. I long to be free, to be able to stand alone, to study, not to be subject to any one, and, above all, *never, never* to be obliged to marry.

But we *must* marry, must, must. Not to marry is the greatest sin which the [Muslim] woman can commit; it is the greatest disgrace which a native girl can bring to her family.

And marriage among us—Miserable is too feeble an expression for it. How can it be otherwise, when the laws have made everything for the man and nothing for the woman? When law and convention both are for the man; when everything is allowed to him?

Love! what do we know here of love? How can we love a man whom we have never known? And how could he love us? That in itself would not be possible. Young girls and men must be kept rigidly apart, and are never allowed to meet.

Using the Evidence:
Claiming Rights

1. **Making comparisons:** In what different ways does the idea of "rights" find expression in these five documents? Which documents speak more about individual rights and which focus attention on collective rights? What common understandings can you identify?

2. **Considering ideas and circumstances:** Historians frequently debate the relative importance of ideas in shaping historical events. What impact do you think the ideas about rights expressed in these documents had on the historical development of the Atlantic world and beyond? And what specific historical contexts or conditions shaped each writer's understanding of "rights"?

3. **Connecting past and present:** Read the Universal Declaration of Human Rights, adopted by the United Nations in 1948 (http://www.un .org/Overview/rights.html). To what extent does this document reflect the thinking about rights spelled out in the French declaration of 1789? What additional rights have been added to the more recent document? How might you account for the changes?

Visual Sources

Considering the Evidence:
Representing the French Revolution

The era of the French Revolution, generally reckoned to have lasted from 1789 to 1815, unfolded as a complex and varied process. Its first several years were relatively moderate, but by 1792 it had become far more radical and violent. After 1795 a reaction set in against the chaos and upheaval that it had generated, culminating in the seizure of power in 1799 by the successful general Napoleon Bonaparte. Nor was the revolution a purely French affair. Conservative opposition in the rest of Europe prompted prolonged warfare, and French efforts under Napoleon to spread the revolution led to a huge French empire in Europe and much resistance to it (see pp. 784–87).

All of this provoked enormous controversy, which found visual expression in paintings, cartoons, drawings, and portraits. The five visual sources that follow suggest something of the changing nature of the revolution and the varied reactions it elicited.

Like all major social upheavals, the French Revolution unleashed both enormous hopes and great fears, largely depending on an individual's position in French society. That society was divided into three legal orders, or estates — the clergy, the nobility, and the commoners. The first two of these estates, the most highly privileged groups of French society, together represented only about 2 percent of the population and were exempt from major forms of taxation in addition to holding much of the country's landed wealth. This generated considerable resentment among the commoners (the third estate) and was a critical motor of the revolution. Nonetheless, in the early stages of the revolution (1789–1791), many people hoped that France could become a constitutional monarchy with a far more limited role for the king and that the three estates could work together in harmony. The high point of this hope for social and national unity occurred during the Festival of the Federation, a massive military pageant featuring troops from all over the country. Watched by close to a million spectators, the festival took place on July 14, 1790, exactly one year after the storming of the Bastille, a large fortress, prison, and armory that had come to symbolize the oppressive old regime. Soldiers swore an oath of allegiance to the king and the National Assembly. Speakers gave public thanks for "this inseparable bond between all the French, regardless of sex, age, station in life or occupation."[25]

Visual Source 17.1 The Early Years of the French Revolution: "The Joyous Accord" (The Bridgeman Art Library)

Visual Source 17.1, entitled "The Joyous Accord," represents this phase of the revolution as it depicts the interaction of members of the three estates. The text reads: "Then Messieur we drink to the health of our good King and the Fatherland, that we may be in agreement, at least this for life. And that virtue may be our guide and we will taste together the true pleasures of life."

- What changes during the first year of the French Revolution does this image reveal? Consider the activity portrayed in the painting and the posture of the three figures. What continuities with the past does it also suggest?

- How does it portray the ideal of national unity?

- How are the representatives of the three estates distinguished from one another?

- Notice the peasants hunting in the background. Keep in mind that before the revolution peasants who hunted on the estates of the nobility were subject to harsh punishment or even death. Why do you suppose the artist chose to include them in the painting?

Despite the hope for harmony, many soon came to see the revolution as a sharp reversal of class roles. Visual Source 17.2, which depicts the three estates of old France as female characters, illustrates this perception of the revolution. The woman on the far right represents the clergy, the one in the middle portrays the nobility, and the figure holding the baby stands for the commoners.

■ What different impressions of the revolution are conveyed by Visual Sources 17.1 and 17.2?

■ How might you interpret the meaning of the caption, which reads: "I really knew we would have our turn."

Visual Source 17.2 A Reversal of Roles: The Three Estates of the Old Regime (Réunion des musées nationaux/Art Resource, NY)

Visual Source 17.3 Revolution and Religion: "Patience, Monsignor, your turn will come." (Musée de la Révolution française, Vizille, France, mfr 89.186)

■ Compare this image with the opening picture of Chapter 17 on page 778. What changes had occurred in the relationship of the classes? How does the woman representing the third estate in Visual Source 17.2 differ from her counterpart in the earlier image?

■ Notice that the woman representing the third estate in this image holds a distaff, a tool used for spinning, as well as a child. What does this suggest about the roles of women in the new order? How might Mary Wollstonecraft (Document 17.2, pp. 808–09) respond to this image?

In its more radical phase, the French Revolution witnessed not only serious class conflict but also a vigorous attack on the Catholic Church and on Christianity itself. The Church was brought under state control, and members of the clergy were required to swear an oath of allegiance to the revolution. The revolutionary government closed many church buildings or sold them to the highest bidder. The government also seized church property to finance France's wars. For a time, revolutionaries tried to establish a Cult of Reason to replace the Christian faith. This de-Christianization policy also involved the closure of monasteries and efforts to force priests to abandon their vocation and even to marry. Visual Source 17.3 suggests some of the reasons why ardent revolutionaries were so opposed to the supernatural religion in general and the Catholic Church in particular.

■ How does this visual source reflect the outlook of the Enlightenment? (See pp. 742–44.)

■ What criticisms of the Church are suggested by this image? Why is the bishop on the left portrayed as a fat, even bloated, figure? What is the significance of efforts to "squeeze" the priests? Based on their dress, what class do you think the pressmen represent?

■ The caption reads: "Patience, Monsignor, your turn will come." What do you imagine was the reaction of devout Catholics to such images and to the policies of de-Christianization?

■ In what ways do Visual Sources 17.1, 17.2, and 17.3 reflect the principles of the Declaration of the Rights of Man and Citizen (Document 17.1, pp. 806–08)?

Attacks on the church and religion in general were among the actions of the Revolution that prompted fear, outrage, and revulsion, both within France and in the more conservative societies of Europe. So too was the execution of Louis XVI and Marie Antoinette, as well as the widespread violence of the Terror. Visual Source 17.4, a British political cartoon, conveys this highly critical, indeed horrified, outlook on the French Revolution. Captioned "Hell Broke

Visual Source 17.4 An English Response to Revolution: "Hell Broke Loose or The Murder of Louis" (Musée de la Révolution française, Vizille, France/The Bridgeman Art Library)

Loose," it depicts the execution of Louis XVI and was printed shortly after his death in January 1793. The flying demonic figures in the image are repeating popular slogans of the revolution: "Vive la nation" ("Long live the nation") and "Ca ira" ("That will go well," or more loosely, "We will win").[26]

■ What is the significance of the demons and dragons in the cartoon? Notice how the soldiers at the bottom of the image are portrayed.

■ What meaning would you attribute to the caption, "Hell Broke Loose"? What disasters might critics of the revolution have imagined coming in its wake?

■ How do you understand the beam of light from heaven that falls on Louis XVI?

■ Why was regicide regarded with such horror in England in the 1790s?

After ten years of upheaval, the French Revolution brought to power in 1799 the much-acclaimed general Napoleon Bonaparte (see p. 787). In the fifteen years that followed, Napoleon launched France into a series of wars that brought the ideas of the revolution, and French control, to much of Europe.

Visual Source 17.5 Revolution, War, and Resistance: A German View of Napoleon (Bridgeman-Giraudon/Art Resource, NY)

Those conquests also aroused much resentment and resistance, which by 1815 brought an end to both Napoleon and the European empire he had created. Visual Source 17.5, a German caricature of Napoleon, illustrates that resistance in visual form. It was created in late 1813 by the German artist J. M. Voltz to mark a major defeat of Napoleon's forces at Leipzig in October of that year. The caption reads: "Triumph of the Year 1813. To the Germans for the New Year 1814." This image was widely reproduced throughout French-occupied Europe in an effort to stimulate further resistance.

- What do the figures embedded in Napoleon's gnarled face represent?

- Notice the Russian-style fur hat with bear claws extending into Napoleon's head. Given the recent Russian military defeats of Napoleon's forces, what do you think this represents?

- How do you understand the hand extending from Napoleon's neck as an epaulet (military insignia worn on the shoulder)?

- What is the meaning of the map depicted on his uniform? The crosses show the location of other defeats for Napoleon's forces. Notice also the red collar, said to represent the blood of Napoleon's many victims.

- How does this German critique of the French Revolution, created in 1813, differ from the British criticism in Visual Source 17.4, which is dated to 1793?

Using the Evidence:
Representing the French Revolution

1. **Considering political art as evidence:** Based on these five visual sources, together with those in the text itself, what are the advantages and limitations of political or satirical art in understanding a complex phenomenon such as the French Revolution?

2. **Making comparisons:** In what different ways was the French Revolution portrayed in these visual sources? How might you account for those differences? Consider issues of class, nationality, religious commitment, time period, and gender.

3. **Defining the French Revolution:** Based on these visual sources, what was revolutionary about the French Revolution? And what earlier patterns of French life persisted?

4. **Identifying opponents of the revolution:** Based on these visual sources and the text narrative, which groups of people likely opposed the revolution? Why?

CHAPTER EIGHTEEN

Revolutions of Industrialization

1750–1914

Explaining the Industrial Revolution
  Why Europe?
  Why Britain?
The First Industrial Society
  The British Aristocracy
  The Middle Classes
  The Laboring Classes
  Social Protest
Variations on a Theme: Comparing
  Industrialization in the United
  States and Russia
  The United States: Industrialization
    without Socialism
  Russia: Industrialization
    and Revolution
The Industrial Revolution and
  Latin America in the
  Nineteenth Century
  After Independence in
    Latin America
  Facing the World Economy
  Becoming like Europe?
Reflections: History and
  Horse Races
Considering the Evidence
  Documents: Varieties of
    European Marxism
  Visual Sources: Art and the
    Industrial Revolution

"Industrialization is, I am afraid, going to be a curse for mankind.... God forbid that India should ever take to industrialism after the manner of the West. The economic imperialism of a single tiny island kingdom (England) is today [1928] keeping the world in chains. If an entire nation of 300 millions took to similar economic exploitation, it would strip the world bare like locusts.... Industrialization on a mass scale will necessarily lead to passive or active exploitation of the villagers.... The machine produces much too fast."[1]

Such were the views of the famous Indian nationalist and spiritual leader Mahatma Gandhi, who subsequently led his country to independence from British colonial rule by 1947, only to be assassinated a few months later. However, few people anywhere have agreed with India's heroic figure. Since its beginning in Great Britain in the late eighteenth century, the idea of industrialization, if not always its reality, has been embraced in every kind of society, both for the wealth it generates and for the power it conveys. Even Gandhi's own country, once it achieved its independence, largely abandoned its founding father's vision of small-scale, village-based handicraft manufacturing in favor of modern industry. As the twenty-first century dawned, India was moving rapidly to develop a major high-technology industrial sector. At that time, across the river from the site in New Delhi where Gandhi was cremated in 1948 a large power plant belched black smoke.

FEW ELEMENTS OF EUROPE'S MODERN TRANSFORMATION HELD A GREATER SIGNIFICANCE for the history of humankind than the Industrial Revolution, which took place initially in the

Industrial Britain: The dirt, smoke, and pollution of early industrial societies are vividly conveyed in this nineteenth-century engraving of a copper foundry in Wales. (Bibliothèque des Arts Décoratifs Paris/Gianni Dagli Orti/The Art Archive)

century and a half between 1750 and 1900. It drew upon the Scientific Revolution and accompanied the unfolding legacy of the French Revolution to utterly transform European society and to propel Europe into a position of global dominance. Not since the breakthrough of the Agricultural Revolution some 12,000 years ago had human ways of life been so fundamentally altered. But the Industrial Revolution, unlike its agricultural predecessor, began independently in only one place, Western Europe, and more specifically Great Britain. From there, it spread far more rapidly than agriculture, though very unevenly, to achieve a worldwide presence in less than 250 years. Far more than Europe's Christian religion, its democratic political values, or its capitalist economic framework, the techniques of its Industrial Revolution have been intensely sought after virtually everywhere.

In any long-term reckoning, the history of industrialization is very much an unfinished story. It is hard to know whether we are at the beginning of a movement leading to worldwide industrialization, stuck in the middle of a world permanently divided into rich and poor countries, or approaching the end of an environmentally unsustainable industrial era. Whatever the future holds, this chapter focuses on the early stages of an immense transformation in the global condition of humankind.

Explaining the Industrial Revolution

The global context for this epochal economic transformation lies in a very substantial increase in human numbers from about 375 million people in 1400 to about 1 billion in the early nineteenth century. Accompanying this growth in population was an emerging energy crisis, most pronounced in Western Europe, China, and Japan, as wood and charcoal, the major industrial fuels, became more scarce and their prices rose. In short, "global energy demands began to push against the existing local and regional ecological limits."[2] In broad terms, the Industrial Revolution marks a human response to that dilemma as fossil fuels replaced the earlier reliance on wind, water, wood, and the muscle power of people and animals. All of those had derived from "recently captured solar energy," but now human ingenuity found the means to tap as well the anciently stored solar energy of coal, oil, and natural gas.[3] It was a breakthrough of unprecedented proportions that made available for human use immensely greater quantities of energy. It also wrought, of course, a mounting impact on the environment with which the world of the twenty-first century is increasingly occupied.

More immediately, however, that access to huge new sources of energy gave rise to an enormously increased output of goods and services. In Britain, where the Industrial Revolution began, industrial output increased some fiftyfold between 1750 and 1900. It was a wholly unprecedented and previously unimaginable jump in the capacity of human societies to produce wealth. Lying behind it was a great acceleration in the rate of technological innovation, not simply this or that invention—the spinning jenny, power loom, steam engine, or cotton gin—but a "culture of innovation," a widespread and almost obsessive belief that things could be endlessly improved.

Early signs of the technological creativity that spawned the Industrial Revolution appeared in eighteenth-century Britain, where a variety of innovations transformed cotton textile production. It was only in the nineteenth century, though, that Europeans in general and the British in particular more clearly forged ahead of the rest of the world. The great breakthrough was the coal-fired steam engine, which provided an inanimate and almost limitless source of power beyond that of wind, water, or muscle and could be used to drive any number of machines as well as locomotives and oceangoing ships. Soon the Industrial Revolution spread beyond the textile industry to iron and steel production, railroads and steamships, food processing, construction, chemicals, electricity, the telegraph and telephone, rubber, pottery, printing, and much more. Agriculture too was affected as mechanical reapers, chemical fertilizers, pesticides, and refrigeration transformed this most ancient of industries. Technical innovation occurred in more modest ways as well. Patents for horseshoes in the United States, for example, grew from fewer than five per year before 1840 to thirty to forty per year by the end of the century. Furthermore, industrialization spread beyond Britain to continental Western Europe and then in the second half of the century to the United States, Russia, and Japan.

In the twentieth century, the Industrial Revolution became global as a number of Asian, African, and Latin American countries developed substantial industrial sectors. Oil, natural gas, and nuclear reactions joined coal as widely available sources of energy, and new industries emerged in automobiles, airplanes, consumer durable goods, electronics, computers, and on and on. It was a cumulative process that, despite periodic ups and downs, accelerated over time. More than anything else, this continuous emergence of new techniques of production and the economic growth that they made possible mark the past 250 years as a distinct phase of human history.

Why Europe?

The Industrial Revolution has long been a source of great controversy among scholars. Why did it occur first in Europe? Within Europe, why did it occur first in Great Britain? And why did it take place in the late eighteenth and nineteenth centuries? Earlier explanations that sought the answer in some unique and deeply rooted feature of European society, history, or culture have been challenged by world historians because such views seemed to suggest that Europe alone was destined to lead the way to modern economic life. This approach not only was Eurocentric and deterministic but also flew in the face of much recent research.

Historians now know that other areas of the world had experienced times of great technological and scientific flourishing. Between 750 and 1100 C.E., the Islamic world generated major advances in shipbuilding, the use of tides and falling water to generate power, papermaking, textile production, chemical technologies, water mills, clocks, and much more.[4] India had long been the world center of cotton textile production, the first place to turn sugarcane juice into crystallized sugar, and the source of many agricultural innovations and mathematical inventions. To the Arabs

■ **Change**
In what respects did the roots of the Industrial Revolution lie within Europe? In what ways did that transformation have global roots?

of the ninth century C.E., India was a "place of marvels."[5] More than either of these, China was clearly the world leader in technological innovation between 700 and 1400 C.E., prompting various scholars to suggest that China was on the edge of an industrial revolution by 1200 or so. For reasons much debated among historians, all of these flowerings of technological creativity had slowed down considerably or stagnated by the early modern era, when the pace of technological change in Europe began to pick up. But their earlier achievements certainly suggest that Europe was not alone in its capacity for technological innovation.

Nor did Europe enjoy any overall economic advantage as late as 1750. Over the past several decades, historians have carefully examined the economic conditions of various Eurasian societies in the eighteenth century and found them surprisingly alike. Economic indicators such as life expectancies, patterns of consumption and nutrition, wage levels, general living standards, widespread free markets, and prosperous merchant communities suggest broadly similar conditions across the major civilizations of Europe and Asia.[6] Thus Europe had no obvious economic lead, even on the eve of the Industrial Revolution. Rather, according to one leading scholar, "there existed something of a global economic parity between the most advanced regions in the world economy."[7]

A final reason for doubting any unique European capacity for industrial development lies in the relatively rapid spread of industrial techniques to many parts of the world over the past 250 years (a fairly short time by world history standards). Although the process has been highly uneven, industrialization has taken root, to one degree or another, in Japan, China, India, Brazil, Mexico, Indonesia, South Africa, Saudi Arabia, Thailand, South Korea, and elsewhere. Such a pattern weakens any suggestion that European culture or society was exceptionally compatible with industrial development.

Thus contemporary historians are inclined to see the Industrial Revolution erupting rather quickly and quite unexpectedly between 1750 and 1850 (see Map 18.1). Two intersecting factors help to explain why this process occurred in Europe rather than elsewhere. One lies in certain patterns of Europe's internal development that favored innovation. Its many small and highly competitive states, taking shape in the twelfth or thirteenth centuries, arguably provided an "insurance against economic and technological stagnation," which the larger Chinese, Ottoman, or Mughal empires perhaps lacked.[8] If so, then Western Europe's failure to re-create the earlier unity of the Roman Empire may have acted as a stimulus to innovation.

Furthermore, the relative newness of these European states and their monarchs' desperate need for revenue in the absence of an effective tax-collecting bureaucracy pushed European royals into an unusual alliance with their merchant classes. Small groups of merchant capitalists might be granted special privileges, monopolies, or even tax-collecting responsibilities in exchange for much-needed loans or payments to the state. It was therefore in the interest of governments to actively encourage commerce and innovation. Thus states granted charters and monopolies to private trading companies, and governments founded scientific societies and offered prizes to promote innovation. In this way, European merchants and other innovators from the fifteenth century onward gained an unusual degree of freedom from state control and in some

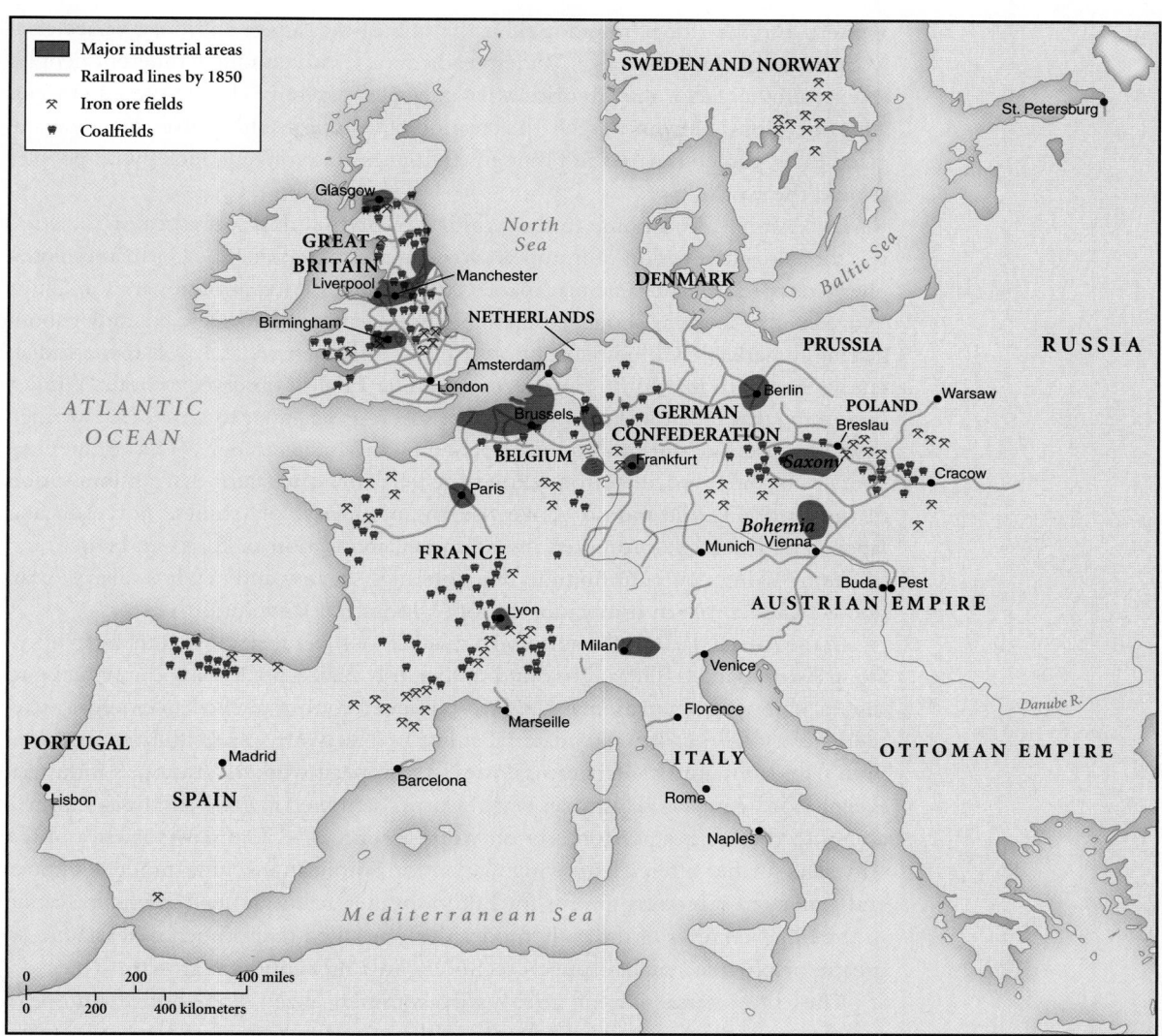

Map 18.1 The Early Phase of Europe's Industrial Revolution
From its beginning in Great Britain, industrialization spread by 1850 across northwestern Europe to include parts of France, Germany, Belgium, Bohemia, and Italy.

places a higher social status than their counterparts in more established civilizations. In Venice and Holland, merchants actually controlled the state. By the eighteenth century major Western European societies were highly commercialized and governed by states generally supportive of private commerce. In short, they were well on their way toward capitalist economies—where buying and selling on the market was a widely established practice—before they experienced industrialization. Such internally competitive economies, coupled with a highly competitive system of rival states, arguably fostered innovation in the new civilization taking shape in Western Europe.

Europe's societies, of course, were not alone in developing market-based economies by the eighteenth century. Japan, India, and especially China were likewise highly commercialized or market driven. However, in the several centuries after 1500,

Western Europe alone "found itself at the hub of the largest and most varied network of exchange in history."[9] Widespread contact with culturally different peoples was yet another factor that historically has generated extensive change and innovation. This new global network, largely the creation of Europeans themselves, greatly energized European commerce and brought Europeans into direct contact with peoples around the world.

For example, Asia, home to the world's richest and most sophisticated societies, was the initial destination of European voyages of exploration. The German philosopher Gottfried Wilhelm Leibniz (1646–1716) encouraged Jesuit missionaries in China "not to worry so much about getting things European to the Chinese but rather about getting remarkable Chinese inventions to us."[10] Inexpensive and well-made Indian textiles began to flood into Europe, causing one English observer to note: "Almost everything that used to be made of wool or silk, relating either to dress of the women or the furniture of our houses, was supplied by the Indian trade."[11] The competitive stimulus of these Indian cotton textiles was certainly one factor driving innovation in the British textile industry. Likewise, the popularity of Chinese porcelain and Japanese lacquerware prompted imitation and innovation in England, France, and Holland.[12] Thus competition from desirable, high-quality, and newly available Asian goods played a role in stimulating Europe's Industrial Revolution.

In the Americas, Europeans found a windfall of silver that allowed them to operate in Asian markets. They also found timber, fish, maize, potatoes, and much else to sustain a growing population. Later, slave-produced cotton supplied an emerging textile industry with its key raw material at low prices, while sugar, similarly produced with slave labor, furnished cheap calories to European workers. "Europe's Industrial Revolution," concluded historian Peter Stearns, "stemmed in great part from Europe's ability to draw disproportionately on world resources."[13] The new societies of the Americas further offered a growing market for European machine-produced goods and generated substantial profits for European merchants and entrepreneurs. None of the other empires of the early modern era enriched their imperial heartlands so greatly or provided such a spur to technological and economic growth.

Thus the intersection of new, highly commercialized, competitive European societies with the novel global network of their own making provides a context for understanding Europe's Industrial Revolution. Commerce and cross-cultural exchange, acting in tandem, provided the seedbed for the impressive technological changes of the first industrial societies.

Why Britain?

■ Comparison
What was distinctive about Britain that may help to explain its status as the breakthrough point of the Industrial Revolution?

If the Industrial Revolution was a Western European phenomenon generally, it clearly began in Britain in particular. The world's first Industrial Revolution unfolded spontaneously in a country that concentrated some of the more general features of European society. It was both unplanned and unexpected.

Britain was the most highly commercialized of Europe's larger countries. Its landlords had long ago "enclosed" much agricultural land, pushing out the small farmers and producing for the market. A series of agricultural innovations—crop rotation, selective breeding of animals, lighter plows, higher-yielding seeds—increased agricultural output, kept food prices low, and freed up labor from the countryside. The guilds, which earlier had protected Britain's urban artisans, had largely disappeared by the eighteenth century, allowing employers to run their manufacturing enterprises as they saw fit. Coupled with a rapidly growing population, these processes ensured a ready supply of industrial workers who had few alternatives available to them. Furthermore, British aristocrats, unlike their counterparts in Europe, had long been interested in the world of business, and some took part in new mining and manufacturing enterprises. British commerce, moreover, extended around the world, its large merchant fleet protected by the Royal Navy. The wealth of empire and global commerce, however, were not themselves sufficient for spawning the Industrial Revolution, especially when we consider that Spain, the earliest beneficiary of American wealth, remained one of the more slowly industrializing European countries into the twentieth century.

British political life encouraged commercialization and economic innovation. Its policy of religious toleration, formally established in 1688, welcomed people with technical skills regardless of their faith, whereas France's persecution of its Protestant minority had chased out some of its most skilled workers. The British government favored men of business with tariffs to keep out cheap Indian textiles, with laws that made it easy to form companies and to forbid workers' unions, with roads and canals that helped create a unified internal market, and with patent laws that served to protect the interests of inventors. Checks on royal authority—trial by jury and the growing authority of parliament, for example—provided a freer arena for private enterprise than elsewhere in Europe.

Europe's Scientific Revolution also took a distinctive form in Great Britain in ways that fostered technological innovation.[14] Whereas science on the continent was largely based on logic, deduction, and mathematical reasoning, in Britain it was much more concerned with observation, experiment, precise measurements, mechanical devices, and practical commercial applications. Discoveries about atmospheric pressure and vacuums, for example, played an important role in the invention and improvement of the steam engine. Even though most inventors were artisans or craftsmen rather than scientists, in eighteenth-century Britain they were in close contact with scientists, makers of scientific instruments, and entrepreneurs, whereas in continental Europe these groups were largely separate. The British Royal Society, an association of "natural philosophers" (scientists) established in 1660, saw its role as one of promoting "useful knowledge." To this end, it established "mechanics' libraries," published broadsheets and pamphlets on recent scientific advances, and held frequent public lectures and demonstrations. The integration of science and technology became widespread and permanent after 1850, but for a century before, it was largely a British phenomenon.

Finally, several accidents of geography and history contributed something to Britain's Industrial Revolution. The country had a ready supply of coal and iron ore, often located close to each other and within easy reach of major industrial centers.

Although Britain took part in the wars against Napoleon, the country's island location protected it from the kind of invasions that so many continental European states experienced during the era of the French Revolution. Moreover, Britain's relatively fluid society allowed for adjustments in the face of social changes without widespread revolution. By the time the dust settled from the immense disturbance of the French Revolution, Britain was well on its way to becoming the world's first industrial society.

The First Industrial Society

Wherever it took hold, the Industrial Revolution generated, within a century or less, an economic miracle, at least in comparison with earlier technologies. The British textile industry, which used 52 million pounds of cotton in 1800, consumed 588 million pounds in 1850. Britain's output of coal soared from 5.23 million tons in 1750 to 68.4 million tons a century later.[15] Railroads crisscrossed Britain and much of Europe like a giant spider web (see Map 18.1, p. 829). Most of this dramatic increase in production occurred in mining, manufacturing, and services. Thus agriculture, for millennia the overwhelmingly dominant economic sector in every civilization, shrank in relative importance. In Britain, for example, agriculture generated only 8 percent of national income in 1891 and employed fewer than 8 percent of working Britons in 1914. Accompanying this vast economic change was an epic transformation of social life. "In two centuries," wrote one prominent historian, "daily life changed more than it had in the 7,000 years before."[16] Nowhere were the revolutionary dimensions of industrialization more apparent than in Great Britain, the world's first industrial society.

Railroads
The popularity of railroads, long a symbol of the Industrial Revolution, is illustrated in this early-nineteenth-century watercolor, which shows a miniature train offered as a paid amusement for enthusiasts in London's Euston Square. (Science Museum, London, UK/The Bridgeman Art Library)

The social transformation of the Industrial Revolution both destroyed and created. Referring to the impact of the Industrial Revolution on British society, historian Eric Hobsbawm said: "[I]n its initial stages it destroyed their old ways of living and left them free to discover or make for themselves new ones, if they could and knew how. But it rarely told them how to set about it."[17] For many people, it was an enormously painful, even traumatic process, full of social conflict, insecurity, and false starts as well as new opportunities, an eventually higher standard of living, and greater participation in public life. Scholars, politicians, journalists, and ordinary people have endlessly debated the gains and losses associated with the

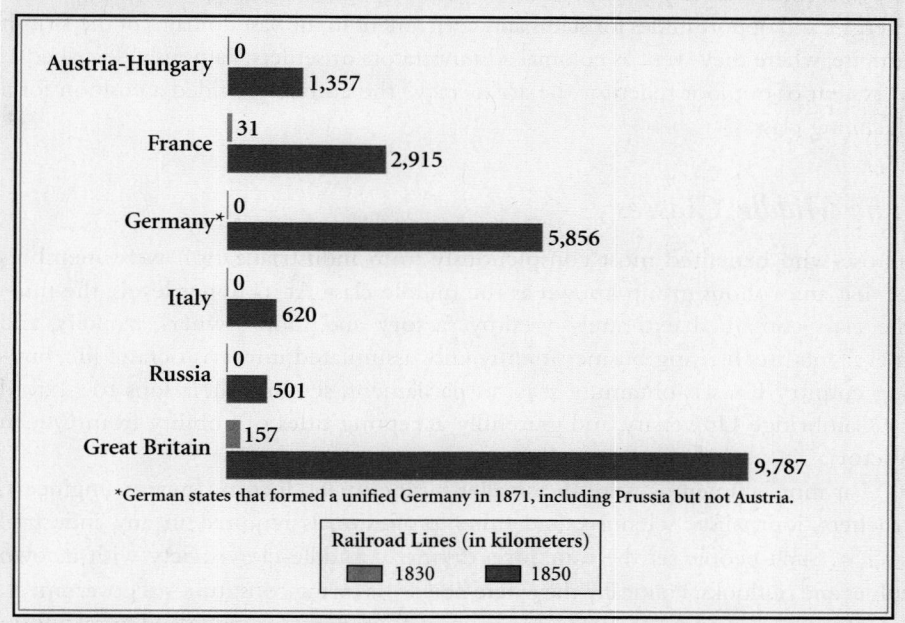

Snapshot   **Measuring the Industrial Revolution**[18]

Railroads are one useful measure of industrial development. This graph illustrates both Britain's head start and the beginning catch-up efforts of other countries.

Country	1830	1850
Austria-Hungary	0	1,357
France	31	2,915
Germany*	0	5,856
Italy	0	620
Russia	0	501
Great Britain	157	9,787

*German states that formed a unified Germany in 1871, including Prussia but not Austria.

Railroad Lines (in kilometers)
☐ 1830   ■ 1850

Industrial Revolution. Amid the controversy, however, one thing is clear: not everyone was affected in the same way. (See Visual Sources: Art and the Industrial Revolution, pp. 867–74, for both celebratory and critical perspectives on industrialization.)

The British Aristocracy

Individual landowning aristocrats, long the dominant class in Britain, suffered little in material terms from the Industrial Revolution. In the mid–nineteenth century, a few thousand families still owned more than half of the cultivated land in Britain, most of it leased to tenant farmers, who in turn employed agricultural wage laborers to work it. Rapidly growing population and urbanization sustained a demand for food products grown on that land. For most of the nineteenth century, landowners continued to dominate the British parliament.

As a class, however, the British aristocracy, like large landowners in every industrial society, declined. As urban wealth became more important, landed aristocrats had to make way for the up-and-coming businessmen, manufacturers, and bankers who had been newly enriched by the Industrial Revolution. The aristocracy's declining political clout was demonstrated in the 1840s when high tariffs on foreign agricultural

■ Change
How did the Industrial Revolution transform British society?

imports, designed to protect the interests of British landlords, were finally abolished. By the end of the century, landownership had largely ceased to be the basis of great wealth, and businessmen, rather than aristocrats, led the major political parties. Even so, the titled nobility of dukes, earls, viscounts, and barons retained great social prestige and considerable personal wealth. Many among them found an outlet for their energies and opportunities for status and enrichment in the vast domains of the British Empire, where they went as colonial administrators or settlers. Famously described as a "system of outdoor relief for the aristocracy," the empire provided a cushion for a declining class.

The Middle Classes

■ **Change**
How did Britain's middle classes change during the nineteenth century?

Those who benefited most conspicuously from industrialization were members of that amorphous group known as the middle class. At its upper levels, the middle class contained extremely wealthy factory and mine owners, bankers, and merchants. Such rising businessmen readily assimilated into aristocratic life, buying country houses, obtaining seats in parliament, sending their sons to Oxford or Cambridge University, and gratefully accepting titles of nobility from Queen Victoria.

Far more numerous were the smaller businessmen, doctors, lawyers, engineers, teachers, journalists, scientists, and other professionals required in any industrial society. Such people set the tone for a distinctly middle-class society with its own values and outlooks. Politically they were liberals, favoring constitutional government, private property, free trade, and social reform within limits. Their agitation resulted in the Reform Bill of 1832, which broadened the right to vote to many men of the middle class, but not to middle-class women. Ideas of thrift and hard work, a rigid morality, and cleanliness characterized middle-class culture. The central value of that culture was "respectability," a term that combined notions of social status and virtuous behavior. Nowhere were these values more effectively displayed than in the Scotsman Samuel Smiles's famous book *Self-Help*, published in 1859. Individuals are responsible for their own destiny, Smiles argued. An hour a day devoted to self-improvement "would make an ignorant man wise in a few years." According to Smiles, this enterprising spirit was what distinguished the prosperous middle class from Britain's poor.

The Industrial Middle Class
This late-nineteenth-century painting shows a prosperous French middle-class family, attended by a servant. (Chateau de Versailles/SuperStock, Inc.)

The misery of the poorer classes was "voluntary and self-imposed—the results of idleness, thriftlessness, intemperance, and misconduct."[19]

Women in such middle-class families were increasingly cast as homemakers, wives, and mothers, charged with creating an emotional haven for their men and a refuge from a heartless and cutthroat capitalist world. They were also the moral center of family life and the educators of "respectability" as well as the managers of consumption as "shopping," a new concept in eighteenth-century Britain, became a central activity. An "ideology of domesticity" defined the home and charitable activities as the proper sphere for women, while paid employment and public life beckoned to men. The English poet Alfred, Lord Tennyson, aptly expressed this understanding in his poem "The Princess":

> Man for the field and woman for the hearth:
> Man for the sword and for the needle she:
> Man with the head and woman with the heart:
> Man to command and woman to obey.
> All else confusion.

Middle-class women played a very different role from women in the peasant farm or the artisan's shop, where wives, though clearly subordinate, worked productively alongside their husbands. By the late nineteenth century, however, some middle-class women began to enter the teaching, clerical, and nursing professions.

As Britain's industrial economy matured, it also gave rise to a sizable lower middle class, which included people employed in the growing service sector as clerks, salespeople, bank tellers, hotel staff, secretaries, telephone operators, police officers, and the like. By the end of the nineteenth century, this growing class represented about 20 percent of Britain's population and provided new employment opportunities for women as well as men. In just twenty years (1881–1901), the number of female secretaries in Britain rose from 7,000 to 90,000. Almost all were single and expected to return to the home after marriage. For both men and women, such employment represented a claim on membership in the larger middle class and a means of distinguishing themselves clearly from a working class tainted by manual labor.

The Laboring Classes

The overwhelming majority of Britain's nineteenth-century population—some 70 percent or more—were, of course, neither aristocrats nor members of the middle classes. They were manual workers in the mines, ports, factories, construction sites, workshops, and farms of an industrializing Britain. Although their conditions varied considerably and changed over time, the laboring classes were the people who suffered most and benefited least from the epic transformations of the Industrial Revolution. Their efforts to accommodate, resist, protest, and change those conditions contributed much to the texture of the first industrial society.

DEATH'S DISPENSARY.
OPEN TO THE POOR, GRATIS, BY PERMISSION OF THE PARISH.

The Urban Poor of Industrial Britain
This 1866 political cartoon shows an impoverished urban family forced to draw its drinking water from a polluted public well, while a figure of Death operates the pump. (The Granger Collection, New York)

The lives of the laboring classes were shaped primarily by the new working conditions of the industrial era. Chief among those conditions was the rapid urbanization of British society. Liverpool's population alone grew from 77,000 to 400,000 in the first half of the nineteenth century. By 1851, a majority of Britain's population lived in towns and cities, an enormous change from the overwhelmingly rural life of almost all previous civilizations. By the end of the century, London was the world's largest city, with more than 6 million inhabitants.

These cities were vastly overcrowded and smoky, with wholly inadequate sanitation, periodic epidemics, endless row houses and warehouses, few public services or open spaces, and inadequate water supplies. This was the environment in which most urban workers lived in the first half of the nineteenth century. Nor was there much personal contact between the rich and the poor of industrial cities. Benjamin Disraeli's novel *Sybil*, published in 1845, described these two ends of the social spectrum as "two nations between whom there is no intercourse and no sympathy; who are ignorant of each other's habits, thoughts and feelings, as if they were dwellers in different zones or inhabitants of different planets."

The industrial factories to which growing numbers of desperate people looked for employment offered a work environment far different from the artisan's shop or the tenant's farm. Long hours, low wages, and child labor were nothing new for the poor, but the routine and monotony of work, dictated by the factory whistle and the needs of machines, imposed novel and highly unwelcome conditions of labor. Also objectionable were the direct and constant supervision and the rules and fines aimed at enforcing work discipline. The ups and downs of a capitalist economy made industrial work insecure as well as onerous. Unlike their middle-class sisters, many girls and young women of the laboring classes worked in mills or as domestic servants in order to supplement meager family incomes, but after marriage they too usually left outside paid employment because a man who could not support his wife was widely considered a failure. Within the home, however, many working-class women continued to earn money by taking in boarders, doing laundry, or sewing clothes.

Social Protest

For workers of the laboring classes, industrial life "was a stony desert, which they had to make habitable by their own efforts."[20] Such efforts took many forms. By 1815, about 1 million workers, mostly artisans, had created a variety of "friendly societies." With dues contributed by members, these working-class self-help groups provided insurance against sickness, a decent funeral, and an opportunity for social life in an otherwise bleak environment. Other skilled artisans, who had been displaced by machine-produced goods and forbidden to organize in legal unions, sometimes wrecked the offending machinery and burned the mills that had taken their jobs. The class consciousness of working people was such that one police informer reported that "most every creature of the lower order both in town and country are on their side."[21]

Others acted within the political arena by joining movements aimed at obtaining the vote for working-class men, a goal that was gradually achieved in the second half of the nineteenth century. When trade unions were legalized in 1824, growing numbers of factory workers joined these associations in their efforts to achieve better wages and working conditions. Initially their strikes, attempts at nationwide organization, and the threat of violence made them fearful indeed to the upper classes. One British newspaper in 1834 described unions as "the most dangerous institutions that were ever permitted to take root, under shelter of law, in any country,"[22] although they later became rather more "respectable" organizations.

Socialist ideas of various kinds gradually spread within the working class, challenging the assumptions of a capitalist society. Robert Owen (1771–1858), a wealthy British cotton textile manufacturer, urged the creation of small industrial communities where workers and their families would be well treated. He established one such community, with a ten-hour workday, spacious housing, decent wages, and education for children, at his mill in New Lanark in Scotland.

Of more lasting significance was the socialism of Karl Marx (1818–1883). German by birth, Marx spent much of his life in England, where he witnessed the brutal conditions of Britain's Industrial Revolution and wrote voluminously about history and economics. His probing analysis led him to the conclusion that industrial capitalism was an inherently unstable system, doomed to collapse in a revolutionary upheaval that would give birth to a classless socialist society, thus ending forever the ancient conflict between rich and poor. (See Document 18.1, pp. 856–59, for Marx's own understanding of industrial-era capitalism.)

In these ideas, the impact of Europe's industrial, political, and scientific revolutions found expression. Industrialization created both the social conditions against which Marx protested so bitterly and the enormous wealth he felt would make socialism possible. The French Revolution, still a living memory in Marx's youth, provided evidence that grand upheavals, giving rise to new societies, had in fact taken place and could do so again. Moreover, Marx regarded himself as a scientist, discovering the laws of social development in much the same fashion as Newton discovered the laws of

■ Change
How did Karl Marx understand the Industrial Revolution? In what ways did his ideas have an impact in the industrializing world of the nineteenth century?

motion. His was therefore a "scientific socialism," embedded in these laws of historical change; revolution was a certainty and the socialist future inevitable.

It was a grand, compelling, prophetic, utopian vision of human freedom and community—and it inspired socialist movements of workers and intellectuals amid the grim harshness of Europe's industrialization in the second half of the nineteenth century. Socialists established political parties in most European states and linked them together in international organizations as well. These parties recruited members, contested elections as they gained the right to vote, agitated for reforms, and in some cases plotted revolution. The so-called workers' hymn, the "Internationale," expressed the visionary possibilities of socialism and the threatening challenge it posed to the triumphant capitalism of industrial Europe (see Document 18.4, pp. 863–64).

In the later decades of the nineteenth century, such ideas echoed among more radical trade unionists and some middle-class intellectuals in Britain, and even more so in a rapidly industrializing Germany and elsewhere. By then, however, the British working-class movement was not overtly revolutionary. When a working-class political party, the Labour Party, was established in the 1890s, it advocated a reformist program and a peaceful democratic transition to socialism, largely rejecting the class struggle and revolutionary emphasis of classical Marxism. (See Document 18.2, pp. 859–61, for an argument favoring a democratic rather than a revolutionary path toward socialism.)

Improving material conditions during the second half of the nineteenth century helped to move the working-class movement in Britain and elsewhere away from a revolutionary posture. Marx had expected industrial capitalist societies to polarize into a small wealthy class and a huge and increasingly impoverished proletariat. However, standing between "the captains of industry" and the workers was a sizable middle and lower-middle class, constituting perhaps 30 percent of the population, most of whom were not really wealthy but were immensely proud that they were not manual laborers. Marx had not foreseen the development of this intermediate social group, nor had he imagined that workers could better their standard of living within a capitalist framework. But they did. Wages rose under pressure from unions; cheap imported food improved working-class diets; infant mortality rates fell; and shops and chain stores catering to working-class families multiplied. As English male workers gradually obtained the right to vote, politicians had an incentive to legislate in their favor, by abolishing child labor, regulating factory conditions, and even, in 1911, inaugurating a system of relief for the unemployed. Sanitary reform considerably cleaned up the "filth and stink" of early-nineteenth-century cities, and urban parks made a modest appearance. Contrary to Marx's expectations, capitalist societies demonstrated some capacity for reform.

Further eroding working-class radicalism was a growing sense of nationalism, which bound workers in particular countries to their middle-class employers and compatriots, offsetting to some extent the economic and social antagonism between them. When World War I broke out, the workers of the world, far from uniting against

Manifestation du Père Lachaise
Parti Socialiste, Section Française de l'Internationale Ouvrière
Groupe de la Villette

their bourgeois enemies as Marx had urged them, instead set off to slaughter one another in enormous numbers on the battlefields of Europe. National loyalty had trumped class loyalty.

Nonetheless, as the twentieth century dawned, industrial Britain could hardly be described as a stable or contented society. Immense inequalities still separated the classes. Some 40 percent of the working class continued to live in conditions then described as "poverty." A mounting wave of strikes from 1910 to 1913 testified to the intensity of class conflict. The Labour Party was becoming a major force in parliament. Some socialists and some feminists were becoming radicalized. "Wisps of violence hung in the English air," wrote Eric Hobsbawm, "symptoms of a crisis in economy and society, which the [country's] self-confident opulence... could not quite conceal."[23] The world's first industrial society remained dissatisfied and conflicted.

It was also a society in economic decline relative to industrial newcomers such as Germany and the United States. Britain paid a price for its early lead, for its businessmen became committed to machinery that became obsolete as the century progressed. Latecomers invested in more modern equipment and in various ways had surpassed the British by the early twentieth century.

Socialist Protest
Socialism, a response to the injustices and inequalities of industrial capitalism, spread throughout Europe in the nineteenth and early twentieth centuries. Here a group of French socialists in 1908 are demonstrating in memory of an earlier uprising, the Paris commune of 1871. (Demonstration at Père-Lachaise for the commemoration of the Paris Commune, by Socialist party, French Section of the International Workingmen's Association, group of La Villette, 1st May 1908 [colored photo], Gondry, [19th–early 20th century]/ Private Collection/The Bridgeman Art Library)

Variations on a Theme: Comparing Industrialization in the United States and Russia

Not for long was the Industrial Revolution confined to Britain. It soon spread to continental Western Europe, and by the end of the nineteenth century, it was well under way in the United States, Russia, and Japan. The globalization of industrialization had begun. Everywhere it took hold, industrialization bore a range of outcomes broadly similar to those in Britain. New technologies and sources of energy generated vast increases in production and spawned an unprecedented urbanization as well. Class structures changed as aristocrats, artisans, and peasants declined as classes, while the middle classes and a factory working class grew in numbers and social prominence. Middle-class women generally withdrew from paid labor altogether, and their working-class counterparts sought to do so after marriage. Working women usually received lower wages than their male counterparts, had difficulty joining unions, and were subject to charges that they were taking jobs from men. Working-class frustration and anger gave rise to trade unions and socialist movements, injecting a new element of social conflict into industrial societies.

Nevertheless, different histories, cultures, and societies ensured that the Industrial Revolution unfolded variously in the diverse countries in which it became established. Differences in the pace and timing of industrialization, the size and shape of major industries, the role of the state, the political expression of social conflict, and many other factors have made this process rich in comparative possibilities. French industrialization, for example, occurred more slowly and perhaps less disruptively than did that of Britain. Germany focused initially on heavy industry—iron, steel, and coal—rather than on the textile industry with which Britain had begun. Moreover, German industrialization was far more highly concentrated in huge companies called cartels, and it generated a rather more militant and Marxist-oriented labor movement than in Britain.

Nowhere were the variations in the industrializing process more apparent than in those two vast countries that lay on the periphery of Europe. To the west across the Atlantic Ocean was the United States, a young, vigorous, democratic, expanding country, populated largely by people of European descent, along with a substantial number of slaves of African origin. To the east was Russia, with its Eastern Orthodox Christianity, an autocratic tsar, a huge population of serfs, and an empire stretching across all of northern Asia. In the early nineteenth century, the French observer Alexis de Tocqueville famously commented on these two emerging giants:

> The Anglo-American relies upon personal interest to accomplish his ends and gives free scope to the unguided strength and common sense of the people; the Russian centers all the authority of society in a single arm.... Their starting-point is different and their courses are not the same; yet each of them seems marked out by the will of Heaven to sway the destinies of half the globe.

By the early twentieth century, his prediction seemed to be coming true. Industrialization had turned the United States into a major global power and in Russia had spawned an enormous revolutionary upheaval that made that country the first outpost of global communism.

The United States: Industrialization without Socialism

American industrialization began in the textile industry of New England during the 1820s but grew explosively in the half century following the Civil War (1861–1865) (see Map 18.2). The country's huge size, the ready availability of natural resources, its growing domestic market, and its relative political stability combined to make the United States the world's leading industrial power by 1914. At that time, it produced 36 percent of the world's manufactured goods, compared to 16 percent for Germany, 14 percent for Great Britain, and 6 percent for France. Furthermore, U.S. industrialization was closely linked to that of Europe. About one-third of the capital investment

■ **Comparison**

What were the differences between industrialization in the United States and that in Russia?

Map 18.2 The Industrial United States in 1900

By the early twentieth century, manufacturing industries were largely in the Northeast and Midwest, whereas mining operations were more widely scattered across the country.

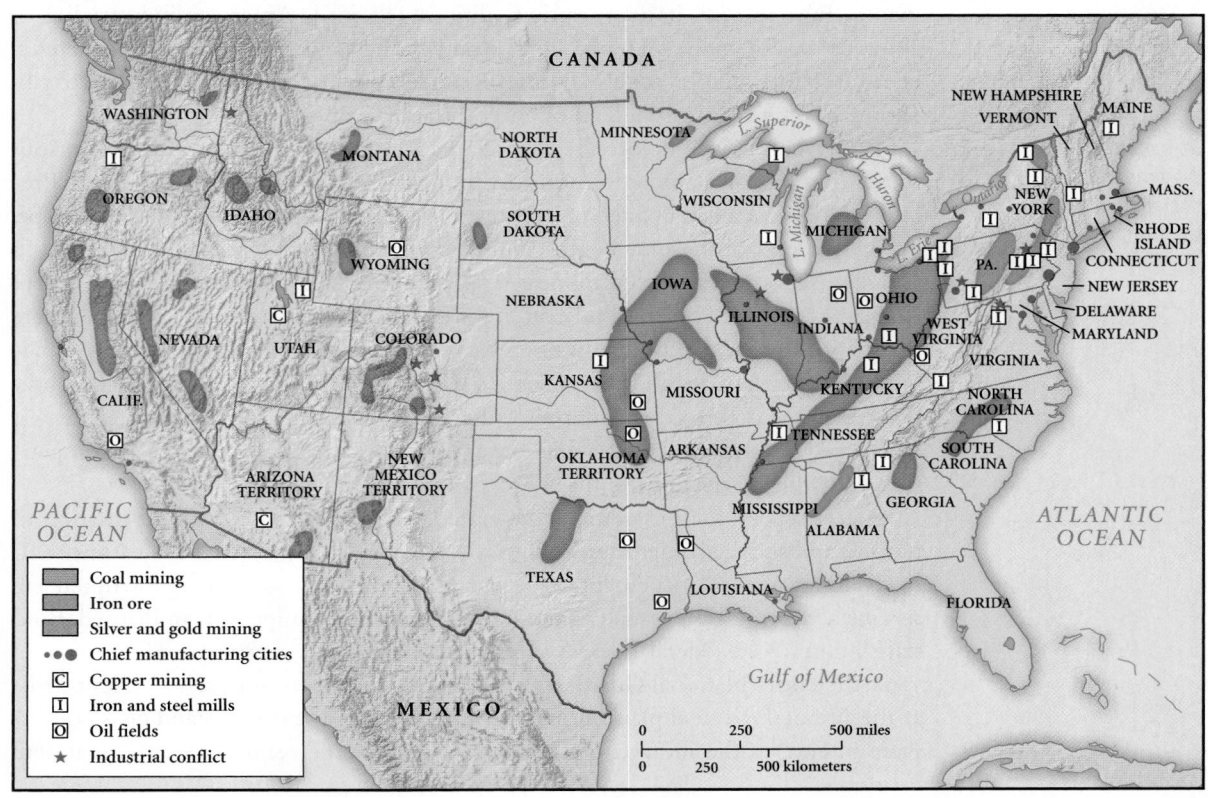

that financed its remarkable growth came from British, French, and German capitalists. But unlike Latin America, which also received much foreign investment, the United States was able to use those funds to generate an independent Industrial Revolution of its own.

As in other second-wave industrializing countries, the U.S. government played an important role, though less directly than in Germany or Japan. Tax breaks, huge grants of public land to the railroad companies, laws enabling the easy formation of corporations, and the absence of much overt regulation of industry all fostered the rise of very large business enterprises. The U.S. Steel Corporation, for example, by 1901 had an annual budget three times the size of the federal government. In this respect, the United States followed the pattern of Germany but differed from that of France and Britain, where family businesses still predominated.

The United States also pioneered techniques of mass production, using interchangeable parts, the assembly line, and "scientific management" to produce for a mass market. The nation's advertising agencies, Sears Roebuck's and Montgomery Ward's mail-order catalogs, and urban department stores generated a middle-class "culture of consumption." When the industrialist Henry Ford in the early twentieth century began producing the Model T at a price that many ordinary people could afford, he famously declared: "I am going to democratize the automobile." More so than in Europe, with its aristocratic traditions, self-made American industrialists of fabulous wealth such as Henry Ford, Andrew Carnegie, and John D. Rockefeller became cultural heroes, widely admired as models of what anyone could achieve with daring and hard work in a land of endless opportunity.

■ **Explanation**
Why did Marxist socialism not take root in the United States?

Nevertheless, well before the first Model T rolled off the assembly line, serious social divisions of a kind common to European industrial societies mounted. Pre-industrial America had boasted of a relative social equality, quite unlike that of Europe, but by the end of the nineteenth century, a widening gap separated the classes. In Carnegie's Homestead steel plant near Pittsburgh, employees worked every day except Christmas and the Fourth of July, often for twelve hours a day. In Manhattan, where millions of European immigrants disembarked, many lived in five- or six-story buildings with four families and two toilets on each floor. In every large city, such conditions prevailed close by the mansions of elite neighborhoods. To some, the contrast was a betrayal of American ideals, while others saw it as a natural outcome of competition and "the survival of the fittest."

As elsewhere, such conditions generated much labor protest, the formation of unions, and strikes, sometimes leading to violence. In 1877, when the eastern railroads announced a 10 percent wage cut for their workers, strikers disrupted rail service across the eastern half of the country, smashed equipment, and rioted. Both state militias and federal troops were called out to put down the movement. In 1892, the entire National Guard of Pennsylvania was sent to suppress a violent strike at the Homestead steel plant near Pittsburgh. Class consciousness and class conflict were intense in the industrial America of the late nineteenth and early twentieth centuries.

Unlike many European countries, however, no major political party emerged in the United States to represent the interests of the working class. Nor did the ideas of socialism, and especially Marxism, appeal to American workers nearly as much as they did in Europe. At its high point, the Socialist Party of America garnered just 6 percent of the vote for its presidential candidate in the 1912 election, whereas socialists at the time held more seats in Germany's parliament than any other party. Even in the depths of the Great Depression of the 1930s, no major socialist movement emerged to champion American workers. How might we explain this distinctive feature of American industrial development?

One answer lies in the relative conservatism of major American union organizations, especially the American Federation of Labor. Its focus on skilled workers excluded the more radical unskilled laborers, and its refusal to align with any party limited its influence in the political arena. Furthermore, the immense religious, ethnic, and racial divisions of American society contrasted sharply with the more homogeneous populations of many European countries. Catholics and Protestants; English, Irish, Germans, Slavs, Jews, and Italians; whites and blacks—such differences undermined the class solidarity of American workers, making it far more difficult to sustain class-oriented political parties and a socialist labor movement. Moreover, the country's remarkable economic growth generated on average a higher standard of living for American workers than their European counterparts experienced. Land was cheaper, and home ownership was more available. Workers with property generally found socialism less attractive than those without. By 1910, a particularly large group of white-collar workers in sales, services, and offices outnumbered factory laborers. Their middle-class aspirations further diluted impulses toward radicalism.

But political challenges to the abuses of capitalist industrialization did arise. Among small farmers in the U.S. South, West, and Midwest, "populists" railed against banks, industrialists, monopolies, the existing money system, and both major political parties, all of which they thought were dominated by the corporate interests of the eastern elites. More successful, especially in the early twentieth century, were the Progressives, who pushed for specific reforms, such as wages-and-hours legislation, better sanitation standards, antitrust laws, and greater governmental intervention in the economy. Socialism, however, came to be defined as fundamentally "un-American" in a country that so valued individualism and so feared "big government." It was a distinctive feature of the American response to industrialization.

Russia: Industrialization and Revolution

As a setting for the Industrial Revolution, it would be hard to imagine two more different environments than the United States and Russia. If the United States was the Western world's most exuberant democracy in the nineteenth century, Russia remained the sole outpost of absolute monarchy, in which the state exercised far greater control over individuals and society than anywhere in the Western world.

Russian Serfdom
This nineteenth-century cartoon by the French artist Gustave Doré shows Russian noblemen gambling with tied bundles of stiff serfs. Serfdom was not finally abolished in Russia until 1861. (The Granger Collection, New York)

At the beginning of the twentieth century, Russia still had no national parliament, no legal political parties, and no nationwide elections. The tsar, answerable to God alone, ruled unchecked. Furthermore, Russian society was dominated by a titled nobility of various ranks, whose upper levels included great landowners, who furnished the state with military officers and leading government officials. Until 1861, most Russians were peasant serfs, bound to the estates of their masters, subject to sale, greatly exploited, and largely at the mercy of their owners. In Russia at least, serfdom approximated slavery. A vast cultural gulf separated these two classes. Many nobles were highly Westernized, some speaking French better than Russian, whereas their serfs were steeped in a backwoods Orthodox Christianity that incorporated pre-Christian spirits, spells, curses, and magic.

A further difference between Russia and the United States lay in the source of social and economic change. In the United States, such change bubbled up from society as free farmers, workers, and businessmen sought new opportunities and operated in a political system that gave them varying degrees of expression. In autocratic Russia, change was far more often initiated by the state itself, in its continuing efforts to catch up with the more powerful and innovative states of Europe. This kind of "transformation from above" found an early expression in the reign of Peter the Great (reigned 1689–1725). His massive efforts included vast administrative changes, the enlargement and modernization of Russian military forces, a new educational system for the sons of noblemen, and dozens of manufacturing enterprises. Russian nobles were instructed to dress in European styles and to shave their sacred and much-revered beards. The newly created capital city of St. Petersburg was to be Russia's "window on the West." One of Peter's successors, Catherine the Great (reigned 1762–1796), followed up with further efforts to Europeanize Russian cultural and intellectual life, viewing herself as heir to the European Enlightenment.

Such state-directed change continued in the nineteenth century with the freeing of the serfs in 1861, an action stimulated by military defeat at the hands of British and French forces in the Crimean War (1854–1856). To many thoughtful Russians, serfdom seemed incompatible with modern civilization and held back the country's overall development, as did its economic and industrial backwardness. Thus, beginning in the 1860s, Russia began a program of industrial development, which was more heavily directed by the state than was the case in Western Europe or the United States.

By the 1890s, Russia's Industrial Revolution was launched and growing rapidly. It focused particularly on railroads and heavy industry and was fueled by a substantial amount of foreign investment. By 1900, Russia ranked fourth in the world in

■ **Change**
What factors contributed to the making of a revolutionary situation in Russia by the beginning of the twentieth century?

steel production and had major industries in coal, textiles, and oil. Its industrial enterprises, still modest in comparison to those of Europe, were concentrated in a few major cities—Moscow, St. Petersburg, and Kiev, for example—and took place in factories far larger than in most of Western Europe.

All of this contributed to the explosive social outcomes of Russian industrialization. A growing middle class of businessmen and professionals increasingly took shape. As modern and educated people, many in the middle class objected strongly to the deep conservatism of tsarist Russia and sought a greater role in political life, but they were also dependent on the state for contracts and jobs and for suppressing the growing radicalism of the workers, which they greatly feared. Although factory workers constituted only about 5 percent of Russia's total population, they quickly developed an unusually radical class consciousness, based on harsh conditions and the absence of any legal outlet for their grievances. Until 1897, a thirteen-hour working day was common. Ruthless discipline and overt disrespect from supervisors created resentment, while life in large and unsanitary barracks added to workers' sense of injustice. In the absence of legal unions or political parties, these grievances often erupted in the form of large-scale strikes.

In these conditions, a small but growing number of educated Russians found in Marxist socialism a way of understanding the changes they witnessed daily and hope for the future in a revolutionary upheaval of workers. In 1898, they created an illegal Russian Social-Democratic Labor Party and quickly became involved in workers' education, union organizing, and, eventually, revolutionary action. By the early twentieth century, the strains of rapid change and the state's continued intransigence had reached the bursting point, and in 1905, following its defeat in a naval war with Japan, Russia erupted in spontaneous insurrection. Workers in Moscow and St. Petersburg went on strike and created their own representative councils, called soviets. Peasant uprisings, student demonstrations, revolts of non-Russian nationalities, and mutinies in the military all contributed to the upheaval. Recently formed political parties, representing intellectuals of various persuasions, came out into the open.

The 1905 revolution, though brutally suppressed, forced the tsar's regime to make more substantial reforms than it had ever contemplated. It granted a constitution, legalized both trade unions and political parties, and permitted the election of a national assembly, called the Duma. Censorship was eased, and plans were under way for universal primary education. Industrial development likewise continued at a rapid rate, so that by 1914 Russia stood fifth in the world in terms of overall output. But in the first half of that year, some 1,250,000 workers, representing about 40 percent of the entire industrial workforce, went out on strike.

Thus the tsar's limited political reforms, which had been granted with great reluctance and were often reversed in practice, failed to tame working-class radicalism or to bring social stability to Russia. In 1906–1907, when a newly elected and radically inclined Duma refused to cooperate with the

The 1905 Revolution in Russia

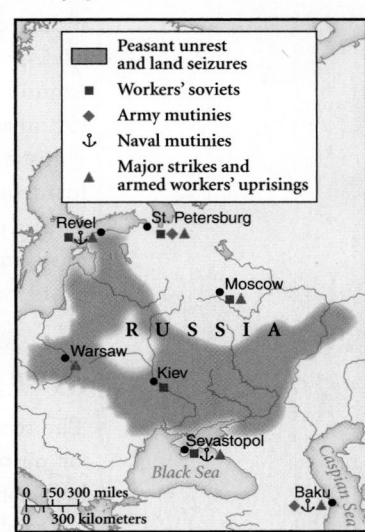

Peasant unrest and land seizures

■ Workers' soviets

◆ Army mutinies

⚓ Naval mutinies

▲ Major strikes and armed workers' uprisings

Revel

St. Petersburg

Moscow

R U S S I A

Warsaw

Kiev

Sevastopol

Black Sea

Baku

Caspian Sea

0   150 300 miles
0   300 kilometers

tsar's new political system, Tsar Nicholas II twice dissolved that elected body and finally changed the electoral laws to favor the landed nobility. Consequently, in Russian political life, the people generally, and even the middle class, had only a limited voice. The representatives of even the privileged classes had become so alienated by the government's intransigence that many felt revolution was inevitable. Various revolutionary groups, many of them socialist, published pamphlets and newspapers, organized trade unions, and spread their messages among workers and peasants. Particularly in the cities, these revolutionary parties had an impact. They provided a language through which workers could express their grievances; they created links among workers from different factories; and they furnished leaders who were able to act when the revolutionary moment arrived.

World War I provided that moment. The enormous hardships of that war, coupled with the immense social tensions of industrialization within a still autocratic political system, sparked the Russian Revolution of 1917 (see Chapter 22). That massive upheaval quickly brought to power the most radical of the socialist groups operating in the country—the Bolsheviks, led by the charismatic Vladimir Ilyich Ulyanov, better known as Lenin. (See Document 18.5, pp. 864–65, for Lenin's view of revolution.) Only in Russia was industrialization associated with violent social revolution, and this was the most distinctive feature of Russia's modern historical development. And only in Russia was a socialist political party, inspired by the teachings of Karl Marx, able to seize power, thus launching the modern world's first socialist society, with enormous implications for the twentieth century.

The Industrial Revolution and Latin America in the Nineteenth Century

Beyond the world of Europe and North America, only Japan underwent a major industrial transformation during the nineteenth century, part of that country's overall response to the threat of European aggression. (See pp. 901–02 for a more detailed examination of Japan's industrialization.) Elsewhere—in colonial India, Egypt, the Ottoman Empire, China, and Latin America—very modest experiments in modern industry were undertaken, but nowhere did they drive the kind of major social transformation that had taken place in Britain, Europe, North America, and Japan. However, even in societies that did not experience their own Industrial Revolution, the profound impact of European and North American industrialization was hard to avoid. Such was the case in Latin America during the nineteenth century.

After Independence in Latin America

The struggle for independence in Latin America had lasted far longer and proved far more destructive than in North America. Decimated populations, diminished herds of livestock, flooded or closed silver mines, abandoned farms, shrinking international trade and investment capital, and empty national treasuries—these were

Snapshot   The Industrial Revolution and the Global Divide[24]

During the nineteenth century, the Industrial Revolution generated an enormous and unprecedented economic division in the world, as measured by the share of manufacturing output. What patterns can you see in this table?

SHARE OF TOTAL WORLD MANUFACTURING OUTPUT (PERCENT)

	1750	1800	1860	1880	1900
Europe as a Whole	**23.2**	**28.1**	**53.2**	**61.3**	**62.0**
UNITED KINGDOM	1.9	4.3	19.9	22.9	18.5
FRANCE	4.0	4.2	7.9	7.8	6.8
GERMANY	2.9	3.5	4.9	8.5	13.2
RUSSIA	5.0	5.6	7.0	7.6	8.8
United States	**0.1**	**0.8**	**7.2**	**14.7**	**23.6**
Japan	**3.8**	**3.5**	**2.6**	**2.4**	**2.4**
The Rest of the World	**73.0**	**67.7**	**36.6**	**20.9**	**11.0**
CHINA	32.8	33.3	19.7	12.5	6.2
SOUTH ASIA (INDIA/PAKISTAN)	24.5	19.7	8.6	2.8	1.7

among the conditions under which Latin American countries greeted independence. Furthermore, the four major administrative units (vice-royalties) of Spanish America ultimately dissolved into eighteen separate countries, and regional revolts wracked Brazil in the early decades of its independent life. A number of international wars in the postindependence century likewise shook these new nations. Peru and Bolivia briefly united and then broke apart in a bitter conflict (1836–1839); Mexico lost huge territories to the United States (1846–1848); and an alliance of Argentina, Brazil, and Uruguay went to war with Paraguay (1864–1870) in a conflict that devastated Paraguay's small population.

Within these new countries, political life was turbulent and unstable. Conservatives favored centralized authority and sought to maintain the social status quo of the colonial era in alliance with the Catholic Church, which at independence owned perhaps half of all productive land. Their often bitter opponents were liberals, who attacked the Church in the name of Enlightenment values, sought at least modest social reforms, and preferred federalism. In many countries, conflicts between these factions, often violent, enabled military strongmen known as *caudillos* to achieve power as defenders of order and property, although they too succeeded one another with great frequency. One of them, Antonio López de Santa Anna of Mexico, was president of his country at least nine separate times between 1833 and 1855. Constitutions too replaced one another with bewildering speed. Bolivia had ten constitutions during the nineteenth century, while Ecuador and Peru each had eight.

Social life did not change fundamentally in the aftermath of independence. Slavery, it is true, was abolished in most of Latin America by midcentury, although it persisted in both Brazil and Cuba until the late 1880s. Most of the legal distinctions among various racial categories also disappeared, and all free people were considered, at least officially, equal citizens. Nevertheless, productive economic resources such as businesses, ranches, and plantations remained overwhelmingly in the hands of creole whites, who were culturally oriented toward Europe. The military provided an avenue of mobility for a few skilled and ambitious mestizo men, some of whom subsequently became caudillos. Other mixed-race people found a place in a small middle class as teachers, shopkeepers, or artisans. The vast majority—blacks, Indians, and many mixed-race people—remained impoverished, working small subsistence farms or laboring in the mines or on the *haciendas* (plantations) of the well-to-do. Only rarely did the poor and dispossessed actively rebel against their social betters. One such case was the Caste War of Yucatán (1847–1901), a prolonged struggle of the Maya people of Mexico, aimed at cleansing their land of European and mestizo intruders.

Facing the World Economy

■ **Connection**
In what ways and with what impact was Latin America linked to the global economy of the nineteenth century?

During the second half of the nineteenth century, a measure of political consolidation took hold in Latin America, and countries such as Mexico, Peru, and Argentina entered periods of greater stability. At the same time, Latin America as a whole became more closely integrated into a world economy driven by the industrialization of Western Europe and North America. The new technology of the steamship cut the sailing time between Britain and Argentina almost in half, while the underwater telegraph instantly brought the latest news and fashions of Europe to Latin America.

The most significant economic outcome of this growing integration was a rapid growth of Latin American exports to the industrializing countries, which now needed the food products, raw materials, and markets of these new nations. Latin American landowners, businessmen, and governments proved eager to supply those needs, and in the sixty years or so after 1850, an export boom increased the value of Latin American goods sold abroad by a factor of ten.

Mexico continued to produce large amounts of silver, supplying more than half the world's new supply until 1860. Now added to the list of raw materials flowing out of Latin America were copper from Chile, a metal that the growing electrical industry required; tin from Bolivia, which met the mounting demand for tin cans; and nitrates from Chile and guano (bird droppings) from Peru, both of which were used for fertilizer. Wild rubber from the Amazon rain forest was in great demand for bicycle and automobile tires, as was sisal from Mexico, used to make binder twine for the proliferating mechanical harvesters of North America. Bananas from Central America, beef from Argentina, cacao from Ecuador, coffee from Brazil and Guatemala, and sugar from Cuba also found eager markets in the rapidly growing and increasingly prosperous world of industrializing countries. In return for these primary products, Latin Americans imported the textiles, machinery, tools, weapons, and luxury goods of Europe and the United States (see Map 18.3).

Accompanying this burgeoning commerce was large-scale investment of European capital in Latin America, $10 billion alone between 1870 and 1919. Most of this capital came from Great Britain, which invested more in Argentina in the late nineteenth century than in its colony of India, although France, Germany, Italy, and the United States also contributed to this substantial financial transfer. By 1910, U.S. business interests controlled 40 percent of Mexican property and produced half of its oil. Much of this capital was used to build railroads, largely to funnel Latin American exports to the coast, where they were shipped to overseas markets. Mexico had only 390 miles of railroad in 1876; it had 15,000 miles in 1910. By 1915, Argentina, with 22,000 miles of railroad, had more track per person than the United States.

Becoming like Europe?

To the economic elites of Latin America, intent on making their countries resemble Europe or the United States, all of this was progress. In some respects, they were surely right. Economies were growing and producing more than ever before. The population also was burgeoning; it increased from about 30 million in 1850 to more than 77 million in 1912 as public health measures (such as safe drinking water, inoculations, sewers, and campaigns to eliminate mosquitoes that carried yellow fever) brought down death rates.

> ■ **Comparison**
> Did Latin America follow or diverge from the historical path of Europe during the nineteenth century?

Urbanization also proceeded rapidly. By the early twentieth century, wrote one scholar, "Latin American cities lost their colonial cobblestones, white-plastered walls, and red-tiled roofs. They became modern metropolises, comparable to urban giants anywhere. Streetcars swayed, telephones jangled, and silent movies flickered from Montevideo and Santiago to Mexico City and Havana."[25] Buenos Aires, Argentina's metropolitan center, boasted 750,000 people in 1900 and billed itself the "Paris of South America." There the educated elite, just like the English, drank tea in the afternoon, while discussing European literature, philosophy, and fashion, usually in French.

To become more like Europe, Latin America sought to attract more Europeans. Because civilization, progress, and modernity apparently derived from Europe, many Latin American countries actively sought to increase their European populations by deliberately recruiting impoverished people with the promise, mostly unfulfilled, of a new and prosperous life in the New World. Argentina received the largest wave of European immigrants (some 2.5 million between 1870 and 1915), mostly from Spain and Italy. Brazil and Uruguay likewise attracted substantial numbers of European newcomers.

Only a quite modest segment of Latin American society saw any great benefits from the export boom and all that followed from it. Upper-class landowners certainly gained as exports flourished and their property values soared. Middle-class urban dwellers—merchants, office workers, lawyers, and other professionals—also

U.S. Interventions

→ Puerto Rico, 1898–on
→ Panama, 1903
→ Cuba, 1898–1902, 1905–09, 1917–21
→ Haiti, 1915–34
→ Mexico, 1914, 1916–17
→ Nicaragua, 1909, 1912–25, 1927–32
→ Dominican Republic, 1916–24

MEXICO
$1329

CUBA
$471

$11 $16 $44

$99 $42
$19 $12
$61 $28

VENEZUELA
$161

COLOMBIA
$77

ECUADOR
$41

PERU
$197

BRAZIL
$1913

BOLIVIA
$59

PARAGUAY
$27

ARGENTINA
$4001

CHILE
$668

URUGUAY
$475

Bananas   ◆ Nitrate
Cacao   Oil
Cattle   Rubber
Coffee   Sheep
Copper and tin   Silver
Cotton   Sugar
Guano   Tobacco
Sisal   Wheat

$161 Foreign investment
(in millions of U.S. dollars around 1914)

← European immigration

Map 18.3 Latin America and the World, 1825–1935
During the nineteenth and early twentieth centuries, Latin American countries interacted with the industrializing world via investment, trade, immigration, and military intervention from the United States.

grew in numbers and prosperity as their skills proved valuable in a modernizing society. As a percentage of the total population, however, these were narrow elites. In Mexico in the mid-1890s, for example, the landowning upper class made up no more than 1 percent and the middle classes perhaps 8 percent of the population. Everyone else was lower-class, and most of them were impoverished.[26]

A new but quite small segment of this vast lower class emerged among urban workers who labored in the railroads, ports, mines, and a few factories. They organized themselves initially in a variety of mutual aid societies, but by the end of the nineteenth century, they were creating unions and engaging in strikes. To authoritarian governments interested in stability and progress, such activity was highly provocative and threatening, and they acted harshly to crush or repress unions and strikes. In 1906, the Mexican dictator Porfirio Díaz invited the Arizona Rangers to suppress a strike at Cananea near the U.S. border, an action that resulted in dozens of deaths. The following year in the Chilean city of Iquique, more than 1,000 men, women, and children were slaughtered by police when nitrate miners protested their wages and working conditions.

The vast majority of the lower class lived in rural areas, where they suffered the most and benefited the least from the export boom. Government attacks on communal landholding and peasant indebtedness to wealthy landowners combined to push many farmers off their land or into remote and poor areas where they could barely make a living. Many wound up as dependent laborers or peons on the haciendas of the wealthy, where their wages were often too meager to support a family. Thus women and children, who had earlier remained at home to tend the family plot, were required to join their menfolk as field laborers. Many immigrant Italian farmworkers in Argentina and Brazil were unable to acquire their own farms, as they had expected, and so drifted into the growing cities or returned to Italy.

Although local protests and violence were frequent, only in Mexico did these vast inequalities erupt into a nationwide revolution. There, in the early twentieth century, middle-class reformers joined with workers and peasants to overthrow the long dictatorship of Porfirio Díaz (1876–1911). What followed was a decade of bloody conflict (1910–1920) that cost Mexico some 1 million lives, or roughly 10 percent of the population. Huge peasant armies under charismatic leaders such as Pancho Villa and Emiliano Zapata helped oust Díaz. Intent on seizing land and redistributing it to the peasants, they then went on to attack many of Mexico's large haciendas. But unlike the later Russian and Chinese revolutions, in which the most radical elements seized state power, Villa and Zapata proved unable to do so, in part because they were hobbled by factionalism and focused on local or regional issues. Despite this limitation and its own internal conflicts, the Mexican Revolution transformed the country. When the dust settled, Mexico had a new constitution (1917) that proclaimed universal suffrage; provided for the redistribution of land; stripped the Catholic Church of any role in public education and forbade it to own land; announced unheard-of rights for workers, such as a minimum wage and an eight-hour workday;

The Mexican Revolution
Women were active participants in the Mexican Revolution. They prepared food, nursed the wounded, washed clothes, and at times served as soldiers on the battlefield, as illustrated in this cover image from a French magazine in 1913. (© Archivo Iconografico, S.A./Corbis)

and placed restrictions on foreign ownership of property. Much of Mexico's history in the twentieth century involved working out the implications of these nationalist and reformist changes. The revolution's direct influence, however, was largely limited to Mexico itself, without the wider international impact of the Russian and Chinese upheavals.

Perhaps the most significant outcome of the export boom lay in what did *not* happen, for nowhere in Latin America did it jump-start a thorough Industrial Revolution, despite a few factories that processed foods or manufactured textiles, clothing, and building materials. The reasons are many. A social structure that relegated some 90 percent of its population to an impoverished lower class generated only a very small market for manufactured goods. Moreover, economically powerful groups such as landowners and cattlemen benefited greatly from exporting agricultural products and had little incentive to invest in manufacturing. Domestic manufacturing enterprises could only have competed with cheaper and higher-quality foreign goods if they had been protected for a time by high tariffs. But Latin American political leaders had thoroughly embraced the popular European doctrine of prosperity through free trade, and many governments depended on taxing imports to fill their treasuries.

Instead of its own Industrial Revolution, Latin Americans developed a form of economic growth that was largely financed by capital from abroad and dependent on European and North American prosperity and decisions. Brazil experienced this kind of dependence when its booming rubber industry suddenly collapsed in 1910–1911, after seeds from the wild rubber tree had been illegally exported to Britain and were used to start competing and cheaper rubber plantations in Malaysia.

Later critics saw this "dependent development" as a new form of colonialism, expressed in the power exercised by foreign investors. The influence of the U.S.-owned United Fruit Company in Central America was a case in point. Allied with large landowners and compliant politicians, the company pressured the governments of these "banana republics" to maintain conditions favorable to U.S. business. This indirect or behind-the-scenes imperialism was supplemented by repeated U.S. military intervention in support of American corporate interests in Cuba, Haiti, the Dominican Republic, Nicaragua, and Mexico. The United States also controlled the Panama Canal and acquired Puerto Rico as a territory in the aftermath of the Spanish-American War (see Map 18.3, p. 850).

Thus, despite its domination by people of European descent and its close ties to the industrializing countries of the Atlantic world, Latin America's historical trajectory in the nineteenth century diverged considerably from that of Europe and North America.

Reflections: History and Horse Races

Historians and students of history seem endlessly fascinated by "firsts"—the first breakthrough to agriculture, the first civilization, the first domestication of horses, the first use of gunpowder, the first printing press, and so on. Each of these firsts presents a problem of explanation: why did it occur in some particular time and place rather than somewhere else or at some other time? Such questions have assumed historical significance both because "first achievements" represent something new in the human journey and because many of them conveyed unusual power, wealth, status, or influence on their creators.

Nonetheless, the focus on firsts can be misleading as well. Those who accomplished something first may see themselves as generally superior to those who embraced that innovation later. Historians too can sometimes adopt a winners-and-losers mentality, inviting a view of history as a horse race toward some finish line of accomplishment. Most first achievements in history, however, were not the result of intentional efforts but rather were the unexpected outcome of converging circumstances.

The Industrial Revolution is a case in point. Understanding the European beginnings of this immense breakthrough is certainly justified by its pervasive global consequences and its global spread over the past several centuries. In terms of our ability to dominate the natural environment and to extract wealth from it, the Industrial Revolution marks a decisive turning point in human history. But Europeans' attempts to explain their Industrial Revolution have at times stated or implied their own unique genius. In the nineteenth century, many Europeans saw their technological mastery as a sure sign of their cultural and racial superiority as they came to use "machines as the measure of men."[27] In attempting to answer the "why Europe?" question, historians too have sometimes sought the answer in some distinct or even superior feature of European civilization.

In emphasizing the unexpectedness of the first Industrial Revolution, and the global context within which it occurred, world historians have attempted to avoid a "history as horse race" syndrome. Clearly the first industrial breakthrough in Britain was not a self-conscious effort to win a race; it was the surprising outcome of countless decisions by many people to further their own interests. Subsequently, however, other societies and their governments quite deliberately tried to catch up, seeking the wealth and power that the Industrial Revolution promised.

The rapid spread of industrialization across the planet, though highly uneven, promises to diminish the importance of the "why Europe?" issue. Just as no one views agriculture as a Middle Eastern phenomenon, even though it occurred first in that region, it seems likely that industrialization will be seen increasingly as a global process rather than one uniquely associated with Europe. If industrial society proves to be a sustainable future for humankind—and this is presently an open question—historians of the future may well be more interested in the pattern of its global spread and in efforts to cope with its social and environmental consequences than with its origins in Western Europe.

Second Thoughts

What's the Significance?

To assess your mastery of the material in this chapter, visit the **Student Center** at bedfordstmartins.com/strayer.

steam engine	Karl Marx	Russian Revolution of 1905
Indian cotton textiles	Labour Party	*caudillos*
British Royal Society	proletariat	Latin American export boom
middle-class values	socialism in the United States	Mexican Revolution
lower middle class	Progressives	dependent development

Big Picture Questions

1. What was revolutionary about the Industrial Revolution?
2. What was common to the process of industrialization everywhere, and in what ways did that process vary from place to place?
3. What did humankind gain from the Industrial Revolution, and what did it lose?
4. In what ways might the Industrial Revolution be understood as a global rather than simply a European phenomenon?

Next Steps: For Further Study

For Web sites and additional documents related to this chapter, see **Make History** at bedfordstmartins.com/strayer.

John Charles Chasteen, *Born in Blood and Fire* (2006). A lively and well-written account of Latin America's turbulent history since the sixteenth century.

Jack Gladstone, *Why Europe? The Rise of the West in World History, 1500–1850* (2009). An original synthesis of recent research provided by a leading world historian.

David S. Landes, *The Wealth and Poverty of Nations* (1998). An argument that culture largely shapes the possibilities for industrialization and economic growth.

Robert B. Marks, *The Origins of the Modern World* (2007). An effective summary of new thinking about the origins of European industrialization.

Peter Stearns, *The Industrial Revolution in World History* (1998). A global and comparative perspective on the Industrial Revolution.

Peter Waldron, *The End of Imperial Russia, 1855–1917* (1997). A brief account of Russian history during its early industrialization.

Bridging World History, Units 18 and 19, http://www.learner.org/channel/courses/worldhistory. An innovative world history Web site that provides pictures, video, and text dealing with "Rethinking the Rise of the West" and "Global Industrialization."

Documents

Considering the Evidence:
Varieties of European Marxism

Among the ideologies and social movements that grew out of Europe's
Industrial Revolution, none was more important than socialism. When
it emerged in the nineteenth century, the word "socialism" referred to public or
state ownership and control of the means of production and distribution (land,
railroads, and factories, for example). Adherents hoped to achieve far greater
equality and cooperation than was possible under the competitive and cutthroat
capitalism of an industrializing Europe. Clearly the most important socialist
ideas derived from the writings of Karl Marx. Known widely as Marxism, those
ideas spawned a variety of interpretations, applications, and debates. For many
people, they also served as a way of understanding the world perhaps akin to
an alternative religion, or an alternative to religion.

The historical significance of Marxist socialism was immense. First, it
offered a devastating critique of the industrializing process as it unfolded during the nineteenth century—its inequalities, its instability, its materialism, its
exploitation of workers. For followers of Marx, however, that critique was
thoroughly modern, embracing the new science, technology, and means of production that the Industrial Revolution had generated, while deploring the
social outcomes of that process and the capitalist economic system in which it
took place. Second, socialists offered an alternative model for industrializing
societies, imagining a future that would more fully realize the promise of modern industry and more equally distribute its benefits. Third, Marxist thinking
gave a sharp edge to the social conflicts that characterized industrializing
Europe. Those conflicts featured two classes, both of which grew substantially
during the nineteenth century (see pp. 833–36). One was the wealthy industrial business class, the bourgeoisie, those who owned and managed the mines,
factories, and docks of an industrializing Europe. The other involved the
proletariat, the workers in those enterprises—often impoverished, exploited,
and living in squalid conditions. Finally, nineteenth-century Marxism provided the foundation for twentieth-century world communism as it took
shape in Russia, China, Vietnam, Cuba, and elsewhere.

By the end of the nineteenth century, socialism had become a major element
of European political and intellectual life, and it enjoyed a modest presence
in the United States and Japan and among a handful of intellectuals elsewhere.
Its spread to the rest of the world would have to await developments in the

twentieth century. The documents that follow illustrate some of the ways that Marxist socialism was expressed and contested within a nineteenth-century European context.

Document 18.1

Socialism According to Marx

The early currents of socialist thinking took shape during the first quarter of the nineteenth century in the minds of various thinkers—the Englishman Robert Owen and the Frenchman Charles Fourier, for example, both of whom were appalled by the social divisions that industrial society generated. As an alternative they proposed small-scale, voluntary, and cooperative communities, and their followers actually established a number of such experimental groups in Europe and the United States. But the most significant expression of modern socialism took shape in the fertile mind of the brilliant German intellectual Karl Marx (1818–1883). His life coincided with perhaps the harshest phase of capitalist industrialization in Europe. At that time an encompassing market economy was rudely shattering older institutions and traditions, but the benefits of this new and highly productive system were not yet widely shared (see pp. 835–36). But in this brutal process, Marx discerned the inevitable approach of a new world. Document 18.1 presents excerpts from the most famous of Marx's writings, the *Communist Manifesto*, first published in 1848. In this effort and throughout much of his life, Marx was assisted by another German thinker, Friedrich Engels (1820–1895), the son of a successful textile manufacturer. Engels became radicalized as he witnessed the devastating social results of capitalist industrialization.

Marx and Engels's *Manifesto* begins with a summary description of the historical process. Much of the document then analyzes what the authors call the "bourgeoisie" or the "bourgeois epoch," terms that refer to the age of industrial capitalism.

- How do Marx and Engels understand the motor of change in human history? How do they view the role of class?

- What are Marx and Engels's criticisms of the existing social system? What do they see as its major achievements?

- Why do Marx and Engels believe that the capitalist system is doomed?

- How does the industrial proletariat differ from the lower class of the preindustrial era? What role do Marx and Engels foresee for the proletariat?

- Which of Marx and Engels's descriptions and predictions ring true even now? In what respects was their analysis disproved by later developments?

■   How do Marx and Engels describe the socialist society that will follow
the collapse of the capitalist system? Why do they believe that only a
revolution, "the forcible overthrow of all existing social conditions," will
enable the creation of a socialist society?

KARL MARX AND FRIEDRICH ENGELS
The Communist Manifesto
1848

The history of all hitherto existing society is the history of class struggles. Freeman and slave, patrician and plebeian, lord and serf, guild-master and journeyman, in a word, oppressor and oppressed, stood in constant opposition to one another, carried on an uninterrupted, now hidden, now open fight, a fight that each time ended, either in a revolutionary reconstitution of society at large, or in the common ruin of the contending classes....

Our epoch, the epoch of the bourgeoisie, possesses, however, this distinct feature: it has simplified class antagonisms. Society as a whole is more and more splitting up into two great hostile camps, into two great classes directly facing each other—bourgeoisie and proletariat....

Modern industry has established the world market, for which the discovery of America paved the way. This market has given an immense development to commerce, to navigation, to communication by land....

[T]he bourgeoisie has at last, since the establishment of Modern Industry and of the world market, conquered for itself, in the modern representative state, exclusive political sway. The executive of the modern state is but a committee for managing the common affairs of the whole bourgeoisie.

The bourgeoisie, historically, has played a most revolutionary part.

The bourgeoisie, wherever it has got the upper hand, has put an end to all feudal, patriarchal, idyllic relations. It has pitilessly torn asunder the motley feudal ties that bound man to his "natural superiors," and has left no other nexus between people than naked self-interest, than callous "cash payment." It has drowned out the most heavenly ecstasies of religious fervor, of chivalrous enthusiasm, of philistine sentimentalism, in the icy water of egotistical calculation. It has resolved personal worth into exchange value, and in place of the numberless indefeasible chartered freedoms, has set up that single, unconscionable freedom—Free Trade. In one word, for exploitation, veiled by religious and political illusions, it has substituted naked, shameless, direct, brutal exploitation.

The bourgeoisie has stripped of its halo every occupation hitherto honored and looked up to with reverent awe. It has converted the physician, the lawyer, the priest, the poet, the man of science, into its paid wage laborers.

The bourgeoisie has torn away from the family its sentimental veil, and has reduced the family relation into a mere money relation....

It has been the first to show what man's activity can bring about. It has accomplished wonders far surpassing Egyptian pyramids, Roman aqueducts, and Gothic cathedrals....

The need of a constantly expanding market for its products chases the bourgeoisie over the entire surface of the globe. It must nestle everywhere, settle everywhere, establish connections everywhere....

All old-established national industries have been destroyed or are daily being destroyed. They are dislodged by new industries, whose introduction becomes a life and death question for all civilized nations, by industries that no longer work up indigenous raw material, but raw material drawn from the

Source: John E. Toews, ed., *The Communist Manifesto by Karl Marx and Frederick Engels with Related Documents* (Boston: Bedford/St. Martin's, 1999), 63–96.

remotest zones; industries whose products are consumed, not only at home, but in every quarter of the globe. In place of the old wants, satisfied by the production of the country, we find new wants, requiring for their satisfaction the products of distant lands and climes. In place of the old local and national seclusion and self-sufficiency, we have intercourse in every direction, universal interdependence of nations....

The bourgeoisie, by the rapid improvement of all instruments of production, by the immensely facilitated means of communication, draws all, even the most barbarian, nations into civilization. The cheap prices of commodities are the heavy artillery with which it forces the barbarians' intensely obstinate hatred of foreigners to capitulate. It compels all nations, on pain of extinction, to adopt the bourgeois mode of production; it compels them to introduce what it calls civilization into their midst, i.e., to become bourgeois themselves. In one word, it creates a world after its own image.

The bourgeoisie has subjected the country to the rule of the towns. It has created enormous cities, has greatly increased the urban population as compared with the rural, and has thus rescued a considerable part of the population from the idiocy of rural life. Just as it has made the country dependent on the towns, so it has made barbarian and semi-barbarian countries dependent on the civilized ones, nations of peasants on nations of bourgeois, the East on the West....

The bourgeoisie, during its rule of scarce one hundred years, has created more massive and more colossal productive forces than have all preceding generations together. Subjection of nature's forces to man, machinery, application of chemistry to industry and agriculture, steam navigation, railways, electric telegraphs, clearing of whole continents for cultivation, canalization or rivers, whole populations conjured out of the ground—what earlier century had even a presentiment that such productive forces slumbered in the lap of social labor?...

It is enough to mention the commercial crises that, by their periodical return, put the existence of the entire bourgeois society on its trial, each time more threateningly.... In these crises, there breaks out an epidemic that, in all earlier epochs, would have seemed an absurdity—the epidemic of over-production....

But not only has the bourgeoisie forged the weapons that bring death to itself; it has also called into existence the men who are to wield those weapons—the modern working class—the proletarians....

These laborers, who must sell themselves piecemeal, are a commodity, like every other article of commerce, and are consequently exposed to all the vicissitudes of competition, to all the fluctuations of the market.

Owing to the extensive use of machinery, and to the division of labor, the work of the proletarians has lost all individual character, and, consequently, all charm for the workman. He becomes an appendage of the machine, and it is only the most simple, most monotonous, and most easily acquired knack, that is required of him....

Masses of laborers, crowded into the factory, are organized like soldiers. As privates of the industrial army, they are placed under the command of a perfect hierarchy of officers and sergeants. Not only are they slaves of the bourgeois class, and of the bourgeois state; they are daily and hourly enslaved by the machine, by the overlooker, and, above all, by the individual bourgeois manufacturer himself....

The lower strata of the middle class—the small tradespeople, shopkeepers, and retired tradesmen generally, the handicraftsmen and peasants—all these sink gradually into the proletariat.... Thus, the proletariat is recruited from all classes of the population....

This organization of the proletarians into a class, and, consequently, into a political party, is continually being upset again by the competition between the workers themselves. But it ever rises up again, stronger, firmer, mightier....

Finally, in times when the class struggle nears the decisive hour,... a small section of the ruling class cuts itself adrift, and joins the revolutionary class, the class that holds the future in its hands....What the bourgeoisie therefore produces, above all, are its own grave-diggers. Its fall and the victory of the proletariat are equally inevitable....

We have seen above that the first step in the revolution by the working class is to raise the proletariat to the position of ruling class, to win the battle of democracy.

The proletariat will use its political supremacy to wrest, by degree, all capital from the bourgeoisie, to centralize all instruments of production in the hands of the state, i.e., of the proletariat organized as the ruling class; and to increase the total productive forces as rapidly as possible.

Of course, in the beginning, this cannot be effected except by means of despotic inroads on the rights of property....

These measures will, of course, be different in different countries.

Nevertheless, in most advanced countries, the following will be pretty generally applicable.

1. Abolition of property in land and application of all rents of land to public purposes.
2. A heavy progressive or graduated income tax.
3. Abolition of all rights of inheritance.
4. Confiscation of the property of all emigrants and rebels.
5. Centralization of credit in the banks of the state, by means of a national bank with state capital and an exclusive monopoly.
6. Centralization of the means of communication and transport in the hands of the state.
7. Extension of factories and instruments of production owned by the state; the bringing into cultivation of waste lands, and the improvement of the soil generally in accordance with a common plan.
8. Equal obligation of all to work. Establishment of industrial armies, especially for agriculture.
9. Combination of agriculture with manufacturing industries; gradual abolition of all the distinction between town and country by a more equable distribution of the populace over the country.
10. Free education for all children in public schools. Abolition of children's factory labor in its present form. Combination of education with industrial production, etc.

When, in the course of development, class distinctions have disappeared, and all production has been concentrated in the hands of a vast association of the whole nation, the public power will lose its political character. Political power, properly so called, is merely the organized power of one class for oppressing another. If the proletariat during its contest with the bourgeoisie is compelled, by the force of circumstances, to organize itself as a class; if, by means of a revolution, it makes itself the ruling class, and, as such, sweeps away by force the old conditions of production, then it will, along with these conditions, have swept away the conditions for the existence of class antagonisms and of classes generally, and will thereby have abolished its own supremacy as a class.

In place of the old bourgeois society, with its classes and class antagonisms, we shall have an association in which the free development of each is the condition for the free development of all....

The Communists disdain to conceal their views and aims. They openly declare that their ends can be attained only by the forcible overthrow of all existing social conditions. Let the ruling classes tremble at a communist revolution. The proletarians have nothing to lose but their chains. They have a world to win.

Document 18.2

Socialism without Revolution

Karl Marx and Friedrich Engels provided the set of ideas that informed much of the European socialist movement during the second half of the nineteenth century. Organized in various national parties and joined together in international organizations as well, socialists usually referred to themselves as social democrats, for they were seeking to extend the principles of democracy from the political arena (voting rights, for example) into the realm of the economy and society. By the 1890s, however, some of them had begun to question at least part of Marx's teachings, especially the need for violent revolution. The chief spokesperson for this group of socialists, known as "revisionists," was Eduard Bernstein (1850–1932), a prominent member of the German Social Democratic Party. His ideas provoked a storm of controversy within European socialist circles. Document 18.2 is drawn from the preface of Bernstein's 1899 book, *Evolutionary Socialism*.

■ In what ways and for what reasons was Bernstein critical of Marx and Engels's analysis of capitalism?

■ Why do you think he refers so often to Engels?

■ What strategy does Bernstein recommend for the German Social Democratic Party?

■ What does he mean by saying that "the movement means everything to me and … 'the final aim of socialism' is nothing"?

■ Why would some of Marx's followers have considered Bernstein a virtual traitor to the socialist cause?

EDUARD BERNSTEIN

Evolutionary Socialism

1899

It has been maintained in a certain quarter that the practical deductions from my treatises would be the abandonment of the conquest of political power by the proletariat organized politically and economically. That [idea] … I altogether deny.

I set myself against the notion that we have to expect shortly a collapse of the bourgeois economy. …

The adherents of this theory of a catastrophe, base it especially on the conclusions of the *Communist Manifesto*. This is a mistake. …

Social conditions have not developed to such an acute opposition of things and classes as is depicted in the *Manifesto*. It is not only useless, it is the greatest folly to attempt to conceal this from ourselves. The number of members of the possessing classes is today not smaller but larger. The enormous increase

of social wealth is not accompanied by a decreasing number of large capitalists but by an increasing number of capitalists of all degrees. The middle classes change their character but they do not disappear from the social scale.

The concentration in productive industry is not being accomplished even today in all its departments with equal thoroughness and at an equal rate. … Trade statistics show an extraordinarily elaborated graduation of enterprises in regard to size. …

In all advanced countries we see the privileges of the capitalist bourgeoisie yielding step by step to democratic organizations. Under the influence of this, and driven by the movement of the working classes which is daily becoming stronger, a social reaction has set in against the exploiting tendencies of capital. … Factory legislation, the democratizing of local government, and the extension of its area of work, the freeing of trade unions and systems of co-operative trading from legal restrictions, the consid-

Source: Eduard Bernstein, *Evolutionary Socialism*, translated by Edith C. Harvey (New York: Schocken Books, 1961), xxiv–xxx.

eration of standard conditions of labor in the work undertaken by public authorities—all these characterize this phase of the evolution.

But the more the political organizations of modern nations are democratized, the more the needs and opportunities of great political catastrophes are diminished....

[Engels] points out in conformity with this opinion that the next task of the party should be "to work for an uninterrupted increase of its votes" or to carry on a slow *propaganda of parliamentary activity....*

Shall we be told that he [Engels] abandoned the conquest of political power by the working classes...?

[F]or a long time yet the task of social democracy is, instead of speculating on a great economic crash, "to organize the working classes politically and develop them as a democracy and to fight for all reforms in the State which are adapted to raise the working classes and transform the State in the direction of democracy."...

[T]he movement means everything for me and that what is *usually* called "the final aim of socialism" is nothing....

The conquest of political power by the working classes, the expropriation of capitalists, are not ends themselves but only means for the accomplishment of certain aims and endeavors.... But the conquest of political power necessitates the possession of political *rights*; German social democracy [must] devise the best ways for the extension of the political and economic rights of the German working classes.

Document 18.3

Socialism and Women

Marxist socialism focused largely on issues of class, but that movement coincided with the emergence of feminism, giving rise to what many socialists called "the woman question." The main theoretical issue was the source of female subjugation. Did it derive from private property and the class structure of capitalist society, or was it the product of deeply rooted cultural attitudes independent of class? While middle-class feminists generally assumed the second view, orthodox Marxist thinking aligned with the first one, believing that the lack of economic independence was the root cause of women's subordination. Their liberation would follow, more or less automatically, after the creation of socialist societies. On a more practical level, the question was whether socialist parties should seek to enroll women by actively supporting their unique concerns—suffrage, equal pay, education, maternity insurance. Or did such efforts divide the working class and weaken the socialist movement? Should socialists treat women as members of an oppressed class or as members of an oppressed sex?

Among the leading figures addressing such issues was Clara Zetkin (1857–1933), a prominent German socialist and feminist. In Document 18.3 Zetkin outlines the efforts of the German Social Democratic Party to reach out to women and describes the party's posture toward middle-class feminism.

- How would you describe Zetkin's view of the relationship between socialism and feminism? Which one has priority in her thinking?

- Why is she so insistent that the Social Democratic Party of Germany address the concerns of women? How precisely did it do so?

- Why does she believe that women's issues will be better served within a socialist framework than in a bourgeois women's rights movement?

- How might critics—both feminist and socialist—argue with Zetkin?

CLARA ZETKIN

The German Socialist Women's Movement

1909

In 1907 the Social-Democratic Party of Germany [SDP] embraced 29,458 women members, in 1908 they numbered 62,257.... One hundred and fifty lecture and study circles for women have been established.... Socialist propaganda amongst the workers' wives and women wage-earners has been carried on by many hundred public meetings, in which women comrades addressed more particularly working-class women....

The women's office works now in conjunction with the Party's Executive.... They are to make a vigorous propaganda that the wage-earning women shall in large numbers exercise the franchise to the administrative bodies of the State Sick-Insurance, the only kind of franchise women possess in Germany. The women comrades were further engaged to form local committees for the protection of children.... Besides this, Socialist women were reminded to found and improve protective committees for women-workers, and collect their grievances on illegal and pernicious conditions of labor, forwarding them to the factory inspector.

Besides their activity in that line, the Socialist women have continued their propaganda in favor of the full political emancipation of their sex. The struggle for universal suffrage...was a struggle for adult suffrage for both sexes, vindicated in meetings and leaflets. Public and factory meetings in great number; and an indefatigable activity in other different forms, have served the trade union organizations of the women workers.... The work

of our trade unions to enlighten, train, and organize wage-earning women is not smaller nor less important than what the S.D.P. has done to induce women to join in political struggles of the working class....

The most prominent feature of the Socialist women's movement in Germany is its clearness and revolutionary spirit as to Socialist theories and principles. The women who head it are fully conscious that the social fate of their sex is indissolubly connected with the general evolution of society, the most powerful moving force of which is the evolution of labor, of economic life. The integral human emancipation of all women depends in consequence on the social emancipation of labor; that can only be realized by the class-war of the exploited majority. Therefore, our Socialist women oppose strongly the bourgeois women righters' credo that the women of all classes must gather into an unpolitical, neutral movement striving exclusively for women's rights. In theory and practice they maintain the conviction that the class antagonisms are much more powerful, effective, and decisive than the social antagonisms between the sexes.... [T]hus the working-class women will [only] win their full emancipation...in the class-war of all the exploited, without difference of sex, against all who exploit, without difference of sex. That does not mean at all that they undervalue the importance of the political emancipation of the female sex. On the contrary, they employ much more energy than the German women-righters to conquer the suffrage. But the vote is, according to their views, not the last word and term of their aspirations, but only a weapon—a means in struggle for a revolutionary aim—the Socialistic order.

Source: Clara Zetkin, *The German Socialist Women's Movement*, Marxists Internet Archive, www.marxists.org.

The Socialist women's movement in Germany... strives to help change the world by awakening the consciousness and the will of working-class women to join in performing the most Titanic deed that history will know: the emancipation of labor by the laboring class themselves.

Document 18.4

Socialism in Song

While European socialists argued theory, debated strategy, and organized workers, they also sang. The hymn of the socialist movement was "The Internationale," composed in 1871 by Eugene Pottier, a French working-class activist, poet, and songwriter. Document 18.4 offers an English translation made in 1900 by Charles Kerr, an American publisher of radical books. The song gave expression to both the oppression and the hopes of ordinary people as they worked for a socialist future.

- What evidence of class consciousness is apparent in the song? What particular grievances are expressed in it?

- How does "The Internationale" portray the struggle and the future?

- What evidence of Marxist thinking can you find in its lyrics?

- How does this song, intended for a mass audience, differ from the more political and intellectual documents above?

EUGENE POTTIER (TRANS. CHARLES KERR)

The Internationale
1871

Arise, ye prisoners of starvation!
Arise, ye wretched of the earth!
For justice thunders condemnation,
A better world's in birth!
No more tradition's chains shall bind us,
Arise ye slaves, no more in thrall!
The earth shall rise on new foundations,
We have been nought, we shall be all.

(Chorus)
'Tis the final conflict,
Let each stand in his place.

The international working class
Shall be the human race.

We want no condescending saviors
To rule us from a judgment hall;
We workers ask not for their favors;
Let us consult for all.
To make the thief disgorge his booty
To free the spirit from its cell,
We must ourselves decide our duty,
We must decide, and do it well.
(Chorus)

The law oppresses us and tricks us,
wage slav'ry drains the workers' blood;

Source: "The Internationale," http://en.wikisource.org/wiki/The_Internationale_(Kerr).

The rich are free from obligations,
The laws the poor delude.
Too long we've languished in subjection,
Equality has other laws;
"No rights," says she, "without their duties,
No claims on equals without cause."
(Chorus)

Behold them seated in their glory
The kings of mine and rail and soil!
What have you read in all their story,
But how they plundered toil?
Fruits of the workers' toil are buried
In the strong coffers of a few;

In working for their restitution
The men will only ask their due.
(Chorus)

Toilers from shops and fields united,
The union we of all who work;
The earth belongs to us, the workers,
No room here for the shirk.
How many on our flesh have fattened;
But if the noisome birds of prey
Shall vanish from the sky some morning,
The blessed sunlight still will stay.
(Chorus)

Document 18.5

Lenin and Russian Socialism

By the late nineteenth century, most West European socialist parties were operating in a more or less democratic environment in which they could organize
legally, contest elections, and serve in parliament. Some of them, following
Eduard Bernstein, had largely abandoned any thoughts of revolution in favor of
a peaceful and democratic path to socialism. For others, this amounted to a
betrayal of the Marxist vision. This was particularly the case for Vladimir Ilyich
Ulyanov, better known as Lenin, then a prominent figure in the small Russian
Social Democratic Labor Party, established in 1898. Lenin was particularly
hostile to what he called "economism" or "trade-unionism," which focused on
immediate reforms such as higher wages, shorter hours, and better working
conditions. He was operating in a still autocratic Russian state, where neither
political parties nor trade unions were legal and where no national parliament
or elections allowed for the expression of popular grievances.

In a famous pamphlet titled *What Is to Be Done?* (1902), Lenin addressed
many of these issues, well before he became the leader of the world's first successful socialist revolution in 1917.

- What were Lenin's objections to economism?

- What kind of party organization did he favor?

- Why did Lenin believe that workers were unlikely to come to a revolutionary consciousness on their own? What was necessary to move them
  in that direction?

- Was Lenin more faithful to the views of Marx himself than the revisionists
  and economists were?

- In what ways did Lenin's views reflect the specific conditions of Russia?

V. I. LENIN
What Is to Be Done?
1902

The history of all countries shows that the working class, exclusively by its own effort, is able to develop only trade union consciousness, *i.e.*, it may itself realize the necessity for combining in unions, for fighting against the employers, and for striving to compel the government to pass necessary labor legislation, etc. The theory of socialism, however, grew out of the philosophic, historical, and economic theories that were elaborated by the educated representatives of the propertied classes, the intellectuals.... [I]n Russia... it arose as a natural and inevitable outcome of the development of ideas among the revolutionary socialist intelligentsia.

It is only natural that a Social Democrat, who conceives the political struggle as being identical with the "economic struggle against the employers and the government," should conceive of an "organization of revolutionaries" as being more or less identical with an "organization of workers."...

[O]n questions of organization and politics, the Economists are forever lapsing from Social Democracy into trade unionism. The political struggle carried on by the Social Democrats is far more extensive and complex than the economic struggle the workers carry on against the employers and the government. Similarly... the organization of a revolutionary Social Democratic Party must inevitably *differ* from the organizations of the workers designed for the latter struggle. A workers' organization... must be as wide as possible; and... it must be as public as conditions will allow.... On the other hand, the organizations of revolutionaries must consist first and foremost of people whose profession is that of a revolutionary.... Such an organization must of necessity be not too extensive and as secret as possible....

I assert:

1. that no movement can be durable without a stable organization of leaders to maintain continuity;
2. that the more widely the masses are spontaneously drawn into the struggle and form the basis of the movement and participate in it, the more necessary is it to have such an organization....
3. that the organization must consist chiefly of persons engaged in revolutionary activities as a profession;
4. that in a country with an autocratic government, the more we restrict the membership of this organization to persons who are engaged in revolutionary activities as a profession and who have been professionally trained in the art of combating the political police, the more difficult will it be to catch the organization....

The centralization of the more secret functions in an organization of revolutionaries will not diminish, but rather increase the extent and the quality of the activity of a large number of other organizations intended for wide membership.... [I]n order to "serve" the mass movement we must have people who will devote themselves exclusively to Social Democratic activities, and that such people must *train* themselves patiently and steadfastly to be professional revolutionaries....

Let no active worker take offense at these frank remarks, for as far as insufficient training is concerned, I apply them first and foremost to myself. I used to work in a circle that set itself great and all-embracing tasks; and every member of that circle suffered to the point of torture from the realization that we were proving ourselves to be amateurs at a moment in history when we might have been able to say, paraphrasing a well-known epigram: "Give us an organization of revolutionaries, and we shall overturn the whole of Russia!"

Source: V. I. Lenin, *What Is to Be Done?* Pamphlet, 1902. Marxist Internet Archives, www.marxists.org.

Using the Evidence:
Varieties of European Marxism

1. **Comparing socialisms:** While the various strands of Marxist socialism in nineteenth-century Europe shared some common views and values, it was also a sharply divided movement. How would you describe those commonalities as well as the divisions and controversies?

2. **Connecting human rights and socialism:** To what extent did socialist thinking reflect the human rights concerns expressed in the documents of Chapter 17? In what ways might socialists have taken issue with human rights advocates?

3. **Understanding class:** In what ways do these documents help you understand the experience of "class" during the first century of the industrial era?

4. **Considering responses to socialism:** With which of the variant forms of socialism might Marx himself been most and least sympathetic? Which of them do you think would have had most appeal in the United States? How might a manager or owner of a modern industrial enterprise respond to these ideas?

Visual Sources

Considering the Evidence:
Art and the Industrial Revolution

The immense economic and social transformations of the Industrial Revolution left almost no one untouched in those societies that experienced it most fully. But its impact varied greatly across social classes; among men, women, and children; and over time. Those variations registered not only in politics but also in the work of artists. Through their eyes and in their images we can find the full range of perceptions and reactions—from celebratory to devastatingly critical—which this epic upheaval generated. From the endless visual representations of the Industrial Revolution that are available to historians, we present six, drawn mostly from Great Britain, where it all began. The first three visual sources highlight positive perceptions of industrialization, while the final three illustrate the enormous cost of that process.

By the mid-nineteenth century, the Industrial Revolution and a growing global empire had generated for many people in Great Britain feelings of enormous pride, achievement, and superiority. Nowhere did that sensibility register more clearly than in the Crystal Palace Exhibition of 1851. Held in London, the exhibition was housed in a huge modernistic structure made of cast iron and glass and constructed in only nine months. It attracted more than 6 million visitors and contained some 14,000 exhibits from all around the world, allowing Britain to contrast its own achievements with those of "lesser" peoples. Visual Source 18.1, an engraving from the exhibition's "machinery department" first published in a London newspaper, illustrates the growing tendency of Europeans to view "technology as the main measure of human achievement."[28]

- What overall impression of Britain's industrial technology was this engraving intended to convey? Notice the building itself as well as the machinery.

- How are the visitors to this exhibit portrayed? What segment of British society do you think they represent? What does their inclusion suggest about the beneficiaries of the Industrial Revolution?

The most prominent symbol of the Industrial Revolution was the railroad (see the photo on p. 832). To industrial-age enthusiasts, it was a thing of wonder, power, and speed. Samuel Smiles, a nineteenth-century British writer and

Visual Source 18.1 The Machinery Department of the Crystal Palace (Mary Evans Picture Library/The Image Works)

advocate of self-help and individualism, wrote rhapsodically of the railroad's beneficent effects:

> The iron rail proved a magicians' road. The locomotive gave a new celerity to time. It virtually reduced England to a sixth of its size. It brought the country nearer to the town and the town to the country.... It energized punctuality, discipline, and attention; and proved a moral teacher by the influence of example.[29]

Visual Source 18.2, dating from the 1870s, shows a family in a railroad compartment, returning home from a vacation.

- What attitude toward the railroad in particular and the industrial age in general does this image suggest?

- Notice the view out the window. What do the telegraph lines and St. Paul's Cathedral, a famous feature of the London landscape, contribute to the artist's message?

- What marks this family as middle class? How would you compare this image with the painting of middle class life on page 834? Do the two families derive from the same segments of the middle class? Do you think they could mix socially?

- What does the poem at the top of the image suggest about the place of "home" in industrial Britain? How does the image itself present the railway car as a home away from home?

And Papa and Mamma took them home the same day,—
They were glad to go home, and yet wanted to stay;
But the train went quite fast, and it seemed a nice change
To be back in their own home, where nothing was strange:

And always they reckon'd that seeing these sights
Was a thing to remember—a week of delights;
And, though they may see them all many times more,
They'll never enjoy them so much, I am sure.

Visual Source 18.2 The Railroad as a Symbol of the Industrial Era (Mary Evans Picture Library/The Image Works)

Visual Source 18.3 Outside the Factory: Eyre Crowe, *The Dinner Hour, Wigan* (© Manchester Art Gallery, UK/The Bridgeman Art Library)

The Industrial Revolution was more than invention and technological innovation, for it also involved a new organization of work, symbolized by the modern factory. The human impact of factory labor was a central feature in the debate about this massive transformation of economic life. Visual Source 18.3, an 1874 painting by English artist Eyre Crowe, shows a number of young women factory workers during their dinner hour outside the cotton textile mill in the industrial town of Wigan. Art critics at the time commented variously on the painting. One wrote, "We think it was a pity Mr. Crowe wasted his time on such unattractive materials." Another suggested, "Crowe has apparently set himself to record the unpictorial lives of the working classes of the manufacturing districts in a prosaic but entirely honest manner." Yet a third declared, "The picture is not a mere romantic invention: it is a veracious [truthful] statement."[30]

- How would you respond to these comments on Crowe's painting? In particular, do you think it was an "entirely honest" portrayal of factory life for women? What was missing?

- Why do you think Crowe set this scene outside the factory rather than within it?

- Notice the details of the painting—the young women's relationship to one another, the hairnets on their heads, their clothing, their activities during this break from work. What marks them as working-class women? What impression of factory life did Crowe seek to convey? Was he trying to highlight or minimize the class differences of industrial Britain?

- Notice the small male figure in a dark coat and carrying a cane. At least one observer of this painting has suggested that he may well be the mill owner, the "figure around which their [the women's] life depends."[31] If so, how would you imagine his relationship to the young women?

Turning to more negative and critical perspectives on industrialization, we begin with a sharply contrasting image of factory life, this time a colorized photograph of women and children at work in a vegetable cannery in Baltimore in 1912 (Visual Source 18.4). It was taken by Lewis W. Hine (1874–1940), a prominent American photographer who spent much of his professional life documenting child labor and factory working life. Often Hine briefly interviewed the children he photographed. When he asked one young girl her age, she replied: "I don't remember. I'm not old enough to work, but do just the same." A twelve-year-old illiterate boy told Hine: "Yes I want to learn, but can't when I work all the time."[32] Hine's photographs played a role in the passage of child labor laws in the United States.

- What impressions of factory life does Hine seek to convey in this photograph?

- How do the women and children in this image compare with those in Visual Source 18.3?

- How would you imagine a conversation between Hine and Crowe discussing these two images?

- Notice the male figure smoking a pipe. What do you think his role in the factory might be?

- Is a photograph necessarily a more truthful image than a painting? Consider the advantages and disadvantages of each as a source of information for historians.

Prominent among the criticisms of the industrialization process was its impact on the environment. The massive extraction of nonrenewable raw

Visual Source 18.4 Inside the Factory: Lewis Hine, *Child Labor, 1912* (Oil over photograph, 1912, by Lewis W. Hine. The Granger Collection, New York)

materials to feed and to fuel industrial machinery — coal, iron ore, petroleum, and much more — altered the landscape in many places. Sewers and industrial waste emptied into rivers, turning them into poisonous cesspools. In 1858, the Thames River running through London smelled so bad that the British House of Commons had to suspend its session. Smoke from coal-fired industries and domestic use polluted the air in urban areas and sharply increased the incidence of respiratory illness. (See the chapter opening image on p. 824.) Against these conditions a number of individuals and small groups raised their voices. Romantic poets such as William Blake and William Wordsworth inveighed against the "dark satanic mills" of industrial England and nostalgically urged a return to the "green and pleasant land" of an earlier time.

Nowhere in Britain were the environmental changes of the early industrial era more visible than in Coalbrookdale, a major center of the iron industry. A visitor wrote of the place in 1768:

Coalbrookdale is a very romantic spot, it is a winding glen between two immense hills..., all thickly covered with wood....Indeed too

Visual Source 18.5 Philip James de Loutherbourg, *Coalbrookdale by Night* (Science Museum/Science & Society Picture Library)

beautiful to be much in unison with that variety of horrors art spread at the bottom: the noises of the forges, mills, etc., with all their vast machinery, the flames bursting from the furnaces with the burning of coal and the smoke of the lime kilns.[33]

In 1801, Philip James de Loutherbourg, an English artist born in France, painted *Coalbrookdale by Night* (Visual Source 18.5), an image that became for many people emblematic of the early Industrial Revolution in Britain.

■ To what extent does that image reflect the description of Coalbrookdale above? Why do you think the artist set the image at night?

■ How would you interpret the flames issuing from the iron foundry? What is conveyed by the industrial debris in the foreground of the image?

■ How are human figures portrayed?

■ What overall impression of the industrial age does this painting suggest? Does the painting strike you as beautiful, horrific, or both?

CAPITAL AND LABOUR.

Visual Source 18.6 John Leech, *Capital and Labour* (The Granger Collection, New York)

In critiques of the industrial era, social issues loomed far larger than environmental concerns. Visual Source 18.6, an image by British artist John Leech, was published in 1843 in *Punch*, a magazine of humor and social satire. It reflects a common theme in the artistic and literary representations of industrial Britain.

- How precisely would you define that theme?

- How are the sharp class differences of industrial Britain represented in this visual source?

- How does this visual source connect the Industrial Revolution with Britain's colonial empire? Notice the figure in the upper right reclining in exotic splendor, perhaps in India.

- To what extent does the image correspond with Karl Marx and Frederick Engels's description of industrial society in Document 18.1 (pp. 856–59)?

- How might you understand the figure of the woman and small angel behind a door at the left?

Using the Evidence:
Art and the Industrial Revolution

1. **Deciphering class:** In what different ways is social class treated in these visual sources?

2. **Celebrating industrialization:** Based on these visual sources, the documents on socialism (pp. 855–66), and the text of Chapter 18, construct an argument in celebration of the Industrial Revolution.

3. **Criticizing industrialization:** Construct another argument based on the evidence in the chapter criticizing the Industrial Revolution.

4. **Considering images as evidence:** What are the strengths and limitations of visual sources such as these in helping historians understand the Industrial Revolution?

5. **Distinguishing capitalism and industrialization:** To what extent are the visual sources in this section actually dealing with the Industrial Revolution itself and in what ways are they addressing the economic system known as capitalism? How useful is this distinction for understanding reactions to the industrial age?

CHAPTER NINETEEN

Internal Troubles, External Threats

China, the Ottoman Empire, and Japan

1800–1914

The External Challenge: European
    Industry and Empire
    New Motives, New Means
    New Perceptions of the "Other"
Reversal of Fortune: China's
    Century of Crisis
    The Crisis Within
    Western Pressures
    The Failure of Conservative
        Modernization
The Ottoman Empire and the West
    in the Nineteenth Century
    "The Sick Man of Europe"
    Reform and Its Opponents
    Outcomes: Comparing China and
        the Ottoman Empire
The Japanese Difference: The Rise
    of a New East Asian Power
    The Tokugawa Background
    American Intrusion and the
        Meiji Restoration
    Modernization Japanese Style
    Japan and the World
Reflections: Success and Failure
    in History
Considering the Evidence
    Documents: Voices from the
        Opium War
    Visual Sources: Japanese
        Perceptions of the West

In the early twenty-first century, Japanese history textbooks became a serious issue in the relationship between Japan and its Chinese neighbor. From a Chinese point of view, those textbooks had minimized or whitewashed Japanese atrocities committed against China during World War II. In particular, many Chinese were outraged at the treatment of the so-called Rape of Nanjing, which witnessed the killing of perhaps 200,000 people, most of them civilians, and the rape of countless women. "Nanjing city was soaked with bloodshed and piles of bodies were everywhere," declared one survivor of those events. "Japanese rightist groups distort history and attempt to cover the truth of Nanjing Massacre. This makes me extremely angry."[1] Another issue was the Japanese use of Chinese "comfort women," perhaps 200,000 of them, sexual slaves forced to service Japanese troops. Japan, they argued, had not sufficiently acknowledged this outrage in their history textbooks, nor had the Japanese government adequately apologized for it.

To an observer from, say, the fifteenth century or even the eighteenth century, all of this—Japanese aggression during World War II, its enormous economic success after the war, and the continuing fear and resentment of Japan reflected in the textbook controversy— would have seemed strange indeed. For many centuries, after all, Japan had lived in the shadow of its giant Chinese neighbor, borrowing many elements of Chinese culture. Certainly it was never a threat to China. Beginning in the mid-nineteenth century, however, a remarkable reversal of roles occurred in East Asia when both China and Japan experienced a series of internal crises and, at the

Carving Up the Pie of China: In this French cartoon from the late 1890s, the Great Powers of the day (from left to right: Great Britain's Queen Victoria, Germany's Kaiser Wilhelm, Russia's Tsar Nicholas II, a female figure representing France, and the Meiji emperor of Japan) participate in dividing China, while a Chinese figure behind them tries helplessly to stop the partition of his country. (Gianni Dagli Orti/The Art Archive)

same time, had to confront the novel reality of an industrialized, newly powerful, intrusive Western world. It was their very different responses to these internal crises and external challenges that led to their changed relationship in the century or more that followed and to the continuing suspicions and tensions that still characterize their relationship.

CHINA AND JAPAN WERE NOT ALONE IN FACING THE EXPANSIVE FORCES OF EUROPE AND THE UNITED STATES. During the nineteenth century, and in some places earlier, most of the peoples of Asia, the Middle East, and Africa, as well as those living in the newly independent states of Latin America, were required to deal with European or American imperialism of one kind or another. Whatever their other differences, this was a common thread that gave these diverse peoples something of a shared history.

But—and this can hardly be emphasized too strongly—dealing with Europe was not the only item on their agendas. Many African peoples were occupied with Islamic revival movements and the rise and fall of their own states; population growth and peasant rebellion wracked China; the great empires of the Islamic world shrank or disappeared; Hindus and Muslims persisted in their sometimes competitive and sometimes cooperative relationship in India; and rivalry among competing elites troubled Latin American societies. Encounters with an expansive Europe were conditioned everywhere by particular local circumstances. Those encounters provided a mirror in which the peoples of Asia and Africa viewed themselves, as they alternately celebrated, criticized, and sought to transform their own cultures.

This chapter examines the experience of societies that confronted these crises while retaining their formal independence, with China, the Ottoman Empire, and Japan as primary examples. The following chapter turns the spotlight on the colonial experience of those peoples who fell under the official control of one or another of the European powers. In both cases, they were dealing with a new thrust of European expansion, one that drew its energy from the Industrial Revolution.

Four dimensions of an expansive Europe confronted these societies. First, they faced the immense military might and political ambitions of rival European states. Second, they became enmeshed in networks of trade, investment, and sometimes migration that radiated out from an industrializing and capitalist Europe to generate a new world economy. Third, they were touched by various aspects of traditional European culture, as some among them learned the French, English, or German language; converted to Christianity; or studied European literature and philosophy. Finally, Asians and Africans engaged with the culture of modernity—its scientific rationalism; its technological achievements; its belief in a better future; and its ideas of nationalism, socialism, feminism, and individualism. In those epic encounters, they sometimes resisted, at other times accommodated, and almost always adapted what came from the West. They were active participants in the global drama of nineteenth-century world history, not simply its passive victims or beneficiaries.

The External Challenge: European Industry and Empire

More than at any other time, the nineteenth century was Europe's age of global expansion. During that century, Europe became the center of the world economy, with ties of trade and investment in every corner of the globe. Between 1812 and 1914, millions of Europeans migrated to new homes outside Europe. Missionaries and explorers penetrated the distant interiors of Asia and Africa. European states incorporated India, Africa, Southeast Asia, and the islands of the Pacific into their overseas colonial empires and seriously diminished the sovereignty and independence of the once proud domains of China, the Ottoman Empire, and Persia. Many newly independent states in Latin America became economically dependent on Europe and the United States (see pp. 846–48). How can we explain such dramatic changes in the scope, character, and intensity of European expansion?

New Motives, New Means

Behind much of Europe's nineteenth-century expansion lay the massive fact of its Industrial Revolution. That process gave rise to new economic needs, many of which found solutions abroad. The enormous productivity of industrial technology and Europe's growing affluence now created the need for extensive raw materials and agricultural products: wheat from the American Midwest and southern Russia, meat from Argentina, bananas from Central America, rubber from Brazil, cocoa and palm oil from West Africa, tea from Ceylon, gold and diamonds from South Africa. This demand radically changed patterns of economic and social life in the countries of their origin.

■ **Change**
In what ways did the Industrial Revolution shape the character of nineteenth-century European imperialism?

Furthermore, Europe needed to sell its own products. One of the peculiarities of industrial capitalism was that it periodically produced more manufactured goods than its own people could afford to buy. By 1840, for example, Britain was exporting 60 percent of its cotton-cloth production, annually sending 200 million yards to Europe, 300 million yards to Latin America, and 145 million yards to India. This last figure is particularly significant because for centuries Europe had offered little that Asian societies were willing to buy. Part of European and American fascination with China during the nineteenth and twentieth centuries lay in the enormous potential market represented by its huge population.

Much the same could be said for capital, for European investors often found it more profitable to invest their money abroad than at home. Between 1910 and 1913, Britain was sending about half of its savings abroad as foreign investment. In 1914, it had about 3.7 billion pounds sterling invested abroad, about equally divided between Europe, North America, and Australia on the one hand and Asia, Africa, and Latin America on the other hand.

Wealthy Europeans also saw social benefits to foreign markets, which served to keep Europe's factories humming and its workers employed. The English imperialist Cecil Rhodes confided his fears to a friend:

Yesterday I attended a meeting of the unemployed in London and having listened to the wild speeches which were nothing more than a scream for bread, I returned home convinced more than ever of the importance of imperialism.... In order to save the 40 million inhabitants of the United Kingdom from a murderous civil war, the colonial politicians must open up new areas to absorb the excess population and create new markets for the products of the mines and factories.... The British Empire is a matter of bread and butter. If you wish to avoid civil war, then you must become an imperialist.[2]

Thus imperialism promised to solve the class conflicts of an industrializing society while avoiding revolution or the serious redistribution of wealth.

But what made imperialism so broadly popular in Europe, especially in the last quarter of the nineteenth century, was the growth of mass nationalism. By 1871, the unification of Italy and Germany made Europe's always competitive political system even more so, and much of this rivalry spilled over into the struggle for colonies or economic concessions in Asia and Africa. Colonies and spheres of influence abroad became a symbol of national "Great Power" status, and their acquisition was a matter of urgency, even if they possessed little immediate economic value. After 1875, it seemed to matter, even to ordinary people, whether some remote corner of Africa or some obscure Pacific island was in British, French, or German hands. Imperialism, in short, appealed on economic and social grounds to the wealthy or ambitious, seemed politically and strategically necessary in the game of international power politics, and was emotionally satisfying to almost everyone. It was a potent mix.

If the industrial era made overseas expansion more desirable or even urgent, it also provided new means for achieving those goals. Steam-driven ships, moving through the new Suez Canal, allowed Europeans to reach distant Asian and African ports more quickly and predictably and to penetrate interior rivers as well. The underwater telegraph made possible almost instant communication with far-flung outposts of empire. The discovery of quinine to prevent malaria greatly reduced European death rates in the tropics. Breech-loading rifles and machine guns vastly widened the military gap between Europeans and everyone else.

The Gatling Gun
The Gatling gun, which was designed by the American Richard Gatling during the Civil War, was one of the earliest machine guns. By the late nineteenth century, this weapon, together with breech-loading rifles, gave European powers and the United States an enormous military advantage. (Courtesy, Royal Artillery Historical Trust)

New Perceptions of the "Other"

Industrialization also occasioned a marked change in the way Europeans perceived themselves and others. In earlier centuries, Europeans had defined others largely in religious terms. "They" were heathen; "we" were Christian. Even as they held on to this sense of religious superiority, Europeans nonetheless adopted many of the ideas and techniques of more advanced societies. They held many aspects of Chinese and Indian civilization in high regard; they freely mixed and mingled with Asian and African elites and often married their women; some even saw the more technologically simple peoples of Africa and America as "noble savages."

■ **Change**
What contributed to changing European views of Asians and Africans in the nineteenth century?

With the advent of the industrial age, however, Europeans developed a secular arrogance that fused with or in some cases replaced their notions of religious superiority. They had, after all, unlocked the secrets of nature, created a society of unprecedented wealth, and used both to produce unsurpassed military power. These became the criteria by which Europeans judged both themselves and the rest of the world.

By such standards, it is not surprising that their opinions of other cultures dropped sharply. The Chinese, who had been highly praised in the eighteenth century, were reduced in the nineteenth century to the image of "John Chinaman," weak, cunning, obstinately conservative, and, in large numbers, a distinct threat, the "yellow peril" of late-nineteenth-century European fears. African societies, which had been regarded even in the slave-trade era as nations and their leaders as kings, were demoted in nineteenth-century European eyes to the status of tribes led by chiefs as a means of emphasizing their "primitive" qualities.

Increasingly, Europeans viewed the culture and achievements of Asian and African peoples through the prism of a new kind of racism, expressed now in terms of modern science. Although physical differences had often been a basis of fear or dislike, in the nineteenth century Europeans increasingly used the prestige and apparatus of science to support their racial preferences and prejudices. Phrenologists, craniologists, and sometimes physicians used allegedly scientific methods and numerous instruments to classify the size and shape of human skulls and concluded, not surprisingly, that those of whites were larger and therefore more advanced. Nineteenth-century biologists, who classified the varieties of plants and animals, applied these notions of rank to varieties of human beings as well. The result was a hierarchy of races, with the whites, naturally, on top and the less developed "child races" beneath them. Race, in this view, determined human intelligence, moral development, and destiny. "Race is everything," declared the British anatomist Robert Knox in 1850; "civilization depends on it."[3] Furthermore, as the germ theory of disease took hold in nineteenth-century Europe, it was accompanied by fears that contact with "inferior" peoples threatened the health and even the biological future of more advanced or "superior" peoples.

These ideas influenced how Europeans viewed their own global expansion. Almost everyone saw it as inevitable, a natural outgrowth of a superior civilization.

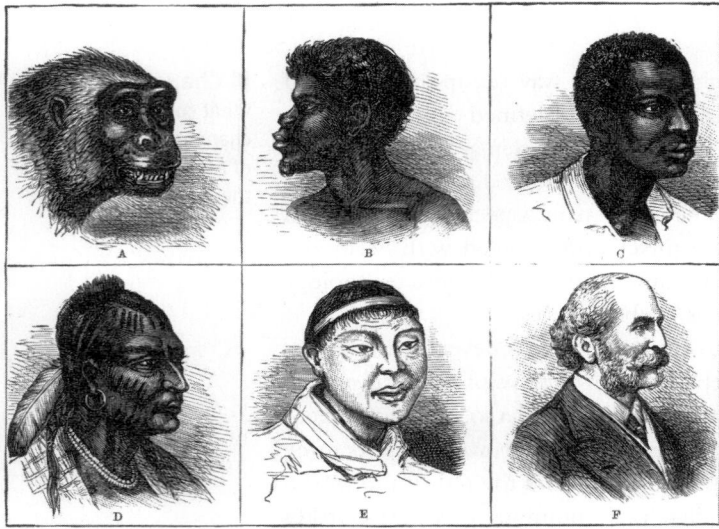

PROGRESSIVE DEVELOPMENT OF MAN.—(2) EVOLUTION ILLUSTRATED WITH THE SIX CORRESPONDING LIVING FORMS.

European Racial Images
This nineteenth-century chart, depicting the "Progressive Development of Man" from apes to modern Europeans, reflected the racial categories that were so prominent at the time. It also highlights the influence of Darwin's evolutionary ideas as they were applied to varieties of human beings. (The Granger Collection, New York)

For many, though, this viewpoint was tempered with a genuine, if condescending, sense of responsibility to the "weaker races" that Europe was fated to dominate. "Superior races have a right, because they have a duty," declared the French politician Jules Ferry in 1883. "They have the duty to civilize the inferior races."[4] That "civilizing mission," as Europeans regarded it, included bringing Christianity to the heathen, good government to disordered lands, work discipline and production for the market to "lazy natives," a measure of education to the ignorant and illiterate, clothing to the naked, and health care to the sick, while suppressing "native customs" that ran counter to Western ways of living. All of this was defined as "progress" and "civilization."

Another, harsher side to the ideology of imperialism derived from an effort to apply, or perhaps misapply, the evolutionary thinking of Charles Darwin to an understanding of human history. The key concept of this "social Darwinism," though not necessarily shared by Darwin himself, was "the survival of the fittest," suggesting that European dominance inevitably involved the displacement or destruction of backward peoples or "unfit" races. Referring to native peoples of Australia, a European bishop declared:

> Everyone who knows a little about aboriginal races is aware that those races which are of a low type mentally and who are at the same time weak in constitution rapidly die out when their country comes to be occupied by a different race much more rigorous, robust, and pushing than themselves.[5]

Such views made imperialism, war, and aggression seem both natural and progressive, for they were predicated on the notion that weeding out "weaker" peoples of the world would allow the "stronger" to flourish. These were some of the ideas with which industrializing and increasingly powerful Europeans confronted the peoples of Asia and Africa in the nineteenth century. Among those confrontations, none was more important than Europe's encounter with China.

Reversal of Fortune: China's Century of Crisis

In 1793 in a famous letter to King George III, the Chinese emperor Qianlong sharply rebuffed British requests for a less restricted trading relationship with his country. "Our Celestial Empire possesses all things in prolific abundance...," he declared. "There was therefore no need to import the manufactures of outside barbarians" (see

Document 19.1, pp. 905–07). Qianlong's snub simply continued the pattern of the previous several centuries, during which Chinese authorities had strictly controlled and limited the activities of European missionaries and merchants. By 1912, little more than a century later, China's long-established imperial state had collapsed, and the country had been transformed from a central presence in the Afro-Eurasian world to a weak and dependent participant in a European-dominated world system. It was a stunning reversal of fortune for a country that in Chinese eyes was the civilized center of the entire world—in their terms, the Middle Kingdom.

The Crisis Within

In many ways, China was the victim of its own earlier success. Its robust economy and American food crops had enabled massive population growth, from about 100 million people in 1685 to some 430 million in 1853. Unlike Europe, though, where a similar population spurt took place, no Industrial Revolution accompanied this vast increase in the number of people, nor was agricultural production able to keep up. The result was growing pressure on the land, smaller farms for China's huge peasant population, and, in all too many cases, unemployment, impoverishment, misery, and starvation.

■ **Causation**
What accounts for the massive peasant rebellions of nineteenth-century China?

Furthermore, China's famed centralized and bureaucratic state did not enlarge itself to keep pace with the growing population. In 1400, the lowest administrative unit, a county, encompassed perhaps 50,000 people and was governed by a magistrate and a small staff. By 1800, that same magistrate had to deal with 200,000 people, with no increase in his staff. Thus the state was increasingly unable to effectively perform its many functions, such as tax collection, flood control, social welfare, and public security. Gradually the central state lost power to provincial officials and local gentry. Among such officials, corruption was endemic, and harsh treatment of peasants was common. According to an official report issued in 1852, "[D]ay and night soldiers are sent out to harass taxpayers. Sometimes corporal punishments are imposed upon tax delinquents; some of them are so badly beaten to exact the last penny that blood and flesh fly in all directions."[6]

This combination of circumstances, traditionally associated with a declining dynasty, gave rise to growing numbers of bandit gangs roaming the countryside and, even more dangerous, to outright peasant rebellion. Beginning in the late eighteenth century, such rebellions drew upon a variety of peasant grievances and found leadership in charismatic figures proclaiming a millenarian religious message. Increasingly they also expressed opposition to the Qing dynasty on account of its foreign Manchu origins. "We wait only for the northern region to be returned to a Han emperor," declared one rebel group in the early nineteenth century.[7]

The culmination of China's internal crisis lay in the Taiping Uprising, which set much of the country aflame between 1850 and 1864. This was a different kind of peasant upheaval. Its leaders largely rejected Confucianism, Daoism, and Buddhism alike, finding their primary ideology in a unique form of Christianity. Its leading figure, Hong Xiuquan (1814–1864), proclaimed himself the younger brother of Jesus, sent to cleanse the world of demons and to establish a "heavenly kingdom of great peace." Nor were these leaders content to restore an idealized Chinese society; instead they insisted on genuinely revolutionary change. They called for the abolition of private property; a radical redistribution of land; the equality of men and women; the end of foot binding, prostitution, and opium smoking; and the organization of society into sexually segregated military camps of men and women. Hong fiercely denounced the Qing dynasty as foreigners who had "poisoned China" and "defiled the emperor's throne." His cousin, Hong Rengan, developed plans for transforming China into an industrial nation, complete with railroads, health insurance for all, newspapers, and widespread public education.

With a rapidly swelling number of followers, Taiping forces swept out of southern China and established their capital in Nanjing in 1853. For a time, the days of the Qing dynasty appeared to be over. But divisions and indecisiveness within the Taiping leadership and their inability to link up with several other rebel groups also operating separately in China provided an opening for Qing dynasty loyalists to rally and by 1864 to crush this most unusual of peasant rebellions. Western military support for pro-Qing forces likewise contributed to their victory. It was not, however, the imperial military forces of the central government that defeated the rebels. Instead provincial gentry landowners, fearing the radicalism of the Taiping program, mobilized their own armies, which in the end crushed the rebel forces.

Thus the Qing dynasty was saved, but it was also weakened as the provincial gentry consolidated their power at the expense of the central state. The intense conservatism of both imperial authorities and their gentry supporters postponed any resolution of China's peasant problem, delayed any real change for China's women, and deferred vigorous efforts at modernization until the communists came to power in the mid-twentieth century. More immediately, the devastation and destruction occasioned by this massive civil war seriously disrupted and weakened China's economy. Estimates of the number of lives lost range from 20 to 30 million. In human terms, it was the most costly conflict in the world of the nineteenth century, and it took China more than a decade to recover from that devastation. China's internal crisis in general and the Taiping Uprising in particular also provided a highly unfavorable setting for the country's encounter with a Europe newly invigorated by the Industrial Revolution.

Western Pressures

■ Connection

How did Western pressures stimulate change in China during the nineteenth century?

Nowhere was the shifting balance of global power in the nineteenth century more evident than in China's changing relationship with Europe, a transformation that registered most dramatically in the famous Opium Wars. Derived from Arab traders in the eighth century or earlier, opium had long been used on a small scale as a drinkable medicine, regarded as a magical cure for dysentery and described by one poet as "fit for Buddha."[8] It did not become a serious problem until the late eighteenth century,

Snapshot   **Chinese/British Trade at Canton, 1835–1836**[9]

What do these figures suggest about the role of opium in British trade with China?
Calculate opium exports as a percentage of British exports to China, Britain's trade deficit
without opium, and its trade surplus with opium. What did this pattern mean for China?

	Item	Value (in Spanish dollars)
British Exports to Canton	Opium	17,904,248
	Cotton	8,357,394
	All other items (sandlewood, lead, iron, tin, cotton yarn and piece goods, tin plates, watches, clocks)	6,164,981
	Total	32,426,623
British Imports from Canton	Tea (black and green)	13,412,243
	Raw silk	3,764,115
	Vermilion	705,000
	All other goods (sugar products, camphor, silver, gold, copper, musk)	5,971,541
	Total	23,852,899

when the British began to use opium, grown and processed in India, to cover their persistent trade imbalance with China. By the 1830s, British, American, and other Western merchants had found an enormous, growing, and very profitable market for this highly addictive drug. From 1,000 chests (each weighing roughly 150 pounds) in 1773, China's opium imports exploded to more than 23,000 chests in 1832.

By then, Chinese authorities recognized a mounting problem on many levels. Because opium importation was illegal, it had to be smuggled into China, thus flouting Chinese law. Bribed to turn a blind eye to the illegal trade, many officials were corrupted. Furthermore, a massive outflow of silver to pay for the opium reversed China's centuries-long ability to attract much of the world's silver supply, and this imbalance caused serious economic problems. Finally, China found itself with many millions of addicts—men and women, court officials, students preparing for exams, soldiers going into combat, and common laborers seeking to overcome the pain and drudgery of their work. Following an extended debate at court in 1836—whether to legalize the drug or to crack down on its use—the emperor decided on suppression (see Documents 19.2 and 19.3, pp. 907–10). An upright official, Commissioner

Addiction to Opium
Throughout the nineteenth century, opium imports created a massive addiction problem in China, as this photograph of an opium den from around 1900 suggests. Not until the early twentieth century did the British prove willing to curtail the opium trade from their Indian colony. (Hulton-Deutsch Collection/Corbis)

Lin Zexu, led the campaign against opium use as a kind of "drug czar." His measures included seizing and destroying, without compensation, more than 3 million pounds of opium from Western traders and expelling them from the country.

The British, offended by this violation of property rights and emboldened by their new military power, sent a large naval expedition to China, determined to end the restrictive conditions under which they had long traded with that country. In the process, they would teach the Chinese a lesson about the virtues of free trade and the "proper" way to conduct relations among countries. Thus began the first Opium War, in which Britain's industrialized military might proved decisive. (See Documents: Voices from the Opium War, pp. 905–13, for more on the origins of that conflict.) The Treaty of Nanjing, which ended the war in 1842, largely on British terms, imposed numerous restrictions on Chinese sovereignty and opened five ports to European traders. Its provisions reflected the changed balance of global power that had emerged with Britain's Industrial Revolution. To the Chinese, that agreement represented the first of the "unequal treaties" that seriously eroded China's independence by the end of the century.

But it was not the last of those treaties. Britain's victory in a second Opium War (1856–1858) was accompanied by the brutal vandalizing of the emperor's exquisite Summer Palace outside Beijing and resulted in further humiliations. Still more ports were opened to foreign traders. Now those foreigners were allowed to travel freely and buy land in China, to preach Christianity under the protection of Chinese authorities, and to patrol some of China's rivers. Furthermore, the Chinese were forbidden to use the character for "barbarians" to refer to the British in official documents. Following military defeats at the hands of the French (1885) and Japanese (1895), China lost control of Vietnam, Korea, and Taiwan. By the end of the century, the Western nations plus Japan and Russia all had carved out spheres of influence within China, granting themselves special privileges to establish military bases, extract raw materials, and build railroads. Many Chinese believed that their country was being "carved up like a melon" (see Map 19.1 and the photo on p. 876).

Coupled with its internal crisis, China's encounter with European imperialism had reduced the proud Middle Kingdom to dependency on the Western powers as it became part of a European-based "informal empire." China was no longer the center of civilization to which barbarians paid homage and tribute, but just one nation

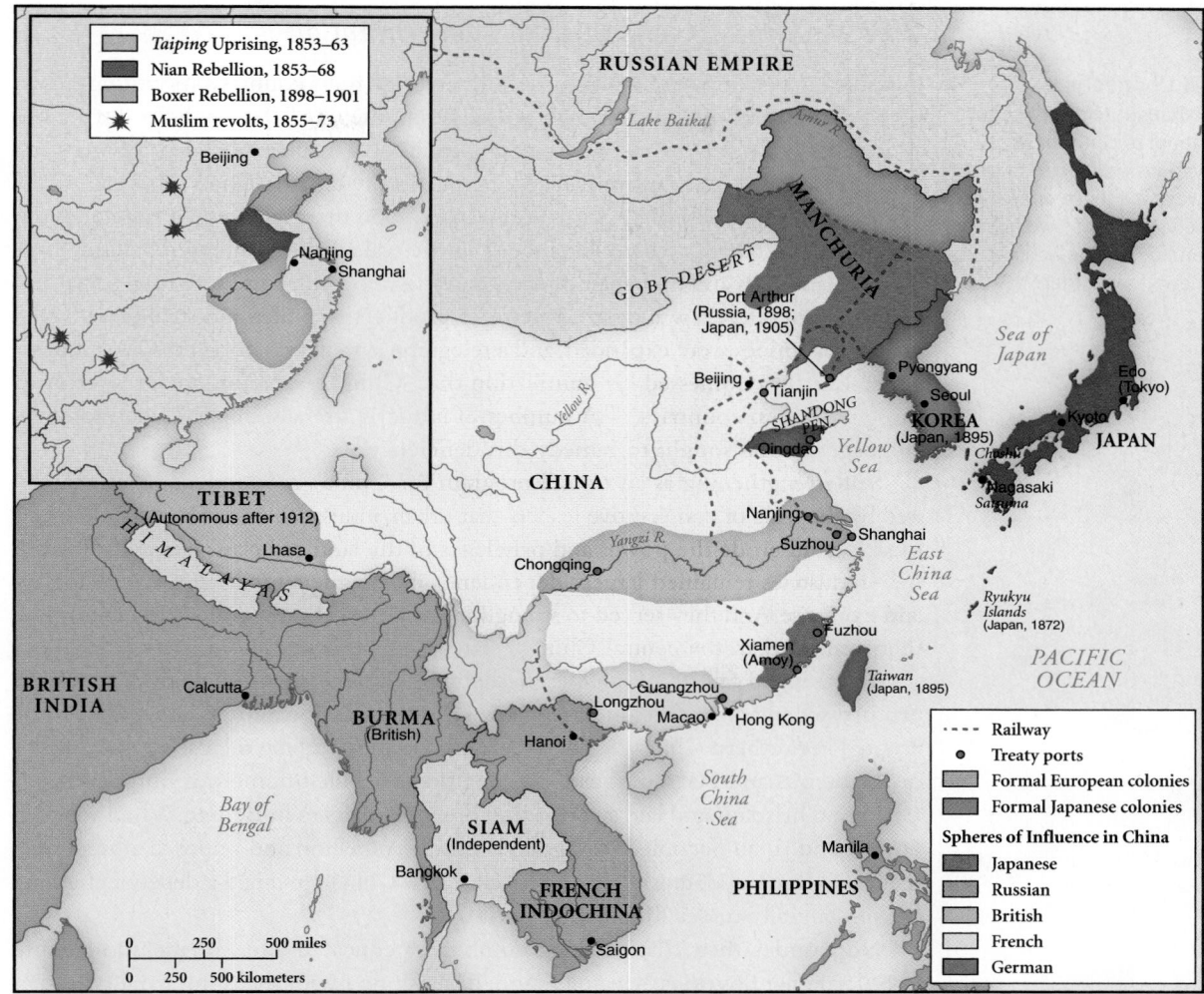

Map 19.1 China and the World in the Nineteenth Century

As China was reeling from massive internal upheavals during the nineteenth century, it also faced external assaults from Russia, Japan, and various European powers. By the end of the century, large parts of China were divided into spheres of influence, each affiliated with one of the major industrial powers of the day.

among many others, and a weak dependent nation at that. The Qing dynasty remained in power, but in a weakened condition, which served European interests well and Chinese interests poorly. Restrictions imposed by the unequal treaties clearly inhibited China's industrialization, as foreign goods and foreign investment flooded the country largely unrestricted. Chinese businessmen mostly served foreign firms, rather than developing as an independent capitalist class capable of leading China's own Industrial Revolution.

The Failure of Conservative Modernization

■ Connection

What strategies did China adopt to confront its various problems? In what ways did these strategies reflect China's own history and culture as well as the new global order?

Chinese authorities were not passive in the face of their country's mounting crises, both internal and external. Known as "self-strengthening," their policies during the 1860s and 1870s sought to reinvigorate a traditional China while borrowing cautiously from the West. An overhauled examination system, designed to recruit qualified candidates for official positions, sought the "good men" who could cope with the massive reconstruction that China faced in the wake of the Taiping rebellion. Support for landlords and the repair of dikes and irrigation helped restore rural social and economic order. A few industrial factories producing textiles and steel were established, coal mines were expanded, and a telegraph system was initiated. One Chinese general in 1863 confessed his humiliation that "Chinese weapons are far inferior to those of foreign countries."[10] A number of modern arsenals, shipyards, and foreign-language schools sought to remedy this deficiency.

Self-strengthening as an overall program for China's modernization was inhibited by the fears of conservative leaders that urban, industrial, or commercial development would erode the power and privileges of the landlord class. Furthermore, the new industries remained largely dependent on foreigners for machinery, materials, and expertise. And they served to strengthen local authorities who largely controlled them, rather than the central Chinese state.

The general failure of "self-strengthening" became apparent at the end of the century, when an antiforeign movement known as the Boxer uprising (1898–1901) erupted in northern China. Led by militia organizations calling themselves the Society of Righteous and Harmonious Fists, the "Boxers" killed numerous Europeans and Chinese Christians and laid siege to the foreign embassies in Beijing. When Western powers and Japan occupied Beijing to crush the rebellion and imposed a huge payment on China as a punishment, it was clear that China remained a dependent country, substantially under foreign control.

No wonder, then, that growing numbers of educated Chinese, including many in official elite positions, became highly disillusioned with the Qing dynasty, which was both foreign and ineffective in protecting China. By the late 1890s, such people were organizing a variety of clubs, study groups, and newspapers to examine China's desperate situation and to explore alternative paths. The names of these organizations reflect their outlook—the National Rejuvenation Study Society, Society to Protect the Nation, and Understand the National Shame Society. They admired not only Western science and technology but also Western political practices that limited the authority of the ruler and permitted wider circles of people to take part in public life. They believed that only a truly unified nation in which rulers and ruled were closely related could save China from dismemberment at the hands of foreign imperialists. Thus was born the immensely powerful force of Chinese nationalism, directed against both the foreign imperialists and the foreign Qing dynasty, which many held responsible for China's nineteenth-century disasters.

The Qing dynasty response to these new pressures proved inadequate. More extensive reform in the early twentieth century, including the end of the old examination system and the promise of a national parliament, was a classic case of too little too late. In 1911, the ancient imperial order that had governed China for two millennia collapsed, with only a modest nudge from organized revolutionaries. It was the end of a long era in China and the beginning of an immense struggle over the country's future.

The Ottoman Empire and the West in the Nineteenth Century

Like China, the Islamic world represented a highly successful civilization that felt little need to learn from the "infidels" or "barbarians" of the West until it collided with an expanding and aggressive Europe in the nineteenth century. Unlike China, though, Islamic civilization had been a near neighbor to Europe for 1,000 years. Its most prominent state, the Ottoman Empire, had long governed substantial parts of the Balkans and posed a clear military and religious threat to Europe in the sixteenth and seventeenth centuries. But if its encounter with the West was less abrupt than that of China, it was no less consequential. Neither the Ottoman Empire nor China fell under direct colonial rule, but both were much diminished as the changing balance of global power took hold; both launched efforts at "defensive modernization" aimed at strengthening their states and preserving their independence; and in both societies, some people held tightly to old identities and values, even as others embraced new loyalties associated with nationalism and modernity.

"The Sick Man of Europe"

In 1750, the Ottoman Empire was still the central political fixture of a widespread Islamic world. From its Turkish heartland of Anatolia, it ruled over much of the Arab world, from which Islam had come. It protected pilgrims on their way to Mecca, governed Egypt and coastal North Africa, and incorporated millions of Christians in the Balkans. Its ruler, the sultan, claimed the role of caliph, successor to the Prophet Muhammad, and was widely viewed as the leader, defender, and primary representative of the Islamic world. But by the middle, and certainly by the end, of the nineteenth century, the Ottoman Empire was no longer able to deal with Europe from a position of equality, let alone superiority. Among the Great Powers of the West, it was now known as "the sick man of Europe." Within the Muslim world, the Ottoman Empire, once viewed as "the strong sword of Islam," was unable to prevent region after region—India, Indonesia, West Africa, Central Asia—from falling under the control of Christian powers.

The Ottoman Empire's own domains shrank considerably at the hands of Russian, British, Austrian, and French aggression (see Map 19.2). In 1798, Napoleon's invasion

■ **Change**
What lay behind the decline of the Ottoman Empire in the nineteenth century?

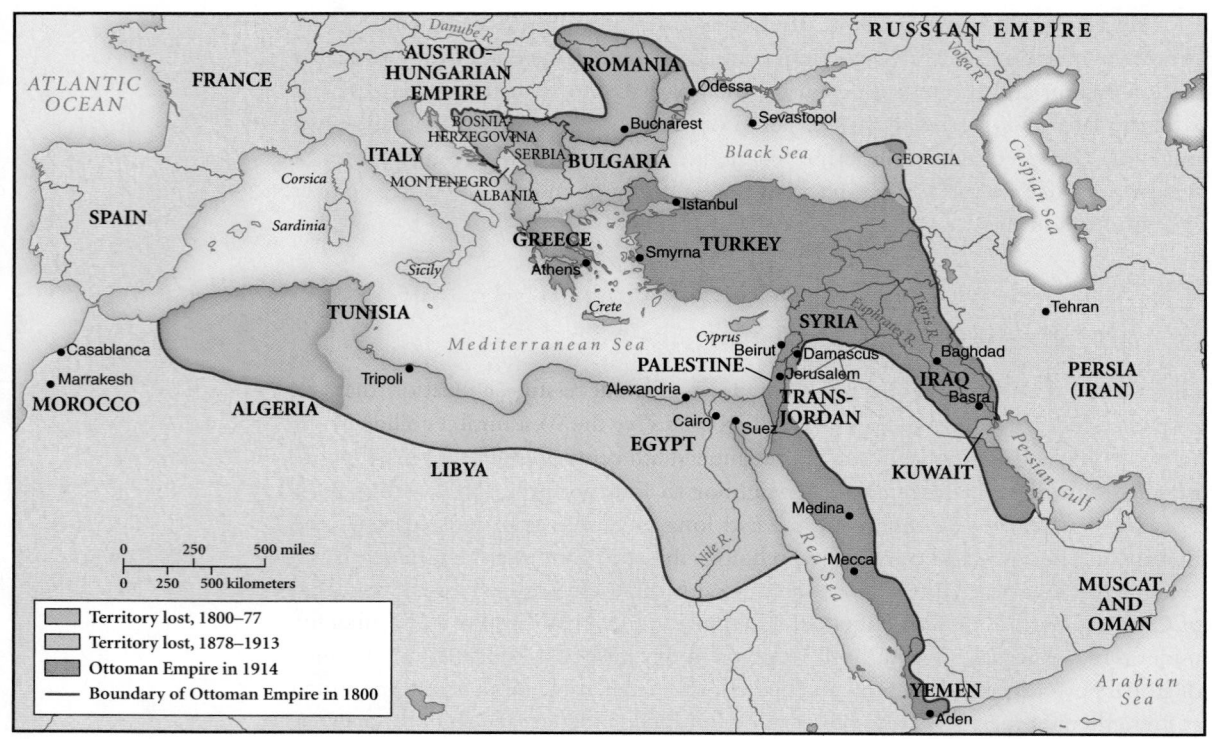

Map 19.2   The Contraction of the Ottoman Empire
Foreign aggression and nationalist movements substantially diminished the Ottoman Empire during the nineteenth century, but they also stimulated a variety of efforts to revive and reform Ottoman society.

of Egypt, which had long been a province of the Ottoman Empire, was a particularly stunning blow. A contemporary observer, Abd al-Rahman al-Jabarti, described the French entry into Cairo:

> [T]he French entered the city like a torrent rushing through the alleys and streets without anything to stop them, like demons of the Devil's army.... And the French trod in the Mosque of al-Azhar with their shoes, carrying swords and rifles.... They plundered whatever they found in the mosque.... They treated the books and Quranic volumes as trash.... Furthermore, they soiled the mosque, blowing their spit in it, pissing and defecating in it. They guzzled wine and smashed bottles in the central court.[11]

When the French left, a virtually independent Egypt pursued a modernizing and empire-building program of its own and on one occasion came close to toppling the Ottoman Empire itself.

Beyond territorial losses to stronger European powers, other parts of the empire, such as Greece, Serbia, Bulgaria, and Romania, achieved independence based on their own surging nationalism and support from the British or the Russians. The continued independence of the core region of the Ottoman Empire owed much to the inability of Europe's Great Powers to agree on how to divide it up among themselves.

Behind the contraction of the Ottoman Empire lay other problems. As in China, the central Ottoman state had weakened, particularly in its ability to raise necessary revenue, as provincial authorities and local warlords gained greater power. Moreover, the Janissaries, once the effective and innovative elite infantry units of the Ottoman Empire, lost their military edge, becoming a highly conservative force within the empire. The technological and military gap with the West was clearly growing.

Economically, the earlier centrality of the Ottoman and Arab lands in Afro-Eurasian commerce diminished as Europeans achieved direct oceanic access to the treasures of Asia. Competition from cheap European manufactured goods hit Ottoman artisans hard and led to urban riots protesting foreign imports. Furthermore, a series of agreements, known as capitulations, between European countries and the Ottoman Empire granted Westerners various exemptions from Ottoman law and taxation. Like the unequal treaties in China, these agreements facilitated European penetration of the Ottoman economy and became widely resented. Such measures eroded Ottoman sovereignty and reflected the changing position of that empire relative to Europe. So too did the growing indebtedness of the Ottoman Empire, which came to rely on foreign loans to finance its efforts at economic development. By 1882, its inability to pay the interest on those debts led to foreign control of much of its revenue-generating system and the outright occupation of Egypt by the British. Like China, the Ottoman Empire had fallen into a position of considerable dependency on Europe.

Reform and Its Opponents

The leadership of the Ottoman Empire recognized many of its "illnesses" and during the nineteenth century mounted increasingly ambitious programs of "defensive modernization" that were earlier, more sustained, and far more vigorous than the timid and half-hearted measures of self-strengthening in China. One reason perhaps lay in the absence of any internal upheaval, such as the Taiping uprising in China, which threatened the very existence of the ruling dynasty. Nationalist revolts on the empire's periphery, rather than Chinese-style peasant rebellion at the center, represented the primary internal crisis of nineteenth-century Ottoman history. Nor did the Middle East in general experience the explosive population growth that contributed so much to China's nineteenth-century crisis. Furthermore, the long-established Ottoman leadership was Turkic and Muslim, culturally similar to its core population, whereas China's Qing dynasty rulers were widely regarded as foreigners from Manchuria.

Ottoman reforms began in the late eighteenth century when Sultan Selim III sought to reorganize and update the army and to draw on European advisers and techniques. Even these modest innovations stirred the hostility of powerful factions among both the *ulama* (religious scholars) and the elite military corps of Janissaries, who saw them in conflict with both Islam and their own institutional interests. Opposition to his measures was so strong that Selim was overthrown in 1807 and then murdered.

■ **Change**
In what different ways did the Ottoman state respond to its various problems?

Subsequent sultans, however, crushed the Janissaries and brought the ulama more thoroughly under state control than elsewhere in the Islamic world.

Then, in the several decades after 1839, more far-reaching reformist measures, known as Tanzimat (reorganization), took shape as the Ottoman leadership sought to provide the economic, social, and legal underpinnings for a strong and newly recentralized state. Factories producing cloth, paper, and armaments; modern mining operations; reclamation and resettlement of agricultural land; telegraphs, steamships, railroads, and a modern postal service; Western-style law codes and courts; new elementary and secondary schools—all of these new departures began a long process of modernization and Westernization in the Ottoman Empire.

Even more revolutionary, at least in principle, were changes in the legal status of the empire's diverse communities, which now gave non-Muslims equal rights under the law. An imperial proclamation of 1839 declared:

> Every distinction or designation tending to make any class whatever of the subjects of my Empire inferior to another class, on account of their religion, language or race shall be forever effaced.... No subject of my Empire shall be hindered in the exercise of the religion that he professes.... All the subjects of my Empire, without distinction of nationality, shall be admissible to public employment.

This declaration represented a dramatic change that challenged the fundamentally Islamic character of the state. Mixed tribunals with representatives from various religious groups were established to hear cases involving non-Muslims. More Christians were appointed to high office. A mounting tide of secular legislation and secular

The Ottoman Empire and the West
The intense interaction of the Ottoman Empire and the world of European powers is illustrated in this nineteenth-century Austrian painting, which depicts an elaborate gathering of Ottoman officials with members of the Austrian royal family around 1850. (Miramare Palace Trieste/Alfredo Dagli Orti/The Art Archive)

schools, drawing heavily on European models, now competed with traditional Islamic institutions.

The reform process raised profound and highly contested questions. What was the Ottoman Empire, and who were its people? To those who supported the reforms, the Ottoman Empire was a secular state whose people were loyal to the dynasty that ruled it, rather than a primarily Muslim state based on religious principles. This was the outlook of a new class spawned by the reform process itself—lower-level officials, military officers, writers, poets, and journalists, many of whom had a modern Western-style education. Dubbed the Young Ottomans, they were active during the middle decades of the nineteenth century, as they sought major changes in the Ottoman political system itself. They favored a more European-style democratic, constitutional regime that could curtail the absolute power of the emperor. Only such a political system, they felt, could mobilize the energies of the country to overcome backwardness and preserve the state against European aggression. Known as Islamic modernism, such ideas found expression in many parts of the Muslim world in the second half of the century. Muslim societies, they argued, needed to embrace Western technical and scientific knowledge, while rejecting its materialism. Islam in their view could accommodate a full modernity without sacrificing its essential religious character. After all, the Islamic world had earlier hosted impressive scientific achievements and had incorporated elements of Greek philosophical thinking.

■ Comparison

In what different ways did various groups define the Ottoman Empire during the nineteenth century?

In 1876, the Young Ottomans experienced a short-lived victory when the Sultan Abd al-Hamid (1876–1909) accepted a constitution and an elected parliament, but not for long. Under the pressure of war with Russia, the Sultan soon suspended the reforms and reverted to an older style of despotic rule for the next thirty years, even renewing the claim that he was the caliph, successor to the Prophet and the protector of Muslims everywhere.

Opposition to this revived despotism soon surfaced among both military and civilian elites known as the Young Turks. Largely abandoning any reference to Islam, they advocated a militantly secular public life, were committed to thoroughgoing modernization along European lines, and increasingly thought about the Ottoman Empire as a Turkish national state. "There is only one civilization, and that is European civilization," declared Abdullah Cevdet, a prominent figure in the Young Turk movement. "Therefore we must borrow western civilization with both its rose and its thorn."[12]

A military coup in 1908 finally allowed the Young Turks to exercise real power. They pushed for a radical secularization of schools, courts, and law codes; permitted elections and competing parties; established a single Law of Family Rights for all regardless of religion; and encouraged Turkish as the official language of the empire. They also opened up modern schools for women, allowed them to wear Western clothing, restricted polygamy, and permitted women to obtain divorces in some situations. But the nationalist conception of Ottoman identity antagonized non-Turkic peoples and helped stimulate Arab and other nationalisms in response. For some, a secular nationality was becoming the most important public loyalty, with Islam relegated to private life. Such nationalist sentiments contributed to the complete disintegration of the Ottoman Empire following World War I, but the secularizing and Westernizing principles of the Young Turks informed the policies of the Turkish republic that replaced it.

Outcomes: Comparing China and the Ottoman Empire

By the beginning of the twentieth century, both China and the Ottoman Empire, recently centers of proud and vibrant civilizations, had experienced the consequences of a rapidly shifting balance of global power. Now they were "semicolonies" within the "informal empires" of Europe, although they retained sufficient independence for their governments to launch catch-up efforts of defensive modernization. But neither was able to create the industrial economies or strong states required to fend off European intrusion and restore their former status in the world. Despite their diminished power, however, both China and the Ottoman Empire gave rise to new nationalist conceptions of society, which were initially small and limited in appeal but of great significance for the future.

In the early twentieth century, that future witnessed the end of both the Chinese and Ottoman empires. In China, the collapse of the imperial system in 1911 was followed by a vast revolutionary upheaval that by 1949 led to a communist regime within largely the same territorial space as the old empire. By contrast, the collapse of the Ottoman Empire following World War I led to the creation of a new but much smaller nation-state in the Turkish heartland of the old empire, having lost its vast Arab and European provinces.

China's twentieth-century revolutionaries rejected traditional Confucian culture far more thoroughly than the secularizing leaders of modern Turkey rejected Islam. Almost everywhere in the Islamic world, traditional religion retained its hold on the private loyalties of most people and later in the twentieth century became a basis for social renewal in many places. Islamic civilization, unlike its Chinese counterpart, had many independent centers and was never so closely associated with a single state. Furthermore, it was embedded in a deeply religious tradition that was personally meaningful to millions of adherents, in contrast to the more elitist and secular outlook of Confucianism. Many rural Chinese, however, retained traditional Confucian values such as filial piety, and Confucianism has made something of a comeback in China over the past several decades. Nonetheless, Islam retained a hold on its civilization in the twentieth century rather more firmly than Confucianism did in China.

The Japanese Difference: The Rise of a New East Asian Power

Like China and the Ottoman Empire, the island country of Japan confronted the aggressive power of the West during the nineteenth century, most notably in the form of U.S. commodore Matthew Perry's "black ships," which steamed into Tokyo Bay in 1853 and forcefully demanded that this reclusive nation open up to more "normal" relations with the world. However, the outcome of that encounter differed sharply from the others. In the second half of the nineteenth century, Japan undertook a radical transformation of its society—a "revolution from above," according to some historians—turning it into a powerful, modern, united, industrialized nation. It was an achievement that neither China nor the Ottoman Empire was able to duplicate. Far from succumbing to Western domination, Japan joined the club of imperialist countries by creating its own East Asian empire, largely at the expense of China. In building a society that was both modern and distinctly Japanese, Japan demonstrated that modernity was not a uniquely European phenomenon. This "Japanese miracle," as some have called it, was both promising and ominous for the rest of Asia. How had it occurred?

The Tokugawa Background

For 250 years prior to Perry's arrival, Japan had been governed by a *shogun* (a military ruler) from the Tokugawa family who acted in the name of a revered but powerless emperor, who lived in Kyoto, 300 miles away from the seat of power in Edo (Tokyo). The chief task of this Tokugawa shogunate was to prevent the return of civil war among some 260 rival feudal lords, known as *daimyo*, each of whom had a cadre of armed retainers, the famed samurai warriors of Japanese tradition.

> ■ **Comparison**
> How did Japan's historical development differ from that of China and the Ottoman Empire during the nineteenth century?

Based on their own military power and political skills, successive shoguns gave Japan more than two centuries of internal peace (1600–1850). To control the restive daimyo, they required these local authorities to create second homes in Edo, the country's capital, where they had to live during alternate years. When they left for their rural residences, families stayed behind, almost as hostages. Nonetheless, the daimyo, especially the more powerful ones, retained substantial autonomy in their own domains and behaved in some ways like independent states with separate military forces, law codes, tax systems, and currencies. With no national army, no uniform currency, and little central authority at the local level, Tokugawa Japan was "pacified... but not really unified."[13] To further stabilize the country, the Tokugawa regime issued highly detailed rules governing occupation, residence, dress, hairstyles, and behavior of the four hierarchically ranked status groups into which Japanese society was divided—samurai at the top, then peasants, artisans, and, at the bottom, merchants.

Much was changing within Japan during these 250 years of peace in ways that belied the control and orderliness of Tokugawa regulations. For one thing, the samurai, in the absence of wars to fight, evolved into a salaried bureaucratic or administrative class amounting to 5 to 6 percent of the total population, but they were still fiercely devoted to their daimyo lords and to their warrior code of loyalty, honor, and self-sacrifice.

> ■ **Change**
> In what ways was Japan changing during the Tokugawa era?

More generally, centuries of peace contributed to a remarkable burst of economic growth, commercialization, and urban development. Entrepreneurial peasants, using fertilizers and other agricultural innovations, grew more rice than ever before and engaged in a variety of rural manufacturing enterprises as well. By 1750, Japan had become perhaps the world's most urbanized country, with about 10 percent of its population living in sizable towns or cities. Edo, with a million residents, was the world's largest city. Well-functioning markets linked urban and rural areas, marking Japan as an emerging capitalist economy. The influence of Confucianism encouraged education and generated a remarkably literate population, with about 40 percent of men and 15 percent of women able to read and write. Although no one was aware of it at the time, these changes during the Tokugawa era provided a solid foundation for Japan's remarkable industrial growth in the late nineteenth century.

These changes also undermined the shogunate's efforts to freeze Japanese society in the interests of stability. Some samurai found the lowly but profitable path of commerce too much to resist. "No more shall we have to live by the sword," declared one of them in 1616 while renouncing his samurai status. "I have seen that great profit can be made honorably. I shall brew *sake* and soy sauce, and we shall prosper."[14] Many merchants, though hailing from the lowest-ranking status group, prospered in the new commercial environment and supported a vibrant urban culture, while not a few daimyo found it necessary, if humiliating, to seek loans from these social inferiors. Thus merchants had money, but little status, whereas samurai enjoyed high status but were often indebted to inferior merchants. Both resented their position.

Despite prohibitions to the contrary, many peasants moved to the cities, becoming artisans or merchants and imitating the ways of their social betters. A decree of 1788 noted that peasants "have become accustomed to luxury and forgetful of their status." They wore inappropriate clothing, used umbrellas rather than straw hats in the rain, and even left the villages for the city. "Henceforth," declared the shogun, "all luxuries should be avoided by the peasants. They are to live simply and devote themselves to farming."[15] This decree, like many others before it, was widely ignored.

More than social change undermined the Tokugawa regime. Corruption was widespread, to the disgust of many. The shogunate's failure to deal successfully with a severe famine in the 1830s eroded confidence in its effectiveness. At the same time, a mounting wave of local peasant uprisings and urban riots expressed the many grievances of the poor. The most striking of these outbursts left the city of Osaka in flames in 1837. Its leader, Oshio Heihachiro, no doubt spoke for many ordinary people when he wrote:

> We must first punish the officials who torment the people so cruelly; then we must execute the haughty and rich Osaka merchants. Then we must distribute the gold, silver, and copper stored in their cellars, and bands of rice hidden in their storehouses.[16]

From the 1830s on, one scholar concluded, "there was a growing feeling that the *shogunate* was losing control."[17]

American Intrusion and the Meiji Restoration

It was foreign intervention that brought matters to a head. Since the expulsion of European missionaries and the harsh suppression of Christianity in the early seventeenth century (see p. 681), Japan had deliberately limited its contact with the West to a single port, where only the Dutch were allowed to trade. By the early nineteenth century, however, various European countries and the United States were knocking at the door. All were turned away, and even shipwrecked sailors or whalers were expelled, jailed, or executed. As it happened, it was the United States that forced the issue, sending Commodore Perry in 1853 to demand humane treatment for castaways, the right of American vessels to refuel and buy provisions, and the opening of ports for trade. Authorized to use force if necessary, Perry presented his reluctant hosts, among other gifts, with a white flag for surrender should hostilities follow. (For a Japanese perception of Perry and his ships, see Visual Sources 19.1 and 19.2, pp. 916 and 917.)

The "Opening" of Japan This nineteenth-century Japanese woodblock print depicts Commodore Perry's meeting with a Japanese official in 1853. It was this encounter that launched Japan on a series of dramatic changes that resulted in the country's modernization and its emergence as one of the world's major industrialized powers by the early twentieth century. (Bettmann/Corbis)

In the end, war was avoided. Aware of what had happened to China in resisting European demands, Japan agreed to a series of unequal treaties with various Western powers. That humiliating capitulation to the demands of the "foreign devils" further eroded support for the shogunate, triggered a brief civil war, and by 1868 led to a political takeover by a group of young samurai from southern Japan. This decisive turning point in Japan's history was known as the Meiji restoration, for the country's new rulers claimed that they were restoring to power the young emperor, then a fifteen-year-old boy whose throne name was Meiji, or Enlightened Rule. But despite his youth, he was regarded as the most recent link in a chain of descent that traced the origins of the imperial family back to the sun goddess Amaterasu. Having eliminated the shogunate, the patriotic young men who led the takeover soon made their goals clear—to save Japan from foreign domination, not by futile resistance, but by a thorough transformation of Japanese society, drawing upon all that the modern West had to offer. "Knowledge shall be sought throughout the world," they declared, "so as to strengthen the foundations of imperial rule."

Japan now had a government committed to a decisive break with the past, and it had acquired that government without massive violence or destruction. By contrast, the defeat of the Taiping Uprising had deprived China of any such opportunity for a fresh start, while saddling it with enormous devastation and massive loss of life. Furthermore, Japan was of less interest to Western powers than either China, with its huge potential market and reputation for riches, or the Ottoman Empire, with its strategic location at the crossroads of Asia, Africa, and Europe. The American Civil War and its aftermath likewise deflected U.S. ambitions in the Pacific for a time, further reducing the Western pressure on Japan.

Modernization Japanese Style

■ Change
In what respects was
Japan's nineteenth-
century transformation
revolutionary?

These circumstances gave Japan some breathing space, and its new rulers moved quickly to take advantage of that unique window of opportunity by directing a cascading wave of dramatic changes that rolled over the country in the last three decades of the nineteenth century. Those reforms, which were revolutionary in their cumulative effect, transformed Japan far more thoroughly than even the most radical of the Ottoman efforts, let alone the modest self-strengthening policies of the Chinese.

The first task was genuine national unity, which required an attack on the power and privileges of both the daimyo and the samurai. In a major break with the past, the new regime soon ended the semi-independent domains of the daimyo, replacing them with governors appointed by and responsible to the emerging national government. The central state, not the local authorities, now collected the nation's taxes and raised a national army based on conscription from all social classes.

Thus the samurai relinquished their ancient role as the country's warrior class and with it their cherished right to carry swords. The old Confucian-based social order with its special privileges for various classes was largely dismantled, and almost all Japanese became legally equal as commoners and as subjects of the emperor. Limitations on travel and trade likewise fell as a nationwide economy came to parallel the centralized state. Although there was some opposition to these measures, including a brief rebellion of resentful samurai in 1877, it was on the whole a remarkably peaceful process in which a segment of the old ruling class abolished its own privileges. Many, but not all, of these displaced elites found a soft landing in the army, bureaucracy, or business enterprises of the new regime, thus easing a painful transition.

Accompanying these social and political changes was a widespread and eager fascination with almost everything Western (see Visual Source 19.3, p. 918). Knowledge about the West—its science and technology; its various political and constitutional arrangements; its legal and educational systems; its dances, clothing, and hairstyles—was enthusiastically sought out by official missions to Europe and the United States, by hundreds of students sent to study abroad, and by many ordinary Japanese at home. Western writers were translated into Japanese; for example, Samuel Smiles's *Self-Help*, which focused on "achieving success and rising in the world," sold a million copies. "Civilization and Enlightenment" was the slogan of the time, and both were to be found in the West. The most prominent popularizer of Western knowledge, Fukuzawa Yukichi, summed up the chief lesson of his studies in the mid-1870s— Japan was backward and needed to learn from the West: "If we compare the knowledge of the Japanese and Westerners, in letters, in technique, in commerce, or in industry, from the largest to the smallest matter, there is not one thing in which we excel.... In Japan's present condition there is nothing in which we may take pride vis-à-vis the West."[18]

After this initial wave of uncritical enthusiasm for everything Western receded, Japan proceeded to borrow more selectively and to combine foreign and Japanese

Snapshot   **Key Moments in the Rise of Japan in the Nineteenth Century and Beyond**

Famines, urban and rural rebellions	1830s
Commodore Perry arrives in Japan	1853
Meiji restoration	1868
Government-run enterprises in railroad construction, manufacturing, and mining	1870s
Western dress prescribed for court and official ceremonies	1872
Samurai rebellion crushed	1877
Government sells state industries to private investors	1880s
Ito Hirobumi travels to Europe to study political systems	1882
Peak of peasant protest against high taxes and prices	1883–1884
Women banned from political parties and meetings	1887
Japan's modern constitution announced	1889
Sino-Japanese War	1894–1895
Japan's labor movement crushed	by 1901
Anglo-Japanese alliance marks Japan's acceptance as Great Power	1902
Russo-Japanese War	1904–1905
Universal primary education	1905
Japanese annexation of Korea	1910
Meiji emperor dies	1912

elements in distinctive ways (see Visual Source 19.4, p. 919). For example, the constitution of 1889, drawing heavily on German experience, introduced an elected parliament, political parties, and democratic ideals, but that constitution was presented as a gift from a sacred emperor descended from the Sun Goddess. The parliament could advise, but ultimate power, and particularly control of the military, lay theoretically with the emperor and in practice with an oligarchy of prominent reformers acting in his name. Likewise, a modern educational system, which achieved universal primary schooling by the early twentieth century, was also laced with Confucian-based moral instruction and exhortations of loyalty to the emperor. Neither Western-style feminism nor Christianity made much headway in Meiji Japan, but Shinto, an ancient religious tradition featuring ancestors and nature spirits, was elevated to the status of an official state cult. Japan's earlier experience in borrowing massively but selectively from Chinese culture perhaps served it better in these new circumstances than either the Chinese disdain for foreign cultures or the reluctance of many Muslims to see much of value in the infidel West.

At the core of Japan's effort at defensive modernization lay its state-guided industrialization program. More than in Europe or the United States, the government itself established a number of enterprises, later selling many of them to private investors. It also acted to create a modern infrastructure by building railroads, creating a postal system, and establishing a national currency and banking system. By the early twentieth century, Japan's industrialization, organized around a number of large firms called *zaibatsu*, was well under way. The country became a major exporter of textiles and was able to produce its own munitions and industrial goods as well. Its major cities enjoyed mass-circulation newspapers, movie theaters, and electric lights. All of this was accomplished through its own resources and without the massive foreign debt that so afflicted Egypt and the Ottoman Empire. No other country outside of Europe and North America had been able to launch its own Industrial Revolution in the nineteenth century. It was a distinctive feature of Japan's modern transformation.

Less distinctive, however, were the social results of that process. Taxed heavily to pay for Japan's ambitious modernization program, many peasant families slid into poverty. Their sometimes violent protests peaked in 1883–1884 with attacks on government offices and moneylenders' homes that were aimed at destroying records of debt. Despite substantial private relief efforts, the Japanese countryside witnessed infanticide, the sale of daughters, and starvation.

As elsewhere during the early stages of industrial growth, urban workers were treated badly. The majority of Japan's textile workers were young women from poor

Japan's Modernization
In Japan, as in Europe, railroads quickly became a popular symbol of the country's modernization, as this woodblock print from the 1870s illustrates. (Visual Arts Library [London]/Alamy)

families in the countryside. Their pay was low and their working conditions terrible. Anarchist and socialist ideas circulated among intellectuals. Efforts to create unions and organize strikes, both illegal in Japan at the time, were met with harsh repression even as corporate and state authorities sought to depict the company as a family unit to which workers should give their loyalty, all under the beneficent gaze of the divine emperor.

Japan and the World

Japan's modern transformation soon registered internationally. By the early twentieth century, its economic growth, openness to trade, and embrace of "civilization and enlightenment" from the West persuaded the Western powers to revise the unequal treaties in Japan's favor. This had long been a primary goal of the Meiji regime, and the Anglo-Japanese Treaty of 1902 now acknowledged Japan as an equal player among the Great Powers of the world.

■ **Connection**
How did Japan's relationship to the larger world change during its modernization process?

Not only did Japan escape from its semicolonial entanglements with the West, but it also launched its own empire-building enterprise, even as European powers and the United States were carving up much of Asia and Africa into colonies or spheres of influence. It was what industrializing Great Powers did in the late nineteenth century, and Japan followed suit. Successful wars against China (1894–1895) and Russia (1904–1905) established Japan as a formidable military competitor in East Asia and the first Asian state to defeat a major European power. Through those victories, Japan also gained colonial control of Taiwan and Korea and a territorial foothold in Manchuria. (See Visual Source 19.5, p. 920, for an image of Japan's new relationship with China and the West.)

Japan's entry onto the broader global stage was felt in many places (see Map 19.3). It added yet one more imperialist power to those already burdening a beleaguered China. Defeat at the hands of Japanese upstarts shocked Russia and triggered the 1905 revolution in that country. To Europeans and Americans, Japan was now an economic, political, and military competitor in Asia.

In the world of subject peoples, the rise of Japan and its defeat of Russia generated widespread admiration among those who saw Japan as a model for their own modern development and perhaps as an ally in the struggle against imperialism. Some Poles, Finns, and Jews viewed the Russian defeat in 1905 as an opening for their own liberation from the Russian Empire and were grateful to Japan for the opportunity. Despite Japan's aggression against their country, many Chinese reformers and nationalists found in the Japanese experience valuable lessons for themselves. Thousands flocked to Japan to study its achievements. Newspapers throughout the Islamic world celebrated Japan's victory over Russia as an "awakening of the East," which might herald Muslims' own liberation. Some Turkish women gave their children Japanese names. Indonesian Muslims from Aceh wrote to the Meiji emperor asking for help in their struggle against the Dutch, and Muslim poets wrote odes in his honor. The Egyptian nationalist Mustafa Kamil spoke for many when he declared:

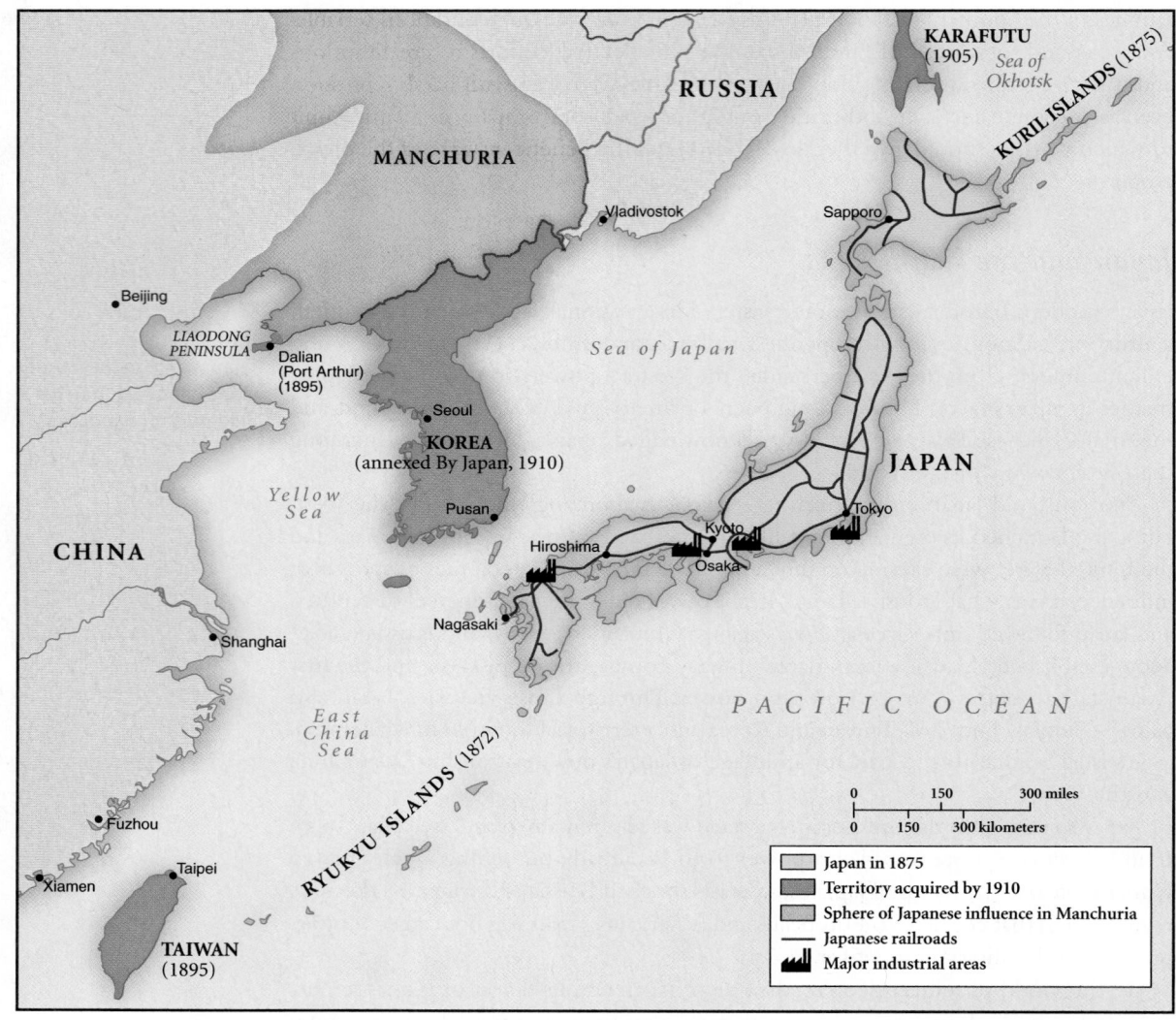

The following labels appear on the map:

KARAFUTU (1905)
Sea of Okhotsk
RUSSIA
KURIL ISLANDS (1875)
MANCHURIA
Vladivostok
Sapporo
Beijing
LIAODONG PENINSULA
Dalian (Port Arthur) (1895)
Sea of Japan
Seoul
KOREA (annexed By Japan, 1910)
JAPAN
Pusan
Yellow Sea
Tokyo
CHINA
Hiroshima
Kyoto
Osaka
Shanghai
Nagasaki
PACIFIC OCEAN
East China Sea
RYUKYU ISLANDS (1872)
Fuzhou
Xiamen
Taipei
TAIWAN (1895)

0   150   300 miles
0   150   300 kilometers

Legend:
Japan in 1875
Territory acquired by 1910
Sphere of Japanese influence in Manchuria
Japanese railroads
Major industrial areas

Map 19.3   The Rise of Japan
As Japan modernized after the Meiji restoration, it launched an empire-building program that provided a foundation for further expansion in the 1930s and during World War II.

"We are amazed by Japan because it is the first Eastern government to utilize Western civilization to resist the shield of European imperialism in Asia."[19]

Those who directly experienced Japanese imperialism in Taiwan or Korea no doubt had a less positive view, for its colonial policies matched or exceeded the brutality of European practices. In the twentieth century, China and much of Southeast Asia suffered bitterly under Japanese imperial aggression. Nonetheless, both the idea of Japan as a liberator of Asia from the European yoke and the reality of Japan as an oppressive imperial power in its own right derived from the country's remarkable modern transformation and its unique response to the provocation of Western intrusion.

⊏⊐ Reflections: Success and Failure in History

Beyond describing what happened in the past and explaining why, historians often find themselves evaluating the events they study. When they make judgments about the past, notions of success and failure frequently come into play. Should Europe's Industrial Revolution and its rise to global power be regarded as a success? If so, does that imply that others were failures? Should we consider Japan more successful than China or the Ottoman Empire during the nineteenth century? Three considerations suggest that we should be very careful in applying these ideas to the complexities of the historical record.

First, and most obviously, is the question of criteria. If the measure of success is national wealth and power, then the Industrial Revolution surely counts as a great accomplishment. But if preservation of the environment, spiritual growth, and the face-to-face relationships of village life are more highly valued, then industrialization, according to some, might be more reasonably considered as a disaster.

Second, there is the issue of "success for whom?" British artisans who lost their livelihood to industrial machines as well as those Japanese women textile workers who suffered through the early stages of industrialization might be forgiven for not appreciating the "success" of their countries' transformation, even if their middle-class counterparts and subsequent generations benefited. In cases such as this, issues of both social and generational justice complicate any easy assessment of the past.

Finally, success is frequently associated with good judgment and wise choices, yet actors in the historical drama are never completely free in making their decisions, and none, of course, have the benefit of hindsight, which historians enjoy. Did the leaders of China and the Ottoman Empire fail to push industrial development more strongly, or were they not in a position to do so? Were Japanese leaders wiser and more astute than their counterparts elsewhere, or did their knowledge of China's earlier experience and their unique national history simply provide them with circumstances more conducive to modern development? Such questions regarding the possibilities and limitations of human action have no clear-cut answers, but they might caution us about any easy use of notions of success and failure.

Second Thoughts

What's the Significance?

social Darwinism	China, 1911	informal empires
Taiping Uprising	"the sick man of Europe"	Tokugawa Japan
Opium Wars	Tanzimat	Meiji restoration
unequal treaties	Young Ottomans	Russo-Japanese War,
self-strengthening movement	Sultan Abd al-Hamid II	1904–1905
Boxer uprising	Young Turks	

To assess your mastery of the material in this chapter, visit the **Student Center** at bedfordstmartins.com/strayer.

Big Picture Questions

1. How did European expansion in the nineteenth century differ from that of the early modern era (see Chapters 14–16)?
2. What differences can you identify in how China, the Ottoman Empire, and Japan experienced Western imperialism and confronted it? How might you account for those differences?
3. "The response of each society to European imperialism grew out of its larger historical development and its internal problems." What evidence might support this statement?
4. What kinds of debates, controversies, and conflicts were generated by European intrusion within each of the societies examined in this chapter?

Next Steps: For Further Study

For Web sites and additional documents related to this chapter, see **Make History** at bedfordstmartins.com/strayer.

William Bowman et al., *Imperialism in the Modern World* (2007). A collection of short readings illustrating the various forms and faces of European expansion over the past several centuries.

Carter V. Finley, *The Turks in World History* (2004). A study placing the role of Turkish-speaking peoples in general and the Ottoman Empire in particular in a global context.

Maurice Jansen, *The Making of Modern Japan* (2000). A well-regarded account of Japan since 1600 by a leading scholar.

Jonathan Spence, *The Search for Modern China* (1999). Probably the best single-volume account of Chinese history from about 1600 through the twentieth century.

E. Patricia Tsurumi, *Factory Girls: Women in the Thread Mills of Meiji Japan* (1990). An examination of the lives of women in Japan's nineteenth-century textile factories.

Arthur Waley, *The Opium War through Chinese Eyes* (1968). An older classic that views the Opium War from various Chinese points of view.

Justin Jesty, "Japanese History from 1868 to the Present," http://ceas.uchicago.edu/outreach/1868%20to%20Present.pdf. A guide to modern Japanese history, with many links to pictures, documents, and further information.

Documents

Considering the Evidence:
Voices from the Opium War

The Opium War of 1839–1842 marked a dramatic turn in China's long history and in its relationship with the wider world. It was also indicative of the new kinds of cross-cultural encounters that were increasingly taking place as Europe's global power mounted. The five documents in this section of the chapter allow us to follow the unfolding of that encounter, largely from a Chinese point of view.

By the early nineteenth century, China had long enjoyed a position of unrivaled dominance in East Asia. Furthermore, its wealth and technological innovations had given it a major role in the world economy of the early modern era, reflected in the flow of much of the world's silver into China. At the same time, the island nation of Great Britain was emerging as a major global economic and military power, thanks to its position as the first site of the Industrial Revolution and its increasingly dominant role in India.

At the heart of the emerging conflict between these two countries was trade rather than territory. From the British point of view, the problem lay in the sharp restrictions that the Chinese had long imposed on commerce between the two nations. The British were permitted to trade only in a single city, Canton, and even there had to deal with an officially approved group of Chinese merchants. This so-called Canton system meant that Europeans had no direct access to the Chinese market. Thus in the early 1790s, the British government sent a major diplomatic mission to China, headed by Lord George Macartney, to seek greater access to the Chinese market.

Document 19.1

A Chinese Response to Lord Macartney

Despite a polite reception at the Chinese court, Macartney's mission was an almost total failure from the British point of view. At its conclusion the Chinese emperor Qianlong sent a message to the British monarch George III replying to Macartney's requests.

■ What reasons does Emperor Qianlong give for rejecting British requests?

- What does this document reveal about the Chinese view of trade in general?

- What does it show about China's relations with foreign "barbarians," and about China's understanding of its place in the world?

- In what historical context does the Chinese emperor understand Macartney's mission?

EMPEROR QIANLONG

Message to King George III
1793

You, O King, from afar have yearned after the blessings of our civilization, and in your eagerness to come into touch with our converting influence have sent an Embassy across the sea bearing a memorial. I have already taken note of your respectful spirit of submission, have treated your mission with extreme favor and loaded it with gifts, besides issuing a mandate to you, O King, and honoring you with the bestowal of valuable presents. Thus has my indulgence been manifested.

Yesterday your Ambassador petitioned my Ministers to memorialize me regarding your trade with China, but his proposal is not consistent with our dynastic usage and cannot be entertained. Hitherto, all European nations, including your own country's barbarian merchants, have carried on their trade with our Celestial Empire at Canton. Such has been the procedure for many years, although our Celestial Empire possesses all things in prolific abundance and lacks no product within its own borders. There was therefore no need to import the manufactures of outside barbarians in exchange for our own produce. But as the tea, silk, and porcelain which the Celestial Empire produces are absolute necessities to European nations and to yourselves, we have permitted, as a signal mark of favor, that foreign hongs°

should be established at Canton, so that your wants might be supplied and your country thus participate in our beneficence. But your Ambassador has now put forward new requests which completely fail to recognize the Throne's principle to "treat strangers from afar with indulgence," and to exercise a pacifying control over barbarian tribes, the world over. Moreover, our dynasty, swaying the myriad races of the globe, extends the same benevolence toward all. Your England is not the only nation trading at Canton. If other nations, following your bad example, wrongfully importune my ear with further impossible requests, how will it be possible for me to treat them with easy indulgence? Nevertheless, I do not forget the lonely remoteness of your island, cut off from the world by intervening wastes of sea, nor do I overlook your excusable ignorance of the usages of our Celestial Empire. I have consequently commanded my Ministers to enlighten your Ambassador on the subject, and have ordered the departure of the mission....

Your request for a small island near Chusan, where your merchants may reside and goods be warehoused, arises from your desire to develop trade. As there are neither foreign hongs nor interpreters in or near Chusan, where none of your ships have ever called, such an island would be utterly useless for your purposes. Every inch of the territory of our Empire is marked on the map and the strictest vigilance is exercised over it all: even tiny islets and far-lying sand-banks are clearly defined as part of the provinces to which they belong. Consider, more-

---

°*hongs:* approved Chinese trading firms.

Source: "Edict on Trade with Great Britain," in J. O. P. Brand, *Annals and Memoirs of the Court of Peking* (Boston: Houghton Mifflin, 1914), 325–31.

over, that England is not the only barbarian land which wishes to establish relations with our civilization and trade with our Empire: supposing that other nations were all to imitate your evil example and beseech me to present them each and all with a site for trading purposes, how could I possibly comply? This also is a flagrant infringement of the usage of my Empire and cannot possibly be entertained....

Regarding your nation's worship of the Lord of Heaven, it is the same religion as that of other European nations. Ever since the beginning of history, sage Emperors and wise rulers have bestowed on China a moral system and inculcated a code, which from time immemorial has been religiously observed by the myriads of my subjects [Confucianism]. There has been no hankering after heterodox doctrines. Even the European officials [missionaries] in my capital are forbidden to hold intercourse with Chinese subjects; they are restricted within the limits of their appointed residences, and may not go about propagating their religion. The distinction between Chinese and barbarian is most strict, and your Ambassador's request that barbarians shall be given full liberty to disseminate their religion is utterly unreasonable....

[Perhaps] you yourself are ignorant of our dynastic regulations and had no intention of transgressing them when you expressed these wild ideas and hopes.... If, after the receipt of this explicit decree, you lightly give ear to the representations of your subordinates and allow your barbarian merchants to proceed to Zhejiang and Tianjin, with the object of landing and trading there, the ordinances of my Celestial Empire are strict in the extreme, and the local officials, both civil and military, are bound reverently to obey the law of the land. Should your vessels touch the shore, your merchants will assuredly never be permitted to land or to reside there, but will be subject to instant expulsion. In that event your barbarian merchants will have had a long journey for nothing. Do not say that you were not warned in due time! Tremblingly obey and show no negligence! A special mandate!

Documents 19.2 and 19.3

Debating the Opium Problem

With Europe engulfed in the Napoleonic wars, Great Britain made no immediate response to China's 1793 rebuff. But in the several decades following Napoleon's 1815 defeat, the issue reemerged. This time the question was not just trade in general but opium in particular. By the early nineteenth century, that addictive drug was providing a solution to another of Great Britain's problems in its trade relations with China—the difficulty of finding Western goods that the Chinese were willing to buy. This had long meant that the British had to pay for much-desired Chinese products with major exports of silver. Now, however, opium grown in British India proved increasingly attractive in China, and imports soared.

But this solution to a British problem had by the mid-1830s provoked a growing and many-sided crisis for China. The country's legal prohibition on the importing of opium was widely ignored, silver was flowing out of the country to pay for the drug, and addiction was increasing, even among the elite. This dire situation prompted the Chinese emperor Daoguang to seek advice from his senior officials. The two documents that follow illustrate the sharp division within Chinese official circles, one side advocating legalization and the other counseling suppression.

- What arguments are made for each position? On what issues did they disagree?

- How might each respond to the arguments of the other?

- What similarities and differences do you see between this debate within the Chinese court of the 1830s and contemporary discussion about the legalization of marijuana in the United States?

Xu Naiji
An Argument for Legalization
1836

Xu Naiji, Vice-President of the Sacrificial Court, presents the following memorial in regard to opium, to show that the more severe the interdicts against it are made, the more widely do the evils arising therefrom spread....

In Keenlung's reign, as well as previously, opium was inserted in the tariff of Canton as a medicine, subject to a duty.... After this, it was prohibited.... Yet the smokers of the drug have increased in number, and the practice has spread almost throughout the whole empire....

Formerly, the barbarian merchants brought foreign money to China; which being paid in exchange for goods, was a source of pecuniary advantage to the people of all the sea-board provinces. But latterly, the barbarian merchants have clandestinely sold opium for money, which has rendered it unnecessary for them to import foreign silver. Thus foreign money has been going out of the country, while none comes into it.

It is proposed entirely to cut off the foreign trade, thus to remove the root, to dam up the source of the evil. The Celestial Dynasty would not, indeed, hesitate to relinquish the few millions of duties arising therefrom. But all the nations of the West have had a general market open to their ships for upward of a thousand years, while the dealers in opium are the English alone; it would be wrong, for the sake of cut-

ting off the English trade, to cut off that of all the other nations. Besides, the hundreds of thousands of people living on the sea-coast depend wholly on trade for their livelihood, and how are they to be disposed of? Moreover, the barbarian ships, being on the high seas, can repair to any island that may be selected as an entrepôt, and the native sea-going vessels can meet them there; it is then impossible to cut off the trade.... Thus it appears that, though the commerce of Canton should be cut off, yet it will not be possible to prevent the clandestine introduction of merchandise.

It will be found, on examination, that the smokers of opium are idle, lazy vagrants, having no useful purpose before them, and are unworthy of regard or even of contempt. And though there are smokers to be found who have overstepped the threshold of age, yet they do not attain to the long life of other men. But new births are daily increasing the population of the empire; and there is no cause to apprehend a diminution therein; while, on the other hand, we cannot adopt too great, or too early, precautions against the annual waste which is taking place in the resources, the very substance of China.

Since then, it will not answer to close our ports against [all trades], and since the laws issued against opium are quite inoperative, the only method left is to revert to the former system, to permit the barbarian merchants to import opium paying duty thereon as a medicine, and to require that, after having passed the Custom-House, it shall be delivered to the Hong merchants only in exchange for merchandise, and

Source: "Memorial from Heu-Naetse," in *Blue Book— Correspondence Relating to China* (London, 1840), 56–59.

that no money be paid for it. The barbarians finding that the amount of dues to be paid on it, is less than what is now spent in bribes, will also gladly comply therein. Foreign money should be placed on the same footing with sycee silver, and the exportation of it should be equally prohibited. Offenders, when caught, should be punished by the entire destruction of the opium they may have, and the confiscation of the money that may be found with them....

It becomes my duty, then, to request that it be enacted, that any officer, scholar, or soldier, found guilty of secretly smoking opium, shall be immediately dismissed from public employ, without being made liable to any other penalty....

Lastly, that no regard be paid to the purchase and use of opium on the part of the people generally....

Besides, the removal of the prohibitions refers only to the vulgar and common people, those who have no official duties to perform. So long as the officers of the Government, the scholars, and the military are not included, I see no detriment to the dignity of the Government. And by allowing the proposed importation and exchange of the drug for other commodities, more than ten millions of money will annually be prevented from flowing out of the Central land.

Yuan Yulin

An Argument for Suppression
1836

I, your minister, believe that the success or failure in government and the prosperity or decay of administration depend largely upon our capacity to distinguish between right and wrong, between what is safe and what is dangerous.... The prevailing evil of to-day is the excuse that things are hard to get done, and the foremost example of such hypocrisy is the proposal to legalize opium....

In my humble opinion, the proposal for legalization has overlooked the distinction between right and wrong.... Further, it fails to appreciate what is safe and what is dangerous....

The prohibition of opium is most solemnly recorded on the statute books.... The proposal to change the established law is thus a violation of an inherited institution and of the imperial edicts.

Uniformity is the most important element in the decrees of the Court. Now it has been proposed that the prohibition of opium-smoking would reach the officers of the Government, the scholars, and the military, but not the common people. But it is forgotten that the common people of to-day will be the officers, scholars, and the military of the future. Should they be allowed to smoke at first and then be prohibited from it in the future? Moreover, the officers, scholars, and the military of to-day may be degraded to the rank of the common people. In that case, are they to be freed from the prohibition once imposed on them? Prohibition was proclaimed because opium is pernicious. It follows then that the ban should not be abolished until it ceases to be an evil. A partial prohibition or partial legalization is a confusion of rules by the government itself; consequently good faith in its observance can hardly be expected. When the law was all for prohibition, decrees had not been followed. How can the people respect the restrictions or punishments should the law be in confusion? The logical consequence will be the ruin of government and demoralization of our culture....

Even if the duties be raised to twofold, it would be only a little over 200,000 taels. Further doubled, the figure will stand at only 500,000 taels.... Hence, if our Government should seek its revenue from the duties on opium, it is to make an enormous sacrifice for a scanty profit....

The drain of silver, to be sure, arouses apprehension. But the point is whether inspection is faithfully

Source: "Memorial from Yuan Yu-lin," in P. C. Kuo, *A Critical Study of the First Anglo-Chinese War* (Shanghai: Commercial Press, 1935), 211–13.

enforced or not. Should the inspection be faithful, opium prohibition will be effective; so also will be the ban on the silver export. If it be not faithful, opium prohibition will come to naught, and so will the ban on silver export. It must not be supposed that inspection will be facilitated by relaxing opium prohibition or that it will be difficult if the prohibition is severe....

It has been argued that since the imported opium costs an enormous sum of money, the cultivation of the poppy should be allowed in the interior of the country.... [But], the farm lands of our country are fixed in number.... The valuable acres yielding crops may easily be turned into a vast field of opium. This means to destroy agriculture and ruin the very foundation of the lives of the people.

If the habit of smoking secretly spreads over the country under the present prohibition, its legalization will mean greater disasters: fathers would no longer be able to teach their sons; husbands would no longer be able to admonish their wives; masters would no longer be able to restrain their servants; and teachers would no longer be able to train their pupils. The habitual smokers would continue it as a regular practice, while others would strive for imitation. The per-

petration of evils will be fathomless. It would mean the end of the life of the people and the destruction of the soul of the nation.

As a result of the smoking of opium, the soldiers of Kwangtung were enfeebled. Your Majesty admonished them on that account during the late rebellion of the mountaineers in the said province. Now should the proposal be adhered to that soldiers, but not the people, be prohibited from smoking opium, then at the future recruitment of the army it would be found that old soldiers had already been spoiled by secret smoking, while fresh recruits would be habitual smokers!... The very trick of the cunning barbarians is to weaken our nation with poison. If they now actually succeed in fooling our people, it means the disintegration of our national defense and the opening up of the same to their penetration....

[W]hat arouses our gravest apprehension is the perpetration of an evil which might completely go out of control. Once opium is legalized, the people will flock to it. When the evil becomes alarming and when we come to repent the wrong of legalization... we will readily find that the country is so heavily saddled with its bad results that recovery is well-nigh impossible....

Document 19.4

A Moral Appeal to Queen Victoria

The Chinese emperor soon decided this debate in favor of suppression and sent a prominent official, Commissioner Lin Zexu, to enforce it. Lin did so vigorously, seizing and destroying millions of pounds of the drug, flushing it out to the sea with a prayer to the local spirit: "[You] who wash away all stains and cleanse all impurities."[20] At the same time (1839), Lin wrote a letter to the British monarch, Queen Victoria, appealing for her assistance in ending this noxious trade.

- On what basis does Commissioner Lin appeal to Queen Victoria?

- How might you compare this letter with that of Document 19.1? What similarities and differences can you notice?

- What assumptions about the West does this letter reveal? Which were accurate and which represented misunderstandings?

- Although there is no evidence of a response to the letter, how might you imagine British reaction to it?

COMMISSIONER LIN ZEXU
Letter to Queen Victoria
1839

A communication: magnificently our great Emperor soothes and pacifies China and the foreign countries, regarding all with the same kindness. If there is profit, then he shares it with the people of the world; if there is harm, then he removes it on behalf of the world....

We find that your country is sixty or seventy thousand *li*° from China. Yet there are barbarian ships that strive to come here for trade for the purpose of making a great profit. The wealth of China is used to profit the barbarians.... By what right do they...use this poisonous drug to injure the Chinese people?...

Let us ask, where is your conscience? I have heard that the smoking of opium is very strictly forbidden by your country; that is because the harm caused by opium is clearly understood. Since it is not permitted to do harm to your country, then even less should you let it be passed on to the harm of other countries—how much less to China! Of all that China exports to foreign countries, there is not a single thing which is not beneficial to people: they are of benefit when eaten, or of benefit when used, or of benefit when resold: all are beneficial. Is there a single article from China which has done any harm to foreign countries? Take tea and rhubarb,° for example; the foreign countries cannot get along for a single day without them. If China cuts off these benefits with no sympathy for those who are to suffer, then what can the barbarians rely upon to keep themselves alive?...On the other hand, articles coming from the outside to China can only be used as toys. We can take them or get along without them....Nevertheless our Celestial Court lets tea, silk, and other goods be shipped without limit and circulated everywhere without begrudging it in the slightest. This is for no other reason but to share the benefit with the people of the whole world....

We have heard heretofore that your honorable ruler is kind and benevolent. Naturally you would not wish to give unto others what you yourself do not want....

Suppose a man of another country comes to England to trade, he still has to obey the English laws; how much more should he obey in China the laws of the Celestial Dynasty?...

Therefore in the new regulations, in regard to those barbarians who bring opium to China, the penalty is fixed at decapitation or strangulation. This is what is called getting rid of a harmful thing on behalf of mankind....

After receiving this dispatch will you immediately give us a prompt reply regarding the details and circumstances of your cutting off the opium traffic? Be sure not to put this off.

°*li:* approximately one-third of a mile.

°**rhubarb:** used as a medicine.

Source: Dun J. Li, ed., *China in Transition, 1517–1911* (London: Wadsworth, 1969), 64–67.

Document 19.5
War and Defeat

While Queen Victoria and British authorities apparently never received Commissioner Lin's letter and certainly did not respond to it, they did react to the commissioner's actions. Citing the importance of free trade and the violation of British property rights, they launched a major military expedition in which their steamships and heavy guns reflected the impact of the Industrial Revolution on the exercise of British power. This was the first Opium War, and the Chinese lost it badly. One prominent scholar has described it as "the most decisive reversal the Manchus [Qing dynasty] had ever received."[21] The Treaty of Nanjing, which ended that conflict in 1842, was largely imposed by the British. It was the first of many "unequal treaties" that China was required to sign with various European powers and the United States in the decades that followed. While Chinese authorities tried to think about the treaty as a means of "subduing and conciliating" the British, as they had done with other barbarian intruders, it represented in fact a new, much diminished, and dependent position for China on the world stage.

■ What were the major provisions of the treaty? Why do you think that opium, ostensibly the cause of the conflict, was rarely mentioned in the treaty?

■ In what respects did the treaty signal an unequal relationship between China and Great Britain? What aspects of Chinese independence were lost or compromised by the treaty?

■ What provisions of the treaty most clearly challenged traditional Chinese understandings of their place in the world?

The Treaty of Nanjing
1842

I.

There shall henceforward be peace and friendship between Her Majesty the Queen of the United Kingdom of Great Britain and Ireland and His Majesty the Emperor of China, and between their respective subjects, who shall enjoy full security and protection for their persons and property within the dominions of the other.

II.

His Majesty the Emperor of China agrees, that British subjects, with their families and establishments, shall be allowed to reside, for the purposes of carrying on their mercantile pursuits, without molestation or restraint, at the cities and towns of Canton, Amoy, Foochowfoo, Ningpo, and Shanghai....

III.

It being obviously necessary and desirable that British subjects should have some port whereat they may [maintain] and refit their ships when required, and keep stores for that purpose, His Majesty the Emperor of China cedes to Her Majesty the Queen of Great Britain, &c., the Island of Hong-Kong....

IV.

The Emperor of China agrees to pay the sum of 6,000,000 of dollars, as the value of the opium which was delivered up at Canton in the month of March,

Source: Treaty of Nanjing, in *Treaties, Conventions, etc., between China and Foreign States* (London: Statistical Department of the Inspectorate General of Customs, 1917), 1:351–56.

1839, as a ransom for the lives of Her Britannic Majesty's Superintendent and subjects, who had been imprisoned and threatened with death by the Chinese High Officers....

V.

The Government of China having compelled the British merchants trading at Canton to deal exclusively with certain Chinese merchants, called Hong merchants (or Co-Hong)...the Emperor of China agrees to abolish that practice in future at all ports where British merchants may reside, and to permit them to carry on their mercantile transactions with whatever persons they please; and His Imperial Majesty further agrees to pay to the British Government the sum of 3,000,000 of dollars, on account of debts due to British subjects by some of the said Hong merchants, who have become insolvent, and who owe very large sums of money to subjects of Her Britannic Majesty.

VI.

The Government of Her Britannic Majesty having been obliged to send out an expedition to demand and obtain redress for the violent and unjust proceedings of the Chinese High Authorities towards Her Britannic Majesty's officer and subjects, the Emperor of China agrees to pay the sum of 12,000,000 of dollars, on account of the expenses incurred....

VIII.

The Emperor of China agrees to release, unconditionally, all subjects of Her Britannic Majesty (whether natives of Europe or India), who may be in confinement at this moment in any part of the Chinese empire.

X.

...[T]he Emperor further engages, that when British merchandise shall have once paid at any of the said ports the regulated customs and dues,...such merchandise may be conveyed by Chinese merchants to any province or city in the interior of the Empire of China....

XI.

It is agreed that Her Britannic Majesty's Chief High Officer in China shall correspond with the Chinese High Officers, both at the capital and in the provinces,...on a footing of perfect equality....

XII.

On the assent of the Emperor of China to this Treaty being received, and the discharge of the first instalment of money, Her Britannic Majesty's forces will retire from Nanking and the Grand Canal, and will no longer molest or stop the trade of China. The military post at Chinhai will also be withdrawn, but the Islands of Koolangsoo, and that of Chusan, will continue to be held by Her Majesty's forces until the money payments, and the arrangements for opening the ports to British merchants, be completed.

Using the Evidence:
Voices from the Opium War

1. **Defining the issues in the Opium War:** The Opium War was about more than opium. How would you support or challenge this statement?

2. **Characterizing the Opium War:** In what ways might the Opium War be regarded as a clash of cultures? In what respects might it be seen as a clash of interests? Was it an inevitable conflict or were there missed opportunities for avoiding it? (Note: You may want to consider the data in the Snapshot on p. 885 as well as Documents 19.1–19.5, pp. 905–13.)

3. **Interpreting the Treaty of Nanjing:** In the context of British and Chinese views of the world, how do you understand the Treaty of Nanjing? Which country's view of the world is more clearly reflected in that treaty?

4. **Exploring Chinese views of the British:** Based on these documents, how well or how poorly did the Chinese understand the British? How might you account for their misunderstandings?

Visual Sources

Considering the Evidence:
Japanese Perceptions of the West

The second half of the nineteenth century witnessed a profound transformation of Japanese life. (See pp. 894–902) The Tokugawa shogunate, which had governed the country for over two centuries, came to an inglorious end in the Meiji restoration of 1868, and the country then embarked on a massive process of modernization and industrialization. Accompanying these upheavals, Japan's political and military relationship to the West changed dramatically, as its government and its people found themselves required to confront both Western power and Western culture, a common feature of nineteenth-century world history in many places. Accordingly, Japanese understanding of the West, and what they had to fear or gain from it, also changed. Those evolving perceptions of the West found artistic expression, especially in Japanese woodblock printing, an art form that reached its high point in the late nineteenth century. Those images provide for historians a window into Japanese thinking about their own society and the larger world impinging upon them during this critical half-century.

The initial occasion for serious Japanese reflection on the West occurred in 1853–1854, in the context of American commodore Matthew Perry's efforts to "open" Japan to regular commercial relationships with the United States. His nine coal-fired steamships, belching black smoke and carrying a crew of some 1,800 men and more than 100 mounted cannons, became known in Japan as the "black ships." Visual Source 19.1, created around 1854, represents perhaps the best known of many such Japanese depictions of the American warships.

■ What general impression of the American intrusion did the artist seek to convey?

■ What specific features of the image help the artist make his case?

■ Why might the artist have chosen to depict the gunfire coming from the American ship as streams of light?

Beyond portraying the American warships, Japanese artists sought to depict their inhabitants, especially Commodore Perry and his top aides. Some Japanese men rowed their small boats out to the black ships, hoping to catch a glimpse of Perry himself. But the commodore remained largely inaccessible, and the

Visual Source 19.1 The Black Ships (Courtesy, Ryosenji Treasure Museum)

Japanese called his secluded on-board cabin "The Abode of His High and Mighty Mysteriousness." Visual Source 19.2 represents one of many portrayals of Perry (on the right), together with his second-in-command, Commander Henry A. Adams.

- What overall impression of the Americans was the artist seeking to communicate?

- What features of this image seem intended to show the Americans as "other" or different from the Japanese?

- The Japanese had long portrayed a particular kind of goblin, known as *tengu*, with long noses and viewed them as dangerous, demonic, and warlike. What aspects of this depiction of the Americans suggest that the artist sought to associate them with *tengu*?

- But not all portrayals of the Americans displayed such gross and negative features. Compare this image with the woodblock print on page 897. How would you describe the difference between the two portrayals of the Americans? How might you account for the difference?

Visual Source 19.2 Depicting the Americans (Courtesy, Ryosenji Treasure Museum)

By the 1880s, Japan was in the midst of an amazing transformation, in part the outcome of Perry's forced "opening" of the country. By then Japan had a new government committed to the country's rapid modernization. Dozens of official missions and thousands of students had been sent abroad to learn from the West. Particularly among the young, there was an acute awareness of the need to create a new culture that could support a revived Japan. "We have no history," declared one of these students; "our history begins today."[22] In this context, much that was Western was enthusiastically embraced. The technological side of this borrowing was illustrated in woodblock print on page 900. But it extended as well to more purely cultural matters. Eating beef became popular, despite Buddhist objections. Many men adopted Western hairstyles and grew beards, even though the facial hair of Westerners had earlier been portrayed as ugly. In 1872, Western dress was ordered for all official ceremonies. Women in elite circles likewise adopted Western ways, as illustrated in Visual Source 19.3, an 1887 woodblock print titled *Illustration of Singing by the Plum Garden*. At the same time, the dress of the woman in the middle seems to reflect

Visual Source 19.3 Women and Westernization (Museum of Fine Arts, Boston, Gift of L. Aaron Lebowich. RES.53.82-4. Photograph © 2010 Museum of Fine Arts, Boston)

earlier Japanese court traditions that encouraged women to wear many layers of kimonos.

- What elements of Western culture can you identify in this visual source?

- In what ways does this print reflect the continuing appeal of Japanese culture? Pay attention to the scenery, the tree, and the flowers.

- Why were so many Japanese so enamored of Western culture during this time? And why did the Japanese government so actively encourage their interest?

Not everyone in Japan was so enthusiastic about the adoption of Western culture, and by the late 1870s and into the next decade numerous essays and images satirized the apparently indiscriminate fascination with all things European. Visual Source 19.4, drawn by Japanese cartoonist Kobayashi Kiyochika in 1879, represents one of those images. Its full English-language caption read as follows: "Mr. Morse [an American zoologist who introduced Darwin's theory of evolution to Japan in 1877] explains that all human beings were monkeys in the beginning. In the beginning—but even now aren't we still monkeys? When it comes to Western things we think the red beards are the most skillful at everything."[23]

- What specific aspects of Japan's efforts at Westernization is the artist mocking?

- Why might the artist have used a Western scientific theory (Darwinian evolution) to criticize excessive Westernization in Japan?

■ Why do you think a reaction set in against the cultural imitation of Europe?

Behind Japan's modernization and Westernization was the recognition that Western imperialism was surging in Asia, and that China was a prime example of what happened to countries unable to defend themselves against it. Accordingly, achieving political and military equality with the Great Powers of Europe and the United States became a central aim of Japan's modernization program.

Strengthening Japan against Western aggression increasingly meant "throwing off Asia," a phrase that implied rejecting many of Japan's own cultural traditions as well as creating an Asian empire of its own. Fukuzawa Yukichi, a popular advocate of Western knowledge, declared:

> We must not wait for neighboring countries to become civilized so that we can together promote Asia's revival. Rather we should leave their ranks and join forces with the civilized countries of the West. We don't have to give China and Korea any special treatment just because they are neighboring countries. We should deal with them as Western people do. Those who have bad friends cannot avoid having a bad reputation. I reject the idea that we must continue to associate with bad friends in East Asia.[24]

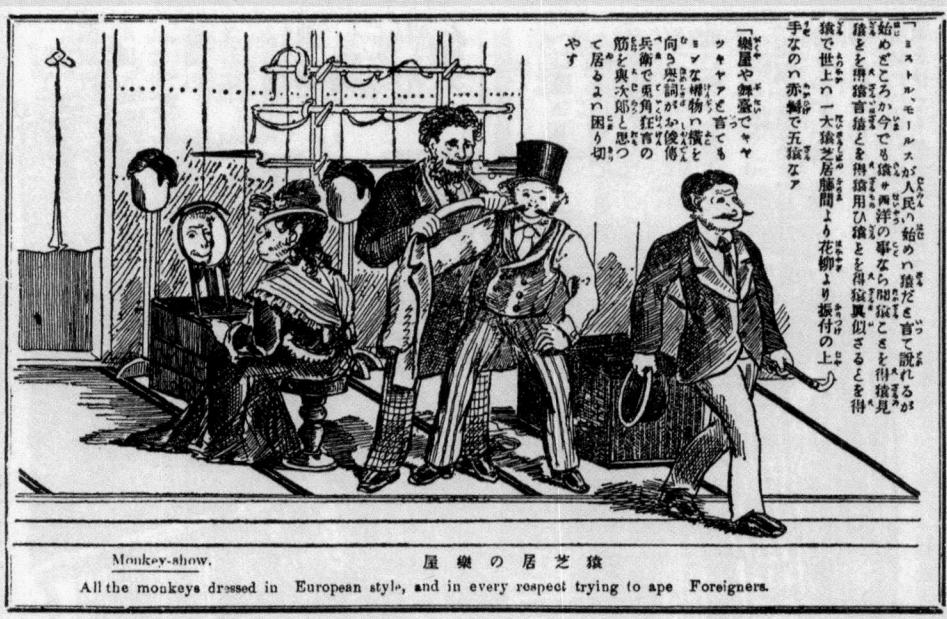

Monkey-show.   　猿芝居の樂屋

All the monkeys dressed in European style, and in every respect trying to ape Foreigners.

Visual Source 19.4 Kobayashi Kiyochika's Critique of Wholesale Westernization (Library of Congress)

Visual Source 19.5 Japan, China, and Europe: A Reversal of Roles (Museum of Fine Arts, Boston, Leonard A. Lauder Collection of Japanese Postcards. 2002.3504. Photograph © 2010 Museum of Fine Arts, Boston)

Historically the Japanese had borrowed a great deal from China—Buddhism, Confucianism, court rituals, city-planning ideas, administrative traditions, and elements of the Chinese script. But Japan's victory in a war with China in 1894–1895 showed clearly that it had thrown off the country in whose cultural shadow it had lived for centuries. Furthermore, Japan had begun to acquire an East Asian empire in Korea and Taiwan. And its triumph over Russia in another war ten years later illustrated its ability to stand up to a major European power. The significance of these twin victories is expressed in Visual Source 19.5, a Japanese image created during the Russo-Japanese War and titled *The Japanese Navy Uses China as Bait to Trap the Greedy Russian.*

■ What overall message did the artist seek to convey in this print?

■ What is the significance of the Chinese figure with a chicken in hand, lying as "bait" at the bottom of the image?

■ How is the Russia character portrayed?

■ What had changed in Japanese thinking about China and Europe during the nineteenth century?

Using the Evidence:
Changing Japanese Perceptions of the West

1. **Explaining change:** How and why had Japanese perceptions of themselves and their relationship to the West changed in the half century since the Meiji restoration? What elements of continuity in Japanese traditions are evident in these visual sources?

2. **Making comparisons:** Based on these visual sources and the documents about the Opium War, how might you compare Japanese and Chinese perceptions of the West during the nineteenth century? What accounts for both the similarities and differences?

3. **Distinguishing modernization and westernization:** Based on a careful reading of Chapter 19, including the documents and images, do you think that technological borrowing (modernization) requires cultural borrowing (westernization) as well? Is it possible to modernize while avoiding the incorporation of western culture at the same time? What do the examples of China, the Ottoman Empire, and Japan in the nineteenth century suggest about this issue?

CHAPTER TWENTY

Colonial Encounters

1750–1914

A Second Wave of
  European Conquests
Under European Rule
  Cooperation and Rebellion
  Colonial Empires with a Difference
Ways of Working: Comparing
  Colonial Economies
  Economies of Coercion: Forced
    Labor and the Power of the State
  Economies of Cash-Crop Agriculture:
    The Pull of the Market
  Economies of Wage Labor:
    Working for Europeans
  Women and the Colonial Economy:
    An African Case Study
  Assessing Colonial Development
Believing and Belonging: Identity
  and Cultural Change in the
  Colonial Era
  Education
  Religion
  "Race" and "Tribe"
Reflections: Who Makes History?
Considering the Evidence
  Documents: Indian Responses
    to Empire
  Visual Sources: The Scramble
    for Africa

In mid-1967, I was on summer break from a teaching assignment with the Peace Corps in Ethiopia and was traveling with some friends in neighboring Kenya, just four years after that country had gained its independence from British colonial rule. The bus we were riding on broke down, and I found myself hitchhiking across Kenya, heading for Uganda. Soon I was picked up by a friendly Englishman, one of Kenya's many European settlers who had stayed on after independence. At one point, he pulled off the road to show me a lovely view of Kenya's famous Rift Valley, and we were approached by a group of boys selling baskets and other tourist items. They spoke to us in good English, but my British companion replied to them in Swahili. He later explained that Europeans generally did not speak English with the "natives." I was puzzled, but reluctant to inquire further.

Several years later, while conducting research about British missionaries in Kenya in the early twentieth century, I found a clue about the origins of this man's reluctance to speak his own language with Kenyans. It came in a letter from a missionary in which the writer argued against the teaching of English to Africans. Among his reasons were "the danger in which such a course would place our white women and girls" and "the danger of organizing against the government and Europeans."[1] Here, clearly displayed, was the European colonial insistence on maintaining distance and distinction between whites and blacks, for both sexual and political reasons. Such monitoring of racial boundaries was a central feature of many nineteenth- and early-twentieth-century colonial societies and, in the case of my new British acquaintance, a practice that persisted even after the colonial era had ended.

The Imperial Durbar of 1903: To mark the coronation of British monarch Edward VII and his installation as the Emperor of India, colonial authorities in India mounted an elaborate assembly, or *durbar*. The durbar was intended to showcase the splendor of the British Empire, and its pageantry included sporting events; a state ball; a huge display of Indian arts, crafts, and jewels; and an enormous parade in which a long line of British officials and Indian princes passed by on bejeweled elephants. (Topham/The Image Works)

FOR MANY MILLIONS OF AFRICANS AND ASIANS, colonial rule—by the British, French, Germans, Italians, Belgians, Portuguese, Russians, or Americans—was the major new element in their historical experience during the nineteenth century. Between roughly 1750 and 1950, much of the Afro-Asian-Pacific world was enveloped within this new wave of European empire building. The encounter with European power in these colonized societies was more immediate, and often more intense, than in those regions that were buffered by their own independent governments, such as Latin America, China, Persia, and the Ottoman Empire. Of course, no single colonial experience characterized these two centuries across this vast region. Much depended on the cultures and prior history of various colonized people. Policies of the colonial powers sometimes differed sharply and changed over time. Men and women experienced the colonial era differently, as did traditional elites, Western-educated classes, urban artisans, peasant farmers, and migrant laborers. Furthermore, the varied actions and reactions of such people, despite their oppression and exploitation, shaped the colonial experience, perhaps as much as the policies, practices, and intentions of their temporary European rulers. All of them—colonizers and colonized alike—were caught up in the flood of change that accompanied the Industrial Revolution and a new burst of European imperialism.

A Second Wave of European Conquests

■ Comparison

In what different ways did the colonial takeover of Asia and Africa occur?

If the sixteenth- and seventeenth-century takeover of the Americas represented the first phase of European colonial conquests, the century and a half between 1750 and 1900 was a second and quite distinct round of that larger process. Now it was focused in Asia and Africa rather than in the Western Hemisphere. It featured a number of new players—Germany, Italy, Belgium, the United States, Japan—who were not at all involved in the earlier phase, while the Spanish and Portuguese now had only minor roles. In mainland Asia and Africa, nineteenth-century European conquests nowhere had the devastating demographic consequences that had so sharply reduced the Native American populations. Furthermore, this second wave of European colonial conquests, at least by the mid-nineteenth century, was conditioned by Europe's Industrial Revolution. In both their formal colonies and their "informal empires" (Latin America, China, the Ottoman Empire, and for a time Japan), European motives and activities were shaped by the military capacity and economic power that the Industrial Revolution conveyed. In general, Europeans preferred informal control, for it was cheaper and less likely to provoke wars. But where rivalry with other European states made it impossible or where local governments were unable or unwilling to cooperate, Europeans proved more than willing to undertake the expense and risk of conquest and outright colonial rule.

The construction of these second-wave European empires in the Afro-Asian world, like empires everywhere, involved military force or the threat of using it. Initially, the European military advantage lay in organization, drill and practice, and command structure. Increasingly in the nineteenth century, the Europeans also pos-

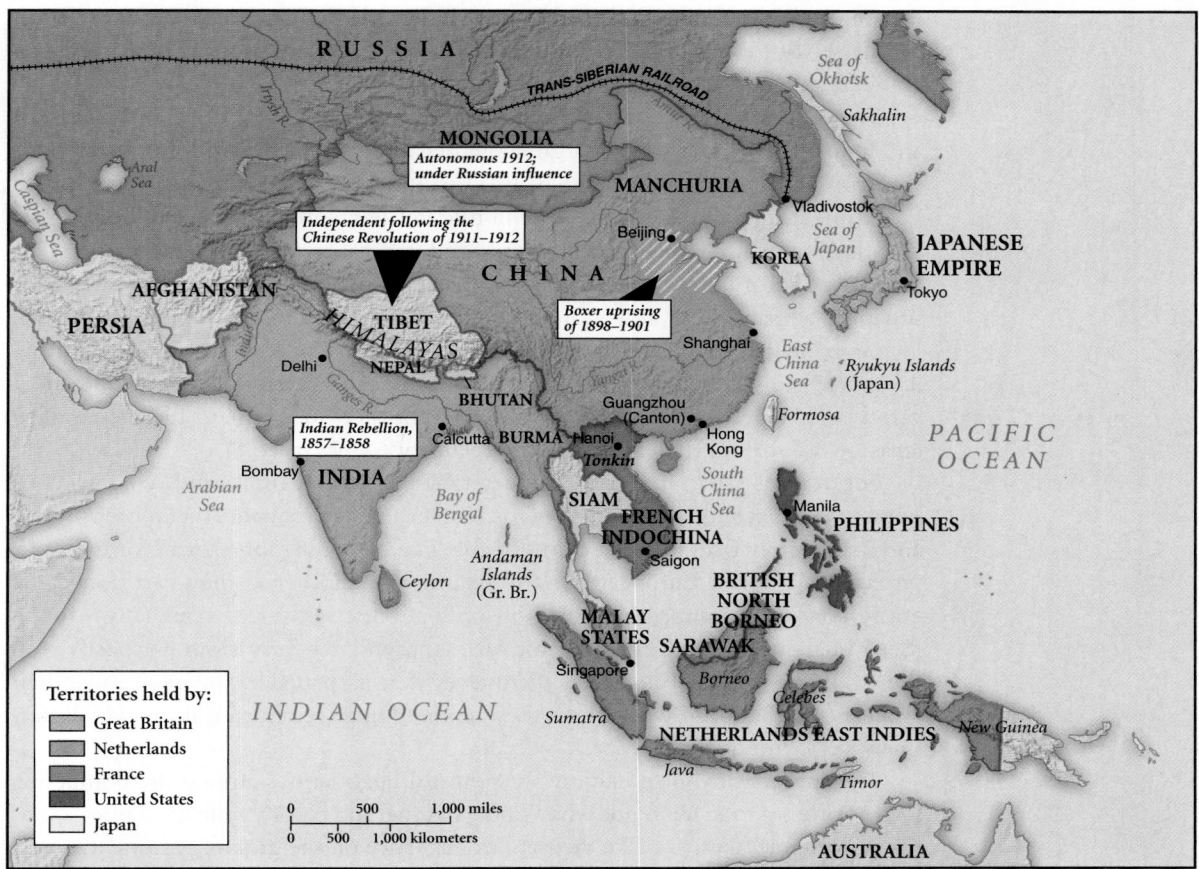

Map 20.1 Colonial Asia in the Early Twentieth Century By the early 1900s, several of the great population centers of Asia had come under the colonial control of Britain, the Netherlands, France, the United States, or Japan.

sessed overwhelming advantages in firepower, deriving from the recently invented repeating rifles and machine guns. A much-quoted jingle by the English writer Hilaire Belloc summed up the situation:

> Whatever happens we have got
> The Maxim gun [an automatic machine gun] and they have not.

Nonetheless, Europeans had to fight, often long and hard, to create their new empires, as countless wars of conquest attest. In the end, though, they prevailed almost everywhere, largely against adversaries who did not have Maxim guns or in some cases any guns at all. Thus were African and Asian peoples of all kinds incorporated within one or another of the European empires. Gathering and hunting bands in Australia, agricultural village societies or chiefdoms on Pacific islands and in Africa, pastoralists of the Sahara and Central Asia, residents of states large and small, and virtually everyone in the large and complex civilizations of India and Southeast Asia—all of them alike lost the political sovereignty and freedom of action they had previously exercised.

For some, such as Hindus governed by the Muslim Mughal Empire, it was an exchange of one set of foreign rulers for another. But now all were subjects of a European colonial state.

The passage to colonial status occurred in various ways. For the peoples of India and Indonesia, colonial conquest grew out of earlier interaction with European trading firms. Particularly in India, the British East India Company, rather than the British government directly, played the leading role in the colonial takeover of South Asia. The fragmentation of the Mughal Empire and the absence of any overall sense of cultural or political unity both invited and facilitated European penetration. A similar situation of many small and rival states assisted the Dutch acquisition of Indonesia. However, neither the British nor the Dutch had a clear-cut plan for conquest. Rather it evolved slowly as local authorities and European traders made and unmade a variety of alliances over roughly a century in India (1750–1850). In Indonesia, a few areas held out until the early twentieth century (see Map 20.1).

For most of Africa, mainland Southeast Asia, and the Pacific islands, colonial conquest came later, in the second half of the nineteenth century, and rather more abruptly and deliberately than in India or Indonesia. The "scramble for Africa," for example, pitted half a dozen European powers against one another as they partitioned the entire continent among themselves in only about twenty-five years (1875–1900). (See Visual Sources: The Scramble for Africa, pp. 960–67, for various perspectives on the "scramble.") European leaders themselves were surprised by the intensity of their rivalries and the speed with which they acquired huge territories, about which they knew very little (see Map 20.2).

That process involved endless but peaceful negotiations among the competing Great Powers about "who got what" and extensive and bloody military action, sometimes lasting decades, to make their control effective on the ground. Among the most difficult to subdue were those decentralized societies without a formal state structure. In such cases, Europeans confronted no central authority with which they could negotiate or that they might decisively defeat. It was a matter of village-by-village conquest against extended resistance. As late as 1925, one British official commented on the process as it operated in central Nigeria: "I shall of course go on walloping them until they surrender. It's a rather piteous sight watching a village being knocked to pieces and I wish there was some other way, but unfortunately there isn't."[2]

The South Pacific territories of Australia and New Zealand, both of which were taken over by the British during the nineteenth century, were more similar to the earlier colonization of North America than to contemporary patterns of Asian and African conquest. In both places, conquest was accompanied by massive European settlement and diseases that reduced native numbers by 75 percent or more by 1900. Like Canada and the United States, these became settler colonies, "neo-European" societies in the Pacific. Aboriginal Australians constituted only about 2.4 percent of their country's population in the early twenty-first century, and the indigenous Maori were a minority of about 15 percent in New Zealand. With the exception of Hawaii, nowhere else in the nineteenth-century colonial world were existing

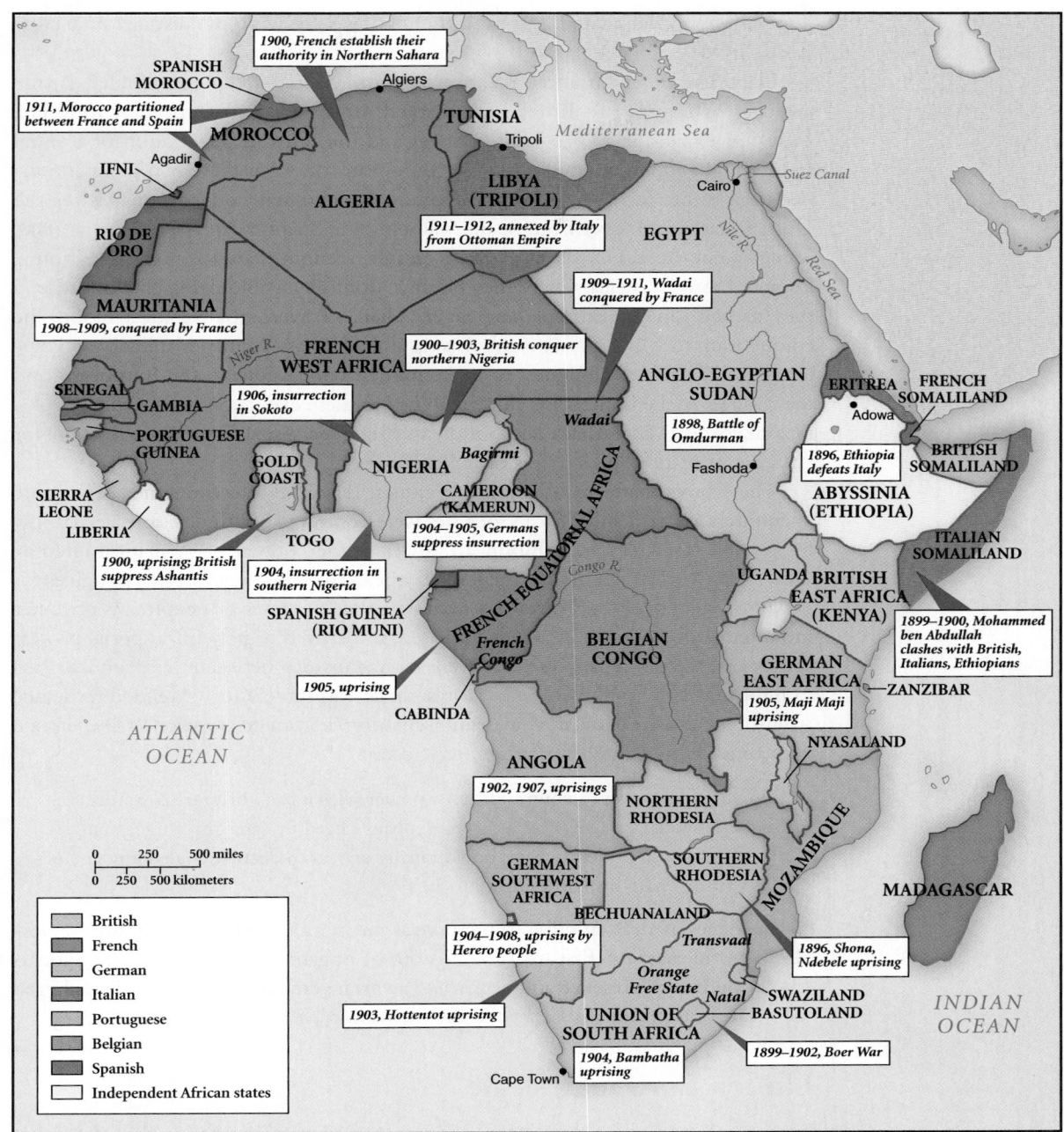

Map 20.2 Conquest and Resistance in Colonial Africa

By the early twentieth century, the map of Africa reflected the outcome of the "scramble for Africa," a conquest that was heavily resisted in many places. The boundaries established during that process still provide the political framework for Africa's independent states.

populations so decimated and overwhelmed as they were in Australia and New Zealand.

Elsewhere other variations on the theme of imperial conquest unfolded. Japan's takeover of Taiwan and Korea bore marked similarities to European actions. The westward expansion of the United States and the Russian penetration of Central Asia brought additional millions under European control as these two states continued their earlier territorial growth. Filipinos acquired new colonial rulers when the United States took over from Spain following the Spanish–American War of 1898. Some 13,000 freed U.S. slaves, seeking greater freedom than was possible at home, migrated to West Africa, where they became, ironically, a colonizing elite in the land they named Liberia. Ethiopia and Siam (Thailand) were notable for avoiding the colonization to which their neighbors succumbed. Those countries' military and diplomatic skills, their willingness to make modest concessions to the Europeans, and the rivalries of the imperialists all contributed to these exceptions to the rule of colonial takeover in East Africa and Southeast Asia. (See Visual Source 20.5, p. 966, for an account of Ethiopia's defeat of Italian forces.)

These broad patterns of colonial conquest dissolved into thousands of separate encounters as Asian and African societies were confronted with decisions about how to respond to encroaching European power in the context of their local circumstances. Many initially sought to enlist Europeans in their own internal struggles for power or in their external rivalries with neighboring states or peoples. As pressures mounted and European demands escalated, some tried to play off imperial powers against one another. Many societies were sharply divided between those who wanted to fight and those who believed that resistance was futile. After extended resistance against French aggression, the nineteenth-century Vietnamese emperor Tu Duc argued with those who wanted the struggle to go on:

> Do you really wish to confront such a power with a pack of [our] cowardly soldiers? It would be like mounting an elephant's head or caressing a tiger's tail.... With what you presently have, do you really expect to dissolve the enemy's rifles into air or chase his battleships into hell?[3]

Others negotiated, attempting to preserve as much independence and power as possible. The rulers of the East African kingdom of Buganda, for example, saw opportunity in the British presence and negotiated an arrangement that substantially enlarged their state and personally benefited the kingdom's elite class.

Under European Rule

In many places and for many people, incorporation into European colonial empires was a traumatic experience. Especially for small-scale societies, the loss of life, homes, cattle, crops, and land was devastating. In 1902, a British soldier in East Africa described what happened in a single village: "Every soul was either shot or bayoneted.... We burned all the huts and razed the banana plantations to the ground."[4]

For the Vietnamese elite, schooled for centuries in Chinese-style Confucian thinking, conquest meant that the natural harmonies of life had been badly disrupted; it was a time when "water flowed uphill." Nguyen Khuyen (1835–1909), a senior Vietnamese official, retired to his ancestral village to farm and write poetry after the French conquest. In his poems he expressed his anguish at the passing of the world he had known:

> Fine wine but no good friends,
> So I buy none though I have the money.
> A poem comes to mind, but I choose not to write it down.
> If it were written, to whom would I give it?
> The spare bed hangs upon the wall in cold indifference.
> I pluck the lute, but it just doesn't sound right.[5]

Many others also withdrew into private life, feigning illness when asked to serve in public office under the French.

Cooperation and Rebellion

Although violence was a prominent feature of colonial life both during conquest and after, various groups and many individuals willingly cooperated with colonial authorities to their own advantage. Many men found employment, status, and security in European-led armed forces. The shortage and expense of European administrators and the difficulties of communicating across cultural boundaries made it necessary for colonial rulers to rely heavily on a range of local intermediaries. Thus Indian princes, Muslim emirs, and African rulers, often from elite or governing families, found it possible to retain much of their earlier status and privileges while gaining considerable wealth by exercising authority, both legally and otherwise, at the local level. For example, in French West Africa, an area eight times the size of France itself and with a population of about 15 million in the late 1930s, the colonial state consisted of just 385 French administrators and more than 50,000 African "chiefs." Thus colonial rule rested upon and reinforced the most conservative segments of Asian and African societies.

■ Explanation
Why might subject people choose to cooperate with the colonial regime? What might prompt them to rebel or resist?

Both colonial governments and private missionary organizations had an interest in promoting a measure of European education. From this process arose a small Western-educated class, whose members served the colonial state, European businesses, and Christian missions as teachers, clerks, translators, and lower-level administrators. A few received higher education abroad and returned home as lawyers, doctors, engineers, or journalists. As colonial governments and business enterprises became more sophisticated, Europeans increasingly depended on the Western-educated class at the expense of the more traditional elites.

If colonial rule enlisted the willing cooperation of some, it provoked the bitter opposition of many others. Thus periodic rebellions, both large and small, punctuated the history of colonial regimes everywhere. The most famous among them was

THE DEVILFISH IN EGYPTIAN WATERS.

An American View of British Imperialism
In this American cartoon dating to 1882, the British Empire is portrayed as an octopus whose tentacles are already attached to many countries, while one tentacle is about to grasp still another one, Egypt. (The Granger Collection, New York)

the Indian Rebellion of 1857–1858, which was triggered by the introduction into the colony's military forces of a new cartridge smeared with animal fat from cows and pigs. Because Hindus venerated cows and Muslims regarded pigs as unclean, both groups viewed the innovation as a plot to render them defiled and to convert them to Christianity. Behind this incident were many groups of people with a whole series of grievances generated by the British colonial presence: local rulers who had lost power; landlords deprived of their estates or their rent; peasants overtaxed and exploited by urban moneylenders and landlords alike; unemployed weavers displaced by machine-manufactured textiles; and religious leaders exposed to missionary preaching. A mutiny among Indian troops in Bengal triggered the rebellion, which soon spread to other regions of the colony and other social groups. Soon much of India was aflame. Some rebel leaders presented their cause as an effort to revive an almost-vanished Mughal Empire and thereby attracted support from those with strong resentments against the British (see Document 20.3, pp. 953–55). Although it was crushed in 1858, the rebellion greatly widened the racial divide in colonial India and eroded British tolerance for those they viewed as "nigger natives" who had betrayed their trust. It made the British more conservative and cautious about deliberately trying to change Indian society for fear of provoking another rebellion. Moreover, it convinced the British government to assume direct control over India, ending the era of British East India Company rule in the subcontinent.

Colonial Empires with a Difference

■ **Comparison**

What was distinctive about European colonial empires of the nineteenth century?

At one level, European colonial empires were but the latest in a very long line of imperial creations, all of which had enlisted cooperation and experienced resistance from their subject peoples, but the nineteenth-century European version of empire differed from the others in several remarkable ways. One was the prominence of race in distinguishing rulers and ruled, as the high tide of "scientific racism" in Europe coincided with the acquisition of Asian and African colonies (see pp. 881–82). In East Africa, for example, white men were referred to as *bwana* (Swahili for "master"), whereas Europeans regularly called African men "boy." Education for colonial subjects was both limited and skewed toward practical subjects rather than scientific and literary studies, which were widely regarded as inappropriate for the "primitive mind" of "natives." Particularly affected by European racism were those whose Western education and aspirations most clearly threatened the racial divide. Europeans were exceedingly reluctant to allow even the most highly educated Asians and Africans to enter the higher ranks of the colonial civil service. A proposal in 1883 to allow Indian judges to hear cases involving whites provoked outrage and massive demonstrations among European inhabitants of India.

In those colonies that had a large European settler population, the pattern of racial separation was much more pronounced than in places such as Nigeria, which had few permanently settled whites. The most extreme case was South Africa, where a large European population and the widespread use of African labor in mines and industries brought blacks and whites into closer and more prolonged contact than elsewhere. The racial fears that were aroused resulted in extraordinary efforts to establish race as a legal, not just a customary, feature of South African society. This racial system provided for separate "homelands," educational systems, residential areas, public facilities, and much more. In what was eventually known as apartheid, South African whites attempted the impossible task of creating an industrializing economy based on cheap African labor, while limiting African social and political integration in every conceivable fashion.

A further distinctive feature of nineteenth-century European empires lay in the extent to which colonial states were able to penetrate the societies they governed. Centralized tax-collecting bureaucracies, new means of communication and transportation, imposed changes in landholding patterns, integration of colonial economies into a global network of exchange, public health and sanitation measures, and the activities of missionaries all touched the daily lives of many people far more deeply than in earlier empires. Not only were Europeans foreign rulers, but they also bore the seeds of a very different way of life, which grew out of their own modern transformation.

Nineteenth-century European colonizers were extraordinary as well in their penchant for counting and classifying their subject people. With the assistance of anthropologists and missionaries, colonial governments collected a vast amount of information, sought to organize it "scientifically," and used it to manage the unfamiliar, complex, varied, and fluctuating societies that they governed. In India, the British found in classical texts and Brahmin ideology an idealized description of the caste system, based on the notion of four ranked and unchanging varnas, which made it possible to bring order out of the immense complexity and variety of caste as it actually operated. Thus the British invented or appropriated a Brahmin version of "traditional India" that they favored and sought to preserve, while scorning as "non-Indian" the new elite educated in European schools and enthusiastic about Western ways of life (see Document 20.2, pp. 951–53). This view of India reflected the great influence of Brahmins on British thinking and clearly served the interests of this Indian upper class.

Likewise within African colonies, Europeans identified, and sometimes invented, distinct tribes, each with its own clearly defined territory, language, customs, and chief. The notion of a "tribal Africa" expressed the Western view that African societies were primitive or backward, representing an earlier stage of human development. It was also a convenient idea, for it reduced the enormous complexity and fluidity of African societies to a more manageable state and thus made colonial administration easier.

Finally, European colonial policies contradicted their own core values and their practices at home to an unusual degree. While nineteenth-century Britain and France were becoming more democratic, their colonies were essentially dictatorships, offering perhaps order and stability, but certainly not democratic government, because few colonial subjects were participating citizens. Empire of course was wholly at odds with European notions of national independence, and ranked racial classifications went against the grain of both Christian and Enlightenment ideas of human equality. Furthermore, many Europeans were distinctly reluctant to encourage within their colonies the kind of modernization—urban growth, industrialization, individual values, religious skepticism—that was sweeping their own societies. They feared that this kind of social change, often vilified as "detribalization," would encourage unrest and challenge colonial rule. As a model for social development, they much preferred "traditional" rural society, with its established authorities and social hierarchies, though shorn of abuses such as slavery and *sati* (widow-burning). Such contradictions between what Europeans preached at home and what they practiced in the colonies became increasingly apparent to many Asians and Africans and played a major role in undermining the foundations of colonial rule in the twentieth century.

Ways of Working: Comparing Colonial Economies

Colonial rule affected the lives of its subject people in many ways, but the most pronounced change was in their ways of working. The colonial state—with its power to tax, to seize land for European enterprises, to compel labor, and to build railroads, ports, and roads—played an important role in these transformations. Even more powerful was the growing integration of Asian and African societies into a world economy that increasingly demanded their gold, diamonds, copper, tin, rubber, coffee, cotton, sugar, cocoa, and many other products. But the economic transformations born of these twin pressures were far from uniform. Various groups—migrant workers and cash-crop farmers, plantation laborers and domestic servants, urban elites and day laborers, men and women—experienced the colonial era differently as their daily working lives underwent profound changes.

To various degrees, old ways of working were eroded almost everywhere in the colonial world. Subsistence farming, in which peasant families produced largely for their own needs, diminished as growing numbers directed at least some of their energies to working for wages or selling what they produced for a cash income. That money was both necessary to pay their taxes and school fees and useful for buying the various products—such as machine-produced textiles, bicycles, and kerosene— that the industrial economies of Europe sent their way. As in Europe, artisans suffered greatly when cheaper machine-manufactured merchandise displaced their own hand-made goods. A flood of inexpensive textiles from Britain's new factories ruined the livelihood of tens of thousands of India's handloom weavers. Iron smelting largely disappeared in Africa, and occupations such as blacksmithing and tanning lost ground. Furthermore, Asian and African merchants, who had earlier handled the trade between their countries and the wider world, were squeezed out by well-financed European commercial firms.

Economies of Coercion: Forced Labor and the Power of the State

Many of the new ways of working that emerged during the colonial era derived directly from the demands of the colonial state. The most obvious was required and unpaid labor on public projects, such as building railroads, constructing government buildings, and transporting goods. In French Africa, all "natives" were legally obligated for "statute labor" of ten to twelve days a year, a practice that lasted through 1946. It was much resented. A resident of British West Africa, interviewed in 1996, bitterly recalled this feature of colonial life: "They [British officials] were rude, and they made us work for them a lot. They came to the village and just rounded us up and made us go off and clear the road or carry loads on our heads."[6]

■ **Connection**
How did the power of colonial states transform the economic lives of colonial subjects?

The most infamous cruelties of forced labor occurred during the early twentieth century in the Congo Free State, then governed personally by Leopold II of Belgium. Private companies in the Congo, operating under the authority of the state, forced villagers to collect rubber, which was much in demand for bicycle and automobile tires, with a reign of terror and abuse that cost millions of lives. One refugee from these horrors described the process:

> We were always in the forest to find the rubber vines, to go without food, and our women had to give up cultivating the fields and gardens. Then we starved. . . . We begged the white man to leave us alone, saying we could get no more rubber, but the white men and their soldiers said "Go. You are only beasts yourselves. . . . " When we failed and our rubber was short, the soldiers came to our towns and killed us. Many were shot, some had their ears cut off; others were tied up with ropes round their necks and taken away.[7]

Eventually such outrages were widely publicized in Europe, where they created a scandal, forcing the Belgian government to take control of the Congo in 1908 and ending Leopold's reign of terror.

A variation on the theme of forced labor took shape in the so-called cultivation system of the Netherlands East Indies (Indonesia) during the nineteenth century. Peasants were required to cultivate 20 percent or more of their land in cash crops such as sugar or coffee to meet their tax obligation to the state. Sold to government contractors at fixed and low prices, those crops, when resold on the world market, proved highly profitable for Dutch traders and shippers as well as for the Dutch state and its citizens. According to one scholar, the cultivation system "performed a

Colonial Violence in the Congo
These young boys with severed hands were among the victims of a brutal regime of forced labor undertaken in the Congo during the late nineteenth and early twentieth centuries. Such mutilation was punishment for their villages' inability to supply the required amount of wild rubber. (Courtesy, Anti-Slavery Organization, London)

■ **Change**
How did cash-crop agriculture transform the lives of colonized peoples?

miracle for the Dutch economy," enabling it to avoid taxing its own people and providing capital for its Industrial Revolution.[8] It also enriched and strengthened the position of those "traditional authorities" who enforced the system, often by using lashings and various tortures, on behalf of the Dutch. For the peasants of Java, however, it meant a double burden of obligations to the colonial state as well as to local lords. Many became indebted to moneylenders when they could not meet those obligations. Those demands, coupled with the loss of land and labor now excluded from food production, contributed to a wave of famines during the mid-nineteenth century in which hundreds of thousands perished.

The forced cultivation of cash crops was widely and successfully resisted in many places. In German East Africa, for example, colonial authorities in the late nineteenth century imposed the cultivation of cotton, which seriously interfered with production of local food crops. Here is how one man remembered the experience:

> The cultivation of cotton was done by turns. Every village was allotted days on which to cultivate.... After arriving you all suffered very greatly. Your back and your buttocks were whipped and there was no rising up once you stooped to dig.... And yet he [the German] wanted us to pay him tax. Were we not human beings?[9]

Such conditions prompted a massive rebellion in 1905 and persuaded the Germans to end the forced growing of cotton. In Mozambique, where the Portuguese likewise brutally enforced cotton cultivation, a combination of peasant sabotage, the planting of unauthorized crops, and the smuggling of cotton across the border to more profitable markets ensured that Portugal never achieved its goal of becoming self-sufficient in cotton production. In such ways did the actions of colonized peoples alter or frustrate the plans of the colonizers.

Economies of Cash-Crop Agriculture: The Pull of the Market

Many Asian and African peoples had produced quite willingly for an international market long before they were enclosed within colonial societies. They offered for trade items such as peanuts and palm oil in West Africa, cotton in Egypt, spices in Indonesia, and pepper and textiles in India. In some places, colonial rule created conditions that facilitated and increased cash-crop production to the advantage of local farmers. British authorities in Burma, for example, acted to encourage rice production among small farmers by ending an earlier prohibition on rice exports, providing irrigation and transportation facilities, and enacting land tenure laws that facilitated private ownership of small farms. Under these conditions, the population of the Irrawaddy Delta boomed, migrants from Upper Burma and India poured into the region, and rice exports soared. Local small farmers benefited considerably because they were now able to own their own land, build substantial houses, and buy imported goods. For several decades in the late nineteenth century, standards of living improved sharply, and huge increases in rice production fed millions of people in other parts of Asia and elsewhere. It was a very different situation from that of peasants forced to grow crops that seriously interfered with their food production.

But that kind of colonial development, practiced also in the Mekong River delta of French-ruled Vietnam, had important environmental consequences. It involved the destruction of mangrove forests and swamplands along with the fish and shellfish that supplemented local diets. New dikes and irrigation channels inhibited the depositing of silt from upstream and thus depleted soils in the deltas of these major river systems. And, unknown to anyone at the time, this kind of agriculture generates large amounts of methane gas, a major contributor to global warming.[10]

Profitable cash-crop farming also developed in the southern Gold Coast (present-day Ghana), a British territory in West Africa. Unlike Burma, it was African farmers themselves who took the initiative to develop export agriculture. Planting cacao trees in huge quantities, they became the world's leading supplier of cocoa, used to make chocolate, by 1911. Cacao was an attractive crop because, unlike cotton, it was compatible with the continued production of foods and did not require so much labor time. In the early twentieth century, it brought a new prosperity to many local farmers. "A hybrid society was taking shape," wrote one scholar, "partly peasant, in that most members farmed their own land with family labor . . . and partly capitalist, in that a minority employed wage laborers, produced chiefly for the market, and reinvested profits."[11]

That success brought new problems in its wake. A shortage of labor fostered the employment of former slaves as dependent and exploited workers and also generated tensions between the sexes when some men married women for their labor power but refused to support them adequately. Moreover, the labor shortage brought a huge influx of migrants from the drier interior parts of West Africa, generating ethnic and class tensions. Furthermore, many colonies came to specialize in one or two cash crops, creating an unhealthy dependence when world market prices dropped. Thus African and Asian farmers were increasingly subject to the uncertain rhythms of the international marketplace as well as to those of the seasons and the weather.

Economies of Wage Labor: Working for Europeans

Yet another new way of working in colonial societies involved wage labor in some European enterprise. Driven by the need for money, by the loss of land adequate to support their families, or sometimes by the orders of colonial authorities, millions of colonial subjects across Asia and Africa sought employment in European-owned

■ Change
What kinds of wage labor were available in the colonies? Why might people take part in it? How did doing so change their lives?

plantations, mines, construction projects, and homes. All across Southeast Asia in the later nineteenth and early twentieth centuries, huge plantations sprouted, which were financed from Europe and which grew sugarcane, rubber, tea, tobacco, sisal (used for making rope), and more. Impoverished workers by the hundreds of thousands came from great distances—India, China, Java—finding their way to these plantations, where they were subject to strict control, often housed in barracks, and paid poorly, with women receiving 50 to 75 percent of a man's wage. Disease was common, and death rates were twice or more that of the colony as a whole. In southern Vietnam in 1927 alone, one in twenty plantation workers died. British colonial authorities in India facilitated the migration of millions of Indians to work sites elsewhere in the British Empire—Trinidad, Fiji, Malaysia, Ceylon, South Africa, Kenya, and Uganda, for example—with some working as indentured laborers and others as independent merchants.

In Africa more than in Asia, people migrated to European farms or plantations because they had lost their own land. In the settler colonies of Africa—Algeria, Kenya, Southern Rhodesia (Zimbabwe), and South Africa, for example—permanent European communities, with the help of colonial governments, obtained huge tracts of land, much of which had previously been home to African societies. A 1913 law in South Africa legally defined 88 percent of the land as belonging to whites, who were then about 20 percent of the population. Much of highland Kenya, an enormously rich agricultural region that was home to the Gikuyu and Kamba peoples, was taken

Economic Change in the Colonial World
These workers on a Ceylon tea plantation in the early twentieth century are moving sacks of tea into a drying house in preparation for export. The Lipton label on the bags is a reminder of the role of large-scale foreign investment in the economic transformations of the colonial era. (Hulton-Deutsch Collection/Corbis)

over by some 4,000 white farmers. In such places, some Africans stayed on as "squatters," working for the new landowners as the price of remaining on what had been their own land. Others were displaced to "native reserves," limited areas that could not support their growing populations, thus forcing many to work for wages on European farms. Most notably in South Africa, such reserved areas, known as Bantustans, became greatly overcrowded: soil fertility declined, hillsides were cleared, forests shrank, and erosion scarred the land. This kind of ecological degradation was among the environmental consequences of African wage labor on European farms and estates.

Mines were another source of wage labor for many. In the British-ruled Malay States (Malaysia), tin mining accelerated greatly in the late nineteenth century, and by 1895 that colony produced some 55 percent of the world's tin. Operated initially by Chinese and later by European entrepreneurs, Malaysian tin mines drew many millions of impoverished Chinese workers on strictly controlled three-year contracts. Appalling living conditions, disease, and accidents generated extraordinarily high death rates. The gold and diamond mines of South Africa likewise set in motion a huge pattern of labor migration that encompassed all of Africa south of the Belgian Congo. With skilled and highly paid work reserved for white miners, Africans were relegated largely to unskilled labor at a fraction of white wages. Furthermore, they were recruited on short-term contracts, lived in all-male prison-like barracks that were often surrounded by barbed wire, and were forced to return home periodically to prevent them from establishing a permanent family life near the mines.

The rapidly swelling cities of the colonial world—Lagos, Nairobi, Cairo, Calcutta, Rangoon, Batavia, Singapore, Saigon—required no coercion to attract would-be wage earners, particularly from the late nineteenth century on. Racially segregated, often unsanitary, and greatly overcrowded, these cities nonetheless were seen as meccas of opportunity for people all across the social spectrum. Traditional elites, absentee landlords, and wealthy Chinese businessmen occupied the top rungs of Southeast Asian cities. Western-educated people everywhere found opportunities as teachers, doctors, and professional specialists, but more often as clerks in European business offices and government bureaucracies. Skilled workers on the railways or in the ports represented a working-class elite, while a few labored in the factories that processed agricultural goods or manufactured basic products such as beer, cigarettes, cement, and furniture. Far more numerous were the construction workers, rickshaw drivers, food sellers, domestic servants, prostitutes, and others who made up the urban poor of colonial cities. In 1955, a British investigating commission described life in Nairobi, the capital of Kenya, one of Britain's richest colonies:

> The wages of the majority of African workers are too low to enable them to obtain accommodation which is adequate to any standard. The high cost of housing relative to wages is in itself a cause of overcrowding, because housing is shared to lighten the cost. This, with the high cost of food in towns, makes family life impossible for the majority.[12]

Thus, after more than half a century of colonial rule, British authorities themselves acknowledged that normal family life in the colony's major urban center proved out of reach for the vast majority. It was quite an admission.

Women and the Colonial Economy: An African Case Study

■ Change
How were the lives of African women altered by colonial economies?

If economic life in European empires varied greatly from place to place, even within the same colony, it also offered a different combination of opportunities and hardships to women than it did to men, as the experience of colonial Africa shows.[13] In precolonial times, African women were almost everywhere active farmers, with responsibility for planting, weeding, and harvesting in addition to food preparation and child care. Men cleared the land, built houses, herded the cattle, and in some cases assisted with field work. Within this division of labor, women were expected to feed their own families and were usually allocated their own fields for that purpose. Many also were involved in local trading activity. Though clearly subordinate to men, African women nevertheless had a measure of economic autonomy.

As the demands of the colonial economy grew, women's lives diverged more and more from those of men. In colonies where cash-crop agriculture was dominant, men often withdrew from subsistence production in favor of more lucrative export crops. Among the Ewe people of southern Ghana, men almost completely dominated the highly profitable cacao farming, whereas women assumed near total responsibility for domestic food production. In neighboring Ivory Coast, women had traditionally grown cotton for their families' clothing; but when that crop acquired a cash value, men insisted that cotton grown for export be produced on their own personal fields. Thus men acted to control the most profitable aspects of cash-crop agriculture and in doing so greatly increased the subsistence workload of women. One study from Cameroon estimated that women's working hours increased from forty-six per week in precolonial times to more than seventy by 1934.

Women in Colonial Africa The movement of many African men into wage labor thrust even more of the domestic responsibilities onto women. Here in a photograph from colonial Kenya in 1936 a woman carries on the ancient craft of making clay pots. (Elspeth Huxley/ Huxley Collection/Images of Empire, British Empire & Commonwealth Museum)

Further increasing women's workload and differentiating their lives from those of men was labor migration. As more and more men sought employment in the cities, on settler farms, or in the mines, their wives were left to manage the domestic economy almost alone. In many cases, women also had to supply food to men in the cities to compensate for very low urban wages. They often took over such traditionally male tasks as breaking the ground for planting, milking the cows, and supervising the herds, in addition to their normal responsibilities. In South Africa, where the demands of the European economy were particularly heavy, some 40 to 50 percent of able-bodied adult men were absent from the rural areas, and women headed 60 percent of households. In Botswana, which supplied much male labor to South Africa, married couples by the 1930s rarely lived together for more than two months at a time. In such situations, the lives and cultures of men and women increasingly diverged, with one focused on the cities and working for wages and the other on village life and subsistence agriculture.

Women coped with these difficult circumstances in a number of ways. Many sought closer relations with their families of birth rather than with their absent husbands' families, as would otherwise have been expected. Among the Luo of Kenya, women introduced laborsaving crops, adopted new farm implements, and earned some money as traders. In the cities, they established a variety of self-help associations, including those for prostitutes and for brewers of beer.

The colonial economy sometimes provided a measure of opportunity for enterprising women, particularly in small-scale trade and marketing. In some parts of West Africa, women came to dominate this sector of the economy by selling foodstuffs, cloth, and inexpensive imported goods, while men or foreign firms controlled the more profitable wholesale and import-export trade. Such opportunities sometimes gave women considerable economic autonomy. By the 1930s, for example, Nupe women in northern Nigeria had gained sufficient wealth as itinerant traders that they were contributing more to the family income than their husbands and frequently lent money to them. Among some Igbo groups in southern Nigeria, men were responsible for growing the prestigious yams, but women's crops—especially cassava—came to have a cash value during the colonial era, and women were entitled to keep the profits from selling it. "What is man? I have my own money" expressed the growing economic independence of such women.[14]

At the other end of the social scale, women of impoverished rural families, by necessity, often became virtually independent heads of household in the absence of their husbands. Others took advantage of new opportunities in mission schools, towns, and mines to flee the restrictions of rural patriarchy. Such challenges to patriarchal values elicited various responses from men, including increased accusations of witchcraft against women and fears of impotence. Among the Shona in Southern Rhodesia, and no doubt elsewhere, senior African men repeatedly petitioned the colonial authorities for laws and regulations that would criminalize adultery and restrict women's ability to leave their rural villages.[15] The control of women's sexuality and mobility was a common interest of European and African men.

Assessing Colonial Development

Beyond the many and varied changes that transformed the working lives of millions in the colonial world lies the difficult and highly controversial question of the overall economic impact of colonial rule on Asian and African societies. Defenders, both then and now, praise it for jump-starting modern growth, but numerous critics cite a record of exploitation and highlight the limitations and unevenness of that

■ Change
Did colonial rule bring "economic progress" in its wake?

growth. Amid the continuing debates, three things seem reasonably clear. First, colonial rule served, for better or worse, to further the integration of Asian and African economies into a global network of exchange, now centered in Europe. In many places, that process was well under way before conquest imposed foreign rule, and elsewhere it occurred without formal colonial control. Nonetheless, it is apparent that within the colonial world far more land and labor were devoted to production for the global market at the end of the colonial era than at its beginning.

Second, Europeans could hardly avoid conveying to the colonies some elements of their own modernizing process. It was in their interests to do so, and many felt duty bound to "improve" the societies they briefly governed. Modern administrative and bureaucratic structures facilitated colonial control; communication and transportation infrastructure (railroads, motorways, ports, telegraphs, postal services) moved products to the world market; schools trained the army of intermediaries on which colonial rule depended; and modest health care provisions fulfilled some of the "civilizing mission" to which many Europeans felt committed. These elements of modernization made an appearance, however inadequately, during the colonial era.

Third, nowhere in the colonial world did a breakthrough to modern industrial society of Japanese dimensions occur. When India became independent after two centuries of colonial rule by the world's first industrial society, it was still one of the poorest of the world's developing countries. The British may not have created Indian poverty, but neither did they overcome it to any substantial degree. Scholars continue to debate the reasons for that failure: was it the result of deliberate British policies, or was it due to the conditions of Indian society? The nationalist movements that surged across Asia and Africa in the twentieth century had their own answer. To their many millions of participants, colonial rule, whatever its earlier promise, had become an economic dead end, whereas independence represented a grand opening to new and more hopeful possibilities. Paraphrasing a famous teaching of Jesus, Kwame Nkrumah, the first prime minister of an independent Ghana, declared, "Seek ye first the political kingdom, and all these other things [schools, factories, hospitals, for example] will be added unto you."

Snapshot   **Long-Distance Migration in an Age of Empire, 1846–1940**[16]

The age of empire was also an age of global migration. Beyond the long-distance migration shown here, shorter migrations within particular regions or colonies set millions more into motion.

Origins	Destination	Numbers
Europe	Americas	55–58 million
India, southern China	Southeast Asia, Indian Ocean rim, South Pacific	48–52 million
Northeast Asia, Russia	Manchuria, Siberia, Central Asia, Japan	46–51 million

Believing and Belonging: Identity and Cultural Change in the Colonial Era

The experience of colonial rule—its racism, its exposure to European culture, its social and economic upheavals—contributed much to cultural change within Asian and African societies. Coping with these enormous disruptions induced many colonized peoples to alter the ways they thought about themselves and their communities. Cultural identities, of course, are never static, but the transformations of the colonial era catalyzed substantial and quite rapid changes in what people believed and in how they defined the societies to which they belonged. Those transformed identities continued to echo long after European rule had ended.

Education

For an important minority, it was the acquisition of Western education, obtained through missionary or government schools, that generated a new identity. To previously illiterate people, the knowledge of reading and writing of any kind often suggested an almost magical power. Within the colonial setting, it could mean an escape from some of the most onerous obligations of living under European control, such as forced labor. More positively, it meant access to better-paying positions in government bureaucracies, mission organizations, or business firms and to the exciting imported goods that their salaries could buy. Moreover, education often provided social mobility and elite status within their own communities and an opportunity to achieve, or at least approach, equality with whites in racially defined societies. An African man from colonial Kenya described an encounter he had as a boy in 1938 with a relative who was a teacher in a mission school:

> Aged about 25, he seems to me like a young god with his smart clothes and shoes, his watch, and a beautiful bicycle. I worshipped in particular his bicycle that day and decided that I must somehow get myself one. As he talked with us, it seemed to me that the secret of his riches came from his education, his knowledge of reading and writing, and that it was essential for me to obtain this power.[17]

Many such people ardently embraced European culture, dressing in European clothes, speaking French or English, building European-style houses, getting married in long white dresses, and otherwise emulating European ways (see Document 20.1, pp. 950–51). Some of the early Western-educated Bengalis from northeastern India boasted about dreaming in English and deliberately ate beef, to the consternation of their elders. In a well-known poem entitled "A Prayer for Peace," Léopold Senghor, a highly educated West African writer and political leader, enumerated the many crimes of colonialism and yet confessed, "I have a great weakness for France." Asian and African colonial societies now had a new cultural divide: between the small number who had mastered to varying degrees the ways of their rulers and the vast majority who had not. Literate Christians in the East African kingdom of Buganda referred with contempt to their "pagan" neighbors as "they who do not read."

■ **Change**
What impact did Western education have on colonial societies?

The Educated Elite
Throughout the Afro-Asian world of the nineteenth century, the European presence generated a small group of people who enthusiastically embraced the culture and lifestyle of Europe. Here King Chulalongkorn of Siam poses with the crown prince and other young students, all of them garbed impeccably in European clothing. (Hulton-Deutsch Collection/Corbis)

Many among the Western-educated elite saw themselves as a modernizing vanguard, leading the regeneration of their societies in association with colonial authorities. For them, at least initially, the colonial enterprise was full of promise for a better future. The Vietnamese teacher and nationalist Nguyen Thai Hoc, while awaiting execution in 1930 by the French for his revolutionary activities, wrote about his earlier hopes: "At the beginning, I had thought to cooperate with the French in Indochina in order to serve my compatriots, my country, and my people, particularly in the areas of cultural and economic development."[18] Senghor too wrote wistfully about an earlier time when "we could have lived in harmony [with Europeans]."

In nineteenth-century India, Western-educated people organized a variety of reform societies, which sought a renewed Indian culture that was free of idolatry, child marriages, caste, and discrimination against women, while drawing inspiration from the classic texts of Hinduism. For a time, some of these Indian reformers saw themselves working in tandem with British colonial authorities. One of them, Keshub Chunder Sen (1838–1884), spoke to his fellow Indians in 1877: "You are bound to be loyal to the British government that came to your rescue, as God's ambassador, when your country was sunk in ignorance and superstition. . . . India in her present fallen condition seems destined to sit at the feet of England for many long years, to learn western art and science."[19] (See Document 20.2, pp. 951–53, for another such view.)

Such fond hopes for the modernization of Asian and African societies within a colonial framework would be bitterly disappointed. Europeans generally declined to treat their Asian and African subjects—even those with a Western education—as equal partners in the enterprise of renewal. The frequent denigration of their cultures as primitive, backward, uncivilized, or savage certainly rankled, particularly among the well-educated. "My people of Africa," wrote the West African intellectual James Aggrey in the 1920s, "we were created in the image of God, but men have made us think that we are chickens, and we still think we are; but we are eagles. Stretch forth your wings and fly."[20] In the long run, the educated classes in colonial societies everywhere found European rule far more of an obstacle to their countries' development than a means of achieving it. Turning decisively against a now-despised foreign imperialism, they led the many struggles for independence that came to fruition in the second half of the twentieth century.

Religion

Religion too provided the basis for new or transformed identities during the colonial era. Most dramatic were those places where widespread conversion to Christianity took place, such as New Zealand, the Pacific islands, and especially non–Muslim Africa. Some 10,000 missionaries had descended on Africa by 1910; by the 1960s, about 50 million Africans, roughly half of the non–Muslim population, claimed a Christian identity. The attractions of the new faith were many. As in the Americas centuries earlier, military defeat shook confidence in the old gods and local practices, fostering openness to new sources of supernatural power that could operate in the wider world now impinging on their societies. Furthermore, Christianity was widely associated with modern education, and, especially in Africa, mission schools were the primary providers of Western education. The young, the poor, and many women—all of them oppressed groups in many African societies—found new opportunities and greater freedom in some association with missions. Moreover, the spread of the Christian message was less the work of European missionaries than of those many thousands of African teachers, catechists, and pastors who brought the new faith to remote

■ Change

What were the attractions of Christianity within some colonial societies?

The Missionary Factor

Among the major change agents of the colonial era were the thousands of Christian missionaries who brought not only a new religion but also elements of European medicine, education, gender roles, and culture. Here is an assembly at a mission school for girls in New Guinea in the early twentieth century. (Rue des Archives/The Granger Collection, New York)

villages as well as the local communities that begged for a teacher and supplied the labor and materials to build a small church or school.

As elsewhere, Christianity in Africa soon became Africanized. Within mission-based churches, many converts continued using protective charms and medicines and consulting local medicine men, all of which caused their missionary mentors to speak frequently of "backsliding." Other converts continued to believe in their old gods and spirits but now deemed them evil and sought their destruction. Furthermore, thousands of separatist movements established a wide array of independent churches, which were thoroughly Christian but under African rather than missionary control and which in many cases incorporated African cultural practices and modes of worship. It was a twentieth-century "African Reformation."

In India, where Christianity made only very modest inroads, leading intellectuals and reformers began to define their region's endlessly varied beliefs, practices, sects, rituals, and schools of philosophy as a more distinct, unified, and separate religion that we now know as Hinduism. It was in part an effort to provide for India a religion wholly equivalent to Christianity, "an accessible tradition and a feeling of historical worth when faced with the humiliation of colonial rule."[21] To Swami Vivekananda (1863–1902), one of nineteenth-century India's most influential religious figures, a revived Hinduism, shorn of its distortions, offered a means of uplifting the country's village communities, which were the heart of Indian civilization. Moreover, it could offer spiritual support to a Western world mired in materialism and militarism, a message that he took to the First World Parliament of Religions held in 1893 in Chicago. Here was India speaking back to Europe:

> Let the foreigners come and flood the land with their armies, never mind. Up, India and conquer the world with your spirituality.... The whole of the Western world is a volcano which may burst tomorrow, go to pieces tomorrow.... Now is the time to work so that India's spiritual ideas may penetrate deep into the West.[22]

This new notion of Hinduism provided a cultural foundation for emerging ideas of India as a nation, but it also contributed to a clearer sense of Muslims as a distinct community in India. Before the British takeover, little sense of commonality united the many diverse communities who practiced Islam—urban and rural dwellers; nomads and farmers; artisans, merchants, and state officials.

■ **Change**

How and why did Hinduism emerge as a distinct religious tradition during the colonial era in India?

Hinduism in the West

The cultural interactions of the colonial era brought Asian traditions such as Hinduism to the attention of small groups in Europe and the United States. The visit of India's Swami Vivekananda to the First World Parliament of Religions in Chicago in 1893 was part of that process, illustrated here by a famous poster that circulated at that event. (Courtesy, Goes Lithographics, Chicago, after photo by Frank Parlato Jr. Image provided by www.vivekananda.net)

But the British had created separate inheritance laws for all Muslims and others for all Hindus; in their census taking, they counted the numbers of people within these now sharply distinguished groups; and they allotted seats in local councils according to these artificial categories. As some anti-British patriots began to cast India in Hindu terms, the idea of Muslims as a separate community, which was perhaps threatened by the much larger number of Hindus, began to make sense to some who practiced Islam. In the early twentieth century, a young Hindu Bengali schoolboy noticed that "our Muslim school-fellows were beginning to air the fact of their being Muslims rather more consciously than before and with a touch of assertiveness."[23] Here were the beginnings of what became in the twentieth century a profound religious and political division within the South Asian peninsula.

"Race" and "Tribe"

In Africa as well, intellectuals and ordinary people alike forged new ways of belonging as they confronted the upheavals of colonial life. Central to these new identities were notions of race and ethnicity. By the end of the nineteenth century, a number of African thinkers, familiar with Western culture, began to define the idea of an "African identity." Previously, few if any people on the continent had regarded themselves as Africans. Rather they were members of particular local communities, usually defined by language; some were also Muslims; and still others inhabited some state or empire. Now, however, influenced by the common experience of colonial oppression and by a highly derogatory European racism, well-educated Africans began to think in broader terms, similar to Indian reformers who were developing the notion of Hinduism. It was an effort to revive the cultural self-confidence of their people by articulating a larger, common, and respected "African tradition," equivalent to that of Western culture.

■ **Change**

In what way were "race" and "tribe" new identities in colonial Africa?

This effort took various shapes. One line of argument held that African culture and history in fact possessed the very characteristics that Europeans exalted. Knowing that Europeans valued large empires and complex political systems, African intellectuals pointed with pride to the ancient kingdoms of Ethiopia, Mali, Songhay, and others. C. A. Diop, a French-educated scholar from Senegal, insisted that Egyptian civilization was in fact the work of black Africans. Reversing European assumptions, Diop argued that Western civilization owed much to Egyptian influence and was therefore derived from Africa. Black people, in short, had a history of achievement fully comparable to that of Europe and therefore deserved just as much respect and admiration.

An alternative approach to defining an African identity lay in praising the differences between African and European cultures. The most influential proponent of such views was Edward Blyden (1832–1912), a West African born in the West Indies and educated in the United States who later became a prominent scholar and political official in Liberia. Blyden accepted the assumption that the world's various races were different but argued that each had its own distinctive contribution to make to world civilization. The uniqueness of African culture, Blyden wrote, lay in its communal, cooperative, and egalitarian societies, which contrasted sharply with Europe's highly individualistic, competitive, and class-ridden societies; in its harmonious relationship with nature as opposed to Europe's efforts to dominate and exploit the natural order; and particularly in its profound religious sensibility, which Europeans had lost in centuries of attention to material gain. Like Vivekananda in India, Blyden argued that Africa had a global mission "to be the spiritual conservatory of the world."[24]

In the twentieth century, such ideas resonated with a broader public. Hundreds of thousands of Africans took part in World War I, during which they encountered other Africans as well as Europeans. Some were able to travel widely. Contact with American black leaders such as Booker T. Washington, W. E. B. DuBois, Marcus Garvey, and various West Indian intellectuals further stimulated among a few a sense of belonging to an even larger pan-African world. Such notions underlay the growing nationalist movements that contested colonial rule as the twentieth century unfolded.

For the vast majority, however, the most important new sense of belonging that evolved from the colonial experience was not the notion of "Africa"; rather, it was the idea of "tribe" or, in the language of contemporary scholars, that of ethnic identity. African peoples, of course, had long recognized differences among themselves based on language, kinship, clan, village, or state, but these were seldom sharp or clearly defined. Boundaries fluctuated and were hazy; local communities often incorporated a variety of culturally different peoples. The idea of an Africa sharply divided into separate and distinct "tribes" was in fact a European notion that facilitated colonial administration and reflected Europeans' belief in African primitiveness. When the British, for example, began to govern the peoples living along the northern side of Lake Tanganyika, in present-day Tanzania, they found a series of communities that were similar to one another in language and customs but that governed themselves separately and certainly had not regarded themselves as a tribe. It was British attempts to rule them as a single people, first through a "paramount chief" and later through a council of chiefs and elders, that resulted in their being called, collectively, the Nyakyusa. A tribe had been born. By requiring people to identify their tribe on applications for jobs, schools, and identity cards, colonial governments spread the idea of tribe widely within their colonies.

New ethnic identities were not simply imposed by Europeans; Africans increasingly found ethnic or tribal labels useful. This was especially true in rapidly growing urban areas. Surrounded by a bewildering variety of people and in a setting where competition for jobs, housing, and education was very intense, migrants to the city found it helpful to categorize themselves and others in larger ethnic terms. Thus, in many colonial cities, people who spoke similar languages, shared a common culture, or came from the same general part of the country began to think of themselves as a single people—a new tribe. They organized a rich variety of ethnic or tribal associations to provide mutual assistance while in the cities and to send money back home to build schools or clinics. Migrant workers, far from home and concerned to protect their rights to land and to their wives and families, found a sense of security in being part of a recognized tribe, with its chiefs, courts, and established authority.

The Igbo people of southeastern Nigeria represent a case in point. Prior to the twentieth century, they were organized in a series of independently governed village groups. Although they spoke related languages, they had no unifying political system and no myth of common ancestry. Occupying a region of unusually dense population, many of these people eagerly seized on Western education and moved in large numbers to the cities and towns of colonial Nigeria. There they gradually discovered what they had in common and how they differed from the other peoples of Nigeria. By the 1940s, they were organizing on a national level and calling on Igbos everywhere to "sink all differences" in order to achieve "tribal unity, cooperation, and progress of all the Igbos." Fifty years earlier, however, no one had regarded himself or herself as an Igbo. One historian summed up the process of creating African ethnic identities in this way: "Europeans believed Africans belonged to tribes; Africans built tribes to belong to."[25]

⊥⊥ Reflections: Who Makes History?

Winners may write history, but they do not make history, at least not alone. Dominant groups everywhere—slave owners, upper classes, men generally, and certainly colonial rulers—have found their actions constrained and their choices limited by the sheer presence of subordinated people and the ability of those people to act. Europeans who sought to make their countries self-sufficient in cotton by requiring colonized Africans to grow it generally found themselves unable to achieve that goal. Missionaries who tried to impose their own understanding of Christianity in the colonies found their converts often unwilling to accept missionary authority or the cultural framework in which the new religion was presented. In the twentieth century, colonial rulers all across Asia and Africa found that their most highly educated subjects became the leaders of those movements seeking to end colonial rule. Clearly this was not what they had intended.

In recent decades, historians have been at pains to uncover the ways in which subordinated people—slaves, workers, peasants, women, the colonized—have been able to act in their own interests, even within the most oppressive conditions. This kind of "history from below" found expression in a famous book about American slavery that was subtitled *The World the Slaves Made*. Historians of women's lives have sought to show women not only as victims of patriarchy but also as historical actors in their own right. Likewise, colonized people in any number of ways actively shaped the history of the colonial era. On occasion, they resisted and rebelled; in various times and places, they embraced, rejected, and transformed a transplanted Christianity; many eagerly sought Western education but later turned it against the colonizers; women both suffered from and creatively coped with the difficulties of colonial life; and everywhere people created new ways of belonging. None of this diminishes the hardships, the enormous inequalities of power, or the exploitation and oppression of the colonial experience. Rather it suggests that history is often made through the struggle of unequal groups and that the outcome corresponds to no one's intentions.

Perhaps we might let Karl Marx have the last word on this endlessly fascinating topic: "Men make their own history," he wrote, "but they do not make it as they please nor under conditions of their own choosing." In the colonial experience of the nineteenth and early twentieth centuries, both the colonizers and the colonized "made history," but neither was able to do so as they pleased.

Second Thoughts

What's the Significance?

To assess your mastery of the material in this chapter, visit the **Student Center** at bedfordstmartins.com/strayer.

scramble for Africa	cash-crop agriculture	European racism
Indian Rebellion, 1857–1858	Western-educated elite	Edward Blyden
Congo Free State/Leopold II	Africanization of Christianity	colonial tribalism
cultivation system	Swami Vivekananda	

Big Picture Questions

1. Why were Asian and African societies incorporated into European colonial empires later than those of the Americas? How would you compare their colonial experiences?
2. In what ways did colonial rule rest upon violence and coercion, and in what ways did it elicit voluntary cooperation or generate benefits for some people?
3. In what respects were colonized people more than victims of colonial conquest and rule? To what extent could they act in their own interests within the colonial situation?
4. Was colonial rule a transforming, even a revolutionary, experience, or did it serve to freeze or preserve existing social and economic patterns? What evidence can you find to support both sides of this argument?

Next Steps: For Further Study

For Web sites and additional documents related to this chapter, see **Make History** at bedfordstmartins.com/strayer.

A. Adu Boahen, *African Perspectives on Colonialism* (1987). An examination of the colonial experience by a prominent African scholar.

Alice Conklin and Ian Fletcher, *European Imperialism, 1830–1930* (1999). A collection of both classical reflections on empire and examples of modern scholarship.

Scott B. Cook, *Colonial Encounters in the Age of High Imperialism* (1996). Seven case studies of the late-nineteenth-century colonial experience.

Adam Hochschild, *King Leopold's Ghost* (1999). A journalist's evocative account of the horrors of early colonial rule in the Congo.

Douglas Peers, *India under Colonial Rule* (2006). A concise and up-to-date exploration of colonial India.

Bonnie Smith, ed., *Imperialism* (2000). A fine collection of documents, pictures, and commentary on nineteenth- and twentieth-century empires.

Margaret Strobel, *Gender, Sex, and Empire* (1994). A brief account of recent historical thinking about colonial life and gender.

"History of Imperialism," http://members.aol.com/TeacherNet/World.html. A Web site with dozens of links to documents, essays, maps, cartoons, and pictures dealing with modern empires.

Documents

Considering the Evidence: Indian Responses to Empire

The European empires of the nineteenth and early twentieth centuries elicited a variety of responses from their colonial subjects—acceptance and even gratitude, disappointment with unfulfilled promises, active resistance, and sharp criticism. The documents that follow present a range of Indian commentary on British rule from the late eighteenth to the early twentieth centuries.

During that roughly 150 years, India was Britain's "jewel in the crown," the centerpiece of its expanding empire in Asia and Africa (see Map 20.1, p. 926). Until the late 1850s, Britain's growing involvement with South Asia was organized and led by the British East India Company, a private trading firm that had acquired a charter from the Crown allowing it to exercise military, political, and administrative functions in India as well as its own commercial operations (see pp. 679–80). As the Mughal Empire decayed, the company assumed a governing role for increasingly large parts of the subcontinent. But after the explosive upheaval of the Indian Rebellion of 1857–1858, the British government itself assumed control of the region. Throughout the colonial era, the British relied heavily on an alliance with traditional elite groups in Indian society—landowners; the "princes" who governed large parts of the region; and the Brahmins, the highest-ranking segment of India's caste-based society.

Document 20.1

The Wonders of British Calcutta

Originally a small village in Bengal, Calcutta grew into a major trading settlement under the British East India Company, becoming the capital of British India in 1772. In the late eighteenth century, a widely traveled Indian Muslim scholar named Nawab Muhabbat Khan described in poetry his impressions of this British city.

■ What features of Calcutta most surprised Muhabbat Khan?

■ What were his attitudes toward the British themselves?

■ What might you infer about his posture toward an emerging British political presence in India?

Nawab Muhabbat Khan

On Calcutta
Late Eighteenth Century

Calcutta is a wonderful city, in the country of Bang.°
It is a specimen of both China and Farang.°
Its buildings are heart-attracting and delightful....
From the beauty of the works of the European artists
The senses of the spectator are overpowered.
The hat-wearing Englishmen who dwell in them
All speak the truth and have good dispositions....
As a multitude of persons like the planets roam in every direction,
The streets take the resemblance of the Milky Way.

°**Bang:** Bengal.

°**Farang:** the West.

Source: Sir H. M. Elliot, *The History of India as Told by Its Own Historians* (London: Trubner and Co., 1877), 8:382–83.

You will see, if you go to the bazaar, all the excellent things of the world.
All things which are produced in any part of the inhabited world
Are found in its bazaar without difficulty.
If I attempt to write in praise of the marvels of the city,
The pen will refuse its office.
But it is well known to all of every degree
That it combines the beauties of China and Farang.
The ground is as level as the face of the sky,
And the roads in it are as straight as the line of the equator.
People go out to walk on them,
And there they meet together like the planets.
Such a city as this in the country of the Bengalis
Nobody has seen or heard of in the world.

Document 20.2

Seeking Western Education

Ram Mohan Roy (1772–1833), born and highly educated within a Brahmin Hindu family, subsequently studied both Arabic and Persian, learned English, came into contact with British Christian missionaries, and found employment with the British East India Company. He emerged in the early nineteenth century as a leading advocate for religious and social reform within India, with a particular interest in ending *sati*, the practice in which widows burned themselves on their husbands' funeral pyres. In 1823, he learned about a British plan to establish a school in Calcutta that was to focus on Sanskrit texts and traditional Hindu learning. Document 20.2 records his response to that school, and to British colonial rule, in a letter to the British governor-general of India.

■ Why was Roy opposed to the creation of this school?

■ What does this letter reveal about Roy's attitude toward Indian and European cultures?

■ What future did Roy imagine for India?

■ How would you describe Roy's attitude toward British colonial rule in India?

RAM MOHAN ROY
Letter to Lord Amherst
1823

The establishment of a new Sanskrit School in Calcutta evinces the laudable desire of Government to improve the natives of India by education, a blessing for which they must ever be grateful.... When this seminary of learning was proposed... we were filled with sanguine hopes that [it would employ] European gentlemen of talent and education to instruct the natives of India in Mathematics, Natural Philosophy, Chemistry, Anatomy, and other useful sciences, which the natives of Europe have carried to a degree of perfection that has raised them above the inhabitants of other parts of the world.... Our hearts were filled with mingled feelings of delight and gratitude; we already offered up thanks to Providence for inspiring the most generous and enlightened nations of the West with the glorious ambition of planting in Asia the arts and sciences of Modern Europe.

We find [however] that the Government are establishing a Sanskrit school under Hindu Pandits° to impart such knowledge as is already current in India. This seminary can only be expected to load the minds of youth with grammatical niceties and metaphysical distinctions of little or no practical use to the possessors or to society. The pupils will there acquire what was known two thousand years ago with the addition of vain and empty subtleties since then produced by speculative men, such as is already commonly taught in all parts of India....

Neither can much improvement arise from such speculations as the following which are the themes suggested by the Vedanta:° in what manner is the soul absorbed in the Deity? What relation does it bear to the Divine Essence? Nor will youths be fitted to be better members of society by the Vedantic doctrines which teach them to believe, that all visible things have no real existence, that as father, brother, etc., have no actual entity, they consequently deserve no real affection, and therefore the sooner we escape from them and leave the world the better....

[T]he Sanskrit system of education would be the best calculated to keep this country in darkness, if such had been the policy of the British legislature. But as the improvement of the native population is the object of the Government, it will consequently promote a more liberal and enlightened system of instruction, embracing Mathematics, Natural Philosophy, Chemistry, Anatomy, with other useful sciences, which may be accomplished with the sums proposed by employing a few gentlemen of talent and learning educated in Europe and providing a College furnished with necessary books, instruments, and other apparatus. In presenting this subject to your Lordship, I conceive myself discharging a solemn duty which I owe to my countrymen, and also to that

°**Pandits:** learned teachers.

Source: Rammohun Roy, *The English Works of Raja Rammohun Roy* (Allahabad, India: Panini Office, 1906), 471–74.

°**Vedanta:** a branch of Hindu philosophy.

enlightened sovereign and legislature which have extended their benevolent care to this distant land, actuated by a desire to improve the inhabitants, and therefore humbly trust you will excuse the liberty I have taken in thus expressing my sentiments to your Lordship.

Document 20.3

The Indian Rebellion

In 1857–1858, British-ruled India erupted in violent rebellion (see pp. 929–30). Some among the rebels imagined that the Mughal Empire might be restored to its former power and glory. Such was the hope that animated the Azamgarh Proclamation, issued in the summer of 1857, allegedly by the grandson of the last and largely powerless Mughal emperor, Bahadur Shah, who controlled little more than the Red Fort in which he lived in Delhi.

■ What grievances against British rule does this document disclose?

■ How does the proclamation imagine the future of India, should the rebellion succeed? How does this compare to Roy's vision of India's future in Document 20.2?

■ To what groups or classes of people was the proclamation directed? What classes were left out in the call to rebellion? Why might they have been omitted?

■ Does the proclamation represent the strength and authority of the Mughal Empire or its weakness and irrelevance?

BAHADUR SHAH

The Azamgarh Proclamation

1857

It is well known to all that in this age the people of Hindustan,° both Hindus and Muslims, are being ruined under the tyranny and oppression of the infidel and the treacherous English. It is therefore the bounden duty of all the wealthy people of India, especially of those who have any sort of connection with any of the Muslim royal families and are considered the pastors and masters of their people, to stake their lives and property for the well-being of the public. . . . I, who am the grandson of Bahadur Shah, have . . . come here to extirpate the infidels residing in the eastern part of the country, and to liberate and protect the poor helpless people now groaning under their iron rule. . . .

Several of the Hindu and Muslim chiefs who . . . have been trying their best to root out the English in India, have presented themselves to me and taken part in the reigning Indian crusade. . . . [B]e it known to all, that the ancient works both of the Hindus and the Muslims, the writings of the miracle-workers, and the calculations of the astrologers, pundits and

°**Hindustan:** northern India.

Source: "The Azamgarh Proclamation," *Delhi Gazette*, September 29, 1857.

rammals,° all agree, asserting that the English will no longer have any footing in India or elsewhere. Therefore it is incumbent on all to give up the hope of the continuation of the British sway, [and to] side with me....

Section I: Regarding Zamindars°

It is evident the British government, in making [land] settlements, have imposed exorbitant jummas,° and have disgraced and ruined several zamindars, by putting up their estates to public auction for arrears of rent, insomuch, that on the institution of a suit by a common ryot° yet, a maidservant, or a slave, the respectable zamindars are summoned into court arrested, put in gaol, and disgraced.... Besides this, the coffers of the zamindars are annually taxed with subscriptions for schools, hospitals, roads, etc. Such extortions will have no manner of existence in the Badshahi government;° but, on the contrary, the jummas will be light, the dignity and honour of the zamindars safe, and every zamindar will have absolute rule in his own zamindary. [A]nd should any zamindar who has been unjustly deprived of his lands during the English government personally join the war, he will be restored to his [property] and excused from paying one-fourth of the revenue.

Section II: Regarding Merchants

It is plain that the infidel and treacherous British government have monopolized the trade of all the fine and valuable merchandise such as indigo, cloth, and other articles of shipping, leaving only the trade of trifles to the people, and even in this they are not without their share of the profits, which they secure by means of customs and stamp fees, etc., in money suits, so that the people have merely a trade in name. Besides this, the profits of the traders are taxed with

postages, tolls, and subscriptions for schools. Notwithstanding all these concessions, the merchants are liable to imprisonment and disgrace at the instance or complaint of a worthless man. When the Badshahi government is established, all these aforesaid fraudulent practices shall be dispensed with, and the trade of every article, without exception both by land and water, shall be open to the native merchants of India, who will have the benefit of the government steam-vessels and steam carriages for the conveyance of their merchandise gratis.... It is therefore the duty of every merchant to take part in the war, and aid the Badshahi government with his men and money....

Section III: Regarding Public Servants

It is not a secret thing, that under the British government, natives employed in the civil and military services have little respect, low pay, and no manner of influence; and all the posts of dignity and emolument in both the departments are exclusively bestowed upon Englishmen.... But under the Badshahi government, [these] posts...will be given to the natives.... Natives, whether Hindus or Muslims, who fall fighting against the English, are sure to go to heaven; and those killed fighting for the English, will, doubtless, go to hell; therefore, all the natives in the British service ought to be alive to their religion and interest, and, abjuring their loyalty to the English, side with the Badshahi government and obtain salaries of 200 or 300 rupees per month for the present, and be entitled to high posts in future.

Section IV: Regarding Artisans

It is evident that the Europeans, by the introduction of English articles into India, have thrown the weavers, the cotton-dressers, the carpenters, the blacksmiths, and the shoemakers, etc., out of employ, and have engrossed their occupations, so that every description of native artisan has been reduced to beggary. But under the Badshahi government the native artisan will exclusively be employed in the services of the kings, the rajahs, and the rich; and this will no doubt insure their prosperity.

°**rammals:** fortune tellers.

°**Zamindars:** large landowners.

°**jummas:** taxes.

°**ryot:** peasant farmer.

°**Badshahi government:** restored imperial government.

Section V: Regarding Pundits,° Fakirs,° and Other Learned Persons

The pundits and fakirs being the guardians of the Hindu and Muslim religions, respectively, and the European being the enemies of both the religions, and as at present a war is raging against the English on account of religion, the pundits and fakirs are bound to present themselves to me and take their share in the holy war, otherwise they will stand condemned... but if they come, they will, when the Badshahi government is well established, receive rent-free lands.

Lastly, be it known to all, that whoever out of the above-named classes, shall... still cling to the British government, all his estates shall be confiscated, and his property plundered, and he himself, with his whole family, shall be imprisoned, and ultimately put to death.

°**Pundits:** scholars.

°**Fakirs:** religious mystics.

Document 20.4

The Credits and Debits of British Rule in India

Dadabhai Naoroji (1825–1917) was a well-educated Indian intellectual, a cotton trader in London, and a founding member of the Indian National Congress, an elite organization established in 1885 to press for a wider range of opportunities for educated Indians within the colonial system. He was also the first Indian to serve in the British parliament. In 1871, while addressing an English audience in London, he was asked about the impact of British rule in India. Representing a "moderate" view within Indian political circles at the time, he organized his response in terms of "credits" and "debits."

- According to Naoroji, what are the chief advantages and drawbacks of British rule?

- What is Naoroji seeking from Britain?

- How does Naoriji's posture toward British rule compare to that of Ram Mohan Roy in Document 20.2 or the Azamgarh Proclamation in Document 20.3?

DADABHAI NAOROJI

Speech to a London Audience

1871

Credit

In the Cause of Humanity: Abolition of *suttee°* and infanticide. Destruction of *Dacoits, Thugs, Pindarees°* and other such pests of Indian society. Allowing remarriage of Hindu widows, and charitable aid in time of famine. Glorious work all this, of which any nation may well be proud....

In the Cause of Civilization: Education, both male and female. Though yet only partial, an inestimable blessing as far as it has gone, and leading gradually to the destruction of superstition, and many moral and social evils. Resuscitation of India's own noble literature, modified and refined by the enlightenment of the West.

Politically: Peace and order. Freedom of speech and liberty of the press. Higher political knowledge and aspirations. Improvement of government in the native states. Security of life and property. Freedom from oppression caused by the caprice or greed of despotic rulers, and from devastation by war. Equal justice between man and man (sometimes vitiated by partiality to Europeans). Services of highly educated administrators, who have achieved the above-mentioned results.

Materially: Loans for railways and irrigation. Development of a few valuable products, such as indigo, tea, coffee, silk, etc. Increase of exports. Telegraphs.

Generally: A slowly growing desire of late to treat India equitably, and as a country held in trust. Good intentions. No nation on the face of the earth has ever had the opportunity of achieving such a glorious work as this.... I appreciate, and so do my countrymen, what England has done for India, and I know that it is only in British hands that her regeneration can be accomplished. Now for the debit side.

Debit

In the Cause of Humanity: Nothing. Everything, therefore, is in your favor under this heading.

In the Cause of Civilization: As I have said already, there has been a failure to do as much as might have been done, but I put nothing to the debit. Much has been done, though.

Politically: Repeated breach of pledges to give the natives a fair and reasonable share in the higher administration of their own country, which has much shaken confidence in the good faith of the British word. Political aspirations and the legitimate claim to have a reasonable voice in the legislation and the imposition and disbursement of taxes, met to a very slight degree, thus treating the natives of India not as British subjects, in whom representation is a birthright. Consequent on the above, an utter disregard of the feelings and views of the natives....

Financially: All attention is engrossed in devising new modes of taxation, without any adequate effort to increase the means of the people to pay; and the consequent vexation and oppressiveness of the taxes imposed, imperial and local. Inequitable financial relations between England and India, i.e., the political debt of £100,000,000 clapped on India's shoulders, and all home charges also, though the British Exchequer contributes nearly £3,000,000 to the expense of the colonies.

Materially: The political drain, up to this time, from India to England, of above £500,000,000, at the lowest computation, in principal alone, which with interest would be some thousands of millions. The further continuation of this drain at the rate, at present, of above £12,000,000 per annum, with a tendency to increase. The consequent continuous impoverishment and exhaustion of the country, ex-

---

°*suttee:* variant spelling of *sati*, the practice of widows burning themselves on their husbands' funeral pyres.

°**Dacoits, Thugs, Pindarees:** thieves, murderers, bands of robbers.

Source: Dadabhai Naoroji, *Essays, Speeches, Addresses and Writings* (Bombay: Caxton Printing Works, 1887), 131–36.

cept so far as it has been very partially relieved and replenished by the railway and irrigation loans, and the windfall of the consequences of the American war, since 1850. Even with this relief, the material condition of India is such that the great mass of the poor have hardly tuppence a day and a few rags, or a scanty subsistence. The famines that were in their power to prevent, if they had done their duty, as a good and intelligent government. The policy adopted during the last fifteen years of building railways, irrigation works, etc., is hopeful, has already resulted in much good to your credit, and if persevered in, gratitude and contentment will follow. An increase of exports without adequate compensation; loss of manufacturing industry and skill. Here I end the debit side.

Summary:

To sum up the whole, the British rule has been: morally, a great blessing; politically, peace and order on one hand, blunders on the other; materially, impoverishment, relieved as far as the railway and other loans go. The natives call the British system "Sakar ki Churi," the knife of sugar. That is to say, there is no oppression, it is all smooth and sweet, but it is the knife, notwithstanding. I mention this that you should know these feelings. Our great misfortune is that you do not know our wants. When you will know our real wishes, I have not the least doubt that you would do justice. The genius and spirit of the British people is fair play and justice.

Document 20.5

Gandhi on Modern Civilization

Mahatma Gandhi, clearly modern India's most beloved leader, is best known for his theories of *satyagraha*. This was an aggressive but nonviolent approach to political action that directly challenged and disobeyed unjust laws, while seeking to change the hearts of their British oppressors (see pp. 1086–90 in Chapter 23). But Gandhi's thinking was distinctive in another way as well, for he objected not only to the foreign and exploitative character of British rule but also more fundamentally to the modern civilization that it carried. In 1908, he spelled out that critique in a pamphlet titled "*Hind Swaraj*" ("Indian Home Rule"). There Gandhi assumes the role of an "editor," responding to questions from a "reader."

■ What is Gandhi's most fundamental criticism of British rule in India?

■ What is the difference between his concept of "civilization" and that which he ascribes to the British?

■ How does Gandhi reconcile the idea of India as a single nation with the obvious religious division between Hindus and Muslims?

■ What kind of future does Gandhi seek for his country?

■ What criticisms do you imagine that Gandhi met as he sought to introduce his ideas into India's increasingly nationalist political life?

Mahatma Gandhi
Indian Home Rule
1908

READER: Now you will have to explain what you mean by civilization.

EDITOR: Let us first consider what state of things is described by the word "civilization."...The people of Europe today live in better-built houses than they did a hundred years ago. This is considered an emblem of civilization....If people of a certain country, who have hitherto not been in the habit of wearing much clothing, boots, etc., adopt European clothing, they are supposed to have become civilized out of savagery. Formerly, in Europe, people ploughed their lands mainly by manual labor. Now, one man can plough a vast tract by means of steam engines and can thus amass great wealth. This is called a sign of civilization. Formerly, only a few men wrote valuable books. Now, anybody writes and prints anything he likes and poisons people's minds. Formerly, men traveled in wagons. Now, they fly through the air in trains at the rate of four hundred and more miles per day. This is considered the height of civilization. It has been stated that, as men progress, they shall be able to travel in airship and reach any part of the world in a few hours....Everything will be done by machinery. Formerly, when people wanted to fight with one another, they measured between them their bodily strength; now it is possible to take away thousands of lives by one man working behind a gun from a hill. This is civilization....Formerly, men were made slaves under physical compulsion. Now they are enslaved by temptation of money and of the luxuries that money can buy....This civilization takes note neither of morality nor of religion. Its votaries calmly state that their business is not to teach religion. Some even consider it to be a superstitious growth....This civilization is irreligion, and it has taken such a hold on the people in Europe that those who are in it appear to be half mad. They lack real physical strength or courage. They keep up their energy by intoxication. They can hardly be happy in solitude. Women, who should be the queens of households, wander in the streets or they slave away in factories. For the sake of a pittance, half a million women in England alone are laboring under trying circumstances in factories or similar institutions.

This civilization is such that one has only to be patient and it will be self-destroyed....I cannot give you an adequate conception of it. It is eating into the vitals of the English nation. It must be shunned.... Civilization is not an incurable disease, but it should never be forgotten that the English are at present afflicted by it.

READER: I now understand why the English hold India. I should like to know your views about the condition of our country.

EDITOR: It is a sad condition....It is my deliberate opinion that India is being ground down, not under the English heel, but under that of modern civilization. It is groaning under the monster's terrible weight. [M]y first complaint is that India is becoming irreligious....We are turning away from God....[W]e should set a limit to our worldly ambition....[O]ur religious ambition should be illimitable....

EDITOR: Railways, lawyers, and doctors have impoverished the country so much so that, if we do not wake up in time, we shall be ruined.

READER: I do now, indeed, fear that we are not likely to agree at all. You are attacking the very institutions which we have hitherto considered to be good.

EDITOR: It must be manifest to you that, but for the railways, the English could not have such a hold on India as they have. The railways, too, have spread the bubonic plague. Without them the masses could not move from place to place. They are the carriers of plague germs. Formerly we had natural segregation. Railways have also increased the frequency of famines because, owing to facility of means of locomotion, people sell out their grain and it is sent to

Source: Mohandas Gandhi, *Indian Home Rule* (Madras: Ganesh and Co., 1922), Parts 6, 8, 9, 10, 13.

the dearest markets. People become careless and so the pressure of famine increases. Railways accentuate the evil nature of man. Bad men fulfill their evil designs with greater rapidity....

READER: You have denounced railways, lawyers, and doctors. I can see that you will discard all machinery. What, then, is civilization?

EDITOR: The answer to that question is not difficult. I believe that the civilization India has evolved is not to be beaten in the world.... India is still, somehow or other, sound at the foundation.... India remains immovable and that is her glory. It is a charge against India that her people are so uncivilized, ignorant, and stolid that it is not possible to induce them to adopt any changes. It is a charge really against our merit. What we have tested and found true on the anvil of experience, we dare not change. Many thrust their advice upon India, and she remains steady. This is her beauty: it is the sheet-anchor of our hope.

Civilization is that mode of conduct which points out to man the path of duty. Performance of duty and observance of morality are convertible terms. To observe morality is to attain mastery over our mind and our passions. So doing, we know ourselves....

If this definition be correct, then India... has nothing to learn from anybody else.... Our ancestors, therefore, set a limit to our indulgences. [They] dissuaded us from luxuries and pleasures. We have managed with the same kind of plough as existed thousands of years ago. We have retained the same kind of cottages that we had in former times and our indigenous education remains the same as before. We have had no system of life-corroding competition. Each followed his own occupation or trade and charged a regulation wage. It was not that we did not know how to invent machinery, but our forefathers knew that, if we set our hearts after such things, we would become slaves and lose our moral fiber.... They were, therefore, satisfied with small villages.... A nation with a constitution like this is fitter to teach others than to learn from others....

The tendency of the Indian civilization is to elevate the moral being; that of the Western civilization is to propagate immorality. The latter is godless; the former is based on a belief in God. So understanding and so believing, it behooves every lover of India to cling to the Indian civilization even as a child clings to the mother's breast.

Using the Evidence:
Indian Responses to Empire

1. **Noticing differences and changes:** What different understandings of British colonial rule are reflected in these documents? In what ways did those understandings change over time? How might you account for those differences and changes?

2. **Describing alternative futures:** What can you infer about the kind of future for India that the authors of these documents anticipate?

3. **Noticing what's missing:** What Indian voices are not represented in these documents? How might such people have articulated a different understanding of the colonial experience?

4. **Responding to Gandhi:** How might each of the other authors have responded to Gandhi's analysis of British colonial role and his understanding of "civilization"? To what extent do you find Gandhi's views relevant to the conditions of the early twenty-first century?

Visual Sources

Considering the Evidence: The Scramble for Africa

The centerpiece of Europe's global expansion during the nineteenth century occurred in the so-called scramble for Africa, when a half dozen or so European countries divided up almost the entire continent into colonial territories (see Map 20.2, p. 927). The "scramble" took place very quickly (between roughly 1875 and 1900), surprising even the European leaders who initiated it, as well as the many African societies which suddenly found themselves confronting highly aggressive and well-armed foreign forces. Each of the rival powers—Britain, France, Germany, Belgium, Portugal, Spain, and Italy—sought to get a piece of a continent that many believed held the promise of great wealth. Given Europe's wars over colonial possessions in the early modern era, it is remarkable that the entire partition of Africa took place without any direct military conflict between the competing countries. But in establishing their control on the ground, Europeans faced widespread African resistance, making the scramble an extremely bloody process of military conquest. The images that follow illustrate some of the distinctive features of the scramble for Africa as well as the differing ways in which it was perceived and represented.

As the Atlantic slave trade diminished over the course of the nineteenth century, Europeans began to look at Africa in new ways—as a source of raw materials, as an opportunity for investment, as a market for industrial products, as a field for exploration, and as an opportunity to spread Christianity. It was not until the last quarter of the nineteenth century that Europeans showed much interest in actually acquiring territory and ruling large populations in Africa. Visual Source 20.1, from a late-nineteenth-century French board game, illustrates the widespread interest in the growing missionary enterprise in Africa as well as in the celebrated adventures of the intrepid explorers who penetrated the dangerous interior of the continent. It enabled ordinary Europeans to participate in exciting events in distant lands. This game featured the travels of David Livingstone and Henry Stanley. Livingstone (1813–1873) was a British missionary and explorer of central Africa whose work in exposing the horrors of the Arab slave trade gave him an almost mythic status among Europeans. That East African commerce in human beings, operating largely in the Islamic world, was growing even as the transatlantic trade was shrinking. Stanley (1841–1904), a British journalist and explorer, gained lasting fame by finding Livingstone, long out of touch with his homeland, deep in the African interior.

Visual Source 20.1 Prelude to the Scramble (Private Collection/Archives Charmet/The Bridgeman Art Library)

- What images of Africa are suggested by this board game? Notice carefully the landscape, the animals, and the activities in which people are engaged.
- How does the game depict European activities in Africa?
- What might be the meaning of the large sun arising at the top of the image?
- What nineteenth-century realities are missing from this portrayal of Africa?

As the scramble for Africa got under way in earnest in the 1880s and 1890s, it became a highly competitive process. French designs on Africa, for example, focused on obtaining an uninterrupted East–West link from the Atlantic Ocean to the Red Sea. But the British, entrenched in Egypt and in

Visual Source 20.2 Conquest and Competition (Alinari/Art Resource, NY)

control of the Suez Canal, were determined that no major European power should be allowed to control the headwaters of the Nile on which Egypt depended. Those conflicting goals came to a head in 1898, when British forces moving south from Egypt met a French expedition moving northeast from the Atlantic coast of what is now Gabon. That encounter took place along the Nile River at Fashoda in present-day Sudan, threatening war between France and Great Britain. In the end, negotiations persuaded the French to withdraw.

Visual Source 20.2, the cover of a French publication, shows the commander of the French expedition, Jean-Baptiste Marchand, who gained heroic stature in leading his troops on an epic journey across much of Africa for more than eighteen months.

- How did the artist portray Marchand? How might a British artist have portrayed him?

- What does this visual source suggest about the role of violence in the scramble for Africa?

- Notice the large number of African troops among Marchand's forces. What does that suggest about the process of colonial conquest? Why might Africans have agreed to fight on behalf of a European colonial power?

- How do you understand the fallen soldier lying between Marchand's legs?

Nowhere did the vaulting ambition of European colonial powers in Africa emerge more clearly than in the British vision of a North–South corridor of British territories along the eastern side of the continent stretching from South Africa to Egypt, or in the more popular phrase of the time, "from the Cape to Cairo." A part of this vision was an unbroken railroad line running the entire length of the African continent. That grand idea was popularized by Cecil Rhodes, a British-born businessman and politician who made a fortune in South African diamonds and became an enthusiastic advocate of British imperialism. Visual Source 20.3, an 1892 cartoon published in the British magazine *Punch*, shows Rhodes bestriding the continent with one foot in Egypt and the other in South Africa.

- Is this famous image criticizing or celebrating Rhodes's Cape-to-Cairo dream? Explain your reasoning.

- What does this visual source suggest about the purpose of the Cape-to-Cairo scheme and the means to achieve it? Notice the telegraph wire in Rhodes's hands and the rifle on his shoulder.

- How did the artist portray the African continent? What does the absence of African people suggest? How does this visual source compare to Visual Source 20.1?

THE RHODES COLOSSUS
STRIDING FROM CAPE TOWN TO CAIRO.

Visual Source 20.3 From the Cape to Cairo (The Granger Collection, NY)

■ Scholars have sometimes argued that the scramble for Africa was driven less by concrete economic interests than by emotional, even romantic, notions of national grandeur and personal adventure. In what ways do Visual Sources 20.2 and 20.3 support or challenge this interpretation?

While late-nineteenth-century public opinion in Europe widely and often enthusiastically supported the acquisition of African territories, there were critics of that process as well. In France, some saw imperialism as contradicting values deriving from the French Revolution (liberty, equality, fraternity), while others argued that adventures in Africa distracted their country from the more serious threat of growing German power in Europe. Visual Source 20.4, published in 1900, represents a critical French commentary on British imperialism during the Boer War. In that conflict, which began in 1899, British colonial authorities in South Africa sought to crush communities of earlier Dutch settlers, known as Boers, who stood in the way of complete British control over South Africa's rich diamond and gold resources. The figure on the left represents Cecil Rhodes, the arch-imperialist business magnate and a prominent politician in South Africa, while the figure on the right portrays Joseph Chamberlain, the British colonial secretary who ardently supported the war as a means of

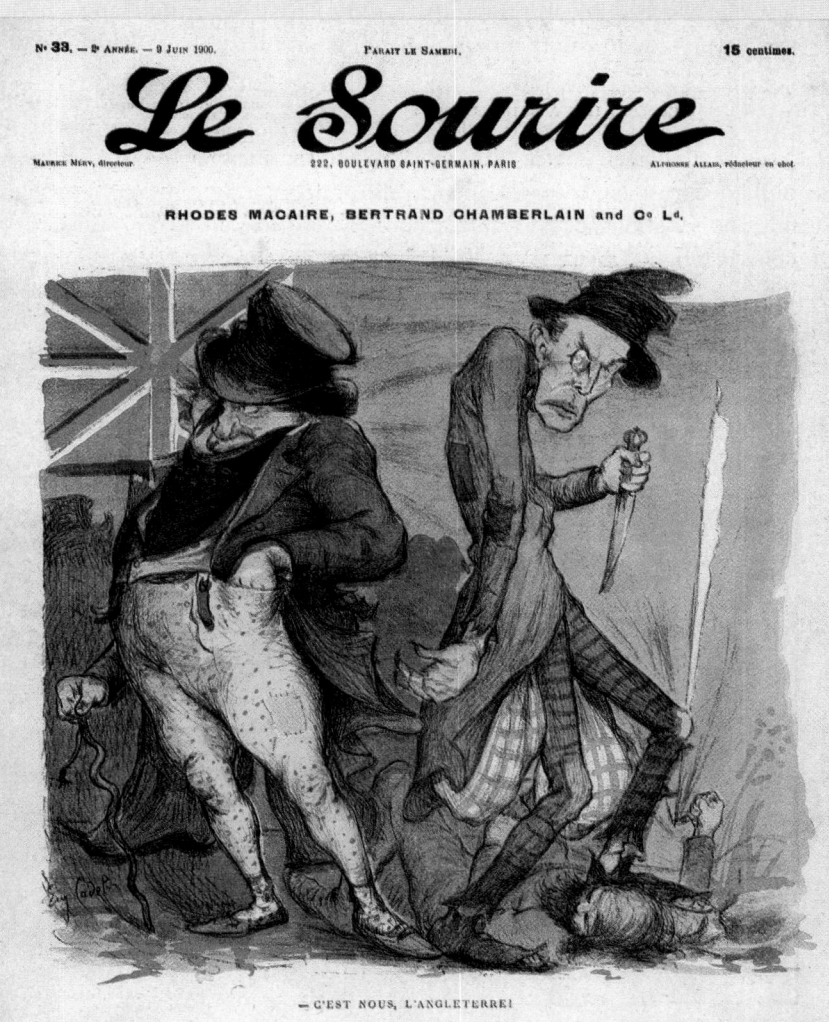

Visual Source 20.4 A French Critique of the Boer War (Mary Evans Picture Library/The Image Works)

ensuring complete British supremacy in South Africa. The figure on the floor is a Boer victim of British imperialism.

- How does this image depict Rhodes and Chamberlain? What motives are implied for British actions in South Africa?

- How does this portrayal of Cecil Rhodes differ from that in Visual Source 20.3?

- Given extensive French conquests in Africa, how might British observers have responded to this cartoon?

- Notice that the victim in this case is white, a Boer descendant of Dutch settlers, who had been in South Africa since 1652. What difference might this have made in the French willingness to criticize their British rivals?

One exception to the general European takeover of Africa during the scramble was the kingdom of Ethiopia. Located in the mountainous highlands of northeastern Africa, Ethiopia boasted an ancient pedigree, a long-established Christian culture, a literate elite, and rich agricultural resources. During the scramble for Africa, that country also had an astute monarch in Menelik II (reigned 1889–1913). Playing various European powers against one another, he acquired from them a considerable arsenal of modern weapons and gained substantial territory for his kingdom, in effect taking part in the scramble. In the famous Battle of Adowa in 1896, Menelik's forces decisively defeated the Italians, who were seeking to add Ethiopia to their country's African empire. By this victory, Ethiopia preserved its independence and became

Visual Source 20.5 The Ethiopian Exception (© Trustees of the British Museum)

a continental symbol of African bravery and resistance in the face of European imperialism.

In Visual Source 20.5, an unknown Ethiopian artist, working during the 1940s, celebrated the victory at Adowa at a time when Ethiopia had just fought off yet another Italian effort at conquest, this time led by Mussolini during World War II. The painting itself replicated in both style and content many earlier artistic celebrations of that earlier victory. In the upper left corner, Emperor Menelik is shown wearing a crown and seated under a royal umbrella. His queen, Empress Taytu, is visible in the lower left on horseback and holding a revolver. The commander of the Ethiopian forces sits on a brown horse, while leading his troops. At the top of the painting, St. George, the patron saint of Ethiopia, presides over the battle scene within a halo of red, yellow, and green, the colors of the Ethiopian flag adopted shortly after the battle.[26]

■ How does this painting represent the Ethiopian triumph at Adowa?

■ What features of the painting might help explain that improbable victory, at least to Ethiopian observers? How does the artist portray the resources available to each side?

■ How did the Ethiopian painter depict the Italian enemy? Keep in mind that Ethiopian artists generally portrayed the forces of good in full face, while the wicked or evil were shown in profile.

■ How do you imagine the news of the Battle of Adowa was received elsewhere in Africa and among peoples of African descent in the Americas? What might this painting have meant to Ethiopians in the wake of Mussolini's invasion of their country during the 1930s?

Using the Evidence:
The Scramble for Africa

1. **Distinguishing viewpoints:** From what different perspectives do these visual sources represent the scramble for Africa? What criticisms of the scramble can you read in them?

2. **Portraying Africans and Europeans:** Both Africans and Europeans are portrayed variously in these visual sources. What differences can you identify?

3. **Using images ... selectively:** In what ways might visual sources such as these be most useful to historians seeking to understand the scramble for Africa? For what kinds of questions about the scramble might they have little to offer?

4. **Considering moral visions:** How do these visual sources deal with issues of morality or visions of right and wrong?

PART SIX

The Most Recent Century

1914–2010

Contents

Chapter 21. The Collapse and Recovery of Europe, 1914–1970s
Chapter 22. The Rise and Fall of World Communism, 1917–Present
Chapter 23. Independence and Development in the Global South, 1914–Present
Chapter 24. Accelerating Global Interaction, Since 1945

The Twentieth Century: A New Period in World History?

Dividing up time into coherent segments—periods, eras, ages—is the way historians mark major changes in the lives of individuals, local communities, social groups, nations, and civilizations and also in the larger story of humankind as a whole. Because all such divisions are artificial, imposed by scholars on a continuously flowing stream of events, they are endlessly controversial and never more so than in the case of the twentieth century. To many historians, that century, and a new era in the human journey, began in 1914 with the outbreak of World War I. That terrible conflict, after all, represented a fratricidal civil war within Western civilization, triggered the Russian Revolution and the beginning of world communism, and stimulated many in the colonial world to work for their own independence. The way it ended set the stage for an even more terrible struggle in World War II.

But do the almost 100 years since 1914 represent a separate phase of world history? Granting them that status has become conventional in many world history textbooks, including this one, but there are reasons to wonder whether future generations will agree. One problem, of course, lies in the brevity of this period—less than 100 years, compared to the many centuries or millennia that comprise earlier eras. Furthermore, an immense overload of information about these decades makes it difficult to distinguish what will prove of lasting significance and what will later seem of only passing importance. Furthermore, because we are so close to the events we study and obviously ignorant of the future, we cannot know if or when this most recent period of world history will end. Or, as some have argued, has it ended already, perhaps with the collapse of the Soviet Union in 1991, with the attacks of September 11, 2001, or with the global economic crisis beginning in 2008? If so, are we now in yet another phase of historical development?

Old and New in the Twentieth Century

Like all other historical periods, this most recent century both carried on from the past and developed distinctive characteristics as well. Whether that combination of the old and new merits the designation of a separate era in world history will likely be debated for a long time to come. For our purposes, it will be enough to highlight both its continuities with the past and the sharp changes that the last 100 years have witnessed.

Consider, for example, the world wars that played such an important role in the first half of the century. They grew out of Europeans' persistent inability to embody their civilization within a single state or empire, as China had long done. They also represent a further stage of European rivalries around the globe that had been going on for four centuries. Nonetheless, the world wars of the twentieth century were also new in the extent to which whole populations were mobilized to fight them and in the enormity of the destruction that they caused. During World War II, for example, Hitler's attempted extermination of the Jews in the Holocaust and the United States' dropping of atomic bombs on Japanese cities marked something new in the history of human conflict.

The communist phenomenon provides another illustration of the blending of old and new. The Russian (1917) and Chinese (1949) revolutions, both of which were enormous social upheavals, brought to power regimes committed to remaking their societies from top to bottom along socialist lines. They were the first large-scale attempts in modern world history to undertake such a gigantic task, and in doing so they broke sharply with the capitalist democratic model of the West. They also created a new and global division of humankind, expressed most dramatically in the cold war between the communist East and the capitalist West. On the other hand, the communist experience also drew much from the past. The great revolutions of the twentieth century derived from long-standing conflicts within Russian and Chinese societies, particularly between impoverished and exploited peasants and dominant landlord classes. The ideology of those communist governments came from the thinking of the nineteenth-century German intellectual Karl Marx. Their intention, like that of their capitalist enemies, was modernization and industrialization. They simply claimed to do it better—more rapidly and more justly.

Another distinguishing feature of the twentieth century lay in the disintegration of its great empires—the Austro-Hungarian, Ottoman, Russian, British, French, Japanese, Soviet, and more—and in their wake the emergence of dozens of new nation-states. At one level, this is simply the latest turn of the wheel in the endless rise and fall of empires, dating back to the ancient Assyrians. But something new occurred this time, for the very idea of empire was rendered illegitimate in the twentieth century, much as slavery lost its international acceptance in the nineteenth century. The superpowers of the second half of the twentieth century—the Soviet Union and the United States—both claimed an anticolonial ideology, even as both of them constructed their own "empires" of a different kind. By the beginning of the twenty-first century, some 200 nation-states, each claiming sovereignty and legal equality with all the others, provided a distinctly new political order for the planet.

The less visible underlying processes of the twentieth century, just like the more dramatic wars, revolutions, and political upheavals, also had roots in the past as well as new expressions in the new century. Perhaps the most fundamental process was explosive population growth, as human numbers more than quadrupled since 1900, leaving the planet with about 6.8 billion people by mid-2009. This was an absolutely unprecedented rate of growth that conditioned practically every other feature of

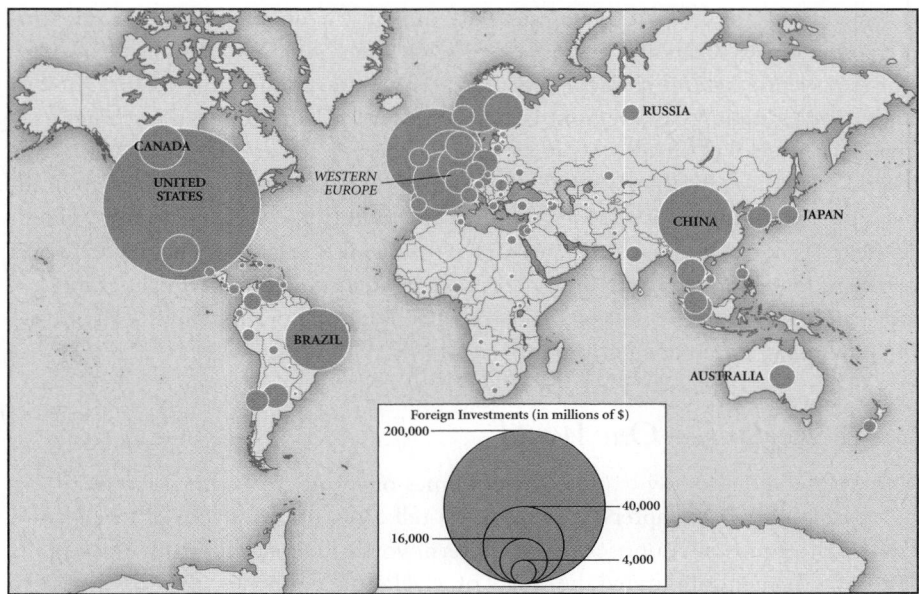

Globalization in Action: Trade and Investment in the Early Twenty-first Century (p. 1136)

the century's history. Still, this new element of twentieth-century world history built upon earlier achievements, most notably the increased food supply deriving from the global spread of American crops such as corn and potatoes. Improvements in medicine and sanitation, which grew out of the earlier Scientific and Industrial revolutions, likewise drove down death rates and thus spurred population growth.

While global population increased fourfold in the twentieth century, industrial output grew fortyfold. This unprecedented economic growth, despite large variations over time and place, was associated with a cascading rate of scientific and technological innovation as well as with the extension of industrial production to many regions of the world. This too was a wholly novel feature of twentieth-century world history and, combined with population growth, resulted in an extraordinary and mounting human impact on the environment. Historian J. R. McNeill wrote that "this is the first time in human history that we have altered ecosystems with such intensity, on such a scale, and with such speed.... The human race, without intending anything of the sort, has undertaken a gigantic uncontrolled experiment on the earth."[1] From a longer-term perspective, of course, these developments represent a continued unfolding of the Scientific and Industrial revolutions. Both began in Europe, but in the twentieth century they largely lost their unique association with the West as they took hold in many cultures. Furthermore, the human impact on the earth itself and other living creatures has a history dating back to the extinction of some large mammals at the hands of Paleolithic hunters.

Much the same might be said about that other grand process of twentieth-century world history—globalization. It too has a genealogy reaching deep into the past, reflected in the Silk Road trading network; Indian Ocean and trans-Saharan commerce; the spread of Buddhism, Christianity, and Islam; and the Columbian exchange. But the twentieth century deepened and extended the connections among the distinct peoples, nations, and regions of the world in ways unparalleled in earlier centuries. A few strokes on a keyboard can send money racing around the planet; radio, television, and the Internet link the world in an unprecedented network of communication; the warming of the lower atmosphere due to the accumulation of greenhouse gases portends radical changes for the whole planet; far more people than ever before produce for and depend on the world market; and global inequalities increasingly surface as sources of international conflict. For good or ill, we live—all of us— in a new phase of an ancient process.

Three Regions—One World

The chapters that follow explore these themes of twentieth-century world history in a particular way. Chapters 21, 22, and 23 tell the separate stories of three major regions or groups of countries—the Western world; the communist world; and the third world, sometimes called the world of developing countries. Chapter 21, which focuses on the Western world of capitalist countries, highlights the dramatic changes that occurred at the center of the global network. The European heartland of the world system collapsed in war and economic depression during the first half of the century but recovered in the second half as leadership of the West passed to the United States.

Accompanying those changes was the emergence of world communism. Chapter 22 addresses four highly significant features of the communist phenomenon: the revolutionary origins of communism, especially in Russia and China; the efforts of those two communist giants to build new and socialist societies; the global conflict of the cold war, which arose from the expansion of communism; and the amazing abandonment of communism as the century ended.

Chapter 23 turns the historical spotlight on the colonial world of Asia and Africa. Two major themes serve to structure the twentieth-century history of this vast region. The first focuses attention on the struggles for independence, the end of colonial empires, and the emergence of dozens of new nations. The second describes the increasingly important role on the global stage that these new states have played in the second half of the century. The assertion of African, Asian, and Middle Eastern peoples, joined by those of Latin America, made the world of the early twenty-first century a very different place from that of a hundred years earlier.

These histories of the Western world, the communist world, and the third world during the past century not only paralleled each other but also frequently intersected and overlapped, as Chapters 21, 22, and 23 repeatedly indicate. However, they were also part of an even larger story, known everywhere now as globalization. The post–World War II acceleration of this much older process is the "big picture" theme of Chapter 24, which examines both its economic and cultural dimensions. Thus it focuses attention on the development of the world economy as well as on the global expressions of feminism, religious fundamentalism, and environmentalism.

Perhaps there is enough that is new about the century following 1914 to treat it, tentatively, as a distinct era in human history, but only what happens next will determine how this period will be understood by later generations. Will it be regarded as the beginning of the end of the modern age, as human demands upon the earth prove unsustainable? Or will it be seen as the midpoint of an ongoing process that extends a full modernity to the entire planet? Like all of our ancestors, every one of them, we too live in a fog when contemplating our futures and see more clearly only in retrospect. In this strange way, our future will shape the telling of the past, even as the past shapes the living of the future.

Landmarks of the Most Recent Century, 1914–2010

1910	1920	1930	1940	1950	

The Western/ Developed World

1919 Treaty of Versailles, ending World War I

1914–1918 World War I

1929 Stock market crash and beginning of Great Depression

1933 Hitler's rise to power in Germany

1937 Japan invades China, beginning World War II in Asia

1939–1945 World War II/Holocaust in Europe

1945 Bombing of Hiroshima/Nagasaki (first use of nuclear weapons in combat)

1957 European Economic Community established

The Communist World

1921 Founding of Chinese Communist Party

1917 Russian Revolution

1929–1953 Stalin in power in USSR

1934–1935 Long March in China

1945–1950 Expansion of communism in Eastern Europe

1949 Communist triumph in Chinese Revolution

1950–1953 Korean War

The Third World/ Developing World

1923–1938 Turkey's secular modernization/Kemal Atatürk

1919 May Fourth movement in China

1928 Muslim Brotherhood established in Egypt

1947 Independence of India/Pakistan

1949 Independence of Indonesia

1959 Cuban Revolution

The Whole World (Markers of Globalization)

1919–1946 League of Nations

1945 Founding of United Nations

1945 World Bank/International Monetary Fund established

1946–1991 Cold war

1960	1970	1980	1990	2000

1960s Civil Rights and anti-Vietnam protests in the U.S.

1968 Student protests in France

1991 End of cold war

1994 European Union established

2001 Attacks on World Trade Center

2002 Introduction of the euro

2003 Iraq War begins

1962 Cuban missile crisis

1964 Emergence of Chinese/Soviet hostility

1976–early 1990s Deng Xiaoping and beginnings of Communist reform in China

1991 Collapse of the Soviet Union

1965–1973 Vietnam War

1968 Prague Spring/Soviet invasion of Czechoslovakia

1989 Fall of communism in Eastern Europe

1985–1990 Gorbachev reforms in USSR

1967 Six-Day War between Arabs and Israel

1970s–present Rise of Islamic renewal movements

1979 Islamic Revolution in Iran

1990s Rapid economic growth in China and India

1957–1975 African independence achieved

1973 OPEC oil embargo

1979–1989 Soviet war in Afghanistan

1994 End of apartheid; African majority rule in South Africa

1960 OPEC established

1970 Greenpeace established

1982 Law of the Sea Convention introduced

1995 World Trade Organization established

1997 Kyoto protocol on global warming introduced

1999 Antiglobalization protests in Seattle, Washington

2000 World population reaches 6 billion

1994 NAFTA established

2001 World Social Forum (alternative globalization group) established

2008 World economic crisis begins

1778   1943

AMERICANS
will always fight for liberty

CHAPTER TWENTY-ONE

The Collapse and Recovery of Europe

1914–1970s

The First World War: European
    Civilization in Crisis, 1914–1918
    An Accident Waiting to Happen
    Legacies of the Great War
Capitalism Unraveling: The Great
    Depression
Democracy Denied: Comparing
    Italy, Germany, and Japan
    The Fascist Alternative in Europe
    Hitler and the Nazis
    Japanese Authoritarianism
A Second World War
    The Road to War in Asia
    The Road to War in Europe
    The Outcomes of Global Conflict
The Recovery of Europe
Reflections: War and Remembrance:
    Learning from History
Considering the Evidence
    Documents: Ideologies of the
        Axis Powers
    Visual Sources: Propaganda and
        Critique in World War I

"I was told that I was fighting a war that would end all wars, but that wasn't the case." Spoken a few years before his death, these were the thoughts of Alfred Anderson, a World War I veteran who died in Scotland in November 2005, at the age of 109. He was apparently the last survivor of the famous Christmas truce of 1914, when British and German soldiers, enemies on the battlefield of that war, briefly mingled, exchanged gifts, and played football in the no-man's land that lay between their entrenchments in Belgium. He had been especially dismayed when in 2003 his own unit, the famous Black Watch regiment, was ordered into Iraq along with other British forces.[1] Despite his disappointment at the many conflicts that followed World War I, Anderson's own lifetime had witnessed the fulfillment of the promise of the Christmas truce. By the time he died, the major European nations had put aside their centuries-long hostilities, and war between Britain and Germany, which had erupted twice in the twentieth century, seemed unthinkable. What happened to Europe, and to the larger civilization of which it was a part, during the life of this one man is the focus of this chapter.

THE "GREAT WAR," WHICH CAME TO BE CALLED THE FIRST WORLD WAR (1914–1918), effectively launched the twentieth century, considered as a new phase of world history. That bitter conflict—essentially a European civil war with a global reach—was followed by the economic meltdown of the Great Depression, by the rise of Nazi Germany and the horror of the Holocaust, and by

The United States and World War II: The Second World War and its aftermath marked the decisive emergence of the United States as a global superpower. In this official 1943 poster, U.S. soldiers march forward to "fight for liberty" against fascism while casting a sideways glance for inspiration at the ragged colonial militiamen of their Revolutionary War. (Library of Congress, LC-USZC4-2119)

an even bloodier and more destructive World War II. During those three decades, Western Europe, for more than a century the dominant and dominating center of the modern "world system," largely self-destructed, in a process with profound and long-term implications far beyond Europe itself. By 1945, an outside observer might well have thought that Western civilization, which for several centuries was in the ascendancy on the global stage, had damaged itself beyond repair.

In the second half of the century, however, that civilization proved quite resilient. Its Western European heartland recovered remarkably from the devastation of war, rebuilt its industrial economy, and set aside its war-prone nationalist passions in a loose European Union. But as Europe revived after 1945, it lost both its overseas colonial possessions and its position as the political, economic, and military core of Western civilization. That role now passed across the Atlantic to the United States, marking a major change in the historical development of the West. The offspring now overshadowed its parent.

Map 21.1   The World in 1914
A map of the world in 1914 shows an unprecedented situation in which one people—Europeans or those of European descent—exercised enormous control and influence over virtually the entire planet.

The First World War: European Civilization in Crisis, 1914–1918

Since 1500, Europe had assumed an increasingly prominent position on the global stage, driven by its growing military capacity and the marvels of its Scientific and Industrial revolutions. By 1900, Europeans, or people with a European ancestry, largely controlled the world's other peoples through their formal empires, their informal influence, or the weight of their numbers (see Map 21.1). That unique situation pro-

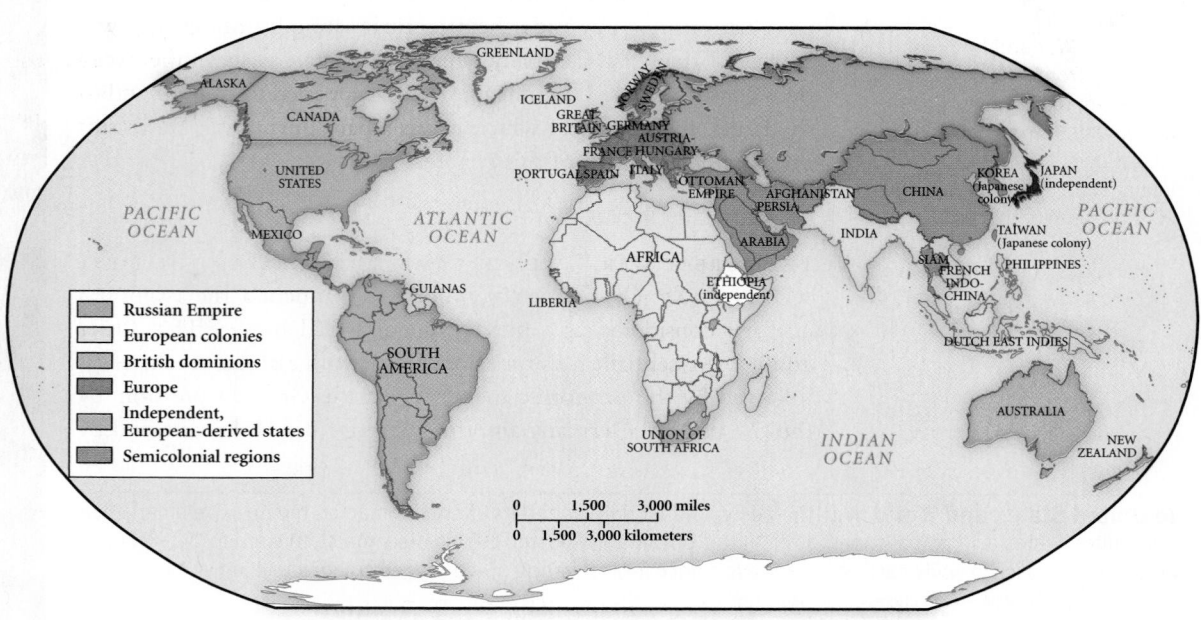

vided the foundation for Europeans' pride, self-confidence, and sense of superiority. Few could have imagined that this "proud tower" of European dominance would lie shattered less than a half century later. The starting point in that unraveling was the First World War.

An Accident Waiting to Happen

Europe's modern transformation and its global ascendancy were certainly not accompanied by a growing unity or stability among its own peoples—quite the opposite. The most obvious division was among its competing states, a long-standing feature of European political life. Those historical rivalries further sharpened as both Italy and Germany joined their fragmented territories into two major new powers around 1870. German unification had occurred in the context of a short war with France (the Franco-Prussian War of 1870–1871), which embittered relations between these two large countries for the next half century. More generally, the arrival on the international scene of a powerful and rapidly industrializing Germany, seeking its "place in the sun" as Kaiser Wilhelm put it, was a disruptive new element in European political life, especially for the more established powers, such as Britain, France, and Russia. Since the defeat of Napoleon in 1815, a fragile and fluctuating balance of power had generally maintained the peace among Europe's major countries. By the early twentieth century, that balance of power was expressed in two rival alliances, the Triple Alliance of Germany, Austria, and Italy and the Triple Entente of Russia, France, and Britain. It was those commitments, undertaken in the interests of national security, that transformed a minor incident in the Balkans into a conflagration that consumed all of Europe.

That incident occurred on June 28, 1914, when a Serbian nationalist assassinated the heir to the Austrian throne, Archduke Franz Ferdinand. To the rulers of Austria, the surging nationalism of Serbian Slavs was a mortal threat to the cohesion of their fragile multinational empire, which included other Slavic peoples as well, and they determined to crush it. But behind Austria lay its far more powerful ally, Germany; and behind tiny Serbia lay Russia, with its self-proclaimed mission of protecting other Slavic peoples; and allied to Russia were the French and the British. Thus a system of alliances intended to keep the peace created obligations that drew the Great Powers of Europe into a general war by early August 1914 (see Map 21.2).

The outbreak of that war was an accident, in that none of the major states planned or predicted the archduke's assassination or deliberately sought a prolonged conflict, but the system of rigid alliances made Europe prone to that kind of accident. Moreover, behind those alliances lay other factors that contributed to the eruption of war and shaped its character. One of them was a mounting popular nationalism (see pp. 796–800). Slavic nationalism and Austrian opposition to it certainly lay at the heart of the war's beginning. More important, the rulers of the major countries of Europe saw the world as an arena of conflict and competition among rival nation-states. The Great Powers of Europe competed intensely for colonies, spheres

■ **Explanation**
What aspects of Europe's nineteenth-century history contributed to the First World War?

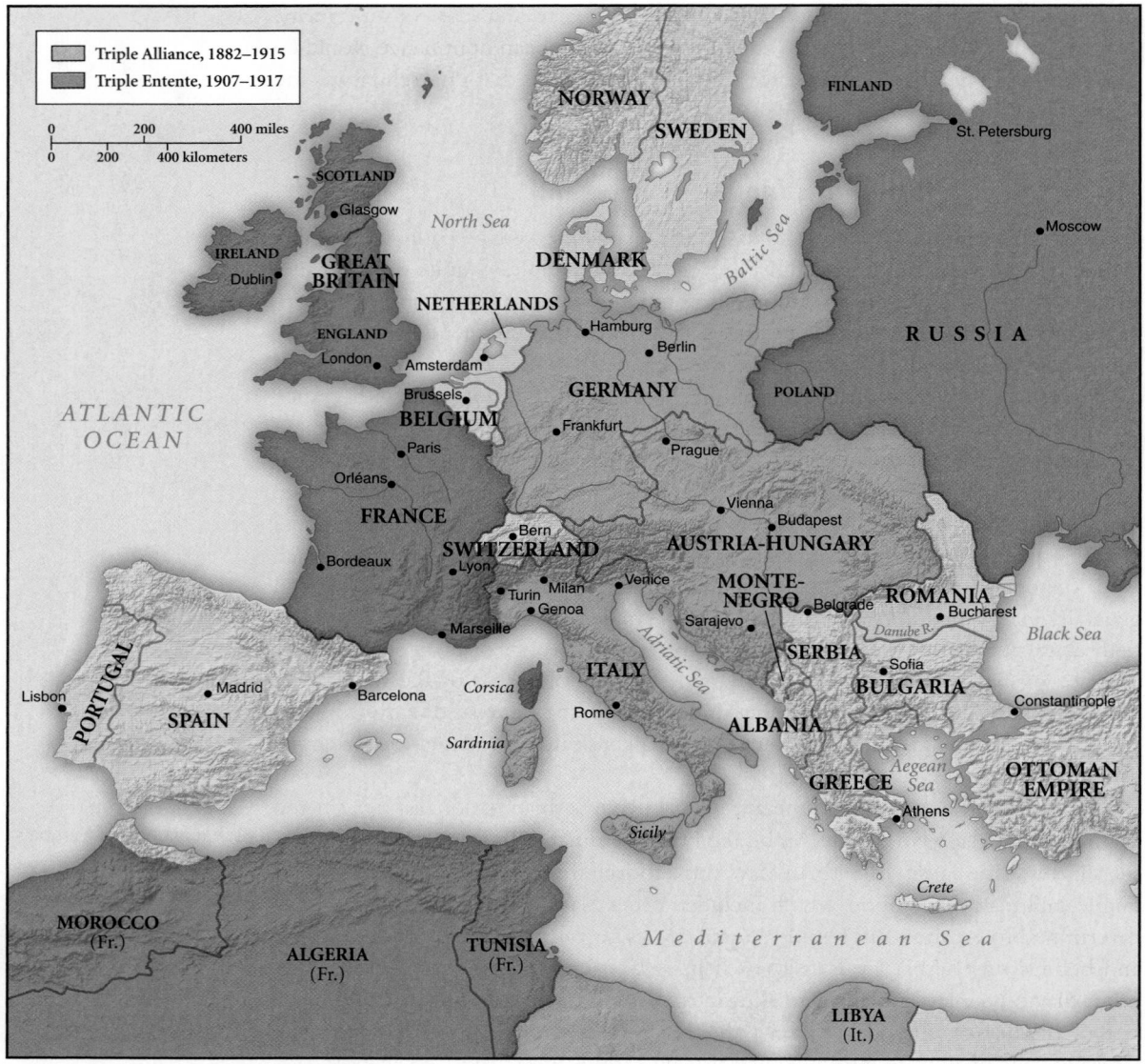

Map 21.2   Europe on the Eve of World War I
Despite many elements of common culture, Europe in 1914 was a powder keg, with its major states armed to the teeth and divided into two rival alliances. In the early stages of the war, Italy changed sides to join the French, British, and Russians.

of influence, and superiority in armaments. Schools, mass media, and military service had convinced millions of ordinary Europeans that their national identities were profoundly and personally meaningful. The public pressure of these competing nationalisms allowed statesmen little room for compromise and ensured widespread popular support, at least initially, for the decision to go to war. Men rushed to recruiting offices, fearing that the war might end before they could enlist. Celebratory parades sent them off to the front. For conservative governments, the prospect of war was a welcome occasion for national unity in the face of the mounting class- and gender-based conflicts of European society.

Also contributing to the war was an industrialized militarism. Europe's armed rivalries had long ensured that military men enjoyed great social prestige, and most heads of state wore uniforms in public. All of the Great Powers had substantial standing armies and, except for Britain, relied on conscription (compulsory military service) to staff them. One expression of the quickening rivalry among these states was a mounting arms race in naval warships, particularly between Germany and Britain. Furthermore, each of the major states had developed elaborate "war plans" spelling out in great detail the movement of men and materials that should occur immediately upon the outbreak of war. Such plans created a hair-trigger mentality, since each country had an incentive to strike first so that its particular strategy could be implemented on schedule and without interruption or surprise. The rapid industrialization of warfare had generated an array of novel weapons, including submarines, tanks, airplanes, poison gas, machines guns, and barbed wire. This new military technology contributed to the staggering casualties of the war, including some 10 million deaths; perhaps twice that number wounded, crippled, or disfigured; and countless women for whom there would be no husbands or children.

Europe's imperial reach around the world likewise shaped the scope and conduct of the war. It funneled colonial troops and laborers by the hundreds of thousands into the war effort, with men from Africa, India, China, Southeast Asia, Australia, New Zealand, Canada, and South Africa taking part in the conflict (see Visual Source 21.3, p. 1023). Battles raged in Africa and the South Pacific as British and French forces sought to seize German colonies abroad. Japan, allied with Britain, took various German possessions in China and the Pacific and made heavy demands on China itself. The Ottoman Empire, which entered the conflict on the side of Germany, became the site of intense military actions and witnessed an Arab revolt against Ottoman control. Finally, the United States, after initially seeking to avoid involvement in European quarrels, joined the war in 1917 when German submarines threatened American shipping. Some 2 million Americans took part in the first U.S. military action on European soil and helped turn the tide in favor of the British and French. Thus the war, though centered in Europe, had global dimensions and certainly merited its familiar title as a "world war."

Legacies of the Great War

The Great War was a conflict that shattered almost every expectation. Most Europeans believed in the late summer of 1914 that "the boys will be home by Christmas," but instead the war ground relentlessly on for more than four years before ending in a German defeat in November 1918. (See Visual Sources: Propaganda and Critique in World War I, pp. 1019–27, for various representations of the war.) At

■ **Change**
In what ways did World War I mark new departures in the history of the twentieth century?

THESE WOMEN ARE DOING THEIR BIT

LEARN TO MAKE MUNITIONS

Women and the Great War
World War I temporarily brought a halt to the women's suffrage movement as well as to women's activities on behalf of international peace. Most women on both sides actively supported their countries' war efforts, as suggested by this British wartime poster, inviting women to work in the munitions industry. (Eileen Tweedy/The Art Archive)

the beginning, most military experts expected a war of movement and attack, but it soon bogged down on the western front into a war of attrition, in which trench warfare resulted in enormous casualties while gaining or losing only a few yards of muddy, blood-soaked ground (see Visual Source 21.4, p. 1025). Extended battles lasting months—such as those at Verdun and the Somme—generated casualties of a million or more each, as the destructive potential of industrialized warfare made itself tragically felt. Moreover, everywhere it became a "total war," requiring the mobilization of each country's entire population. Thus the authority of governments expanded greatly. The German state, for example, assumed such control over the economy that its policies became known as "war socialism." Vast propaganda campaigns sought to arouse citizens by depicting a cruel and inhuman enemy who killed innocent children and violated women. In factories, women replaced the men who had left for the battle-front, while labor unions agreed to suspend strikes and accept sacrifices for the common good.

No less surprising were the outcomes of the war. In the European cockpit of that conflict, unprecedented casualties, particularly among elite and well-educated groups, and physical destruction, especially in France, led to a widespread disillusionment among intellectuals with their own civilization (see Visual Source 21.5, p. 1026). The war seemed to mock the Enlightenment values of progress, tolerance, and rationality. Who could believe any longer that the West was superior or that its vaunted science and technology were unquestionably good things? In the most famous novel to emerge from the war, the German veteran Erich Remarque's *All Quiet on the Western Front*, one soldier expressed what many no doubt felt: "It must all be lies and of no account when the culture of a thousand years could not prevent this stream of blood being poured out."

Furthermore, from the collapse of the German, Russian, and Austrian empires emerged a new map of Central Europe with an independent Poland, Czechoslovakia, Yugoslavia, and other nations (see Map 21.3). Such new states were based on the principle of "national self-determination," a concept championed by the U.S. president Woodrow Wilson, but each of them also contained dissatisfied ethnic minorities, who claimed the same principle. In Russia, the strains of war triggered a vast revolutionary upheaval that brought the radical Bolsheviks to power in 1917 and took Russia out of the war. Thus was launched world communism, which was to play such a prominent role in the history of the twentieth century (see Chapter 22).

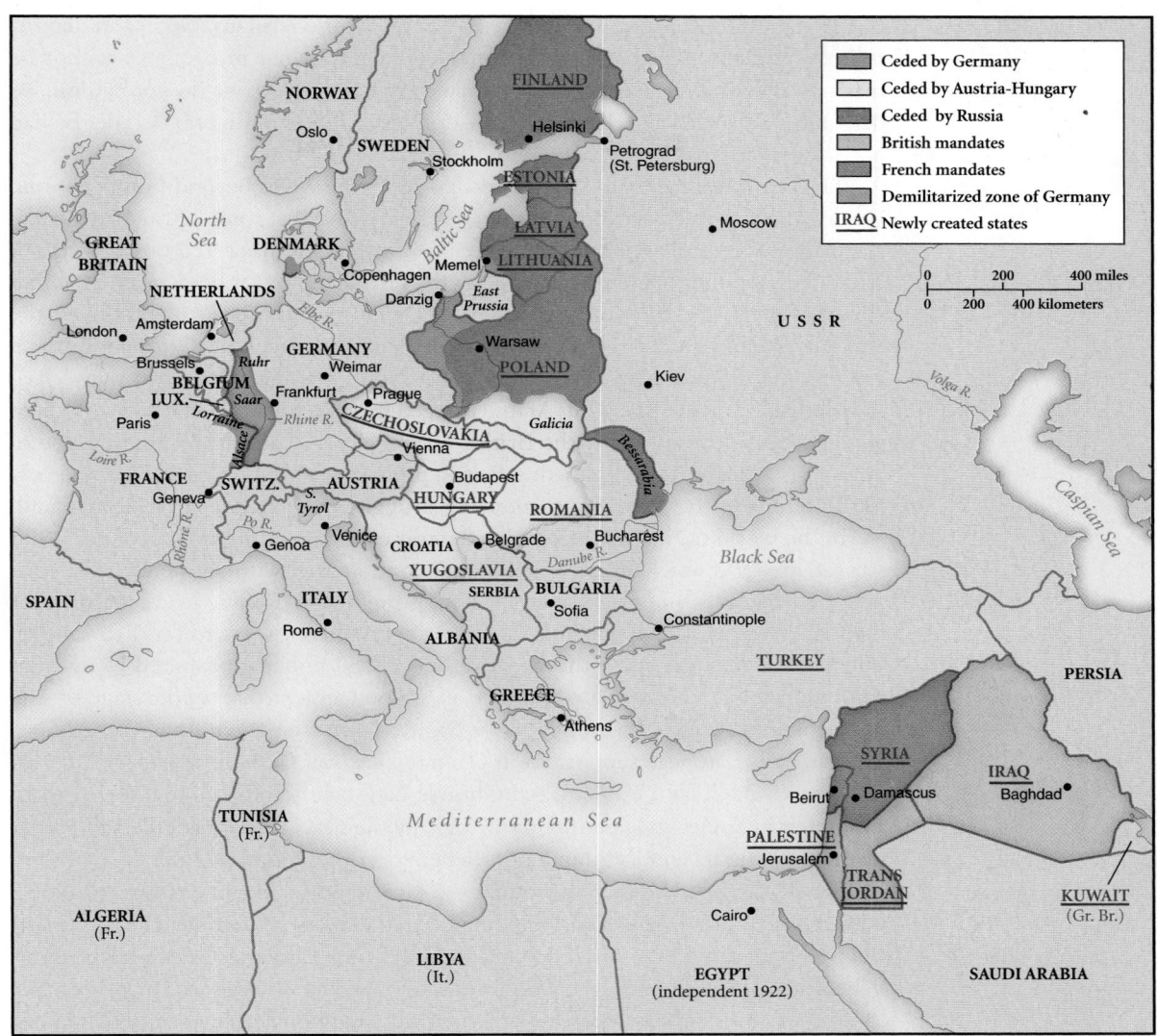

Map 21.3   Europe and the Middle East after World War I

The Great War brought into existence a number of new states that were carved out of the old German, Austro-Hungarian, Russian, and Ottoman empires. Turkey and the new states in Europe were independent, but those in the Middle East — Syria, Palestine, Iraq, and Transjordan — were administered by Britain or France as mandates of the League of Nations.

The Treaty of Versailles, which formally concluded the war in 1919, proved in retrospect to have established conditions that generated a second world war only twenty years later. In that treaty, Germany lost its colonial empire and 15 percent of its European territory, was required to pay heavy reparations to the winners, had its military forces severely restricted, and had to accept sole responsibility for the outbreak of the war. All of this created immense resentment in Germany. One of the country's many demobilized and disillusioned soldiers declared in 1922: "It cannot be that two million Germans should have fallen in vain. . . . No, we do not pardon, we demand—vengeance."[2] His name was Adolf Hitler, and within two decades he had begun to exact that vengeance.

The Great War generated profound changes in the world beyond Europe as well. During the war itself, Ottoman authorities, suspecting that some of their Armenian population were collaborating with the Russian enemy, massacred or deported an estimated 1 million Armenians. Although the term had not yet been invented, those atrocities merit the label of "genocide" and established a precedent on which the Nazis later built. The war also brought a final end to a declining Ottoman Empire, creating the modern map of the Middle East, with the new states of Turkey, Syria, Iraq, Jordan, and Palestine. Thus Arabs emerged from Turkish rule, but many of them were governed for a time by the British or French, as "mandates" of the League of Nations (see Map 21.3). Conflicting British promises to both Arabs and Jews regarding Palestine set the stage for an enduring struggle over that ancient and holy land.

In the world of European colonies, the war echoed loudly. Millions of Asian and African men had watched Europeans butcher one another without mercy, had gained new military skills and political awareness, and returned home with less respect for their rulers and with expectations for better treatment as a reward for their service. To gain Indian support for the war, the British had publicly promised to put that colony on the road to self-government, an announcement that set the stage for the independence struggle that followed. In East Asia, Japan emerged strengthened from the war, with European support for its claim to take over German territory and privileges in China. That news enraged Chinese nationalists and among a few sparked an interest in Soviet-style communism, for only the new communist rulers of Russia seemed willing to end the imperialist penetration of China.

Finally, the First World War brought the United States to center stage as a global power. Its manpower had contributed much to the defeat of Germany, and its financial resources turned the United States from a debtor nation into Europe's creditor. When the American president Woodrow Wilson arrived in Paris for the peace conference in 1919, he was greeted with an almost religious enthusiasm. His famous Fourteen Points seemed to herald a new kind of international life, one based on moral principles rather than secret deals and imperialist machinations. Particularly appealing to many was his idea for the League of Nations, a new international peacekeeping organization based on the principle of "collective security" and intended to avoid any repetition of the horrors that had just ended. Wilson's idealistic vision largely failed, however. Germany was treated more harshly than he had wished. And in his own country, the U.S. Senate refused to join the League, on which he had pinned his hopes for a lasting peace. Its opponents feared that Americans would be forced to bow to "the will of other nations." That refusal seriously weakened the League of Nations as a vehicle for a new international order.

Capitalism Unraveling: The Great Depression

The aftermath of war brought substantial social and cultural changes to the European and American victors in that conflict. Integrating millions of returning veterans into ordinary civilian life was no easy task, for they had experienced horrors almost beyond imagination. Governments sought to accommodate them—for example, with housing programs called "homes for heroes" and with an emphasis on traditional family values. French authorities proclaimed Mother's Day as a new holiday designed to encourage childbearing and thus replace the millions lost in the war.

Nonetheless, the war had loosened the hold of tradition in many ways. Enormous casualties promoted social mobility, allowing commoners to move into positions previously dominated by aristocrats. Women increasingly gained the right to vote. Young middle-class women, sometimes known as "flappers," began to flout convention by appearing at nightclubs, smoking, dancing, drinking hard liquor, cutting their hair short, wearing revealing clothing, and generally expressing a more open sexuality. A new consumerism encouraged those who could to acquire cars, washing machines, vacuum cleaners, electric irons, gas ovens, and other newly available products. Radio and the movies now became vehicles of popular culture, transmitting American jazz to Europe and turning Hollywood stars into international celebrities.

Far and away the most influential change of the postwar decades lay in the Great Depression. If World War I represented the political collapse of Europe, this catastrophic downturn suggested that its economic system was likewise failing. During the nineteenth century, European industrial capitalism had spurred the most substantial economic growth in world history and had raised the living standards of millions, but to many people it was a troubling system. Its very success generated an individualistic materialism that seemed to conflict with older values of community and spiritual life. To socialists and many others, its immense social inequalities were unacceptable. Furthermore, its evident instability—with cycles of boom and bust, expansion and recession—generated profound anxiety and threatened the livelihood of both industrial workers and those who had gained a modest toehold in the middle class.

■ **Connection**

In what ways was the Great Depression a global phenomenon?

Never had the flaws of capitalism been so evident or so devastating as during the decade that followed the outbreak of the Great Depression in 1929. All across the Euro-American heartland of the capitalist world, this vaunted economic system seemed to unravel. For the rich, it meant contracting stock prices that wiped out paper fortunes almost overnight. On the day that the American stock market initially crashed (October 24, 1929), eleven Wall Street financiers committed suicide, some by jumping out of skyscrapers. Banks closed, and many people lost their life savings. Investment dried up, world trade dropped by 62 percent within a few years, and businesses contracted when they were unable to sell their products. For ordinary people, the worst feature of the Great Depression was the loss of work. Unemployment soared everywhere, and in both Germany and the United States it

The Great Depression
This famous photograph of an impoverished American mother of three children, which was taken in 1936, came to symbolize the agonies of the Depression and the apparent breakdown of capitalism in the United States. (Library of Congress)

reached 30 percent or more by 1932 (see the Snapshot on p. 987). Vacant factories, soup kitchens, bread lines, shantytowns, and beggars came to symbolize the human reality of this economic disaster.

Explaining its onset, its spread from America to Europe and beyond, and its continuation for a decade has been a complicated task for historians. Part of the story lies in the United States' booming economy during the 1920s. In a country physically untouched by the war, wartime demand had greatly stimulated agricultural and industrial capacity. By the end of the 1920s, its farms and factories were producing more goods than could be sold because a highly unequal distribution of income meant that many people could not afford to buy the products that American factories were churning out. Nor were major European countries able to purchase those goods. Germany and Austria had to make huge reparation payments and were able to do so only with extensive U.S. loans. Britain and France, which were much indebted to the United States, depended on those reparations to repay their loans. Furthermore, Europeans generally had recovered enough to begin producing some of their own goods, and their expanding production further reduced the demand for American products. Meanwhile, a speculative stock market frenzy had driven up stock prices to an unsustainable level. When that bubble burst in late 1929, this intricately connected and fragile economic network across the Atlantic collapsed like a house of cards.

Much as Europe's worldwide empires had globalized the war, so too its economic linkages globalized the Great Depression. Countries or colonies tied to exporting one or two products were especially hard-hit. Chile, which was dependent on copper mining, found the value of its exports cut by 80 percent. In an effort to maintain the price of coffee, Brazil destroyed enough of its coffee crop to have supplied the world for a year. Colonial Southeast Asia, the world's major rubber-producing region, saw the demand for its primary export drop dramatically as automobile sales in Europe and the United States were cut in half. In Britain's West African colony of the Gold Coast (present-day Ghana), farmers who had staked their economic lives on producing cocoa for the world market were badly hurt by the collapse of commodity prices. Depending on a single crop or product rendered these societies extraordinarily vulnerable to changes in the world market.

The Great Depression sharply challenged the governments of capitalist countries, which generally had believed that the economy would regulate itself through the market. The market's apparent failure to self-correct led many people to look twice at the Soviet Union, a communist state whose more equal distribution of income and state-controlled economy had generated an impressive growth with no unemployment in the 1930s, even as the capitalist world was reeling. No Western country opted for the dictatorial and draconian socialism of the USSR, but in Britain, France, and Scandinavia, the Depression energized a "democratic socialism" that sought greater regulation of the economy and a more equal distribution of wealth through peaceful means and electoral politics.

The United States' response to the Great Depression came in the form of President Franklin Roosevelt's New Deal (1933–1942), an experimental combination of reforms seeking to restart economic growth and to prevent similar calamities in the future. These measures reflected the thinking of John Maynard Keynes, a prominent British economist who argued that government actions and spending programs could moderate the recessions and depressions to which capitalist economies were prone. Although this represented a departure from standard economic thinking, none of it was really "socialist," even if some of the New Deal's opponents labeled it as such.

Nonetheless, Roosevelt's efforts permanently altered the relationship among government, the private economy, and individual citizens. Through immediate programs

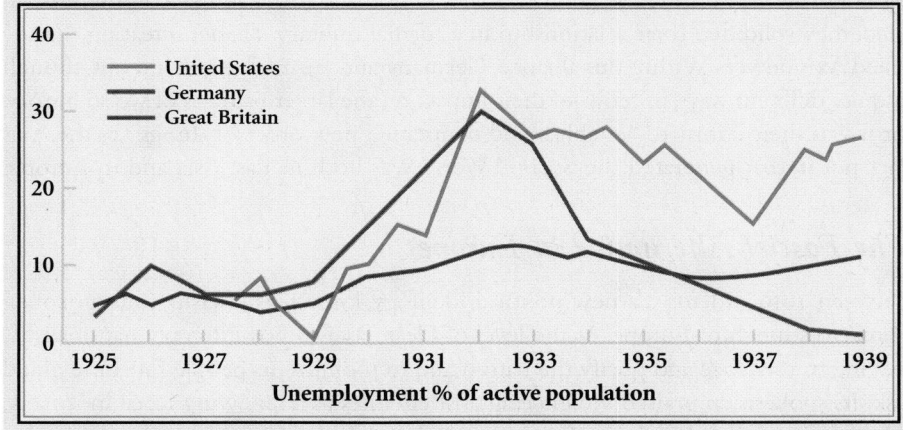

$\mathcal{S}$napshot   **Comparing the Impact of the Depression**[3]

As industrial production dropped during the Depression, unemployment soared. Yet the larger Western capitalist countries differed considerably in the duration and extent of this unemployment. Note especially the differences between Germany and the United States. How might you account for this difference?

Unemployment % of active population

of public spending (for dams, highways, bridges, and parks), the New Deal sought to prime the pump of the economy and thus reduce unemployment. The New Deal's longer-term reforms, such as the Social Security system, the minimum wage, and various relief and welfare programs, attempted to create a modest economic safety net to sustain the poor, the unemployed, and the elderly. By supporting labor unions, the New Deal strengthened workers in their struggles with business owners or managers. Subsidies for farmers gave rise to a permanent agribusiness that encouraged continued production even as prices fell. Finally, a mounting number of government agencies marked a new degree of federal regulation and supervision of the economy.

Ultimately, none of the New Deal's programs worked very well to end the Great Depression. Not until the massive government spending required by World War II kicked in did that economic disaster abate in the United States. The most successful efforts to cope with the Depression came from unlikely places—Nazi Germany and an increasingly militaristic Japan.

Democracy Denied: Comparing Italy, Germany, and Japan

Despite the victory of the democratic powers in World War I—Britain, France, and the United States—their democratic political ideals and their cultural values celebrating individual freedom came under sharp attack in the aftermath of that bloody conflict. One challenge derived from communism, which was initiated in the Russian Revolution of 1917 and expressed most fully in the cold war during the second half of the twentieth century (see Chapter 22). In the 1920s and 1930s, however, the more immediate challenge to the victors in the Great War came from highly authoritarian, intensely nationalistic, territorially aggressive, and ferociously anticommunist regimes, particularly those that took shape in Italy, Germany, and Japan. (See Documents: Ideologies of the Axis Powers, pp. 1010–18, for the ideas underlying these regimes.) The common features of these three countries drew them together by 1936–1937 in a political alliance directed against the Soviet Union and international communism. In 1940, they solidified their relationship in a formal military alliance, creating the so-called Axis powers. Within this alliance, Germany and Japan clearly stand out, though in quite different ways, in terms of their impact on the larger patterns of world history, for it was their efforts to "establish and maintain a new order of things," as the Axis Pact put it, that generated the Second World War both in East Asia and in Europe.

The Fascist Alternative in Europe

■ Change

In what ways did fascism challenge the ideas and practices of European liberalism and democracy?

Between 1919 and 1945, a new political ideology, known as fascism, found expression across much of Europe. At the level of ideas, fascism was intensely nationalistic, seeking to revitalize and purify the nation and to mobilize its people for some grand task. Its spokesmen praised violence against enemies as a renewing force in society, celebrated action rather than reflection, and placed their faith in a charismatic leader.

Fascists also bitterly condemned individualism, liberalism, feminism, parliamentary democracy, and communism, all of which, they argued, divided and weakened the nation. In their determination to overthrow existing regimes, they were revolutionary; in their embrace of traditional values and their opposition to much of modern life, however, they were conservative or reactionary.

Such ideas appealed to aggrieved people all across the social spectrum. In the devastation that followed the First World War, the numbers of such people grew substantially. In the aftermath of the Russian Revolution of 1917, some among the middle and upper classes saw the rise of socialism and communism as a dire threat; small-scale merchants, artisans, and farmers feared the loss of their independence to either big business or socialist revolution; demobilized soldiers had few prospects and nursed many resentments; and intellectuals were appalled by the materialism and artificiality of modern life. Such people had lost faith in the capacity of liberal democracy and capitalism to create a good society and to protect their interests. Some among them proved a receptive audience for the message of fascism.

Small fascist movements appeared in many Western European countries, including France, Great Britain, and the Netherlands, but they had little political impact. More substantial movements took shape in Austria, Hungary, and Romania. In Spain, the rise of a fascist movement led to a bitter civil war (1936–1939) and a dictatorial regime that lasted into the 1970s. But in Italy and Germany, such movements achieved prolonged power in major states, with devastating consequences for Europe and the world.

The fascist alternative took shape first in Italy. That nation had become a unified state only in 1870 and had not yet developed a modern democratic culture. In the early twentieth century, conservative landlords still dominated much of the countryside. Northern Italy, however, had begun to industrialize in the late nineteenth century, generating the characteristic tension between a factory working class and a substantial middle class. The First World War gave rise to resentful veterans, many of them unemployed, and to patriots who believed that Italy had not gained the territory it deserved from the Treaty of Versailles. During the serious economic downturn after World War I, trade unions, peasant movements, and various communist and socialist parties threatened the established social order with a wave of strikes and land seizures.

Into this setting stepped a charismatic orator and a former journalist with a socialist background, Benito Mussolini (1883–1945). With the help of a private army of disillusioned veterans and jobless men known as the Black Shirts, Mussolini swept to power in 1922, promising an alternative to both communism and ineffective democratic rule. Considerable violence accompanied Mussolini's rise to power as bands of Black Shirts destroyed the offices of socialist newspapers and attacked striking workers. Fearful of communism, big business threw its support to Mussolini, who promised order in the streets, an end to bickering party-based politics, and the maintenance of the traditional social order. That Mussolini's government allegedly made the trains run on time became evidence that these promises might be fulfilled. The symbol of this

The Faces of European Fascism
Benito Mussolini (left) and Adolf Hitler came to symbolize fascism in Europe in the several decades between the two world wars. In this photograph from September 1937, they are reviewing German troops in Munich during Mussolini's visit to Germany, a trip that deepened the growing relationship between their two countries.
(Luce/Keystone/Getty Images)

■ **Comparison**

What was distinctive about the German expression of fascism? What was the basis of popular support for the Nazis?

movement was the *fasces*, a bundle of birch rods bound together around an axe, which represented power and strength in unity and derived from ancient Rome. Thus fascism was born. (See Document 22.1, pp. 1010–12, for Mussolini's understanding of fascism.)

Mussolini promised his mass following major social reforms, though in practice he concentrated instead on consolidating the power of the central state. Democracy in Italy was suspended, and opponents were imprisoned, deported, or sometimes executed. Independent labor unions and peasant groups were disbanded, as were all political parties except the Fascist Party. In economic life, a "corporate state" took shape, at least in theory, in which workers, employers, and various professional groups were organized into "corporations" that were supposed to settle their disagreements and determine economic policy under the supervision of the state.

Culturally, fascists invoked various aspects of traditional Italian life. Mussolini, though personally an atheist, embraced the Catholic culture of Italy in a series of agreements with the Church (the Lateran Accords of 1929) that made the Vatican a sovereign state and Catholicism Italy's national religion. In fascist propaganda, women were portrayed in highly traditional terms as domestic creatures, particularly as mothers creating new citizens for the fascist state, with no hint of equality or liberation. Nationalists were delighted when Italy invaded Ethiopia in 1935, avenging the embarrassing defeat that Italians suffered at the hands of Ethiopians in 1896. In the eyes of Mussolini and fascist believers, all of this was the beginning of a "new Roman Empire" that would revitalize Italian society and give it a global mission.

Hitler and the Nazis

Far more important in the long run was the German expression of European fascism, which took shape as the Nazi Party under the leadership of Adolf Hitler (1889–1945). In many respects, it was similar to its Italian counterpart. Both espoused an extreme nationalism, openly advocated the use of violence as a political tool, generated a single-party dictatorship, were led by charismatic figures, despised parliamentary democracy, hated communism, and viewed war as a positive and ennobling experience.[4] The circumstances that gave rise to the Nazi movement were likewise broadly similar to those of Italian fascism, although the Nazis did not achieve national power until 1933.

The end of World War I witnessed the collapse of the German imperial government, itself less than a half century old. It was left to the democratic politicians of a new government—known as the Weimar Republic—to negotiate a peace settlement with the victorious allies. Traditional elites, who had withdrawn from public life in disgrace, never explicitly took responsibility for Germany's defeat; instead they attacked the democratic politicians who had the unenviable task of signing the Treaty of Versailles and enforcing it. In this setting, some began to argue that German military forces had not really lost the war but that civilian socialists, communists, and Jews had betrayed the nation, "stabbing it in the back."

As in postwar Italy, liberal or democratic political leaders during the 1920s faced considerable hostility. Paramilitary groups of veterans known as the Freikorps assassinated hundreds of supporters of the Weimar regime. Gradually, some among the middle classes as well as conservative landowners joined in opposition to the Weimar regime, both groups threatened by the ruinous inflation of 1923 and then the Great Depression. The German economy largely ground to a halt in the early 1930s amid massive unemployment among workers and the middle class alike. Everyone demanded decisive action from the state. Many industrial workers looked to socialists and communists for solutions; others turned to fascism. Large numbers of middle-class people deserted moderate political parties in favor of conservative and radical right-wing movements.

This was the context in which Adolf Hitler's National Socialist, or Nazi, Party gained growing public support. Founded shortly after the end of World War I, the Nazi Party under Hitler's leadership proclaimed a message of intense German nationalism cast in terms of racial superiority, bitter hatred for Jews as an alien presence, passionate opposition to communism, a determination to rescue Germany from the humiliating requirements of the Treaty of Versailles, and a willingness to decisively tackle the country's economic problems. Throughout the 1920s, the Nazis were a minor presence in German politics, gaining only 2.6 percent of the vote in the national elections of 1928. Just four years later, however, in the wake of the Depression's terrible impact and the Weimar government's inability to respond effectively, the Nazis attracted 37 percent of the vote. In 1933, Hitler was legally installed as the chancellor of the German government. Thus did the Weimar Republic, a democratic regime that never gained broad support, give way to the Third Reich.

Once in power, Hitler moved quickly to consolidate Nazi control of Germany. All other political parties were outlawed; independent labor unions were ended; thousands of opponents were arrested; and the press and radio came under state control. Far more thoroughly than Mussolini in Italy, Hitler and the Nazis established their control over German society.[5]

By the late 1930s, Hitler apparently had the support of a considerable majority of the population, in large measure because his policies successfully brought Germany out of the Depression. The government invested heavily in projects such as superhighways, bridges, canals, and public buildings and, after 1935, in rebuilding and rearming the country's diminished military forces. These policies drove down the number of unemployed Germans from 6.2 million in 1932 to fewer than 500,000 in 1937. Two years later Germany had a labor shortage. Erna Kranz, a teenager in the 1930s, later remembered the early years of Nazi rule as "a glimmer of hope...not just for the unemployed but for everybody because we all knew that we were downtrodden.... It was a good time...there was order and discipline."[6] Millions agreed with her.

Other factors as well contributed to Nazi popularity. Like Italian fascists, Hitler too appealed to rural and traditional values that many Germans feared losing as their country modernized. In Hitler's thinking and in Nazi propaganda, Jews became the symbol of the urban, capitalist, and foreign influences that were undermining traditional German culture. Thus the Nazis reflected and reinforced a broader and long-established current of anti-Semitism that had deep roots in much of Europe. In his book *Mein Kampf* (*My Struggle*), Hitler outlined his case against the Jews and his call for the racial purification of Germany in vitriolic terms. (See Document 21.2, pp. 1012–15, for a statement of Hitler's thinking.)

Far more than elsewhere, this insistence on a racial revolution was a central feature of the Nazi program and differed from the racial attitudes in Italy, where Jews were a tiny minority of the population and deeply assimilated into Italian culture. Early on, Mussolini had ridiculed Nazi racism, but as Germany and Italy drew closer together, Italy too began a program of overt anti-Semitism, though nothing approaching the extremes that characterized Nazi Germany.

Upon coming to power, Hitler implemented policies that increasingly restricted Jewish life. Soon Jews were excluded from universities, professional organizations, and civil employment. In 1935, the Nuremberg Laws ended German citizenship for Jews and forbade marriage or sexual relations between Jews and Germans. On the night of November 9, 1938, known as Kristallnacht, persecution gave way to terror, when Nazis smashed and looted Jewish shops. Such actions made clear the Nazis' determination to rid Germany of its Jewish population, thus putting into effect the most radical element of Hitler's program. Still, it was not yet apparent that this "racial revolution" would mean the mass killing of Europe's Jews. That horrendous development emerged only in the context of World War II.

Also sustaining Nazi rule were massive torchlight ceremonies celebrating the superiority of the

Nazi Hatred of the Jews
This picture served as the cover of a highly anti-Semitic book of photographs entitled *The Eternal Jew*, published by the Nazis in 1937. It effectively summed up many of the themes of the Nazi case against the Jews, showing them as ugly and subhuman, as the instigators of communism (the hammer and sickle on a map of Russia), as greedy capitalists (coins in one hand), and as seeking to dominate the world (the whip). (akg-images)

German race and its folk culture. In these settings, Hitler was the mystical leader, the Führer, a mesmerizing orator who would lead Germany to national greatness and individual Germans to personal fulfillment.

If World War I and the Great Depression brought about the political and economic collapse of Europe, the Nazi phenomenon represented a moral collapse within the West, deriving from a highly selective incorporation of earlier strands of European culture. On the one hand, the Nazis actively rejected some of the values—rationalism, tolerance, democracy, human equality—that for many people had defined the core of Western civilization since the Enlightenment. On the other hand, they claimed the legacy of modern science, particularly in their concern to classify and rank various human groups. Thus they drew heavily on the "scientific racism" of the nineteenth century and its expression in phrenology, which linked the size and shape of the skull to human behavior and personality. Moreover, in their effort to purify German society, the Nazis reflected the Enlightenment confidence in the perfectibility of humankind and in the social engineering necessary to achieve it.

Japanese Authoritarianism

In various ways, the modern history of Japan paralleled that of Italy and Germany. All three were newcomers to great power status, with Japan joining the club of industrializing and empire-building states only in the late nineteenth century as its sole Asian member (see pp. 898–901). Like Italy and Germany, Japan had a rather limited experience with democratic politics, for its elected parliament was constrained by a very small electorate (only 1.5 million men in 1917) and by the exalted position of a semidivine emperor and his small coterie of elite advisers. During the 1930s, Japan too moved toward authoritarian government and a denial of democracy at home, even as it launched an aggressive program of territorial expansion in East Asia.

Despite these broad similarities, Japan's history in the first half of the twentieth century was clearly distinctive. In sharp contrast to Italy and Germany, Japan's participation in World War I was minimal, and its economy grew considerably as other industrialized countries were engaged in the European war. At the peace conference ending that war, Japan was seated as an equal participant, allied with the winning side of democratic countries such as Britain, France, and the United States.

During the 1920s, Japan seemed to be moving toward a more democratic politics and Western cultural values. Universal male suffrage was achieved in 1925; cabinets led by leaders of the major parties, rather than bureaucrats or imperial favorites, governed the country; and a two-party system began to emerge. Supporters of these developments generally embraced the dignity of the individual, free expression of ideas, and greater gender equality. Education expanded; an urban consumer society developed; middle-class women entered new professions; young women known as *moga* (modern girls) sported short hair and short skirts, while dancing with *mobo* (modern boys) at jazz clubs and cabarets. To such people, the Japanese were becoming world citizens and their country was becoming "a province of the world" as they participated increasingly in a cosmopolitan and international culture.

■ Comparison

How did Japan's experience during the 1920s and 1930s resemble that of Germany, and how did it differ?

In this environment, the accumulated tensions of Japan's modernizing and industrializing processes found expression. "Rice riots" in 1918 brought more than a million people into the streets of urban Japan to protest the rising price of that essential staple. Union membership tripled in the 1920s as some factory workers began to think in terms of entitlements and workers' rights rather than the benevolence of their employers. In rural areas, tenant unions multiplied, and disputes with landowners increased amid demands for a reduction in rents. A mounting women's movement advocated a variety of feminist issues, including suffrage and the end of legalized prostitution. "All the sleeping women are now awake and moving," declared Yosano Akiko, a well-known poet, feminist, and social critic. Within the political arena, a number of "proletarian parties"—the Labor-Farmer Party, the Socialist People's Party, and a small Japan Communist Party—promised in various ways to "bring about the political, economic and social emancipation of the proletarian class."[7]

To many people in established elite circles—bureaucrats, landowners, industrialists, military officials—all of this was alarming, even appalling, and suggested echoes of the Russian Revolution of 1917. A number of political activists were arrested, and a few were killed. A Peace Preservation Law, enacted in 1925, promised long prison sentences, or even the death penalty, to anyone who organized against the existing imperial system of government or private property.

As in Germany, however, it was the impact of the Great Depression that paved the way for harsher and more authoritarian action. That worldwide economic catastrophe hit Japan hard. Shrinking world demand for silk impoverished millions of rural dwellers who raised silkworms. Japan's exports fell by half between 1929 and 1931, leaving a million or more urban workers unemployed. Many young workers returned to their rural villages only to find food scarce, families forced to sell their daughters to urban brothels, and neighbors unable to offer the customary money for the funerals of their friends. In these desperate circumstances, many began to doubt the ability of parliamentary democracy and capitalism to address Japan's "national emergency." Politicians and business leaders alike were widely regarded as privileged, self-centered, and heedless of the larger interests of the nation.

Such conditions energized a growing movement in Japanese political life known as Radical Nationalism or the Revolutionary Right. Expressed in dozens of small groups, it was especially appealing to younger army officers. The movement's many separate organizations shared an extreme nationalism, hostility to parliamentary democracy, a commitment to elite leadership focused around an exalted emperor, and dedication to foreign expansion. The manifesto of one of those organizations, the Cherry Blossom Society, expressed these sentiments clearly in 1930:

> As we observe recent social trends, top leaders engage in immoral conduct, political parties are corrupt, capitalists and aristocrats have no understanding of the masses, farming villages are devastated, unemployment and depression are serious. . . . The rulers neglect the long term interests of the nation, strive to win only the pleasure of foreign powers and possess no enthusiasm for external expansion. . . . The people are with us in craving the appearance of a vigorous

and clean government that is truly based upon the masses, and is genuinely centered around the Emperor.[8]

Members of such organizations managed to assassinate a number of public officials and prominent individuals, in the hope of provoking a return to direct rule by the emperor, and in 1936 a group of junior officers attempted a military takeover of the government, which was quickly suppressed. In sharp contrast to developments in Italy and Germany, however, no right-wing party gained wide popular support, nor was any such party able to seize power in Japan. Although individuals and small groups sometimes espoused ideas similar to those of European fascists, no major fascist party emerged. Nor did Japan produce any charismatic leader on the order of Mussolini or Hitler. People arrested for political offenses were neither criminalized nor exterminated, as in Germany, but instead were subjected to a process of "resocialization" that brought the vast majority of them to renounce their "errors" and return to the "Japanese way." Japan's established institutions of government were sufficiently strong, and traditional notions of the nation as a family headed by the emperor were sufficiently intact, to prevent the development of a widespread fascist movement able to take control of the country.[9]

In the 1930s, though, Japanese public life clearly changed in ways that reflected the growth of right-wing nationalist thinking. Parties and the parliament continued to operate, and elections were held, but major cabinet positions now went to prominent bureaucratic or military figures rather than to party leaders. The military in particular came to exercise a more dominant role in Japanese political life, although military men had to negotiate with business and bureaucratic elites as well as party leaders. Censorship limited the possibilities of free expression, and a single news agency was granted the right to distribute all national and most international news to the country's newspapers and radio stations. An Industrial Patriotic Federation replaced independent trade unions with factory-based "discussion councils" to resolve local disputes between workers and managers.

Established authorities also adopted many of the ideological themes of the Radical Right. In 1937, the Ministry of Education issued a new textbook, *The Cardinal Principles of Our National Polity*, for use in all Japanese schools (see Document 21.3, pp. 1015–17). That document proclaimed the Japanese to be "intrinsically quite different from the so-called citizens of Occidental [Western] countries." Those nations were "conglomerations of separate individuals" with "no deep foundation between ruler and citizen to unite them." In Japan, by contrast, an emperor of divine origin related to his subjects as a father to his children. It was a natural, not a contractual, relationship, expressed most fully in the "sacrifice of the life of a subject for the Emperor." In addition to studying this text, students were now required to engage in more physical training, in which Japanese martial arts replaced baseball in the physical education curriculum.

The erosion of democracy and the rise of the military in Japanese political life reflected long-standing Japanese respect for the military values of its ancient samurai warrior class as well as the relatively independent position of the military in Japan's

Meiji constitution. The state's success in quickly bringing the country out of the Depression likewise fostered popular support. As in Nazi Germany, state-financed credit, large-scale spending on armaments, and public works projects enabled Japan to emerge from the Depression more rapidly and more fully than major Western countries. "By the end of 1937," noted one Japanese laborer, "everybody in the country was working."[10] By the mid-1930s, the government increasingly assumed a supervisory or managerial role in economic affairs that included subsidies to strategic industries; profit ceilings on major corporations; caps on wages, prices, and rents; and a measure of central planning. Private property, however, was retained, and the huge industrial enterprises called *zaibatsu* continued to dominate the economic landscape.

Although Japan during the 1930s shared some common features with fascist Italy and Nazi Germany, it remained, at least internally, a less repressive and more pluralistic society than either of those European states. Japanese intellectuals and writers had to contend with government censorship, but they retained some influence in the country. Generals and admirals exercised great political authority as the role of an elected parliament declined, but they did not govern alone. Political prisoners were few and were not subjected to execution or deportation as in European fascist states. Japanese conceptions of their racial purity and uniqueness were directed largely against foreigners rather than an internal minority. Nevertheless, like Germany and Italy, Japan developed extensive imperial ambitions. Those projects of conquest and empire building collided with the interests of established world powers such as the United States and Britain, launching a second, and even more terrible, global war.

A Second World War

World War II, even more than the Great War, was a genuinely global conflict with independent origins in both Asia and Europe. Their common feature lay in dissatisfied states in both continents that sought to fundamentally alter the international arrangements that had emerged from World War I. Many Japanese, like their counterparts in Italy and Germany, felt stymied by Britain and the United States as they sought empires that they regarded as essential for their national greatness and economic well-being.

The Road to War in Asia

■ **Comparison**
In what ways were the origins of World War II in Asia and in Europe similar to each other? How were they different?

World War II began in Asia before it occurred in Europe. In the late 1920s and the 1930s, Japanese imperial ambitions mounted as the military became more powerful in Japan's political life and as an earlier cultural cosmopolitanism gave way to more nationalist sentiments. An initial problem was the rise of Chinese nationalism, which seemed to threaten Japan's sphere of influence in Manchuria, acquired after the Russo–Japanese War of 1904–1905. Acting independently of civilian authorities in Tokyo, units of the Japanese military seized control of Manchuria in 1931 and established a puppet state called Manchukuo. This action infuriated Western powers, prompting Japan to withdraw from the League of Nations, to break politically with its Western allies, and in 1936 to align more closely with Germany and Italy. By that time, relations with an increasingly nationalist China had deteriorated further, leading to a full-scale attack on heartland China in 1937 and escalating a bitter conflict that would last another eight years. World War II in Asia had begun (see Map 21.4).

As the war with China unfolded, the view of the world held by Japanese authorities and many ordinary people hardened. Increasingly, they felt isolated, surrounded, and threatened. A series of international agreements in the early 1920s that had granted Japan a less robust naval force than Britain or the United States as well as anti-Japanese immigration policies in the United States convinced some Japanese that European racism prevented the West from acknowledging Japan as an equal power. Furthermore, Japan was quite dependent on foreign and especially American sources of strategic goods. By the late 1930s, some 73 percent of Japan's scrap iron, 60 percent of its imported machine tools, 80 percent of its oil, and about half of its copper came from the United States, which was becoming increasingly hostile to Japanese ambitions in Asia. Moreover, Western imperialist powers—the British, French, and Dutch—controlled resource-rich colonies in Southeast Asia. Finally, the Soviet Union, proclaiming an alien communist ideology, loomed large in northern Asia. To growing numbers of Japanese, their national survival was at stake.

Thus in 1940–1941, Japan extended its military operations to the French, British, Dutch, and American colonies of Indochina, Malaya, Burma, Indonesia, and the Philippines in an effort to acquire those resources that would free it from dependence on the West. In carving out this Pacific empire, the Japanese presented themselves as liberators and modernizers, creating an "Asia for Asians" and freeing their continent from European dominance. Experience soon showed that Japan's concern was far more for Asia's resources than for its liberation and that Japanese rule exceeded in brutality even that of the Europeans.

A decisive step in the development of World War II in Asia lay in the Japanese attack on the United States at Pearl Harbor in Hawaii in December 1941. Japanese authorities undertook that attack with reluctance and only after negotiations to end American hostility to Japan's empire-building enterprise proved fruitless and an American oil embargo was imposed on Japan in July 1941. American opinion in the 1930s increasingly saw Japan as aggressive, oppressive, and a threat to U.S. economic interests in Asia. In the face of this hostility, Japan's leaders felt that the alternatives for their country boiled down to either an acceptance of American terms, which they feared would reduce Japan to a second- or third-rank power, or a war with an uncertain outcome. Given those choices, the decision for war was made more with foreboding than with enthusiasm. A leading Japanese admiral made the case for war in this way in late 1941: "The government has decided that if there were no war the fate of the nation is sealed. Even if there is a war, the country may be ruined. Nevertheless a nation that does not fight in this plight has lost its spirit and is doomed."[11]

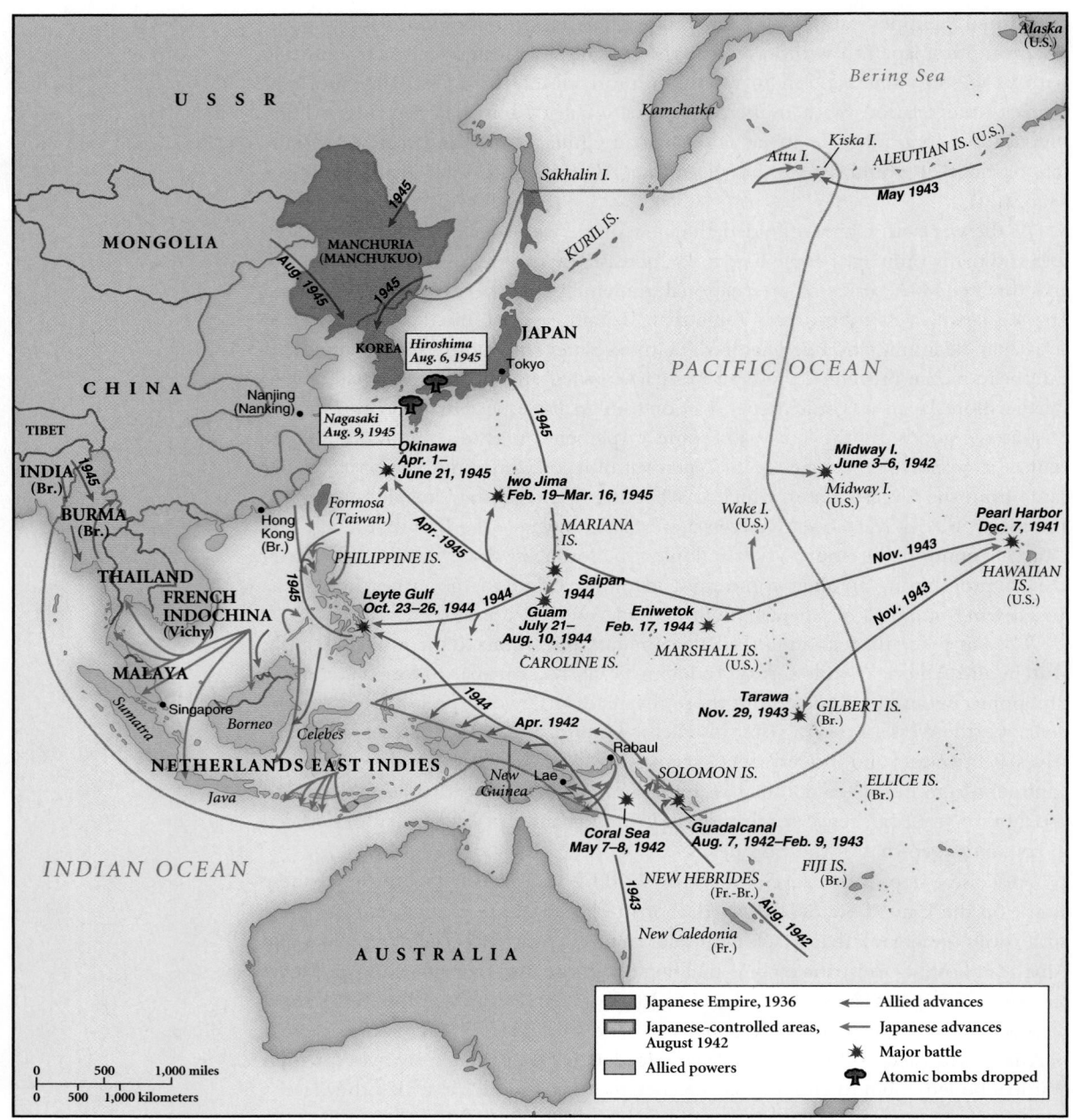

Map 21.4 World War II in Asia
Japanese aggression temporarily dislodged the British, French, Dutch, and Americans from their colonial possessions in Asia, while inflicting vast devastation on China.

As a consequence of the attack on Pearl Harbor, the United States entered the war in the Pacific, beginning a long and bloody struggle that ended only with the use of atomic bombs against Hiroshima and Nagasaki in 1945. The Pearl Harbor action also joined the Asian theater of the war and the ongoing conflict in Europe into a single global struggle that pitted Germany, Italy, and Japan (the Axis powers) against the United States, Britain, and the Soviet Union (the Allies).

The Road to War in Europe

If Japan was the dissatisfied power in Asia, Nazi Germany occupied that role in Europe even more sharply. As a consequence of its defeat in World War I and the harsh terms of the Treaty of Versailles, many Germans harbored deep resentments about their country's position in the international arena. Taking advantage of those resentments, the Nazis pledged to rectify the treaty's perceived injustices. Thus, to most historians, the origins of World War II in Europe lie squarely in German aggression, although with many twists and turns and encouraged by the initial unwillingness of Britain, France, and the Soviet Union to confront that aggression forcefully and collectively. If World War I was accidental and unintended, World War II was more deliberate and planned, perhaps even desired by the German leadership and by Hitler in particular.

War was central to the Nazi phenomenon in several ways. Nazism was born out of World War I, the hated treaty that ended it, and the disillusioned ex-soldiers who emerged from it. Furthermore, the celebration of war as a means of ennobling humanity and enabling the rise of superior peoples was at the core of Nazi ideology. "Whoever would live must fight," Hitler declared. "Only in force lies the right of possession." He consistently stressed the importance for Germany of gaining *lebensraum* (living space) in the east, in the lands of Slavic Poland and Russia. Inevitably, this required war (see Document 21.2, pp. 1012–15).

Slowly at first and then more aggressively, Hitler prepared the country for war and pursued territorial expansion. A major rearmament program began in 1935. The next year, German forces entered the Rhineland, which the Treaty of Versailles had declared demilitarized. In 1938, Germany annexed Austria and the German-speaking parts of Czechoslovakia. At a famous conference in Munich in that year, the British and the French gave these actions their reluctant blessing, hoping that this "appeasement" of Hitler could satisfy his demands and avoid all-out war. But it did not. In the following year, 1939, Germany unleashed a devastating attack on Poland, an action that triggered the Second World War in Europe, as Britain and France declared war on Germany. Quickly defeating France, the Germans launched a destructive air war against Britain and in 1941 turned their war machine loose on the Soviet Union. By then, most of Europe was under Nazi control (see Map 21.5).

Although Germany was central to both world wars, the second one was quite different from the first. It was not welcomed with the kind of mass enthusiasm that

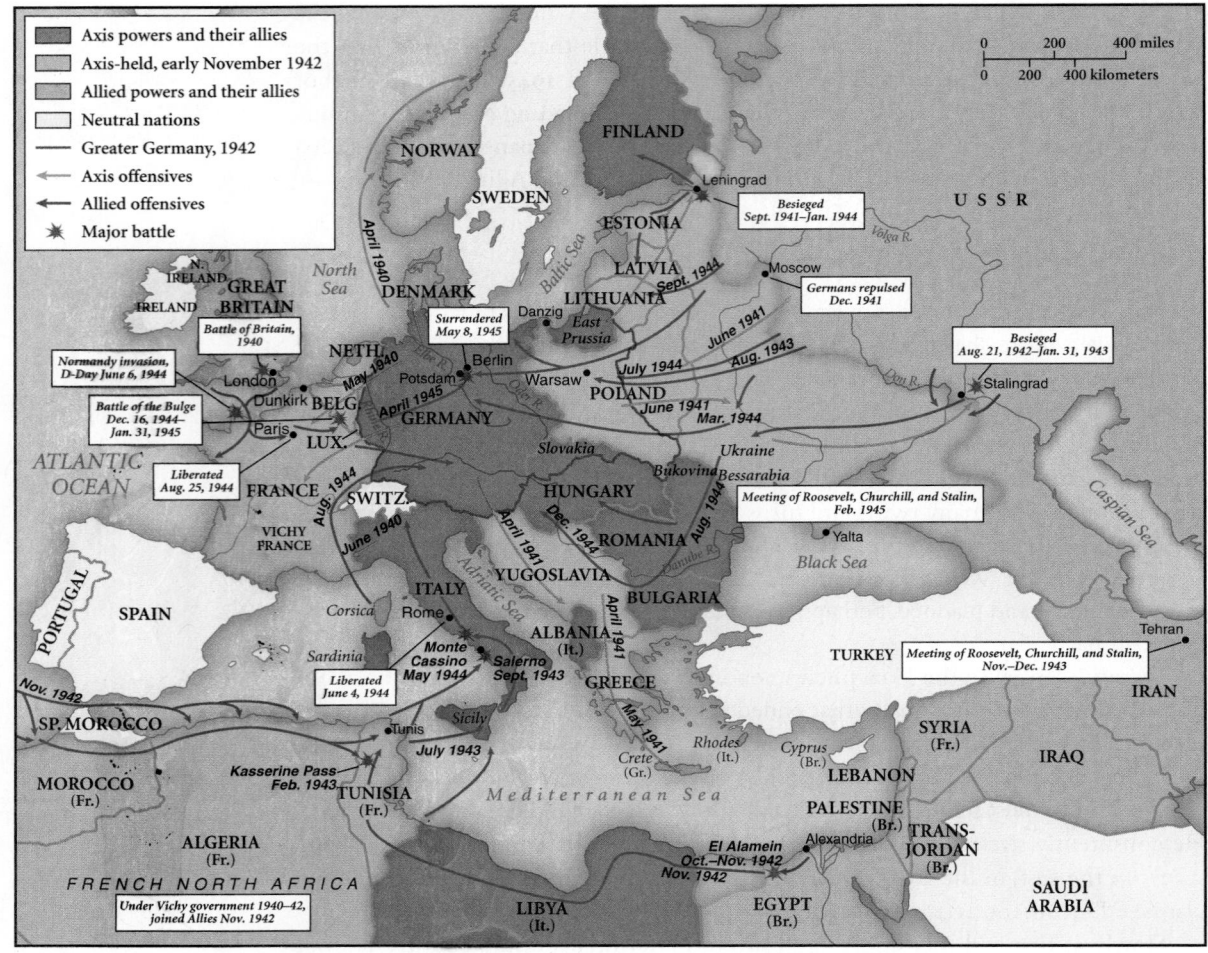

Map 21.5 World War II in Europe

For a brief moment during World War II, Nazi Germany came close to bringing all of Europe and much of the Mediterranean basin under its rule.

had accompanied the opening of World War I in 1914. The bitter experience of the Great War suggested to most people that only suffering lay ahead. The conduct of the two wars likewise differed. The first war had quickly bogged down in trench warfare that emphasized defense, whereas in the second war the German tactic of *blitzkrieg* (lightning war) coordinated the rapid movement of infantry, tanks, and airpower over very large areas.

Such military tactics were initially successful and allowed German forces, aided by their Italian allies, to sweep over Europe, the western Soviet Union, and North Africa. The tide began to turn in 1942 when the Soviet Union absorbed the German onslaught and then began to counterattack, slowly and painfully moving westward toward the German heartland. The United States, with its enormous material and human resources, fully joined the struggle against Germany in 1942. Three more years of bitter fighting ensued before the German defeat in May 1945.

The Outcomes of Global Conflict

The Second World War was the most destructive conflict in world history, with total deaths estimated at around 60 million, some six times the deaths in World War I. More than half of those casualties were civilians. Partly responsible for this horrendous toll were the new technologies of warfare—heavy bombers, jet fighters, missiles, and atomic weapons. Equally significant, though, was the almost complete blurring of the traditional line between civilian and military targets, as entire cities and whole populations came to be defined as the enemy.

Nowhere was that blurring more complete than in the Soviet Union, which accounted for more than 40 percent of the total deaths in the war—probably around 25 million, with an equal number made homeless and thousands of towns, villages, and industrial enterprises destroyed. German actions fulfilled Hitler's instructions to his leading generals: "The war against Russia will be such that it cannot be conducted in a knightly fashion; the struggle is one of ideologies and racial differences and will

■ Comparison
How did World War II differ from World War I?

Snapshot   **Key Moments in the History of World War II**

Japanese invasion of Manchuria	1931
Hitler's rise to power	1933
Italian invasion of Ethiopia	1935
Anti-Comintern Pact (alliance of Germany, Japan, and Italy)	1936–1937
Japanese invasion of China/Rape of Nanjing	1937–1938
German takeover of Austria and Sudetenland in Czechoslovakia	1938
German invasion of Poland (beginning of World War II in Europe)	1939
The fall of France and German air war on Britain	1940
Japanese seizure of French, British, Dutch, and U.S. colonies in Asia	1940–1942
German invasion of USSR; Japanese attack on Pearl Harbor, Hawaii	1941
The Holocaust	1941–1945
U.S. victory in Battle of Midway (turning point in the Pacific war)	1942
Soviet victory in Battle of Stalingrad (turning point in the European war)	1943
D-day: Allied forces invade France	1944
Yalta Conference (Britain, United States, Soviet Union) to determine fate of postwar Europe	1945
Soviets capture Berlin; atomic bombing of Hiroshima and Nagasaki; Germany and Japan surrender	1945

have to be conducted with unprecedented, unmerciful, and unrelenting harshness.... German soldiers guilty of breaking international law...will be excused."[12]

In China as well, perhaps 15 million deaths and uncounted refugees grew out of prolonged Chinese resistance and the shattering Japanese response, including the killing of every person and every animal in many villages. During the infamous Rape of Nanjing in 1937–1938, some 200,000 to 300,000 Chinese civilians were killed and often mutilated within a few months, and countless women were sexually assaulted. Indiscriminate German bombing of British cities and the Allied firebombing of Japanese and German cities likewise reflected the new morality of total war, as did the dropping of atomic bombs on Hiroshima and Nagasaki, which in a single instant vaporized tens of thousands of people. This was total war with a scale, intensity, and indiscriminate brutality that exceeded even the horrors of World War I.

A further dimension of total war lay in governments' efforts to mobilize their economies, their people, and their propaganda machines even more extensively than before. Colonial resources were harnessed once again. The British in particular made extensive use of colonial troops and laborers from India and Africa. Japan compelled several hundred thousand women from Korea, China, and elsewhere to serve the sexual needs of Japanese troops as "comfort women," who often accommodated twenty to thirty men a day.

Everywhere, the needs of the war drew large numbers of women into both industry and the military, although in Britain and the United States this was regarded as

Hiroshima
The dropping of atomic bombs on Hiroshima (August 6, 1945) and a few days later on Nagasaki marked the end of World War II in the Pacific and the opening of a nuclear arms race that cast an enormous shadow on the world ever since. In this photograph from an utterly devastated Hiroshima, a group of survivors waits for help in the southern part of the city a few hours after the bomb was dropped. (AP Images/ Wide World Photos)

a temporary necessity. In the United States, "Rosie the Riveter" represented those women who now took on heavy industrial jobs, which previously had been reserved for men. In the USSR, women constituted more than half of the workforce by 1945. A much smaller percentage of Japanese women were mobilized for factory work, but a Greater Japan Women's Society enrolled some 19 million members, who did volunteer work and promised to lay aside their gold jewelry and abandon extravagant weddings. As always, war heightened the prestige of masculinity, and given the immense sacrifices that men had made, few women were inclined to directly challenge the practices of patriarchy immediately following the war.

Among the most haunting outcomes of the war was the Holocaust. The outbreak of that war closed off certain possibilities, such as forced emigration, for implementing the Nazi dream of ridding Germany of its Jewish population. It also brought millions of additional Jews in Poland and Russia under German control and triggered among Hitler's enthusiastic subordinates various schemes for a "final solution" to the Jewish question. From this emerged the death camps that included Auschwitz, Dachau, and Bergen-Belsen. Altogether, some 6 million Jews perished in a technologically sophisticated form of mass murder that set a new standard for human depravity. Millions more whom the Nazis deemed inferior, undesirable, or dangerous—Russians, Poles, and other Slavs; Gypsies, or the Roma; mentally or physically handicapped people; homosexuals; communists; and Jehovah's Witnesses—likewise perished in Germany's efforts at racial purification.

Although the Holocaust was concentrated in Germany, its significance in twentieth-century world history has been huge. It has haunted postwar Germany in particular and the Western world in general. How could such a thing have occurred in a Europe bearing the legacy of both Christianity and the Enlightenment? More specifically, it sent many of Europe's remaining Jews fleeing to Israel and gave urgency to the establishment of a modern Jewish nation in the ancient Jewish homeland. That action outraged many Arabs, some of whom were displaced by the arrival of the Jews, and has fostered an enduring conflict in the Middle East. Furthermore, the Holocaust defined a new category of crimes against humanity—genocide, the attempted elimination of entire peoples. Universal condemnation of the Holocaust, however, did not end the practice, as cases of mass slaughter in Cambodia, Rwanda, Bosnia, and the Sudan have demonstrated.

On an even larger scale than World War I, this second global conflict rearranged the architecture of world politics. As the war ended, Europe was impoverished, its industrial infrastructure shattered, many of its great cities in ruins, and millions of its people homeless or displaced. Within a few years, this much-weakened Europe was effectively divided, with its western half operating under an American umbrella and the eastern half subject to Soviet control. It was clear that Europe's dominance in world affairs was finished.

Over the next two decades, Europe's greatly diminished role in the world registered internationally as its Asian and African colonies achieved independence. Not only had the war weakened both the will and the ability of European powers to hold onto their colonies, but it had also emboldened nationalist and anticolonial movements everywhere (see Chapter 23). Japanese victories in Southeast Asia had certainly damaged European prestige, for British, Dutch, and American military forces fell to Japanese conquerors, sometimes in a matter of weeks. Japanese authorities staged long and brutal marches of Western prisoners of war, partly to drive home to local people that the era of Western domination was over. Furthermore, tens of thousands of Africans had fought for the British or the French, had seen white people die, had enjoyed the company of white women, and had returned home with very different ideas about white superiority and the permanence of colonial rule. Colonial subjects everywhere were very much aware that U.S. president Franklin Roosevelt and British prime minister Winston Churchill had solemnly declared in 1941 that "we respect the right of all peoples to choose the form of government under which they will live." Many asked whether those principles should not apply to people in the colonial world as well as to Europeans.

A further outcome of World War II lay in the consolidation and extension of the communist world. The Soviet victory over the Nazis, though bought at an unimaginable cost in blood and treasure, gave immense credibility to that communist regime and to its leader, Joseph Stalin. In the decades that followed, Soviet authorities nurtured a virtual cult of the war: memorials were everywhere; wedding parties made pilgrimages to them, and brides left their bouquets behind; May 9, Victory Day, saw elaborately orchestrated celebrations; veterans were honored and granted modest privileges. Furthermore, communist parties, largely dominated by the Soviet Union and supported by its armed forces, took power all across Eastern Europe, pushing the communist frontier deep into the European heartland. Even more important was a communist takeover in China in 1949. The Second World War allowed the Chinese Communist Party to gain support and credibility by leading the struggle against Japan. By 1950, the communist world seemed to many in the West very much on the offensive (see Chapter 22).

The horrors of two world wars within a single generation prompted a renewed interest in international efforts to maintain the peace in a world of competing and sovereign states. The chief outcome was the United Nations (UN), established in 1945 as a successor to the moribund League of Nations. As a political body dependent on agreement among its most powerful members, the UN proved more effective as a forum for international opinion than as a means of resolving the major conflicts of the postwar world, particularly the Soviet/American hostility during the cold war decades. Further evidence for a growing internationalism lay in the creation in late 1945 of the World Bank and International Monetary Fund, whose purpose was to regulate the global economy, prevent another depression, and stimulate economic growth, especially in the poorer nations.

What these initiatives shared was the dominant presence of the United States. Unlike the aftermath of World War I, when an isolationist United States substantially withdrew from world affairs, the half century following the end of World War II witnessed the emergence of the United States as a global superpower. This was one of the major outcomes of the Second World War and a chief reason for the remarkable recovery of a badly damaged and discredited Western civilization.

The Recovery of Europe

The tragedies that afflicted Europe in the first half of the twentieth century—fratricidal war, economic collapse, the Holocaust—were wholly self-inflicted, and yet despite the sorry and desperate state of heartland Europe in 1945, that civilization had not permanently collapsed. In the twentieth century's second half, Europeans rebuilt their industrial economies and revived their democratic political systems, while the United States, a European offshoot, assumed a dominant and often dominating role both within Western civilization and in the world at large.

■ Change
How was Europe able to recover from the devastation of war?

Three factors help to explain this astonishing recovery. One is the apparent resiliency of an industrial society, once it has been established. The knowledge, skills, and habits of mind that enabled industrial societies to operate effectively remained intact, even if the physical infrastructure had been largely destroyed. Thus even the most terribly damaged countries—Germany, the Soviet Union, and Japan—had substantially recovered, both economically and demographically, within a quarter of a century. A second factor lay in the ability of the major Western European countries to integrate their recovering economies. After centuries of military conflict climaxed by the horrors of the two world wars, the major Western European powers were at last willing to put aside some of their prickly nationalism in return for enduring peace and common prosperity.

Perhaps most important, Europe had long ago spawned an overseas extension of its own civilization in what became the United States. In the twentieth century, that country served as a reservoir of military manpower, economic resources, and political leadership for the West as a whole. By 1945, the center of gravity within Western civilization had shifted decisively, relocated now across the Atlantic. With Europe diminished, divided, and on the defensive against the communist threat, leadership of the Western world passed, almost by default, to the United States. It was the only major country physically untouched by the war. Its economy had demonstrated enormous productivity during that struggle and by 1945 was generating fully 50 percent of total world production. Its overall military strength was unmatched, and it was in sole possession of the atomic bomb, the most powerful weapon ever constructed. Thus the United States became the new heartland of the West as well as a global superpower. In 1941, the publisher Henry Luce had proclaimed the twentieth century as "the American century." As the Second World War ended, that prediction seemed to be coming true.

An early indication of the United States' intention to exercise global leadership took shape in its efforts to rebuild and reshape shattered European economies. Known as the Marshall Plan, that effort funneled into Europe some $12 billion, at the time a very large amount, together with numerous advisers and technicians. It was motivated by some combination of genuine humanitarian concern, a desire to prevent a new depression by creating overseas customers for American industrial goods, and an interest in undermining the growing appeal of European communist parties. This economic recovery plan was successful beyond anyone's expectations. Between 1948 and the early 1970s, Western European economies grew rapidly, generating a widespread prosperity and improving living standards; at the same time, Western Europe became both a major customer for American goods and a major competitor in global markets.

The Marshall Plan also required its European recipients to cooperate with one another. After decades of conflict and destruction almost beyond description, many Europeans were eager to do so. That process began in 1951 when Italy, France, West Germany, Belgium, the Netherlands, and Luxembourg created the European Coal and Steel Community to jointly manage the production of these critical items. In 1957, these six countries deepened their level of cooperation by establishing the European Economic Community (EEC), more widely known as the Common Market, whose members reduced their tariffs and developed common trade policies. Over the next half century, the EEC expanded its membership to include almost all of Europe, including many former communist states. In 1994, the EEC was renamed the European Union, and in 2002 twelve of its members adopted a common currency, the euro (see Map 21.6). All of this sustained Europe's remarkable economic recovery and expressed a larger European identity, although it certainly did not erase deeply rooted national loyalties. Nor did it lead, as some had hoped, to a political union, a United States of Europe.

Beyond economic assistance, the American commitment to Europe soon came to include political and military security against the distant possibility of renewed German aggression and the more immediate communist threat from the Soviet Union. Without that security, economic recovery was unlikely to continue. Thus was born the military and political alliance known as the North Atlantic Treaty Organization (NATO) in 1949. It committed the United States and its nuclear arsenal to the defense of Europe against the Soviet Union, and it firmly anchored West Germany within the Western alliance. Thus, as Western Europe revived economically, it did so under the umbrella of U.S. political and military leadership, which Europeans generally welcomed. It was perhaps an imperial relationship, but to historian John Gaddis, it was "an empire by invitation" rather than by imposition.[13]

A parallel process in Japan, which was under American occupation between 1945 and 1952, likewise revived that country's devastated but already industrialized economy. In the two decades following the occupation, Japan's economy grew at the remarkable rate of 10 percent a year, and the nation became an economic giant on the world stage. This "economic miracle" received a substantial boost from some $2 billion in American aid during the occupation and even more from U.S. military purchases in Japan during the Korean War (1950–1953). Furthermore, the democratic

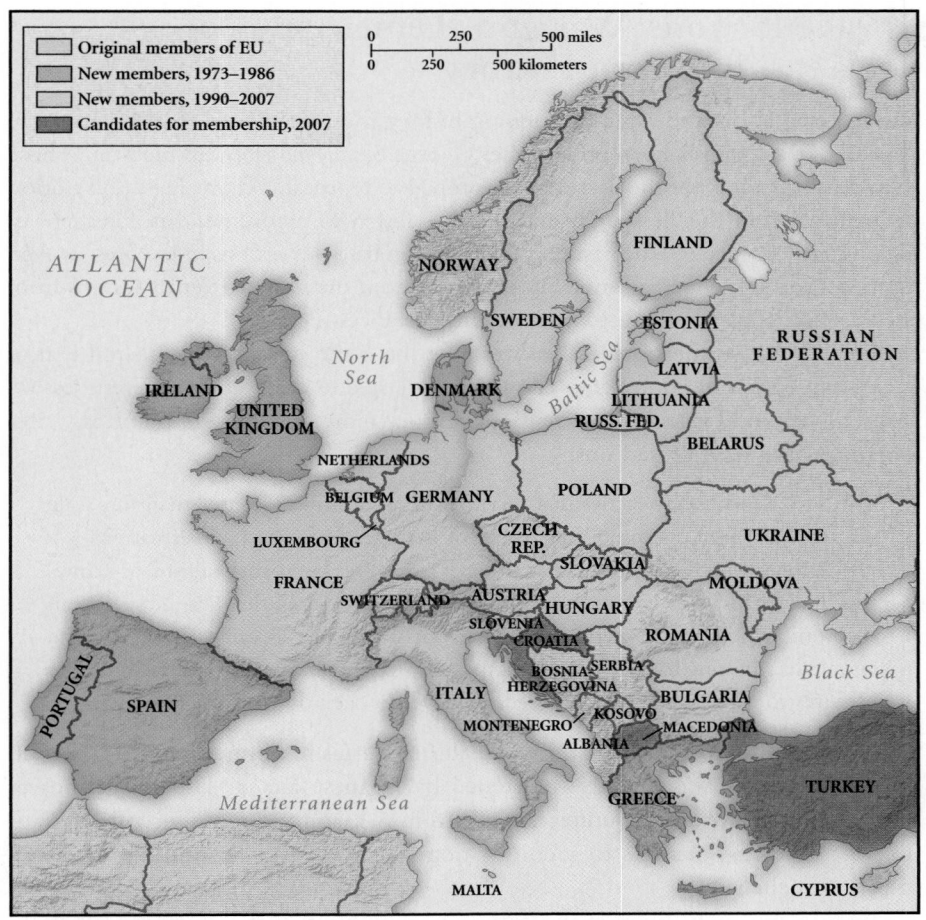

Map legend:
- Original members of EU
- New members, 1973–1986
- New members, 1990–2007
- Candidates for membership, 2007

Map 21.6   The Growth of European Integration
Gradually during the second half of the twentieth century, Europeans put aside their bitter rivalries and entered into various forms of economic cooperation with one another, although these efforts fell short of complete political union. This map illustrates the growth of what is now called the European Union (EU). Notice the eastward expansion of the EU following the collapse of communism in Eastern Europe and the Soviet Union.

constitution imposed on Japan by American occupation authorities required that "land, sea, and air forces, as well as other war potential, will never be maintained." This meant that Japan, even more so than Europe, depended on the United States for its military security. Because it spent only about 1 percent of its gross national product on defense, more was available for productive investment.

The Western world had changed dramatically during the twentieth century. It began that century with its European heartland clearly the dominant imperial center of a global network. That civilization substantially self-destructed in the first half of the century, but it revived during the second half in a changed form—without its Afro-Asian colonies and with a new and powerful core in the United States. Accompanying this process and intersecting with it was another major theme of twentieth-century world history—the rise and fall of world communism, which is the focus of the next chapter.

⊔ Reflections: War and Remembrance: Learning from History

When asked about the value of studying history, most students respond with some version of the Spanish-born philosopher George Santayana's famous dictum: "Those who cannot remember the past are condemned to repeat it." At one level, this notion of learning from the "lessons of history" has much to recommend it, for there is, after all, little else except the past on which we can base our actions in the present. And yet historians in general are notably cautious about drawing particular lessons from the past and applying them to present circumstances.

For one thing, the historical record, like the Bible or any other sacred text, is sufficiently rich and complex to allow many people to draw quite different lessons from it. The world wars of the twentieth century represent a case in point, as writer Adam Gopnik has pointed out:

> The First World War teaches that territorial compromise is better than full-scale war, that an "honor-bound" allegiance of the great powers to small nations is a recipe for mass killing, and that it is crazy to let the blind mechanism of armies and alliances trump common sense. The Second teaches that searching for an accommodation with tyranny by selling out small nations only encourages the tyrant, that refusing to fight now leads to a worse fight later on. . . . The First teaches us never to rush into a fight, the Second never to back down from a bully.[14]

Did the lessons of the First World War lead Americans to ignore the rise of fascism until the country was directly threatened by Japanese attack? Did the lessons of World War II contribute to unnecessary wars in Vietnam and more recently in Iraq? There are no easy answers to such questions, for the lessons of history are many, varied, and changing.

Behind any such lesson is the common assumption that history repeats itself. This too is a notion to which historians bring considerable skepticism. They are generally more impressed with the complexity and particularity of major events such as wars rather than with their common features. Here is a further basis for caution in easily drawing lessons from the past.

But the wars of the past century perhaps share one broad similarity: all of them led to unexpected consequences. Few people expected the duration and carnage of World War I. The Holocaust was literally unimaginable when Hitler took power in 1933 or even at the outbreak of the Second World War in 1939. Who would have expected an American defeat at the hands of the Vietnamese? And the invasion of Iraq in 2003 generated a long list of surprises for the United States, including the absence of weapons of mass destruction and a prolonged insurgency. History repeats itself most certainly only in its unexpectedness.

Second Thoughts

What's the Significance?

World War I

Treaty of Versailles

Woodrow Wilson/Fourteen
  Points

Great Depression

New Deal

fascism

Mussolini

Nazi Germany/Hitler

Revolutionary Right (Japan)

World War II in Asia

World War II in Europe

total war

Holocaust

Marshall Plan

European Economic
  Community

NATO

To assess your mastery of the material in this chapter, visit the **Student Center** at bedfordstmartins.com/strayer.

Big Picture Questions

1. What explains the disasters that befell Europe in the first half of the twentieth century?

2. In what ways were the world wars a motor for change in the history of the twentieth century?

3. To what extent were the two world wars distinct and different conflicts, and in what ways were they related to each other? In particular, how did the First World War and its aftermath lay the foundations for World War II?

4. In what ways did Europe's internal conflicts between 1914 and 1945 have global implications?

Next Steps: For Further Study

Michael Burleigh, *The Third Reich: A New History* (2001). A fresh and thorough look at the Nazi era in Germany's history.

John Keegan, *The Second World War* (2005). A comprehensive account by a well-known scholar.

Bernd Martin, *Japan and Germany in the Modern World* (1995). A comparative study of these two countries' modern history and the relationship between them.

Mark Mazower, *Dark Continent* (2000). A history of Europe in the twentieth century that views the era as a struggle among liberal democracy, fascism, and communism.

Michael S. Nieberg, *Fighting the Great War: A Global History* (2006). An exploration of the origins and conduct of World War I.

Dietman Rothermund, *The Global Impact of the Great Depression, 1929–1939* (1996). An examination of the origins of the Depression in America and Europe and its impact in Asia, Africa, and Latin America.

First World War.com, http://www.firstworldwar.com. A Web site rich with articles, documents, photos, diaries, and more that illustrate the history of World War I.

"Nazi Rule," http://www.ushmm.org/outreach/nrule.htm. A great Web site, sponsored by the U.S. Holocaust Memorial Museum, for exploring various aspects of the Nazi experience.

For Web sites, images, and additional documents related to this chapter, see **Make History** at bedfordstmartins.com/strayer.

Documents

Considering the Evidence:
Ideologies of the Axis Powers

Even more than the Great War of 1914–1918, the Second World War was a conflict of ideas and ideologies as well as a struggle of nations and armies. Much of the world was immensely grateful that the defeat of Italy, Germany, and Japan discredited the ideas that underlay those regimes. Yet students of history need to examine these ideas, however repellant they may be, to understand the circumstances in which they arose and to assess their consequences. Described variously as fascist, authoritarian, right-wing, or radically nationalist, the ideologies of the Axis powers differed in tone and emphasis. But they shared a repudiation of mainstream Western liberalism, born of the Enlightenment, as well as an intense hatred of Marxist communism. The three documents that follow provide an opportunity to define their common features and to distinguish among them.

Document 21.1

Mussolini on Fascism

In 1932, after ten years in power, the Italian fascist leader Benito Mussolini wrote a short article for an Italian encyclopedia outlining the political and social ideas that informed the regime that he headed. It was an effort to provide some philosophical coherence for the various measures and policies that had characterized the first decade of his rule. (See pp. 988–90 for background on Italian fascism.)

- To what ideas and historical circumstances is Mussolini reacting in this document?

- What is his criticism of pacifism, socialism, democracy, and liberalism?

- How does Mussolini understand the state? What is its relationship to individual citizens?

- Why might these ideas have been attractive to many in Italy in the 1920s and 1930s?

BENITO MUSSOLINI

The Political and Social Doctrine of Fascism

1933

Above all, Fascism... believes neither in the possibility nor the utility of perpetual peace. It thus repudiates the doctrine of Pacifism—born of a renunciation of the struggle and an act of cowardice in the face of sacrifice. War alone brings up to its highest tension all human energy and puts the stamp of nobility upon the peoples who have the courage to meet it.... This anti-Pacifist spirit is carried by Fascism even into the life of the individual;... it is the education to combat, the acceptance of the risks which combat implies, and a new way of life for Italy. Thus the Fascist... conceives of life as duty and struggle and conquest, life which should be high and full, lived for oneself, but above all for others— those who are at hand and those who are far distant, contemporaries, and those who will come after....

Fascism repudiates any universal embrace, and in order to live worthily in the community of civilized peoples watches its contemporaries with vigilant eyes....

Such a conception of Life makes Fascism the complete opposite of... Marxian Socialism, the materialist conception of history; according to which the history of human civilization can be explained simply through the conflict of interests among the various social groups and by the change and development in the means and instruments of production.... Fascism, now and always, believes in holiness and in heroism; that is to say, in actions influenced by no economic motive, direct or indirect.... It follows that the existence of an unchangeable and unchanging class war is also denied.... And above all Fascism denies that class-war can be the preponderant force in the transformation of society.... Fascism repudiates the conception of "economic" happiness, to be realized by Socialism.... Fascism denies the validity of the equation, well-being = happiness, which

would reduce men to the level of animals, caring for one thing only—to be fat and well-fed and would thus degrade humanity to a purely physical existence.

After Socialism, Fascism combats the whole complex system of democratic ideology, and repudiates it.... Fascism denies that the majority, by the simple fact that it is a majority, can direct human society; it denies that numbers alone can govern by means of a periodical consultation, and it affirms the immutable, beneficial, and fruitful inequality of mankind, which can never be permanently leveled through the mere operation of a mechanical process such as universal suffrage. The democratic regime may be defined as from time to time giving the people the illusion of sovereignty, while the real effective sovereignty lies in the hands of other concealed and irresponsible forces....

The foundation of Fascism is the conception of the State, its character, its duty, and its aim. Fascism conceives of the State as an absolute, in comparison with which all individuals or groups are relative, only to be conceived of in their relation to the State.... [T]he Fascist State is itself conscious, and has itself a will and a personality.... For us Fascists, the State is not merely a guardian, preoccupied solely with the duty of assuring the personal safety of the citizens; nor is it an organization with purely material aims, such as to guarantee a certain level of well-being and peaceful conditions of life.... The State, as conceived of and as created by Fascism, is a spiritual and moral fact in itself.... The State is the guarantor of security, both internal and external, but it is also the custodian and transmitter of the spirit of the people, as it has grown up through the centuries in language, in customs and in faith.... [I]t represents the immanent spirit of the nation.... It is the State which educates its citizens in civic virtue, gives them a consciousness of their mission, and welds them into unity.... It leads men from primitive tribal life to that highest expression of human power which is Empire.

Source: Benito Mussolini, *The Political and Social Doctrine of Fascism*, translated by Jane Soames (London: Leonard and Virginia Woolf at the Hogarth Press, 1933).

[T]he Fascist State... is not reactionary, but revolutionary, in that it anticipates the solution of the universal political problems which elsewhere have to be settled in the political field by the rivalry of parties, the excessive power of the Parliamentary regime and the irresponsibility of political assemblies; while it meets the problems of the economic field by a system of syndicalism°... and in the moral field enforces order, discipline, and obedience to that which is the determined moral code of the country. Fascism desires the State to be a strong and organic body, at the same time reposing upon broad and popular support....The Fascist State organizes the nation, but leaves a sufficient margin of liberty to the individual; the latter is deprived of all useless and possibly harmful freedom, but retains what is essential; the deciding power in this question cannot be the individual, but the State alone. The Fascist State is not indifferent to the fact of religion in general, or to that particular

—————————
°**syndicalism:** federations of trade unions under state direction.

and positive faith which is Italian Catholicism. The State professes no theology, but a morality, and in the Fascist State religion is considered as one of the deepest manifestations of the spirit of man, thus it is not only respected but defended and protected.

For Fascism the growth of Empire, that is to say the expansion of the nation, is an essential manifestation of vitality, and its opposite a sign of decadence. Peoples which are rising, or rising again after a period of decadence, are always imperialist; any renunciation is a sign of decay and of death. Fascism is the doctrine best adapted to represent the tendencies and the aspirations of a people, like the people of Italy, who are rising again after many centuries of abasement and foreign servitude. But Empire demands discipline, the coordination of all forces and a deeply felt sense of duty and sacrifice: this fact explains...the necessarily severe measures which must be taken against those who would oppose this spontaneous and inevitable movement of Italy in the twentieth century... for never before has the nation stood more in need of authority, of direction, and of order.

Document 21.2

Hitler on Nazism

Unlike Mussolini, Adolph Hitler published his political views well before he came to power. Born in Austria, Hitler absorbed a radical form of German nationalism, which he retained as a profoundly disillusioned veteran of World War I. In 1919, he joined a very small extremist group called the German Workers Party, where he rose quickly to a dominant role based on his powerful oratorical abilities. Inspired by Mussolini's recent victory in Italy, Hitler launched in 1923 an unsuccessful armed uprising in Munich for which he was arrested and imprisoned. During his brief stay in prison (less than a year), he wrote *Mein Kampf* (*My Struggle*), part autobiography and part an exposition of his political and social philosophy. Armed with these ideas, Hitler assumed the leadership of Germany in 1933 (see pp. 990–93).

■ What larger patterns in European thinking does Hitler's book reflect and what elements of European thought does he reject? Consider in particular his use of social Darwinism, then an idea with wide popularity in Europe.

ing. Every man in a position of responsibility will have councilors at his side, but the decision is made by that individual person alone....

[T]he principle of parliamentarian democracy, whereby decisions are enacted through the majority vote, has not always ruled the world. On the contrary, we find it prevalent only during short periods of history, and those have always been periods of decline in nations and States....

Eastern Orientation or Eastern Policy

[W]e National Socialists must hold unflinchingly to our aim in foreign policy, namely, to secure for the German people the land and soil to which they are entitled on this earth.... If we speak of soil in Europe today, we can primarily have in mind only Russia and her vassal border states....

The National Socialist movement must strive to eliminate the disproportion between our population and our area—viewing this latter as a source of food as well as a basis for power politics—between our historical past and the hopelessness of our present impotence. And in this it must remain aware that we, as guardians of the highest humanity on this earth, are bound by the highest obligation, and the more it strives to bring the German people to racial awareness..., the more it will be able to meet this obligation....

State boundaries are made by man and changed by man.... And in this case, right lies in this strength alone.... Just as our ancestors did not receive the soil on which we live today as a gift from Heaven, but had to fight for it at the risk of their lives, in the future no folkish grace will win soil for us... but only the might of a victorious sword....

Never forget that the most sacred right on this earth is a man's right to have earth to till with his own hands, and the most sacred sacrifice the blood that a man sheds for this earth.

Document 21.3

The Japanese Way

In the Japanese language the word *kokutai* is an evocative term that refers to the national essence or the fundamental character of the Japanese nation and people. Drawing both on long-established understandings and on recently developed nationalist ideas, the Ministry of Education in 1937 published a small volume, widely distributed in schools and homes throughout the country, entitled the *Kokutai No Hongi* (*Cardinal Principles of the National Entity of Japan*). That text, excerpted in Document 21.3, defined the uniqueness of Japan and articulated the philosophical foundation of its authoritarian regime. (See pp. 993–96 for the background to this document.) When the Americans occupied a defeated and devastated Japan in 1945, they forbade the further distribution of the book.

- According to *Cardinal Principles*, what was *kokutai*? How did the document define the national essence of Japan? How did its authors compare Japan to the West?

- What was the ideal role of the individual in Japanese society?

- What were the major tasks confronting Japan in the 1930s, according to the document?

- How might this document have been used to justify Japan's military and territorial expansion?

- Why do you think the American occupation authorities banned the document?

- What aspects of this document might Hitler have viewed with sympathy, and what parts of it might he have found distasteful or offensive?

Cardinal Principles of the National Entity of Japan
1937

The various ideological and social evils of present-day Japan are the result of ignoring the fundamental and running after the trivial, of lack of judgment, and a failure to digest things thoroughly; and this is due to the fact that since the days of *Meiji* so many aspects of European and American culture, systems, and learning, have been imported, and that, too rapidly. As a matter of fact, the foreign ideologies imported into our country are in the main ideologies of the [European] Enlightenment that have come down from the eighteenth century, or extensions of them. The views of the world and of life that form the basis of these ideologies...lay the highest value on, and assert the liberty and equality of, individuals....

We have already witnessed the boundless Imperial virtues. Wherever this Imperial virtue of compassion radiates, the Way for the subjects naturally becomes clear. The Way of the subjects exists where the entire nation serves the Emperor united in mind....That is, we by nature serve the Emperor and walk the Way of the Empire....

We subjects are intrinsically quite different from the so-called citizens of the Occidental countries....

When citizens who are conglomerations of separate individuals independent of each other give support to a ruler,...there exists no deep foundation between ruler and citizen to unite them. However, the relationship between the Emperor and his sub-jects arises from the same fountainhead, and has prospered ever since the founding of the nation as one in essence....

Our country is established with the Emperor.... For this reason, to serve the Emperor and to receive the Emperor's great august Will as one's own is the rationale of making our historical "life" live in the present....

Loyalty means to reverence the Emperor as [our] pivot and to follow him implicitly....Hence, offering our lives for the sake of the Emperor does not mean so-called self-sacrifice, but the casting aside of our little selves to live under his august grace and the enhancing of the genuine life of the people of a State....An individual is an existence belonging to the State and her history, which forms the basis of his origin, and is fundamentally one body with it....

We must sweep aside the corruption of the spirit and the clouding of knowledge that arises from setting up one's "self" and from being taken up with one's "self" and return to a pure and clear state of mind that belongs intrinsically to us as subjects, and thereby fathom the great principle loyalty....

Indeed, loyalty is our fundamental Way as subject, and is the basis of our national morality. Through loyalty are we become Japanese subjects; in loyalty do we obtain life and herein do we find the source of all morality....

In our country filial piety is a Way of the highest importance. Filial piety originates with one's family as its basis, and in its larger sense has the nation for its foundation....

Our country is a great family nation, and the Imperial Household is the head family of the sub-

Source: J. O. Gauntlett, trans., and R. K. Hall, ed., *Kokutai No Hongi* (*Cardinal Principles of the National Entity of Japan*) (Cambridge: Harvard University Press, 1949), 53–183.

jects and the nucleus of national life. The subjects revere the Imperial Household, which is the head family, with the tender esteem they have for their ancestors; and the Emperor loves his subjects as his very own....

When we trace the marks of the facts of the founding of our country and the progress of our history, what we always find there is the spirit of harmony....The spirit of harmony is built upon the concord of all things. When people determinedly count themselves as masters and assert their egos, there is nothing but contradictions and the setting of one against the other; and harmony is not begotten....That is, a society of individualism is one of the clashes between [masses of] people... and all history may be looked upon as one of class wars....

And this, this harmony is clearly seen in our nation's martial spirit. Our nation is one that holds bushido° in high regard, and there are shrines deifying warlike spirits....Bushido may be cited as showing an outstanding characteristic of our national morality....That is to say, though a sense of obligation binds master and servant, this has developed in a spirit of self-effacement and meeting death with a perfect calmness. In this, it was not that death was made light of so much as that many tempered himself to death and in a true sense regarded it with esteem. In effect, man tried to fulfill true life by the way of death....

_____

°**bushido:** the way of the warrior.

To put it in a nutshell, while the strong points of Occidental learning and concepts lie in their analytical and intellectual qualities, the characteristics of Oriental learning and concepts lie in their intuitive and aesthetic qualities. These are natural tendencies that arise through racial and historical differences; and when we compare them with our national spirits, concepts, or mode of living, we cannot help recognizing further great and fundamental differences. Our nation has in the past imported, assimilated, and sublimated Chinese and Indian ideologies, and has therewith supported the Imperial Way, making possible the establishment of an original culture based on her national polity....

Since the *Meiji* restoration our nation has adapted the good elements of the advanced education seen among European and American nations, and has exerted efforts to set up an educational system and materials for teaching. The nation has also assimilated on a wide scale the scholarship of the West, not only in the fields of natural science, but of the mental sciences, and has thus striven to see progress made in our scholastic pursuits and to make education more popular....

However, at the same time, through the infiltration of individualistic concepts, both scholastic pursuits and education have tended to be taken up with a world in which the intellect alone mattered....

In order to correct these tendencies, the only course open to us is to clarify the true nature of our national polity, which is at the very source of our education, and to strive to clear up individualistic and abstract ideas.

Using the Evidence:
Ideologies of the Axis Powers

1. **Making comparisons:** What similar emphases can you find in these three documents? What differences can you identify? Consider especially the relationship of individuals and the state.

2. **Criticizing the West:** In what ways did Mussolini, Hitler, and the authors of *Cardinal Principles* find fault with mainstream Western societies and their political and social values?

3. **Considering ideas and circumstances:** From what concrete conditions did the ideas expressed in these documents arise? Why did they achieve such widespread popularity? You might even consider using these documents to make the case in favor of fascist or authoritarian government from the viewpoint of the 1930s.

4. **Considering ideas and action:** To what extent did the ideas articulated in these documents find expression in particular actions or policies of political authorities?

5. **Noticing continuity and change:** To what extent were the ideas in these documents new and revolutionary? In what respects did they draw on long-standing traditions in their societies? In what ways did they embrace modern life and what aspects of it did they reject? Have these ideas been completely discredited or do they retain some resonance in contemporary political discourse?

Visual Sources

Considering the Evidence:
Propaganda and Critique in World War I

More than any other conflict before it, World War I was represented visually and publically in many ways. Newspapers competed to print the most sensational pictures, many taken by soldiers themselves using handheld cameras. The war also offered a highly popular theme for the new technology of cinema and the emerging motion picture industry. One of the most pervasive uses of art and artists involved the prolific creation, under government auspices, of posters designed to generate public support for the war. Independent artists, many of whom participated in the war, tried to depict its horror and devastation, both during the conflict and after it finally ended. The first three visual sources illustrate the official propaganda dimension of the war's representation, while the final two provide examples of how that enormous conflict and its outcomes were subjected to artistic scrutiny.

The "total" character of World War I ensured that women would be mobilized for the struggle in many ways. In Russia, after the revolution of early 1917, a number of all-female combat units were created to shame or inspire the war-weary male soldiers into greater action. Some British women even presented men not in uniform with a white feather, symbolizing cowardice, to encourage them to enlist. More widely, women were recruited into war-related industries to replace the men who were away fighting, as the British poster on page 982 indicates. American women were strongly encouraged to save food, especially wheat, to support the war effort. Posters also gave the great struggle a feminine face. Visual Source 21.1 is a 1917 U.S. poster meant to encourage people to buy Liberty Bonds, which raised money for the war effort and demonstrated the buyer's patriotism.

- How would you describe the posture of the woman in this poster? What image of a woman does it seek to convey?

- What message does the backdrop of the poster communicate? Notice the church and city in flames.

- In appealing for sacrifice or public support in time of war, why might a feminine image be more effective than a masculine image?

- Compare this poster with the British one shown on page 982 in this chapter. What different message about the role of women does this image convey? To what kind of audience did each of these posters appeal?

Visual Source 21.1 Women and the War (Library of Congress, LC-USZCA-9462)

Among the chief uses of wartime propaganda posters was to portray the enemy in the most despicable terms. German posters, for example, often depicted the country's enemies as animals or misbehaving children, suggesting that they were something less than fully human. They usually showed Russians as alcoholics. Visual Source 21.2 is a French poster from around 1915.

It pictures Germany as Thor, an ancient pagan Germanic god of thunder, who had been turned into a demonic figure as Christianity took hold in Europe. The caption at the top of the image reads: "The god Thor—the most barbaric of the barbarian divinities of old Germany."

- What does the poster convey by presenting Germany as Thor?

- Note the Prussian imperial eagle standing on a bomb. What impression of German goals does that convey?

- How do you understand the religious imagery of this French print? Notice Thor preparing to destroy a church with his hammer as well as the broken cross between his feet at the bottom.

- To whom do you think such images were directed and for what purpose?

A distinctive feature of World War I was the extensive use of troops drawn from the colonies of the contending powers. Many thousands of African and Asian men took part in that struggle, both in their homelands and in Europe. The French, for example, were initially reluctant to employ colonial troops, fearing to arm black men and perhaps uncertain of their loyalty. But the desperate need for manpower finally overcame these reservations, and France recruited large numbers of men from its North and West African colonies as well as from Southeast Asia. Some 71,000 French colonial soldiers died in the war. Visual Source 21.3 shows a French wartime poster; the French translates as "Day of the African Army and Colonial Troops."

- What image of African soldiers does the poster suggest? How might this image be at variance with that of earlier European stereotypes of their African subjects?

- What is conveyed by the juxtaposition of an African soldier and his French counterpart fighting together?

- Why might the French have set aside a special day to honor colonial troops?

- How might the experience of fighting in Europe have affected the outlook of a West African soldier?

The destructiveness of the Great War was almost beyond the imagination of contemporary Europeans. Among its most notable and horrific features was the long period of trench warfare, in which lines of entrenched men, often not far apart, periodically went "over the top," only to gain a few yards of bloody ground before being thrown back with enormous causalities. Visual Source 21.4 shows a particular instance of this process by the British painter John Nash (1893–1977), who was an official war artist. Nash was also part of an eighty-man British unit that was sent over the top in late 1917 and one of only twelve

Visual Source 21.2 Defining the Enemy (The Art Archive)

Visual Source 21.3 War and the Colonies (Private collection/Barbara Singer/The Bridgeman Art Library

survivors of that attack. Three months later he painted this haunting picture from his memory of that experience.

- What posture toward the war does this image convey? Do you think Nash's military superiors were pleased by the painting?

- How does the painting portray the attitude of the soldiers?

- What does war do to human beings? What answer to this question does this image suggest?

- How might you imagine the response of those who created the first three images to John Nash and this portrayal of trench warfare?

Among the many outcomes of the Great War was the presence in every European country of disillusioned, maimed, and disfigured veterans, many of them literally "men without faces." For some intellectuals and artists, they represented the fundamentally flawed civilization that had given rise to such carnage. Often neglected or overlooked, such men were reminders of a terrible past that others wanted to forget. The German artist Otto Dix (1891–1969), who served in his country's military forces throughout the war and was seriously wounded, portrayed this situation in a 1920 painting called *Prague Street* (Visual Source 21.5). In 1924, he joined with other artists to mount an exhibition entitled No More War. His antiwar activism later earned Dix the enmity of the Hitler regime, which fired him from his academic position and destroyed some of his paintings. Artistically, Dix worked in a style known as the "new objectivity," which focused heavily on the horrendous outcomes of the war. It deliberately included subject matter that was upsetting and even ugly, and it made little attempt to create a unified image, preferring to present disconnected "particles of experience."

- How does the painting describe the situation of the veterans?

- On the left, the arm of a wealthy man drops a coin into the outstretched hand of a maimed veteran, while on the right, a well-dressed woman in a pink dress and high heels walks by with her dog. What do these features add to the portrayal of the plight of the veterans?

- Notice the leaflet on the skateboard of the legless cripple at the bottom. It reads *"Juden raus"* (Jews out)." What does this suggest about the political views of these veterans? Keep in mind that Hitler, although not maimed, was a disillusioned veteran of World War I, as were many of his early followers.

- What do the images in the store windows suggest?

- What commentary does this painting make on German society after the country's defeat in World War I? How does it foreshadow what was to come?

Visual Source 21.4 The Battlefield (Imperial War Museum, London/The Bridgeman Art Library)

Visual Source 21.5 The Aftermath of War (Kunstmuseum-Stuttgart © 2010 Artist's Rights Society (ARS), New York/VG Bildkunst, Bonn)

Using the Evidence:
Propaganda and Critique in World War I

1. **Describing the war:** Based on these visual sources, how would you define the novel or distinctive features of World War I compared to earlier European conflicts?

2. **Considering war and progress:** How do you think Otto Dix and John Nash might have responded to the ideas of Condorcet contained in Document 16.2, pages 752–54?

3. **Images as propaganda and criticism:** This selection of visual sources contains a mix of those that express essentially government-sponsored messages and those that convey the outlook of individual artists. What ideas about the war did governments seek to inculcate in their citizens? How do the paintings of John Nash and Otto Dix respond to those ideas?

4. **Seeking further evidence:** What other kinds of visual sources would be useful in constructing a visual history of World War I?

ЛЕНИН —
ЖИЛ,
ЛЕНИН —
ЖИВ,
ЛЕНИН —
БУДЕТ ЖИТЬ

ВЛ. МАЯКОВСКИЙ.

CHAPTER TWENTY-TWO

The Rise and Fall of World Communism

1917—PRESENT

Global Communism
Comparing Revolutions as a Path to Communism
 Russia: Revolution in a Single Year
 China: A Prolonged Revolutionary Struggle
Building Socialism in Two Countries
 Communist Feminism
 Socialism in the Countryside
 Communism and Industrial Development
 The Search for Enemies
East versus West: A Global Divide and a Cold War
 Military Conflict and the Cold War
 Nuclear Standoff and Third World Rivalry
 The United States: Superpower of the West, 1945–1975
 The Communist World, 1950s–1970s
Comparing Paths to the End of Communism
 China: Abandoning Communism and Maintaining the Party
 The Soviet Union: The Collapse of Communism and Country
Reflections: To Judge or Not to Judge
Considering the Evidence
 Documents: Experiencing Stalinism
 Visual Sources: Poster Art in Mao's China

"I was living in Germany on the day the wall came down and well remember talking to my German neighbour. With tears streaming down his face he kept saying in English and German: 'I never thought I would live to see this.'

"For anyone who didn't experience the Wall, it will be hard to imagine what an overwhelming feeling of relief, of joy, of unreality filled one that this monster was dead, and people had conquered it."[1]

Both of these eyewitness comments referred to that remarkable day, November 9, 1989, when the infamous Berlin Wall in Germany was breached. Built in 1961 to prevent the residents of communist East Berlin from escaping to the West, that concrete barrier had become a potent symbol of communist tyranny. Its fall, amid the overthrow of communist governments all across Eastern Europe, was part of a larger process that marked the collapse or the abandonment of communism as the twentieth century entered its final decade. In the midst of that euphoria, it was hard to remember that earlier in the century communism had been greeted with enthusiasm by many people—in Russia, China, Cuba, Vietnam, and elsewhere—as a promise of liberation from inequality, oppression, exploitation, and backwardness.

COMMUNISM WAS A PHENOMENON OF ENORMOUS SIGNIFICANCE IN THE WORLD OF THE TWENTIETH CENTURY. Communist regimes came to power almost everywhere in the tumultuous wake of war, revolution, or both. Once established, those regimes set about a thorough and revolutionary transformation of their societies—"building socialism," as they so often put it. Internationally, world communism

Lenin: Vladimir Ulyanov, better known as Lenin, was the Bolshevik leader of the Russian Revolution. He became the iconic symbol of world communism and in his own country was the focus of a semireligious cult. This widely distributed Soviet propaganda poster reads "Lenin lived; Lenin lives; Lenin will live." (David King Collection)

posed a profound military and political/ideological threat to the Western world of capitalism and democracy, particularly during the decades of the cold war (1946–1991). That struggle divided continents, countries, and cities into communist and non-communist halves. It also prompted a global rivalry between the United States and the Soviet Union (USSR) for influence in the third world. Most hauntingly, it spawned an arms race in horrendously destructive nuclear weapons that sent school-children scrambling under their desks during air raid drills, while sober scientists speculated about the possible extinction of human life, and perhaps all life, in the event of a major war.

Then, to the amazement of everyone, it was over, more with a whimper than a bang. The last two decades of the twentieth century witnessed the collapse of communist regimes or the abandonment of communist principles practically everywhere. The great global struggle of capitalism and communism, embodied in the United States and the Soviet Union, was resolved in favor of the former far more quickly and much more peacefully than anyone had imagined possible.

Global Communism

■ Description
When and where did communism exercise influence during the twentieth century?

Modern communism found its political and philosophical roots in nineteenth-century European socialism, inspired by the teachings of Karl Marx. (See p. 837 and Chapter 18's Documents: Varieties of European Marxism, pp. 855–66.) Although most European socialists came to believe that they could achieve their goals peacefully and through the democratic process, those who defined themselves as communists in the twentieth century disdained such reformism and advocated uncompromising revolution as the only possible route to a socialist future. Russia was the first country to experience such a revolution. Other movements that later identified or allied with the Soviet Union, as the Russian Empire was renamed after its 1917 revolution, likewise defined themselves as communist. In Marxist theory, communism also referred to a final stage of historical development when social equality and collective living would be most fully developed, wholly without private property. Socialism was an intermediate stage along the way to that final goal.

By the 1970s, almost one-third of the world's population lived in societies governed by communist regimes. By far the most significant were the Soviet Union, the world's largest country in size, and China, the world's largest country in population. This chapter focuses primarily on a comparison of these two large-scale experiments in communism and their global impact.

Beyond the Soviet Union and China, communism also came to Eastern Europe in the wake of World War II and the extension of the Soviet military presence there. In Asia, following Japan's defeat in that war, its Korean colony was partitioned, with the northern half coming under Soviet and therefore communist control. In Vietnam, a much more locally based communist movement, under the leadership of Ho Chi Minh, embodied both a socialist vision and Vietnamese nationalism as it battled Japanese, French, and later American invaders and established communist control first in the northern half of the country and after 1975 throughout the whole country. The victory of the Vietnamese communists spilled over into neighboring Laos and Cambodia, where communist parties took power in the mid-1970s. In Latin America, Fidel Castro led a revolutionary nationalist movement against a repressive and American-backed government in Cuba. On coming to power in 1959, he moved toward communism and an alliance with the Soviet Union. Finally, a shaky communist regime took power in Afghanistan in 1979, propped up briefly only by massive Soviet military support. None of these countries had achieved the kind of advanced industrial capitalism that Karl Marx had viewed as a prerequisite for revolution and socialism. In one of history's strange twists, the great revolutions of the twentieth century took place instead in largely agrarian societies.

In addition to those countries where communist governments exercised state power, communist parties took root in still other places, where they exercised various degrees of influence. In the aftermath of World War II, such parties played important political roles in Greece, France, and Italy. In the 1950s, a small communist party in the United States became the focus of an intense wave of fear and political repression known as McCarthyism. Revolutionary communist movements threatened established governments in the Philippines, Malaya, Indonesia, Bolivia, Peru, and elsewhere, sometimes provoking brutal crackdowns by those governments. A number of African states in the 1970s proclaimed themselves Marxist for a time and aligned with the Soviet Union in international affairs. All of this was likewise part of global communism.

These differing expressions of communism were linked to one another in various ways. They shared a common ideology derived from European Marxism, although it was substantially modified in many places. That ideology minimized the claims of national loyalty and looked forward to an international revolutionary movement of the lower classes and a worldwide socialist federation. The Russian Revolution of 1917 served as an inspiration and an example to aspiring revolutionaries elsewhere, and the new Soviet Communist Party and government provided them aid and advice. Through an organization called Comintern (Communist International), Soviet authorities also sought to control their policies and actions.

During the cold war decades, the Warsaw Pact brought the Soviet Union and Eastern European communist states together in a military alliance designed to counter the threat from the Western capitalist countries of the NATO alliance. A parallel organization called the Council on Mutual Economic Assistance tied Eastern European economies tightly to the economy of the Soviet Union. A Treaty of Friendship between the Soviet Union and China in 1950 joined the two communist giants in an alliance that caused many in the West to view communism as a unified international movement aimed at their destruction. Nevertheless, rivalry, outright hostility, and on occasion military conflict marked the communist world as much or more than solidarity and cooperation. Eastern European resentment of their Soviet overlords was expressed in periodic rebellions, even as the Soviet Union and China came close to war in the late 1960s.

Although the globalization of communism found expression primarily in the second half of the twentieth century, that process began with two quite distinct and different revolutionary upheavals—one in Russia and the other in China—in the first half of that century.

Comparing Revolutions as a Path to Communism

■ **Comparison**
Identify the major differences between the Russian and Chinese revolutions.

Communist movements of the twentieth century quite self-consciously drew on the mystique of the earlier French Revolution, which suggested that new and better worlds could be constructed by human actions. Like their French predecessors, communist revolutionaries ousted old ruling classes and dispossessed landed aristocracies. Those twentieth-century upheavals also involved vast peasant upheavals in the countryside and an educated leadership with roots in the cities. All three revolutions—French, Russian, and Chinese—found their vision of the good society in a modernizing future, not in some nostalgic vision of the past. Communists also worried lest their revolutions end up in a military dictatorship like that of Napoleon following the French Revolution.

But the communist revolutions were distinctive as well. They were made by highly organized parties guided by a Marxist ideology, were committed to an industrial future, pursued economic as well as political equality, and sought the abolition of private property. In doing so, they mobilized, celebrated, and claimed to act on behalf of society's lower classes—exploited urban workers and impoverished rural peasants. The middle classes, who were the chief beneficiaries of the French Revolution, numbered among the many victims of the communist upheavals. The Russian and Chinese revolutions shared these features, but in other respects they differed sharply from each other.

Russia: Revolution in a Single Year

In Russia, communists came to power on the back of a revolutionary upheaval that took place within a single year, 1917. The immense pressures of World War I, which was going very badly for the Russians, represented the catalyst for that revolution as the accumulated tensions of Russian society exploded (see pp. 843–46). Much exploited and suffering from wartime shortages, workers, men and women alike, took to the streets to express their outrage at the incompetence and privileges of their social betters. Activists from various parties, many of them socialist, recruited members, organized demonstrations, published newspapers, and plotted revolution. By February 1917, Tsar Nicholas II had lost almost all support and was forced to abdicate the throne, thus ending the Romanov dynasty, which had ruled Russia for more than three centuries.

That historic event opened the door to a massive social upheaval. Ordinary soldiers, seeking an end to a terrible war and despising their upper-class officers, deserted in substantial numbers. In major industrial centers such as St. Petersburg

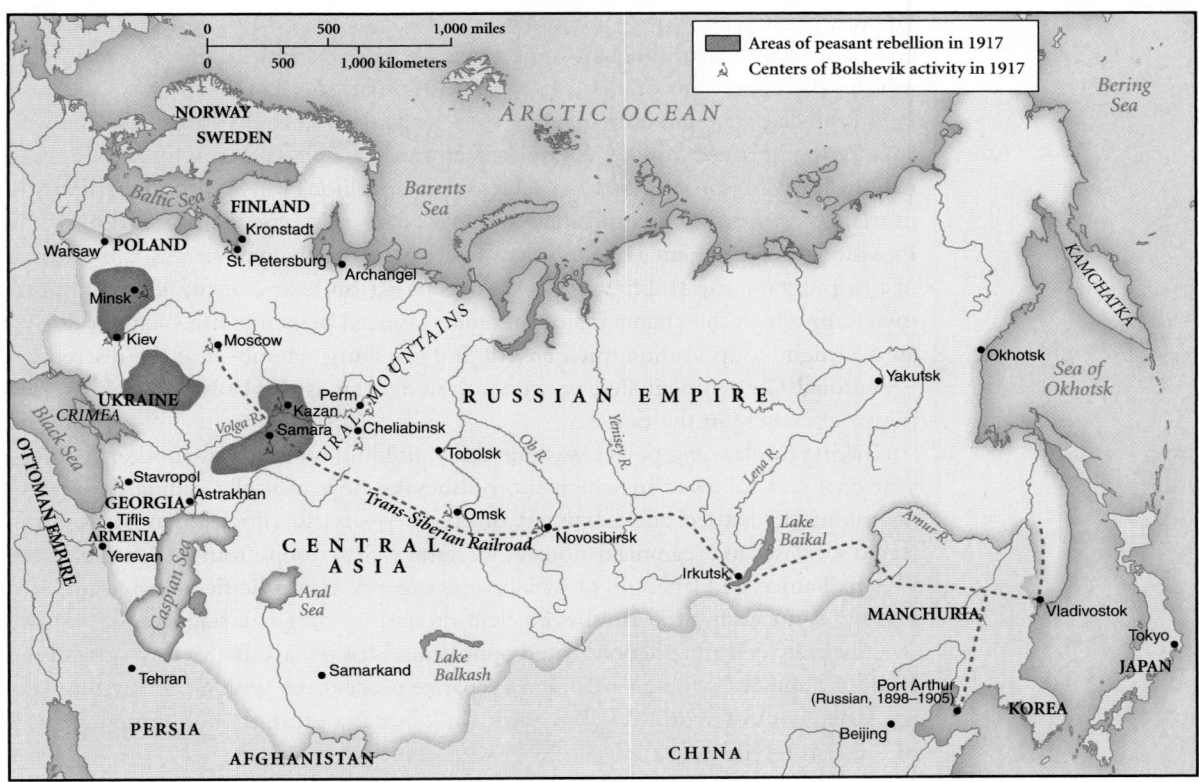

Map 22.1   Russia in 1917
During the First World War, the world's largest state, bridging both Europe and Asia, exploded in revolution in 1917. The Russian Revolution brought to power the twentieth century's first communist government and launched an international communist movement that eventually incorporated about one-third of the world's people.

and Moscow, new trade unions arose to defend workers' interests, and some workers seized control of their factories. Grassroots organizations of workers and soldiers, known as soviets, emerged to speak for ordinary people. Peasants, many of whom had been serfs only a generation or two ago, seized landlords' estates, burned their manor houses, and redistributed the land among themselves. Non-Russian nationalists in Ukraine, Poland, Muslim Central Asia, and the Baltic region demanded greater autonomy or even independence (see Map 22.1).

This was social revolution, and it quickly demonstrated the inadequacy of the Provisional Government, which had come to power after the tsar abdicated. Consisting of middle-class politicians and some socialist leaders, that government was divided and ineffectual, unable or unwilling to meet the demands of Russia's revolutionary masses. Nor was it willing to take Russia out of the war, as many were now demanding. Impatience and outrage against the Provisional Government provided an opening for more radical groups. The most effective were the Bolsheviks, a small socialist party with a determined and charismatic leader, Vladimir Ilyich Ulyanov, more commonly known as Lenin. He had long believed that Russia, despite its industrial backwardness, was nonetheless ready for a socialist revolution that would, he expected, spark further revolutions in the more developed countries of Europe (see

■ Change
Why were the Bolsheviks able to ride the Russian Revolution to power?

Document 18.5, pp. 864–65). Thus backward Russia would be a catalyst for a more general socialist breakthrough. It was a striking revision of Marxist thinking to accommodate the conditions of a largely agrarian Russian society.

In the desperate circumstances of 1917, his party's message—an end to the war, land for the peasants, workers' control of factories, self-determination for non-Russian nationalities—resonated with an increasingly rebellious public mood, particularly in the major cities. Lenin and the Bolsheviks also called for the dissolution of the Provisional Government and a transfer of state power to the new soviets. On the basis of this program, the Bolsheviks—claiming to act on behalf of the highly popular soviets, in which they had a major presence—seized power in late October during an overnight coup in the capital city of St. Petersburg. Members of the discredited Provisional Government fled or were arrested, even as the Bolsheviks also seized power elsewhere in the country.

Taking or claiming power was one thing; holding on to it was another. A three-year civil war followed in which the Bolsheviks, now officially calling their party "communist," battled an assortment of enemies—tsarist officials, landlords, disaffected socialists, and regional nationalist forces, as well as troops from the United States, Britain, France, and Japan, all of which were eager to crush the fledgling communist regime. Remarkably, the Bolsheviks held on and by 1921 had staggered to victory over their divided and uncoordinated opponents. That remarkable victory was assisted by the Bolsheviks' willingness to sign a separate peace treaty with Germany, thus taking Russia out of World War I in early 1918, but at a great, though temporary, loss of Russian territory.

During the civil war (1918–1921), the Bolsheviks had harshly regimented the economy, seized grain from angry peasants, suppressed nationalist rebellions, and perpetrated bloody atrocities, as did their enemies as well. But they also had integrated many lower-class men into the Red Army, as Bolshevik military forces were known, and into new local governments, providing them an avenue of social mobility not previously available. By battling foreign troops from the United States, Britain, France, and Japan, the Bolsheviks claimed to be defending Russia from imperialists and protecting the downtrodden masses from their exploiters. The civil war exaggerated even further the Bolsheviks' authoritarian tendencies and their inclination to use force. Shortly after that war ended, they renamed their country the Union of Soviet Socialist Republics and set about its transformation.

For the next twenty-five years, the Soviet Union remained a communist island in a capitalist sea. The next major extension of communist control occurred in Eastern Europe in the aftermath of World War II, but it took place quite differently than in Russia. The war had ended with Soviet military forces occupying much of Eastern Europe. Furthermore, Stalin, the USSR's longtime leader, had determined that Soviet security required "friendly" governments in the region so as to permanently end the threat of invasion from the West. When the Marshall Plan seemed to suggest American plans to incorporate Eastern Europe into a Western economic network,

Stalin acted to install fully communist governments, loyal to himself, in Poland, East Germany, Czechoslovakia, Hungary, Romania, and Bulgaria. Backed by the pressure and presence of the Soviet army, communism was largely imposed on Eastern Europe from outside rather than growing out of a domestic revolution, as had happened in Russia itself.

Local communist parties, however, had some domestic support, deriving from their role in the resistance against the Nazis and their policies of land reform. In Hungary and Poland, for example, communist pressures led to the redistribution of much land to poor or landless peasants, and in free elections in Czechoslovakia in 1946, communists received 38 percent of the vote. Furthermore, in Yugoslavia, a genuinely popular communist movement had played a leading role in the struggle against Nazi occupation and came to power on its own with little Soviet help. Its leader, Josef Broz, known as Tito, openly defied Soviet efforts to control it, claiming that "our goal is that everyone should be master in his own house."[2]

China: A Prolonged Revolutionary Struggle

Communism triumphed in the ancient land of China in 1949, about thirty years after the Russian Revolution, likewise on the heels of war and domestic upheaval. But that revolution, which was a struggle of decades rather than a single year, was far different from its earlier Russian counterpart. The Chinese imperial system had

■ **Change**
What was the appeal of communism in China before 1949?

collapsed in 1911, under the pressure of foreign imperialism, its own inadequacies, and mounting internal opposition (see pp. 888–89). Unlike Russia, where intellectuals had been discussing socialism for half a century or more before the revolution, the ideas of Karl Marx were barely known in China in the early twentieth century. Not until 1921 was a small Chinese Communist Party (CCP) founded, aiming its efforts initially at organizing the country's minuscule urban working class.

Over the next twenty-eight years, that small party, with an initial membership of only sixty people, grew enormously, transformed its strategy, found a charismatic leader in Mao Zedong, engaged in an epic struggle with its opponents, fought the Japanese heroically, and in 1949 emerged victorious as the rulers

Mao Zedong and the Long March
An early member of China's then minuscule Communist Party, Mao rose to a position of dominant leadership during the Long March of 1934–1935, when beleaguered communists from southeastern China trekked to a new base area in the north. This photograph shows Mao on his horse during that epic journey of some 6,000 miles. (Collection J.A. Fox/Magnum Photos)

of China. The victory was all the more surprising because the CCP faced a far more formidable foe than the weak Provisional Government over which the Bolsheviks had triumphed in Russia. That opponent was the Guomindang (Nationalist Party), which governed China after 1928. Led by a military officer, Chiang Kai-shek, that party promoted a measure of modern development (railroads, light industry, banking, airline services) in the decade that followed. However, the impact of these achievements was limited largely to the cities, leaving the rural areas, where most people lived, still impoverished. The Guomindang's base of support was also narrow, deriving from urban elites, rural landlords, and Western powers.

Chased out of China's cities in a wave of Guomindang-inspired anticommunist terror in 1927, the CCP groped its way toward a new revolutionary strategy, quite at odds with both classical Marxism and Russian practice. Whereas the Bolsheviks had found their primary audience among workers in Russia's major cities, Chinese communists increasingly looked to the country's peasant villages for support. Thus European Marxism was adapted once again, this time to fit the situation in a mostly peasant China. Still, it was no easy sell. Chinese peasants did not rise up spontaneously against their landlords, as Russian peasants had. However, years of guerrilla warfare, experiments with land reform in areas under communist control, efforts to empower women, and the creation of a communist military force to protect liberated areas from Guomindang attack and landlord reprisals—all of this slowly gained for the CCP a growing measure of respect and support among China's peasants. In the process, Mao Zedong, the son of a prosperous Chinese peasant family and a professional revolutionary since the early 1920s, emerged as the party's leader.

It was Japan's brutal invasion of China that gave the CCP a decisive opening, for that attack destroyed Guomindang control over much of the country and forced it to retreat to the interior, where it became even more dependent on conservative landlords. The CCP, by contrast, grew from just 40,000 members in 1937 to more than 1.2 million in 1945, while the communist-led People's Liberation Army mushroomed to 900,000 men, supported by an additional 2 million militia troops (see Map 22.2). Much of this growing support derived from the vigor with which the CCP waged war against the Japanese invaders. Using guerrilla warfare techniques learned in the struggle against the Guomindang, communist forces established themselves behind enemy lines and, despite periodic setbacks, offered a measure of security to many Chinese faced with Japanese atrocities. The Guomindang, by contrast, sometimes seemed to be more interested in eliminating the communists than in actively fighting the Japanese. Furthermore, in the areas it controlled, the CCP reduced rents, taxes, and interest payments for peasants; taught literacy to adults; and mobilized women for the struggle. As the war drew to a close, more radical action followed. Teams of activists, called cadres, encouraged poor peasants to "speak bitterness" in public meetings, to "struggle" with landlords, and to "settle accounts" with them.

Thus the CCP frontally addressed both of China's major problems—foreign imperialism and peasant exploitation. It expressed Chinese nationalism as well as a demand for radical social change. It gained a reputation for honesty that contrasted

Map 22.2   The Rise of Communism in China
Communism arose in China at the same time as the country was engaged in a terrible war with Japan and in the context of a civil war with Guomindang forces.

sharply with the massive corruption of Guomindang officials. It put down deep roots among the peasantry in a way that the Bolsheviks never did. And whereas the Bolsheviks gained support by urging Russian withdrawal from the highly unpopular First World War, the CCP won support by aggressively pursuing the struggle against Japanese invaders during World War II. In 1949, four years after the war's end, the Chinese communists swept to victory over the Guomindang, many of whose followers fled to Taiwan. Mao Zedong announced triumphantly in Beijing's Tiananmen Square that "the Chinese people have stood up."

Building Socialism in Two Countries

Once they came to power, the communist parties of the Soviet Union and China set about the construction of socialist societies. In the Soviet Union, this massive undertaking occurred under the leadership of Joseph Stalin in the 1920s and 1930s. The corresponding Chinese effort took place during the 1950s and 1960s with Mao Zedong at the helm.

To communist regimes, building socialism meant first of all the modernization and industrialization of their backward societies. In this respect, they embraced many of the material values of Western capitalist societies and were similar to the new nations of the twentieth century, all of which were seeking development. The communists, however, sought a distinctly socialist modernity. This involved a frontal attack on long-standing inequalities of class and gender, an effort to prevent the making of new inequalities as the process of modern development unfolded, and the promotion of cultural values of selflessness and collectivism that could support a socialist society.

Those imperatives generated a political system thoroughly dominated by the Communist Party. Top-ranking party members enjoyed various privileges but were expected to be exemplars of socialism in the making by being disciplined, selfless, and utterly loyal to their country's Marxist ideology. The party itself penetrated society in ways that Western scholars called "totalitarian," for other parties were forbidden, the state controlled almost the entire economy, and political authorities ensured that the arts, education, and the media conformed to approved ways of thinking. Mass organizations for women, workers, students, and various professional groups operated under party control, with none of the independence that characterized civil society in the West.

In undertaking these tasks, the Soviet Union and China started from different places, most notably their international positions. In 1917 Russian Bolsheviks faced a hostile capitalist world alone, while Chinese communists, coming to power over thirty years later, had an established Soviet Union as a friendly northern neighbor and ally. Furthermore, Chinese revolutionaries had actually governed parts of their huge country for decades, gaining experience that the new Soviet rulers had altogether lacked, since they had come to power so quickly. And the Chinese communists were firmly rooted in the rural areas and among the country's vast peasant population, while their Russian counterparts had found their support mainly in the cities.

If these comparisons generally favored China in its efforts to "build socialism," in economic terms, that country faced even more daunting prospects than did the Soviet Union. Its population was far greater, its industrial base far smaller, and the availability of new agricultural land far more limited than in the Soviet Union. China's literacy and modern education as well as its transportation network were likewise much less developed. Even more than the Soviets, Chinese communists had to build a modern society from the ground up.

Communist Feminism

Among the earliest and most revolutionary actions of these new communist regimes were efforts at liberating and mobilizing their women. Communist countries in fact pioneered forms of women's liberation that only later were adopted in the West. This communist feminism was largely state-directed, with the initiative coming from the top rather than bubbling up from grassroots movements as in the West. In the Soviet Union, where a small women's movement had taken shape in pre–World War I Russia, the new communist government almost immediately issued a series of laws and decrees regarding women. These measures declared full legal and political equality for women; marriage became a civil procedure among freely consenting adults; divorce was legalized and made easier, as was abortion; illegitimacy was abolished; women no longer had to take their husbands' surnames; pregnancy leave for employed women was mandated; and women were actively mobilized as workers in the country's drive to industrialization.

In 1919, the party set up a special organization called Zhenotdel (Women's Department), whose radical leaders, all women, pushed a decidedly feminist agenda in the 1920s. They organized numerous conferences for women, trained women to run day-care centers and medical clinics, published newspapers and magazines aimed at a female audience, provided literacy and prenatal classes, and encouraged Muslim women to take off their veils. Much of this encountered opposition from male communist officials and from ordinary people as well, and Stalin abolished Zhenotdel in 1930. While it lasted, though, it was a remarkable experiment in women's liberation by means of state action, animated by an almost utopian sense of new possibilities set loose by the revolution.

Similar policies took shape in communist China. The Marriage Law of 1950 was a direct attack on patriarchal and Confucian traditions. It decreed free choice in marriage, relatively easy divorce, the end of concubinage and child marriage, permission for widows to remarry, and equal property rights for women. A short but intense campaign by the CCP in the early 1950s sought to implement these changes, often against strenuous opposition. The party also launched a Women's Federation, a mass organization that enrolled millions of women. Its leadership, however, was far less radical than that of the Bolshevik feminists who led Zhenotdel in the 1920s. In China,

■ **Change**
What changes did communist regimes bring to the lives of women?

Mobilizing Women for Communism
As the Soviet Union mobilized for rapid economic development in the 1930s, women entered the workforce in great numbers. Here two young women are mastering the skills of driving a tractor on one of the large collective farms that replaced the country's private agriculture. (Sovfoto/Eastfoto)

there was little talk of "free love" or the "withering away of the family," as there had been in the USSR. Nevertheless, like their Soviet counterparts, Chinese women became much more actively involved in production outside the home. By 1978, 50 percent of agricultural workers and 38 percent of nonagricultural laborers were female. "Women can do anything" became a famous party slogan in the 1960s (see Visual Source 22.3, p. 1075).

Still, communist-style women's liberation had definite limits. Fearing that the women's question would detract from his emphasis on industrial production, Stalin declared it "solved" in 1930. Little direct discussion of women's issues was permitted in the several decades that followed. In neither the Soviet Union nor China did the Communist Party undertake a direct attack on male domination within the family. Thus the double burden of housework and child care plus paid employment continued to afflict most women. Moreover, women appeared only very rarely in the top political leadership of either country.

Socialism in the Countryside

■ **Comparison**
How did the collectivization of agriculture differ between the USSR and China?

In their efforts to build socialism, both the Soviet Union and China first expropriated landlords' estates and redistributed that land on a much more equitable basis to the peasantry. Such actions, although clearly revolutionary, were not socialist, for peasants initially received their land as private property. In Russia, the peasants had spontaneously redistributed the land among themselves, and the victorious Bolsheviks merely ratified their actions. In China after 1949, it was a more prolonged and difficult process. Hastily trained land reform teams were dispatched to the newly liberated areas, where they mobilized the poorer peasants in thousands of separate villages to confront and humiliate the landlords or the more wealthy peasants and seized their land, animals, tools, houses, and money for redistribution to the poorer members of the village. In the villages, the land reform teams encountered the age-old deference that peasants traditionally had rendered to their social superiors. One young woman activist described the confrontational meetings intended to break this ancient pattern:

> "Speak bitterness meetings," as they were called, would help [the peasants] to understand how things really had been in the old days, to realize that their lives were not blindly ordained by fate, that poor peasants had a community of interests, having suffered similar disasters and misery in the past—and that far from owing anything to the feudal landlords, it was the feudal landlords who owed them a debt of suffering beyond all reckoning.[3]

It was, as Mao Zedong put it, "not a dinner party." Approximately 1 to 2 million landlords were killed in the process, which was largely over by 1952.

A second and more distinctly socialist stage of rural reform sought to end private property in land by collectivizing agriculture. In China, despite brief resistance from richer peasants, collectivization during the 1950s was a generally peaceful process, owing much to the close relationship between the Chinese Communist Party and the peasantry, which had been established during three decades of struggle. This contrasted markedly with the experience of the Soviet Union from 1928 to 1933, when peasants were forced into collective farms and violence was extensive. Russian peasants slaughtered and consumed hundreds of thousands of animals rather than surrender them to the collectives. Stalin singled out the richer peasants, known as *kulaks*, for exclusion from the new collective farms. Some were killed, and many others were deported to remote areas of the country. With little support or experience in the countryside, Soviet communists, who came mostly from the cities, were viewed as intrusive outsiders in Russian peasant villages. A terrible famine ensued, with some 5 million deaths from starvation or malnutrition. (See Document 22.2, pp. 1062–64, for a firsthand account of the collectivization process.)

China pushed collectivization even further than the Soviet Union did, particularly in huge "people's communes" during the Great Leap Forward in the late 1950s. It was an effort to mobilize China's enormous population for rapid development and at the same time to move toward a more fully communist society with an even greater degree of social equality and collective living. (See Visual Source 22.2, p. 1073, for more on communes.) Administrative chaos, disruption of marketing networks, and bad weather combined to produce a massive famine that killed an amazing 20 million people or more between 1959 and 1962, dwarfing even the earlier Soviet famine.

Communism and Industrial Development

Both the Soviet Union and China defined industrialization as a fundamental task of their regimes. That process was necessary to end humiliating backwardness and poverty, to provide the economic basis for socialism, and to create the military strength that would enable their revolutions to survive in a hostile world. Though strongly anticapitalist, communists everywhere were ardent modernizers.

■ **Change**
What were the achievements of communist efforts at industrialization? What problems did these achievements generate?

When the Chinese communists began their active industrialization efforts in the early 1950s, they largely followed the model pioneered by the Soviet Union in the late 1920s and the 1930s. That model involved state ownership of property, centralized planning embodied in successive five-year plans, priority to heavy industry, massive mobilization of the nation's human and material resources, and intrusive Communist Party control of the entire process. (See Document 22.1, pp. 1060–62, and Document 22.3, pp. 1064–67, for more on Soviet industrialization.) Both countries experienced major—indeed unprecedented—economic growth. The Soviet Union constructed the foundations of an industrial society in the 1930s that proved itself in the victory over Nazi Germany in World War II and which by the 1960s and 1970s generated substantially improved standards of living. China too quickly expanded its output (see the Snapshot on p. 1042). In addition, both countries achieved massive improvements in their literacy rates and educational opportunities, allowing far greater social mobility for millions of people than ever before. In both countries, industrialization fostered a similar set of social outcomes: rapid urbanization, exploitation of the countryside to provide resources for modern industry in the cities, and

Snapshot   **China under Mao, 1949–1976**

The following table reveals some of the achievements, limitations, and tragedies of China's communist experience during the era of Mao Zedong.[4]

Steel production	from 1.3 million to 23 million tons
Coal production	from 66 million to 448 million tons
Electric power generation	from 7 million to 133 billion kilowatt-hours
Fertilizer production	from 0.2 million to 28 million tons
Cement production	from 3 million to 49 million tons
Industrial workers	from 3 million to 50 million
Scientists and technicians	from 50,000 to 5 million
"Barefoot doctors" posted to countryside	1 million
Annual growth rate of industrial output	11 percent
Annual growth rate of agricultural output	2.3 percent
Total population	from 542 million to 1 billion
Average population growth rate per year	2 percent
Per capita consumption of rural dwellers	from 62 to 124 yuan annually
Per capita consumption of urban dwellers	from 148 to 324 yuan
Overall life expectancy	from 35 to 65 years
Counterrevolutionaries killed (1949–1952)	between 1 million and 3 million
People labeled "rightists" in 1957	550,000
Deaths from famine during Great Leap Forward	20 million or more
Deaths during Cultural Revolution	500,000
Officials sent down to rural labor camps during Cultural Revolution	3 million or more
Urban youth sent down to countryside (1967–1976)	17 million

the growth of a privileged bureaucratic and technological elite intent on pursuing their own careers and passing on their new status to their children.

Perhaps the chief difference in the industrial histories of the Soviet Union and China lies in the leadership's response to these social outcomes. In the Soviet Union under Stalin and his successors, they were largely accepted. Industrialization was centered in large urban areas, which pulled from the countryside the most ambitious and talented people. A highly privileged group of state and party leaders emerged in the

Stalin era and largely remained the unchallenged ruling class of the country until the 1980s. Even in the 1930s, the outlines of a conservative society, which had discarded much of its revolutionary legacy, were apparent. Stalin himself endorsed Russian patriotism, traditional family values, individual competition, and substantial differences in wages to stimulate production, even as an earlier commitment to egalitarianism was substantially abandoned. Increasingly the invocation of revolutionary values was devoid of real content, and by the 1970s the perception of official hypocrisy was widespread.

The unique feature of Chinese history under Mao Zedong's leadership was a recurrent effort to combat these perhaps inevitable tendencies of any industrializing process and to revive and preserve the revolutionary spirit, which had animated the Communist Party during its long struggle for power. By the mid-1950s, Mao and some of his followers had become persuaded that the Soviet model of industrialization was leading China away from socialism and toward new forms of inequality, toward individualistic and careerist values, and toward an urban bias that privileged the cities at the expense of the countryside. The Great Leap Forward of 1958–1960 marked Mao's first response to these distortions of Chinese socialism. It promoted small-scale industrialization in the rural areas rather than focusing wholly on large enterprises in the cities; it tried to foster widespread and practical technological education for all rather than relying on a small elite of highly trained technical experts; and it envisaged an immediate transition to full communism in the "people's communes" rather than waiting for industrial development to provide the material basis for that transition. The disruptions and resentments occasioned by this Great Leap Forward, coupled with a series of droughts, floods, and typhoons, threw China into a severe crisis, including a massive famine that brought death and malnutrition to some 20 million people between 1959 and 1962.

In the mid-1960s, Mao launched yet another campaign—the Great Proletarian Cultural Revolution—to combat the capitalist tendencies that he believed had penetrated even the highest ranks of the Communist Party itself. The Cultural Revolution also involved new policies to bring health care and education to the countryside and to reinvigorate earlier efforts at rural industrialization under local rather than central control. In these ways, Mao struggled, though without great success, to

Substituting Manpower for Machinery
Lacking sophisticated equipment, Chinese communist leaders pursued a labor-intensive form of development, mobilizing the country's huge population in constructing the economic infrastructure for its industrial development. Here thousands of workers using ancient techniques participate in the building of a modern dam during China's Great Leap Forward in 1958. (Henry Cartier-Bresson/Magnum Photos)

overcome the inequalities associated with China's modern development and to create a model of socialist modernity quite distinct from that of the Soviet Union.

The Search for Enemies

■ Explanation
Why did communist regimes generate terror and violence on such a massive scale?

Despite their totalitarian tendencies, the communist societies of the Soviet Union and China were laced with conflict. Under both Stalin and Mao, those conflicts erupted in a search for enemies that disfigured both societies. An elastic concept of "enemy" came to include not only surviving remnants from the prerevolutionary elites but also, and more surprisingly, high-ranking members and longtime supporters of the Communist Party who allegedly had been corrupted by bourgeois ideas. Refracted through the lens of Marxist thinking, these people became class enemies who had betrayed the revolution and were engaged in a vast conspiracy, often linked to foreign imperialists, to subvert the socialist enterprise and restore capitalism. In the rhetoric of the leadership, the class struggle continued and in fact intensified as the triumph of socialism drew closer.

In the Soviet Union, that process culminated in the Terror, or the Great Purges, of the late 1930s, which enveloped tens of thousands of prominent communists, including virtually all of Lenin's top associates, and millions of more ordinary people. (See Document 22.4, pp. 1067–69, for personal experiences of the Terror.) Based on suspicious associations in the past, denunciations by colleagues, connections to foreign countries, or simply bad luck, such people were arrested, usually in the dead of night, and then tried and sentenced either to death or to long years in harsh and remote labor camps known as the gulag. Many of the accused were linked, almost always falsely, to the Nazis, who were then a real and growing external threat to the Soviet Union. A series of show trials publicized the menace that these "enemies of the people" allegedly posed to the country and its revolution. Close to 1 million people were executed between 1936 and 1941. Perhaps an additional 4 or 5 million were sent to the gulag, where they were forced to work in horrendous conditions and died in appalling numbers. Victimizers too were numerous: the Terror consumed the energies of a huge corps of officials, investigators, interrogators, informers, guards, and executioners, many of whom themselves were arrested, exiled, or executed in the course of the purges.

In the Soviet Union, the search for enemies occurred under the clear control of the state. In China, however, it became a much more public process, escaping the control of the leadership, particularly during the Cultural Revolution of 1966–1969. Mao had become convinced that many within the Communist Party had been seduced by capitalist values of self-seeking and materialism and were no longer animated by the idealistic revolutionary vision of earlier times. Therefore, he called for rebellion, against the Communist Party itself. Millions of young people responded, and, organized as Red Guards, they set out to rid China of those who were "taking the capitalist road." Following gigantic and ecstatic rallies in Beijing, they fanned out across the country and attacked local party and government officials, teachers, intellectuals, factory managers, and others they defined as enemies. (See Visual Sources 22.1 and 22.4, pp. 1072 and 1077). Rival revolutionary groups soon began fighting with one another, violence erupted throughout the country, and civil war threatened China. Mao found himself forced to call in the military to restore order and Communist Party control. Both the Soviet Terror and the Chinese Cultural Revolution badly discredited the very idea of socialism and contributed to the ultimate collapse of the communist experiment at the end of the century.

East versus West: A Global Divide and a Cold War

Not only did communist regimes bring revolutionary changes to the societies they governed, but they also launched a global conflict that restructured international life and touched the lives of almost everyone, particularly in the twentieth century's second half. That rift began soon after the Russian Revolution when the new communist government became the source of fear and loathing to many in the Western capitalist world. The common threat of Nazi Germany temporarily made unlikely allies of the Soviet Union, Britain, and the United States, but a few years after World War II ended, that division erupted again in what became known as the cold war. Underlying that conflict were the geopolitical and ideological realities of the postwar world. The Soviet Union and the United States were now the major political/military powers, replacing the shattered and diminished states of Western Europe, but they represented sharply opposed views of history, society, politics, and international relations. Conflict, in retrospect, seemed almost inevitable.

Military Conflict and the Cold War

The initial arena of the cold war was Europe, where Soviet insistence on security and control in Eastern Europe clashed with American and British desires for open and democratic societies with ties to the capitalist world economy. What resulted were rival military alliances (NATO and the Warsaw Pact), a largely voluntary American sphere of influence in Western Europe, and an imposed Soviet sphere in Eastern Europe. The heavily fortified border between Eastern and Western Europe came to be known as the Iron Curtain. Thus Europe was bitterly divided. But although tensions flared across this dividing line, particularly in Berlin, no shooting war occurred between the two sides (see Map 22.3).

■ **Connection**
In what different ways was the cold war expressed?

By contrast, the extension of communism into Asia—China, Korea, and Vietnam—globalized the cold war and led to its most destructive and prolonged "hot wars." A North Korean invasion of South Korea in 1950 led to both Chinese and American involvement in a bitter three-year war (1950–1953), which ended in an essential standoff that left the Korean peninsula still divided in the early twenty-first century. Likewise in Vietnam, military efforts by South Vietnamese communists and the already communist North Vietnamese government to unify their country prompted massive American intervention in the 1960s, peaking at some 550,000 U.S. troops. To American authorities, a communist victory opened the door to further communist expansion in Asia and beyond. Armed and supported by the Soviets and Chinese and willing to endure enormous losses, the Vietnamese communists bested

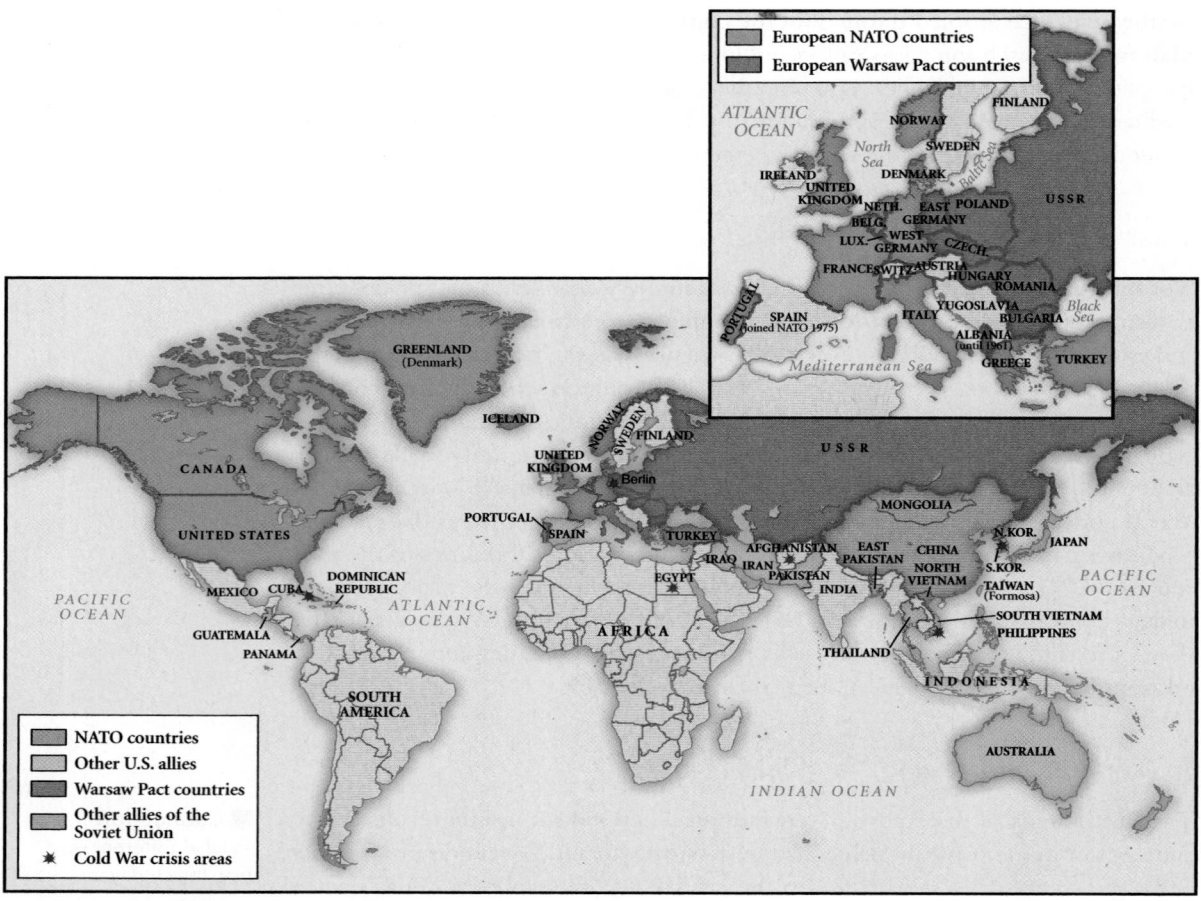

Map 22.3   The Global Cold War

The cold war sharply divided the world as a whole as well the continent of Europe; the countries of Korea, Vietnam, and Germany; and the city of Berlin. In many places, it also sparked crises that brought the nuclear-armed superpowers of the United States and the USSR to the brink of war, although in every case they managed to avoid direct military conflict between themselves.

the Americans, who were hobbled by growing protest at home. The Vietnamese united their country under communist control by 1975.

A third major military conflict of the cold war era occurred in Afghanistan, where a Marxist party had taken power in 1978. Soviet leaders were delighted at this extension of communism on their southern border, but radical land reforms and efforts to liberate Afghan women soon alienated much of this conservative Muslim country and led to a mounting opposition movement. Fearing the overthrow of a new communist state and its replacement by Islamic radicals, Soviet forces intervened militarily and were soon bogged down in a war they could not win. For a full decade (1979–1989), that war was a "bleeding wound," sustained in part by U.S. aid to Afghan guerrillas. Under widespread international pressure, Soviet forces finally withdrew in 1989, and the Afghan communist regime soon collapsed. In Vietnam and Afghanistan, both superpowers painfully experienced the limits of their power.

The most haunting battle of the cold war era was one that never happened. The setting was Cuba. When the revolutionary Fidel Castro came to power in 1959, his nationalization of American assets provoked great U.S. hostility and efforts to over-throw his regime. Such pressure only pushed this revolutionary nationalist closer to the Soviet Union, and gradually he began to think of himself and his revolution as Marxist. Soviet authorities were elated. "You Americans must realize what Cuba means to us old Bolsheviks," declared one high-ranking Soviet official. "We have been waiting all our lives for a country to go communist without the Red Army. It has hap-pened in Cuba, and it makes us feel like boys again."[5] Fearing the loss of their new-found Caribbean ally to American aggression, the Soviet leader Nikita Khrushchev, who had risen to power after Stalin's death in 1953, secretly deployed nuclear-tipped Soviet missiles to Cuba, believing that this would deter further U.S. action against Castro. When the missiles were discovered in October 1962, the world held its breath for thirteen days as American forces blockaded the island and prepared for an inva-sion. A nuclear exchange between the superpowers seemed imminent, but that catas-trophe was averted by a compromise between Khrushchev and U.S. president John F. Kennedy. Under its terms, the Soviets removed their missiles from Cuba in return for an American promise not to invade the island.

Nuclear Standoff and Third World Rivalry

The Cuban missile crisis gave concrete expression to the most novel and dangerous dimension of the cold war—the arms race in nuclear weapons. An American monop-oly on those weapons when World War II ended prompted the Soviet Union to redouble its efforts to acquire them, and in 1949 it succeeded. Over the next forty years, the world moved from a mere handful of nuclear weapons to a global arsenal of close to 60,000 warheads. Delivery systems included bomber aircraft and missiles that could rapidly propel numerous warheads across whole continents and oceans with accuracies measured in hundreds of feet. During those decades, the world's many peoples lived in the shadow of weapons whose destructive power is scarcely within the bounds of human imagination. A single bomb in a single instant could have obliterated any major city in the world. The detonation of even a small fraction of the weapons then in the arsenals of the Soviet Union and the United States could have reduced the target countries to radioactive rubble and social chaos. Responsible scientists seriously discussed the possible extinction of the human species under such conditions.

Awareness of this possibility is surely the primary reason that no shooting war of any kind occurred between the two superpowers. During the two world wars, the participants had been greatly sur-prised by the destructiveness of modern

The Hydrogen Bomb During the 1950s and early 1960s, tests in the atmos-phere of ever larger and more sophisticated hydro-gen bombs made images of enormous fireballs and mushroom-shaped clouds the universal symbol of these weapons, which were immensely more powerful than the atomic bombs dropped on Japan. The American test pictured here took place in 1957. (Image courtesy The Nuclear Weapon Archive)

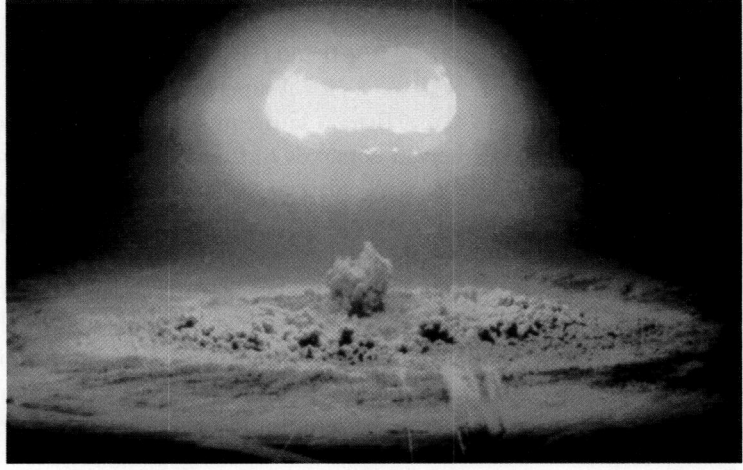

weapons. During the cold war, however, the leaders of the two superpowers knew beyond any doubt that a nuclear war would produce only losers and utter catastrophe. Already in 1949, Stalin had observed that "atomic weapons can hardly be used without spelling the end of the world."[6] Furthermore, the deployment of reconnaissance satellites made it possible to know with some clarity the extent of the other side's arsenals. Particularly after the frightening Cuban missile crisis of 1962, both sides carefully avoided further nuclear provocation, even while continuing the buildup of their respective arsenals. Moreover, because they feared that a conventional war would escalate to the nuclear level, they implicitly agreed to sidestep any direct military confrontation at all.

Still, opportunities for conflict abounded as the U.S.-Soviet rivalry spanned the globe. Using military and economic aid, educational opportunities, political pressure, and covert action, both sides courted countries just emerging from colonial rule. (These became known as "third-world" countries—distinct from the "first world" of the developed West and the "second world" of communist countries.) Cold war fears of communist penetration prompted U.S. intervention, sometimes openly and often secretly, in Iran, the Philippines, Guatemala, El Salvador, Chile, the Congo, and elsewhere. In the process the United States frequently supported anticommunist but corrupt and authoritarian regimes. However, neither superpower was able to completely dominate its supposed third-world allies, many of whom resisted the role of pawns in superpower rivalries. Some countries, such as India, took a posture of non-alignment in the cold war, while others tried to play off the superpowers against each other. Indonesia received large amounts of Soviet and Eastern European aid, but that did not prevent it from destroying the Indonesian Communist Party in 1965, butchering half a million suspected communists in the process. When the Americans refused to assist Egypt in building the Aswan Dam in the mid-1950s, that country developed a close relationship with the Soviet Union. Later, in 1972, Egypt expelled 21,000 Soviet advisers and again aligned more clearly with the United States.

The United States: Superpower of the West, 1945–1975

■ Connection
In what ways did the United States play a global role after World War II?

World War II and the cold war provided the context for the emergence of the United States as a global superpower, playing a role that has often been compared to that of Great Britain in the nineteenth century. Much of that effort was driven by the perceived demands of the cold war, during which the United States spearheaded the Western effort to contain a worldwide communist movement that seemed to be advancing. A series of global alliances and military bases sought to create a barrier against further communist expansion and to provide launching pads for military action should it become necessary. By 1970, one writer observed, "the United States had more than 1,000,000 soldiers in 30 countries, was a member of four regional defense alliances and an active participant in a fifth, had mutual defense treaties with 42 nations, was a member of 53 international organizations, and was furnishing military or economic aid to nearly 100 nations across the face of the globe."[7]

The need for quick and often secret decision making gave rise in the United States to a strong or "imperial" presidency and a "national security state," in which defense and intelligence agencies acquired great power within the government and were often unaccountable to Congress. With power so focused in the executive branch, critics charged that democracy itself was undermined. Fear of internal subversion produced an intense anticommunism in the 1950s and in general narrowed the range of political debate in the country as both parties competed to appear tough on communism. All of this served to strengthen the influence of what U.S. president Dwight Eisenhower (1953–1961) called the "military-industrial complex," a coalition of the armed services, military research laboratories, and private defense industries that both stimulated and benefited from increased military spending and cold war tensions.

Sustaining this immense military effort was a flourishing U.S. economy and an increasingly middle-class society. The United States, of course, was the only major industrial society to escape the physical devastation of war on its own soil. As World War II ended with Europe, the Soviet Union, and Japan in ruins, the United States was clearly the world's most productive economy. "The whole world is hungry for American goods," wrote one American economist in 1945. "Everyone would like to have the opportunity of riding in American automobiles, of drinking American fruit juices, and of possessing electric refrigerators and other conveniences of life."[8] Americans were a "people of plenty," ready and willing "to show to other countries the path that may lead them to plenty like our own."[9] Beyond their goods, Americans sent their capital abroad in growing amounts—from $19 billion in 1950 to $81 billion in 1965. Huge American firms such as General Motors, Ford, Mobil, Sears, General Electric, and Westinghouse established factories, offices, and subsidiaries in many countries and sold their goods locally. The U.S. dollar replaced the British pound as the most trusted international currency.

Accompanying the United States' political and economic penetration of the world was its popular culture. In musical terms, first jazz, then rock-and-roll, and most recently rap have found receptive audiences abroad, particularly among the young. Blacks in South Africa took up American "Negro spirituals." In the Soviet Union, American rock-and-roll became the music of dissent and a way of challenging the values of communist culture. Muslim immigrants to France as well as young Japanese have developed local traditions of rap. By the 1990s, American movies took about 70 percent of the market in Europe, and some 20,000 McDonald's restaurants in 100 countries served 30 million customers every day. Various American brand names— Kleenex, Coca-Cola, Jeep, Spam, Nike, Kodak—became common points of reference around the world. English became a global language, while American slang terms— "groovy," "crazy," "cool"—were integrated into many of the world's languages.

The Communist World, 1950s–1970s

On the communist side, the cold war was accompanied by considerable turmoil both within and among the various communist states. Joseph Stalin, Soviet dictator and

■ **Description**
What were the strengths and weaknesses of the communist world by the 1970s?

acknowledged leader of the communist world in general, died in 1953 as that global conflict was mounting. His successor, Nikita Khrushchev, stunned his country and communists everywhere with a lengthy speech delivered to a party congress in 1956 in which he presented a devastating account of Stalin's crimes, particularly those against party members. "Everywhere and in everything, he [Stalin] saw 'enemies,' 'two-facers,' and 'spies,'" declared Khrushchev. "Possessing unlimited power, he indulged in great willfulness and choked a person morally and physically."[10] These revelations shocked many of the party faithful, for Stalin had been viewed as the "genius of all time." Now he was presented as a criminal.

In the Soviet Union, the superpower of the communist world, the cold war justified a continuing emphasis on military and defense industries after World War II and gave rise to a Soviet version of the military-industrial complex. Sometimes called a "metal-eater's alliance," this complex joined the armed forces with certain heavy industries to press for a weapons buildup that benefited both. Soviet citizens, even more than Americans, were subject to incessant government propaganda that glorified the Soviet system and vilified that of their American opponents.

As the communist world expanded, so too did divisions and conflicts among its various countries. Many in the West had initially viewed world communism as a monolithic force whose disciplined members meekly followed Soviet dictates in cold war solidarity against the West. And Marxists everywhere contended that revolutionary socialism would erode national loyalties as the "workers of the world" united in common opposition to global capitalism. Nonetheless, the communist world experienced far more bitter and divisive conflict than did the Western alliance, which was composed of supposedly warlike, greedy, and highly competitive nations.

In Eastern Europe, Yugoslav leaders early on had rejected Soviet domination of their internal affairs and charted their own independent road to socialism. Fearing that reform might lead to contagious defections from the communist bloc, Soviet

Czechoslovakia, 1968
In August 1968, Soviet forces invaded Czechoslovakia, where a popular reform movement proclaiming "socialism with a human face" threatened to erode established communist control. The Soviet troops that crushed this so-called Prague Spring were greeted by thousands of peaceful street demonstrators begging them to go home. (Bettmann/Corbis)

forces actually invaded their supposed allies in Hungary (1956–1957) and Czechoslovakia (1968) to crush such movements. In the early 1980s, Poland was seriously threatened with a similar action. The brutal suppression of these reform movements gave credibility to Western perceptions of the cold war as a struggle between tyranny and freedom and badly tarnished the image of Soviet communism as a reasonable alternative to capitalism.

Even more startling, the two communist giants, the Soviet Union and China, found themselves sharply opposed, owing to territorial disputes, ideological differences, and rivalry for communist leadership. The Chinese bitterly criticized Khrushchev for backing down in the Cuban missile crisis, while to the Soviet leadership, Mao was insanely indifferent to the possible consequences of a nuclear war. In 1960, the Soviet Union backed away from an earlier promise to provide China with the prototype of an atomic bomb and abruptly withdrew all Soviet advisers and technicians, who had been assisting Chinese development. By the late 1960s, China on its own had developed a modest nuclear capability, and the two countries were at the brink of war, with the Soviet Union hinting at a possible nuclear strike on Chinese military targets. Their enmity certainly benefited the United States, which in the 1970s was able to pursue a "triangular diplomacy," easing tensions and simultaneously signing arms control agreements with the USSR and opening a formal relationship with China. Beyond this central conflict, a communist China in fact went to war against a communist Vietnam in 1979, while Vietnam invaded a communist Cambodia in the late 1970s. Nationalism, in short, proved more powerful than communist solidarity, even in the face of cold war hostilities with the West.

Despite its many internal conflicts, world communism remained a powerful global presence during the 1970s, achieving its greatest territorial reach. China was emerging from the chaos of the Cultural Revolution. The Soviet Union had matched U.S. military might; in response, the Americans launched a major buildup of their own military forces in the early 1980s. Despite American hostility, Cuba remained a communist outpost in the Western Hemisphere, with impressive achievements in education and health care for its people. Communism triumphed in Vietnam, dealing a major setback to the United States. A number of African countries affirmed their commitment to Marxism. Few people anywhere expected that within two decades most of the twentieth century's experiment with communism would be gone.

Comparing Paths to the End of Communism

More rapidly than its beginning, and far more peacefully, the communist era came to an end during the last two decades of the twentieth century. It was a drama in three acts. Act One began in China during the late 1970s, following the death of its towering revolutionary leader Mao Zedong in 1976. Over the next several decades, the CCP gradually abandoned almost everything that had been associated with Maoist communism, even as the party retained its political control of the country. Act Two took place in Eastern Europe in the "miracle year" of 1989, when popular movements toppled despised communist governments one after another all across the region. The climactic act in this "end of communism" drama occurred in 1991 in the Soviet Union, where the entire "play" had opened seventy-four years earlier. There the reformist leader Mikhail Gorbachev had come to power in 1985 intending to revive and save Soviet socialism from its accumulated dysfunctions. Those efforts, however, only exacerbated the country's many difficulties and led to the political disintegration of the Soviet Union on Christmas Day of 1991. The curtain had fallen on the communist era and on the cold war as well.

■ Change
What explains the rapid end of the communist era?

Behind these separate stories lay two general failures of the communist experiment, measured both by their own standards and by those of the larger world. The first was economic. Despite their early successes, communist economies by the late 1970s showed no signs of catching up to the more advanced capitalist countries. The highly regimented Soviet economy in particular was largely stagnant; its citizens were forced to stand in long lines for consumer goods and complained endlessly about their poor quality and declining availability. This was enormously embarrassing, for it had been the proud boast of communist leaders everywhere that they had found a better route to modern prosperity than their capitalist rivals. Furthermore, these comparisons were increasingly well known, thanks to the global information revolution. They had security implications as well, for economic growth, even more than military capacity, was the measure of state power as the twentieth century approached its end.

The second failure was moral. The horrors of Stalin's Terror and the gulag, of Mao's Cultural Revolution, of something approaching genocide in communist Cambodia— all of this wore away at communist claims to moral superiority over capitalism. Moreover, this erosion occurred as global political culture more widely embraced democracy and human rights as the universal legacy of humankind, rather than the exclusive possession of the capitalist West. In both economic and moral terms, the communist path to the modern world was increasingly seen as a road to nowhere.

Communist leaders were not ignorant of these problems, and particularly in China and the Soviet Union, they moved aggressively to address them. But their approach to doing so varied greatly, as did the outcomes of those efforts. Thus, much as the Russian and Chinese revolutions differed and their approaches to building socialism diverged, so too did these communist giants chart distinct paths during the final years of the communist experiment.

China: Abandoning Communism and Maintaining the Party

As the dust settled from the political shakeout following Mao's death in 1976, Deng Xiaoping emerged as China's "paramount leader," committed to ending the periodic upheavals of the Maoist era while fostering political stability and economic growth. Soon previously banned plays, operas, films, and translations of Western classics reappeared, and a "literature of the wounded" exposed the sufferings of the Cultural Revolution. Some 100,000 political prisoners, many of them high-ranking communists, were released and restored to important positions. A party evaluation of Mao severely criticized his mistakes during the Great Leap Forward and the Cultural Revolution, while praising his role as a revolutionary leader.

Even more dramatic were Deng's economic reforms. In the rural areas, these reforms included a rapid dismantling of the country's system of collectivized farming and a return to something close to small-scale private agriculture. Impoverished Chinese peasants eagerly embraced these new opportunities and pushed them even further than the government had intended. Industrial reform proceeded more gradually. Managers of state enterprises were given greater authority and encouraged to act like private owners, making many of their own decisions and seeking profits. China opened itself to the world economy and welcomed foreign investment in special enterprise zones along the coast, where foreign capitalists received tax breaks and other inducements. Local governments and private entrepreneurs joined forces in thousands of flourishing "township and village enterprises" that produced food, clothing, building materials, and much more.

The outcome of these reforms was stunning economic growth, the most rapid and sustained in world history, and a new prosperity for millions. Better diets, lower mortality rates, declining poverty, massive urban construction, and surging exports accompanied China's rejoining of the world economy, contributed to a much-improved material life for many of its citizens, and prompted much commentary about China as the economic giant of the twenty-first century. On the other hand, the country's burgeoning economy also generated massive corruption among Chinese officials, sharp inequalities between the coast and the interior, a huge problem of urban overcrowding, terrible pollution in major cities, and periodic inflation as the state loosened its controls over the economy. Urban vices such as street crime, prostitution, gambling, drug addiction, and a criminal underworld, which had been largely eliminated after 1949, surfaced again in China's booming cities. Nonetheless, something remarkable had occurred in China: an essentially capitalist economy had been restored, and by none other than the Communist Party itself. Mao's worst fears had been realized, as China "took the capitalist road." (See Visual Source 22.5, p. 1078, and Visual Source 24.2, p. 1183.)

Although the party was willing to largely abandon communist economic policies, it was adamantly unwilling to relinquish its political monopoly or to promote democracy at the national level. "Talk about democracy in the abstract," Deng Xiaoping declared, "will inevitably lead to the unchecked spread of ultra-democracy and anarchism, to the complete disruption of political stability, and to the total failure of our modernization program.... China will once again be plunged into chaos, division, retrogression, and darkness."[11] Such attitudes associated democracy with the chaos and uncontrolled mass action of the Cultural Revolution. Thus, when a democracy movement spearheaded by university and secondary school students surfaced in the late 1980s, Deng ordered the brutal crushing of its brazen demonstration in Beijing's Tiananmen Square before the television cameras of the world.

After Communism in China Although the Communist Party still governed China in the early twenty-first century, communist values of selflessness, community, and simplicity had been substantially replaced for many by Western-style consumerism. Here a group of young people in Shanghai are eating at a Kentucky Fried Chicken restaurant, drinking Pepsi, wearing clothing common to modern youth everywhere, and using their ubiquitous cell phones. (Mike Kemp/Corbis)

China entered the new millennium as a rapidly growing economic power with an essentially capitalist economy presided over by an intact and powerful Communist Party. Culturally, some combination of nationalism, consumerism, and a renewed respect for ancient traditions had replaced the collectivist and socialist values of the Maoist era. It was a strange and troubled hybrid.

The Soviet Union: The Collapse of Communism and Country

■ Comparison

How did the end of communism in the Soviet Union differ from communism's demise in China?

By the mid-1980s, the reformist wing of the Soviet Communist Party, long squelched by an aging conservative establishment, had won the top position in the party as Mikhail Gorbachev assumed the role of general secretary. Like Deng Xiaoping in China, Gorbachev was committed to aggressively tackling the country's many problems—economic stagnation, a flourishing black market, public apathy, and cynicism about the party. His economic program, launched in 1987 and known as *perestroika* (restructuring), paralleled aspects of the Chinese approach by freeing state enterprises from the heavy hand of government regulation, permitting small-scale private businesses called cooperatives, offering opportunities for private farming, and cautiously welcoming foreign investment in joint enterprises.

Heavy resistance to these modest efforts from entrenched party and state bureaucracies persuaded Gorbachev to seek allies outside of official circles. The vehicle was *glasnost* (openness), a policy of permitting a much wider range of cultural and intellectual freedoms in Soviet life. He hoped that glasnost would overcome the pervasive, long-standing distrust between society and the state and would energize Soviet society for the tasks of economic reform. "We need *glasnost*," Gorbachev declared, "like we need the air."[12]

In the late 1980s, glasnost hit the Soviet Union like a bomb. Newspapers and TV exposed social pathologies—crime, prostitution, child abuse, suicide, corruption, and homelessness—that previously had been presented solely as the product of capitalism. Films broke the ban on nudity and explicit sex. TV reporters climbed the wall of a secluded villa to film the luxurious homes of the party elite. Soviet history was also reexamined as revelations of Stalin's crimes poured out of the media. The Bible and the Quran became more widely available, atheistic propaganda largely ceased, and thousands of churches and mosques were returned to believers and opened for worship. Plays, poems, films, and novels that had long been buried "in the drawer" were now released to a public that virtually devoured them. "Like an excited boy reads a note from his girl," wrote one poet, "that's how we read the papers today."[13]

Beyond glasnost lay democratization and a new parliament with real powers, chosen in competitive elections. When those elections occurred in 1989, dozens of leading communists were rejected at the polls. And when the new parliament met and actually debated controversial issues, its televised sessions were broadcast to a transfixed audience of 100 million or more. In foreign affairs, Gorbachev moved to end the cold war by making unilateral cuts in Soviet military forces, engaging in arms control negotiations with the United States, and refusing to intervene as communist governments in Eastern Europe were overthrown. Thus the Soviet reform program was far more broadly based than that of China, for it embraced dramatic cultural and political changes, which Chinese authorities refused to consider.

Despite his good intentions, almost nothing worked out as Gorbachev had anticipated. Far from strengthening socialism and reviving a stagnant Soviet Union, the reforms led to its further weakening and collapse. In a dramatic contrast with China's booming economy, that of the Soviet Union spun into a sharp decline as its planned economy was dismantled before a functioning market-based system could emerge. Inflation mounted; consumer goods were in short supply, and ration coupons reappeared; many feared the loss of their jobs. Unlike Chinese peasants, few Soviet farmers were willing to risk the jump into private farming, and few foreign investors found the Soviet Union a tempting place to do business.

Furthermore, the new freedoms provoked demands that went far beyond what Gorbachev had intended. A democracy movement of unofficial groups and parties now sprang to life, many of them seeking a full multiparty democracy and a market-based economy. They were joined by independent labor unions, which actually went on strike, something unheard of in the "workers' state." Most corrosively, a multitude of nationalist movements used the new freedoms to insist on greater autonomy, or even independence, from the Soviet Union. In the Baltic republics of Latvia, Lithuania, and Estonia, nationalists organized a human chain some 370 miles long, sending the word "freedom" along the line of a million people. Even in Russia, growing numbers came to feel that they too might be better off without the Soviet Union. In the face of these mounting demands, Gorbachev resolutely refused to use force to crush the protesters, another sharp contrast with the Chinese experience.

Events in Eastern Europe now intersected with those in the Soviet Union. Gorbachev's reforms had lit a fuse in these Soviet satellites, where communism had been imposed and maintained from outside. If the USSR could practice glasnost and hold competitive elections, why not Eastern Europe as well? This was the background for the "miracle year" of 1989. Massive demonstrations, last-minute efforts at reforms, the breaching of the Berlin Wall, the surfacing of new political groups—all of this and more quickly overwhelmed the highly unpopular communist regimes of Poland, Hungary, East Germany, Bulgaria, Czechoslovakia, and Romania, which were quickly swept away. This success then emboldened nationalists and democrats in the Soviet Union. If communism had been overthrown in Eastern Europe, perhaps it could be overthrown in the USSR as well. Soviet conservatives and patriots, however, were outraged. To them, Gorbachev had stood idly by while the political gains of World War II, for which the Soviet Union had paid in rivers of blood, vanished before their eyes. It was nothing less than treason.

A brief and unsuccessful attempt to restore the old order through a military coup in August 1991 triggered the end of the Soviet Union and its communist regime.

From the wreckage there emerged fifteen new and independent states, following the internal political divisions of the USSR (see Map 22.4). Within Russia itself, the Communist Party was actually banned for a time in the place of its origin.

The Soviet collapse represented a unique phenomenon in the world of the late twentieth century. Simultaneously, the world's largest state and its last territorial empire vanished; the first Communist Party disintegrated; a powerful command economy broke down; an official socialist ideology was repudiated; and a forty-five-year global struggle between the East and the West ended. In Europe, Germany was reunited, and a number of former communist states joined NATO and the European Union, ending the division of that continent. At least for the moment, capitalism and democracy seemed to triumph over socialism and authoritarian governments. In many places, the end of communism allowed simmering ethnic tensions to explode into open conflict. Beyond the disintegration of the Soviet Union, both Yugoslavia and Czechoslovakia fragmented, the former amid terrible violence and the latter peacefully. Chechens in Russia, Abkhazians in Georgia, Russians in the Baltic states and Ukraine, Tibetans and Uighurs in China—all of these minorities found themselves in opposition to the states in which they lived.

As the twenty-first century dawned, the communist world had shrunk considerably from its high point just three decades earlier. In the Soviet Union and East-

Map 22.4 The Collapse of the Soviet Empire
Soviet control over its Eastern European dependencies vanished as those countries threw off their communist governments in 1989. Then, in 1991, the Soviet Union itself disintegrated into fifteen separate states, none of them governed by communist parties.

ern Europe, communism had disappeared entirely as the governing authority and dominant ideology, although communist parties continued to play a role in some countries. China had largely abandoned its communist economic policies as a market economy took shape. Like China, Vietnam and Laos remained officially communist, even while they pursued Chinese-style reforms, though more cautiously. Even Cuba, which was beset by economic crisis in the 1990s after massive Soviet subsidies ended, allowed small businesses, private food markets, and tourism to grow, while harshly repressing opposition political groups. An impoverished North Korea remained the most unreformed and repressive of the remaining communist countries.

International tensions born of communism remained only in East Asia and the Caribbean. North Korea's threat to develop nuclear weapons posed a serious international issue. Continuing tension between China and Taiwan as well as between the United States and Cuba were hangovers from the cold war era. But either as a primary source of international conflict or as a compelling path to modernity and social justice, communism was effectively dead. The communist era in world history had ended.

⊢⊣ Reflections: To Judge or Not to Judge

Should historians or students of history make moral judgments about the people and events they study? On the one hand, some would argue, scholars do well to act as detached and objective observers of the human experience, at least as much as possible. The task is to describe what happened and to explain why things turned out as they did. Whether we approve or condemn the outcomes of the historical process is, in this view, beside the point. On the other hand, all of us, scholars and students alike, stand somewhere. We are members of particular cultures; we have values and outlooks on the world that inevitably affect the way we write or think about the past. Perhaps it is better to recognize and acknowledge these limitations than to pretend some unattainable objectivity that places us above it all. Furthermore, making judgments is a way of connecting with the past, of affirming our continuing relationship with those who have gone before us. It shows that we care.

The question of making judgments arises strongly in any examination of the communist phenomenon. In a United States without a strong socialist tradition, sometimes saying anything positive about communism or even noting its appeal to millions of people has brought charges of whitewashing its crimes. Within the communist world, even modest criticism was usually regarded as counterrevolutionary and was largely forbidden and harshly punished. Certainly few observers were neutral in their assessment of the communist experiment.

Were the Russian and Chinese revolutions a blow for human freedom and a cry for justice on the part of oppressed people, or did they simply replace one tyranny with another? Was Stalinism a successful effort to industrialize a backward country or a ferocious assault on its moral and social fabric? Did Chinese reforms of the late twentieth century represent a return to sensible policies of modernization, a continued denial of basic democratic rights, or an opening to capitalist inequalities, corruption, and acquisitiveness? Passionate debate continues on all of these questions.

Communism, like many human projects, has been an ambiguous enterprise. On the one hand, communism brought hope to millions by addressing the manifest injustices of the past; by providing new opportunities for women, workers, and peasants; by promoting rapid industrial development; and by ending Western domination. On the other hand, communism was responsible for mountains of crimes—millions killed and wrongly imprisoned; massive famines partly caused by radical policies; human rights violated on an enormous scale; lives uprooted and distorted by efforts to achieve the impossible.

Studying communism challenges our inclination to want definitive answers and clear moral judgments. Can we hold contradictory elements in some kind of tension? Can we affirm our own values while acknowledging the ambiguities of life, both past and present? Doing so is arguably among the essential tasks of growing up and achieving a measure of intellectual maturity. That is the gift, both painful and enormously enriching, that the study of history offers to us all.

Second Thoughts

What's the Significance?

To assess your mastery of the material in this chapter, visit the **Student Center** at bedfordstmartins.com/strayer.

Russian Revolution (1917)	Stalin	Nikita Khrushchev
Bolsheviks/Lenin	Zhenotdel	Mikhail Gorbachev
Guomindang	collectivization	Deng Xiaoping
Chinese Revolution	Cultural Revolution	perestroika/glasnost
Mao Zedong	Great Purges/Terror	
building socialism	Cuban missile crisis	

Big Picture Questions

1. What was the appeal of communism, in terms of both its promise and its achievements? To what extent did it fulfill that promise?
2. Why did the communist experiment, which was committed to equality and a humane socialism, generate such oppressive, brutal, and totalitarian regimes?
3. What is distinctive about twentieth-century communist industrialization and modernization compared to the same processes in the West a century earlier?
4. What was the global significance of the cold war?
5. "The end of communism was as revolutionary as its beginning." Do you agree with this statement?
6. In what different ways did the Soviet Union and China experience communism during the twentieth century?

Next Steps: For Further Study

Archie Brown, *The Gorbachev Factor* (1996). A careful examination of Gorbachev's role in the collapse of the Soviet Union.

Jung Chang, *Wild Swans* (2004). A compelling view of twentieth-century Chinese history through the eyes of three generations of women in a single family.

Timothy Check, *Mao Zedong and China's Revolutions* (2002). A collection of documents about the Chinese Revolution and a fine introduction to the life of Mao.

John L. Gaddis, *The Cold War: A New History* (2005). An overview by one of the most highly regarded historians of the cold war.

Peter Kenez, *A History of the Soviet Union from the Beginning to the End* (1999). A thoughtful overview of the entire Soviet experience.

Maurice Meisner, *Mao's China and After* (1999). A provocative history of Mao's China and what followed.

Robert Strayer, *The Communist Experiment: Revolution, Socialism, and Global Conflict in the Twentieth Century* (2007). A comparative study of Soviet and Chinese communism.

"Mao Zedong Reference Archive," http://www.marxists.org/reference/archive/mao. A Web site offering the translated writings of Mao, including poetry and some images.

"Soviet Archives Exhibit," http://www.ibiblio.org/expo/soviet.exhibit/entrance.html. A rich Web site from the Library of Congress, focusing on the operation of the Soviet system and relations with the United States.

For Web sites and additional documents related to this chapter, see **Make History** at bedfordstmartins.com/strayer.

Documents

Considering the Evidence: Experiencing Stalinism

For the Soviet Union, the formative period in establishing communism encompassed the years of Joseph Stalin's rule (1929–1953). Born in Georgia in 1878 rather than in Russia itself, the young Stalin grew up with a brutal and abusive father, trained for the priesthood as a young man, but slowly gravitated toward the emerging revolutionary movement of the time. He subsequently joined the Bolsheviks, led by Lenin, though he played only a modest role in the Russian Revolution of 1917. After Lenin's death in 1924, Stalin rose to the dominant position in the Communist Party amid a long and bitter struggle among the Bolsheviks. By 1929 he had consolidated his authority and exercised enormous personal power until his death in 1953.

To Stalin and the Soviet leadership, the 1930s was a time of "building socialism," that is, creating the modern, abundant, and just society that would replace an outdated, corrupt, and exploitative capitalism. Undertaking that gigantic task meant social upheaval on an enormous scale, offering undreamed-of opportunities for some and disruption and trauma beyond imagination for others. The documents that follow allow us to see something of the Stalinist vision for the country as well as to gain some insight into the lives of ordinary people—peasants, workers, women, ethnic minorities, the young, and the upwardly mobile—as they experienced what scholars have come to call simply "Stalinism."

Document 22.1

Stalin on Stalinism

In January 1933, Stalin appeared before a group of high-ranking party officials to give a report on the achievements of the country's first five-year plan for overall development. The years encompassed by that plan, roughly 1928–1932, coincided with Stalin's rise to the position of supreme leader within the governing Communist Party of the Soviet Union.

■ What larger goals for the country underlay Stalin's report? Why did he feel those goals had to be achieved so rapidly?

■ To what indications of success did Stalin point? Which of these claims do you find most/least credible?

■ What criticisms of Stalin's policies can you infer from the document?

■ What do you think Stalin meant when he referred to the "world-wide historic significance" of the Soviet Union's achievement? Keep in mind what was happening in the capitalist world at the time.

JOSEPH STALIN

The Results of the First Five-Year Plan

1933

The fundamental task of the five-year plan was to convert the U.S.S.R. from an agrarian and weak country, dependent upon the caprices of the capitalist countries, into an industrial and powerful country, fully self-reliant and independent of the caprices of world capitalism, ... to completely oust the capitalist elements, to widen the front of socialist forms of economy, and to create the economic basis for the abolition of classes in the U.S.S.R., for the building of a socialist society....

The fundamental task of the five-year plan was to transfer small and scattered agriculture on to the lines of large-scale collective farming, so as to ensure the economic basis of socialism in the countryside....

[O]nly a modern large-scale industry... can serve as a real and reliable foundation for the Soviet regime....

Let us pass now to the results of the fulfillment of the five-year plan....

We did not have an iron and steel industry, the basis for the industrialization of the country. Now we have one.

[Stalin follows with a long list of new industries developed during the first five-year plan: tractors, automobiles, machine tools, chemicals, agricultural machinery, electric power, oil and coal, metals.]

And we have not only created these new great industries, but have created them on a scale and in dimensions that eclipse... European industry.

And as a result of all this the capitalist elements have been completely and irrevocably ousted from industry, and socialist industry has become the sole form of industry in the U.S.S.R....

Finally, as a result of all this the Soviet Union has been converted from a weak country, unprepared for defense, into a country mighty in defense..., a country capable of producing on a mass scale all modern means of defense and of equipping its army with them in the event of an attack from abroad.

We are told: This is all very well; many new factories have been built, and the foundations for industrialization have been laid; but it would have been far better... to produce more cotton fabrics, shoes, clothing, and other goods for mass consumption.... Then we would now have more cotton fabrics, shoes, and clothing. But we would not have a tractor industry or an automobile industry; we would not have anything like a big iron and steel industry; we would not have metal for the manufacture of machinery—and we would remain unarmed while encircled by capitalist countries armed with modern technique....

It was necessary to urge forward a country which was a hundred years behindhand and which was faced with mortal danger because of its backwardness....

The five-year plan in the sphere of agriculture was a five-year plan of collectivization.... [I]t was

Source: Joseph Stalin, "The Results of the First Five-Year Plan," *Pravda*, January 10, 1933.

necessary in addition to industrialization, to pass from small, individual peasant farming to…large collective farms, equipped with all the modern implements of highly developed agriculture, and to cover unoccupied land with model state farms….

The Party has succeeded in routing the kulaks° as a class, although they have not yet been dealt the final blow; the laboring peasants have been emancipated from kulak bondage and exploitation, and the Soviet regime has been given a firm economic basis in the countryside, the basis of collective farming.

In our country, the workers have long forgotten unemployment….Look at the capitalist countries: what horrors result there from unemployment! There

°**kulaks:** relatively rich peasants.

are now no less than 30–40 million unemployed in those countries….

The same thing must be said of the peasants…. It has brought them into the collective farms and placed them in a secure position. It has thus eliminated the possibility of the differentiation of the peasantry into exploiters—kulaks—and exploited—poor peasants—and abolished destitution in the countryside…. Now the peasant is in a position of security, a member of a collective farm which has at its disposal tractors, agricultural machinery, seed funds, reserve funds….

[W]e have achieved such important successes as to evoke admiration among the working class all over the world; we have achieved a victory that is truly of world-wide historic significance.

Document 22.2

Living through Collectivization

For Russian peasants, and those of other nationalities as well, the chief experience of Stalinism was that of collectivization—the enforced bringing together of many small-scale family farms into much larger collective farms called *kolhozy*. Thus private ownership of land was largely ended, except for some small plots, which peasants could till individually. That process generally began with the arrival of outside "agitators" or Community Party officials who sought to persuade, or if necessary to force, the villagers to enter the *kolhoz*. They divided peasants (*muzhiks*) into class categories: rich peasants (*kulaks*) were to be excluded from the collective farms as incipient capitalists; poor (*bedniak*) and middle (*seredniak*) peasants were expected to join.

One witness to this process was Maurice Hindus, a Russian-born American writer who returned to his country of origin in 1929, when Soviet collectivization was beginning in earnest. There he roamed on foot around the countryside, recording conversations with those he met. The extract that follows begins with a letter he received from "Nadya," a young activist who was among many sent to the rural areas to encourage, or enforce, collectivization. Then Hindus records a discussion between peasants objecting to collectivization and an "agitator," like Nadya, seeking to convince them of its benefits.

■ How do Nadya and the agitator understand collectivization and their role in this process? Why do they believe that it was so critical to building socialism?

- How do village peasants view collectivization? On what grounds do they object to it? How might they view the role of the agitators?

- How did the peasants understand themselves and their village community? How did they respond to the communists' insistence on defining them in rigid class terms? Why do you think they finally entered the collective farms?

- Why were Stalin and the Communist Party so insistent on destroying the *kulaks*?

MAURICE HINDUS
Red Bread
1931

Nadya Speaks

I am off in villages with a group of other brigadiers organizing *kolhozy*. It is a tremendous job, but we are making amazing progress. It would do you worlds of good to be with us and watch us draw the stubborn peasant into collectivization. Contrary to all your affirmations and prophecies, our *muzhik* is yielding to persuasion. He is joining the *kolhozy*, and I am confident that in time not a peasant will remain on his own land. We shall yet smash the last vestiges of capitalism and forever rid ourselves of exploitation. Come, join us; see with your own eyes what is happening, how we are rebuilding the Russian villages. The very air here is afire with a new spirit and a new energy.

Nadya

The Peasants Speak

"There was a time,"... began Lukyan, who had been a blacksmith,... "when we were just neighbors in this village. We quarreled, we fooled, sometimes we cheated one another. But we were neighbors. Now we are *bedniaks, seredniaks, koolacks*.° I am a *seredniak*,

°**koolacks:** variant spelling of "kulaks."

Source: Maurice Hindus, *Red Bread: Collectivization in a Russian Village* (Bloomington: Indiana University Press, 1988), 1, 22–34.

Boris here is a *bedniak*, and Nisko is a *koolack*, and we are supposed to have a class war—pull each other's hair or tickle each other on the toes, eh? One against the other, you understand?...

"But it is other things that worry us," continued the flat-faced *muzhik*..., "it is the *kolhoz*. That, citizen, is a serious matter—the most serious we have ever encountered. Who ever heard of such a thing—to give up our land and our cows and our horses and our tools and our farm buildings, to work all the time and divide everything with others? Nowadays members of the same family get in each other's way and quarrel and fight, and here we, strangers, are supposed to be like one family. Can we—dark, beastly *muzhiks*—make a go of it without scratching each other's faces, pulling each other's hair or hurling stones at one another?"...

"We won't even be sure," someone else continued the lament, "of having enough bread to eat. Now, however poor we may be, we have our own rye and our own potatoes and our own cucumbers and our own milk. We know we won't starve. But in the *kolhoz*, no more potatoes of our own, no more anything of our own. Everything will be rationed out by orders; we shall be like mere *batraks*° on the landlord's estates in the old days. Serfdom—that is what it is—and who wants to be a serf?"...

°**batraks:** hired help.

"Dark-minded beasts we may be," wailed another *muzhik*...."We are not learned; we are not wise. But a little self-respect we have, and we like the feeling of independence. Today we feel like working, and we work; tomorrow we feel like lying down, and we lie down; the next day we feel like going to town, and we go to town. We do as we please. But in the *kolhoz*, brother, it is do-as-you-are-told, like a horse—go this way and that, and don't dare turn off the road or you get it hard, a stroke or two of the whip on bare flesh....We'll just wither away on the socialist farm, like grass torn out by the roots."...

The Communist Party Official Speaks

At this point a new visitor arrived, a tall youth, in boots, in a black blouse and with a shaved head.... A stranger in the village, he was the organizer of the *kolhoz*, therefore a person of stern importance....

"Everything is possible, grandfather, if we all pool our resources and our powers together," replied the visitor.

More laughter and more derisive comment....

"Tell me, you wretched people, what hope is there for you if you remain on individual pieces of land? Think, and don't interrupt.... From year to year as you increase in population you divide and subdivide your strips of land. You cannot even use machinery on your land because no machine man ever made could stand the rough ridges that the strip system creates. You will have to work in your own old way and stew in your old misery. Don't you see that under your present system there is nothing ahead of you but ruin and starvation?...You do not think of a future, of ten, twenty, a hundred years from now, and we do. That's the difference between you and us. The coming generations mean nothing to you. Else you would see a real deliverance in the *kolhoz*, where you will work with machinery in a modern organized way, with the best seeds obtainable and under the direction of experts.... Isn't it about time you stopped thinking each one for himself, for his own piggish hide? You *koolacks* of course will never become reconciled to a new order. You love to fatten on other people's blood. But we know how to deal with you. We'll wipe you off the face of the earth, even as we have the capitalists in the city. Make no mistake about our intentions and our powers. We shan't allow you to profit from the weakness of the *bedniak*. And we shan't allow you to poison his mind, either! Enough. But the others here—you *bedniaks* and you *seredniaks*—what have you gained from this stiff-necked individualism of yours? What? Look at yourselves, at your homes—mud, squalor, fleas, bedbugs, cockroaches, *lapti*.° Are you sorry to let these go? Oh, we know you *muzhiks*—too well....You can whine eloquently and pitifully.... But we know you—you cannot fool us. We have grown hardened to your wails. Remember that. Cry all you want to, curse all you want to. You won't hurt us, and I warn you that we shan't desist. We shall continue our campaign for the *kolhozy* until we have won our goal and made you free citizens in a free land."

°**lapti:** cheap wooden shoes.

Document 22.3

Living through Industrialization

A second major feature of the Stalinist era was rapid state-controlled industrialization. "We are fifty to a hundred years behind the advanced countries," declared Stalin. "We must make good this distance in ten years. Either we shall do it or we shall go under." During the 1930s, that enormous process brought huge numbers of peasants from the countryside to the cities, sent many of them to new and distant industrial sites such as Magnitogorsk—a huge new iron and steel enterprise—and thrust millions into recently established technical institutes where they learned new skills and nurtured new ambitions. The brief excerpts in Document 22.3 disclose the voices of some of these workers as they celebrated the new possibilities and lamented the disappointments and injustices of Stalinist industrialization. These sources come from letters written to newspapers or to high government officials, from private letters and diaries, or from reports filed by party officials based on what they had heard in the factories.

■ In what respects might Soviet workers have benefited from Stalinist industrialization?

■ What criticisms were voiced in these extracts? Do they represent fundamental opposition to the idea of socialism or disappointments in how it was implemented?

■ Which of these selections do you find most credible?

■ Through its control of education and the media, the Stalinist regime sought to instill a single view of the world in its citizens. Based on these selections, to what extent had they succeeded or failed?

Personal Accounts of Soviet Industrialization
1930s

Letter in a Newspaper from a Tatar Electrician

I am a Tatar.° Before October, in old tsarist Russia, we weren't even considered people. We couldn't even dream about education, or getting a job in a state enterprise. And now I'm a citizen of the USSR. Like all citizens, I have the right to a job, to education, to leisure. I can elect and be elected to the soviet [legislative council]. Is this not an indication of the supreme achievements of our country?...

Two years ago I worked as the chairman of a village soviet in the Tatar republic. I was the first person there to enter the kolhoz and then I led the collectivization campaign. Collective farming is flourishing with each year in the Tatar republic.

In 1931 I came to Magnitogorsk. From a common laborer I have turned into a skilled worker. I was elected a member of the city soviet. As a deputy, every day I receive workers who have questions or need help. I listen to each one like to my own brother, and try to do what is necessary to make each one satisfied.

I live in a country where one feels like living and learning. And if the enemy should attack this country, I will sacrifice my life in order to destroy the enemy and save my country.

°**Tatar:** a Turkic ethnic group.

Source: First and second selections: Stephen Kotkin, *Magnetic Mountain* (Berkeley: University of California Press, 1995), 221–22, 349–50; third through seventh selections: Sarah Davies, *Popular Opinion in Stalin's Russia* (New York: Cambridge University Press, 1997), 39, 72, 134–35, 139, 173–74.

Newspaper Commentary by an Engineer, 1938

Soon it will be seven years that I'm working in Magnitogorsk [a huge new iron and steel enterprise]. With my own eyes I've seen the pulsating, creative life of the builders of the Magnitogorsk giant. I myself have taken an active part in this construction with great enthusiasm. Our joy was great when we obtained the first Magnitogorsk steel from the wonderful open-hearth ovens. At the time there was no greater happiness for me than working in the open-hearth shop.... Here I enriched my theoretical knowledge and picked up practical habits... of work. Here as well I grew politically, acquired good experience in public-political work. I came to Magnitogorsk nonparty. The party organization... accepted me into a group of sympathizers. Not long ago I entered the ranks of the Leninist-Stalinist [communist] party.... I love my hometown Magnitka with all my heart. I consider my work at the Magnitogorsk factory to be a special honor and high trust shown to me, a Soviet engineer, by the country.

Letter to a Soviet Official from a Worker, 1938

In fact, there's been twenty years of our [Soviet] power. Fifteen to sixteen of these have been peaceful construction.... The people struggled with zeal, overcame difficulties. Socialism has been built in the main. As we embark on the third five-year plan we shout at meetings, congresses, and in newspapers "Hurray, we have reached a happy, joyful life!" However, incidentally, if one is to be honest, those shouts are mechanical, made from habit, pumped by social organizations. The ordinary person makes such speeches like a street newspaper-seller. In fact, in his heart, when he comes home, this bawler, eulogist, will agree with his family, his wife who reproaches him that today she has been torturing herself in queues and did not get anything—there are no suits, no coats, no meat, no butter.

Letter from a Student to His Teacher, No Date

I worked at a factory for five years. Now I'll have to leave my studies at the institute. Who will study? Very talented Lomonosovs° and the sons of Soviet rulers,

°**Lomonosovs:** i.e., brilliant students (Mikhal Lomonosov, 1711–1765, was a Russian scientist and writer).

since they have the highest posts and are the best paid. In this way education will be available only to the highest strata (a sort of nobility), while for the lowest strata, the laboring people, the doors will be closed.

Two Comments from Factory Workers Found in Soviet Archives, 1930s

What is there to say about the successes of Soviet power? It's lies. The newspapers cover up the real state of things. I am a worker, wear torn clothes, my four children go to school half-starving, in rags. I, an honest worker, am a visible example of what Soviet power has given the workers in the last twenty years.

How can we liquidate classes, if new classes have developed here, with the only difference being that they are not called classes? Now there are the same parasites who live at the expense of others. The worker produces and at the same time works for many people who live off him. From the example of our factory it is clear that there is a huge apparat of factory administrators, where idlers sit. There are many administrative workers who travel about in cars and get three to four times more than the worker. These people live in the best conditions and live at the expense of the labor of the working class.

Entry from a Worker's Diary, 1936

[T]he portraits of party leaders are now displayed the same way icons used to be: a round portrait framed and attached to a pole. Very convenient, hoist it onto your shoulder and you're on your way. And all these preparations are just like what people used to do before church holidays.... They had their own activists then, we have ours now. Different paths, the same old folderol.

Comment from an Anonymous Communist in Soviet Archives, 1938

Do you not think that comrade Stalin's name has begun to be very much abused? For example:

Stalin's people's commissar…
Stalin's canal…
Stalin's harvest…
Stalin's five-year plan…
Stalin's constitution…
Stalin's Komsomol°…

———————

°**Komsomol:** youth organization.

I could give a hundred other examples, even of little meaning. Everything is Stalin, Stalin, Stalin. You only have to listen to a radio program about our achievements, and every fifth or tenth word will be the name of comrade Stalin. In the end this sacred and beloved name—Stalin—may make so much noise in people's heads that it is very possible that it will have the opposite effect.

Document 22.4

Living through the Terror

More than anything else, it was the Terror—sometimes called the Great Purges—that came to define Stalinism as a distinctive phenomenon in the history of Soviet communism (see p. 1038). Millions of people were caught up in this vast process of identifying and eliminating so-called "enemies of the people," many of them loyal communist citizens. The three selections that follow, all from women, provide a small taste of what it meant to experience arrest and interrogation, life in the camps of the Gulag, and the agony of those left behind waiting for loved ones who had vanished into the Terror.

- What might you infer from these selections about purposes of the Terror, the means by which it was implemented, and its likely outcomes, whether intended or not?

- Many innocent people who were arrested believed that others were guilty as charged, while in their own case a mistake had been made. How might you account for this widespread response to the Terror?

- In what different ways did people experience the Stalinist Terror? What do you think motivated each of these women who wrote about it?

- The extent of the Terror did not become widely known until well after Stalin's death in 1953. How do you imagine that knowledge was used by critics of communism? What impact might it have had on those who had ardently believed in the possibilities of a socialist future?

- How might you compare the Soviet terror and the Nazi Holocaust?

Personal Accounts of the Terror

1930s

[The first excerpt is from the memoirs of Irina Kakhovskaya, an ardent revolutionary, though not a party member, who was arrested in 1937 and spent seventeen years either in prison or in a labor camp. Here she describes her arrest and interrogation.]

Early on the morning of February 8, 1937, a large group of men appeared at the door of our quiet apartment in Ufa. We were shown a search warrant and warrants for our arrest. The search was carried out in violent, pogrom-like fashion and lasted all day. Books went pouring down from the shelves; letters and papers, out of boxes. They tapped the walls and, when they encountered hollow spots, removed the bricks. Everything was covered with dust and pieces of brick....

At the prison everything was aimed at breaking prisoners' spirits immediately, intimidating and stupefying them, making them feel that they were no longer human, but "enemies of the people," against whom everything was permitted. All elementary human needs were disregarded (light, air, food, rest, medical care, warmth, toilet facilities)....

In the tiny, damp, cold, half-lit cell were a bunk and a half bunk. The bunk was for the prisoner under investigation and on the half bunk, their legs drawn up, the voluntary victims, the informers from among the common criminals, huddled together. Their duty was never to let their neighbor out of their sight, never to let the politicals communicate with one another... and above all to prevent the politicals from committing suicide.... The air was fouled by the huge wooden latrine bucket....

The interrogation began on the very first night.... Using threats, endearments, promises and enigmatic hints, they tried to confuse, wear down, frighten, and break the will of each individual, who was kept totally isolated from his or her comrades.... Later stools were removed and the victim had to simply stand for hours on end....

At first it seemed that the whole thing was a tremendous and terrible misunderstanding, that it was our duty to clear it up.... But it soon became apparent that what was involved was deliberate ill will and the most cynical possible approach to the truth....

In the interrogation sessions, I now had several investigators in a row, and the "conveyor belt" questioning would go on for six days and nights on end.... Exhaustion reached the ultimate limit. The brain, inadequately supplied with blood, began to misfunction.... "Sign! We won't bother you anymore. We'll give you a quiet cell and a pillow and you can sleep...." That was how the investigator would try to bribe a person who was completely debilitated and stupefied from lack of sleep.

Each of us fought alone to keep an honest name and save the honor of our friends, although it would have been far easier to die than to endure this hell month after month. Nevertheless the accused remained strong in spirit and, apart from the unfortunate Mayorov, not one real revolutionary did they manage to break.

[The second selection comes from the memoirs of Eugenia Ginsberg, a woman who survived many years in perhaps the most notorious of the gulag camps—Kolyma in the frigid northeastern corner of the Soviet Union. In this selection, Ginsberg recounts an ordinary day in camps.]

The work to which I was assigned...went by the imposing name of "land improvement." We set out before dawn and marched in ranks of five for about three miles, to the accompaniment of shouts from the guards and bad language from the common criminals who were included in our party as a punish-

Source: First selection: Irina Kakhovskaya, "Our Fate" in *An End to Silence*, translated by George Saunders and edited by Stephen Cohen (New York: Norton, 1982), 81–90; second selection: Eugenia Semyonovna Ginzburg, *Journey into the Whirlwind* (New York: Harcourt, Brace Jovanovich, 1967), 366–67; third selection: Anna Akhnatova, *Poems*, selected and translated by Lyn Coffin (New York: Norton, 1983), 82, 85.

ment for some misdeed or other. In time we reached a bleak, open field where our leader, another common criminal called Senka—a disgusting type who preyed on the other prisoners and made no bones about offering a pair of warm breeches in return for an hour's "fun and games"—handed out picks and iron spades with which we attacked the frozen soil of Kolyma until one in the afternoon. I cannot remember, and perhaps I never knew, the rational purpose this "improvement" was supposed to serve. I only remember the ferocious wind, the forty-degree frost, the appalling weight of the pick, and the wild, irregular thumping of one's heart. At one o'clock we were marched back for dinner. More stumbling in and out of snowdrifts, more shouts and threats from the guards whenever we fell out of line. Back in the camp we received our longed-for piece of bread and soup and were allowed half an hour in which to huddle around the stove in the hope of absorbing enough warmth to last us halfway back to the field. After we had toiled again with our picks and spades till late in the evening, Senka would come and survey what we had done and abuse us for not doing more. How could the assignment ever be completed if we spoiled women fulfilled only thirty percent of the norm?... Finally a night's rest, full of nightmares, and the dreaded banging of a hammer on an iron rail which was the signal for a new day to begin.

[The third selection is from the poetry of Anna Akhmatova, probably Russia's most famous modern poet. In this poem, "Requiem," Akhmatova writes passionately about endlessly standing in line, either seeking information about her imprisoned son or trying to send him parcels, an experience that paralleled that of countless other mothers and wives during the Terror.]

In the awful years of Yezhovian horror,° I spent seventeen months standing in line in front of various prisons in Leningrad. One day someone "recognized" me. Then a woman with blue lips, who was standing behind me, and who, of course, had never heard my name, came out of the stupor which typified all of us, and whispered into my ear (everyone there spoke only in whispers):

—Can you describe this?

And I said:

—I can.

Then something like a fleeting smile passed over what once had been her face.

For months I've filled the air with pleas,
Trying to call you back.
I've thrown myself at the hangman's knees,
You are my son and my rack....
I've seen how a face can fall like a leaf,
How, from under the lids, terror peeks,
I've seen how suffering and grief
Etches hieroglyphs on cheeks,
How ash-blonde hair, from roots to tips,
Turns black and silver overnight.
How smiles wither on submissive lips,
And in a half-smile quivers fright.
Not only for myself do I pray,
But for those who stood in front and behind me,
In the bitter cold, on a hot July day
Under the red wall that stared blindly.

°**Yezhovian horror:** i.e., the Terror (Nikolay Yezhov, 1895–1939, a communist official, administered the most severe stage of the purges).

Using the Evidence:
Experiencing Stalinism

1. **Defending Stalinism:** Develop an argument that the fundamental goals of Stalinism (building socialism) were largely achieved during the 1930s.

2. **Criticizing Stalinism:** Develop an argument that genuine socialism was essentially betrayed or perverted by the developments of the Stalin era.

3. **Assessing change:** In what ways did the Stalin era represent a revolutionary transformation of Soviet society? In what ways did it continue older patterns of Russian history?

4. **Considering moral judgments:** Why do you think that historians have found it so difficult to write about the Stalin era without passing judgment on it? Does this represent a serious problem for scholars? Should students of the past seek to avoid moral judgments or is it an inevitable, perhaps even useful, part of the historian's craft?

Visual Sources

Considering the Evidence:
Poster Art in Mao's China

"I wanted to be the girl in the poster when I was growing up. Every day I dressed up like that girl in a white cotton shirt with a red scarf around my neck, and I braided my hair in the same way. I liked the fact that she was surrounded by revolutionary martyrs whom I was taught to worship since kindergarten."[14] As things turned out, this young girl, Anchee Min, did become the subject of one of the many thousands of propaganda posters with which the Chinese communist government flooded the country during the thirty years or so following the Chinese Revolution of 1949.

In China, as in other communist countries, art served the state and the Communist Party. Nowhere was this more apparent than in these propaganda posters, which were found in homes, schools, workplaces, railway stations, and elsewhere. The artists who created these images were under the strict control of Communist Party officials and were expected to use their skills to depict the party's leaders and achievements favorably, even grandly. They were among the "engineers of the human soul" who were reshaping the consciousness of individuals and remaking their entire society. One young man, born in 1951, testified to the effectiveness of these posters: "They... were my signposts through life. They made sure we did not make mistakes.... [M]y life is reflected in them."[15]

The posters that follow illustrate the kind of society and people that the communist leadership sought to create during the years that Mao Zedong ruled the country (1949–1976). The realities behind these images, of course, were often far different.

Coming to power in 1949, Chinese Communist Party leaders recognized that their enemies were by no means totally defeated. A persistent theme throughout the years of Mao's rule was an effort to eliminate those enemies or convert them to the communist cause. Spies, imperialist sympathizers, those infected with "bourgeois values" such as materialism and individualism, landowners or capitalists yearning for the old life—all of these had to be identified and confronted. So too were many "enemies" within the Communist Party itself, people who were suspected of opposition to the radical policies of Mao. Some of these alleged enemies were killed, others imprisoned, and still others—millions of them—were subjected to endless self-criticism sessions or sent down to remote rural areas to "learn from the peasants." This need to demolish the

Visual Source 22.1 Smashing the Old Society (Courtesy, Centre for the Study of Democracy, University of Westminster, London, Chinese Poster Collection)

old society and old values is reflected in Visual Source 22.1, a poster from 1967, the height of the Cultural Revolution (see pp. 1043–44). Its caption reads: "Destroy the Old World; Establish the New World."

■ Notice the various items beneath this young revolutionary's feet. What do they represent to the ardent revolutionaries seeking to "destroy the old world"? What groups of people were most likely to be affected by such efforts?

■ What elements of a new order are being constructed in this image?

■ How does the artist distinguish visually between the old and the new? Note the use of colors and the size of various figures and objects in the poster.

The centerpiece of Mao's plans for the vast Chinese countryside lay in the "people's communes." Established during the so-called Great Leap Forward in the late 1950s, these were huge political and economic units intended to work the land more efficiently and collectively, to undertake large-scale projects such as building dams and irrigation systems, to create small-scale industries in the rural areas, and to promote local self-reliance. They also sought to move China more rapidly toward genuine communism by eliminating virtually every form of private property and emphasizing social equality and shared living. Commune members ate together in large dining halls, and children were cared for during the day in collective nurseries rather than by their own families. Visual Source 22.2, a poster created in 1958 under the title "The People's Communes Are Good," shows a highly idealized image of one such commune.

■ What appealing features of commune life and a communist future are illustrated in this poster? Notice the communal facilities for eating and washing clothes as well as the drill practice of a "people's militia" unit at the bottom of the picture.

■ One of Mao's chief goals was to overcome the sharp division between industrial cities and the agricultural countryside. How is this effort illustrated in the poster?

The actual outcomes of the commune movement departed radically from their idealistic goals. Economic disruption occasioned by the creation of communes contributed a great deal to the enormous famines of the late 1950s, in which many millions perished. Furthermore, efforts to involve the peasants in iron and steel production through the creation of much-heralded "backyard furnaces," illustrated in this image, proved a failure. Most of the metal produced in these primitive facilities was of poor quality and essentially unusable. Such efforts further impoverished the rural areas as peasants were encouraged to contribute their pots, pans, and anything made of iron to the smelting furnaces.

Among the core values of Maoist communism were human mastery over the natural order, rapid industrialization, and the liberation of women from ancient limitations and oppressions in order to mobilize them for the task of building socialism. Visual Source 22.3, a 1975 poster, illustrates these values. Its caption reads: "Women Can Hold Up Half the Sky; Surely the Face of Nature Can Be Transformed."

Visual Source 22.2 Building the New Society: The People's Commune (Shanghai Educational Publishing House/Coll. SL (Stefan Landsberger)/IISH)

- In what ways does this poster reflect Maoist communism's core values?

- How is the young woman in this image portrayed? What does the expression on her face convey? Notice her clothing and the shape of her forearms, and the general absence of a feminine figure. Why do you think she is portrayed in this largely sexless fashion? What does this suggest about the communist attitude toward sexuality?

Visual Source 22.3 Women, Nature, and Industrialization (Courtesy, Centre for the Study of Democracy, University of Westminster, London, Chinese Poster Collection)

- What does this image suggest about how the party sought to realize gender equality? What is the significance of the work the young woman is doing?

- Notice the lights that illuminate a nighttime work scene. What does this suggest about attitudes toward work and production?

A central feature of Chinese communism, especially during the Cultural Revolution of 1966–1976, was the growing veneration, even adoration, of Chairman Mao. Portraits, statues, busts, and Mao badges proliferated. Everyone was expected to read repeatedly the "Red Treasured Book," which offered a selection of quotations from Mao's writings and which was widely believed to facilitate solutions to almost all problems, both public and private. Many families erected "tablets of loyalty" to Mao, much like those previously devoted to ancestors. People made pilgrimages to "sacred shrines" associated with key events in his life. Schoolchildren began the day by chanting, "May Chairman Mao live ten thousand times ten thousand years."

And Mao was the centerpiece of endless posters. Visual Source 22.4, a poster created in 1968, portrays a familiar scene from the Cultural Revolution. Millions of young people, organized as Red Guards and committed to revolutionary action, flocked to Beijing, where enormous and ecstatic rallies allowed them to catch a glimpse of their beloved leader and to unite with him in the grand task of creating communism in China. The poster's caption reads: "The reddest, reddest, red sun in our heart, Chairman Mao, and us together."

- What relationship between Mao and his young followers does the poster suggest? Why might some scholars have seen a quasi-religious dimension to that relationship?

- How do you understand the significance of the "Red Treasured Book" of quotations from Mao, which the young people are waving?

- How might you account for the unbridled enthusiasm expressed by the Red Guards? In this case, the poster portrays the realities of these rallies with considerable accuracy. Can you think of other comparable cases of such mass enthusiasm?

After Mao's death in 1976, the Communist Party backed away from the disruptive radicalism of the Cultural Revolution and initiated the market-based reforms that have generated such spectacular economic growth in China in recent decades (see pp. 1052–54). In this new era, the poster tradition of the Maoist years faded, and party control over the arts loosened. Visual Source 22.5 reflects the new values of the post-Mao era. Dating from 1993, it is a New Year's "good luck" print featuring the traditional gods of wealth, happiness, and longevity. Its caption reads: "The Gods of wealth enter the home from everywhere; wealth, treasures, and peace beckon." Another poster reflecting the post-Mao era in China can be found in Visual Source 24.2 on page 1183.

我们心中最红最红的红太阳毛主席和我们在一起

Visual Source 22.4 The Cult of Mao (Zhejiang People's Art Publishing House/Coll. SL (Stefan Landsberger)/IISH)

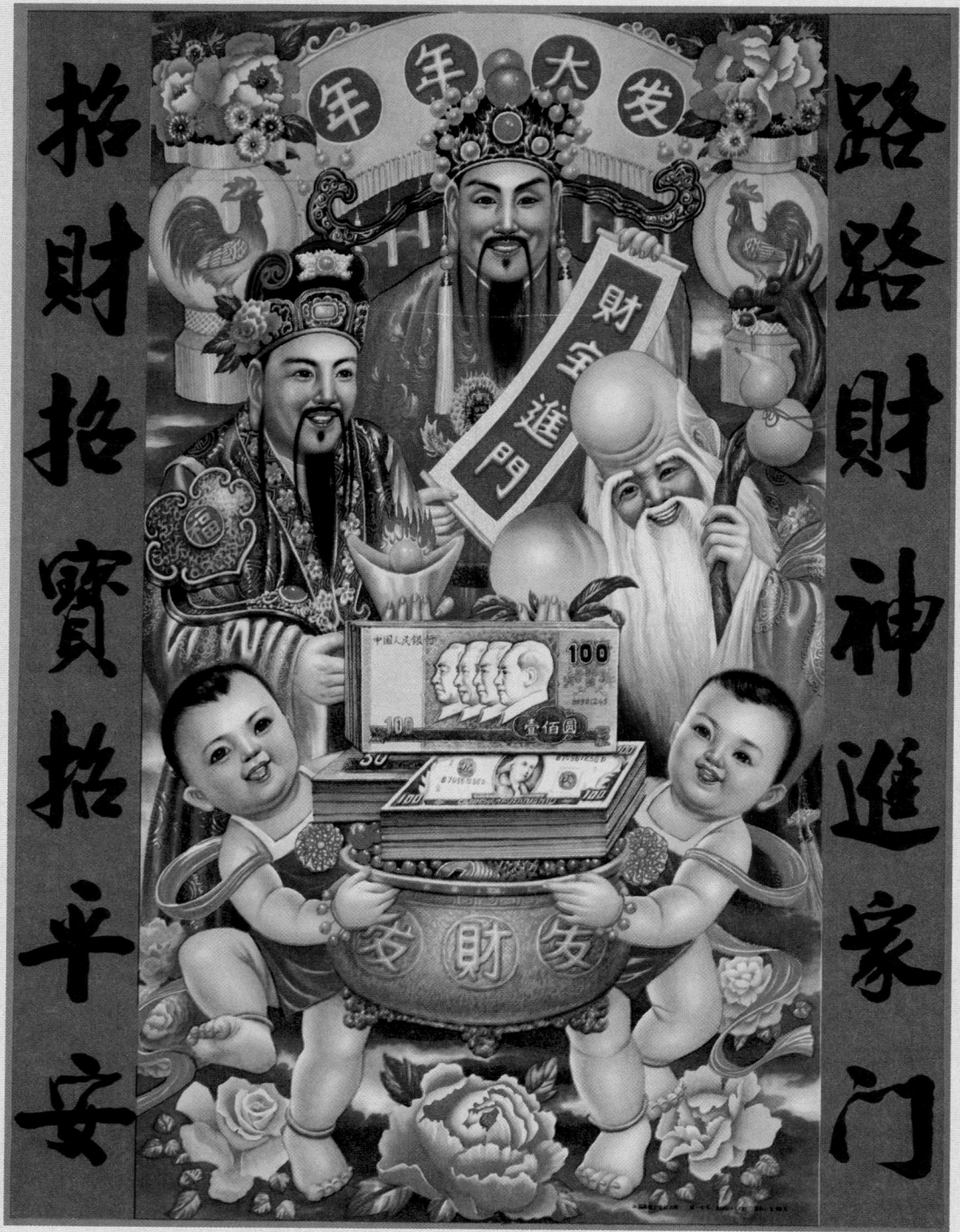

Visual Source 22.5 Propaganda Posters after Mao (Zhejiang People's Art Publishing House/Coll. SL (Stefan Landsberger)/IISH)

- In what specific ways do these posters reflect the changed policies and values of the post-Mao era in China? Pay attention to the role of tradition, material values, and foreign contact. What, if any, points of similarity with the earlier posters can you find?

- How might ardent advocates of Maoist communism respond to these posters?

- How do these posters represent the good life? How is wealth portrayed? What is the significance of the American currency?

Using the Evidence:
Poster Art in Mao's China

1. **Reading communist intentions:** Based on the first four visual sources, how would you describe the kind of society that the Chinese Communist Party sought to create in China during Mao's lifetime?

2. **Distinguishing image and reality:** Based on the narrative of this chapter and especially on what happened after Mao's death, assess the realities that lay behind these visual sources. To what extent do the posters accurately represent the successes of Maoist communism? What insights do they shed on its failures?

3. **Defining audience and appeal:** To whom do you think these posters were directed? What appeal might they have for the intended audience?

4. **Noticing change:** How could you use these posters to define the dramatic changes that transformed China since 1949? How might a traditional Chinese official from the nineteenth century respond to them?

5. **Assessing posters as evidence:** What are the strengths and limitations of poster art for understanding Chinese communism under Mao and after his death?

CHAPTER TWENTY-THREE

Independence and Development in the Global South

1914–PRESENT

Toward Freedom: Struggles
   for Independence
   The End of Empire in World History
   Explaining African and
      Asian Independence
Comparing Freedom Struggles
   The Case of India: Ending
      British Rule
   The Case of South Africa:
      Ending Apartheid
Experiments with Freedom
   Experiments in Political Order:
      Comparing African Nations
      and India
   Experiments in Economic
      Development: Changing Priorities,
      Varying Outcomes
   Experiments with Culture: The Role
      of Islam in Turkey and Iran
Reflections: History in the Middle
   of the Stream
Considering the Evidence
   Documents: Debating Development
      in Africa
   Visual Sources: Representing
      Independence

"During my lifetime I have dedicated myself to this struggle of the African people. I have fought against white domination, and I have fought against black domination. I have cherished the ideal of a democratic and free society in which all persons live together in harmony and with equal opportunity. It is an ideal which I hope to live for and to achieve. But, if need be, it is an ideal for which I am prepared to die."[1]

Nelson Mandela, South Africa's nationalist leader, first uttered these words in 1964 at his trial for treason, sabotage, and conspiracy to overthrow the apartheid government of his country. Convicted of those charges, he spent the next twenty-seven years in prison, sometimes working at hard labor in a stone quarry. Often the floor was his bed, and a bucket was his toilet. For many years, he was allowed one visitor a year for thirty minutes and permitted to write and receive one letter every six months. When he was finally released from prison in 1990 under growing domestic and international pressure, he concluded his first speech as a free person with the words originally spoken at his trial. Four years later in 1994, South Africa held its first election in which blacks and whites alike were able to vote. The outcome of that election made Mandela the country's first black African president, and it linked South Africa to dozens of other countries all across Africa and Asia that had thrown off European rule or the control of white settlers during the second half of the twentieth century.

VARIOUSLY CALLED THE STRUGGLE FOR INDEPENDENCE OR DECOLONIZATION, that process carried an immense significance

Nelson Mandela: In April 1994, the long struggle against apartheid and white domination in South Africa came to an end in the country's first democratic and nonracial election. The symbol of that triumph was Nelson Mandela, long a political prisoner, head of the African National Congress, and the country's first black African president. He is shown here voting in that historic election. (Peter Turnley/Corbis)

for the history of the twentieth century. It marked a dramatic change in the world's political architecture, as nation-states triumphed over the empires that had structured much of African and Asian life in the nineteenth and early twentieth centuries. It mobilized millions of people, thrusting them into political activity and sometimes into violence and warfare. Decolonization signaled the declining legitimacy of both empire and race as credible bases for political or social life. It promised not only national freedom but also personal dignity, abundance, and opportunity.

What followed in the decades after independence was equally significant. Political, economic, and cultural experiments proliferated across these newly independent nations, which during the cold war were labeled as the third world and now are often referred to as developing countries or the Global South. Their peoples, who represented the vast majority of the world's population, faced enormous challenges: the legacies of empire; their own deep divisions of language, ethnicity, religion, and class; their rapidly growing numbers; the competing demands of the capitalist West and the communist East; the difficult tasks of simultaneously building modern economies, stable politics, and coherent nations; and all of this in a world still shaped by the powerful economies and armies of the wealthy, already industrialized nations. The emergence of the developing countries onto the world stage as independent and assertive actors has been a distinguishing feature of world history in this most recent century.

Toward Freedom: Struggles for Independence

In 1900, European colonial empires in Africa and Asia appeared as permanent features of the world's political landscape. Well before the end of the twentieth century, they were gone. The first major breakthroughs occurred in Asia and the Middle East in the late 1940s, when the Philippines, India, Pakistan, Burma, Indonesia, Syria, Iraq, Jordan, and Israel achieved independence. The period from the mid-1950s through the mid-1970s was the age of African independence as colony after colony, more than fifty in total, emerged into what was then seen as the bright light of freedom.

The End of Empire in World History

■ Comparison
What was distinctive about the end of Europe's African and Asian empires compared to other cases of imperial disintegration?

At one level, this vast process was but the latest case of imperial dissolution, a fate that had overtaken earlier empires, including those of the Assyrians, Romans, Arabs, and Mongols. But never before had the end of empire been so associated with the mobilization of the masses around a nationalist ideology; nor had these earlier cases generated a plethora of nation-states, each claiming an equal place in a world of nation-states. More comparable perhaps was that first decolonization, in which the European colonies in the Americas threw off British, French, Spanish, or Portuguese rule during the late eighteenth and early nineteenth centuries (see Chapter 17). Like their twentieth-century counterparts, these new nations claimed an international status equivalent to that of their former rulers. In the Americas, however, many of the colonized people were themselves of European origin, sharing much of their culture with their colonial rulers. In that respect, the African and Asian struggles of the twentieth century were very different, for they not only asserted political independence but also affirmed the vitality of their cultures, which had been submerged and denigrated during the colonial era.

The twentieth century witnessed the demise of many empires. The Austrian and Ottoman empires collapsed following World War I, giving rise to a number of new states in Europe and the Middle East. The Russian Empire also unraveled, although it was soon reassembled under the auspices of the Soviet Union. World War II ended the German and Japanese empires. African and Asian movements for independence shared with these other end-of-empire stories the ideal of national self-determination. This novel idea—that humankind was naturally divided into distinct peoples or nations, each of which deserved an independent state of its own—was loudly proclaimed by the winning side of both world wars. The belief in national self-determination gained a global following in the twentieth century and rendered empire illegitimate in the eyes of growing numbers of people.

Empires without territory, such as the powerful influence that the United States exercised in Latin America and elsewhere, likewise came under attack from highly nationalist governments. An intrusive U.S. presence was certainly one factor stimulating the Mexican Revolution, which began in 1910. One of the outcomes of that upheaval was the nationalization in 1937 of Mexico's oil industry, much of which was owned by American and British investors. Similar actions accompanied Cuba's revolution of 1959–1960 and also occurred in other places throughout Latin America and elsewhere. National self-determination likewise lay behind the disintegration of the Soviet Union in 1991, when the last of the major territorial empires of the twentieth century came to an inglorious end with the birth of fifteen new states. Although the winning of political independence for Europe's African and Asian colonies was perhaps the most spectacular challenge to empire in the twentieth century, that achievement was part of a larger pattern in modern world history (see Map 23.1).

Explaining African and Asian Independence

As the twentieth century closed, the end of European empires seemed an almost "natural" phenomenon, for colonial rule had lost any credibility as a form of political order. What could be more natural than for people to seek to rule themselves? Yet at the beginning of the century, few observers were predicting the collapse of these empires, and the idea that "the only legitimate government is self-government" was not nearly so widespread as it subsequently became. This situation has presented historians with a problem of explanation—how to account for the fall of European colonial empires and the emergence of dozens of new nation-states.

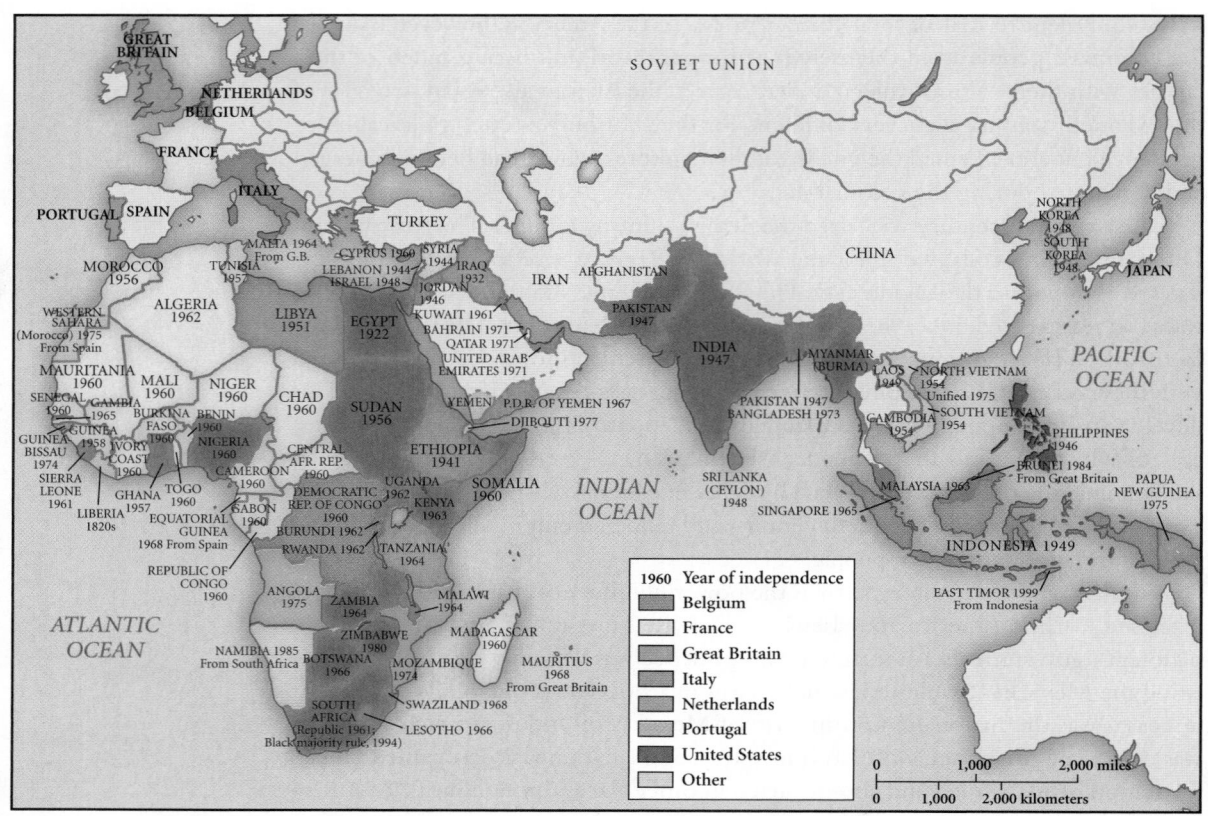

Map 23.1 The End of European Empires
In the second half of the twentieth century, under pressure from nationalist movements, Europe's Asian and African empires dissolved into dozens of new independent states.

■ **Change**
What international circumstances and social changes contributed to the end of colonial empires?

One approach to explaining the end of colonial empires focuses attention on fundamental contradictions in the entire colonial enterprise that arguably rendered its demise more or less inevitable. The rhetoric of both Christianity and material progress sat awkwardly with the realities of colonial racism, exploitation, and poverty. The increasingly democratic values of European states ran counter to the essential dictatorship of colonial rule. The ideal of national self-determination was profoundly at odds with the possession of colonies that were denied any opportunity to express their own national character. The enormously powerful force of nationalism, having earlier driven the process of European empire building, now played a major role in its disintegration. Colonial rule, in this argument, dug its own grave.

But why did this "fatal flaw" of European colonial rule lead to independence in the post–World War II era rather than earlier or later? In explaining the timing of the end of empire, historians frequently use the notion of "conjuncture," the coming together of several separate developments at a particular time. At the international level, the world wars had weakened Europe, while discrediting any sense of European moral superiority. Both the United States and the Soviet Union, the new global superpowers, generally opposed the older European colonial empires. Meanwhile, the

United Nations provided a prestigious platform from which to conduct anticolonial agitation. All of this contributed to the global illegitimacy of empire, a transformation of social values that was enormously encouraging to Africans and Asians seeking political independence.

At the same time, social and economic circumstances within the colonies themselves generated the human raw material for anticolonial movements. By the early twentieth century in Asia and the mid-twentieth century in Africa, a second or third generation of Western-educated elites, largely male, had arisen throughout the colonial world. These young men were thoroughly familiar with European culture, were deeply aware of the gap between its values and its practices, no longer viewed colonial rule as a vehicle for their peoples' progress as their fathers had, and increasingly insisted on independence now. Moreover, growing numbers of ordinary people also were receptive to this message. Veterans of the world wars; young people with some education but no jobs commensurate with their expectations; a small class of urban workers who were increasingly aware of their exploitation; small-scale traders resentful of European privileges; rural dwellers who had lost land or suffered from forced labor; impoverished and insecure newcomers to the cities—all of these groups had reason to believe that independence held great promise.

A third approach to explaining the end of colonial empires puts the spotlight squarely on particular groups or individuals whose deliberate actions brought down the colonial system. Here the emphasis is on the "agency"—the deliberate initiatives—of historical actors rather than on impersonal contradictions or conjunctures. But which set of actors were most important in this end-of-empire drama?

Particularly in places such as West Africa or India, where independence occurred peacefully and through a negotiated settlement, the actions of colonial rulers have received considerable attention from historians. As the twentieth century wore on, these rulers were increasingly on the defensive and were actively planning for a new political relationship with their Asian and African colonies. With the colonies integrated into a global economic network and with local elites now modernized and committed to maintaining those links, outright colonial rule seemed less necessary to many Europeans. It was now possible to imagine retaining profitable economic interests in Asia and Africa without the expense and bother of formal colonial government. Deliberate planning for decolonization included gradual political reforms; investments in railroads, ports, and telegraph lines; the holding of elections; and the writing of constitutions. To some observers, it seemed as if independence was granted by colonial rulers rather than gained or seized by nationalist movements.

But these reforms and, ultimately, independence itself occurred only under considerable pressure from mounting nationalist movements. Creating such movements was no easy task. Political leaders, drawn from the ranks of the educated few, organized political parties, recruited members, plotted strategy, developed an ideology, and negotiated with one another and with the colonial state. The most prominent among them became the "fathers" of their new countries as independence dawned— Mahatma Gandhi and Jawaharlal Nehru in India, Sukarno in Indonesia, Ho Chi

■ Description
What obstacles confronted the leaders of movements for independence?

Minh in Vietnam, Kwame Nkrumah in Ghana, and Nelson Mandela in South Africa. In places where colonial rule was particularly intransigent—settler-dominated colonies and Portuguese territories, for example—leaders also directed military operations and administered liberated areas.

Agency within nationalist movements was not limited to leaders and the educated few. Millions of ordinary people decided to join Gandhi's nonviolent campaigns; tens of thousands of freedom fighters waged guerrilla warfare in Algeria, Kenya, Mozambique, and Zimbabwe; workers went on strike; market women in West Africa joined political parties, as did students, farmers, and the unemployed. In short, the struggle for independence did not happen automatically. It was deliberately made by the conscious personal choices of innumerable individuals across Asia and Africa.

In some places, that struggle, once begun, produced independence within a few years, four in the case of the Belgian Congo. Elsewhere it was measured in decades. But everywhere it was a contested process. Those efforts were rarely if ever cohesive movements of uniformly oppressed people. More often they were fragile alliances of conflicting groups and parties representing different classes, ethnic groups, religions, or regions. Beneath the common goal of independence, they struggled with one another over questions of leadership, power, strategy, ideology, and the distribution of material benefits, even as they fought and negotiated with their colonial rulers. The very notion of "national self-government" posed obvious but often contentious questions: What group of people constituted the "nation" that deserved to rule itself? And who should speak for it?

Comparing Freedom Struggles

Two of the most extended freedom struggles—in India and South Africa—illustrate both the variations and the complexity of this process, which was so central to twentieth-century world history. India was among the first colonies to achieve independence and provided both a model and an inspiration to others, whereas South Africa, though not formally a colony, was among the last to throw off political domination by whites.

The Case of India: Ending British Rule

■ Change
How did India's nationalist movement change over time?

Surrounded by the Himalayas and the Indian Ocean, the South Asian peninsula, commonly known as India, enjoyed a certain geographic unity. But before the twentieth century few of its people thought of themselves as "Indians." Cultural identities were primarily local and infinitely varied, rooted in differences of family, caste, village, language, region, tribe, and religious practice. In earlier centuries—during the Mauryan, Gupta, and Mughal empires, for example—large areas of the subcontinent had been temporarily enclosed within a single political system, but always these were imperial overlays, constructed on top of enormously diverse Indian societies.

So too was British colonial rule, but the British differed from earlier invaders in ways that promoted a growing sense of Indian identity. Unlike previous foreign rulers, the British never assimilated into Indian society because their acute sense of racial and cultural distinctiveness kept them apart. This served to intensify Indians' awareness of their collective difference from their alien rulers. Furthermore, British railroads, telegraph lines, postal services, administrative networks, newspapers, and schools as well as the English language bound India's many regions and peoples together more firmly than ever before and facilitated communication among its educated elite. Early-nineteenth-century cultural nationalists, seeking to renew and reform Hinduism, registered this sense of India as a cultural unit.

The most important political expression of an all-Indian identity took shape in the Indian National Congress (INC), which was established in 1885. This was an association of English-educated Indians—lawyers, journalists, teachers, businessmen—drawn overwhelmingly from regionally prominent high-caste Hindu families. Its founding represented the beginning of a new kind of political protest, quite different from the rebellions, banditry, and refusal to pay taxes that had periodically erupted in the rural areas of colonial India. The INC was largely an urban phenomenon and quite moderate in its demands. Initially, its well-educated members did not seek to overthrow British rule; rather they hoped to gain greater inclusion within the political, military, and business life of British India. From such positions of influence, they argued, they could better protect the interests of India than could their foreign-born rulers. The British mocked their claim to speak for ordinary Indians, referring to them as "babus," a derogatory term that implied a semiliterate "native" with only a thin veneer of modern education.

Even in the first two decades of the twentieth century, the INC remained largely an elite organization; as such, it had difficulty gaining a mass following among India's vast peasant population. That began to change in the aftermath of World War I. To attract Indian support for the war effort, the British in 1917 had promised "the gradual development of self-governing institutions," a commitment that energized nationalist politicians to demand more rapid political change. Furthermore, British attacks on the Islamic Ottoman Empire antagonized India's Muslims. The end of the war was followed by a massive influenza epidemic, which cost the lives of millions of Indians. Finally, a series of repressive actions antagonized many, particularly the killing of some 400 people who had defied a ban on public

Mahatma Gandhi
The most widely recognized and admired figure in the global struggle against colonial rule was India's Mahatma Gandhi. In this famous photograph, he is sitting cross-legged on the floor, clothed in a traditional Indian garment called a *dhoti*, while nearby stands a spinning wheel, symbolizing the independent and nonindustrial India that Gandhi sought. (Margaret Bourke-White/Time Life Pictures/Getty Images)

meetings to celebrate a Hindu festival in the city of Amritsar. This was the context in which Mohandas Gandhi (1869–1948) arrived on the Indian political scene and soon transformed it.

■ Change
What was the role of Gandhi in India's struggle for independence?

Gandhi was born in the province of Gujarat in western India to a pious Hindu family of the Vaisya, or business, caste. He was married at the age of thirteen, had only a mediocre record as a student, and eagerly embraced an opportunity to study law in England when he was eighteen. He returned as a shy and not very successful lawyer, and in 1893 he accepted a job with an Indian firm in South Africa, where a substantial number of Indians had migrated as indentured laborers during the nineteenth century. While in South Africa, Gandhi personally experienced overt racism for the first time and as a result soon became involved in organizing Indians, mostly Muslims, to protest that country's policies of racial segregation. He also developed a concept of India that included Hindus and Muslims alike and pioneered strategies of resistance that he would later apply in India itself. His emerging political philosophy, known as *satyagraha* (truth force), was a confrontational, though nonviolent, approach to political action. As Gandhi argued,

> Non-violence means conscious suffering. It does not mean meek submission to the will of the evil-doer, but it means the pitting of one's whole soul against the will of the tyrant....[I]t is possible for a single individual to defy the whole might of an unjust empire to save his honour, his religion, his soul.[2]

Returning to India in 1914, Gandhi quickly rose within the leadership ranks of the INC. During the 1920s and 1930s, he applied his approach in periodic mass campaigns that drew support from an extraordinarily wide spectrum of Indians—peasants and the urban poor, intellectuals and artisans, capitalists and socialists, Hindus and Muslims. The British responded with periodic repression as well as concessions that allowed a greater Indian role in political life. Gandhi's conduct and actions—his simple and unpretentious lifestyle, his support of Muslims, his frequent reference to Hindu religious themes—appealed widely in India and transformed the INC into a mass organization. To many ordinary people, Gandhi possessed magical powers and produced miraculous events. He was the Mahatma, the Great Soul.

His was a radicalism of a different kind. He did not call for social revolution but sought the moral transformation of individuals. He worked to raise the status of India's untouchables (the lowest and most ritually polluting groups within the caste hierarchy), although he launched no attack on caste in general and accepted support from businessmen and their socialist critics alike. His critique of India's situation went far beyond colonial rule. "India is being ground down," he argued, "not under the English heel, but under that of modern civilization"—its competitiveness, its materialism, its warlike tendencies, its abandonment of religion.[3] Almost alone among nationalist leaders in India or elsewhere, Gandhi opposed a modern industrial future for his country, seeking instead a society of harmonious self-sufficient villages drawing on ancient Indian principles of duty and morality. (See Document 20.5, pp. 957–59, for a more extended statement of Gandhi's thinking.)

Gandhi and the INC or Congress Party leadership had to contend with a wide range of movements, parties, and approaches, whose very diversity tore at the national unity that they so ardently sought. Whereas Gandhi rejected modern industrialization, his own chief lieutenant, Jawaharlal Nehru, thoroughly embraced science, technology, and industry as essential to India's future. Nor did everyone accept Gandhi's nonviolence or his inclusive definition of India. A militant Hindu organization preached hatred of Muslims and viewed India as an essentially Hindu nation. To some in the Congress Party, movements to improve the position of women or untouchables seemed a distraction from the chief task of gaining independence from Britain. Whether to participate in British-sponsored legislative bodies without complete independence also became a divisive issue. Furthermore, a number of smaller parties advocated on behalf of particular regions or castes. India's nationalist movement, in short, was beset by division and controversy. (For an image that illustrates these divisions, see Visual Source 23.1, p. 1124.)

By far the most serious threat to a unified movement derived from the growing divide between the country's Hindu and Muslim populations. As early as 1906, the formation of an All-India Muslim League contradicted the Congress Party's claim to speak for all Indians. As the British allowed more elected Indian representatives on local councils, the League demanded separate electorates, with a fixed number of seats on local councils for Muslims. As a distinct minority within India, some Muslims feared that their voice could be swamped by a numerically dominant Hindu population, despite Gandhi's inclusive philosophy. Some Hindu politicians confirmed those fears when they cast the nationalist struggle in Hindu religious terms, hailing their country, for example, as a goddess, Bande Mataram (Mother India). When elections in 1937 gave the Congress Party control of many provincial governments, some of those governments began to enforce the teaching of Hindi in schools and to protect cows from slaughter, both of which antagonized Muslims.

As the movement for independence gained ground, the Muslim League and its leader, Muhammad Ali Jinnah, increasingly argued that those parts of India that had a Muslim majority should have a separate political status. They called it Pakistan, the land of the pure. In this view, India was not a single nation, as Gandhi had long argued. Jinnah put his case succinctly:

> The Muslims and Hindus belong to two different religious philosophies, social customs, and literatures. They neither intermarry nor interdine [eat] together and, indeed, they belong to two different civilizations.[4]

With great reluctance and amid mounting violence, Gandhi and the Congress Party finally agreed to partition as the British declared their intention to leave India after World War II.

Thus colonial India became independent in 1947 as two countries—a Muslim Pakistan, itself divided into two wings 1,000

■ **Description**
What conflicts and differences divided India's nationalist movement?

The Independence of British South Asia

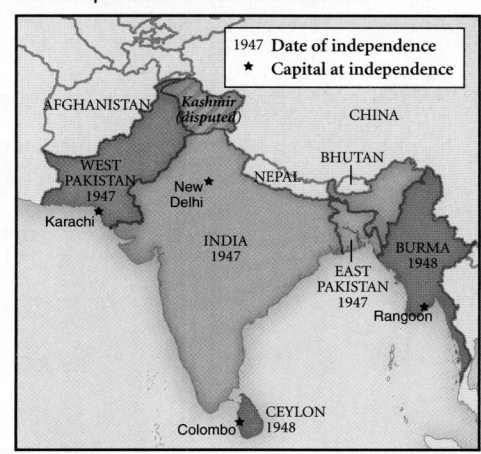

miles apart, and a mostly Hindu India governed by a secular state. Dividing colonial India in this fashion was horrendously painful. A million people or more died in the communal violence that accompanied partition, and some 12 million refugees moved from one country to the other to join their religious compatriots. Gandhi himself, desperately trying to stem the mounting tide of violence in India's villages, refused to attend the independence celebrations. He was assassinated in 1948 by a Hindu extremist. The great triumph of independence, secured from the powerful British Empire, was shadowed by an equally great tragedy in the violence of partition.

The Case of South Africa: Ending Apartheid

■ Comparison
Why was African majority rule in South Africa delayed until 1994, whereas the overthrow of European colonialism had occurred much earlier in the rest of Africa and Asia?

The setting for South Africa's freedom struggle was very different from the situation in India. In the twentieth century, that struggle was not waged against an occupying European colonial power, for South Africa had in fact been independent of Great Britain since 1910. That independence, however, had been granted to a government wholly controlled by a white settler minority, which represented less than 20 percent of the total population. The country's black African majority had no political

Snapshot   **Key Moments in South African History**

Earliest humans in South Africa	by 50,000 years ago
Arrival of iron-using, Bantu-speaking agricultural peoples	by 500 C.E.
First Dutch settlement	1652
Shaka and creation of a Zulu state	early 19th century
British takeover of South Africa	1806
Great Trek: Afrikaner migration to the interior to escape more liberal British rule	1830s
European conquest of interior African societies	mid- to late 19th century
Gold and diamond mining begins	late 19th century
Great Britain defeats Afrikaners in Boer War	1899–1902
South Africa independent under white minority government	1910
African National Congress established	1912
National Party comes to power; apartheid formally established	1948
Sharpville massacre	1960
ANC launches armed struggle	1961
Black Consciousness movement; urban insurrection	1970s
Nelson Mandela released from prison	1990
ANC comes to power following first all-race elections	1994

rights whatsoever within the central state. Black South Africans' struggle therefore was against this internal opponent rather than against a distant colonial authority, as in India. Economically, the most prominent whites were of British descent. They or their forebears had come to South Africa during the nineteenth century, when Great Britain was the ruling colonial power. But the politically dominant section of the white community, known as Boers or Afrikaners, was descended from the early Dutch settlers, who had arrived in the mid-seventeenth century. The term "Afrikaner" reflected their image of themselves as "white Africans," permanent residents of the continent rather than colonial intruders. They had unsuccessfully sought independence from a British-ruled South Africa in a bitter struggle (the Boer War, 1899–1902), and a sense of difference and antagonism lingered. Despite a certain hostility between white South Africans of British and Afrikaner background, both felt that their way of life and standard of living were jeopardized by any move toward black African majority rule. The intransigence of this sizable and threatened settler community helps explain why African rule was delayed until 1994, while India, lacking any such community, had achieved independence almost a half century earlier.

Unlike a predominantly agrarian India, South Africa by the early twentieth century had developed a mature industrial economy, based initially in gold and diamond mining, but by midcentury including secondary industries such as steel, chemicals, automobile manufacturing, rubber processing, and heavy engineering. Particularly since the 1960s, the economy benefited from extensive foreign investment and loans. Almost all black Africans were involved in this complex modern economy, working in urban industries or mines, providing labor for white-owned farms, or receiving payments from relatives who did. The extreme dependence of most Africans on the white-controlled economy rendered individuals highly vulnerable to repressive action, but collectively the threat to withdraw their essential labor also gave them a powerful weapon.

A third unique feature of the South African situation was the overwhelming prominence of race, expressed most clearly in the policy of apartheid, which attempted to separate blacks from whites in every conceivable way while retaining Africans' labor power in the white-controlled economy. An enormous apparatus of repression enforced that system. Rigid "pass laws" monitored and tried to control the movement of Africans into the cities, where they were subjected to extreme forms of social segregation. In the rural areas, a series of impoverished and overcrowded "native reserves," or Bantustans, served as ethnic homelands that kept Africans divided along tribal lines. Even though racism was present in colonial India, nothing of this magnitude developed there.

As in India, various forms of opposition—resistance to conquest, rural rebellions, urban strikes, and independent churches—arose to contest the manifest injustices of South African life. There too an elite-led political party provided an organizational umbrella for many of the South African resistance efforts in the twentieth century. Established in 1912, the African National Congress (ANC), like its Indian predecessor, was led by educated, professional, and middle-class Africans who sought not to overthrow the existing order, but to be accepted as "civilized men" within it. They

■ **Change**
How did South Africa's struggle against white domination change over time?

appealed to the liberal, humane, and Christian values that white society claimed. For four decades, its leaders pursued peaceful and moderate protest—petitions, multiracial conferences, delegations appealing to the authorities—even as racially based segregationist policies were implemented one after another. By 1948, when the Afrikaner-led National Party came to power on a platform of apartheid, it was clear that such "constitutional" protest had produced nothing.

During the 1950s, a new and younger generation of the ANC leadership, which now included Nelson Mandela, broadened its base of support and launched non-violent civil disobedience—boycotts, strikes, demonstrations, and the burning of the hated passes that all Africans were required to carry. All of these actions were similar to and inspired by the tactics that Gandhi had used in India twenty to thirty years earlier. The government of South Africa responded with tremendous repression, including the shooting of sixty-nine unarmed demonstrators at Sharpville in 1960, the banning of the ANC, and the imprisonment of its leadership. This was the context in which Mandela was arrested and sentenced to his long prison term.

At this point, the freedom struggle in South Africa took a different direction than it had in India. Its major political parties were now illegal. Underground nationalist leaders turned to armed struggle, authorizing selected acts of sabotage and assassination, while preparing for guerrilla warfare in camps outside the country. Active opposition within South Africa was now primarily expressed by student groups that were part of the Black Consciousness movement, an effort to foster pride, unity, and political awareness among the country's African majority. Such young people were at the center of an explosion of protest in 1976 in a sprawling, segregated, impoverished black neighborhood called Soweto, outside Johannesburg, in which hundreds were killed. The initial trigger for the uprising was the government's decision to enforce education for Africans in the hated language of the white Afrikaners rather than English. However, the momentum of the Soweto rebellion persisted, and by the mid-1980s, spreading urban violence and the radicalization of urban young people had forced the government to declare a state of emergency. Furthermore, South Africa's black labor movement, legalized only in 1979, became increasingly active and political. In June 1986, to commemorate the tenth anniversary of the Soweto uprising, the Congress of South African Trade Unions orchestrated a general strike involving some 2 million workers.

Independence in Kenya, East Africa
Almost everywhere in the colonial world, the struggle for independence climaxed in a formal and joyful ceremony in which power was transferred from the colonial authority to the leader of the new nation. Here a jubilant Jomo Kenyatta takes the oath of office in 1964 as Kenya's first president, while a dour and bewigged British official looks on. (Bettmann/Corbis)

Beyond this growing internal pressure, South Africa faced mounting international demands to end apartheid as well. Exclusion from most international sporting events, including the Olympics; the refusal of many artists and entertainers to perform in South Africa; economic boycotts; the withdrawal of private investment funds—all of this isolated South Africa from a Western world in which its white rulers claimed membership. This was another feature of the South African freedom movement that had no parallel in India.

The combination of these internal and external pressures persuaded many white South Africans by the late 1980s that discussion with African nationalist leaders was the only alternative to a massive, bloody, and futile struggle to preserve white privileges. The outcome was the abandonment of key apartheid policies, the release of Nelson Mandela from prison, the legalization of the ANC, and a prolonged process of negotiations that in 1994 resulted in national elections, which brought the ANC to power. To the surprise of almost everyone, the long nightmare of South African apartheid came to an end without a racial bloodbath (see Map 23.2).

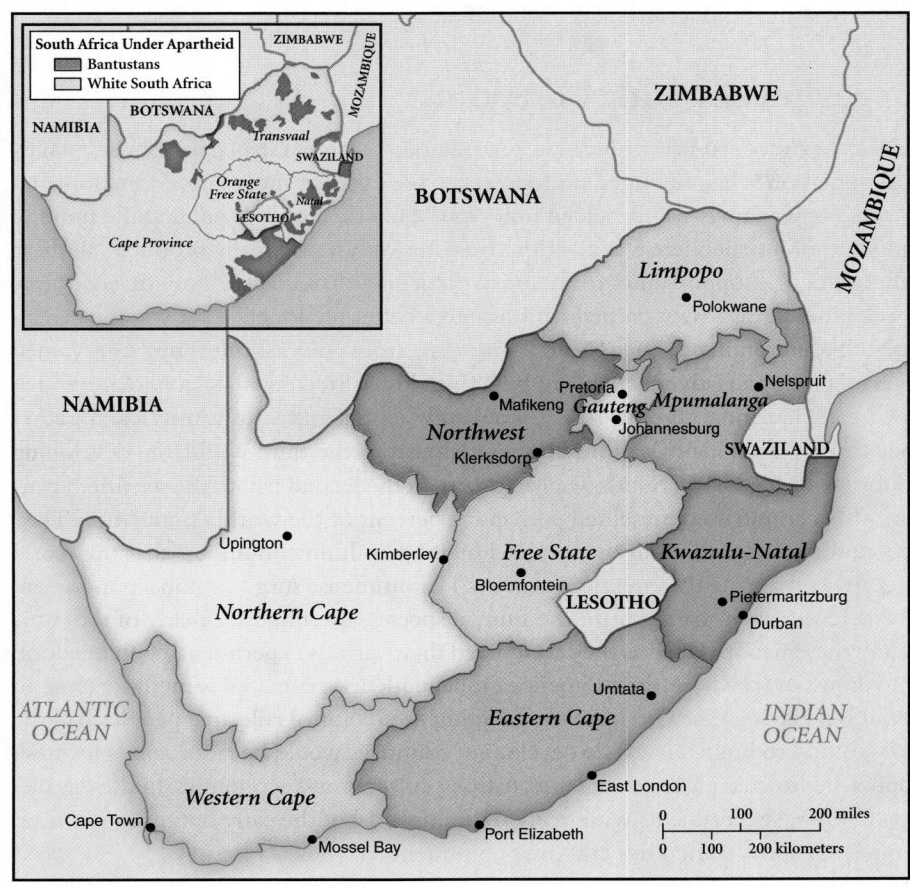

Map 23.2 South Africa after Apartheid
Under apartheid, all black Africans were officially designated as residents of small, scattered, impoverished Bantustans, shown on the inset map. Many of these people, of course, actually lived in white South Africa, where they worked. The main map shows the new internal organization of the country as it emerged after 1994, with the Bantustans abolished and the country divided into nine provinces. Lesotho and Swaziland had been British protectorates during the colonial era and subsequently became separate independent countries, although surrounded by South African territory.

As in India, the South African nationalist movement that finally won freedom was divided and conflicted. Unlike India, though, these divisions did not occur along religious lines. Rather it was race, ethnicity, and ideology that generated dissension and sometimes violence. Whereas the ANC generally favored a broad alliance of everyone opposed to apartheid (black Africans, Indians, "coloreds" or mixed-race people, and sympathetic whites), a smaller group known as the Pan Africanist Congress rejected cooperation with other racial groups and limited its membership to black Africans. During the urban uprisings of the 1970s and 1980s, young people supporting the Black Consciousness movements and those following Mandela and the ANC waged war against each other in the townships of South African cities. Perhaps most threatening to the unity of the nationalist struggle were the separatist tendencies of the Zulu-based Inkatha Freedom Party. Its leader, Gatsha Buthelezi, had cooperated with the apartheid state and even received funding from it. As negotiations for a transition to African rule unfolded in the early 1990s, considerable violence between Inkatha followers, mostly Zulu migrant workers, and ANC supporters broke out in a number of cities. None of this, however, approached the massive killing of Hindus and Muslims that accompanied the partition of India. South Africa, unlike India, acquired its political freedom as an intact and unified state.

Experiments with Freedom

Africa's first modern nationalist hero, Kwame Nkrumah of Ghana, paraphrased a biblical quotation when he urged his followers, "Seek ye first the political kingdom and all these other things will be added unto you." However, would winning the political kingdom of independence or freedom from European rule really produce "all these other things"—opportunity for political participation, industrial growth, economic development, reasonably unified nations, and a better life for all? That was the central question confronting the new nations emerging from colonial rule. They were joined in that quest by already independent but nonindustrialized countries and regions such as China, Thailand, Ethiopia, Iran, Turkey, and Central and South America. Together they formed the bloc of nations known variously as the third world, the developing countries, or the Global South (see Map 23.3). In the second half of the twentieth century, these countries represented perhaps 75 percent of the world's population. They accounted for almost all of the fourfold increase in human numbers that the world experienced during the twentieth century. That immense surge in global population, at one level a great triumph for the human species, also underlay many of the difficulties these nations faced as they conducted their various experiments with freedom.

Almost everywhere, the moment of independence generated something close to euphoria. Having emerged from the long night of colonial rule, free peoples had the opportunity to build anew. The developing countries would be laboratories for fresh approaches to creating modern states, nations, cultures, and economies. In the decades that followed, experiments with freedom multiplied, but the early optimism was soon tempered by the difficulties and disappointments of those tasks.

Experiments in Political Order: Comparing African Nations and India

All across the developing world, efforts to create political order had to contend with a set of common conditions. Populations were exploding. Expectations for independence ran very high, often exceeding the available resources. Most developing countries were culturally diverse, with little loyalty new to the central state. Nonetheless, public employment mushroomed as the state assumed greater responsibility for economic development. In conditions of widespread poverty and weak private economies, groups and individuals sought to capture the state, or parts of it, both for the salaries and status it offered and for the opportunities for private enrichment that political office provided.

This was the formidable setting in which developing countries had to hammer out their political systems. The range of that effort was immense: Communist Party control in China, Vietnam, and Cuba; multiparty democracy in India and South Africa; one-party democracy in Tanzania and Senegal; military regimes for a time in much of Latin America and Africa; personal dictatorships in Uganda and the Philippines. In many places, one kind of political system followed another in kaleidoscopic succession. The political evolution of postindependence Africa illustrates the complexity and the difficulty of creating a stable political order in developing countries.

Map 23.3   The "Worlds" of the Twentieth Century During the cold war, the term "third world" referred to those countries not solidly in either the Western or the Communist bloc of nations. Gradually it came to designate developing countries, those less wealthy and less industrialized societies seeking to catch up to the more developed countries of Europe, North America, and Japan. China, Vietnam, and Cuba, although governed by communist regimes, have been widely regarded as part of the developing world as well.

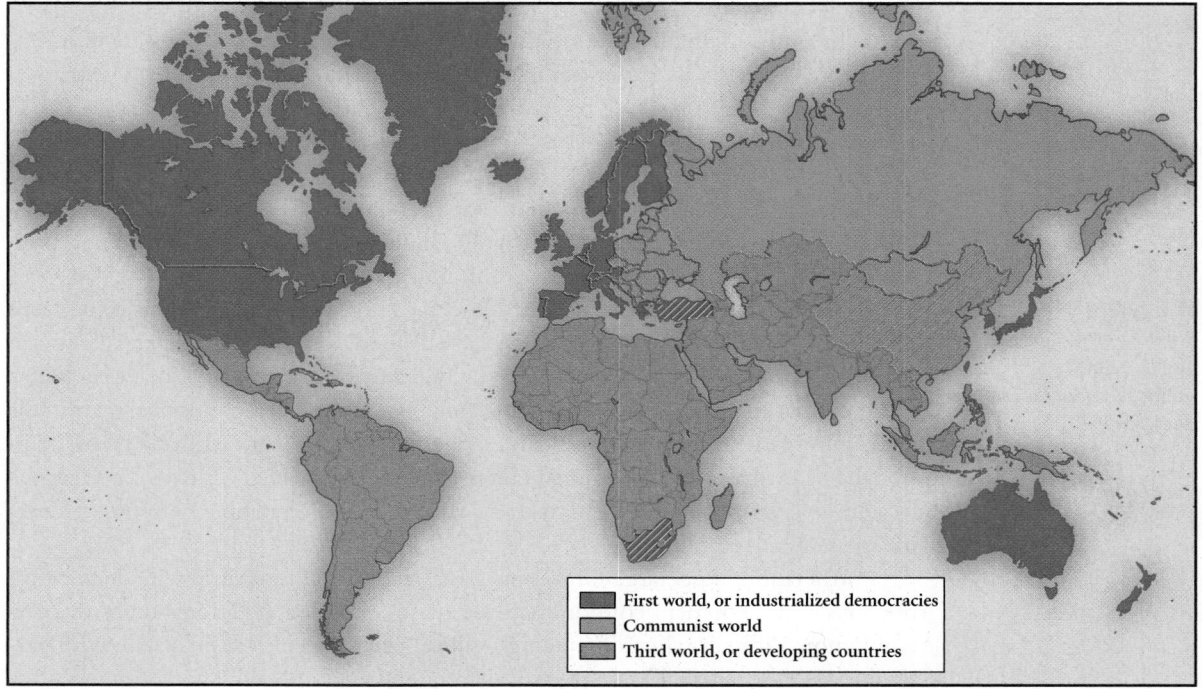

- ■ First world, or industrialized democracies
- ■ Communist world
- ■ Third world, or developing countries

Although colonial rule had been highly authoritarian and bureaucratic with little interest in African participation, during the 1950s the British, the French, and the Belgians attempted, rather belatedly, to transplant democratic institutions to their colonies. They established legislatures, permitted elections, allowed political parties to operate, and in general anticipated the development of constitutional, parliamentary, multiparty democracies similar to their own. It was with such institutions that most African states greeted independence.

By the early 1970s, however, few such regimes were left among the new states of Africa. Many of the apparently popular political parties that had led the struggle for independence lost mass support and were swept away by military coups. When the army took power in Ghana in 1966, no one lifted a finger to defend the party that had led the country to independence only nine years earlier. Other states evolved into one-party systems, sometimes highly authoritarian and bureaucratic and sometimes more open and democratic. Still others degenerated into personal tyrannies or dictatorships. Freedom from colonial rule certainly did not automatically generate the internal political freedoms associated with democracy.

■ **Comparison**

Why was Africa's experience with political democracy so different from that of India?

The contrast between Africa's political evolution and that of India has been particularly striking. In India, Western-style democracy, including regular elections, multiple parties, civil liberties, and peaceful changes in government, has been practiced almost continuously since independence. The struggle for independence in India had been a far more prolonged affair, thus providing time for an Indian political leadership to sort itself out. Furthermore, the British began to hand over power in a gradual way well before complete independence was granted in 1947. Thus a far larger number of Indians had useful administrative or technical skills than was the case in Africa. In sharp contrast to most African countries, the nationalist movement in India was embodied in a single national party (the Congress Party), which encompassed a wide variety of other parties and interest groups. Its leadership was genuinely committed to democratic practice. Even the tragic and painful partition of colonial India into two countries eliminated a major source of internal discord as independent India was born. Moreover, Indian statehood could be built on cultural and political traditions that were far more deeply rooted than in most African states.

■ **Change**

What accounts for the ups and downs of political democracy in postcolonial Africa?

Explaining the initial rejection of democracy in Africa has been a major concern of politicians and scholars alike. Some have argued, on the basis of paternalistic or even racist assumptions, that Africans were not ready for democracy or that they lacked some crucial ingredient for democratic politics—an educated electorate, a middle class, or perhaps a thoroughly capitalist economy. Others suggested that Africa's traditional culture, based on communal rather than individualistic values and concerned to achieve consensus rather than majority rule, was not compatible with the competitiveness of party politics.

Furthermore, some argued, Western-style democracy was simply inadequate for the tasks of development confronting the new states. Creating national unity was certainly more difficult when competing political parties identified primarily with particular ethnic or "tribal" groups, as was frequently the case in Africa. Similarly, the immense problems that inevitably accompany the early stages of modern economic development were compounded by the heavy demands of a political system based on universal suffrage. Certainly Europe did not begin its modernizing process with such a system. Why, many Africans asked, should they be expected to do so?

Beyond these general considerations, more immediate conditions likewise undermined the popular support of many postindependence governments in Africa and discredited their initial democracies. One was widespread economic disappointment. By almost any measure, African economic performance since independence has been the poorest in the developing world. This has translated into students denied the white-collar careers they expected, urban migrants with little opportunity for work, farmers paid low prices for their cash crops, consumers resentful about shortages and inflation, and millions of impoverished and malnourished peasants pushed to the brink of starvation. These were people for whom independence was unable to fulfill even the most minimal of expectations, let alone the grandiose visions of a better life that so many had embraced in the early 1960s. Since modern governments everywhere staked their popularity on economic performance, it is little wonder that many Africans became disaffected and withdrew their support from governments they had enthusiastically endorsed only a few years earlier.

Nevertheless, economic disappointment did not affect everyone to the same extent, and for some, independence offered great opportunities for acquiring status, position, and wealth. Unlike the situation in Latin America and parts of Asia, those who benefited most from independence were not large landowners, for most African societies simply did not have an established class whose wealth was based in landed estates. Rather they were members of the relatively well-educated elite who had found high-paying jobs in the growing bureaucracies of the newly independent states. The privileges of this dominant class were widely resented. Government ministers in many countries earned the title "Mr. Ten Percent," a reference to the bribes or "gifts" they received from private contractors working for the state. This kind of resentment broke out in Zaire between 1964 and 1968 in the form of a widespread peasant rebellion calling for a "second independence" against the "new whites" of the elite class.

Frequently, however, the resentments born of inequality and of competition for jobs, housing, educational opportunities, development projects, and political position found expression in ethnic conflict, as Africa's immense cultural diversity became intensely politicized. In many places, a judicious balancing of appointments and budgetary allocations among major ethnic groups contained conflict within a peaceful political process. Elsewhere it led to violence. An ethnically based civil war in Nigeria during the late 1960s cost the lives of millions, while in the mid-1990s ethnic hatred led Rwanda into the realm of genocide.

Thus economic disappointment, class resentments, and ethnic conflict eroded support for the transplanted democracies of the early independence era. The most common alternative involved government by soldiers, a familiar pattern in Latin America as well. By the early 1980s, the military had intervened in at least thirty of Africa's forty-six independent states and actively governed more than half of them.

Usually, the military took power in a crisis, after the civilian government had lost most of its popular support. The soldiers often claimed that the nation was in grave danger, that corrupt civilian politicians had led the country to the brink of chaos, and that only the military had the discipline and strength to put things right. And so they swept aside the old political parties and constitutions and vowed to begin anew, while promising to return power to civilians and restore democracy at some point in the future.

Since the early 1980s, a remarkable resurgence of Western-style democracy has brought popular movements, multiparty elections, and new constitutions to a number of African states, including Ghana, Kenya, Mali, Senegal, and Zambia. It was part of a late-twentieth-century democratic revival of global dimensions that included Southern and Eastern Europe, most of Latin America, and parts of Asia and the Middle East. How can we explain this rather sudden, though still fragile, resumption of democracy in Africa? Perhaps the most important internal factor was the evident failure of authoritarian governments to remedy the disastrous economic situation. Disaffected students, religious organizations, urban workers, and women's groups joined in a variety of grassroots movements to demand democratic change as a means to a better life. This pressure from below for political change reflected the growing strength of civil society in many African countries as organizations independent of the state provided a social foundation for the renewal of democracy.

Such movements found encouragement in the demands for democracy that accompanied the South African struggle against apartheid and the collapse of Soviet and Eastern European communism. The end of the cold war reduced the willingness of the major industrial powers to underwrite their authoritarian client states. For many Africans, democracy increasingly was viewed as a universal political principle to which they could also aspire rather than an alien and imposed system deriving from the West. None of this provided an immediate solution for the economic difficulties, ethnic conflicts, and endemic corruption of African societies, but it did suggest a willingness to continue the political experiments that had begun with independence.

Experiments in Economic Development: Changing Priorities, Varying Outcomes

■ Change

What obstacles impeded the economic development of third-world countries?

At the top of the agenda everywhere in the Global South was economic development, a process that meant growth or increasing production as well as distributing the fruits of that growth to raise living standards. This quest for development, now operating all across the planet, represented the universal acceptance of beliefs unheard of not many centuries earlier—that poverty was no longer inevitable and that it was possible to deliberately improve the material conditions of life for everyone. Economic development was a central promise of all independence struggles, and it was increasingly the standard by which people measured and granted legitimacy to their governments.

Achieving economic development, however, proved immensely difficult. It took place in societies sharply divided by class, religion, ethnic group, and gender and in the face of explosive population growth. In many places, colonial rule had provided only the most slender foundations for modern development to these newly independent nations, which had low rates of literacy, few people with managerial experience, a weak private economy, and transportation systems oriented to export rather than national integration. Furthermore, the entire effort occurred in a world split by rival superpowers and economically dominated by the powerful capitalist economies of the West. Despite their political independence, most developing countries had little leverage in negotiations with the wealthy nations of the Global North and their immense transnational corporations. It was hardly an auspicious environment in which to seek a fundamental economic transformation.

Beyond these structural difficulties, it was hard for leaders of developing countries to know what strategies to pursue. The academic field of "development economics" was new; its experts disagreed and often changed their minds; and conflicting political pressures, both internal and international, only added to the confusion. All of this resulted in considerable controversy, changing policies, and much experimentation. (See Documents: Debating Development in Africa, pp. 1110–21, for various African views about development.)

One fundamental issue lay in the role of the state. All across the developing world and particularly in newly independent nations, most people expected that state authorities would take major responsibility for spurring the economic development of their countries. After all, the private economy was weakly developed; few entrepreneurs had substantial funds to invest; the example of rapid Soviet industrialization under state direction was hopeful; and state control held the promise of protecting vulnerable economies from the ravages of international capitalism. Some state-directed economies had real successes. China launched a major industrialization effort and massive land reform under the leadership of the Communist Party. A communist Cuba, even while remaining dependent on its sugar production, wiped out illiteracy and provided basic health care to its entire population, raising life expectancy to seventy-six years by 1992, equivalent to that of the United States. Elsewhere as well—in Turkey, India, South Korea, and much of Africa—the state provided tariffs, licenses, loans, subsidies, and overall planning, while most productive property was owned privately.

Yet in the last several decades of the twentieth century, an earlier consensus in favor of state direction largely collapsed, replaced by a growing dependence on the market to generate economic development. This was most apparent in the abandonment of much communist planning in China and the return to private farming (see pp. 1052–54). India and many Latin American and African states privatized their state-run industries and substantially reduced the role of the state in economic affairs. In part, this sharp change in economic policies reflected the failure, mismanagement, and corruption of many state-run enterprises, but it also was influenced by the collapse in the Soviet Union of the world's first state-dominated economy. Western pressures, exercised through international organizations such as the World Bank, likewise pushed developing countries in a capitalist direction. In China and India, the new approach generated rapid economic growth, but also growing inequalities and social conflict. As the new millennium dawned, a number of Latin American countries—Venezuela,

■ Change
In what ways did thinking about the role of the state in the economic life of developing countries change? Why did it change?

Snapshot   **Economic Development in the Global South by the Early Twenty-first Century**[5]

This table samples the economic performance of fourteen developing countries and five major regions of the Global South by the early twenty-first century. Similar data for the United States, Japan, and Russia are included for comparative purposes. Which indicators of development do you find most revealing? What aspects

Regions/Countries	Population Growth Rate Average Annual 2000–2007 (%)	Gross National Income per Capita, 2007 (U.S. $)	Purchasing Power per Capita, 2007 (U.S. $)
East Asia	0.8	2,180	4,937
China	0.6	2,360	5,370
Philippines	2.0	1,620	3,370
Latin America	1.3	5,540	9,321
Mexico	1.0	8,340	12,580
Brazil	1.4	5,910	9,370
Guatemala	2.5	2,440	4,520
Middle East and North Africa	1.8	2,794	7,385
Egypt	1.8	1,580	5,400
Turkey	1.3	8,020	12,090
Iran	1.5	3,470	10,800
Saudi Arabia	2.3	15,440	22,910
South Asia	1.6	880	2,537
India	1.4	950	2,470
Indonesia	1.3	1,650	3,580
Sub-Saharan Africa	2.5	952	1,870
Nigeria	2.4	930	1,770
Congo	3.0	140	290
Tanzania	2.5	400	1,200
For comparison			
High-income countries	0.7	37,566	36,100
United States	0.9	46,040	45,850
Japan	0.1	37,670	34,600
Russia	−0.5	7,560	14,400

of development does each of them measure? Based on these data, which countries or regions would you consider the most and the least successful? Does your judgment about "success" vary depending on which measure you use?

Life Expectancy in years, 2003–2006		Adult Literacy (%) 2005	Infant Mortality (Deaths under Age 5 per 1,000)		CO$_2$ Emission per Capita, 2004 (Metric Tons)
MALE	FEMALE		1990	2006	
69	73	91	56	29	3.3
70	74	91	45	24	3.9
69	74	93	62	32	1.0
70	76	90	55	20	2.7
72	77	92	53	35	4.3
69	76	89	57	20	1.8
66	74	69	82	41	1.0
68	72	73	78	42	4.2
69	73	71	91	35	2.2
69	74	87	82	26	3.2
69	72	82	72	34	6.4
71	75	83	44	25	13.7
63	66	58	123	83	1.1
63	66	61	115	76	1.2
66	70	90	91	34	1.7
49	52	59	184	157	0.9
46	47	69	230	191	0.8
45	47	67	205	205	0.0
51	53	69	161	118	0.1
76	82	99	12	7	13.1
75	81	99	11	8	20.6
79	86	99	6	4	9.8
59	73	99	27	16	10.6

Microloans
Bangladesh's Grameen Bank pioneered an innovative approach to economic development by offering modest loans to poor people, enabling them to start small businesses. Here a group of women who received such loans meet in early 2004 to make an installment payment to an officer of the bank. (Rafiqur Rahman/Reuters/Corbis)

Brazil, and Bolivia, for example—once again asserted a more prominent role for the state in their quests for economic development and social justice.

Other issues as well inspired debate. In many places, an early emphasis on city-based industrial development, stirred by visions of a rapid transition to modernity, led to a neglect or exploitation of rural areas and agriculture. This "urban bias" subsequently came in for much criticism and some adjustment in spending priorities. A growing recognition of the role of women in agriculture led to charges of "male bias" in development planning and to mounting efforts to assist women farmers directly (see Document 23.4). Women also were central to many governments' increased interest in curtailing population growth. Women's access to birth control, education, and employment, it turned out, provided powerful incentives to limit family size. Another debate pitted the advocates of capital- and technology-driven projects (dams and factories, for example) against those who favored investment in "human capital," such as education, technical training, health care, and nutrition. The benefits and drawbacks of foreign aid, investment, and trade have likewise been contentious issues. Should developing countries seek to shield themselves from the influences of international capitalism, or are they better off vigorously engaging with the global economy?

Economic development was never simply a matter of technical expertise or deciding among competing theories. Every decision was political, involving winners and losers in terms of power, advantage, and wealth. Where to locate schools, roads, factories, and clinics, for example, provoked endless controversies, some of them expressed in terms of regional or ethnic rivalries. It was an experimental process, and the stakes were high.

The results of those experiments have varied considerably, as the Snapshot on pages 1100–01 indicates. East Asian countries in general have had the strongest record of economic growth. South Korea, Taiwan, Singapore, and Hong Kong were dubbed "newly industrialized countries," and China boasted the most rapid economic growth in the world by the end of the twentieth century, replacing Japan as the world's second-largest economy. In the 1990s, Asia's other giant, India, opened itself more fully to the world market and launched rapid economic growth with a powerful high-tech sector and an expanding middle class. Oil-producing countries reaped a bonanza when they were able to demand much higher prices for that essential commodity in the 1970s and after. Several Latin American states (Chile and Brazil, for example) entered the world market vigorously and successfully with growing industrial sectors. Limited principally to Europe, North America, and Japan in the nineteenth century, industrialization had become a global phenomenon in the twentieth century.

Elsewhere, the story was very different. In most of Africa, much of the Arab world, and parts of Asia—regions representing about one-third of the world's population— there was little sign of catching up and frequent examples of declining standards of living since the end of the 1960s. Between 1980 and 2000, the average income in forty-three of Africa's poorest countries dropped by 25 percent, pushing living standards for many below what they had been at independence.

Scholars and politicians alike argue about the reasons for such sharp differences. Variables such as geography and natural resources, differing colonial experiences, variations in regional cultures, the degree of political stability and social equality, state economic policies, population growth rates, and varying forms of involvement with the world economy have been invoked to explain the widely diverging trajectories among developing countries.

Experiments with Culture: The Role of Islam in Turkey and Iran

The quest for economic development represented the embrace of an emerging global culture of modernity—with its scientific outlook, its technological achievements, and its focus on material values. It also exposed developing countries to the changing culture of the West, including feminism, rock and rap, sexual permissiveness, consumerism, and democracy. But the peoples of the Global South also had inherited cultural patterns from the more distant past—Hindu, Confucian, or Islamic, for example. A common issue all across the developing world involved the uneasy relationship between these older traditions and the more recent outlooks associated with modernity and the West. This tension provided the raw material for a series of cultural experiments in the twentieth century, and nowhere were they more consequential than in the Islamic world. No single answer emerged to the question of how Islam and modernity should relate to each other, but the experience of Turkey and Iran illustrate two quite different approaches to this fundamental issue.

In the aftermath of World War I, modern Turkey emerged from the ashes of the Ottoman Empire, led by an energetic general, Mustafa Kemal Atatürk (1881–1938), who fought off British, French, Italian, and Greek efforts to dismember what was left of the old empire. Often compared to Peter the Great in Russia (see p. 844), Atatürk then sought to transform his country into a modern, secular, and national state. Such ambitions were not entirely new, for they built upon the efforts of nineteenth-century

■ **Comparison**
In what ways did cultural revolutions in Turkey and Iran reflect different understandings of the role of Islam in modern societies?

Iran, Turkey, and the Middle East

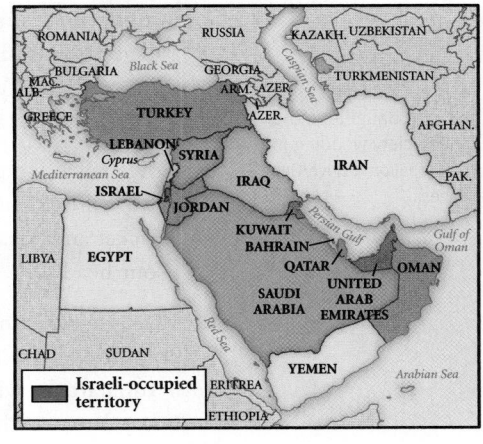

Westernization in Turkey Mustafa Kemal Atatürk, the founder of modern Turkey, often appeared in public in elegant European dress, symbolizing for his people a sharp break with traditional Islamic ways of living. Here he is dancing with his adopted daughter at her high-society wedding in 1929. (Hulton Archive/Getty Images)

Ottoman reformers, who, like Atatürk, greatly admired European Enlightenment thinking and sought to bring its benefits to their country.

To Atatürk and his followers, to become modern meant "to enter European civilization completely." They believed that this required the total removal of Islam from public life, relegating it to the personal and private realm. In doing so, Atatürk argued that "Islam will be elevated, if it will cease to be a political instrument." In fact, he sought to broaden access to the religion by translating the Quran into Turkish and issuing the call to prayer in Turkish rather than Arabic.

Ataturk largely ended, however, the direct political role of Islam. The old sultan or ruler of the Ottoman Empire, whose position had long been sanctified by Islamic tradition, was deposed as Turkey became a republic. Furthermore the caliphate, by which Ottoman sultans had claimed leadership of the entire Islamic world, was abolished. Various Sufi organizations, sacred tombs, and religious schools were closed and a number of religious titles abolished. Islamic courts were likewise dissolved, while secular law codes, modeled on those of Europe, replaced the *sharia*. In history textbooks, pre-Islamic Turkish culture was celebrated as the foundation for all ancient civilizations. The Arabic script in which the Turkish language had long been written was exchanged for a new Western-style alphabet that made literacy much easier but rendered centuries of Ottoman culture inaccessible to these newly literate people. (See Document 24.1, pp. 1167–68, for an example of Atatürk's thinking.)

The most visible symbols of Atatürk's revolutionary program occurred in the realm of dress. Turkish men were ordered to abandon the traditional headdress known as the *fez* and to wear brimmed hats. According to Atatürk,

> A civilized, international dress is worthy and appropriate for our nation, and we will wear it. Boots or shoes on our feet, trousers on our legs, shirt and tie, jacket and waistcoat—and of course, to complete these, a cover with a brim on our heads.[6]

Although women were not forbidden to wear the veil, many elite women abandoned it and set the tone for feminine fashion in Turkey.

In Atatürk's view, the emancipation of women was a cornerstone of the new Turkey. In a much-quoted speech, he declared:

If henceforward the women do not share in the social life of the nation, we shall never attain to our full development. We shall remain irremediably backward, incapable of treating on equal terms with the civilizations of the West.[7]

Thus polygamy was abolished; women were granted equal rights in divorce, inheritance, and child custody; and in 1934 Turkish women gained the right to vote and hold public office, a full decade before French women gained that right. Public beaches were now opened to women as well.

These reforms represented a "cultural revolution" unique in the Islamic world of the time, and they were imposed against considerable opposition. After Atatürk's death in 1938, some of them were diluted or rescinded. The call to prayer returned to the traditional Arabic in 1950, and various political groups urged a greater role for Islam in the public arena. In 1996, a moderate Islamic political party came to power, and in early 2008 the Turkish parliament voted to end the earlier prohibition on women wearing headscarves in universities. Nevertheless, the essential secularism of the Turkish state, backed by a powerful military establishment, remained an enduring legacy of the Atatürk revolution. But elsewhere in the Islamic world, other solutions to the question of Islam and modernity took shape.

A very different answer emerged in Iran in the final quarter of the twentieth century. By that time all across the Islamic world, disappointments abounded with the social and economic results of political independence and secular development, while hostility to continuing Western cultural, military, and political intrusion grew apace. These conditions gave rise to numerous movements of Islamic revival or renewal that cast the religion as a guide to public as well as private life. If Western models of a good society had failed, it seemed reasonable to many people to turn their attention to distinctly Islamic solutions.

Iran seemed an unlikely place for an Islamic revolution. Under the government of Shah Mohammad Reza Pahlavi (ruled 1941–1979), Iran had undertaken what many saw as a quite successful modernization effort. The country had great wealth in oil, a powerful military, a well-educated elite, and a solid alliance with the United States. Furthermore, the shah's so-called White Revolution, intended to promote the country's modernization, had redistributed land to many of the Iran's impoverished peasantry, granted women the right to vote, invested substantially in rural health care and education, initiated a number of industrial projects, and offered workers a share in the profits of those industries. But beneath the surface of apparent success, discontent and resentment were brewing. Traditional merchants, known as *bazaaris*, felt threatened by an explosion of imported Western goods and by competition from large-scale businesses. Religious leaders, the *ulama*, were offended by secular education programs that bypassed Islamic schools and by state control of religious institutions. Educated professionals found Iran's reliance on the West disturbing. Rural migrants to the country's growing cities, especially Tehran, faced rising costs and uncertain employment.

A repressive and often brutal government allowed little outlet for such grievances. Thus, opposition to the shah's regime came to center on the country's many mosques, where Iran's Shi'ite religious leaders invoked memories of earlier perse-cution and martyrdom as they mobilized that opposition and called for the shah's removal. The emerging leader of that movement was the high-ranking Shia cleric Ayatollah Ruholla Khomeini (1902–1989), who in 1979 returned from long exile in Paris to great acclaim. By then, massive urban demonstrations, strikes, and defections from the military had eroded support for the shah, who abdicated the throne and left the country.

What followed was also a cultural revolution, but one that moved in precisely the opposite direction from that of Atatürk's Turkey—toward, rather than away from, the Islamization of public life. The new government defined itself as an Islamic repub-lic, with an elected parliament and a constitution, but in practice it represented the rule of Islamic clerics, in which conservative ulama, headed by Khomeini, exercised dominant power. The Council of Guardians, composed of leading legal scholars, was empowered to interpret the constitution, to supervise elections, and to review legislation—all designed to ensure compatibility with a particular vision of Islam. Opposition to the new regime was harshly crushed, with some 1,800 executions in 1981 alone for those regarded as "waging war against God."[8]

Khomeini, whose ideas are illustrated more fully in Document 24.3 on pages 1171–73, believed that the purpose of government was to apply the law of Allah as expressed in the sharia. Thus all judges now had to be competent in Islamic law, and those lacking that qualification were dismissed. The secular law codes under which the shah's government had operated were discarded in favor of those based solely on Islamic precedents. Islamization likewise profoundly affected the domain of education and culture. In June 1980 the new government closed some 200 uni-versities and colleges for two years while textbooks, curricula, and faculty were "purified" of un-Islamic influences. Elementary and secondary schools, largely sec-ular under the shah, now gave priority to religious instruction and the teaching of Arabic, even as about 40,000 teachers lost their jobs for lack of sufficient Islamic piety. Pre-Islamic Persian literature and history were now out of favor, while the history of Islam and Iran's revolution predominated in schools and the mass media. Western loan words were purged from the Farsi language, replaced by their Arabic equivalents.

As in Turkey, the role of women became a touchstone of this Islamic cultural revolution. By 1983, all women were required to wear the modest head-to-toe cov-ering known as *hijab*, a regulation enforced by roving groups of militants or "revo-lutionary guards." Those found with "bad hijab" were subject to harassment and sometimes lashings or imprisonment. Sexual segregation was imposed in schools, parks, beaches, and public transportation. The legal age of marriage for girls, set at eighteen under the shah, was reduced to nine with parental consent and thirteen, later raised to fifteen, without it. Married women could no longer file for divorce or attend school. Yet, despite such restrictions, many women supported the revolution and over the next several decades found far greater opportunities for employment

and higher education than before. By the early twenty-first century, almost 60 percent of university students were women. And women's right to vote was left intact.

While Atatürk's cultural revolution of Westernization and secularism was largely an internal affair that freed Turkey from the wider responsibilities of the caliphate, Khomeini clearly sought to export Iran's Islamic revolution. He openly called for the replacement of insufficiently Islamic regimes in the Middle East and offered training and support for their opponents. In Lebanon, Syria, Bahrain, Saudi Arabia, Iraq, and elsewhere, Khomeini appealed to Shi'ite minorities and other disaffected people, and Iran became a model to which many Islamic radicals looked. An eight-year war with Saddam Hussein's highly secularized Iraq (1980–1988) was one of the outcomes and generated enormous casualties. That conflict reflected the differences between Arabs and Persians, between Sunni and Shia versions of Islam, and between a secular Iraqi regime and Khomeini's revolutionary Islamic government.

After Khomeini's death in 1989, some elements of this revolution eased a bit. For a time enforcement of women's dress code was not so stringent, and a more moderate government came to power in 1997, raising hopes for a loosening of strict Islamic regulations. By 2005, however, more conservative elements were back in control and a new crackdown on women's clothing soon surfaced. A heavily disputed election

Women and the Iranian Revolution
One of the goals of Iran's Islamic Revolution was to enforce a more modest and traditional dress code for the country's women. In this photo from 2004, a woman clad in hijab and talking on her cell phone walks past a poster of the Ayatollah Khomeini, who led that revolution in 1979. (AP Images)

in 2009 revealed substantial opposition to the country's rigid Islamic regime. Iran's ongoing Islamic revolution, however, did not mean the abandonment of economic modernity. The country's oil revenues continued to fund its development, and by the early twenty-first century, Iran was actively pursuing nuclear power and perhaps nuclear weapons, in defiance of Western opposition to these policies.

Reflections: History in the Middle of the Stream

Historians are usually more at ease telling stories that have clear endings, such as those that describe ancient Egyptian civilization, Chinese maritime voyages, the collapse of the Aztec Empire, or the French Revolution. There is a finality to these stories and a distance from them that makes it easier for historians to assume the posture of detached observer, even if their understandings of those events change over time. Finality, distance, and detachment are harder to come by when historians are describing the events of the past century, for many of its processes are clearly not over. The United States' role as a global superpower and its war in Iraq, the fate of democracy in Latin America and Africa, the rise of China and India as economic giants, the position of Islam in Turkey and Iran—all of these are unfinished stories, their outcomes unknown and unknowable. In dealing with such matters, historians write from the middle of the stream, often uncomfortably, rather than from the banks, where they might feel more at ease.

In part, that discomfort arises from questions about the future that such issues inevitably raise. Can the spread of nuclear weapons be halted? Will democracy flourish globally? Are Islamic and Christian civilizations headed for a global clash? Can African countries replicate the economic growth experience of India and China? Historians in particular are uneasy about responding to such questions because they are so aware of the unexpectedness and surprising quality of the historical process. Yet those questions about the future are legitimate and important, for as the nineteenth-century Danish philosopher Søren Kierkegaard remarked: "Life can only be understood backward, but it is lived forward." History, after all, is the only guide we have to the possible shape of that future. So, like everyone before us, we stumble on, both individually and collectively, largely in the dark, using analogies from the past as we make our way ahead.

These vast uncertainties about the future provide a useful reminder that although we know the outcomes of earlier human stories—the Asian and African struggles for independence, for example—those who lived that history did not. Such awareness can perhaps engender in us a measure of humility, a kind of sympathy, and a sense of common humanity with those whose lives we study. However we may differ from our ancestors across time and place, we share with them an immense ignorance about what the future holds.

Second Thoughts

What's the Significance?

decolonization

Indian National Congress

Mahatma Gandhi

satyagraha

Muslim League

Muhammad Ali Jinnah

African National Congress

Nelson Mandela

Black Consciousness

Soweto

democracy in Africa

economic development

Kemal Atatürk

Ayatollah Khomeini

To assess your mastery of the material in this chapter, visit the **Student Center** at bedfordstmartins.com/strayer.

Big Picture Questions

1. In what ways did the colonial experience and the struggle for independence shape the agenda of developing countries in the second half of the twentieth century?
2. To what extent did the experience of the former colonies and developing countries in the twentieth century parallel that of the earlier "new nations" in the Americas in the eighteenth and nineteenth centuries?
3. How would you compare the historical experiences of India and China in the twentieth century?
4. From the viewpoint of the early twenty-first century, to what extent had the goals of nationalist or independence movements been achieved?

Next Steps: For Further Study

Chinua Achebe, *Anthills of the Savannah* (1989). A brilliant fictional account of postindependence Nigeria by that country's foremost novelist.

Fredrick Cooper, *Africa since 1940* (2002). A readable overview of the coming of independence and efforts at development by a leading historian of Africa.

Ramachandra Guha, *India after Gandhi: The History of the World's Largest Democracy* (2007). A thoughtful account of India's first six decades of independence.

John Isbister, *Promises Not Kept* (2006). A well-regarded consideration of the obstacles to and struggles for development in the Global South.

Nelson Mandela, *Long Walk to Freedom: The Autobiography of Nelson Mandela* (1995). Mandela's account of his own amazing life as nationalist leader and South African statesman.

W. David McIntyre, *British Decolonization, 1946–1997* (1998). A global history of the demise of the British Empire.

Complete site on Mahatma Gandhi, http://www.mkgandhi.org. A wealth of resources for exploring the life of Gandhi.

For Web sites and additional documents related to this chapter, see **Make History** at bedfordstmartins.com/strayer.

Documents

Considering the Evidence: Debating Development in Africa

Nowhere were the expectations for national independence greater than in Africa during the 1950s through the 1970s as country after country broke free from colonial rule. "We shall achieve in a decade what it took others a century," declared Kwame Nkrumah, who had led Ghana to freedom in 1957 as black Africa's first independent country. "[W]e shall not rest content until we demolish these miserable colonial structures and erect in their place a veritable paradise."[9] But nowhere have the disappointments of the postindependence era been more acute than in Africa. Despite some scattered successes, Africa after independence experienced the slowest rate of economic growth among the various regions of the developing world. Famine, civil war, genocide, failed states, endemic corruption, the AIDS epidemic, massive poverty, frequent military coups—all of this and more accompanied, and surely contributed to, the economic disappointments of the past half-century.

Such conditions have generated a sharp debate about development among African political and intellectual leaders as well as among disillusioned citizens. Why have African nations performed so poorly in improving the living standards of their impoverished people? What strategies should African states adopt in their continuing search for development? The documents presented here offer a sample of African thinking about development.

Document 23.1

The Colonial Legacy for Modern Development

The starting point for much discussion about African development is the legacy of colonial rule. How well or how poorly had the colonial experience prepared these new countries for modern economic development? To varying degrees, most recent African assessments have been highly critical, even while acknowledging some positive developments. One such account comes from the well-known Ghanaian historian A. Adu Boahen. He recognized some benefits of colonial rule: a measure of "peace and stability" for a time; "an infrastructure of roads, railways, harbors"; the "spread of cash crop agriculture... and western education"; and opportunities for social mobility. But the overall thrust of his judgment was negative.

- What were Boahen's chief criticisms of the colonial economy?

- What problems or challenges did the colonial economic legacy present to newly independent states?

- How might European defenders of colonial rule respond to Boahen's critique?

- How does Boahen's assessment of colonial rule in Africa compare to that of Indian critics of colonial rule as reflected in Documents 20.3, 20.4, and 20.5?

A. ADU BOAHEN
African Perspectives on Colonialism
1987

Had African states been in control of their own destinies—as say, Japan was…—there is no reason why…they could not also have followed the Japanese model, as indeed some of their educated sons…were advocating.… It is in this loss of sovereignty and the consequent isolation from the outside world that one finds one of the most pernicious impacts of colonialism on Africa and one of the fundamental causes of its present underdevelopment and technological backwardness.…

The transportation and communication infrastructure that was provided [by colonial rule] was not only inadequate but was also very unevenly distributed.… The roads and railways were by and large constructed to link areas with the potential for cash crops and mineral deposits with the sea or the world commodity market. [They] were meant to facilitate the exploitation of natural resources, but not to promote…the development of all regions of the colony. The outcome…has been uneven regional economic development.…

[T]he colonial system led to the delay of industrial and technological developments in Africa.… One of the typical features of the colonial political economy was the total neglect of industrialization and of the processing of locally produced raw materials and agricultural products in the colonies.… [P]reexisting industries were almost all eradicated by the importation of cheap and even better substitutes from Europe and India.… This…further explains Africa's present technological backwardness.…

[C]olonialism saddled most colonies with monocrop economies.… Each colony was made to produce a single cash crop or two, and no attempts were made to diversify the agricultural economy.… The other consequence of this concentration on the production of cash crops for export was the neglect of the internal sector of the economy and, in particular, of the production of food for internal consumption. Thus, during the colonial period, Africans were encouraged to produce what they did not consume and to consume what they did not produce, a clear proof of the exploitative nature of the colonial political economy.…

Colonialism also put an end to inter-African trade.… The new artificial boundaries not only divided peoples but also blocked the centuries-old transregional and regional caravan routes.… The flow of trade in each colony was now oriented to the relevant metropolitan country.…

[A]ll the colonial currencies were tied to those of the metropolitan countries, and all their foreign exchange earnings were kept in the metropolitan countries and not used for internal development.

Source: A. Adu Boahen, *African Perspectives on Colonialism* (Baltimore: The Johns Hopkins University Press, 1987), pp. 99–108.

The expatriate commercial banks and companies were also allowed to repatriate their deposits, savings, and profits instead of reinvesting them in the colonies for further development. The consequence of all this was that at the time of independence, no African state apart from the Union of South Africa had the strong economic or industrial base needed for a real economic takeoff....

[I]t was the colonial system that initiated the gap that still exists between the urban and rural areas. All of the modern facilities—schools, hospitals, street lights, radio, postal services—and above all most of the employment opportunities were concentrated in the urban centers. The combination of modern life and employment pulled rural dwellers, especially the young one and those with schooling, in the direction of the cities.

[T]he social services provided by colonialism were grossly inadequate and unevenly distributed.... University education was totally ignored in all the colonies until the 1940s, and only one university was subsequently established for each colony.... In practically every colony only a very small percentage of school-age children could gain admission into schools....

The effects of colonial education were really unfortunate.... Because of its inadequacy, large numbers of Africans remained illiterate.... The elite produced by these colonial educational institutions were with few exceptions people who were alienated from their own society in terms of their dress, outlook, and tastes in food, music, and even dance. They were people who worshiped European culture and looked down on their own culture....

Another negative social impact of colonialism was the downgrading of the status of women in Africa.... [T]here were far fewer facilities for girls than for boys. Women could not therefore gain access into the professions.... The colonial world was definitely a man's world, and women were not allowed to play any meaningful role in it except as petty traders and farmers.

The colonial administrators and their allies, the European missionaries, condemned everything African in culture—African names, music, dance, art, religion, marriage, the system of inheritance—and completely discouraged the teaching of these things in their schools and colleges....

[This has resulted in] the creation of a colonial mentality among educated Africans in particular and also among the populace in general. This mentality manifests itself in the condemnation of anything traditional, in the preference for imported goods to locally manufactured goods (since independence), and in the style of dress—such as the wearing of three piece suits in a climate where temperatures routinely exceed eighty degrees Farenheit. Above all, it manifests itself in the belief...that government and all public property and finance belong, not to the people, but to the colonial government, and could and should therefore be taken advantage of at the least opportunity, a belief which leads to the often reckless dissipation and misuse of public funds and property.

Document 23.2

Development and African Unity

One of the most important legacies of the colonial era was the African continent's division into more than fifty separate countries, many of them quite small. And yet the common experience of colonial rule and the sharp racial divisions of the colonial era had also given rise to the notion of an overall African identity, especially among educated people. As independence dawned across the continent, some leaders sought to translate that pan-African ideal into a concrete political and economic union. The chief spokesman for that idea in the early years of independence was Ghana's nationalist leader and its first president, Kwame Nkrumah. He was convinced that only in union could the African continent achieve genuine and substantial economic development. Nkrumah's pan-African ideal has achieved some very modest successes in the form of several regional groupings of African states trying to coordinate their economic policies and in an African Union in which all African states seek to address common problems. But nothing approaching the kind of larger economic and political union that Nkrumah envisaged has emerged.

- Why did Nkrumah think that union was so essential? What benefits would it bring to Africa in its efforts at development?

- What kind of union did Nkrumah seek?

- What challenges does Nkrumah identify to his soaring vision of a United States of Africa? Which of these do you think was most daunting?

- Why do you think the thirteen separate colonies of British North America were able to form a United States of America in the late eighteenth century while their twentieth-century counterparts in Africa have not created a more substantial union?

KWAME NKRUMAH
Africa Must Unite
1963

There are those who maintain that Africa cannot unite because we lack the three necessary ingredients for unity, a common race, culture, and language. It is true that we have for centuries been divided. The territorial boundaries dividing us were fixed long ago, often quite arbitrarily, by the colonial powers. Some of us are Moslems, some Christians; many believe in traditional, tribal gods. Some of us speak French, some English, some Portuguese, not to mention the millions who speak only one of the hundreds of different African languages. We have acquired cultural differences which affect our outlook and condition our political development....

In the early flush of independence, some of the new African states are jealous of their sovereignty and tend to exaggerate their separatism in a historical period that demands Africa's unity in order that their independence may be safeguarded....

[A] united Africa—that is, the political and economic unification of the African Continent—should seek three objectives:

Firstly, we should have an overall economic planning on a continental basis. This would increase the industrial and economic power of Africa. So long as we remain balkanized, regionally or territorially, we shall be at the mercy of colonialism and imperialism. The lesson of the South American Republics vis-à-vis the strength and solidarity of the United States of America is there for all to see.

The resources of Africa can be used to the best advantage and the maximum benefit to all only if they are set within an overall framework of a continentally planned development. An overall economic plan, covering an Africa united on a continental basis, would increase our total industrial and economic

Source: Kwame Nkrumah, *Africa Must Unite* (London: Heinemann, 1963), 132, 148, 218–21.

power. We should therefore be thinking seriously now of ways and means of building up a Common Market of a United Africa and not allow ourselves to be lured by the dubious advantages of association with the so-called European Common market....

Secondly, we should aim at the establishment of a unified military and defense strategy....

For young African States, who are in great need of capital for internal development, it is ridiculous—indeed suicidal—for each State separately and individually to assume such a heavy burden of self-defense, when the weight of this burden could be easily lightened by sharing it among themselves....

The third objective: [I]t will be necessary for us to adopt a unified foreign policy and diplomacy to give political direction to our joint efforts for the protection and economic development of our continent.... The burden of separate diplomatic

representation by each State on the Continent of Africa alone would be crushing, not to mention representation outside Africa. The desirability of a common foreign policy which will enable us to speak with one voice in the councils of the world, is so obvious, vital and imperative that comment is hardly necessary....

Under a major political union of Africa there could emerge a United Africa, great and powerful, in which the territorial boundaries which are the relics of colonialism will become obsolete and superfluous, working for the complete and total mobilization of the economic planning organization under a unified political direction. The forces that unite us are far greater than the difficulties that divide us at present, and our goal must be the establishment of Africa's dignity, progress, and prosperity.

Document 23.3

Development, Socialism, and Self-Reliance

In the early postindependence decades, a number of African states expressed their plans for development in terms of socialism. After all, capitalism was associated with a despised colonial rule, and the communist countries of the Soviet Union and China had made significant economic progress within a socialist framework. One of the most prominent expressions of this socialist approach to development came from Tanzania, in East Africa. There Julius Nyerere, the country's nationalist leader and its first president, articulated a distinctly African and non-Marxist version of socialism, known as *ujamaa* ("familyhood" in the Swahili language). Ujamaa found expression in the nationalization of businesses and rental housing in the cities, while in the countryside socialist villages were supposed to encourage the cooperative working of the land and the creation of small local manufacturing industries. Document 23.3 presents excerpts from the Arusha Declaration of 1967, which spelled out the basic principles of ujamaa socialism.

■ What kind of development does the declaration foresee for Tanzania?

■ What criticisms does it make about other formulas for development?

■ What is socialist about the Arusha Declaration? How does it differ from Marxist socialism (see Documents, Chapter 18, pp. 855–66)?

In an economic sense, ujamaa socialism in Tanzania was largely a failure and was later abandoned. Farmers herded into communal villages did not have much personal incentive to produce, and state-run businesses were inefficient and badly managed.

■ What features of the Arusha Declaration might have contributed to this failure?

JULIUS NYERERE

The Arusha Declaration
1967

We are trying to overcome our economic weakness by using the weapons of the economically strong—weapons which in fact we do not possess.... It is stupid to rely on money as the major instrument of development when we know only too well that our country is poor. It is... even more stupid, for us to imagine that we shall rid ourselves of our poverty through foreign financial assistance rather than our own financial resources....

We are mistaken when we imagine that we shall get money from foreign countries, firstly because, to say the truth, we cannot get enough money for our development and, secondly, because even if we could get it, such complete dependence on outside help would have endangered our independence and the other policies of our country.

We have put too much emphasis on industries.... The mistake we are making is to think that development *begins* with industries. It is a mistake because we do not have the means to establish many modern industries in our country. We do not have either the necessary finances or the technical know-how.... And even if we could get the necessary assistance [from foreigners], dependence on it could interfere with our policy of socialism. The policy of inviting a chain of capitalists to come and establish industries in our country might succeed in giving us all the industries we need, but it would also succeed in preventing the establishment of socialism unless we believe that without first building capitalism, we cannot build socialism.

Our emphasis on money and industries has made us concentrate on urban development.... The largest proportion of the [foreign] loans will be spent in, or for, the urban areas, but the largest proportion of the repayment will be made through the efforts of the farmers [through the sale of their agricultural products].... We must not forget that people who live in towns can possibly become the exploiters of those who live in the rural areas....

A great part of Tanzania's land is fertile and gets sufficient rains. Our country can produce various crops for home consumption and for export. We can produce food crops such as maize, rice, wheat, beans, and groundnuts. And we can produce such cash crops as sisal, cotton, coffee, tobacco, pyrethrum, and tea. Our land is also good for grazing cattle, goats, sheep, and for raising chickens; we can get plenty of fish from our rivers, lakes, and from the sea.... [O]ur purpose must be to increase production of these agricultural crops. This is in fact the only road through which we can develop our country....

Everybody wants development, but not everybody understands and accepts the basic requirements for development. The biggest requirement is hard work.... In towns, for example, the average paid worker works... for 45 hours a week in 48 to 50 weeks a year.

For a country like ours, these are really quite short working hours.... By starting with such short

Source: From "The Policy of Self-Reliance: Excerpts from the Arusha Declaration of February 5, 1967," *Africa Report* (March 1967): 11–13.

working hours and asking for even shorter hours, we are in fact imitating the more developed countries....

It would be appropriate to ask our farmers, especially the men, how many hours a week and how many weeks a year they work. Many do not even work for half as many hours as the wage-earner does. The truth is that in the villages the women work very hard. At times they work for 12 or 14 hours a day. They even work on Sundays and public holidays. Women who live in the villages work harder than anybody else in Tanzania. But the men who live in villages (and some of the women in towns) are on leave for half of their life. The energies of the millions of men in the villages and thousands of women in the towns which are at present wasted in gossip, dancing, and drinking, are a great treasure which could contribute more toward the development of our country than anything we could get from rich nations....

The second condition of development is the use of intelligence. Unintelligent hard work would not bring the same good results as the two combined. Using a big hoe instead of a small one; using a plough pulled by oxen instead of an ordinary hoe; the use of fertilizers; the use of insecticides; knowing the right crop for a particular season or soil; choosing good seeds for planting; knowing the right time for planting, weeding, etc.; all these things show the use of knowledge and intelligence. And all of them combine with hard work to produce more and better results.

The money and time we spend on passing on this knowledge to the peasants are better spent and bring more benefits to our country than the money and the great amount of time we spend on other things which we call development....

None of this means that from now on we will not need money or that we will not start industries or embark upon development projects which require money.... What we are saying, however, is that from now on we shall know what is the foundation and what is the fruit of development. Between *money* and *people* it is obvious that the people and their *hard work* are the foundation of development, and money is one of the fruits of that hard work.... This is the meaning of self-reliance.

Document 23.4

Development and Women

When deliberate planning for African economic development began in earnest following independence, it was focused almost wholly on men, for women had little presence in the modern sector of the economy toward which development was aimed. By the 1980s and 1990s, however, that was changing as scholars and policymakers alike focused more attention on the role of women in the modern development of African countries. In part, this was a consequence of international feminism, which turned the spotlight on issues of gender in all fields of study and practice. Furthermore, the importance of agriculture, in which African women were centrally involved, became increasingly apparent. This new perspective on development is reflected in a 1981 essay written by Mildred Malineo Tau from Lesotho in southern Africa, who was then her country's ambassador to the United States, Mexico, and Brazil.

■ What obstacles to women's active participation in economic development does this document emphasize? How does Ambassador Tau understand the sources of sexual inequality?

- Why does Ambassador Tau believe that development planning should focus explicitly on the needs of women? How would attention to women alter the priorities of development planning?

- What features of Ambassador Tau's development plan might coincide with the priorities of the Arusha Declaration? In what respects might they differ?

- What do the visions of development laid out by Ambassador Tau and the Arusha Declaration tell us about the lives of women in modern Africa? Are these issues unique to Africa or are they common to women everywhere?

MILDRED MALINEO TAU
Women: Critical to African Development
1981

Women, especially rural women, are the core of development in most African countries. Most of them are faced with a disproportionate level of responsibility for which they are ill prepared. Development efforts have had the tendency to "plan *for* instead of *with* women."

Recognition of the role of women in development is critical. There are many efforts to introduce women into the process of development, but these efforts must not be mere gestures to make them appear useful....

One striking characteristic of African women is their multiplicity of roles. African women's contribution to an active involvement in subsistence farming and wage activities, their critical presence in marketing, food distribution networks, and their continued responsibilities as wives and mothers combine to make their role in the survival of the family and the community most important....The majority of African women are engaged in agriculture.

Several factors have mitigated against developmental programs having a positive impact on these women. First, development planning has been based largely on male conceptualizations of life, which most often fail to take into account the activities of, and socioeconomic pressures impinging upon, women.

Second, they are often designed from an urban viewpoint rather than from an understanding of the dynamics of rural life.

The heavy dependence in Africa on subsistence agriculture, which is largely the province of women, makes policies affecting land, its distribution, and ownership critical to development....Assuming that men were the primary factors in agricultural production, improved technology and training were offered to men, but not to women....

[T]he increasing monetization of economies in developing countries puts an extra demand on women to raise cash for food, transportation, shelter, school fees, and household supplies. The opportunities for women's entry into the cash economy are severely limited, but it is they who need the cash since incidental cash earned by men is less likely to go into the basic needs of the family than that earned by women.... Improving their productive capacity even within these spheres of activity has been limited by their lack of access to training, intermediate and advanced technology, and capital resources.

...The long hours African women labor and the near impossibility of cutting out any of this work

Source: Mildred Malineo Tau, "Women: Critical to African Development," *Africa Report* (March/April, 1981): 4–6.

which is so necessary for daily survival, hinder their ability to participate in development activities, take advantage of training, health services, political forums, etc.

Environmental conditions present in many African countries have imposed heavy burdens on women. Fetching water and collecting fuel can consume a large portion of a woman's time each day. Improving the productive capacity of women as a means of enhancing general development gains will need to include attention to access to water and fuel. . . .

Among the potential resources for development in Africa are a strong tradition of cooperative work and diverse and often strong women's organizations, both formal and informal. . . .

[W]omen may be denied credit as a policy of the bank although by law discrimination is prohibited.

We need support for projects which analyze existing legislation, monitor implementation, or disseminate information and education to grass-roots women on their legal rights and responsibilities.

The issue of women's access to wage work and other sources of cash income in the African continent is more than one of equity. It goes beyond the question of equal rights for women to become one of economic survival for them and their children. Because women in Africa are not secondary earners, neither ideologically nor in reality as are many women in Latin America, for example, but are providers of food, clothing, and shelter, their increased dependence on the monetary economy may have a more immediate negative impact on African women. If their role as main provider continues to go unacknowledged in development planning, the consequences could be serious.

Document 23.5

Development, Elites, and the State

In the aftermath of independence, many African explanations for the continent's mounting economic problems focused on external factors such as the colonial legacy and an unjust world economy dominated by the rich countries. Many argued that the solution to these problems lay in state control or direction of the economy. By the 1980s and 1990s, however, many African economies had deteriorated badly in sharp contrast to the growth patterns of Asian countries, such as South Korea, China, India, and Indonesia. In this context, a number of African intellectuals and some political leaders began to rethink the task of development with a more self-critical focus on the continent's internal problems and with a greater appreciation for the possibilities of private enterprise. Document 23.5, drawn from two of the writings by prominent Ghanaian economist George Ayittey in the 1990s, represents this line of thinking.

■ How does Ayittey understand the major obstacles to development in Africa?

■ How does he view the role of post-independence African elites and the states they govern?

■ What prescriptions for African development are stated or implied in this document?

■ In what ways might Ayittey's prescriptions for development be seen as a rejection of the ideas contained in the first three selections in this feature? To what extent does his thinking build upon, or evolve from, those earlier ideas?

GEORGE B. N. AYITTEY
Africa Betrayed
1992

Africa in Chaos
1998

By the beginning of the 1990s economic and political conditions in Africa had become intolerable....

It is easy for African leaders to put the blame somewhere else; for example, on Western aid donors or on an allegedly hostile international economic environment,... but in my view the internal factors have played far greater roles than the external ones.

True freedom never came to much of Africa after independence. Despite the rhetoric and vituperations against colonialism, very little changed in the years immediately following independence. For many countries independence meant only a change in the color of the administrators from white to black. The new leaders began to act in the same manner as the colonialists. In fact in many places they were worse than the colonialists.

Inchoate democratic structures, hastily erected by the departing colonialists, were perceived by the new leaders as "Western." They were quickly uprooted and replaced with systems that were, in many cases, far more repressive than the hated colonial system....

In most African countries, the elites as a group make up less than 10 percent of the population. Yet they regard political power as their prerogative and government as their property. Political power is not to be shared with the "backward masses," who are too uneducated to understand such esoterica as "constitutional rights." The elites deem it the responsibility of the government to provide and care for themselves. The government must provide them not only jobs but also everything from houses, cars, refrigerators, television sets, to even their own funerals at subsidized rates. Naturally, to win their political support, African governments have been obliged to grant many of these demands. Moreover, governments themselves are run by the elites. Therefore, providing perks and subsidies to one section of the elite class enables the super elites to grab an even larger piece of the pie for themselves....

Dishonesty, thievery, and speculation pervade the public sector. Public servants embezzle state funds; high-ranking ministers are on the take. The chief bandit is the head of state himself. President Mobutu Sese Seko of Zaire was not satisfied with his personal fortune of $10 billion; he stole an entire gold-mining region, Kilo-motor, which covers 32,000 square miles and reportedly has reserves of 100 tons of gold....

[I]n Africa, government officials do not serve the people. The African state has been reduced to a mafia-like bazaar, where anyone with an official designation can pillage at will. In effect, it is a "state" that has been hijacked by gangsters, crooks, and scoundrels. They have seized and monopolized both political and economic power to advance their own selfish and criminal interests, not to develop their economies. Their overarching obsession is to amass

---

Source: George B. N. Ayittey, *Africa Betrayed* (New York: St. Martin's Press, 1992), 100, 335–36; George B. N. Ayittey, *Africa in Chaos* (New York: St. Martin's Press, 1998), 120–21, 150–52, 248, 343–44.

personal wealth, gaudily displayed in flashy automobiles, fabulous mansions, and a bevy of fawning women. Helping the poor, promoting economic growth, or improving the standard of living of their people is anathema to the ruling elites. "Food for the people!" "People's power!" "Houses for the masses!" are simply empty slogans that are designed to fool the people and the international community....

... [V]irtually all the internal problems emanate from two deadly diseases: sultanism° and statism.° While acknowledging that the state or government has a role to play in the development process, the state, as it is conventionally understood, does not exist in Africa. Rather what exists in many African countries is a vampire state—a government hijacked by gangsters, con artists, and scrofulous bandits.... Its driving motivation is self-perpetuation in power and self-aggrandizement. Poverty reduction and promotion of economic growth are the least among its priorities. It operates by extracting resources from the productive sections of the population (the peasant majority) and spends it in the urban areas and on the elites—a non-productive, parasitic class.

In country after country, the state has been captured or monopolized by one tiny group—an ethnic group, professional (soldiers), or a religious group—and the instruments of state power and government machinery have been used to advance the economic interests of the ruling group....

In other words, the state vehicle that currently exists in many African countries cannot take Africans on the "development journey" into the twenty-first century....

In the postcolonial period, African governments... arrogated onto themselves the power to intervene in almost every conceivable aspect of their economies, ostensibly for "national development" and [to] protect the New African nations against "foreign exploitation." Subsequently, state controls were used for the benefit of a tiny ruling elite. State hegemony in the economy became pervasive. The bureaucracy swelled with payrolls padded with government/party supporters. State controls created shortages and opportunities for illicit enrichment by the elites and bred a culture of bribery and corruption. In addition, they killed off the incentive to produce. The state sector became grotesquely inefficient and wasteful. The rot at the government house propelled the military to intervene in politics....

The pervasive control African governments wield over their economies needs to be rolled back. Peasants who produce foodstuffs and cash crops should be allowed to keep a larger portion of their proceeds. Countries that move away from a state-controlled economy toward greater reliance on the private sector generally do better economically....

Privatization (economic reform) seeks to place the vehicle in the hands of the people or the private sector for the simple reason that it would be better taken care of. Evidence for this fact abounds in Africa. In West Africa some of the privately owned "mammy lories,"° called *trotros* in Ghana and *mutates* in East Africa, that regularly ply the roads, have been in operation for the past 40 years. By contrast, brand-new buses ordered by African governments barely last six months....

[T]here are a number of ways that aid resources Africa desperately needs can be found in Africa itself....

First, in 1989 Africa was spending $12 billion annually to import arms and to maintain the military. Second, the elites illegally transferred from Africa at least $15 billion annually during the latter part of the 1980s. Third, at least $5 billion annually could be saved if Africa could feed itself. Foreign exchange saved is foreign exchange earned. Fourth, another $5 billion could be saved from waste and inefficiencies in Africa's 3,200-odd state enterprises. This might entail selling off some of them or placing them under new management. Fifth, the civil wars raging in Africa exact a heavy toll in lost output, economic development, and destroyed property.

°**sultanism:** one-man rule.

°**statism:** government control of the economy.

°**mammy lories:** mini-buses.

Using the Evidence:
Debating Development in Africa

1. **Defining a controversy:** Based on these documents, identify the major issues that constitute the development debate in post–independence Africa. How do these documents define "development"?

2. **Explaining African economic performance:** What alternative explanations for Africa's poor economic performance over the past half-century are apparent in these documents? To what extent are those explanations at odds with one another? How might you combine them into a single comprehensive understanding of Africa's post–independence economic difficulties? What other factors, not mentioned in these documents, might have contributed to those difficulties?

3. **Comparing prescriptions:** What different policy suggestions or overall approaches to African development are suggested or implied by these documents? How might critics challenge the effectiveness or feasibility of these proposals?

4. **Noticing change:** What differences do you see between Documents 23.2 and 23.3, written during the 1960s and 1970s, and the last two documents, composed in the 1980s and 1990s? How would you explain the changes in tone and emphasis?

Visual Sources

Considering the Evidence: Representing Independence

For millions of people in Africa and Asia, the achievement of political independence from European or American domination marked a singular moment in their personal and collective histories. That moment represented a triumph against great odds and an awakening to the possibility of building new lives and new societies. In the words of India's nationalist leader and first prime minister, Jawaharlal Nehru, it was a "tryst with destiny." Both during the struggle and after, the various meanings attributed to independence found visual expression in a proliferation of poster art. Such images served to inspire and mobilize large numbers of people for the tasks ahead, to articulate a vision of the future, and sometimes to celebrate success. Those grand hopes became a baseline from which future generations measured the realities of the post-independence period.

India's independence movement, embodied in the Congress Party and led by the iconic figure of Mahatma Gandhi, was among the first to achieve success as it broke the hold of British colonialism in 1947. It subsequently became an inspiration and a model for many others all across the colonial world and beyond. That success, however, was the product of long decades of hard struggle against British repression, for the colonial power was reluctant to fully accommodate the increasingly forceful demands of the movement. The Indian nationalist struggle was likewise accompanied by serious internal divisions and controversies, and the moment of its greatest victory also witnessed its greatest tragedy—the bloody partition of the country into two states: a Muslim Pakistan and a largely Hindu India (see pp. 1089–90).

Visual Source 23.1 shows a Congress Party poster from the early 1930s in support of Gandhi's policy of nonviolence and noncooperation with British authorities. In "reading" this richly detailed image, it will be useful to notice a number of its major features. In the center is the Tree of Noncooperation; slightly to the right, a British soldier is trying to shake Gandhi's followers out of the tree using a rope labeled "Policy of Repression" with a British colonial jail prominent in the upper right. In the tree are two rival groups of Gandhi's followers, one labeled the "Swarajya (Independence) Party" and the other called the "No-Change Party," a critical reference to those who thought Gandhi was moving too rapidly and aggressively. Two bridges cross the "Gulf of Differences" at left. One leads to the Council Chamber, representing cooperation with British-created political institutions, while the other leads to the Swarajya Ashram, a center for training young freedom fighters in Gandhi's philosophy of noncooperation. At the bottom left are several blood-stained and quarreling figures labeled "Hindu-Mohammedan friction," while at the upper left three earlier figures in India's nationalist movement overlook the scene below from the clouds.

In the lower right, the female figure labeled Bharat Mata (Mother India) is a Hindu goddess image widely used in Congress Party circles to represent the Indian nation. Her male companion is Krishna, a major Hindu deity, shown pointing toward Gandhi. The quotation above Krishna's head comes from a famous speech that the god made, as recorded in the sacred Hindu text known as the Bhagavad Gita:

> The virtuous people to protect, and to destroy the sinful ones,
> To set up firmly righteousness, from age to age, I enter birth.

Finally, the red-clad Goddess of Unity in the Tree of Noncooperation seeks to hold together the several factions of Gandhi's movement.

- How does the poster portray British colonial authorities in relationship to Gandhi's movement?

- What kinds of divisions within India's nationalist movement does the poster suggest?

- What does the poster disclose about the role of religion, and particularly Hinduism, in the Indian nationalist movement? How might Muslims have responded to the Hindu religious imagery of the poster?

- How does the poster portray Gandhi and his wife, Kasturbai, the woman in white sitting in front of the small red house? According to the poster, what kind of India was Gandhi seeking after independence?

The freedom struggle in South Africa was led by the African National Congress (ANC), a political organization that was founded in 1912 and finally came to power in 1994. Over those decades, its strategy evolved from polite elite protest to confrontational mass campaigns and from a commitment to open and peaceful means to a selective embrace of underground organization and armed struggle. Throughout its history, the ANC held generally to the goal of a democratic and multiracial society. Visual Source 23.2, an undated ANC poster, shows the organization's flag and various symbols of its long struggle. The colors of the flag depict South Africa's resources: black for the vast majority of its population, green for its rich land, and yellow for the gold that had long provided a basis for the country's wealth.

- Does the poster reflect the ANC's earlier, more peaceful and elite-based politics or its later, more aggressive posture? On what do you base your conclusion?

Visual Source 23.1 *Non-Co-operation Tree and Mahatma Gandhi* (© British Library Board, PIB 170/2)

■ How might you understand the wheel, the fist, the spear, and the shield shown on the poster? Why do you think the poster used these traditional weapons rather than modern rifles?

■ Notice the mass march that provides the background to the poster's primary images. What message does this convey?

■ Pay attention to the several red flags, representing the South African Communist Party, among the crowd. What posture toward communism is suggested by these flags? Keep in mind that the Communist Party was a longtime ally of the ANC.

■ How might white, Indian, and mixed-race ("colored") supporters of the ANC react to this poster? How might white advocates of apartheid respond to it?

Visual Source 23.2 African National Congress (Special Collections, Senate House Library, University of London)

In Vietnam, the struggle for independence was a prolonged process and took place against a variety of enemies. French colonial rule had prompted various kinds of resistance since the late nineteenth century. Then Japanese occupation of the country during World War II stimulated the formation of a nationalist party known as the Viet Minh, dominated by a communist party and led by Ho Chi Minh. After Japan's defeat in World War II, that movement continued as an effort to oust the French, which succeeded by 1954. At that point, Vietnam was divided between the communist-dominated North Vietnam and the U.S.-backed South Vietnam. What followed was a twenty-year effort by North Vietnam and communist supporters in the south to reunify their country and to drive out the American military forces, which numbered over a half million by the mid-1960s.

By 1975, the North Vietnamese had succeeded (see Map 23.1, p. 1084). It was a stunning reversal for the American superpower and an equally stunning triumph for the small Southeast Asian country. While the reasons for this

Visual Source 23.3 Vietnamese Independence and Victory over the United States (Laurie Steelink/Track16/ SmartArt, Inc.)

surprising turn of events have been debated ever since, it was clearly of enormous significance for Vietnamese understandings of their national independence. Visual Source 23.3 presents a Vietnamese poster, dating from somewhere between 1965 and 1975, that celebrates one aspect of that unlikely achievement. The caption reads: "Bravo for Hanoi's Tremendous Victory When 23 B–52s Were Shot Down!"

- How does this poster present the struggle against the United States?

- In what way does it anticipate or celebrate the victory over the United States? What meaning does it attach to that victory? How might you understand the flowers that the soldier is holding and the small pagoda in the upper left?

- What other perspectives on this victory for national independence can you imagine? Consider various viewpoints within the United States as well as those of the anticommunist elements in Vietnamese society.

The establishment of the independent state of Israel in 1948 marked an enormous victory for Jewish people that took on rich meaning for them in many contexts. The most historically significant context no doubt lay in the return of widely scattered Jewish people to the ancient biblical homeland from which so many Jews had fled or been expelled by various foreign rulers — Babylonian, Assyrian, Roman, Byzantine, and Crusader European. Since the first century C.E., the majority of the world's Jews had lived in diaspora in the Middle East, North Africa, or Europe, with smaller numbers retaining a Jewish presence in what was then called Palestine. For those whose families had long lived in exile, the opportunity to return to an authentically Jewish state in the area comprising the ancient Land of Israel must have seemed miraculous.

A more immediate context for the establishment of Israel was that of the Zionist movement, formally initiated in Europe in 1897 with the goal of creating a "home for the Jewish people in Palestine." It was a response to the racism and anti-Semitism of European culture, and it drew upon currents of nationalist thinking then surging across Europe. A major expression of Zionism lay in growing Jewish emigration to their ancient homeland, especially during the 1920s and 1930s and even more so in the several years following World War II. During that war some 6 million Jews perished in Nazi death camps as Hitler sought to rid Europe of a Jewish presence. Many among those who survived the Holocaust sought refuge and security in a land of their own.

Two major obstacles confronted these Jewish emigrants. One was British control of Palestine, granted to Great Britain as a mandate of the League of Nations following World War I. While the British favored the eventual creation of a Jewish state, they also feared antagonizing their Arab allies by allowing unfettered Jewish immigration. The second obstacle was opposition from the Arab majority of Palestine, who feared not only the loss of their land as Jewish settlers bought up growing amounts of it but also the loss of their cultural identity as Muslims in what they feared would become a Jewish land. The creation of Israel in 1948, with support from the United Nations, marked the triumph of Zionism and a victory over both British imperialism and Arab resistance.

Visual Source 23.4 shows a Zionist poster created around 1940 and intended to encourage emigration to the Land of Israel and to persuade donors to contribute money for the purchase of land in Palestine. It was titled "Redeem the Land," a reference to the Zionist goal of using up-to-date farming techniques to provide the agricultural basis for a modern society.[10]

- What features of the poster contributed to the Zionists' message?

- Why do you think the land is shown without any people?

- How do you understand the contrast between the richly plowed land and the adjacent barren areas? What image of the new Israel does this poster project?

Visual Source 23.4 Winning a Jewish National State (The Central Zionist Archives, Jerusalem)

- The fruits on the left side of the poster reflect the biblical description of "promised land" as recorded in Deuteronomy 8:7–10. What is their function in the poster?

If the establishment of Israel as an independent state was a great triumph for Jewish nationalism, it was a disaster for Arabs in general and Palestinian Arabs in particular. In the decades that followed, Israel and various Arab states (Egypt, Jordan, and Syria, for example) went to war repeatedly. The so-called Six Day War of 1967 brought under Israeli control additional Palestinian land, including the West Bank, the Gaza Strip, and East Jerusalem, areas now known as the Palestinian Territories.

At the same time, the Arabs of Palestine, both within Israel and in the adjacent territories, were developing a distinct national identity of their own. Many of them had lost their land and had lived for several generations as refugees in overcrowded camps in neighboring countries or territories where they were dependent on services provided by the United Nations. Almost all Palestinians felt oppressed, constrained, or discriminated against by Israeli authorities. Their emerging national identity found expression in the Palestinian Liberation Organization (PLO), founded in 1964. Initially the PLO called for the complete liberation of Palestine from Zionist colonialism, but by the late 1980s the organization had implicitly recognized the right of Israel to exist and sought a "two-state solution" with an independent Palestine and Israel living side by side.

Achieving even a limited Palestinian state, however, has proved extraordinarily difficult. In pursuit of their national goals, Palestinians have conducted raids, suicide bombing missions, and rocket attacks on Israel from camps in neighboring territories and on several occasions have organized large-scale violent resistance movements known as *intifada*. For its part, Israel has launched highly destructive large-scale military actions in the Palestinian territories, imposed economic blockades that have brought immense suffering to Palestinians, built walls and fences that have disrupted the normal movement of Palestinians, and continued to enlarge the Jewish settlements, especially in the West Bank. Both sides have presented their actions as largely defensive and reactive to the provocations of the other. They have also engaged in periodic negotiations with each other, but those efforts have thus far foundered on unbridgeable differences as to the size and nature of a future Palestinian state, the status of Jerusalem, and the right of Palestinian refugees to return to their lands in Israel. Divisions among Palestinians have also hampered their movement, particularly the recent rivalry between the PLO and Hamas, an Islamic organization with both welfare and political/military functions.

Like other peoples seeking an independent state, Palestinians have represented their struggles in posters such as Visual Source 23.5, created by the Palestinian artist Abdel Rahman Al Muzain in 1984. Featuring a Palestinian

Visual Source 23.5 A Palestinian Nation in the Making (Palestine Poster Project Archives/ Visual Connection Archive)

farmer, it was undertaken to commemorate Land Day, an annual observance of the occasion in 1976 when six Palestinians were killed in demonstrations against Israeli confiscation of their land.[11]

■ How might you read this poster as a response to the Israeli poster in Visual Source 23.4?

■ What significance would you attach to the posture and the traditional clothing of the farmer? Why do you think the artist depicted him with a pickax rather than a rifle?

■ What message is conveyed by the rows of traditional houses on the hillside behind the farmer?

■ What expectations for the future does the poster imply? Consider the meaning of the doves between the feet and on the shoulder of the farmer as well as the sun's swirling rays that seem to link the earth and sky.

Using the Evidence:
Representing Independence

1. **Making comparisons:** Movements of national independence can be defined by the conditions they were opposing as well as the kind of future they were seeking. With these two criteria in mind, what similarities and what differences can you identify among these visual sources and the movements they represented?

2. **Defining points of view:** How would you identify the point of view that each of these visual sources conveys? Can you imagine a visual source with an alternative point of view for each of them?

3. **Seeking meaning in visual sources:** How do visual sources such as these help to illuminate the meaning of national independence? In what ways are they limited as sources of evidence for historians?

CHAPTER TWENTY-FOUR

Accelerating Global Interaction

SINCE 1945

The Transformation of the
  World Economy
    Reglobalization
    Growth, Instability, and Inequality
    Globalization and an
      American Empire
The Globalization of Liberation:
  Comparing Feminist Movements
    Feminism in the West
    Feminism in the Global South
    International Feminism
Religion and Global Modernity
  Fundamentalism on a Global Scale
  Creating Islamic Societies:
    Resistance and Renewal in the
    World of Islam
  Religious Alternatives to
    Fundamentalism
The World's Environment and the
  Globalization of Environmentalism
    The Global Environment
    Transformed
    Green and Global
Final Reflections: Pondering the
  Uses of History
Considering the Evidence
  Documents: Contending for Islam
  Visual Sources: Experiencing
    Globalization

"I think every Barbie doll is more harmful than an American missile," declared Iranian toy seller Masoumeh Rahimi in early 2002. To Rahimi, Barbie's revealing clothing, her shapely appearance, and her close association with Ken, her longtime unmarried companion, were "foreign to Iran's culture." Thus Rahimi warmly welcomed the arrival of Sara and Dara, two Iranian Muslim dolls meant to counteract the negative influence of Barbie and Ken, who had long dominated Iran's toy market. Sara and her brother, Dara, depicted eight-year-old twins. Sara came complete with a headscarf to cover her hair in modest Muslim fashion and a full-length white chador enveloping her from head to toe. They were described as helping each other solve problems, while looking to their loving parents for guidance, hardly the message that Barbie and Ken conveyed.[1]

The widespread availability of Barbie in Muslim Iran provides one small example of the power of global commerce in the world of the early twenty-first century. The creation of Sara and Dara illustrates resistance to the cultural values associated with this American product. Still, Sara and Barbie had something in common: both were manufactured in China. This triangular relationship of the United States, Iran, and China neatly symbolized the growing integration of world economies and cultures as well as the divergences and conflicts that this process generated. Those linked but contrasting patterns are the twin themes of this final chapter.

DURING THE TWENTIETH CENTURY, AN INCREASINGLY DENSE WEB OF POLITICAL RELATIONSHIPS, economic transactions, and

One World: This NASA photograph, showing both the earth and the moon, reveals none of the national, ethnic, religious, or linguistic boundaries that have long divided humankind. Such pictures have both reflected and helped create a new planetary consciousness among growing numbers of people. (Image created by Reto Stockli, Nazmi El Saleous, and Marit Jentoft-Nilsen, NASA GSFC)

cultural influences cut across the world's many peoples, countries, and regions, binding them together more tightly, but also more contentiously. By the 1990s, this process of accelerating engagement among distant peoples was widely known as globalization.

Although the term was relatively new, the process was not. From the viewpoint of world history, the genealogy of globalization reaches far into the past. The Arab, Mongol, Russian, Chinese, and Ottoman empires; the Silk Road, Indian Ocean, and trans-Saharan trade routes; the spread of Buddhism, Christianity, and especially Islam—all of these connections had long linked the societies of the Eastern Hemisphere, bringing new rulers, religions, products, diseases, and technologies to many of its peoples. Later, in the centuries after 1500, European maritime voyages and colonizing efforts launched the Columbian exchange, incorporating the Western Hemisphere and inner Africa firmly and permanently into a genuinely global network of communication, exchange, and often exploitation. During the nineteenth century, as the Industrial Revolution took hold and Western nations began a new round of empire building in Asia and Africa, that global network tightened further, and its role as generator of social and cultural change only increased.

These were the foundations on which twentieth-century globalization was built. A number of prominent developments of the past century, explored in the previous three chapters, operated on a global scale: the world wars, the Great Depression, communism, the cold war, the end of empire. But global interaction, while continuing earlier patterns, vastly accelerated its pace after World War II. Those contacts and interactions among geographically and culturally distant peoples gave rise to a world more densely connected and converging than ever before, but also to a world deeply divided, unequal, conflicted, and violent. To illustrate this accelerating globalization, this chapter examines four major processes: the transformation of the world economy, the emergence of global feminism, the confrontation of world religions with modernity, and the growing awareness of humankind's enormous impact on the environment.

The Transformation of the World Economy

■ **Change**

What factors contributed to economic globalization during the twentieth century?

When most people speak of globalization, they are referring to the immense acceleration in international economic transactions that took place in the second half of the twentieth century and has continued into the twenty-first. Many have come to see this process as almost natural, certainly inevitable, and practically unstoppable. Yet the first half of the twentieth century, particularly the decades between the two world wars, witnessed a deep contraction of global economic linkages as the aftermath of World War I and then the Great Depression wreaked havoc on the world economy. International trade, investment, and labor migration dropped sharply as major states turned inward, favoring high tariffs and economic autonomy in the face of a global economic collapse.

The aftermath of World War II was very different. The capitalist victors in that conflict, led by the United States, were determined to avoid any return to such

Depression-era conditions. At a conference in Bretton Woods, New Hampshire, in 1944, they forged a set of agreements and institutions (the World Bank and the International Monetary Fund) that laid the foundation for postwar globalization. This "Bretton Woods system" negotiated the rules for commercial and financial dealings among the major capitalist countries, while promoting relatively free trade, stable currency values linked to the U.S. dollar, and high levels of capital investment.

A World Economy
Indian-based call centers that serve North American or European companies and customers have become a common experience of globalization for many. Here employees in one such call center in Patna, a major city in northeastern India, undergo voice training in order to communicate more effectively with their English-speaking callers. (Indiapicture/Alamy)

Technology also contributed to the acceleration of economic globalization. Containerized shipping, huge oil tankers, and air express services dramatically lowered transportation costs, while fiber-optic cables and later the Internet provided the communication infrastructure for global economic interaction. In the developing countries, population growth, especially when tied to growing economies and modernizing societies, further fueled globalization as dozens of new nations entered the world economy.

What kind of economic globalization was taking shape? In the 1970s and after, major capitalist countries such as the United States and Great Britain abandoned many earlier political controls on economic activity as their leaders and businesspeople increasingly viewed the entire world as a single market. Known as neo-liberalism, this approach to the world economy favored the reduction of tariffs, the free global movement of capital, a mobile and temporary workforce, the privatization of many state-run enterprises, the curtailing of government efforts to regulate the economy, and both tax and spending cuts. Powerful international lending agencies such as the World Bank and the International Monetary Fund imposed such free-market and pro-business conditions on many poor countries if they were to qualify for much-needed loans. The collapse of the state-controlled economies of the communist world only furthered such unrestricted global capitalism. In this view, the market, operating both globally and within nations, was the most effective means of generating the holy grail of economic growth. By the end of the twentieth century, as economic historian Jeffrey Frieden put it, "capitalism was global and the globe was capitalist."[2]

Reglobalization

These were the foundations for a dramatic quickening of global economic transactions after World War II, a "reglobalization" of the world economy following the contractions of the 1930s. This immensely significant process was expressed in the accelerating circulation of goods, capital, and people.

■ **Connection**
In what ways has economic globalization linked the world's peoples more closely together?

Map 24.1   Globalization in Action: Foreign Direct Investment in the Late Twentieth Century
Investment across national borders has been a major expression of globalization. This map shows the global distribution of investment inflows as of 1998. Notice which countries or regions were receiving the most investment from abroad and which received the least. How might you account for this pattern? Keep in mind that some regions, such as the United States, Western Europe, and Japan, were major sources of such investment as well as recipients of it.

World trade, for example, skyrocketed from a value of some $57 billion in 1947 to well over $13 trillion in 2007. Department stores and supermarkets around the world stocked their shelves with goods from every part of the globe. Twinings of London marketed its 120 blends of tea in more than 100 countries, and the Australian-based Kiwi shoe polish was sold in 180 countries. In 2005, about 70 percent of Walmart products reportedly included components from China. And the following year, Toyota replaced General Motors as the world's largest auto maker with manufacturing facilities in at least eighteen countries.

Money as well as goods achieved an amazing global mobility in three ways. The first was "foreign direct investment," whereby a firm in, say, the United States opens a factory in China or Mexico (see Map 24.1 and Visual Source 24.1, p. 1181). Such investment exploded after 1960 as companies in the rich countries sought to take advantage of cheap labor, tax breaks, and looser environmental regulations in the developing countries. A second form of money in motion has been the short-term movement of capital, in which investors annually spent trillions of dollars purchasing foreign currencies or stocks likely to increase in value and often sold them quickly thereafter, with unsettling consequences. A third form of money movement involved the personal funds of individuals. By the end of the twentieth century, international

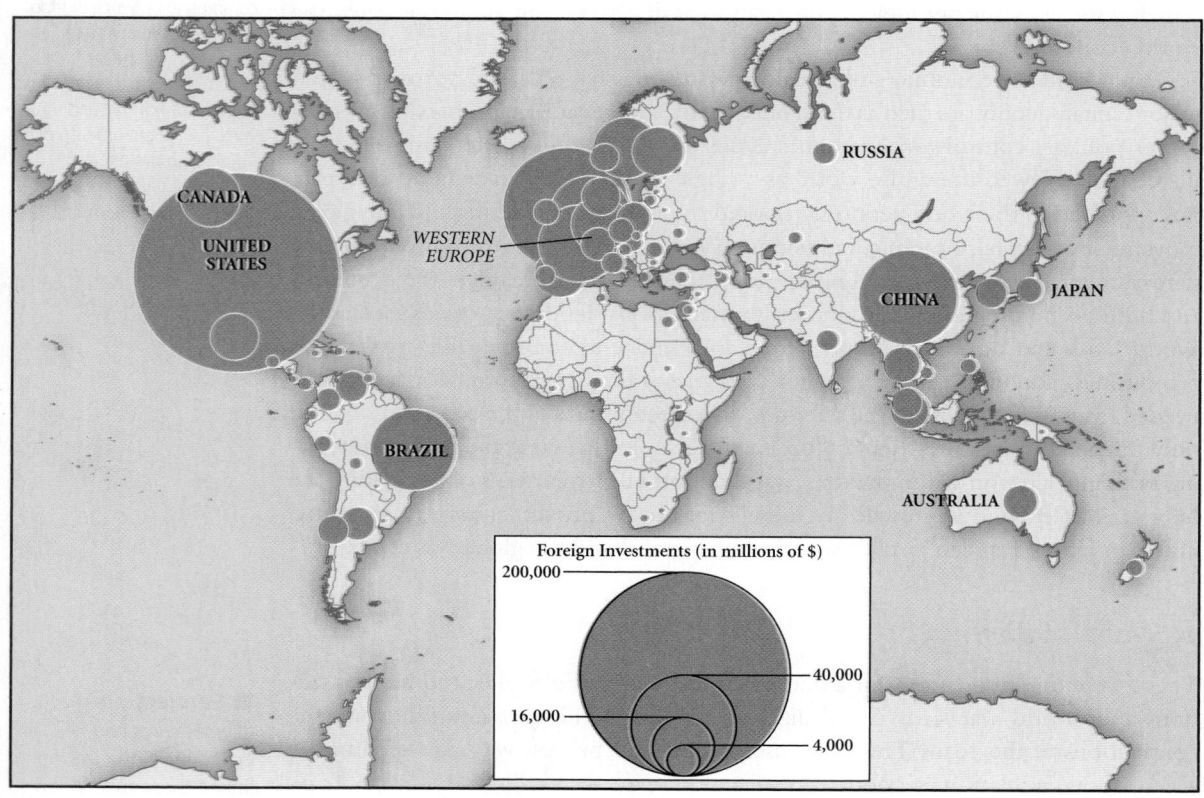

Map 24.1   Globalization in Action: Foreign Direct Investment in the Late Twentieth Century

credit cards had taken hold almost everywhere, allowing for easy transfer of money across national borders. In 2003, MasterCard was accepted at some 32 million businesses in 210 countries or territories.

Central to the acceleration of economic globalization have been huge global businesses known as transnational corporations (TNCs), which produce goods or deliver services simultaneously in many countries. For example, Mattel Corporation produced Barbie, that quintessentially American doll, in factories located in Indonesia, Malaysia, and China, using molds from the United States, plastic and hair from Taiwan and Japan, and cotton cloth from China. From distribution centers in Hong Kong, more than a billion Barbies were sold in 150 countries by 1999. Burgeoning in number since the 1960s, those TNCs, such as Royal Dutch Shell, Sony, and General Motors, often were of such an enormous size and economic clout that they dwarfed many countries. By 2000, 51 of the world's 100 largest economic units were in fact TNCs, not countries. In the permissive economic circumstances of recent decades, such firms have been able to move their facilities quickly from place to place in search of the lowest labor costs or the least restrictive environmental regulations. Nike, for example, during one five-year period closed twenty factories and opened thirty-five others, often thousands of miles apart.

More than ever workers too were on the move in a rapidly globalizing world economy. Examples included South Asians and West Indians seeking work and a better life in Great Britain; Algerians and West Africans in France; Yugoslavs in Germany and Switzerland; Mexicans, Cubans, and Haitians in the United States. By 2003, some 4 million Filipino domestic workers were employed in 130 countries. Young women by the hundreds of thousands from poor countries have been recruited as sex workers in wealthy nations, sometimes in conditions approaching slavery. Many highly educated professionals—doctors, nurses, engineers, computer specialists—left their homes in the Global South in a "brain drain" that clearly benefited the Global North. These migrating workers often represented a major source of income to their home countries. They also provided an inexpensive source of labor for their adopted countries, even as their presence generated mounting political and cultural tensions (see Visual Source 24.3, p. 1184). Beyond those seeking work, millions of others sought refuge in the West from political oppression or civil war at home, and hundreds of millions of short-term international travelers and tourists joined the swelling ranks of people in motion.

Growth, Instability, and Inequality

What was the impact of these tightening economic links for nations and peoples around the world? That question has prompted enormous debate and controversy. Amid the swirl of contending opinion, one thing seemed reasonably clear: economic globalization accompanied, and arguably helped generate, the most remarkable spurt of economic growth in world history. On a global level, total world output grew from a value of $7.1 trillion in 1950 to $55.9 trillion in 2003 and on a per capita basis

■ **Connection**
What new or sharper divisions has economic globalization generated?

Snapshot   **Indicators of Reglobalization**[3]

Telephone lines	from 150 million in 1965 to 1.5 billion in 2000
Mobile telephones	from 0 in 1978 to more than 1 billion in 2004
Internet users	from 0 in 1985 to 934 million in 2004
International air travelers	from 25 million in 1950 to 400 million in 1996
Export processing zones	from 0 in 1957 to 3,000 in 2002
Daily foreign exchange turnover	from $15 billion in 1973 to $1.9 trillion in 2004
International bank loans	from $9 billion in 1972 to $1.465 trillion in 2000
World stock of foreign direct investment	from $66 billion in 1960 to $7.1 trillion in 2002
Value of international trade	from $629 billion in 1960 to $13.6 trillion in 2007
Number of transnational companies	from 7,000 in the late 1960s to 65,000 in 2001

from $2,835 to $8,753.[4] This represents an immense, rapid, and unprecedented creation of wealth with a demonstrable impact on human welfare. Life expectancies grew almost everywhere, infant mortality declined, and literacy increased. The UN Human Development Report in 1997 concluded that "in the past 50 years, poverty has fallen more than in the previous 500."[5]

Far more problematic have been the stability of this emerging world economy and the distribution of the wealth it has generated. Amid overall economic growth, periodic crises and setbacks have likewise shaped recent world history. Soaring oil prices contributed to a severe stock market crash in 1973–1974 and especially great hardship for many developing countries. Inability to repay mounting debts triggered a major financial crisis in Latin America during the 1980s and resulted in a "lost decade" in terms of economic development. Another financial crisis, this time in Asia during the late 1990s, resulted in the collapse of many businesses, widespread unemployment, and political upheaval in Indonesia and Thailand.

But nothing since the Great Depression more clearly illustrated the unsettling consequences of global connectedness in the absence of global regulation than the worldwide economic contraction that began in 2008. When an inflated housing market, or "bubble," in the United States collapsed—triggering millions of home foreclosures, growing unemployment, the tightening of credit, and declining consumer spending—the results rippled around the world. Iceland's rapidly growing economy collapsed almost overnight as three major banks failed, the country's stock market dropped by 80 percent, and its currency lost more than 70 percent of its value—all in a single week. In Africa, reduced demand for exports threatened to halt a promising decade of economic progress. In Sierra Leone, for example, some 90 percent of the country's diamond-mine workers lost their jobs. The slowing of China's once-booming economy led to unemployment for one in seven of the country's urban migrants, forcing them to return to already overcrowded rural areas. Impoverished Central American and Caribbean families, dependent on money sent home by family members working abroad, suffered further as those remittances dropped sharply. Calls for both protectionism and greater regulation suggested that the wide-open capitalist world economy of recent decades was perhaps not as inevitable as some had thought. Whatever the overall benefits of the modern global system, economic stability and steady progress were not among them.

Nor was equality. Since Europe's Industrial Revolution took hold in the early nineteenth century, a wholly new division appeared within the human community—between the rich industrialized countries, primarily in Europe and North America, and everyone else. In 1820, the ratio between the income of the top and bottom 20 percent of the world's population was three to one. By 1991, it was eighty-six to one.[6] The accelerated economic globalization of the twentieth century did not create this global rift, but it arguably has worsened the North/South gap and certainly has not greatly diminished it. Even the well-known capitalist financier and investor George Soros, a billionaire many times over, acknowledged this reality in 2000: "The global capitalist system has produced a very uneven playing field. The gap between the rich and the poor is getting wider."[7] That gap has been evident, often tragically, in great disparities in incomes, medical care, availability of clean drinking water, educational and employment opportunities, access to the Internet, and dozens of other ways. It has shaped the life chances of practically everyone (see Map 24.2 and Visual Source 24.5, p. 1186).

These disparities were the foundations for a new kind of global conflict. As the East/West division of capitalism and communism faded, differences between the rich nations of the Global North and the developing countries of the Global South assumed greater prominence in world affairs. Highly contentious issues have included the rules for world trade, availability of and terms for foreign aid, representation in international economic organizations, the mounting problem of indebtedness, and environmental and labor standards. Such matters surfaced repeatedly in international negotiations during the last half of the twentieth century and into the twenty-first. In the 1970s, for example, a large group of developing countries joined together to demand a "new international economic order" that was more favorable to the poor countries. Not much success attended this effort. More recently, developing countries have contested protectionist restrictions on their agricultural exports imposed by the rich countries seeking to protect their own politically powerful farmers.

Beyond active resistance by the rich nations, a further obstacle to reforming the world economy in favor of the poor lay in growing disparities among the developing countries themselves (see Chapter 23). The oil-rich economies of the Middle East had little in common with the banana-producing countries of Central America. The rapidly industrializing states of China, India, and South Korea had quite different economic agendas than impoverished African countries. These disparities made common action difficult to achieve.

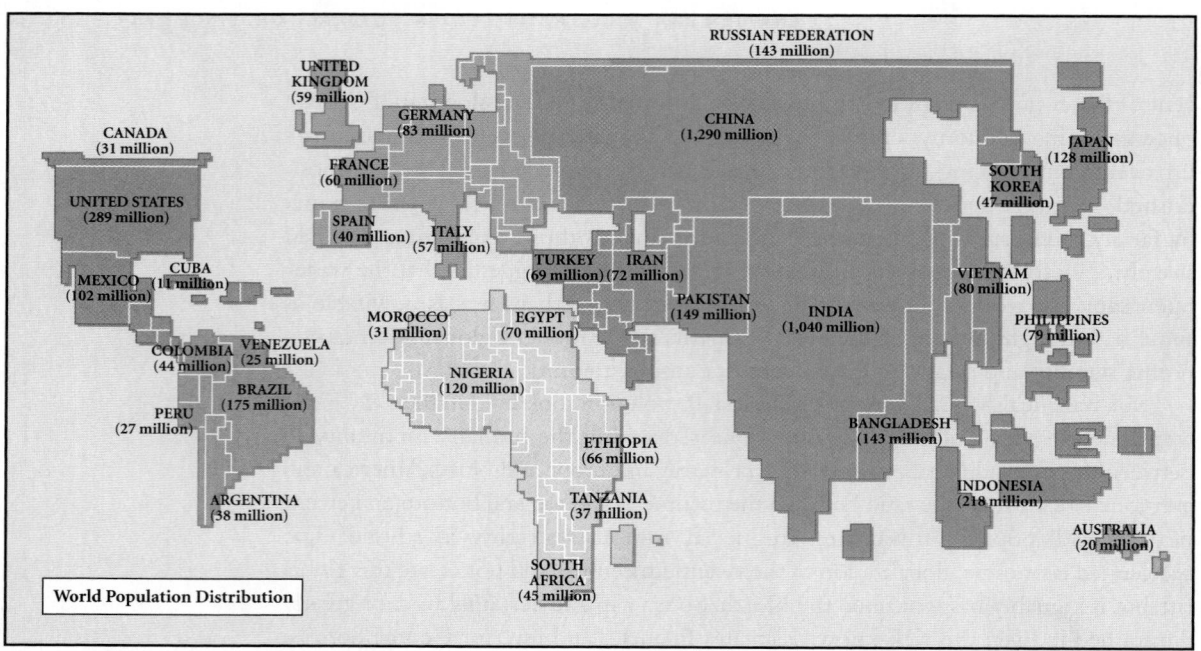

World Population Distribution

Country	Population
RUSSIAN FEDERATION	(143 million)
UNITED KINGDOM	(59 million)
GERMANY	(83 million)
FRANCE	(60 million)
CHINA	(1,290 million)
JAPAN	(128 million)
CANADA	(31 million)
SOUTH KOREA	(47 million)
UNITED STATES	(289 million)
SPAIN	(40 million)
ITALY	(57 million)
TURKEY	(69 million)
IRAN	(72 million)
VIETNAM	(80 million)
MEXICO	(102 million)
CUBA	(11 million)
PAKISTAN	(149 million)
INDIA	(1,040 million)
PHILIPPINES	(79 million)
MOROCCO	(31 million)
EGYPT	(70 million)
COLOMBIA	(44 million)
VENEZUELA	(25 million)
NIGERIA	(120 million)
BRAZIL	(175 million)
BANGLADESH	(143 million)
PERU	(27 million)
ETHIOPIA	(66 million)
INDONESIA	(218 million)
TANZANIA	(37 million)
ARGENTINA	(38 million)
AUSTRALIA	(20 million)
SOUTH AFRICA	(45 million)

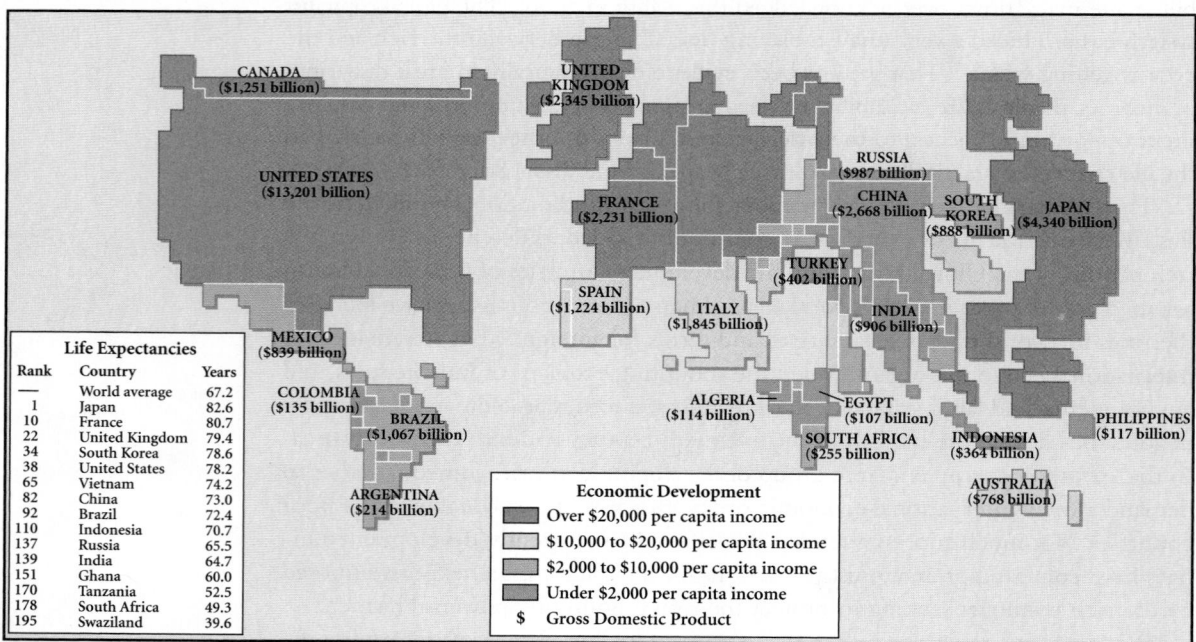

Life Expectancies		
Rank	Country	Years
—	World average	67.2
1	Japan	82.6
10	France	80.7
22	United Kingdom	79.4
34	South Korea	78.6
38	United States	78.2
65	Vietnam	74.2
82	China	73.0
92	Brazil	72.4
110	Indonesia	70.7
137	Russia	65.5
139	India	64.7
151	Ghana	60.0
170	Tanzania	52.5
178	South Africa	49.3
195	Swaziland	39.6

Economic Development

- Over $20,000 per capita income
- $10,000 to $20,000 per capita income
- $2,000 to $10,000 per capita income
- Under $2,000 per capita income
- $ Gross Domestic Product

Country GDP values:
CANADA ($1,251 billion), UNITED KINGDOM ($2,345 billion), RUSSIA ($987 billion), CHINA ($2,668 billion), SOUTH KOREA ($888 billion), JAPAN ($4,340 billion), UNITED STATES ($13,201 billion), FRANCE ($2,231 billion), TURKEY ($402 billion), SPAIN ($1,224 billion), ITALY ($1,845 billion), INDIA ($906 billion), MEXICO ($839 billion), COLOMBIA ($135 billion), BRAZIL ($1,067 billion), ALGERIA ($114 billion), EGYPT ($107 billion), SOUTH AFRICA ($255 billion), INDONESIA ($364 billion), PHILIPPINES ($117 billion), AUSTRALIA ($768 billion), ARGENTINA ($214 billion)

Map 24.2 Global Inequality: Population and Economic Development

These two maps illustrate in graphic form the global inequalities of the early twenty-first century. The first shows the relative size of the world's population by region and country; the second shows the size of the economy measured by total gross domestic product and per capita income. Illustrating yet another indication of the global economic divide are figures for overall life expectancy, an indicator that has narrowed more sharply than have others.

Economic globalization has generated inequalities not only at the global level and among developing countries but also within individual nations, rich and poor alike. In the United States, for example, a shifting global division of labor required the American economy to shed millions of manufacturing jobs. With recent U.S. factory wages perhaps thirty times those of China, many companies moved their manufacturing operations offshore to Asia or Latin America. This left many relatively unskilled American workers in the lurch, forcing them to work in the low-wage service sector, even as other Americans were growing prosperous in emerging high-tech industries. Even some highly skilled work, such as computer programming, was outsourced to lower-wage sites in India, Ireland, Russia, and elsewhere.

Globalization divided Mexico as well. The northern part of the country, with close business and manufacturing ties to the United States, grew much more prosperous than the south, which was largely a rural agricultural area and had a far more slowly growing economy. Beginning in 1994, southern resentment boiled over in the Chiapas rebellion, which featured a strong antiglobalization platform. Its leader, Subcomandante Marcos, referred to globalization as a "process to eliminate that multitude of people who are not useful to the powerful."[8] China's rapid economic growth likewise fostered mounting inequality between its rural households and those in its burgeoning cities, where income by 2000 was three times that of the countryside. Economic globalization may have brought people together as never before, but it also divided them sharply.

The hardships and grievances of those left behind or threatened by the march toward economic integration have fueled a growing popular movement aimed at criticizing and counteracting globalization. Known variously as an antiglobalization, alternative globalization, or global justice movement, it emerged in the 1990s as an international coalition of political activists, concerned scholars and students, trade unions, women's and religious organizations, environmental groups, and others, hailing from rich and poor countries alike. Thus opposition to neo-liberal globalization was itself global in scope. That opposition, though reflecting a variety of viewpoints, largely agreed that free-trade, market-driven corporate globalization had lowered labor standards, fostered ecological degradation, prevented poor countries from protecting themselves against financial speculators, ignored local cultures, disregarded human rights, and enhanced global inequality, while favoring the interests of large corporations and the rich countries.

This movement appeared dramatically on the world's radar screen in late 1999 in Seattle at a meeting of the World Trade Organization (WTO) (see Visual Source 24.4, p. 1185). An international body representing 149 nations and charged with negotiating the rules for global commerce and promoting free trade, the WTO had become a major target of globalization critics. "The central idea of the WTO," argued one such critic, "is that *free trade*—actually the values and interests of global corporations—should supersede all other values."[9] Tens of thousands of protesters—academics, activists, farmers, labor union leaders from all over the world—descended on Seattle in what became a violent, chaotic, and much-publicized protest. At the city's harbor, protest organizers created a Seattle Tea Party around the slogan "No globalization without representation," echoing the Boston Tea Party of 1773. Subsequent meetings of the WTO and other high-level international economic gatherings were likewise greeted with large-scale protest and a heavy police presence. In 2001, alternative globalization activists created the World Social Forum, an annual gathering to coordinate strategy, exchange ideas, and share experiences, under the slogan "Another world is possible." It was an effort to demonstrate that neo-liberal globalization was not inevitable and that the processes of a globalized economy could and should be regulated and subjected to public accountability.

Globalization and an American Empire

For many people, opposition to this kind of globalization also expressed resistance to mounting American power and influence in the world. An "American Empire," some have argued, is the face of globalization (see Map 24.3), but scholars, commentators, and politicians have disagreed about how best to describe the United States' role in the postwar world. Certainly it has not been a colonial territorial empire such as that of the British or the French in the nineteenth century. Americans generally, seeking to distinguish themselves from Europeans, have vigorously denied that they are an empire at all.

In some ways, the U.S. global presence might be seen as an "informal empire," similar to the ones that Europeans exercised in China and the Middle East during the nineteenth century. In both cases, economic penetration, political pressure, and periodic military action sought to create societies and governments compatible with the values and interests of the dominant power, but without directly governing large populations for long periods. In its economic dimension, American dominance has been termed an "empire of production," which uses its immense wealth to entice or intimidate potential collaborators.[10] Some scholars have emphasized the United States' frequent use of force around the world, while others have focused attention on the "soft power" of its cultural attractiveness, its political and cultural freedoms, the economic benefits of cooperation, and the general willingness of many to follow the American lead voluntarily.

With the collapse of the Soviet Union and the end of the cold war by the early 1990s, U.S. military dominance was now unchecked by any equivalent power. When the United States was attacked by Islamic militants on September 11, 2001, that power was unleashed first against Afghanistan (2001), which had sheltered the al-Qaeda instigators of that attack, and then against Iraq (2003), where Saddam Hussein allegedly had been developing weapons of mass destruction. In the absence of the Soviet Union, the United States could act unilaterally without fear of triggering a conflict with another major power. Although the Afghan and Iraqi regimes were quickly defeated, establishing a lasting peace and rebuilding badly damaged Muslim countries have proved difficult tasks. Thus, within a decade of the Soviet collapse, the United States found itself in yet another global struggle, an effort to contain or eliminate Islamic terrorism.

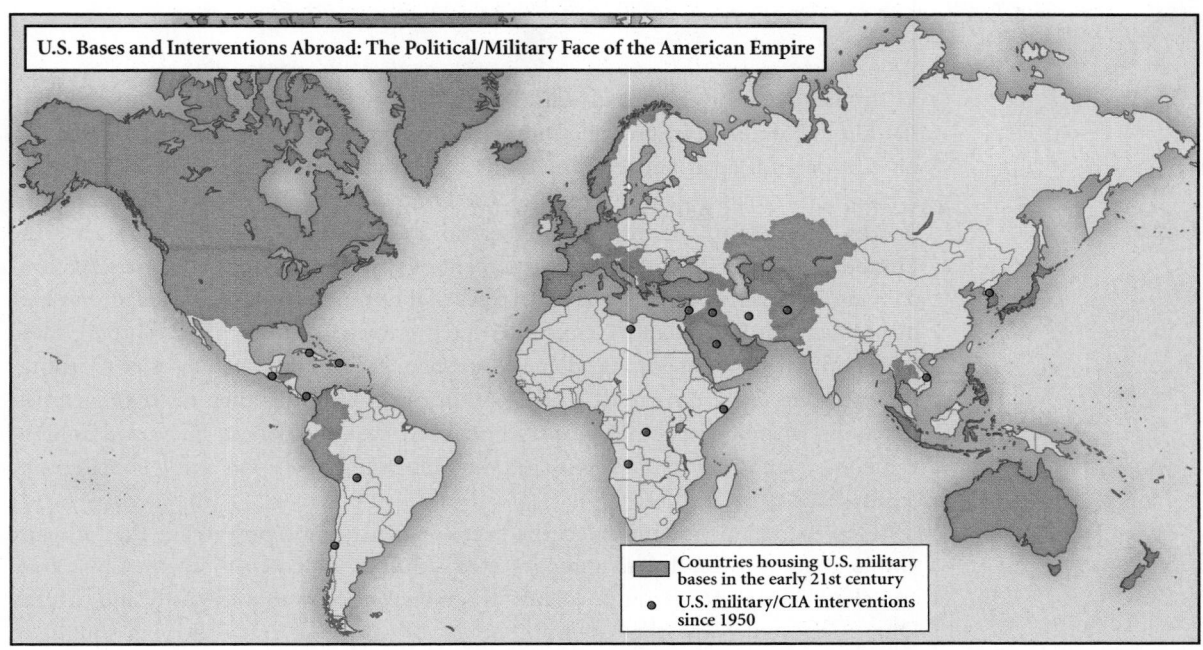

U.S. Bases and Interventions Abroad: The Political/Military Face of the American Empire

Countries housing U.S. military bases in the early 21st century

• U.S. military/CIA interventions since 1950

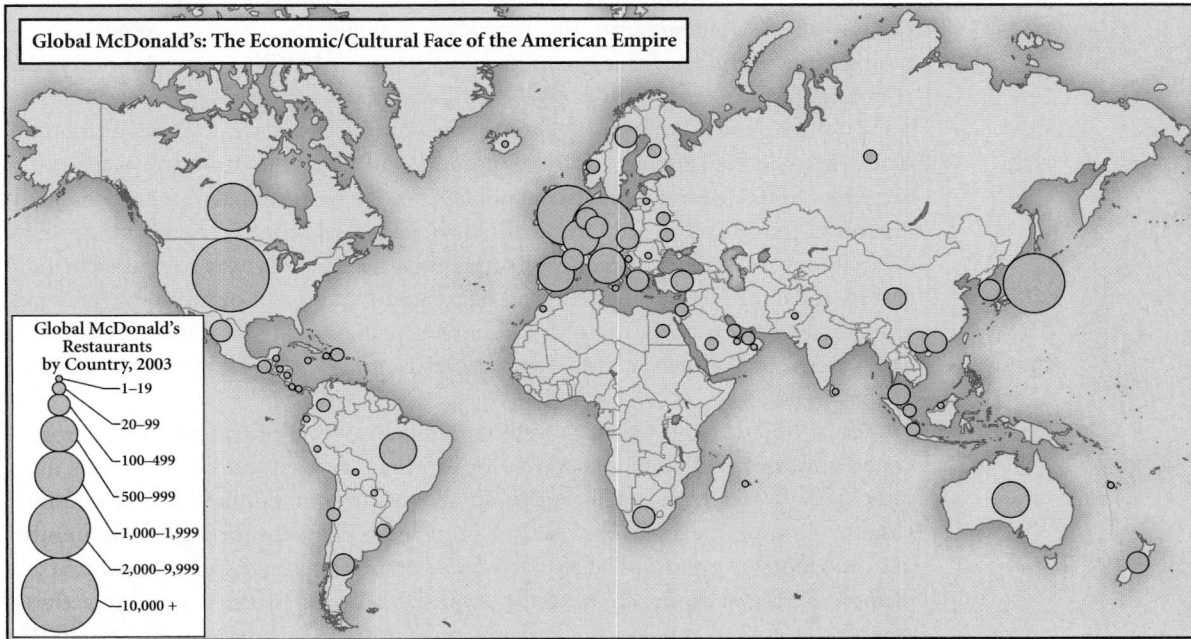

Global McDonald's: The Economic/Cultural Face of the American Empire

Global McDonald's Restaurants by Country, 2003

1–19
20–99
100–499
500–999
1,000–1,999
2,000–9,999
10,000 +

Map 24.3 Two Faces of an "American Empire"

Those who argue that the United States constructed an empire in the second half of the twentieth century point both to its political/military alliances and interventions around the world and to U.S. economic and cultural penetration of many countries. The distribution of U.S. military bases, a partial indication of its open and covert interventions, and the location of McDonald's restaurants indicates something of the scope of America's global presence in the early twenty-first century.

In the final quarter of the twentieth century, as its relative military strength peaked, the United States faced growing international economic competition. The recovery of Europe and Japan and the emergent industrialization of South Korea, Taiwan, China, and India substantially reduced the United States' share of overall world production from about 50 percent in 1945 to 20 percent in the 1980s. By 2008 the United States accounted for just 8.1 percent of world merchandise exports. Accompanying this relative decline was a sharp reversal of the country's trade balance as U.S. imports greatly exceeded its exports. Once the world's leading creditor, the United States now became its leading debtor. Lee Iacocca, president of Chrysler Corporation, registered the dismay that many Americans felt at this turn in their fortunes: "We send Japan low-value soybeans, wheat, corn, coal, and cotton. They send us high-value autos, motorcycles, TV sets, and oil well casings. It's 1776 and we're a colony again."[11]

However it might be defined, the exercise of American power, like that of many empires, was resisted abroad and contested at home. In Korea, Vietnam, Cuba, Iraq, and elsewhere, armed struggle against U.S. intervention was both costly and painful. During the cold war, the governments of India, Egypt, and Ethiopia sought to diminish American influence in their affairs by turning to the Soviet Union or playing off the two superpowers against each other. Even France, resenting U.S. domination, withdrew from the military structure of NATO in 1967 and expelled all foreign-controlled troops from the country. Many intellectuals, fearing the erosion of their own cultures in the face of well-financed American media around the world, have decried American "cultural imperialism." By the early twenty-first century, the United States' international policies—such as its refusal to accept the jurisdiction of the International Criminal Court; its refusal to ratify the Kyoto protocol on global warming; its doctrine of preemptive war, which was exercised in Iraq; and its apparent use of torture—had generated widespread opposition. However, when Barack Obama became the country's first African-American president in 2009, promising a different global posture, his election was greeted warmly in much of the world.

Within the United States as well, the global exercise of American power generated controversy. The Vietnam War, for example, divided the United States more sharply than at any time since the Civil War. It split families and friendships, churches and political parties. The war provided a platform for a growing number of critics, both at home and abroad, who had come to resent American cultural and economic dominance in the post-1945 world. It stimulated a new sense of activism among students in the nation's colleges and universities. Finally, the Vietnam War gave rise to charges that the cold war had undermined American democracy by promoting an overly powerful, "imperial" presidency, by creating a culture of secrecy and an obsession with national security, and by limiting political debate in the country. Not a few came to see America itself as an imperialist power. A similar set of issues, protests, and controversies followed the American invasion of Iraq in 2003.

The Globalization of Liberation: Comparing Feminist Movements

More than goods, money, and people traversed the planet during the twentieth century. So too did ideas, and none was more powerful than the ideology of liberation. Communism promised workers and peasants liberation from capitalist oppression. Nationalism offered subject peoples liberation from imperialism. Advocates of democracy sought liberation from authoritarian governments.

The 1960s in particular witnessed an unusual convergence of protest movements around the world, suggesting the emergence of a global culture of liberation. Within the United States, the civil rights demands of African Americans and Hispanic Americans; the youthful counterculture of rock music, sex, and drugs; the prolonged and highly divisive protests against the war in Vietnam—all of this gave the 1960s a distinctive place in the country's recent history. Across the Atlantic, swelling protests against unresponsive bureaucracy, consumerism, and middle-class values likewise erupted, most notably in France in 1968. There a student-led movement protesting conditions in universities attracted the support of many middle-class people, who were horrified at the brutality of the police, and stimulated an enormous strike among some 9 million workers. France seemed on the edge of another revolution. Related but smaller-scale movements took place in Germany, Italy, and elsewhere.

The communist world too was rocked by protest. In 1968, the new Communist Party leadership in Czechoslovakia, led by Alexander Dubcek, initiated a sweeping series of reforms aimed at creating "socialism with a human face." Censorship ended, generating an explosion of free expression in what had been a highly repressive regime; unofficial political clubs emerged publicly; victims of earlier repression were rehabilitated; secret ballots for party elections were put in place. To the conservative leaders of the Soviet Union, this "Prague Spring" seemed to challenge communist rule itself, and they sent troops and tanks to crush it. Across the world in communist China, another kind of protest was taking shape in that country's Cultural Revolution (see Chapter 22).

In the developing countries, a substantial number of political leaders, activists, scholars, and students developed the notion of a "third world." Their countries, many of which had only recently broken free from colonial rule, would offer an alternative to both a decrepit Western capitalism and a repressive Soviet communism. They claimed to pioneer new forms of economic development, of grassroots democracy, and of cultural renewal. By the late 1960s, the icon of

Che Guevara
In life, Che was an uncompromising but failed revolutionary, while in death he became an inspiration to third-world liberation movements and a symbol of radicalism to many in the West. His image appeared widely on T-shirts and posters, and in Cuba itself a government-sponsored cult featured schoolchildren chanting each morning "We will be like Che." This billboard image of Che was erected in Havana in 1988. (Tim Page/Corbis)

this third-world ideology was Che Guevara, the Argentine-born revolutionary who had embraced the Cuban Revolution and subsequently attempted to replicate its experience of liberation through guerrilla warfare in parts of Africa and Latin America. Various aspects of his life story—his fervent anti-imperialism, cast as a global struggle; his self-sacrificing lifestyle; his death in 1967 at the hands of the Bolivian military, trained and backed by the American CIA—made him a heroic figure to third-world revolutionaries. He was popular as well among Western radicals, who were disgusted with the complacency and materialism of their own societies.

No expression of the global culture of liberation held a more profound potential for change than feminism, for it represented a rethinking of the most fundamental and personal of all human relationships—that between women and men. Feminism had begun in the West in the nineteenth century with a primary focus on suffrage and in several countries had achieved the status of a mass movement by the outbreak of World War I (see pp. 800–803). The twentieth century, however, witnessed the globalization of feminism as organized efforts to address the concerns of women took shape across the world. Communist governments—in the Soviet Union, China, and Cuba, for example—mounted vigorous efforts to gain the support of women and to bring them into the workforce by attacking major elements of older patriarchies (see pp. 1039–40). But feminism took hold in many cultural and political settings, where women confronted different issues, adopted different strategies, and experienced a range of outcomes.

Feminism in the West

■ **Comparison**
What distinguished feminism in the industrialized countries from that of the Global South?

In the West, organized feminism had lost momentum by the end of the 1920s, when most countries had achieved universal suffrage. When it revived in the 1960s in both Western Europe and the United States, it did so with a quite different agenda. In France, for example, the writer and philosopher Simone de Beauvoir in 1949 had published *The Second Sex*, a book arguing that women had historically been defined as "other," or deviant from the "normal" male sex. The book soon became a central statement of a reviving women's movement. French feminists dramatized their concerns publicly in the early 1970s when some of them attempted to lay a wreath at the tomb of the unknown soldier in Paris, declaring, "Someone is even more unknown than the soldier: his wife." They staged a counter–Mother's Day parade under the slogan "Celebrated one day; exploited all year." To highlight their demand to control their own bodies, some 343 women signed a published manifesto stating that they had undergone an abortion, which was then illegal in France.

Across the Atlantic, millions of American women responded to Betty Friedan's book *The Feminine Mystique* (1963), which disclosed the identity crisis of educated women who were unfulfilled by marriage and motherhood. Some adherents of this second-wave feminism took up the equal rights agenda of their nineteenth-century predecessors, but with an emphasis now on employment and education rather than voting rights.

A more radical expression of American feminism took shape from the experience of women who had worked in other kinds of radical politics, such as the civil rights movement. Widely known as "women's liberation," this approach took broader aim at patriarchy as a system of domination, similar to those of race and class. One manifesto from 1969 declared:

> We are exploited as sex objects, breeders, domestic servants, and cheap labor. We are considered inferior beings, whose only purpose is to enhance men's lives.... Because we live so intimately with our oppressors, we have been kept from seeing our personal suffering as a political condition.[12]

Thus liberation for women meant becoming aware of their own oppression, a process that took place in thousands of consciousness-raising groups across the country. Many such women preferred direct action rather than the political lobbying favored by equal rights feminists. They challenged the Miss America contest of 1968 by tossing stink bombs in the hall, crowning a live sheep as their Miss America, and disposing of girdles, bras, high-heeled shoes, tweezers, and other "instruments of oppression" in a Freedom Trashcan. They also brought into open discussion issues involving sexuality, insisting that free love, lesbianism, and celibacy should be accorded the same respect as heterosexual marriage.

Yet another strand of Western feminism emerged from women of color. For many of them, the concerns of white, usually middle-class, feminists were hardly relevant to their oppression. Black women had always worked outside the home and so felt little need to be liberated from the chains of homemaking. Whereas white women might find the family oppressive, African American women viewed it as a secure base from which to resist racism. Solidarity with black men, rather than separation from them, was essential in confronting a racist America. Viewing mainstream feminism as "a family quarrel between White women and White men," many women of African descent in the United States and Britain established their own organizations, with a focus on racism and poverty.[13]

Feminism in the Global South

As women mobilized outside of the Western world during the twentieth century, they faced very different situations than did white women in the United States and Europe. For much of Asia, Africa, and Latin America, the predominant issues—colonialism, racism, the struggle for independence, poverty, development, political oppression, and sometimes revolution—were not directly related to gender. Women were affected by and engaged with all of these efforts and were welcomed by nationalist and communist leaders, mostly men, who needed their support. Once independence or the revolution was achieved, however, the women who had joined those movements often were relegated to marginal positions.

The different conditions within developing countries sometimes generated sharp criticism of Western feminism. To many African feminists in the 1970s and beyond, the concerns of their American or European sisters were too individualistic, too focused on sexuality, and insufficiently concerned with issues of motherhood, marriage, and poverty to be of much use. Furthermore, they resented Western feminists' insistent interest in cultural matters such as female genital mutilation and polygamy, which sometimes echoed the concerns of colonial-era missionaries and administrators. Western feminism could easily be seen as a new form of cultural imperialism. Moreover, many African governments and many African men defined feminism of any kind as "un-African" and associated with a hated colonialism.

Women's movements in the Global South took shape around a wide range of issues, not all of which were explicitly gender based. In the East African country of Kenya, a major form of mobilization was the women's group movement. Some 27,000 small associations of women, which were an outgrowth of traditional self-help groups, had a combined membership of more than a million by the late 1980s. They provided support for one another during times of need, such as weddings, births, and funerals; they took on community projects, such as building water cisterns, schools, and dispensaries; in one province, they focused on providing permanent iron roofing for their homes. Some became revolving loan societies or bought land or businesses. One woman testified to the sense of empowerment she derived from membership in her group:

> I am a free woman. I bought this piece of land through my group. I can lie on it, work on it, keep goats or cows. What more do I want? My husband cannot sell it. It is mine.[14]

Elsewhere, other issues and approaches predominated. In the North African Islamic kingdom of Morocco, a more centrally directed and nationally focused feminist movement targeted the country's Family Law Code, which still defined women as minors. In 2004, a long campaign by Morocco's feminist movement, often with the help of supportive men and a liberal king, resulted in a new Family Law Code, which recognized women as equals to their husbands and allowed them to initiate divorce and to claim child custody, all of which had previously been denied.

In Chile, a women's movement emerged as part of a national struggle against the military dictatorship of General Augusto Pinochet, who ruled the country from 1973 to 1990. Because they were largely regarded as "invisible" in the public sphere, women were able to organize extensively, despite the repression of the Pinochet regime. From

Mothers of Missing Children

This group of Brazilian mothers in Rio de Janeiro gathered every week during the mid-1990s to bring pressure on the government to find their missing children, generally believed to have been seized by criminal gangs engaged in child prostitution and illegal adoption. Often seeking loved ones who probably were executed by government or paramilitary death squads, such "mothers of the disappeared" have been active in many Latin American countries.

(AP Images/Diego Guidice)

this explosion of organizing activity emerged a women's movement that crossed class lines and party affiliations. Human rights activists, most of them women, called attention to the widespread use of torture and to the "disappearance" of thousands of opponents of the regime, while demanding the restoration of democracy. Poor urban women by the tens of thousands organized soup kitchens, craft workshops, and shopping collectives, all aimed at the economic survival of their families. Smaller numbers of middle-class women brought more distinctly feminist perspectives to the movement and argued pointedly for "democracy in the country and in the home." This diverse women's movement was an important part of the larger national protest that returned Chile to democratic government in 1990.

In South Korea as in Chile, women's mobilization contributed to a "mass people's movement" that brought a return to democracy by the late 1980s, after a long period of highly authoritarian rule. The women's movement in South Korea drew heavily on the experience of young female workers in the country's export industries. In those factories, they were poorly paid, were subjected to exhausting working conditions and frequent sexual harassment, and lived in crowded company dormitories, often called "chicken coops." Such women spearheaded a democratic trade union movement during the 1970s, and in the process many of them developed both a feminist and a class consciousness.

International Feminism

Perhaps the most impressive achievement of feminism in the twentieth century was its ability to project the "woman question" as a global issue and to gain international recognition for the view that "women's rights are human rights."[15] Like slavery and empire before it, patriarchy lost at least some of its legitimacy during this most recent century, although clearly it has not been vanquished.

Feminism registered as a global issue when the United Nations, under pressure from women activists, declared 1975 as International Women's Year and the next ten years as the Decade for Women. The United Nations also sponsored a series of World Conferences on Women over the next twenty years. By 2006, 183 nations had ratified a UN Convention to Eliminate Discrimination against Women, which committed them to promote women's legal equality, to end discrimination, to actively encourage women's development, and to protect women's human rights. Clearly this international attention to women's issues was encouraging to feminists operating in their own countries and in many places stimulated both research and action.

This growing international spotlight on women's issues also revealed sharp divisions within global feminism. One issue was determining who had the right to speak on behalf of women at international gatherings—the official delegates of male-dominated governments or the often more radical unofficial participants representing various nongovernmental organizations. North/South conflicts also surfaced at these international conferences. In preparing for the Mexico City gathering in 1975, the United States attempted to limit the agenda to matters of political and civil rights for women, whereas delegates from third-world and communist countries wanted to include issues of economic justice, decolonization, and disarmament. Feminists from the South resented the dominance and contested the ideas of their Northern sisters. One African group highlighted the differences:

> While patriarchal views and structures oppress women all over the world, women are also members of classes and countries that dominate others and enjoy privileges in terms of access to resources. Hence, contrary to the best intentions of "sisterhood," not all women share identical interests.[16]

Nor did all third-world groups have identical views. Some Muslim delegates at the Beijing Conference in 1995 opposed a call for equal inheritance for women, because Islamic law required that sons receive twice the amount that daughters inherit. In contast, Africans, especially in non–Muslim countries, were aware of how many children had been orphaned by AIDS and felt that girls' chances for survival depended on equal inheritance.

Beyond such divisions within international feminism lay a global backlash among those who felt that its radical agenda had undermined family life, the proper relationship of men and women, and civilization generally. To Phyllis Schlafly, a prominent American opponent of the Equal Rights Amendment, feminism was a "disease" that brought in its wake "fear, sickness, pain, anger, hatred, danger, violence, and all manner of ugliness."[17] In the Islamic world, Western-style feminism, with its claims of gender equality and open sexuality, was highly offensive to many and fueled movements of religious revivalism that invited or compelled women to wear the veil and sometimes to lead highly restricted lives. The Vatican, some Catholic and Muslim countries, and at times the U.S. government took strong exception to aspects of global feminism, particularly its emphasis on reproductive rights, including access to abortion and birth control. Thus feminism was global as the twenty-first century dawned, but it was very diverse and much contested.

Religion and Global Modernity

Beyond liberation and feminism, a further dimension of cultural globalization took shape in the challenge that modernity presented to the world's religions. To the most "advanced" thinkers of the past several hundred years—Enlightenment writers in the eighteenth century, Karl Marx in the nineteenth, socialist intellectuals and secular-minded people in the twentieth—supernatural religion was headed for extinction in the face of modernity, science, communism, or globalization. In some places—Britain, France, the Netherlands, and the Soviet Union, for example—religious belief and practice had declined sharply. Moreover, the spread of a scientific culture around the world persuaded small minorities everywhere, often among the most highly educated, that the only realities worth considering were those that could be measured with the techniques of science. To such people, all else was superstition, born of ignorance. Nevertheless, the far more prominent trends of the last century have been those that involved the further spread of major world religions, their resurgence in new forms, their opposition to elements of a secular and global modernity, and their political role as a source of community identity and conflict. Contrary to earlier expectations, religion has played an unexpectedly powerful role in this most recent century.

Buddhism, Christianity, and Islam had long functioned as transregional cultures, spreading far beyond their places of origin. That process continued in the twentieth century. Buddhist ideas and practices such as meditation found a warm reception in the West, as did yoga, originally a mind-body practice of Indian origin. Christianity of various kinds spread widely in non-Muslim Africa and South Korea and less extensively in parts of India. By the end of the century, it was growing even in China, where perhaps 7 to 8 percent of China's population—some 84 to 96 million people—claimed allegiance to the faith. No longer a primarily European or North American religion, Christianity by the early twenty-first century found some 62 percent of its adherents in Asia, Africa, and Latin America. In some instances missionaries from those regions have set about the "re-evangelization" of Europe and North America. Moreover, millions of migrants from the Islamic world planted their religion solidly in the West. In the United States, for example, a substantial number of African Americans and smaller numbers of European Americans engaged in Islamic practice. For several decades the writings of the thirteenth-century Islamic Sufi poet Rumi have been bestsellers in the United States. Religious exchange, in short, has been a two-way street, not simply a transmission of Western ideas to the rest of the world. More than ever before, religious pluralism characterized many of the world's societies, confronting people with the need to make choices in a domain of life previously regarded as given and fixed.

Fundamentalism on a Global Scale

Religious vitality in the twentieth century was expressed not only in the spread of particular traditions to new areas but also in the vigorous response of those traditions to the modernizing and globalizing world in which they found themselves. One such response has been widely called "fundamentalism," a militant piety—defensive, assertive, and exclusive—that took shape to some extent in every major religious tradition. Many features of the modern world, after all, appeared threatening to established religion. The scientific and secular focus of global modernity directly challenged the core beliefs of supernatural religion. Furthermore, the social upheavals connected with capitalism, industrialization, and globalization thoroughly upset customary class, family, and gender relationships that had long been sanctified by religious tradition. Nation-states, often associated with particular religions, were likewise undermined by the operation of a global economy and challenged by the spread of alien cultures. In much of the world, these disruptions came at the hands of foreigners, usually Westerners, in the form of military defeat, colonial rule, economic dependency, and cultural intrusion.

■ Change
In what respect did the various religious fundamentalisms of the twentieth century express hostility to global modernity?

To such threats, fundamentalism represented a religious response, characterized by one scholar as "embattled forms of spirituality...experienced as a cosmic war between the forces of good and evil."[18] Although fundamentalisms everywhere have looked to the past for ideals and models, their rejection of modernity was selective, not wholesale. What they sought was an alternative modernity, infused with particular religious values. Most, in fact, made active use of modern technology to communicate their message and certainly sought the potential prosperity associated with modern life. Extensive educational and propaganda efforts, political mobilization of their followers, social welfare programs, and sometimes violence ("terrorism" to their opponents) were among the means that fundamentalists employed.

The term "fundamentalism" derived from the United States, where religious conservatives in the early twentieth century were outraged by critical and "scientific" approaches to the Bible, by Darwinian evolution, and by liberal versions of Christianity that accommodated these heresies. They called for a return to the "fundamentals" of the faith, which included the literal truthfulness of the scriptures, the virgin birth and physical resurrection of Jesus, and a belief in miracles. After World War II, American Protestant fundamentalism came to oppose political liberalism and "big government," the sexual revolution of the 1960s, homosexuality and abortion rights, and secular humanism generally. Many fundamentalists saw the United States on the edge of an abyss. For one major spokesman, Francis Schaeffer (1912–1984), the West was about to enter

> an electronic dark age, in which the new pagan hordes, with all the power of technology at their command, are on the verge of obliterating the last strongholds of civilized humanity. A vision of darkness lies before us. As we leave the shores of Christian Western man behind, only a dark and turbulent sea of despair stretches endlessly ahead...unless we fight.[19]

And fight they did! At first, fundamentalists sought to separate themselves from the secular world in their own churches and schools, but from the 1970s on, they entered the political arena as the "religious right," determined to return America to a "godly path." "We have enough votes to run this country," declared Pat Robertson, a major fundamentalist evangelist and broadcaster who ran for president in 1988. Conservative fundamentalist Christians, no longer willing to restrict their attention to personal conversion, had emerged as a significant force in American political life well before the end of the century.

In the very different setting of independent India, another fundamentalist movement—known as Hindutva (Hindu nationalism)—took shape during the 1980s. Like American fundamentalism, it represented a politicization of religion within a democratic context. To its advocates, India was, and always had been, an essentially Hindu land, even though it had been overwhelmed in recent centuries by Muslim invaders, then by the Christian British, and most recently by the secular state of the postindependence decades. The leaders of modern India, they argued, and particularly its first prime minister, Jawaharlal Nehru, were "the self-proclaimed secularists who...seek to remake India in the Western image," while repudiating its basically Hindu religious character. The Hindutva movement took political shape in an increasingly popular party called the Bharatiya Janata Party (BJP), with much of its support coming from urban middle-class or upper-caste people who resented the state's efforts to cater to the interests of Muslims, Sikhs, and the lower castes. Muslims in particular were defined as outsiders, potentially more loyal to a Muslim Pakistan than to India. The BJP became a major political force in India during the 1980s and 1990s, winning a number of elections at both the state and national levels and promoting a distinctly Hindu identity in education, culture, and religion.

Creating Islamic Societies: Resistance and Renewal in the World of Islam

The most prominent of the fundamentalisms that emerged in the late twentieth century was surely that of Islam, which was permanently etched in Americans' memory in the image of Osama bin Laden and the destruction of the World Trade Center on September 11, 2001. However, this violent event was only one expression of a much larger phenomenon—an effort among growing numbers of Muslims to create a new religious/political order centered on a particular understanding of Islam.

■ **Change**
From what sources did Islamic renewal movements derive?

Emerging strongly in the last quarter of the century, this Islamic renewal gained strength from the enormous disappointments that had accumulated in the Muslim world by the 1970s. Political independence had given rise to major states—Egypt, Iran, Algeria, and others—that pursued essentially Western and secular policies of nationalism, socialism, and economic development, often with only lip service to an Islamic identity. These policies, however, were not very successful. A number of endemic problems—vastly overcrowded cities with few services, widespread unemployment, pervasive corruption, slow economic growth, a mounting gap between the rich and poor—flew in the face of the great expectations that had accompanied the struggle against European domination. Despite independence from a century or more of humiliating Western imperialism, foreign intrusion still persisted. Israel, widely regarded as an outpost of the West, had been reestablished as a Jewish state in the very center of the Islamic world in 1948. In 1967, Israel inflicted a devastating defeat on Arab forces in the Six-Day War and seized various Arab territories, including the holy city of Jerusalem. Furthermore, broader signs of Western cultural penetration—secular schools, alcohol, Barbie dolls, European and American movies, scantily clad women—appeared frequently in the Muslim world.

This was the context in which the idea of an Islamic alternative to Western models of modernity began to take hold (see Document 24.2, pp. 1169–71). The intellectual and political foundations of this Islamic renewal had been established earlier in the century. Its leading figures, such as the Indian Mawlana Mawdudi and the Egyptian Sayyid Qutb, insisted that the Quran and the *sharia* (Islamic law) provided a guide for all of life—political, economic, and spiritual—and a blueprint for a distinctly Islamic modernity not dependent on Western ideas. It was the departure from Islamic principles, they argued, that had led the Islamic world into decline and subordination to the West, and only a return to the "straight path of Islam" would ensure

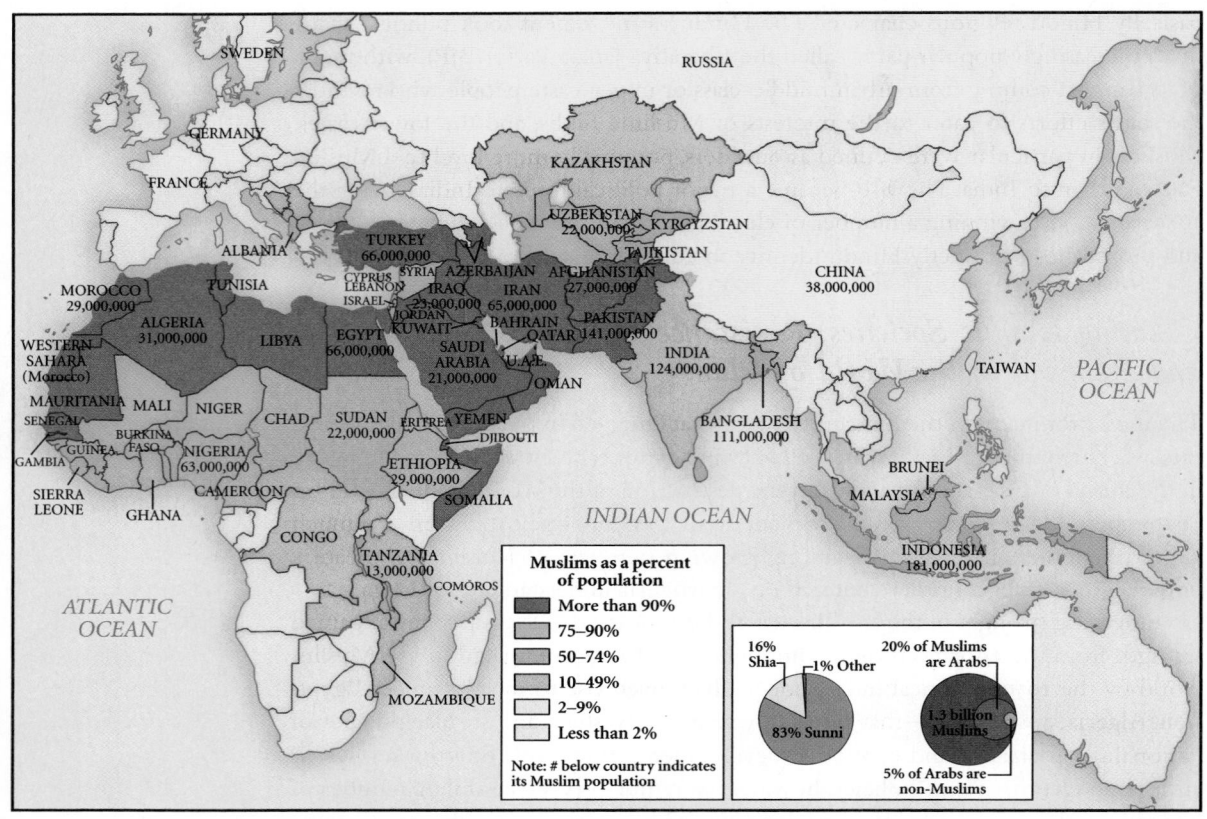

Map 24.4 The Islamic World in the Early Twenty-first Century

An Islamic world of well over a billion people incorporated much of the Afro-Asian landmass but was divided among many nations and along linguistic and ethnic lines as well. The long-term split between the majority Sunnis and the minority Shias also sharpened in the new millennium.

a revival of Muslim societies. That effort to return to Islamic principles was labeled *jihad*, an ancient and evocative religious term that refers to "struggle" or "striving" to please God. In its twentieth-century political expression, jihad included the defense of an authentic Islam against Western aggression and vigorous efforts to achieve the Islamization of social and political life within Muslim countries. It was a posture that would enable Muslims to resist the seductive but poisonous culture of the West. Sayyid Qutb had witnessed that culture during a visit to the United States in the late 1940s, and was shocked by what he saw:

> Look at this capitalism with its monopolies, its usury…at this individual freedom, devoid of human sympathy and responsibility for relatives except under force of law; at this materialistic attitude which deadens the spirit; at this behavior like animals which you call "free mixing of the sexes"; at this vulgarity which you call "emancipation of women"; at this evil and fanatical racial discrimination.[20]

■ **Comparison**

In what different ways did Islamic renewal express itself?

Such ideas soon echoed widely all across the Islamic world and found expression in many ways. At the level of personal life, many people became more religiously observant, attending mosque, praying regularly, and fasting. Substantial numbers of women, many of them young, urban, and well educated, adopted modest Islamic dress and the veil quite voluntarily. Participation in Sufi mystical practices increased. Furthermore, many governments sought to anchor themselves in Islamic rhetoric and practice. Under pressure from Islamic activists, the government of Sudan in the 1980s adopted Quranic punishments for various crimes (such as amputating the hand of a thief) and announced a total ban on alcohol, dramatically dumping thousands of bottles of beer and wine into the Nile. During the 1970s, President Anwar Sadat of Egypt claimed the title of "Believer-President," referred frequently to the Quran, and proudly displayed his "prayer mark," a callus on his forehead caused by touching his head to the ground in prayer.

All over the Muslim world, from North Africa to Indonesia, Islamic renewal movements spawned organizations that operated legally to provide social services—schools, clinics, youth centers, legal-aid centers, financial institutions, publishing houses—that the state offered inadequately or not at all. Islamic activists took leadership roles in unions and professional organizations of teachers, journalists, engineers, doctors, and lawyers. Such people embraced modern science and technology but sought to embed these elements of modernity within a distinctly Islamic culture. Some served in official government positions or entered political life where it was possible to do so. The Algerian Islamic Salvation Front was poised to win elections in 1992, when a frightened military government intervened to cancel the elections, an action that plunged the country into a decade of bitter civil war. In Turkey, Egypt, Jordan, Iraq, Palestine, and Lebanon, Islamic parties made impressive electoral showings in the 1990s and the early twenty-first century.

Hamas in Action
The Palestinian militant organization Hamas, founded in 1987 as an offshoot of Egypt's Muslim Brotherhood, illustrates two dimensions of Islamic radicalism. On the one hand, Hamas repeatedly sent suicide bombers to target Israeli civilians and sought the elimination of the Israeli state. A group of would-be suicide bombers are shown here in white robes during the funeral of colleagues killed by Israeli security forces in late 2003. On the other hand, Hamas ran a network of social services, providing schools, clinics, orphanages, summer camps, soup kitchens, and libraries for Palestinians. The classroom pictured here was part of a school founded by Hamas. (Andrea Comas/Reuters/Corbis; Abid Katib/Getty Images)

Another face of Islamic renewal, however, sought the violent overthrow of what they saw as compromised regimes in the Muslim world. One such group, the Egyptian Islamic Jihad, assassinated President Sadat in 1981, following Sadat's brutal crackdown on both Islamic and secular opposition groups. One of the leaders of Islamic Jihad explained:

> We have to establish the Rule of God's Religion in our own country first, and to make the Word of God supreme.... There is no doubt that the first battlefield for jihad is the extermination of these infidel leaders and to replace them by a complete Islamic Order.[21]

Two years earlier in Mecca, members of another radical Islamic group sought the overthrow of the Saudi government. They despised its alliance with Western powers, the corrupt and un-Islamic lifestyle of its leaders, and the disruptive consequences of its oil-fueled modernization program. They even invaded the Grand Mosque, Islam's most sacred shrine. In Iran (1979), Afghanistan (1996), parts of Northern Nigeria (2000), and a section of Pakistan (2009), Islamic movements succeeded in coming to power and began to implement a program of Islamization based on the sharia. (See pp. 1105–08 in Chapter 23 for Iran and Documents 24.2 and 24.3, pp. 1169–73.)

Islamic revolutionaries also took aim at hostile foreign powers. Hamas in Palestine and Hezbollah in Lebanon, supported by the Islamic regime in Iran, targeted Israel with popular uprisings, suicide bombings, and rocket attacks in response to the Israeli occupation of Arab lands. For some, Israel's very existence was illegitimate. The Soviet invasion of Afghanistan in 1979 prompted widespread opposition aimed at liberating the country from atheistic communism and creating an Islamic state. Sympathetic Arabs from the Middle East flocked to the aid of their Afghan compatriots.

Among them was the young Osama bin Laden, a wealthy Saudi Arab, who created an organization, al-Qaeda (meaning "the base" in Arabic), to funnel fighters and funds to the Afghan resistance. At the time, bin Laden and the Americans were on the same side, both opposing Soviet expansion into Afghanistan, but they soon parted ways. Returning to his home in Saudi Arabia, bin Laden became disillusioned and radicalized when the government of his country allowed the stationing of "infidel" U.S. troops in Islam's holy land during and after the first American war against Iraq in 1991. By the mid-1990s, he had found a safe haven in Taliban-ruled Afghanistan, from which he and other leaders of al-Qaeda planned their now infamous attack on the World Trade Center and other targets. Although they had no standing as Muslim clerics, in 1998 they issued a *fatwa* (religious edict) declaring war on America:

> [F]or over seven years the United States has been occupying the lands of Islam in the holiest of places, the Arabian Peninsula, plundering its riches, dictating to its rulers, humiliating its people, terrorizing its neighbors, and turning its bases in the Peninsula into a spearhead through which to fight the neighboring Muslim peoples.... [T]he ruling to kill the Americans and their allies—civilians and military—is an individual duty for every Muslim who can do it in any country in which it is possible to do it, in order to liberate the al-Aqsa Mosque in Jerusalem

and the holy mosque (in Mecca) from their grip, and in order for their armies to move out of all the lands of Islam, defeated and unable to threaten any Muslim.[22]

Elsewhere as well—in East Africa, Indonesia, Great Britain, Spain, Saudi Arabia, and Yemen—al-Qaeda or groups associated with it launched scattered attacks on Western interests. At the international level, the great enemy was not Christianity itself or even Western civilization, but irreligious Western-style modernity, U.S. imperialism, and an American-led economic globalization so aptly symbolized by the World Trade Center. Ironically, al-Qaeda itself was a modern and global organization, many of whose members were highly educated professionals from a variety of countries. Despite their focus on the West, the struggles undertaken by politicized Islamic activists were as much within the Islamic world as they were with the external enemy. If Islamic fundamentalism represented a clash of cultures or civilizations, that collision took place among different conceptions of Islam at least as sharply as with the outlook and practices of the modern West.

Religious Alternatives to Fundamentalism

Militant revolutionary fundamentalism has certainly not been the only religious response to modernity and globalization within the Islamic world. Many who shared a concern to embed Islamic values more centrally in their societies have acted peacefully and within established political structures. Considerable debate among them has raised questions about the proper role of the state, the difference between the eternal law of God (sharia) and the human interpretations of it, the rights of women, the possibility of democracy, and many other issues (see Documents 24.4 and 24.5, pp. 1173–78). Some Muslim intellectuals and political leaders have called for a dialogue between civilizations; others have argued that traditions can change in the face of modern realities without losing their distinctive Islamic character. In 1996, Anwar Ibrahim, a major political and intellectual figure in Malaysia, insisted that

> [Southeast Asian Muslims] would rather strive to improve the welfare of the women and children in their midst than spend their days elaborately defining the nature and institutions of the ideal Islamic state. They do not believe it makes one less of a Muslim to promote economic growth, to master the information revolution, and to demand justice for women.[23]

And in many places Sufi devotionalism stands as a strong alternative to a legalistic Islamic fundamentalism.

Within other religious traditions as well, believers found various ways of responding to global modernity. More liberal or mainstream Christian groups spoke to the ethical issues arising from economic globalization. Many Christian organizations, for example, were active in agitating for debt relief for poor countries. Pope John Paul II was openly concerned about "the growing distance between rich and poor, unfair competition which puts the poor nations in a situation of ever-increasing inferiority." "Liberation theology," particularly in Latin America, sought a Christian basis for action in the areas of social justice, poverty, and human rights, while viewing Jesus as liberator as well as savior. In Asia, a growing movement known as "socially engaged Buddhism" addressed the needs of the poor through social reform, educational programs, health services, and peacemaking action during times of conflict and war. The Dalai Lama has famously advocated a peaceful resolution of Tibet's troubled relationship with China. Growing interest in communication and exchange among the world's religions was expressed at a World Peace Summit in 2000, when more than 1,000 religious and spiritual leaders met to explore how they might more effectively confront the world's many conflicts. In short, religious responses to global modernity were articulated in many voices.

The World's Environment and the Globalization of Environmentalism

Even as world religions, fundamentalist and otherwise, challenged global modernity on cultural or spiritual grounds, burgeoning environmental movements in the 1960s and after did so with an eye to the human impact on the earth and its many living creatures, including ourselves. Among the distinctive features of the twentieth century, none has been more pronounced than humankind's growing ability to alter the natural order and the mounting awareness of this phenomenon. When the wars, revolutions, and empires of this most recent century have faded from memory, environmental transformation and environmental consciousness may well seem to future generations the decisive feature of that century.

The Global Environment Transformed

■ Change

How can we explain the dramatic increase in the human impact on the environment in the twentieth century?

Underlying the environmental changes of the twentieth century were three other factors that vastly magnified the human impact on earth's ecological systems far beyond anything previously known.[24] One was the explosion of human numbers, an unprecedented quadrupling of the world's population in a single century. Another lay in the amazing new ability of humankind to tap the energy potential of fossil fuels—coal in the nineteenth century and oil in the twentieth. Hydroelectricity, natural gas, and nuclear power added to the energy resources available to our species. These new sources of energy made possible a third contribution to environmental transformation—phenomenal economic growth—as modern science and technology immensely increased the production of goods and services. None of this occurred evenly across the planet. An average North American in the 1990s, for example, used 50 to 100 times more energy than an average Bangladeshi. But almost everywhere—in capitalist, communist, and developing countries alike—the idea of economic growth as something possible and desirable took hold as a part of global culture.

These three factors were the foundations for the immense environmental transformations of the twentieth century. Human activity had always altered the natural order, usually on a local basis, but now the scale of those disruptions assumed global

Snapshot   **World Population Growth, 1950–2005**[25]

The great bulk of the world's population growth in the second half of the twentieth century occurred in the developing countries of Asia, Africa, the Middle East, and Latin America.

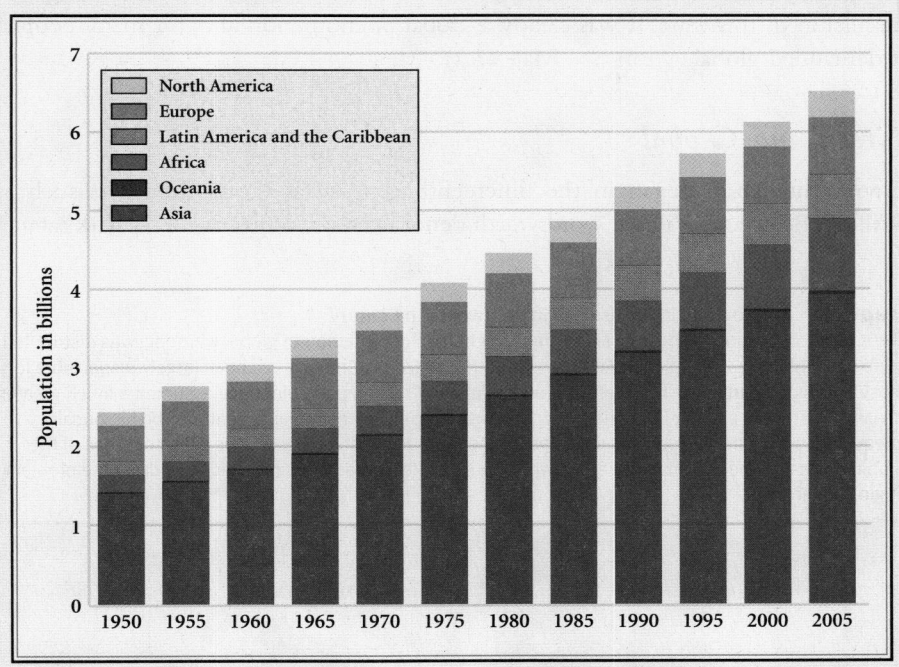

proportions. The growing numbers of the poor and the growing consumption of the rich led to the doubling of cropland and a corresponding contraction of the world's forests and grasslands. With diminished habitats, numerous species of plants and animals either disappeared or were threatened with extinction. The human remaking of the environment also greatly increased the population of cattle, pigs, chickens, rats, and dandelions.

The global spread of modern industry, which was heavily dependent on fossil fuels, created a pall of air pollution in many major cities. By the 1970s, traffic police in Tokyo frequently wore face masks. In Mexico City, officials estimated in 2002 that air pollution killed 35,000 people every year. Industrial pollution in the Soviet Union rendered about half of the country's rivers severely polluted by the late 1980s, while fully 20 percent of its population lived in regions defined as "ecological disasters." The release of chemicals known as chlorofluorocarbons thinned the ozone layer, which protects the earth from excessive ultraviolet radiation.

The most critical and intractable environmental transformation was global warming. By the end of the twentieth century, a worldwide scientific consensus had emerged that the vastly increased burning of fossil fuels, which emit heat-trapping greenhouse gases, as well as the loss of trees that would otherwise remove carbon dioxide from the air, had begun to warm the atmosphere significantly. Although considerable disagreement existed about the rate and likely consequences of this process, concern about melting glaciers and polar ice caps, rising sea levels, thawing permafrost, extreme hurricanes, further species extinctions, and other ecological threats punctuated global discussion of this issue. It was clearly a global phenomenon and, for many people, it demanded global action (see Map 24.5).

Green and Global

Environmentalism began in the nineteenth century as Romantic poets such as William Blake and William Wordsworth denounced the industrial era's "dark satanic

Map 24.5   Carbon Dioxide Emissions in the Twentieth Century
The source of carbon dioxide emissions, the chief human contribution to global warming, was distributed quite unevenly across the planet. Although the industrialized countries have been largely responsible for those emissions during the twentieth century, India and China in particular have assumed a much greater role in this process as their industrialization boomed in the early twenty-first century. The historically unequal distribution of those emissions has prompted much controversy between the countries of the Global North and the Global South about who should make the sacrifices required to address the problem of global warming.

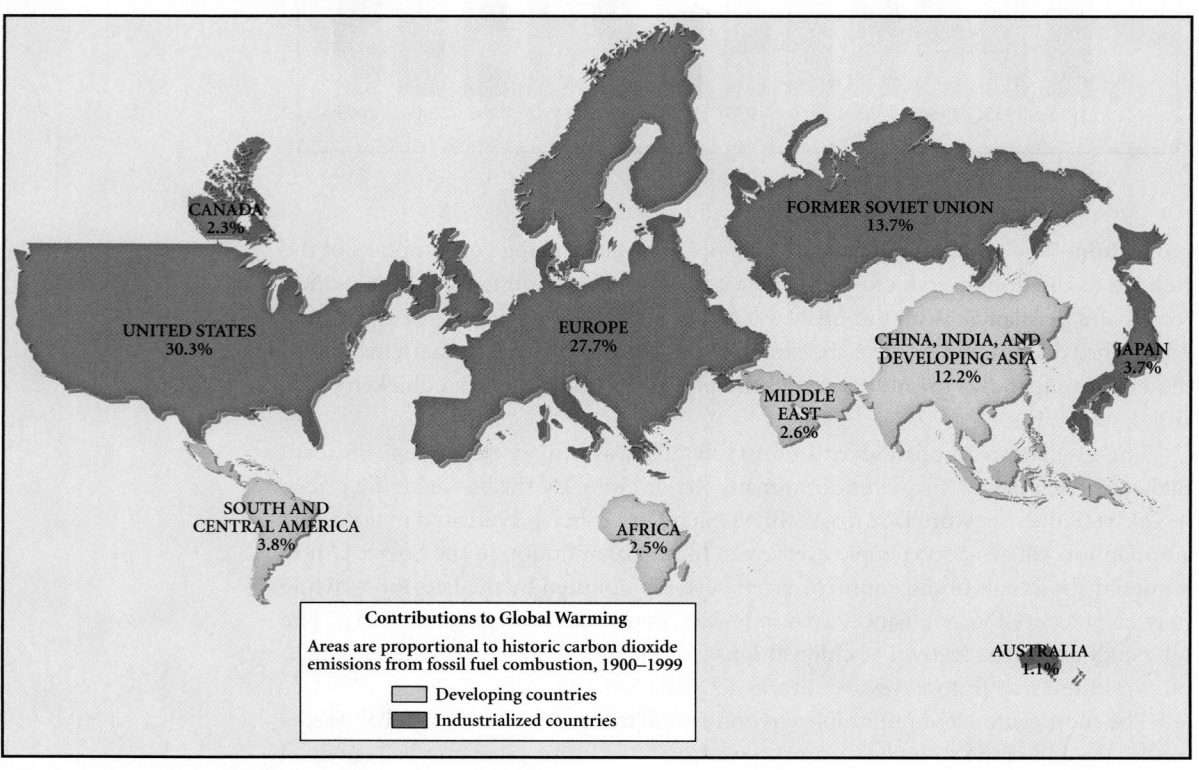

CANADA
2.3%

FORMER SOVIET UNION
13.7%

UNITED STATES
30.3%

EUROPE
27.7%

CHINA, INDIA, AND
DEVELOPING ASIA
12.2%

JAPAN
3.7%

MIDDLE
EAST
2.6%

SOUTH AND
CENTRAL AMERICA
3.8%

AFRICA
2.5%

AUSTRALIA
1.1%

Contributions to Global Warming

Areas are proportional to historic carbon dioxide
emissions from fossil fuel combustion, 1900–1999

☐ Developing countries
■ Industrialized countries

mills," which threatened the "green and pleasant land" of an earlier England. The "scientific management" of nature, both in industrializing countries and in European colonies, represented another element of emerging environmental awareness among a few. So did the "wilderness idea," which aimed to preserve untouched areas from human disruption,[26] as, for example, in the U.S. national parks. None of these strands of environmentalism attracted a mass following or provoked a global response. Not until the second half of the twentieth century, and then quite rapidly, did environmentalism achieve a worldwide dimension, although it was expressed in many quite different ways.

This second-wave environmentalism began in the West with the publication in 1962 of Rachel Carson's *Silent Spring*, an exposure of the chemical contamination of the environment that threatened both human health and the survival of many other species. She wrote of a "strange stillness" in a world where the songs of birds might no longer be heard. The book touched a nerve, generating an enormous response and effectively launching the environmental movement in the United States. Here, as virtually everywhere else, the impetus for action came from the grass roots and citizen protest. By the early 1990s, some 14 million Americans, one in seven adults, had joined one of the many environmental organizations—national or local—that aimed much of their effort at lobbying political parties and businesses. In Europe, the Club of Rome, a global think tank, issued a report in 1972 called *Limits to Growth*, which warned of resource exhaustion and the collapse of industrial society in the face of unrelenting economic growth. The German environmental movement was distinctive in that its activists directly entered the political arena as the Green Party, which came to have a substantial role in German national politics. One of the Greens' main concerns was opposition to nuclear energy. Beyond addressing environmental pollution, Western activists focused much attention on wilderness issues, opposing logging, road building, and other development efforts in remaining unspoiled areas.

■ **Comparison**

What differences emerged between environmentalism in the Global North and that in the Global South?

Quite quickly, during the 1970s and 1980s, environmentalism took root in the developing countries as well. There it often assumed a different character: it was more locally based and had fewer large national organizations than in the West; it involved poor people rather than affluent members of the middle class; it was less engaged in political lobbying and corporate strategies; it was more concerned with issues of food security, health, and basic survival than with the rights of nature or wilderness protection; and it was more closely connected to movements for social justice.[27] Thus, whereas Western environmentalists defended forests where few people lived, the Chikpo, or "tree-hugging," movement in India sought to protect the livelihood of farmers, artisans, and herders living in areas subject to extensive deforestation. A massive movement to prevent or limit the damming of India's Narmada River derived from the displacement of local people; similar anti-dam protests in the American Northwest were more concerned with protecting salmon runs.

Western environmentalists often called on individuals to change their values by turning away from materialism toward an appreciation of the intricate and fragile web of life that sustains us all. In the Philippines, by contrast, environmental activists

Environmentalism in Action These South Korean environmental activists are wearing death masks and holding crosses representing various countries during an anti-nuclear protest in Seoul in 1996, exactly ten years after a large-scale nuclear accident at Chernobyl in the Soviet Union. The lead protester holds a placard reading "Don't forget Chernobyl!" (AP Images/Yun Hai-Huoung)

confronting the operation of foreign mining companies have sought fundamental changes in the political and social structure of their country. There, environmental protest has overlapped with other movements seeking to challenge established power structures and social hierarchies. Coalitions of numerous local groups—representing various religious, women's, human rights, indigenous peoples', peasant, and political organizations—frequently mobilized large-scale grassroots movements against the companies rather than seeking to negotiate with them. These movements have not been entirely nonviolent; occasionally they have included guerrilla warfare actions by "green armies." Such mass mobilization contributed to the decision of the Australian-based Western Mining Corporation in 2000 to abandon its plans for developing a huge copper mine in Mindanao.

By the late twentieth century, environmentalism had become a matter of global concern. That awareness motivated legislation aimed at pollution control in many countries; it pushed many businesses in a "green" direction; it fostered research on alternative and renewable sources of energy; it stimulated UN conferences on global warming; it persuaded millions of people to alter their way of life; and it generated a number of international agreements addressing matters such as whaling, ozone depletion, and global warming.

The globalization of environmentalism also disclosed sharp conflicts, particularly between the Global North and South. Both activists and governments in the developing countries have often felt that Northern initiatives to address atmospheric pollution and global warming would curtail their industrial development, leaving the North/South gap intact. "The threat to the atmospheric commons has been building over centuries," argued Indian environmentalist Vandana Shiva, "mainly because of industrial activity in the North. Yet . . . the North refuses to assume extra responsibility for cleaning up the atmosphere. No wonder the Third World cries foul when it is asked to share the costs." A Malaysian official put the dispute succinctly: "The developed countries don't want to give up their extravagant lifestyles, but plan to curtail our development."[28] Western governments argued that newly industrializing countries such as China and India must also sharply curtail their growing emissions if further global warming is to be prevented. Such deep disagreements between industrialized and developing countries contributed to the failure of the United Nations Copenhagen climate conference in late 2009 to reach legally binding agreements to substantially reduce greenhouse gas emissions.

Beyond these and other conflicts, global environmentalism, more than any other widespread movement, came to symbolize "one-world" thinking, a focus on the common plight of humankind across the artificial boundaries of nation-states. It also marked a challenge to modernity itself, particularly its consuming commitment to endless growth. The ideas of sustainability and restraint, certainly not prominent in any list of modern values, entered global discourse and marked the beginnings of a new environmental ethic. This change in thinking was perhaps the most significant achievement of global environmentalism.

Final Reflections: Pondering the Uses of History

The end of a history book is an appropriate place to ask the fundamental question: just what is it good for, this field of study we call history? What, in short, are the uses of the past, and particularly of the global past?

At one level, philosophers, scholars, and thoughtful people everywhere have long used history to probe the significance of human experience. Does an examination of the past disclose any purpose, meaning, or pattern, or is it "just one damned thing after another"? Some sages, of course, have discerned divine purpose in the unfolding of the human story. To Saint Augustine, an early Christian thinker and writer, that purpose was the building of the "heavenly city," while events in this world were but steps in God's great plan. Chinese thinkers often viewed history as the source of moral lessons and related the behavior of rulers to the rise and fall of their dynasties. Europeans and others operating within the Enlightenment tradition have seen history in secular terms as a record of progress toward greater freedom or rationality in human affairs. Karl Marx viewed the past as a succession of economic changes and class struggles culminating in the creation of socialism, a secular utopia that would forever banish war, inequality, and social conflict.

Most contemporary historians are skeptical of such grand understandings of the human past, especially those that depend on some unseen hand directing the course of history to a defined end or those that reflect a particular set of values. But if "purpose" is hard to detect in the human story, some general "directions" over the long run are perhaps more evident.

One such trend lies in growing human numbers, which are linked to greater control over the natural environment as our ways of living moved from gathering and hunting, to agriculture, and most recently to industrial societies. Accompanying this broad direction in world history has been the growing complexity of human societies. Small hunting bands of a few dozen people gave way to agricultural villages of several thousands, to cities populated by tens or hundreds of thousands, to states and empires consisting of many millions. As the scale of human communities enlarged, so too did the pace of change in human affairs. In recent centuries, change has become both expected and valued in ways that would surely seem strange to most of the world's earlier inhabitants. A final possible direction in world history has been toward greater connection among the planet's diverse cultures and peoples. To early links among neighboring settlements or villages were later added networks of exchange and communication that operated among distant civilizations, across whole hemispheres, and after 1500 on a genuinely global level.

A word of caution, however, about finding direction in world history. None of this happened smoothly, evenly, or everywhere, and all of it was accompanied by numerous ups and downs, reversals, and variations. Furthermore, the notion of direction in history is quite different from that of progress. It is an observation rather than a judgment. One might consider growing populations, control over nature, increasing complexity, more rapid change, and global integration as great achievements and evidence of human "success." Alternatively, one might regard them as a burden or a curse, more of a disease than a triumph. We do well in studying the past to separate as much as possible our descriptions about what happened from our opinions about those events and processes.

In addition to discovering meaning or, even more modestly, direction in history, the uses of the past have long included efforts by political authorities to inculcate national, religious, civic, patriotic, or other values in their citizens. Furious debates in recent decades about history curricula in the schools of the United States, Japan, China, and elsewhere testify to the continuing impulse to use history in this way. In democratic societies, many people also express the hope that grounding in history will generate wiser public policies and more informed and effective participation by citizens. It is not always easy to find evidence for such outcomes of historical study, for the lessons of the past are many, varied, and conflicting, and the world, as always, hovers on the knife edge of possibility and disaster. Nonetheless, advocates for historical study continue to believe that probing the past enhances public life.

On a more personal level, many people have found in the study of history endless material for musing, for pondering those matters of the heart and spirit that all of us must confront as we make our way in the world. Consider, for example, the question of suffering. History is, among other things, a veritable catalog of the varieties of human suffering. It provides ample evidence, should we need it, that suffering is a common and bedrock human experience—and that none of us is exempt. But the study of history also highlights the indisputable fact that much of human suffering has come at our own hands in the shape of war, racism, patriarchy, exploitation, inequality, oppression, and neglect.

Is it possible that some exposure to the staggering sum of human suffering revealed in the historical record can soften our hearts, fostering compassion for our own suffering and that of others? In short, can the study of history generate kindness, both at the level of day-to-day personal interactions and at the wider level of acting to repair the brokenness of the world?

For those who choose to practice kindness or to seek justice in public life—overcoming global poverty, promoting equality between men and women, seeking understanding among religious traditions, encouraging environmental sustainability—history offers some encouragement. For one thing, it provides a record of those who have struggled long, hard, and on occasion with some success. Abolitionists contributed to the ending of slavery. Colonized peoples broke free of empire. Women secured the vote and confronted patriarchy. Socialists and communists challenged the inequities of capitalism, while popular protest brought repressive communist regimes to their knees in the Soviet Union and Eastern Europe. Brave people have spoken truth to power. In short, things changed, and sometimes people changed things.

There is yet another way in which history might assist our personal journeys through life. We are, most of us, inclined to be insular, to regard our own ways as the norm, to be fearful of difference. Nor is this tendency largely our own fault. We all have limited experience. Few of us have had much personal encounter with cultures beyond our own country, and none of us, of course, knows personally what life was like before our birth. But we do know that a rich and mature life involves opening up to a wider world. If we base our understanding of life only on what we personally experience, we are impoverished indeed.

In this task of opening up, history in general and world history in particular have much to offer. They provide a marvelous window into the unfamiliar. They confront us with the whole range of human achievement, tragedy, and sensibility. They give context and perspective to our own limited experience. They allow us some modest entry into the lives of people far removed from us in time and place. They offer us company for the journeys of our own lives. If we take it seriously, historical study can assist us in enlarging and enriching our sense of self. In helping us open up to the wider experience of "all under heaven," as the Chinese put it, history can assist us in becoming wiser and more mature people. What more might one ask from any field of study?

Second Thoughts

What's the Significance?

neo-liberalism

reglobalization

transnational corporations

North/South gap

antiglobalization

Prague Spring

Che Guevara

second-wave feminism

fundamentalism

Hindutva

Islamic renewal

Osama bin Laden/al-Qaeda

global warming

environmentalism

Big Picture Questions

1. To what extent did the processes discussed in this chapter (economic globalization, feminism, fundamentalism, environmentalism) represent something new in the twentieth century? In what respects did they have roots in the more distant past?
2. In what ways did the global North/South divide find expression in the twentieth and early twenty-first centuries?
3. What have been the benefits and drawbacks of globalization since 1945?
4. Do the years since 1914 confirm or undermine Enlightenment predictions about the future of humankind?
5. "The twentieth century marks the end of the era of Western dominance in world history." What evidence might support this statement? What evidence might contradict it?
6. To what extent do you think the various liberation movements of the twentieth and early twenty-first centuries — communism, nationalism, democracy, feminism, internationalism — have achieved their goals?
7. Based on material in Chapters 21, 22, and 24, how might you define the evolving roles of the United States in the twentieth and early twenty-first centuries?

For Further Study

Karen Armstrong, *The Battle for God* (2000). A comparison of Christian, Jewish, and Islamic fundamentalism in historical perspective.

Nayan Chanda, *Bound Together: How Traders, Preachers, Adventurers, and Warriors Shaped Globalization* (2007). An engaging, sometimes humorous, long-term view of the globalization process.

Jeffrey Frieden, *Global Capitalism: Its Fall and Rise in the Twentieth Century* (2006). A thorough, thoughtful, and balanced history of economic globalization.

Michael Hunt, *The World Transformed* (2004). A thoughtful global history of the second half of the twentieth century.

J. R. McNeill, *Something New under the Sun: An Environmental History of the Twentieth Century World* (2001). A much-acclaimed global account of the rapidly mounting human impact on the environment during the most recent century.

Bonnie Smith, ed., *Global Feminisms since 1945* (2000). A series of essays about feminist movements around the world.

"No Job for a Woman," http://www.iwm.org.uk/upload/package/30/women/index.htm. A Web site illustrating the impact of war on the lives of women in the twentieth century.

Documents

Considering the Evidence:
Contending for Islam

L ike all religious traditions, Islam has never been a single body of thought and practice. Various legal traditions, leadership issues, rituals, understandings of the Quran, attitudes toward human reason, and more have long divided the Islamic world. Other divisions arose as Muslims confronted the growing intrusion of Western imperialism and modern secular culture. Which ideas and influences flowing from the West could Muslims safely utilize and which should they decisively reject? In the twentieth century, and especially during its second half, the issue prompted acute and highly visible controversy among Muslims as they debated the meaning of Islam and its implications for social and political life (see pp. 1153–57). The documents that follow illustrate something of the sharp controversies and variations in the understanding of Islam during the past century.

Document 24.1

A Secular State for an Islamic Society in Turkey

Modern Turkey emerged from the ashes of the Ottoman Empire after World War I and adopted a distinctive path of modernization, Westernization, and secularism under the leadership of Mustafa Kemal Atatürk (see pp. 1103–05). Such policies sought to remove Islam from any significant role in public life and included abolition of the caliphate, by which Ottoman rulers had claimed leadership of the entire Islamic world. In a speech delivered in 1927, Atatürk explained and justified these policies, which went against the grain of much Islamic thinking.

■ On what grounds did Atatürk justify the abolition of the caliphate?

■ What additional actions did he take to remove Islam from a public or political role in the new Turkish state?

■ What can you infer about Atatürk's view of Islam?

■ How did Atatürk's conception of a Turkish state differ from that of Ottoman authorities? In what ways did he build upon Ottoman reforms of the nineteenth century? (See pp. 891–94 in Chapter 19.)

MUSTAFA KEMAL ATATÜRK
Speech to the General Congress of the Republican Party
1927

[Our Ottoman rulers] hoped to unite the entire Islamic world in one body, to lead it and to govern it. For this purpose, [they] assumed the title of Caliph.°... It is an unrealizable aim to attempt to unite in one tribe the various races existing on the earth, thereby abolishing all boundaries.... There is nothing in history to show how [such] a policy of Pan-Islamism could have succeeded....

If the Caliph and the Caliphate were to be invested with a dignity embracing the whole of Islam,... a crushing burden would be imposed on Turkey.... I gave the people to understand that neither Turkey nor the handful of men she possesses could be placed at the disposal of the Caliph so that he might fulfill the mission attributed to him, namely, to found a state comprising the whole of Islam....

[Furthermore], will Persia or Afghanistan, which are [Muslim] states, recognize the authority of the Caliph in a single matter? No, and this is quite justifiable, because it would be in contradiction to the independence of the state, to the sovereignty of the people.

[The current constitution] laid down as the first duty of the Grand National Assembly that "the prescriptions of the Shari'a° should be put into force...." [But] if a state, having among its subjects elements professing different religions and being compelled to act justly and impartially toward all of them..., it is obliged to respect freedom of opinion and conscience.... The Muslim religion includes freedom of religious opinion.... Will not every grownup person in the new Turkish state be free to select his own religion?... When the first favorable opportunity arises, the nation must act to eliminate these superfluities [the enforcement of sharia] from our Constitution....

Under the mask of respect for religious ideas and dogmas, the new Party [in opposition to Atatürk's reformist plans] addressed itself to the people in the following words: "We want the re-establishment of the Caliphate; we are satisfied with the religious law; we shall protect the Medressas,° the Tekkes,° the pious institutions, the Softahs,° the Sheikhs,° and their disciples.... The party of Mustapha Kemal, having abolished the Caliphate, is breaking Islam into ruins; they will make you into unbelievers... they will make you wear hats." Can anyone pretend that the style of propaganda used by the Party was not full of these reactionary appeals?...

Gentlemen, it was necessary to abolish the fez,° which sat on our heads as a sign of ignorance, of fanaticism, of hatred to progress and civilization, and to adopt in its place the hat, the customary headdress of the whole civilized world, thus showing that no difference existed in the manner of thought between the Turkish nation and the whole family of civilized mankind.... [Thus] there took place the closing of the Tekkes, of the convents, and of the mausoleums, as well as the abolition of all sects and all kinds of [religious] titles....

Could a civilized nation tolerate a mass of people who let themselves be led by the nose by a herd of Sheikhs, Dedes, Seids, Tschelebis, Babas, and Emirs°.... Would not one therewith have committed the greatest, most irreparable error to the cause of progress and awakening?

°**Caliph:** successor to the prophet Muhammad.

°**Shari'a:** Islamic law.

Source: *A Speech Delivered by Ghazi Mustapha Kemal, October 1927* (Leipzig: K. F. Koehler, 1929), 377–79, 591–93, 595–98, 717, 721–22.

°**Medressas:** Islamic schools.

°**Tekkes:** places for Sufi worship.

°**Softahs:** students in religious schools.

°**Sheikhs:** Sufi masters.

°**fez:** a distinctive Turkish hat with no brim.

°**Sheikhs...Emirs:** various religious titles.

Document 24.2

Egypt's Muslim Brotherhood

While Kemal Atatürk was building a secular state in a largely Muslim Turkey, an Egyptian organization known as the Muslim Brotherhood sought to move in precisely the opposite direction. Founded in 1928 by an impoverished school-teacher named Hassan al-Banna (1906–1949), the Muslim Brotherhood believed that Egypt's many problems—poverty, political factionalism, social unrest—derived from the neglect of Islamic principles that followed from British colonial rule and the penetration of Western values. The solution was a return to the original prescriptions of Islam. The Muslim Brotherhood quickly attracted a mass following, including many poor urban residents recently arrived from the countryside. In 1936, the organization spelled out the kind of reforms that it sought for Egypt.

■ How did the Muslim Brotherhood understand the proper role of government as well as the appropriate relationship of individuals and the state?

■ What problems in Egyptian society did the Muslim Brotherhood seek to correct?

■ How does this document understand the proper relationship of the sexes?

■ What aspects of Western and modern culture did the Muslim Brotherhood reject and which might it have embraced?

■ How might Atatürk (Document 24.1) have responded to the Muslim Brotherhood's vision of a good society?

HASSAN AL-BANNA

Toward the Light

1936

The following are chapter headings for a reform based upon the true spirit of Islam:

I. In the political, judicial, and administrative fields:
    1st. To prohibit political parties and to direct the forces of the nation toward the formation of a united front;

2nd. To reform the law in such a way that it will be entirely in accordance with Islamic legal practice;

3rd. To build up the army, to increase the number of youth groups; to instill in youth the spirit of holy struggle, faith, and self-sacrifice;

4th. To strengthen the ties among Islamic countries and more particularly among Arab countries which is a necessary step toward serious examination of the question of the defunct "Caliphate";

Source: Robert G. Landon, ed., *The Emergence of the Modern Middle East* (New York: Van Nostrand Reinhold, 1970), 261–64; translated, probably by the editor, from Hasan al-Banna, *Nahw al-Nur* (*Toward the Light*) (Cairo: 1936), 38–48.

5th. To propagate an Islamic spirit within the civil administration so that all officials will understand the need for applying the teachings of Islam;

6th. To supervise the personal conduct of officials because the private life and the administrative life of these officials forms an indivisible whole;...

9th. Government will act in conformity to the law and to Islamic principles; the carrying out of ceremonies, receptions, and official meetings, as well as the administration of prisons and hospitals should not be contrary to Islamic teachings. The scheduling of government services ought to take account of the hours set aside for prayer....

II. In the fields of social and everyday practical life:...

2nd. To find a solution for the problems of woman, a solution that will allow her to progress and which will protect her while conforming to Islamic principles....

3rd. To root out clandestine or public prostitution and to consider fornication as a reprehensible crime, the authors of which should be punished;

4th. To prohibit all games of chance (gaming, lotteries, races, golf);

5th. To stop the use of alcohol and intoxicants—these obliterate the painful consequences of people's evil deeds;

6th. To stop attacks on modesty, to educate women, to provide quality education for female teachers, school pupils, students, and doctors;

7th. To prepare instructional programs for girls; to develop an educational program for girls different than the one for boys;

8th. Male students should not be mixed with female students—any relationship between unmarried men and women is considered to be wrong until it is approved;...

10th. To close dance halls; to forbid dancing;

11th. To censor theater productions and films; to be severe in approving films;

12th. To supervise and to approve music;

13th. To approve programs, songs, and subjects before they are released, to use radio to encourage national education;

14th. To confiscate malicious articles and books as well as magazines displaying a grotesque character or spreading frivolity;...

16th. To change the hours when public cafés are opened or closed, to watch the activities of those who habituate them—to direct these people toward wholesome pursuits, to prevent people from spending too much time in these cafés;

17th. To use the cafés as centers to teach reading and writing to illiterates, to seek help in this task from primary school teachers and students;...

19th. To bring to trial those who break the laws of Islam, who do not fast, who do not pray, and who insult religion;...

21st. Religious teaching should constitute the essential subject matter to be taught in all educational establishments and faculties;

22nd. To memorize the Koran in state schools—this condition will be essential in order to obtain diplomas with a religious or philosophical specialty—in every school students should learn part of the Koran;...

24th. Interested support for teaching the Arabic language in all grades—absolute priority to be given to Arabic over foreign languages (primary teaching);

25th. To study the history of Islam, the nation, and Muslim civilization;

26th. To study the best way to allow people to dress progressively and in an identical manner;

27th. To combat foreign customs (in the realm of vocabulary, customs, dress, nursing) and to Egyptianize all of these (one finds these customs among the well-to-do members of society);

28th. To orient journalism toward wholesome things, to encourage writers and authors who should study specifically Muslim and Oriental subjects;

29th. To safeguard public health through every kind of publicity—increasing the number of hospitals, doctors, and out-patient clinics;

30th. To call particular attention to the problems of village life (administration, hygiene, water supply, education, recreation, morality).

III. The economic field:

1st. Organization of the "zakat tax" according to Islamic precepts, using zakat proceeds for welfare projects such as aiding the indigent, the poor, orphans; the zakat should also be used to strengthen the army;

2nd. To prevent the practice of usury, to direct banks to implement this policy; the government should provide an example by giving up the "interest" fixed by banks for servicing a personal loan or an industrial loan, etc.;

3rd. To facilitate and to increase the number of economic enterprises and to employ the jobless there, to employ for the nation's benefit the skills possessed by the foreigners in these enterprises;

4th. To protect workers against monopoly companies, to require these companies to obey the law, the public should share in all profits;

5th. Aid for low-ranking employees and enlargement of their pay, lowering the income of high-ranking employees;...

7th. To encourage agricultural and industrial works, to improve the situation of the peasants and industrial workers;

8th. To give special attention to the technical and social needs of the workers, to raise their level of life and aid their class;

9th. Exploitation of certain natural resources (unworked land, neglected mines, etc.).

Document 24.3

The Ideas of the Ayatollah Khomeini

While the Muslim Brotherhood was never able to seize control of the state in Egypt, an Islamic Revolution in Iran brought to power in 1979 a government committed to the thorough Islamization of public life (see the map on p. 1154, and see pp. 1105–08). That revolution had been inspired and led by the Ayatollah Khomeini (1902–1989), an Iranian religious scholar, who became the rallying point for those opposed to the regime of the Shah of Iran, which was strongly backed by the United States. Document 24.3 provides the flavor of Khomeini's thinking. As the Supreme Leader of Iran during the 1980s, he was in a position to put many of those ideas into practice.

■ How does Khomeini define the enemies of Islam?

■ How would you summarize his case against European imperialism and the Shah's government?

■ In what ways does Khomeini seek to apply Islamic principles in the public life of Iran? What is his view of Iranian popular culture? How do his prescriptions for an Islamic society compare with those of Hassan al-Banna in Document 24.2?

- What kind of government does Khomeini foresee for Iran? Why does he believe that a proper Islamic government "cannot be totalitarian or despotic but is constitutional and democratic"?

- To whom might Khomeini's views be most appealing?

AYATOLLAH KHOMEINI

Sayings of the Ayatollah Khomeini
1980

Islam is a religion of those who struggle for truth and justice, of those who clamor for liberty and independence. It is the school of those who fight against colonialism.

Islamic faith and justice demand that within the Muslim world, anti-Islamic governments not be allowed to survive.... Any nonreligious power, whatever form or shape it may take, is necessarily an atheistic power, the tool of Satan; ... [W]e have no recourse other than to overthrow all governments that do not rest on pure Islamic principles.... That is not only our duty in Iran, but it is also the duty of all Muslims in the world, in all Muslim countries, to carry the Islamic political revolution to its final victory....

The homeland of Islam, one and indivisible, was broken up by the doings of the Imperialists and despotic and ambitious leaders.... And when the Ottoman Empire struggled to achieve Islamic unity, it was opposed by a united front of Russian, English, Austrian, and other imperialist powers, which split it up among themselves.

Western missionaries, carrying out secret plans drawn up centuries ago, have created religious schools of their own within Muslim countries.... These missionaries infiltrated our villages and our countrysides, to turn our children into Christians or atheists!

The Islamic movement met its first saboteur in the Jewish people, who are at the source of all the anti-Islamic libels and intrigues current today. Then came the turn of those even more damnable repre-

sentatives of Satan, the imperialists. Within the last three centuries or more, they have invaded every Muslim country, with the intention of destroying Islam.

Their plan is to keep us in our backward state, to preserve our backward state, to preserve our pathetic way of life, so they can exploit the tremendous wealth of our underground resources, of our land, and our manpower. They want us to stay destitute, distracted by niggling day-to-day problems of survival, our poor living in misery, so that we will never become aware of the laws of Islam—which contain the solution to misery and poverty! All of this they have done so they can sit in their big palaces, living their stupid shallow lives!

Many of these corruptions have their origin in the gang that is in power, and in the family of a despotic and capricious ruler [the Shah of Iran]. These are the rulers who create hotbeds of lust, prostitution, and drugs, who devote the revenues of the mosque to building cinemas!

What do you understand of the harmony between social life and religious principles? And more important, just what is the social life we are talking about? Is it those hotbeds of immorality called theaters, cinemas, dancing, and music? Is it the promiscuous presence in the streets of lusting young men and women with arms, chests, and thighs bared? Is it the ludicrous wearing of a hat like the Europeans or the imitation of their habit of wine drinking? We are convinced that you have been made to lose your ability to distinguish between good and evil, in exchange for a few radio sets and ludicrous Western hats. Your attention has been attracted to the disrobed women to be seen on thoroughfares and in swim-

Source: *Sayings of the Ayatollah Khomeini* (New York: Bantam Books, 1980), 3–4, 7–12, 15–17, 29–30, 35–36.

ming pools. Let these shameful practices come to an end, so that the dawn of a new life may break!

We [clergy] forcefully affirm that refusal to wear the veil is against the law of Allah and the Prophet, and a material and moral affront to the entire country. We affirm that the ludicrous use of the Western hat stands in the way of our independence and is contrary to the will of Allah. We affirm that coeducational schools are an obstacle to a wholesome life; they are a material and moral affront to the country and contrary to the divine will. We affirm that music engenders immorality, lust, and licentiousness, and stifles courage, valor, and the chivalrous spirit; it is forbidden by Qur'anic law and must not be taught in the schools. Radio Tehran, by broadcasting Western, Oriental, and Iranian music, plays a nefarious role by introducing immorality and licentiousness into respectable families.

An Islamic government cannot be totalitarian or despotic, but is constitutional and democratic. In this democracy, however, the laws are not made by the will of the people, but only by the Qur'an and the Sunnah° of the Prophet. The constitution, the civil code, and the criminal code should be inspired only by Islamic laws contained in the Qur'an and transcribed by the Prophet. Islamic government is the government of divine right, and its laws cannot be changed, modified, or contested....

It is often proclaimed that religion must be separated from politics, and that the ecclesiastical world should keep out of affairs of state. It is proclaimed that high Muslim clerical authorities have no business mixing into the social and political decisions of the government. Such proclamations can come only from atheists; they are dictated and spread by imperialists....Think of it—a political clergy! Well, why not? The Prophet was a politician!...

Islam has precepts for everything that concerns man and society....There is no subject upon which Islam has not expressed judgment.

The Islamic republic is a government according to the Law and the wise men and theological experts of the clergy are therefore responsible for it. It is they who must watch over all aspects of administration and planning. In administering the laws of God in such matters as taxes and property for example, they must be trusted....If the punitive laws of Islam were applied for only one year, all the devastating injustices and immoralities would be uprooted. Misdeeds must be punished by the law of retaliation: cut off the hands of the thief; kill the murderer instead of putting him in prison; flog the adulterous woman or man....

We have a duty to create an Islamic republic and to that end our first obligation is the creation of a system of propaganda....Radio and television are allowed if they are used for the broadcasting of news or sermons, for the spreading of good educational material for publicizing the products and curiosities of the planet; but they must prohibit singing, music, anti-Islamic laws, the lauding of tyrants, mendacious words, and broadcasts which spread doubt and undermine virtue.

°**Sunnah:** traditions.

Document 24.4

A Liberal Viewpoint from an Islamic Woman

Islamic renewal movements such as the Muslim Brotherhood and Islamic governments in Iran and even more radically in Taliban-governed Afghanistan have sought to impose sharp restrictions on the public activities and private behavior of women as well as maintaining their seclusion from and subordination to men. For them, this was a crucial element of an effort to bring society into alignment with Islamic law. Yet this element of Islamic thought and practice has been sharply contested. While Iran was implementing a largely male-dominated Islamic society during the last two decades of the twentieth century, the Muslim country of Pakistan twice selected the same woman, Benazir Bhutto, as prime minister. Both times she was removed from power on charges of corruption and spent many years in exile. During her third attempt to achieve the political leadership of Pakistan in 2007, she was assassinated. In 1985, Bhutto gave an address at Radcliffe College in the United States in which she laid out an argument for women's equality within an Islamic context.

- On what basis does Bhutto argue that "Islam provides justice and equality for women"?

- How does she account for the manifest inequality of women in so many Muslim societies?

- How do you think Kemal Atatürk, Hasan al-Banna, and the Ayatollah Khomeini might respond to her ideas?

Benazir Bhutto
Politics and the Muslim Woman
1985

I think one of the first things that we must appreciate about the religion of Islam is that there is no one interpretation to it....

I would describe Islam in two main categories: reactionary Islam and progressive Islam. We can have a reactionary interpretation of Islam which tries to uphold the status quo, or we can have a progressive interpretation of Islam which tries to move with a changing world, which believes in human dignity, which believes in consensus, and which believes in giving women their due right....

I believe that Islam within it provides justice and equality for women, and I think that those aspects of Islam which have been highlighted by the *mullas* [religious scholars] do not do a service to our religion.... Christianity has a clergy. Islam does not have a clergy. The relationship between a Muslim and God is direct. There is no need for somebody to intervene. The *mullas* try to intervene. The *mullas*

give their own interpretation. But I think there are growing movements, as more and more people in Muslim countries, both men and women, achieve education and begin to examine the Qur'an in the light of their education, they are beginning not to agree with the *mullas* on their orthodox or reactionary version of Islam.

Let us start with the story of the Fall. Unlike Christianity, it is not Eve who tempts Adam into tasting the apple and being responsible for original sin. According to Islam—and I mention this because I believe that Islam is an egalitarian religion—both Adam and Eve are tempted, both are warned, both do not heed the warning, and therefore the Fall occurs.

As far as opportunity is concerned, in Islam there is equal opportunity for both men and women. I refer to the Sura *Ya Sin* [Sura 36, Verses 34–35], which says: "We produce orchids and date gardens and vines, and we cause springs to gush forth, that they may enjoy the fruits of it." God does not give fruits, orchids, or the fruit of the soil just for men to enjoy or men to plow; he gives it for both men and women. What, in terms of income and opportunity, is avail-

Source: Benazir Bhutto, "Politics and the Muslim Woman," transcript of audio recording, April 11, 1985, in Charles Kurzman, ed., *Liberal Islam: A Sourcebook* (New York: Oxford University Press, 1998), 107–11.

able, is available to both man and woman. Sura *an-Nisa* [Sura 4, Verse 32]: "To men is allotted what they earn, and to women to what they earn."...

The references [in the Quran] are to men and women. The references are not to men as being characteristic of certain qualities and separate qualities for women. It is not a reference to the male sex as being endowed with some superior attributes and to the woman as being endowed with inferior attributes. The attributes are the same. Both are the creatures of God. Both have certain rights. Both have certain duties. Both have certain obligations. If they want to go to Heaven, thay have to behave in a special manner. If they want to do good in this earth, they have to give alms to the needy, they have to help orphans—the behavior is applicable to both men and women. It is not religion which makes the difference. The difference comes from man-made law. It comes from the fact that soon after the Prophet died, it was not the Islam of the Prophet that remained. What took place was the emergence or the reassertiveness of the partiarchal society, and religion was taken over to justify the norms of the tribal society, rather than the point that the Prophet had made in replacing the tribal society with a religion that aimed to cut across narrow loyalties and sought to create a new community, or *umma*, on the basis of Islam and the message of God.

[About] the right of divorce and polygamy. It is often said that Islam provides for four wives for a man. But in my interpretation of this, and in the interpretation of many other Muslims, that is simply not true.

What the Qur'an does say, and I quote: "Marry as many women as you wish, wives two or three or four. If you fear not to treat them equally, marry only one. [...] I doubt you will be able to be just between your wives, even if you try" [Sura 4, Verses 3 and 129]. So if God Himself and His message says that He doubts that you can be equal, I don't know how any man can turn around and say that "God has given me this right to get married more than once."

I would like to say that within Islamic history there are very strong roles for women. For instance, the Prophet's wife, Bibi Khadija, was a woman of independent means. She had her own business, she traded, she dealt with society at large, she employed the Prophet Muhammad, peace be upon him, when he was a young boy, and subsequently, Bibi Khadija herself sent a proposal [of marriage] to the Prophet. So she is the very image of somebody who is independent, assertive, and does not conform to the passive description of women in Muslim societies that we have grown accustomed to hearing about....

[T]here is Bibi 'A'isha [wife of the Prophet, circa 614–678], who is also put forward as a politically astute woman, who, after the death of the Prophet, was responsible for many of the Traditions that have been handed down to us, who was the one who proposed the caliphate of Hazrat 'Uthman, and held out the shirt of the Prophet Muhammad, and said that, "Even before this shirt has decayed, you have to ordain someone like Hazrat 'Uthman." She made her views known. She was an extremely bold person. Not only did she make her views known; when she opposed something, she went to the battlefield and fought against it.

So when we have such powerful role models of women...then one must ask, why is it that today in Muslim countries, one does not see that much of women? One does not hear that much of women. Why is it that women are secluded? Why is it that women are subject to social control? Why is it that women are not given their due share of property?... It has got nothing to do with the religion, but it has got very much to do with material or man-made considerations....

Before I conclude on this aspect of the powerful role within Islam of women, I would like to quote from the Qur'an, the Sura "The Ant" [Sura 27, Verse 23]: "I found a woman ruling over them, and she has been given abundance of all things, and hers is a mighty throne." It is not Islam which is averse to women rulers, I think—it is men.

Document 24.5

Islam and 9/11

In the early twenty-first century, the international face of an assertive Islamic fundamentalism was that of Osama bin Laden, whose al-Qaeda organization launched the attacks on the United States on September 11, 2001, and called for the overthrow of compromised governments in Saudi Arabia and elsewhere in the Islamic world (see pp. 1156–57). Substantial numbers of Muslims no doubt shared bin Laden's outrage at the sorry state of many Muslim societies as well as his opposition to heavy U.S. backing for the state of Israel and to American military interventions in Iraq and Afghanistan. Addressing fellow Muslims, bin Laden lashed out against those who interacted with American economic interests: "The money you pay to buy American goods will be transformed into bullets and used against our brothers in Palestine."

But bin Laden and his followers were certainly not the only voices laying claim to Islam in the aftermath of 9/11. All across the Islamic world, others argued that Muslims could retain their distinctive religious sensibility while embracing democracy, women's rights, technological progress, freedom of thought, and religious pluralism. Just a month after the 9/11 attacks, the well-known Malaysian intellectual and political figure Anwar Ibrahim pondered the meaning of those attacks: "One wonders how, in the twenty-first century, the Muslim world could have produced an Osama bin Laden. In the centuries when Islam forged civilizations, men of wealth created pious foundations supporting universities and hospitals, and princes competed with one another to patronize scientists, philosophers, and men of letters."[29] Muslims like Anwar Ibrahim were following in the tradition of nineteenth-century Islamic modernism (see pp. 891–94), even as they recalled earlier centuries of Islamic intellectual and scienific achievement and religious tolerance. That viewpoint was expressed in a pamphlet composed by a leading American Muslim scholar, translator, and Sufi teacher, Sheikh Kabir Helminski, in 2009.

■ Against what charges does Sheikh Kabir seek to defend Islam? How does this document reflect the experience of 9/11?

■ In what ways are Sheikh Kabir's views critical of radical or "fundamentalist" ideas and practices?

■ How does this document, together with Document 24.4, articulate the major features of a more progressive or liberal Islam? What kinds of arguments are employed to make their case?

■ To whom might these arguments appeal? What obstacles do they face in being heard within the Islamic world?

■ How might the Muslim Brotherhood (Document 24.2), Ayatollah Khomeini (Document 24.3), or Osama bin Laden respond to the arguments in this document? In what ways does this vision of a "liberal" or "moderate" Islam differ from those of Kemal Atatürk (Document 24.1)?

KABIR HELMINSKI
"Islam and Human Values"
2009

If the word "Islam" gives rise to fear or mistrust today, it is urgent that American Muslims clarify what we believe Islam stands for in order to dispel the idea that there is a fundamental conflict between the best values of Western civilization and the essential values of Islam....

Islamic civilization, which developed out of the revelation of the Qur'an in the seventh century, affirms the truth of previous revelations, affirms religious pluralism, cultural diversity, and human rights, and recognizes the value of reason and individual conscience....

[One issue] is the problem of violence.... Thousands of Muslim institutions and leaders, the great majority of the world's billion or more Muslims, have unequivocally condemned the hateful and violent ideologies that kill innocents and violate the dignity of all humanity....

Islamic civilizations have a long history of encouraging religious tolerance and guaranteeing the rights of religious minorities. The reason for this is that the Qur'an explicitly acknowledges that the diversity of religions is part of the Divine Plan and no religion has a monopoly on truth or virtue....

Jerusalem, under almost continuous Islamic rule for nearly fourteen centuries, has been a place where Christians and Jews have lived side by side with Muslims, their holy sites and religious freedom preserved. Medieval Spain also created a high level of civilization as a multi-cultural society under Islamic rule for several centuries. The Ottoman Empire, the longest lived in history, for the more than six centuries of its existence encouraged ethnic and religious minorities to participate in and contribute to society. It was the Ottoman sultan who gave sanctuary to the Jews expelled from Catholic Spain. India was governed for centuries by Muslims, even while the majority of its people practiced Hinduism....

[T]he acceptance of Islam must be an act of free will. Conversion by any kind of coercion was universally condemned by Islamic scholars....

There are many verses in the Qur'an that affirm the actuality and even the necessity of diversity in ways of life and religious belief: [For example] *O mankind, truly We [God] have created you male and female, and have made you nations and tribes that ye may know one another.* [Surah 49:13]....

In general, war is forbidden in Islam, except in cases of self-defense in response to explicit aggression. If there is a situation where injustice is being perpetrated or if the community is being invaded, then on a temporary basis permission is given to defend oneself. This principle is explained in the following verses: *And fight in God's cause against those who war against you, but do not commit aggression—for, verily, God does not love aggressors.* [Surah 2:190]

The general principle established throughout the Qur'an is that the relationship between Muslims and non-Muslims should be based on peace and fairness. So that there is no ambiguity, it clearly and unequivocally states: *Allah does not forbid you from dealing kindly and justly with those who do not fight you for (your) Faith nor drive you out of your homes: for Allah loves those who are just.* [Surah 60:8]

Source: Selections from Kabir Helminski, "Islam and Human Values," unpublished pamphlet, 2009.

[I]n recent decades...an intolerant ideology has been unleashed. A small minority of the world's one and a half billion Muslims has misconstrued the teachings of Islam to justify their misguided and immoral actions. It is most critical at this time for Muslims to condemn such extreme ideologies and their manifestations. It is equally important that non-Muslims understand that this ideology violates the fundamental moral principles of Islam and is repugnant to the vast majority of Muslims in the world.... So-called "suicide-bombers" did not appear until the mid-1990s. Such strategies have no precedent in Islamic history. The Qur'an says quite explicitly: *Do not kill yourselves*. [4:29]...

Muslims living in pluralistic societies have no religious reasons to oppose the laws of their own societies as long as they are just, but rather are encouraged to uphold the duly constituted laws of their own societies.... Islam and democracy are compatible and can coexist because Islam organizes humanity on the basis of the rule of law and human dignity.

The first four successors to the Prophet Muhammad were chosen by the community through consultation, i.e., a representative democracy. The only principle of political governance expressed in the Qur'an is the principle of Consultation (Shura), which holds that communities will "*rule themselves by means of mutual consultation*." [Surah 42:38]

Following the principles of the Qur'an, Muslims are encouraged to cooperate for the well-being of all. The Qur'an emphasizes three qualities above all others: peace, compassion, and mercy. The standard greeting in Islam is "As-Salam alaykum (Peace be with you)."

An American Muslim scholar, Abdul Aziz Sachedina, expresses it this way: "Islam does not encourage turning God into a political statement since humans cannot possess God. They can simply relate themselves to God by emulating God's compassion and forgiveness."...

[T]here is nothing in the Qur'an that essentially contradicts reason or science.... Repeatedly the Qur'an urges human beings to "reflect" and "use their intelligence."

Islam is not an alien religion. It does not claim a monopoly on virtue or truth. It follows in the way of previous spiritual traditions that recognized One Spirit operating within nature and human life. It continues on the Way of the great Prophets and Messengers of all sacred traditions.

Using the Evidence:
Voices of Islam

1. **Understanding the uses of history:** How does each of these authors use history to make his or her arguments? To what different historical contexts do they appeal?

2. **Identifying "fundamentalist" themes:** What common emphases do you see in the two more "fundamentalist" authors represented here in Documents 24.2 and 24.3? To what extent do they reflect or diverge from themes articulated in the mid-eighteenth century by Abd al Wahhab (Document 16.4, pp. 756–57)?

3. **Comparing Islamic modernists:** How do you think Kemal Atatürk would respond to later Islamic modernists such as Benazir Bhutto and Sheikh Kabir?

4. **Imagining an Islamic conversation:** Construct a dialog between the Islamic fundamentalists and the Islamic moderates. Can you identify any points of contact or similarity on which they might be able to agree? On which points would they probably never agree?

5. **Considering religion and politics:** How does each of these documents understand the relationship of religion and political life? How do they view the division between the public and private spheres of life?

Visual Sources

Considering the Evidence: Experiencing Globalization

A lthough a few people in the world of the early twenty-first century may remain untouched by globalization, surely they are not many. For most of humankind, the pervasive processes of interaction among distant peoples has shaped the clothing we wear, the foods we eat, the products we consume, the ways we work, the music we listen to, the religions we practice, and the identities we assume. Globalization has bound the various peoples of the planet more tightly together and in some respects has made us more alike. Almost all of us, for example, live in nation-states and seek the wealth and prosperity that modern science and technology promise. And yet in other ways we are very different, divided, and conflicted. The enormous gap in wealth between the rich countries of the Global North and the poor nations of the Global South represents a sharp and quite recent rift in the human community. The visual sources that follow illustrate just a few of the ways in which the world's peoples have experienced globalization in recent decades and have responded to it.

Among the common experiences of globalization for some people living in Asia, Africa, or Latin America has been that of working in foreign-owned production facilities. Companies in wealthier countries have often found it advantageous to build such facilities in places where labor is less expensive or environmental regulations are less strict. China, Vietnam, Indonesia, Bangladesh, the Philippines, Mexico, Brazil, and various African states are among the countries that have hosted foreign-owned manufacturing operations. The worst of them—in terms of child labor, low pay, few benefits, and dangerous working conditions—have been called "sweatshops." Such abuses have generated an international movement challenging those conditions. Visual Source 24.1 illustrates an interesting twist on this common feature of a globalized world economy—a Chinese-owned company producing Western-style blue jeans in Lesotho, a small country in southern Africa.

■ Why might China, itself the site of many foreign-owned factories, place such a factory in Africa? What does this suggest about the changing position of China in the world economy? What is the significance of the blue jeans for an understanding of contemporary globalization?

■ Does this photograph conform to your image of a sweatshop? Why or why not?

Visual Source 24.1 Globalization and Work (brianafrica/Alamy)

■ Why might many developing countries accept foreign-owned production facilities, despite the criticisms of the working conditions in them?

■ Why do you think most of the workers in this photo are women? How might you imagine their motivations for seeking this kind of work? Keep in mind that the unemployment rate in Lesotho in the early twenty-first century was 45 percent.

■ What differences can you observe between the workers in this ass[embly] factory and those in the Indian call center shown on page 11[?] similarities might you identify?

If globalization offered employment opportunities—albeit conditions—to some people in the developing countries worldwide culture of consumerism. That culture placed material goods, many of them of western origin, above attainment or social responsibility. Nowhere has this been more prominent than in China, where the fading the country's massive economic growth, and its new op world combined to generate an unabashed materialism in and early twenty-first centuries. A popular slogan suggested th

China required the "eight bigs": color TV, refrigerator, stereo, camera, motorcycle, a suite of furniture, washing machine, and an electric fan. Visual Source 24.2 illustrates this culture of consumerism as well as one of the "eight bigs" in a poster from the post-Mao era. The photograph on page 1053 in Chapter 22 provides further illustration of Chinese consumerism, as does Visual Source 22.5 on page 1078.

- In what ways might these images be used to illustrate Westernization, modernization, globalization, and consumerism?

- How might the young people on the motorcycle and those in the KFC restaurant understand their own behavior? Do you think they are conscious of behaving in Western ways or have these ways become Chinese? What is the significance of a Chinese couple riding a Suzuki motorcycle, a Japanese product probably manufactured in China under a license agreement?

- Beyond consumerism, how does this poster reflect changes in relationships between men and women in China after Mao? Is this yet another face of globalization or does it remain a distinctly Western phenomenon?

- How might these images be read as a celebration of Chinese success? How might they be used to criticize contemporary Chinese society?

Beyond changes in the working lives and consumption habits of individuals, globalization in the second half of the twentieth century reversed earlier patterns of global migration. In the nineteenth century, Europeans had moved in huge numbers to the Americas, Australia, New Zealand, and South Africa. That flow largely stopped by the 1920s, replaced by a massive movement of people from the so-called third world to the West. Pakistanis, Indians, and West Indians moved to Great Britain; Algerians and West Africans to France; Filipinos, Koreans, Mexicans, and Haitians to the United States. These new patterns of migration disrupted the lives of many, both in their countries of origin and in their new homelands. A poem by a young Moroccan wife whose husband left for work in Europe during the 1970s reflects the pain of separation:

> With you he stays one year, with me just one month,
> to you he gives his health and sweat,
> to me he only comes to recuperate.
> Then he leaves again to work for you, to beautify
> you as a bride, each day anew.
> And I, I wait; I am like a flower that
> withers, more each day....
> ask you: give him back to me.[30]

人勤春早

Visual Source 24.2 Globalization and Consumerism (Coll. SL [Stefa

Visual Source 24.3 Globalization and Migration (Owen Franken/Corbis)

North African migrants to France, almost all of them Muslims, have injected new controversies in their adopted country. One of them has been the issue of girls wearing headscarves in school. A French law passed in 2004 forbade the practice on the grounds that it compromised the secularism of French education and represented the repression of women. But many Muslim women strongly objected to that law, arguing that it undermined their freedom of religion and violated their cultural traditions. Visual Source 24.3 captures one such protest. The first line of the large banner in the front reads: "The veil is a choice," but the second line is more ambiguous, for "frace" is not a word in the French language. Does it contain a misspelling of "France" with the letter "n" omitted? If so, it could be translated as "France is my right." Or is it a pun on "face" or "race," both of which are French words that carry the same meaning as their English equivalents? If so, perhaps it implies that the protesters have a right to their facial appearance or to culture of their racial or ethnic group. Or does it contain a deliberate le or triple meaning?

- How might different readings of "la frace" convey different meanings of the poster? On what principles do you think this protest is based? Do they derive from France or from the world of Islam?

- The smaller sign behind the banner says, "The ignorance of people is the door that undermines our freedom." How might you understand this statement?

- In what respect do these young women seem to be "French" or "European" and in what ways are they Muslim and North African?

- What groups of people might find the demands of these protesters unacceptable? How might such critics have responded to the protesters?

- What outcomes and tensions of globalization does this image reflect?

During the last several decades of the twentieth century, the process of economic globalization spawned various movements of resistance and criticism (see pp. 1141–42). In dozens of developing countries, protesters demonstrated or rioted against government policies that removed subsidies, raised prices on essential products, froze salaries, or cut back on social services. Because such policies were often required by the World Bank or the International Monetary Fund as a condition for receiving much-needed loans, protesters often directed their anger at these international financial institutions. In the wealthier countries of the world as well, activists have mounted large-scale protests against what they see as the abuses of unregulated corporate power operating in the world economy. Visual Source 24.4 shows a display of this anger that occurred during the protests in Seattle that coincided with the 1999 gathering of the World Trade Organization in that city.

- How does this image reflect the concerns of globalization's many critics? What political message does it convey? Do you think it expresses more clearly the political agenda of the Global North or the Global South?

Visual Source 24.4 Globalization and Protest (Michael McGuerty)

Visual Source 24.5 Globalization: One World or Many? (NASA/GSFC Digital Archive)

■ Why have these criticisms come to focus so heavily on the activities of the World Trade Organization?

■ To what groups of people might such images be most compelling? How might advocates of corporate globalization respond to these protesters?

Visual Source 24.5, a composite satellite photograph of the world at night taken in late 2000, reflects three aspects of the globalization process. The first is the growing consciousness of the earth as a single place, the common home of humankind. Such thinking has been fostered by and expressed in those many remarkable images of the earth taken from space or from the moon (see the photo on p. 1132). In such photographs no artificial boundaries of state or nation are visible; just a single solitary planet cast against the immeasurable vastness of space. Second, this photograph shows the globalization of electricity, a central feature of modern life, which has taken place since the late nineteenth century. Finally, this image discloses sharp variations in modern development across the planet as the twenty-first century dawned.

■ To what extent has your thinking about the earth and its inhabitants been shaped by images such as this?

- Based on the electrification evident in this photo, what does this image show about the economic divisions of the world in the early twenty-first century?

- Does this image support or contradict Map 24.2, page 1140? What features of this image do you find surprising?

Using the Evidence:
Experiencing Globalization

1. **Defining differences:** Based on these visual sources and the text of Chapter 24, in what different ways have various groups of people experienced globalization since the end of World War II?

2. **Noticing change:** Based on these visual sources and those in the text of Chapter 24 as well, in what respects does contemporary globalization differ from that of earlier times? What continuities might you observe? Consider in particular the question of who is influencing who. Does recent globalization represent largely the impact of the West on the rest of the world or is it more of a two-way street?

3. **Making assessments:** Opinions about contemporary globalization depend heavily on the position of observers—their class, gender, or national locations. How might you illustrate this statement from the visual sources in this chapter?

4. **Seeking further evidence:** What additional visual sources might add to this effort to illustrate visually the various dimensions of globalization? What visual sources do you think might be added to it fifty or a hundred years from now?

Notes

Prologue

1. Adapted from Carl Sagan, *The Dragons of Eden* (New York: Random House, 1977), 13–17.
2. See David Christian, *Maps of Time* (Berkeley: University of California Press, 2004).
3. Voltaire, *Treatise on Toleration*, chap. 22.
4. See David Christian, "World History in Context," *Journal of World History* 14, no. 4 (December 2003), 437–58.

Part One

Chapter 1

1. Richard Rainsford, "What Chance, the Survival Prospects of East Africa's Last Hunting and Gathering Tribe," 1997, http://www.ntz.info/gen/n00757.html.
2. What follows comes from Sally McBreatry and Alison S. Brooks, "The Revolution That Wasn't: A New Interpretation of the Origin of Modern Human Behavior," *Journal of Human Evolution* 39 (2000): 453–563.
3. Peter Bogucki, *The Origins of Human Society* (Oxford: Blackwell, 1999), 94–95.
4. Paul G. Bahn and Jean Vertut, *Images of the Ice Age* (New York: Facts on File, 1988), chap. 7.
5. John Mulvaney and Johan Kaminga, *Prehistory of Australia* (Washington, D.C.: Smithsonian Institution Press, 1999), 93–102.
6. For a recent summary of this debate, see Charles C. Mann, *1491: New Revelations of the Americas before Columbus* (New York: Alfred Knopf, 2005), chap. 5.
7. Brian M. Fagan, *Ancient North America* (London: Thames and Hudson, 1995), 77–87.
8. Ben Finney, "The Other One-Third of the Globe," *Journal of World History* 5, no. 2 (Fall 1994): 273–85.
9. David Christian, *Maps of Time* (Berkeley: University of California Press, 2004), 143.
10. Richard B. Lee, *The Dobe Ju/'hoansi* (New York: Harcourt Brace, 1993), 58.
11. J. C. Beaglehole, *The Journals of Captain James Cook* (Cambridge: Hakluyt Society, 1968), 1:399.
12. Inga Clendinnen, *Dancing with Strangers* (Cambridge: Cambridge University Press, 2005), 159–67.
13. Marshall Sahlins, *Stone Age Economics* (London: Tavistock, 1972), 1–39.

14. Christopher Ehret, *The Civilizations of Africa* (Charlottesville: University of Virginia Press, 2002), chap. 2.
15. Marija Gimbutas, *The Language of the Goddess* (San Francisco: HarperCollins, 1989), 316–18.
16. Derived from Christian, *Maps of Time*, 208.
17. D. Bruce Dickson, *The Dawn of Belief* (Tucson: University of Arizona Press, 1990), 210.
18. Brian Fagan, *People of the Earth* (New York: HarperCollins, 1992), 200–201.
19. Jan Platvoet, "At War with God: Ju/'hoan Curing Dances," *Journal of Religion in Africa* 29, no. 1 (1999): 5.
20. J. David Lewis-Williams, *Believing and Seeing: Symbolic Meaning in Southern San Rock Paintings* (London: Academic Press, 1981).
21. Lee, *The Dobe Ju/'hoansi*. Unless otherwise noted, all information and quotes about the Ju/'hoansi come from this book.
22. Elizabeth Marshall Thomas, *The Harmless People* (New York: Vintage Books, 1989), 180.
23. For a contemporary account of a curing dance, see Bradford Keeney, "Ropes to God: Experiencing the Bushman Spiritual Universe," *Parabola* 27, no. 3 (2002): S1–S16.
24. Platvoet, "At War with God."
25. Brian Fagan, *Before California* (New York: Rowman and Littlefield, 2003), 153–55, 341–44.
26. Jeanne E. Arnold, *The Origins of a Pacific Coast Chiefdom* (Salt Lake City: University of Utah Press, 2001), 14.
27. Chester King, "Chumash Inter-Village Economic Exchange," in *Native Californians*, edited by Lowell John Bean and Thomas C. Blackburn (Menlo Park: Ballena Press, 1976), 289–318. The quote is on p. 297.
28. http://www.lonker.net/art_aboriginal_1.htm (accessed April 1, 2009).
29. Elaine Godden and Jutta Malnic, *Rock Paintings of Aboriginal Australia* (London: New Holland Publishers, 2001), preface.

Chapter 2

1. "Population 1: The Town That's Been Reclaimed by the Prairie," *International Observer*, November 20, 2005, http://observer.guardian.co.uk/international/story/0,6903,1646659,00.html?gusrc=rss.
2. Peter Bellwood, *First Farmers* (London: Blackwood, 2005), 7.

3. Mark Nathan Cohen, *The Food Crisis in Prehistory* (New Haven: Yale University Press, 1977).

4. Bruce Smith, *The Emergence of Agriculture* (New York: Scientific American Library, 1995), 206–14.

5. Jared Diamond, *Guns, Germs, and Steel* (New York: Vintage, 1997), 132, 157–75.

6. Bellwood, *First Farmers*, 54–55.

7. Steven Mithen, *After the Ice: A Global Human History, 20,000–50,000 B.C.* (Cambridge, Mass.: Harvard University Press, 2004), 87.

8. Neil Roberts, *The Holocene: An Environmental History* (Oxford: Blackwell, 1998), 116.

9. Nina V. Federoff, "Prehistoric GM Corn," *Science* 302 (November 2003): 1158.

10. Diamond, *Gun, Germs, and Steel*, 367.

11. The most recent summary of an immense literature on the spread of languages is found in Bellwood, *First Farmers*.

12. Many of these dates are much debated. See John Staller et al., *Histories of Maize* (Boston: Academic Press, 2006).

13. John A. Mears, "Agricultural Origins in Global Perspective," in *Agricultural and Pastoral Societies in Ancient and Classical History*, edited by Michael Adas (Philadelphia: Temple University Press, 2001), 63–64.

14. Elizabeth Wayland Barber, *Women's Work: The First 20,000 Years* (New York: W. W. Norton, 1994), chap. 3.

15. Andrew Sherrat, "The Secondary Exploitation of Animals in the Old World," *World Archeology* 15, no. 1 (June 1983): 90–104.

16. Clive Ponting, *A Green History of the World* (New York: St. Martin's Press, 1991), 69.

17. Anatoly M. Khazanov, *Nomads and the Outside World* (Madison: University of Wisconsin Press, 1994), 15.

18. Ian Hodder, "Women and Men at Catalhoyuk," *Scientific American* 15, no. 1 (2005): 35–41.

19. Allen W. Johnson and Timothy Earle, *The Evolution of Human Societies* (Stanford, Calif.: Stanford University Press, 2000), 281–94.

20. Ian Hodder, "Discussions with the Goddess Community," Catalhöyük: Excavations of a Neolithic Anatolian Höyük, http://www.catalhoyuk.com/library/goddess.html (accessed April 1, 2009).

21. Ian Hodder, "A Journey to 9,000 Years Ago," January 17, 2008, http://sci.tech-archive.net/Archive/sci.archaeology/2008-01/msg00519.html (accessed April 1, 2009).

22. http://www.reuters.com/article/scienceNews/idUSLM62397220080922 (accessed April 15, 2009).

23. Reuters, "Stonehenge May Have Been Pilgrimage Site for Sick," September 22, 2008, http://uk.reuters.com/article/scienceNews/idUKTRE48M0R320080923 (accessed April 15, 2009).

Chapter 3

1. Utah Outventures, http://www.utahoutventures.com/multiactivity/raftoffroadtours.htm (accessed April 1, 2009).

2. Charles C. Mann, 1491: *New Revelations of the Americas before Columbus* (New York: Alfred A. Knopf, 2005), 174–91; Proyecto Arqueológico Norte Chico, Project Description, 2005, http://www.fieldmuseum.org/research_collections/anthropology/anthro_sites/PANC/proj_desc.htm.

3. Jonathan Mark Kenoyer, *Ancient Cities of the Indus Valley Civilization* (Oxford: Oxford University Press, 1998), 83–84.

4. For a summary of many theories, see Stephen K. Sanderson, *Social Transformations* (Oxford: Blackwell, 1995), chap. 3.

5. Robert Carneiro, "A Theory of the Origin of the State," *Science* 169 (1970): 733–38.

6. Susan Pollock, *Ancient Mesopotamia* (Cambridge: Cambridge University Press, 1999), 48.

7. *The Epic of Gilgamesh*, translated and edited by Benjamin R. Foster (New York: W. W. Norton, 2001), 10, Tablet 1:226–32.

8. Samuel Noah Kramer, *History Begins at Sumer* (Philadelphia: University of Pennsylvania Press, 1981), 3–4.

9. James Legge, trans., *The Chinese Classics* (London: Henry Frowde, 1893), 4:171–72.

10. Marija Gimbutas, *The Living Goddess* (Berkeley: University of California Press, 1999).

11. Margaret Ehrenberg, *Women in Prehistory* (London: British Museum Publications, 1989), 107.

12. David Christian, *Maps of Time* (Berkeley: University of California Press, 2004), 256–57, 263–64.

13. Sherry Ortner, "Is Female to Male as Nature Is to Culture?" in *Women, Culture, and Society*, edited by Michelle Rosaldo and Louise Lamphere (Stanford, Calif.: Stanford University Press, 1974), 67–88.

14. Gerda Lerner, *The Creation of Patriarchy* (New York: Oxford University Press, 1986), 70.

15. Miriam Lichtheim, *Ancient Egyptian Literature* (Berkeley: University of California Press, 1975), 2:184–85.

16. Ibid., 2:168–75.

17. Prologue to *The Code of Hammurabi*, http://www.wsu.edu/~dee/MESO/CODE.HTM.

18. Gary Urton, "From Knots to Narratives: Reconstructing the Art of Historical Record-Keeping in the Andes from Spanish Transcriptions of Inka Khipus," *Ethnohistory* 45, no. 3 (1998): 409–38.

19. Adolf Erman, *The Literature of the Ancient Egyptians*, translated by Aylward M. Blackman (London: Methuen, 1927), 136–37.

20. Henri Frankfort, H. A. Frankfort, John A. Wilson, and Thorkild Jacobsen *Before Philosophy: The Intellectual Adventure of Ancient Man* (Baltimore: Penguin Books, 1963), 39, 138.

21. Quoted in Peter Stearns et al., *World Civilizations* (New York: Longman, 1996), 1:30.

22. See Clive Ponting, *A Green History of the World* (New York: St. Martin's Press, 1991), chap. 5.

23. Samuel Kramer, *The Sumerians* (Chicago: University of Chicago Press, 1963), 142.

24. Cyril Aldred, *The Egyptians* (London: Thames and Hudson, 1998), 138.

25. For a recent summary of a long debate about the relationship of Egypt and Africa, see David O'Connor and Andrew Reid, eds., *Ancient Egypt in Africa* (London: UCL Press, 2003).

26. James B. Pritchard, ed., *Ancient Near Eastern Texts Relating to the Old Testament* (Princeton: Princeton University Press, 1969), 647–48.

27. Lichtheim, *Ancient Egyptian Literature*, 1:25–27.

28. Joan Oates, *Babylon* (London: Thames and Hudson, 1986), 91.

29. Marvin Harris, ed., *Cannibals and Kings* (New York: Vintage, 1978), 102.

30. Lichtheim, *Ancient Egyptian Literature*, 2:177.

31. Jonathan M. Kenoyer, *Ancient Cities of the Indus Valley Civilization* (Karachi: Oxford University Press, 1998), 84.

32. Ibid., 100.

33. Gregory L. Possehl, *The Indus Civilization: A Contemporary Perspective* (Walnut Creek, Calif.: AltaMira Press, 2002), 114.

Part Two

1. Stephen K. Sanderson, *Social Transformation* (Oxford: Blackwell, 1995), chap. 4.

2. From ibid., 103.

3. Colin Ronan and Joseph Needham, *The Shorter Science and Civilization in China* (Cambridge: Cambridge University Press, 1978), 58.

4. Sidney W. Mintz, *Sweetness and Power* (New York: Penguin Books, 1985), chap. 2.

5. William H. McNeill, *Plagues and Peoples* (New York: Doubleday, 1977), 94.

6. See world population estimates by region in Paul Adams et al., *Experiencing World History* (New York: New York University Press, 2000), 334.

Chapter 4

1. Cullen Murphy, *Are We Rome? The Fall of an Empire and the Fate of America* (Boston: Houghton Mifflin, 2007).

2. J. M. Cook, *The Persian Empire* (London: J. M. Dent & Sons, 1983), 76.

3. George Rawlinson, trans., *The Histories of Herodotus* (London: Dent, 1910), 1:131–40.

4. Erich F. Schmidt, *Persepolis I: Structures, Reliefs, Inscriptions*, OIP 68 (Chicago: University of Chicago Press, 1953), 63.

5. Quoted in Thomas R. Martin, *Ancient Greece from Prehistoric to Hellenistic Times* (New Haven: Yale University Press, 1996), 86.

6. Christian Meier, *Athens* (New York: Metropolitan Books, 1993), 93.

7. Arrian, *The Campaigns of Alexander*, translated by Aubrey de Selincourt, revised by J. R. Hamilton (London: Penguin, 1971), 395–96.

8. Stanley Burstein, *The Hellenistic Period in World History* (Washington, D.C.: American Historical Association, 1996), 12.

9. Norman F. Cantor, *Antiquity* (New York: HarperCollins, 2003), 25.

10. Greg Woolf, "Inventing Empire in Ancient Rome," in *Empires: Perspectives from Archeology and History*, edited by Susan Alcock et al. (Cambridge: Cambridge University Press, 2001), 314.

11. S. A. M. Adshead, *China in World History* (London: McMillan Press, 1988), 4–21.

12. See Padma Manian, "Harappans and Aryans: Old and New Perspectives on Ancient Indian History," *The History Teacher* 32, no. 1 (November 1998): 17–32.

13. Roger Boesche, *The First Great Political Realist: Kautilya and His Arthashastra* (Lanham, Md.: Lexington Books, 2002), 17.

14. Stanley Wolpert, *A New History of India* (New York: Oxford University Press, 1993), chap. 5.

15. Zhengyuan Fu, *Autocratic Tradition and Chinese Politics* (New York: Cambridge University Press, 1993), 188.

16. Jane Portal, ed., *The First Emperor: China's Terracotta Army* (London: The British Museum Press, 2007), 110.

17. Quoted in Anders Blixt, "Qin Shi Huang Di, 'The Tiger Emperor': The First Emperor of China," http://biphome.spray.se/coif/history/qin/shie09.html (accessed Feb. 1, 2009).

18. Portal, *First Emperor*, 21.

Chapter 5

1. S. N. Eisenstadt, ed., *The Origins and Diversity of Axial Age Civilizations* (Albany: SUNY Press, 1986), 1–4; Karen Armstrong, *The Great Transformation* (New York: Alfred A. Knopf, 2006).

2. Quoted in Arthur Waley, *Three Ways of Thought in Ancient China* (Garden City, N.Y.: Doubleday, 1956), 159–60.

3. Nancy Lee Swann, trans., *Pan Chao: Foremost Woman Scholar of China* (New York: Century, 1932), 111–14.

4. Quoted in Huston Smith, *The Illustrated World's Religions* (San Francisco: HarperCollins, 1994), 123.

5. Lao Tsu, *Tao Te Ching*, translated by Gia-Fu Feng and Jane English (New York: Vintage Books, 1972), 80.

6. George Bühler, trans., *The Laws of Manu*, 5:148, http://www.sacred-texts.com/hin/manu/manu05.htm (accessed Feb. 1, 2009).

7. Quoted in Karen Andrews, "Women in Theravada Buddhism," http://www.enabling.org/ia/vipassana/ Archive/A/Andrews/womenTheraBudAndrews.html (accessed Feb. 1, 2009).

8. A. L. Basham, *The Wonder That Was India* (London: Sidgwick and Jackson, 1967), 309.

9. S. A. Nigosian, *The Zoroastrian Faith: Tradition and Modern Research* (Montreal: McGill–Queen's University Press, 1993), 95–97.

10. Isaiah 1:11–17.

11. Plato, *Apologia*.

12. Hippocrates, *On the Sacred Disease*, http://classics.mit.edu/ Hippocrates/sacred.html.

13. Thanissaro Bhikkhu, trans., "Karaniya Metta Sutta, 2004," http://www.accesstoinsight.org/tipitaka/kn/snp/snp.1.08 .than.html (accessed Feb. 1, 2009).

14. Matthew 5:43–44.

15. See Marcus Borg, ed., *Jesus and Buddha: The Parallel Sayings* (Berkeley, Calif.: Ulysses Press, 1997).

16. For a popular summary of the voluminous scholarship on Jesus, see Stephen Patterson et al., *The Search for Jesus: Modern Scholarship Looks at the Gospels* (Washington, D.C.: Biblical Archeological Society, 1994).

17. Galatians 3:28.

18. Ephesians 5:22; 1 Corinthians 14:35.

19. Ekkehard W. Stegemann and Wolfgang Stegemann, *The Jesus Movement: A History of Its First Century* (Minneapolis: Fortress Press, 1999), 291–96.

20. Ramsay MacMullen, *Christianizing the Roman Empire* (New Haven: Yale University Press, 1984), chap. 4.

21. Peter Brown, *The Rise of Western Christendom* (London: Blackwell, 2003), 69–71.

22. Mary Ann Rossi, "Priesthood, Precedent, and Prejudice: On Recovering the Women Priests of Early Christianity," *Journal of Feminist Studies* 7, no. 1 (1991): 73–94.

23. Chai-Shin Yu, *Early Buddhism and Christianity* (Delhi: Motilal Banarsidass, 1981), 211.

24. "Footprints of the Buddha," http://www.sacred-texts.com/ shi/igj/igj09.htm.

Chapter 6

1. Po Chu-I, "After Passing the Examination," in Arthur Waley, *More Translations from the Chinese* (New York: Alfred A. Knopf, 1919), 37.

2. Quoted in Michael Lowe, *Everyday Life in Early Imperial China* (New York: Dorset, 1968), 38.

3. Selected Poems from Tang Dynasty: http://shixuewang.com/ xlib/lingshidao/hanshi/tang1.htm.

4. A. L. Basham, *The Wonder That Was India* (London: Sidgwick and Jackson, 1967), 138.

5. Karl Jacoby, "Slaves by Nature: Animals and Human Slaves," *Slavery and Abolition* 15 (1994): 89–97.

6. Orlando Patterson, *Slavery and Social Death* (Cambridge, Mass.: Harvard University Press, 1982).

7. Basham, *The Wonder That Was India*, 152.

8. Sarah Pomeroy et al., *Ancient Greece* (New York: Oxford University Press, 1999), 63, 239.

9. R. Zelnick-Abramovitz, *Not Wholly Free* (Leiden: Brill, 2005), 337, 343.

10. Keith Bradley, *Slavery and Society at Rome* (Cambridge: Cambridge University Press, 1994), 30.

11. 1 Peter 2:18.

12. Milton Meltzer, *Slavery: A World History* (New York: Da Capo Press, 1993), 189.

13. Quoted in Bret Hinsch, *Women in Early Imperial China* (Oxford: Rowman and Littlefield, 2002), 155.

14. Nancy Lee Swann, trans., *Pan Chao: Foremost Woman Scholar of China* (New York: Century, 1932), 111–14.

15. Lisa Raphals, *Sharing the Light: Representations of Women and Virtue in Early China* (Albany: SUNY Press, 1998).

16. Valerie Hansen, *The Open Empire* (New York: Norton, 2000), 183–84; Thomas Barfield, *The Perilous Frontier* (Cambridge: Blackwell, 1989), 140.

17. Vivian-Lee Nyitray, "Confucian Complexities," in *A Companion to Gender History* edited by Teresa A. Meade and Merry E. Weisner-Hanks (Oxford: Blackwell, 2004), 278.

18. Aristotle, *Politica*, ed. Loeb Classical Library, 1254b10–14.

19. Quoted in Pomeroy et al., *Ancient Greece*, 146.

20. "The Destruction of Pompeii, 79 AD," EyeWitness to History, www.eyewitnesstohistory.com/pompeii.htm (accessed April 1, 2009).

21. August Mau, *Pompeii: Its Life and Art* (New Rochelle: Caratzas Brothers, 1982), 16.

22. "Graffiti from Pompeii," http://www.pompeiana.org/ Resources/Ancient/Graffiti%20from%20Pompeii.htm (accessed April 1, 2009).

Chapter 7

1. Rethinking Schools *Online*, Fall 1999, http://www.rethinkingschools.org/archive/14_01/ poor141.shtml.

2. Thomas Benjamin, "A Time of Reconquest: History, the Maya Revival, and the Zapatista Rebellion in Chiapas," *American Historical Review* 105, no. 2 (April 2000): 417.

3. Population figures are taken from Paul Adams et al., *Experiencing World History* (New York: New York University Press, 2000), 334.

4. Roderick J. McIntosh, *Ancient Middle Niger* (Cambridge: Cambridge University Press, 2005), 10.

5. Roderick J. McIntosh, *The Peoples of the Middle Niger* (Oxford: Blackwell, 1998), 177.

6. Kairn A. Klieman, *"The Pygmies Were Our Compass": Bantu and Batwa in the History of West Central Africa, Early Times to C. 1900 C.E.* (Portsmouth, N.H.: Heinemann, 2003), chaps. 4, 5.

7. Christopher Ehret, *The Civilizations of Africa* (Charlottesville: University of Virginia Press, 2002), 175.

8. See Jan Vansina, *Paths in the Rainforest* (Madison: University of Wisconsin Press, 1990), 95–99.

9. Richard E. W. Adams, *Prehistoric Mesoamerica* (Norman: University of Oklahoma Press, 2005), 16.

10. Richard E. W. Adams, *Ancient Civilizations of the New World* (Boulder, Colo.: Westview Press, 1997), 53–56; T. Patrick Culbert, "The New Maya," Archeology 51, no. 5 (September–October 1998): 47–51.

11. William Haviland, "State and Power in Classic Maya Society," *American Anthropologist* 94, no. 4 (1992):937.

12. Jared Diamond, *Collapse: How Societies Choose to Fail or Succeed* (New York: Viking, 2005), chap. 5.

13. Esther Pasztory, *Teotihuacan: An Experiment in Living* (Norman: University of Oklahoma Press, 1997), 193.

14. George L. Cowgill, "The Central Mexican Highlands . . . ," in *The Cambridge History of the Native Peoples of the Americas*, vol. 2, part 1, Mesoamerica, edited by Richard E. W. Adams and Murdo J. MacLeod (Cambridge: Cambridge University Press, 2000), 289.

15. Karen Olsen Bruhns, *Ancient South America* (Cambridge: Cambridge University Press, 1994), 126–41; Sylvia R. Kembel and John W. Rick, "Building Authority at Chavín de Huántar," in *Andean Archeology*, edited by Helaine Silverman (Oxford: Blackwell, 2004), 59–76.

16. Garth Bawden, *The Moche* (Oxford: Blackwell, 1996), chaps. 9, 10.

17. John E. Kicza, *The Peoples and Civilizations of the Americas before Contact* (Washington, D.C.: American Historical Association, 1998), 43–44.

18. Much of this section draws on Brian M. Fagan, *Ancient North America* (London: Thames and Hudson, 2005), chaps. 14, 15. The quote is on p. 345.

19. George R. Milner, *The Moundbuilders: Ancient Peoples of Eastern North America* (London: Thames and Hudson, 2004).

20. David Hurst Thomas, *Exploring Ancient Native America* (New York: Routledge, 1999), 137–42.

21. Stephen H. Lekson and Peter N. Peregrine, "A Continental Perspective for North American Archeology," *The SAA Archeological Record* 4, no. 1 (January 2004): 15–19.

22. Fagan, *Ancient North America*, 475.

23. Quoted in Lynda Norene Shaffer, *Native Americans before 1492* (Armonk, N.Y.: M. E. Sharpe, 1992), 70.

24. See Stanley Burstein, *Ancient African Civilizations: Kush and Axum* (Princeton: Markus Weiner Publishers, 1998), 14–20. I am grateful to Professor Burstein and this book for references to many of the documents in this section.

25. Mary Ellen Miller, *Maya Art and Architecture* (London: Thames & Hudson, 1999), 8–11.

26. Linda Schele and Mary Ellen Miller, *The Blood of Kings* (London: Thames & Hudson, 1992), 176.

27. Mary Miller and Simon Martin, *Courtly Art of the Ancient Maya* (New York: Thames & Hudson, 2004), 63.

Part Three

1. Marshall G. S. Hodgson, *The Venture of Islam* (Chicago: University of Chicago Press, 1974), 1:71.

2. Lynda Shaffer, "Southernization," *Journal of World History* 5, no. 1 (Spring 1994): 7.

Chapter 8

1. Somini Sengupta, "Sahara Journal," *New York Times*, November 25, 2003.

2. Seneca the Younger, *Declamations*, vol. 1.

3. Liu Xinru, "Silks and Religion in Eurasia, A.D. 600–1200," *Journal of World History* 6, no. 1 (Spring 1995): 25–48.

4. Jerry Bentley, "Hemispheric Integration, 500–1500 C.E.," *Journal of World History* 9, no. 2 (Fall 1998): 241–44.

5. See Jerry Bentley, *Old World Encounters* (New York: Oxford University Press, 1993), 42–53, 69–84.

6. Liu Xinru, *The Silk Road* (Washington, D.C.: American Historical Association, 1998), 10.

7. See William H. McNeill, *Plagues and Peoples* (New York: Doubleday, 1977), chaps. 3, 4.

8. Boccaccio, *The Decameron*, translated by M. Rigg (London: David Campbell, 1921), 1:5–11.

9. Kenneth McPherson, *The Indian Ocean* (Oxford: Oxford University Press, 1993), 15.

10. Janet L. Abu-Lughod, *Before European Hegemony* (Oxford: Oxford University Press, 1989), 269.

11. Nigel D. Furlonge, "Revisiting the Zanj and Revisioning Revolt," *Negro History Bulletin* 62 (December 1999).

12. Patricia Risso, *Merchants and Faith: Muslim Commerce and Culture in the Indian Ocean* (Boulder, Colo.: Westview, 1995), 54.

13. McPherson, *The Indian Ocean*, 97.

14. Kenneth R. Hall, *Maritime Trade and State Development in Early Southeast Asia* (Honolulu: University of Hawaii Press, 1985), 101.

15. Lynda Norene Shaffer, *Maritime Southeast Asia to 1500* (Armonk, N.Y.: M. E. Sharpe, 1996), 37, 46.

16. M. C. Horton and T. R. Burton, "Indian Metalwork in East Africa: The Bronze Lion Statuette from Shanga," *Antiquities* 62 (1988): 22.

17. Ross Dunn, *The Adventures of Ibn Battuta* (Berkeley: University of California Press, 1986), 124.

18. Christopher Ehret, *The Civilizations of Africa* (Charlottesville: University of Virginia Press, 2002), 255.

19. Ibid., 227–32.

20. Nehemia Levtzion and Jay Spaulding, eds., *Medieval West Africa: Views from Arab Scholars and Merchants* (Princeton, N.J.: Marcus Wiener, 2003), 5.

21. Quoted in John Iliffe, *Africans: The History of a Continent* (Cambridge: Cambridge University Press, 1995), 75–76.

22. J. R. McNeill and William McNeill, *The Human Web* (New York: W. W. Norton, 2003), 160.

23. Lauren Ristvet, *In the Beginning* (New York: McGraw-Hill, 2007), 165.

24. Maria Rostworowski de Diez Canseco, *History of the Inca Realm* (Cambridge: Cambridge University Press, 1999), 209–12.

25. Michael Haederle, "Mystery of Ancient Pueblo Jars Is Solved," *New York Times*, February 4, 2009.

26. Anthony Andrews, "America's Ancient Mariners," *Natural History*, October 1991, 72–75.

27. Richard Blanton and Gary Feinman, "The Mesoamerican World System," *American Anthropologist* 86, no. 3 (September 1984): 677.

28. Li Rongxi (trans.), *A Biography of the Tripitaka Master of the Great Ci'en Monastery of the Great Tang Dynasty* (Berkeley: Numata Center for Buddhist Translation, 1995), 31.

29. For a brief account of Xuanzang's life and travels, see Stephen S. Gosch and Peter N. Stearns, *Premodern Travel in World History* (New York: Routledge, 2008), 75–101.

30. Craig Benjamin, "The Kushans in World History," *World History Bulletin*, XXV:1 (Spring 2009), 30.

31. Xinru Liu and Lynda N. Shaffer, *Connections across Eurasia* (Boston: McGraw-Hill, 2007), 56–63.

32. Quoted in David Christian, *Inner Eurasia from Prehistory to the Mongol Empire* (Oxford: Blackwell Publishers, 1998), 267.

33. Hans-Joachim Klimkeit, *Manichaean Art and Calligraphy* (Leiden: E. J. Brill, 1982), 38

34. Carter Findley, *The Turks in World History* (Oxford: Oxford University Press, 2005), 61–64.

35. Bahodir Sidikov, "Sufism and Shamanism" in Eva Fridman and Mariko Walter (eds), *Shamanism* (ABC-Clio, 2004), 241.

Chapter 9

1. *The Guardian*, June 15, 2006.

2. John K. Fairbank, ed., *The Chinese World Order* (Cambridge, Mass.: Harvard University Press, 1968).

3. Quoted in Mark Elvin, *The Retreat of the Elephants* (New Haven: Yale University Press, 2004), chap. 1. The quote is on p. 19.

4. Mark Elvin, *The Pattern of the Chinese Past* (London: Eyre Methuen, 1973), 55.

5. Samuel Adshead, *T'ang China: The Rise of the East in World History* (New York: Palgrave, 2004), 30.

6. Elvin, *The Pattern of the Chinese Past*, part 2; William McNeill, *The Pursuit of Power* (Chicago: University of Chicago Press, 1984), 50.

7. See "The Attractions of the Capital," in *Chinese Civilization: A Sourcebook* edited by Patricia B. Ebrey (New York: Free Press, 1993), 178–85.

8. Marco Polo, "The Glories of Kinsay," *Medieval Sourcebook*, http://www.fordham.edu/halsall/source/polo-kinsay.html.

9. John K. Fairbank, *China: A New History* (Cambridge, Mass.: Harvard University Press, 1992), 89.

10. J. R. McNeill and William H. McNeill, *The Human Web* (New York: W. W. Norton, 2003), 123.

11. Francesca Bray, *Technology and Gender: Fabrics of Power in Late Imperial China* (Berkeley: University of California Press, 1997), 116.

12. Patricia Ebrey, *The Inner Quarters* (Berkeley: University of California Press, 1993), 207.

13. Ibid., 37–43.

14. Ibid., 6.

15. See Nicolas DiCosmo, *Ancient China and Its Enemies* (Cambridge: Cambridge University Press, 2002), chap. 6.

16. Ibid., 94.

17. Quoted in Thomas J. Barfield, "Steppe Empires, China, and the Silk Route," in *Nomads in the Sedentary World*, edited by Anatoly M. Khazanov and Andre Wink (Richmond: Kurzon Press, 2001), 237.

18. Quoted in Edward H. Shafer, *The Golden Peaches of Samarkand* (Berkeley: University of California Press, 1963), 28.

19. Susan Mann, "Women in East Asia," in *Women's History in Global Perspective*, edited by Bonnie Smith (Urbana: University of Illinois Press, 2005), 2:53–56.

20. Joseph Buttinger, *A Dragon Defiant: A Short History of Vietnam* (New York: Praeger, 1972), 32–34; Jerry Bentley, *Old World Encounters* (New York: Oxford University Press, 1993), 85–86.

21. Cited in "Trung Trac and Trung Nhi," http://www.viettouch.com/trungsis.

22. Liam C. Kelley, *Beyond the Bronze Pillars: Envoy Poetry and the Sino-Vietnamese Relationship* (Honolulu: University of Hawai'i Press, 2005).

23. H. Paul Varley, "Japan, 550–838," in *Asia in Western and World History*, edited by Ainslee T. Embrey and Carol Gluck (Armonk, N.Y.: M. E. Sharpe, 1997), 353.

24. Quoted in McNeill, *The Pursuit of Power*, 40.

25. John K. Fairbank et al., *East Asia: Tradition and Transformation* (Boston: Houghton Mifflin, 1978), 353.

26. Arnold Pacey, *Technology in World Civilization* (Cambridge, Mass.: MIT Press, 1991), 50–53.

27. McNeill, *The Pursuit of Power*, 24–25.

28. Hugh Clark, "Muslims and Hindus in the Culture and Morphology of Quanzhou from the Tenth to the Thirteenth Century," *Journal of World History* 6, no. 1 (Spring 1995): 49–74.

29. Quoted in Arthur F. Wright, *Studies in Chinese Buddhism* (New Haven: Yale University Press, 1990), 16.

30. Arthur F. Wright, *Buddhism in Chinese History* (Stanford, Calif.: Stanford University Press, 1959), 36–39.

31. Quoted in Wright, *Buddhism in Chinese History*, 67.

32. Quoted in Eric Zurcher, *The Buddhist Conquest of China* (Leiden: E. J. Brill, 1959), 1:262.

33. Jacquet Gernet, *A History of Chinese Civilization* (Cambridge: Cambridge University Press, 1996), 291–96.

34. Edwin O. Reischauer, *Ennin's Travels in T'ang China* (New York: Ronald Press, 1955), 221–24.

35. William Theodore de Bary et al., *Sources of Japanese Tradition* (New York: Columbia University Press, 2001), 1:42.

36. Kenneth Henshall, *A History of Japan* (New York: Palgrave Macmillan, 2004), 17.

37. Donald Keene, *Seeds in the Heart* (New York: Henry Holt, 1993), 477–78.

38. Quoted in China History Forum, http://www.chinahistoryforum.com/index.php?showtopic=17789&st=30&start=30.

39. I Lo-fen, "Dialogue Between the 'Fatuous Emperor' and the 'Treacherous Minister': Song Hui Zong's 'Literary Gathering' Painting (Wen-Hui Tu) and Its Poetic Inscriptions," *Literature and Philosophy* 8 (June 2006): 253–78.

40. Quoted at Charles Hartman's site for SUNY–Albany students in his Chinese Painting course, http://www.albany.edu/faculty/hartman/eac280/25.html.

Chapter 10

1. "East and West Churches Reconcile," http://chi.gospelcom.net/DAILYF/2002/12/daily-12-07-2002.shtml.

2. Paul R. Spickard and Kevin M. Cragg, *A Global History of Christians* (Grand Rapids, Mich.: Baker Academic, 1994), chap. 6.

3. Leonora Neville, *Authority in Byzantine Provincial Society, 950–1100* (Cambridge: Cambridge University Press, 2004), 2.

4. Quoted in Deno John Geanakoplos, *Byzantium: Church, Society, and Civilization Seen through Contemporary Eyes* (Chicago: University of Chicago Press, 1984), 389.

5. Quoted in ibid., 143.

6. Quoted in A. A. Vasiliev, *History of the Byzantine Empire* (Madison: University of Wisconsin Press, 1978), 79–80.

7. Quoted in Geanakoplos, *Byzantium*, 362.

8. Quoted in ibid., 369.

9. Rowena Loverance, *Byzantium* (Cambridge, Mass.: Harvard University Press, 2004), 43.

10. Daniel H. Kaiser and Gary Marker, *Reinterpreting Russian History* (Oxford: Oxford University Press, 1994), 63–67.

11. Quoted in Patrick J. Geary, *Before France and Germany* (New York: Oxford University Press, 1988), 79.

12. Quoted in Stephen Williams, *Diocletian and the Roman Recovery* (London: Routledge, 1996), 218.

13. Peter Brown, *The Rise of Western Christendom* (London: Blackwell, 1996), 305.

14. Quoted in John M. Hobson, *The Eastern Origins of Western Civilization* (New York: Cambridge University Press, 2004), 113.

15. Clive Ponting, *A Green History of the World* (New York: St. Martin's, 1991), 121–23.

16. Christopher Tyerman, *Fighting for Christendom: Holy Wars and the Crusades* (Oxford: Oxford University Press, 2004), 16.

17. Edward Peters, "The Firanj Are Coming—Again," *Orbis* 48, no. 1 (Winter 2004), 3–17.

18. Quoted in Peter Stearns, *Western Civilization in World History* (New York: Routledge, 2003), 52.

19. Quoted in Jean Gimple, *The Medieval Machine* (New York: Holt, 1976), 178.

20. Quoted in Stuart B. Schwartz, ed., *Victors and Vanquished* (Boston: Bedford/St. Martins, 2000), 147.

21. Quoted in Carlo Cipolla, *Before the Industrial Revolution* (New York: Norton, 1976), 207.

22. Quoted in S. Lilley, *Men, Machines, and History* (New York: International, 1965), 62.

23. See Toby Huff, *The Rise of Early Modern Science* (Cambridge: Cambridge University Press, 1993).

24. Quoted in Edward Grant, *Science and Religion from Aristotle to Copernicus* (Westport, Conn.: Greenwood Press, 2004), 158.

25. Quoted in L. Thorndike, *A History of Magic and Experimental Science* (New York: Columbia University Press, 1923), 2:58.

26. Quoted in Edward Grant, *God and Reason in the Middle Ages* (Cambridge: Cambridge University Press, 2001), 70.

27. Grant, *Science and Religion*, 228–29.

28. Marcia L. Colish, *Medieval Foundations of the Western Intellectual Tradition* (New Haven: Yale University Press, 1997), 128.

29. Charles G. Herbermann, ed., *The Catholic Encyclopedia* (New York: The Encyclopedia Press, 1913), 7:668.

30. Simon Morsink, *The Power of Icons* (Ghent: Snoek, 2006), 12; Robin Cormack, *Icons* (London: The British Museum Press, 2007), 29.

Chapter 11

1. Al-Hajj Malik El-Shabazz (Malcolm X), "The Pilgrimage to Mecca," Islam Online, http://www.islamonline.net/English/hajj/2002/01/Experience/article2.shtml.

2. Reza Aslan, *No God but God* (New York: Random House, 2005), 14.

3. Quoted in Karen Armstrong, *A History of God* (New York: Ballantine Books, 1993), 146.

4. Quran 1:5.

5. Quran 3:110.

6. Quran 9:71.

7. "The Prophet's Farewell Sermon," Islam Online, http://www.islamonline.net/English/In_Depth/mohamed/1424/kharitah/article02.shtml.

8. Quoted in Patricia Crone, "The Rise of Islam in the World," in *Cambridge Illustrated History of the Islamic World*, edited by Francis Robinson (Cambridge: Cambridge University Press, 1996), 11.

9. Richard Bulliet, *Conversion to Islam in the Medieval Period* (Cambridge, Mass.: Harvard University Press, 1979), 33.

10. Nehemiah Levtzion, ed., *Conversion to Islam* (New York: Holmes and Meier, 1979), chap. 1.

11. Jerry Bentley, *Old World Encounters* (New York: Oxford University Press, 1993), 93.

12. Bernard Lewis, *Islam and the West* (New York: Oxford University Press, 1993), 157.

13. Quoted in Crone, "The Rise of Islam in the World," 14.

14. Quoted in Margaret Smith, *Readings from the Mystics of Islam* (London: Luzac, 1972), 11.

15. Aslan, *No God but God*, 201.

16. Quran 33:35.

17. Quran 4:34.

18. Quoted in Judith Tucker, "Gender and Islamic History," in *Islamic and European Expansion*, edited by Michael Adas (Philadelphia: Temple University Press, 1993), 46.

19. Nikki R. Keddie, "Women in the Middle East since the Rise of Islam," in *Women's History in Global Perspective*, edited by Bonnie G. Smith (Urbana: University of Illinois Press, 2005), 74–75.

20. Quoted in William T. de Bary, ed., *Sources of Indian Tradition* (New York: Columbia University Press, 1958), 2:355–57.

21. V. L. Menage, "The Islamization of Anatolia," in *Conversion to Islam*, edited by Nemehia Levtzion (New York: Holmes and Meier, 1979), chap. 4.

22. Ira M. Lapidus, *A History of Islamic Societies* (Cambridge: Cambridge University Press, 1988), 304–6.

23. Quoted in Keddie, "Women in the Middle East," 81.

24. Ross Dunn, *The Adventures of Ibn Battuta* (Berkeley: University of California Press, 1986), 300.

25. Jane I. Smith, "Islam and Christendom," in *The Oxford History of Islam*, edited by John L. Esposito (Oxford: Oxford University Press, 1999), 317–21.

26. Richard Eaton, "Islamic History as Global History," in *Islamic and European Expansion*, edited by Michael Adas (Philadelphia: Temple University Press, 1993), 12.

27. Francis Robinson, "Knowledge, Its Transmission and the Making of Muslim Societies," in *Cambridge Illustrated History of the Islamic World*, edited by Francis Robinson (Cambridge: Cambridge University Press, 1996), 230.

28. Janet L. Abu-Lughod, *Before European Hegemony* (Oxford: Oxford University Press, 1989), 216–24.

29. Andrew Watson, *Agricultural Innovation in the Early Islamic World* (Cambridge: Cambridge University Press, 1983); Michael Decker, "Plants and Progress: Rethinking the Islamic Agricultural Revolution," *Journal of World History* 20; no. 2 (June 2009): 187–206.

30. Arnold Pacey, *Technology in World History* (Cambridge, Mass.: MIT Press, 1991), 8, 74.

31. Robinson, "Knowledge, Its Transmission," 215.

32. Ahmad Dallal, "Science, Medicine, and Technology: The Making of a Scientific Culture," in *The Oxford History of Islam*, edited by John Esposito (Oxford: Oxford University Press, 1999), chap. 4.

33. David W. Tschanz, "The Arab Roots of European Medicine," *Aramco World*, May–June 1997, 20–31.

34. Bertold Spuler. *The Muslim World*, vol. 1, *The Age of the Caliph* (Leiden: E. J. Brill, 1960), 29.

35. Oleg Grabar, *Mostly Miniatures: An Introduction to Persian Painting* (Princeton: Princeton University Press, 2000), 2.

36. The commentary on both Visual Sources 11.1 and 11.2 draws on Oleg Grabar and Mika Natif, "Two Safavid

Paintings: An Essay in Interpretation," *Muqarnas* 18 (2001): 173–202.

Chapter 12

1. Jack Weatherford, *Genghis Khan and the Making of the Modern World* (New York: Crown, 2004), xv.
2. Data derived from Thomas J. Barfield, "Pastoral Nomadic Societies," in *Berkshire Encyclopedia of World History* (Great Barrington: Berkshire, 2005), 4:1432–37.
3. Giovanni Carpini, *The Story of the Mongols*, translated by Erik Hildinger (Boston: Braden, 1996), 54.
4. Quoted in Peter B. Golden, "Nomads and Sedentary Societies in Eurasia," in *Agricultural and Pastoral Societies in Ancient and Classical History*, edited by Michael Adas (Philadelphia: Temple University Press, 2001), 73.
5. Thomas J. Barfield, *The Nomadic Alternative* (Englewood Cliffs, N.J.: Prentice Hall, 1993), 12.
6. Anatoly Khazanov, "The Spread of World Religions in Medieval Nomadic Societies of the Eurasian Steppes," in *Nomadic Diplomacy, Destruction and Religion from the Pacific to the Adriatic*, edited by Michael Gervers and Wayne Schlepp (Toronto: Joint Center for Asia Pacific Studies, 1994), 11.
7. Quoted in Gregory Guzman, "Were the Barbarians a Negative or Positive Factor in Ancient and Medieval History?" *The Historian* 50 (August 1988): 558–72.
8. Carter Finley, *The Turks in World History* (Oxford: Oxford University Press, 2005), 28–37.
9. Ibid., 40.
10. Thomas Spear and Richard Waller, eds., *Being Maasai* (London: James Curry, 1993), 6, 12.
11. Richard Waller, ""Ecology, Migration, and Expansion in East Africa," *African Affairs* 84 (1985): 347–70; Thomas Spear, *Kenya's Past* (London: Longman, 1981), 107.
12. Godfrey Muriuki, *A History of the Kikuyu* (Nairobi: Oxford University Press, 1974), chap. 4.
13. David Christian, *A History of Russia, Central Asia, and Mongolia* (London: Blackwell, 1998), 1:385.
14. Quoted in ibid., 389.
15. David Morgan, *The Mongols* (Oxford: Blackwell, 1986), 63–67.
16. Weatherford, *Genghis Khan*, 86.
17. Chinggis Khan, "Letter to Changchun" in E. Bretschneider, *Mediaeval Researches from Eastern Asiatic Sources* (London: Kegan, Paul, Trench, Trübner, 1875), 37–39.
18. Thomas T. Allsen, *Mongol Imperialism* (Berkeley: University of California Press, 1987), 6.
19. Chinggis Khan, "Letter to Changchun."
20. Quoted in Weatherford, *Genghis Khan*, 111.
21. Barfield, *The Nomadic Alternative*, 166.

22. Peter Jackson, "The Mongols and the Faith of the Conquered," in *Mongols, Turks, and Others*, edited by Reuven Amitai and Michael Biran (Leiden: Brill, 2005), 262.
23. Quoted in Christian, *A History of Russia*, 425.
24. Quoted in David Morgan, *Medieval Persia* (London: Longman, 1988), 79.
25. Morgan, *Medieval Persia*, 82.
26. Charles J. Halperin, *Russia and the Golden Horde* (Bloomington: Indiana University Press, 1985), 126.
27. Charles H. Halperin, "Russia in the Mongol Empire in Comparative Perspective," *Harvard Journal of Asiatic Studies* 43, no. 1 (June 1983): 261.
28. Quoted in Kevin Reilly, ed., *Worlds of History* (Boston: Bedford, 2004), 1:420.
29. Thomas Allsen, *Culture and Conquest in Mongol Eurasia* (Cambridge: Cambridge University Press, 2001), 211.
30. Quoted in ibid., 121.
31. John Aberth, *From the Brink of the Apocalypse* (New York: Routledge, 2000), 122–131.
32. Quoted in John Aberth, *The Black Death: The Great Mortality of 1348–1350* (Boston: Bedford/St. Martin's, 2005), 84–85.
33. Michael Dols, *The Black Death in the Middle East* (Princeton: Princeton University Press, 1977), 212, 223.
34. Quoted in John Aberth, *A Knight at the Movies: Medieval History on Film* (New York: Routledge, 2003), 225.
35. Aberth, *The Black Death*, 72.
36. Quoted in Dols, *The Black Death in the Middle East*, 67.
37. Andre Gunder Frank, *ReOrient* (Berkeley: University of California Press, 1998), 256.
38. Arnold Pacey, *Technology in World Civilization* (Cambridge, Mass.: MIT Press, 1990), 62.
39. Quoted in Golden, "Nomads and Sedentary Societies," 72–73.
40. Quoted in Guzman, "Were the Barbarians a Negative or Positive Factor?" 558–72.
41. Quoted in Barfield, *The Nomadic Alternative*, 3.
42. Quoted in Aberth, *The Black Death*, 99.
43. Quoted in David Herlihy, *The Black Death and the Transformation of the West* (Cambridge: Harvard University Press, 1997), 65.
44. Quoted in ibid., 62.
45. Quoted in Aberth, *The Black Death*, 79.
46. Quoted in ibid., 174.
47. "Lübeck's Dance of Death," http://www.dodedans.com/Etext2.htm.
48. Quoted in Norman Cantor, *In the Wake of the Plague* (New York: The Free Press, 2001), 6.
49. Quoted in Aberth, *The Black Death*, 73–74.

Chapter 13

1. Brian Fagan, *Ancient North America* (London: Thames and Hudson, 2005), 503.

2. Quoted in Charles C. Mann, *1491: New Revelations of the Americas before Columbus* (New York: Alfred A. Knopf, 2005), 334.

3. Louise Levanthes, *When China Ruled the Seas* (New York: Simon and Schuster, 1994), 175.

4. Niccolò Machiavelli, *The Prince* (New York: New American Library, 1952), 90, 94.

5. Frank Viviano, "China's Great Armada," *National Geographic*, July 2005, 34.

6. Quoted in John J. Saunders, ed., *The Muslim World on the Eve of Europe's Expansion* (Englewood Cliffs, N.J.: Prentice Hall, 1966), 41–43.

7. Leo Africanus, *History and Description of Africa* (London: Hakluyt Society, 1896), 824–25.

8. Quoted in Craig A. Lockhard, *Southeast Asia in World History* (Oxford: Oxford University Press, 2009), 67.

9. Quoted in Patricia Risso, *Merchants and Faith* (Boulder, Colo.: Westview Press, 1995), 49.

10. Quoted in Stuart B. Schwartz, ed., *Victors and Vanquished* (Boston: Bedford/St. Martin's, 2000), 8.

11. Quoted in Michael E. Smith, *The Aztecs* (London: Blackwell, 2003), 108.

12. Smith, *The Aztecs*, 220.

13. Miguel Leon-Portilla, *Aztec Thought and Culture*, translated from the Spanish by Jack Emory Davis (Norman: University of Oklahoma Press, 1963), 7; Miguel Leon-Portilla, *Fifteen Poets of the Aztec World* (Norman: University of Oklahoma Press, 1992), 80–81.

14. Terence N. D'Altroy, *The Incas* (London: Blackwell, 2002), chaps. 11, 12.

15. For a summary of this practice among the Aztecs and Incas, see Karen Vieira Powers, *Women in the Crucible of Conquest* (Albuquerque: University of New Mexico Press, 2005), chap. 1.

16. Ibid., 25.

17. Louise Burkhart, "Mexica Women on the Home Front," in *Indian Women of Early Mexico*, edited by Susan Schroeder et al. (Norman: University of Oklahoma Press, 1997), 25–54.

18. The "web" metaphor is derived from J. R. McNeill and William H. McNeill, *The Human Web* (New York: W. W. Norton, 2003).

19. Graph from David Christian, *Map of Time* (Berkeley: University of California Press, 2004), 343.

20. Andrew Spicer and Sarah Hamilton, eds., *Defining the Holy: Sacred Space in Medieval and Early Modern Europe* (Farnham, U.K.: Ashgate Publishing, 2006), Chap. 1.

21. Oleg Grabar, "The Umayyad Dome of the Rock in Jerusalem," in Eva R. Hoffman, ed., *Late Antique and Medieval Art of the Mediterranean World* (London: John Wiley and Sons, 2007), 166.

22. Ibid., 161.

23. Trudy Ring, ed., *International Dictionary of Historic Places*, vol. 4, *Middle East and Africa* (Chicago: Fitzroy Dearborn, 1994–96), 444.

24. Francisco Alvarez, *The Prester John of the Indies* (Cambridge: Hakluyt Society, 1961), 226.

Part Four

1. Victor Lieberman, "Transcending East–West Dichotomies," *Modern Asian Studies* 31 (1997): 463–546; John Richards, *The Unending Frontier* (Berkeley: University of California Press, 2003), 22–24.

Chapter 14

1. *Taipei Times*, October 11, 1999, http://uyghuramerican.org/articles/145/1/Fight-for-East-Turkestan/Fight-for-East-Turkestan.html.

2. Winona LaDuke, "We Are Still Here: The 500 Year Celebration," *Sojourners Magazine*, October 1991.

3. Quoted in Thomas E. Skidmore and Peter H. Smith, *Modern Latin America* (New York: Oxford University Press, 2001), 15.

4. George Raudzens, ed., *Technology, Disease, and Colonial Conquest* (Boston: Brill Academic, 2003), xiv.

5. Alfred W. Crosby, "The Columbian Voyages, the Columbian Exchange, and Their Historians," in *Islamic and European Expansion*, edited by Michael Adas (Philadelphia: Temple University Press, 1993), 160.

6. Quoted in Noble David Cook, *Born to Die: Disease and the New World Conquest* (Cambridge: Cambridge University Press, 1998), 202.

7. Quoted in ibid., 206.

8. Quoted in Charles C. Mann, *1491* (New York: Alfred A. Knopf, 2005), 56.

9. Felipe Fernandez-Armesto, "Empires in Their Global Context," in *The Atlantic in Global History*, edited by Jorge Canizares-Esguerra and Erik R. Seeman (Upper Saddle River, N.J.: Prentice-Hall, 2007), 105.

10. Quoted in Anthony Padgen, "Identity Formation in Spanish America," in *Colonial Identity in the Atlantic World, 1500–1800*, edited by Nicholas Canny and Anthony Padgen (Princeton, N.J.: Princeton University Press, 1987), 56.

11. Quoted in Marjorie Wall Bingham, *An Age of Empire, 1200–1750* (Oxford: Oxford University Press, 2005), 116.

12. Derived from Skidmore and Smith, *Modern Latin America*, 25.

13. Quoted in James Lockhart and Stuart B. Schwartz, *Early Latin America* (Cambridge: Cambridge University Press, 1983), 206.

14. From Kevin Reilly et al., eds., *Racism: A Global Reader* (Armonk, N.Y.: M. E. Sharpe, 2003), 136–37.

15. Felipe Fernandez-Armesto, *The Americas: A Hemispheric History* (New York: Modern Library, 2003), 58–59.

16. Willard Sutherland, *Taming the Wild Fields: Colonization and Empire on the Russian Steppe* (Ithaca, N.Y.: Cornell University Press, 2004), 223–24.

17. Quoted in Michael Khodarkovsky, *Russia's Steppe Frontier* (Bloomington: Indiana University Press, 2002), 216.

18. Andreas Kappeler, *The Russian Empire* (New York: Longman, 2001), 115–17, 397–99.

19. Khodarkovsky, *Russia's Steppe Frontier*, 222.

20. Geoffrey Hosking, "The Freudian Frontier," *Times Literary Supplement*, March 10, 1995, 27.

21. Peter Perdue, *China Marches West: The Qing Conquest of Central Eurasia* (Cambridge: Harvard University Press, 2005), 10–11.

22. Quoted in Stephen F. Dale, "The Islamic World in the Age of European Expansion," in *The Cambridge Illustrated History of the Islamic World*, edited by Francis Robinson (Cambridge: Cambridge University Press, 1996), 80.

23. Quoted in Stanley Wolpert, *A New History of India* (New York: Oxford University Press, 1993), 160.

24. Jane I. Smith, "Islam and Christendom," in *The Oxford History of Islam*, edited by John Esposito (Oxford: Oxford University Press, 1999), 342.

25. Charles Thornton Forester and F. H. Blackburne Daniell, *The Life and Letters of Ogier Ghiselin de Busbecq* (London: C. Kegan Paul & Co., 1881), 1:405–6.

26. Jean Bodin, "The Rise and Fall of Commonwealths," chap. 7, http://www.constitution.org/bodin/bodin_4.htm.

27. Lord Wharncliffe, ed., *The Letters and Works of Lady Mary Wortley Montagu* (London: Henry G. Bohn, 1861), 1:298–300.

28. Quoted in Stuart B. Schwartz, ed., *Victors and Vanquished* (Boston: Bedford/St. Martin's, 2000), 31.

29. Schwartz, *Victors and Vanquished*, 29.

30. Quoted in ibid., 164.

31. Miguel Leon-Portilla, *The Broken Spears* (Boston: Beacon Press, 1992), 80–81.

Chapter 15

1. Jacob Wheeler, "From Slave Post to Museum," *Christian Science Monitor*, December 31, 2002.

2. Quoted in Paul Lunde, "The Coming of the Portuguese," *Saudi Aramco World*, July–August 2005, 56.

3. Philip Curtin, *Cross Cultural Trade in World History* (Cambridge: Cambridge University Press, 1984), 144.

4. Quoted in Patricio N. Abinales and Donna J. Amoroso, *State and Society in the Philippines* (Lanham: Rowman and Littlefield, 2005), 50.

5. Anthony Reid, *Southeast Asia in the Age of Commerce, 1450–1680* (New Haven: Yale University Press, 1993), 2:274, 290.

6. Anthony Reid, *Charting the Shape of Early Modern Southeast Asia* (Chiang Mai: Silkworm Books, 1999), 227.

7. Andre Gunder Frank, *ReOrient: Global Economy in the Asian Age* (Berkeley: University of California Press, 1998), 131.

8. Quoted in Richard von Glahn, "Myth and Reality of China's Seventeenth Century Monetary Crisis," *Journal of Economic History* 56, no. 2 (June 1996): 132.

9. Kenneth Pomeranz and Steven Topik, *The World That Trade Created* (Armonk, N.Y.: M. E. Sharpe, 2006), 151–54.

10. Dennis O. Flynn and Arturo Giraldez, "Born with a 'Silver Spoon,'" *Journal of World History* 6, no. 2 (Fall 1995): 210.

11. Quoted in Mark Elvin, *The Retreat of the Elephant* (New Haven: Yale University Press, 2004), 37.

12. Quoted in Robert Marks, *The Origins of the Modern World* (Lanham: Rowman and Littlefield, 2002), 81.

13. See John Richards, *The Endless Frontier* (Berkeley: University of California Press, 2003), part 4. Much of this section is drawn from this source.

14. Elspeth M. Veale, *The English Fur Trade in the Later Middle Ages* (Oxford: Clarendon Press, 1966), 141.

15. Quoted in Richards, *The Endless Frontier*, 499.

16. Richards, *The Endless Frontier*, 504.

17. Quoted from "The Iroquois Confederacy," Portland State University, 2001, http://www.iroquoisdemocracy.pdx.edu/html/furtrader.htm.

18. These figures derive from the Trans-Atlantic Slave Trade Database, http://www.slavevoyages.org/tast/assessment/estimates.faces.

19. David Brion Davis, *Challenging the Boundaries of Slavery* (Cambridge, Mass.: Harvard University Press, 2003), 13.

20. Quoted in Bernard Lewis, *Race and Slavery in the Middle East* (New York: Oxford University Press, 1990), 52–53.

21. Audrey Smedley, *Race in North America* (Boulder, Colo.: Westview Press, 1993).

22. Kevin Reilly et al., eds., *Racism: A Global Reader* (Armonk, N.Y.: M. E. Sharpe, 2003), 131.

23. Quoted in Donald R. Wright, *The World and a Very Small Place in Africa* (Armonk, NY: M. E. Sharpe, 1997), 109–10.

24. John Thornton, *Africa and Africans in the Making of the Atlantic World* (Cambridge: Cambridge University Press, 1998), 72.

25. Thomas Phillips, "A Journal of a Voyage Made in the Hannibal of London in 1694," in *Documents Illustrative of the History of the Slave Trade to America*, edited by Elizabeth Donnan (Washington, D.C.: Carnegie Institute, 1930), 399–410.

26. Erik Gilbert and Jonathan T. Reynolds, *Africa in World History* (Upper Saddle River, N.J.: Pearson, 2004), 160.

27. Trans-Atlantic Slave Trade Database, http://www.slavevoyages.org/tast/assessment/estimates.faces.

28. Paul Adams et al., *Experiencing World History* (New York: New York University Press, 2000), 334.

29. Anne Bailey, *African Voices in the Atlantic Slave Trade* (Boston: Beacon Press, 2005), 153–54.

30. The present-day state of Benin is where the earlier kingdom of Dahomey once was. The ancient kingdom of Benin was located within present-day Nigeria.

31. Erik Gilbert and Jonathan Reynolds, *Trading Tastes: Commodity and Cultural Exchange to 1750* (Upper Saddle River, N.J.: Pearson Prentice Hall, 2006), 9.

32. Alex Szogyi, ed., *Chocolate: Food of the Gods* (Santa Barbara: Greenwood Press, 1997), 166.

33. James Grehan, "Smoking and 'Early Modern' Sociability: The Great Tobacco Debate in the Ottoman Middle East (Seventeenth to Eighteenth Centuries)," *The American Historical Review*, December 2006, http://www.historycooperative.org/journals/ahr/111.5/grehan.html.

34. Uzi Baram and Lynda Carroll, eds., *A Historical Archeology of the Ottoman Empire* (New York: Springer, 2000), 172–74.

Chapter 16

1. Andrew Rice, "Mission from Africa," *New York Times Magazine*, April 8, 2009; "African Missionaries Take Religion to the West," *Church Shift*, August 7, 2006, (http://www.churchshift.org).

2. Dr. Peter Hammond, "The Reformation," http://www.frontline.org.za/articles/thereformation_lectures.htm.

3. Glenn J. Ames, *Vasco da Gama: Renaissance Crusader* (New York: Pearson Education, 2005), 50.

4. Cecil Jane, ed. and trans., *Selected Documents Illustrating the Four Voyages of Columbus* (London: Hakluyt Society, 1930–1933), 2:2–18.

5. Kenneth Mills, *Idolatry and Its Enemies* (Princeton, N.J.: Princeton University Press, 1997), chap. 9.

6. Quoted in U.S. Library of Congress, "Country Studies: Peru," http://countrystudies.us/peru/5.htm.

7. Quoted in Nicolas Griffiths, *The Cross and the Serpent* (Norman: University of Oklahoma Press, 1996), 263.

8. See James Lockhart, *The Nahuas after Conquest* (Stanford, Calif.: Stanford University Press, 1992), chap. 6.

9. Quoted in Joanna Waley-Cohen, *The Sextants of Beijing* (New York: W. W. Norton, 1999), 76–77.

10. Richard M. Eaton, "Islamic History as Global History," in *Islamic and European Expansion*, edited by Michael Adas (Philadelphia: Temple University Press, 1993), 25.

11. Robert Bly and Jane Hirshfield, trans., *Mirabai: Ecstatic Poems* (Boston: Beacon Press, 2004), ix–xi.

12. Quoted in Steven Shapin, *The Scientific Revolution* (Chicago: University of Chicago Press, 1996), 66.

13. This section draws heavily on Toby E. Huff, *The Rise of Early Modern Science* (Cambridge: Cambridge University Press, 2003), 48, 52, 76.

14. Huff, *The Rise of Early Modern Science*, 87, 288.

15. Jerome Cardano, *The Book of My Life*, translated by Jean Stoner (London: J. M. Dent, 1931), 189.

16. Quoted in Shapin, *The Scientific Revolution*, 28.

17. Quoted in ibid., 61.

18. Quoted in ibid., 33.

19. Quoted in ibid., 68.

20. Stillman Drake, trans., *Discoveries and Opinions of Galileo* (Garden City, N.Y.: Doubleday, 1957).

21. H. S. Thayer, ed., *Newton's Philosophy of Nature: Selections from His Writings* (New York: Hafner Library of Classics, 1953), 42.

22. Immanuel Kant, "What Is Enlightenment?" translated by Peter Gay, in *Introduction to Contemporary Civilization in the West* (New York: Columbia University Press, 1954), 1071.

23. Voltaire, *A Treatise on Toleration* (1763), chap. 22, http://www.constitution.org/volt/tolerance.htm.

24. Quoted in Margaret C. Jacob, *The Enlightenment* (Boston: Bedford/St. Martin's, 2001), 103.

25. Quoted in Jonathan Spence, *The Search for Modern China* (New York: Norton, 1999), 104.

26. Waley-Cohen, *The Sextants of Beijing*, 105–14.

27. Benjamin A. Elman, *On Their Own Terms: Science in China, 1550–1900* (Cambridge, Mass.: Harvard University Press, 2005).

28. Quoted in David R. Ringrose, *Expansion and Global Interaction, 1200–1700* (New York: Longman, 2001), 188.

29. Ekmeleddin Ihsanoglu, *Science, Technology, and Learning in the Ottoman Empire* (Burlington, Vt.: Ashgate, 2004).

30. Quoted in Sergiusz Michalski, *The Reformation and the Visual Arts* (New York: Routledge, 1993), 7.

31. Quoted in Angela Vanhalaen, "Iconoclasm and the Creation of Images in Emanuel de Witte's Old Church in Amsterdam," *The Art Bulletin* (June 2005): 5.

32. David Brett, *The Plain Style* (Cambridge: Letterworth Press, 2004), 61–62.

33. Gauvin Alexander Bailey, *Art on the Jesuit Missions in Asia and Latin America* (Toronto: University of Toronto Press, 1999), 102–4.

34. John W. O'Malley et al., *The Jesuits* (Toronto: University of Toronto Press, 1999), 381.

Part Five

1. Quoted in Ross Dunn, *The New World History* (Boston: Bedford/St. Martin's, 2000), 17.

2. William H. McNeill, "*The Rise of the West* after 25 Years," *Journal of World History* 1, no. 1 (Spring 1990): 7.

Chapter 17

1. Quoted in Keith M. Baker, "A World Transformed," *Wilson Quarterly* (Summer 1989): 37.

2. Quoted in Thomas Benjamin et al., *The Atlantic World in the Age of Empire* (Boston: Houghton Mifflin, 2001), 205.

3. Jack P. Greene, "The American Revolution," *American Historical Review* 105, no. 1 (February 2000): 96–97.

4. Quoted in ibid., 102.

5. Quoted in Susan Dunn, *Sister Revolutions* (New York: Faber and Faber, 1999), 11, 12.

6. Quoted in ibid., 9.

7. Quoted in Lynn Hunt et al., *The Making of the West* (Boston: Bedford/St. Martin's, 2003), 625.

8. From James Leith, "Music for Mass Persuasion during the Terror," a collection of texts, tapes, and slides, copyright James A. Leith, Queen's University Kingston.

9. Franklin W. Knight, "The Haitian Revolution," *American Historical Review* 105, no. 1 (February 2000): 103.

10. Quoted in David P. Geggus, *Haitian Revolutionary Studies* (Bloomington: Indiana University Press, 2002), 27.

11. John C. Chasteen, *Born in Blood and Fire* (New York: Norton, 2006), 103.

12. Peter Winn, *Americas: The Changing Face of Latin America and the Caribbean* (Berkeley: University of California Press, 2006), 83.

13. Quoted in Thomas E. Skidmore and Peter H. Smith, *Modern Latin America* (New York: Oxford University Press, 2001), 33.

14. James Walvin, "The Public Campaign in England against Slavery," in *The Abolition of the Atlantic Slave Trade*, edited by David Eltis and James Walvin (Madison: University of Wisconsin Press, 1981), 76.

15. Michael Craton, "Slave Revolts and the End of Slavery," in *The Atlantic Slave Trade*, edited by David Northrup (Boston: Houghton Mifflin, 2002), 200.

16. Joseph Dupuis, *Journal of a Residence in Ashantee* (London: Henry Colburn, 1824),162–64

17. Eric Foner, *Nothing but Freedom* (Baton Rouge: Louisiana State University Press, 1983).

18. Quoted in Daniel Moran and Arthur Waldron, eds., *The People in Arms: Military Myth and National Mobilization since the French Revolution* (Cambridge: Cambridge University Press, 2003), 14.

19. Barbara Winslow, "Feminist Movements: Gender and Sexual Equality," in *A Companion to Gender History*, edited by Teresa A. Meade and Merry E. Weisner-Hanks (London: Blackwell, 2004), 186.

20. Bonnie S. Anderson, *Joyous Greetings: The First International Women's Movement, 1830–1860* (Oxford: Oxford University Press, 2000).

21. Quoted in Claire G. Moses, *French Feminism in the Nineteenth Century* (Albany: SUNY Press, 1984), 135.

22. See Lynn Hunt, ed., *The French Revolution and Human Rights* (Boston: Bedford/St. Martin's, 1996), 1–31.

23. Quoted in "The Rights of Women," http://www.pinn.net/~sunshine/book-sum/gouges.html.

24. Jean-Denis Lanjuinais, "Discussion of Citizenship under the Proposed New Constitution" in *The French Revolution and Human Rights*, edited by Lynn Hunt (Boston: Bedford/St. Martin's, 1996), 133.

25. Quoted in Lynn Hunt, *Politics, Culture, and Class in the French Revolution* (Berkeley: University of California Press, 2004), 35.

26. Modern History Sourcebook, "Ca ira," http://www.fordham.edu/halsall/mod/caira.html.

Chapter 18

1. "Mahatma Gandhi on Industrialization," http://www.tinytechindia .com/gandhi3.htm#1.

2. Edmund Burke III and Kenneth Pomeranz, eds., *The Environment and World History* (Berkeley: University of California Press, 2009), 41.

3. David Christian, *Maps of Time* (Berkeley: University of California Press, 2004), 346–47.

4. Joel Mokyr, *The Lever of Riches* (New York: Oxford University Press, 1990), 40–44.

5. Lynda Shaffer, "Southernization," *Journal of World History* 5, no. 1 (Spring 1994): 1–21.

6. Kenneth Pomeranz, *The Great Divergence* (Princeton, N.J.: Princeton University Press, 2000). See also Jack Goldstone, *Why Europe? The Rise of the West in World History* (Boston: McGraw-Hill, 2009).

7. Pier Vries, "Are Coal and Colonies Really Crucial?" *Journal of World History* 12, no. 2 (Fall 2001): 411.

8. Christian, *Maps of Time*, 390.

9. E. L. Jones, *The European Miracle* (Cambridge: Cambridge University Press, 1981), 119.

10. Quoted in Mokyr, *The Lever of Riches*, 188.

11. Quoted in Prasannan Parthansaranthi, "Rethinking Wages and Competitiveness in the Eighteenth Century," *Past and Present* 158 (February 1998): 79.

12. Maxine Berg, *Luxury and Pleasure in Eighteenth-Century Britain* (Oxford: Oxford University Press, 2005), 79–84.

13. Peter Stearns, *The Industrial Revolution in World History* (Boulder, Colo.: Westview Press, 1998), 36.

14. Goldstone, *Why Europe?* Ch. 8.

15. Eric Hopkins, *Industrialization and Society* (London: Routledge, 2000), 2.

16. Mokyr, *The Lever of Riches*, 81.

17. Eric Hobsbawm, *Industry and Empire* (New York: New Press, 1999), 58. This section draws heavily on Hobsbawm's celebrated account of British industrialization.

18. Lynn Hunt et al., *The Making of the West* (Boston: Bedford/St. Martin's, 2009), 656.

19. Samuel Smiles, *Thrift* (London: John Murray, 1875), 30–40.

20. Hobsbawm, *Industry and Empire*, 65.

21. Peter Stearns and John H. Hinshaw, *Companion to the Industrial Revolution* (Santa Barbara: ABC-CLIO, 1996), 150.

22. Workers' Liberty, http://www.workersliberty.org/node/view/3359?PHPSESSID=93d.

23. Hobsbawm, *Industry and Empire*, 171.

24. Derived from Paul Kennedy, *The Rise and Fall of the Great Powers* (New York: Random House, 1987), 149.

25. John Charles Chasteen, *Born in Blood and Fire* (New York: W. W. Norton, 2006), 181.

26. Peter Bakewell, *A History of Latin America* (Oxford: Blackwell, 1997), 425.

27. Michael Adas, *Machines as the Measure of Men* (Ithaca, N.Y.: Cornell University Press, 1990).

28. Ibid., 133.

29. Quoted in Francis D. Klingender, *Art and the Industrial Revolution* (New York: Augustus M. Kelley Publishers, 1968), 139.

30. See Kathryn J. Summerwill, "Eyre Crowe A.R.A. (1824–1910)," http://www.geocities.com/eyre_crowe/1874.html.

31. "*The Dinner Hour: Wigan*, Eyre Crowe," Images of the Industrial Revolution, http://www.netnicholls.com/neh2000/paper/pages/txt07.htm#.

32. "Child Labor in America: Photographs of Lewis W. Hine, 1908–1912," The History Place, http://www.historyplace.com/unitedstates/childlabor/.

33. Quoted in Albert Boime, *Art in an Age of Bonapartism, 1800–1815* (Chicago: University of Chicago Press, 1990), 120–21.

Chapter 19

1. People's Daily, April 6, 2001, http://english.peopledaily.com.cn/english/200104/06/eng20010406_66955.html.

2. Quoted in Heinz Gollwitzer, *Europe in the Age of Imperialism* (London: Thames and Hudson, 1969), 136.

3. Robert Knox, *Races of Man* (Philadelphia: Lea and Blanchard, 1850), v.

4. Quoted in Ralph Austen, ed., *Modern Imperialism* (Lexington, Mass.: D. C. Heath, 1969), 70–73.

5. Quoted in Julian Burger, "Echoes of History," *New Internationalist*, August 1988, http://www.newint.org/issue186/echoes.htm.

6. Dun J. Li, ed., *China in Transition, 1517–1911* (New York: Van Nostrand Reinhold, 1969).

7. Quoted in Jonathan D. Spence, *The Search for Modern China* (New York: W. W. Norton, 1999), 169.

8. Hsin-Pao Chang, ed., *Commissioner Lin and the Opium War* (New York: Norton, 1970), 226–27.

9. Barbara Hodgson, *Opium: A Portrait of the Heavenly Demon* (San Francisco: Chronicle Books, 1999), 32.

10. Quoted in Teng Ssu and John K. Fairbanks, eds. and trans., *China's Response to the West* (New York: Atheneum, 1963), 69.

11. Quoted in Magali Morsy, *North Africa: 1800–1900* (London: Longman, 1984), 79.

12. Quoted in M Sukru Hanioglu, *The Young Turks in Opposition* (New York: Oxford University Press, 1995), 17.

13. Marius B. Jansen, *The Making of Modern Japan* (Cambridge, Mass.: Harvard University Press, 2002), 33.

14. Quoted in Carol Gluck, "Themes in Japanese History," in *Asia in Western and World History*, edited by Ainslie T. Embree and Carol Gluck (Armonk, N.Y.: M. E. Sharpe, 1997), 754.

15. Quoted in S. Hanley and K. Yamamura, *Economic and Demographic Change in Pre-Industrial Japan* (Princeton, N.J.: Princeton University Press, 1977), 88–90.

16. Quoted in Harold Bolitho, "The Tempo Crisis," in *The Cambridge History of Japan*, vol. 5, *The Nineteenth Century*, edited by Maurice B. Jansen (Cambridge: Cambridge University Press, 1989), 230.

17. Kenneth Henshall, *A History of Japan* (New York: Palgrave, 2004), 67.

18. Quoted in James L. McClain, *Japan: A Modern History* (New York: W. W. Norton, 2002), 177.

19. Selcuk Esenbel, "Japan's Global Claim to Asia and the World of Islam," *American Historical Review* (October 2004), par. 1, 9, http://www.historycooperative.org/journals/ahr/109.4/esenbel.html.

20. Jonathan Spence, *The Search for Modern China* (New York: W. W. Norton, 1999), 154.

21. Ibid., 159.

22. Quoted in Marius B. Jensen, *The Making of Modern Japan* (Cambridge: Harvard University Press, 2000), 460.

23. Quoted in Julia Meech-Pekarik, *The World of the Meiji Print: Impressions of a New Civilization* (New York: Weatherhill, 1986), 182.

24. Quoted in Oka Yoshitake, Prologue to Marlene Mayo, ed., *The Emergence of Imperial Japan* (Lexington: Heath, 1970).

Chapter 20

1. Quoted in Robert Strayer, *The Making of Mission Communities in East Africa* (London: Heinemann, 1978), 89.

2. Quoted in John Iliffe, *Africans: The History of a Continent* (Cambridge: Cambridge University Press, 1995), 191.

3. Quoted in Nicholas Tarling, "The Establishment of Colonial Regimes," in *The Cambridge History of Southeast Asia*, edited by Nicholas Tarling (Cambridge: Cambridge University Press, 1992), 2:76.

4. R. Meinertzhagen, *Kenya Diary* (London: Oliver and Boyd, 1957), 51–52.

5. Quoted in Neil Jamieson, *Understanding Vietnam* (Berkeley: University of California Press, 1993), 49–57.

6. Quoted in Donald R. Wright, *The World and a Very Small Place in Africa* (Armonk, N.Y.: M. E. Sharpe, 2004), 170.

7. Quoted in Scott B. Cook, *Colonial Encounters in the Age of High Imperialism* (New York: HarperCollins, 1996), 53.

8. D. R. SarDesai, *Southeast Asia: Past and Present* (Boulder, Colo.: Westview Press, 1997), 95–98.

9. Quoted in G. C. K. Gwassa and John Iliffe, *Records of the Maji Maji Rising* (Nairobi: East African Publishing House, 1967), 1: 4–5.

10. Michael Adas, "Continuity and Transformation: Colonial Rice Frontiers and Their Environmental Impact…," in *The Environment and World History*, edited by Edmund Burke III and Kenneth Pomeranz (Berkeley: University of California Press, 2009), 191–207.

11. Iliffe, *Africans*, 216.

12. Quoted in Basil Davidson, *Modern Africa* (London: Longmans, 1983), 79, 81.

13. This section draws heavily on Margaret Jean Hay and Sharon Stichter, eds., *African Women South of the Sahara* (London: Longmans, 1984), especially chaps. 1–5.

14. Quoted in Robert A. Levine, "Sex Roles and Economic Change in Africa," in *Black Africa*, edited by John Middleton (London: Macmillan, 1970), 178.

15. Elizabeth Schmidt, *Peasants, Traders, and Wives: Shona Women in the History of Zimbabwe, 1870–1939* (Portsmouth, N.H.: Heinemann, 1992), chap. 4.

16. Derived from Adam McKeown, "Global Migration, 1846–1940," *Journal of World History* 15, no. 2 (June 2004): 156.

17. Josiah Kariuki, *Mau Mau Detainee* (London: Oxford University Press, 1963), 5.

18. Quoted in Harry Benda and John Larkin, *The World of Southeast Asia* (New York: Harper and Row, 1967), 182–85.

19. William Theodore de Bary, *Sources of Indian Tradition* (New York: Columbia University Press, 1958), 619.

20. Quoted in Edward W. Smith, *Aggrey of Africa*, (London: SCM Press, 1929).

21. C. A. Bayly, *The Birth of the Modern World* (Oxford: Blackwell, 2004), 343.

22. de Bary, *Sources of Indian Tradition*, 652.

23. Nirad Chaudhuri, *Autobiography of an Unknown Indian* (London: John Farquharson, 1968), 229.

24. Edward Blyden, *Christianity, Islam, and the Negro Race* (Edinburgh: Edinburgh University Press, 1967), 124.

25. John Iliffe, *A Modern History of Tanganyika* (Cambridge: Cambridge University Press, 1979), 324.

26. British Museum, http://ww.britishmuseum.org/explore/highlights/ highlight_objects/aoa/b/the_battle_of_adwa, _painting.aspx.

Part Six

1. J. R. McNeill, *Something New under the Sun* (New York: W. W. Norton, 2000), 3–4.

Chapter 21

1. "Scotland's Oldest Man Turns 107," *Scotsman*, June 25, 2003, http://www.aftermathww1.com/oldestscot.asp; MSNBC, November 21, 2005, http://www.msnbc.msn.com/id/10138446/

2. Quoted in John Keegan, *The First World War* (New York: Vintage Books, 1998), 3.

3. Adapted from Lynn Hunt et al., *The Making of the West: Peoples and Cultures* (Boston: Bedford/St. Martin's, 2001), 1024.

4. Stanley Payne, *History of Fascism, 1914–1945* (Madison: University of Wisconsin Press, 1995), 208.

5. Richard Bessel, ed., *Fascist Italy and Nazi Germany: Comparisons and Contrasts* (Cambridge: Cambridge University Press, 1996), 8.

6. Quoted in Laurence Rees, *The Nazis: A Warning from History* (New York: New Press, 1997), 62.

7. James L. McClain, *Japan: A Modern History* (New York: W. W. Norton, 2002), 378.

8. Quoted in ibid., 414.

9. Bernd Martin, *Japan and Germany in the Modern World* (Providence: Berghahn Books, 1995), 155–81.

10. Quoted in Marius B. Jansen, *The Making of Modern Japan* (Cambridge, Mass.: Harvard University Press, 2000), 607.

11. Quoted in ibid., 639.

12. Quoted in John Keegan, *The Second World War* (New York: Viking Penguin, 1989), 186.

13. John Lewis Gaddis, *We Now Know: Rethinking Cold War History* (Oxford: Oxford University Press, 1997), 52.

14. Adam Gopnik, "The Big One: Historians Rethink the War to End All Wars," *The New Yorker*, August 23, 2004, 78.

Chapter 22

1. BBC, "On this Day," November 9, 1989, http://news.bbc.co.uk/onthisday/hi/witness/november/9/newsid_3241000/3241641.stm.

2. Quoted in Ronald Suny, *The Soviet Experiment* (Oxford: Oxford University Press, 1998), 357.

3. Yuan-tsung Chen, *The Dragon's Village* (New York: Penguin Books, 1980), 85.

4. Such figures are often highly controversial. See Maurice Meisner, *Mao's China and After* (New York: Free Press, 1999), 413–25; Roderick MacFarquhar, ed., *The Politics of China* (Cambridge: Cambridge University Press, 1997), 243–45.

5. Quoted in Richard Rusk, *As I Saw It* (New York: Norton, 1990), 245.

6. Quoted in John L. Gaddis, *The Cold War: A New History* (New York: Penguin Press, 2005), 57.

7. Ronald Steel, *Pax Americana* (New York: Viking Press, 1970), 254.

8. Quoted in Donald W. White, *The American Century* (New Haven: Yale University Press, 1996), 164.

9. David Potter, *People of Plenty* (Chicago: University of Chicago Press, 1954), 139.

10. Quoted in John M. Thompson, *A Vision Unfulfilled* (Lexington, Mass.: D. C. Heath, 1996), 383.

11. Deng Xiaoping, "The Necessity of Upholding the Four Cardinal Principles in the Drive for the Four Modernizations," in *Major Documents of the People's Republic of China* (Beijing: Foreign Language Press, 1991), 54.

12. Mikhail Gorbachev, *Perestroika: New Thinking for Our Country and the World* (New York: Harper and Row, 1987), 64.

13. Quoted in Abraham Brumberg, *Chronicle of a Revolution* (New York: Pantheon Books, 1990), 225–26.

14. Quoted in *Chinese Propaganda Posters* (Koln: Taschen, 2003), 5.

15. Quoted in ibid., 10.

Chapter 23

1. Nelson Mandela, "I Am Prepared to Die," statement at the Rivonia trial, April 20, 1964, http://www.anc.org.za/ancdocs/history/rivonia.html.

2. Quoted in Jim Masselos, *Nationalism on the Indian Subcontinent* (Melbourne: Nelson, 1972), 122.

3. Mohandas Gandhi, *Hind Swaraj*, 1909, http://www.mkgandhi-sarvodaya.org/hindswaraj.htm.

4. Quoted in Stanley Wolpert, *A New History of India* (Oxford: Oxford University Press, 1993), 331.

5. This information is drawn from the World Bank, *World Development Report 2009* (Oxford: Oxford University Press, 2008), Tables 1, 2.

6. Quoted in Bernard Lewis, *The Emergence of Modern Turkey* (London: Oxford University Press, 1968), 268–69.

7. Quoted in Patrick B. Kinross, *Ataturk: A Biography of Mustafa Kemal* (New York: Morrow, 1965), 390.

8. Sandra Mackey, *The Iranians* (New York: Penguin, 1998), 306.

9. Kwame Nkrumah, *Ghana: An Autobiography* (London: Nelson, 1957), 34.

10. Liberation Graphics, "Palestine Poster Project," http://www.liberationgraphics.com/ppp/Redeem_the_Land.html.

11. Ibid., http://www.liberationgraphics.com/ppp/landday.html.

Chapter 24

1. BBC News, March 5, 2002, http://news.bbc.co.uk/2/hi/middle_east/1856558.stm.

2. Jeffrey Frieden, *Global Capitalism* (New York: W. W. Norton, 2006), 476.

3. Jan Aart Scholte, *Globalization: A Critical Introduction* (New York: Palgrave, 2005), 117.

4. Based on constant 2004 U.S. dollars. Earth Policy Institute, "Eco-Economy Indicators," http://www.earth-policy.org/Indicators/Econ/Econ_data.htm.

5. United Nations, *Human Development Report, 1997*, 2, http://hdr.undp.org/reports/global/1997/en.

6. Michael Hunt, *The World Transformed* (Boston: Bedford/St. Martin's, 2004), 442.

7. Quoted in Frieden, *Global Capitalism*, 408.

8. Quoted in Manfred B. Steger, *Globalization: A Very Short Introduction* (Oxford: Oxford University Press, 2003), 122.

9. Quoted in Frieden, *Global Capitalism*, 459.

10. Charles S. Maier, *Among Empires: American Ascendancy and Its Predecessors* (Cambridge, Mass.: Harvard University Press, 2006), chap. 5.

11. Quoted in Donald W. White, *The American Century: The Rise and Decline of the United States as a World Power* (New Haven: Yale University Press, 1996), 395.

12. Quoted in Sarah Shaver Hughes and Brady Hughes, *Women in World History* (Armonk, N.Y.: M. E. Sharpe, 1997), 2:268.

13. Susan Kent, "Worlds of Feminism," in *Women's History in Global Perspective*, edited by Bonnie G. Smith (Urbana: University of Illinois Press, 2004), 1:305–6.

14. Quoted in Wilhelmina Oduol and Wanjiku Mukabi Kabira, "The Mother of Warriors and Her Daughters: The Women's Movement in Kenya," in *Global Feminisms since 1945*, edited by Bonnie Smith (London: Routledge, 2000), 111.

15. Elisabeth Jay Friedman, "Gendering the Agenda," *Women's Studies International Forum* 26, no. 4 (2003): 313–31.

16. Quoted in Mary E. Hawkesworth, *Globalization and Feminist Activism* (New York: Rowman and Littfield, 2006), 124.

17. Phyllis Schlafly, *The Power of the Christian Woman* (Cincinnati: Standard, 1981), 117.

18. Karen Armstrong, *The Battle for God* (New York: Alfred A. Knopf, 2000), xi.

19. Quoted in Armstrong, *The Battle for God*, 273.

20. Quoted in John Esposito, *Unholy War* (Oxford: Oxford University Press, 2002), 57.

21. Quoted in ibid., 63.

22. "Fatwah Urging Jihad against Americans," http://www.ict.org.il/articles/fatwah.htm.

23. Anwar Ibrahim, "The Ardent Moderates," *Time*, September 23, 1996, 24.

24. See J. R. McNeill, *Something New under the Sun: An Environmental History of the Twentieth Century World* (New York: Norton, 2001).

25. Adapted from Lynn Hunt et *al., The Making of the West: Peoples and Cultures* (Bedford/St. Martin's, 2009), 968.

26. Ramachandra Guha, *Environmentalism: A Global History* (New York: Longman, 2000), part 1.

27. Timothy Doyle, *Environmental Movements in Minority and Majority Worlds: A Global Perspective* (New Brunswick, N.J.: Rutgers University Press, 2005).

28. Quoted in Shiraz Sidhva, "Saving the Planet: Imperialism in a Green Garb," *The UNESCO Courier*, April 2001, 41–43.

29. Anwar Ibrahim, "Who Hijacked Islam?" *Time Magazine*, October 8, 2001.

30. *Bulletin of the Committee of Moroccan Workers in Holland*, 1978, quoted in *Third World Lives of Struggle*, edited by Hazel Johnson and Henry Bernstein (London: Heinemann, 1982), 173-74.

Acknowledgments

Chapter 3

Benjamin R. Foster. "Come then, Enkidu, to ramparted Uruk." Excerpt (7 lines) from *The Epic of Gilgamesh*, translated by Benjamin R. Foster, p. 10. Tablet 1: 226–232. Copyright © 2001 by W.W. Norton & Company. Used by permission of W.W. Norton & Company, Inc.

Miriam Lichtheim. "Seven days to yesterday, I have not seen the 'sister.'" As appears in *Ancient Egyptian Literature*, volume 2, pp. 184–185 by Miriam Lichtheim, translator. Copyright © 1976 by University of California Press. Reproduced with permission of University of California Press, in the format Textbook via Copyright Clearance Center.

Miriam Lichtheim. "Now the scribe lands on the shore." From *Ancient Egyptian Literature*, volume 2, translated by Miriam Lichtheim, pp. 168–175. As appears in *A Book of Readings: the New Kingdom* by Miriam Lichtheim, translator. Copyright © 1976 by University of California Press. Reproduced with permission of University of California Press, in the format textbook via Copyright Clearance Center.

N. K. Sandars. "You will never find that life for which you are looking...." Excerpts from *The Epic of Gilgamesh*, translated with an introduction by N. K. Sandars (Penguin Classics 1960, Third Edition 1972). Copyright © N.K. Sandars, 1960, 1964, 1972. Reproduced by permission of Penguin Books, Ltd.

Miriam Lichtheim. "The gatekeeper comes out to you." From *Ancient Egyptian Literature*, volume 2, translated by Miriam Lichtheim, pp. 124–126. As appears in *A Book of Readings: the New Kingdom* by Miriam Lichtheim, translator. Copyright © 1976 by University of California Press. Reproduced with permission of University of California Press, in the format textbook via Copyright Clearance Center.

Samuel Kramer. "After your city had been destroyed, how now can you exist!" From *The Sumerians*, translated by Samuel Kramer, p. 142. Copyright © 1963 by University of Chicago Press. Used by permission of University of Chicago Press.

Samuel Kramer. "In those days the dwellings of Agade were filled with gold." Translated by Samuel Kramer. As appears in *Ancient Near Eastern Texts Relating to the Old Testament* by James Pritchard, ed., pp. 647–648. Copyright © 1969 Princeton University Press. Used by permission of Princeton University Press.

Chapter 5

Lao Tsu. "A small country has few people." From *Tao Te Ching* by Lau Tsu, translated by Gia-Fu Feng and Jane English, p. 80. Copyright © 1972 by Gia-Fu Feng and Jane English. Translation copyright © 1997 by Jane English. Used by permission of Alfred A. Knopf, a division of Random House, Inc.

Sappho. "If you will come, I shall put out new pillows for you to rest on." From *Sappho: A New Translation* by Mary Bernard, translator. Copyright © 1958 by University of California Press. Reproduced with permission of University of California Press, in the format Textbook via Copyright Clearance Center.

Ovid. "Add gifts of mind to bodily language...." From *The Art of Love and Other Poems*, translated by H. H. Mozley. Published by William Heinemann, 1929, pp. 73, 75.

Chapter 9

Yuan Chen. "Ever since the Western horsemen began raising smut and dust." Quoted in *The Golden Peaches of Samarkand: A Study of T'ang Exotics*, by Edward H. Shafer, translator. Copyright © 1963 by University of California Press. Reproduced by permission of University of California Press in the format Textbook via Copyright Clearance Center.

Chapter 11

Visual Source 11.1. Attributed to Mir Sayyid 'Ali, *Nomadic Encampment*, folio from a manuscript of the *Khamsa* (quintet) of Nizami, mid-16th century. Opaque watercolor, gold, and silver on paper, 28.4 x 20 cm. Harvard Art Museum, Arthur M. Sackler Museum, Gift of John Goelet, formerly in the collection of Louis J. Cartier, 1958.75. Photo: Katya Kallsen. © President and Fellows of Harvard College.

Visual Source 11.2. Attributed to Mir Sayyid 'Ali, *Nighttime in a Palace*, folio from a manuscript, c. 1539–1543. Opaque watercolor, gold, and silver on paper; 28.6 x 20 cm. Harvard Art Museum, Arthur M. Sackler Museum, Gift of

John Goelet, formerly in the collection of Louis J. Cartier, 1958.76. Photo: Katya Kallsen. © President and Fellows of Harvard College.

Chapter 13

Miguel Leon-Portilla. "Like a painting, we will be erased." From *Fifteen Poets of the Aztec World* by Miguel Leon-Portilla, editor and translator. Copyright © 1992 by the University of Oklahoma Press, Norman. Reprinted by permission.

Chapter 15

Mark Elvin. "Rarer too their timber grew." Excerpt (4 lines) from *Retreat of the Elephants* by Mark Elvin. Copyright © 2004 by Mark Elvin. Used by permission of Yale University Press.

Chapter 16

Mirabai. "What I paid was my social body…." From *Mirabai: Ecstatic Poems* by Robert Bly and Jane Hirshfeld. Copyright © by Robert Bly and Jane Hirshfield. Reprinted by Beacon Press, Boston.

Chapter 20

Neil Jamieson. "Fine wine but no good friends." From *Understanding Vietnam* by Neil Jamieson, translator. Copyright © 1993 by University of California Press. Reproduced with permission of University of California Press in the format Textbook via Copyright Clearance Center.

Chapter 24

Map 24.3 (bottom) is adapted from http://www.princeton.edu/~ina/infographics/starbucks.html (2003).

Index

Note: Names of individuals are in **boldface** and: (f) figures, including charts and graphs; (i) illustrations, including photographs and artifacts in the narrative portion of the book only, not in the docutext sections; (m) maps; (t) tables; (v) visual sources, including all illustrations in the docutext portion of the book; (d) documents in the docutext portion of the book

Abbasid caliphate, 484–485
  Baghdad and, 497
  maritime trade and, 344
  Mongol conquest of, 489, 538
  Turks in, 528
Abd al-Hamid II (Ottoman Empire, r. 1876–1909), 893
Abd al-Malik (Umayyad caliph), 612–613
Abd al-Rahman al-Jabarti, 890
Abd al-Rahman III (Spain, 912–961), 495
Abd al-Wahhab (1703–1792), 734, 756–757(d)
abolition of slavery, 793–796, 794(i)
  manumission and, 248(t), 251
Aboriginal people (Australia), 17, 21(i), 571–572
  mythology of, 39, 40–41(d)
abortion rights, 1150
Abraham (Old Testament), 204
Abu Amir al-Mansur (981–1002), 495
Abu Bakr (caliph), 483
Abyssinia. See Axum; Ethiopia
Academy (Plato), 208, 451
Achaemenid dynasty (Persia, 558–330 B.C.E.), 203
acupuncture, 544
Addams, Jane, 801
Adelard of Bath (1080–1142), 451
administration. See government
Adowa, Battle of (1896), 966–967, 966(v)

Adulis (port of Axum), 287
Aelius Aristides (ca. 117–181 C.E.), 172–173, 173–174(d)
Affonso I (Kongo), 706, 706–707(d)
Afghanistan
  Bactria in, 153
  Buddha and, 228
  communism in, 1031
  Islamic militants in, 1142
  Islamization in, 1156
  Soviet war in, 1046
  Taliban in, 1156
  trade in, 108
Africa. See also specific locations
  agricultural village societies in, 572–573
  agriculture in, 51, 52(t), 55
  ancient historical landmarks in, 8–9(f)
  Asia and, 111
  Bantu speakers in, 290–292
  Christianity in, 943–944
  civilizations of, 86, 282, 283–292
  in classical era, 283–292, 285(m)
  colonial development in, 939–940
  colonial rule in, 772(m), 795, 924–925, 926, 927(m), 960–967, 961(v), 962(v), 964(v), 965(v), 966(v)
  colonial societies in, 931–932, 943–944
  communism in, 1031, 1051
  cultural traditions in, 732–733
  democracy in, 1096–1097, 1098
  diaspora from, 690
  early humans in, 3
  economic development in, 1097, 1099, 1100–1101(t), 1110–1120, 1111–1112(d), 1113–1114(d), 1115–1116(d), 1117–1118(d), 1119–1120(d), 1138–1139
  Egypt and, 110
  elites and state in, 1118, 1119–1120(d)
  ethnic identities in, 946–947
  European racism in, 930–931

  feminists in, 1147–1148
  in 15th century, 570(t), 571, 582(m)
  France and, 961–963, 962(v)
  gold in, 348, 349
  in Great Depression, 986
  Ibn Battuta in, 363–365(d)
  imperialism in, 880
  independence and, 1083, 1094
  India compared with, 1095–1098
  Islam in, 575, 586–588
  lineage system in, 64
  migrations from, 12–16, 14–15(m)
  missionaries in, 960
  nationalism in, 800, 1081
  pastoral societies in, 79(v), 575
  political evolution in, 1096–1098
  population in classical era, 282
  Portuguese trade and, 674
  postindependence period in, 1095–1098
  race, tribe, and, 945–947
  religious wars in, 733
  rock art in, 10(i), 25, 28
  scramble for, 926, 960–967, 961(v), 962(v), 964(v), 965(v), 966(v)
  settler colonies in, 936
  slave trade in, 636, 672(i), 690–697
  socialism in, 1114–1115, 1115–1116(d)
  trade across, 346–351
  wage labor in colonies, 935–938
  women in, 938–939, 1116–1117, 1117–1118(d)
  after World War II, 1003, 1004
African Americans. See also slave trade
  civil rights for, 1145
  as Muslims, 473
  Obama as, 1144
African identity, 1112
Africanization, of Christianity, 943–944
African National Congress (ANC), 1091–1092, 1093, 1123, 1125(v)
African unity, Nkrumah on, 1112–1113, 1113–1114(d)

Afrikaners, 1091

Afro-Eurasia, 284, 334, 340, 344, 351, 352(m), 354, 732–737
  in 15th century, 584–588
  Islamic exchange and, 497
  religion and commerce in, 596(m)

afterlife
  Confucianism on, 195
  in Egypt, 105, 121–122(d)
  in First Civilizations, 121, 122–123(d)

"After Passing the Examination"
  (Po Chu-I), 239

age-grade systems, in Africa, 528

age of warring states. *See* warring states period (China)

Aggrey, James, 943

agrarianism. *See also* Agricultural
  Revolution; agriculture
  in early modern era, 620–621

Agricultural era, 23

Agricultural Revolution, 5–6, 50–56, 282, 522. *See also* agriculture
  in Americas, 304
  art, artifacts, and, 76–83, 77(v), 78(v), 79(v), 81(v), 82(v)
  civilization origins in, 91–92
  disease and, 61
  in Fertile Crescent, 60
  locations of, 51–53
  in New Guinea, 60
  pastoral societies and, 525
  societies in, 62–66, 68–75, 69–71(d), 72–73(d), 74–75(d)
  technology and, 61–62
  variations in, 53–56
  world population and, 135(f)

agriculture. *See also* Agricultural
  Revolution; farms and farming;
  irrigation; plantations; sugar
  industry
  in Africa, 289, 291, 349
  in Andes, 297
  in Australia, 572
  breakthroughs in, 52(t)
  cash-crop, 934–935, 938
  in China, 61, 577, 584, 888, 1052
  collectivization of, 1040–1041
  in colonial Latin America, 632
  culture of, 61–62
  decline of farming and, 49–50
  development of, 5

diffusion of, 57
  in Dutch East Indies, 933–934
  in Egypt, 103–104, 106, 108
  in England, 832
  in Europe, 584
  gender and, 96
  globalization of, 58–59(m), 60
  hoe-based, 53
  imperialism and, 879
  innovations in, 831
  intensification of, 51, 62
  Islamic exchange and, 497
  legacies of, 66–67
  Masai, 528–529
  of Maya, 294
  in Meroë, 286
  in Mesoamerica, 294
  of Mound Builders, 303–304
  Pacific migrations and, 19
  vs. pastoralism, 528
  plow, gender, and, 96–97
  population growth and, 61
  in Russian Empire, 641
  in southwestern North America, 301
  Soviet, 1039(i)
  three-field system of, 447
  in Vietnam, 393
  villages and, 64–65, 64(i), 68–83, 572–574
  women in, 1039(i), 1040

Ahkmatova, Anna, 1069(d)

Ahura Mazda (god, Persia), 145, 147, 203

Ain Ghazal, Jordan, statues of, 48(i)

Ain Jalut, Palestine, battle at, 533

Aisha (wife of Muhammad), 487, 517

Aja-speaking peoples, slave trade and, 696

Akbar (Mughal Empire, r. 1556–1605), 645–646, 767

Akiko, Yosano, 994

Akkad and Akkadians, 105(m), 106

alcohol, Native Americans and, 687–688

Alexander the Great (Macedonia, d. 323 B.C.E.), 152–154, 152(m), 153(i), 166

Alexandria, Egypt, 153

Algeria, 153, 1086
  Islamic Salvation Front in, 1155
  rock art from, 80

Algonquian peoples, Europeans and, 687

Ali (caliph), 483

Allah, 475, 476, 502–503. *See also*
  Islam; Muhammad; Muslims

alliances. *See also* specific alliances
  Japanese, 997
  military, 1045
  before World War I, 979
  in World War II, 1002

All-India Muslim League, 1089

All Quiet on the Western Front
  (Remarque), 982

Alopen (Persian Christian monk), 462

alphabet. *See also* writing systems
  Cyrillic, 433
  Korean, 392
  Phoenician, 109

al-Qaeda, 1142, 1156, 1157, 1176

Alvarez, Francisco, 616

Amaterasu (goddess), 897

Amazon River region, 298, 353
  agricultural village societies in, 572

American Empire, globalization and, 1142–1144, 1143(m)

American Federation of Labor, 843

American Indians. *See* Native
  Americans

Americanos, 792

American Revolution (1775–1783), 779, 781–784. *See also* United States
  French Revolution compared with, 787

Americas. *See also* civilization(s);
  Mesoamerica; North America;
  plantations; slave trade; South
  America; Western Hemisphere;
  specific locations
  agriculture in, 51, 52(t), 55
  ancient historical landmarks in, 8–9(f)
  Christian missionaries in, 727
  classical era in, 292–304
  colonial societies in, 631–639
  decolonization in, 1082
  in early modern era, 622–623(t)
  European empires in, 626–631
  in 15th century, 570(t), 571, 588–594, 589(m)
  gathering and hunting peoples of, 18, 29–31, 60

after independence, 793
Islam and, 733
metallurgy in, 283
migrations to, 14–15(m), 18
mixed-race peoples in, 715–718, 717(v)
population in classical era, 282
slavery in, 95–96, 248(t), 591, 690, 695
sugar industry in, 634–637
Amida Buddha/Amitabha (deity, Buddhism), 234(v), 235, 408
Amos (prophet, Judaism), 190, 191(t), 205
Amritsar
Golden Temple of, 737
massacre in, 1087–1088
Anabaptists, 725
Analects, The (Confucius), 193, 217, 218–219(d)
Anasazi people. *See* Ancestral Pueblo people
Anatolia, 172, 428. *See also* Ottoman Empire; Turkey
Greek settlements in, 151, 207
Hittites in, 110
Islam and, 491–492
Ottoman Empire in, 647, 647(m), 648
population of, 491
trade of, 108
ancestors
in Bantu religions, 292
Chinese veneration of, 194
in Dreamtime Australia, 17–18
human, 4
Ancestral Pueblo people (Anasazi), 301
ancient régime. *See* Old Regime
anda (Mongol custom), 550, 551(d)
al-Andalus. *See* Spain
Andes Mountains region, 293, 327. *See also* specific countries and societies
agriculture in, 51, 52(t), 55
civilizations of, 87, 297–300, 589(m)
cross-cultural interaction in, 328
after First Civilizations, 297
Inca Empire in, 592–594
Mesoamerican interaction with, 353–354
religion in, 728–729
writing in, 101(t), 102
Angkor, 346
Anglicanism, 725

Anglo-Japanese Treaty (1902), 901
Anglo-Saxons, 457, 458(d)
Angola, 693, 695. *See also* Kongo, kingdom of
Angra Mainyu (supernatural figure, Persia), 203
animal husbandry, 63, 522
animals. *See also* specific animals
in Americas, 18, 55
in Columbian exchange, 630, 630(i)
depictions of, 16–17, 16(i)
domestication of, 5–6, 50, 63(i), 282–283, 522
habitats of, 1159
after Ice Age, 53
textiles and, 62
An Lushan rebellion (755–763), 403
Anselm, 450
anticolonialism, 1083–1086. *See also* colonies and colonization; decolonization; empires
antiglobalization movements, 1141–1142
anti-Semitism, 445. *See also* Jews and Judaism
Nazi Germany and, 992, 993(i)
antislavery movement. *See* abolition of slavery
Aotearoa (New Zealand), 19
apartheid (South Africa), 1090–1094, 1093(m)
Apedemek (Meroë god), 286
Apology (Plato), 222–223(d)
appeasement, of Hitler, 999
Appian Way, 252
Arabia, 475, 475(m)
Islam in, 478–480, 733–734
nomadic peoples of, 513, 514(v)
Wahhabi movement in, 734, 756
Arabic language
Islam and, 483, 493
in Persia, 512
in Swahili cities, 348
Arabs and Arab Empire, 328, 344, 474, 480–488, 481(m). *See also* Islam
Byzantine Empire and, 432
Islam and, 480–495
Israel and, 1003, 1153
learning from, 446, 451
mission of, 482
nomadic pastoralism in, 526–527
Palestine and, 1127, 1129–1131, 1130(v)

Persian miniatures and, 512
sugar production in, 635
technology in, 827–828
trade and, 137, 329, 482, 675
Turks and, 526–528
West Africa and, 362–363, 363–365(d)
after World War I, 984
architecture
in Axum, 287, 287(i)
Baroque, 762–764, 763(v)
Byzantine, 430(i)
in Neolithic age, 76
in Russia, 641(i)
in Teotihuacán, 296
Arctic regions, in 15th century, 571
Argentina, 847, 848
Aristides, Aelius, 172, 173–174(d)
aristocracy. *See also* nobility
Byzantine, 429
in China, 160, 380, 382
in England, 833–834
in Korea, 391, 392
Roman, 155
in Vietnam, 394
Aristotle (384–322 B.C.E.), 191(t), 208, 451
science and, 738
on slavery, 249
on women, 256
worldview of, 739
Arius and Arianism, 430, 456
armed forces. *See* military; navy
Armenia
Christianity in, 426, 761
merchants from, 681
Ottomans and, 984
arms and armaments. *See* weapons; specific weapons
arms race, in cold war, 1047–1048, 1047(i)
art(s). *See also* architecture; literature; painting; poetry; rock art
in Australia, 42–46, 43(v), 45(v), 46(v)
Benin sculpture and, 573, 573(i)
Buddhist, 154
in Central Asia, 367–376, 369(v), 370(v), 372(v), 374(v), 376(v)
of Chavín de Huántar, 298
in China, 417, 1071–1079, 1072(v), 1074(v), 1075(v), 1077(v), 1078(v)

art(s) (*continued*)
Industrial Revolution and, 867–874, 868(v), 869(v), 870(v), 872(v), 873(v), 874(v)
Maya people and, 316–323, 317(v), 319(v), 320(v), 321(v), 322(v)
of Moche craftsmen, 299
Neolithic, 76–83, 77(v), 78(v), 79(v), 81(v), 82(v)
of Nok culture, 82–83, 82(v)
Paleolithic, 10(i), 17
in Renaissance, 579–580
Romantic movement in, 744
of San peoples, 10(i), 25
of Teotihuacán, 296
as World War I propaganda, 1019
Arthashastra (The Science of Worldly Wealth), 166
Arusha Declaration, The (Nyerere), 1115–1116(d)
Aryan peoples, 165, 243
Asante kingdom (West Africa), and slave trade, 708–709(d)
ascetics, Hindu, 198, 198(i)
Ashoka (India, r. 268–232 B.C.E.), 153, 167, 167(i), 168, 176, 177–178(d), 200, 212
Aspasia (Greece, ca. 470–400 B.C.E.), 257
assimilation
in Chinese and Roman empires, 161, 162, 164
in Hinduism, 202
of Jews, 204
Assyria and Assyrians, 105(m), 106–107
Egypt and, 107(t)
Israel and, 204
Astarte (goddess, Phoenicia), 109
astronomy, 740–741
of Ancestral Pueblo people, 302–303
in China, 378(i), 745
in India, 167
Islamic, 739, 739(i)
Muslim, 544, 739(i)
Stonehenge and, 81
Aswan Dam (Egypt), 1048
Atahualpa (Inca), 628
Atatürk, Mustafa Kemal (1881–1938), 1103–1105, 1104(i), 1167, 1168(d)
Athaulf (Visigoths, r. 410–415), 435
Athenagoras (Patriarch), 425

Athens. *See also* Greece
democracy in, 149, 150, 151, 170, 171–172(d)
diseases spread to, 340
Greco-Persian wars and, 151
patriarchy contrasted with Sparta, 255–258, 259
Plato's Academy in, 208
slaves in, 249
women in, 255–257, 256(i)
Atlantic Ocean region. *See also* Atlantic Revolutions
European empire in, 626–631
networks in, 631
slave trade in, 672(i), 673–674, 689–697, 689(m)
Atlantic Revolutions (1750–1914), 779–781, 781(t)
atman (individual soul), 198
atomic bomb, 1005
in Hiroshima and Nagasaki, 999, 1002, 1002(i)
Attila (Huns), 164(i)
Augustine (Saint, 354–430 C.E.), 191(t), 250, 284
Augustus (Rome, r. 27 B.C.E.–14 C.E.), 142, 157–158
Aurangzeb (Mughal Empire, 1658–1707), 646
Auschwitz, 1003
Australia
Aboriginal people in, 17, 21(i), 39, 40–41(d)
Aboriginal rock art painting in, 42–46, 43(v), 45(v), 46(v)
colonization of, 926–928
Dreamtime in, 17–18
early humans in, 3
Europeans in, 21
farming in, 572
in 15th century, 571–572
migrations into, 14–15(m), 17–18
Austria
fascism in, 989
German annexation of, 999
Habsburgs in, 650
Hungarian uprising against, 797(t)
Ottoman Empire and, 889
Poland and, 799(i)
reparations after World War I, 986
World War I and, 979

Austrian Empire
end of, 1083
independence movements in, 797
Austro-Hungarian Empire, 798(m), 970, 983(m). *See also* Austria; Hungary
Austronesian-speaking peoples, migration of, 19–20, 19(m), 60
authoritarianism
in Japan, 993–996, 1015, 1016–1017(d)
in Russia, 1034
after World War I, 988
automobile industry, 842
Avalokitesvara (bodhisattva), 231
Averroës. *See* Ibn Rushd
Avicenna. *See* Ibn Sina
awakenings, religious, 744
Axis powers (Italy, Germany, Japan), 988
ideologies of, 1010–1017, 1011–1012(d), 1013–1015(d), 1016–1017(d)
Axum, 282, 286–288, 307–314. *See also* Ethiopia
Byzantine view of, 312, 313(d)
Christianity in, 310, 311–312(d)
Church of St. George in, 614–615, 615(v)
columns of, 287, 287(i)
empire of, 309–310(d)
gold trade and, 313–314, 314(d)
Ayittey, George, 1118, 1119–1120
Azamgarh Proclamation (1857), 953–954
Aztec Empire, 293, 297, 326–327, 446, 588–592, 589(m), 712
culture of, 591–592
Spanish conquest of, 626, 628, 632–634
Spanish view of, 601–602(d), 602–603(d), 603–604(d)
trade and, 353–354, 590–591
women in, 591(i)

Babylon and Babylonians, 89(m), 105(m), 106, 110
Jews and, 146, 204
Bacon, Francis (1561–1626), 740(t)
Bacon, Roger, 448
Bactria, 153, 154
Baghdad, 484, 497
House of Wisdom in, 498
Mongol sack of, 489, 538

Bahadur Shah (Mughal Empire), 953–955(d)
balance of power
    global, 631
    before World War I, 979
Balkan region
    Byzantine Empire and, 428, 432
    Ottoman Empire and, 648
    World War I and, 979
ball games, of Maya, 320–322, 321(v)
Baltic region
    in Christendom, 444
    Crusades and, 444
    independence in, 1055
    Russia and, 1033
al-Banna, Hassan, 1169–1171(d)
Banpo, China, 61
Bantu speakers (Africa), 25, 284, 285(m), 290–292, 291(i)
    expansion of, 290
    migrations of, 60, 60(m)
    San people and, 290
    Swahili civilization and, 347
Bantustans, South Africa, 937, 1091, 1093(m)
Ban Zhao (China, 45–116 C.E.), 194, 253, 263–264, 264–266(d)
barbarians
    in China, 160, 161, 163–164, 380, 389
    nomadic peoples as, 547
    slaves as, 250
barley, 105–106
Baroque architecture, in churches, 762–764, 763(v)
Batavia, 937
battles. See wars and warfare; specific battles and wars
Batwa (Pygmy) people, 291
B.C./B.C.E. defined, 6–7
Beauvoir, Simone de, 1146
beaver, in fur trade, 685, 686
Bede (Venerable), 457
Bedouins, 474, 527
Beguines, 441
Beijing, 577. See also Khanbalik
    Temple of Heaven in, 577, 609, 610(v)
    Tiananmen Square demonstrations in (1989), 779
Belgian Congo, 1086

Belgium
    Congo and, 933
    imperialism of, 924
Belorussia, Russia and, 642
Bengal, 490
Benin, 83, 573, 573(i)
    slave trade and, 696, 703, 704–705(d)
Berber peoples, 483, 526
Bergen-Belsen, 1003
Bering Strait, migrations across, 18
Berlin, division of, 1045
Berlin Wall, fall of, 1029, 1055
Bernal, Martin, 110
Bernard of Clairvaux, 450
Bernstein, Eduard (1850–1932), 860, 860–861(d)
Bhagavad Gita, 201–202, 219–221(d)
bhakti (worship), 202, 736
Bharatiya Janata Party (BJP, India), 1153
Bhutto, Benazir, on Islamic women, 1174, 1174–1175(d)
Bible. See also New Testament; Old Testament
    Cain and Abel in, 63
    icons and, 468, 469(v)
    Luther on, 723, 750–751(d)
    in Protestantism, 725
    sciences and, 742
"big men" (clan leaders), 572
Bill of Rights (U.S.), 784
Bini people, 573–574
bin Laden, Osama, 473, 1153, 1156, 1176
birth control, 1150
al-Biruni (973–1048), 499(t), 739(i)
bishop of Rome. See popes
Black Athena (Bernal), 110
Black Consciousness movement (South Africa), 1092, 1094
Black Death, 329, 335, 545–547, 545(i)
    culture of death and, 563–567, 564(v), 566(v)
    European recovery after, 674
    flagellants and, 561, 562(v)
    religion in Western Europe and, 560–567, 562(v), 563(v), 564(v), 566(v)
"blackness"
    African slavery and, 691–692
    Haitian Revolution and, 789

black people. See also Africa; African Americans
    achievements of, 945
Black Sea region, 427
    Greek settlements and, 149
"black ships," 894–895, 915–916, 916(v)
Black Shirts (Italy), 989
Blake, William, 872, 1160
blitzkrieg, 1000
bloodletting, by Maya, 318–320, 319(v)
Blyden, Edward (1832–1912), 945
Boahen, A. Adu (Ghana), 1110–1111, 1111–1112(d)
boats. See navigation; ships and shipping
Boccaccio, Giovanni (Italy), 340, 563
bodhisattvas, 231, 339
Bodin, Jean, 649–650
Boers, 1091
Boer War (1899–1902), 965, 965(v), 1091
Bolívar, Simón (1783–1830), 780, 781, 784, 792(i), 810, 810–811(d)
Bolivia, 847
    communism in, 1031
    constitutions in, 847–848
    cultural blending in, 764, 765(v)
    economic development in, 1102
    in 19th century, 848
    silver in, 675, 682, 683
Bolsheviks, 846, 982, 1028(i), 1033–1035, 1038. See also Russian Revolution
Bombay, India, 680
bombings. See also atomic bomb
    World War II firebombings, 1002
Bonampak, Mexico, 318
Bonaparte. See Napoleon Bonaparte
Boniface (Saint, 672–754), 460, 466–467(d)
Book of the Dead (Egypt), 122–123(d)
Borobudur, Java, 345, 346(i)
Bosnia, genocide in, 1003
Botswana, 939
Boudica (Celts), 158(i)
Bouillon, Godefroi de, 444(i)
bourgeoisie, Marx and Engels on, 856, 857–859(d)
bows and arrows, 24
Boxer uprising (1899–1901), 888
Bradford, William (Plymouth), 629
Brahman (World Soul), 198
Brahmins (priests), 197, 243, 245

Brazil
    Candomble and Macumba in, 732
    economic development in, 1102, 1103
    independence of, 781(t)
    industry in, 852
    mothers of missing children in,
        1148(i)
    Muslims in, 733
    Portugal and, 626
    race in, 636
    slavery in, 636, 695, 795
    sugar production in, 635
    war with Paraguay, 847
    women's rights in, 802
Bretton Woods system, 1135
Britain. See British Empire; England
        (Britain)
British East India Company, 679, 680,
        926, 950
British Empire, 168, 626, 831. See also
        specific locations
    Gandhi on, 957, 958–960(d)
    India and, 680, 942, 950–959, 951(d),
        952–953(d), 953–955(d),
        956–957(d), 958–959(d),
        1086–1089
    labor in, 936
    North American colonies of,
        637–638, 685, 782–783
British Royal Africa Company, 693–694
British Royal Society, 831
British West Indies, 794
broad spectrum diet, 52
bronze
    Benin arts and, 573(i)
    from Shang China, 91(i)
    spread of metallurgy and, 110
Brotherhood of the Tomol, 30, 31
Broz, Josef. See Tito
Bruno, Giordano, 741
bubonic plague. See plague
Buddha, 154, 190, 199, 215, 259–260
    footprints of, 228, 229(v)
    Hinduism and, 20
    interpretations of teachings, 214
    Jesus compared with, 209–214
    representations of, 227–235, 229(v),
        230(v), 232(v), 233(v)
Buddhism, 595
    Ashoka conversion to, 167, 176
    in Asia, 399, 400(m)

in China, 161, 162, 189, 255, 338, 339,
        399–403, 735
    Chinese Buddhist in India and,
        356–357, 357–358(d), 358–359(d)
    Confucian thought and, 402
    Diamond Sutra and, 399
    disagreements within, 214
    in early modern era, 722
    Greek culture and, 369(v)
    Hinduism and, 199–200
    India and, 167, 190, 199–201, 339–340
    Islam and, 490
    in Japan, 394, 395
    in Korea, 399
    Mahayana, 211, 231–235, 402
    Mongols and, 537
    organization of, 200
    practices of, 1151
    Pure Land, 235, 408
    silk trade and, 337, 338
    socially engaged, 1158
    spread of, 213(m), 335, 344
    in Srivijaya, 345
    Temple of the Golden Pavilion and,
        611–612, 612(v)
    Theravada, 214, 402
    women as nuns in, 200
    Zen, 408–409, 409–410(d)
Buganda, East Africa, 928, 941
buildings. See architecture; specific
        buildings
al-Bukhari (810–870), 505, 505–506(d)
Bulgaria
    communism in, 1035, 1055
    independence of, 890
Bulgars, 432
bureaucracy. See also government;
        political systems
    in China, 162, 164, 194, 238–239,
        382, 883
    in European colonies, 931
    European society and, 165
    in Japan, 395
    in Mauryan India, 166
    Mongol, 535
    in Persia, 146, 539
    writing and, 102
burials
    in Cahokia, 304
    of Chinese rulers, 160
    of kings, 102–103

Paleolithic, 24
    of plague victims, 563, 563(v)
    Stonehenge and, 81
    terra-cotta army and, 182–186, 183(v),
        184(v), 185(v), 186(v)
Burma, 677
    colonial cash crops in, 935
    Japan and, 997
    temples in, 346
Busbecq, Ogier Ghiselin de, 657,
        658–659(d)
bushido (Japanese way of the warrior),
        395, 414, 415–416(d)
Buthelezi, Gatsha, 1094
Byzantine Empire, 163, 326, 426,
        427–433, 427(t), 428(m)
    Anatolia and, 491
    Arabia and, 475
    architecture of, 430(i)
    Axum and, 312, 313(d)
    Christianity and, 427–433
    Crusades and, 431–432
    Eastern Orthodox Christianity in,
        426
    emperors in, 429
    Greek language in, 431
    Greek learning and, 208
    icons in, 430, 431, 466–471, 468(v),
        469(v), 470(v)
    Islam and, 480, 491
    learning in, 451
    Muslims and, 429
    Ottoman Empire and, 491, 492(m)
    political system in, 428–429
    silk in, 337
Byzantium. See Byzantine Empire;
        Constantinople

Cabrera, Miguel, 633(i), 715, 717(v)
cacao, 935, 938
cacique (hierarchy of chiefs), 73
Caesar, Julius (Rome), 157
Caesar Augustus. See Augustus
caesaropapism, 429, 449
Cahokia, 66, 66(i), 94, 304, 353
Cain (Bible), 63
Cairo, 937
Calcutta, 680, 937
    British, 950–951, 951(d)
calendars, 394
    in French Revolution, 785–786

caliphs, 483–485
  Abbasid, 484–485
  in Turkey, 1107
  Umayyad, 484
calligraphy. *See also* writing
  in Islamic world, 397
Calvinism, 725
Cambodia
  communism in, 1031
  genocide in, 1003, 1052
camels, 63, 349, 527
Canada, 926. *See also* North America
canals
  in China, 380–381, 383
  between Nile and Red Sea, 147
Candomble (Brazil), 732
cannibalism, in Chaco canyon, 303
cannons, 398
canoes, 595
  Chumash, 29–30, 30(i)
Canton, China
  Chinese/British trade in, 885(t)
  Islamic trade and, 497
  massacre of foreigners in, 399
Canton system, 905
Cao Xueqin, 735
capital (financial)
  European investment and, 879
  free movement of, 1135
  globalization of, 1136–1137
  U.S. industrialization and, 841–842
capitalism
  in China, 887, 1053
  communism and, 1052
  globalization of, 1135
  in Global South, 1099–1102
  Great Depression and, 985–988
  industrial, 879
  Marx and, 838
Caral, Peru, 87
caravan trade, 137, 286
carbon dioxide emissions, 1160, 1160(m)
Cardano, Girolamo (1501–1576), 739
*Cardinal Principles of Our National
  Polity, The* (Japan), 995
Caribbean region. *See also* specific
  locations
  communism and, 1057
  economy in, 1139
  European diseases in, 629
  religion in, 73, 74–75(d)

slaves in, 695
sugar production in, 635
trade in, 353
Carnegie, Andrew, 842
Carolingian Empire, 436, 436(m)
Carpini, Giovanni DiPlano, 524
Carson, Rachel, 1161
cartaz (trading license/pass), 677
Carthage, 136, 156–157
  Punic Wars and, 155, 268(d)
cash-crop agriculture. *See also* agriculture
  in colonies, 934–935, 938
cassava (manioc), 630, 630(i), 696
casta paintings, in Mexico, 715–718,
  717(v)
caste system. *See also* classes
  Hinduism and, 198, 201–202
  in India, 167, 237, 242–246, 243(i),
    260–261, 359(d)
  Islamic equality and, 490
  in Niger River region, 289
Caste War of Yucatán (1847–1901), 848
castiza, 633(i)
Castro, Fidel (Cuba), 1031, 1046–1047
casualties, in World War II, 1001
Catalan Atlas, 351(i)
Çatalhüyük, Turkey, 64(i), 76–80, 77(v),
  78(v)
Catherine the Great (Russia, r. 1762–
  1796), 641, 844
Catholic Counter-Reformation,
  725–726
Catholicism. *See* Roman Catholic
  Church
cattle, domestication of, 55
caudillos (Latin American strongmen),
  847
cave paintings, 16, 16(i), 339(i)
Cayuga people, 574
Celtic peoples, 158(i)
Central America. *See also* Mesoamerica
  economy in, 1139
Central Asia. *See also* Silk Roads
  art, religion, and cultural exchange
    in, 367–376, 369(v), 370(v), 372(v),
    374(v), 376(v)
  bubonic plague in, 341
  China, Russia, and, 645
  culture in, 575
  in 15th century, 570(t)
  Huns from, 164

nomads of, 63, 527
religions in, 426
Russia and, 1033
silk in, 337
Turks in, 375, 376(v)
Xiongnu and, 526, 526(m)
Central Europe, after World War I, 982
Cevdet, Abdullah, 893
Ceylon (Sri Lanka), 578, 936(i)
Chaco Phenomenon, 302–303
Chalcedon, Council of (451 C.E.), 214
Chamberlain, Joseph, 965–966, 965(v)
Chan Buddhism. *See* Zen Buddhism
Chang'an, China, 391, 394
Changchun (Daoist master), 553–554(d)
chariot technology, 110
Charlemagne (Franks, r. 772–814),
  424(i), 436, 458–459, 459–460(d)
Charles V (Habsburg), 764
Chavín culture, 87, 298, 592
Cherry Blossom Society (Japan),
  994–995
Chiapas rebellion (Mexico), 1141
chiefdoms, 65–66(i), 73
Chikpo movement, 1161
child labor, 838, 871, 872(v)
Chile, 593, 851
  economic growth in, 1103
  in Great Depression, 986
  humans in, 18
  in 19th century, 848
  women's movement in, 1148–1149
Chimu kingdom, 297(m), 300, 592
China, 158–163. *See also* Chinese
    Empire; Chinese Revolutions;
    Mao Zedong; specific rulers and
    empires
  agriculture in, 51, 52(t), 577, 584
  astronomy in, 378(i)
  Austronesian languages and, 19
  Boxer uprising in, 888
  Buddhism in, 161, 162, 189, 255, 338,
    339, 399–403, 735
  cannons in, 398
  capitalism in, 1099
  Christianity in, 730–732, 731(i),
    766–767, 767(v), 1151
  civilization (early) in, 89(m), 90
  classes in, 94–95, 238, 242
  classical period in, 158–165, 159(m),
    162(t), 192–197, 238–242

China (*continued*)
  collectivization in, 1040–1041
  communes in, 1041, 1073, 1074(v)
  communism in, 1004, 1030,
    1035–1037, 1037(m), 1045,
    1052–1054, 1057, 1099
  Confucianism in, 160, 165, 180, 384,
    401, 403, 734–735, 894
  consolidation of empire in, 160–163
  consumerism in, 1181–1182, 1183(v)
  cultural borrowings by, 399
  Cultural Revolution in, 1145
  Daoism in, 195–197
  dating system in, 7
  East Asia and, 390–391
  economy in, 382, 577, 682–683,
    684–685, 1052–1053, 1099, 1139,
    1141
  elite leisure in, 417–422, 418(v),
    419(v), 420(v), 421(v), 422(v)
  as empire, 643–645
  environment in, 1160(m)
  Eurasian world economy and,
    397–399
  Europe, Europeans, and, 359–360,
    360–362(d), 575–576, 580–584,
    585(t), 620, 881
  examination system in, 162, 164,
    194–195, 238–239, 255, 382, 402
  expansion of, 644–645
  external interactions by, 404
  feminism in, 1039–1040
  in 15th century, 575–578, 580–584
  as First Civilization, 90, 158
  foot binding in, 384–385, 385(i)
  golden age in, 380–384
  government of, 195, 577, 883–884
  Great Leap Forward in, 1041, 1043,
    1043(i)
  gunpowder in, 383–384
  Indian Ocean region and, 399, 578,
    584
  industrialization and, 828, 888,
    1041–1044, 1052–1053, 1073,
    1075(v), 1139, 1160(m)
  industry in, 383, 846
  Japan and, 378(i), 394–397, 406–407,
    407–408(d), 877, 901, 920, 920(v),
    997, 1035, 1036
  Jesuits in, 730–732, 731(i), 745, 830

Jesus Sutras in, 462, 463–464(d)
  kaozheng movement in, 735
  kingship in, 100
  Korea and, 391–392
  landlords in, 240
  Macartney's mission and, 905–906
  Malay sea route to, 345
  maritime voyages by, 577–578, 580,
    581–584
  merchants in, 242
  migration from, 940(t)
  military in, 383
  Mongols and, 370(v), 373, 374(v),
    536–538, 537(i), 544, 555–556,
    556–557(d), 644
  nationalism in, 800, 888–889, 1036
  northern nomads in, 385–390
  opium trade and, 885–886, 885(t),
    886(i), 907–908, 908–909(d),
    909–910(d), 910, 911(d)
  Opium Wars and, 884–885, 886, 905
  Ottoman Empire compared with,
    894
  painting in, 195(i)
  partition of, 876(i)
  patriarchy in, 253–255, 262, 263
  peasants in, 95, 240–242, 241(i),
    1040–1041
  poster art in, 1071–1079, 1072(v),
    1074(v), 1075(v), 1077(v), 1078(v)
  printing in, 383
  products for Europe from, 712
  reforms in, 1052–1053
  religions in, 189, 390, 426
  reunification of, 192
  revival of, 344
  Roman Empire compared with,
    160–165
  Russia and, 644
  scholar-officials (scholar-gentry) in,
    196, 240, 259
  sciences and, 738–739
  self-strengthening in, 888–889
  silk in, 337
  silver and, 683, 684–685
  socialism in, 1038–1045
  Soviet Union and, 1031, 1038–1045,
    1050–1051
  Taiwan and, 886, 1037, 1057
  technology in, 137

Temple of Heaven in, 577, 609,
    610(v)
  terra-cotta army in, 182–186, 183(v),
    184(v), 185(v), 186(v)
  as third-wave civilization, 379–380
  Tiananmen Square demonstrations
    in (1989), 779
  trade in, 675, 684–685
  tribute system in, 387–389, 388(i)
  Uighurs and, 625
  unification of, 380–385
  urban areas in, 382–383
  Vietnam and, 392–394
  warring states period in, 158
  waterways in, 380–381, 383
  Western pressures in, 876(i),
    884–887, 887(m)
  Western science in, 745
  women in, 194, 253–255, 263–264,
    264–266(d), 384–385, 803
    after World War I, 984
    in World War II, 1037
    writing in, 90, 101(t)
  Zheng He voyages and, 569
"china" (porcelain), 697
Chinese Bureau of Astronomy, Jesuits
  in, 731
Chinese Communist Party (CCP), 1004,
  1035, 1040–1041, 1051, 1053, 1076
Chinese Empire, 158–165, 180–186,
  181(v), 183(v), 184(v), 185(v), 186(v)
  collapse of, 1035
  governing of, 174, 175(d)
  after Han dynasty, 164
  languages in, 160, 162
  under Manchu dynasty (1644–1912),
    643–645
Chinese language, 162
Chinese people, in Philippines, 679
Chinese Revolutions
  of 1911, 1035
  of 1949, 970, 1035–1037
Chinggis Khan (1162–1227), 373,
  520(i), 521, 525, 532–533, 550–551,
  551–552(d), 553–554(d)
  military organization of, 533
  Persian invasion by, 538
Chinookan peoples, 572
chocolate, 712–713, 714(v)
Christ. *See* Jesus of Nazareth

Christianity, 595. *See also* Jesus of
    Nazareth; specific groups
  Africa and, 284, 943–944
  in Americas, 634
  Andean, 729
  in Arabia, 475
  in Asia, 678
  in Axum, 286–288, 310, 311–312(d)
  Black Death and, 560–567
  bubonic plague and, 340
  in Byzantine Empire, 427–433
  in China, 189, 730–732, 731(i),
    766–767, 767(v), 883–884
  conversion to, 212, 460–461(d)
  Coptic, 286, 287
  Crusades and, 442–445, 443(m)
  Eastern vs. Western, 452–453
  Ethiopian, 284, 343, 614–616, 615(v)
  in European colonies, 929, 941,
    943–945
  European exploration and, 581
  in 15th century, 570(t)
  fundamentalist, 1152
  globalization of, 722–732, 761–768
  global modernity and, 1157–1158
  hierarchy of, 212–214
  in India, 761, 767–769, 768(v)
  Islam and, 477(i), 479, 483
  in Islamic Spain, 495
  in Japan, 681, 728(i)
  Jesus and Buddha compared,
    209–214
  Jesus Sutras and, 462, 463–464(d)
  Judaism and, 205
  in Latin America, 764–766, 765(v)
  in Mexico, 664, 729–730
  Middle Eastern monotheism and,
    477(i)
  missionaries and, 727–728
  Nestorian, 426, 462, 463–464(d)
  Ottoman Empire and, 585, 648–650,
    889, 892–893
  Protestant Reformation and,
    723–727, 726(m)
  in Roman Empire, 161, 162, 276–279
  in Russia, 433–434, 642
  sacred sites of, 614
  sciences and, 742
  silk and, 338
  slavery and, 250

  in Spanish America, 727–730
  spread of, 211–212, 213(m), 455–456,
    456–457(d), 727–728, 878, 1151
  Western dating system based on, 6–7
  in Western Europe, 437–438
  women in, 211, 211(i), 213
  writings on love, 209
  Zoroastrianism and, 204
Chumash peoples (California), 24,
    29–31, 29(m), 94
chu nom (writing, Vietnam), 394
churches. *See also* specific religions
  Baroque architecture in, 762
  Christian, 212–213, 479
  in Latin America, 764–766, 765(v)
  Protestant and Catholic, 761–762,
    762(v), 763(v)
Churchill, Winston, 1004
Church of St. George (Lalibela,
    Ethiopia), 614–615, 615(v)
Cieza de Leon, Pedro, 605,
    605–607(d)
circumcision, 488, 528, 1148
cities and towns. *See also* state (nation);
    urbanization; specific locations
  in Axum, 287
  in China, 382–383, 1053
  of colonial world, 937
  crowding in, 836
  in Egypt, 107–108
  in Europe, 440, 674
  in First Civilizations, 92–94
  Hellenistic, 153
  in Indus Valley region, 92–93
  in Latin America, 849
  in Mesoamerica, 294–297
  in Mesopotamia, 92–93, 106–107
  in Niger River region, 288–289
  in Norte Chico, 87
  on Silk Roads, 339
citizenship
  in Athens, 150
  in Roman Empire, 157, 161
  slaves and, 249, 251
  in Sparta, 149
city-states
  Greek, 149, 150, 153
  in Italy, 442, 578
  of Maya, 294
  Rome as, 155

  Sumer as, 86, 106–107
  Swahili, 347
  in West Africa, 350–351
  Yoruba, 573
civic nationalism, 799
civilization(s), 67. *See also* specific
    groups and locations
  in Africa, 86, 282, 283–292
  in Americas, 87
  of Andes mountains region, 87,
    297–300, 592–594, 593(i)
  changes in, 135–138
  in China, 90
  classical, 138–141, 144–145
  connections among, 594–595
  continuities in, 134–135
  in Egypt, 86, 107(t)
  emergence of, 86–94
  "escaping" from, 85
  European perceptions of, 881–882
  external interactions by, 404
  First Civilizations, 85–107, 88–89(m)
  in India, 165–166
  Indus Valley, 87–90, 89(m)
  Islam as, 474, 495–499
  in Japan, 406–417
  of Maya people, 281–282, 294–295
  of Mesoamerica, 292–297, 293(m)
  in Mesopotamia, 86
  of Niger River region, 282, 284,
    288–289
  in Nile River region, 107(t)
  origins of, 91–92
  Persian, 145–147
  in Peru, 87, 297, 298–300
  second wave of, 134, 136–138, 238
  slavery and, 95, 247–249
  social hierarchies in, 94–98
  third wave of, 325–329, 330–331(t)
  turning point of, 6
  use of term, 86, 111–113
  in Western Europe, 327
civil rights movement, in United
    States, 1145
civil service system. *See also* bureaucracy;
    examination system
  in China, 162, 164, 255, 382
  colonial, 931
civil wars
  in Athens (431–404 B.C.E.), 151

civil wars (*continued*)
  in Japan, 681, 895, 897
  in Nigeria (1960s), 1097
  in Russia, 1034
  in United States, 777(f), 793, 795
classes. *See also* caste system; estates
    (classes); social hierarchies; specific
    classes
  in Africa, 1097
  in China, 240–242
  Chumash, 31
  conflict among, 842
  in England, 833–836
  in First Civilizations, 91, 94–98
  in France, 785
  gender and, 96
  in Greece, 149
  in Haiti, 787–790
  Hammurabi on, 120(d)
  hierarchies of, 94–96
  in India, 167, 242–246, 1087
  in Japan, 898
  in Latin America, 633–634, 637,
    849–850
  Marx on, 744
  in Mesoamerica, 294
  punishments by, 95
  in Rome, 155
classical era, 138–139, 238. *See also*
    specific locations
  Africa during, 281–283, 283–292
  in Americas, 292–304
  in Andes region, 297–300
  in China, 158–165, 159(m), 162(t),
    192–197, 404
  empires of, 144–145
  globalization in, 326, 336
  in Greece, 147–154, 148(m), 150(t),
    205–209, 255–259
  in India, 197–202, 242–246, 244(t)
  in North America, 301–304, 301(m)
  patriarchy in, 252–259, 262,
    263–264(d)
  in Persian Empire, 145–147
  political authority in, 170–179,
    171–172(d), 173–174(d), 175(d),
    177–178(d)
  population during, 282
  slavery in Roman Empire, 247–252
  in South Asia, 165–167
  thinkers and philosophies of, 191(t)

20th century and, 167–168
  Xiongnu people and, 526
"Classic of Filial Piety" (China), 193(i)
class structure. *See* apartheid; caste system;
    classes; elites
class struggle, 838–839, 1163–1164. *See*
    also Marx, Karl
Cleisthenes (Athens), 150
clergy
  Christian, 213
  as first estate, 449
Climacus, John (Saint), 470(v), 471
climate. *See also* environment
  in Africa, 284
  agriculture and, 51
  in Ice Age, 16
  Maya and, 295
climate change. *See also* global warming
  over time, 23–24
clitorectomy, Islamic, 488
Clovis (Franks, r. 485–511), 455–456,
    456–457(d)
Clovis points and culture, 18
Club of Rome, 1161
Coalbrookdale, England, 872–873, 873(v)
Code of Hammurabi, 95, 100, 102
coffee
  from Ethiopia, 712
  in Ottoman Empire, 714–715, 716(v)
  trade in, 714–715
cofradías, 729
Colbert, Jean-Baptiste (France), 660,
    662(d)
cold war (1946–1991), 1030,
    1045–1047, 1049–1051. *See also*
    Soviet Union; United States
  authoritarian states after, 1098
  Cuba in, 1046–1047
  ending of, 1055
  global, 1046(m)
  in 1950s-1970s, 1049–1051
  superpowers in, 1144
  third world and, 1095(m)
collective security, after World War I, 984
collectivization
  in China, 1040–1041, 1052
  in Soviet Union, 1039(i), 1041,
    1062–1063, 1063–1064(d)
colonies and colonization. *See also*
    decolonization; empires; imperial-
    ism; specific locations

  in Africa, 772(m), 795, 924–925, 926,
    927(m), 938–939, 960–967, 961(v),
    962(v), 964(v), 965(v), 966(v),
    1110–1111, 1111–1112(d)
  in Asia, 924–928, 925(m)
  cash-crop agriculture in, 934–935
  cooperation and rebellion in,
    929–93
  dependent development and, 852–853
  economies of, 932–940, 936(i)
  education in, 941–943
  Ethiopia and, 928, 966–967, 966(v)
  ethnicity in Latin America, 636(t)
  European empires and, 626–631,
    627(m), 773–774, 880, 922(i),
    923–947
  European rule in, 928–932
  forced labor in, 933–934
  Great Power competition for,
    979–980
  in Haiti, 789
  identity and culture in, 941–947
  independence for, 1082–1086
  in India, 926
  in Latin America, 790–793
  migration and, 940(t)
  in North America, 637–639,
    782–783
  in Philippines, 678–679
  race and, 772, 930–931, 945–947
  religion in, 728–729, 943–945
  rights in, 814–816(d)
  scramble for Africa and, 926,
    960–967, 961(v), 962(v), 964(v),
    965(v), 966(v)
  societies in Americas, 631–639
  sugar industry in, 634–637
  trading post empires and, 680
  Western education in, 941–943,
    951–952, 952–953(d)
  women in, 938–939
  after World War I, 983–984, 983(m)
  after World War II, 1003–1004, 1007
  World War I troops from,
    1021–1024, 1023(v)
Columbian exchange, 629–631
Columbus, Christopher
  Christianity spread by, 727
  in Hispaniola, 568(i)
  Taino peoples and, 73
  voyages of, 568(i), 571, 577(i), 580, 581

comfort women, in World War II, 877, 1002

Comintern (Communist International), 1031

commerce. *See* trade

Committee of Public Safety (France), 785

Common Market, 1006

communes, in China, 1041, 1073, 1074(v)

communism, 1029–1030, 1095(m). *See also* cold war; Communist Party entries
  in Afghanistan, 1031
  in Asia, 1045–1046, 1057
  Atlantic revolutions and, 780
  in China, 68, 984, 1030, 1035–1037, 1037(m), 1045, 1099
  collapse of, 1051–1057, 1056(m)
  in Cuba, 1031
  in Eastern Europe, 1034–1035, 1055–1057, 1056(m)
  economic collapse and, 1135
  feminism and, 1039–1040
  global, 1030–1032
  in Indonesia, 1048
  industrialization and, 1041–1044
  in Korea, 1045
  Nazis and, 1003
  in 1950s–1970s, 1049–1051
  revolutions leading to, 1032–1037
  in Soviet Union, 984, 987, 1030, 1054–1057, 1056(m)
  in twentieth century, 970
  in United States, 1031
  in Vietnam, 1045
  after World War II, 1004, 1005
  worldwide, 982

Communist Manifesto (Marx and Engels), 856–857, 857–859(d)

Communist Party (China), 1004, 1040–1041, 1051, 1053, 1076
  economic growth and, 1099

Communist Party (Czechoslovakia), 1145

Communist Party (Russia), 1056, 1060

concentration camps. *See* death camps

Condorcet (Marquis de) (1743–1794), 743, 752, 752–754(d), 800

Confucianism. *See also* Neo-Confucianism
  Buddhism and, 401
  in China, 160, 165, 180, 384, 401, 403, 420, 420(v), 734–735, 894
  Christianity and, 730–731
  debate over, 754, 755–756(d)
  in Japan, 394, 896
  Korea and, 391
  Mongols and, 538
  Neo-Confucianism and, 734–735
  science and, 737

Confucius (551–479 B.C.E.)
  anniversary of birth, 189, 190, 191(t)
  classical era and, 193–195
  state officials and, 238
  writings of, 193, 217, 218–219(d)

Congo. *See* Belgian Congo

Congo Free State, 933, 934(i)

Congress of South African Trade Unions, 1092

Congress Party (India). *See* Indian National Congress (INC, Congress Party)

conscription
  mass (France), 796
  in World War I, 981

Constantine (Rome)
  Constantinople and, 427
  conversion to Christianity, 212

Constantinople
  bubonic plague and, 340
  Crusaders and, 431–432
  Ottoman seizure of, 429, 585, 648, 722
  population of, 440

Constantinople, Council of (533 C.E.), 214

constitution(s)
  in Africa, 1098
  in Japan, 899, 1006–1007
  in Latin America, 847–848
  in United States, 784

Constitutional Convention (U.S., 1787), 781(t)

consumerism
  in China, 1181–1182, 1183(v)
  globalization and, 1183(v)

conversion
  to Christianity, 212, 460–461(d), 728–729, 731
  of Clovis, 455–457
  to Islam, 482–483, 544

Cook, James, 21

Copenhagen climate conference (2009), 1163

Copernicus, Nicolaus (1473–1543), 737, 739, 740, 740(t), 745

Coptic Christianity, 286, 287

corn (maize), 5, 5(i), 55, 56, 57(t), 630
  African slave trade and, 696
  Mound Builders and, 303–304
  Norte Chico and, 87

Cortés, Hernán, 590, 628, 633, 666–667, 666(v), 669, 669(v), 671, 713

Cosmas (Greek merchant), 309–310(d), 313–314, 314(d)

Cossacks, 641(i)

cotton, 870(v)
  China and, 885(t)
  in German East Africa, 934
  in India, 167, 685, 830

cotton gin, 826

Council of Guardians (Iran), 1106

Council on Mutual Economic Assistance, 1031

councils (Christian),
  of Chalcedon, Constantinople, Nicaea, 214
  of Trent (1545–1563), 725–726

Counter-Reformation, 725–726, 762

Cranach, Lucas, 723(i)

Creek Indians, 687

creoles, 633, 790, 791, 792

Crimean War (1854–1856), 844

crops. *See also* food(s); specific crops
  in Americas, 630
  ancient, 5, 51
  cash-crop agriculture and, 934–935, 938
  in colonies, 934–935
  Masai, 528–529
  in Mesopotamia, 105–106
  in plantation colonies, 636–637
  industrialization and, 830

crucifixion, of Jesus, 210

Crusades, 442–445, 443(m)
  cultural contacts in, 329
  Eastern Orthodox Christianity and, 431–432
  Jews and, 445

Crystal Palace Exhibition (London, 1851), 867, 868(v)

Cuba
  in Cold War, 1046–1047

Cuba (*continued*)
  communism in, 1031, 1051
  economic growth in, 1099
  Guevara and, 1145(i), 1146
  missile crisis in, 1047, 1048
  Santeria in, 732
  slavery in, 795
  Taino peoples and, 73
  United States and, 852, 1057
Cuban missile crisis, 1047, 1048
cultivation system, in Dutch East
    Indies, 933–934
Cultural Revolution (China), 1043–1045,
    1052, 1072(v), 1076, 1145
culture. *See also* language(s); religion;
    specific locations and groups
  in Africa, 732–733, 945–947
  of agriculture, 61–62
  in Americas, 18, 292–304, 352,
    629–630
  in Anatolia, 491–492
  Arabic, 480, 483
  Aztec, 591–592, 664
  Bantu, 291
  Byzantine, 432–433
  in China, 195, 254–255, 381–382, 389,
    537–538
  Christian, 425–426
  Clovis, 18
  in colonial era, 941–947
  connections among, 594–595
  in early modern world, 621, 722,
    749–760
  in Egypt, 104–106, 110–111
  environment and, 104
  in Eurasia, 188(i), 189–192, 191(t)
  European, 578–580, 878
  European perceptions of "other,"
    881–882
  around 500 B.C.E., 190–192
  in former Roman Empire, 164
  Greek, 110, 147–150, 151, 153, 161–162
  Inca, 593
  in India, 167, 197–202, 490, 942
  interactions among, 327–329
  Islamic encounters with, 488–495
  in Japan, 395, 397
  in Korea, 391–392
  Maya, 295
  in Mesopotamia, 104–106
  Moche, 299–300
  modernity in, 1103–1108
  Mongols and, 530–531, 544
  of Mound Builders, 303–304
  in Mughal Empire, 646
  non-Western, 773
  Olmec, 91
  Paleolithic, 22–23
  of pastoral nomads, 525–526
  Persian, 146, 512–519
  religious, 1151
  in Renaissance, 579–580
  Roman, 161–162
  of San peoples, 25
  science and, 739–742
  Swahili, 347–348
  trade and, 338–340
  Turkic, 527–528
  of Vietnam, 392–394
  wisdom traditions in, 137
cuneiform
  Sumerian, 109
  as writing system, 101(t)
currency
  Chumash, 30
  euro as, 1006
  globalization of, 1136
  paper money in China as, 384
Cuzco, Peru, 593
Cyril (missionary), 432–433
Cyrillic alphabet, 433
Cyrus (Persia, r. 557–530 B.C.E.), 145
Czechoslovakia
  communism in, 1035, 1055, 1145
  Germany and, 999
  Prague Spring uprising in, 1050,
    1050(i), 1145
Czech people, autonomy for, 797

Dachau, 1003
Dahomey, slave trade and, 696–697,
    718–719, 718(v)
daimyo (Japanese feudal lords), 414, 681,
    895
Dakar, slave trade in, 672(i)
Dalai Lama, 1158
Dalit caste (India), 243
Damascus, Syria, 484
"dancing girl," 130(v)
dao (the way), 401
Daodejing (The Way and Its Power)
    (Laozi), 195
Daoism, 188(i)
  in China, 195–197, 384, 401, 403
  Mongols and, 535
  women's roles and, 255
Darius I (Persia, r. 522–486 B.C.E.),
    145, 147
Darius III (Persia), 153(i)
Darwin, Charles (1809–1882), 3, 744,
    745, 882, 882(i)
dating systems, 6–7
David, Jacques-Louis, 206(i)
Davison, Emily, 801
death. *See also* mortality rates
  culture of, during plague, 563–567,
    564(v), 566(v)
  in European colonies, 936
  from pollution, 1159
death camps, Nazi, 1003
de Bry, Theodore, 568(i)
Declaration of Independence (U.S.),
    781(t), 784
Declaration of the Rights of Man and
    Citizen (France), 784, 807–808(d)
*Declaration of the Rights of Woman and the
    Female Citizen* (de Gouges), 808
decolonization, 1082–1086
deforestation, 62, 105
Deists, 743
deities. *See* gods and goddesses; religion
Delhi, Sultanate of, 490, 490(m), 576(m)
democracy
  in Africa, 1096–1097, 1098
  in Athens, 150, 151, 170, 171–172(d)
  collapse of communism and, 1055
  denial of in Italy, Germany, and
    Japan, 988
  in Japan, 995
  nationalism and, 799
  in Soviet Union, 1054–1055
  in United States, 784
democratic socialism, 987
Democritus (Greek philosopher), 207
demography. *See* population
Deng Xiaoping (China), 1052–1053
dependent development, as colonialism,
    852–853
depressions. *See* economy; Great
    Depression
dervishes, 509
Descartes, René (1596–1650), 737,
    740(t), 741

Descent of Man, The (Darwin), 744
Dessalines, Jean-Jacques, 789
detribalization, 932
developing countries, 446, 1082,
    1095–1108, 1095(m). *See also*
    dependent development; Global
    South
  decolonization in, 1082
  environmentalism in, 1161
  protests against globalization in, 1185
devshirme, 648–649
dharma, 245, 401
dhimmis (Islamic protected subjects), 482
diamonds, 937
Diamond Sutra, 399
diaspora, African, 690
Díaz, Porfirio (1876–1911), 851
Diego, Juan, 720(i)
diet (foods)
  broad spectrum, 52
  of Ju/'hoansi peoples, 26
  Paleolithic, 32
diffusion
  of agriculture, 57
  of technologies, 329
Dionysus (god, Greece), 208
  cult of, 278–279, 278(v)
Diop, C. A., 945
diplomacy. *See also* alliances; specific
    alliances
  between Egypt and Mesopotamia,
    108–109
  in Eurasia, 542–544
  in Mongol Empire, 542
  U.S. triangular, 1051
diseases. *See also* Black Death; plague;
    specific diseases
  in Africa, 284, 290
  Arab physicians and, 499
  in Asia and African colonies, 936
  Aztecs and, 670, 670(v)
  contact with animals and, 61
  in 14th century, 543(m)
  globalization of, 619–620
  lack of immunity to, 60
  Native Americans and, 628, 687
  in North American colonies, 638
  in Roman and Chinese empires, 163
  slave trade and, 692
  trade and, 137–138, 335, 335(m),
    340–341

Disraeli, Benjamin, 836
divine rights of kings, 742, 780
divinity. *See also* gods and goddesses;
    specific divinities
  of Egyptian kings, 108
  in Islam, 477
  Jewish conception of, 205
division of labor
  in African colonies, 938
  in Europe, 440
  gender-based, 21
divorce
  in Islam, 487
  in Sparta, 258
  in Turkey, 893
Dix, Otto (1891–1969), 1024, 1026(v)
Dogen (Japanese monk, 1200–1253),
    409–410(d)
Doll's House, A (Ibsen), 801–802
Dome of the Rock (Jerusalem),
    612–614, 613(v)
domestication. *See also* Agricultural
    Revolution
  of animals, 5, 50, 53, 55, 63(i),
    282–283, 522
  of plants, 5, 50, 53, 55, 63(i), 522
Dominican missionary order, 727
Dominican Republic, 73, 852
donkeys, 55
Donne, John, 327
Douglass, Frederick, 794, 812,
    812–813(d)
draft (military). *See* conscription
drama. *See* specific works
Dream of the Red Chamber, The (Cao
    Xueqin), 735
Dreamtime (Australia), 17–18,
    40–41(d)
Dubcek, Alexander, 1145
DuBois, W. E. B., 946
Duma (Russia), 845–846
Dunhuang, China, 338, 339(i), 369
Dupuis, Joseph, 708–709(d)
Duran, Diego, 601–602, 602–603(d),
    603–604(d)
Duran Codex, 665, 665(v), 668–669,
    668(v)
Dutch
  fur trade and, 685
  in Indonesia, 926
  Japan and, 745, 897

slave trade and, 693
  trade by, 679–680, 681
Dutch East India Company, 679
Dutch Empire, 626
Dutch Reformed Church, 762(v)
dynasties. *See* specific dynasties and
    countries

East Africa. *See also* specific locations
  Bantu speakers in, 290–292
  colonization of, 928
  cotton in German colonies, 934
  economic exchange in, 675
  Gikuyu people of, 64
  Masai of, 528–529, 528(m)
  Sea Roads and, 346–348
  slave trade in, 344
  Swahili civilization of, 325–326, 328,
    346–348, 347(m)
East Asia. *See also* specific locations
  Buddhism in, 399, 400(m)
  China and, 390–391
  communism and, 1057
  economic development in,
    1100–1101(t), 1102
  in 15th century, 570(t)
  Japanese power in, 894–902
Easter Island, 20
Eastern Europe. *See also* Europe and
    Europeans
  in Cold War, 1050–1051
  communism in, 1030, 1034–1035,
    1051, 1055–1056, 1056(m)
  Mongols in, 533, 539–541, 540(i),
    542
  Ottomans and, 584
  Soviets and, 1004, 1031, 1045
Eastern Orthodox Christianity,
    213–214, 595, 722, 726(m). *See also*
    Russian Orthodox Church
  in Byzantine Empire, 426, 427–433
  Crusades and, 431–432
  icons of, 430, 431, 466–471, 468(v),
    469(v), 470(v)
  organization of, 429–430
  patriarch of, 425, 429
  Roman Catholic Church and, 425
  in Russia, 433–434
  in Slavic world, 433–434
eastern Roman Empire, 211, 427. *See
    also* Byzantine Empire

eastern woodlands (North America), 51,
52(t), 303–304
East Germany, fall of communism in,
1055
East India companies, 679–680
East/West divide, 151
Ecclesiastes (Old Testament), 259
economic development
in Africa, 939–940, 1097, 1110–1120,
1111–1112(d), 1113–1114(d),
1115–1116(d), 1117–1118(d),
1119–1120(d)
African unity and, 1112–1113,
1113–1114(d)
Chinese Great Leap Forward and,
1041, 1043(i)
in fascist Italy, 990
globalization and, 1137–1138, 1186,
1186 (m)
in Global South, 1098–1103,
1100–1101(t)
microloan programs and, 1102(i)
state-directed, 1099
economic systems. See agriculture;
capitalism; communism; economy;
gathering and hunting peoples;
industrialization; pastoral societies
economy. See also capitalism; cash-crop
agriculture; globalization; trade;
specific locations
after abolition of slavery, 795
in Africa, 1097
anticolonialism and, 1085
in Axum, 287
in China, 382–384, 385, 398–399,
577, 682–683, 684–685,
1052–1053, 1139
China and Eurasian, 397–399
Chumash, 30
Cold War ending and, 1052
colonial, 932–940
contraction in 2008, 1138–1139
in Dutch East Indies, 933–934
in early modern era, 620
in England, 831, 832, 839
in Europe, 440, 446, 1005–1006,
1007(m)
after First Civilizations, 134
global, 354–355, 697–698, 848–849,
1134–1144
in Great Depression, 985–988

Hammurabi on, 119–120(d)
Inca, 593
in India, 167
in Indian Ocean basin, 343–344, 343(t)
Industrial Revolution and, 828, 847(t)
Islam on, 508–509(d)
Italian fascism and, 990
in Japan, 900, 1006
of Ju/'hoansi peoples, 27
labor in European colonies, 935–938
in Latin America, 632, 848–849
of Maya, 294
of Meroë, 286
in Mesoamerica, 294
under Mongol Empire, 542
of Native Americans, 574
in Niger River urban areas, 288–289
of Norte Chico, 87
in oil-producing countries, 1102–1103
Olmec, 90
in Paleolithic era, 21–22
of Persia under Mongols, 539
in Russian Empire, 641
of San peoples, 25
silver and, 682–685
slavery and, 250–251
slave trade and, 690
in South Africa, 1091
in Soviet Union, 1054, 1055
trade and, 338
United States and, 1049, 1142
in World War II, 1002–1003
Ecuador, 593, 848
Edict of Nantes, 725
Edo (Tokyo), Japan, 620, 895–896
education. See also literacy; scholarship;
universities and colleges
in China, 193, 194, 238–239, 739
in colonial era, 941–943
Confucianism and, 193–194
Islamic, 496
in Japan, 899
Muslim scholarship and, 444,
451–452, 499(t)
Protestantism and, 725
Rousseau on, 744
of Spartan women, 257
Western in colonial era, 941–943,
951–952, 952–953(d)
for women, 742
Edward VII (England), 922(i)

EEC. See European Economic
Community (EEC)
Egypt, 1153. See also Nile River region
afterlife in, 105, 121–122(d)
agriculture in, 108
Alexandria in, 153
animal husbandry in, 63(i)
British occupation of, 891
Christianity and, 286, 761
cities in, 107–108
civilization of, 86, 89(m)
culture in, 104–106, 110–111
empire of, 111, 112(m)
England and, 961–963
feminism in, 803
Hellenistic, 154
Hyksos invasion of, 110, 111
industry in, 846
Islam and, 483, 1155, 1156
Jewish exodus from, 204
kingship in, 100
Mesopotamia compared with,
103–111, 105(m), 107(t)
Mongols and, 533
Muslim Brotherhood in, 1155(i),
1169–1171(d)
Napoleon in, 890
nationalism in, 799
Nubia and, 91, 284–285
occupations of, 123
plague in, 545
Ptolemaic empire in, 153
Roman Empire and, 107(t)
scribes in, 84(i), 123, 124–125(d)
slavery in, 95
Soviet Union and, 1048
trade of, 108–109
women in, 98
writing in, 101(t)
Eisenhower, Dwight, 1049
electricity, globalization of, 1186(v)
elites, 19. See also aristocracy; caste system;
classes
in Africa, 1097, 1118, 1119–1120(d)
in American colonies, 783
in Cahokia, 304
in Chaco canyon, 302–303
in China, 163–164, 194–195,
238–239, 389, 417–422, 418(v),
419(v), 420(v), 421(v), 422(v), 643
Chumash, 31

in colonies, 937, 942, 942(i)
in early modern era, 620–621
in India, 1087
in industrial cities, 842
in Iran, 1105
in Japan, 898, 994
in Latin America, 791, 849–851
Maya people and, 294
in Mesoamerica, 294
Moche, 299
trade and, 334
in Vietnam, 393
Western-educated, 924, 929, 937, 942–943, 942(i)
El Niño, Moche society and, 300
emperors. *See* specific empires and emperors
empires. *See also* colonies and colonization; imperialism; specific empires
of Alexander the Great, 152–154, 152(m)
American, 1142–1144, 1143(m)
in Asia, 643–650
British, 831
in China, 159–165, 643–645, 653–654(d), 886–887, 894
collapse of Chinese and Roman, 163–165
comparison of, 650
cross-cultural interaction in, 328
cultural diffusion and, 336
decline of, 1082–1086, 1084(m)
defined, 144–145
disintegration in twentieth century, 970
early modern, 621
Egyptian, 110(m), 112
Eurasian, 144, 145
European, 626–631, 627(m), 771, 773–774, 880, 922(i), 923–947
growth of, 652
in India, 165–167
informal, 894, 924
infrastructure of, 147
Islamic, 480–488, 585(m)
Japanese, 902(m), 997
of Maya, 294–295
in Mesopotamia, 107
rise of, 6
Roman compared with Chinese, 160–165

Russian, 639
second-wave, 136, 924–925
trade and, 328
trading post empires, 677
after World War I, 982
enclosure, of British agricultural land, 830–831
Engels, Friedrich, 856–857, 857–859(d), 859
England (Britain), 578. *See also* British Empire; World War II
American Revolution and, 781–783
aristocracy in, 833–834
Asian colonial rule by, 925(m)
Asian trade and, 680
China and, 885, 885(t), 886
Christianity in, 457, 458(d)
classes in, 833–836
economic globalization and, 1135
exports of, 879
Hundred Years' War and, 578–579
in Ice Age, 16
Industrial Revolution in, 824(i), 829(m), 830–832
Irish home rule and, 797
Japan and, 901
mandates governed by, 983(m)
Nazi Germany and, 999
Nigeria and, 926
opium trade and, 885–886, 885(t), 886(i), 907–908
Ottoman Empire and, 889
Palestine and, 984, 1127
Rome and, 155
slave trade and, 693
trade by, 679, 680
women in, 801, 835, 836
World War I and, 979
English language, as global language, 1049
Enlightenment, 752
in France, 785
revolutions and, 780, 783, 785
rights and, 806–807(d), 807–808(d)
sciences and, 742–744
women and, 800
environment. *See also* climate; environmentalism
in Africa, 284
agriculture and, 60, 62
in Columbian exchange, 630

and culture, 104
deforestation and, 62, 105
in Egypt, 103–104
in French Vietnam, 935
fur trade and, 685
human migrations and, 19–20
industrialization and, 872–873, 873(v)
in Mesopotamia, 103–104
in Paleolithic era, 22
population expansion and, 24
transformation of, 1158–1160
environmentalism
in Germany, 1161
globalization of, 1158–1163
origins of, 1160–1161
past peoples and, 32
second-wave, 1161
in South Korea, 1162(i)
Epic of Gilgamesh, 93, 104, 115–116, 116–118(d)
Equal Rights Amendment (U.S.), 1150
Equiano, Olaudah, 700, 701–703(d)
Eritrea, 287
Estates General, in France, 784
Estonia, 1055
Ethiopia. *See also* Axum
agriculture in, 55
Christianity in, 284, 343, 426, 761
Church of St. George in, 614–615, 615(v)
coffee from, 712, 715
colonization and, 928, 966–967, 966(v)
Italian invasion of, 990
ethnicity
in Africa, 946–947
in Latin America, 633–634, 633(i), 636, 636(t)
Roman slavery and, 250
in Russian Empire, 643
Euripides, 256
euro (currency), 1006
Eurocentrism, 650, 771–775
countering, 772–775
Western dating systems and, 6–7
European Coal and Steel Community (1951), 1006
Europe and Europeans. *See also* empires; Eurasia; Great Powers; state (nation); specific locations
agriculture and, 584

Europe and Europeans (*continued*)
American empires of, 626–631
Asian commerce and, 674–682, 676(m)
in Australia, 21
China and, 359–360, 360–362(d), 580–584, 876(i), 882–887
colonial rule by, 928–929
colonization by, 626, 923, 924–928
Crusades and, 442–445, 443(m)
in early modern era, 620, 622–623(t)
economic integration and, 1006, 1007(m)
end of empires of, 1083–1086, 1084(m)
exchange of diseases and, 341
fascism and, 988–990
in 15th century, 570(t), 578–584
fur trade and, 685–688, 686(m)
Germanic societies in, 68–71(d)
globalization of Christianity and, 722–732
Great Depression and, 985–987
in High Middle Ages, 438–442, 439(m)
imperialism by, 876(i), 878
Industrial Revolution and, 827–830, 829(m)
industry, empire, and, 879–882
Islam and, 723
Latin America and, 849–853
maritime voyages by, 568(i), 580–584
migration from, 940(t)
Native Americans and, 574, 628
Ottomans and, 649–650
population of, 438, 674, 685
printing in, 397–398
Protestant Reformation in, 723–727, 726(m)
recovery after World War II, 1005–1007
religion and Black Death in, 560–567, 562(v), 563(v), 564(v), 566(v)
Renaissance and, 579–580
Scientific Revolution and, 737–746
scramble for Africa by, 926, 960–967, 961(v), 962(v), 964(v), 965(v), 966(v)
slave trade and, 692–695
socialism and, 855–856
technology of, 446–447, 447(i)

as third-wave civilization, 426
universities and, 738
World War I and, 977–984, 980(m), 982(i), 983(m)
World War II and, 976(i), 999–1001, 1000(m), 1003–1004
European Economic Community (EEC), 1006
European Union (EU), 1006, 1007(m), 1056
evangelicals, antislavery sentiments and, 794
evolution (human)
Darwin and, 882, 882(i)
fundamentalism on, 1152
evolutionary socialism, Bernstein on, 860–861(d)
Ewe people, 938
Ewuare (Benin king), 573
examination system
in China, 162, 164, 194–195, 238–239, 255, 382, 402, 537
Korea and, 392
Vietnam and, 394
exchange networks, 13. *See also* trade
Islamic, 497–499
exodus, of Jews, 204
exploration, 570(t), 580–584, 581(t), 582(m). *See also* navigation; specific countries and explorers
Chinese, 577–578
by Columbus, 568(i), 580
European, 568(i), 580–584, 581(t)
by Portugal, 580–581, 584, 674
Spanish, 677–678
Viking, 442
exports. *See* trade; specific products
extinction, 18
of plants and animals, 1159
Ezana (Axum), 287

factories, 870(v), 871, 872(v)
in England, 836
regulation of, 838
fairs. *See* trading fairs
families
in China, 193(i)
in Japan, 684
in Korea, 392
of !Kung people, 35–36(d)
Family Law Code (Morocco), 1148

famines
in China, 1041, 1043
in Soviet Union, 1041
farms and farming. *See also* agriculture
in Africa, 55, 290
in African and Asian colonies, 935
decline of, 49–50
domestication, cultivation, and, 5–6
frontier of, 572
herders and, 63–64
Inca, 593
in Latin America, 851
fascism. *See also* Nazi Germany
in Europe, 988–990
in Italy, 989–990
Mussolini on, 1010, 1011–1012(d)
Fashoda, 963
fatwa (religious edict), 1156
Federalist Papers, 784
Feminine Mystique, The (Friedan), 1146
feminism
beginnings of, 800–803
communist, 1039–1040
divisions in, 1149–1150
globalization of, 1145–1150
in Global South, 1147–1149
international, 1149–1150
in Japan, 994
opposition to, 802
Paleolithic peoples and, 32
second-wave, 1146
socialism and, 861
in Western world, 1146–1147
Ferdinand VII (Spain), 791
Ferdowsi (Persian poet), 512
Ferry, Jules, 882
Fertile Crescent, 51, 52(t), 53–55, 54(m), 56
Festival of the Federation (France), 817
feudalism. *See also* Middle Ages
in France, 785
in Western Europe, 436–437
fez, in Turkey, 1104
Fiji, 595
filial piety, in China, 193(i), 194
Filipinos. *See* Philippines
"final solution," by Nazis, 1003
Finland, women's voting rights in, 801
fire altar, Zoroastrian, 203(i)
firebombings, in World War II, 1002
"firestick farming," in Australia, 572

First Civilizations, 85–107, 88–89(m).
  See also specific civilizations
  assessments of, 112–113
  classes in, 94–95
  interactions among, 108–112
  invasions of, 133
  Mesopotamia and Egypt compared,
    103–106
  slavery in, 95
  states in, 99–103
  writing and accounting in, 100–102,
    101(t), 115
First Emperor. *See* Qin Shihuangdi
First World Parliament of Religions
    (1893), 944
First World War. *See* World War I
Five-Year Plans (Soviet Union),
    1061–1062
flagellants, Black Death and, 561, 562(v)
"flappers," 985
Florence, 440, 578
  causes of Black Death and, 560
Florentine Codex, 591(i), 664, 667–668,
    670, 670(v)
Flores man, 22
flu. *See* influenza
food(s). *See also* agriculture; crops;
    specific foods
  from Americas, 630–631
  in China, 382–383
  grains as, 23
  population growth and, 24
  revolution in, 5–6
  of San peoples, 26
  spread of, 329, 343
foot binding, in China, 384–385, 385(i)
Forbidden City (Beijing), 577, 609
forced labor
  in European colonies, 933–934
  for rubber crops, 933, 934(i)
  in World War II, 1002
Ford, Henry, 842
foreign investment. *See* investment
forests
  in Africa, 349
  in China, 684
  environment and, 1160, 1161
  in Europe, 438–439
  in Japan, 684
fossil fuels. *See also* oil and oil industry
  environment and, 1158

Fourier, Charles, 856
Fourteen Points, 984
France, 578. *See also* French Empire;
    French Revolution
  Africa and, 961–963, 962(v)
  Asian colonial rule by, 925(m)
  China and, 886
  estates in, 449, 778(i), 817, 819(v)
  feminism in, 801, 1146
  fur trade and, 685
  headscarves in schools in, 1184
  Huguenots in, 725
  Hundred Years' War and, 578–579
  imperialism by, 964–965, 965(v)
  Islam and, 480
  Lascaux caves in, 16(i)
  under Louis XIV, 659–660, 661(d)
  mandates governed by, 983(m)
  middle class in, 834(i)
  missionaries from, 727
  NATO and, 1144
  North African migrants to,
    1183–1185, 1184(v)
  Old Regime in, 778(i)
  Ottomans and, 650, 889–890
  Rome and, 155
  slave trade and, 693
  socialists in, 839(i)
  student protests in, 1145
  trading company from, 679
  women's voting rights in, 801
  World War I and, 979
Franciscans, 542–543, 727
Franco-Prussian War (1870–1871),
    979
Franks, 435
  Charlemagne and, 424(i)
Franz Ferdinand (Austria), 979
Freetown, Sierra Leone, 794
Freikorps (Germany), 991
French Empire, 626
  in Africa, 962–963(i)
  of Napoleon, 788(m)
French Revolution (1789–1815), 781,
    784–787, 817–823, 818(v), 819(v),
    820(v), 821(v), 822(v)
  American Revolution compared
    with, 787
  Enlightenment and, 785
  religion in, 820(v)
  rights of man and, 806–807(d)

  Terror and, 785
  women and, 800
French West Africa, 929
Freud, Sigmund (1856–1939), 745
Friedan, Betty, 1146
Fukuzawa Yukichi, 898, 919
Fulbe people, 575
fundamentalism
  global, 1151–1153
  Islamic, 500, 1153–1157, 1176,
    1177–1178(d)
  religious alternatives to Islamic,
    1157–1158
Funeral Oration (Pericles), 171–172(d)
fur trade
  global 685–688, 686 (m)
  in Russia, 639, 688, 688(i)
Fu Xuan (China), 262, 263(d)

Gabon, 963
Galilei, Galileo (1564–1642), 737,
    740(t), 741–742
Gama, Vasco da, 580–581, 584, 674, 727
Gambia, 692–693
Gandhara, 228
Gandhi, Mohandas (Mahatma)
    (1869–1948), 237, 825, 957,
    958–960(d), 1085, 1087(i),
    1088–1090, 1122–1123
Ganges River region, 165
Gao, 351
Garvey, Marcus, 946
gathering and hunting peoples, 11–12,
    20. *See also* agriculture
  of Americas, 18, 29–31, 60, 301, 572
  of Australia, 17
  Chumash people as, 24–25
  Clovis people and, 18
  San people as, 25–29
Gatling gun, 880(i)
Gaza Strip, 1129
Gelasius (Pope), 213
gender and gender issues. *See also* men;
    patriarchy; women
  division of labor and, 21
  Hammurabi on, 120–121(d)
  hierarchies and, 96–97
  in Islamic society, 486–488
  of Ju/'hoansi peoples, 27
  in Mesoamerican and Andean
    societies, 594

gender and gender issues (*continued*)
  in Paleolithic societies, 20
  patriarchies of classical era and,
    252–259
General Motors, 1137
genetic engineering, of corn, 56
genital mutilation, 488, 1148
Genoa, 440
genocide
  in Armenia, 984
  in Bosnia, 1003
  in Cambodia, 1003, 1052
  Holocaust as, 1003
  in Rwanda, 1003, 1097
  in Sudan, 1003
Gentiles (non-Jews), 211
George III (England), China and,
  882–883, 905–906, 906–907(d)
German East Africa, 934
German Empire, end of, 1083
Germanic peoples
  agricultural village societies of, 68,
    69–71(d)
  Carolingian Empire and, 436, 436(m)
  Roman Empire and, 164, 435–436
  Western European societies and, 327
German Social Democratic Party, 861,
  862–863(d)
Germany, 578. *See also* Berlin Wall;
    Nazi Germany
  flagellants in, 561
  Great Depression in, 985–986
  Green Party in, 1161
  imperialism of, 924
  industrialization in, 840
  Japan and, 997
  Otto I in, 436
  peasant revolts in, 724(t)
  Reformation in, 723, 725
  reparations after World War I, 983,
    986
  Russian treaty with (1918), 1034
  unification of, 797(t), 798(m), 979
  after World War I, 983–984, 988, 991
  World War I and, 979, 981, 982
Ghana (modern), 708. *See also* Gold
    Coast (Ghana)
  cacao farming in, 935, 938
  constitution in, 1098
  independence of, 1110

nationalist movement in, 1112–1113,
    1113–1114(d)
  slavery and, 696
Ghana (West African kingdom), 289,
    350, 350(m), 492
al-Ghazali (1058–1111), 486, 488
Ghazan (Mongol ruler of Persia,
    1295–1304), 539, 544
Gikuyu peoples, 64, 71, 72–73(d), 529,
    936
Gilgamesh. *See* Epic of Gilgamesh
Ginsberg, Eugenia, 1068–1069(d)
gladiators, revolt by, 251–252
glasnost (openness), 1054
globalization, 972–973, 1134,
    1180–1187, 1186 (m)
  of agriculture, 58–59(m), 60
  American Empire and, 1142–1144,
    1143(m)
  antiglobalization movements and,
    1141–1142
  call centers and, 1135(i)
  of Christianity, 722–732, 761–768
  of civilization, 326
  in classical era, 326
  of commerce, 674
  consumerism and, 1183(v)
  distribution of wealth and, 1138
  in early modern era, 619, 697–698
  in early twenty-first century,
    971–972, 971(m)
  economic, 354–355, 697–698, 940,
    1085, 1110–1111, 1111–1112(d),
    1134–1144
  economic development and, 1186,
    1186 (m)
  of electricity, 1186(v)
  of environmentalism, 1162–1163
  of feminist movements, 1146–1150
  foreign direct investment and,
    1136(m)
  of fundamentalism, 1151–1153
  of humankind, 4–5
  of industrialization, 827, 828, 1103
  inequities in, 1139–1141, 1140(m)
  of investment, 1136, 1136(m)
  Islamic trade and, 498
  Mexico and, 1141
  migration and, 1182–1185, 1184(v)
  under Mongol Empire, 542

neo-liberal, 1141, 1142
  protests against, 1185–1186, 1185(v)
  reglobalization and, 1135–1137
  religion and, 1150–1158
  sweatshops and, 1180–1181, 1181(v)
  of trade, 1133
  U.S. influences and, 1142–1144,
    1143(m)
  work and, 1181(v)
Global North
  environmentalism and, 1163
  gap with South, 1139, 1140(m)
Global South, 1082. *See also* developing
    countries
  economic development in,
    1098–1103, 1100–1101(t)
  environmentalism and, 1163
  feminism in, 1147–1149
  gap with North, 1139, 1140(m)
  older vs. modern outlooks in, 1103
global warming, 1160, 1160(m), 1162
  French Vietnamese agriculture and,
    935
  after Ice Age, 23–24, 52–53
  interruption in, 53–54
  Kyoto protocol on, 1144
  UN conferences on global warming,
    1162
Goa, 237, 676
gods and goddesses. *See also* religion
  Aztec, 591, 603–604(d)
  Buddha and, 339
  of Chavín de Huántar, 298
  Greek, 205, 208
  of Hebrews, 98, 109, 204–205
  of Ju/'hoansi peoples, 28
  Mesopotamian, 98
  Paleolithic, 22–23
  rulers and, 100
  women's roles and, 98
gold
  in Africa, 348, 349
  Axum and, 313, 314(d)
  of Mali, 351(i)
  in South Africa, 937
  trade and, 675
Gold Coast (Ghana), 708, 935, 986
Golden Horde. *See also* Kipchak
    Khanate
  Mongols of, 540, 541

Golden Temple (Amritsar), 737
Gorbachev, Mikhail (Soviet Union),
　1051, 1054–1055
Goree, 672(i)
Gospel of Matthew, The, 224–225(d)
Goths, 435
de Gouges, Olympe, 808
government
　in Athens, 150
　of British India, 930
　of Byzantine Empire, 428–429
　chiefdoms as, 65–66
　in China, 158–160, 162, 174, 175(d),
　　195, 238–239, 254, 577
　in colonial Latin America, 632–633
　in early modern era, 652–662
　economy and, 1097
　in Egypt, 108
　of England, 831
　European, 442
　European colonial, 928–932
　in Great Depression, 987
　Greek thought on, 207
　Inca, 592–593
　of Indian Empire, 176, 177–178(d)
　of Indus Valley civilization, 90
　of Iran, 1105–1106
　Islamic, 508(d)
　of Japan, 394, 895–896, 897, 996
　of Maya, 294
　in Mexico, 851
　of Persian Empire, 146
　of Roman Empire, 158, 162–163
　of Russia, 843–844
　by soldiers, 1097–1098
　in Sparta, 149
　of state, 99–100
　of Teotihuacán, 296–297
　of village-based societies, 64–65
Grand Canal (China), 381(m)
Grand Mosque, 1156
Great Britain. *See* England (Britain)
Great Depression (1930s), 986(i)
　capitalism and, 985–988
　comparing impact of, 987(f)
　Japan and, 994
　New Deal in, 987–988
　socialism in U.S. and, 843
great dying, the, 629
Greater Japan Women's Society, 1003

Great Khans. *See* Mongols and Mongol
　Empire
Great Law of Peace, 574
Great Leap Forward (China, 1958–
　1960), 1041, 1043, 1043(i), 1073
Great Proletarian Cultural Revolution
　(China). *See* Cultural Revolution
Great Purges, in Soviet Union, 1044
Great Wall (China), 160, 163, 381(m)
Great War, the, 977. *See also* World War I
Great Zimbabwe, 348
Greco-Persian wars, 150–151
Greco-Roman traditions
　Christianity and, 161–162, 327
　Indian Buddhism and, 340
　slavery and, 248(t)
Greece. *See also* Athens; specific locations
　Byzantine Empire and, 428
　city-states of, 149, 150, 153
　classical era in, 147–154, 148(m),
　　150(t), 205–209
　classical intellectual thought from,
　　429, 451, 579–580
　communism in, 1031
　culture of, 147–150, 161–162, 369(v)
　diseases spread to, 340
　Egyptian influence on, 111
　Golden Age in, 151
　Hellenistic culture of, 153
　independence of, 797, 890
　India and, 154, 166
　legacy of, 208
　rationalism in, 190, 205–208
　religion in, 205–206
　slavery in, 95, 249, 690
　wars with Persia, 150–151
　writings on love, 209
Greek fire, 432
Greek language
　in Byzantine Empire, 431
　in Coptic Christianity, 286
greenhouse gases, 1159–1160
Greenland, Viking colony in, 442
Green Party (Germany), 1161
Gregory I (pope, r. 590–604), 457,
　458(d)
Gregory II (Pope), 466
Gregory of Tours (538–594), 455,
　456–457(d)
Guam, 595

guano, 848
Guanyin (bodhisattva), 231
Guatemala, 280(i), 353
guerrilla warfare
　in Afghanistan, 1046
　in China, 1036
　independence movements and, 1086
Guevara, Che, 1145, 1146
Gu Hongzhong (Chinese painter),
　422, 422(v)
guilds
　in England, 831
　in Europe, 440
　in India, 167
guillotine, 785, 786(i), 821(v)
gulag (Soviet Union), 1044, 1052
gunpowder
　in China, 383–384, 398, 399
　in Europe, 447
　Native American weapons and, 687
Guomindang (Chinese Nationalist
　Party), 1036
Gupta dynasty (India, 320–550 C.E.),
　167, 236(i)
Guru Granth (Sikh sacred text), 737
Guru Nanak. *See* Nanak (founder of
　Sikhism)
Gutenberg, Johannes, 397
Guyuk (Great Khan), 543
Gypsies, Nazis and, 1003

Habsburgs (Austria)
　Hungarian uprising against, 797(t)
　Ottomans and, 650
haciendas (plantations), 848, 851
hadith, 505–506(d)
　women portrayed in, 488, 502
Hafiz (Sufi poet), 485, 496, 515
Haiti, 73, 787. *See also* Haitian
　Revolution; Hispaniola
　equality in, 795
　revolution in, 774
　slavery in, 789–790
　United States and, 852
　Vodou in, 732
Haitian Revolution (1791–1804), 252,
　779, 781(t), 787–790, 789(i), 794
hajj (pilgrimage to Mecca), 472(i), 473,
　478, 484(i), 595
Hamas, 1129, 1155(i)

Hammurabi (r. 1792–1750 B.C.E.), law code of, 95, 100, 102, 118–119, 119–121(d)

Han dynasty (China, 206 B.C.E.–220 C.E.), 160, 162, 163, 238, 241(m)
  Buddhism and, 401
  collapse of, 163–164, 380
  Confucius and, 193
  diseases spread to, 340
  merchants and, 242
  peasants and, 241
  slavery and, 248
  tribute system and, 387
  Xiongnu people and, 388–389, 526

Han Fei (China), 174, 175(d), 192

hangul (Korean language writing), 392

Hangzhou, 383, 440

Han Kuan (Chinese scholar), 524, 547

Hannibal (Carthage), 268

Han Yu (China), 403

Harappa, 89(m), 93, 126, 127(v), 165

Harijan. See untouchables caste

Haruko (Japanese empress), 803

Harvey, William (1578–1657), 740(t)

Hatshepsut (Egypt, r. 1472–1457 B.C.E.), 98, 107(t)

Hausa people, 350, 350(m)

Hawaii, 926
  Pearl Harbor attack in, 997–999
  society in, 19

Hazda people (Tanzania), 11

headscarves
  in French schools, 1184
  in Turkey, 1105

health and health care. See also diseases; medicine
  farming and, 61
  Ju/'hoansi peoples healers and, 28–29

Hebrews, 109, 204. See also Jews and Judaism
  god of, 109
  prophets of, 190, 191(t)

Heian (Kyoto), Japan, 394, 396

Hellenes, 147–148

Hellenistic world, 153–154. See also Greece

Helminski, Kabir (Sheikh), 1176–1177, 1177–1178(d)

helots, in Greece, 149, 258

Henry IV (France), 725

herding, 5–6, 63–64, 522, 574–575

heresy
  Arian, 430
  Crusades and, 444
  Nestorian, 430

Herodotus, 146, 147, 207

Hidalgo-Morelos rebellion (Mexico; 1810–1813), 781(t), 791, 792

hieroglyphics, as writing system, 101(t)

High Middle Ages, 438–445, 439(m), 446–448

hijab, in Iran, 1106, 1107

hijra, 478

Hildegard of Bingen, 441

Himyarite kingdom (Arabia), 312

Hinduism, 722
  ascetics of, 198, 198(i)
  in Asian commerce, 681–682
  Bhagavad Gita and, 201–202, 219–221(d)
  bhakti, 736
  Buddhism and, 199–200
  in colonial era, 944–945, 944(i)
  duty and devotion in, 201–202
  fundamentalism in, 1152–1153
  in India, 167, 197–198, 326
  Indian independence and, 1123
  Indian Muslims and, 1089
  Islam and, 490–491, 645, 736–737
  in Mughal Empire, 645–646
  spread of, 329, 338, 344

Hindutva (Hindu nationalism), 1152

Hine, Lewis W. (1874–1940), 871, 872(v)

Hippocrates, 207

Hiroshima bombing, 999, 1002, 1002(i)

Hispanic Americans, civil rights for, 1145

Hispaniola, 73, 568(i). See also Haiti

Hitler, Adolf (Germany, 1889–1945), 984, 990–993, 990(i). See also Nazi Germany
  on Nazism, 1012–1013, 1013–1015(d)

Hittites, 111

Hobsbawm, Eric, 832, 839

Ho Chi Minh (Vietnam), 784, 1030, 1086

Holland. See Dutch; Netherlands

Holocaust, in World War II, 1003

Holy Land. See Middle East; specific regions

Holy Roman Empire, 436, 726(m)
  Catholic-Protestant struggle in, 725

holy wars, Crusades as, 442–445, 443(m)

Homestead steel, strike against, 842

hominid family, 3, 12

Homo habilis, 3

Homo sapiens, 3, 12, 22

homosexuality
  Nazis and, 1003
  in Sparta, 258

Hong Rengan, 884

Hong Xiuquan (1814–1864), 884

Hopewell culture, 303

hoplites (infantrymen), in Greece, 149

Hormuz, 676

Horn of Africa, 287

horses
  domestication of, 63
  in Europe, 447
  nomadic peoples and, 525–526
  in pastoral societies, 525–526

horticulture, Agricultural Revolution and, 53

House of Wisdom (Baghdad), 498

housing
  of Ancestral Pueblo peoples, 301–303, 302(i)
  Chumash, 30
  collapse of "bubble" in, 1138
  of nomadic pastoralists, 524
  in Teotihuacán, 296

Huari kingdom, 297(m), 300

Huáscar (Inca), 628

Huck Finn (Twain), 85

Hudson Bay region, 685

Huguenots, 725

Huitzilopochtli (Aztec god), 591, 667

Huizong (Chinese emperor, 1082–1135), 417–418

Hulegu (Mongol il-khan), 538, 539

Human Development Report (UN), on life expectancies, 1138

humanists, 580

human rights, 806–807(d), 806–808, 807–808(d)
  feminists and, 1149

human sacrifice
  Aztec, 591, 603–604(d)
  in China, 182
  in First Civilizations, 103
  Inca, 593

Hundred Years' War (1337–1453), 578–579

Hungary
communism in, 1035, 1055
fascism in, 989
independence movement and, 797
uprising against Austrian Habsburgs, 797(t)
uprising in (1956–1957), 1050

Huns, 164, 164(i)
Huron peoples, 687
Hussein, Saddam, 1107, 1142
hydrogen bomb, 1047(i)
Hyksos, 107(t), 111, 112

Iacocca, Lee, 1144
Ibn Battuta (1304–1368), 351, 492
travels of, 362–363, 363–366(d), 494
Ibn Khaldun (1332–1406), 499(t), 546, 547
Ibn Rushd (Averroës, 1126–1198), 499(t)
Ibn Sina (Avicenna, 980–1037), 498–499, 499(t)
Ibrahim, Anwar, 1157, 1176
Ibsen, Henrik, 801–802
Ice Age, 16, 17
Agricultural Revolution and, 51
Little Ice Age and, 685
warming after, 23–24
Iceland
economy in, 1138
Viking colony in, 442
icons
Byzantine, 466–471, 468(v), 469(v), 470(v)
Eastern Orthodox, 430, 431
ideology. *See also* specific ideologies
of Axis powers, 1010–1017, 1011–1012(d), 1013–1015(d), 1016–1017(d)
communist, 970, 1031
Confucianism as, 160, 165, 194
of Daoism, 197
of fascism, 988–989
of Hinduism, 201–202
of Hitler, 992, 1012, 1013–1015(d)
independence movements and, 1086
in Japan, 1015, 1016–1017(d)
Nazi, 999
Ife people, 83
Igbo peoples, 65, 573, 939, 947

il-khans
Ghazan, 539, 544
in Persia, 538, 543–544
Imagawa Ryoshun (Japan, 1325–1420), 414, 415–416(d)
immigrants and immigration. *See* migrations; specific groups
immortality. *See* afterlife; eternal life
imperialism. *See also* decolonization
in Asia and Africa, 924–928, 925(m), 927(m)
British, 930(i)
China and, 876(i), 1036
European, 774, 878–880
French, 964–965, 965(v)
of Japan, 901, 902(m)
nationalism and, 774, 880
in Southeast Asia, 997
by United States, 852–853, 878, 1144
Inca Empire, 87, 293, 297, 327, 328, 592–594
conquest of, 626
economy of, 593
government of, 592–593
society of, 592–594
Spain and, 601, 605–607(d), 628
trade and, 354
indentured servants, as labor, 795
independence. *See also* specific countries
in Africa, 1083–1086, 1122
in Asia, 1083–1086, 1122
in Baltic region, 1055
decolonization and, 1082–1086
experiments in, 1095–1108
India and, 957, 958–960(d), 1085, 1086–1090, 1089(m), 1122–1123, 1124(v)
of Korea, 392
in Latin America, 791–793, 791(m), 846–848
leaders and, 1085–1086
in less developed countries, 1095, 1095 (m)
nationalism and, 797
in South Africa, 1080(i), 1086, 1090–1094, 1123–1124, 1125(v)
in Spanish America, 781(t), 790–793, 791(m)
struggles for, 1082–1086
of U.S. colonies, 781(t)
of Vietnam, 1125–1126, 1126(v)

in West Africa, 1085
after World War I, 983(m)
India. *See also* Gandhi, Mohandas; Indus Valley civilization; Pakistan; South Asia; specific rulers and empires
Africa compared with, 1095–1098
alternative to patriarchy in, 266–267, 267–268(d)
Asian commerce and, 681–682
British Empire in, 680, 926, 942, 950–959, 951(d), 952–953(d), 953–955(d), 956–957(d), 958–959(d)
Buddhism and, 167, 190, 212, 230(v), 339–340, 400
caste system in, 167, 237, 242–246, 260–261
Chinese Buddhists in, 356–357, 357–359(d)
Christianity in, 761, 767–769, 768(v)
civilization of, 326
classical period in, 197–202, 242–246, 244(t)
colonial economy in, 933, 935
colonial society in, 931
cotton production in, 830
culture of, 167, 197–202
da Gama voyage to, 580–581
economy in, 167, 1099, 1102
empires in, 165–167, 166(m)
European culture in, 941, 942
in 15th century, 570(t)
after First Civilizations, 165
fundamentalism in, 1152–1153
Greek culture in, 154, 166
Hinduism in, 167, 197–198, 736–737, 944–945, 944(i), 1089
independence and, 957, 958–960(d), 1085, 1086–1090, 1089(m), 1122–1123, 1124(v)
industrialization and, 825, 846, 1139
innovations in, 137
Islam and, 489–491, 497, 528, 733
jatis in, 245–246
Malay sea route to, 345
migration from, 940(t)
Mughal Empire in, 587, 624(i), 645–646, 645(m)
Muslims in, 736–737, 944–945, 1153
Naramada River dam in, 1161

India (*continued*)
  nationalism in, 800
  opium from, 907
  partition of, 1089–1090, 1122
  Persian Empire and, 166
  political evolution in, 1096
  rebellions against colonialism in, 930
  religion in, 167
  slavery in, 248–249
  Southeast Asia and, 345–346
  Srivijaya and, 345
  technology in, 827–828
  textiles in, 685, 830
  trade and, 675
  Upanishads in, 190
  use of term, 310
  after World War I, 984
Indian Empire, governing of, 176,
  177–178(d)
Indian National Congress (INC,
  Congress Party), 800, 955, 1087,
  1089, 1096, 1122–1123, 1124(v)
Indian Ocean region
  China and, 399, 578, 584
  Europe and, 582, 675
  Islam and, 497, 588
  migrations across, 19
  monsoons in, 342, 343
  Portuguese commerce in, 675–676
  trade in, 307–308, 308(d), 341–344,
  342(m), 628, 675, 677(i)
  trading companies in, 679
Indian Rebellion (1857–1858), 930,
  950, 953–955(d)
Indians. *See* Native Americans
Indo-Europeans, 109
  languages of, 57, 111
  Persians as, 145
Indonesia. *See also* specific locations
  Cold War and, 1048
  colonial rule and, 926
  Dutch in, 680, 926, 933–934
  financial crisis in, 1138
  Flores man from, 22
  Islam and, 588
  Japan and, 997
  migrations from, 19
industrialization, 824(i), 829(m). *See also*
  Industrial Revolution
  abuses and, 843

  in China, 888, 1041–1044,
  1052–1053, 1073, 1075(v)
  in early modern era, 620–621
  European, 879–882
  in Germany, 840
  globalization of, 827, 828, 854, 1103
  in Global South, 1102
  in Japan, 846, 897(i), 900–901, 994
  in Latin America (1825–1935),
  846–853, 850(m)
  in Russia, 843–846
  in Soviet Union, 1041–1044,
  1064–1065, 1065–1067(d)
  in twentieth century, 971
  in United States, 840–843, 841(m)
  of warfare, 981
Industrial Patriotic Federation (Japan),
  995
Industrial Revolution, 825–832
  aristocracy and, 833–834
  arts and, 867–874, 868(v), 869(v),
  870(v), 872(v), 873(v), 874(v)
  colonial wealth and, 631
  in England, 824(i), 829(m), 830–832
  in Europe, 827–830, 829(m)
  explanation of, 826–832
  global divide over, 847(t)
  imperialism and, 879–882
  in Japan, 684
  Latin America and, 846–853
  railroads and, 832(i), 833(f)
  in Russia, 844–846
  spread of, 840–841, 853–854
industry
  military and, 1049
  pollution from, 1159
  in South Africa, 1091
  in United States, 1049
Indus Valley civilization, 87–90, 89(m),
  126–131, 127(v), 128(v), 129(v),
  130(v)
  cities and towns in, 92–93
  Mohenjo Daro, 89(m), 93, 93(i)
  seal from, 128(v)
  slaves in, 95
  trade of, 108, 127
  writing in, 101(t)
infanticide, female, 487
influenza, 629, 687
  epidemic in India, 1087

informal empires, 894, 924
Inkatha Freedom Party (South Africa),
  1094
Inner Asia. *See* Central Asia, Inner
  Eurasia
Inner Eurasia, 336, 531
intellectual thought. *See also* sciences
  in Africa, 945
  in China, 745
  classical Greek learning and, 429,
  451, 579–580
  in classical period, 191(t)
  in Enlightenment, 742–744
  Eurasian culture and, 190
  in Europe, 449–452
  Europeans in China and, 730–731
  Greek, 153, 206–208, 256, 451–452
  of humanists, 580
  in India, 167
  Islamic, 444, 451–452, 498–499,
  499(t), 733
  in Japan, 745–746
  Reformation and, 727
  in Renaissance, 579
  sciences and, 737–746
  after World War I, 982
intendants, in France, 660
International Criminal Court, 1144
Internationale, The, 838, 863–864(d)
International Monetary Fund, 1004,
  1135, 1185
international organization. *See* League of
  Nations; United Nations; specific
  groups
intifada, 1129
inventions. *See also* technology
  in China, 383, 397
  in England, 831
  in High Middle Ages, 446–448
  industrial, 826, 827
  of printing, 383, 397–398
Ionia, Greek settlements in, 151, 207
Iran, 1103(m), 1153. *See also* Persia
  Khomeini, Ruholla (Ayatollah)
  Iraq war with, 1107
  Islam and, 483, 1105–1108, 1156
  revolution in, 1106–1107
  trade in, 108
  women in, 1106–1107, 1107(i)
Iranian Revolution (1979), 473

Iraq. *See also* Mesopotamia
  Iran war with, 1107
  Islam and, 483
  Islamic parties in, 1155
  Saddam Hussein in, 1107, 1142
  after World War I, 983(m), 984
Iraq War (2003–), 1142, 1144
Ireland
  home rule in, 797
  potatoes in, 630
  slaves in, 351
iron and iron industry
  in Africa, 290
  in China, 383
  European empire and, 628
  industrialization and, 872–873,
    873(v)
  in Niger Valley, 289
  San peoples and, 25
Iron Curtain, 1045
Iroquois League of Five Nations, 574
Iroquois peoples, European alcohol
  sales to, 687–688
irrigation
  First Civilizations and, 91–92
  Indus Valley civilization and, 90
  in Sumer, 106
Isaiah (prophet, Judaism), 190, 191(t),
  205
Ishtar (goddess, Egypt), 109
Isis (goddess, Egypt), 162, 277
Islam, 431, 595. *See also* Mongols and
    Mongol Empire; Mughal Empire;
    Muhammad; Muslims; Ottoman
    Empire; Quran; Safavid Empire;
    Songhay Empire; Sufism
  in Africa, 575, 586–588
  in Anatolia, 491–492
  Arab Empire and, 328
  Arabic language and, 483, 493
  astronomy in, 739, 739(i)
  Berbers and, 483
  birth of, 474–480
  in Borobudur, 346(i)
  calligraphy in, 397
  as civilization, 495–499
  conversion to, 482–483
  Crusades and, 444
  dating system in, 7
  divisions in, 483–485

  Dome of the Rock and, 612–614,
    613(v)
  in early 21st century, 1154(m)
  in early modern era, 620,
    622–623(t), 722
  on economy, 508–509(d)
  empires of, 585(m)
  Europeans and, 444, 723
  exchange networks of, 497–499
  expansion of, 480–483, 481(m),
    733–734
  feminism and, 1150
  in 15th century, 584–588
  fundamentalist, 500
  government in, 508(d)
  Greek learning and, 208
  growth of, 473–474, 489(m)
  hajj in, 472(i), 473, 478
  Hinduism and, 490, 645, 736–737
  historic role of, 500
  in India, 489–491, 497, 528, 587
  in Iran, 1105–1108
  jihad in, 478
  jizya in, 482, 646
  Judaism and, 205
  laws of, 479, 506–507, 507–509(d)
  marriage in, 487, 508(d)
  men in, 486–488, 487(i)
  mysticism in, 485–486
  among nomads, 526–527
  in Nubia, 286
  organization of, 479
  in Ottoman Empire, 643, 647, 648,
    889–894
  Persian Mongols and, 544
  in Philippines, 678
  Pillars of, 477–478
  reconquest in Spain and, 495
  religious alternatives to fundamental-
    ism in, 1157–1158
  renewal of, 1153
  sciences and, 498–499, 499(t),
    738–739, 739(i), 746
  second flowering of, 587–588
  September 11, 2001, and, 1176–1177,
    1177–1178(d)
  Shia, 483–485, 488, 500, 586
  slave trade and, 690, 692
  Songhay Empire and, 586–587
  in Southeast Asia, 346, 587–588

  Spain and, 480, 483, 494–495
  spread of, 329
  Sunni, 483–485, 500, 586
  Swahili civilization and, 347–348
  technology in, 827
  as third-wave civilization, 326
  trade and, 675
  Turkey and, 1103–1105, 1167, 1168(d)
  Turks' conversion to, 375
  in 20th century, 894
  ulama and, 484, 486, 496
  umma in, 477, 478
  urbanization in, 497, 515, 516(v)
  Wahhabi, 734, 734(m), 756–757(d)
  in the West, 1151
  in West Africa, 289, 351, 492–494,
    493(m)
  Western culture and, 1153
  women in, 477, 486–488, 487(i), 494,
    508(d), 803, 1173–1174,
    1174–1175(d)
  world of, 1153–1157
  Zoroastrianism and, 204
Islamic empire. *See* Arabs and Arab
  Empire
Islamic Jihad, 1156
Islamic law. *See sharia*
Islamic modernism, 893
Islamic Salvation Front (Algeria), 1155
Islamic terrorism, U.S. attack and, 1142
Israel
  ancient, 204, 204(m)
  Arabs and, 1003, 1153
  Muslims and, 1153
  state of, 1127–1129, 1128(v)
  World War II and, 1003
Issus, Battle of (333 B.C.E.), 153(i)
Istanbul, 648. *See also* Constantinople
Italy, 578. *See also* Roman Empire
  city-states in, 442
  Ethiopia and, 990
  fascism in, 989–990
  immigrant farm workers from, 851
  imperialism of, 924
  Japan and, 997
  plague in, 545–546
  Rome and, 155, 161
  trade in, 440
  unification of, 797(t), 798(m)
  after World War I, 988

Ivan III (Russia), 614
Ivory Coast, women in, 938

Jahan (Shah), 624(i)
Jahangir (Mughal Empire), 645, 655, 655–657(d), 767
Jamaica, 790
    after slavery, 795
    Taino peoples and, 73
Janissaries, in Ottoman Empire, 586(i), 648, 891, 892
Japan, 394(m). *See also* Pearl Harbor attack; samurai warriors
    Asian colonial rule by, 925(m)
    authoritarianism in, 993–996, 1015, 1016–1017(d)
    Buddhist temple in, 611–612, 612(v)
    bushido (way of the warrior) in, 395, 414, 414–415(d), 415–416(d)
    China and, 378(i), 380, 394–397, 406–407, 407–408(d), 877, 886, 901, 920, 920(v), 997, 1035, 1036
    Christianity in, 681, 728(i)
    as a civilization, 406–416
    civil wars in, 681, 895, 897
    Confucianism in, 394, 896
    constitution in, 899
    Dutch and, 681, 745
    economy in, 900, 1100–1101(t), 1102
    education in, 899
    Europeans and, 620
    Great Depression and, 994
    imperialism of, 924
    industrialization in, 684, 846
    Jomon society in, 24
    League of Nations and, 997
    Meiji restoration in, 897
    modernization in, 898–901, 900(i)
    Mongols and, 533
    nationalism in, 799
    opening of, 897(i)
    Pearl Harbor attack by, 997–999
    peasants in, 896
    population in, 684
    Portugal and, 677, 681
    religion in, 394, 395
    right-wing nationalism in, 995
    rise of, 894–902, 898(t), 902(m)
    Russia and, 901
    samurai warriors in, 395, 396(i)
    silver in, 682, 684

    Taiwan and, 901
    Tokugawa shogunate in, 681, 684, 895–896
    trade in, 745, 897
    treaties with West, 897
    uniqueness of, 410, 411–412(d)
    United States and, 896–897, 1006
    Western science in, 745–746
    West perceived by, 915–920, 916(v), 917(v), 918(v), 919(v), 920(v)
    women in, 396–397, 803, 896, 918–919, 918(v), 1003
    workers in, 900–901
    World War I and, 984, 988
    World War II and, 996–999, 998(m), 1004
    Zen Buddhism in, 408–409, 409–410(d)
Jasaw Chan K'awiil I (Maya, r. 682–734), 280(i)
jati, 245–246
Java, 345, 588, 934
Jefferson, Thomas, 780, 784
Jehovah's Witnesses, Nazis and, 1003
Jenne-jeno, 288–289, 351
Jeremiah (prophet, Judaism), 190, 191(t)
Jericho, 89(m)
Jerome (Saint, 340–420 C.E.), 191(t), 547
Jerusalem, 1129, 1153
    Crusades and, 443, 444(i)
    Dome of the Rock in, 612–614, 613(v)
    temple in, 146
Jesuits, 726, 727
    in China, 730–732, 731(i), 745, 830
    in India, 767–768
Jesus of Nazareth, 191(t), 215, 425, 768(v)
    Buddha compared with, 209–214
    as Christ Pantokrator, 467, 468(v)
    date adopted as birthday, 437–438
    nature of, 214
    reflections from, 223, 224–225(d)
Jesus Sutras, in China, 462, 463–464(d)
Jews and Judaism. *See also* Arabs and Arab Empire; Israel; Palestine; Zionism
    in Arabia, 475
    in Babylon, 204
    Black Death and, 560
    Christianity and, 162, 210

    Crusades and, 443, 443(m), 445
    Greek culture and, 153
    Holocaust and, 1003
    Indian Ocean trade and, 344
    Islam and, 477(i), 478–479, 1153
    monotheism and, 190, 202, 204–205, 477(i)
    nationalism in, 799
    Nazi Germany and, 992, 993(i)
    in Ottoman Empire, 648
    in Persian Empire, 146
    Spanish reconquest and, 495
    writings on love, 209
    Zoroastrianism and, 203–204
Jie people, 339
jihad, 478, 1154
Jin Empire (China), 381(m), 389
Jinnah, Muhammad Ali, 1089
jizya (Islamic tax), 482, 646
John Paul II (Pope), 1157–1158
Jomon society, 24
Jordan
    Ain Ghazal statues in, 48(i)
    Islamic parties in, 1155
Jordan River region, settlements in, 54–55
Judaea, 209
Judah, state of, 204
Judaism. *See* Jews and Judaism
Ju/'hoansi peoples, 26–29. *See also* San peoples
Julian (Byzantine emissary), 312, 313–314(d)
Julian of Norwich, 441
Jurchen people (1115–1234), 389
Justinian (Byzantine Empire, r. 527–565), 312, 428, 451
    Axum and, 312, 313(d)
Juwayni (Persian historian), 538

Kaaba (shrine), 475, 479, 484(i)
Kabir (Indian poet), 491, 758, 758–759(d)
kaghan (Turkic ruler), 527–528
Kaifeng, China, 383(i)
Kakhovskaya, Irina, 1068–1068(d)
Kalahari Desert region, 284, 290
    San peoples of, 10(i), 24, 25–29
Kaleb of Axum, 312
Kamba peoples, 936
Kamchatka Peninsula, 641(i)

kami (Japanese sacred spirits), 395
Kamil, Mustafa (Egypt), 901–902
Kaminalijuyu (Maya city), 297
Kanem-Bornu, 350, 492
Kangxi (Chinese emperor, r. 1661–1722), 653, 653–654(d), 732
Kannon (bodhisattva), 231, 232(v)
Kano, 351
Kant, Immanuel (1724–1804), 742
kaozheng movement (China), 735, 745
Karakorum, 534, 535, 544
karma, 198, 245
Kartini, Raden Adjeng (Java), 814, 814–816(d)
Kazakhstan, 524(i)
Kemal, Mustafa. *See* Atatürk, Mustafa Kemal
Kennedy, John F., 1047
Kenya, 72–73(d), 923, 936–937. *See also* Gikuyu peoples
  Bantu speakers in, 292
  democracy in, 1098
  independence in, 1086, 1092(i)
  Masai in, 528
  urban poor in, 937–938
  wage labor in, 938(i), 939
  women's group movement in, 1148
Kenyatta, Jomo, 71, 72–73(d), 1092(i)
Kepler, Johannes (1571–1630), 740(t), 741
Kerala, India, Christianity in, 343
Kerr, Charles, 863–864(d)
Khadija, 475
Khan, Nawab Muhabbat, 950–951, 951(d)
khanates, in Mongol Empire, 530(m), 537
Khanbalik (China), 536. *See also* Beijing
Khayyam, Omar (1048–1131), 499(t)
Khitan people (907–1125), 389
Khmer people, 346
Khoikhoi people, 291(i)
Khoisan-speaking peoples, 25
Khomeini, Ruholla (Ayatollah), 1106, 1171–1172, 1172–1173(d)
Khrushchev, Nikita (Soviet Union), 1047, 1050
Khubilai Khan (China), 360, 373, 532, 537, 537(i)
al- Khwarazim (790–840), 499(t)
Khwarizm, Central Asia, 534–535

Kievan Rus, 326, 328, 433, 539. *See also* Russia
Kilwa, East Africa, 347
kings and kingdoms, 108. *See also* pharaohs (Egypt); specific kings and kingdoms
  divine right and, 742
  of First Civilizations, 100
  Germanic, 436, 436(m)
  in Korea, 391–392, 391(m)
  lifestyles of, 102–103
  in Persian Empire, 145
Kinkakuji (Temple of the Golden Pavilion), 611–612, 612(v)
kinship
  in Africa, 573
  in China, 386
  of Germanic peoples, 435
  Paleolithic, 20, 24
  in pastoral societies, 522
  state and, 99
Kipchak Khanate, 540–541
Kitabatake Chikafusa (Japan, 1293–1354), 410, 411–412(d)
kivas, 301
knights, 436–437
Knox, Robert, 881
Kobayashi Kiyochika, 918, 919(v)
kokutai (Japan), 1015
Kong Fuzi. *See* Confucius
Kongo, kingdom of, slave trade and, 693, 697, 705–706, 706–707(d)
Koran. *See* Quran
Korea
  Buddhism in, 399
  China and, 380, 381, 391–392, 886
  communism in, 1045
  dynasties in, 391
  Japan and, 920
  kingdoms of, 391(m)
Korean War (1950–1953), 1006–1007, 1045
Koryo dynasty (Korea, 918–1392), 391
Kremlin (Moscow), 614
Krishna (god, India), 201–202, 219–220, 220–221(d)
Kristallnacht (1938), 992
Kshatriya (warrior) caste, 154, 243
kulaks (Russia peasants), 1041, 1062
!Kung people, lifestyle of, 34–35, 35–39(d)

Kush, Nubian kingdom of, 107(t)
Kushan culture, 367–368, 369(v)
Kyoto, Japan, 394
Kyoto protocol, 1144

labor. *See also* slaves and slavery; strikes; workers
  Africa and, 631, 935, 938–939
  Asian and African colonial, 935–938
  in China, 1043, 1043(i)
  civilization and, 92
  colonial, 932–933
  in England, 831, 835–836
  in Europe, 440–441, 441(i)
  forced, 933–934
  for fur trade, 685
  gender-based division of, 21
  globalization and, 1181(v)
  in Haiti, 787
  Inca, 593
  in Japan, 900–901, 994
  of Ju/'hoansi peoples, 26
  in Latin America, 632, 851
  in Mesoamerica, 294
  migration of, 938–939, 1137, 1141
  after slavery, 795
  slaves as, 250–251
  in Soviet Union, 1055
  women as, 96, 254(i), 1040
  in World War II, 1002–1003
labor unions
  conservatism of, 843
  in Japan, 901, 994, 995
  in Mexico, 851
Labour Party (Great Britain), 838, 839
LaDuke, Winona, 625
Lafayette (Marquis de), 806–807(d)
Lagash, 89(m), 100
Lalibela (Zagwe king), 615
Lalibela, Ethiopia, Church of St. George in, 614–615, 615(v)
land bridges, in Ice Age, 16
landowners
  classes and, 95
  in classical China, 240
  in England, 834
  after Roman Empire, 163
  in Western Europe, 436
land ownership. *See* property ownership
landscape painting, in China, 195(i)

languages. *See also* writing systems
  Arabic, 483
  Austronesian, 19, 19(m)
  of Bantu peoples, 290–291
  in Chinese Empire, 160, 162
  diffusion of, 57
  English as global, 1049
  Greek, 153, 431
  hangul, 392
  identity and, 796
  Indo-European, 57
  in Japan, 394
  in Korea, 392
  Latin, 162, 426, 431
  Marathi, 237
  in Mongol Empire, 535
  of Olmecs, 90
  Pali, 200
  Persian, 485
  Quechua, 593
  in Roman Empire, 162
  Sanskrit, 197
  Swahili, 347
  in Vietnam, 393
Laos, 1031, 1057
Laozi, 188(i), 190, 191(t), 195, 196
Las Casas, Bartolomé de, 73, 74–75(d)
Lascaux caves (France), 16(i)
Lateran Accords (1929), 990
latifundia (estates), 250
Latin America. *See also* Americas;
    Bolívar, Simón; slave trade; Spanish
    America; specific locations
  capitalism in, 1099–1102
  Christian churches in, 764–766, 765(v)
  communism in Cuba, 1031
  economic development in,
    1100–1101(t), 1103
  ethnicity in (1825), 636(t)
  Europe and, 849–853
  exports from, 848–849
  financial crises in, 1138
  government by soldiers in, 1097
  independence in, 791–793, 791(m),
    846–848
  Industrial Revolution in, 846–853,
    850(m), 852
  investment in, 842, 849
  liberation theology in, 1158
  national self-determination in, 1083

revolutions in, 779–780, 790–793,
    791(m)
  silver from, 683–684, 683(i)
  slavery abolished in, 794
  slaves in, 636–637, 695
Latin Christendom. *See* Roman
    Catholic Church; Western world
Latin language, 162, 426, 431
Latvia, 1055
law(s). *See also* law codes; *sharia*
  Aztec, 602–603(d)
  in China, 158–159, 255
  European study of, 450
  of historical development, 744
  Islamic, 479, 506–507, 507–509(d)
  in Mesopotamia, 118–121(d)
  in Mongol Empire, 537–538
  natural, 741, 742
  Quranic, 1155
  in Roman Empire, 163
law codes
  of Hammurabi, 95, 100, 102,
    119–121(d)
  in Japan, 394
  Napoleonic, 787
  patriarchy in, 97
  in Rome, 155
Law of Family Rights (Turkey), 893
Laws of Manu, The, 200, 266
League of Nations, 984, 1004
  Japanese withdrawal from, 997
  mandates of, 983(m), 984, 1127
Leakey, Mary, 3
leather industry, 685
Lebanon, Islamic parties in, 1155
lebensraum (living space), 999
Lee, Richard, 25–26
Legalism (China), 158–159, 160, 174,
    192–193
legions (Roman), 161
Leibniz, Gottfried Wilhelm
    (1646–1716), 830
Leipzig, battle at, 823(v)
leisure
  of Chinese elites, 417–422, 418(v),
    419(v), 420(v), 421(v), 422(v)
  in gathering and hunting societies, 21
Lenin (Vladimir Ilyich Ulyanov),
    846, 864, 865(d), 1028(i), 1033–1034
Leo I (Pope), 164

Leo Africanus, 587
Leonardo da Vinci, 580
Leopold II (Belgium), 933
Lerner, Gerda, 97, 98
Lesbos. *See* Sappho
Lesotho, 1093(m), 1180, 1181(v)
Lessons for Women (Ban Zhao), 194, 253,
    263–264, 264–266(d)
levée en masse (mass conscription), 796,
    797(t)
liberalism. *See* neo-liberalism
liberation, globalization of, 1145–1150
liberation theology, 1158
Liberia, 928
Liberty Bonds, in World War I, 1019,
    1020(v)
life expectancy
  globalization and, 1138
  in Paleolithic era, 22
Lima, Peru, 683
Limits to Growth (Club of Rome), 1161
lineage system, in Africa, 64, 65, 292, 528
Lin Zexu, 886, 910, 911(d)
Li Shen (China), 241
literacy. *See also* education
  in China, 1041
  in Cuba, 1099
  in First Civilizations, 100–102
  in modern societies, 598
  printing and, 397–398
  Protestantism and, 725
  in Soviet Union, 1041
literature. *See also* specific authors and
    works
  in China, 735, 1052
  Epic of Gilgamesh and, 93
  in Renaissance, 579–580
  Romantic movement in, 744
  in Vietnam, 394
Lithuania, 1055
Little Ice Age, 685
Liu Guandao (China), 373
Liu Zongyuan (China), 380
Livingstone, David (1813–1873), 960
Livy (Rome), 268, 269–271(d)
Li Yu (Chinese emperor), 422
llama, 351
Locke, John (1632–1704), 742, 780–781
Lombards, 435
long-distance trade. *See* trade

Long March (China, 1934–1935), 1035(i)
Lords of Sipan (Moche culture), 299, 300(i)
Lotus Sutra, 231
Louis XIV (France), 659–660, 661(d)
Louis XVI (France), 781(t), 784, 785, 821(v)
Louisiana Purchase, 790
Loutherbourg, Philip James de, 873, 873(v)
Louverture, Toussaint, 789
lower middle class, 835
Luce, Henry, 1005
Luo people, 939
Luther, Martin (1483–1546), 723, 723(i), 750, 750–751
　Bible and, 725, 750–751(d)
　on churches, 761
　protest by, 749–751(d)
　on salvation, 723, 735, 751(d)
Lutheranism, 725
luxury products, trade in, 336–337, 674
Lycurgus, 258

Macao, 676
Macartney (Lord), mission to China, 905–906
Macedonia, growth of, 151
Machiavelli, Niccolò (1469–1527), 580
machine guns, 880, 880(i)
Machu Picchu, 593(i)
Macumba (Brazil), 732
Madagascar, 19, 343
Madison, James, 784
madrassas (Islamic schools), 496
Magao Caves (China), 369
Magellan, Ferdinand, 678
Mahabharata, 201, 219
Mahabodhi Temple (India), 199(i)
Mahatma. *See* Gandhi, Mohandas
Mahavira, 191(t)
Mahayana Buddhism, 211, 231–235, 402
mail-order catalogs, 842
Maitreya Buddha, 233, 233(v)
maize. *See* corn (maize)
Malacca, 576(m), 588, 676
malaria, 290, 629
Malaya
　communism in, 1031
　Japan and, 997

sailors from, 343, 345
Srivijaya kingdom and, 345
trade and, 675
Malay Peninsula, 345
Malaysia, 852, 937
Malcolm X, 473
Mali (kingdom), 289, 350, 350(m), 351
　gold of, 351(i)
　Ibn Battuta in, 363
　Islam and, 492
Mali (modern), democracy in, 1098
Malinche, La, 667
Mamluks, 614
mammoths, 18
al-**Mamun** (Abbasid caliph), 498
Manchu dynasty. *See* Qing dynasty
Manchukuo, 997
Manchuria, 526
　Japanese acquisition of, 996
　Qing dynasty from, 643
Mandate of Heaven (China), 90, 100, 160, 192, 393
mandates, of League of Nations, 983(m), 984, 1127
Mandela, Nelson (South Africa), 1080(i), 1086, 1092, 1093, 1094
Mani, 371
Manichaeism, 371, 372(v), 525
Manila, Philippines, 679
manioc. *See* cassava (manioc)
Mansur (caliph, r. 754–775), 487
Manufacturing *See also* industrialization
　in England, 831, 841
　in Germany, 841
　Ottomans and, 891
　overproduction and, 879
　in United States, 841
manumission, 248, 251. *See also* slaves and slavery
Maori people, 926
Mao Zedong (China), 1042(t), 1043–1044
　collectivization by, 1040–1041
　communist revolution and, 1035–1037, 1035(i)
　compared to Shihuangdi, 168, 180
　Confucianism and, 189
　Cultural Revolution and, 1043–1045
　death of, 1051

Great Leap Forward and, 1041, 1043, 1043(i), 1073
　Long March of, 1035(i)
　poster art in China under, 1071–1079, 1072(v), 1074(v), 1075(v), 1077(v), 1078(v)
　search for enemies by, 1044–1045
　socialist society under, 1038–1045
　veneration of, 1076, 1077(v)
Marathi language, 237
Marathon, Battle of (490 B.C.E.), 151
Marchand, Jean-Baptiste, 963
Marduk (god, Babylon), 100
Marie Antoinette (France), 785, 821(v)
Marina (Doña), 667
maritime voyages
　Chinese, 577–578
　by Columbus, 568(i), 580
　European, 568(i), 580–584, 581(t)
　by Portugal, 580–581, 674
　Viking, 442
　of Zheng He, 569, 571
Marius (Rome), 157
marriage. *See also* gender and gender issues
　in India, 245, 359(d)
　in Islam, 487, 508(d)
　in Japan, 396–397
　in Korea, 392
　of !Kung people, 36–37(d)
　in Sparta, 258
Marriage Law (China, 1950), 1039
Marshall, John, 783
Marshall Plan, 1005–1006, 1034
martyrs, Christian, in Japan, 728(i)
Marx, Karl (1818–1883), 744, 745, 837–839, 948, 970
　Chinese communism and, 1035
　socialism and, 744, 837–839, 856–857, 857–859(d), 859–860, 1030
　view of history, 1163–1164
Marxism. *See also* communism
　in Africa, 1031
　in Europe, 855–856
　Lenin and, 846, 1033–1034
Mary (mother of Jesus), 468, 469(v), 720(i), 765(v), 766, 767(v), 768, 768(v)
Masai people, 528–529, 528(m), 529(i)
Massachusetts, Puritans in, 638

mass conscription, 796, 797(t)
MasterCard, globalization of,
  1137–1138
maternal feminism, 800–801
mathematics
  in China, 745
  spread of, 329
Mathnawi (Rumi), 509
Mattel Corporation, 1137
Mauritania, 695
Mauryan Empire (India, 326–184 B.C.E.),
  166, 176
Mawdudi, Mawlana, 1153
Maya people, 281–282, 294–295, 712
  agriculture of, 294
  arts of, 316–323, 317(v), 319(v), 320(v),
    321(v), 322(v)
  Caste War of Yucatán and, 848
  collapse of, 295, 326
  economy of, 294
  government of, 294
  Olmec influence on, 91
  population of, 136, 295
  Temple of Great Jaguar, 103, 280(i)
  trade and, 353
  warfare and, 318
  writing systems of, 294
Ma Yuan (Chinese painter, 1160–1225),
  421, 421(v)
McCarthyism, 1031
McDonald's, 1049
  global locations of, 1143(m)
measles, 340, 629
Mecca, 478
  commerce and, 497
  hajj to, 472(i), 473
  hijra from, 478
  Kaaba in, 475, 479, 484(i)
  Wahhabi movement in, 734, 756
medicine. *See also* diseases; health and
    health care
  Arab scholarship and, 498–499
  in China, 745
  European study of, 450
  Greek, 207
Medina, Arabia, 478
Mediterranean region
  bubonic plague in, 340
  Byzantine Empire and, 428
  Greco-Roman-Christian traditions
    of, 327

Greek settlements in, 149
Islamic trade in, 497
Rome and, 155, 158
sea trade in, 341, 677
megafaunal extinction, 18
Meiji emperor (Japan), 876(i)
Meiji restoration (Japan), 897
Mein Kampf (My Struggle) (Hitler), 992,
  1012, 1013–1015(d)
Mellaart, James, 77, 78
men. *See also* gender and gender issues;
    male suffrage; patriarchy
  as African workers, 938–939
  Aztec, 594
  in Chinese society, 194
  in Christian Church, 212–214
  gender hierarchies and, 97–98
  in Ghana, 938
  Inca, 594
  Islamic, 486–488, 487(i)
  patriarchy and, 96
Menander (Greek writer), 256
Menander (Indo-Greek king), 154
Menelik II (Ethiopia, r. 1889–1913),
  966
Menggu (Mongol official), Chinese on,
  555, 556–557(d)
mercantilism, 632
merchants
  Asian, 681–682
  in China, 242, 399
  in Europe, 449
  Indian Ocean basin and, 343
  Islam and, 492
  in Mongol Empire, 542
  Muslim, 497–499
  as social group, 334
  state control by, 829
  as third estate, 449
Meroë, Kingdom of, 282, 284–286,
  285(m), 286(i)
  Axum and, 287–288, 309
Mersankh, 84(i)
Mesoamerica, 282, 326–327, 589(m).
    See also Americas; specific regions
  agriculture in, 51, 52(t), 55, 56, 294
  Andes interaction with, 353–354
  chocolate from, 712–713
  classical civilizations of, 292–297,
    293(m)
  Maya peoples in, 294–295

Olmec civilization in, 88(m), 90–91,
  103, 103(i)
  religion in, 728–729
  Teotihuacán in, 93, 295–297
Mesopotamia, 104(t), 105(m). *See also*
    Iraq; Sumer
  Akkadians in, 106
  Assyrians in, 106–107
  Babylonians in, 106
  chiefdoms in, 65
  cities in, 106–107
  civilizations of, 86, 89(m)
  culture in, 104–106
  East African slave trade and, 344
  Egypt compared with, 103–112,
    105(m), 107(t)
  environment in, 103–104
  kingship in, 100
  law and justice in, 118, 119–121(d)
  trade of, 108
  Uruk in, 92–93
  women in, 98
  ziggurat in, 92–93, 100(i)
mestizos, 633, 633(i), 634, 792, 848
metallurgy
  in Americas, 283
  Phoenician, 111
  spread of, 111
  and trade, 675
Methodius (missionary), 432–433
Metochites, Theodore, 451
Mevlevi Sufi order, 509
Mexican Revolution (1910–1920), 851,
  852(i)
Mexica people, 588–590. *See also* Aztec
    Empire
Mexico, 353. *See also* Maya people;
    Mesoamerica; North America;
    Olmec civilization; Teotihuacán,
    Mexico
  Aztec Empire in, 588–592, 589(m)
  casta paintings in, 715–718, 717(v)
  Christianity in, 729–730
  elites in, 851
  European diseases in, 629
  globalization and, 1141
  independence movement in, 791
  labor in, 851
  nationalization of oil in, 1083
  in 19th century, 848
  silver in, 631, 675

Spanish conquest of, 628, 664–671, 665(v), 666(v), 668(v), 669(v), 670(v)
Teotihuacán and, 93, 295–297, 296(i)
United States and, 847, 849, 852
Virgin of Guadalupe in, 720(i)
women's rights in, 802
pollution deaths in, 1159
Michelangelo, 580
microloan programs, 1102(i)
Micronesia, trade in, 595
Middle Ages (European), 438–445, 439(m)
feudalism and, 436–437
universities in, 450, 450(i)
middle classes
communism and, 1032
in England, 834–835
in France, 834(i)
Marx and, 838
in Mexico, 851
in Russia, 845
in United States, 843, 1049
values of, 834
women and, 800–801
Middle East, 1103(m). *See also* Islam; Ottoman Empire
Christianity in, 431
civilizations in, 86
Crusades and, 443–444, 444(i)
economic development in, 1100–1101(t)
Fertile Crescent in, 53–55, 54(m)
in 15th century, 570(t)
Indian Ocean trade and, 344
monotheism in, 190, 202–205, 477(i)
Ottoman Empire and, 584
Persian Empire in, 145–147, 146(m)
plague in, 545
after World War I, 983(m), 984
middle kingdom, China as, 387, 404
Middle Passage, 689, 691(i), 695. *See also* slave trade
migrations
Africa and, 12–16, 14–15(m), 935
in age of empire, 940(t)
agriculture and, 51
to Americas, 18
ancient, 282
to Australia, 14–15(m), 17–18

of Austronesian-speaking people, 19–20, 19(m)
of Bantu speakers, 60(m), 290–291
into Eurasia, 13, 14–15(m), 16–17
Germanic, 435
globalization and, 1182–1185, 1184(v)
of labor, 938–939, 1141
into Pacific Ocean region, 19–20
Paleolithic, 4
to Philippines, 679
of workers, 938–939, 1137, 1141
Milan, 578
militarism, World War I and, 981
military. *See also* navy; nuclear weapons; wars and warfare; weapons; specific battles and wars
chariots and, 111
in China, 383, 644
in Cold War, 1051
European weapons and, 880, 880(i)
in French Revolution, 786
gender and, 97
in Germany, 992
government by, 1097–1098
in India, 166
in Japan, 995–996
of Mississippi chiefdoms, 304
Mongol, 533–535, 534(i)
of nomadic pastoralists, 525
Roman, 155, 161
of United States, 1005, 1142, 1144
World War I and, 981
World War II and, 1000
military-industrial complex, 1049, 1050
military technology, 981
European advantage in, 924–925
Mongol, 534
in World War I, 981
in World War II, 1001
Mindanao island, 678, 1162
Ming dynasty (China, 1368–1644), 538, 576–580, 576(m)
Jesuits and, 730
Neo-Confucianism and, 735
miniatures. *See* Persian miniatures
mining
colonial wage laborers and, 937
in England, 831
nitrate, 851
of silver, 683
Mirabai (1498–1547), 736

missiles. *See* nuclear weapons
missions and missionaries, 1151
in Africa, 960
Catholic, 437
in China, 730–732, 731(i)
colonization and, 929
in European colonies, 943–945, 943(i)
in Japan, 681
in Mexico, 664
in Philippines, 678
spread of Christianity and, 727–728
Mississippi River region
agriculture in, 55
fur trade in, 685
Mound Builders of, 303–304
Mithra (god, Persia), 162
mixed-race peoples in Americas, 637, 715–718, 717(v), 848
mobility. *See* social mobility
Moche civilization, 87, 282, 297(m), 298–300, 592
Moctezuma I (Aztecs), 601, 602–603(d), 633, 666–667, 666(v)
Model T Ford, 842
Modun (Xiongnu, r. 210–174 B.C.E.), 526
Mohawk people, 574
Mohenjo Daro, 89(m), 93, 93(i), 128, 129(v)
moksha (liberation), 198
Mombasa, East Africa, 347, 676–677
monasteries and monasticism. *See also* nuns; specific orders
Buddhism and, 338–339, 401, 402
Confucian classics and, 402
in Eastern Orthodox Christianity, 430
European, 441
money. *See* currency
Mongke (Mongol Empire), 532, 535
Mongolia, 389, 526, 643. *See also* Mongols and Mongol Empire
Mongols and Mongol Empire, 328, 373, 374(v), 524, 526, 529–535, 530(m), 531(t), 534(i), 550–551, 551–552(d), 553–554(d)
Baghdad sacked by, 489, 538
Black Death spread by, 340–341, 560
China and, 370(v), 374(v), 536–538, 537(i), 555–556, 556–557(d), 644

Mongols and Mongol Empire (*continued*)
Chinggis Khan and, 373, 520(i), 521, 525, 532–533
cultural exchange by, 544
in Eastern Europe, 533
Egypt and, 533
end of, 546
as Eurasian network, 541–547
growth of, 533–534
Japan and, 533
movement of peoples in, 544
Persia and, 534, 538–539
religion and, 535
rise of, 532–533
Russia and, 539–541, 540(i), 554–555(d)
Silk Roads and, 336
warfare in, 533–535
women, 557–559(d)
Zunghars and, 644
monks. *See* monasteries and monasticism
monotheism
in Arab world, 475
of Christianity, 212
of Islam, 734
of Judaism, 109, 202, 204–205
in Middle East, 190, 202–205, 477(i)
in Paleolithic societies, 22
of Zoroastrianism, 202, 203–204
monsoons, 342, 343
Monte Alban, 297
Montgomery Ward, 842
Morocco
Family Law Code in, 1148
migration from, 1182
Moscow, 541, 639
mosques, in United States, 473
Mother's Day (France), 985
Mound Builders, 303–304
movable type, in China, 383, 397
movies, as World War I propaganda, 1019
Mozambique, 347, 934, 1086
Mozarabs, 494–495
Mughal Empire (India), 587, 624(i), 643, 645(m), 677, 926, 930, 950
Christianity in, 761, 767–769, 768(v)
England and, 680
Hindu/Muslim interaction in, 736–737

Islam and, 587, 645–646, 733
Jahangir in, 645, 655–657(d)
religion in, 645–646
Muhammad (Islam) (570–632 C.E.), 215, 475–478, 480, 517, 518(v). *See also* Islam; Muslims
Arabia and, 475, 475(m)
Axum and, 287–288
hadith of, 488, 502, 505–506(d)
hijra of, 478
on *umma*, 477
mulattoes, 636, 637
mullahs (Islamic teachers), 488
Munich conference (1938), 999
munitions. *See* weapons; specific weapons
Murasaki Shikibu (Japan), 396
music
Internationale, The, and, 863–864(d)
of San peoples, 25
in United States, 1049
Muslim Brotherhood (Egypt), 1155(i), 1169–1171(d)
Muslim League, 1089
Muslims. *See also* Arabs and Arab Empire; Islam; Shia Muslims; Sunni Muslims
in Americas, 733
astronomy and, 739(i)
Byzantine Empire and, 429
Crusades and, 443
Europeans and, 445
in France, 1183–1185, 1184(v)
in India, 944–945, 1089, 1153
intellectual thought of, 451–452
Middle Eastern monotheism and, 477(i)
in Mongol Empire, 537–538
in Mughal Empire, 645–646
in Ottoman Empire, 647, 648, 892–893
in Russian Empire, 641
Turkic peoples as, 528
in United States, 473
Mussolini, Benito (Italy, 1883–1945), 168, 989
on fascism, 1010, 1011–1012(d)
Mutazalites, 498
mutual defense treaties, U.S., 1048
mystery religions, 277–279, 278(v)
mysticism, in Islamic practice, 485–486

mythology
of Australian Aboriginal people, 39, 40–41(d)
Greek, 205

Nagasaki, Japan, 745, 999, 1002
Nalanda University (monastic complex), 357
Nanak (Indian guru, 1469–1539), 491, 736, 736(i)
Nanjing
Rape of Nanjing (Nanjing Massacre, 1937–1938) and, 877, 1002
Taiping Uprising and, 884
Treaty of (1842), 886, 912–913(d)
Nantes, Edict of, 725
Naoroji, Dadabhai, 955, 956–957(d)
Napoleon Bonaparte (France, r. 1799–1814), 781(t), 787, 822–823, 822(v)
Egypt and, 890
empire of, 788(m)
Haitian Revolution and, 789, 790
law code of, 787
national resistance to, 796, 797(t)
Spain, Portugal, and, 791
NASA (National Aeronautics and Space Administration), 1132(i)
Nash, John (1893–1977), 1021–1023, 1025(v)
Natchez people, 304
National American Woman Suffrage Association, 801
National Assembly (France), 784, 785, 817
nationalism, 774, 796–800. *See also* independence
Atlantic revolutions and, 780
in China, 800, 888–889, 984, 1036
in Europe, 787, 799
in Germany, 990–991
growth of, 797(t)
Hindu, 1152
imperialism and, 880
in India, 800, 1096, 1123–1124, 1124(v)
Italian, 990
in Japan, 799, 995
in Ottoman Empire, 800, 890(m), 891, 893–894
in Poland, 799(i)
in Russia, 1033
Slavic, 979

in South Africa, 1081, 1090–1094
in Soviet Union, 1055
in Vietnam, 1030
Nationalist Party (China), 1036
nationalization, of Mexican oil, 1083
National Party (South Africa), 1092
National Rejuvenation Study Society
   (China), 888
national self-determination, after World
   War I, 982, 1083
Native Americans, 574, 625. *See also*
   specific groups
   Christianity and, 728
   in classical North America, 301–304
   in colonial Americas, 632
   demography of, 629, 687
   disease and, 628, 629, 687
   fur trade and, 685, 687
   as hunter/gatherers, 572
   in Latin America, 633, 634
   in North America, 638
   in silver mines, 683, 683(i)
"native reserves," in South Africa, 1091
Nativity, 469(v)
NATO. *See* North Atlantic Treaty
   Organization (NATO)
natural laws
   in Enlightenment, 742
   Newton on, 741
natural philosophy
   Arabic, 451–452
   in England, 831
   European study of, 450–451
nature, 1160–1161. *See also* environment;
   environmentalism
   Daoism on, 196
   European study of, 450
   women identified with, 97
naval technologies, European, 676, 681
navigation
   Chinese, 383
   European, 447–448, 546–547
   human migrations and, 19
   Swahili, 347
   trade and, 342
navy
   Chinese, 578
   Japanese, 997
   Roman, 155
   U.S., 894–895
Nayambolmi, 43

Nazca civilization, 87, 297(m), 300, 592
Nazi Germany. *See also* Hitler, Adolf
   anti-Semitism and, 992, 993(i)
   communism and, 1003
   England and, 999
   in World War II, 990–993, 990(i),
      992(i), 999–1001, 1000(m)
Neanderthals, 22
Negative Confession *(Book of the Dead)*,
   122–123(d)
Nehru, Jawaharlal (India), 1085, 1122,
   1152–1153
Neo-Confucianism, 382, 734–735
neo-liberalism, 1135
   globalization and, 1141, 1142
Neolithic age, 76
   art and artifacts in, 76–83, 77(v),
      78(v), 79(v), 81(v), 82(v)
   pastoral societies in, 80
Neolithic Revolution, 50. *See also*
   Agricultural Revolution
Nerchinsk, Treaty of (1689), 644
Nestorianism, 426, 462, 463–464(d)
Nestorius, 430
Netherlands. *See also* Dutch
   Asian colonial rule by, 925(m)
   merchants in, 829
Netherlands East Indies (Indonesia),
   933–934
New Deal (1933–1942), 987–988
Newfoundland, Viking colony in, 442
New Guinea, 17, 19, 943(i)
   agriculture in, 51, 52(t), 60, 572
New Kingdom Egypt, 98, 110(m)
New Lanark community, Scotland, 837
newly industrialized countries, economic
   growth in, 1102
New Netherlands, 629
"New Rome," Constantinople as, 427
New Stone Age. *See* Neolithic
   Revolution
New Testament, 210, 211, 725
Newton, Isaac (1642–1727), 737,
   740(t), 741
New Zealand
   colonization of, 926–928, 943
   settlement of, 19
   women's voting rights in, 801
Nezahualcoyotl (1402–1472), 591
Nguyen Khuyen (1835–1909), 929
Nguyen Thai Hoc (Vietnam), 942

Nicaea Council (325 C.E.), 214
Nicaragua, United States and, 852
Nicholas II (Russia), 846, 876(i), 1032
Nigeria
   British in, 926
   Christianity in, 721
   civil war in (1960s), 1097
   in 15th century, 573
   horses in, 595
   Igbo peoples of, 65, 573, 939, 947
   Islamization in, 1156
   Nok culture of, 82–83, 82(v)
   racism and, 931
   slave trade and, 696, 700
   Tiv peoples of, 64–65
   women in, 939
Niger Valley region, civilizations of,
   282, 284, 288–289
Nightingale, Florence, 801
Nike, 1137
Nile River region, 106, 108, 963. *See
   also* Egypt; specific locations
   civilizations of, 86, 89(m), 107(t),
      284–285
   Meroë and, 286
Ninety-five Theses (Luther), 723, 723(i)
Ninevah, 89(m)
Nippur, 89(m)
nirvana, 200, 228, 408
Nisa (!Kung woman), 34–35, 35–39(d)
nitrate mining, 851
Niumi, Gambia, 692–693
Nkrumah, Kwame (Ghana), 940, 1086,
   1110, 1112–1113, 1113–1114(d)
nobility. *See also* aristocracy
   in Europe, 438, 449
   in French Revolution, 785
   in Russia, 844, 846
   as second estate, 449
"noble savage" concept, 881
Noche Triste, La, 669, 669(v)
Nok culture (Nigeria), 82–83, 82(v)
nomadic peoples, 63. *See also* pastoral
   societies
   in Americas, 301
   in Arabia, 474–475, 513, 514(v)
   China and, 163, 254–255, 380,
      385–390, 388–389, 645
   empires and, 328–329
   in 15th century, 574–575
   images of, 547–548

nomadic peoples (*continued*)
  in Russian Empire, 640, 645
  societies of, 522–526, 523(t)
  Xiongnu as, 526, 526(m)
Norte Chico civilization, 87, 88(m), 297
North Africa
  Berbers of, 483
  camels in, 349
  Christianity in, 431
  commerce in, 348
  economic development in,
    1100–1101(t)
  Islam and, 480, 483
  migrants to France from, 1183–1185,
    1184(v)
  Ottoman Empire and, 584
  religions in, 426
  Rome and, 136, 155, 284
  slaves in, 351
  in World War II, 1000
North America. *See also* American
    Revolution; Americas; Canada;
    Mesoamerica; Mexico; slave trade;
    United States; specific regions
  agricultural village societies in, 572,
    574
  British colonies in, 637–638
  chiefdoms in, 66, 66(i)
  Christianity in, 727
  classical era in, 301–304, 301(m)
  European diseases in, 629
  European rivalry over, 687
  15th century societies of, 572
  fur trade in, 685–688, 686(m)
  gathering and hunting peoples in, 60
  interactions with, 352, 352(m)
  migrations to, 18
  Mound Builders of, 303–304
  settler colonies in, 637–639
  trade in, 595
  world role of, 771
North Atlantic Treaty Organization
    (NATO), 1006, 1031, 1045, 1056,
    1144
North Korea, 1057
North/South gap, 1139
Notke, Berndt, 564, 564(v)
Notre Dame Cathedral (Paris), 786
Nubia, 86, 89(m), 91, 107(t), 109, 109(i)
  Egypt and, 109(i), 110(m), 112
  Islam and, 286

Meroë and, 284–286, 285(m)
  religions in, 426
nuclear power, 1158
nuclear weapons
  in China, 1051
  in cold war, 1047–1048, 1047(i)
  in Cuba, 1047
  in Iran, 1108
  NATO and, 1006
  in North Korea, 1057
  in World War II, 999, 1001, 1002,
    1002(i), 1005
numerals, from India, 329
nuns
  Buddhist, 200
  European, 441
Nupe people, 939
Nuremberg Laws (1935), 992
nursing profession, 801
nutrition, Paleolithic diet and, 32
Nyakyusa people, 946
Nyerere, Julius (Tanzania), 1114–1115,
    1115–1116(d)

oases
  cities in Central Asia, 338
  in Sahara, 349
Obama, Barack, U.S. global role and,
    1144
obelisks, in Axum, 287, 287(i)
occupation (military), of Japan,
    1006–1007
oceangoing canoes. *See* canoes
Oceania
  agriculture in, 60
  British settlement in, 926
  colonization of, 943
  El Niño currents and, 300
  in 15th century, 570(t)
  imperialism in, 880
  Japanese empire in, 997
  migrations into, 14–15(m), 16, 19–20
  trade in, 595, 682–683, 682(m)
  in World War II, 999
oceans. *See also* maritime voyages; specific
    ocean regions
  trade and, 341–348, 546–547
Octavian (Rome). *See* Augustus
Odoacer (Germanic peoples), 435
Ogodei (Mongol Empire), 532, 536,
    542, 550, 552–553(d)

Ohio River region, Hopewell culture
    in, 303
oil and oil industry
  environment and, 1158
  Mexican nationalization of, 1083
  Middle East economies and, 1139
  oil-producing economies and,
    1102–1103
Old Regime (France), 778(i), 784
old stone age. *See* Paleolithic era
Old Testament, 109, 204, 259
Olmec civilization, 88(m), 90–91, 293, 712
  carvings by, 103, 103(i)
  writing by, 101(t)
Olympic Games, in ancient Greece,
    148–149
Olympus, Mount, 205, 208
Oman, 677
Oneida people, 574
Onondaga people, 574
*On the Revolutions of the Heavenly
    Spheres* (Copernicus), 740
opium trade, 885–886, 885(t), 886(i),
    907–908, 908–909(d), 909–910(d),
    910, 911(d)
Opium Wars, 884–885, 886, 905, 912
Oppian Laws (Rome), 268
oracle bones, 90
  as writing system, 101(t)
Origin of Species, The (Darwin), 744
Orinoco River, 353
Orthodox Christianity. *See* Eastern
    Orthodox Christianity
Osaka, Japan, 896
Osei Bonsu (Asante kingdom), 708,
    708–709, 795
Oshio Heihachiro, 896
Osiris (god, Egypt), 108
Otto I (Saxony, r. 936–973), 436
Ottoman Empire, 492(m), 626, 643,
    647–650, 647(m). *See also*
    Crusades; Turkey; specific countries
  Anatolia in, 491
  Armenians and, 984
  Byzantine Empire and, 432
  China compared with, 894
  coffee in, 714–715, 716(v)
  collapse of, 893–894
  Constantinople seized by, 429
  contraction of, 890(m)
  in 15th century, 584–585

industry in, 846
Janissaries in, 586(i)
religion in, 647–650, 892–893
Russian furs and, 688
under Suleiman I, 649, 657,
    658–659(d)
Sunni Muslims in, 595
Turkey after, 1103–1105
Turkic creation of, 528
West and, 892(i)
World War I and, 984
Ottoman Turks, 326. *See also* Ottoman
    Empire
Outline of the World's History, An
    (Swinton), 772
Ovid, on love, 209
Owen, Robert (1771–1858), 837, 856
Oxford, 450
    University of, 738
Oyo, kingdom of, 696
ozone depletion, 1162

pagans (non-Christians), 457, 458(d)
Pahlavi, Muhammad Reza (Shah of
    Iran, r. 1941–1979), 1105–1106
painting. *See also* art(s); rock art; specific
    locations and works
    casta paintings, 715–718, 717(v)
    in Çatalhüyük, 77(v), 79(v)
    in China, 195(i)
    Persian miniatures and, 485, 512–519,
        514(v), 516(v), 518(v)
Pakistan, 87, 1089–1090. *See also* India;
    Indus Valley civilization
    Islam and, 483, 1156
Palau, 595
Palembang, Srivijaya kingdom, 345
Paleolithic era, 23. *See also* gathering
    and hunting peoples
    in Australia, 17–18
    criticisms of contemporary life and, 32
    gathering and hunting peoples in, 12
    human migrations in, 4
    in Ice Age, 17
    lifestyle in, 34–35, 35–39(d), 40–41(d)
    persistence of, 570(t), 571–572
    religion in, 22–23
    societies in, 20–22, 24–31
Palestine, 983(m), 1129–1131, 1130(v)
    Egypt and, 112, 113(m)
    Hamas in, 1155(i)

Islamic parties in, 1155
Jews in, 204, 1127–1129, 1128(v)
settlements in, 54–55
after World War I, 984
Zionism and, 797
Palestinian Liberation Organization
    (PLO), 1129
Palestinian Territories, 1129
Pali language, 200
Pan Africanist Congress, 1094
Panama Canal, United States and, 853
pantheists, 743
papacy. *See also* popes
    European nobility and, 438
    in Rome, 430
paper, printing and, 397–398
papermaking, 397, 498
paper money, in China, 384
Paraguay, 847
Paris, 440, 450
    Huguenot massacre in, 725
    University of, 738
Parsis, 203
Parthian dynasty (Persia. 247
    B.C.E.–224 C.E.), 203
partition, of India, 1089–1090, 1122
Pascal, Blaise (1623–1662), 741
pastoral societies, 5–6, 11, 63–64, 79(v),
    282, 522–529, 523(t), 525
    in Africa, 575
    agriculture and, 525, 528
    cultural diffusion through, 336
    Egypt, Mesopotamia, and, 111
    empires and, 328–329
    Fulbe, 575
    Masai, 528–529
    religion and, 525
    varieties of, 523(t)
    women in, 523–524
pathogens, spread via trade, 335
patriarch, of Eastern Orthodox
    Christianity, 425, 429
patriarchy, 96–98, 259–260
    in Africa, 939
    in Athens and Sparta, 255–259
    in China, 253–255, 262, 263(d), 384,
        1039
    in Christianity, 211
    in classical era, 252–259
    feminist opposition to, 800–803,
        808–809(d), 1146–1150

Indian alternative to, 266–267,
    267–268(d)
Islamic, 488
social hierarchies and, 96–98
patricians, in Rome, 155
Paul (Saint, 10–65 C.E.), 191, 191(t), 209,
    211, 250
Paul VI (Pope), 425
pax Romana, 158, 172
Peace of Westphalia, 725
Peace Preservation Law (Japan, 1925), 994
Pearl Harbor attack (1941), 997–999
peasant revolts
    in China, 163, 241, 241(m)
    in Germany, 724(t)
    plague and, 546
peasants. *See also* peasant revolts; serfs
    and serfdom
    in China, 95, 240–242, 241(i), 1036,
        1040–1041, 1052
    in France, 785
    in India, 1087
    in Japan, 896, 900
    in Russia, 795, 1033
Peloponnesian War (431–404 B.C.E.), 170
peninsulares, 633
Pennsylvania, Quakers in, 638
People's Liberation Army (China), 1036
pepper, trade in, 674
perestroika (restructuring), 1054
Pericles (Athens), 150, 151, 170,
    171–172(d), 257
Perry, Matthew, 894, 897, 897(v),
    915–917, 916(v)
Persepolis, Persia, 147, 147(i)
Persia
    culture of, 512–519
    Egypt and, 107(t)
    Greco-Persian wars and, 150–151
    il-khans in, 538, 543–544
    India and, 646
    Islam and, 483, 484–485, 516(v)
    Manichaeism from, 371, 372(v)
    Mongols and, 534, 538–539
    Safavid Empire and, 586
    Seleucid empire in, 153
    trade and, 675, 677
Persian church, 430
Persian Empire, 145–147, 146(m)
    Alexander the Great and, 152
    Byzantine Empire and, 432

Persian Empire (*continued*)
  India and, 166
  Zoroastrianism in, 203–204
Persian Gulf region, 676
  England and, 680
Persian miniatures, 485, 512–519, 514(v),
  516(v), 518(v)
Peru. *See also* Inca Empire
  Chavín culture of, 87, 298
  civilizations of, 87, 297, 298–300
  colonization of, 632–634
  communism in, 1031
  constitutions in, 848
  First Civilizations in, 297
  Moche peoples in, 87, 282, 298–300
  Nazca in, 300
  in 19th century, 848
  religious movements in, 298
  silver in, 631
  Taki Onqoy in, 729
  Tupac Amaru revolt in, 634, 781(t), 792
Perun (Rus god), 433
Peter the Great (Russia, r. 1689–1725),
  844
Petrarch, Francesco, on Black Death,
  546, 565
pharaohs (Egypt), 105, 108. *See also*
  kings and kingdoms; monarchs
  and monarchies
  afterlife and, 121–122(d)
Pharisees, 153
Philip II (Macedonia), 152
Philip II (Spain), 677
Philippines
  communism in, 1031
  environmentalists in, 1161–1162
  global trade and, 682
  Japan and, 997
  migrations from, 19
  Spain and, 677–679
  Spanish-American War and, 928
Phillips, Thomas, 703, 704–705(d)
philosophy. *See also* Aristotle;
  Enlightenment; intellectual
  thought; Plato; Socrates; specific
  philosophers
  of Buddhism, 199–200
  of classical era, 137, 191(t)
  Greek, 206–208
  of Hinduism, 198
  Legalism (China) as, 192–193

Phoenicians, 109–111
physical science, Newton and, 741
physicians. *See also* medicine
  Arab, 498–499
pictographs
  of Maya, 294
  as writing system, 101(t)
pilgrimage
  hajj as, 472(i), 473, 497
  by Sufis, 496
Pilgrimage Church of Mariazell, 762,
  763(v)
Pillars of Islam, 477–478
Pillow Book (Sei Shonagon), 396, 412,
  412–414(d)
Pinochet, Augusto (Chile), 1148–1149
plague, 329. *See also* Black Death
  bubonic, 340
  in Eurasia, 545–547, 545(i)
plantations, 631
  in Latin America, 634–637, 635(i)
  slavery for, 690, 691, 693, 794–795
  Southeast Asian colonial, 936
plants
  in Columbian exchange, 630, 630(i)
  cultivation of, 5–6
  domestication of, 5, 50, 53, 55, 63(i),
  522
  habitats of, 1159
  textiles and, 61–62
Plato (429–348 B.C.E.), 191(t), 207, 208
  Academy of, 208, 451
  on Socrates, 221, 222–223(d)
plebeians, in Rome, 155
Pliny the Younger (Rome), 272
plow, 446–447
  gender hierarchies and, 96
Plutarch, 258
pochteca (Aztec merchants), 353,
  590–591
Po Chu-I (China, 772–846 C.E.), 239
poetry. *See also* literature; specific poets
  bhakti, 736
  in China, 239, 241
  Japanese *tanka* and, 396
Poland
  communism in, 1035, 1055
  division of, 799(i)
  German attack on, 999
  Jews in, 561
  nationalism and, 799(i)

Russia and, 797, 797(t), 1033
  uprising in (1980s), 1051
political parties. *See also* specific parties
  in Asia and Africa, 1085
  in England, 838, 839
  in Germany, 1161
  in Japan, 994
  for workers, 843
political systems. *See also* specific
  locations
  in Africa, 1096–1098
  Arab Empire as, 344
  in Athens, 149, 150
  in Byzantine Empire, 428–429
  in China, 158–159, 162, 382
  in developing countries, 1095
  in India, 1096–1098
  Industrial Revolution and, 828–830
  in Japan, 395, 993
  of Maya, 294
  in Mesoamerica, 294
  of Moche, 299
  in Ottoman Empire, 893
  in Roman Empire, 155, 162–163
  in Sparta, 149
  in United States, 783–784
  in West, 448–449
  in Western Europe, 164–165
pollution. *See also* environment
  from industry, 1159
Polo, Marco, 329, 446
  on China, 359–360, 360–362(d)
  on Hangzhou, 383
  Khubilai Khan and, 537, 537(i)
  Mongols and, 535, 542, 555
  travel narratives by, 359–360,
  360–362(d)
Polybius, 160
polygamy, 487, 1105, 1148
Polynesia, chiefdoms in, 65
Polytheism
  Bantu, 292
  Christian ban on, 212
  Greek, 205–206
  Mesopotamian, 118 (d)
  Persian, 203
Pompeii, 272–276, 273(v), 274(v)
Pompey (Rome), 157
popes. *See also* papacy; specific popes
  Eastern Orthodox Christianity
  and, 431

Luther on, 751(d)
  in Western Church, 213–214
popular sovereignty, 780, 796
  in Spanish America, 790
population. *See also* food
  in age of agricultural civilization,
    135(f)
  agriculture and, 61
  of American colonies, 628
  of Anatolia, 491
  ancient, 4
  Aztec, 590
  of Chumash peoples, 29
  civilization and, 92
  in classical era, 282
  in Common Era, 282
  continental in classical era, 283(t)
  of Edo (Tokyo), 620, 896
  environment and, 1158
  of Europe, 438, 674, 685
  of European cities, 440
  expansion of, 11–20, 14–15(m)
  from 1400–1800, 619
  of French West Africa, 929
  in Global South, 1102
  growth in twentieth century, 970–971
  in Japan, 684
  in Latin America, 849
  of Maya, 136, 295
  in Meroë, 286
  in Mexico, 629, 633
  Mongol, 533, 534
  Native American, 687
  in Roman Empire, 163
  of Roman slaves, 249
  world growth of, 597(t), 1159(t)
porcelain, 713(v). *See also* pottery
  from China, 697, 830
Portugal, 578. *See also* Portuguese
    Empire
  Brazil and, 626, 781(t)
  empire of, 626, 675–677
  Japan and, 677, 681
  Kongo and, 705–706
  missionaries from, 727
  Mozambique colony of, 934
  Napoleon and, 791
  slave trade and, 693
  sugar colonies and, 635
  trade and, 675, 681
  voyages by, 580–581, 674

post-classical civilizations, 325–329,
    330–331(t), 332–376
  Afro-Eurasia changes and, 344
  China as, 379–385, 381(m)
  Christianity and, 425–432
  cultural borrowings by, 446
  Europe as, 426
  globalization of, 326
  innovations of, 137
  landmarks of, 330–331(f)
  nomadic peoples and, 526–528
  Russia as, 433
  transregional interaction by,
    327–329
poster art
  in China under Mao, 1071–1079,
    1072(v), 1074(v), 1075(v), 1077(v),
    1078(v)
  for independence movements,
    1122–1131, 1124(v), 1125(v),
    1126(v), 1128(v), 1130(v)
  as World War I propaganda,
    1019–1021, 1020(v), 1022(v)
potatoes, 53, 351, 630
Potosí, Bolivia, 683, 683(i), 765(v)
Pottier, Eugene, 863, 863–864(d)
poverty
  in African colonies, 937–939
  in England, 836, 836(i), 839
  during Great Depression, 985–986
  in Japan, 994
power loom, 826
Prague Spring (Czechoslovakia), 1050,
    1050(i), 1145
Prague Street (Dix), 1024, 1026(v)
pre-Columbian Americas, 292–297,
    301–304, 301(m), 629
Prince, The (Machiavelli), 580
printing, in China, 383, 397, 399
progress
  Condorcet on, 752–754(d)
  Darwin and Marx on, 745
  Enlightenment belief in, 743–744
Progressives (U.S.), 843
proletariat, 838
propaganda
  Italian fascist, 990
  Nazi, 992
  in World War I, 982, 1019–1026,
    1020(v), 1022(v), 1023(v), 1025(v),
    1026(v)

prophets
  Hebrew, 190, 191(t), 204, 205
  Muhammad as, 477
protectionism, 1139
protest(s). *See also* revolts and rebellions;
    revolution(s)
  in Chile, 851
  against Czech Communist Party, 1145
  against damming rivers, 1161
  against globalization, 1185–1186,
    1185(v)
  by Japanese peasants, 900
  in 1960s, 1145
  19th-century social, 837–839
  by Roman women, 268, 269–271(d)
  socialist, 839(i)
  Tiananmen Square demonstrations
    and (1989), 779, 1053
  against WTO, 1141–1142, 1185(v)
Protestantism. *See also* Protestant
    Reformation
  Catholic differences with, 724(t), 761
  churches in, 725
  fundamentalist, 1152
  in North American colonies, 638, 727
  women in, 725
Protestant Reformation, 723–727,
    723(i), 726(m), 749–750(d),
    750–751(d). *See also* Protestantism
  Catholic Counter-Reformation and,
    725–726
Provisional Government (Russia), 1033,
    1034
Prussia, Poland and, 799(i)
Ptolemaic empire (Egypt), 153
Ptolemy (astronomer/mathematician),
    739–740
pueblo peoples. *See* Ancestral Pueblo
    people (Anasazi)
pueblos, Pueblo Bonito, 302, 302(i)
Puerto Rico
  Taino peoples and, 73
  United States and, 853
Punch magazine
  on English industrialization, 874,
    874(v)
  on Rhodes, 963, 964(v)
Punic Wars, 155, 268
Punjab, 490
Punt, 109
Pure Land Buddhism, 235, 408

purges, in Soviet Union, 1044
Puritans, 638, 727
Pygmy people. *See* Batwa (Pygmy) people
pyramids
    in Cahokia, 304
    in Egypt, 105
    Moche, 299
    in Teotihuacán, 295–296
    ziggurats as, 92–93, 100(i)
Pythagoras (Greek philosopher), 207

Qadiriya order (Sufi), 496
Qianlong (Chinese emperor), 882–883, 905–906, 906–907(d)
Qin dynasty (China, 221–206 B.C.E.), 160, 174, 192–193, 240
Qing dynasty (Manchu dynasty, China, 1644–1912), 626, 644(m)
    Chinese Empire under, 643–645
    collapse of, 889
    missionaries and, 730, 732
    Neo-Confucianism and, 735
    Taiping Uprising and, 883–884
    Western imperialism and, 884–887, 887(m)
Qin Shihuangdi (Chinese emperor, r. 221–210 B.C.E.), 102, 158–160, 168, 174, 180–186, 181(v), 183(v), 184(v), 185(v), 186(v), 192
Quakers, 638, 725, 794, 794(i)
Quanzhou, China, 399
Quechua language, 593
Queen Mother of the West (Chinese deity), 384
quipu (Inca counting device), 87, 354, 593
Quran (Koran), 338, 476, 477–478, 502, 503–504(d)
    on equality of men and women, 486–487
    laws based on, 1155
    sciences and, 738
    in Turkish, 1104
    women and, 486–488
Quraysh (Arabian tribe), 475, 478
Qutb, Sayyid, 1153, 1154

Rabia (Sufi master), 485
race and racism
    African culture and, 945–947
    in Brazil, 636, 637

colonialism and, 772, 930–931, 945–947
    decolonization and, 1082
    in European colonies, 923, 930–931, 937
    European perceptions of, 881–882, 882(i)
    feminism and, 1147
    in Haiti, 787–788, 789–790, 789(i)
    in India, 242–243
    toward Japan, 997
    in Latin America, 633(i), 790
    in Nazi Germany, 992, 1003
    slavery and, 248, 250, 691–692
    in South Africa, 931, 1091
radical reconstruction (U.S.), 795
Raherka, 84(i)
railroads, 773(i), 832(i), 869(v)
    in Latin America, 849
    in Russia, 844
    strikes against, 842
Ramadan, 478
Ramayana, 201, 646
Ramisht (Persian merchant), 338
Rapa Nui, forests of, 20
rape, gender issues and, 97
Rape of Nanjing (1937–1938), 877, 1002
Raphael, 580
rationalism, 780. *See also* Enlightenment
    in Greece, 190, 205–208
al-Razi (Arab physician), 498–499, 499(t)
rebellions. *See* revolts and rebellions
reconquest, of Spain, 495
Record of the Western Regions (Xuanzang), 357
Red Army (Russia), 1034
Redeemed Christian Church of God, 721
Red River region, in Vietnam, 393
Red Sea trade, 677
    Axum and, 287
Reformation. *See* Protestant Reformation
Reform Bill (England, 1832), 834
reglobalization, 1135–1137, 1138(t)
reincarnation, in Hinduism, 198, 245
relics, 369, 430
religion. *See also* cults; gods and goddesses; intellectual thought; philosophy; specific groups
    in Africa, 493–494

Andes civilizations and, 594, 728–729
    awakenings in, 744
    Aztec, 594
    of Bantu-speaking peoples, 292
    and Black Death in Western Europe, 560–567, 562(v), 563(v), 564(v), 566(v)
    Buddhism and, 199–200
    Buddhism and Christianity compared, 209–214
    in Caribbean region, 73
    in central Asia, 367–376, 369(v), 370(v), 372(v), 374(v), 376(v)
    of Chavín culture, 298
    in China, 160, 161, 189, 390
    colonial rule and, 943–945, 943(i)
    contacts among, 595, 596(m)
    Daoism and, 196–197
    in Europe, 449–450, 723–727
    in European colonies, 943–945
    European women in, 441
    in fascist Italy, 990
    freedom of, 780
    in French Revolution, 820(v)
    global fundamentalism and, 1151–1153
    global modernity and, 1150–1158
    in Greece, 205–206
    history and, 214–215, 305
    identity and, 796
    Inca, 594
    in India, 167, 176, 177–178(d), 197, 201–202, 212
    Islamic networks of, 495–497
    in Japan, 394, 395
    of Ju/'hoansi peoples, 28
    in Mesoamerica, 728–729
    Mongols and, 530–531, 535
    in Mughal Empire, 645–646
    in Ottoman Empire, 647–650
    in Paleolithic era, 22
    pastoral nomads and, 525
    Protestant Reformation and, 722–732, 723(i), 726(m)
    reinvigoration of Christianity and, 721
    Roman Christianity and, 212
    in Roman Empire, 161, 276–279, 277(v), 278(v)
    in Russia, 433–434, 641
    sacred places and, 608–616, 610(v), 612(v), 613(v), 615(v)
    of San peoples, 25

science and, 743
Silk Roads and, 337–338
social order and, 100
syncretic, 732–733
of Taino peoples, 73, 74(d)
trade and, 137
in Vietnam, 392
Zoroastrianism and, 203–204
religious orders
Dominicans, 727
Franciscans, 542–543
Jesuits, 726–727
Reformation and, 726–727
spread of Christianity and, 727–728
Sufi, 496, 509
religious toleration, 780
in France, 725
by Mongols, 535, 540
in Russian Empire, 641
religious wars. See Crusades; jihad
Remarque, Erich, 982
Renaissance, in Europe, 579–580
reparations, German after World War I, 983, 986
reproductive rights, 1150
republic
in France, 786
in Rome, 155, 158
Republic, The (Plato), 207
republicanism, 780, 783, 793
resistance. See protest(s); revolts and rebellions
revolts and rebellions
in British West Indies, 794
in China, 883–884
in colonies, 929–930
in Eastern Europe, 1050
against European dominance, 773–774
by European peasants, 546
by German peasants, 724(t)
in Haiti, 252, 789–790
Indian Rebellion and, 930, 950, 953–955(d)
in Philippines, 679
by Roman slaves, 251–252, 251(m)
by Tupac Amaru (Peru), 634, 781(t), 792
Yellow Turban Rebellion (China), 163, 197, 241, 241(m)
in Zaire, 1097

revolution(s). *See also* specific revolutions
abolition of slavery and, 793–796
in Americas, 779–780
assessments of, 803–804
in Atlantic region (1750–1914), 779–781, 781(t)
in China, 1035–1037
communism after, 1038–1045
Enlightenment and, 744, 780, 783, 785
feminism and, 800–803
in Iran, 1106–1107
nationalism after, 796–800
in Russia, 845(m), 1032–1035
smaller-scale, 793
socialism without, 859–860, 860–861(d)
in twentieth century, 970
Rhodes, Cecil, 879–880, 963, 964(v), 965(v)
Rhodesia, 939
Ricci, Matteo, 730
Rightly Guided Caliphs (632–661), 483
rights
in colonial world, 814–816(d)
of former slaves, 795
gender-based, 252, 255–259
human, 806–807(d), 807–808(d)
national independence and, 810–811(d)
in Ottoman Empire, 892–893
reproductive, 1150
of slaves, 793–794, 811–812, 812–813(d)
of women, 487, 808, 809(d), 1039–1040
Robertson, Pat, 1152
Robespierre, Maximilien (France), 785, 786(i)
rock-and-roll music, 1049
rock art, 10(i), 22
from Algeria, 80
Australian aboriginal, 42–46, 43(v), 45(v), 46(v)
Paleolithic, 10(i), 22, 25, 28
of San peoples, 25
of southern Africa, 28
Rockefeller, John D., 842
Roman Catholic Church, 595, 722, 726(m). *See also* Protestant Reformation
Black Death and, 560

Byzantine Empire, Crusaders and, 431–432
Chinese culture compared with, 165
Eastern Orthodox Christianity and, 425
in fascist Italy, 990
in France, 785, 786, 787, 820(v)
hierarchy of organization in, 212–213, 751(d)
intellectual life and, 449–450
Mexico and, 720(i), 851
Protestant differences with, 724(t), 761
on scientific thinking, 741–742
and Western European society, 436–438
Roman Empire, 136, 136(m), 154–158, 156(m), 157(t), 172, 173–174(d). *See also* Byzantine Empire
Charlemagne and, 424(i)
Chinese Empire compared with, 160–165
Christianity and, 161, 162, 211
citizenship in, 157, 161
collapse of, 163, 164–165, 435
consolidation of, 160–163
culture in, 161–162
diseases in, 340
Egypt and, 107(t)
Germanic peoples and, 164
Greek influence on, 161–162, 208
Huns in, 164, 164(i)
innovations in, 137
laws in, 163
military in, 435
religion in, 161, 276–279, 277(v), 278(v)
slavery in, 95, 247, 249–252, 249(i)
Western European civilization after, 327
women's protests in, 268, 269–271(d)
writings on love in, 209
Romania
communism in, 1035, 1055
fascism in, 989
independence of, 890
Romanov dynasty (Russia), 1032. *See also* specific rulers
Roman Republic, 155
Romantic movement, 744
Romantic poets, environment and, 1160–1161

Roma people. *See* Gypsies
Rome. *See also* Roman Empire
  as city-state, 155, 161
  papacy in, 430
  population of, 435
Roosevelt, Franklin D., 987–988
"Rosie the Riveter," 1003
Rousseau, Jean-Jacques (1712–1778), 744, 785
Roy, Ram Mohan (1772–1833), 951–952, 952–953(d)
Royal Dutch Shell, 1137
"royal road," in Persian Empire, 147
rubber, 9, 848, 852
  forced labor and, 933, 934(i)
Rufinus (345–410 C.E.), 310–311, 311–312(d)
rum, 697
Rumi (Sufi poet), 375, 485, 496, 509, 510(d), 1151
Russia, 578. *See also* Kievan Rus; Russian Revolution entries; Soviet Union
  Bolsheviks in, 982
  Byzantium and, 446
  China and, 644, 886
  Christianity in, 433–434
  communism in, 1033–1035
  Eastern Orthodox Christianity in, 433–434
  economic development in, 1100–1101(t)
  industrialization in, 843–846
  migration from, 940(t)
  Mongols and, 539–541, 540(i), 554–555(d)
  as multiethnic empire, 642–643
  nationalism in, 798
  in 1917, 1033(m)
  Ottoman Empire and, 889
  Poland and, 799(i)
  Polish revolts against, 797(t)
  serfs in, 794, 795, 844(i)
  society in, 845–846
  steppes in, 540, 639–643
  trade and, 328
  World War I and, 979, 984
Russian Empire, 639–643, 640(m). *See also* Russia; Soviet Union
  Asia and, 642
  Christianity in, 727

  collapse of, 643, 1083
  end of, 1083
  expansion of, 644, 645
  fur trade in, 639, 688, 688(i)
  multiethnic nature of, 642–643
  Siberia in, 626, 639, 640(m)
  as Soviet Union, 1030
Russian Orthodox Church, 541. *See also* Eastern Orthodox Christianity
  missionaries from, 727
  Mongols and, 540
Russian Revolution (1905), 845(m)
Russian Revolutions (1917), 846, 970, 988, 1032–1035, 1033(m). *See also* Lenin
  Lenin and, 1033–1034
  Provisional Government and, 1033, 1034
  revolutionary movements and, 1031
  World War I and, 1034
Russo-Japanese War (1904–1905), 901, 920, 996
Rwanda, genocide in, 1003, 1097

sacrifices
  Aztec, 591, 603–604(d)
  in China, 182
  in First Civilizations, 103
  in Hinduism, 197
  by Inca, 593
  by Moche people, 299
Sadat, Anwar, 1155, 1156
Saddam Hussein. *See* Hussein, Saddam
Safavid Empire, 586
  Shia Muslims in, 595, 648
Safi al-Din (1252–1334), 586
Sahagun, Bernardino de, 664
Sahara Desert, 284
  camels in, 349
  pastoralism in, 575
  trade across, 333, 334, 348–351, 350(m), 690
Sahul supercontinent, 16
Saigon, 937
Sailendra kingdom (Java), 345
Saint Domingue, 787–788. *See also* Haiti
St. Lawrence River region, fur trade in, 685
St. Mark's Basilica (Venice), 430(i)

St. Petersburg, Russia, 844
  Russian Revolution and, 1032–1033, 1034
saints (Christian). *See also* specific saints
  in Mexico, 729–730
  veneration of, 725
Samarkand, Central Asia, 338, 575
Samoa, 595
samsara (rebirth/reincarnation), 198
samurai warriors, 395, 396(i), 414, 415(d), 681, 896, 898
Sand Roads, long-distance trade and, 348–351
San Martín, José, 792
San peoples, 10(i), 24, 25–29, 25(m), 34–35, 35–39(d), 290
Sanskrit language, 197, 951
Santa Anna, Antonio López de, 847
Santeria (Cuba), 732
Sanxingdui, China, 91
Sappho, 209
Sassanid Empire (Persia, 224–651 C.E.), 203
  Arabia and, 475, 480
sati, 646, 736, 932, 951
satraps (Persia), 146
satyagraha, 957, 1088
Saxons, 435
  Charlemagne and, 458–459, 459–460(d)
Scandinavia, Vikings from, 442
Schaeffer, Francis (1912–1984), 1152
Schlafly, Phyllis, 1150
scholar-officials (scholar-gentry)
  in China, 196, 240, 259
  in Vietnam, 394
sciences. *See also* technology
  in Arab world, 451
  Catholic Church on, 741–742
  in China, 745
  culture and, 739–742
  in England, 831
  Enlightenment and, 742–744
  Europe and, 446, 450, 737–746
  in India, 167
  Islamic, 499(t)
  in Japan, 745–746
  modern, 737–746
  in 19th century, 744–745
  racism and, 881
  religion and, 743

scientific racism, 930–931, 993
Scientific Revolution, 722, 737, 752
  English technology and, 831
  thinkers and achievements of, 740(t)
scramble for Africa, 926, 960–967, 961(v), 962(v), 964(v), 965(v), 966(v)
scribes, in Egypt, 84(i), 123, 124–125(d)
Scythians, 524(i)
Sea Roads, 341–348
  East Africa, Swahili civilization, and, 346–348
  in Indian Ocean region, 343–344
  Southeast Asia, Srivijaya, and, 344–346
Sears Roebuck, 842
Seattle, WTO protests in, 1141–1142, 1185, 1185(v)
secondary products revolution, 62
Second Sex, The (Beauvoir), 1146
second-wave civilizations, 134, 136–138, 238. See also classical era
second-wave feminism, 1146
Second World War. See World War II
secularism
  antislavery thinking and, 794
  in Iran, 1106
  in Ottoman Empire, 892–893
  in Turkey, 1105, 1167, 1168(d)
Sei Shonagon (Japan), 396, 412, 412–414(d)
Seleucid dynasty (Persia, 330–155 B.C.E.), 153, 203
Self-Help (Smiles), 834, 898
self-strengthening movement, in China, 888–889
Selim III (Ottoman Empire), 891
Sen, Keshub Chunder, 942
Seneca people, 574
Senegal
  democracy in, 1098
  slave trade in, 672(i)
Senghor, Léopold, 941, 942
seppuku (ritual suicide), 414
September 11, 2001, attacks, 1153
  Islam and, 1176–1177, 1177–1178(d)
Serbia
  independence of, 890
  World War I and, 979
serfs and serfdom, 437. See also peasants
  plague and, 546
  in Russia, 794, 795, 844(i)

Sermon on the Mount (Jesus), 223, 224–225(d)
settler colonies, 637–638
  in Africa, 936
Seventeen Article Constitution (Japan), 394, 407–408(d)
sex and sexuality
  feminism and, 1147, 1148, 1150
  fundamentalists on, 1152
  gender hierarchies and, 97
  in Greece, 258
  in Islam, 487
  of Maya, 322–323, 322(v)
  Paleolithic rules about, 21
  patriarchy and, 97–98
  women's movement and, 1147
  after World War I, 985
sex workers, women recruited as, 1137
Shahnama (The Book of Kings, Ferdowsi), 512
Shah of Iran. See Pahlavi, Muhammad Reza
shamans, 298
  Mongol, 531
  Sufis and, 375, 376(v), 492
Shang dynasty (China, 1766–1122 B.C.E.), 90, 91, 91(i), 158
Sharawi, Huda, 803
sharecroppers, 795
sharia (Islamic law), 479, 485, 496, 502, 506–507, 507–509(d)
  Islamization and, 1156
Sharpville, shootings at (1960), 1092
shaykhs (Sufi teachers), 496
Shia Muslims, 483–485, 488, 500, 586
  in Iran, 1106, 1107
  in Safavid Empire, 595, 648
Shiba Yoshimasa (Japan, 1349–1410), 414, 415(d)
Shihuangdi. See Qin Shihuangdi
Shi Le (Jie people), 339
Shinto, 410, 899
ships and shipping
  Chinese, 577, 577(i)
  Chumash canoe and, 29–30, 30(i)
  European, 447–448, 577(i)
  human migrations and, 19
  in Indian Ocean, 342
  Swahili, 347
  in World War I, 981
Shiva, Vandana, 1163

shoguns and shogunate, 414, 681, 895
Shona people, 939
Shotoku Taishi (572–622), 394, 406–407, 407–408(d)
Siam (Thailand)
  colonization and, 928
  European-educated elite in, 942(i)
Siberia
  in 15th century, 571
  fur trade in, 685, 688
  human migration to, 18
  in Ice Age, 16
  in Russian Empire, 626, 639, 640(m), 641
  trade and, 595
Sicily, in Christendom, 444
Siddhartha Gautama, 190, 191(t), 199. See also Buddha
Sierra Leone, 794, 1138–1139
Sikhism, 491, 736–737, 749, 758
Silent Spring (Carson), 1161
silk and silk industry
  in China, 385, 685, 885(t)
  spread of trade and, 329, 337
Silk Roads, 328, 332(i), 335(m), 595
  Buddhism and, 400
  China and, 387
  cultural exchange along, 338–340, 367–376
  disease spread along, 340–341
  economic exchange along, 337(t)
  Eurasia and, 335–341
  growth of, 336
  Islamic trade and, 497
  in Mongol Empire, 542
Silla dynasty (Korea, 688–900), 391
silver. See also mining
  in Americas, 631, 675
  from Bolivia, 675, 682, 683, 683(i)
  China and, 683–685
  Europe and, 830
  global commerce and, 682–685, 682(m)
  in Japan, 682, 684
  slave trade and, 693
Sima Guang (China, 1019–1086), 384
Singapore, 937, 1102
Six-Day War (1967), 1129, 1153
Skagit peoples, 572
slaves and slavery. See also abolition of slavery; slave trade
  abolition of, 793–796

slaves and slavery (*continued*)
African, 636
in Americas, 690, 783
in Athens, 249
Aztec, 591
destinations of slaves, 694(f)
in First Civilizations, 95–96
in France, 785
Greco-Roman, 248(t)
in Greece, 95, 249, 690
in Haiti, 787, 789–790
Hammurabi on, 120(d)
in India, 248–249
in Korea, 392
in Latin America, 636–637
Liberia and, 928
plantations and, 690, 691
revolts by, 251–252, 251(m)
rights and, 793–794, 811–812,
812–813(d)
Roman Empire and, 95, 247–252,
249(i)
serfdom and, 437
sexual, 877
in United States, 248(t)
West Africa and, 350–351, 691,
696–697, 718–719, 718(v)
slave trade, 794–795
African, 636, 672(i), 689–697, 689(m)
Asante kingdom and, 708–709(d)
business of, 703, 704–705(d)
in East Africa, 344
end of, 794, 960
Equiano and, 700, 701–703(d)
Kongo and, 693, 697, 705–706,
706–707(d)
numbers involved in, 693, 694(f)
practice of, 692–695
Roman, 250
trans-Saharan, 351
Slavic world
Byzantine culture in, 432–433
origin of term, 351
Orthodox Christianity in, 433–434
World War I and, 979
smallpox, 340, 629, 670, 670(v), 687
Smiles, Samuel, 834, 867–868, 898
Smith, Adam (1723–1790), 742, 783
social classes. *See* classes; specific classes
social contract, 780–781
social Darwinism, 882

Social Democratic Labor Party (Russia),
864
socialism. *See also* communism
in Africa, 1114–1115, 1115–1116(d)
Atlantic revolutions and, 780
in China, 1038–1045
communism and, 1030, 1038
democratic, 859–861(d), 987
in England, 837
in France, 839(i)
Marx and, 744, 837–839, 856–857,
857–859(d), 1030
protests and, 839(i)
in Russia, 846, 864, 864(d)
in song, 863–865(d)
in Soviet Union, 1038–1045
in United States, 843
women and, 802, 861–862,
862–863(d)
after World War I, 985
Socialist Party of America, 843
socially engaged Buddhism movement,
1158
social work, women in, 801
Society of Jesus. *See* Jesuits
Society of Righteous and Harmonious
Fists. *See* Boxer uprising
Socrates (469–399 B.C.E.), 191(t), 206–
207, 206(i), 208, 221, 222–223(d)
Sofala, East Africa, 347
soldiers. *See also* military
from colonies in World War I,
1021–1024, 1023(v)
government by, 1097–1098
Roman, 155
Russian Revolution and, 1032–1033
Solon (Athens), 150
Somalia, 347
Somme, battle at, 982
Song dynasty (China, 960–1279), 164,
193(i), 241(i), 344, 381, 381(m), 382
economic revolution in, 382–384
foot binding in, 384–385
Kaifeng during, 383(i)
women during, 384–385
Songhay Empire, 289, 350, 573,
586–587
Islam and, 492
Song of Solomon, 209
Sonni Ali (Songhay, r. 1465–1492),
494, 587

Son of Heaven (China), 90, 100, 160
Sony, 1137
sorghum, 55
Soros, George, 1139
South Africa, 1090(t)
apartheid and, 1090–1094
colonial labor in, 937
Gandhi in, 1088
independence for, 1080(i), 1086,
1090–1094, 1123–1124, 1125(v)
labor in, 939
Mandela in, 1080(i)
racism in, 931
white land ownership in, 936
South America. *See also* Americas; civi-
lization(s); Mesoamerica; specific
regions and groups
agriculture in, 55
interactions with, 352, 352(m)
migrations to, 18
trade in, 353, 595
South Asia. *See also* India; Indus Valley
civilization; specific locations
civilizations in, 165–167, 166(m)
economic development in,
1100–1101(t)
in 15th century, 570(t)
religions in, 197–198
Southeast Asia, 345(m)
agricultural village societies in, 572
colonial economies in, 936
colonization of, 926, 928
in 15th century, 570(t)
in Great Depression, 986
Hinduism in, 197
India and, 345–346
Islam in, 346, 587–588
Mongols and, 533
Sea Roads and, 344–346
after World War II, 1004
Southern Rhodesia, 939
South Korea
economic growth in, 1099, 1102
environmental activists in, 1162(i)
industrialization and, 1139
women's movement in, 1149
Southwest Asia, agriculture in, 51,
52(t), 55
Soviet Union, 1034–1035. *See also*
Russia; specific leaders
Afghanistan war and, 1046

China and, 1031, 1038–1045, 1050–1051
cold war and, 1030, 1049–1051
collapse of, 625, 1051–1052, 1054–1057, 1083
collectivization in, 1039(i), 1041, 1062–1063, 1063–1064(d)
colonial empires and, 1084–1085
communism in, 987, 1030, 1031
economy in, 1052, 1054, 1055
feminism in, 1039–1040
industrialization and, 1041–1044, 1064–1065, 1065–1067(d)
Russian Empire and, 643
socialism in, 1038–1045
society in, 1054–1057
Stalinism in, 1060–1069, 1061–1062(d), 1063–1064(d), 1065–1067(d), 1068–1069(d)
Terror in, 1044, 1052, 1067, 1068–1069(d)
after World War II, 1004, 1006
in World War II, 999, 1000, 1001–1002
Soweto, 1092
Spain, 578. *See also* Spanish Empire
American empire of, 631–639
Aztec conquest by, 632–634
Aztecs and Incas viewed by, 601–602(d), 602–603(d), 603–604(d), 605–607(d)
chocolate drink in, 712, 713, 714(v)
in Christendom, 444
Christianity in colonies of, 727–730
conquest of Mexico by, 664–671, 665(v), 666(v), 668(v), 669(v), 670(v)
fascism in, 989
Islam and, 480, 483, 494–495
missionaries from, 727
Napoleon and, 791
Philippines and, 677–679, 928
reconquest of, 495
Rome and, 155
silver and, 682, 683–684, 683(i)
Spanish America. *See also* Americas; Latin America; Spain; specific locations
vice-royalties in, 847
Spanish-American Revolutions (1810–1825), 781(t), 790–793

Spanish-American War (1898), 678, 853
Philippines and, 928
Spanish Empire, 626, 683–684
Sparta, 149
homosexuality in, 258
patriarchy contrasted with Athens, 257–259
women in, 257–259, 258(i)
Spartacus, rebellion by, 251, 251(m)
Spice Islands, 680
spice trade, 328, 588, 674, 677(i), 679–680
East India Companies in, 679–680
spinning jenny, 826
Sri Lanka. *See* Ceylon
Srivijaya civilization, 328, 345
Stalin, Joseph (Soviet Union), 1004, 1034, 1041–1042
death of, 1047, 1049
on nuclear weapons, 1048
search for enemies by, 1044–1045
Stalinism under, 1060–1069, 1061–1062(d), 1063–1064(d), 1065–1067(d), 1068–1069(d)
Stanley, Henry (1841–1904), 960
Stanton, Elizabeth Cady, 801
stateless societies, 65
status. *See* classes
steam engine, 826
steppes
nomads from, 386, 387, 389–390, 527
in Russia, 540, 640–641
stock markets
economic decline and, 1138–1139
Great Depression and, 985, 986
Stonehenge, 80–81, 81(v)
strikes (labor)
industrial, 842
in Japan, 901
laboring classes and, 837
submarines, in World War I, 981
Sudan
agriculture in, 55
genocide in, 1003
Quranic law in, 1155
states of, 351
trade in, 349, 350
Sudra caste, 243, 244
Suez Canal, 880, 963
suffrage. *See* voting rights; women's suffrage

Sufism, 375, 376(v), 485–486, 496, 509, 510(d)
in Anatolia, 491
bhakti and, 736
in India, 490
vs. Islamic fundamentalism, 1157
Wahhabi movement and, 734
women in, 488
sugar industry, 137
in colonial Americas, 634–637
rum production and, 697
slavery and, 691
Sui dynasty (China 589–618), 164, 326, 380–381
Sukarno (Indonesia), 1085
Suleiman I (Ottoman Empire, 1520–1566), 649, 657, 658–659(d)
Sulla (Rome), 157
sultans and sultanates, 485, 496
of Delhi, 490, 490(m)
in Ottoman Empire, 889
Safavids and, 586
Turkic peoples and, 527–528
Sumatra (Indonesia), 588
Sumer (southern Mesopotamia), 105(m), 106
environment in, 105–106
trade of, 108
writing in, 86, 89(m), 101(t), 109
Sunni Muslims, 483–485, 500, 586, 595, 1107
in Ottoman Empire, 648
colonial empires and, 1084–1085
Swahili civilization (East Africa), 325–326, 347(m)
Islam and, 347–348
Sea Roads and change in, 346–348
trade and, 328
Swaziland, 1093(m)
sweatshops, 1180–1181, 1181(v)
Swinton, William O., 772
Sybil (Disraeli), 836
Syria, 983(m)
Egypt and, 112
after World War I, 984

Tacitus (56–117), 68–69, 69–71(d)
Taino peoples, 73, 74(d), 568(i), 789
Taiping Uprising (1850–1864), 883–884
Taiwan
China and, 886, 1037, 1057

Taiwan (*continued*)
economic growth in, 1102
Japan and, 901, 920
Taizon (Tang emperor), 462
Taki Onqoy (Peru), 729
Tale of Genji, The (Murasaki Shikibu),
396
Taliban, 1156
Talleyrand, Charles, 808
Tamerlane. *See* Timur
Tang dynasty (China, 618–907), 326,
332(i), 344, 381, 381(m), 382, 389
printing in, 399
Vietnam and, 393–394
women in, 255, 384
tanka (Japanese writing), 396
Tanzania
humans in, 3
socialism in, 1114–1115, 1115–1116(d)
Tanzimat reforms, 892
Tartars, 554–555(d)
Ta-Seti, Nubian kingdom of, 107(t)
Tassili-n-Ajjer, Algeria, 80
Tau, Mildred Malineo, 1116–1117,
1117–1118(d)
taxation
in China, 683
in Europe, 674
in French Revolution, 817
in India, 646
Islamic *jizya* as, 482
in Japan, 394
by Mongols, 535, 539
in Ottoman Empire, 648
in Philippines, 679
tea
China trade and, 885(t)
colonial economies and, 936(i)
as European beverage, 712, 713(v)
technology. *See also* industrialization;
Industrial Revolution; sciences;
tools
advances in, 827–828
agriculture and, 61–62
ancient, 5
chariot, 111
in China, 137, 397–398
Chinese in Mongol society, 544
Chumash canoe as, 29–30, 30(i)
in classical era, 192
Clovis point, 18

from East, 446
in England, 831
environment and, 1158
European, 446–447, 447(i)
European seafaring, 628
European women and, 440–441
after First Civilizations, 134–135
human migrations and, 12–13
Islamic trade and, 498
military, 981
miniaturization and, 23
naval, 676
of Nazca people, 300
of nomadic peoples, 525–526
Paleolithic, 20
in pastoral societies, 525
permanent settlements and, 24,
52–53
of San peoples, 25
Scientific Revolution and, 737
spread of, 329, 335(m)
telegraph, 880, 888
telescope, 741
temples. *See also* mosques; ziggurats
in Chavín culture, 298
of Feathered Serpent (Teotihuacán),
296
of the Golden Pavilion (Kyoto,
Japan), 611–612, 612(v)
Golden Temple of Amritsar, 737
of Great Jaguar (Maya), 103, 280(i)
of Heaven (Beijing), 577, 609, 610(v)
in Java, 345–346, 346(i)
in Jerusalem, 146
of Jews, 146
Maya people and, 103, 280(i)
of Reason (Cathedral of Notre
Dame), 786
Temujin. *See* Chinggis Khan
Ten Commandments, 204, 467
Tengri (Mongol god), 531
Tenochtitlán, 590
Cortés in, 666–667, 666(v), 671
massacre of the nobles in, 668–669
population of, 440, 590
teosinte, 5(i), 56
Teotihuacán, Mexico, 93, 295–297,
296(i), 353, 590
collapse of, 326
government of, 296–297
Olmec influence on, 91

terra-cotta army, in Xian, China,
182–186, 183(v), 184(v), 185(v),
186(v)
Terror, the
in France, 1793–1794, 781(t), 785
Islamic, 1142
in Soviet Union, 1044, 1052, 1067,
1068–1069(d)
Tertullian (150–225 C.E.), 449
Teti (Egypt, r. 2345–2333 B.C.E.), 121
Texcoco
city-state, 591
Lake, 588
textiles and textile industry, 870(v)
African slave trade and, 693
in Agricultural Revolution, 61–62
in China, 385, 888
in England, 831
India and, 685, 830, 933
Industrial Revolution and, 827, 841
in Japan, 900–901
Thailand, 928, 1138
Thales (Greek philosopher), 207
Theodosius (Rome, r. 379–395 C.E.),
212
theology
Eastern Orthodox, 430
of Eastern vs. Latin Christianity,
430–431
Greek thought and, 208
liberation, 1158
in West, 450
Theravada Buddhism, 214, 402
third Rome doctrine, in Russia, 434
third-wave civilizations. *See* post-classical
civilizations
third world, 1048, 1082, 1095(m). *See
also* Global South
concept of, 1145–1146
environment and, 1163
migration to West from, 1182–1185,
1184(v)
Thirty Years' War (1618–1648), 214, 725
three-field system, 447
three obediences, 253
Thucydides, 138, 171–172(d)
Tiananmen Square demonstrations
(1989), 779, 1053
Tibet, 380, 643, 645
Tigris-Euphrates river valley, 65,
103–104

Tikal (Maya city), 103, 280(i), 294, 297
Timbuktu, 351, 493, 587
Timur (Tamerlane), 574, 576(m)
tin mines, in Malaysia, 937
"title societies," 65
Tito (Yugoslavia), 1035
Tiv peoples, 64–65
Tiwanaku civilization, 297(m), 300
Tlacaelel (1398–1480), 591
tlacuilo (artist-scribes), 664
Tlatelolco, Aztec market in, 590
Tlaxcala people, 667, 669, 669(v)
tobacco
    slavery and, 691
    spread of, 714–715
Tocqueville, Alexis de, 840–841
Tokugawa shogunate (Japan), 681, 684,
    895–896
Tokyo, Japan. *See* Edo (Tokyo)
Toltec civilization, 590
tomol (Chumash canoe), 29–30, 30(i)
Tonga, 595
tools. *See also* technology
    early, 3, 12–13, 53
    miniaturization of, 23
    of San peoples, 25
totalitarianism, in communism, 1038
total war
    in World War I, 982, 1019
    in World War II, 1002
trade. *See also* opium trade; roads and
        highways; slave trade; spice trade;
        specific types
    in Africa, 573
    in Americas, 351–354, 352(m)
    in Arab world, 137, 475, 482
    Armenian, 681
    in Asia, 681–682
    in Australia, 572
    Buddhism and, 335
    in Cahokia, 353
    in China, 399, 577, 684–685, 712,
        885(t)
    cross-cultural interaction and,
        328–329, 334–335, 595, 596(m)
    in Dutch East Indies, 933–934
    by ecological zones, 334
    Egypt and, 108–109
    in England, 831
    in Eurasia, 645
    European, 442, 674–680, 676(m)

exports and, 879
in First Civilizations, 127
in 14th century, 543(m)
fur, 639, 685–688, 686(m)
global, 940, 1133, 1134
Greek, 149
by Hopewell people, 303
in Indian Ocean region, 307, 308(d),
    341–344, 342(m)
industrialization and, 830
Islamic, 492, 497–499
in Italy, 440
in Japan, 745–746, 897
in Jenne-jeno, 289
Latin American, 848–849, 852
long-distance routes, 137–138
of Maya, 295
of Meroë, 286
Mesoamerican, 293
in Mongol Empire, 542, 546
Native Americans and, 685–688
in Northern Europe, 439–440
Ottoman, 891
in Persian Empire, 147
in products from Europe, 879–880
in Rome, 435
in Russia, 433
on Sea Roads, 341–348, 342(m)
on Silk Roads, 335–341
silver and, 631, 682–685, 682(m)
social impact of, 334–335
Spanish, 677–679
state control of, 780
status and, 711–719, 713(v), 714(v),
    716(v), 717(v), 718(v)
in sugar, 137
in third-wave civilizations, 328
trans-Saharan, 348–349, 350(m), 586
U.S. role in, 1144
in Venice, 341
in West Africa, 326, 692–693
in Western Europe, 434
in Western Hemisphere, 351–354,
    352(m), 353(i)
after World War II, 1006
worldwide, 1136
trade-unionism
    in England, 837
    Lenin on, 864
    in USA, 842–843
trading post empires, 677, 680

trance-dance healers, 28–29
transatlantic slave trade. *See* slave trade
transnational corporations (TNCs), 1137
transportation
    in China, 384
    expansion and, 880
trans-Saharan trade
    routes, 348–351, 586
    in slaves, 690
travel. *See also* trade
    cultural connections and, 328–329
    in Sahara, 349–350, 350(m)
Travels of Marco Polo, The, 360–362(d)
treaties
    Anglo-Japanese (1902), 901
    European-Ottoman, 891
    Japanese with West, 897
    mutual defense, 1048
    of Nanjing (1842), 886, 912–913(d)
    NATO, 1006
    of Nerchinsk (1689), 644
    Russia-German (1918), 1034
    Unequal with China, 886, 887, 891,
        897, 901
    of Versailles (1919), 983–984, 989
Treatise on Toleration (Voltaire), 743
trench warfare, in World War I, 1000
Trent, Council of (1545–1563),
    725–726
tribes and tribalism. *See also* kinship
    in Africa, 946–947
    in Central Asia, 63
    in China, 386
    colonialism and, 931–932
tribunes, in Rome, 155
tribute system
    in China, 387–389, 388(i), 577
    Korean tributes to China, 391
    in Russian Empire, 641
    Spanish colonial, 634
    Xiongnu Empire and, 526
Trinity, doctrine of, 214, 430, 431
Triple Alliance
    of Mexica (1428), 590
    in World War I, 979
Triple Entente, 979
Trojan Women, The (Euripides), 256
Trung sisters, 393, 393(i)
tsar (Russia), 844. *See also* specific rulers
    abdication of, 1032, 1033
Tu Duc (Vietnam), 928

Tulalip peoples, 572
Turkey, 893–894, 983(m), 1103(m). *See also* Anatolia; Atatürk, Mustafa Kemal
   agricultural village society in, 64(i)
   economic growth in, 1099
   Islam and, 483, 1103–1105
   Islamic parties in, 1155
   modern, 1103–1105
   nationalism in, 800
   secular state in, 1167, 1168(d)
   women in, 893, 1104–1105
   after World War I, 984
Turkmenistan, 336
Turks, 527. *See also* Ottoman Empire
   Arabs and, 526–528
   in Central Asia, 375, 376(v), 645
   culture of, 527–528
   Islam and, 444, 489, 490, 492, 492(m), 528
   nomadic pastoralism of, 526, 527
   Ottoman, 326, 584, 649
   Timur and, 575
   Young Turk movement and, 893–894
al-Tusi, Nasir al-Din (1201–1274), 499(t)
Twain, Mark, 85
typhus, 629
tyrants, in Greece, 149

Uighur peoples, 371, 372(v), 389, 625
ujama (familyhood), 1114
Ukraine
   nationalism in, 797(t)
   Russia and, 642, 797, 797(t), 1033
ulama (Islamic scholars), 484, 486, 496, 891, 892, 1105
Ulyanov, Vladimir. *See* Lenin
Umar (caliph), 487
Umayyad caliphate (661–750), 484, 612–613
umma (Islamic community), 477, 478, 481
unemployment, in Great Depression, 985–986, 987(f)
unequal treaties, 886, 887, 891, 897, 901
Union of Soviet Socialist Republics (USSR). *See* Soviet Union
unions. *See* labor unions
United Kingdom. *See* England (Britain)

United Nations (UN), 1004
   conferences on global warming, 1162
   Copenhagen climate conference (2009), 1163
   Human Development Report, 1138
   Universal Declaration of Human Rights (1948), 780
United States. *See also* American Revolution; North America
   abolition and, 795
   anti-Japanese immigration policy in, 997
   Asian colonial rule by, 925(m)
   black leaders in, 946
   civil rights movement in, 1145
   Civil War in, 777(f), 793, 795
   cold war and, 1030
   colonial empires and, 1084–1085
   communism in, 1031
   cultural imperialism by, 1144
   economic globalization and, 1135
   economy in, 1049, 1100–1101(t)
   "empire" of, 1142–1144, 1143(m)
   feminism in, 801, 1146–1147
   as global power, 984
   Great Depression in, 985–988
   imperialism of, 852–853, 878, 924
   industrialization in, 840–843, 841(m)
   investment in, 842
   Japan and, 896–897, 915–917, 916(v), 917(v), 997
   Latin America and, 639
   Mexico and, 847, 849
   Muslims in, 473
   national parks in, 1161
   as new Roman Empire, 143
   Pearl Harbor attack and, 997–999
   Postal Service in, 147
   slavery in, 248(t)
   as superpower, 1048–1049
   triangular diplomacy of, 1051
   wealth and power of, 793
   women's voting rights in, 801
   as world power, 1005–1007
   in World War I, 981
   after World War II, 1004–1005
   in World War II, 1000
U.S. Steel Corporation, 842
Universal Declaration of Human Rights (UN, 1948), 780

universal suffrage. *See* voting rights; women's suffrage
universities and colleges. *See also* specific schools
   in Europe, 738
   in Middle Ages, 450, 450(i)
   women in, 801
untouchables (caste) 237, 243(i), 245, 490
Upanishads, 190, 191(t), 197–198
Ur, Mesopotamia, 89(m), 100(i), 106
urbanization. *See also* cities and towns; specific areas
   in China, 382–383, 1041
   in East Africa, 347
   in Europe, 440
   in First Civilizations, 92–93
   in Global South, 1102
   Islamic, 497, 515, 516(v)
   in Japan, 895–896
   in Latin America, 849
   of modern societies, 597
   in Niger River region, 288–289
   in Soviet Union, 1041
   in Sumer, 106
Uruguay, 847
Uruk, Mesopotamia, 92
Urukagina (Mesopotamia), 100
USSR. *See* Soviet Union
Uthman (caliph), 483
Uzbekistan, 336

Vaisya caste, 243–244
Vajrapani (Buddhist deity), 340
varna (caste system), 242–244, 244(t)
Vedas, 197, 198
veils
   in Egypt, 98, 803
   in France, 1184, 1184(v)
   in Islamic societies, 1155
   in Mesopotamia, 98
Venice, 578
   merchants in, 829
   population of, 440
   St. Mark's Basilica in, 430(i)
   trade in, 341, 440, 675
Venus figurines, 17, 22
Veracruz, Mexico, 90
Verdun, battle at, 982
Versailles, Treaty of (1919), 983–984, 989

Vesalius, Andreas (1514–1564), 740(t), 743(i)

Victoria (England), 876(i), 910, 911(d), 911–912(d), 912–913(d)

Victoria, Lake, 292

Vienna, Ottoman sieges of, 585, 649, 649(m), 722

Vietnam, 392(m)
  China and, 380, 886, 1051
  colonial cash crops in, 935
  colonization of, 929
  communism in, 1030–1031, 1045, 1057
  culture of, 392–394
  independence of, 1125–1126, 1126(v)
  religion in, 392

Vietnam War
  protests against, 1145
  U.S. imperialism and, 1144

Vijayanagara kingdom, 576(m), 587

Vikings, 442

Villa, Pancho, 851

Vindication of the Rights of Women, A (Wollstonecraft), 800, 808, 809(d)

Virgin Mary. *See* Mary (mother of Jesus)

Virgin of Guadalupe, 720(i)

Vishnu (god, India), 201–202

Visigoths, 435
  Athaulf of, 435–436

Vivekandanda (Swami), 944

Vladimir (Kievan prince), 433

Vodou (Haiti), 732

Voltaire (1694–1778), 743, 780

voting rights
  in England, 834
  in France, 786
  for men, 786, 993
  for women, 801, 802(i), 985, 1105

Wahhab, Abdullah, 756–757(d)

Wahhabi movement (Islamic renewal), 734, 734(m), 756–757(d)

Waldseemüller, Martin, 583(m)

Wall Street crash (October 24, 1929), 985

Wang Dayue, 684

Wang Mang (China), 240

Wang Shugu (China, 1649–1730), 188(i)

Wang Yangming (1472–1529), 735, 754, 755(d)

warring states period (China), 158, 192, 404

warriors
  Aztec, 602–604(d)
  Japanese samurai as, 395, 396(i), 414(d), 415(d), 681, 896, 898
  Kshatriya caste as, 244
  Moche, 299
  in Sparta, 257
  in Western Europe, 436

wars and warfare, 678, 853, 928. *See also* cold war; guerrilla warfare; revolts and rebellions; revolution(s); weapons; specific battles and wars
  in Africa, 733
  in American Revolution, 779, 781–784
  Arab-Israeli, 1129
  Aztec, 591
  blitzkrieg and, 1000
  Boer War (1899–1902), 965, 965(v), 1091
  in China, 158
  Crimean War (1854–1856), 844
  Crusades and, 442–445, 443(m)
  in Europe, 448
  Franco-Prussian War (1870–1871), 979
  in French Revolution, 781, 784–787, 812–823, 818(v), 819(v), 820(v), 821(v), 822(v)
  Greco-Persian, 150–151
  Hundred Years' War and, 578–579
  Islamic empire and, 480–482
  Korean War (1950–1953), 1006–1007, 1045
  for Latin American independence, 790–793, 791(m), 847
  Maya, 318
  in Mongol Empire, 533–535
  naval, 676
  in Norte Chico civilization, 87, 88(m), 297
  Opium Wars, 884–885, 886, 905, 912
  patriarchy and, 97
  Peloponnesian War, 170
  Punic Wars, 155, 268, 268(d)
  religious, in West Africa, 733

Russo-Japanese, 901
  Spanish-American War (1898), 678
  Thirty Years' War (1618–1648), 214, 725
  total war and, 982, 1002
  trade and, 680
  trench warfare in World War I, 1000
  U.S.-Mexico, 847
  of Xiongnu, 526

Warsaw Pact, 1045

war socialism, in Germany, 982

Washington, Booker T., 946

wealth. *See also* aristocracy
  in Bolivia, 683, 683(i)
  of Chinese Buddhism, 402
  Chumash, 30, 31
  classes and, 94–95
  colonial, 631
  European exploration for, 581, 583
  exchange, status, and, 711–719, 713(v), 714(v), 716(v), 717(v), 718(v)
  gap between North and South, 1139, 1140(m)
  in Meroë, 286, 286(i)
  of Moche elites, 299
  in modern societies, 598
  of Mongols, 534
  in Roman Empire, 157
  from trade, 334, 338

weapons. *See also* nuclear weapons; wars and warfare; specific weapons
  cannons as, 398
  in China, 383
  European, 447, 880, 880(i)
  European expansion and, 628
  Gatling gun, 880(i)
  Greek fire, 432
  iron, 383
  of mass destruction, 1142
  Native Americans and, 687
  paleolithic, 24
  in World War I, 980, 981
  in World War II, 999, 1002, 1002(i), 1005

weaving
  in Agricultural Revolution, 62
  women and, 62(i)

Weimar Republic, 991

Wen (Chinese emperor), 526

Wendi (Chinese emperor, r. 581–604 C.E.), 386(t), 402
West Africa, 284, 326. *See also* Niger Valley region; specific countries
agricultural village societies in, 573
agriculture in, 55
arts in, 82–83, 82(v)
city-states in, 350–351
European culture in, 941
French, 929
Ibn Battuta in, 362–363, 363–365(d), 494
independence in, 1085
Islam in, 351, 492–494, 493(m)
nationalism in, 800
Portuguese voyages and, 675
religious wars in, 733
Sand Roads to, 348
slavery and, 350–351, 691, 695, 696–697, 718–719, 718(v)
Songhay Empire in, 586–587
states (empires) in, 289
trade and, 328, 349–351, 350(m)
traditions from, 732
women in, 364(d), 939
West Bank, 1129
Western Christendom. *See* Roman Catholic Church
Western-educated elites, 924, 929, 937, 942–943, 942(i)
Western Europe, 434–445. *See also* Europe and Europeans; Roman Catholic Church; Western world; specific locations
American sphere of influence in, 1045
change in (1000–1300), 438–442
comparison of empires and, 650
culture of, 164
fascism in, 989
global dominance by, 354
Industrial Revolution in, 830
in 9th century, 436(m)
political life in (500–1000), 435–436
religion and Black Death in, 560–567, 562(v), 563(v), 564(v), 566(v)
Roman Catholic Church and, 436–438
after Roman Empire, 327, 426
silk in, 338

trade of, 711–719
women in, 437
world role of, 771
after World War II, 1005–1007
world wars in, 977–978
Western Hemisphere. *See also* Americas; empires; specific groups and regions
agriculture in, 55
civilizations of, 326–327
Eurasian diseases in, 341
in 15th century, 570(t)
migrations to, 18
trade in, 351–354, 352(m), 353(i)
West Indies
Britain and, 782, 794
intellectuals from, 946
Westphalia, Peace of, 725
whaling, 1162
"What is Enlightenment?" (Kant), 742
What Is to Be Done? (Lenin), 864, 865(d)
wheat, 5, 105
whirling dervishes, 509
whiskey. *See* alcohol
White Revolution (Iran), 1105
Whydah, kingdom of, 703
wilderness idea, 1161
Wilhelm (Germany), 876(i), 979
Willendorf Venus, 22(i)
William of Conches, 450
William of Rubruck, 557, 558–559(d)
Willibald, on Boniface, 460–461(d)
Wilson, Woodrow, 982, 984
windmills, 399
winds
in Atlantic, 626–628
monsoons as, 342
witches and witchcraft, Bantu speakers and, 292
Woden (god of war), 435
Wollstonecraft, Mary, 800, 808, 809(d)
women. *See also* feminism; gender and gender issues; patriarchy; specific individuals
in Africa, 938–939, 1116–1117, 1117–1118(d)
in Athens, 255–257, 256(i)
Aztec, 591(i), 594

in Buddhism, 200
in Çatalhüyük, 77–79, 78(v)
in China, 194, 253–255, 263–264, 263(d), 264–266(d), 384–385, 419, 419(v), 1073, 1075(v)
in Christianity, 211, 211(i), 213
in communist world, 1039–1040
education for, 742
in England, 835, 836
in Europe, 440–441, 441(i)
in fascist Italy, 990
in Ghana, 938
in Global South, 1102
in *hadiths*, 488
Inca, 593, 594
industrialization and, 840
in Indus Valley civilization, 130–131, 130(v)
in Iran, 1106–1107, 1107(i)
Islam and, 477, 486–488, 487(i), 494, 508(d), 1154–1155, 1173–1174, 1174–1175(d)
in Japan, 396–397, 412, 412–414(d), 896, 918–919, 918(v)
in Korea, 392
in Latin American colonies, 637
Moche, 299
Mongol, 538, 557, 558–559(d)
mothers of missing children and, 1148(i)
Paleolithic, 19–20, 34–35, 35–39(d)
in pastoral societies, 523–524
professions for, 801
in Protestantism, 724–725
protests in Rome, 268, 269–271(d)
in religious life, 441
rights of, 808, 809(d)
San, 26–28, 35–39(d)
as sex workers, 1137
socialism and, 861–862, 862–863(d)
in Sparta, 257–259, 258(i)
in Turkey, 893, 1104–1105
Turkic traditions and, 492
voting rights for, 985
weaving and, 62(i)
in Western Europe, 437
as workers, 254(i)
in World War I, 982(i), 1019
in World War II, 1002–1003
Women's Federation (China), 1039
women's liberation, 1147

women's movements
   in Africa, 1147–1148
   in Chile, 1148–1149
   during nineteenth century, 800–803
   in South Korea, 1149
   in United States, 1147, 1148
   women's group movement (Kenya),
      1148
women's rights. *See also* feminism
   spread of, 802–803
women's rights conference (Seneca
   Falls, NY), 801
Women's Social and Political Union,
   801
women's suffrage, 801, 802(i), 985, 1105
Wordsworth, William, 872, 1160
workers. *See also* labor
   from Africa, 631
   in Japan, 900–901
   in Mexico, 851
   migrations of, 938–939, 1137, 1141
   in modern societies, 597–598
   in Russia, 845, 1032
   women as, 840, 1002–1003, 1039
World Bank, 1004, 1099, 1135, 1185
world economy, 354–355, 697–698, 940,
   1085, 1110–1111, 1111–1112(d),
   1134–1144, 1186, 1186 (m). *See also*
   economy; globalization
   antiglobalization movements and,
      1141–1142
   consumerism and, 1183(v)
   distribution of wealth and, 1138
   in early modern era, 619, 697–698
   Mongols and, 535
   in third-wave civilizations, 327–329
World Peace Summit (2000), 1158
World Social Forum, 1142
World Trade Center attacks, 1153, 1156
World Trade Organization (WTO),
   Seattle protests against, 1141–1142,
   1185, 1185(v)
World War I (1914–1918), 977–984,
   980(m), 982(i), 983(m). *See also*
   specific countries
   Africans in, 946
   battles in, 982
   destructiveness of, 1021–1024,
      1025(v)
   empires after, 982
   Europe after, 983(m)

Europe before, 980(m)
Germany after, 991
intellectual thought after, 982
Japan in, 993
legacies of, 981–984
Middle East after, 983(m)
nationalism and, 797, 979–980
propaganda in, 982, 1019–1026,
   1020(v), 1022(v), 1023(v), 1025(v),
   1026(v)
reparations after, 983, 986
Russian Revolution and, 1034
total war in, 982, 1019
trench warfare in, 1000
United States and, 981, 1004
veterans after, 989, 991, 1024,
   1026(v)
women in, 982(i), 1019
workers and, 838–839
World War II, 976(i), 996–1005. *See also*
   Germany; World War II; specific
   countries
   in Asia, 988, 996, 997–999, 998(m)
   Axis Powers and, 988
   bombings in, 999, 1002, 1002(i)
   in Europe, 999–1001, 1000(m)
   global economy after, 1134–1137
   Hitler on, 1012, 1013–1015(d)
   Holocaust and, 1003
   Japan and, 996–999, 998(m)
   key moments in, 1001(t)
   Nazis and, 990–993, 990(i), 992(i),
      999–1001, 1000(m)
   outcomes of, 1001–1005
   in Soviet Union, 1001–1002
   total war in, 1002
   United States after, 1004–1005
   Western Europe after, 1005–1007
   world politics after, 1003–1004
writing systems. *See also* alphabet
   in ancient Egypt, 84(i)
   Andes civilizations and, 297
   Chinese, 90, 160, 162
   cuneiform, 101(t), 109
   in First Civilizations, 100–102,
      101(t), 115
   in Japan, 396
   in Korea, 392
   of Maya, 294
   of Olmecs, 90
   Peruvian *quipu* and, 87

sacred, 109
spread of Buddhism and, 339
of Teotihuacán, 296
in Vietnam, 393
Wu (Chinese Empress, r. 690–705 C.E.),
   255
Wu (Xia dynasty), 90
Wudi (China, r. 141–87 B.C.E.), 162,
   238

Xenophon, 258
Xia dynasty (China, 2200–1766 B.C.E.),
   90, 158
Xian, China, terra-cotta army in,
   182–186, 183(v), 184(v), 185(v),
   186(v)
Xinjiang, 643, 645
Xiongnu people, 159(m), 163, 336,
   388–389, 526, 526(m), 547
Xuanzang (China), 356–357,
   358–359(d)
Xu Naiji (China), 908–909(d)

Yahweh, 98, 109, 204, 205, 475
yams, 291
Yap, Micronesia, 595
Yathrib. *See* Medina, Arabia
yellow fever, 629
"yellow peril," 881
Yellow Turban Rebellion (China,
   184 C.E.), 163, 197, 241, 241(m)
Yemen, 287, 474, 715
Yi dynasty (Korea, 1392–1910), 391
Yi Jing (Chinese monk), 345
yin/yang, 196, 253
yoga, 1151
Yongle (Chinese emperor, r. 1402–
   1422), 577, 578, 609
Yoruba people, 573–574
Young Ireland movement, 797(t)
Young Ottomans, 893
Young Turks, 893–894
Yuan dynasty (China), 536
Yuan Yulin (China), 909–910(d)
Yucatán area, 353, 848
Yugoslavia, communism in, 1035, 1050

Zagwe dynasty (Ethiopia), 615
zaibatsu, 900, 996
Zaire, rebellions in, 1097
Zakat (alms), 507–508(d)

Zambia, democracy in, 1098

Zapata, Emiliano, 851

Zapatista Army of National Liberation, 281–282

Zapotec people, Monte Alban and, 297

Zarathustra. *See* Zoroaster

Zen Buddhism, in Japan, 408–409, 409–410(d)

zero, Indian concept of, 329

Zetkin, Clara (1857–1933), 861–862, 862–863(d)

Zheng He (Chinese admiral), voyages of, 569, 571, 581, 582–583, 643

Zhenotdel (Women's Department, USSR), 1039

Zhou dynasty (China, 1122–256 B.C.E.), 100, 158, 192

Zhou Enlai (China), 803

Zhou Wenju (Chinese painter), 420, 420(v)

Zhuangzi (369–286 B.C.E.), 191(t)

ziggurats, 92–93, 100(i)

Zimbabwe, 292, 1086. *See also* Great Zimbabwe

Zionism, 797, 1127–1129, 1128(v)

Zoroaster, 190, 191(t), 203

Zoroastrianism, 190, 202, 203–204
in Arabia, 475
fire altar of, 203(i)
Islam and, 483
spread of, 338

Zulus, in South Africa, 1094

Zunghars, 644

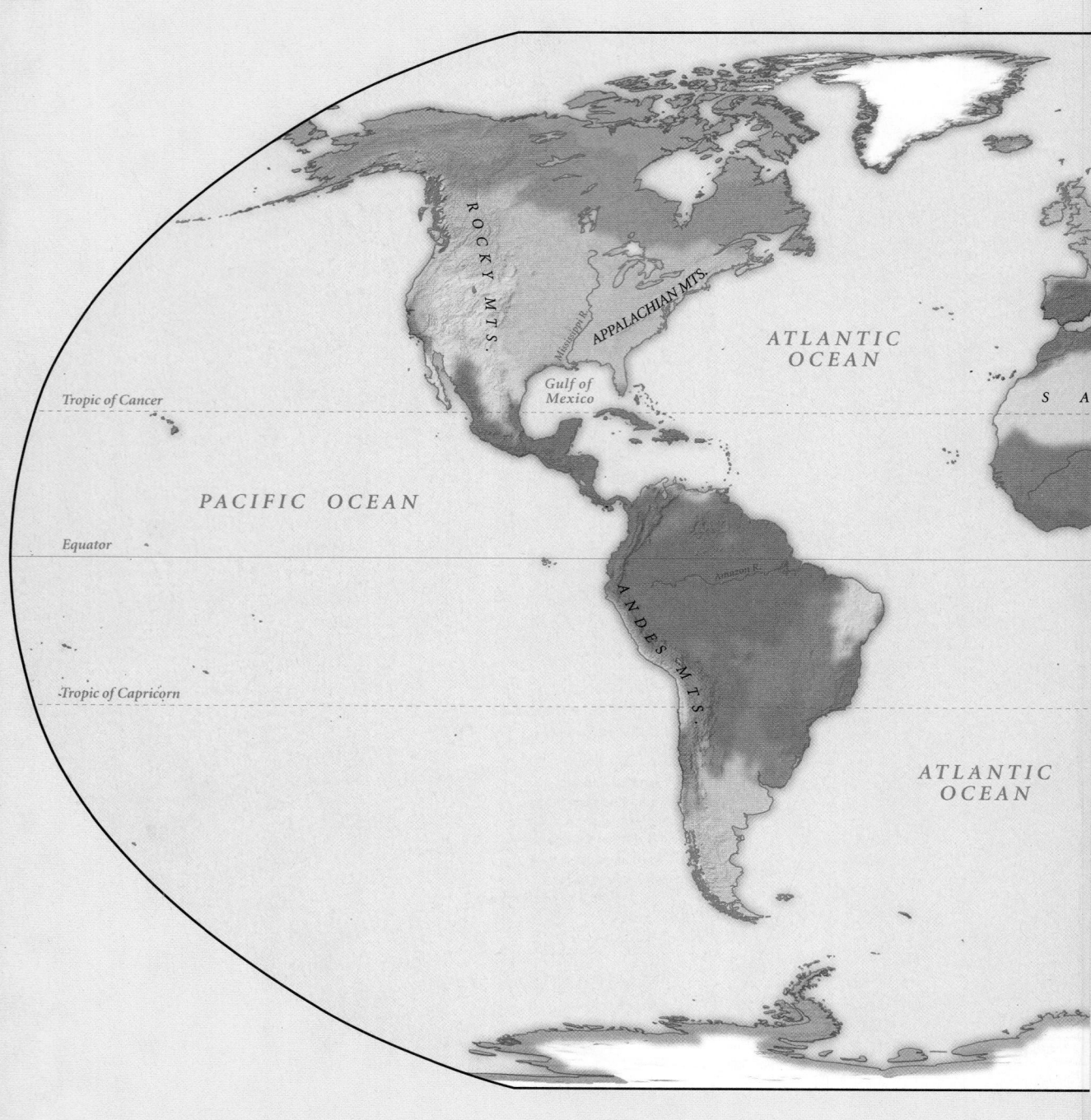

ROCKY MTS.

Mississippi R.

APPALACHIAN MTS.

ATLANTIC
OCEAN

Tropic of Cancer

Gulf of
Mexico

S A

PACIFIC OCEAN

Equator

Amazon R.

A N D E S   M T S.

Tropic of Capricorn

ATLANTIC
OCEAN

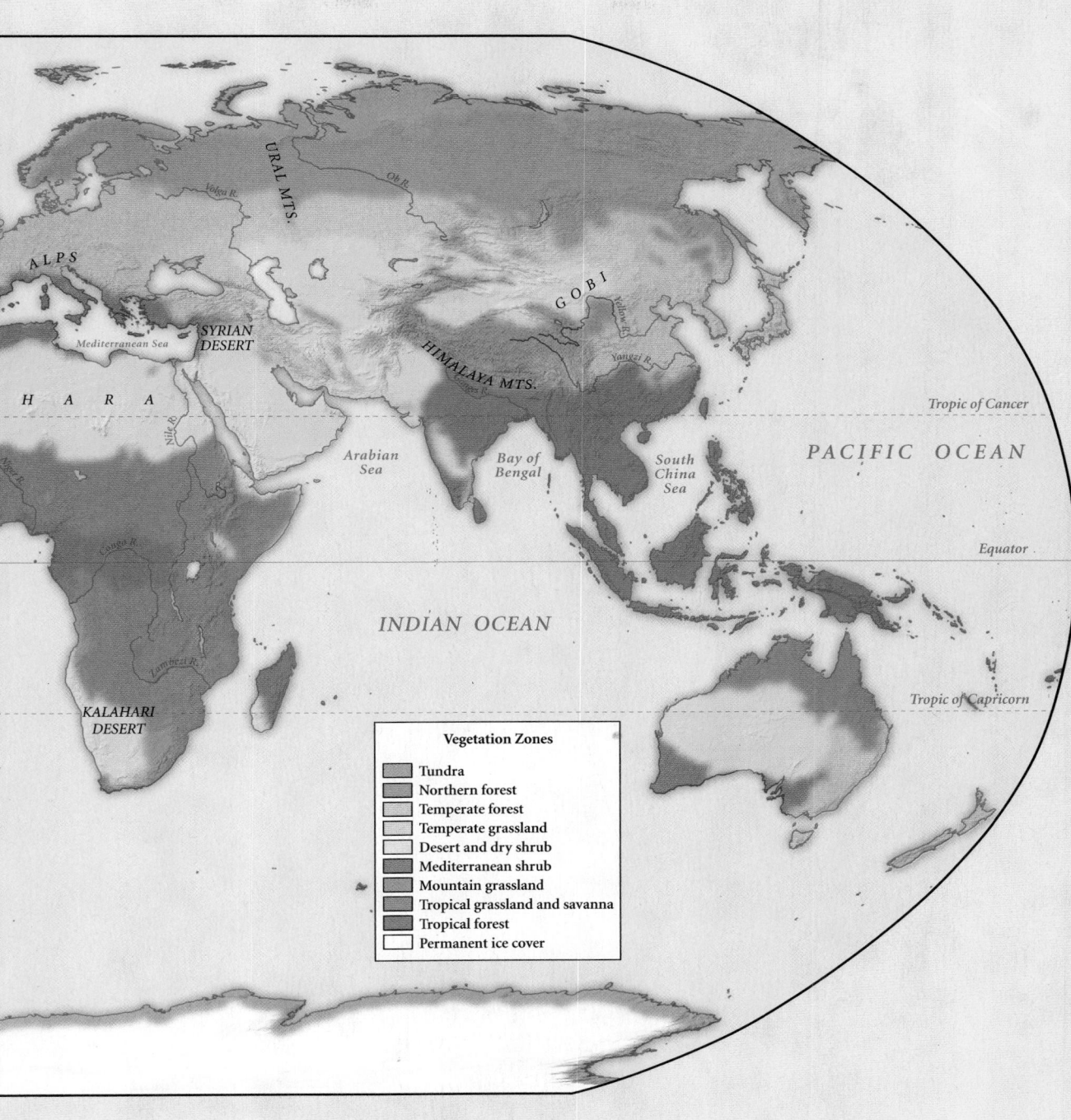

ALPS

URAL MTS.

Volga R.

Ob R.

G O B I

Yellow R.

HIMALAYA MTS.

Yangzi R.

SYRIAN
DESERT

Mediterranean Sea

H A R A

Nile R.

Niger R.

Congo R.

Zambezi R.

KALAHARI
DESERT

Arabian
Sea

Bay of
Bengal

South
China
Sea

Tropic of Cancer

PACIFIC OCEAN

Equator

INDIAN OCEAN

Tropic of Capricorn

Vegetation Zones

- Tundra
- Northern forest
- Temperate forest
- Temperate grassland
- Desert and dry shrub
- Mediterranean shrub
- Mountain grassland
- Tropical grassland and savanna
- Tropical forest
- Permanent ice cover

About the Author

Robert W. Strayer (Ph.D., University of Wisconsin) brings wide experience in world history to the writing of this text. His teaching career began with two years of high school instruction in Ethiopia as part of the Peace Corps. At the university level, he taught African, Soviet, and world history for many years at SUNY College at Brockport, where he received Chancellor's Awards for Excellence in Teaching and for Excellence in Scholarship. In 1998 he was visiting professor of world and Soviet history at the University of Canterbury in Christchurch, New Zealand. Since moving to California in 2002, he has taught world history at the University of California, Santa Cruz; California State University, Monterey Bay; and Cabrillo College. He is a long-time member of the World History Association and served on its Executive Committee.

His publications include *Kenya: Focus on Nationalism* (1975), *The Making of Mission Communities in East Africa* (1978), *The Making of the Modern World* (1988, 1995), *Why Did the Soviet Union Collapse?* (1998), and *The Communist Experiment* (2007). He has also published in a number of academic journals, including the *Journal of World History*.

"Strayer writes beautifully and clearly about complicated issues."

–Deborah Gerish, *Emporia State University*